HEALTH PSYCHOLOGY

HEALTH PSYCHOLOGY

SECOND EDITION

Shelley E. Taylor

University of California, Los Angeles

McGRAW-HILL, INC.

New York   St. Louis   San Francisco   Auckland   Bogotá
Caracas   Lisbon   London   Madrid   Mexico City   Milan
Montreal   New Delhi   San Juan   Singapore
Sydney   Tokyo   Toronto

HEALTH PSYCHOLOGY

5 6 7 8 9 0 DOH DOH 9 5 4

ISBN 0-07-063195-6

This book was set in Palatino by the
College Composition Unit in cooperation with
Waldman Graphics, Inc.
The editors were Jane Vaicunas and Tom Holton;
the production supervisor was Kathryn Porzio.
The cover was designed by Karen K. Quigley.
The photo editor was Elyse Rieder.
R. R. Donnelley & Sons Company was printer
and binder.
Cover photo: Franco Fontana/The Image Bank.

Acknowledgments appear on page v, and on this
page by reference.

Library of Congress Cataloging-in-Publication Data

Taylor, Shelley E.
      Health psychology/Shelley E. Taylor.—2nd ed.
         p.   cm.
      Includes bibliographical references (p.   ) and
      index.ISBN 0-07-063195-6
      1. Clinical health psychology.   2. Health
   attitudes.   I. Title.
   R726.7.T39   1991
   616'.0019—dc20   90-13552

This book is printed on acid-free paper.

COPYRIGHT ACKNOWL- EDGMENTS

ABOUT
THE AUTHOR

Shelley E. Taylor is Professor of Psychology at the University of California, Los Angeles. She received her Ph.D. in social psychology from Yale University. After a visiting professorship at Yale and assistant and associate professorships at Harvard University, she joined the faculty of UCLA in 1979. Her research interests are in health psychology, especially the factors that promote long-term psychological adjustment, and in social cognition. In the former capacity, she is the director of the Health Psychology program at UCLA. Professor Taylor is the recipient of a number of awards, most notably the American Psychological Association's Distinguished Scientific Award for an Early Career Contribution to Psychology, and a 10-year Research Scientist Development Award from the National Institute of Mental Health. She is the author of over 100 publications in journals and books and is also the author of *Social Cognition* and *Positive Illusions*.

CONTENTS

PREFACE

When I wrote the first edition of *Health Psychology* over five years ago, the task was much simpler than is now the case. Health psychology was new and relatively small. In the last few years, the field has mushroomed, and great research advances have been made. Chief among these developments has been the increasing use and refinement of the biopsychosocial model: the study of health issues from the standpoint of biological, psychological, and social factors acting together. Increasingly, research has attempted to identify the physiological pathways by which such psychosocial factors as stress may exert an adverse effect on health, and by which such potentially protective factors as social support may buffer the impact of stress. My goal in the second edition of this text is to convey the increasing sophistication and complexity of the field in a manner that makes it accessible, comprehensible, and exciting to undergraduates, without compromising the scientific nature of the field.

My goals guiding the preparation of this edition were several. The first concerns the nature of the content. Like any science, health psychology is cumulative, building on past research advances to develop new ones. Accordingly, I have tried to present not only the fundamental contributions to the field, but the current form research on these issues takes. Because health psychology is developing and changing so rapidly, it is essential that a text be current. Therefore, I have reviewed not only the recent research in health psychology, but sought to obtain information about many research projects that will not be available in the general literature for several years. In so

doing, I believe this edition is both up to date and oriented toward the future.

A second goal is to portray health psychology appropriately as intimately involved with the problems of our times. AIDS is now a major medical reality, having become one of the leading causes of death among young adults in the United States. The need for such health measures as condom use is readily apparent, if we are to stop the spread of this disease. The aging of the population and the shift in numbers toward the later years create unprecedented health needs to which health psychology must respond. Such efforts include the need for a campaign of health promotion for these aging cohorts, and an understanding of the psychosocial issues that arise in response to chronic disorders. Research that increasingly implicates health habits in the development of the most prevalent disorders in this country underscores more than ever the importance of modifying problematic health behaviors such as smoking and alcohol consumption. Increasingly, research documents the importance of a healthy diet, regular exercise, and breast self-examination, among other positive health habits for maintaining good health. By expanding the coverage of health promotion issues and integrating them more fully into the later chapters on seeking treatment and managing illness, this edition highlights these developments, forging an integrated presentation of the complex relations among health habits, psychosocial resources, stress and coping, and health and illness outcomes.

Fields that were only just developing when the first edition of this book was prepared now boast substantial and sophisticated research traditions, and these are covered in the new edition. There is now extensive coverage of the developing field of psychoneuroimmunology (Chapter 15). We know more about coping techniques and coping resources for dealing with stressful events than we did a mere five years ago (Chapter 8). Research on the psychosocial factors contributing to the development of coronary artery disease and hypertension has mushroomed (Chapter 14). The second edition of *Health Psychology* especially chronicles and highlights the places where research has advanced the most.

Health psychology is both an applied field and a basic research field. Accordingly, in highlighting the research accomplishments of the field, I have not only tried to present a comprehensive picture of the scientific progress, but also tried to portray the very important applications that have been derived from that body of knowledge. The chapters on health promotion, for example, put particular emphasis on the most promising methods and venues for changing health behaviors in the population. The chapters on chronic diseases highlight how knowledge about the psychosocial causes and consequences of these disorders may be used to intervene with these populations, first to reduce the likelihood that such disorders will develop, and second, to deal effectively with the psychosocial issues that do arise. These applications of the science center around intervention implications for those having difficulty managing the implications of their disorders.

The fact that health psychology has so many direct applications to daily life has led to another important feature of the second edition, namely the effort to make the issues addressed in this book relevant to the lives of the student readers. For example, the presentation of of stress management is tied directly to how students might manage the stresses associated with college life. The presentation of alcoholism and problem drinking includes sections on college students' alcohol consumption and its modification. Health habits relevant to this age group, such as breast self-examination, testicular self-examination, exercise, and diet, among others, are highlighted for their relevance to the college population. By providing students with anecdotes, case histories, and specific research examples that are relevant to their own lives, I have attempted to show the students how important this body of knowledge is, not only to their growth as developing students, but also to their lives as young adults. The success of any text depends ultimately upon its ability to communicate clearly to student readers and to spark interest in the field.

Health psychology is a science, and consequently it is important to communicate not only the research itself, but some understanding of how studies were designed and why they were designed that way. The role of research methods and theories to understanding health-related issues is consequently a major theme in the book. Throughout the text, particular studies are singled out and illustrated so that the student may have a sense of how researchers make decisions about how to gather the best data on a problem or how to intervene most effectively.

Special Features of the Second Edition

I have made several major organizational and content-based changes in the second edition.

- A greatly expanded section on health promotion
- The addition of specific chapters on health-enhancing and health-compromising behaviors
- The addition of a new chapter on heart disease, hypertension, stroke, and diabetes
- The addition of a new chapter on psychoimmunology, AIDS, cancer, and arthritis
- A revised chapter on physiology

Certain features of the first edition that worked successfully have been retained in this edition. For example, the introduction of general principles and concepts in chapters which are then followed up with chapters on specific applications have been retained. Thus, for example, Chapters 3 and 4 discuss general strategies of health promotion, and Chapters 5 and 6 discuss those issues with specific reference to particular health habits, such as alcoholism, smoking, accident prevention, and weight control. Chapters 12 and 13 discuss broad issues that arise in the context of managing chronic and terminal illness. In Chapters 14 and 15, these issues are addressed more concretely with reference to specific disorders, such as heart disease, cancer, and AIDS.

The flexibility in orientation has also been preserved. Because health psychology is taught within all areas of psychology (clinical, social, cognitive, physiological, learning, developmental), material from each of these areas is included in the text, so that it can be accommodated to the orientation of each instructor. Consequently, not all material in the book is relevant for all courses. Successive chapters of the book build on each other but do not depend on each other. Thus, each instructor can accommodate the use of the text to his or her needs, giving some chapters more attention than others and omitting some chapters altogether, without undermining the integrity of the presentation. The book also makes no commitment to a particular theory, but instead reviews a variety of theoretical perspectives as they become relevant to the particular health problems under discussion.

Instructor's Manual and Study Guide

The second edition is now accompanied by a comprehensive Instructor's Manual with tests, prepared by Cheryl Rickabaugh. The manual outlines each chapter and provides detailed suggestions for lectures. Also included are ideas for classroom discussion, student projects, paper topics, and other activities. There is extensive presentation of the methodologies of health psychology, including epidemiology, experiments, surveys, and the like. There is also a listing of annotated readings and other materials to enrich the course, and an extensive test bank of multiple-choice questions that test students' recall of material as well as their ability to comprehend and apply the concepts in the text.

Acknowledgments

My extended gratitude goes to Garrett Duncan Songhawke for the many hundreds of hours he put in on the manuscript, for innumerable hours of overtime, and for the crises he weathered successfully to be certain that the manuscript would be on time. In addition, I thank Michelle Nieto, who gathered materials and made countless trips to the library. In the preparation of this book, I wrote to members of the Society of Behavioral Medicine and the Academy of Behavioral Medicine Research to ask for reprints and preprints relating to their most current research that might otherwise not be available through a search of the literature. Many dozens of you responded to this request, making my task enormously more time-consuming and complex. Ultimately, however, it will greatly enrich the text, making it more comprehensive and up-to-date. I thank you for your efforts in this regard. I thank Jane Vaicunas, my editor, and Renee Shively Leonard, Tom Holton, and Kathy Bendo at McGraw-Hill, who devoted much time and help to the preparation of the book. I am grateful to Christine Dunkel-Schetter and John Lydon for test-marketing the book in their courses. I also wish to thank the following reviewers who commented on all or part of the book: Kelly Brownell, University of Pennsylvania; Lynn Durel, University of Miami; Dennis Elsenrath, University of Wisconsin at Stevens Point; Barry Hurwitz, University of Miami; Margaret Kemeny, University of California at Los Angeles; John Liebeskind, University of California at Los Angeles; Mary Obear, State University of New York at Buffalo; Ann O'Leary, Rutgers University; Cheryl Rickabaugh, University of Redlands; Wolfgang Stroebe, Universität Tübingen; Neil Weinstein, Rutgers University; and Deborah Wiebe, University of Utah.

Shelley E. Taylor

PART 1

INTRODUCTION TO HEALTH PSYCHOLOGY

1

WHAT IS HEALTH PSYCHOLOGY?

Health involves the general condition of the body. Psychology is concerned with the state of the mind. Because the mind and body work together, producing physical and mental health, the field of health psychology is a logical and important contributor to both the health sciences and the discipline of psychology.

In this chapter, we consider how philosophers have conceived of the **mind–body relationship,** and we see why our current state of knowledge has virtually demanded development of the field of health psychology. After describing health psychology, we contrast it with related fields in different disciplines and examine what health psychologists actually do. We then consider the many factors that have given rise to health psychology. Next, we consider the dominant clinical and research model in health psychology: the biopsychosocial model. Finally, we end the chapter with an overview of the field as presented in this book.

THE MIND–BODY RELATIONSHIP: A BRIEF HISTORY

Historically, philosophers have vacillated between the view that the mind and body are part of the same system and the idea that they are two separate ones. When we look at ancient history, it becomes clear that we have come full circle in our beliefs about the mind–body relationship.

Although we do not have direct access to many ancient cultures, what evidence there is suggests that in the earliest times the mind and body were considered a unit. Early cultures believed that disease arose when evil spirits entered the body and that these spirits could be exorcised through the treatment process. Archeologists have found Stone Age skulls with small holes in them that are believed to have been made intentionally with sharp stone tools. This procedure, called trephination, allowed the evil spirit to leave the body while the "physician," or shaman, performed his treatment ritual (Kaplan, 1975).

The Greeks were among the earliest civilizations to identify the role of bodily functioning in health and illness. Rather than ascribing illness to evil spirits, they developed a humoral theory of illness that was first proposed by Hippocrates (*ca.* 460–*ca.* 377 B.C.) and later expanded by Galen (A.D. 129–*ca.* 199). According to this view, disease arises when the four circulating fluids of the body—blood, black bile, yellow bile, and phlegm—are out of balance. The function of treatment is to restore balance among the humors. Specific personality types were believed to be associated with bodily temperaments in which one of the four humors predominated.

In the Middle Ages, mysticism and demonology dominated concepts of disease, which was seen as God's punishment for evildoing. Cure often consisted of driving out evil by torturing the body. Later, this "therapy" was replaced by penance through prayer and good works. Throughout this time, the Church was the guardian of medical knowledge; as a re-sult, medical practice took on religious over-tones, including religiously based but unscientific generalizations about the body and the mind–body relationship. Not surprisingly, as the functions of the physician were absorbed by the priest, healing and the practice of religion became indistinguishable (Kaplan, 1975).

Beginning in the Renaissance and continuing up to the present day, great strides have been made in the technological basis of medical practice. Most notable among these were Anton van Leeuwenhoek's (1632–1723) work in microscopy and Giovanni Morgagni's (1682–1771) contributions to autopsy, both of which laid the groundwork for the rejection of the humoral theory of illness. The humoral approach was finally put to rest by the theory of cellular pathology, which maintains that all disease is disease of the cell rather than a matter of fluid imbalance (Kaplan, 1975).

As a result of such advances, medicine looked more and more to the medical laboratory and bodily factors, rather than to the mind, as a basis for medical progress. In an effort to break with the superstitions of the past, the dualistic conception of mind and body was

Sophisticated—though not always successful—techniques for the treatment of illness were developed during the Renaissance. This woodcut from the 1570s depicts a surgeon drilling a hole in a patient's skull, with the patient's family and pets looking on.

strongly reinforced, so that physicians became the guardians of the body while philosophers and theologians became the caretakers of the mind. For the next 300 years, as physicians focused primarily on organic and cellular changes and pathology as a basis for their medical inferences, physical evidence became the sole basis for diagnosis and treatment of illness (Kaplan, 1975).

This view began to change with the rise of modern psychology, in particular, with Sigmund Freud's (1856–1939) early work on **conversion hysteria.** According to Freud, specific unconscious conflicts can produce particular physical disturbances that symbolize the repressed psychological conflicts. In conversion hysteria, the patient converts the conflict into a symptom via the voluntary nervous system; he or she then becomes relatively free of the anxiety the conflict would otherwise produce (Cameron, 1963).

The conversion hysteria literature is full of intriguing but biologically impossible disturbances, such as glove anesthesia (in which the hand, but not other parts of the arm, loses sensation) in response to highly stressful events. Other problems—including sudden loss of speech, hearing, or sight; tremors; muscular paralysis; and eating disorders such as anorexia nervosa and bulimia—have also been interpreted as forms of conversion hysteria. True conversion responses are now less frequent than they were in Freud's time.

Nonetheless, the idea that specific illnesses are produced by individuals' internal conflicts was perpetuated in the work of Flanders Dunbar in the 1930s (Dunbar, 1943) and Franz Alexander in the 1940s (Alexander, 1950). Unlike Freud, these researchers linked patterns of personality rather than a single specific conflict to specific illnesses. For example, Alexander developed a profile of the ulcer-prone personality as someone whose disorder was caused primarily by excessive needs for dependency and love.

A more important departure from Freud concerned the physiological mechanism postulated to account for the link between conflict and disorder. Whereas Freud believed that conversion reactions occurred via the voluntary nervous system with no necessary physiological changes, Dunbar and Alexander argued that conflicts produce anxiety that becomes unconscious and takes a physiological toll on the body via the autonomic nervous system. The continuous physiological changes eventually produce an actual organic disturbance. In the case of the ulcer patient, for example, repressed emotions resulting from frustrated dependency and love-seeking needs were said to increase the secretion of acid in the stomach, eventually eroding the stomach lining and producing ulcers (Alexander, 1950).

Dunbar's and Alexander's works helped shape the emerging field of **psychosomatic medicine** by offering profiles of particular disorders believed to be psychosomatic in origin—that is, bodily disorders caused by emotional conflicts: ulcers, hyperthyroidism, rheumatoid arthritis, essential hypertension, neurodermatitis (a skin disorder), colitis, and bronchial asthma. Many of the early ideas generated by the psychosomatic medicine perspective persist today (Engel, 1986). Nonetheless, several important criticisms of this movement have been ventured. First, the work on which many of these formulations was based was methodologically problematic, not conforming to the highest scientific standards of the day. Second and more important, researchers now believe that a particular conflict or personality type is not sufficient to produce illness. Rather, the onset of disease requires the interaction of a variety of factors; these include a possible genetic weakness in the organism, the presence of environmental stressors, early learning experiences and conflicts, current ongoing learning and conflicts, and individual cognitions and coping efforts. A third criticism of the psychosomatic movement was that it cordoned off a particular set of diseases as caused by psychological factors, thereby restricting the range of medical problems to which psychological and social factors were deemed to apply.

Despite the criticisms of the early psychosomatic movement, it laid the groundwork for a profound change in beliefs about the relation of the mind and the body (Engel, 1986). It is now known that physical health is inextricably interwoven with the psychological and social environment: All conditions of health and illness, not just the diseases identified by the early psychosomatic theorists, are influenced by psychological and social factors. The treatment of illness and prognosis for recovery are substantially affected by such factors as the relationship between patient and practitioner and expectations about pain and discomfort. Staying well is heavily determined by good health habits, all of which are under one's personal control, and by such socially determined factors as stress and social support. The mind and the body cannot be meaningfully separated in matters of health and illness. An adequate understanding of what keeps people healthy or makes them get well is impossible without knowledge of the psychological and social context within which health and illness are experienced. This current conception of the mind–body interaction is one of the many factors that have spawned the rapidly growing field of health psychology.

DEFINITION OF HEALTH PSYCHOLOGY

Health psychology is the field within psychology devoted to understanding psychological influences on how people stay healthy, why they become ill, and how they respond when they do get ill. Health psychologists both study such issues and promote interventions to help people stay well or get over illness. For example, a health psychology researcher might be interested in why people continue to smoke even though they know that smoking increases their risk of cancer and heart dis-

ease. Information about why people smoke would help the researcher both to understand this poor health habit and to design interventions to help people stop smoking.

Health psychology is concerned with all psychological aspects of health and illness across the life span (Maddux, Roberts, Sledden, & Wright, 1986). Health psychologists focus on *health promotion and maintenance,* which includes such issues as how to get children to develop good health habits, how to promote regular exercise, and how to design a media campaign to get people to improve their diets.

Health psychologists also study the psychological aspects of the *prevention and treatment of illness.* A health psychologist might try to teach people in a high-stress occupation how to manage stress effectively so that it will not adversely affect their health. A health psychologist might work with people who are already ill to help them adjust more successfully to their illness or to learn to follow their treatment regimen.

Health psychologists also focus on the *etiology and correlates of health, illness, and dysfunction.* **Etiology** refers to the origins or causes of illness, and health psychologists are especially interested in behavioral and social factors that contribute to health or illness and dysfunction. Such factors can include health habits such as alcohol consumption, smoking, exercise, the wearing of seat belts, and ways of coping with stress.

Finally, health psychologists analyze and attempt to improve *the health care system and the formulation of health policy.* They study the impact of health institutions and health professionals on people's behavior and develop recommendations for improving health care. Putting it all together:

Health psychology is the aggregate of the specific educational, scientific and professional contributions of the discipline of psychology to the promotion and maintenance of health, the prevention and treatment of illness, the identification of etiologic and diagnostic correlates of health, illness, and related dysfunction and the improvement of the health care system and health policy formation. (Matarazzo, 1980, p. 815)

Distinguishing "Health Psychology" from Related Terms

Exposure to health psychology inevitably also exposes an individual to related fields. These include medical sociology, medical psychology, medical anthropology, behavioral medicine, and behavioral health. The ability to distinguish among these is important not only for understanding these related disciplines but also for refining the definition of health psychology itself.

Medical sociology is a subfield within sociology devoted to a sociological perspective on health and illness (see Bloom, 1986). What is the sociological perspective, and, more importantly, how does it differ from the psychological perspective? Sociologists are concerned with society, social institutions, and social relationships—that is, the big picture. In contrast, psychologists are more concerned with individual behavior, personality, and small-group influences on behavior. Thus, for example, a medical sociologist might study the structure of the hospital, whereas a health psychologist might study the impact of the hospital on its patients. A medical sociologist might study cultural factors that contribute to poor health habits, whereas a health psychologist might study what influences a person to practice good health habits and how such habits can be instilled.

Medical psychology is a subfield within health psychology devoted primarily to the study of psychological factors in the illness experience. Historically, medical psychology preceded the development of health psychology. Medical psychologists were individuals within medical departments whose primary function was the psychological assessment of medical and psychiatric patients. Individuals who call themselves medical psychologists are still often located in medical settings and apply expertise from the discipline of psychology, especially psychological tests, to problems that are posed by the medical environment.

Medical anthropology is a subfield within the general field of anthropology. It is a "biocultural discipline concerned with both the biological and sociocultural aspects of human behavior, and particularly with the ways in which the two interact and have interacted throughout history to influence health and disease" (Foster & Anderson, 1978, p. 3). What differentiates medical anthropology from health psychology? Medical anthropologists are more concerned with differences in the nature and definition of health and illness *across cultures* than are health psychologists. They are also interested in cultural differences in the interpretation and treatment of illness, whereas health psychologists have less interest in these issues. For example, medical anthropologists explore primitive rituals, religion, and magic in the context of disease, whereas health psychologists generally do not (Foster & Anderson, 1978). Medical anthropologists are also more interested in historical patterns of health and illness and in the interplay of cultural development with health and illness than are health psychologists. In general, then, medical anthropologists tend to look for cultural explanations for health and illness, whereas health psychologists focus more on individual behavior.

Two terms frequently heard in conjunction with health psychology are *behavioral medicine* and *behavioral health.* Historically, **behavioral medicine** was an outgrowth of the theoretical tradition of learning theory. Consequently, behavioral medicine focused on overt health and illness behaviors, the conditions that maintain them, and the conditions that can modify them. In practice, behavioral medicine employed behavior therapy and behavior modification for the evaluation, prevention, management, and treatment of physical disease or physiological dysfunction (Pomerleau & Brady, 1979). As a research discipline, behavioral medicine contributed to "the functional analysis and understanding of behavior associated with medical disorders and problems in health care" (Pomerleau & Brady, 1979, p. xii).

Today, however, behavioral medicine has transcended these early behaviorist origins. Both overt behaviors (such as smoking, for example) and covert behaviors (such as attitudes and emotions) are considered legitimate objects of study. Behavioral medicine is now defined as a broad interdisciplinary field concerned with health, illness, and related dysfunction (Matarazzo, 1980). It draws on the professional contributions of psychology, as well as many other disciplines, including anthropology, sociology, epidemiology, physiology, pharmacology, nutrition, neuroanatomy, endocrinology, immunology, dentistry, medicine, nursing, social work, health education, and public health, among others (Miller, 1983). **Behavioral health** is a "new interdisciplinary subspecialty within behavioral medicine specifically concerned with the maintenance of health and the prevention of illness and dysfunction in currently healthy persons" (Matarazzo, 1980, p. 807). Consequently, behavioral medicine and behavioral health can be distinguished from health psychology by one main factor: Behavioral medicine and behavioral health are interdisciplinary in nature, and health psychology is one of the specific disciplines that makes contributions to the larger collective enterprise of behavioral health and behavioral medicine.

A Synthesis of Many Definitions

The frustrated reader, now overwhelmed with a variety of seemingly overlapping definitions, may legitimately ask, "Why are there so many terms?" The answer is that any good idea invents itself a number of times, and this has

been true of the idea that psychological and behavioral factors influence health and illness. It has been reinvented within each of the social and behavioral sciences. But each incarnation of an idea will be slightly different, depending partly on the nature of the discipline that spawned it. Consequently, each effort to study the role of psychological and behavioral factors in health and illness has had an emphasis that is slightly different from the others.

The important point to take away from this discussion is that psychologists, other social scientists, and professionals in the health sciences are increasingly sharing a common vision: the view of health and illness as determined by a variety of biological, psychological, and social factors. At the core of this vision is the belief that, by working together, these professionals can help people maintain a higher level of health, modify many of the behavioral factors that give rise to disease, and ameliorate many of the adverse consequences of disease (see Matarazzo, 1980, 1982).

WHAT DO HEALTH PSYCHOLOGISTS DO?

Students who are trained in health psychology on the undergraduate level go on to many different occupations. Some go into medicine, becoming physicians and nurses who, because of their training in health psychology, are better able to understand and manage the social and psychological aspects of the health problems they treat. Others go into allied health fields such as social work, occupational therapy, dietetics, physical therapy, or public health, where their work with healthy or ill populations is likewise enlightened by their understanding of the social and psychological bases of prevention, illness, and treatment.

A third group of students go on to graduate school in psychology, where they learn the research, teaching, and intervention skills necessary to practice health psychology. As health psychologists, they may be responsible for educating physicians, nurses, other health workers, or fellow psychologists. They may conduct research programs to try to uncover the factors associated with the maintenance of health and the onset of illness. They may develop interventions to improve the health or health behavior of particular populations. Or they may do clinical work in which they may be allied with a hospital or other treatment setting. This last group of health psychologists often deals individually with patients who need help in managing health problems. Solutions can be as varied as establishing a biofeedback program to control pain, initiating individual psychotherapy to control depression, or working with family members to help set up a self-care treatment regimen for a chronically ill patient. In short, then, health psychologists explore an exciting and wide array of issues associated with health, illness, and recovery.

WHY IS THE FIELD OF HEALTH PSYCHOLOGY NEEDED?

A number of trends within medicine, psychology, and the health care system have combined to make the emergence of health psychology inevitable. It is safe to say that health psychology is one of the most important developments within the field of psychology in the last 50 years. Some of the factors that have contributed to its emergence are the following.

Changing Patterns of Illness

The most important factor giving rise to health psychology has been the change in illness patterns that has occurred in the United States and other technologically advanced societies. As Figure 1.1 shows, until the twentieth cen-

tury, the major causes of illness and death in the United States were **acute disorders**—especially tuberculosis, pneumonia, and other infectious diseases. Acute disorders are short-term medical illnesses, often the result of a viral or bacterial invader and usually amenable to cure. Now, however, **chronic illnesses**—especially heart disease, cancer, and diabetes—are the main contributors to disability and death. Chronic illnesses are typically diseases that cannot be cured, but rather only managed by patient and practitioner together. Why have they helped spawn the field of health psychology? First, these are diseases in which psychological and social factors are implicated as causes. Second, because these are illnesses with which people may live for many years, psychological issues arise in connection with them. Thus, the prevalence of chronic illness has increased the number of psychological questions that health psychology is now beginning to answer, as will shortly be seen.

Expanded Health Care Services

Another set of factors that has contributed to the rise of health psychology relates to the expansion of health care services. Health care is the largest service industry in the United States, and it is still growing rapidly. Americans spend over $500 billion annually on health—more than 11% of their total income. As an economic force, then, health care is formidable. The health care industry also has an enormous impact on people. It employs many millions of individuals in a variety of jobs and has direct contact with nearly every individual in the country as a recipient of services. Health is an important value to Americans, since without good health, little else in life can be enjoyed. For all these reasons, then, health has a substantial social and psychological impact on people, an impact that is addressed by health psychologists.

FIGURE 1.1   Death Rates for the 10 Leading Causes of Death per 100,000 Population, United States, 1900 and 1988

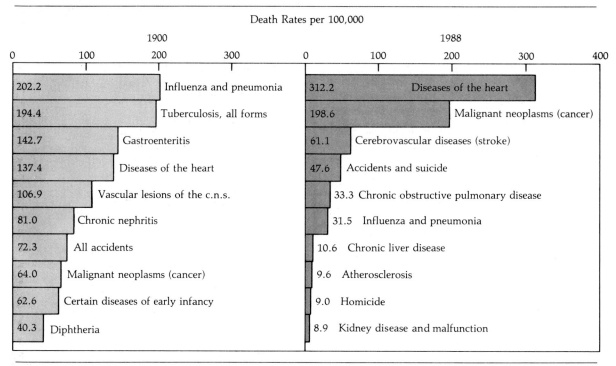

(From Sexton, 1979, and the National Center for Health Statistics, 1988)

Increased Medical Acceptance

Another reason for the development of health psychology is the increasing acceptance of health psychologists within the medical community. Although health psychologists have been employed in health settings for many years, their value is increasingly recognized by physicians and other health care professionals. At one time, the role of health psychologists in health care was largely confined to the task of administering tests and interpreting the test results of individuals who were suspected of being psychologically disturbed. Like psychiatrists in health settings, psychologists usually saw only the "problem patients" who were difficult for medical staff to manage or whose physical complaints were believed to be entirely psychological in origin. Patients who had complaints that could be readily at-

tributed to medical problems and who were easy to manage were considered not to have psychological problems and were therefore thought to be outside the psychologist's province of expertise. Now, however, caregivers are increasingly recognizing that psychological and social factors are always important in health and illness. Accordingly, the role of the psychologist in changing patients' health habits and contributing to treatment is increasingly acknowledged (Nethercut & Piccione, 1984).

Demonstrated Contributions to Health

Health psychology is also an important field because it has already demonstrated that it can make substantial contributions to health. Although these contributions form the substance of later chapters in this book, a few brief examples here can illustrate this point. As previously noted, psychologists have been involved in the development of behavior-change programs to teach people to practice better health habits, including not smoking, getting exercise, eating a balanced diet, practicing safe sex, reducing alcohol consumption, avoiding accidents, and managing stress. Such programs may well contribute to the fact that the incidence of some diseases, especially coronary heart disease, has now actually declined. To take another example, psychologists learned many years ago that preparing patients to undergo unpleasant medical procedures, such as surgery, improves their adjustment to those procedures (Janis, 1958; Johnson, 1984). As a consequence of these studies, many hospitals and other treatment centers now routinely prepare patients for such procedures. Ultimately, if a discipline is to flourish, it must demonstrate a strong track record, and health psychology has done precisely that.

Methodological Contributions

An additional basis for the increasing medical acknowledgment of health psychologists is the important methodological contribution they make to issues of health and illness. Many of the issues that arise in medical settings demand rigorous research investigation. Although physicians and nurses receive some methodological and statistical education, their training may be inadequate to conduct research on the issues they wish to address unless they make research their specialty. The health psychologist can be a valuable member of the research team by providing the methodological and statistical expertise that is the hallmark of good training in psychology.

In this section, we have maintained that health psychology is important because the major health problems of the day, especially the origin and treatment of chronic illness, can increasingly be understood substantially in terms of psychological and social factors; the field of health psychology addresses an issue of paramount economic and social importance, namely, health care; the field has a demonstrated track record of ameliorating important health problems; and health psychology provides methodological and statistical guidance in research. This last function has been an extremely important one and, in this context, it is useful to consider the general model of health and illness that forms the basis for much health psychology research.

THE BIOPSYCHOSOCIAL MODEL IN HEALTH PSYCHOLOGY RESEARCH

The idea that the mind and the body together determine health and illness logically implies a model for studying these issues. This model is called the **biopsychosocial model.** As its name implies, its fundamental assumption is that any health or illness outcome is a consequence of the interplay of biological, psychological, and social factors (Engel, 1977, 1980; Schwartz, 1982). Because the biopsychosocial model figures so prominently in the research examples in this book, we consider it in some detail here.

The Biopsychosocial Model versus the Biomedical Model

Perhaps the best way to understand the biopsychosocial model is to contrast it with the **biomedical model,** which is still the dominant model in medicine today. The biomedical model, which has governed the thinking of most health practitioners for the last 300 years, maintains that all illness can be explained on the basis of aberrant somatic processes, such as biochemical imbalances or neurophysiological abnormalities. The biomedical model assumes that psychological and social processes are largely independent of the disease process.

The biomedical model has several important implications. First, it is a *reductionistic* model. This means that it reduces illness to low-level processes, such as disordered cells and chemical imbalances, rather than recognizing the role of more general social and psychological processes. The biomedical model is also essentially a *single-factor* model of illness. That is, it explains illness in terms of a biological malfunction rather than recognizing that a variety of factors, only some of which are biological, may be responsible for the development of illness. The biomedical model clearly incorporates the assumption of a *mind–body dualism*, maintaining that mind and body are separate entities. Finally, the biomedical model clearly *emphasizes illness over health*. That is, it is focused on aberrations that lead to illness rather than on the conditions that might promote health (Engel, 1977).

There are several obvious problems with the biomedical model. First, it has difficulty

accounting for why a particular set of somatic conditions need not inevitably lead to illness. Why, for example, if six people are exposed to measles, do only three develop the disease? There are psychological and social factors that influence the development of illness, and these are ignored by the biomedical model. Whether a treatment will cure a disease is also substantially affected by psychological and social factors, and this cannot be explained by the biomedical model. Finally, even with the most competent of diagnoses and treatment, the practitioner-patient relationship substantially influences the therapeutic outcome. All these factors are outside the biomedical model; as a consequence, the biomedical model has proven to be scientifically and clinically inadequate in explaining the disease process (Engel, 1977).

Advantages of the Biopsychosocial Model

How, then, does the biopsychosocial model of health and illness overcome the disadvantages of the biomedical model? The biopsychosocial model, as previously noted, maintains that biological, psychological, and social factors are all-important determinants of health and illness. As such, both *macrolevel processes* (such as the existence of social support, the presence of depression) and *microlevel processes* (such as cellular disorders or chemical imbalances) interact to produce a state of health or illness. The biopsychosocial model maintains that *health and illness are caused by multiple factors and produce multiple effects*. The model further maintains that the *mind and body cannot be distinguished* in matters of health and illness because both so clearly influence an individual's state of health. The biopsychosocial model *emphasizes both health and illness* rather than regarding illness as a deviation from some steady state. From this viewpoint, health becomes something that one achieves through attention to biological, psychological, and social needs rather than something that is taken for granted.

In the nineteenth and twentieth centuries, great strides were made in the technical basis of medicine. As a result, physicians looked more and more to the medical laboratory and less to the mind as a way of understanding the onset and progression of illness.

The Biopsychosocial Model as a Tool of Research

How does the biopsychosocial model translate into a research model? At its most basic, the biopsychosocial model maintains that to understand health outcomes, one must consider the operation of biological, psychological, and social processes simultaneously. Therefore, research investigators must try to measure all three classes of variables (see Peterson, 1984). Alternatively, if researchers do not intend to study biological, psychological, or social processes and their interactions in concert, they must understand that any generalization about any one variable assumes a certain set of biological, psychological, and social conditions. For example, the argument that a high level of stress in a person's life produces illness presupposes that the biological conditions necessary to produce illness are present. Similarly, the argument that a particular **pathogen** will produce a particular disease assumes that the social and psychological conditions conducive to the development of illness also exist.

Good biopsychosocial research must also be conducted in the context of state-of-the-art methodology in the relevant fields. Often this will mean that health psychologists must become familiar with methodological and statistical tools from related disciplines. Some, for example, have called for an understanding of biostatistics and epidemiology (Palinkas & Hoiberg, 1982), as well as the more traditional experimental, interview, and survey methodologies associated with conventional research of psychology.

The Interaction of Biopsychosocial Variables

But how do biological, social, and psychological variables interact, particularly if biological factors are microlevel processes and psychological and social factors are macrolevel pro-

cesses? To address this question, researchers have adopted a **systems theory** approach to health and illness. Systems theory maintains that all levels of organization in any entity are linked to each other hierarchically, and that change in any one level will effect change in all the other levels. This means that the microlevel processes (such as cellular changes) are nested within the macrolevel processes (such as societal values), and that changes on the microlevel can have macrolevel effects (and vice versa). Consequently, health, illness, and medical care are all interrelated processes involving interacting changes within the individual and on these various levels. To address these issues impels researchers toward interdisciplinary thinking and collaboration. It also requires researchers to be sophisticated in multivariate approaches to testing problems and to the often complex statistics needed to analyze them (Schwartz, 1982).

Clinical Implications of the Biopsychosocial Model

There are several implications of the biopsychosocial model for clinical practice with patients. First, the biopsychosocial model maintains that the process of diagnosis should always consider the interacting role of biological, psychological, and social factors in assessing an individual's health or illness. Therefore, an interdisciplinary team approach may be the best way to make a diagnosis (Schwartz, 1982). Second, the biopsychosocial model maintains that recommendations for treatment must also examine all three sets of factors. By doing this, it should be possible to target therapy uniquely to a particular individual, consider a person's health status in toto, and make treatment recommendations that can deal with more than one problem simultaneously. Again, a team approach may be most appropriate (Schwartz, 1982). Third, the biopsychosocial model makes explicit the significance of the relationship between patient and practitioner.

An effective patient–practitioner relationship can improve a patient's use of services as well as the efficacy of treatment and the rapidity with which illness is resolved.

In summary, the biopsychosocial model clearly implies that the practitioner must understand the social and psychological factors that contribute to an illness in order to treat it appropriately. In the case of a healthy individual, the biopsychosocial model suggests that one can understand health habits only in their psychological and social contexts. These contexts may maintain a poor health habit, or, with appropriate modifications, can facilitate the development of healthy ones. In the case of the ill individual, biological, psychological, and social factors all contribute to recovery.

To take a specific example, consider a high-powered business executive in his early 40s who has a heart attack. A traditional medical approach to this problem would emphasize control of the problem through the regular administration of drugs. The biopsychosocial approach to this man's problem would also identify his health practices that may have contributed to the early heart attack. Treatment efforts might focus on exercise, rehabilitation, training in techniques for stress management, and a recommendation to a program to help him stop smoking. In addition, such an assessment might look at his social environment, recognize that he spends relatively little time with his wife and children, and recommend that he make positive social interaction with his family an additional goal for his rehabilitation.

HEALTH PSYCHOLOGY: AN OVERVIEW

Having examined some of the general reasons why health psychology is an important developing field and having examined the biopsychosocial model that forms the basis of re-search, we can now turn to a number of specific problems to see how health psychologists have addressed them. In so doing, we provide a brief overview of the forthcoming chapters in this book.

In Part 1, "Introduction to Health Psychology," we provide an overview of the field, covering both its history and the reasons for its development as well as its breadth and limits (Chapter 1). Chapter 2, "The Systems of the Body," provides a brief look at human physiology, so that these systems and processes will be familiar when they are introduced in later chapters.

Part 2, "Health Behavior and Primary Prevention," acknowledges the important role that psychological and social factors play, both in the health habits that predispose people to be healthy or ill and in the environmental context that contributes to the onset of illness.

The two major causes of death in the United States, heart disease and cancer, are both now known to be affected by behavioral factors. It is estimated, for example, that 25% of all cancer deaths could be avoided simply by getting people to stop smoking. Heart disease is affected by a host of behavioral factors, including smoking, diet, and exercise patterns. Dietary factors and stress are implicated in both the onset and management of diabetes. Breast cancer, the main cause of cancer deaths among American women, can be successfully treated if it is detected early, and breast self-examination, an important health habit, is one of the best methods currently available for doing this.

Chapter 3, "Health Promotion and the Practice of Health Behaviors," focuses on the general issue of health promotion and determinants of the practice of health habits. In Chapter 4, "The Modification of Health Behaviors," we examine attitudinal and cognitive-behavioral approaches to the modification of poor health habits. Chapter 5 considers "Health-Enhancing Behaviors," such as exercise, accident prevention, breast and testicular self-examination, weight control, and diet. Chapter 6 considers "Health-Compromising Behaviors," especially alcoholism and smoking. Together, these two chapters illustrate the applications of the concepts from Chapters 3 and 4 regarding the practice of appropriate health behaviors. We will see illustrated repeatedly in these two chapters the principle that health promotion is the personal responsibility of each individual.

In Part 3, "Stress and Coping," we examine the important role that stress plays in good health. Chapter 7, "Stress and the Development of Illness," points out that stress is an important contributing factor in illness. Individuals who do not feel they have the capabilities to meet the demands of their environment more frequently fall prey to illnesses ranging from the simple cold to heart disease. A particularly poignant example of this fact comes from the life of former President Lyndon Johnson. During each of his major election battles, Johnson developed a serious illness for which he had to be hospitalized. The most dramatic such event came after he left public life. As president, Johnson considered his major accomplishment to be the Great Society, a series of social programs, and he once remarked that if the program were abandoned, it would kill him. In fact, on the day that his successor, President Richard Nixon, signed into law the legislation disbanding the Great Society, Lyndon Johnson died (Kearns, 1976). Although few examples are as dramatic as this one, stress is now implicated in the onset of both acute and chronic disease.

In Chapter 8, "Coping with Stress," we consider factors that moderate the stress–illness relationship, making it stronger or weaker. Such factors can include personality variables such as optimism or "hardiness," individual coping patterns such as vigilance or avoidance, and the presence or absence of environmental supports. In this last category, perhaps the most intriguing discovery is the finding that people with strong personal relationships with others are less likely to become ill and tend to recover more quickly when they do get sick. Social support appears to be a buffer against the strains of illness.

In Part 4, "The Patient in the Treatment Setting," we examine the psychological and social factors that prompt people to seek treatment, that determine the nature of their interaction with medical practitioners, and that influence whether or not they follow through on treatment recommendations. Many people never seek treatment for conditions that should get medical attention. Chapter 9, "The Use of Health Services," looks at how people detect and appraise their symptoms and, once they have decided they have a problem, what leads them to seek or neglect treatment. As we shall see, the processes of interpreting disorders and seeking treatment are substantially guided by cultural and social factors, as well as by idiosyncratic responses to particular symptoms or pain. Treatment institutions themselves can affect health by altering patients' beliefs about the quality of care they receive. Overcrowded waiting rooms with long waits, short consultations, and seemingly endless referrals can discourage patients from seeking treatment in the future. Hospitals, with their complex structure and often impersonal care, can inadvertently exacerbate stress in patients who are already disoriented by their illness.

"Patient–Practitioner Interaction," Chapter 10, discusses what is often an important stumbling block in the search for a cure. Communication problems are rampant in the treatment setting, as demonstrated by the fact that as many as two-thirds of all patients are unable to repeat simple facts about their illness and its treatment after meeting with a physician. The consequences of such poor communication can be severe, including nonadherence to treatment and the initiation of malpractice suits.

In Chapter 11, "The Management of Pain and Discomfort," we tackle the question of pain directly. We examine the elusive nature of pain, why it is so heavily psychological, and why it has been so difficult to study. In this context, we examine developments in the physiology of pain, especially the existence of natural pain-combating substances, called endorphins, within the body. We also consider the control of pain and examine the many technologies that have been used to combat it, including biofeedback, relaxation, acupuncture, and hypnosis. In particular, we consider the problems of the patient with chronic pain—one who suffers from continual, seemingly unavoidable distress—and examine the promising new regimens that have been developed to ease such suffering.

Part 5 is entitled "Management of Chronic and Terminal Illness." It was noted earlier that chronic illness raises more issues of psychological interest than does acute illness. Some of these issues arise because chronic illness is often caused at least partly by behavioral factors that can be modified. Another set of psychological issues is raised by the fact that chronic illness is a condition with which people may live for many years; therefore, they must often become actively involved in their own care. This latter set of issues constitutes the content of Chapter 12, "The Management of Chronic Illness." Consider, for example, the situation of a male juvenile diabetic who learns at age 13 that he has this serious, chronic illness. His life will never be the same. It now includes strict diet control, daily injections of insulin, and the lurking fear of a progressively worsening condition, including a high risk of blindness, heart disease, and early death. As might be expected, his reaction to such information might be far from calm. It comes at a time when the young man is just beginning adolescence, struggling to find his own identity, and trying to come to terms with the authorities around him. Not surprisingly, the juvenile diabetic is often a problem patient. He may take his medication irregularly, break his diet, or fail to cooperate in

other ways. This is one kind of serious problem that health psychologists face when working with the chronically ill.

"Psychological Issues in Advancing and Terminal Illness," Chapter 13, presents a strong challenge to the health psychologist. The topic of death is often avoided by medical staff, families, and patients alike, but it is clear that patients need support and guidance in their efforts to die with dignity. One of the more promising recent developments in this area is the creation of hospices, institutions that are designed especially to care for the terminally ill. Hospices seek to create a warm, homelike environment in which dying patients can spend their last weeks free of pain and in the company of family and medical staff who care.

We next turn to the development, management, and treatment of several major specific disorders. We consider both the behavioral lifestyle factors that are associated with their etiology and issues raised by their management. Chapter 14 considers factors that predict the development of coronary heart disease, hypertension, diabetes, and stroke; Chapter 15 addresses psychoimmunology, AIDS, cancer, and arthritis. In this pair of chapters, we see the application of the knowledge from the previous thirteen chapters concerning the practice of health habits, the roles of stress and coping mechanisms in the development of disease, the determinants of use of services, patient–practitioner interaction, adherence to treatment, the management of pain, and the control of chronic and terminal illness.

The last chapter, "Health Psychology: Past, Present, and Future" (Chapter 16), examines anticipated trends in the field of health psychology. Some of these trends stem from changes within the field of medicine. For example, psychologists will need to address questions that arise from our increasingly complex medical technology and its social effects. Other changes are inevitable consequences of social patterns in our country. For example, from the year 2010 on, when members of the post–World War II baby boom start to turn 65, the number of elderly people in our country will be enormous, creating extensive shifts in illness patterns, an unprecedented need for medical services, and other health-related demands such as needs for geriatric health promotion, psychological services, chronic care, and housing. If health psychologists are to fulfill the vital role that such changes open up for them, they must begin to anticipate these trends now.

Other changes are more difficult to anticipate. Additional behavior patterns implicated in the onset of illness may be identified, and psychologists may be asked to promote or modify these behaviors. New techniques for the control of pain and discomfort will be developed, and psychologists will have a role in

their implementation. Potentially adverse effects of institutional health care may increasingly be recognized, with the result that psychologists may be asked to help design new, more psychologically supportive health services. And the role of psychologists in chronic care will no doubt be expanded to address the broad array of rehabilitative needs of chronically ill patients, an increasing challenge now that AIDS patients are living longer.

The field of health psychology is a vibrant, dynamic one, constantly changing in response to the health environment. As a discipline, it has already made important contributions to health, illness prevention, medicine, and medical practice. The only aspect of health psychology that is more exciting than its distinguished past and its impressive present is its promising future.

SUMMARY

1. The interaction of the mind and the body has concerned philosophers and scientists for centuries. Different models of the relationship have predominated at different times in history, but current emphasis is on the inextricable unity of the two, which has spawned the field of health psychology.

2. Health psychology is the field within psychology devoted to understanding psychological influences on how people stay healthy, why they become ill, and how they respond when they do get ill. It focuses on health promotion and maintenance; prevention and treatment of illness; the etiology and correlates of health, illness, and dysfunction; and improvement of the health care system and the formulation of health policy.

3. Related endeavors probing the mind–body relationship exist in sociology, anthropol-

ogy, medicine, and other fields concerned with health and illness. Behavioral medicine is the interdisciplinary field to which all of these disciplines make active contributions.

4. Health psychologists do research, examining the interaction of biological, psychological, and social factors in producing health and illness, and they also help treat patients suffering from a variety of disorders.

5. The developing field of health psychology can be tied to several factors, including the rise of chronic or lifestyle-related illnesses, the expanding role of health care in the economy, the realization that psychological and social factors contribute to health and illness, the demonstrated importance of psychological interventions to improving people's health, and the rigorous methodological contributions of expert researchers.

6. The biomedical model, which dominates medicine, is a reductionistic, single-factor model of illness that regards the mind and body as separate entities and emphasizes illness concerns over health.

7. The biomedical model is currently being replaced by the biopsychosocial model, which regards any health or illness outcome as a complex interplay of biological, psychological, and social factors. The biopsychosocial model recognizes the importance of both macrolevel and microlevel processes in producing health and illness, and considers that the mind and body cannot be distinguished in matters of health and illness. Under this model, health is regarded as an active achievement.

8. The biopsychosocial model guides health psychologists in their research efforts to uncover factors that predict states of health and illness and in their clinical interventions with patients.

KEY TERMS

acute disorders
behavioral health
behavioral medicine
biomedical model
biopsychosocial model
chronic illnesses
conversion hysteria
etiology

health psychology
medical anthropology
medical psychology
medical sociology
mind–body relationship
pathogen
psychosomatic medicine
systems theory

2

THE SYSTEMS OF THE BODY

An understanding of health problems requires a working knowledge of human physiology. This knowledge makes it possible to understand, among others, such issues as how good health habits make illness less likely, how stress affects bodily functioning, how repeated stress can lead to hypertension or coronary artery disease, and how cell growth is radically altered by cancer.

Physiology is the study of the body's functioning. The body is made up of many millions of cells that, grouped together, form organs whose functions overlap to produce the body's systems. In this chapter, we consider the nervous system, the endocrine system, the cardiovascular system, the respiratory system, the digestive system, the renal system, the reproductive system, and the immune system. In each case, we detail how the system functions normally to maintain health while also considering some of the disorders to which the system may be vulnerable.

THE NERVOUS SYSTEM

Overview

The **nervous system** is a complex network of interconnected nerve fibers. Sensory nerve fibers provide input to the brain and spinal cord by carrying signals from sensory receptors; motor nerve fibers provide output from the brain or spinal cord to muscles and other organs, resulting in voluntary and involuntary movement. The nervous system as a whole is made up of the central nervous system and the peripheral nervous system. The central nervous system consists of the brain and the spinal cord. The rest of the nerves in the body, including those that connect to the brain and spinal cord, constitute the peripheral nervous system.

The peripheral nervous system is itself made up of two parts: the somatic nervous system and the autonomic nervous system. The somatic, or voluntary, nervous system connects nerve fibers to voluntary muscles and provides the brain with feedback in the form of sensory information about voluntary movement. The autonomic, or involuntary, nervous system connects the central nervous system with all internal organs over which individuals do not customarily have control.

Regulation of the autonomic nervous system occurs via the **sympathetic nervous system** and the **parasympathetic nervous system.** The sympathetic nervous system mobilizes the body for action, as when a person perceives a threat or experiences stress. The parasympathetic system is responsible for normal vegetative functions (such as digestion) and conservation of energy. The components of the nervous system are summarized in Figure 2.1. We consider several of these in greater detail below.

The Brain

The brain might best be thought of as the command center of the body. It receives afferent (sensory) impulses from the peripheral nerve endings and sends efferent (motor) impulses to the extremities and to internal organs to carry out necessary movement. The brain con-

sists of three sections: the hindbrain, the midbrain, and the forebrain. The parts of the brain are shown in Figure 2.2.

The Hindbrain and the Midbrain   The hindbrain has three main parts: the medulla, the pons, and the cerebellum. The **medulla** is located just above the point where the spinal cord enters the skull. Vital centers in the medulla control the reflex activities of the body. For example, the medulla receives information about the rate at which the heart is contracting and is responsible for speeding up or slowing down the heart rate as required. The medulla also receives sensory information about blood pressure and then, based on this feedback, regulates constriction or dilation of the blood vessels. Sensory information about the levels of carbon dioxide and oxygen in the body also come to the medulla, which, if necessary, sends motor impulses to respiratory muscles to alter the rate of breathing. Thus, the medulla is heavily responsible for the regulation of heart rate, blood pressure, and respiration.

The pons serves as a link between the hindbrain and the midbrain. It also includes a center that helps control respiration. The **cere-**

FIGURE 2.1   The Components of the Nervous System

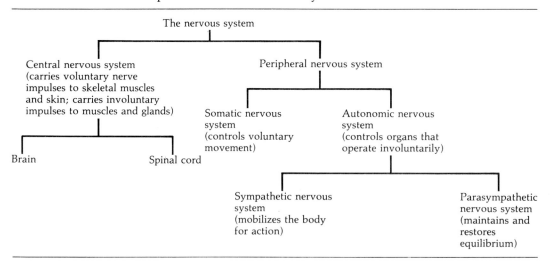

FIGURE 2.2   The Brain

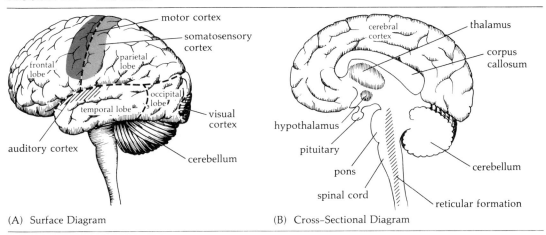

(A) Surface Diagram   (B) Cross–Sectional Diagram

bellum, the second largest part of the brain, is partly responsible for the coordination of voluntary muscle movement, the maintenance of balance and equilibrium, and the maintenance of muscle tone and posture. Therefore damage to this area makes it hard for a person to coordinate muscles effectively; such damage produces lack of muscle tone, tremors, and disturbances in posture or gait.

The midbrain is the major pathway for sensory and motor impulses moving between the forebrain and the hindbrain. It is also responsible for the coordination of visual and auditory reflexes.

The Forebrain   The forebrain has two main sections: the diencephalon and the telencephalon. The diencephalon is composed of the thalamus and the hypothalamus. The **thalamus** is responsible for the recognition of sensory stimuli and the relay of sensory impulses to the appropriate areas in the upper portions of the brain—that is, to the cerebral cortex.

The **hypothalamus** acts as a command post to several centers in the medulla, helping to control cardiac functioning, blood pressure, and respiration. It is also responsible for regulating water balance in the body and for regulating appetites, including hunger and sexual desire. It is an important transition center between the thoughts generated in the cerebral cortex of the brain and their impact on internal organs. Thus, embarrassment, for example, can lead to blushing via instruction from the hypothalamus through the vasomotor center in the medulla to the blood vessels. Or, anxiety may be manifested by the secretion of hydrochloric acid in the stomach via impulses from the hypothalamus. Together with the pituitary gland, the hypothalamus helps regulate the endocrine system, which releases hormones, influencing functioning in target organs throughout the body.

The other portion of the forebrain, the telencephalon, is composed of the two hemispheres (left and right) of the cerebral cortex. This largest portion of the brain, the cerebral cortex, is responsible for intelligence, memory, and personality. The sensory impulses that are conducted from the peripheral areas of the body, up the spinal cord, and through the hindbrain and midbrain are finally received and interpreted in the cerebral cortex. Motor impulses, in turn, pass down from the cortex to the lower portions of the brain and from there to other parts of the body.

The **cerebral cortex** consists of four lobes: frontal, parietal, temporal, and occipital. Each lobe appears to have its own memory storage area or area of association. Through a complex network of associations, the brain is able to re-late current sensations to past ones, giving the cerebral cortex formidable interpretive capabil-ities. In addition to its role in associative mem-ory, each lobe is generally associated with par-ticular functions. The frontal lobe contains the motor cortex, which coordinates voluntary movement. The left part of the motor cortex controls activities of the voluntary muscles on the right side of the body, while the right part of the motor cortex controls voluntary activi-ties on the left side of the body. The parietal lobe contains the somatosensory cortex, in which sensations of touch, pain, temperature, and pressure are registered and interpreted. The temporal lobe contains the cortical areas responsible for auditory and olfactory (smell) impulses, and the occipital lobe contains the visual cortex, which receives visual impulses. Finally, the basal ganglia, four round masses embedded deep in the cerebrum (the main portion of the brain), help make muscle con-tractions orderly, smooth, and purposeful.

The Reticular Activating System and the Limbic System   The last sections of the brain that we will discuss are the reticular ac-tivating system and the limbic system. The reticular activating system runs from the me-dulla through the midbrain into the hypothal-amus. This system is responsible for activating all regions of the brain for incoming sensory impulses. If the reticular activating system is blocked, unconsciousness will result; in cases of severe damage to this system, coma will en-sue. In contrast, stimulation to this area will cause the brain to be hyperalert.

The structures of the limbic system, which border the midline of the brain, play an impor-tant role in emotional experience. It is believed to be made up of three circuits. One includes the amygdala and the hippocampus, and in-volves behaviors essential for self-preserva-tion, which can include aggression. The sec-ond circuit involves the cigulate gyrus, the

septum, and areas in the hypothalamus, and appears to be related to pleasurable emotions, including sexual excitement. The third sys-tem, composed of the anterior portion of the thalamus and some nuclei within the hypo-thalamus, are believed to be important for socially relevant behaviors (MacLean, 1970).

The Spinal Cord

The other portion of the central nervous sys-tem is the **spinal cord,** which transmits sen-sory and motor information to and from the brain and other parts of the body. Sensory in-formation received from peripheral nerve end-ings is conducted up the spinal cord to the brain. Information about motor responses is transmitted down the spinal cord from the brain to the peripheral nerve endings.

Because the spinal cord plays such a critical role in the transmission of sensory and motor impulses, damage to it has severe repercus-sions. Disorders of the spinal cord include po-liomyelitis, paraplegia, and quadriplegia. Po-liomyelitis is a viral disease that attacks the spinal nerves and destroys the cell bodies of motor neurons, so that motor impulses cannot be carried from the spinal cord outward to the effectors. Consequently, the individual is par-alyzed. Paraplegia is paralysis of the lower ex-tremities of the body; it results from an injury to the lower portion of the spinal cord. Quad-riplegia is paralysis of all four extremities and the trunk of the body; it occurs when the up-per portion of the spinal cord is severed. Once the spinal cord has been severed, no motor impulses can descend to tissues below the cut, nor can sensory impulses from the tissues be-low the cut ascend to the brain. As a conse-quence, a person usually loses bladder and bowel control in both paraplegia and quadri-plegia. Moreover, the muscles below the cut area may well lose their tone, becoming weak and flaccid. In Chapter 12, we examine inter-ventions that health psychologists have devel-oped to deal with the physical and psychological rehabilitation of patients with injuries to the spinal cord.

The Autonomic Nervous System

As just noted, the voluntary regulation of muscle tissue by the brain is mediated by the voluntary, or somatic, nervous system. The **autonomic nervous system,** in contrast, controls the activities of the visceral organs, whose functions cannot typically be controlled voluntarily. As previously noted, the autonomic nervous system is divided into the sympathetic and parasympathetic systems.

The sympathetic nervous system prepares the body to respond to emergencies, to strong emotions such as anger or fear, and to strenuous activity. As such, it plays an important role in reactions to stress. Because it is concerned with the mobilization and exertion of energy, it is called a catabolic system. In contrast, the parasympathetic nervous system controls the activities of organs under normal circumstances and acts antagonistically to the sympathetic nervous system. When an emergency has passed, the parasympathetic nervous system restores the body to a normal state. Because it is concerned with the conservation of body energy, it is called an anabolic system.

The functioning of the autonomic nervous system is very similar to that of the somatic nervous system. Sensory autonomic nerves carry impulses from the visceral organs to the medulla and the hypothalamus. These nerves travel alongside the somatic afferent nerves to the brain. The medulla and hypothalamus integrate this sensory information and send out motor impulses, which travel down the spinal cord alongside the somatic efferent nerves to the internal organs.

The Role of Neurotransmitters

The nervous system also has chemicals, called **neurotransmitters,** that regulate nervous sys-

tem functioning. For example, stimulation of the sympathetic nervous system prompts the secretion of large quantities of two neurotransmitters, epinephrine and norepinephrine, together termed the **catecholamines.** These substances enter the bloodstream and are carried throughout the body to promote the activity of sympathetic stimulation. As we shall see, arousal of the sympathetic nervous system and the production and release of catecholamines are critically important in individual responses to stressful circumstances. Moreover, it is believed that repeated arousal of the sympathetic nervous system may have implications for the development of several chronic disorders, such as coronary artery disease and hypertension, which will be considered in greater detail in Chapter 14.

Arousal of the body via the sympathetic nervous system and the release of catecholamines prompt a variety of important bodily changes. Heart rate increases and the heart's capillaries dilate; also, blood vessels constrict, increasing blood pressure. More blood is diverted into muscle tissue. Respiration rate goes up, and the amount of air flowing into the lungs is increased. The functioning of the **metabolic system** (digestion and urination) is generally decreased. The pupils of the eyes dilate, and sweat glands are stimulated to produce more sweat. These changes are familiar to everyone who has experienced a strong emotion such as fear or embarrassment. After the emergency has passed, the cessation of sympathetic stimulation, aided by the parasympathetic system, helps reverse each of these changes. Thus, the heart rate decreases, the heart's capillaries constrict, blood vessels dilate, respiration rate decreases, the metabolic system resumes its activities, and the pupils of the eye contract to their normal state.

Disorders of the Nervous System

Approximately 20 million Americans have some disorder of the nervous system, which together account for 20% of hospitalizations each year and 12% of deaths. The most common forms of neurological dysfunction are epilepsy and Parkinson's disease. Cerebral palsy, multiple sclerosis, Huntington's disease, and myasthenia gravis also affect a substantial number of individuals.

Epilepsy   A disease of the central nervous system affecting more than 4 million people in the U.S., epilepsy is often idiopathic in nature, which means that no specific cause for the symptoms can be identified. Heredity may be a factor in some cases. Symptomatic epilepsy may be traced to such factors as injury during birth, severe injury to the head, infectious disease such as meningitis or encephalitis, and metabolic or nutritional disorders. Epilepsy is marked by seizures, which may range from barely noticeable staring or purposeless motor movements (such as chewing and lip smacking) to violent convulsions accompanied by irregular breathing, drooling, and loss of consciousness. Epilepsy cannot be cured, but it can often be successfully controlled through medication and behavioral interventions designed to manage stress (see Chapters 8 and 12).

Cerebral Palsy   Affecting approximately 750,000 Americans, cerebral palsy is a chronic, nonprogressive disorder marked by lack of muscle control. It stems from brain damage caused by an interruption in the brain's oxygen supply, usually during a difficult childbirth. In older children, a severe accident or physical abuse can produce the condition. There are three main types of cerebral palsy: spastic, athetoid, and ataxic. The person with spastic palsy has difficulty moving and moves very stiffly. Athetoid palsy involves involuntary and uncontrolled muscular movements. The victim of ataxic palsy has a disturbed sense of balance and poor depth perception. Apart from being unable to control motor

functions, sufferers may (but need not) also have seizures, spasms, mental retardation, difficulties of sensation and perception, and problems with sight, hearing, or speech.

Parkinson's Disease   Patients with Parkinson's disease suffer from progressive degeneration of the basal ganglia, the group of nuclei that control smooth motor coordination. Such people show tremors, rigidity, and slowness of movement. Approximately 1 million Americans are affected, usually late in life, and men are more likely than women to develop the disease. Although the cause of Parkinson's is not fully known, depletion of dopamine—a substance in the brain that aids in the transmission of nerve impulses—may be involved. Although Parkinson's patients may be treated with medication, massive doses, which can cause undesirable side effects, are often required for control of the symptoms.

Multiple Sclerosis   Approximately 250,000 Americans are affected by multiple sclerosis, a degenerative disease of certain brain tissues that can cause paralysis as well as, occasionally, blindness, deafness, and mental deterioration. Early symptoms include numbness, double vision, dragging of the feet, loss of bladder or bowel control, speech difficulties, and extreme fatigue. Symptoms may appear and disappear over a period of years; after that, deterioration is steady. The effects of multiple sclerosis are the result of the disintegration of myelin, a fatty membrane that surrounds the nerve fibers and facilitates the conduction of nerve impulses. The causes of multiple sclerosis are unknown, but they may include autoimmunity, in which an individual develops an allergic reaction to his or her own tissues.

Myasthenia Gravis   In the United States, approximately 30,000 people suffer from myasthenia gravis, a muscle disease that stems from a defect in the transmission of nerve impulses to the muscles. Deficiencies in the production of neurotransmitters is one possible cause. Symptoms of myasthenia gravis include drooping eyelids, blurred vision, and difficulty in chewing and swallowing. All the symptoms of the disease are aggravated by activity. Myasthenia gravis used to have a high mortality rate, but this has been substantially reduced by the use of medication. Most patients are now able to recover 80 to 90% of their normal strength.

Huntington's Disease   Another hereditary disorder of the central nervous system, Huntington's disease, is characterized by chronic physical and mental deterioration and stems from genetically based damage to the brain cells. Symptoms include involuntary muscle spasms, loss of motor abilities, personality changes, and other signs of mental disintegration. Because some of the symptoms are similar, Huntington's disease is sometimes mistaken for epilepsy. Approximately 50,000 people carry the gene that can produce the disease. Although no treatment for Huntington's disease has been found, proper medication can alleviate some of the symptoms.

Hundreds of thousands of individuals live with these and other diseases of the nervous system for many years. Therefore they must face many problems of physical as well as emotional and social functioning. We explore many of these difficulties and adjustments in Chapter 12.

THE ENDOCRINE SYSTEM

Overview

The systems of the body are multiple and complex, requiring a high degree of coordination and control. Two systems in particular are chiefly responsible for this coordination. The first is the nervous system, which we have just considered. The second is the **endocrine**

system, diagrammed in Figure 2.3, which complements the nervous system in controlling bodily activities. The endocrine system is made up of a number of ductless, or endocrine, glands, which secrete hormones into the blood. These hormones then stimulate changes in target organs. The endocrine and nervous systems depend on each other, stimulating and inhibiting each other's activities. The nervous system is chiefly responsible for fast-acting, short-duration responses to changes in the body, while the endocrine system mainly governs slow-acting responses of long duration.

The endocrine system is regulated by the hypothalamus and the **pituitary gland,** located at the base of the brain. Regulated by the brain, the pituitary produces a number of hormones that affect other glands and prompts

FIGURE 2.3   The Endocrine System

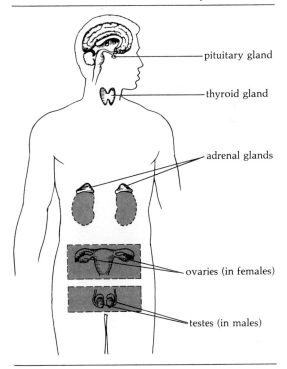

- pituitary gland
- thyroid gland
- adrenal glands
- ovaries (in females)
- testes (in males)

(After Lankford, 1979, p. 232)

the production of other hormones. The anterior pituitary lobe secretes a number of hormones responsible for growth: somatotropic hormone (STH), which regulates bone, muscle, and other organ development; gonadotropic hormones, which control the growth, development, and secretion of the gonads (testes and ovaries); thyrotropic hormone (TSH), which controls the growth, development, and secretion of the thyroid gland; and adrenocorticotropic hormone (ACTH), which controls the growth and secretions of the cortex region of the adrenal glands (to be described below). The posterior pituitary lobe produces oxytocin, which controls contractions during labor, and antidiuretic hormone (ADH), which controls the water-absorbing ability of the kidneys.

The Adrenal Glands

A major component of the endocrine system is the **adrenal glands,** which are important in re-

actions to stress (Figure 2.4). These two small glands are located on top of each of the kidneys. Each adrenal gland consists of an adrenal medulla and an adrenal cortex. The hormones of the adrenal medulla are the neurotransmitters epinephrine and norepinephrine, which we described earlier. The adrenal cortex is stimulated by adrenocorticotropic hormone (ACTH) from the anterior pituitary lobe, and it releases hormones known as steroids. These steroids include mineralocorticoids, glucocorticoids, androgens, and estrogens. Of the mineralocorticoids, aldosterone, which facilitates the absorption of sodium by the kidneys, is especially important. Of the glucocorticoids, cortisol may be important in responses to stress. Cortisol acts to conserve stores of carbohydrates and helps reduce inflammation in case of injury. Cortisol is released in large quantities during times of stress, but exactly how it helps in stress situations is not clear.

To summarize, then, the endocrine system

FIGURE 2.4   Adrenal Gland Activity in Response to Stress

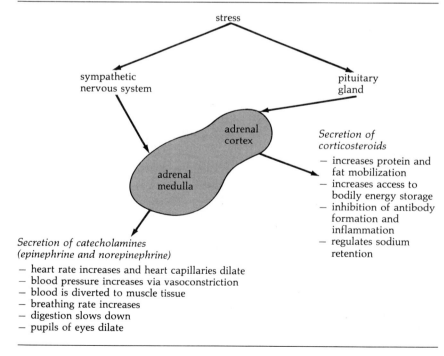

works in coordination with the nervous system to control bodily activities. The hormones released by the endocrine system produce slow-acting changes that augment nervous system functioning. The endocrine system is particularly important in reactions to stress, as Figure 2.4 illustrates. The release of catecholamines by the nervous system mobilizes the organism in response to stress, and the release of corticosteroids via the adrenal cortex is also implicated in the stress response. In addition, the endocrine system helps regulate growth.

Diabetes

Diabetes is a chronic disorder of the endocrine system, in which the body is not able to manufacture or properly use insulin. It is the third most common chronic illness in this country and one of the leading causes of death. It directly causes about 38,000 deaths per year and may contribute to as many as 300,000 deaths annually, including many from heart disease and kidney failure. Currently there are between 5 and 6 million diagnosed diabetics and a suspected 5 to 6 million who are as-yet undiagnosed. Moreover, the number of new cases is increasing at approximately 6% a year, making diabetes an increasingly important and formidable health problem.

Insulin, the hormone secreted by the Islets of Langerhans in the pancreas, controls the conversion of sugar and carbohydrates into energy. In diabetes, either enough insulin is not produced (Type I) or the body is not sufficiently responsive to insulin (Type II). This condition can be caused by viral or bacterial damage to the pancreas and to the insulin-producing cells; there also appears to be a hereditary component to diabetes. In diabetes, there is an excess of glucose in the blood, which is discharged into the urine. This is how diabetes acquired its name: *diabetes mellitus*, the scientific name, literally means "honey passing through," referring to the high sugar content of the urine (American Diabetes Association, 1976).

There are two major types of diabetes, insulin-dependent (or Type I) diabetes and non-insulin-dependent (or Type II) diabetes. Type I diabetes usually develops relatively early in life, earlier for girls than for boys. Type I diabetes is by far the more serious of the two; fortunately, it accounts for only 10% of all diabetes. It is managed primarily through direct injections of insulin; hence the name insulin-dependent diabetes (American Diabetes Association, 1976).

Type II (or non-insulin-dependent) diabetes typically occurs after age 40 and is milder than the insulin-dependent type. In Type II diabetes, insulin is produced by the body, but it is not used properly. The majority of Type II diabetics are obese (60%) and Type II diabetes is more common in women, whites, and individuals of low socioeconomic status (American Diabetes Association, 1976).

The diabetic is vulnerable to two blood sugar problems, hypoglycemia (a blood sugar level that is too low) and hyperglycemia (a blood sugar level that is too high). Hypoglycemia results when a person takes too much insulin, causing an excessive decline in blood sugar. This reaction is typically sudden. The skin turns pale and moist and the individual feels excited, nervous, irritable, and confused. Breathing can be rapid and shallow, and the tongue may have a moist, numb, tingling sensation. The person will be hungry and may be in pain, and there will be little or no sugar in the urine. When signs of possible insulin reaction occur, something containing sugar should be eaten immediately. The reaction of hyperglycemia is more gradual. The skin is flushed and dry, while the individual feels drowsy and has deep labored breathing. Vomiting may be present and the tongue will be dry; feelings of hunger are unlikely, but thirst is common. Abdominal pain may occur, and large amounts of sugar will be detectable in the urine. If a diabetic coma follows, the individual should be taken to a hospital for carefully controlled doses of insulin.

Despite these potential problems, the reason diabetes is such a major health problem stems less from the consequences of insufficient insulin production per se than from complications that may develop. Diabetes is associated with a thickening of the arteries due to the buildup of wastes in the blood. As a consequence, diabetic patients show high rates of coronary heart disease. Diabetes is also the leading cause of blindness among adults, and it accounts for 50% of all the patients who require renal dialysis for kidney failure. Diabetes may also be associated with nervous system damage, including pain and loss of sensation. In severe cases, amputation of the extremities, such as toes and feet, is often required. As a consequence of these manifold complications, diabetics have a considerably shorter life expectancy than do nondiabetic individuals (American Diabetes Association, 1976). In Chapter 14, we consider diabetes and the issues associated with its management more fully.

THE CARDIOVASCULAR SYSTEM

Overview

The heart, blood vessels, and blood form the **cardiovascular system,** which acts as the transport system of the body. Blood carries oxygen from the lungs to the tissues and carbon dioxide from the tissues to the lungs so that it may be excreted as expired air. It also carries nutrients from the digestive tract to the individual cells so that the cells may extract the materials they need for growth and energy. The blood carries waste products from the cells to the kidneys from which the waste is excreted in the urine. It also carries hormones from the endocrine glands to other organs of the body and transports heat to the surface of the skin to control body temperature.

Several types of blood vessels conduct blood throughout the body. The arteries carry blood from the heart to other organs and tissues, where oxygen and nutrients are withdrawn. The arterioles are tiny branches of the arteries, and the capillaries are smaller vessels that branch off from the arteries and carry blood to individual cells. Veins return the blood to the heart after the oxygen has been used up. Taken together, these vessels control peripheral circulation, dilating or constricting in response to a variety of bodily events.

The Heart

The heart functions as a pump, and its pumping action causes the blood to circulate throughout the body. The left side of the heart, consisting of the left atrium and left ventricle, takes in heavily oxygenated blood from the lungs and pumps it out into the aorta (the major artery leaving the heart) from which the blood passes into the smaller vessels (the arteries, arterioles, and capillaries) to reach the cell tissues. As the blood exchanges its oxygen and nutrients for the waste materials of the cells, it changes in color from bright red to dark blue. The blood is then returned to the right side of the heart (right atrium and right ventricle), which pumps it back to the lungs via the pulmonary artery. Once oxygenated, it returns to the left side of the heart through the pulmonary veins. The anatomy and functioning of the heart are pictured in Figure 2.5.

The heart performs these functions through regular rhythmic phases of contraction and relaxation known as the cardiac cycle. There are two phases in the cardiac cycle, systole and diastole. During systole, blood is pumped out of the heart, and blood pressure in the blood vessels increases. As the muscle relaxes during diastole, blood pressure drops and blood is taken into the heart. A number of factors influence the rate at which the heart contracts and relaxes. During exercise, emotional excitement, or stress, for example, the heart speeds

FIGURE 2.5 The Heart

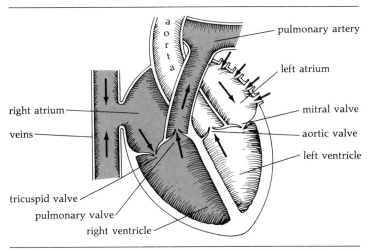

(Arrows indicate flow of blood in and out of the heart.)

up and the cardiac cycle is completed in a shorter time. Most of this speedup comes out of the diastolic or rest period, so that a chronically rapid heart rate reduces overall time for rest. Consequently, a chronically or excessively rapid heart rate can decrease the heart's strength, which may reduce the volume of blood that is pumped. The heart rate is also regulated by the amount of blood flowing into the veins. The larger the quantity of blood available, the harder the heart will have to pump. A lower supply of blood, on the other hand, leads to a weaker and less frequent heartbeat.

The flow of blood in and out of the heart is controlled by valves at the inlet and outlet of each ventricle. These heart valves ensure that blood flows in one direction only. The sound that one hears when listening to the heart is the sound of these valves closing. The first heart sound is the sound of the atrioventricular valves closing. These valves (the tricuspid valve and the mitral valve) control blood flow between the atria and the ventricles; their closing marks the beginning of systole. The second heart sound is the closing of the aortic and pulmonary (semilunar) valves. These valves lead from the ventricles into the arteries; their closing marks the end of systole and the beginning of diastole. These heart sounds, then, make it possible to time the cardiac cycle to determine how rapidly or slowly blood is being pumped in and out of the heart. So-called heart murmurs occur when a valve fails to open or close completely; this condition acts as an obstruction to blood flow.

Diseases of the Heart

The heart and its functioning are subject to a number of disorders, some due to infection and disease and others stemming from congenital defects (that is, defects present at birth). Still other disorders are due to damage acquired over the course of life that produces cumulative cardiac injury.

Atherosclerosis and Other Disorders of the Blood Vessels   The major cause of heart disease in this country is atherosclerosis, a problem that becomes worse with age. **Atherosclerosis** is caused by deposits of cholesterol and other substances on the arterial walls, which then form plaques that narrow the arteries. The presence of atherosclerotic plaques reduces the flow of blood through the arteries and interferes with the passage of nutrients from the capillaries into the cells—a process that can lead to substantial tissue damage. As we shall see, damaged arterial walls are also potential sites for the formation of blood clots, which in themselves can completely obstruct a vessel and cut off the flow of blood. Atherosclerosis is a disease of lifestyle, as we see in Chapter 14. It is associated with a number of poor health habits such as smoking and a high-fat diet. Moreover, it is a very common health problem. These two factors make it of paramount interest to health psychologists, and explain why there is such an emphasis in the field on changing these poor health behaviors.

Atherosclerosis is associated with two primary clinical manifestations: (1) **angina pectoris,** or chest pain, which occurs because the muscle tissue of the heart must continue its activity without a sufficient supply of oxygen or adequate removal of carbon dioxide and other waste products, and (2) myocardial infarction (MI), which is most likely to occur when a clot has developed in a coronary vessel and blocks the flow of blood to the heart. A **myocardial infarction,** otherwise known as a heart attack, can cause death if the heart stops functioning.

Other disorders of the blood vessels include aneurysms, phlebitis, varicose veins, and arteriosclerosis. An aneurysm is a bulge in a section of the wall of an artery or vein; it is the reaction of a weak region to pressure. When an aneurysm ruptures, it can produce instantaneous death from internal hemorrhaging and loss of blood pressure. Aneurysms may be caused by arteriosclerosis and syphilis. Phlebitis is an inflammation of a vein wall; it may be accompanied by water retention and pain. The condition typically results from an infection surrounding the vein, from varicose veins, from pregnancy-related bodily changes, or from the pressure of a tumor on the vein. The chief threat posed by phlebitis is that it

can encourage the production of blood clots that then block circulation. If the clot (or thrombus) breaks loose, becoming an embolus, it may block one of the important blood vessels.

Varicose veins are superficial veins that have become dilated or swollen. Typically, veins in the lower extremities of the body are most susceptible because they are subjected to a tremendous amount of pressure from the force of gravity. As noted above, varicose veins may themselves produce phlebitis.

Arteriosclerosis (or hardening of the arteries) results when calcium, salts, and scar tissue react with the elastic tissue of the arteries. The consequence is to decrease the elasticity of the arteries, making them rigid and hard. Blood pressure then increases because the arteries cannot dilate and constrict to help blood move, and hypertension (high blood pressure) may result.

Rheumatic Fever Rheumatic fever is a bacterial infection that originates in the connective tissue and can spread to the heart, possibly affecting the functioning of the heart valves. The flaps of the valves may be changed into rigid, thickened structures that interfere with the flow of blood between the atrium and the ventricle. Endocarditis is an infection that results in inflammation of the heart muscle tissue. People with rheumatic fever, or with congenital heart disease, are particularly vulnerable to endocarditis, which is caused by staphylococcus or streptococcus organisms.

Blood Pressure

Blood pressure is the force that blood exerts against the blood vessel walls. During systole, the force on the blood vessel walls is greatest; during diastole, it falls to its lowest point. The measurement of blood pressure consists of a ratio of these two pressures. Blood pressure is influenced by several factors, the first of which is cardiac output. Pressure against the arterial walls will be greater as the volume of blood flow increases. A second factor influencing blood pressure is peripheral resistance, or the resistance to blood flow in the small arteries of the body (arterioles). Peripheral resistance is influenced by the viscosity (thickness) of the blood and the structure of the arterial walls. The viscosity of blood depends on the number of red blood cells and the amount of plasma the blood contains. Highly viscous blood produces higher blood pressure. In addition, blood pressure is influenced by the structure of the arterial walls: If the walls have been damaged, if they are clogged by deposits of waste, or if they have lost their elasticity, blood pressure will be higher.

Hypertension is the consequence of too high a cardiac output or too high a peripheral resistance. There are several methods of treating hypertension. If cardiac output is too high, a chemical called a beta-blocking agent can be used to block sympathetic activity. This agent will reduce the heart rate and the force of ventricular contractions. Alternatively, diuretics (which cause a person to excrete more than the usual volume of water) can be used to reduce blood volume; this step, in turn, will reduce cardiac output. We consider the psychosocial issues involved in the management and treatment of hypertension in Chapter 14.

Blood

An adult's body contains approximately 5 liters of blood. Blood consists of plasma and cells. Plasma, the fluid portion of blood, occupies approximately 55% of the blood volume. The blood cells are suspended in the plasma, which consists of plasma proteins and plasma electrolytes (salts) plus the substances that are being transported by the blood (oxygen and nutrients or carbon dioxide and waste materials). The remaining 45% of blood volume is made up of cells.

Blood cells are manufactured in the bone marrow, in the hollow cavities of bones. The bone marrow contains five types of blood-forming cells: myeloblasts and monoblasts, both of which produce white blood cells; lymphoblasts, which produce lymphocytes; erythroblasts, which produce red blood cells; and megakaryocytes, which produce platelets. Each of these types of blood cells has an important function.

White blood cells play an important role in healing by absorbing and removing foreign substances from the body. The white blood cells produced by myeloblasts contain granules that secrete digestive enzymes; these, in turn, are able to dissolve foreign particles. White cells produced by both myeloblasts and monoblasts engulf bacteria and foreign particles, converting them into a form conducive to excretion. Lymphocytes also play an important role in combating foreign substances. They produce antibodies, agents that destroy foreign substances through the antigen-antibody reaction. Together, then, these groups of cells play an important role in fighting infection and disease. We shall consider them more fully in our discussion of the immune system. Red blood cells are chiefly important because they contain hemoglobin, which is needed to carry oxygen and carbon dioxide throughout the body. **Platelets** serve several important functions. They are able to clump together to block small holes that develop in blood vessels, and they also play an important role in blood clotting. When an injury occurs and tissues are damaged, platelets help form thromboplastin, which, in turn, acts on a substance in the plasma known as fibrinogen and changes it to fibrin. The formation of fibrin produces blood clots.

Blood flow is also responsible for the regulation of body temperature. When the body temperature is too high, skin blood vessels dilate and blood is sent to the skin, so that heat will be lost. When the body temperature is too low, skin blood vessels constrict and blood is kept away from the skin, so that heat will be conserved and body temperature maintained. Alterations in skin blood flow are caused partly by the direct action of heat on skin blood vessels and partly by the temperature-regulating mechanism located in the hypothalamus, which alters the sympathetic impact on the skin blood vessels. Blood flow to the skin is also regulated by the catecholamines, epinephrine and norepinephrine. Norepinephrine generally constricts blood vessels (vasoconstriction), whereas epinephrine constricts skin blood vessels while dilating muscle blood vessels. These changes, in turn, increase the force of the heart's contractions.

Blood-Related Disorders

Blood is vulnerable to a number of disorders.

Disorders of White Cell Production   Some blood disorders affect the production of white blood cells; they include leukemia, leukopenia, and leukocytosis. Leukemia is a malignant disease of the bone marrow. It causes the production of an excessive number of white blood cells, thus overloading the blood plasma and reducing the number of red blood cells that can circulate in the plasma. In the short term, anemia (a shortage of red blood cells) will result. In the long term, if left untreated, leukemia will cause death.

Leukopenia is a deficiency of white blood cells; it may accompany diseases like tuberculosis, measles, and viral pneumonia. Leukopenia leaves an individual susceptible to diseases because it reduces the number of white blood cells available to combat infection. Leukocytosis is an excessive number of white blood cells. It is a response to many infections such as leukemia, appendicitis, and infectious mononucleosis. Infection stimulates the body to overproduce these infection-combating cells.

Disorders of Red Cell Production   Other blood disorders involve the production of red blood cells. One of the most common is ane-

mia, a condition in which the number of red blood cells or amount of hemoglobin is below normal. A temporary anemic condition experienced by many women is a consequence of menstruation; through loss of blood, much vital iron (essential for the production of hemoglobin) is lost. Iron supplements must sometimes be taken to offset this problem. Other forms of anemia, including aplastic anemia, may occur because the bone marrow is unable to produce a sufficient number of red blood cells. The result is a decrease in the blood's transport capabilities, causing tissues to receive too little oxygen and to be left with too much carbon dioxide. When it is not checked, anemia can cause permanent damage to the nervous system and produce chronic weakness. In contrast, erythrocytosis is characterized by an excess of red blood cells. It can result from a lack of oxygen in the tissues or as a secondary manifestation of other diseases. Erythrocytosis increases the viscosity of the blood and reduces the rate of blood flow.

Sickle-cell anemia is another disease of the red blood cells. Most common among blacks, it is a genetically transmitted inability to produce normal red blood cells. These cells are sickle-shaped instead of flattened spheres, and they contain abnormal hemoglobin protein molecules. They are vulnerable to rupture, leaving the individual susceptible to anemia. The sickle cell appears to be a genetic adaptation promoting resistance to malaria among African blacks. Unfortunately, although these cells are effective in the short term against malaria, the long-term implications are life-threatening (Diamond, 1989).

Clotting Disorders   A third group of blood disorders involves clotting dysfunctions. Hemophilia affects individuals who are unable to produce thromboplastin and, accordingly, fibrin. Therefore their blood cannot clot naturally in response to injury and they may bleed to death unless they receive medication.

As noted earlier, clots (or thromboses) may sometimes develop in the blood vessels. This is most likely to occur if arterial or venous walls have been damaged or roughened due to the buildup of cholesterol. Platelets then adhere to the roughened area, leading to the formation of a clot. A clot formed in this manner may have very serious consequences if it occurs in the blood vessels leading to the heart (coronary thrombosis) or brain (cerebral thrombosis) because it will block the vital flow of blood to these organs. When a clot occurs in a vein, it may become detached and form an embolus that may finally become lodged in the blood vessels to the lungs, causing pulmonary obstruction. Death is a likely consequence of all of these conditions.

THE RESPIRATORY SYSTEM

Overview: The Structure and Functions of the Respiratory System

Respiration, or breathing, has three main functions: to take in oxygen, to excrete carbon dioxide, and to regulate the relative composition of the blood. The body needs oxygen to metabolize food. During the process of metab-olism, oxygen combines with carbon atoms in food, producing carbon dioxide (CO_2). The respiratory system brings in air, including oxygen, through inspiration; it eliminates carbon dioxide through expiration.

The **respiratory system** involves a number of organs, including the nose, mouth, pharynx, trachea, diaphragm, abdominal muscles, and lungs. Air is inhaled through the nose and mouth and then passes through the pharynx and larynx to the trachea. The trachea, a muscular tube extending downward from the larynx, divides at its lower end into two branches called the primary bronchi. Each bronchus enters a lung, where it then subdivides into secondary bronchi, still-smaller bronchioles, and finally microscopic alveolar ducts, which contain many tiny, clustered sacs called alveoli. The alveoli and the capillaries are responsible for the exchange of oxygen and carbon dioxide. A diagram of the respiratory system appears in Figure 2.6.

The inspiration of air is an active process, brought about by the contraction of muscles. Inspiration causes the lungs to expand inside the thorax (the chest wall). Expiration, in con-

FIGURE 2.6   The Respiratory System

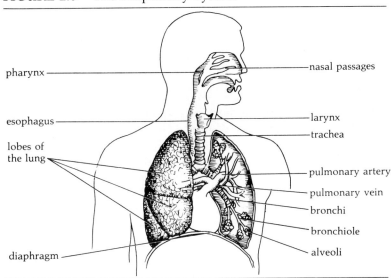

pharynx

esophagus

lobes of
the lung

diaphragm

nasal passages

larynx

trachea

pulmonary artery

pulmonary vein

bronchi

bronchiole

alveoli

(After Lankford, 1979, p. 467)

trast, is a passive function, brought about by the relaxation of the lungs, which reduces the volume of the lungs within the thorax. The lungs fill most of the space within the thorax, called the thoracic cavity, and are very elastic, depending on the thoracic walls for support. Therefore, if air were to get into the space between the thoracic wall and the lungs, one or both lungs would collapse.

Respiratory movements are controlled by a respiratory center in the medulla of the brain. The functions of this center depend partly on the chemical composition of the blood. For example, if the blood's carbon dioxide level rises too high, the respiratory center will be stimulated and respiration will be increased. If the carbon dioxide level falls too low, the respiratory center will slow down until the carbon dioxide level is back to normal.

The respiratory system is also responsible for coughing. A large amount of dust and other foreign material is inhaled with every breath. Some of these substances are trapped in the mucus of the nose and the air passages and are then conducted back toward the throat, where they are swallowed. When a large amount of mucus collects in the large airways, it is removed by coughing (a forced expiratory effort).

Disorders of the Respiratory System

Asphyxia, Anoxia, and Hyperventilation   Of the various potential disorders of the respiratory system, there are several—including asphyxia, anoxia, and hyperventilation—that have little significance when they are short-lived. When they occur on a long-term basis, however, these same disorders can have severe effects.

Asphyxia, a condition of oxygen lack and carbon dioxide excess, can occur when there is a respiratory obstruction, when breathing occurs in a confined space so that expired air is reinhaled, or when respiration is insufficient

for the body's needs. Asphyxia produces increased respiratory activity.

Anoxia, a shortage of oxygen alone, is more serious. People suffering from anoxia may rapidly become disoriented, lose all sense of danger, and pass into a coma without increasing their breathing. This is a danger to which many test pilots are exposed when they take their planes to very high altitudes. Therefore they are carefully trained to be alert to the signs of anoxia so that they can take immediate corrective steps.

Another disruption of the carbon dioxide–oxygen balance results from hyperventilation. During periods of intense emotional excitement, people often breathe deeply, reducing the carbon dioxide content of the blood. Since carbon dioxide is a vasodilator (that is, it dilates the blood vessels), a consequence of hyperventilation is constriction of blood vessels and reduced blood flow to the brain. As a result, the individual may experience impaired vision, difficulty in thinking clearly, and dizziness.

Severe problems occur when a person stops breathing and becomes unconscious. If artificial respiration is not initiated within 2 minutes, brain damage and even death may result.

Hay Fever and Asthma   Hay fever is a seasonal allergic reaction to foreign bodies—including pollens, dust, and other airborne allergens—that enter the lungs. These irritants prompt the body to produce substances called histamines, which cause the capillaries of the lungs to become inflamed and to release large amounts of fluid. The result is violent sneezing.

Asthma is a somewhat more severe allergic reaction that can be caused by a variety of foreign substances, including dust, dog or cat dander, pollens, and fungi. An asthma attack can also be touched off by emotional stress or exercise. These attacks may sometimes be so serious that they produce bronchial spasms, hyperventilation, and excessive secretion of mucus. This may then obstruct the bronchioles, reducing the supply of oxygen and increasing the amount of carbon dioxide.

Viral Infections   The respiratory system is vulnerable to a number of infections and chronic disorders. Perhaps the most familiar of these is the common cold, a viral infection of the upper and sometimes the lower respiratory tract. The infection that results causes discomfort, congestion, and excessive secretion of mucus. The incubation period for a cold—that is, the time between exposure to the virus and onset of symptoms—is 12 to 72 hours, and the typical duration of a cold is a few days. Secondary bacterial infections may complicate the illness. These occur because the primary viral infection causes inflammation of the mucous membranes, reducing their ability to prevent secondary infection.

A somewhat more serious viral infection of the respiratory system is influenza, which can occur in epidemic form. Flu viruses attack the lining of the respiratory tract, killing healthy cells. Fever and inflammation of the respiratory tract may result. A common complication is a secondary bacterial infection such as pneumonia.

A third infection, bronchitis, is an inflammation of the mucosal membrane inside the bronchi of the lungs. Large amounts of mucus are produced in bronchitis, leading to persistent coughing.

Bacterial Infections   The respiratory system is also vulnerable to bacterial attack by, for example, strep throat, whooping cough, and diphtheria. Strep throat, an infection of the throat and soft palate, is characterized by edema (swelling) and reddening. Whooping cough invades the upper respiratory tract and moves down to the trachea and bronchi. The associated bacterial growth leads to the production of a viscous fluid, which the body attempts to expel through violent coughing. Although diphtheria is an infection of the upper respiratory tract, its bacterial organisms secrete a toxic substance that is absorbed by the blood and is thus circulated throughout the body. Therefore this disease can damage nerves, cardiac muscle, kidneys, and the adrenal cortex.

For the most part, strep throat, whooping cough, and diphtheria do not cause permanent damage to the upper respiratory tract. Their main danger is the possibility of secondary infection, which results from lowered resistance. However, these bacterial infections can cause more permanent damage to other tissues, including heart tissue.

Pneumonia and Emphysema   The respiratory system is also vulnerable to several lung diseases. Chief among these is pneumonia, of which there are two main types. Lobar pneumonia is a primary infection of the entire lobe of a lung. The alveoli become inflamed, and normal oxygen–carbon dioxide exchange between the blood and alveoli can be disrupted. Spread of infection to other organs is also likely. Bronchial pneumonia, which is confined to the bronchi, is typically a secondary infection that may result from complications of other disorders. It is not as serious as lobar pneumonia.

Pulmonary emphysema involves a persistent obstruction of the flow of air. It occurs when the alveoli become dilated, atrophied, and thin, so that they lose their elasticity and cannot constrict during exhalation. As a result, exhalation becomes difficult and forced, so that carbon dioxide is not readily eliminated. Emphysema is caused by a variety of factors, including asthma and long-term smoking.

Tuberculosis and Pleurisy   Tuberculosis is an infectious disease caused by bacteria that invade lung tissue. When the invading bacilli are surrounded by macrophages (white blood cells of a particular type), they form a clump called a tubercle, which is the typical manifestation of this disease. Eventually, through a process called caseation, the center of the tubercle turns into a cheesy mass, which can produce cavities in the lung. Such cavities, in turn, can give rise to permanent scar tissue, causing chronic difficulties in oxygen and carbon dioxide exchange between the blood and the alveoli.

Pleurisy is an inflammation of the pleura, the membrane that surrounds the organs in the thoracic cavity. The inflammation, which produces a sticky fluid, is usually a consequence of pneumonia or tuberculosis. It can be extremely painful.

Lung Cancer   Lung cancer, or carcinoma of the lung, is an increasingly common disease. It is caused by smoking and other factors as yet unknown, including possible environmental carcinogens (air pollution) or cancer-causing substances encountered in the workplace (such as asbestos). The affected cells in the lungs begin to divide in a rapid and unrestricted manner, producing a tumor. Malignant cells grow faster than healthy cells; they crowd the healthy cells out and rob them of nutrients, causing them to die. The tumor then spreads into surrounding tissue.

Alleviating Respiratory Diseases

A number of the diseases of the respiratory system we have just described are tied directly to health problems that can be addressed by health psychologists. For example, smoking is a major health problem that is implicated in both pulmonary emphysema and lung cancer, and the spread of tuberculosis can be reduced by encouraging people to obtain regular chest x-rays. Faulty methods of infection control, dangerous substances in the workplace, and air pollution are also factors that contribute to the incidence of respiratory problems. As we see in Chapters 3 to 6, health psychologists

have addressed a variety of these problems. In addition, some of the respiratory disorders we have considered are chronic conditions with which an individual may live for some time. Consequently, issues of long-term physical, vocational, social, and psychological rehabilitation become crucial, and we cover these issues as well in Chapters 12, 14, and 15.

THE DIGESTIVE SYSTEM AND THE METABOLISM OF FOOD

Overview

Food, essential for survival, is converted by the process of metabolism into heat and energy, and it also supplies nutrients for growth and the repair of tissues. But before food can be used by cells, it must be changed into a form suitable for absorption into the blood. This conversion process is called *digestion.*

Digestion begins in the mouth, where enzymes in the saliva begin to break food down. Food then passes from the mouth down the esophagus to the stomach. From the stomach it proceeds through the duodenum, jejunum, and ileum of the small intestine. Food that is not absorbed passes on through the large intestine to the rectum and the anus, from which it is excreted. At each phase along the way, digestion is brought about by protein substances known as enzymes, which are named for the substance on which they act. Thus, for example, the enzyme in the small intestine that acts on sucrose (sugar) is named sucrase, and the one that acts on lactose (milk) is called lactase.

The Functioning of the Digestive System

Food is first lubricated by saliva in the mouth, where it forms a soft, rounded lump called a bolus. It passes through the esophagus by means of peristalsis, a unidirectional muscular movement toward the stomach. The stomach produces various gastric secretions, including pepsin and hydrochloric acid, to further the digestive process. Gastric secretions are controlled by the vagus nerve. The sight or even the thought of food starts the flow of gastric juices.

As food progresses from the stomach to the duodenum, the pancreas becomes involved in the digestive process. The pancreatic juices, which are secreted into the duodenum, contain several enzymes that break down proteins, carbohydrates, and fats. A critical function of the pancreas is the production of the hormone insulin, which is important because it facilitates the entry of glucose into the bodily tissues. The liver also plays an important role in metabolism. It produces bile, which enters the duodenum and helps break down fats. The bile is stored in the gallbladder and is secreted into the duodenum as it is needed.

Most metabolic products are water-soluble and can be transported easily in the blood. However, other substances are not soluble in water and therefore must be transported in the blood plasma as complex substances combined with plasma protein. Known as lipids, these substances include fats, cholesterol, and lecithin. An excess of lipids in the blood is called hyperlipidemia, a condition common in diabetes, some kidney diseases, hyperthyroidism, and alcoholism. It is also a causal factor in heart disease (see Chapter 14).

The absorption of food takes place primarily in the small intestine, which produces a variety of enzymes that complete the breakdown of proteins to amino acids. The motility of the small intestine is under the control of the sympathetic and parasympathetic nervous systems. Parasympathetic activity speeds up metabolism, whereas sympathetic nervous system activity reduces it.

Food then passes into the large intestine (whose successive segments are known as the cecum and the ascending, transverse, descending, and sigmoid colon), which acts largely as a storage organ for the accumulation of food residue and helps in the reabsorption of water. The entry of feces into the rectum then brings about the urge to defecate, or expel the solid waste from the body via the anus. The organs involved in the metabolism of food are pictured in Figure 2.7.

Disorders of the Digestive System

The digestive system is susceptible to a number of disorders, some of which are only mildly uncomfortable and temporary and others of which are more serious and chronic.

Gastroenteritis, Diarrhea, and Dysentery Gastroenteritis is an inflammation of the lining of the stomach and small intestine. It may be caused by such factors as excessive amounts of food or drink, contaminated food or water, or food poisoning. Symptoms appear approximately 2 to 4 hours after the ingestion of food;

FIGURE 2.7 The Digestive System

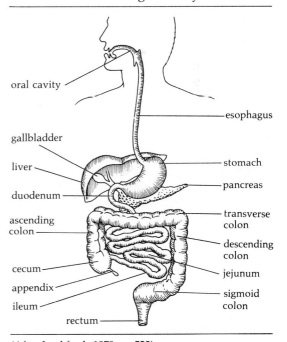

(After Lankford, 1979, p. 523)

they include vomiting, diarrhea, abdominal cramps, and nausea. Diarrhea, characterized by watery and frequent bowel movements, occurs when the lining of the small and large intestines cannot properly absorb water or digested food. Chronic diarrhea can result in serious disturbances of fluid and electrolyte (sodium, potassium, magnesium, calcium) balance. Dysentery is similar to diarrhea except that mucus, pus, and blood are also excreted. It may be caused by a protozoan that attacks the large intestine (amoebic dysentery) or by a bacterial organism.

Peptic Ulcer   A peptic ulcer is an open sore in the lining of the stomach or the duodenum. It results from the hypersecretion of hydrochloric acid and occurs when pepsin, a protein-digesting enzyme secreted in the stomach, digests a portion of the stomach wall or duodenum. The causes of ulcers are not fully known. As we shall see, there is some speculation that ulcers may result from particular psychological problems, although the evidence on this point is equivocal. Ulcers do seem to develop in people between the ages of 20 and 40 who are experiencing considerable tension.

Diseases of the Gallbladder   The gallbladder is susceptible to several disorders. One is gallstones, made up of a combination of cholesterol, calcium, bilirubin, and inorganic salts. When gallstones move into the duct of the gallbladder, they may cause painful spasms; such stones must often be removed surgically. Infection and inflammation of the gallbladder is called cholecystitis and may be a precondition for gallstones.

Appendicitis, a common condition, occurs when wastes and bacteria accumulate in the appendix. If the small opening of the appendix becomes obstructed, bacteria can easily proliferate. Soon this condition gives rise to pain, increased peristalsis, and nausea. If the appendix ruptures and the bacteria are re-

leased into the abdominal cavity or peritoneum, they can cause further infection (peritonitis) or even death.

Hepatitis   Inflammation of the liver, or hepatitis, damages the liver, preventing it from doing its normal job. When the liver is inflamed, bilirubin, a product of the breakdown of hemoglobin, cannot easily pass into the bile ducts. It remains in the blood, causing a yellowing condition of the skin known as jaundice. There are two types of hepatitis. The infectious type, caused by viruses, is transmitted through foods and liquids. It can be spread by poorly cooked seafood or through unsanitary preparation or storage of food. Serum hepatitis, the second type, is also caused by a virus and is transmitted by transfusion of infected blood or by use of improperly sterilized needles and syringes. It is one of the risks of drug use.

The digestive system, then, is responsible for the conversion of food into heat and energy, which enables cells to grow and repair themselves. But the digestive system is also vulnerable to many disorders. Some of these are a function of poor eating habits, which we cover in the next chapters. Others may be due to genetic or acquired abnormalities in metabolic processes.

THE RENAL SYSTEM

Overview

The **renal system**—consisting of the kidneys, ureters, urinary bladder, and urethra—is also critically important in metabolism. The kidneys are chiefly responsible for the regulation of the bodily fluids; their principal function is to produce urine. The ureters contain smooth muscle tissue that contracts, causing peristaltic waves to move urine to the bladder, a muscular bag that acts as a reservoir for urine. The urethra then conducts urine from the bladder out of the body. The anatomy of the renal system is pictured in Figure 2.8.

Urine contains surplus water, surplus electrolytes, waste products from the metabolism of food, and surplus acids or alkalis. By carrying these products out of the body, it maintains water balance, electrolyte balance, and blood pH. Of the electrolytes, sodium and potassium are the most important because they are involved in the normal chemical reactions of the body, muscular contractions, and the conduction of nerve impulses. Thus, an important function of the kidneys is to maintain an adequate balance of sodium and potassium ions. In the case of certain diseases, the urine will also contain abnormal amounts of some constituents; therefore, urinalysis offers important diagnostic clues to many disorders. For example, an excess of glucose may indicate diabetes, an excess of red blood cells may indicate a kidney disorder, and so on. This is one of the reasons why a medical checkup often includes a urinalysis.

As noted above, one of the chief functions of the kidneys is to control the water balance in the body. For example, on a hot day when one has been active and has perspired pro-fusely, relatively little urine will be produced so that the body may retain more water. This is because much water has already been lost through the skin. On the other hand, on a cold day when one is relatively inactive and during which a good deal of liquid has been consumed, urine output will be higher so as to prevent overhydration.

To summarize, then, the urinary system regulates bodily fluids by removing surplus water, surplus electrolytes, and the waste products generated by the metabolism of food. Unfortunately, a number of diseases of the urinary system can interfere with these vital functions. Several of these are chronic conditions, and the conditions themselves as well as the technologies designed to treat them often call upon individuals to make substantial long-term adjustments in their lives. We discuss some of these conditions below.

Disorders of the Renal System

The renal system is vulnerable to a number of disorders. Among the most common are urinary tract infections, to which women are especially vulnerable, and which can result in considerable pain, especially upon urination. If untreated, they can lead to more serious infection.

Acute glomerular nephritis is a disease that results from an antigen-antibody reaction in which the gomeruli of the kidneys become markedly inflamed. These inflammatory reactions can cause total or partial blockage of a large number of glomeruli, which may lead to increased permeability of the glomerular membrane, allowing large amounts of protein to leak in. When there is rupture of the membrane, large numbers of red blood cells may also pass into the glomerular filtrate. In severe cases, total renal shutdown occurs. Acute glomerular nephritis is usually a secondary response to a streptococcus infection. The infection itself does not damage the kidneys, but when antibodies develop, the antibodies and

FIGURE 2.8   The Renal System

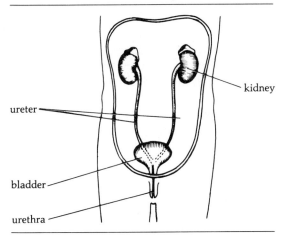

(After Lankford, 1979, p. 585)

the antigen react with each other to form a precipitate that becomes entrapped in the middle of the glomerular membrane. This infection usually subsides within 2 weeks.

Another common cause of acute renal shutdown is tubular necrosis, which involves destruction of the epithelial cells in the tubules of the kidneys. Poisons that destroy the tubular epithelial cells or severe circulatory shock are most common causes of tubular necrosis.

Nephrons are the basic structural and functional unit of the kidneys. In many types of kidney disease, such as that caused by hypertension, large numbers of nephrons are destroyed or damaged so severely that the remaining nephrons simply cannot perform their normal functions. Kidney failure is a severe disorder because the inability to produce an adequate amount of urine will cause the waste products of metabolism as well as surplus inorganic salts and water to be retained in the body. An artificial kidney, a kidney transplant, or **kidney dialysis** may be required in order to rid the body of its wastes. Although these technologies can cleanse the blood to remove the excess salts, water, and metabolites, they are highly stressful medical procedures. Kidney transplants carry many health risks, and kidney dialysis can be extremely stressful for patients. Consequently, health psychologists have been increasingly involved in addressing the problems of the kidney patient and in attempting to find new ways of dealing with these disorders.

THE REPRODUCTIVE SYSTEM AND AN INTRODUCTION TO GENETICS

The development of the reproductive system is substantially controlled by the pituitary gland at the base of the brain. The anterior pituitary lobe produces the gonadotropic hormones, which control development of the ovaries in females and the testes in males. The gonadotropic hormones in the female are the follicle-stimulating hormone (FSH), the luteinizing hormone (LH), and a hormone associated with lactation (milk production) known as prolactin. FSH is also present in the male. Whereas hormones are released cyclically in the female on approximately a 28-day basis, they are released intermittently in the male. The release of hormones appears to be under the control of the hypothalamus via the pituitary gland.

The Ovaries and Testes

A diagrammatic representation of the human reproductive system appears in Figure 2.9.

The female has two ovaries located in the pelvis. Each month, one or the other of the ovaries produces an ovum (egg), which is discharged at ovulation into the Fallopian tubes. If the ovum is not fertilized (if it does not meet a sperm), it remains in the uterine cavity for about 14 days and is then flushed out of the system with the uterine endometrium and its blood vessels (during menstruation). The ovaries also produce the hormones estrogen and progesterone. Estrogen leads to the development of secondary sex characteristics in the female, including breasts and female distribution of both body fat and body hair. Progesterone, which is produced during the second half of the menstrual cycle to prepare the body for pregnancy, declines if pregnancy fails to occur.

Testosterone is produced by the interstitial cells of the testes under the control of the anterior pituitary lobe. It brings about the production of sperm and the development of secondary sex characteristics in the male, including growth of the beard, deepening of the voice, male distribution of body hair, and both skeletal and muscular growth.

FIGURE 2.9   The Reproductive System

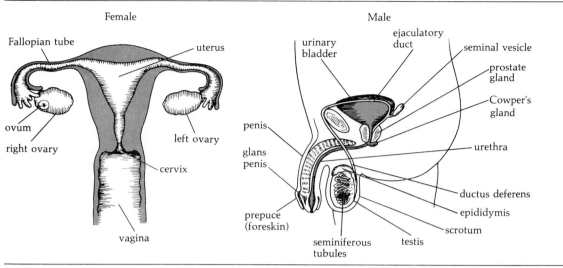

(After Green, 1978, p. 122, and Lankford, 1979, p. 688)

Fertilization and Gestation

When sexual intercourse takes place and ejaculation occurs, sperm are released into the vagina. These sperm, which have a high degree of motility, proceed upward through the uterus into the Fallopian tubes, where one sperm may fertilize an ovum. The fertilized ovum then travels down the Fallopian tube into the uterine cavity, where it embeds itself in the uterine wall and develops over the next 9 months into a human being.

Genetics and Health

The fetus starts life as a single cell that contains all the inherited information from both parents that will determine its characteristics. The genetic code regulates such factors as color of eyes and color of hair as well as behavioral factors. Genetic material for inheritance lies in the nucleus of the cell in the form of 46 chromosomes, 23 from the mother and 23 from the father. Two of these 46 are sex chromosomes, which are an X from the

mother and either an X or a Y from the father. If the father provides an X chromosome, a female child will result; if he provides a Y chromosome, a male child will result.

Charles Darwin, the evolutionary theorist (1809–1882), proposed that the variations seen within any given species result from efforts to adapt to the environment. These adaptations, he argued, appear in successive generations via the principle of survival of the fittest. This principle maintains that those individuals who are best suited to a given environment are most likely to survive and to pass their genetic material on to offspring. Successive generations are thus increasingly well suited to particular environments (the principle of natural selection). Gregor Mendel (1822–1884), who worked experimentally with plants, later illustrated some of the principles that Darwin had proposed in his theoretical model.

Eugenics   The principle of natural selection gave rise to a movement known as eugenics, the effort to develop a superrace of human beings with maximally desirable characteristics. In the early part of the twentieth century in the United States, so-called unfit individuals (such as the mentally retarded, alcoholics, drug addicts, and other "degenerates") could legally be sterilized to prevent them from passing on their genes to offspring. An even more massive and horrible campaign of this sort was mounted in Germany in the 1930s, when Adolf Hitler's government murdered millions of Jews, gypsies, homosexuals, mentally retarded people, and members of other groups that the Nazis considered genetically inferior to the Aryan "master race."

The Inheritance of Susceptibility to Disease
Although much of the eugenics movement was based on misinformation about which attributes are hereditary and which are not, it is now known that a number of health-related and behavioral characteristics can be inherited. Scientists make use of this principle in breeding strains of rats, mice, and other laboratory animals that are sensitive or insensitive to the onset of particular diseases. Thus, for example, a strain of rats that is particularly susceptible to cancer may be used to study the development of this disease, since their initial susceptibility will ensure that many of the rats will develop malignancies when implanted with carcinogenic (cancer-causing) materials.

Although people are obviously not bred for particular attributes, it is clear that a variety of both desirable and undesirable characteristics are transmitted genetically. Some of these characteristics have strong health implications. For example, hemophilia, described earlier, is a genetically based inability to produce the fibrinogen required for the blood to clot after an injury. The disease is carried by females in a recessive form and passed on to their male offspring. There is some suspicion that susceptibilities to particular diseases, such as coronary artery disease or cancer, may also be inherited, although the specific mechanisms by which this might occur are not yet fully understood.

Genetics and Psychology   As we shall see in later chapters, the increasing implication of genetics in a number of serious health disorders can create substantial psychological issues. In extreme cases, when a genetic factor may lead to the premature death or substantial disability of a child, prospective parents may need genetic counseling, which incorporates the inputs of psychologists. Increasingly, too, clinical psychologists who work with chronically ill patients have recognized the problems that genetically based disorders may create for family functioning. Offspring may blame their parents for the conditions that have left them disabled—a problem that may require psychological intervention.

Several types of research help demonstrate whether a characteristic is genetically acquired or not. Studies of families, for example, can reveal whether or not members of the same family are statistically more likely to develop a disorder such as heart disease than are unrelated individuals within a similar environment. If a factor is genetically determined, family members would be expected to show it more frequently than would unrelated individuals.

Twin research is another method for examining the genetic basis of a characteristic. If a characteristic is genetically transmitted, identical twins should share it more commonly than would fraternal twins or other brothers and sisters. This is because identical twins share the same genetic makeup, whereas other brothers and sisters have only partially overlapping genetic makeup. Examining the characteristics of twins reared together as opposed to twins reared apart is also informative regarding genetics. Attributes that emerge for twins reared apart are suspected to be genetically determined, especially if the rate of occurrence between twins reared together and those reared apart is the same. Finally, studies of adopted children also help identify which characteristics are genetic and which are environmentally produced. Adopted children should not manifest genetically transmitted characteristics from their adopted parents, but they would very likely manifest environmentally transmitted characteristics.

For example, if we are able to ascertain that heart disease occurs in families to a greater extent than would be expected by chance and that it affects both members of a set of twins even more often (including twins reared apart), and, further, that adopted children fail to develop heart disease as a consequence of being raised in a family prone to heart disease, then the suspicion of a genetic predisposition for heart disease would be great.

Increasingly, these kinds of methods are being employed to help clarify the potential role of genetics in other health-related behavioral risk factors. These methods can be useful, for example, in identifying possible genetic components in obesity and alcoholism.

THE IMMUNE SYSTEM

As we have seen, disease can be caused by a variety of factors including genetic defects, hormone imbalances, nutritional deficiencies, and infection. In this section, we are primarily concerned with the transmission of disease by infection, that is, the invasion of microbes and their growth in the body. The microbes that cause infection are transmitted to people in one of four ways: direct transmission, indirect transmission, biological transmission, and mechanical transmission.

Direct transmission involves bodily contact, such as handshaking, kissing, and sexual intercourse. For example, genital herpes is generally contracted by direct transmission. *Indirect transmission* (or environmental transmission) occurs when microbes are passed to an individual via airborne particles, dust, water, soil, or food. Legionnaire's disease is an example of an environmentally transmitted disease. *Biological transmission* occurs when a transmitting agent, such as a mosquito, picks up microbes, changes them into a form condu-

cive to growth in the human body, and passes the disease on to the human. The transmission of yellow fever, for example, occurs by this biological method. Finally, *mechanical transmission* is the passage of a microbe to an individual by means of a carrier that is not directly involved in the disease process. Transmission of an infection by dirty hands, bad water, rats, mice, or flies are methods of mechanical transmission. For example, hepatitis can be acquired through mechanical transmission. Box 2.1 tells about two people who were carriers of deadly diseases.

Once a microbe has reached the body, it penetrates into bodily tissue via any of several routes, including the skin, the throat and respiratory tract, the digestive tract, or the genitourinary system. Whether or not the invading microbes gain a foothold in the body and produce infection depends on three factors: the number of organisms, the body's defensive powers, and the virulence of the organisms. The virulence of an organism is determined by its aggressiveness (that is, its ability to resist the body's defenses) and by its toxigenicity (that is, its ability to produce poisons that invade other parts of the body).

The Course of Infection

Assuming that the invading organism does gain a foothold, the natural history of infection follows a specific course. First, there is an incubation period between the time the infection is contracted and the time the symptoms appear. Next, there is a period of nonspecific symptoms, such as headaches and general discomfort, which precedes the onset of the disease. During this time, the microbes are actively colonizing and producing toxins. The next stage is the acute phase, when the disease and its symptoms are at their height. Unless the infection proves fatal, a period of decline follows the acute phase. During this period the organisms are expelled from the mouth and nose in saliva and respiratory se-

---

Box 2.1
Portraits of Two Carriers

Carriers are people who transmit a disease to others without actually contracting that disease themselves. They are especially dangerous because they are not ill and are therefore not removed from society. Thus, it is possible for a carrier to infect dozens, hundreds, or even thousands of individuals as he or she goes about the business of everyday life.

"Typhoid Mary"

Perhaps the most famous carrier in history was "Typhoid Mary," a young Swiss immigrant to the United States who apparently infected thousands of people during her lifetime. During her ocean crossing, Mary was taught how to cook, and eventually some 100 individuals aboard the ship died of typhoid, including the cook who trained her. Once Mary arrived in New York, she obtained a series of jobs as a cook, continually passing the disease on to those for whom she worked without contracting it herself.

Typhoid is precipitated by a *Salmonella* bacterium that can be transmitted through water, food, and physical contact. Mary carried a virulent form of the infection in her body but was herself immune to the disease. It is believed that Mary was unaware that she was a carrier for many years. Toward the end of her life, however, she began to realize that she was responsible for the many deaths around her.

Her status as a carrier also became known to medical authorities, and in the latter part of her life she was in and out of institutions in a vain attempt to isolate her from others. In 1930, Mary died not of typhoid but of a brain hemorrhage (Federspiel, 1983).

"Helen"

The CBS News program *60 Minutes* profiled an equally terrifying carrier: a prostitute, "Helen," who is a carrier of AIDS (acquired immune deficiency syndrome). Helen has never had AIDS, but her baby was born with the disease. As a prostitute and heroin addict, she is not only at risk for developing the illness herself but also poses a substantial threat to her clients and anyone with whom she shares a needle. Helen represents a dilemma for medical and criminal authorities. She is a known carrier of AIDS, yet there is no legal basis for preventing her from coming into contact with others. Although she can be arrested for prostitution or drug dealing, such incarcerations are usually short term and would have a negligible impact on her ability to spread the disease to others. For as-yet incurable diseases like AIDS, the carrier poses a frustrating nightmare of complications. Although he or she can augment the incidence of the disease, medical and legal authorities have been almost powerless to intervene (Moses, 1984).

---

cretions as well as through the digestive tract and the genitourinary system in feces and urine.

Infections may be localized, focal, or systemic. Localized infections remain at their original site and do not spread throughout the body. Although a focal infection is confined to a particular area, it sends toxins to other parts of the body, causing other disruptions. Systemic infections, by contrast, affect a number of different areas or body systems.

The primary infection initiated by the microbe can also lead to secondary infections. These occur because the body's resistance is lowered from fighting the primary infection, leaving it susceptible to other invaders. In many cases, secondary infections such as pneumonia pose a greater risk than primary ones.

Immunity

Immunity is the body's resistance to injury from invading organisms. It can develop either naturally or artificially. Some natural immunity is passed from the mother to the child at birth and through breast feeding, although this type of immunity is only temporary. Natural immunity is also acquired through disease. For example, if you have measles once, it is unlikely that you will develop it a second time; you will have built up an immunity to it. Artificial immunity is acquired through vaccinations and inoculations. For example, most children receive shots for a variety of diseases—among them, diphtheria, whooping cough, smallpox, and poliomyelitis—so that they will not contract them should they ever be exposed.

How does immunity work? The body has a number of different responses to invading organisms, some nonspecific and others specific. **Nonspecific immune mechanisms** are a general set of systemic responses to any kind of infection or disorder; **specific immune mechanisms,** which are always acquired after birth, fight particular microorganisms and their toxins.

Nonspecific Immunity   Nonspecific immunity is mediated in four main ways: through anatomical barriers, phagocytosis, antimicrobial substances, and inflammatory reactions.

Anatomical barriers prevent the passage of microbes from one section of the body to another. For example, the skin functions as an extremely effective anatomical barrier to many infections, and the mucous membranes lining the nose and mouth (as well as other cavities

that are open to the environment) also provide protection.

Phagocytosis is the process by which certain white blood cells (called phagocytes) ingest microbes. Phagocytes are usually overproduced when there is a bodily infection, so that sufficient numbers can be sent to the site of infection to ingest the foreign particles.

Antimicrobial substances are chemicals mobilized by the body itself to kill invading microorganisms. One that has received particular attention in cancer research is interferon, an antiviral protein secreted by cells exposed to a viral antigen to protect neighboring uninfected cells from invasion. Hydrochloric acid and enzymes such as lysozyme are other antimicrobial substances that help destroy invading microorganisms.

The *inflammatory response* is a local reaction to infection. At the site of infection, the blood capillaries first enlarge, and a chemical called histamine is released into the area. It causes an increase in capillary permeability, allowing white blood cells and fluids to leave the capillaries and enter the tissues; consequently, the area becomes reddened and fluids accumulate. The white blood cells attack the microbes, resulting in the formation of pus. Temperature increases at the site of inflammation because of the increased flow of blood. Usually, a clot then forms around the inflamed area, isolating the microbes and keeping them from spreading to other parts of the body. A familiar example of the inflammatory response is the reddening, swelling, discharge, and clotting that result when you accidentally lacerate your skin.

Specific Immunity   Specific immunity is acquired after birth and differs from nonspecific immunity in that it protects against particular microorganisms and their toxins. Specific immunity may be acquired by contracting a disease or through artificial means such as vaccinations and operates through the antigen-antibody reaction. Antigens are foreign substances whose presence stimulates the production of antibodies in the cell tissues, and these antibodies then combine chemically with the antigens to activate them.

There are two types of specific immunity: cell-mediated immunity and humoral immunity. *Cell-mediated immunity* occurs at the cellular level. T cells originate in the red bone marrow, mature in the thymus gland, and are carried by the blood to the lymphatic tissue (the lymph nodes, spleen, and tonsils). Some mature T cells produce specific antibodies to combat specific antigens. Cell-mediated immunity is particularly effective in defending the body against fungi, viral infections that have invaded the cells, parasites, foreign tissue, and cancer. *Humoral immunity* is primarily mediated by lymphocytes, termed B cells, that are produced in the bone marrow and carried to the lymph nodes, spleen, and tonsils. When they are stimulated by specific antigens, these cells produce and secrete specific antibodies into the blood, thereby neutralizing the antigens. Certain T cells (called helper and suppressor T cells) also contribute to the regulation of humoral immunity. Humoral immunity is particularly effective in defending the body against bacterial infections and against viral infections that have not yet invaded the cells. We consider these processes more fully in Chapter 15.

The Lymphatic System's Role in Immunity
The **lymphatic system,** which is a drainage system of the body, is involved in important ways in immune functioning. There is lymphatic tissue throughout the body; it consists of lymphatic capillaries, vessels, and nodes. Lymphatic capillaries drain water, proteins, microbes, and other foreign materials from spaces between the cells into lymph vessels. This material is then conducted in the lymph vessels to the lymph nodes, which filter microbes and foreign materials out for ingestion by lymphocytes. The lymphatic vessels

then drain any remaining substances into the blood.

The spleen, tonsils, and thymus gland are also important organs in the lymphatic system. The spleen aids in the production of B cells and T cells and removes worn-out red blood cells from the body. The spleen also helps filter bacteria and is responsible for the storage and release of blood. Tonsils are patches of lymphoid tissue in the pharynx which filter out microorganisms that enter the respiratory tract. Finally, the thymus gland is responsible for helping T cells mature; it also produces a hormone, thymosin, that appears to stimulate T cells and lymph nodes to produce the plasma cells which, in turn, produce antibodies.

To summarize, then, disease can be caused by direct, environmental, biological, or mechanical transmission. Once an invading microbe has been transmitted to an individual, it follows a natural history of infectious spread. A primary infection can, in turn, prompt the appearance of secondary infections. Immunity is the body's resistance to these invading organisms. Nonspecific immune mechanisms are a general set of systemic responses to any kind of infection or disorder. They include anatomical barriers, phagocytosis, antimicrobial substances, and inflammatory reactions. Specific immune mechanisms include cell-mediated immunity and humoral immunity.

The preceding has been a brief consideration of immunity. A more extended discussion is included in Chapter 15, where we consider the rising and rapidly developing field of psychoneuroimmunology and the role of immunity in the development of AIDS (acquired immune deficiency syndrome). As we shall see in that context, increasingly, health psychologists are identifying the importance of social and psychological factors in the functioning of the immune system. Specifically, there is increasing evidence that highly stressful events can alter immune functioning, in some cases to increase resistance and in other cases to substantially decrease it.

Diseases of the Immune System

The immune system and the tissues of the lymphatic system are subject to a number of disorders and diseases. One very important one is AIDS, which is a progressive impairment of immunity. Another is cancer, which is now believed to depend heavily on immunocompromise. We defer extended discussion of AIDS and cancer to Chapter 15.

Some diseases of the immune system result when bacteria are so virulent that the lymph node phagocytes are not able to ingest all of the foreign matter. These include lymphangitis, an inflammation of the lymphatic vessels that results from interference in the drainage of the lymph into the blood; and lymphadenitis, an inflammation of the lymph nodes associated with the phagocytes' efforts to destroy microbes.

A number of infections attack lymphatic tissue. Elephantiasis is a condition produced by worms; it stems from blockage in the flow of lymph into the blood. Massive retention of fluid results, especially in the extremities. Splenomegaly is an enlargement of the spleen that can result from various infectious diseases. It hinders the ability of the spleen to produce phagocytes, antibodies, and lymphocytes. Tonsillitis is an inflammation of the tonsils that interferes with their ability to filter out bacteria. Infectious mononucleosis is a viral disorder marked by an unusually large number of monocytes; it can cause enlargement of the spleen and lymph nodes as well as fever, sore throat, and general lack of energy.

Lymphoma is a tumor of the lymphatic tissue. Hodgkin's disease, a malignant lymphoma, involves the progressive, chronic enlargement of the lymph nodes, spleen, and other lymphatic tissues. As a consequence, the nodes cannot effectively produce antibodies and the phagocytic properties of the nodes are lost. Untreated Hodgkin's disease can be fatal.

Autoimmunity is a condition characterized by a specific humoral or cell-mediated immune response that attacks the body's own tissues. It may result in hypersensitivity reactions, such as allergic responses, or, if severe, in autoimmune disease. Autoimmunity is implicated in certain forms of arthritis, a condition characterized by inflammatory lesions in the joints that produce pain, heat, redness, and swelling. We discuss arthritis more fully in Chapter 15. Multiple sclerosis is also believed by some to be an autoimmune disorder. One of the most severe autoimmune disorders is systemic lupus erythematosis, a generalized disorder of the connective tissue, that primarily affects women and which in its severe forms can lead to eventual heart or kidney failure, causing death.

SUMMARY

1. The nervous system and the endocrine system act as the control systems of the body, mobilizing it in times of threat and maintaining equilibrium and normal functioning otherwise.

2. The nervous system operates primarily through the exchange of nerve impulses between the peripheral nerve endings and internal organs and the brain, thereby providing the integration necessary for voluntary and involuntary movement.

3. The endocrine system operates chemically via the release of hormones stimulated by centers in the brain. It controls growth and development and augments the functioning of the nervous system.

4. The cardiovascular system is the transport system of the body, carrying oxygen and

nutrients to cell tissues and taking carbon dioxide and other wastes away from the tissues for expulsion from the body.

5. The heart acts as a pump to keep the circulation going and is responsive to regulation via the nervous system and the endocrine system.

6. The cardiovascular system is implicated in stress, with cardiac output speeding up during times of threat and slowing down when threat has passed.

7. The heart, the blood vessels, and the blood are vulnerable to a number of problems, most notably atherosclerosis, which makes diseases of the cardiovascular system the major cause of death in this country.

8. The respiratory system is responsible for taking in oxygen, expelling carbon dioxide, and controlling the chemical composition of the blood.

9. The digestive system is responsible for

producing heat and energy, which—along with essential nutrients—are needed for the growth and repair of cells. Through digestion, food is broken down to be used by the cells for this process.

10. The renal system aids in metabolic processes by regulating water balance, electrolyte balance, and blood acidity-alkalinity. Water-soluble wastes are flushed out of the system in the urine.

11. The reproductive system, under the control of the endocrine system, leads to the development of primary and secondary sex characteristics. Through this system, the species is reproduced and genetic material is transmitted from parents to their offspring.

12. The immune system is responsible for warding off infection from invasion by foreign substances. It does so through the production of infection-fighting cells and chemicals.

KEY TERMS

adrenal glands
angina pectoris
atherosclerosis
autonomic nervous system
blood pressure
cardiovascular system
catecholamines
cerebellum
cerebral cortex
digestive system
endocrine system
hypothalamus
immunity
kidney dialysis
lymphatic system

medulla
metabolic system
myocardial infarction
nervous system
neurotransmitters
nonspecific immune mechanisms
parasympathetic nervous system
pituitary gland
platelets
renal system
respiratory system
specific immune mechanisms
spinal cord
sympathetic nervous system
thalamus

PART 2

HEALTH BEHAVIOR AND PRIMARY PREVENTION

3

HEALTH PROMOTION AND THE PRACTICE OF HEALTH BEHAVIORS

Historically in medical practice, good health is something that has been taken for granted, as a steady state against which disturbances can be assessed and corrected by medical intervention. In the last few decades, however, good health has been recognized as something that is actively achieved by people through a healthy lifestyle. In this context, the terms *health promotion* and *wellness* become important.

Health promotion has been defined as the process of enabling people to increase control over, and to improve, their health (Ottowa Charter, 1986). From the individual's standpoint, health promotion and wellness refer to the practice of good health behaviors, such as a balanced diet that is low in cholesterol and fat, regular exercise, and the practice of preventive health behaviors, such as breast and testicular self-examination and regular checkups. They also involve the avoidance of health-compromising behaviors, such as excessive alcohol consumption, smoking, and drug use. From the standpoint of psychologists and health practitioners, health promotion and wellness refer to efforts to intervene with healthy rather than ill populations for the purpose of enhancing and maximizing their good health. An examination of the health goals for the nation for the 1990s clearly shows the increasing importance attached to health promotion (Table 3.1).

A number of factors have fueled the movement toward health promotion. The self-care, civil rights, and women's movements of the 1960s laid the groundwork for shifting the basis of power from authorities to clients themselves, and thus provided a philosophical rationale for the change regarding who is responsible for health. Another origin of the concept of health promotion is the long-standing commitment of public health to health education programs for the public. Community development and mass communication movements, which attempt to educate the public about health risks and the benefits

TABLE 3.1   FIFTEEN SPECIFIC AND MEASURABLE HEALTH OBJECTIVES TO PRODUCE HEALTHIER AMERICANS BY THE YEAR 1990

I. *Preventive Health Services*
   1. High blood pressure control
   2. Family planning
   3. Pregnancy and infant health
   4. Immunization
   5. Sexually transmitted diseases

II. *Health Protection*

   6. Toxic agent control
   7. Occupational safety and health
   8. Accident prevention and injury control
   9. Fluoridation and dental health
   10. Surveillance and control of infectious diseases

III. *Health Promotion*
   11. Smoking and health
   12. Misuse of alcohol and drugs
   13. Nutrition
   14. Physical fitness and exercise
   15. Control of stress and violent behavior

(Source: Matarazzo, 1984; based on Harris, 1980)

TABLE 3.2   THE SPIRALING COSTS OF HEALTH CARE, 1960–1986

YEAR	HEALTH CARE AS A PERCENTAGE OF GNP	TOTAL HEALTH CARE EXPENDITURES (BILLIONS)
1960	5.3	$ 27
1965	6.0	42
1970	7.5	75
1975	8.6	133
1980	9.5	249
1986	10.9	458

(Source: Adapted from Gibson & Waldo, 1982; American Hospital Association, 1987)

of good health behaviors, laid the groundwork for the health promotion enterprise. In addition, certain sources of disenchantment within traditional medicine have fueled an interest in health promotion. The enormous rise in health costs (Table 3.2) and pressures toward cost containment have led researchers and policy-makers to seek ways to improve health rather than to wait until people develop chronic and often expensive diseases and then try to cure them. The growing recognition that lifestyle factors relate to these diseases and the belief that medical care makes only a marginal dent in them have also been important. In addition, as the scientific basis of social, behavioral, and educational interventions has improved, receptivity to health promotion has increased (Green & Raeburn, 1988).

A concern with health promotion leads directly to the question of preventive health behavior. In Chapter 1, we discussed the biomedical model of illness, which emphasizes the role of genetically based factors, hormones and other bodily changes, and specific pathogens such as viruses and bacteria, as critical agents in the development of illness. For the most part, the biomedical model ignores behavioral factors that contribute to illness. Behavioral factors have now proven to be so important, however, that they must be addressed.

Health beliefs appear to develop relatively early in life. By the age of 11 or 12, most children have fairly stable health beliefs that resemble those of adults (Lau & Klepper, 1988). Good health is an important value for most people. In a study that asked people to rank nine values, including physical appearance, inner harmony, security, and wisdom, health was ranked the highest. Women rated good health more highly than men did, and older people ranked health higher than children did, presumably because they have more experience with what happens when good health is compromised. Among all who rated health highly, the belief that preventive health

The foundations for health promotion develop in early childhood, when children are taught to practice good health behaviors, such as tooth-brushing.

behaviors is important was also high (Lau, Hartmann, & Ware, 1986).

In this chapter, we begin by documenting the important role that health behaviors play in terms of health and illness. We then consider some of the barriers to health promotion and some of the factors that determine health habits. Finally, we look at who practices good health behavior and who does not. In Chapter 4, we turn our attention to general strategies for changing health habits, including traditional methods of attitude and behavior change, such as operant and classical conditioning, and more recent cognitive-behavioral techniques, such as self-monitoring and self-reinforcement. In Chapter 5, we consider health-enhancing behaviors such as exercising, avoiding accidents, practicing breast and testicular self-examination, controlling weight,

and managing diet. In Chapter 6, we consider the health-compromising problems of excessive alcohol consumption and smoking.

AN INTRODUCTION TO HEALTH BEHAVIORS

Role of Behavioral Factors in Disease and Disorder

In the past 90 years, patterns of disease in the United States have changed substantially. The prevalence of such acute infectious disorders as tuberculosis, influenza, measles, and poliomyelitis has declined because of treatment innovations and changes in public health standards, such as improvements in waste control and sewage. Simultaneously, there has been an increase in what have been called the "preventable" disorders, including lung cancer, cardiovascular disease, alcohol and drug abuse, and vehicular accidents (Matarazzo, 1982).

The role of behavioral factors in the development of these disorders is increasingly clear. For example, 25% of all cancer deaths and a large number of deaths from heart attack could be avoided by modifying just one behavior: smoking. A mere 10% in weight reduction among men aged 35 to 55 would produce an estimated 20% decrease in coronary heart disease (Kannel & Eaker, 1986); it would also lower the rate of degenerative arthritis, gastrointestinal cancer, diabetes, strokes, and heart attacks. A diet that is high in cholesterol has been tied to reduction in the size of the arteries, whereas a low-cholesterol diet can reduce cholesterol buildup (American Heart Association, 1988). Overall, it is estimated that 50% of the deaths from the ten leading causes of death in this country are due to modifiable lifestyle factors (Centers for Disease Control, 1980). Moreover, the percentage of the gross national product that goes for health care has been climbing steadily (see Table 3.2), in large part because the diseases that are currently most prevalent are chronic in nature and require continual treatment and monitoring. Thus, successful modification of health behaviors may help reduce both the number of deaths and the incidence of preventable disease, as well as make a dent in the more than $500 billion that is spent yearly on health and illness.

What Are Health Behaviors?

Health behaviors are behaviors undertaken by people to enhance or maintain their health (Kasl & Cobb, 1966; Stone, 1979). Poor health behaviors are important not only because they are implicated in illness but also because they may easily become poor health habits. A **health habit** is a health-related behavior that is firmly established and often performed automatically, without awareness. Although it may have developed initially because it was reinforced by specific positive outcomes, it eventually becomes independent of the reinforcement process and is maintained by the environmental factors with which it is customarily associated. As such, it can be highly resistant to change. Consequently, it is important to establish good health behaviors and eliminate poor ones as early as possible.

A dramatic illustration of the importance of good health habits in maintaining good health is provided by a classic study of people living in Alameda County, California, conducted by Belloc and Breslow (1972). These scientists began by defining seven important good health habits: sleeping 7 to 8 hours a night, not smoking, eating breakfast each day, having no more than one or two alcoholic drinks each day, getting regular exercise, not eating between meals, and being no more than 10% overweight. They then asked each of nearly 7,000 county residents to indicate which of these behaviors they practiced. Residents were also asked to indicate how many illnesses they had had, which illnesses they had had, how much energy they had, and how

disabled they had been (for example, how many days of work they had missed) over the previous 6- to 12-month period. The researchers found that the more good health habits people practiced, the fewer illnesses they had, the better they felt, and the less disabled they were. A follow-up of these individuals 9½ years later found that mortality rates were dramatically lower for both men and women practicing the seven health habits. Specifically, men following these practices had a mortality rate only 28% that of men following zero to three of the health practices, and women following the seven health habits had a mortality rate 43% that of women following zero to three of the health practices (Breslow & Enstrom, 1980).

A health behavior may or may not depend on access to the health care system. Some health behaviors clearly do. For example, using a tuberculosis screening program, obtaining a regular Pap smear, and receiving immunizations for childhood diseases such as polio and diphtheria are examples of health behaviors that cannot be practiced on one's own; they require the aid of a health practitioner. Other health behaviors may be recommended by health professionals, but people may not seek professional help to acquire them. These include exercise, dietary control, reduction of alcohol consumption, and stopping smoking. Another type of health behavior is typically encouraged by health practitioners but is enacted privately with little help from the health care system. An example is brushing one's teeth on a regular basis. Finally, people practice some health behaviors without any training by or access to the medical system at all. An example of such a behavior is wearing a seat belt in an automobile. Whether or not a health behavior requires access to the health care system influences who practices it, as we will soon see.

Instilling good health habits and changing poor ones is the task of **primary prevention.** This means taking measures to combat risk factors for illness before an illness ever has a chance to develop. There are two general strategies of primary prevention. The first and most common has been to employ behavior-change methods to get people to alter their problematic health behaviors. The many programs that have been developed to help people lose weight are an example of this approach. The second, more recent approach is to keep people from developing poor health habits in the first place. Smoking prevention programs with young adolescents are an example of this approach, which we consider in Chapter 6. Of the two types of primary prevention, it is obviously far preferable to keep people from developing problematic behaviors than to try to help them stop the behaviors once they are already in place.

Intervening with Children and Adolescents

Health promotion and primary prevention efforts capitalize on educational opportunities to prevent poor health habits from developing. The concept of a **teachable moment** refers to the fact that certain times are better for teaching particular health practices than others. In some cases, a teachable moment develops because the health care delivery system creates it. For example, a large percentage of infants in the United States are covered by some kind of well-baby care. Pediatricians often make use of these early visits to teach motivated new parents the basics of accident prevention and safety in the home. In other cases, a teachable moment may develop because a particular health habit becomes relevant. For example, there appears to be a **window of vulnerability** for beginning smoking that occurs in junior high school when students are first exposed to regular smoking among their peers. Health promotion specialists develop intervention programs that can be implemented in the school system to help students avoid the temptations that may lead to smok-

ing and learn how to resist peer pressure to smoke.

Many school systems require a physical at the beginning of the school year, or at certain points during elementary school. The fact that children come into early regular contact with medical practitioners makes this an appropriate teaching opportunity in several respects. First, these regular visits can be used as opportunities to discuss and prevent the problems of greatest hazard to children. In addition, intervening in childhood can help prevent poor health habits from developing.

But what can children really learn about health habits? Certainly very young children have cognitive limitations that keep them from fully comprehending the difficult and often highly abstract concepts of health promotion (Maddux, Roberts, Sledden, & Wright, 1986). Yet intervention programs with children clearly indicate that they are capable of developing personal responsibility for certain aspects of their health. Such behaviors as choosing nutritionally sound foods, brushing teeth regularly, using car seats and seat belts, participating in exercise, crossing the street safely, and behaving appropriately in real or simulated emergencies (such as earthquake drills) are clearly within the comprehension of children as young as 3 or 4, as long as the behaviors are explained in highly concrete and specific terms and the implications for action are clear and put into practice (Maddux et al., 1986).

Interventions with At-Risk People

Health promotion and primary prevention involve working not only with healthy populations but also with those who are **at risk,** or vulnerable to particular problems by virtue of heredity, health practices, or family environment (Becker & Janz, 1987). For example, a pediatrician may work with obese parents to control the diet of their offspring, in the hopes that obesity in the children can be avoided. If

---

Box 3.1
Health Promotion and the Elderly

One of the U.S. national health objectives of the 1980s was to improve the health and quality of life of the elderly. Specifically, the Public Health Service identified the need to increase the number of older adults who can function independently and to reduce the number of premature deaths among the elderly from influenza and pneumonia. Despite these objectives, health promotion efforts have not been systematically directed at the elderly (Green, 1986; Straus, 1988). Reasons may stem from false beliefs that such efforts would be useless in old age or from stereotypes of the elderly suggesting that they will not engage in health behaviors reliably. Yet to have a healthy, well-functioning, and relatively independent cohort of elderly people demands effective health behavior (Ory, 1988).

Health promotion efforts with the elderly need to focus on several specific health behaviors: developing a healthy, balanced diet; maintaining mobility through exercise; taking steps to reduce accidents; controlling alcohol consumption; eliminating smoking; and reducing the inappropriate use of drugs (e.g., Kaplan, Seeman, Cohen, Knudsen, & Guralnik, 1987). Of these behaviors, lack of exercise shows the highest relationship to illness and mortality among the elderly (Palmore, 1970), so increasing this important but underperformed health behavior is a high priority.

Health problems related to alcohol consumption make this another important target behavior. Some elderly people develop drinking problems in response to age-related difficulties, such as retirement, loneliness, or widowhood. Others try to maintain the drinking habits they have held throughout their lives, which may now be more risky in old age. Specifically, older people who try to maintain their usual drinking habits in the face of metabolic changes related to age may reduce their capacity to drink safely. Moreover, many older people are on medications that interact in dangerous ways with alcohol. Alcohol consumption increases the risk of accidents in the elderly, also a substantial problem facing this population, and it may interfere with adequate nutrition. Finally, drunk driving among the elderly represents a problem, inasmuch as diminished capacities to drive effectively can be further impaired by alcohol.

In short, then, health promotion efforts need to be targeted not only to the young but also to the elderly. Health promotion is a goal that requires the active involvement of all age segments of the populations in planning and enacting of healthy behavior.

---

the dietary changes produce the additional consequence of reducing the parents' weight, so much the better. Daughters of women who have had breast cancer are another vulnerable population that needs to be taught early how to practice breast self-examination and monitor themselves for any changes in the breast tissue. Thus, health promotion involves not only helping people to achieve a maximally healthy lifestyle but also teaching them to be aware of the risks to which they are potentially vulnerable and to take steps early to offset those risks.

There are several advantages to working with people who are at risk for particular health disorders. By identifying these people as early as possible, one may be able to pre-vent or eliminate poor health habits that can contribute to the likelihood of the problem. For example, among males at risk for heart disease, preventing smoking onset or getting them to stop at relatively young ages is desir-able (Schieken, 1988). Even if no intervention is available to reduce risk, knowledge of risk can provide people with information about their current status (Swavely, Silverman, & Falek, 1987). In addition, working with at-risk populations provides a specific focus for health interventions that may achieve good re-sults. When particular risk factors are identi-fied that are important only for particular seg-ments of the population, there is little reason to implement a general health intervention policy regarding that risk factor that targets all elements of the population for behavior mod-ification. It makes more sense to target only those for whom the risk factor is relevant. Thus, for example, some years ago, there were strenuous efforts to induce people to re-duce their salt intake, yet salt is implicated only for a specific subgroup of people prone to hypertension. Consequently, it makes much more sense to direct efforts to modify salt con-sumption to this at-risk group and it does not make much sense to try to get the entire pop-ulation to change salt consumption (McGuire, 1984). Moreover, by doing research on the group that is vulnerable to the particular dis-order, it may be easier to see the other factors that interact with the risk factor (such as salt) in producing the undesirable outcome (e.g., hypertension). Research on the general popu-lation could obscure these important relation-ships.

Clearly, however, there are ethical prob-lems involved in working with populations at risk. Research on risk factor testing suggests several adverse effects that may result from the perception that one is at risk for a disor-der. Some studies suggest that testing positive on a risk factor for a disease leads people into hypervigilant and needlessly restrictive behav-

ior, whereas other research suggests that peo-ple may minimize the significance of their risk factor status or avoid using appropriate screening services (e.g., Booth, Safer, & Leventhal, 1986; Evans, Love, Meyerowitz, Leventhal, & Nerenz, 1985). As yet, the con-ditions under which these two problematic sets of responses occur have not been fully de-lineated (Croyle & Jemmott, in press).

Another ethical issue in working with at-risk populations concerns whether it is appro-priate to alarm at-risk individuals when their risk may be limited. Among people at risk for a particular disorder, only a small proportion may develop the problem and, then, only many years later. For example, alerting daugh-ters of breast cancer patients to their risk in ad-olescence may alarm them at a time when they are attempting to come to terms with their emerging sexuality and needs for self-esteem, which can be compromised by feelings of vul-nerability to this disorder. Inasmuch as only some of these daughters will develop breast cancer and will likely not do so for decades, one may create psychological disturbance in exchange for instilling risk-reduction behav-iors. In some cases, intervention may not work. For example, identifying men at risk for coronary artery disease and teaching them how to manage stress effectively may be un-successful. One may alert the population to its risk without effectively reducing that risk. In other cases, we may have little idea as to what constitutes an effective intervention for an at-risk population. For example, alcoholism is now believed to have a substantial genetic component, particularly among males, and yet exactly how and when one should inter-vene with the offspring of adult alcoholics is not yet clear.

Finally, emphasizing risks that are inherited through the family can raise complicated prob-lems in family dynamics, potentially pitting parents and children against each other and raising issues of who is to blame for the risk (Hastrup, 1985). Daughters of breast cancer patients may suffer considerable stress and behavior problems, due in part to the enhanced recognition of their risk (Taylor, Lichtman, & Wood, 1984a; Wellisch, Gritz, Schain, Wang, & Siau, 1990). For example, one must balance the family's need for privacy against the offsprings' right to know (Hastrup, 1985).

Health promotion programs also need to take account of ethnic and gender differences in health risks to direct programs effectively to vulnerable groups in the population. As Figure 3.1 indicates, different groups may be at risk for different disorders as a result of their health habits or genetic predispositions. For example, black and Hispanic women appear to get less exercise than Anglo women and are somewhat more likely to be overweight. In terms of smoking, however, Anglo and black women are clearly at greater risk than Hispanic women. Alcohol consumption is a substantially greater problem among men than women, and smoking is a somewhat greater problem for Anglo men than for other groups.

Health promotion programs for ethnic groups also need to take account of co-occurring risk factors. The combined effects of low socioeconomic status and a biologic predisposition to particular illnesses puts certain groups at substantially greater risk, as is the case for diabetes among Hispanics and hypertension among blacks, which we consider in more detail in Chapter 14. While ethnic and gender differences in health habits are complex and not yet fully understood, the evidence suggests that this is a valuable source of information for identifying at-risk populations and developing programs targeted to these particular groups.

In summary, then, as research identifies particular individuals or groups that may be at elevated risk for particular disorders, this creates an opportunity to intervene directly with those most likely to develop a disorder in order to reduce their risk. Yet there are potential problems with this approach as well, which include the anxiety and stress that may come from knowledge of one's risk status, problems in family dynamics that may result from heritable disorders, such as alcoholism or breast cancer; the potential for interventions to be overkill, given the small number of people in the at-risk population who may actually develop the disorder; and the fact that in some cases we may know a population is at risk but do not yet have effective interventions for helping them reduce or control that risk.

Health Promotion: An Overview

In short, then, health promotion is a general philosophy that has at its core the idea that good health, or wellness, is a personal and collective achievement. Its methods and goals are illustrated in Figure 3.2. It is an individual concern, a medical and psychological concern, a community concern, and a national concern. On the individual level, it involves developing a program of good health habits early in life and carrying them through adulthood and old age. From the standpoint of the medical practitioner, health promotion involves teaching people how best to achieve this healthy lifestyle, making use of particular teachable moments and particular vulnerabilities to help people at risk for certain health problems incorporate measures to offset or monitor those risks early in life (Maddux et al., 1986). From the standpoint of the psychologist, health promotion involves the development of interventions to help people maximize their practice of healthy behaviors and to change poor health habits when they have developed. From the standpoint of the community and the nation, health promotion involves a general emphasis on good health, the availability of information that people can use to develop and maintain healthy lifestyles, and the availability of resources and facilities that can help them in developing or changing health habits appropriately. The mass media have much to contribute in the way of health promotion by educating people about risks to their health

FIGURE 3.1   Ethnic and Gender Differences in Lifestyle Health Behavior

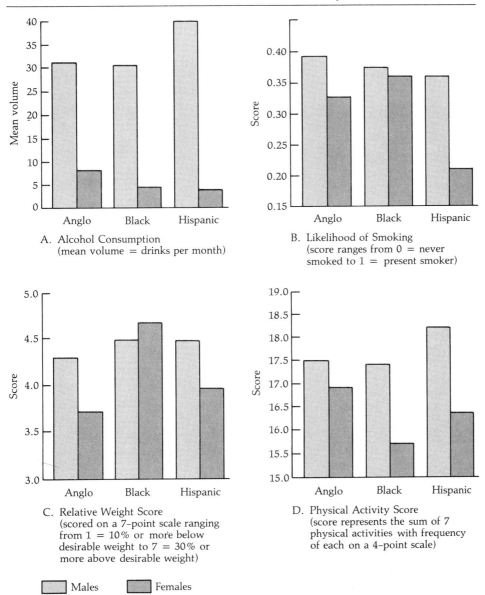

A. Alcohol Consumption
   (mean volume = drinks per month)

B. Likelihood of Smoking
   (score ranges from 0 = never
   smoked to 1 = present smoker)

C. Relative Weight Score
   (scored on a 7-point scale ranging
   from 1 = 10% or more below
   desirable weight to 7 = 30% or
   more above desirable weight)

D. Physical Activity Score
   (score represents the sum of 7
   physical activities with frequency
   of each on a 4-point scale)

☐ Males   ☐ Females

(Based on Gottlieb & Green, 1988)

posed by certain behaviors such as smoking or excessive alcohol consumption. Legislation also has much to contribute to health promotion, by mandating certain activities that may reduce risks, such as the use of child-restraining seats and seat belts.

WHY HAS HEALTH PROMOTION BEEN IGNORED?

Despite the clear importance of health promotion in combating disease, preventive health care accounts for a small percentage of health care dollars spent in the United States. More-over, despite some advances in inducing people to change risky health behaviors (such as smoking), the majority of the population still engages in a number of poor health habits and fails to practice good ones to the maximum extent possible.

Why do we not have a more effective program of health promotion? The first set of factors comes from the medical establishment and its attitudes toward prevention. A second set of barriers focuses on problems within the field of psychology in applying techniques of attitude and behavior change to health behaviors (Stachnik, Stoffelmayr, & Hoppe, 1983). A third set of factors revolves around individual personalities and values. A fourth set of factors has to do with the difficulty of getting people to change poor health habits. We will consider each of these in turn.

Barriers to Health Promotion Within the Structure of Medicine

As we noted in Chapter 1, medicine has traditionally adopted a biomedical approach to illness that underemphasizes behavioral factors. Although it is now widely acknowledged that certain behavioral factors such as smoking, obesity, and lack of exercise can contribute to major chronic diseases, that recognition has not led to a focus on prevention. Because medicine has historically corrected conditions once they have occurred rather than prevented them, it is difficult to shift attention to risk factors. Thus, a formidable change in the perceptions of the medical establishment must be enacted before health promotion can achieve real momentum in medical practice.

Another factor impeding the effective development of health promotion programs is the absence of a formal diagnostic process for health. Because medicine focuses on treating conditions after they have developed, risk factors may go undetected or unacknowledged in the health care process. Individuals who are

not ill are not motivated to seek treatment for potential risk factors, and physicians who see patients are typically oriented toward conditions that should be corrected rather than disorders that might be anticipated. Thus, a major factor that contributes to the lack of effective prevention is the absence of an appropriate method for identifying people who are at risk, for determining the nature of their risk factors, and for teaching them what to modify (Stachnik et al., 1983).

Recently, formal risk assessment efforts have been initiated. An example is the **health risk appraisal,** a formal strategy by which health educators attempt to promote changes in individuals' health behaviors (Becker & Janz, 1987). It involves the assessment of health habits and a quantified, personalized, computerized report indicating which health habits should be modified and what successful modification would mean in terms of impact on mortality. Thus, for example, an individual might be shown approximately how many years he or she could expect to live longer by stopping smoking at age 32. Through this feature, people are able to see the relationships between their lifestyle and their mortality risk, as well as the relative risks of different health behaviors (Becker & Janz, 1987).

Although useful as a teaching tool, the health risk appraisal format has some problems. First, by concentrating on mortality and the threat of death, it may create a negative climate for education, one that does not foster the positive values associated with health that health educators may wish to promote. On the other hand, by providing specific, scientifically based, quantitative data concerning an individual's own risk factors and mortality outcomes, it should encourage belief in the benefits of beginning and maintaining a healthy lifestyle by enumerating specific behaviors to be changed. These efforts are still preliminary, but ultimately formal health risk appraisal may come to be integrated into medical practice.

Other barriers to incorporating preventive care and health promotion into standard medical practice include the fact that prevention is typically ignored in medical education, both formally and in hands-on experience, and consequently, physicians have little training in effective health promotion with their patients. Some **third-party reimbursement programs** do not yet reimburse for preventive programs or counseling, and, consequently, the inability to bill for such programs reduces the likelihood that they will be adopted.

Some physicians are themselves skeptical about the medical evidence that underlies preventive care, such as whether or not changing a poor health habit in an individual patient would actually have any direct impact on health. Preventive care takes up time from other kinds of care, and may also require coordination with community agencies, such as exercise programs, dietary modification programs, smoking prevention programs, and the like. This may go beyond the resources that an individual physician has at his or her

disposal. Many physicians simply believe that prevention is an inappropriate role for them, that they are not effective in giving this kind of training, and that patients would not comply with it anyway (Demak & Becker, 1987).

Individual Barriers to Health Promotion

An important barrier to preventing poor health habits is the fact that health behaviors are learned in the child's most powerful learning environment, the home, from the child's most powerful models, the parents. For example, parents who smoke are significantly more likely to have children who smoke (Leventhal & Cleary, 1980), obese parents are more likely to have obese children (Stunkard, 1979), and the children of problem drinkers are more susceptible to alcoholism (Moos, Cronkite, & Finney, 1982). Although genetic susceptibility is clearly implicated in some of these relationships, learning is also an important factor. Thus, the prevention of poor health habits in a given individual sometimes calls, first, for

Health-compromising behaviors are often learned in the child's most powerful environment, namely the home, from the child's most powerful models, namely the parents.

changes in the health habits of the most influential people in that individual's environment: the parents. Parents generally play an important role in deciding what their children will and will not do; if they are not interested in teaching their children good health habits, other educational efforts may prove ineffective.

Another reason why poor health habits are hard to prevent is that people often have little immediate incentive for practicing good health behavior. At the time when initial health habits develop during childhood and adolescence, most people are healthy. Smoking, drinking, poor nutrition, and lack of exercise have no apparent effect on health and physical functioning. The cumulative damage that these behaviors cause may not become apparent for years, and few children or adolescents are concerned about what their health will be like when they are 40 or 50 years old.

Moreover, research demonstrates that people hold an **unrealistic optimism** about the likelihood that they will develop major health problems (Weinstein, 1982, 1983, 1987). This is true for several reasons. First, people appear to have an exaggerated sense of their ability to control their health; therefore, they may ignore potential health threats. They may believe that the threat does not exist or that they will be able to offset it somehow when it develops. Second, they may have little direct experience with health threats and so underestimate their own vulnerability. The person who has never had a serious illness may find it difficult to imagine what it would be like. Finally, people sometimes erroneously believe that health threats manifest themselves in childhood. If, therefore, they have not already noted signs of a particular health problem, they may imagine that they never will. Unfortunately, unrealistic optimism undermines legitimate worry about risk; it may reduce the likelihood that such people will engage in good health behavior or accept health-habit interventions (Lee, 1989; Weinstein, 1982, 1987).

Despite the fact that health is an important value for most people, people do not seem to have very good assessments of their health risks. Most people either do not acknowledge or cannot see the relationship between their actions and psychological qualities and their risk for poor health. People do understand that a family history of a health problem increases their own susceptibility. Except for smoking, however, relationships between one's own preventive health behaviors and judgments of susceptibility to illness are quite weak (Weinstein, 1984). Generally, then, people seem to be aware of the uncontrollable influences on their health, such as genetics or environmental risk, but they minimize the importance of their own behavior in increasing risk. Because they regard their behavior as under personal control, they may falsely believe that they can modify it before it has an adverse effect on health (Weinstein, 1984).

The tendency to underestimate health risks is robust and is shared by most people in the population. There is, however, one set of circumstances under which people become more pessimistic about their health. People who have had experience with an accident, a crime, a natural hazard, or a heart attack generally view their hazards as more common and see themselves as more likely to be potential future victims. They think about their risk more often and with greater clarity, and, generally speaking, they take at least some precautions. However, relatively small changes in behavior occur and appear to take place only during a window of vulnerability immediately after the experience. For example, there is no general increase in seat belt use among people who have had significant automobile injuries, although there is often a brief increase in the use of seat belts immediately after those injuries (Weinstein, 1989). Similarly, when people are sick, their estimates of their health become more realistic, not only concerning the disorder they have but also for other health risks. Unfortunately, this increased perception of vulnerability is not accompanied by a desire for information about preventive health behavior, and so it may have very little impact on subsequent health behavior (Kulik & Mahler, 1987).

Another factor that may contribute to the relative complacency with which people view their health is the perception that their poor health behaviors are widely shared but that their healthy behaviors are more distinctive. For example, smokers tend to overestimate the numbers of others who smoke; however, people who exercise somewhat underestimate how much other people exercise. One implication of these findings is that people who practice unhealthy behaviors may resist campaigns directed at behavior change because they perceive that there are so many other people engaging in the behavior as well. People who perceive that others are engaging in an unhealthy practice may perceive a lower health risk (Suls, Wan, & Sanders, 1988).

Interventions can reduce these biased perceptions. Weinstein (1983) found that he was able to reduce unrealistic optimism about health risks substantially by providing information about the relation of risk factors to particular health problems and about the standing of typical students on these risk factors. When students were aware that other students had risk factors similar to their own, their unrealistically optimistic perceptions receded substantially.

Health-Habit Factors That Undermine Health Practices

A third set of factors that has interfered with the development of effective health promotion involves the nature of health habits themselves and the people who must practice them. In particular, three aspects of health habits make them hard to modify effectively. The first problem is that we still know so little about them. We have relatively little information about how and when poor health habits

develop. Some of these habits—such as poor diet or lack of exercise—may develop slowly. For example, the young child typically gets sufficient exercise, but as he or she gets older, sluggishness may gradually set in. The exact point when one should intervene to offset this developing poor health habit and how one should go about it are not clear.

Second, health habits are only modestly related to each other. Knowing one health habit does not necessarily enable you to predict another (Harris & Guten, 1979; Mechanic, 1979; Steele, Gotmann, Leventhal, & Easterling, 1983; Zimmerman, 1983). The person who exercises faithfully is not necessarily the person who wears a seat belt. The person who controls her weight may continue to smoke. Health and risk behaviors form some clusters, so that they are highly associated in certain subgroups. For example, the relevant health behaviors of people at risk for cardiac disease may cluster more strongly than those for populations that are not at risk. People who are risk takers generally practice fewer health behaviors overall, and "health nuts" have higher levels of health practices overall (Leventhal, Prohaska, & Hirschman, 1985). The health behaviors of health care providers cluster more strongly than those of nonproviders (Salovey, Rudy, & Turk, 1987). Health habits that by their nature influence each other tend to be related to each other. Physical activity, for example, is positively associated with weight control, whereas physical activity and smoking are somewhat negatively associated (Blair, Jacobs, & Powell, 1985). Beyond these common-sense clusterings, however, health habits retain a fair degree of autonomy. This means that achieving a concerted program of good health behavior, whether for an individual or for a nation, is no small feat.

A third important characteristic of health habits is that they are unstable over time (Mechanic, 1979). Thus, a person may stop smoking for a year but take it up again during a period of stress. A dieter may lose 50 pounds, only to regain them a few months later. A problem drinker may remain abstinent for a period of time and then suddenly revert to his old ways.

Why are health habits autonomous and unstable? There are a variety of reasons. First, *different health habits are controlled by different factors.* For example, smoking may be related to stress, whereas exercise may depend on ease of access to sports facilities. Second, *different factors may control the same health behavior for different people.* Thus, one person's overeating may be "social," and she may eat primarily in the presence of other people. In contrast, another individual's overeating may depend on levels of tension, and he may overeat only when under stress. Third, *factors controlling a health behavior may change over the history of the behavior* (Leventhal, Prohaska, & Hirschman, 1985). The initial instigating factors may no longer be significant, and new maintaining factors may develop to replace them. Although peer group pressure (social factors) is important in initiating the smoking habit, over time, smoking may be maintained because it reduces craving and feelings of stress. One's peer group in adulthood may actually oppose smoking. Fourth, *factors controlling the health behavior may change across a person's lifetime.* Regular exercise occurs almost automatically in childhood, for example, because it is built into the school curriculum. In adulthood, however, this automatic habit must be practiced consciously. Fifth and finally, *health behavior patterns, their developmental course, and the factors that change them across a lifetime will vary substantially between individuals* (Leventhal, Prohaska, & Hirshman, 1985). Thus, one individual may have started smoking for social reasons but continue smoking to control stress; the reverse pattern may characterize the smoking of another individual.

The lack of motivation to change health habits can also act as a barrier. Unhealthy behaviors can be pleasurable, often automatic, sometimes addictive, and maintained by a variety of factors that are already in place in one's life. Consequently, many people simply do not want to develop a preventive health orientation toward the care of their bodies and may resist interventions urging them to do so. Some people feel that a life that focuses heavily on good health habits is a life devoted to the fear of illness. Such a life may be considered dull and not worth the sacrifices. Risky behaviors are fun, and many people are unwilling to give them up. Many say they have other "more important" priorities and cannot allocate time to health. The common recognition that one has to die anyway can undermine the modification of a particular risk factor, since people may feel that if one thing does not get them, another will (Stachnik et al., 1983).

In summary, health behaviors are elicited and maintained by different factors for different people, and these factors change over the lifetime as well as during the course of the health habit. Motivational factors also contribute to poor health habits. Such complexity inevitably means that health habits are very difficult to change. Given the high variability in the causes of a particular health behavior and given that those causes are sometimes unstable, it is impossible to develop an intervention focus that will deal with all of these factors simultaneously. These factors have all acted as barriers to effective primary prevention.

Barriers to Health Promotion Within the Field of Psychology

Psychology can contribute to prevention of disease and disorders by helping to find the best ways to get healthy people to practice good health behavior (Matarazzo, 1982). Yet, an examination of current primary prevention programs reveals that only a small fraction of this promise has been realized. Clearly, there are barriers within the field of psychology that have also contributed to the ineffective development of health promotion in this country.

Historically, psychologists have been concerned with mental health rather than physical health. Thus newness to the area may prompt a reluctance to treat health disorders. In particular, it may be hard to recognize that attitude-change and behavior-change techniques that have been developed for the treatment of emotional disorders are equally applicable to health problems (Stachnik et al., 1983). There may also be a gap between the scientific development of effective change technologies and the practitioner's use of them. Because they feel unskilled in the practice of behavior change, scientist-researchers may be reluctant to translate technologies that are known to work in the laboratory into behavioral methods for changing real people's behavior (Stachnik et al., 1983). These sources of reluctance must be overcome.

In addition, psychologists may bring their habit-change technologies to the general public in the wrong way. Typically, psychologists practice in private offices and treat individual difficulties on a one-to-one or small-group basis. Although this model can be effective for dealing with emotional problems, it is undesirable for changing health behaviors. The most effective programs of primary prevention are those that reach the largest possible number of people simultaneously (Stachnik et al., 1983). Thus, psychologists need to learn a new type of service delivery. They need to develop interventions that are not only effective but are designed for mass consumption.

This goal means, first, reorienting the search for effective behavior-change methods toward approaches that are suitable for large numbers of people. Second, psychologists must rethink their use of already-existing behavior-change techniques and make them more suitable for mass consumption. For example, training lay counselors to use behavior-change methods in groups will reach more people and be less expensive than continuing to focus on training professionals in private practice to use these principles on a one-to-one basis. Third, psychologists need to trans-

port interventions to environments in which large numbers of individuals are found. Exporting interventions to the physician's office, the workplace, schools, and community organizations means that large numbers of people can be influenced simultaneously. Moreover, this change in venue (location) means that health behaviors can be modified in situ—that is, in the environments in which they occur. What is the advantage of an in situ approach? Bringing people into laboratories and offices in order to change their behavior creates an artificial situation; it removes health behaviors from the environments in which they normally occur. By moving into workplaces, schools, and community organizations, one can see how behaviors function in their normal environments and can modify them in the settings in which they occur.

FACTORS INFLUENCING THE PRACTICE OF HEALTH BEHAVIORS

Most people know that health behaviors are good things to do. They cite exercise, rest, diet, control of stress, and not smoking or drinking to excess as valuable for good health. Consistent with these beliefs, virtually every individual performs some health behaviors. Most commonly, people report that they eat regular balanced meals, get enough sleep, engage in some physical activity, and enjoy relaxing leisure-time activities (Harris & Guten, 1979). Interestingly enough, these health behaviors are not the sort that require access to the health care system, as do using preventive screening programs or obtaining a Pap smear, for instance. Rather, they are behaviors that individuals practice on their own. Despite the fact that nearly everyone practices some healthy behaviors, some individuals are more likely to practice good health behavior than others. What are some of the determinants of practicing good health behavior?

Determinants of Health Behavior: An Overview

A variety of factors influence the practice of health behaviors, including social factors, emotional factors, cognitive factors, perceived symptoms, and factors relating to access to medical care (cf. Leventhal, Leventhal, & Nguyen, 1985). We will provide a brief overview of them here.

Health habits differ reliably by *demographic variables.* In a study of five health habits (smoking, physical activity, weight, alcohol consumption, and sleep), Gottlieb and Green (1984) found that health behaviors were commonly practiced by younger, more affluent, better-educated people under low levels of stress and with available social support (assessed by whether or not they were married and whether or not they attended church). Higher levels of stress and/or fewer resources, as may be the case for individuals of low socioeconomic status, are associated with more health-compromising behaviors, such as smoking or alcohol abuse, and with reduced time available for certain health-enhancing behaviors, such as exercise or adequate sleep.

Health habits are strongly affected by early **socialization,** especially the influence of parents as social models (Lau, Quadrel, & Hartman, in press). Parents instill certain habits in their children that become virtually automatic. Health habits that are typically under the control of socialization include wearing a seat belt, brushing one's teeth regularly, and eating breakfast every day. Once students leave home and go off to college, peers have a strong impact on changes in health attitudes. Nonetheless, overall, parents are still much more important determinants of health beliefs and behaviors. Consequently, these early influences are critical, exerting a long, perhaps lifelong, influence on the behavior of their offspring.

Other social factors also influence the practice of health habits, such as *values* associated with a particular culture or socioeconomic

group (Green, 1970; Langlie, 1977). For example, exercise for women may be considered undesirable in one culture but highly desirable in another. Thus, the number of women getting regular exercise would vary substantially between the two cultures as a function of these values. A third category of social factors influencing the development of health behaviors includes *peer influence.* For example, peer pressure is known to be highly significant in the development of smoking behavior in adolescents (see Leventhal & Cleary, 1980). Social factors can also function as maintainers of poor or good health habits. Thus, an individual who smokes socially will find that her smoking behavior is increased when she is around other individuals who smoke and is decreased around individuals who dislike smoking.

Emotional factors play an important role in the practice of some health habits. For example, overeating is linked to stress for some obese people, and they are more likely to overeat when they are under stress than when stress is absent. Positive health behaviors may also be under the control of emotional factors. For example, some individuals exercise when they are under stress, a far more constructive method of coping with the problem than, say, overeating would be. Self-esteem also relates to the practice of health behaviors. In both children and adults, those with higher self-esteem are more likely to practice a variety of good health habits than those with low self-esteem (Lau & Klepper, 1988). Generally, good health behaviors are more likely to be practiced by people with a sense of psychological well-being and a belief that their health is generally good (Mechanic & Cleary, 1980). Mechanic and Cleary (1980) argue that positive health behavior is part of a complex lifestyle that reflects the ability to anticipate problems, to mobilize to meet them, and to cope actively. As such, health behaviors are similar to other aspects of life that require planful problem-solving activity.

Many poor health habits, such as binge eating, meet emotional needs, such as reducing anxiety and inducing relaxation.

Health behaviors are also integrally tied into people's *personal goals*. A study by Eiser and Gentle (1988), for example, found that the extent to which people valued and engaged in behaviors such as smoking, drinking, eating, exercising, and relaxing was related to whether or not they perceived these behaviors as facilitating the attainment of their goals. The overall goal of simply staying healthy was only a partial predictor of these health habits. Moreover, the intention to modify a particular behavior in a healthier direction was somewhat undermined when the health-compromising habit served other goals, such as the ability to lead an exciting life.

Some health habits are controlled by *perceived symptoms*. For example, a smoker may control smoking behavior on the basis of sensations in his throat. If the smoker wakes up with the typical smoker's cough and raspy throat, he may reduce smoking in the belief that he is vulnerable to health problems at this time. But, if there is no smoker's cough or scratchy throat, he may smoke as usual.

Access to the health care system also influences the practice of some health behaviors. Earlier we noted that health behaviors are highly autonomous. For example, such behaviors as the use of seat belts, exercise, good nutritional habits, personal hygiene, checkups, and immunizations do not predict each other very well (Belloc & Breslow, 1972; Harris & Guten, 1979; Langlie, 1977). However, medically oriented preventive health behaviors are correlated fairly well (Langlie, 1977; Slesinger, 1976). Thus, the person who obtains a regular checkup is more likely to use a preventive screening service (such as chest x-ray mobiles) and is more likely to obtain immunizations.

The reason that medically oriented health behaviors are modestly related is that all of them are influenced by a common factor: access to medical services. Thus, in predicting medically oriented health behaviors, we need to know who uses health services more generally. Although this topic is covered more fully in Chapter 9, we take a brief look at the relevant factors here. Individuals who are low in socioeconomic status (SES), who are male, who do not have a regular physician, and who do not have convenient medical services are less likely to use health services generally and to practice health behaviors that require medical intervention than individuals who are high in SES, who are female, who have a regular physician, and who have easy access to medical services (Kirscht, 1983). Research reveals that people with more education and higher income are more likely to receive immunizations, have regular physicals when they have no symptoms, obtain preventive dental care, get Pap tests, and respond to breast cancer screening programs (for a review, see Kirscht, 1983). Even when screening programs or other preventive services are specifically designed for low-SES groups, the more advantaged individuals within that group will use the program more than the less advantaged (Kirscht, 1983). To summarize, then, access to medical care prompts the practice of a variety of medically oriented health behaviors. Unhappily, however, access to medical facilities does not necessarily improve nonmedical health behaviors such as smoking, overeating, and so on.

Finally, *cognitive factors* also determine whether or not individuals practice health behaviors. The belief that a particular health practice is beneficial and that it can help stave off a particular illness, as well as a feeling of vulnerability to that illness, may all contribute to the practice of a particular health behavior. We now turn to this issue in depth and examine the effects of health beliefs on health behaviors.

The Health Belief Model

The most highly influential and widely researched theory of why people practice health behavior is the **health belief model** (Hochbaum, 1958; Rosenstock, 1966). This model states that whether or not a person practices a particular health behavior can be understood by knowing two factors: the degree to which the person perceives a personal health threat and the perception that a particular health practice will be effective in reducing that threat.

The perception of a personal health threat is itself influenced by at least three factors: general health values, which include interest and concern about health; specific beliefs about vulnerability to a particular disorder; and beliefs about the consequences of the disorder (that is, whether or not they are serious). Thus, for example, a person may change his diet to include low-cholesterol foods if he values health, feels threatened by the possibility of heart disease, and perceives that the threat of heart disease is severe.

Whether or not the perception of a threat leads to changing health behavior also depends on whether a person believes a health measure will reduce that threat, as just noted. This factor also breaks down into two subcomponents: whether or not the individual thinks a particular health practice will be effective against the disorder in question and whether or not the cost of undertaking that measure exceeds the benefits of the measure (Rosenstock, 1974a). For example, the man who feels vulnerable to a heart attack and is considering changing his diet may believe that dietary change alone would not reduce the risk of a heart attack and that changing his diet would interfere with his enjoyment of life too much to justify taking the action. Thus, although his belief in his personal vulnerability to heart disease may be great, his faith that a change of diet would reduce his risk is low and he would probably not make any changes. A diagram of the health belief model applied to smoking is presented in Figure 3.2.

A large number of studies suggest that the health belief model explains people's practice of health habits quite well (for reviews, see Janz & Becker, 1984; Kirscht, 1983). For example, the health belief model helps predict who will make use of free health examinations,

FIGURE 3.2 The Health Belief Model Applied to the Health Behavior of Stopping Smoking

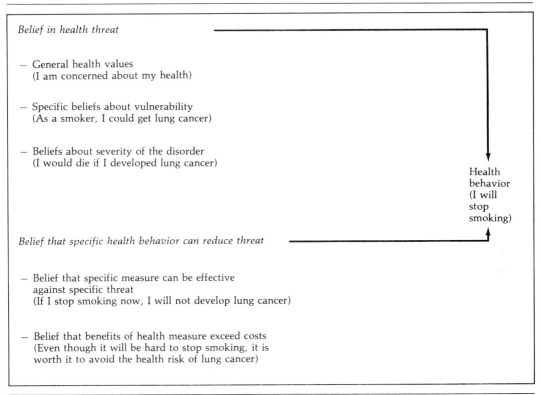

yearly medical checkups, vaccines, and disease-specific screening programs (Kasl, 1975; Rosenstock, Derryberry, & Carriger, 1959); participants in these disease-prevention programs were more likely to value their health highly (general health values), feel susceptible to the particular disorder in question, believe in the power of modern medicine to cure disease if detected early, and believe in the importance of medical research. The health belief model has also been applied to participation in flu immunization programs (e.g., Cummings, Jette, & Rosenstock, 1978), preventive dental care (Kegeles, 1963), smoking (Swinehart & Kirscht, 1966), asymptomatic checkups (Haefner & Kirscht, 1970), genetic screening (Becker, Kaback, Rosenstock, & Ruth, 1975), breast self-examination (Calnan & Moss, 1984), and dieting for obesity (Uzark, Becker, Dielman, & Rocchini, 1987), among many others. Typically, results indicate that health beliefs are a modest determinant of intentions to practice these health measures.

Janz and Becker (1984) examined forty-six studies using the health belief model to identify which components best predict the practice of health behaviors. Overall, perceived barriers to the practice of the health behavior was the most powerful dimension influencing whether or not people actually practiced a particular health behavior. Perceived susceptibility to a health problem was also a strong contributor. Some components of the model predicted sick role behavior (such as taking care of oneself or seeking medical attention), but did not predict health behaviors very well. In particular, perceived benefits of a practice and perceived severity of the problem were both associated with sick role behavior, but these factors were less important in explaining preventive health behavior, such as not smoking or weight control.

Not all research supports the health belief model, however (e.g., Haefner, Kegeles, Kirscht, & Rosenstock, 1967; Weisenberg, Kegeles, & Lund, 1980). One of the problems that has plagued tests of the health belief model is that different questions are used in different studies to tap the same beliefs; consequently, it is difficult both to design appropriate tests of the health belief model and to compare results across studies. Another reason why research does not always support the health belief model is that factors other than health beliefs also heavily influence the practice of health behaviors. As we have seen, these factors include social influences, cultural factors, experience with a particular health behavior or symptom, and SES (Kirscht, 1983).

Overall, the health belief model seems to best explain the preventive health behaviors of high-SES people who are knowledgeable about health matters (Anderson & Bartkus, 1973; Gochman, 1972; Wolinsky, 1978). That is, people who have financial resources and people who are knowledgeable about health issues are more likely to practice good health habits than other people. Thus, the health belief model appears to predict health behavior best when other demographic factors, such as SES and education, have already been considered.

Theory of Reasoned Action

Another cognitive theory that attempts to integrate attitudinal and behavioral factors is Fishbein and Ajzen's **Theory of Reasoned Action** (Ajzen & Fishbein, 1977, 1980; Fishbein, 1965, 1972, 1980). According to this theory, a health behavior is a direct result of a behav-

ioral intention—that is, of whether or not one intends to perform a health behavior. Behavioral intentions are made up of two components: attitudes toward the action and subjective norms about the appropriateness of the action.

Attitudes toward the action are based on beliefs about the likely outcomes of the action and evaluations of those outcomes. Subjective norms derive from what one believes *others* think one should do (normative beliefs) and the motivation to comply with those normative references. These factors combine to produce a behavioral intention and, ultimately, behavior change. Thus, to take a simple example, a smoker who believes that smoking causes serious health outcomes, who believes that other people think he or she should stop smoking, and who is motivated to comply with those normative beliefs will be more likely to intend to stop smoking than an individual who does not have these attitudes and normative beliefs.

What is the value of thinking about health habits from the standpoint of this theory? A strong element of Fishbein and Ajzen's approach is that behavioral intentions are measured at a very specific rather than at a general level. That is, when people are asked about very specific attitudes and normative beliefs, it is possible to obtain a fine-grained picture of their intentions with respect to a particular health habit. The advantages of this specific assessment can be seen in considering a college student's attitudes and practices regarding birth control. She might be favorable toward birth control in general and have a general intention to practice contraception. At the same time, however, she might be highly resistant to certain specific methods of birth control that are available to her. For example, she might be fearful of using birth control pills because of potential side effects, and she may not wish to use a barrier method, such as condoms, because she values spontaneity in her sexual relationships. Consequently, a general assessment of her intention to practice birth control would suggest that she might engage in these behaviors, whereas the specific assessment of her intention to use particular methods would highlight the sources of resistance to these specific methods of making good on that general intention.

The Fishbein-Ajzen approach to health behavior has been found to predict exercise (Valois, Desharnais, & Godin, 1988), use of child safety restraint devices (Gielen, Eriksen, Daltroy, & Rost, 1984), family planning behavior (Davidson & Jaccard, 1975), weight loss (Saltzer, 1978), smoking (Fishbein, 1980), and alcohol and drug use (Bentler & Speckart, 1979), among others. Thus, this approach has proven useful for understanding a number of health behaviors.

Recently, Ajzen and his associates (Ajzen, 1985; Ajzen & Madden, 1986) undertook a revision of Fishbein and Ajzen's theory, which they call the **Theory of Planned Behavior.** They argue that in addition to knowing a person's attitudes, subjective norms, and behavioral intentions with respect to a given behavior, one needs to know his or her perceived behavioral control over that action (cf. Bandura, 1986). In a test of the revised model, they found that people need not only hold a behavioral intention toward a particular attitude object but also feel that they are capable of performing the action contemplated and that the action undertaken will have the intended effect. Thus, feelings of perceived control and **self-efficacy** also appear to be important in demonstrating attitude-behavior consistency, even when there is a clear behavioral intention to act on an attitude.

The theory of reasoned action as originally formulated applies well to behaviors that are under personal control. However, if a behavior is influenced by factors over which people have only limited control, then their perceived self-efficacy, or ability to carry out the recommendations, becomes an important predictive factor. The theory of planned behavior, then, adds this additional element to cover behaviors that may be only partially under personal control.

Inclusion of the normative component in the Fishbein-Ajzen model is an important element in the theory, because normative influences are known to have such a profound effect on health behaviors. For example, the influence of peers on beginning smoking in adolescence is well known, whereas the climate among adults that opposes smoking has been important in leading smokers to develop the motivation to quit.

In summary, then, the theory of planned behavior maintains that people will perform a health behavior if they believe that the advantages of success outweigh the disadvantages of failure, if they believe that other people with whom they are motivated to comply think they should perform the behavior, and if they have sufficient control over internal and external factors that influence the attainment of the behavioral goal. Figure 3.3 presents a diagram of the theory of planned behavior applied to dieting.

In this section, we introduced two of the main attitudinal theories regarding the practice of health behaviors, namely the health belief model and the theory of planned behavior. Both theories highlight the beliefs that may contribute to the practice of preventive health behaviors; the theory of planned behavior also highlights the importance of normative influences, behavioral intentions, and beliefs in self-efficacy as additional factors that will influence the practice of a health behavior. The theories differ in that the focus of the Fishbein-Ajzen model is directly on the specific behaviors associated with a behavioral intention, whereas the health belief model assesses beliefs at a somewhat more general level that is less concretely tied to intentions to perform the behavior. A more complete evaluation of the usefulness of attitudinal theories in understanding health behaviors and how to change them is deferred to Chapter 4, but these issues are introduced here because they

FIGURE 3.3   The Theory of Planned Behavior Applied to the Health Behavior of Dieting

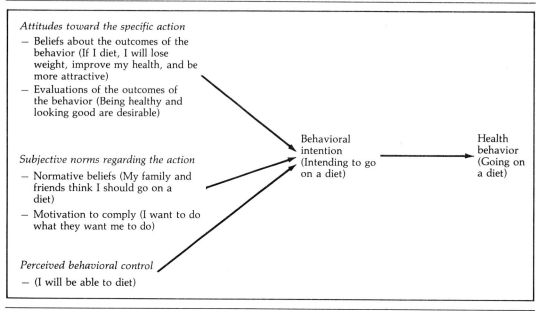

(Ajzen & Fishbein, 1980; Ajzen & Madden, 1986)

constitute some of the cognitive influences on people's practices of health behaviors.

Individual Differences in the Practice of Good Health Behavior

Recently, researchers have tried to find out whether there are particular types of people who are more likely to practice preventive health behaviors than others. That is, are there factors in an individual's personality or general psychological makeup that predispose him or her to engage in healthy behaviors?

One factor that seems to influence the practice of good health behaviors is age. Generally speaking, health behaviors are fairly good in childhood but tend to deteriorate over time. In adolescence and during people's 20s, good health behaviors are at a marked low. After that, however, healthy behaviors improve again, with older people practicing somewhat better health behaviors than younger people (Leventhal, Prohaska, & Hirshman, 1985). Exactly why these age trends exist is not entirely clear. It may be that children who are in the care of their parents and who receive continuous pediatric care are a captive population who practice good health behavior because their environment is structured that way. Adolescents and young adults, in contrast, are at their peak physical performance, and may feel no need to practice good health behaviors (Hershey, 1974). Older people may practice good health behavior because they begin to recognize their legitimate health risks. However, individuals in adolescence and young adulthood may feel invulnerable to health problems and therefore neglect their health.

Personality variables have also been explored for their impact on the practice of preventive health behavior. One such variable that has received attention is **locus of control** (Lau, 1988; Rotter, 1966; Strickland, 1978). This concept grew out of social learning theory and maintains that behavior occurs as a function of chronic expectations about reinforcements in a given situation. The internal-external dimension defines an individual's generalized belief about the source of reinforcements. Individuals with an _internal_ locus of control are more likely to believe that reinforcements are consequents of their own behavior, whereas individuals with an _external_ locus of control tend to see their reinforcements as under the control of external agents—that is, as less dependent on their own actions and more dependent on other people or chance (Rotter, 1954, 1966). Locus of control is similar to the self-efficacy and perceived control beliefs that we discussed in the context of the Fishbein and Ajzen model of health behavior, except that self-efficacy concerns beliefs about the practice of a specific health behavior, whereas locus of control refers to a more general expectation regarding one's impact on the environment.

Researchers have hypothesized that "internal" individuals are more likely than "external" individuals to engage in preventive health behaviors because they see these steps as helping to protect them against poor health. A review of these studies (Strickland, 1978) indicates that this belief is not misplaced. Most research suggests that individuals with an internal locus of control are more likely to assume responsibility for their own health. They may practice better health behaviors, guard more carefully against accidents, and gather more health information than individuals with an external locus. However, results are not always strong, and measurement problems plague the locus-of-control construct. Consequently, the relationship between the locus-of-control variable and preventive health behavior is modest.

There is some evidence that internals who value health seek more information than

internals who do not value health (Strickland, 1978). As a consequence of these kinds of findings, researchers have attempted to examine locus of control more precisely in the health context (Lau & Ware, 1981; Wallston, Wallston, & DeVellis, 1978). For example, the **Health Locus of Control** Scale, developed by Wallston et al. (1978), measures three factors. (1) The internal health locus of control subscale is measured by such items as "I am in control of my health" and "The main thing that affects my health is what I myself do." (2) The powerful others' control over health subscale is measured by such items as "Whenever I don't feel well, I should consult a medically trained professional" and "Whenever I recover from illness, it's usually because other people (for example, doctors, nurses, family, friends) have been taking good care of me." (3) The third subscale, chance health locus of control, is measured by such items as "No matter what I do, if I am going to get sick, I will get sick" and "Luck plays a big part in determining how soon I will recover from an illness."

One might expect that high scorers on the internal health locus of control subscale would practice preventive health behaviors because they would see their health as under their own control. Conversely, one might expect that individuals who scored high on the powerful others' scale or the chance scale would be less likely to practice preventive health behaviors because they would see their health as substantially under the control of external forces. Despite the plausibility of these conjectures, research evidence has not consistently supported them.

Wallston and Wallston (1984) reviewed a number of studies examining the relationship between health locus of control and preventive health behavior. Although high scorers on the internal subscale may be more likely to seek out health information at least on some issues, there are no strong relationships between health locus of control and health behaviors. However, Wallston and Wallston noted that such a relationship would be expected only among persons with strong health values, and rarely has this relationship been tested.

Using a modified health locus of control measure (Lau & Ware, 1981), Jacobs and Lau (1989) found, however, that people with high internal health locus of control beliefs may respond to health promotion messages differently than do those with low internal health locus of control beliefs. Consistent with the Wallston and Wallston hypothesis, internal locus of control people who placed a high value on health retained greater information 3 months after a persuasive health communication than did people without this combination of attributes. Moreover, those high in internal control were somewhat more receptive to persuasive communications consistent with their health control beliefs. Results like these suggest that additional research should examine the possibility of matching types of control appeals in persuasive messages to the health locus of control beliefs of the target audience.

Although thus far the health locus of control variable has not proven to discriminate individuals who practice health behaviors from those who do not, its promise may yet be realized. Moreover, the coming years will undoubtedly offer other individual-difference approaches to understanding the complex factors that go into the practice of preventive health behavior.

HEALTH PROMOTION: A PRELIMINARY EVALUATION

Having focused on the importance of health habits in this chapter and their determinants and factors that have impeded their development, health promotion would seem to be a benefit without concomitant risk. Who could quarrel with the importance of good health and the achievement of a healthy lifestyle to maintain it? Some have argued, however, that the heavy emphasis on health promotion that currently exists in our culture places too much responsibility on people for their health. We are trained virtually from infancy to watch out for every conceivable risk and to take effective action to avoid it. We are alerted regularly to the risks of foods in our diets that may cause this or that disease. Some have argued (Becker, 1986; Evans, 1988) that health promotion is becoming tyrannical, turning into an ideology rather than a science. We may expect people to monitor their lives more than is comfortable for them and more than is necessary. We may be recommending changes in food consumption, for example, that bear trivial relationships to health outcomes. The scientific evidence may not fully justify the enthusiastic zealotry with which some are committed to health promotion. We address this concern again in Chapter 16, but it is worth raising as a countervailing caution here.

SUMMARY

1. Health promotion is the process of enabling people to increase control over and improve their health. It involves the practice of good health behaviors and the avoidance of health-compromising ones.

2. The impetus for health promotion has

come from recognizing the impact of lifestyle factors, such as smoking, drinking, and controlling weight, on chronic health disorders.

3. Health promotion efforts target children and adolescents before bad health habits

are in place. They also focus on individuals and groups at risk for particular disorders to prevent those disorders from occurring.

4. Individual barriers to health promotion consist of unrealistic optimism about health risks, lack of knowledge about the importance of proper health habits, children's modeling of adult health-compromising behavior such as smoking, and little immediate incentive for practicing good health behavior.

5. Medicine has underemphasized health promotion because of a traditional orientation toward treatment and cure, and because of the absence of systematic technology for assessing health risk and developing programs of primary prevention.

6. Health-habit factors that undermine health promotion include the facts that health habits are only modestly related to each other and that they are highly unstable over time.

7. Psychological efforts in health promotion include the need to apply technologies of attitude and behavior change to health problems and the need to find appropriate venues for bringing interventions to the public.

8. Health habits are determined by demographic factors, emotional factors such as stress, social factors such as early socialization and peer group influence, cultural background, perceived symptoms, access to medical care, and cognitive factors such as health beliefs.

9. Health behaviors also depend on whether a person perceives a personal health threat, whether the person believes that a particular health measure will substantially reduce the threat, and whether he or she believes that he or she is able to perform the behavior. Behavioral intentions are also strong determinants of behavior.

10. Individual differences, such as locus of control or health locus of control, may also predict the practice of health behaviors.

11. Although health promotion is an important goal, critics of the health promotion movement have suggested that it places too much responsibility on people for their health, expects them to monitor their lives more than may be comfortable or appropriate, and may overstate the relation between risk factors and health outcomes.

KEY TERMS

at risk
health behaviors
health belief model
health beliefs
health habit
Health Locus of Control
health promotion
health risk appraisal
locus of control
primary prevention

self-efficacy
socialization
teachable moment
Theory of Planned Behavior
Theory of Reasoned Action
third-party reimbursement programs
unrealistic optimism
wellness
window of vulnerability

4

THE MODIFICATION OF HEALTH BEHAVIORS

Habit is habit, and not to be flung out of the window by any man, but coaxed downstairs a step at a time.

—Mark Twain

In the previous chapter, we examined health promotion—the philosophy that health is an active achievement rather than a steady state to be taken for granted. We also identified the health habits that are important for maintaining good health and avoiding major diseases and specified some of the factors that determine whether or not a person will practice a particular health habit. In this chapter, we consider one of the major tasks facing health psychologists: How do we get people to give up the risky behaviors that damage their health and develop good health habits? First, we examine attitude-change approaches that attempt to change health behaviors by changing health beliefs. In this context, we explore the efficacy of fear appeals and informational appeals, the use of the health belief model and protection motivation theory in changing health behaviors, and the success of mass media efforts in changing both health beliefs and health behaviors. As we will see, attitude change campaigns can be successful in inducing the desire to change behaviors, but may not be successful in teaching people exactly how to do so.

Consequently, a therapeutic emphasis is needed to bring about actual behavior change. In this context, we examine cognitive-behavioral approaches to health-habit modification. First we look at self-observation and self-monitoring; then classical conditioning and its offshoot, systematic desensitization; operant conditioning, including behavioral shaping; modeling; and stimulus control. We then turn to therapeutic techniques that integrate the person's specific health cognitions into the behavior-change process and illustrate the important involvement of the client in the behavior-change process. Self-control is essential to behavior change because it instills feelings of competence or efficacy. In this context, we consider the specific techniques of self-observation and self-monitoring, stimulus control, covert self-control, self-reinforcement, and contingency contracting.

Next, we turn to broad-spectrum, or multi-modal, cognitive-behavior therapy. This approach brings a wide range of cognitive and behavior-change techniques to the modification of a particular health habit. In addition, broad-spectrum approaches to habit change analyze the context in which the target behavior occurs and attempt to modify the environment to help maintain behavior change. This attention to the total environment has led to the integration of social-skills training and the involvement of family and peers in the behavior change effort. We also consider the development of relapse prevention techniques that help people maintain health behavior change successfully over the long term. Then, we round out our coverage of health-habit modification by considering the role of social engineering in changing health behaviors and the most appropriate venue for changing health behavior.

CHANGING HEALTH BEHAVIORS BY CHANGING HEALTH BELIEFS

An important step in the modification of health behavior is motivating an individual to want to change the behavior. Thus, for example, a smoker will not stop smoking until she is persuaded that there is a need to stop. An overweight individual will not lose weight until he develops the motivation to lose weight. Accordingly, researchers have initiated a variety of efforts to change health beliefs with the goal of ultimately changing health behaviors.

Attitude Change and Health Behavior

Attitude-change approaches to changing health behaviors implicitly assume that if people can

be persuaded that their current health habits are poor, they will be motivated to change those health habits. In particular, research has focused on the usefulness of appeals to fear or to information, or both, in changing health habits.

Fear Appeals   An extensive program of research in the 1950s and 1960s examined whether fear is an effective motivating factor to get people to change their health behavior (for reviews of the research, see Higbee, 1969; Janis, 1967; Leventhal, 1970). This research was predicated on the assumption that if people become fearful that a particular habit is hurting their health or that the absence of a particular health habit is bad for their health, they will change their behavior to reduce the fear.

Common sense indicates that the relationship between fear and behavior should be a direct one: The more fearful an individual is, the more likely he or she will be to change the relevant health behavior. However, research suggests that this straightforward relationship is not valid (Higbee, 1969; Leventhal, 1970). Although fear-arousing messages that portray strong health threats sometimes produce greater attitude change and intentions to change behavior than do less fear-arousing messages, these changes in attitudes and behavioral intentions often do not persist over time. In some cases, strong fear-arousing messages can lead people to avoid the threatening situation, as when they refuse to expose themselves to x-rays (Leventhal & Watts, 1966) or to obtain information about a screening service. Moreover, if personal vulnerability and high levels of threat are combined, the attitude-change benefits of the threatening messages may be undermined. People may come to feel fearful without believing that they can take any positive action (Leventhal & Cleary, 1980). In other cases, fear appeals may be ignored, because as a population, we have

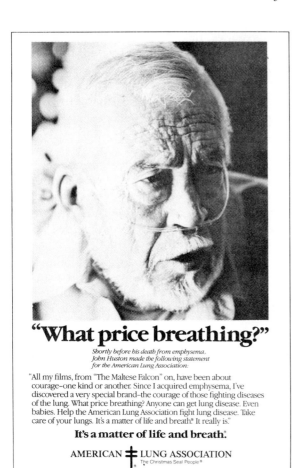

"**What price breathing?**"

*Shortly before his death from emphysema,
John Huston made the following statement
for the American Lung Association:*

"All my films, from "The Maltese Falcon" on, have been about
courage—one kind or another. Since I acquired emphysema, I've
discovered a very special brand—the courage of those fighting diseases
of the lung. What price breathing? Anyone can get lung disease. Even
babies. Help the American Lung Association fight lung disease. Take
care of your lungs. It's a matter of life and breath.® It really is."

It's a matter of life and breath.®

AMERICAN ✚ LUNG ASSOCIATION
The Christmas Seal People ®

*Fear appeals often alert people to a health problem but
do not necessarily change behavior.*

hibit behavior change (Becker & Janz, 1987).
Other attitude-change techniques, such as information alone or information coupled with a
positive appeal (as to good health or physical
attractiveness), can be more effective motivators to get people to change their behavior
(e.g., Evans, Rozelle, Lasater, Dembroski, &
Allen, 1970; Leventhal, Singer, & Jones, 1965).
Fear can sometimes affect intentions to change
health habits (e.g., Sutton & Eiser, 1984; but
see Sutton & Hallett, 1988); however, it may
not produce lasting change in health habits
unless it is coupled with recommendations for
action or information about the efficacy of preventive health behavior (Leventhal, 1970).
This more limited view of the role of fear in
producing health-habit change has been implicitly incorporated into the health belief
model, as we saw in Chapter 3.

**Informational Appeals   Informational ap-
peals** have also been developed to educate
people about the effects of their health habits.
Attitude-change research has demonstrated a
number of important principles for how best
to persuade people to change their behavior
through informational campaigns, including
the following:

1. Communications should be colorful and
   vivid rather than steeped in statistics and
   jargon. If possible, they should also use
   case histories (Taylor & Thompson, 1982).
   For example, a communication that highlights the concrete advantages of exercise
   coupled with a positive, convincing case
   history of an individual who changed from
   a sedentary to an active way of life is typically more persuasive than statistics dron-
   ing out the relationship between lack of exercise and the incidence of heart attacks.

2. The communication source should be expert, prestigious, and trustworthy. Thus, a
   health message will be more persuasive if it
   comes from a highly respected, credible

become inoculated against them. There are so
many messages designed to scare us that fear
appeals may now produce little more than a
yawn (Becker, 1987).

It is now believed that fear appeals are neither necessary nor sufficient to change behavior. Although fear appeals can be successful,
their effects are sometimes short-lived and
helpful mainly for nonrepetitive (or one-time)
behaviors rather than for behavior change that
must be maintained over the long term or that
involves repeated exposure to temptation.
Fear levels that are too high may actually in-

physician than from a proponent of the latest health fad. Communicators are also more persuasive if they are likable, similar to the audience, and familiar to the audience (McGuire, 1964).

3. A communication should discuss both sides of the issue if the audience is not inclined to accept the communicator's viewpoint, but only one side of the issue otherwise. This is because people opposed to an issue need to hear the positive reasons for changing their beliefs as well as the arguments against the position they currently hold. People who favor a health message only need to hear supportive arguments to be persuaded; they do not need to hear a rebuttal of arguments they do not accept anyway. For example, smokers who want to stop smoking should be exposed to communications that uniformly stress the advantages of not smoking and the disadvantages of smoking; smokers who have not yet decided to stop might be better persuaded by a communication that points out the risks of smoking while acknowledging and rebutting the pleasurable effects as well.

4. Strong arguments should be presented at the beginning and end of a health message rather than being buried in the middle. Because people are better able to remember arguments that they hear first and last, they are more likely to retain arguments placed at the beginning or end of a health message.

5. Messages should be short, clear, and direct. Lengthy, unclear, indirect, or ambiguous messages are likely to be tuned out and thus will have only a weak effect on audience attitudes and behavior.

6. Messages should state conclusions explicitly rather than leaving them implicit. For example, a message extolling the virtues of a low-cholesterol diet should explicitly conclude that the audience should alter their diets to include less cholesterol.

7. More extreme messages produce more attitude change, but only up to a point; very extreme messages will be discounted. Thus, a message that urges people to exercise for half an hour 3 days a week may be more effective than one that vaguely urges only "occasional exercise"; however, a message that urged 2 hours of exercise a day would probably be ignored. (McGuire, 1964; Zimbardo, Ebbesen, & Maslach, 1977)

Despite the careful construction of health messages along the lines outlined above, it is clear that the informational approach to changing health behaviors has had only modest effects. What are some of the reasons? First, several decades of attitude-change research have revealed that the attitude-change process is considerably more complex than had initially been thought. Early researchers in attitude change assumed that by exposing individuals to an appropriately constructed health message, they could change attitudes and behavior. However, McGuire's (1969) classic analysis of the persuasion process indicates that attitude change is composed of at least five distinct processes: attention, comprehension, yielding, retention, and action.

Let us elaborate on McGuire's analysis. To be effective, a communication must initially grab an individual's *attention*. In the hectic confusion of the modern world, many messages are lost. Thus, a health message must be able to compete effectively with other demands on an individual's attention before it can have any effect. Second, a communication must be *comprehensible* to the person. As noted above, communications that draw on statistics, medical jargon, or other types of unfamiliar information may not be comprehensible; as a consequence, they may be ignored, dismissed, or forgotten. Third, the communication must persuade its audience to *yield* to the position recommended by the message. This component of the attitude-change process most clearly relates to the message characteristics we described above. Messages that are effectively constructed will lead more people to yield than those that are not well constructed. Fourth, people must *retain* a health communication in order to act on it. Since the quantity of information to which each individual is exposed is so great, any single communication is easily forgotten. Thus, retention becomes a critical component in the attitude-change process. It can be influenced by such factors as frequency of message repetition, the vividness of the message (Taylor & Thompson, 1982), and integration of the health message into aspects of daily life. Finally, if the communication includes specific *action recommendations* that are easy to implement, persuasion and ultimate behavior change will be enhanced.

Behavioral instruction is one of the components that has been most heavily stressed in attitude-change research on health habits, because research has consistently demonstrated that health-habit change depends heavily on specific instructions concerning how, when, and where to act (Leventhal, 1970). Thus, a communication urging the use of a breast self-examination training program is more successful in changing behavior if it includes specific instructions about where the program is held, the time at which instruction is provided, and how a woman can schedule an appointment. Providing the recipients of the message with an opportunity to develop specific action plans with reference to the health habit can also produce behavior change. For example, if a student is given information about a hypertension screening program and is then urged to plan to fit a visit into his schedule, he will be more likely to use the program. The process of developing a specific action plan may also instill a feeling of competence, which itself makes behavior change more likely (Leventhal & Cleary, 1980).

To summarize, then, research on informational appeals has highlighted a number of important characteristics of persuasive communications. However, it is also clear that a competently designed message that communicates health information is not in and of itself sufficient to produce behavior change. Rather, the links between attitudes and behavior are very complex. At a minimum, a persuasive communication is required. However, for action to follow, more attention to the determinants of actual behavior is necessary, as we now discuss.

The Health Belief Model   In Chapter 3, we introduced the health belief model (Rosenstock, 1966). This model maintains that health habits are a function of

1. Perceived vulnerability to a disorder.

2. The belief that a particular health measure will be sufficient to overcome this vulnerability.

The health belief model enables us not only to understand why people practice health behaviors but also to predict some of the circumstances under which people's health behaviors will change. Specifically, if something happens in a person's life that alters the sense of vulnerability to a disorder or the belief that a particular health measure will suffice to overcome that vulnerability, one would expect to see a corresponding change in health behavior (Janz & Becker, 1984; Kirscht, 1983).

A good illustration of this point comes from the experience of a student in the author's psychology class a few years ago. This student (call him Bob) was the only person in the class who smoked, and he was the object of some pressure from both the instructor and students to quit. He was familiar with the Surgeon General's Report (USPHS, 1964) indicating the health risks of smoking. Although he acknowledged a link between lung cancer and smoking and between heart disease and smoking, he believed that the relationships were quite tenuous. Moreover, because he was in very good health and played a number of sports, his feelings of vulnerability were quite low.

Over Thanksgiving vacation, Bob went home, as he always did, to a large family gathering, and discovered to his shock that his favorite uncle, a chain smoker all his adult life, had lung cancer and was not expected to live more than a few months. Suddenly, health became a more salient value for Bob, because it had now struck his own family. Bob's perceived susceptibility to the illness changed both because a member of his own family had been struck down and because the link between smoking and cancer had been graphically illustrated. Bob's perceptions of stopping smoking changed as well. He concluded that this step might suffice to ward off the threat of the disease and that the costs of quitting smoking were not as great as he had thought. When Bob returned from Thanksgiving vacation, he had stopped smoking.

The implications of the health belief model for intervention in health habits should be clear. According to this model, in order to develop an effective intervention, one must increase perceived vulnerability and simultaneously increase the perception that a particular health behavior will be successful in reducing the threat. In fact, several studies support this point. People are more likely to engage in preventive health behaviors (e.g., Becker, Maiman, Kirscht, Haefner, & Drachman, 1977; Kirscht, Becker, Haefner, & Maiman, 1978) and to use health screening services such as x-rays and physical exams if they are exposed to interventions that highlight personal vulnerability and point out the efficacy of a particular health measure in overcoming the vulnerability (Haefner & Kirscht, 1970). Elements of the health belief model have also been incorporated in studies attempting to modify smoking (Eiser, van der Pligt, Raw, & Sutton, 1985; Kaufert, Rabkin, Syrotuik, Boyko, & Shane, 1986).

However, other studies do not support the model. Health beliefs can be very resistant to change, and in other cases changes in health beliefs do not necessarily lead to corresponding behavior changes (Weisenberg et al., 1980). Thus, the health belief model represents one possible, but by no means always successful, attack on the modification of poor health habits.

Self-Efficacy and Health Behaviors The health belief model emphasizes perceptions of vulnerability and beliefs about the importance of particular health behaviors. But undertaking many health behaviors also requires a sense of personal control—a belief that one can actually perform the health behavior. The impact of personal control on health behaviors has been most clearly demonstrated in the research of Albert Bandura (1977; 1986).

Bandura reasoned that an important determinant of the practice of health behaviors is a sense of self-efficacy: the belief that one is able to control one's practice of a particular behavior. For example, a smoker who believes she will not be able to break her habit probably will not try to quit, however much she thinks that smoking is risky and that stopping smoking is desirable. Similarly, an overweight man may have more success with his diet if he is convinced that he has the self-control to restrict his eating. Research has shown that self-efficacy affects health behaviors as varied as abstinence from smoking (Prohaska & DiClemente, 1984b), the intention to try to stop smoking (Eiser et al., 1985), weight control (Strecher, DeVellis, Becker, & Rosenstock, 1986), and the use of condoms by gay men to avoid exposure to the AIDS virus (Coates, Morin, & McKusick, 1987). A recent review of the role of self-efficacy in achieving health behavior change found strong relationships between self-efficacy and both health behavior change and maintenance. Perhaps more important, experimental manipulations designed to increase feelings of self-efficacy found that such manipulations can be successful and that enhancement of self-efficacy is related to subsequent behavior change (Strecher et al., 1986).

In summary, then, whether or not a person practices a particular health behavior depends on several beliefs and attitudes:

1. The perceived threat to one's health;

2. The perceived effectiveness, ease, and desirability of a particular health practice;

3. A sense of self-efficacy that one can actually undertake the health practice.

Protection Motivation Model   A more recent approach to understanding health behaviors developed by Rogers (1984) integrates all of these factors. The **protection motivation model** maintains that the motivation to protect one's self from a health threat is based on four beliefs:

1. The threat is severe (magnitude of threat);

2. One is personally vulnerable to the threat (i.e., its occurrence is likely);

3. One is able to perform the response needed to reduce the threat (self-efficacy);

4. The response will be effective in overcoming the threat (response efficacy).

According to the model, when beliefs about these four factors are strong, then protection motivation is aroused, and an individual is more likely to change his or her attitudes toward a health behavior. An important point in Rogers's protection motivation theory is the assumption that fear is not an essential element in this process. One must instead direct communications toward changing attitudes

about the severity of the threat, personal vulnerability, self-efficacy, and response efficacy.

To apply the protection motivation model toward improving a person's health attitudes and behavior, one needs to identify an individual's attitudes on these four variables, determine which if any need to be changed, and direct communications to the individual that will alter the relevant beliefs. Thus, for example, if a smoker believes that smoking produces serious consequences such as cancer or heart disease, perceives himself as personally vulnerable to it, believes that stopping smoking will be effective in overcoming this threat, but doubts his or her ability to stop smoking, then a relevant attitude-change communication would be to increase perceptions of self-efficacy for stopping smoking (e.g., Maddux & Rogers, 1983; Rippetoe & Rogers, 1987).

In summary, recent attitudinal approaches to understanding and modifying health behaviors have examined four factors now thought to be important in changing health behavior: perception of a health threat, perception of personal vulnerability to that health threat, the belief that a particular health behavior will reduce that threat, and a sense of self-efficacy that one can undertake the behavior.

Through understanding the determinants of health behaviors, it may be easier to see why so few people actually practice good health behaviors overall. The obese individual may not perceive that being overweight is actually a threat to health (perceived threat). The problem drinker may not perceive that he is damaging his health (personal vulnerability). The nonexerciser may believe that exercise alone would not reduce the risk of a particular disease (response efficacy). The smoker may decide that it is too hard to change (low self-efficacy). For a health behavior to occur, all four of these factors must fall into place, and there are any number of beliefs or rationalizations a given person may have for not undertaking a particular health behavior.

Mass Media Appeals and Health Behavior Change One of the reasons attitude-change approaches to health-habit modification are so important is that the mass media draw on these principles in constructing health messages for mass appeal. One of the goals of effective preventive health behavior is to reach as many people as possible. Consequently, if the mass media can communicate persuasive messages that can change attitudes and behavior, they can alter the health practices of large numbers of people simultaneously.

Unfortunately, evaluations of the efficacy of mass media health appeals suggest fairly limited results (Atkin, 1979; Lau, Kane, Berry, Ware, & Roy, 1980). Generally, mass media communications bring about modest attitude changes and even more modest behavior changes. For example, evaluation of a 6-month mass media campaign to encourage the use of seat belts found no increase in seat belt use after the campaign (Robertson et al., 1974). Similarly, a mass media effort to encourage family planning had no effect on several relevant factors, including the sale of contraceptives, the number of unwanted pregnancies, the birthrate in the area, or attendance at family planning clinics (Udry, Clark, Chase, & Levy, 1972). Antismoking campaigns likewise appear to produce transitory decreases in smoking (Warner, 1977) but no long-term decrease. The promise of mass media campaigns to change health behaviors, then, appears to be limited. Box 4.1 tells the story of one such campaign.

The limited effectiveness of mass media health campaigns has a variety of causes. First, it is impossible to control exposure to the message. People may tune out a message when they encounter it, or they may never encounter the message if they do not make use of a particular medium (for example, if they do not read newspapers or watch television). Second, mass media messages are often abstract and may not focus on the concrete experiences that are important to an audience. As we have

already seen, concrete messages are more persuasive than abstract ones. Third, mass appeals sometimes fail to include specific action recommendations that individuals can easily translate into behavior. As we have seen, inducing successful behavior change is often as much a matter of knowing how, when, and where to take advantage of the recommendation as it is of developing the motivation to change the behavior. Alternatively, a mass media appeal may suggest a behavioral measure that some individuals cannot make use of (for example, recommending an intervention that is available only during working hours) and thereby may inadvertently discourage adoption of the recommended health measure.

Fourth, mass media messages are often developed by advertisers on the basis of their hunches as to what will work rather than on the basis of research findings. Careful construction of persuasive messages on the basis of research, such as that just described, is likely to produce more successful attitude and behavior change than messages constructed on hunch. Fifth, the media often inject themselves into people's lives when other influences on behavior are simultaneously present and more influential. Thus, if people are watching a televised health message while they are also chatting over dinner, the impact of that message will be lowered. Finally, it is impossible for any particular message to tap all the complex factors that lead people to practice a particular health behavior (Leventhal & Cleary, 1980). Mass appeals are precisely that: directed toward the masses; as a consequence, the individual factors maintaining each person's health habits cannot be addressed.

Before we conclude that mass media appeals to change health habits are totally ineffective, some important benefits should be underscored. First, mass media communications can alert people to health risks that they might not otherwise have known about (Lau et al., 1980). For example, the attention given to the

---

Box 4.1
Portrait of a Media Campaign to Reduce Cardiovascular Risk

Several years ago, an ambitious undertaking to reduce cardiovascular risk was mounted by a team of researchers at Stanford University (Meyer, Maccoby, & Farquhar, 1980). The Stanford Heart Disease Prevention Program, as it was called, was designed to test a potential model for mass media intervention in communities to get people to change their health habits so as to reduce their risk for cardiovascular disease.

Three communities similar in size and socioeconomic status were identified and compared on risk factors associated with coronary heart disease both before and after the study. One town served as a control town and received no campaign. The second and third towns were both exposed to a massive media campaign on the effects of smoking, diet, and exercise over a 2-year period via television, radio, newspapers, posters, billboards, and printed materials sent by mail. In one of these two towns, the media campaign was supplemented by face-to-face instruction, directed at participants at highest risk for coronary heart disease, on how to modify specific risk factors. This intervention was heralded as a potential major breakthrough in the modification of health habits because it employed an experimental design to examine health-habit modification efforts via the mass media and interpersonal interaction.

Only modest attitude and behavior changes were found in the community that was exposed only to the mass media campaign. As a consequence of the campaign, the participants became more knowledgeable about cardiovascular risk factors and reported that they had reduced their consumption of dietary cholesterol and fats relative to the control group. There was some evidence that systolic blood pressure and plasma cholesterol were reduced. More dramatic and lasting effects, however, were found when the mass media campaign was coupled with behavioral instruction of individuals at risk. These individuals did modify their cardiovascular risk status somewhat compared to the other two groups, primarily through reduced smoking (Leventhal, Safer et al., 1980).

The Stanford study was a valuable step in employing solid experimental data to evaluate mass media and face-to-face campaigns. The conclusions suggest that the mass media alone are relatively unsuccessful in modifying risk status. Because mass media efforts like the Stanford intervention are very expensive, it seems unlikely that future research efforts will employ a media-only campaign to address health habits. Rather, it is more likely that subsequent community studies will use mass media campaigns as only one component of a more complex, concerted approach to health-habit modification.

Surgeon General's 1964 report on the health risks of smoking alerted millions of people to the problem far faster than did other forms of communication. In this way, the mass media does contribute to the motivation to change behavior. As we see in Chapter 6, virtually ev- ery American now knows that smoking is a risky habit, and the majority of smokers want to change their behavior (Leventhal & Cleary, 1980). These motivations have been instilled in large part by mass media publicity on the risks of smoking.

"I'll do a lot for love, but I'm not ready to die for it."

Mass media appeals can change the attitudes of the general public toward particular health-related concerns.

Second, the mass media can have a cumulative effect over time in changing the values associated with health practices (Leventhal & Cleary, 1980). Consistent mass media messages that emphasize the importance of a health habit gradually change opinions, so that the cultural climate shifts in the direction of message recommendations. Again, smoking is a good example. Although mass media messages have been largely ineffective in getting particular individuals to stop smoking, the cumulative effects of antismoking mass media messages have been substantial, and the climate of opinion is now quite clearly on

the side of the nonsmoker. This shifting climate of opinion has induced a number of people who would otherwise be smoking or smoking more to change their behavior (Lau et al., 1980). In the absence of mass media publicity against smoking, we would have a higher rate of smoking in this country than currently exists.

Finally, the mass media can highlight and reinforce trends that are going on in the community through other channels. Although mass media interventions alone are not necessarily effective in modifying health behavior, when they are coupled with organizational, economic, and environmental changes, as well as individual communications that reinforce the behavior-change objectives, they may keep health habits in the public consciousness. Thus, mass media interventions, in conjunction with community interventions that underscore their points, can be more effective than either type of intervention alone (Green & McAlister, 1984).

COGNITIVE-BEHAVIORAL APPROACHES TO HEALTH BEHAVIOR CHANGE

Attitudinal approaches to the modification of health behaviors appear to be most useful in predicting when people will be motivated to change a health behavior and when they will make use of a health behavior opportunity that is offered through the medical health care system (Kirscht, 1983). These attitudinal approaches do not really explain the voluntary practice of good health behavior across a long time period, nor do they indicate which individuals modify their health behaviors successfully and which do not (Kirscht, 1983). A better understanding of these problems requires an approach that integrates cognitions with behavior. Cognitive-behavioral models of health habits stress the fact that the behavior, the environment in which it is embedded, and the possession of necessary skills of behavior change and maintenance all influence whether or not a health behavior will be practiced or changed.

As we have seen, health habits are often deeply ingrained and strongly resistant to change. Attitude-change procedures, such as instilling fear or providing information, do not suffice to alter health habits. These techniques may instill the motivation to change a health habit, but they may not provide the skills necessary to actually alter behavior and maintain that behavior change. Accordingly, psychologists have turned to the principles of learning theory in an effort to modify health behaviors. Learning theory is a particularly appropriate framework for health behavior modification. The behaviors that are important to good health usually involve either poor habits that must be changed or desirable responses that must be learned and incorporated into a person's behavioral repertoire. Accordingly, the principles by which learning is acquired and maintained are useful in understanding these processes (Bandura, 1969, 1986).

Cognitive-behavior therapy approaches to health-habit change focus on the target behavior itself: the conditions that elicit it and maintain it and the factors that reinforce it. Cognitive-behavioral therapists also recognize the significance of people's cognitions about their behavior. People actively interpret their environments and cognitively construct their world. As a consequence, their behavior is a result both of external events, such as controlling stimuli and reinforcements that regulate behavior, and of internal events, such as how one thinks about the world and one's own behavior in that world (Ellis, 1962; Meichenbaum, 1977; see Abel, Rouleau, & Coyne, 1987, for a review).

In particular, cognitive-behavioral therapists have recognized that maladaptive behavior patterns can be the consequence of irrational patterns of thinking. People may generate internal monologues about their habits that can interfere with their ability to change their behavior (Meichenbaum & Cameron, 1974). For example, a patient who wishes to give up smoking may interfere with the quitting process by generating self-doubts. Internal monologues along the lines of "I will never be able to give up smoking," "I'm one of those people who simply depend on cigarettes," and "I've tried before, and I've never been successful" undermine the ability to quit. Unless these internal monologues are modified, cognitive-behavioral therapists argue, the person is less likely to initiate behavior change and cannot maintain it over time.

An additional assumption of cognitive-behavioral therapy is that covert processes, such as thoughts and images, follow the same laws of learning and reinforcement as do external, observable behaviors (Mahoney, Thoresen, & Danaher, 1972). Just as behavior can be modified by controlling the stimulus conditions that give rise to it and the reinforcements that follow it, so too can cognitions be modified. Thus, in this section, we will see that cognitions are frequently targeted to be modified in a program of health-habit changes.

Recognition that people's cognitions about their health habits are important in producing behavior change has led to another insight: the importance of involving the patient as a co-therapist in the behavior-change intervention. Early behavioral approaches to health-habit modification implicitly treated behavior-change techniques as things done to or for the client and implicitly overlooked the client's important role in this process. Increasingly, cognitive-behavior change methods are incorporating the idea that clients must become active co-managers. Most behavior-change programs begin with the client as the object of behavior-change efforts, but in the therapeutic process, control over behavior change shifts gradually from the therapist to the client, so that by the end of the formal intervention stage, clients are monitoring their own behaviors, applying the techniques of cognitive-behavior interventions to their behavior, and rewarding themselves or not appropriately.

This shift in philosophy that enlists the cooperative efforts of the client is an extremely significant one. As research has increasingly acknowledged the importance of client beliefs, especially self-efficacy in the behavior-change process, the realization has come that simply doing things to a client to try to change behavior can inadvertently undermine these feelings of personal control or self-efficacy. Bringing the client actively into the behavior-change process, then, can help build on feelings of personal control and self-efficacy, thus increasing the likelihood that behavior-change efforts will be successful.

The cognitive-behavioral change perspective highlights another important quality of health habits: the distinction between initiating a change in behavior and maintaining that change. As we see in this chapter and in Chapter 5, it is often easy to get people to change a health behavior initially, but it can be extremely difficult to get them to maintain behavior change over time. Thus, for example, a smoker can be induced to quit—but for how long? An obese person may begin a diet—but will weight loss be maintained? After seeing to change health habits, many people backslide and stop complying with their behavior-change regimens. As we see in Chapter 10, nonadherence to health-habit change regimens can be as high as 95%. The cognitive-behavioral therapy perspective acknowledges this problem and builds in techniques aimed at relapse prevention. But maintenance of behavior change continues to be the most formidable problem of health-habit modification.

In the following sections, we examine the important principles of cognitive-behavioral therapy and how they can be applied to health-habit modification. We begin our discussion with self-observation/self-monitoring, which is the first step in most programs of behavior change. We then turn to three basic principles derived from learning theory on

which many health-habit modification programs are based: (1) classical conditioning and its offshoot, systematic desensitization; (2) operant conditioning procedures, including behavioral shaping; and (3) modeling, whereby an individual learns new behaviors by observing another person. Next, we consider stimulus control and the modification of environmental stimuli that help maintain behavior change. Then we turn to the self-control of behavior and the methods by which people help change their own deleterious behaviors and accompanying cognitions. Next, we examine behavioral assignments and skills training that can amplify and maintain behavior change. Finally, we examine broad-spectrum or multimodal behavior change, which is the use of multiple cognitive and behavioral modification techniques to modify a target problem.

It should be noted from the outset that *broad-spectrum, or multimodal, cognitive-behavioral therapy* is the most common method of modifying health habits at the present time. Rarely is one technique employed in isolation. Rather, a number of efficacious techniques are combined to address any given problem. The studies that evaluate particular cognitive-behavioral modification methods in isolation do so for research purposes to identify which components of a cognitive-behavioral change program are most likely to work. For therapeutic purposes, however, any one technique would almost certainly be combined with other methods to achieve the best possible outcome.

Self-Observation and Self-Monitoring

Many programs of cognitive-behavioral modification use **self-observation and self-monitoring** as the first steps toward behavior change. The rationale is that one must understand the dimensions of a target behavior before change can be initiated. Self-observation and self-monitoring assess the frequency of a target behavior and the antecedents and consequents of that behavior (Abel et al., 1987;

Thoresen & Mahoney, 1974). Introducing self-observation and self-monitoring at the outset of the behavior-change process also sets the stage for enlisting the patient's joint participation early in the effort to modify health behaviors.

The first step in self-observation is to learn to discriminate the target behavior. For some behaviors, this step is easy. A smoker obviously can tell whether she is smoking, and an obese individual knows when he is overeating. However, other target behaviors such as the urge to smoke or the urge to overeat may be somewhat less easily discriminated; therefore, an individual may be trained to monitor internal sensations closely so as to identify the target behavior more readily. Sometimes a person can be taught how to monitor a target behavior by observing another person (modeling). For example, the individual who is trying to reduce tension may profit from observing another person who is attempting to understand his or her own tension. Learning that such symptoms as mild headache and tight shoulder muscles are associated with the model's experience of tension, the individual may then more successfully attend to internal cues to recognize signs of his or her own tension.

A second stage in self-observation is recording and charting the behavior. Techniques range from very simple counters with which an individual records the target behavior each time it occurs to complex records documenting the circumstances under which the behavior was enacted as well as the feelings it aroused. Sometimes an individual is trained to plot a graphic display of the behavior so that it will be possible to observe changes in its frequency and in the stimuli that control it over time (e.g., McKennell, 1973; Stunkard, 1979). For example, a smoker may be trained to keep a detailed behavioral record of all smoking events. She may record each time a cigarette is smoked, the time of day, the situation in which the smoking occurred, and whether or not anyone else was present. She may also record the subjective feelings of craving that were present when the cigarette was lighted, the emotional responses that preceded the lighting of the cigarette (such as anxiety or tension), and the feelings that were generated by the actual smoking of the cigarette. She may then graph the behavior to get a picture of her smoking patterns. In this way, the person can begin to get a sense of the circumstances in which she is most likely to smoke, and can then initiate a structured behavior-change program that deals with these contingencies.

Although self-observation is usually considered to be only a beginning step in behavior change, some researchers have suggested that it may itself produce behavior change (McFall, 1970). Simply attending to one's own smoking may lead people to decrease the number of cigarettes they smoke. Typically, however, behavior change that is produced by self-observation or self-monitoring is short-lived and needs to be coupled with other techniques, to be described below, if lasting behavior change is to be produced (Thoresen & Mahoney, 1974).

Classical Conditioning

Classical conditioning was one of the earliest principles of behavior change identified by researchers. It was first described by Russian physiologist Ivan Pavlov in the early twentieth century. At the time, Pavlov was using dogs in his research on the digestive system. He observed that many of his laboratory dogs began to salivate in anticipation of food merely upon hearing the footsteps of the laboratory assistant who fed them. Pavlov reasoned that a behavior (salivating) that normally occurs as a reflexive, automatic consequence of a particular stimulus (food) had become conditioned to a new stimulus—the sound of the laboratory assistant's footsteps. Or, to put it another way, an unconditioned reflex (salivating in response to food) became tied to a new stimulus (the assistant's footsteps) to produce a conditioned reflex (salivating in response to the assistant's footsteps).

Let us examine this phenomenon more closely. *Unconditioned reflexes* are responses that occur automatically as a reaction to a specific stimulus. Such reflexes do not have to be learned. For example, when a physician taps your knee during a medical examination, your leg kicking up is an automatic, unconditioned response to the stimulus of the knee tap. Similarly, sneezing, coughing, and blinking the eyes are all unconditioned reflex responses to particular stimuli—perhaps the irritation produced by dust, pollen, mucus, or some other foreign substance. The exciting aspect of Pavlov's observations was the implication that these unconditioned reactions could be *conditioned responses* to *new* stimuli, with which they were not initially associated. Through continual pairing with a new stimulus, the automatic response could come to be evoked by the new stimulus as well.

Pavlov (1927) demonstrated this phenomenon in a now classic series of experiments. As we have already noted, dogs salivate (unconditioned response) in response to food (unconditioned stimulus). In his experiments, Pavlov rang a bell (conditioned stimulus) just before food was presented to the dogs. As a consequence, the dogs began to associate the bell with the appearance of food. Over time, they learned to salivate on hearing the bell (conditioned response) even when no food was present. Thus, from the unconditioned reflex (salivating in response to food), Pavlov created a conditioned reflex (salivating in response to the bell). This procedure is called classical conditioning; it is a learned association between two stimuli, one a reflex and the other a stimulus to which that reflex has been conditioned. Classical conditioning is also sometimes called *respondent conditioning* because an automatic response is conditioned to a new stimulus.

The principle of classical conditioning has been used extensively in the modification of health habits. For illustration, we can consider a classical conditioning approach to the treatment of alcoholism. Antabuse (unconditioned stimulus) is a drug that produces extreme nausea, gagging, and vomiting (unconditioned response) when it is taken orally by an individual. In theory, one can condition this reflexive response of nausea, gagging, and vomiting to alcohol alone if it is consistently paired with the ingestion of Antabuse. Thus, an alcoholic may be given his favorite alcoholic beverages to sip at the same time that he ingests the Antabuse. Over time, the alcohol will become associated with the nausea and vomiting caused by the Antabuse. After a number of such pairings, alcohol by itself (conditioned stimulus) should come to elicit the same nausea, gagging, and vomiting response (conditioned response). Thus, the rationale of classical conditioning in the treatment of poor health habits is to induce the patient to develop a reflexive response of aversion to a stimulus that was previously associated with pleasurable consequences. Classical conditioning is represented diagrammatically in Figure 4.1.

Although classical conditioning approaches to health-habit modification are often successful, there is a very real problem in inducing patients to make use of them. Ethical guidelines require the informed consent of the patient: He or she must be told ahead of time what will take place during the program and what unpleasant consequences to expect. Thus, although Antabuse is effective in conditioning an aversive response to alcohol, patients know that if they do not take the drug, they will not vomit when they consume alcohol. Therefore, patients often simply refuse to take the drug consistently. Even if classical conditioning has successfully produced a conditioned response to alcohol, the patient knows that if he drinks and gets sick a number of times while not taking Antabuse, eventu-

FIGURE 4.1   A Classical Conditioning Approach to the Treatment of Alcoholism

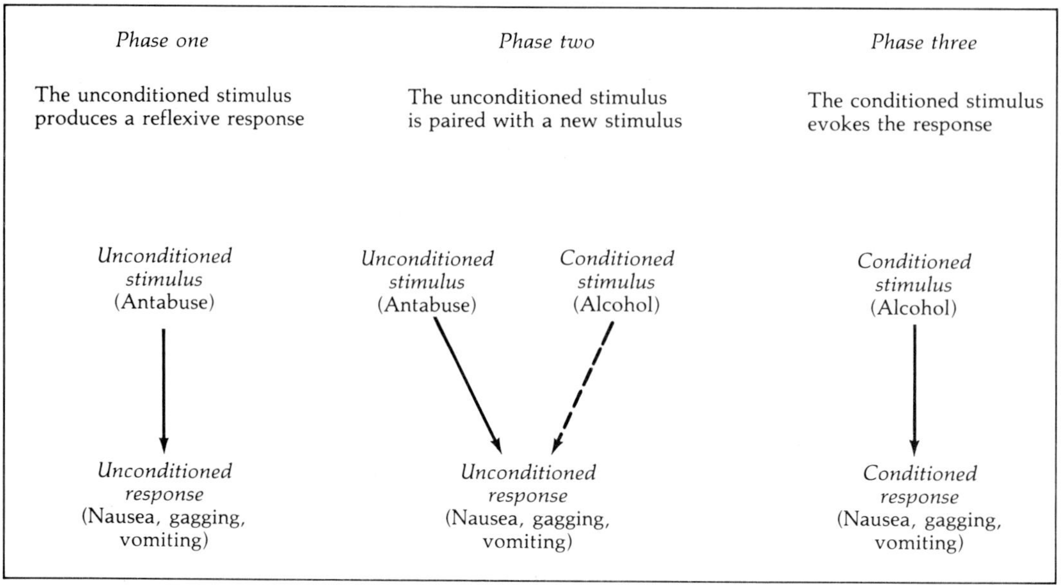

Phase one	*Phase two*	*Phase three*
The unconditioned stimulus produces a reflexive response	The unconditioned stimulus is paired with a new stimulus	The conditioned stimulus evokes the response

ally he will be able to drink without experiencing the conditioned response. Thus, although classical conditioning represents an important behavioral approach to health problems, it has serious limitations as well.

Systematic Desensitization

Classical conditioning procedures have provided the basis for a widely used technique of behavior change known as **systematic desensitization.** It was developed by Joseph Wolpe in 1958 to treat anxiety disorders, in which an individual experiences heightened anxiety in response to a particular stimulus or set of stimuli. A phobic reaction to spiders or snakes is an example of an anxiety disorder. Wolpe's systematic desensitization procedure proposed that classical conditioning could alleviate such anxiety-based responses if an individual learns to emit a response that is antagonistic to anxiety when in the presence of the anxiety-arousing stimulus.

On the basis of this principle, Wolpe trained individuals to substitute relaxation instead of anxiety for the stimuli that produced anxiety. **Relaxation training** typically has two components: deep breathing and progressive muscle relaxation. In deep breathing, a person takes deep, controlled breaths (between six and eight a minute). Deep breathing produces a number of physiological changes such as decreased heart rate, decreased blood pressure, and increased concentration of oxygen in the blood. This is the kind of breathing in which people typically engage when they are relaxed, in contrast to the rapid, shallow breathing they exhibit when they are highly anxious. In progressive muscle relaxation, the individual learns to relax all the muscles in the body and to discharge any tension that is felt, in contrast to the state of muscle tension that usually exists when a person is anxious. (We discuss progressive muscle relaxation more fully in Chapter 11.) Together, deep breathing and progressive muscle relaxation induce an overall feeling of relaxation.

How is relaxation used to alleviate anxiety?

In systematic desensitization therapy, the individual works with a therapist to construct a graduated series of anxiety-arousing situations (a hierarchy). Low items in the hierarchy arouse very little anxiety and are relatively distant from the actual feared situation. For example, a person suffering from fear of social situations might designate dinner with a good friend as an item that is low on the hierarchy of anxiety-arousing situations. Subsequent items in the hierarchy become progressively more anxiety-arousing until the target situation itself becomes the focus. For example, this individual might identify being at a cocktail party with strangers as an element high in the hierarchy.

The person is then trained to relax while imagining scenes from the hierarchy. He or she moves progressively from imagining the low-anxiety scenes to imagining the self in the target situation. This process is called **counterconditioning,** because an antagonistic response (relaxation) is conditioned to the stimulus that initially produced anxiety. As the client moves through the hierarchy of anxiety-arousing situations, she signals the therapist any time anxiety is experienced. Since the goal of the therapy is not to arouse any anxiety during the process, the individual is asked to stop imagining the anxiety-arousing item for the present, if any anxiety is in fact experienced. The individual then moves back to a less anxiety-provoking item in the hierarchy and tackles the other item at some later time (Rimm & Masters, 1974). An example of the use of systematic desensitization in the treatment of a health problem is presented in Box 4.2.

Although systematic desensitization has not been widely used in the modification of health habits, counterconditioning, its underlying principle, has. Researchers have noted that many deleterious health habits, such as smoking and drinking, represent destructive ways of coping with anxiety. The individual who is socially anxious may drink or smoke to combat feelings of rising tension. As a conse-

quence, interventions to alter these destructive health habits often include counterconditioning procedures, so that such people will learn more acceptable ways of coping with their anxiety. For example, a smoker may be trained in progressive relaxation so that when he feels anxious, he will substitute relaxation for smoking. Similarly, the alcoholic may participate in relaxation training or social skills training so that situations that normally arouse anxiety and lead to drinking will instead induce relaxation or other more socially appropriate responses. We will see this point illustrated repeatedly in the next chapter, which examines the modification of specific health habits.

Operant Conditioning

As we have seen, classical conditioning involves conditioning some automatic behavior to a new stimulus. **Operant conditioning,** in contrast, involves conditioning a voluntary, nonautomatic behavior by applying consequences systematically to the behavior. Operant conditioning was originally formulated by E. L. Thorndike (1898) and was more systematically developed by B. F. Skinner (1938). The key to operant conditioning is reinforcement. When an individual emits a behavior and that behavior is followed by reinforcement, the behavior is more likely to occur again. Over time, continued reinforcement of a behavior will increase the likelihood that the behavior will occur. Similarly, if an individual emits a behavior and is punished, the behavior is less likely to be repeated. Over time, punishment of a behavior reduces the likelihood that that behavior will be emitted (at least in that situation and so long as the punishing agent remains present). Thus, whereas classical conditioning involves modifying the antecedent stimuli that control a reflexive behavior, operant conditioning involves modifying the consequents of a behavior (reinforcements or punishments) to systematically increase or decrease its likelihood of occurrence. Operant

---

Box 4.2
Systematic Desensitization Used to Treat Gastric Ulcers

Miss T. was a 46-year-old unmarried dressmaker who was referred for psychotherapy by her physician. A year before, she had developed gastric pains and other digestive symptoms, and x-ray had revealed a peptic ulcer. Although medical treatment had reduced the pain somewhat, there was still radiological evidence of activity in the ulcer, and she complained of distress at the slightest emotional disturbance. Psychotherapy revealed that she showed exceeding sensitivity to social situations, resulting in extreme social anxiety. This social anxiety was successfully treated through systematic desensitization. In particular, over a 2-month period, Miss T. practiced relaxing in response to the following hierarchy of anxiety-arousing social situations, which proceeded from least anxiety-arousing (1) to most anxiety-arousing (13).

1. Having an interview with any doctor or lawyer (her own doctor was the stimulus figure used in the desensitization).

2. Unexpectedly finding a strange man present when visiting at her brother's house.

3. Being phoned by a man to whom she had recently been introduced.

4. Speaking, in company, to a man to whom she had just been introduced.

5. Meeting her girlfriend's boyfriend.

6. Making a speech to the employees of her firm at the end-of-the-year party.

7. Going up to receive a prize at the end-of-the-year party.

8. Having an interview with the representative of the Industrial Council because of sick pay not received from her employer.

9. Telling her employer that an error of which she had been accused was due to someone else's wrong instruction.

10. Being told by her employer that a hem she had made was not straight.

11. Receiving criticisms from members of her family.

12. Receiving criticisms from fellow workers.

13. Being at a party with other women who work with her.

(Based on Wolpe, 1958, pp. 148–152)

---

conditioning, then, involves the manipulation of environmental contingencies so that the frequency of certain target behaviors will be increased while the frequency of other target behaviors will be decreased.

An important feature of operant conditioning is the reinforcement schedule. A continuous reinforcement schedule means that a be-

havior is reinforced each and every time it occurs. Continuous reinforcement, for example, means reinforcing an individual each time a target behavior occurs, whereas continuous punishment involves punishing an individual each time a behavior is emitted. However, continuous reinforcement schedules are highly vulnerable to extinction: If a behavior is occasionally not reinforced, the individual may cease performing the behavior, having come to anticipate reinforcement every time. Psychologists have learned that behavior is often more resistant to extinction if it is maintained by a variable or intermittent reinforcement schedule rather than a continuous reinforcement schedule.

Many health habits can be thought of as operant responses. For example, drinking may be maintained because mood is improved by alcohol, or smoking may occur because peer approval is associated with it. In both of these cases, consequent reinforcement maintains the poor health behavior.

Shaping

Operant conditioning usually occurs by means of a process known as **shaping.** Successful behavior change does not occur all at once. Instead, it usually occurs gradually over time. Reinforcements can be systematically employed to change the behavior gradually to the desired form. Behavioral shaping usually occurs as a series of successive approximations to the target behavior.

Let us take the target behavior of smoking as an example. Many people who try to stop smoking are unable to do it all at once. Instead, they gradually modify their smoking behavior over a series of steps (successive approximations) until they are able to reach the target behavior (not smoking). How might operant conditioning be used in this shaping process? Let us assume that John smokes twenty cigarettes a day. He might first define a set of reinforcers that can be administered when particular smoking-reduction targets are met—reinforcements such as going out to dinner or seeing a popular movie. John may then set a particular reduction in his smoking behavior as a target (such as fifteen cigarettes a day). When that target is reached, he would administer a reinforcement (for example, a movie or a dinner out). The next approxima-

tion might be reducing smoking to ten cigarettes a day, when he would receive another reinforcement. The figure then might be cut progressively to five, three, one, and none. Thus, through the series of successive approximations, the target behavior of abstinence would eventually be reached. We see the principle of operant conditioning (that is, the use of reinforcement to control behavior) illustrated repeatedly in the modification of health habits (e.g., Dworkin, 1982; Lund & Kegeles, 1982).

Modeling

Modeling is learning that occurs by virtue of witnessing another person perform a behavior. Modeling is sometimes called vicarious learning or observational learning, and it is marked by the fact that it occurs without obvious direct reinforcement (Bandura, 1969). Modeling is an important mechanism by which children acquire habits, skills, and other behaviors. For example, the child who parades around in her mother's high heels is not explicitly reinforced for the behavior; indeed, quite the contrary may be true. She performs this behavior because she has seen her mother do the same thing.

Observation and subsequent modeling can be effective approaches to changing health habits. For example, these principles are implicit in some self-help programs that treat destructive health habits such as alcoholism (Alcoholics Anonymous) or drug addiction (Synanon). In these programs, a person who is newly committed to changing his or her addictive behavior joins the company of individuals who have had the same problem and who have had at least some success in solving it. In meetings, such people often share the methods that helped them to overcome their health problem. By listening to these accounts, the new convert can learn how to do likewise and model effective techniques in his or her own rehabilitation.

Modeling can also be used as a technique

for reducing anxiety: A person's fears can be reduced by observing a model engaging in the feared activity. The goal of having fearful people observe models going through the same situations is to help them see exactly how the model is dealing with the problem so that they can imitate those coping techniques. The model may be observed personally (e.g., Shipley, Butt, Horwitz, & Farbry, 1978), or through film (e.g., Melamed & Siegel, 1975).

One study that demonstrates this point (Vernon, 1974) used modeling in an attempt to reduce children's fears about receiving inoculations. Before they received injections, one group of children saw an unrealistic film of children receiving injections without experiencing any pain or expressing any emotion. A second group saw a realistic film that showed children responding to the injections with short-lived, moderate pain and emotion. A third group of children (the control group) saw no film. The results indicated that children who saw the realistic film experienced the least pain when they subsequently received injections. In contrast, those viewing the unrealistic film appeared to experience the most pain.

The results of this study illustrate another important point about modeling. When modeling is used as a procedure for reducing fear or anxiety, it is better to observe models who are also fearful but are able to control their distress rather than models who are demonstrating no fear in response to the situation. Because fearful models provide a realistic portrayal of the experience, the observer may be better able to identify with them than with models who are unrealistically calm in the face of the threat. This identification process may enable the person to learn and model the coping techniques more successfully (Kazdin, 1974; Meichenbaum, 1971).

Variations on these modeling procedures have also been employed in the reduction of anxiety. In a process known as vicarious counterconditioning (Bandura, 1969), individuals are repeatedly exposed to a model engaging in a feared activity. The rationale for this technique is that repeatedly observing someone perform a behavior that does not lead to negative consequences will lead to the extinction of anxiety. For this reason, the procedure is also called vicarious extinction.

In a second variation on modeling, **vicarious systematic desensitization,** or **guided mastery,** an individual copes with anxiety by observing a model progressively moving through a hierarchy of anxiety-arousing situations similar to those that arouse fear in the observer. Thus, for example, observing a socially anxious model successfully negotiate a hierarchy of progressively more anxiety-arousing social situations may help the socially anxious individual cope with these same fears. She may observe the coping techniques the model used and thereby have a set of coping techniques to use when she actually encounters these situations (Bandura, 1969).

In some cases, guided mastery is coupled with actual desensitization experiences. In this instance, the patient first observes a model moving through the hierarchy of behaviors and then is led through each step of the graduated hierarchy as well. However, relaxation training is not used in this particular variant on desensitization training. Instead, an individual's anxiety is reduced by observing the model successfully negotiating the hierarchy and then copying those behaviors rather than by engaging in such relaxation-inducing procedures as deep breathing or progressive relaxation (Bandura, Blanchard, & Ritter, 1969; Ritter, 1968).

To summarize, then, modeling, or imitative learning, has an important role in the modification of health habits and the anxiety that may surround them. Indeed, modeling may be one of the important mechanisms whereby group behavior–change approaches are often successful, inasmuch as members of such groups can potentially observe and adopt each other's successful methods. More formal incorporation of modeling principles into behavior-change efforts could be highly useful in the quest for methods that both bring about behavior change initially and maintain it over time.

Stimulus Control

As we have already seen in this chapter, the successful modification of behavior involves understanding the antecedents as well as the consequences of a target behavior. In this section, we consider stimulus control, a technique aimed at modification of the antecedents of a target behavior.

Individuals who practice poor health habits, such as smoking, drinking, and overeating, develop ties between those behaviors and stimuli in their environments. Each of these stimuli can come to act as a **discriminative stimulus** that is capable of eliciting the target behavior. For example, the sight and smell of food act as discriminative stimuli for eating. The sight of a pack of cigarettes and the smell of coffee may act as discriminative stimuli for smoking. This stimulus is significant because it indicates that a reinforcing response or behavior will occur. **Stimulus-control interventions** with patients who are attempting to alter their health habits take two approaches: ridding the environment of discriminative stimuli that evoke the problem behavior and creating new discriminative stimuli signaling that some new response will be reinforced.

How might stimulus control work in the treatment of a particular health problem? Since stimulus-control methods have been used extensively in the treatment of obesity (e.g., Stuart, 1967), this condition provides an effective example. Eating is typically under the control of a large number of discriminative stimuli, including the presence of desirable foods and activities with which eating is frequently paired (such as talking on the phone or watching television). As an early step in the treatment of obesity, the individual might be encouraged to reduce and eliminate these dis-

criminative stimuli for eating. Thus, he would be urged to rid his home of rewarding and enjoyable fattening foods, to restrict his eating to a single place in the home, and to not eat while engaged in other activities, such as talking on the phone or watching television. Other stimuli might be introduced in the environment to indicate that controlled eating will now be followed by reinforcement. For example, the person might place signs in strategic locations around the home reminding him of reinforcements to be obtained after successful behavior change.

Stimulus-control procedures have generally been found to be useful in the control of problematic behaviors, including health habits (e.g., Bootzin, 1975), but, typically, they are not sufficient to produce behavior change. Cognitions such as beliefs or attitudes that accompany a target behavior may also need to be modified—an issue to which we will shortly turn.

The Self-Control of Behavior

Increasingly, cognitive-behavioral therapists are recognizing that people's behavior is also pulled toward goals which they define and self-consciously move toward by planning and engaging in actions that get them closer to their personal goals (Leventhal, Zimmerman, & Guttmann, 1984). A consequence of this shift in perspective is that the person has increasingly been brought into the behavior-change process (Abel et al., 1987; Hollon & Beck, 1986; Thoresen & Mahoney, 1974). Many behavior therapies implicitly ignore the person by focusing on target behaviors, their antecedents and consequents, without taking a person's cognitions into account. Once cognitions themselves are admitted as a legitimate object of study and modification, the person almost automatically becomes more actively involved in the behavior-change process. He or she must talk about cognitions, indicate when they are present, and help in the modification process. Thus, as we shall see, cognitive behavior therapy has moved increasingly toward a therapeutic model that requires the **self-control** of behavior.

A second reason for the increasing involvement of the self in the therapeutic endeavor is that traditional behavioral approaches to health problems may inadvertently undermine important feelings of self-control and self-efficacy (Bandura, 1986). An individual who turns the self over to a therapist to produce behavior change is tacitly communicating that he or she is unable to control the behavior. Likewise, the therapist who externally imposes therapeutic interventions is communicating the same message back to the client. Increasingly, cognitive-behavioral therapists are recognizing that therapy can be more successful when an individual's capacity for self-help is enlisted in the therapeutic process (Thoresen & Mahoney, 1974).

Research on psychological control suggests that the setting of goals leads to planning and specific action (Leventhal, Zimmerman, & Gutman, 1984). These goals and plans, taken together, may help an individual regard a problem as manageable, leading to specific coping actions that can be evaluated for their effectiveness in terms of progress toward the goal. The presence of an explicit goal also provides the basis for evaluating the efficacy of any action and substituting a new action if the previous one is judged to fail.

Evidence for the importance of enlisting a sense of psychological control in the behavior-change process is plentiful. Some psychologists (e.g., White, 1959) maintain that feelings of personal control may be fundamental to mental health. People have a need to believe that they are active agents of change in their lives (Averill, 1973), and they cope better with aversive events when they believe that they have some control over them (Thompson, 1981). The ability to regulate one's environment is intrinsically reinforcing (Thoresen & Mahoney, 1974). Considerable research demonstrates that people perform better if they can control their own reinforcement schedules rather than having the reinforcements controlled externally by another agent (Lovitt & Curtiss, 1969).

For the above reasons, we will increasingly see *self-control* methods of behavior change incorporated into cognitive-behavioral therapy: The individual whose behavior is the target of intervention acts at least partly as his or her own therapist and, together with outside guidance, learns to control the antecedents and consequents of the target behavior to be modified.

Self-Reinforcement   **Self-reinforcement** is a cognitive-behavioral management technique that draws on the fundamental principle of learning theory: reinforcement. Self-reinforcement involves systematically either rewarding or punishing the self to increase or decrease the occurrence of some target behavior.

There are two kinds of self-reward (Thoresen & Mahoney, 1974). Positive self-reward involves reinforcing oneself with something desirable after successful modification of a target behavior. An example of positive self-reward is allowing oneself to go to a movie following successful weight loss. Negative self-reward involves removing some aversive factor in the environment after successful modification of the target behavior. An example of negative self-reward is taking the Miss Piggy poster off the refrigerator once regular controlled eating has been achieved.

A study by Mahoney (1974b) examined the effects of positive self-reward on weight loss. Mahoney created four experimental conditions: (1) a control condition in which no intervention occurred; (2) a condition in which subjects monitored their own weight; (3) a condition in which self-monitoring was accompanied by self-reinforcement with money or gift certificates for successful weight loss; and (4) a condition in which self-monitoring was coupled with gift certificates or money for successful changes in eating behavior. The two self-reward conditions produced greater weight loss than the control or self-observation conditions. Interestingly, of the two types of self-reward, self-reward for habit change (that is, altered eating behavior) produced more weight loss than self-reward for weight loss. This result appears to have occurred because self-reward for habit change led these obese individuals to modify their eating habits, whereas self-reward for weight loss was associated only with losing weight and not with any behavior change that produced the weight loss.

An example of negative self-reward was used in a study to control obesity (Penick, Filion, Fox, & Stunkard, 1971). In this study, individuals who were overweight were instructed to keep large bags of suet (animal fat) in their refrigerators to remind themselves of their excess weight. Each time they succeeded in losing a certain amount of weight, they were permitted to remove a portion of the suet from the bag, thereby reducing this unattractive stimulus. Techniques such as these can be very effective in maintaining commitment to a behavior change program.

Overall, self-reward has proven to be a useful technique in the modification of behavior. It appears to be at least as good at maintaining behavior change as external reward systems are (Thoresen & Mahoney, 1974). Moreover, self-reward techniques have intrinsic advantages in that no change agent, such as a therapist, is required to monitor and reinforce the behavior; the individual acts as his or her own therapist. Despite the success of self-reward, some questions remain. For example, is intermittent self-reward more effective in changing behavior than continuous self-reward? What kinds of self-reward are more valuable for producing lasting behavior change? Should one use an already existing positive reinforcer (such as television viewing) or create a new reward (such as a gift certificate)? Is positive

self-reward better than negative self-reward? Is there any disadvantage to creating an aversive stimulus in the environment, such as the Miss Piggy poster or the suet, in making use of negative self-reward techniques? These and other questions remain to be addressed by future research (Thoresen & Mahoney, 1974).

Like self-reward, self-punishment is of two types. Negative self-punishment involves the administration of some unpleasant stimulus to punish an undesirable behavior. For example, an individual might self-administer a mild electric shock each time she experiences a desire to smoke. Positive self-punishment consists of withdrawing some positive reinforcer in the environment each time an undesirable behavior is performed. For example, a smoker might rip up a dollar bill each time he had a cigarette that exceeded a predetermined quota (Axelrod, Hall, Weis, & Rohrer, 1974).

Research suggests that self-punishment is not as effective as self-reward in changing behavior (Thoresen & Mahoney, 1974). Studies that have evaluated the efficacy of self-punishment suggest two conclusions: (1) positive self-punishment works somewhat better than negative self-punishment and (2) self-punishment works better if it is also coupled with self-rewarding techniques. To take a specific example, a smoker is less likely to stop smoking if he rips up a dollar bill each time he smokes than if he self-administers electric shock; these principles are even more likely to reduce smoking if the smoker also rewards himself for not smoking.

Contingency Contracting One reason why self-punishment is not always effective in modifying behavior stems from what has been called the contract problem (Mahoney, 1970). This problem involves the fact that individuals' successful behavior modification through self-punishment works only if they actually perform the activities. People may cease self-punishment activities if they become too aversive and thus undermine the efficacy of self-punishment.

One form of self-punishment that works well and has been used widely in behavior modification is **contingency contracting** (Thoresen & Mahoney, 1974; Turk & Meichenbaum, in press). In contingency contracting, an individual forms a contract with another person, such as a therapist, detailing what rewards or punishments are contingent upon the performance or nonperformance of some behavior. For example, a person who wanted to stop drinking might deposit a sum of money with a therapist and arrange to be fined each time she had a drink and to be rewarded each day that she abstained. A particularly interesting example of contingency contracting reported by Thoresen and Mahoney (1974) involved a black woman who was attempting to control her abuse of amphetamines. She deposited a large sum of money with her therapist and authorized the therapist to give $50 to the Ku Klux Klan each time she abused amphetamines. Not surprisingly, this contract was effective in inducing the patient to reduce her amphetamine intake.

Contingency contracting appears to be successful in promoting behavior change. Why has this technique succeeded where other efforts at self-punishment have failed? One reason is that contingency contracting brings self-presentation into play: When an individual makes a contract with another person, the desire to look good and not lose face becomes important. More significantly, contingency contracting is rarely used alone in efforts to modify behavior. Rather, it is combined with other techniques in successful modification of behavior.

Covert Self-Control   **Covert self-control** is the manipulation and alteration of private events. These events include thoughts, images, and internal monologues, such as self-praise and self-instruction. The goal of covert self-control is to train an individual to become his or her own therapist by recognizing and modifying these internal monologues (Hollon & Beck, 1986; Thoresen & Mahoney, 1974).

There are at least three conditions under which one might want to modify cognitions about health behaviors. The cognitions could act as antecedents to a to-be-modified target behavior. For example, if an individual's urge to smoke is preceded by cognitions that he is weak and unable to control smoking urges, these beliefs could undermine his efforts to stop smoking. The smoker might then be trained to develop antecedent cognitions that would help him stop smoking, such as refocusing thoughts on the benefits of not smoking. Cognitions can also act as the consequents of a target behavior and thereby contribute to its maintenance. For example, an obese individual who is trying to lose weight might undermine the weight loss process by reacting with hopelessness to every small dieting setback. This individual might be trained to engage in self-reinforcing cognitions following successful resistance to temptation and constructive self-criticism following setbacks. These revised cognitions would then act as reinforcements for successful behavior change. Cognitions may also themselves be target behaviors for modification. For example, an individual's internal monologues about stress may aggravate the experience of stress. By adopting cognitions that foster a sense of relaxation and control, the experience of stress might be reduced.

Considerable research supports the assumption that covert behaviors, such as images or internal dialogues, can be modified through standard techniques of reinforcement (Mahoney et al., 1972). For example, in one study (Homme, 1965), clients who wished to stop smoking were trained to respond to smoking urges by thinking antismoking thoughts (''Smoking causes cancer'') and thoughts that favored nonsmoking (''My food will taste better if I stop smoking"). To increase the frequency of these cognitions, the clients were trained to reinforce them with a rewarding activity, such as coffee drinking. Following target cognitions with reinforcements reliably increases their frequency (Mahoney et al., 1972).

Research also suggests that covert responses can themselves be employed as positive and negative reinforcements for target behaviors. For example, Miller (1959) treated an alcoholic patient using methods of covert self-control. The patient was trained to develop a graphic image of his worst hangover, including the nausea, vomiting, and pain that accompanied it. Once the patient was able to retrieve this image at will, he was further trained to recall it in conjunction with the smell and taste of alcohol. Over time, the image functioned successfully as a punishment for alcohol consumption.

Overall, then, the results of studies that evaluate covert self-control indicate that internal monologues can be modified by reinforcement principles; they can act as positive reinforcements or punishments for other target behaviors; and they can function as controlling antecedents of a target behavior (Thoresen & Mahoney, 1974). These techniques appear to be most successful in changing behavior when they are repeatedly practiced (Hollon & Beck, 1986).

There are several specific techniques of covert self-control. **Cognitive restructuring,** developed by Meichenbaum (Meichenbaum & Cameron, 1974), is a method for modifying internal monologues that has been widely used in the treatment of anxiety and stress disorders. In a typical intervention, clients are first trained to monitor their monologues in stress-producing situations. In this way, they come to recognize what they say to themselves during times of stress. They are then taught to modify their self-instructions to include adaptive cognitions. Frequently, modeling is used to train a client in cognitive restructuring

The therapist may first demonstrate adaptive **self-talk.** She may identify a target stress-producing situation and then self-administer positive instructions (such as "Relax, you're doing great"). The client then attempts to deal with his stressful situation while the therapist teaches him positive self-instruction. In the next phase of training, the client attempts to cope with the stress-producing situation, instructing himself out loud. Following this phase, self-instruction may become a whisper and, finally, the client performs the anxiety-reducing self-instruction internally. This training procedure uses modeling and behavioral shaping to influence the internal dialogues that an individual has in response to stress.

Thought stopping, a technique developed by Wolpe (1958), is designed to eliminate undesired and often obsessive thoughts or images. In this procedure, target cognitions are first identified and the client signals to the therapist when the cognition enters the head. The therapist then shouts, "Stop!" (Some other loud noise may be substituted.) In theory, the loud noise disrupts the cognitions by startling the client. After this modeling phase, the client is trained to shout "Stop!" in response to the appearance of the target cognitions. Finally, the client is trained to say "Stop!" internally, as a self-control method of terminating the thoughts or images. Thought stopping has been widely used with clients who have obsessive, self-defeating cognitions (Rimm & Masters, 1974), but it can also be used in the modification of health behaviors. For example, clients may learn to disrupt self-destructive rumination about the difficulty of modifying obesity or smoking behavior by shouting "Stop!" to themselves.

Earlier, we considered systematic desensitization, in which a person learns to relax in the presence of a stimulus that was once anxiety arousing. In **self-employed desensitization,** the client constructs his own hierarchy of anxiety-arousing situations and then receives written instructions about how to engage in deep breathing and progressive muscle relaxation. He conducts his own systematic desensitization by moving up the hierarchy of progressively more anxiety-arousing situations, learning to relax in the presence of these stimuli. Just as when a therapist practices systematic desensitization, self-administered desensitization programs instruct clients to move up the hierarchy when no anxiety is experienced and to move back down to a less-threatening situation when some anxiety develops (Kahn & Baker, 1968; Migler & Wolpe, 1967; Suinn, 1971). Although these techniques may be useful in combating anxiety disorders, unfortunately patients tend to drop out of self-administered programs (Phillips, Johnson, & Geyer, 1972).

Most commonly, the **flooding** technique (Thoresen & Mahoney, 1974) is directed by a therapist, but individuals can learn to use the technique themselves (self-flooding). In this technique, patients are trained to let anxiety-arousing cognitions engulf, or flood, them. They are encouraged to expose themselves repeatedly to feared situations through extensive or even exaggerated imagery. The rationale behind this technique is that repeated contact with a fearful image in the absence of actual aversive consequences will reduce the anxiety that the image causes. Ultimately, the anxiety associated with the image should be extinguished. Flooding and self-flooding have not been widely employed in the modification of health habits. However, they are promising as techniques that can help control the anxiety that sometimes give rise to self-destructive health habits, such as smoking or alcoholism.

Various other forms of covert self-control, including self-hypnosis and imaging, also offer promise; we cover them more fully in Chapter 11.

Behavioral Assignments   As we have seen, most health problems are solved with the aid of a therapist. However, as we have also seen,

cognitive-behavioral therapists increasingly realize that an individual must be actively involved in the therapeutic process for it to be effective. **Behavioral assignments** are one way of increasing patient involvement. These assignments are home-practice activities that are integrated into a therapeutic intervention (Shelton & Levy, 1981).

Behavioral assignments are designed to provide continuity in the treatment of a behavior problem. Some part of every behavior-change session is devoted to preparing homework assignments. Typically, these assignments follow up points in the therapeutic session. For example, if an early therapy session with an obese client involved training in self-monitoring, the client would be encouraged to practice systematic recording at home. She might keep a log of her eating behavior, including the circumstances in which it occurred. This log could then be used by the therapist and the patient at the next session to plan future behavioral interventions.

Figure 4.2 provides an example of a behavioral assignment for an obese client. As can be seen in this figure, Tom, the obese patient, has several target activities that he is to perform at home. In addition, at the bottom of the homework assignment is the notation "Homework for John—reread articles on obesity." John is the therapist, and his homework is to develop greater familiarity with Tom's problem. Such bilateral homework assignments are sometimes included so that both client and therapist are committed to the treatment process (Shelton & Levy, 1981). Written agreements for behavioral homework appear to be more successful than verbal agreements, inasmuch as they provide a clear record of the arrangements and may be used as reminders for both patient and therapist (Cox, Tisdelle, & Culbert, 1988).

The value of systematic homework assignments has increasingly been recognized in the treatment of behaviors. A survey of programs for the treatment of health problems (Shelton

FIGURE 4.2 Example of a Systematic Behavioral Assignment for an Obese Client

Homework for Tom [client]

Using the counter, count bites taken.

Record number of bites, time, location, and what you ate.

Record everything eaten for one week.

Call for an appointment.

Bring your record.

Homework for John [therapist]

Reread articles on obesity.

(From Shelton & Levy, 1981, p. 6)

& Levy, 1981) indicated that 75% of obesity programs, 71% of physical illness and rehabilitation programs, and 54% of smoking programs included behavioral assignments.

To summarize, then, the chief advantages of behavioral assignments are that (1) the client becomes involved in the treatment process, (2) the client produces an analysis of the behavior that is useful in planning further interventions, (3) the client becomes committed to the treatment process through a contractual agreement to discharge certain responsibilities, (4) the responsibility for behavior change is gradually shifted to the client, and (5) the use of homework assignments increases the client's sense of self-control.

Skills Training Increasingly, psychologists have realized that some poor health habits de-velop in response to or are maintained by the anxiety people experience in social situations (Chaney, O'Leary, & Marlatt, 1978). For example, adolescents often begin to smoke in order to reduce their social anxiety by communicating a cool, sophisticated image. Drinking and overeating may also be responses to social anxiety.

Research from learning theory consistently demonstrates that extinguishing a problem behavior is easier if a new response is substituted for the maladaptive response. For example, if social anxiety acts as a cue for maladaptive eating behavior, it should be most effective to give an individual some other way of coping with the anxiety while simultaneously attempting to modify eating. As a consequence, a number of programs designed to alter health habits include either **social-skills training** or **assertiveness training,** or both, as part of the intervention package. Individuals are trained in methods that will help them deal more effectively with social anxiety.

The goals of social-skills programs as an ancillary technique in a program of health behavior change are (1) to reduce anxiety that occurs in social situations, (2) to introduce new skills for dealing with situations that previously aroused anxiety, and (3) to provide an alternative behavior for the poor health habit that arose in response to social anxiety.

Broad-Spectrum, or Multimodal, Cognitive-Behavioral Therapy

In our discussion until now, we have considered individual cognitive and behavioral techniques for modifying health behavior in isolation. However, as noted earlier, the most effective approach to health-habit modification often comes from combining multiple behavior-change techniques. This more eclectic approach, which draws on the full range of available cognitive-behavioral techniques, has been termed **broad-spectrum, or multimodal,**

cognitive-behavior therapy (Lazarus, 1971). The terms "broad-spectrum" and "multimodal" refer to the fact that, from an array of available techniques, a therapist selects several complementary methods to intervene in the modification of a target problem and its context.

To see how this approach works, let us use the example of a chronically obese woman who is 50 pounds overweight and who may be at risk for heart disease. First, one needs to understand her eating behavior, the factors that give rise to eating, when it occurs, and the discriminative stimuli that are associated with it. To address these questions, a therapist might begin the intervention with a *self-observation and self-monitoring* phase. The patient would be trained to chronicle her eating behavior and the circumstances in which it occurred. The therapist might then initiate a *stimulus-control intervention* to alter the discriminative stimuli that elicit eating behavior for this individual. For example, if the client eats while watching television, she might be trained to eat only at the kitchen table with the television off. The presence of desirable fattening foods might also act as discriminative stimuli for eating, so she would be urged to clear her refrigerator and shelves of these items. Next, the therapist might wish to alter the patterns of *self-reinforcement* that maintain eating. Accordingly, the client might be encouraged to set up a schedule of projected eating behavior goals and be trained to reinforce herself with a pleasurable activity such as going to a movie each time a goal was met. *Behavioral assignments* might be included to keep the reinforcement schedule as stable as possible.

As we have already noted, eating is related to anxiety in some obese individuals. If our hypothetical client were anxious about social interactions with other people and used her obesity in part as a method for keeping people at a distance, her behavior-change program would need to include some kind of *skills training.* The therapist might recommend social-skills training or assertiveness training so that she would be better able to manage her social anxiety. In summary, this hypothetical multimodal intervention with an obese client draws on several techniques: self-observation/ self-monitoring, stimulus control, self-reinforcement, behavioral assignments, and social skills training. Another example of such a broad-spectrum therapy is shown in Box 4.3.

The advantages of a multimodal approach to health behavior change are several. First, a carefully selected set of techniques can deal with all aspects of a problem: Self-observation and self-monitoring define the dimensions of a problem; stimulus control enables a person to modify antecedents of behavior; self-reinforcement controls the consequents of a behavior; and social-skills training may be added to replace the maladaptive behavior once it has been brought under some degree of control. Thus, a combination of techniques can be more effective in dealing with all phases of a problem than is one technique alone.

A second advantage is that the therapeutic plan can be tailored to each individual's problem. Often, cognitive-behavioral therapy is employed individually with patients; consequently, a therapist can use what he knows about a particular patient to make the treatment regimen maximally effective. Such knowledge might include information about the patient's personality, the determinants of the health habit itself, and the particular life circumstances of the patient. The particular package identified for our hypothetical obese client might not be the same as that developed for another obese client. Another obese individual, for example, might not eat in response to social anxiety but, rather, in response to tension. Thus, instead of a social-skills training program, he might require a stress-management intervention. Similarly, the self-monitoring phase might reveal that his obesity problem was marked by binge eating rather than by multiple small meals, which would require different reinforcement contingencies.

Broad-Spectrum Cognitive Behavioral Change Programs: A Cautionary Note Broad-spectrum or multimodal approaches to health behavior problems have often achieved successful change when more limited programs have not. The intelligent use of such programs involves a detailed analysis of a particular individual's health problem and the identification of the sets of behavior-modification techniques and skills that may bear on that particular individual's problem. Unfortunately, individually tailored programs have not always been the rule. Instead, overzealous interventionists have sometimes assumed that more is better and tried to include as many components as possible into their programs in the hopes that at least a few of them will be successful. In fact, this technique will sometimes backfire (Brownell, Marlatt, Lichtenstein, & Wilson, 1986).

The assumption underlying the addition of elements to multimodal or broad-spectrum approaches has been that they will deal with components of the health habit that other aspects of the intervention may not address. For example, relaxation therapy, social-skills training, or assertiveness training is assumed to attack part of the health behavior problem that cognitive behavior-change techniques alone may not affect. But, as we see in Chapter 10, adherence to lifestyle-modification treatment programs is often very low and declines as the complexity of a treatment regimen increases (Turk & Meichenbaum, in press). Thus, as clients in behavior-change programs find that they must take more and more specific actions, monitor multiple behaviors, and analyze substantial numbers of situations for their implications for the health habit, their motivation in pursuing the program may decline, and they may gradually show lower rates of adherence to the behavior-change program.

Consequently, it is essential that, when a broad-spectrum or multimodal program is employed, it be guided by an intelligent, well-informed selection of the techniques deemed to be potentially effective for a particular individual's problem, rather than an unrealistically optimistic belief that, by adding more to the program, greater success will be achieved.

Another caution that should be raised regarding the efficacy of broad-spectrum or multimodal behavior change programs involves the role of the practitioner. While a concerted program of behavior-change efforts that an individual engineers on his or her own can sometimes be successful in modifying a health behavior problem, the therapeutic relationship is also an important aspect of the success of such programs (Brownell, Marlatt et al., 1986). That is, much valuable behavior change can come about simply from the presence of an enthusiastic, committed practitioner in conjunction with generally efficacious techniques. We address this issue more fully in Chapter 10, but it is an important point to raise in this context as well.

Relapse Prevention

As the previous section implies, one of the biggest problems faced in health-habit modification programs is the tendency for people to relapse to their previous behavior after a behavior-change program has terminated. Relapse is a particular problem with the addictive disorders of alcoholism, smoking, drug addiction, and obesity (Brownell, Marlatt et al., 1986), which are in the range of 50 to 90% (Marlatt & Gordon, 1985). This is not to suggest that people relapse in their health habits immediately after dropping out of programs, or that an occasional lapse in vigilance, such as a single cigarette smoked at a cocktail party or the consumption of an entire cheesecake on a lonely Saturday night, necessarily leads to permanent relapse. However, over time, as initial vigilance fades, relapse rates are high.

Box 4.3
Cognitive-Behavioral Therapy in the Treatment of Alcoholism

Mary was a 32-year-old executive who came in for treatment, saying she thought she was an alcoholic. She had a demanding, challenging job, which she handled very conscientiously. While her husband, Don, was supportive of her career, he felt it was important that evenings be spent in shared activities. They had had several arguments recently because Mary was drinking before coming home and had been hiding liquor around the house. Don was threatening to leave if she did not stop drinking altogether, and Mary also was feeling alarmed by her behavior. Mary was seen over a 3-month period, with follow-up contact over the following year.

Mary's first week's assignment was to complete an autobiography of the history and development of her drinking problem—her parents' drinking behavior, her first drinking experience and first "drunk," the role of drinking in her adult life, her self-image, any problems associated with her drinking, and her attempts to control her drinking. She also self-monitored her drinking for 2 weeks, noting the exact amounts of alcohol consumed each day, the time, and the antecedents and consequences.

At the third session, the following patterns were identified. Mary started work at 8:30, typically had a rushed business lunch, and often did not leave work until 6:00, by which time she was tense and wound up. Because she knew Don did not approve of her drinking, she had begun to pick up a pint of vodka after work and to drink half of it during the 20-minute drive home so that she could get relaxed for the evening. She had also begun stashing liquor away in the house just in case she wanted a drink. She realized that drinking while driving was dangerous, that she was drinking too much too quickly, and that she

was feeling very guilty and out of control. Her husband's anger seemed to increase her urges to drink.

Mary agreed to abstain from any drinking during the third and fourth weeks of treatment. During this period it became apparent that drinking was her only means for reducing the tension that built up during the day and also represented the one indulgence she allowed herself in a daily routine of obligations to external job demands and commitments to her husband and friends. A plan to modify her general lifestyle was worked out that included alternative ways of relaxing and indulging that were not destructive.

Mary joined a local health club and began going for a swim and a sauna every morning on the way to work. She also set aside 2 days a week to have lunch alone or with a friend. She learned a meditation technique, which she began using at the end of the day after getting home from work. She negotiated with Don to spend one evening a week doing separate activities so that she could resume her old hobby of painting.

Mary also decided that she wanted to continue drinking in a moderate way and that Don's support was essential so that she could drink openly. Don attended the sixth session with Mary, the treatment plan was explained to him, his feelings and concerns were explored, and he agreed to support Mary in her efforts to alter her lifestyle as well as to be more accepting of her drinking.

During the next few sessions Mary learned a number of controlled drinking techniques, including setting limits for herself and pacing her drinks by alternating liquor with soft drinks. She also developed strategies for dealing with high-risk situations, which for her were primarily the buildup of tension at work and feelings of guilt or anger toward Don. She learned to become more aware of these situations as they were developing and began to practice more direct ways of communicating with Don. She also was instructed to use any urges to return to old drinking patterns as cues to pay attention to situational factors and use alternative responses rather than to interpret them as signs that she was an alcoholic.

The final two sessions were spent planning and rehearsing what to do if a relapse occurred. Strategies included slowing herself down, cognitive restructuring, a decision-making exercise to review the consequences and relative merits of drinking according to both old and new patterns, analysis of the situation that led to the relapse, problem solving to come up with a better coping response to use next time, and the possibility of scheduling a booster session with her therapist.

At the final follow-up a year later, Mary reported that she was feeling better about herself and more in control, was drinking moderately on social occasions, and was communicating better with Don. She had had a couple of slips but had managed to retrieve the situation, in one case by being more assertive with a superior, and in the other by simply deciding that she could accept some mistakes on her part without having to punish herself by continuing the mistake.

(From Gordon & Marlatt, 1981, pp. 182–183. Reprinted by permission.)

Although there are many differences among the addictive disorders, there are also similarities. Among those seeking professional help, both relapse rates and patterns of relapse over time are very similar for alcohol, drug addiction, and smoking (see Brownell, Marlatt et al., 1986). Research has suggested that relapse rates tend to stabilize approximately 3 months after an intervention, implying that most of the people who relapse will do so within the first 3 months. Closer examination of individual studies suggests that these figures are misleading, however. Although overall relapse rates may remain relatively constant after 3 months, the people who are abstaining from a particular health habit at 3 months are not necessarily the same people who are abstaining at a year. Some people go from abstinence to relapse, and others go from relapse to abstinence.

At present, our knowledge of what factors determine relapse is limited, but a few factors, both internal and external to the individual, have been identified. Genetic factors appear to be implicated in alcoholism, smoking, and obesity, and may form the underpinnings of a propensity to relapse (McClearn, 1981; Pomerleau, 1984; Schuckitt, 1981; Stunkard et al., 1986). Moreover, withdrawal effects occur in response to abstinence from alcohol and cigarettes and may prompt some relapse, especially shortly after efforts to change behavior. There are conditioned associations between cues and physiological responses that may lead to urges or cravings to engage in the habit. All of these factors can promote relapse, particularly if there has already been a lapse.

Relapse is more likely in the presence of negative emotional states such as depression or anxiety, or under stressful circumstances.

For example, when people are moving, breaking off a relationship, or encountering difficulties at work, they may have greater need for their addictive habits than is true at less stressful times. Relapse is also more likely when there has been a decline in motivation to pursue the health habit or when there is an absence of specific goals for maintaining behavior change. Over time, vigilance over the health habit decreases, and people are more vulnerable to situational cues that can induce them to lapse into their previous bad habits. Relapse is less likely if a person has social support from family and friends to maintain the behavior change, and it is more likely if the person lacks social support or is involved in a conflictual interpersonal situation. Relapse is especially likely to occur when one finds oneself in situations that were previously associated with the behavior. For example, going to a smoke-filled bar to have a beer may remind an individual that he used to smoke in these circumstances and may either elicit the behavior or provide a strong temptation to engage in it.

What are the consequences of relapse? Clearly, relapse produces negative emotional effects, such as disappointment or frustration, unhappiness or anger. A relapse could also lead people to feel that they can never control the habit, that it is simply beyond their efforts. Relapse may also be a deterrent to successful behavior change in other ways, as well. For example, among the obese, repeated cycles of weight loss and regain make subsequent dieting more difficult (Brownell, Greenwood, Stellar, & Shrager, 1986).

Alternatively, at least in some cases, relapse may lead people to perceive that they can control their habit, at least under some circumstances. Moreover, in the smoking area, multiple efforts to stop smoking often occur before people succeed (Schachter, 1982), suggesting that initial experiences with stopping smoking may prepare people for later success. The person who relapses may nonetheless acquire

useful information about the habit and learn ways to prevent relapse in the future. At present, relatively little is known about these alternative views, and as implied above, the implications of relapse may vary for different health habits.

Traditionally, behavioral interventions to control relapse have centered on three techniques. Booster sessions following the termination of the initial treatment phase have been one method. Several weeks or months after the end of a formal intervention, smokers may be brought in for an additional smoking-prevention session or dieters may return to their group situation to be weighed in and to brush up on their weight-control techniques. Unfortunately, however, booster sessions have been generally unsuccessful as a method for maintaining behavior change and preventing relapse (Brownell, Marlatt et al., 1986). Another approach has been to add more components to the behavioral intervention, such as relaxation therapy or assertiveness training, but, as just noted, the addition of components does not appear reliably to increase adherence rates and, at least under some circumstances, may actually reduce them. A third approach to relapse prevention is to consider abstinence a lifelong treatment process, as is done in such programs as Alcoholics Anonymous and other well-established lay treatment programs. Though this approach has certainly been successful in some cases, as we see in Chapter 6, it also has certain disadvantages. The philosophy can leave people with the perception that they are constantly vulnerable to relapse, potentially creating the expectation of relapse when vigilance wanes. Moreover, the philosophy implies that people are not in control of their habit, and research on health-habit modification suggests that self-efficacy is an important component in initiating and maintaining behavior change (Bandura, 1986; Brownell, Marlatt et al., 1986).

Marlatt and Gordon (1985) and their associates (e.g., Brownell, Greenwood et al., 1986;

Brownell, Marlatt et al., 1986) argued that relapse prevention must be integrated into treatment programs from the outset. Changing a health habit is not a simple action that is undertaken once a decision is made, but a process that may occur in stages (Brownell, Marlatt et al., 1986b; Prohaska & DiClemente, 1984a). Several factors are relevant during the time when people are first admitted to treatment programs. People who are initially highly committed to the program and motivated to engage in behavior change are less likely to relapse. These observations imply that one important focus of programs must be on methods of increasing motivation and maintaining commitment. For example, programs may create a contingency management procedure in which people are required to deposit money, which is returned if they successfully attend meetings or change their behavior. Another more controversial possibility is the use of screening techniques to weed out from programs those people who are not truly committed to behavior change and who are therefore vulnerable to relapse. There are problems involved in applying screening criteria. Denying people access to a treatment designed to induce healthy behavior change creates certain ethical dilemmas (Brownell, Marlatt et al., 1986). On the other hand, for at least some health behaviors such as dieting, unsuccessful efforts to change the behavior may interfere with the ability to bring about successful behavior change in the future. For example, failed dieters may see themselves as chronically so. There may also be advantages for practitioners in having a highly motivated clientele that is less likely to relapse. Failure of clients in behavior-change programs erodes the morale of those who run them and takes up positions in programs that could go to more motivated clients who are likely to be more successful.

Once motivation and commitment to follow through have been instilled, techniques must be developed in the behavior-change program itself that are designed to maintain behavior change and act as relapse prevention skills once the program terminates. One such strategy involves having people identify the likely situations that might promote a relapse and then develop coping skills that will enable them to manage that stressful event successfully or to reappraise the event in a way that will make relapse less likely. This strategy draws on the principle of self-control, assuming that successful adherence promotes feelings of self-control and that having available coping techniques can enhance feelings of control still further (Marlatt & George, 1988). The initiation of coping responses in a high-risk situation can promote feelings of self-efficacy, decreasing the likelihood of relapse. For example, some programs train participants to engage in constructive self-talk that will enable them to talk themselves through tempting situations (Brownell, Marlatt et al., 1986). The rationale for these coping skills is that people in a high-risk situation who lack coping responses may see themselves as lacking the self-efficacy to restrain and thus use the substance involved, whether alcohol, food, or cigarettes. Cue elimination, or the restructuring of one's environment to avoid all situations that evoke the target behavior, may be required for some people with some habits. When there are no cues present that evoke the target behavior, then relapse is less likely.

There may be self-efficacy advantages to an emphasis on skill-based relapse prevention techniques as well. Previously, the ability to maintain behavior change over time was thought to involve willpower or the sheer effort to maintain behavior change. From this standpoint, lapses and relapses may be threatening to cognitions of self-efficacy, yielding the perception that one lacks the ability to change. An emphasis on skill acquisition for dealing with threatening situations diverts concern away from sheer will to the appropriate use of skills, and, consequently, lapses or relapses may be conceptualized as only temporarily threatening to long-term behavior change. Relapse prevention techniques, then, may contribute to feelings of self-efficacy in the behavior-change process.

Finally, long-term maintenance of behavior change can be promoted by making other health-oriented changes in lifestyle, a technique termed **lifestyle rebalancing** (Marlatt & George, 1988). Initiating lifestyle change, such as adding exercise to one's activities or learning stress-management techniques such as relaxation, may promote a healthy lifestyle more generally and help reduce the likelihood of relapse. Returning to smoking or excessive alcohol consumption could be seen as highly inappropriate in the context of a generally healthier lifestyle. Since adherence to treatment programs is enhanced by social support, promoting long-term social support for behavior change would seem to be desirable. Unfortunately, at present, studies evaluating the efficacy of enlisting the aid of a spouse or other family members in behavior-change efforts have been equivocal (Brownell, Marlatt et al., 1986). It is possible, however, that research has not yet identified the most successful ways of enlisting available social support over the long term.

Long-term monitoring of the behavior may also increase maintenance, in that it promotes vigilance and may guard against lapses. However, since booster sessions themselves are not successful in promoting long-term behavior change, it is not clear exactly what kinds of monitoring may be most successful in promoting behavior change over the long term (Brownell, Marlatt et al., 1986). Relapse prevention techniques that focus on identification of high-risk situations and techniques for coping with them have now been tested with a variety of health behaviors, including exercise adherence (Belisle, Roskies, & Levesque, 1987), alcohol abstinence (Litman, 1980), and smoking abstinence (Shiffman, Read, Maltese, Rapkin, & Jarvik, 1985). They have been found to produce higher rates of adherence

than programs with no relapse prevention components. Moreover, because they are inexpensive to implement, they are potentially more cost-effective than alternative long-term maintenance interventions (Belisle et al., 1987).

In short, then, the last 5 years have seen substantial changes in the treatment of health behaviors, particularly those involving addiction. The focus has changed from inducing people to change their health habits initially toward developing technologies to help them maintain behavior change over time. While previously the problem of maintenance was thought to be best solved by adding additional treatment sessions or additional components to the treatment program, it is now believed that relapse prevention involves processes that must be concretely addressed and integrated from the outset of a behavioral intervention program.

CHANGING HEALTH BEHAVIORS THROUGH SOCIAL ENGINEERING

Lest the reader conclude that all health behaviors are a matter of appropriate psychological intervention, it should be pointed out that a tremendous amount of health behavior change can be effected through social engineering. Indeed, many health psychologists have come to the conclusion that social engineering solutions may be more successful in bringing about behavior change than any attitude techniques or therapeutic interventions. **Social engineering** involves modifying the environment in ways that affect an individual's ability to practice a particular health behavior. These measures are called passive because they do not require an individual to take personal action (Williams, 1982). For example, wearing seat belts is an active measure that an individual must take to control possible injury from an automobile accident, whereas the controversial air bag, which inflates automatically on impact, is a passive measure. A full consideration of social engineering solutions to health problems is beyond the scope of this book, so we will discuss the topic only briefly here.

Many health behaviors are already determined by social engineering. Using seat belts and child-safety seats, banning the use of certain drugs, such as heroin and cocaine, and regulating the disposal of toxic wastes are examples of health measures that have been mandated by legislation. The private sector also sometimes becomes involved in social engineering solutions. For example, private lobbying groups composed of parents have attempted to get junk food commercials off children's television programs and otherwise pressure the networks to modify the advertising during children's programming (McGuire, 1984). Legislation restricting the advertisement of cigarettes and alcohol on TV represents another successful lobbying effort by citizens' groups.

Many times, social engineering solutions to health problems are more successful than individual ones. Consider the example of water purification. One could attempt to instill good water purification habits in individuals by constructing attitudinal and behavioral interventions to persuade each person to boil his or her own water. However, purifying the water at its source is a far better solution (Robertson, 1975). One could intervene with parents to get them to reduce accident risks in the home, but approaches such as using safety containers for medications and making children's clothing with fire-retardant fabrics are more successful (Fielding, 1978). Lowering the speed limit has had far more impact on death and disability from motor vehicle accidents than interventions to get people to change their driving habits (Fielding, 1978). The efficacy of New Mexico's helmet law in reducing motorcycle accident deaths is illustrated in Figure 4.3. Current campaigns to raise the drinking age from 18 to 21 in all the states will ultimately be more successful in reducing alcohol-related vehicular fatalities than will programs designed to help the drunk driver. Raising the price of alcohol and cigarettes to prohibitive levels may have a greater effect on consumption of these substances than therapeutic interventions will have.

But social engineering solutions to health problems may still intersect with psychological principles. Even health problems that can be effectively solved through social engineering contain a psychological element. For example, some group of individuals must feel strongly about a preventive health behavior and coalesce to lobby for it before appropriate social engineering will be initiated. Then, techniques of attitude change can be employed to construct mass media messages that will instill the interest in social engineering solutions in the general population.

Of course, there are limits on social engineering. Even though smoking has been banned in many public areas, it is still not illegal to smoke; if this were to occur, most smokers and a substantial number of nonsmokers would find such mandatory interference unacceptable to civil liberties. Clearly, social engineering raises important ethical questions. Even when the health advantages of social engineering can be dramatically illustrated, the sacrifice in personal liberty may be considered too great (Warwick & Kelman, 1973). Thus, many health habits will remain at the discretion of the individual. It is to such behaviors that psychological interventions most persuasively speak.

THE APPROPRIATE VENUE FOR HEALTH-HABIT MODIFICATION

Now that we have reviewed a variety of techniques aimed at changing health habits, it becomes important to consider how best to use them. In other words, where is the best place to attempt to intervene in people's health hab-

FIGURE 4.3   Legislation can sometimes effect health-related change that behavioral interventions cannot. This figure reveals how institution of New Mexico's mandatory helmet law reduced the death rate among motorcyclists by half.

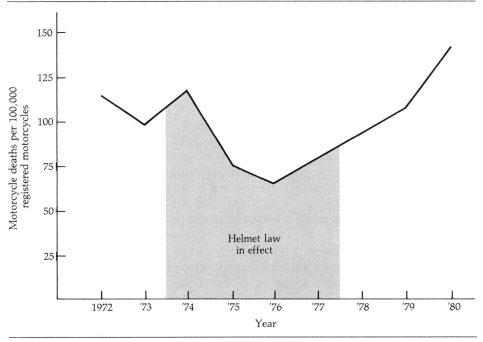

(Berger, 1981).

---

its: the private therapist's office, the physician's office, schools, the workplace, or the community setting?

The Private Therapist's Office

As our previous discussion has implied, some health-habit modification is conducted by psychologists, psychiatrists, and other clinicians privately on a one-to-one basis. These professionals are carefully trained in the techniques of cognitive-behavioral modification that seem to work best in altering health habits. There are two striking advantages of the one-to-one therapeutic experience for the modification of health habits. First, precisely because it is one-to-one, the extensive individual treatment a person receives may make success more likely. Second, because of the individual na-

ture of the experience, the therapist can tailor the behavior-change package to the needs of the particular individual.

In many cases, this package includes psychotherapy. Individual psychotherapy alone has often proven to be ineffective in modifying health habits. However, for some patients, psychotherapy may be a necessary component of treatment to obtain the best results. Some therapists believe that cognitive-behavioral change efforts attack only symptoms of a problem and not the underlying problem itself. For example, an individual who eats because he feels worthless may require therapy to combat these feelings if efforts to modify his eating behavior are to be successful. Otherwise, he may repeatedly fail in his efforts to diet. Traditional psychotherapy, then, clearly has a role in health-habit modification.

However, there is a major disadvantage of initiating changes in health behavior in the therapist's office, and this often overrules its advantages: Only one individual's behavior can be changed at a time. If the modification of health habits is to make any dent in rates of disease, we must find ways of modifying health behaviors that do not require this very expensive one-to-one attention.

The Physician's Office

Health-habit modification can also be undertaken in the physician's office. As we noted in Chapter 3, prevention has not been a strong component of traditional medical practice. Increasingly, however, medical school curricula emphasize the value of diagnosing healthy people's risky behaviors to help get them to modify them.

An influential article in the *New England Journal of Medicine* some years ago (Breslow & Somers, 1977) proposed a lifetime health-monitoring program to be achieved through the physician's office. In this program, a physician assesses a patient's status on particular health goals appropriate for the patient's age group and then recommends health practices to achieve those goals. For example, the health goals for the first year of life include establishing immunity against specific infectious diseases and detecting and preventing other diseases and problems early. In this context, several specific tests and immunizations are recommended. The health risk appraisal profile described in Chapter 3 (Janz & Becker, 1987) represents another approach to the same problem. If these kinds of programs were adopted by every physician, the health status of the population could be substantially improved. Although such a concerted effort may be a long way off, some modest efforts in this regard have begun already. For example, some health maintenance organizations make prevention and the modification of their clientele's health habits a primary concern. Some pediatricians hold classes for parents to teach them how to keep their children healthy and safe and instill health behaviors in their children.

What are the advantages and disadvantages of intervention in the physician's office? Some of the disadvantages are similar to those of private therapy as a vehicle for changing health habits. The one-to-one approach is expensive and reduces only one person's risk status at a time. On the other hand, many people see a physician on at least a semi-regular basis; therefore, reaching people through this venue will affect a substantial proportion of the population. Moreover, as we see in Chapter 10, the physician is a particularly credible agent for instituting health-habit change, and such changes are often more successful when the process is overseen by a physician than when the patient attempts to change the habit alone.

The interventions we have described so far tend to be individually oriented, and indeed, until relatively recently, those who would modify health behaviors have tended to focus on one individual at a time. But, clearly, health habits are embedded in the larger social and environmental context. Social and psychological benefits to health habits can conceivably be highlighted to increase their development and adherence to their practice. There are many naturally occurring social environments that could be enlisted in support of healthy behavior change, such as social groups, schools, and work groups. There are many benefits that people can extract from these kinds of social situations. They may feel more pressure to maintain behavior change, having made a commitment to a group. They may feel that it is important not to let the group down. They may experience social support from similar others trying to achieve the same kind of behavior change. We next examine group efforts to change health behaviors.

Self-Help Groups

Substantially more people attempt to modify their health habits through self-help groups than through contact with private therapists or physicians. These self-help groups bring together a number of individuals with the same health-habit problem and, often with the help of a counselor, they attempt to solve their problem collectively. Some prominent self-help groups include Overeaters Anonymous and TOPS (Take Off Pounds Sensibly) for obesity; Alcoholics Anonymous for alcoholics; and Smokenders for smokers. Many of the leaders of these groups employ cognitive-behavioral principles in their programs. The social support and understanding of mutual sufferers provided by such groups are also important factors in producing successful outcomes. At the present time, self-help groups constitute the major venue for health-habit modification in this country. We examine the self-help group experience more specifically in Chapter 6.

Schools

Interventions to encourage health behaviors have increasingly been implemented through the school system. A number of factors make schools a desirable venue for health-habit modification. First, everyone has to go to school; therefore, virtually all of the population can be reached, at least in their early years. Second, the school population is young. Consequently, we can intervene before children have developed poor health habits rather than wait until poor habits have already developed. For example, in Chapter 6, we give examples of smoking prevention programs that were initiated with schoolchildren before they began smoking. Moreover, when young people are taught good health behaviors early, these behaviors may become habitual and stay with them for their whole lives. Third, schools have a natural intervention ve-

hicle, namely classes of approximately an hour's duration; many health interventions can fit into this format. Finally, certain sanctions can be employed in the school environment to promote health behaviors. For example, many school systems have required that children receive a series of inoculations before they attend school but have not in any way enforced the regulation. Recently, however, the State of New York began denying admission to those who had not received their shots, and this has been extremely successful in increasing compliance with this requirement (McGuire, 1984). For these reasons, then, we are likely to see the schools used increasingly as a venue for influencing health habits.

Worksite Interventions

Very young children and the elderly can be reached through the health care system to aid in the modification of target health behaviors. Schoolchildren and adolescents can be contacted through the schools. The bulk of the adult population, however, is often difficult to reach. They do not use traditional medical services on as regular a basis as children or the elderly, and it is difficult to reach them through other organizational means. However, approximately 70% of the adult population is employed, and, consequently, there is no better place than the workplace to reach such a large percentage of the population (Cataldo, Green, Herd, Parkinson, & Goldbeck, 1986).

There are at least three ways in which the worksite has typically dealt with employees' health habits. The first is the provision of on-the-job programs that help employees practice better health behaviors. Smoking clinics and weight-loss programs are examples. Some of these programs use employee work groups in competition with each other to provide additional incentives for achieving health-related goals. As we see in Chapter 5, weight-loss work-group competitions have been commonly undertaken in employment settings. A second way in which industry has promoted good health habits is by structuring the environment to help people engage in healthy activities. For instance, a company can provide health clubs and spas to employees or provide restaurants that serve balanced meals that are low in fats, sugar, and cholesterol. Third, some industries have provided special incentives, such as reduced insurance premiums for individuals who successfully modify their health habits (for example, individuals who stop smoking).

Of these health programs, health promotion programs are perhaps the most common. Programs designed to help employees stop smoking, reduce stress (Roskies, Spevack, Surkis, Cohen, & Gilman, 1978), change their diet, exercise regularly, lose weight, control hypertension (Alderman & Schoenbaum, 1975), or control problem drinking are in existence in many industries across the country. Overall, employee programs to stop smoking are the most common (Orleans & Shipley, 1982).

The last two decades have seen an evolution in health promotion, or wellness, programs in the worksite. Initially, programs focused on particular diseases or particular aspects of the corporate environment, such as executives prone to stress. Others aimed at a particular health issue, such as hypertension control or antismoking. Current programs are more likely to involve a total wellness program, involving comprehensive health-oriented programs employing multiple behavioral science principles (Cataldo et al., 1986).

In addition to being the main venue through which the adult population can be contacted, the worksite has other advantages for intervention. First, large numbers of individuals can be informed about a program simultaneously. Second, the worksite can provide sanctions for participating in a program. For example, workers may get time off if they agree to take part. Third, the worksite has a built-in social support system of fellow em-

ployees who can provide encouragement for the modification of health habits. Finally, because people spend so much of their lives at work, changing the reinforcements and discriminative stimuli in the environment can help maintain good health habits instead of poor ones (Stachnik & Stoffelmayr, 1982).

How successful are worksite interventions? The answer depends in part upon how one evaluates success. Participation rates in programs, employee satisfaction with the programs, management satisfaction, changes in productivity, long-term health status, cost of the program, and unintended positive side effects, such as improved self-image or job satisfaction, are all potential outcomes that can be formally evaluated (DeMuth, Fielding, Stunkard, & Hollander, 1986). Unfortunately, the majority of health improvement programs at the worksite have not been formally evaluated (Orleans & Shipley, 1982). Of those that have, modest success has been documented in several areas. Hypertension control programs implemented at the worksite appear to be moderately successful in reducing blood pressure (Fielding, 1982). Smoking cessation programs achieve 6 to 12 months of abstinence in 15 to 30% of participants; occasionally the figures are as high as 40 to 60% (Fielding, 1982). The most intensively studied and evaluated programs are those involving weight loss. Those that employ principles of competition between work groups, where each group tries to lose the most weight have been the most successful (Brownell, Cohen, Stunkard, Felix, & Cooley, 1984; DeMuth et al., 1986).

Health promotion interventions at the worksite may have cost savings benefits for organizations. It is estimated that nearly 500 million workdays are lost annually because of health and disability (*Los Angeles Times*, 1984). For example, it is estimated that 57% of all industrial accidents are associated with alcohol, and so an intervention designed to reduce alcohol consumption could reduce costs due to accidents. Successful worksite promotion efforts may also reduce mortality and morbidity due to chronic disorders. The National Heart, Lung, and Blood Institute has estimated that more than $1 billion a year is lost in earnings due to cardiovascular disease related to high blood pressure. Moreover, as has previously been noted, smoking has been related to thousands of unnecessary deaths per year (see Cataldo et al., 1986) and may be implicated in days lost from work due to illness as well. Consequently, interventions that successfully address poor health habits have the potential to save costs for the organization.

However, a major dilemma in inducing corporations to invest in health promotion activities is that the cost-benefit data are not yet encouraging. Nor will it be easy to demonstrate that preventive programs are cost-effective in reducing health care costs (Cataldo et al., 1986). Thus, the incentives to corporations for engaging in health promotion at present rely largely on corporate image, employee morale, quality of life, employee recruitment, good community relations, and a sense of corporate social responsibility rather than on documented health benefits.

Generally, we have little idea how successful worksite intervention programs are or what components of these programs are most successful (Felix, Stunkard, Cohen, & Cooley, 1985; Fielding, 1982). Thus, careful, planned evaluation is essential for worksite interventions of the future. Moreover, if such interventions are to continue to be implemented, it is important to demonstrate cost-effectiveness, not merely success. At present, then, worksite interventions for health promotion are another strategy in the comprehensive arsenal for developing and maintaining health behaviors through multiple means of intervention (DeMuth et al., 1986).

Community-Based Interventions

In order to reach the largest number of people possible, researchers are increasingly turning to community-based interventions to modify health habits. Community-based intervention is a term that encompasses a variety of approaches. A community-based intervention could be a door-to-door campaign informing people of the availability of a breast cancer screening program, a media blitz alerting people to the risks of smoking, a diet-modification program that recruits through community institutions, or a mixed intervention involving both media and interventions directed to high-risk community members.

There are several important reasons why community-based interventions may be effective in modifying health behavior. First, such interventions reach more people than individually based interventions or interventions in limited environments, such as a single workplace or classroom. Second, community-based interventions have the potential to build on social support in reinforcing compliance with recommended health changes. For example, if all your neighbors have agreed to switch to a low-cholesterol diet, you are more likely to do so as well. Third, the community-based intervention tackles one of the most formidable problems of health-habit modification: the maintenance of behavior change. One reason people show only short-term success in changing risk factors is because they return to their old environments and to the discriminative stimuli and reinforcements that maintained their old, risky behavior patterns. Community-based interventions attempt to restructure the environment so that the cues and reinforcements for risky behaviors are replaced by cues and reinforcements for healthy behaviors (Cohen, Stunkard, & Felix, 1986).

Several prominent community-based interventions have been developed to reduce risk factors associated with heart disease. For example, the Multiple Risk Factor Intervention Trial (MRFIT), the North Karelia project in Finland, and the Stanford Heart Disease Prevention Program (Box 4.1) were all designed to modify cardiovascular risk factors such as smoking, dietary cholesterol level, and blood pressure through a combination of media interventions and behavior-change efforts targeted to high-risk groups (see also Alexandrov et al., 1988). As we noted earlier, media interventions alone do not appear to modify health behaviors; when they are coupled with behavior-change instruction specifically targeted to high-risk residents, however, they can achieve modest success in changing behavior. Evidence is now emerging that these community interventions may actually produce declines in cardiovascular mortality as well (Tuomilehto et al., 1986).

These interventions have been the subject of considerable debate, however, with some researchers arguing that the community focus is a valuable one, and others arguing that it is far too expensive for the modest change it brings about. To intervene on a face-to-face basis with people in a designated community is a very costly way to bring about behavior change. Yet, as noted earlier, cheaper alternatives such as mass media appeals alone are less successful.

To address this issue, Cohen, Stunkard, and their colleagues recently initiated CHIP (County Health Improvement Program) that attempted to intervene at a community level but at relatively low cost. The CHIP project, implemented in Lycoming County, Pennsylvania, involved a county of 118,000 people in reducing smoking, hypertension, cholesterol, and overweight and increasing physical activity. The goal of the program was to make use of existing community resources for implementing health-behavior change. Interventions were carried out through the mass media, worksites, health organizations, volunteer organizations, and the schools. For example, smoking prevention programs were introduced into adult church study groups and local schools. Weight-control programs were initiated at local worksites that served a large portion of the working population. Existing social service and voluntary health organiza-

To reach the largest number of people most effectively, researchers are increasingly designing interventions to be implemented on a community basis through existing community resources.

tions were provided with health behavior–change information to distribute to community residents. By using existing community resources, one not only keeps down the costs of community interventions but also embeds the intervention in the community so that it is more likely to be self-sustaining when the research portion of the project is terminated (Cohen, Stunkard et al., 1986; Stunkard, Felix, & Cohen, 1985). Comparisons of risk factors, health promotion activities, and morbidity and mortality from cardiovascular disease were made between the target county and a comparison county and are still continuing. One immediate outcome was a doubling of health promotion activities in the target county, compared to a 42% decrease in the comparison county (Stunkard et al., 1985). The study is still going on.

An ongoing issue in community interventions is how to evaluate them. Does one look at knowledge of health habits, change in health habits, change in risk-factor status, or change in health status? (Kasl, 1980; Leventhal, Safer, Cleary & Gutmann, 1980; Meyer, Nash, McAllister, Maccoby, & Farquhar, 1980). The use of different outcome measures may suggest differential rates of success. For example, it has yet to be demonstrated that any of these community studies has led to substantial declines in morbidity and mortality, although, as just noted, data from the North Karelia project now suggest some impact on mortality (Tuomilehto et al., 1986). Weak effects may be due to the fact that the studies may enroll too few people to see any significant effects. On the other hand, several of these programs have shown substantial changes in the modification of risk factors. For example, the Stanford study produced a 50% decline in smoking over 3 years for those in the counseling plus behavior therapy program, and a 21% reduction in the control community. Similar results were found in the MRFIT project. Dietary modification has not been as impressive (see Cooper, Soltero et al., 1982; Marlotte, Fielding, & Danaher, 1981; Meyer, Nash et al., 1980; Multiple Risk Factor Intervention Trial Research Group, 1982; World Health Organization European Collective Group, 1982).

Most health researchers believe that the community will continue to be a major point of intervention for health habits (Kasl, 1980; Meyer, Maccoby, & Farquhar, 1980). At this point, we have simply scratched the surface of the potential available community strategies for inducing people to give up their poor health habits in favor of good ones.

Conclusions Regarding the Venue for Health-Habit Change

It is clear that the issue of venue is an important one in the modification of health habits. Although psychologists have achieved some success by working with patients individually, health psychologists have increasingly recognized that this is not a viable way to address the issue. Rather, we must look for less expensive methods that reach more people simulta-

neously. As a consequence, health promotion interventions have moved increasingly into physicians' offices, schools, worksites, and communities. In addition, self-help groups address many major health problems. It is clear that the modification of health habits in the future must take a variety of courses simultaneously. Each of the venues examined has particular advantages and disadvantages. By working through all of these approaches, we may ultimately find the most successful means for modifying health habits.

CHANGING HEALTH BEHAVIORS: A NOTE OF CAUTION

In this chapter, we have described a number of techniques for the modification of health behaviors. Attitudinal appeals appear to be effective in changing people's knowledge about health problems and their attitudes about health behavior, but they may have less impact on the behavior itself. In contrast, intensive behavioral approaches may alter risky behaviors in a substantial proportion of people who finish those programs (Leventhal & Cleary, 1980; Lichtenstein & Danaher, 1975; Stunkard, 1979). Taken together, these points suggest that psychologists have technologies to address the full complexity of health habits: the motivation to change, the ability to initiate change, and the ability to maintain behavior change. Consequently, we might expect to see reductions in the incidence of related diseases. However, that has not yet been the case.

To date, few programs of health-habit modification have been able to maintain behavioral changes over long periods of time for the majority of participants (Hunt & Matarazzo, 1973; Kaplan, 1984; Leventhal & Cleary, 1980). Moreover, even in those circumstances when we do successfully modify behavior, we may not see the effects of risk-factor reduction on incidence of disease. To date, evidence relating change in health behaviors to health status has been weak (Kaplan, 1984). There is some evidence that an emphasis on risk reduction overall can increase intercorrelations among health habits (e.g., Langlie, 1977; Leventhal, Prohaska, & Hirschman, 1985), making health habits less independent of each other. However, health status, the outcome that we ultimately wish to modify, is determined by a va-

riety of factors, onlysome of which are risky behaviors. Therefore, if we expect to see major changes in rates of disease as a consequence of changes in health habits, we may be disappointed at least at present. However, as our knowledge of how best to change health habits improves, we may ultimately come to have a greater effect on health status.

SUMMARY

1. Efforts to change health habits have focused primarily on efforts to change attitudes via attitude-change appeals and efforts to change behavior via cognitive-behavioral interventions.

2. Although fear appeals and information appeals have had somewhat limited effects on behavior change, research on the health belief model, Bandura's self-efficacy framework, and protection motivation theory has identified the attitudes needed to be targeted for health-habit modification.

3. These attitudes are the belief that a threat to health is severe, that one is personally vulnerable to the threat, that one is able to perform the response needed to reduce the threat (self-efficacy), and that the response will be effective in overcoming the threat (response efficacy).

4. Mass media appeals alone achieve limited success in changing behavior. However, the mass media do alert people to health risks and over time can change attitudes toward health practices. In conjunction with behavior-change efforts, mass media can reinforce health campaigns implemented via other means.

5. Cognitive-behavioral approaches to health-habit change draw on principles of learning theory designed to modify the antecedents and the consequences of the target behavior.

6. Cognitive behavioral efforts often begin with self-observation or self-monitoring, in which an individual charts the target behavior. Basic principles of behavior change, such as classical conditioning, systematic desensitization, operant conditioning, shaping, modeling, and stimulus control, are then employed to modify the behavior.

7. Cognitive-behavior therapy has brought patients into the treatment process by enlisting them as co-therapists and training them in principles of behavioral self-control and self-modification. Self-reinforcement, contingency contracting, and behavioral assignments underscore the critical role of the patient as co-therapist.

8. Social skills training and relaxation training methods are often incorporated into broad-spectrum, or multimodal, cognitive-behavioral interventions to deal with the anxiety or social deficits that underlie some health problems.

9. Increasingly, research and intervention have focused on relapse prevention: the need to train clients early in methods they can use to avoid the temptations to relapse. Learning coping techniques to be used in high-risk-for-relapse situations is a major component of such programs.

10. Some health habits are better changed through social engineering than through behavior-change methods, such as mandating childhood immunizations or purifying water at its source.

11. The venue for changing health habits is receiving increasing attention. Although modification of behavior in the private therapist's office and the physician's office may be successful, these techniques are expensive and reach only one individual at a time. Self-help groups continue to be the major method of modifying health habits.

12. Increasingly, researchers are introducing health promotion interventions into natural environments, such as schools, worksites, and the community. These efforts currently hold the most promise for modifying the health habits of the largest number of people simultaneously.

KEY TERMS

assertiveness training
behavioral assignments
broad-spectrum, or multimodal,
    cognitive-behavioral therapy
classical conditioning
cognitive-behavior therapy
cognitive restructuring
contingency contracting
counterconditioning
covert self-control
discriminative stimulus
fear appeals
flooding
informational appeals
lifestyle rebalancing
modeling
operant conditioning

protection motivation model
relapse prevention
relaxation training
self-control
self-employed desensitization
self-observation and self-monitoring
self-reinforcement
self-talk
shaping
social engineering
social-skills training
stimulus-control interventions
systematic desensitization
thought stopping
vicarious systematic desensitization, or
    guided mastery

5

HEALTH-ENHANCING BEHAVIORS

In the previous chapter, we examined some of the factors that determine whether or not people practice good health behaviors. We also considered some determinants of attitude and behavior change. These principles of attitude and behavior change can be applied to help people adopt behaviors that increase the likelihood of wellness (Chapter 5) and give up health-compromising behaviors that pave the way to illness (Chapter 6). In this chapter, we focus on several health-enhancing behaviors, including exercise, accident prevention, breast and testicular self-examination, weight control, and consuming a healthy diet. Each of these behaviors is relevant to a major cause of illness, disability, and death in industrialized countries. As noted in earlier chapters, obesity, poor diet, and lack of exercise are implicated in cardiovascular disease. Breast and testicular self-examination can lead to the early detection of cancer. Accident prevention addresses one of the major causes of death among children, adolescents, and young adults.

As we shall see, a focus on these particular health issues also illustrates the broad variety of specific problems that can be addressed by successful behavior change. In this chapter and in Chapter 6, we see the specific principles of attitude and behavior change considered in Chapter 4 applied to these health-enhancing and health-compromising behaviors.

Another reason for focusing on these particular health issues is that they represent the problems to which principles of attitude change and cognitive-behavioral change have most frequently been applied. As we consider each health issue in detail, we will see a progression of approaches that typically takes the following form.

To start, researchers attempted to find the single best way to modify the relevant health behavior. Just as medical researchers have traditionally sought the "magic bullet" that will eradicate a particular disease, so have behavioral researchers sought "magic bullet" solutions for poor health behaviors. However, decades of research have now conclusively shown that there are no "magic bullets" for poor health behaviors for a number of reasons. As we saw in the previous chapter, health behavior change is an enormously complex process; it involves changing attitudes, instilling motivation, gaining adherence to a desirable health practice, and maintaining adherence over time (relapse prevention). Moreover, every health behavior has a developmental course, so that factors that successfully modify the behavior at one stage in its development cycle may not do so at another stage. To make the picture more complex, there is a wide variety of causes for any particular health problem: The factors influencing one person's weight problem may be very different from those influencing another person's weight problem, and, similarly, the onset and history of one person's smoking may be very different from that of another. For all these reasons, the effort to find a single best approach to behavior modification has largely been abandoned.

Instead, researchers have incorporated a broad-spectrum, or multimodal, approach to intervention that combines a variety of techniques designed to modify health behavior. As we saw in the preceding chapter, this viewpoint maintains that no single technique is sufficient in its own right to modify behavior but, combined with other techniques, each can facilitate behavior change when tailored to the particular individual's health habit. We will see this principle illustrated repeatedly as we examine specific health behaviors.

Two consequences of this eclectic approach to behavior change should be noted. First, the theoretical principles that we discussed in the last chapter are no longer applied to health behaviors in a pure form. For example, an intervention to change eating habits might combine information appeals, operant conditioning, contracting, and covert self-control. Theoretical distinctions are important in principle because they can help explain why a par-

ticular technique works, but when it comes to behavior change, interventions make use of whatever works, regardless of its theoretical origins. In the second place, when an intervention is successful in changing a health behavior, we will not know exactly why. We will not be able to point to a particular behavior-change technique and say confidently, "That factor produced the change." Rather, often we must conclude that the combination of factors produced the change without knowing which particular aspects of the intervention were more or less powerful in bringing it about.

The current approach to health behavior change thus begins with a careful analysis of the nature of the problem. What is the target behavior? Do people have the right information about it? Are they motivated to change their behavior? Efforts to change health behavior then turn to the behavior itself. Can the individual change the behavior and, if so, what are the best methods? How can behavior change be maintained over time? How can relapse be avoided? The health researcher or practitioner selects from the arsenal of attitude- and behavior-change techniques those methods that are most effective in dealing with the particular issues posed by the analysis of the target behavior. Let us turn to these target behaviors and see how receptive they are to modification.

EXERCISE

Recently, the medical community and health psychologists have turned their attention to the role of aerobic exercise in maintaining mental and physical health. **Aerobic exercises** include jogging, bicycling, jumping rope, running, and swimming, all of which are marked by their high intensity, long duration, and need for high endurance. Other forms of exercise—such as isokinetic exercises (weight lifting, for example) or high-intensity, short-duration, low-endurance exercises (like sprinting)—may be satisfying but have less effect on fitness. This is because these latter forms of exercise draw on short-term stores of glycogen rather than on the long-term energy conversion system associated with aerobics (McArdle, Katch, & Katch, 1981; Morehouse & Miller, 1976).

Benefits of Exercise

A number of benefits of aerobic exercise have been documented. Aerobic exercise has been tied to increases in cardiovascular fitness and endurance (Alpert, Field, Goldstein, & Perry, 1990; Serfass & Gerberich, 1984) and to reduced risk for heart attack (Paffenbarger, Hyde, Wing, & Steinmetz, 1984; Shephard, 1986). Other benefits include increased efficiency of the cardiorespiratory system, improved physical work capacity, the optimiza-

tion of body weight, the improvement or maintenance of muscle tone and strength, an increase in soft tissue and joint flexibility, the reduction or control of hypertension, improved cholesterol level, improved glucose tolerance, improved tolerance of stress, and reduction in poor health habits, including cigarette smoking, alcohol consumption, and poor diet (Leon 1983; Leon & Fox, 1981). Some cardiovascular benefits have been found even for preschoolers (Alpert et al., 1990). These effects of exercise translate directly into increased longevity. One study estimated that by age 80, the amount of additional life attributable to aerobic exercise is between 1 and 2 years (Paffenbarger, Hyde, Wing, & Hsieh, 1986). Pause for thought is prompted by the observation that in order to achieve these extra 2 years of life, one will need to devote them entirely to exercise over the lifetime (Jacoby, 1986).

Regular aerobic exercise produces many physical and emotional benefits, including reduced risk for cardiovascular disease.

The typical exercise prescription for a normal individual is aerobic exercise just short of maximal intensity. In particular, performing at 70 to 85% of maximal heart rate nonstop for no less than 15 minutes three times a week has been tied to reduced risk for coronary heart disease (Dishman, 1982; Zohman, 1981). A person with low cardiopulmonary fitness may derive benefits with even less exercise each week (Serfass & Gerberich, 1984). Exercise is also a useful way of rehabilitating those already suffering from cardiovascular disorders; consequently, exercise recommendations are frequently made for patients who have had myocardial infarctions (Blackburn, 1983a, 1983b).

Some have maintained that exercise has a beneficial effect on cognitive processes by focusing attention and concentration. However, results suggest that although exercise may initially facilitate attention, as its intensity increases, these effects may be canceled by the debilitating effects of muscle fatigue (Tomporowski & Ellis, 1986).

Researchers have examined the effect of aerobic exercise on psychological factors, such as mood, anxiety, depression, and tension. The results have been cautiously positive, suggesting a beneficial role of exercise on mental as well as physical health. It appears that exercise may have a modest effect on mood and feelings of well-being immediately after a workout; there may also be some improvement in general mood and well-being as a result of long-term participation in an exercise program, although the results are not as strong as those demonstrating an immediate beneficial effect (Rodin & Plante, 1989). Hughes (1984; Hughes, Casal, & Leon, 1986) suggested that at least some of the positive effects of exercise on mood may stem from factors associated with exercise, such as social activity and a feeling of involvement with others. For example, bicycling with friends, swimming with a companion, or running with others may improve mood in part because of the companionship the exercise provides. Alternatively, people may report that they feel good because they are satisfied with their performance, or expect that they should feel an improvement in their mood (Hughes, 1984).

Mood may also improve after exercise because it makes people feel efficacious. To examine this possibility, Rodin (Rodin & Plante, 1989) had subjects attend an exercise group and manipulated the experience of self-efficacy during the program by emphasizing how difficult regular exercise is and how few people are able to achieve physical fitness. Results indicated that, compared to a control group, subjects in the efficacy condition had significantly higher levels of perceived self-efficacy, and these perceptions were associated with improvements in mood and psychological well-being. Rodin also suggests that exercise may facilitate a sense of optimism, leading to fewer physical symptoms and more positive psychological well-being, although the evidence for this mechanism has yet to be provided (Rodin, in press).

Being involved with and committed to an exercise program also appears to have positive effects on self-concept, self-esteem (Rodin & Plante, 1989), and well-being (Hayes & Ross, 1986). Exercise has also been used as a treatment intervention for depression. One study assigned depressed women to either an exercise condition, a relaxation training session, or a no-treatment session. Results indicated that the exercise group improved their mood significantly more than the other two groups (McCann & Holmes, 1984). In addition to mood effects, regular exercise appears to reduce stress, anxiety, and depression (Rodin & Plante, 1989).

A recent review of employee fitness programs, which are now a part of over 50,000 United States businesses, suggests that such programs can reduce absenteeism, increase job satisfaction, and reduce health care costs, especially among women employees (see Rodin & Plante, 1989, for a review). Exercise also appears to buffer people against the adverse health effects of stress. Brown and Siegel (1988) conducted a longitudinal study to see if adolescents who exercised were better able to cope with stress and avoid illness than those who did not. Results indicated that the negative impact of stressful life events on health declined as exercise levels increased. Thus, exercise may be a useful resource for combating stress.

One possible mechanism whereby exercise may buffer the adverse health effects of stress involves the impact of exercise on the immune system. In one study (Fiatarone et al., 1988), exercise produced a rise in natural killer cell activity and an increase in the percentage of lymphocytes bearing natural killer cell surface markers. An increase in endogenous opioids (natural pain inhibitors; see Chapter 11) stimulated by exercise may play a role in the modulation of immune activity during periods of psychological stress.

One puzzle is why exercise, which produces the release of adrenalin and other hormones, has a beneficial effect on heart functioning, whereas stress, which also produces these hormones, has an adverse effect, associated with lesions in the heart tissue (Wright, 1988). One theory maintains that infrequent activation and discharge of adrenalin may have beneficial effects, whereas chronically enhanced discharge of adrenalin may not. Another possibility is that adrenalin discharged under conditions for which it was intended (such as running or fighting) is metabolized differently from adrenalin that occurs in response to stress, which is not expressed physically in the same ways. That is, hormones may be metabolized differently depending on whether one is engaged in large-muscle or small-muscle activity.

Determinants of Regular Exercise

Although the health and mental health benefits of exercise have been established, most people's participation in exercise programs is erratic. Evaluations of exercise programs indicate that 6-month participation levels range from 11 to 87%, averaging at about 50% (Dishman, 1982). That is, on the average, only half of those who initiate a voluntary exercise program are still participating in that program after 6 months. People may be induced to begin an exercise program but find it difficult to make exercise a regular activity (Dishman, 1982). Accordingly, research has attempted to identify the factors that lead people to participate in exercise programs over the long term. Some researchers have emphasized individual characteristics, others have examined the exercise setting, and still others have looked at characteristics of the intervention to see what factors promote exercise. We will consider each in turn.

Individual Characteristics The effort to identify what kinds of people exercise regularly has yielded few generalizations. People who come from families where exercise is practiced (Sallis, Patterson, Buono, Atkins, & Nader, 1988), who have positive attitudes toward physical activity, who perceive themselves as athletic or as the type of person who exercises (Kendzierski, 1990), and who believe that people should take responsibility for their health are more likely to get involved in exercise programs initially than people who do not have these attitudes (Dishman, 1982). However, these factors do not predict participation in exercise programs over the long term. Those who have positive attitudes toward exercise and health are as likely to drop out as those who do not (Dishman, 1982). Dishman (1982) has suggested that, in order to understand exercise adherence more fully, future research should examine an individual's underlying exercise goals and his or her motivation to engage in exercise.

Some physical discriminators predict participation in exercise programs. Overweight people are less likely to participate in exercise programs than are those who are not overweight. It may be that exercise is harder for the overweight or that leaner people who had more active lifestyles before getting involved in exercise are better able to incorporate exercise into their activities (Dishman, 1982). The effects of health status on participation in exercise programs are still unclear. Individuals at risk for cardiovascular disease do show greater adherence to exercise programs than do those who are not (Dishman, 1981; Oldridge, 1979). However, outside of the cardiovascular area, there is no general relationship between health status and participation in exercise (Dishman, 1982).

Characteristics of the Setting   Research has attempted to identify the characteristics of exercise programs that promote adherence. One consistent finding is that convenient and easily accessible exercise settings lead to higher rates of adherence (for a review, see Dishman, 1982). Thus, if you have a tennis court in your backyard, you are more likely to play tennis than if you must compete with fifty other people all trying to schedule the same court at your health club 5 miles from your home.

Research has also examined whether there is an ideal "behavioral dosage" for exercise. That is, are people more likely to adhere to exercise if a given amount of exercise has been prescribed for them? As noted earlier, the usual prescribed dosage of exercise is no less than 15 minutes of sustained activity at 70 to 85% of maximal heart rate three times a week. To date, however, research suggests there is no ideal behavioral dosage that improves adherence (Dishman, 1982). An exercise regimen that is consistently near the maximal heart rate (90%), however, tends to produce noncompliance, perhaps because the regimen is too demanding to be sustained on a regular basis (Martin & Dubbert, 1982).

Perhaps the best predictor of regular exercise is regular exercise. Studies that have assessed attitudinal and motivational predictors of exercise have found that although exercise intentions are influenced by attitudes, long-term practice of regular exercise is heavily determined by habit (Godin, Desharnais, Jobin, & Cook, 1987; Valois et al., 1988). The first 3 to 6 months appear to be critical. People who will drop out appear to do so in that time period. Those who have adhered that long are significantly more likely to continue to do so (Dishman, 1982).

Characteristics of Intervention Strategies Some researchers have focused on aspects of intervention strategies that may increase adherence. Their work indicates that when exercise is made more convenient, as by being performed in the home, and when exercise is tied to one's social system (for example, if one's spouse is involved in the program), adherence is higher (e.g., Wilhelmson et al., 1975). Cognitive-behavioral strategies—including contingency contracting, self-reinforcement, self-monitoring, and goal setting—have been employed in exercise interventions and appear to promote adherence (Dishman, 1982; Martin & Dubbert, 1982; Serfass & Gerberich, 1984).

As with other good health habits, the motivation to engage in regular exercise may be enhanced through a variety of interventions but may fail to be sustained over the long term (Godin et al., 1987). Valois et al. (1988) found that habit (the number of times a person had previously engaged in exercise) was the best predictor of the intention to exercise, but habit alone does not determine exercise. Unlike such habitual behaviors as wearing a seat belt or not lighting a cigarette, exercise requires additional thoughtfulness and planning. Exercising takes will, the recognition that hard work is involved, and a belief in personal responsibility in order to be enacted on a regular basis (Valois et al., 1988).

Because research has identified few reliable individual factors, exercise-setting characteristics, or intervention strategies that predict adherence, an individualized model tailored to encourage exercise adherence may be appropriate for the present (Dishman, 1982). An assessment of an individual's motivation and attitudes can provide the basis for an exercise program that fits the person well, so that exercise will be initiated and maintained. If people participate in activities that they like, that are convenient, for which they can develop goals, and that they are highly motivated to pursue, exercise adherence will be greater (Dishman, 1982).

Recently, Marlatt and Gordon's relapse prevention approach has been used to increase adherence to exercise programs. One study (Belisle et al., 1987) compared adherence to exercise among participants in a 10-week exercise group that either did or did not receive training in relapse prevention. Relapse prevention techniques in this intervention centered around increasing awareness of the obstacles people experience in obtaining regular exercise and developing appropriate techniques for coping with them, such as methods of resisting temptation not to exercise. The results indicated superior adherence in the relapse prevention group.

Do the benefits and results of exercise programs generalize to behavior in nonexercise settings? This intriguing question was studied unobtrusively among sixty Hispanic and Anglo families, half of whom had participated in a 1-year intervention program to modify diet in a healthy direction and to increase physical activity. During a trip to the San Diego Zoo, these families were surreptitiously observed and their dietary intake and amount of walking were recorded. Results indicated that the families participating in the intervention consumed fewer calories, ate less sodium, and walked further than the control families, suggesting that the intervention had been integrated into their lifestyle to the point that it predicted behavior in a novel setting (Patterson et al., 1988).

In conclusion, it is important to underscore the role that cultural values have played and may continue to play in the exercise level of the American population. The number of people who participate in regular exercise has increased by more than 50% over the last few decades (American Running & Fitness Association, 1981). This fact underscores an important point from the previous chapter: that media and other modes of cultural transmission are significant methods of changing attitudes toward a particular health practice. Moreover, these attitudes may ultimately filter down to real behavior change.

ACCIDENT PREVENTION

Accidents represent one of the major causes of preventable death in this country. Approximately one death out of every forty is related to a motor vehicle, and this is one of the greatest causes of death among children, adolescents, and young adults. Between 2 and 10 million people are poisoned each year in the United States, 85% of whom are children. Bicycle accidents cause about 1,300 deaths per year, prompt more than 574,000 emergency room visits, and constitute the major cause of head injury (Thompson, Rivara, & Thompson, 1989), thereby making helmet use an important issue. Occupational accidents and their consequent impact on disability are a major health problem among working men. Consequently, strategies to reduce accidents have increasingly been a focus of health psychology research and interventions.

Accidents in the home, such as accidental poisonings or falls, are one of the most common causes of death and disability among children under age 5. To date, relatively little research has been devoted to reducing these risks. What research has been conducted has, of necessity, focused on parental attitudes and parental instruction. A study by Peterson, Farmer, and Kashani (1990) found that parents were most likely to undertake injury prevention activities if they believed that those steps really would avoid injuries, if they felt knowledgeable and competent to teach safety skills to their children, and if they had a realistic sense of how much time would actually be involved in so doing. Increasingly, pediatricians incorporate such training into their interactions with new parents (Roberts & Turner, 1984). Parent classes can be used to teach parents to identify the most common poisons in their household and how to keep these safeguarded or out of reach of young children. A study evaluating training to childproof a home suggested that such interventions can be successful (Matthews Friman, Barone, Ross, & Christophersen, 1987). Yet more work on this problem is clearly needed.

Motorcycle and Automobile Accidents

"You know what I call a motorcyclist who doesn't wear a helmet? An organ donor."
                    —*Emergency room physician*

The single greatest cause of accidental death is motorcycle and automobile accidents (Califano, 1979a, 1979b). To date, relatively little psychological research has gone into helping people learn to avoid vehicular traffic accidents (Matarazzo, 1982). Instead, efforts have concentrated on such factors as the maintenance of roadways, the volume of travel, and safety standards in automobiles. However, psychological research can address factors associated with accidents, including the way people drive, the speed at which they drive, and the use of preventive measures to increase safety (Sleet, 1984).

It is clear that safety measures such as reducing highway driving speed to 55 miles per hour (Califano, 1979a), requiring seat belts, and placing young children in safety restraint seats reduces the number of severe injuries and vehicular fatalities (McGinnis, 1984; O'Day & Scott, 1984; Sleet, 1984). The use of helmets among bicycle and motorcycle riders reduces the severity of accidents by a substan-

tial degree, particularly preventing serious head injury (Thompson, Rivara, & Thompson, 1989).

Yet, to date, the evidence suggests that getting people to follow these safety measures has been difficult. For example, it is estimated that between 60 to 90% of Americans rarely use seat belts (McGinnis, 1984). In developing strategies to promote the use of seat belts, a combination of social engineering, health education, and psychological intervention may be most appropriate. For example, most states now require that infants and toddlers up to age 3 or 4 be restrained in safety seats and children up to age 6 wear seat belts. This requirement can lay the groundwork for proper safety behavior in automobiles, making people more likely to use seat belts in adolescence and adulthood.

Community-wide health education programs aimed at increasing seat belt usage can be successful. One such program increased the use from 24 to 41%, sustaining at 36% over a 6-month follow-up period (Gemming, Runyan, Hunter, & Campbell, 1984). In terms of improving seat belt use, one program involving high school students found that frequent but small monetary awards coupled with an educational campaign stressing the importance of accident prevention substantially increased seat belt use from approximately 25 to nearly 50% (Campbell, Hunter, & Stutts, 1984).

In the last two decades, accident prevention strategies have focused heavily on the risk of vehicular accidents to infants and young children as well. As just noted, most states now require that infants and toddlers up to age 3 or 4 be restrained in safety seats. Initial evaluations of programs designed to get parents to voluntarily use child safety restraint seats properly produced dismal conclusions. Several studies evaluated interventions designed to increase the use and correct use of child restraint devices, and found that persuasive pamphlets, films, and demonstrations often

Automobile accidents represent a major cause of death, especially among the young. Legislation requiring child safety restraint devices has reduced fatalities dramatically.

produced very low levels of adherence (e.g., Reisinger & Williams, 1978).

However, in recent years, both use and correct use of child restraint devices have increased dramatically. For example, Christophersen, Sosland-Edelman, and LeClaire (1985) found a 90% correct usage of infant restraint devices with more than 80% adherence over the following year. Consistent with these results, Colletti (1984) found in 4 years, the rate of correct car seat usage for newborns increased from 16 to 71%. These dramatic increases appear to be attributable to several factors. They include the increasing availability of car seats, direct educational and mass media interventions promoting the need for their use, and educational influences in the community. Many hospitals now discharge a mother and her newborn only if a car seat for the newborn has been correctly installed in the car. Similarly, Christophersen et al. (1985) found that nursing staff's insistence that seat belts be used following discharge from the hospital

may create a climate conducive to use and provide a model for vehicular safety behavior in the future.

The increase in child safety-related behaviors, then, appears to be attributable to several factors. Social engineering requiring the use of safety restraints lays a basis for high levels of adherence. Mass media interventions and education of prospective parents in the obstetrician's and pediatrician's office create the motivation and intention to comply with these requirements. And the availability of car seats and their increasing use themselves contribute to the high level of use.

To date, interventions to improve safety measures related to automobile and motorcycle accidents have represented an area not fully investigated by psychologists. It is likely that in the coming years we will see more such interventions, coupled with the social engineering solutions (such as laws) that promote a basis for these important behaviors.

BREAST AND TESTICULAR SELF-EXAMINATION

Breast Self-Examination

Breast cancer is one of the leading causes of cancer deaths among American women, striking one out of every eleven women at some point during her life (American Cancer Society, 1989). Although breast cancer does not usually develop until after age 45, its age of onset is decreasing, and more young women than ever are affected. Despite medical advances in technology to detect cancerous lumps, 90% of all breast cancer is still self-detected through self-examination. **Breast self-examination (BSE)** is the practice of checking the breasts to detect alterations in the underlying tissue. Ideally, the breasts are palpated once a month, approximately 10 days into the menstrual cycle, in both a standing-up and lying-down position. Breast self-examination during a shower or a warm bath sometimes improves the ability to detect lesions. The correct practice of breast self-examination involves checking all of the breast tissue, including the nipple and the area under the armpits.

Finding the best method of teaching women how and when to practice BSE has long been a concern of the American Cancer Society and the National Cancer Institute. Despite the widespread availability of pamphlets designed to teach BSE and numerous magazine and newspaper articles on the topic, only about 35% of women do it regularly, and many of these do not use the correct method (National Cancer Institute, 1980).

Several factors may act as deterrents to the regular practice of BSE: not being certain that one is doing it correctly (Gallup, 1979; Kegeles, 1985), having difficulty detecting changes in the breast tissue (Hall et al., 1980; Kegeles, 1985; Trotta, 1980) and fearing what might happen if a lump were detected (Gallup, 1979; Trotta, 1980). However, each of these concerns can be addressed by proper intervention techniques. For instance, it appears that the instructions given in pamphlets and magazine articles are not usually effective in showing women how to practice BSE correctly. Lack of knowledge concerning how to practice BSE is one of the main factors that discriminates consistently between those who practice regularly and irregularly (Alagna & Reddy, 1984; Kegeles, 1985). Women who have been trained by their physicians or other medical professionals are more likely to practice BSE than are women who have learned it in other ways (Gallup, 1979). Thus, personal instruction appears to be a critical factor. However, surveys reveal that not all physicians instruct their patients in BSE (Gallup, 1979). Thus, intervening with physicians would help reduce this barrier (Kegeles, 1985).

Many women who practice BSE are discouraged by the fact that it is hard to detect lumps (Kegeles, 1985). Self-confidence in the

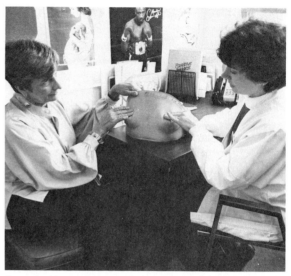

Breast self-examination is a major way of detecting breast cancer, but many women fail to practice it appropriately. Training can improve the quality and frequency of BSE.

efficacy of BSE is a strong predictor of proficient as well as frequent breast self-examination (Alagna & Reddy, 1984). From the standpoint of health attitudes, then, the self-efficacy component should be a focus of intervention (Alagna & Reddy, 1984). Breast tissue tends to be lumpy by nature, and beginners seem to find suspicious lumps all the time. However, research reveals that when women practice BSE on synthetic models that do and do not contain lumps, their ability to discriminate lumps improves. Thus, BSE self-confidence can be augmented by practice on models (e.g., Hall et al., 1980; Stephenson, Adams, Hall, & Pennypacker, 1979).

The fear of detecting an abnormality is also a deterrent to practice among some women (Gallup, 1979; Trotta, 1980). To combat this fear, statistics regarding the successful treatment of breast cancer should be publicized. At the present time, breast cancers that are detected early have an 85 to 90% chance of being cured (American Cancer Society, 1989). Moreover, mastectomies involving the removal of the entire breast and of adjacent tissue are no longer routine. Many women can be treated by means of a minimal procedure, called a lumpectomy, that involves the removal of the malignant lump and surrounding tissue only, not the entire breast. This procedure is not very disfiguring and is associated, for some breast cancers, with cure rates comparable to those for mastectomies.

One of the dilemmas with practicing breast self-examination on a regular basis is that it is often difficult to remember to engage in a habit once a month at the particular time when it is recommended for practice (approximately 10 days into the menstrual cycle) (Strauss, Solomon, Costanza, Worden, & Foster, 1987). In a study examining several approaches to increasing breast self-exam frequency (Craun & Deffenbacher, 1987), women were provided with education about breast cancer and breast self-examination, a demonstration of breast self-examination, or prompt reminders each month to self-examine. The results indicated that, of the three conditions, the prompt was most successful in increasing the frequency of breast self-examination. Although it may be impractical to mail monthly prompts to all adolescent and adult women in the United States, by providing calendars or some other stimulus aid indicating when BSE should be practiced, frequency can be improved (Kegeles, 1985). Phone prompts may be slightly more successful than mail prompts, although any prompt appears to improve the frequency of BSE over no prompt at all (Mayer & Frederiksen, 1986).

Another study (Grady, Goodenow, & Borkin, 1988) compared two types of reward on the frequency of BSE practice: external reinforcement and self-reward. External rewards were either lottery tickets or a Susan B. Anthony dollar, and self-rewards were chosen by the women themselves from a suggested list of twenty-five rewards, including such things as "buy a desired book," "listen to the radio,"

or "don't do the dishes." Participants returned monthly records of BSE practice. Because external reward was more effective than self-reward in increasing the practice of BSE, when the study came to a close and the external reward was withdrawn, BSE practice dropped sharply.

To further address the problem of how to best increase the frequency of a monthly habit, a study by Kemeny, Hovell, Mewborn, Dockter, and Chin (1988) instructed women to practice BSE either weekly, every 2 weeks, or every month. They found that BSE frequency could be enhanced by prescribing it more frequently. Presumably, the more the health habit was practiced, the more women remembered that they should practice it, and, consequently, the dilemma of having to remember each month was at least partially avoided in this study.

As Kegeles (1985) noted, however, increasing the frequency of BSE does not necessarily increase how capably it is done, and an incompetent breast examination may fail to reveal lumps that a more careful examination would. Successful lesion detection has been related not only to a high frequency of BSE practice, but also to a more proficient technique (Alagna & Reddy, 1984).

What, then, is the best way to teach breast self-examination? The best method is personal instruction from a health care agent such as a physician or nurse that involves practice both on oneself and on synthetic models. Such training should increase the proficiency of BSE. By clarifying some of the myths about breast cancer, its detection, and treatment, we can increase the willingness to practice BSE. Finally, prompts or more than monthly practice clearly increase the frequency of practice.

Testicular Self-Examination

Testicular cancer is the most common cancer in men between the ages of 15 and 35, and it is also the leading cause of cancer death and the second leading cause of all deaths of men in this age group. Though not a common cause of death, it is a preventable cause of premature death, and thus merits intervention. In particular, the likelihood of surviving testicular cancer, which is very high, improves with early detection. In its early stages, the disease is entirely curable (Friman & Christophersen, 1986).

The symptoms of testicular cancer are typically a small, usually painless lump on the front or sides of one or both testicles, a feeling of heaviness in the testes, a dragging sensation in the groin, accumulation of fluid or blood in the scrotal sac, and pain in advanced cases (Hongladrom & Hongladrom, 1982). Despite the fact that early detection markedly improves survival rates, young men are generally unaware of either their risk or the appropriate health measures to take to reduce it.

In many ways, effective **testicular self-examination (TSE)** is quite similar to effective breast self-examination. It involves becoming familiar with the surface, texture, and consistency of the testicles, examination during a warm bath or shower, and examination of both testicles rotated between the thumb and forefinger to determine that the entire surface is free of lumps (Hongladrom & Hongladrom, 1982).

Relatively few studies have examined or conducted interventions to assess or improve the frequency and proficiency of testicular self-examination. One study (Friman, Finney, Glasscock, Weigel, & Christophersen, 1986) provided young men with a brief checklist of TSE skills, and found that the educational intervention produced substantial increases in the efficacy of TSE. When contacted later by phone, subjects indicated that they had continued to practice the skill. Consistent with research exploring the attitudinal determinants of health habits, Brubaker and Wickersham (1990) found that men more likely to perform

TSE were more likely to believe that it would be effective in reducing their risk and that others would approve of their practice of the exam (subjective norms). More attention to increasing the frequency and proficiency of this health behavior is clearly needed.

WEIGHT CONTROL

In this section, we consider weight control as a health-enhancing behavior. However, because obesity is a health risk, our discussion begins to cross the line into the area of health-compromising behaviors. Thus, our discussion centers around both the question of controlling and maintaining weight and weight reduction techniques that may be required for those who are already obese.

The Regulation of Eating

Animals, including people, have very sensitive and complex systems for regulating food. Taste has been called the chemical gatekeeper of eating. It is the most ancient of sensory systems and plays an important role in selecting certain foods and rejecting others. The regulation of eating is under the control of manifold biochemical processes, in particular, the monoamines and neurotransmitters. Neuroregulatory agents in eating can be divided into two systems, the peripheral satiety system and the central feeding mechanism. The *peripheral satiety system* regulates eating through the release of gastrointestinal and pancreatic hormones when food passes through the gastrointestinal tract. The *central feeding mechanism* controls eating through a concentration of neuropeptides and other neurotransmitters.

Why Obesity Is a Health Risk

What is **obesity?** Obesity is an excessive accumulation of body fat. What makes an accumulation excessive varies, but, generally speaking, fat should constitute about 20 to 27% of body tissue for women and about 15 to 22% in men. The Metropolitan Life Insurance Company has for years published tables of ideal weight ranges for people of particular heights (Table 5.1). When body weight is in the range of 20% above one's ideal weight, one is said to be overweight; in excess of 20%, one is said to be obese.

Obesity is a risk factor for many disorders, both in its own right and because it affects other risk factors such as blood pressure and plasma cholesterol level (Hubert, Feinleib, McNamara, & Castelli, 1983). It has been associated with atherosclerosis, hypertension, diabetes, some forms of cancer, gall bladder dis-

ease, and arthritis. Obesity also increases risks in surgery, anesthesia administration, and childbearing (Bray, 1976; Dawber, 1980; Kannel & Gordon, 1979; Van Itallie, 1979). As a consequence of its links to chronic disease (especially cardiovascular disease, kidney disease, and diabetes), obesity is associated with early mortality. A recent study of women found that those who were 30% overweight were more than three times as likely to develop heart disease as women who were of normal or slightly under weight (Manson et al., 1990). The risk increased to five times that of normal weight women among the overweight women who were also smokers (Manson et al., 1990).

Obesity is not only a major health problem,

TABLE 5.1   HEIGHT-WEIGHT TABLES FOR ADULTS

	MEN			WOMEN	
HEIGHT	IDEAL WEIGHT (IN POUNDS)	OVERWEIGHT (IN POUNDS)	HEIGHT	IDEAL WEIGHT (IN POUNDS)	OVERWEIGHT (IN POUNDS)
5'1"	131	157	4'9"	112	134
5'2"	133	160	4'10"	114	137
5'3"	135	162	4'11"	117	140
5'4"	138	165	5'0"	119	143
5'5"	140	168	5'1"	122	146
5'6"	143	172	5'2"	125	150
5'7"	146	175	5'3"	128	154
5'8"	149	179	5'4"	131	157
5'9"	152	182	5'5"	134	161
5'10"	155	186	5'6"	137	164
5'11"	159	190	5'7"	140	168
6'0"	162	194	5'8"	143	172
6'1"	166	199	5'9"	146	175
6'2"	170	203	5'10"	149	179
6'3"	174	209	5'11"	152	182

Figures are for adults of average frame size, without shoes or clothing. Height-weight tables reflect the average weights at which large groups of people lived longest. Because healthy individuals can vary widely, height-weight tables cannot specify a precise ideal weight for any one person. In these tables, "overweight" reflects an arbitrary standard of 20 percent above ideal weight.

(Source: Adapted from Metropolitan Life Insurance Company Height and Weight Tables, 1983)

it is also a common one. Estimates indicate that in the United States approximately 14% of adult men and 24% of adult women are at least 20% above the recommended weight for their height. An additional 18% of men and 13% of women are at least 10% overweight, and these figures are considerably higher in poverty-level populations (Stunkard, 1975). Thus, the health implications of obesity are substantial.

Factors Associated with Obesity

Obesity is a function of both the number and size of an individual's bodily fat cells. Among moderately obese people, fat cells are typically large, but there is not an unusual number of them. Among the severely obese, there is both a large number of fat cells and the fat cells themselves are exceptionally large (Brownell, 1982). What determines the number and size of fat cells? Although many of these answers

are not yet known (Hirsch, Fried, Edens, & Leibel, 1989), certain factors clearly contribute.

Family history is clearly implicated in obesity. Overweight parents are more likely to produce overweight offspring than are normal-weight parents. This relationship appears to be due to both genetic and dietary factors. Evidence for genetic factors comes from twin studies, demonstrating that twins reared apart show a tendency toward obesity when both natural parents were obese, even when the twins' environments were very different (Stunkard, 1988). The impact of genetics on weight may be exerted, in part, through feeding style. In a study of healthy infants observed from birth to 2 years, Agras and his associates (Agras, Kraemer, Berkowitz, Korner, & Hammer, 1987) found that children who were later to become obese were distinguished by a vigorous feeding style, consisting of sucking more rapidly, more intensely, and longer, with shorter bursts between sucking. This

Over one-fifth of the adult population in the United States is overweight, putting them at risk for heart disease, kidney disease, hypertension, diabetes, and other health problems.

style produced a higher caloric intake and greater overweight. The fact that the feeding style emerged very early suggests that it may be a genetically endowed behavior and one of the mediators by which a genetic predisposition to obesity leads to obesity. Identifying the role of genetics in obesity has been an important research development, because it helps pinpoint those individuals for whom weight-management interventions are especially important.

Family size and the number of obese persons in the home are also related to childhood obesity and the ability to lose weight in childhood (Epstein, Koeske, Wing, & Valoski, 1986). In particular, the size of a family may influence the extent to which parents can actively manage their children; with fewer children, it may be possible to bring about concerted weight loss in any one child. But a family history of obesity does not necessarily implicate genetics. For example, one study found that 44% of the dogs of obese people were obese, as compared with only 25% of the dogs of those with normal weight (Mason, 1970). There are many environmental factors in a home, such as the type of diet consumed and exercise level, that also contribute to obesity that may run in families.

Early eating and exercise experiences contribute to obesity. Children who are encouraged to overeat in infancy and childhood are more likely to become obese adults, as are children whose daytime activity level is low (Berkowitz, Agras, Korner, Kraemer, & Zeanah, 1985). In fact, 80% of all people who were overweight as children are overweight as adults (Abraham, Collins, & Nordsieck, 1971). One basis for this fact is that the number of fat cells an individual has is typically determined in the first few years of life, as by genetic factors or by early eating habits. A high number of fat cells leads to a marked propensity for fat storage, thus promoting obesity in adulthood. In contrast, poor eating habits in adolescence and adulthood are more likely to affect the size of fat cells but not their number.

Socioeconomic status predicts obesity. Low-SES women are heavier than high-SES women, and black women in particular appear to be vulnerable to obesity (Sobal & Stunkard, 1989). Although SES differences in weight have previously been attributed to high carbohydrate diets early in life, this account does not explain why SES is not associated with obesity in men and children. Values appear to be implicated in the relationship, so that among women in developed countries, an emphasis is placed on the importance of thinness, dietary restraint, and physical activity (Sobal & Stunkard, 1989). Interestingly, in developing countries, obesity among men, women, and children is rare, possibly because of insufficient food; in these countries, the prevalence of obesity rises with SES and increasing wealth.

Paradoxically, obesity is also a risk factor for obesity. That is, the obese are at risk to become even more so. Many obese individuals have a high basal insulin level, which promotes overeating due to increased hunger. Moreover, the obese have large fat cells, which have a greater capacity for producing and storing fat than do small fat cells.

Ironically, dieting may contribute to the propensity for obesity. Successive cycles of dieting and weight gain enhance the efficiency of food use and lower the metabolic rate in rats (Brownell, Greenwood et al., 1986; Reed, Contreras, Maggio, Greenwoods, & Rodin, 1988) and humans (Brownell, 1988). When dieters begin to eat normally again, their metabolic rate may stay low, and it will be easier for them to put on weight again even though they eat less food. Unfortunately, too, these decreases in metabolic rate appear to be more problematic with successive diets. Thus, people who alternate chronically between dieting and regular eating, so-called **yo-yo dieters** (Brownell, 1988), actually increase their chances of becoming obese.

In the last decade, evidence has accumulated for a **"set point" theory of weight** level:

the idea that each individual has an ideal biological weight that cannot be greatly modified. According to the theory, the set point acts like a thermometer regulating heat in a home. The organism eats if its weight gets too low and stops eating as its weight reaches its ideal point. Some individuals may simply have a higher set point than other people, leading them to be obese (see Brownell, 1982). If this is true, this internal regulatory system also contributes to the propensity for the obese to remain so.

Prior diet influences subsequent diet in ways that may contribute to a propensity for obesity. For example, the consumption of particular nutrients may affect how many calories an individual absorbs at a later time. In one study (Spitzer & Rodin, 1987), subjects were given glucose, fructose, or water, and approximately 2 hours later were permitted to choose foods from a buffet. Subjects in the glucose condition ate more calories than those in the water condition who, in turn, ate more than those in the fructose condition. Fructose and glucose may differ in their effects on food intake because they provoke different amounts of insulin secretion. Insulin response to glucose and its subsequent effect on increasing food intake is especially strong for obese subjects (Rodin, Reed, & Jamner, 1988). Conceivably, then, preferences for particular types of nutrients (such as foods high in sugar) may have a gradual impact on long-term body weight.

Early research had suggested the existence of an obese personality characterized by dependency and a proneness to negative affect, such as depression or anxiety. These ideas have been called into question in recent years, and virtually no evidence supports them (Herman, 1987; Rodin, Schank, & Striegel-Moore, 1989). Rodin and her associates (Rodin, Silberstein, & Striegel-Moore, in press) conclude that negative affect, externality, and lack of impulse control, all factors once thought to be components of the obesity-prone personality, may be consequences rather than causes of obesity. However, there may be some individual differences, such as the ability to be aroused easily by food cues, that may be involved in the development of some forms of obesity.

Consistent with this idea, a once-popular theory of obesity maintained that the eating behavior of obese persons is under the control of different stimuli than that of normal-weight individuals. In particular, research evidence suggested that the eating behavior of obese individuals is heavily controlled by external stimuli such as the presence of food, the presence of a lot of food, a clock on the wall indicating that it is time to eat, or easy access to food. In contrast, normal-weight individuals were said to be responsive to internal stimuli of gastric motility that had come to be associated with hunger. Although this theory received some support (Pliner, 1974; Schachter, 1968, 1971; Schachter, Goldman, & Gordon, 1968), later evidence (see Rodin, 1981, for a review) suggested that the theory of externality has limited value in explaining obesity. Some obese people's eating behavior is indeed particularly sensitive to external, food-related cues. However, the obese are generally not more external than normal-weight individuals (Rodin, 1981). One possible reconciliation proposed by Herman and his associates (see Herman, 1987) is that obese people and those on diets require more external information to determine what is appropriate eating, because their prior internal regulatory guidelines, such as using hunger as a cue for eating, no longer provide useful guidelines. This would render externality a consequence of obesity and dieting, rather than a cause. As yet, it has proven difficult to disentangle the possibilities (Herman, 1987).

Studies with rats have suggested a possible brain mechanism for the control of at least some eating behavior and its external regulation. Rats who have a damaged ventromedial hypothalamus behave like obese humans:

They eat excessive amounts of food, show little sensitivity to internal cues related to hunger (for example, how long it has been since they last ate), and respond to food-related external cues such as the presence of food. On the basis of such evidence, it has been suggested that at least some obese humans may have a malfunctioning ventromedial hypothalamus that interferes with normal eating habits. Further research will assess the usefulness of this approach to eating behavior as well.

Finally, eating behavior is also under the control of certain emotional factors, such as anxiety. Humans' eating behavior responds variously to distress, with about half of the population eating more when they are stressed and about half eating less (Willenbring, Levine, & Morley, 1986). In the case of nondieting and nonobese normal eaters, the experience of stress or anxiety may suppress physiological cues suggesting hunger, leading to lower consumption of food. Stress and anxiety, however, can disinhibit the dieter, removing the self-control that usually guards against eating, thus leading to an increase in food intake both among dieters and the obese.

Certain foods and tastes appear to be better at alleviating stress than others. Under stress, stress eaters eat more low-calorie foods and salty foods, although when not under stress, stress eaters show a preference for high-caloric foods. Stress eaters appear to choose foods containing more water, which gives the food a chewier texture (Willenbring et al., 1986). Anxiety and depression appear to figure into **stress eating** as well, especially binge eating. One study found that bingers experience greater fluctuations of anxiety and depression than nonbingers. Overweight individuals also had greater fluctuations in anxiety, hostility, and depression than normal individuals (Lingsweiler, Crowther, & Stephens, 1987).

It is not clear whether stress-induced eating is ever regular enough or massive enough to produce obesity in its own right, even though the phenomenon has been documented. More-over, it appears to be primarily dieters who show increased emotional reactivity to stressors and eat in response to stress. The perception of stress or the experience of psychological distress may also simply be psychological markers of the physiologically based need to restore weight to its set point level (Herman, 1987).

Treatment of Obesity

More people are treated for obesity in the United States than for all other health habits or conditions combined (Stunkard, 1979). Over 400,000 people attend weight-loss clinics alone. Some people attempt to lose weight because they perceive obesity to be a health risk; most, however, are motivated by the fact that being overweight is considered to be unattractive, and it carries a social stigma (Hayes & Ross, 1987; see Box 5.1). The Duchess of Windsor's classic statement "You can never be too thin or too rich" captures the importance that society generally places on physical appearance and, in particular, on weight control. Therefore, the obese are more likely than the nonobese to have a poor self-image. Unlike other groups of people with handicaps, the obese are often blamed for their problem; they are derogated by others because they are seen as lacking sufficient will power or initiative to lose weight (Brownell, 1982; Millman, 1980; Young & Powell, 1985). As a result, obese people are often distressed about their weight problem and are highly motivated to change it.

Obesity is a very difficult disorder to treat (Brownell, 1982; Hall & Hall, 1982). Even initially successful weight-loss programs show a high rate of relapse. In this section, we review the most common approaches to treatment of obesity and consider the reasons why weight control is so difficult.

Dieting   Treating obesity through dieting has historically been the most common ap

Box 5.1
The Stigma of Obesity: Comments of the Obese

"People are always making loud remarks about me in the street, like, 'Look at that woman. She should be in a circus,' or, 'Look at that fat elephant.' It's amazing how insensitive people can be to fat people. You wouldn't walk up to a cripple in the street and say, 'How did you lose the use of your legs?' So I don't know why people think it's all right to say these things to us."

"One day I was in the supermarket and a 4-year-old kid was marching around and around me in circles, screaming at the top of his lungs, 'You are fat. You are fat. You are fat.'—over and over again. I wanted to choke that kid, or say to his mother, 'You should teach your child some manners.' But it's complicated. Sometimes children are only stating a fact, and by saying they shouldn't say it, it's like agreeing that being fat is bad."

"When I was a teenager my mother told me, 'Look how fat you are. Even your father said he thinks you're getting repulsive.' I screamed back at her, 'He didn't say that!' But I believed

her, and it hurt me so much because I loved my father. After my mother told me that, I avoided my father for years afterwards and didn't talk to him, and I never asked him about it. Now, when I think about it, I'm not sure he ever said such a thing to her; she may have said it to frighten me into dieting. And if I asked her now if it were true, she probably wouldn't remember."

"I don't know when the first awareness hit me that I was chubby and different from other children. When I was 3½ my mother took me somewhere without a bathing suit and she wanted me to swim in my underpants, and even at 3½ I resisted physical exposure. I recall being called, 'Hey, fat,' 'Hey, blimp,' 'Hey, you with the headlight.' I was the only child in nursery school who was not allowed chocolate milk at lunch time. In the first grade we put on a play about an Eskimo who was supposed to get stuck in the door to the igloo, and I was chosen for the part."

(From Millman, 1980, pp. 9–10, 38)

---

proach, and most weight-loss programs still begin with dietary treatment (Brownell, 1982). In this approach, people are trained to restrict their caloric and/or carbohydrate intake through education about the caloric values and dietary characteristics of foods. Generally, weight losses produced through dietary methods are small and rarely long maintained. Therefore, those who treat obesity now feel that dietary intervention is a necessary but insufficient condition for producing lasting weight loss (Straw, 1983).

Fasting   Fasting is usually employed with other techniques as a treatment for obesity (Brownell, 1982). In fasting, the individual severely restricts food intake over a period of a few days, sometimes consuming little besides low-calorie liquids. The protein-sparing modified fast has gained considerable popularity as a first step in a multimodal treatment program (Lindner & Blackburn, 1976; Wadden, Stunkard, & Brownell, 1983). In this supplemented fast, an individual typically consumes between 400 and 800 calories per day of foods consisting primarily of protein and some carbohydrates with carefully balanced vitamins and minerals. Typically, fasting produces dramatic early weight losses. However, people cannot fast indefinitely without damaging their health. Moreover, if normal eating habits are resumed, the weight lost through fasting can be rapidly regained (Wadden et al., 1983). Therefore, fasting is typically supplemented with maintenance strategies designed to help the person keep weight off. It should be noted that the term "fasting" may be somewhat misleading; appropriate use of this technique virtually never involves eliminating food and liquid intake altogether. In addition, this technique should never be attempted without medical supervision.

Surgery   Surgical procedures, especially gastric surgeries, represent a radical way of controlling extreme obesity. In the most common surgical procedure, the stomach is literally stapled up to reduce its capacity to hold food, so that the overweight individual must restrict his or her intake. As with all surgeries, there is some risk, and side effects such as gastric and intestinal distress are common. Consequently, this procedure is usually reserved for people who are at least 100% overweight, who have failed repeatedly to lose weight through other methods, and who have complicating health problems that make weight loss urgent.

Appetite-Suppressing Drugs   Drugs, both prescription and over-the-counter types, are often used to reduce appetite and restrict food consumption. In some weight-loss programs, they may be employed in conjunction with a cognitive-behavioral intervention. Such programs often produce substantial weight loss, but sometimes also show greater recidivism, with participants regaining more weight than in a cognitive-behavioral intervention alone. Rodin and her colleagues (Rodin, Elias, Sil-

berstein, & Wagner, 1988) suggested that the impact of drug treatment on weight loss may depend in part on feelings of self-efficacy. If people attribute their weight loss to the drug rather than to their own efforts, they may be more likely to regain the weight when the drug is terminated. Thus, inclusion of drugs in combination with other interventions must be accomplished in such a way that it does not undermine the feelings of self-efficacy necessary for people to maintain weight loss.

Behavior Modification   The techniques for modifying obesity discussed thus far are all fairly radical or limited in their success. Therefore, behavior-modification techniques have come into increasing use in weight-loss programs. These methods, coupled with initial fasting or dieting, now represent the most common approach to the control of obesity.

The behavioral approach to the control of obesity began with the landmark work of Stuart (1967). Using the principle of stimulus control, Stuart trained his obese clients to alter the stimuli in their environments that elicited and maintained maladaptive eating behavior. Clients were trained to restrict their eating to particular places and times of day and not to eat while they were engaged in other pleasurable activities, such as watching television or reading the newspaper. They were urged to eliminate fattening foods from their diet and to support these changes by stocking up on low-calorie groceries and throwing away all the high-calorie foods in their kitchens. Stuart's program produced substantial weight losses, averaging between 26 and 46 pounds, that were maintained over a 1-year period. Although subsequent efforts have not been equally successful, Stuart's landmark contribution was a pioneering step in behavioral interventions for the obese (Stunkard, 1979).

The Multimodal Approach   Many current interventions with the obese use a multimodal approach to maladaptive eating behavior (McReynolds, Green, & Fisher, 1983; Stunkard, 1979). One such program, developed at the University of Pennsylvania (Penick et al., 1971), begins with an analysis of the behavior to be controlled. Obese clients are trained in self-monitoring and are taught to keep careful records of what they eat, when they eat it, how much they eat, where they eat it, and other dimensions of eating behavior. This kind of record keeping simultaneously defines the behavior and makes clients more aware of their eating patterns. Many patients are surprised to discover what, when, and how much they actually eat.

Behavioral analysis then focuses on influencing the antecedents of the target behavior, namely those stimuli that affect eating behavior. As in Stuart's intervention, clients are trained to modify the stimuli in their environment that have previously elicited and maintained overeating. Such steps include purchasing low-calorie foods such as raw vegetables, making access to them easy, and limiting the high-calorie foods kept in the house. Behavioral control techniques are also used to train patients to change the circumstances of eating. Clients are taught to confine eating to one place at particular times of day. They may also be trained to develop new discriminative stimuli that will be associated with eating. For example, they may be encouraged to use a particular place setting, such as a special place mat or napkin, and to eat only when those stimuli are present (Stunkard, 1979).

The next step in this multimodal behavioral intervention is to train patients to gain control over the eating process itself. For example, clients may be urged to count each mouthful of food, each chew, or each swallow. They may be told to put down eating utensils after every few mouthfuls until the food in their mouths is chewed and swallowed. Longer and longer delays are introduced between mouthfuls so as to encourage slow eating (which tends to reduce intake). Such delays are first introduced at the end of the meal, when the client is already satiated, and progressively moved closer to the beginning of the meal. Finally, clients are urged to enjoy and savor their food and to make a conscious effort to appreciate it while they are eating. The goal is to teach the obese person to eat less and enjoy it more (Stunkard, 1979).

Clients are also trained to gain control over the consequents of the target behavior and are accordingly trained to reward themselves for activities they successfully carry out. For example, record keeping, counting of chews, pausing during the meal, or eating only in a specific place might be reinforced by a tangible positive reinforcement, such as going to a movie or making a long-distance phone call to a friend.

Developing a sense of self-control over eating has also been an important part of behavioral treatments of obesity. As an integrated part of relapse prevention programs, self-control is thought to help people override the impact of urges or temptations. Building on this concept, McReynolds et al. (1983) employed choice management strategies with the obese to modify their eating. Choice management is conceptualized as the ability to make choices before temptations ever become so attractive or compelling as to provide a realistic threat for relapse. Strategies may include changing the environment so that temptations are no longer available, reducing the attractiveness of temptations, increasing the attractiveness of alternatives, or managing stimuli associated with temptations in such a way as to diminish their attractiveness.

Over several years, researchers at the University of Pennsylvania have evaluated the success of their program and attempted to identify which aspects are most successful. These analyses have prompted the development of additional elements in the program (Brownell, 1982; Brownell & Kramer, 1989).

Approximately 400,000 Americans participate in organized weight-reduction programs. Many of these now include exercise.

One important component is exercise. Physical activity predicts successful weight loss and maintenance of weight loss. Consequently, individuals in the program are urged to develop a regular program of physical activity that is interesting and convenient for them. Second, cognitive restructuring has become an increasingly important part of the program. As we noted in the last chapter, poor health habits can often be maintained through dysfunctional monologues (for example, "I'll never lose weight—I've tried before and failed so

many times"). Participants in the Pennsylvania program are urged to identify the maladaptive thoughts they have regarding weight loss and its maintenance and to substitute positive self-instruction. A third factor that consistently predicts successfully maintained weight loss is the presence of social support. Because participants with high degrees of social support are more successful than those with little social support, all participants are now trained in methods in eliciting effective support from their families, friends, and co-workers (Brownell and Kramer, 1989; Brownell & Stunkard, 1981).

As is the case with so many health behaviors, successful weight loss necessitates long-term maintenance, and maintaining weight loss is difficult. It is essential, then, that relapse prevention techniques be incorporated into treatment programs, including better screening of applicants to weight-loss programs, matching of treatments to the eating problems of particular clients, the restructuring of the environment to remove temptation, and the rehearsal of high-risk situations for relapse and the development of coping strategies to deal with them. One program has even provided clients with a small portable microcomputer that assists them in maintaining long-term adherence to therapeutic goals. For example, after a meal, the client types in what was consumed, and the computer displays feedback on the caloric value of the meal, the total caloric intake for the day, the percentage of daily calories eaten, and how many calories remain to be consumed during the rest of the day. If caloric intake is at a low level, the computer will provide a positive message congratulating the client on his or her self-control (Burnett, Taylor, & Agras, 1985).

The description of the University of Pennsylvania's program to modify obesity illustrates the multimodal behavioral interventions that are currently in use. Such skills as self-monitoring, stimulus control, and self-reinforcement not only help people lose weight initially but also instill habits that may help them maintain those weight losses. As we have seen, this emphasis on maintenance is well placed. In addition, this program explicitly acknowledges the role of the total environment for initiating and maintaining weight loss. The attention to exercise and social support as lifestyle rebalancing efforts may be particularly well advised, and researchers are increasingly including these components in their interventions (Brownell & Kramer, 1989).

Worksite Weight-Loss Interventions   Worksite weight-loss programs have recently been initiated in the hope that the social support provided by co-workers will help individuals maintain their weight loss (Brownell, 1986; Brownell & Felix, 1987). Although traditional behavioral therapy interventions at the worksite are not very effective (Brownell, Stunkard, & McKeon, 1985), when these programs are coupled with techniques to instill motivation, like competition between work groups to see which group can lose the most weight, more successful weight loss and maintenance can result (Brownell et al., 1984, 1985). One study by Stunkard, Cohen, and Felix (1989) found that team competitions at work were more effective than either cooperation or individual competition on several grounds: enrolling participants initially, keeping them in the program throughout its duration, and producing weight loss.

Exactly why team competitions are successful is unknown. It may be that team competitions draw effectively on social support, or that the arousal produced by a competitive spirit motivates people to work harder to maintain weight loss. Although the effective ingredient is not yet known (Brownell & Felix, 1987), it is clear that worksite competitions can be valuable efforts for intervening in obesity. Whether weight losses engaged through such team competitions can be maintained over time, however, remains at issue (Brownell & Felix, 1987; Stunkard et al., 1988).

Commercial Weight-Loss Programs   More than 500,000 people each week are exposed to behavioral methods of controlling obesity through commercial clinics such as TOPS (Take Off Pounds Sensibly) and Weight Watchers (Stunkard, 1986). These self-help organizations have rarely been formally evaluated. Yet, because they reach thousands more obese individuals than the behavior-modification programs of research psychologists, formal evaluation of their techniques and success rates is essential.

One study of the TOPS program demonstrated the value of behavioral approaches to weight loss (Levitz & Stunkard, 1974). TOPS is a self-help program for obese people that has been in existence for 35 years. The evaluation study involved 298 female members of sixteen TOPS chapters who were exposed to one of four treatments over a 12-week period: behavior modification by psychiatrists; behavior modification by lay TOPS chapter leaders; nutrition education carried out by TOPS chapter leaders; and a control intervention that involved social pressure to lose weight, regular weighing, goal setting, and discussion of techniques for losing weight. Striking differences in dropout rates and in weight loss were observed among the four conditions. The two behavior-modification programs produced lower dropout rates during treatment; as long as a year later, participants in the behavior-modification programs had lost more weight. Because of studies like this, commercial weight-loss organizations, including TOPS, have increasingly adopted behavioral techniques in the effort to help their members find the most effective weight-loss methods.

Evaluation of Cognitive-Behavioral Weight-Loss Techniques

Early evaluations of the efficacy of cognitive behavioral programs for obesity suggested modest weight losses of perhaps a pound a week for up to 20 weeks, and modest maintenance of weight losses of perhaps a pound a week for up to 20 weeks, and modest maintenance of weight losses for up to a year (Brownell, 1982; Hall & Hall, 1982). More recent cognitive behavioral programs for obesity, however, have produced more substantial weight losses, approximating nearly 2 pounds a week for up to 20 weeks. These weight losses can be maintained for up to 2 years by many participants when self-monitoring and other relapse prevention strategies are used (Brownell, 1982; Brownell & Kramer, 1989). These improved effects have been attributed to the fact that the newer programs are both longer and better, and include relapse prevention techniques specifically designed to deal with long-term maintenance (Brownell & Jeffrey, 1987; Brownell and Kramer, 1989).

Responses to behavioral programs, however, are quite variable. One individual may lose a great deal of weight and keep it off successfully, whereas another may revert to his or her original weight almost immediately. Those whose obesity has been associated with binge eating may be particularly vulnerable to drop-out from behavioral programs and to weight regain following their termination (Marcus, Wing, & Hopkins, 1988). Cognitive-behavioral weight-loss programs also appear to be more useful for mildly than severely obese individuals (Foreyt, 1987).

Concerns have recently been expressed as to whether cognitive-behavioral programs alone are sufficient to help the severely obese. Brownell and Jeffrey (1987), for example, suggested that scientists have not been aggressive enough in what they consider to be sufficient weight loss. Obese patients are sometimes enrolled in programs that produce a weight loss of perhaps 10 to 12 pounds over a 12-week period; then they are trained in complex maintenance strategies for maintaining this weight loss. In the context of the overall obesity, how-

ever, the 12 pounds may be a trivial change. Brownell and Jeffrey, therefore, recommended that interventions with the obese set higher goals and be more aggressive. Thus, for those who need to lose substantial amounts of weight, a cognitive-behavioral program can be a necessary but not a sufficient method for so doing. A method that produces more dramatic weight losses, like the modified fast, can be coupled with a behavioral modification program to increase the chances of sustained loss (Foreyt, 1987). Table 5.2 describes some of the promising leads that current research suggests for enhancing long-term weight loss in cognitive-behavioral programs.

An additional remaining question concerns whether cognitive-behavioral programs are superior to other methods. Hall and Hall (1982), for example, concluded that weight losses in live-in clinics are considerable, but in the outpatient clinics more commonly used to treat obesity, weight losses are modest and similar to those found in other types of programs. Such results suggest that behavioral interventions are not necessarily superior to other interventions. However, they may still have a number of attributes that give them intrinsic advantages over other approaches. Cognitive-behavioral interventions show lower drop-out rates than other programs partly because such techniques as contingency contracting elicit financial commitments from participants (Brownell, 1982; Stunkard, 1979). Compared to programs such as surgery or drugs, behavioral programs produce fewer negative side effects. Moreover, they appear to have beneficial effects on psychological functioning, such as improved mood (Brownell, 1982). As such, cognitive-behavioral interventions are at present one of the best technologies available for dealing with obesity.

Before leaving this topic, one curious aspect of obesity should be pointed out. Like people with other addictive disorders, such as alcoholism and smoking, some once-obese people are able to cure themselves. Schachter (1982)

TABLE 5.2 *TECHNIQUES IN A COMPREHENSIVE PROGRAM FOR WEIGHT CONTROL*

Lifestyle techniques	Exercise techniques	Attitude techniques	Relationship techniques	Nutrition techniques
1. Keep an eating diary.	32. Keep an exercise diary.	46. Weigh advantages and disadvantages of dieting.	65. Identify and select partner.	75. Eat less than 1,200 calories per day.
2. Maximize awareness of eating.	33. Understand benefits of exercise.	47. Realize complex causes of obesity.	66. Tell your partner how to help.	76. Be aware of calorie values of foods.
3. Examine patterns in your eating.	34. Increase walking.	48. Distinguish hunger from cravings.	67. Make specific and positive requests of partner.	77. Know the four food groups.
4. Prevent automatic eating.	35. Maximize pleasure of walking.	49. Confront or ignore cravings.	68. Reward your partner.	78. Eat a balanced diet.
5. Identify triggers for eating.	36. Increase life-style activity.	50. Set realistic goals.	69. Do shopping with your partner.	79. Get adequate protein in diet.
6. Weigh yourself regularly.	37. Use stairs whenever possible.	51. Use the shaping concept for habit change.	70. Have partner do shopping for you.	80. Get adequate carbohydrate in diet.
7. Keep a weight graph.	38. Know the calorie values of exercise.	52. Counter food and weight fantasies.	71. Have partner and family read this manual.	81. Increase complex carbohydrates.
8. Examine what occurs before, during, and after eating.	39. Use the pulse test for fitness feedback.	53. Ban perfectionist attitudes.	72. Exercise with partner.	82. Limit fat to 30% of total calories.
9. Alter the antecedents to eating.	40. Choose and use a programmed activity.	54. Beware of attitude traps.	73. Refuse pressures to eat.	83. Make low calorie foods appetizing.
10. Do nothing else while eating.	41. Always warm up and cool down.	55. Stop dichotomous thinking.	74. Use pleasurable partner activities.	84. Consume adequate vitamins.
11. Follow an eating schedule.	42. Experiment with jogging.	56. Counter impossible dream thinking.		85. Take no more than recommended doses of vitamins.
12. Eat in one place.	43. Experiment with cycling.	57. Focus on behavior rather than weight.		86. Increase fiber in diet.
13. Do not clean your plate.	44. Experiment with aerobics.	58. Banish imperatives from vocabulary.		
14. Put your fork down between bites.	45. Remember that any exercise helps.	59. Be aware of high-risk situations.		
15. Pause during the meal.		60. Distinguish lapse and relapse.		
16. Shop on a full stomach.		61. Outlast urges to eat.		
17. Shop from a list.		62. Cope positively with slips and lapses.		
18. Buy foods that require preparation.		63. Take steps to gain control during lapses.		
19. Keep problem foods out of sight.		64. Be a forest ranger for urges and lapses.		
20. Keep healthy foods visible.				
21. Remove serving dishes from the table.				
22. Leave the table after eating.				
23. Serve and eat one portion at a time.				
24. When hungry, wait 5 minutes before eating.				
25. Avoid being a food dispenser.				
26. Use alternatives to eating.				
27. Use techniques for eating away from home.				
28. Prepare in advance for special events.				
29. Plan in advance for high-risk situations.				
30. Identify your behavior chains.				
31. Interrupt your behavior chains.				

(*Source: Brownell, 1990*)

originally suggested this idea and showed, in a study of community residents, that the majority of once-obese individuals were no longer overweight. In a study of obese diabetic patients, Orme and Binik (1987) found that approximately one-third of obese diabetic outpatients had "cured" themselves. As yet, the numbers of self-cures and the factors that lead people to cure their own obesity are unknown. Perhaps as we learn more about self-cure, the treatment of obesity can profit from this knowledge.

Prevention and Weight Control

Clearly, weight-loss programs do not constitute a sufficient attack on obesity. We must also consider prevention. In particular, we must intervene with families that are at risk for producing obese children (Brownell, Kelman, & Stunkard, 1983). If these parents can be trained early to adopt meal-planning and eating habits that they can pass on to their children, the incidence of obesity may ultimately decline (Kirscht et al., 1978).

Weight-gain prevention programs for normal-weight adults have also been undertaken in the hopes that skills can be instilled before weight gain becomes a problem (e.g., Forster, Jeffrey, Schmid, & Kramer, 1988). In one study, normal-weight participants received newsletters relating to weight management, and educational course about weight management, and financial incentives for not gaining weight. Compared to the control group, participants actually lost an average of 1.8 pounds. Programs for weight-gain prevention appear to be feasible, of interest to adults, and potentially more effective than weight-loss treatment programs by preventing weight gain before it ever becomes a problem.

Obesity: An Evaluation

Obesity, then, is a highly complex issue. It is affected by such factors as genetic predisposi-

tion, childhood eating habits, and the resulting size and number of fat cells. It may be complicated by emotional factors such as anxiety or depression and the relationship of emotions to eating. Neurophysiological factors (such as the possibility of hypothalamic damage) and individual differences (such as attitudes toward weight or weight loss) influence weight and the ability to lose weight. And the environment within which weight loss is attempted may contain numerous cues that promote or discourage proper eating behavior. All these factors must be recognized if any headway is to be made against this health issue.

Although research over the last two decades has focused heavily on the health risks of obesity and on strategies to help people reduce their weight, increasingly cautions regarding the cultural values of thinness and dieting have figured into these efforts. The thin physique that is currently valued in American society, especially for women, may actually have health risks. In a report derived from the Framingham study of cardiovascular risk, there was a higher mortality rate found among the thinnest people than among the fattest, although both groups had higher mortality rates than persons of average weight. Moderately overweight people, however, died at about the same rate as normal or moderately underweight people (Sorlie, Gordon, & Kannel, 1980). However, more recent research on women (Manson et al., 1990) suggests that even mildly overweight women experience increased risk for heart disease and heart attack compared to women who are underweight. Obese women who smoke are five times as likely to suffer from heart disease as obese women who do not smoke. The research evidence identifying the risks of obesity for general mortality, coronary heart disease, hypertension, and serum cholesterol is not altogether consistent then (see Polivy & Herman, 1985a, for a review).

Moreover, the risks of dieting are becoming

increasingly evident. Diet pills and other medications often have serious side effects. Fad diets may deprive people of badly needed nutrients. Modified fasting can seriously disrupt metabolism, and yo-yo dieting may actually contribute to long-term obesity by making it increasingly difficult to lose weight with each successive weight-loss attempt.

Dieting has also been reliably related to bouts of overeating and excessive caloric intake, which are themselves risk factors for cardiovascular disease, hypertension, elevated triglyceride levels, and diabetes (see Polivy & Herman, 1985a, for a review). As the cultural value on thinness has taken firm hold, increasing levels of anorexia and bulimia have been observed. Moreover, the judgmental normative climate that surrounds weight can contribute to the psychological stress experienced by the obese. Thus, dieting and overeating may be severe dangers to health, in some cases more so than simply being overweight (see Polivy & Herman, 1985b).

Eating Disorders

Recent years have seen a dramatic increase in the incidence of eating disorders in the adolescent female population of Western countries. Chief among these are anorexia nervosa and bulimia.

Anorexia   **Anorexia nervosa** is a condition amounting to self-starvation, in which an individual diets and exercises to the point that body weight is grossly below optimum level, threatening health and even mortality. Nearly all sufferers are adolescent females from the upper social classes. Several factors have been identified in the development of the illness. Physiological explanations have been spurred by estimates that amenorrhea (cessation of menstruation, a common symptom of anorexia) often precedes weight loss (Fries, 1977; Morimoto et al., 1988). There also appears to be an association between anorexia

and Turner's syndrome (a disorder among females who lack a second X chromosome). Hypothalamic abnormalities may also be involved. However, the direction of causality in these relationships is not entirely clear.

Other researchers have stressed personality characteristics and family interaction patterns as causal in the development of anorexia. Personality factors may include a feeling of personal inefficacy, a need for approval, conscientiousness, perfectionism, and the perception of pressure to succeed. Body image distortions are also common among anorectic females, although it is not clear whether this is a consequence or a cause of the disorder. Frequently, these individuals see themselves as still overweight when they have long since dropped below their ideal weight. Family characteristics, such as parental psychopathology or alcoholism or an extremely close or interdependent family with poor skills for communicating emotion or dealing with conflict, have also been suggested as pivotal in the development of anorexia (Garfinkel & Garner, 1983; Rakoff, 1983).

Increasingly, research is focusing on the conditions that may trigger anorexia in those at risk. Weiner (1977) suggested that the disease may be initiated by a failure to adapt to environmental demands involving a threat to loss of control and a feeling of reduced self-worth. Anorexia may occur when issues of personal identity and autonomy become paramount at puberty, and the fear of separation or unwillingness to assert oneself may produce the self-destructive response of anorexia rather than direct confrontation of these conflicts.

Initially, the chief target of therapy is to bring the patient's weight back up to a safe level, a goal that must often be undertaken in a residential treatment setting such as a hospital. To achieve weight gain, most therapies use behavioral approaches such as operant conditioning. Usually, operant conditioning provides positive reinforcements such as so-

---

Box 5.2
You Can *Be Too Thin*

In the last decade, preoccupation with weight control among adolescents has reached epidemic proportions. In one study conducted in a high school (Rosen & Gross, 1987), 63% of the girls and 16% of the boys reported being on weight-reducing regimens. Virtually all of these students were already of normal weight. Much of this behavior can be attributed to the shift in societal preference toward a thin physique. This ideal may be difficult for normal women to obtain except by dieting, and, consequently, dieting has now become a "normal" eating pattern for North American women (Polivy & Herman, 1987).

Athletes often engage in dietary and weight control efforts. For example, high school wrestlers may feel the need to "cut weight" for matches. Recent research, however, suggests that these weight-gain and -loss cycles may have adverse health consequences. One result is a lowered metabolic rate, which can lead to a general propensity for weight gain. There may also be changes in fat distribution and risk factors for cardiovascular disease. For example, weight loss is associated with decreased blood pressure and gains with increased blood pressure, and successive gains appear also to produce successive gains in blood pressure.

Consequently, these weight loss–regain bouts may have an adverse long-term effect on blood pressure. Among female athletes who maintain a low body weight overall (such as gymnasts and figure skaters), the low percentage of fat distribution may lead to amenorrhea (cessation of menstrual periods) and problems in the ability to reproduce (Brownell, Steen, & Wilmore, 1987; Steen, Oppliger, & Brownell, 1988).

The cultural emphasis on thinness is a norm not only for women, but among homosexual men. One study compared homosexual and heterosexual men's perceptions of their appearance. Homosexual men were more dissatisfied with their bodies and considered appearance more central to their self-image. Their exercise regimen was motivated more by a desire to become more attractive than by a desire to be healthy. Moreover, the homosexual men who wanted to be thinner showed more attitudes and behaviors associated with disordered eating. These findings suggest that a male subculture that emphasizes appearance so heavily may heighten vulnerability of its members to body dissatisfaction and disordered eating, just as is true for women in the culture (Silberstein, Striegel-Moore, & Rodin, 1987)

---

cial visits in return for eating or weight gain. However, behavioral treatments in a hospital setting alone may fail to generalize to the home setting (Garfinkel & Garner, 1982), because of family and environmental factors that may induce or maintain the behavior. Thus, once weight has been restored to a safe level, additional therapies are used. Because of the important role that family dynamics appear to play in the onset of anorexia, family therapy

may be initiated to help families learn more positive methods of communicating emotion and conflict (Minuchen, Rosman, & Baker, 1978). Psychotherapy to improve self-esteem and to communicate skills for adjusting to stress and social pressure may also be incorporated into treatments (Hall & Crisp, 1983). Although some have criticized behavioral treatments on the grounds that the technique is somewhat coercive, taking control away from a patient who is already feeling a lack of control (Bruch, 1973), the outlook for anorectic patients receiving therapy appears generally to be good, with one behavioral therapy intervention reporting success rates of 86% (Minuchen et al., 1978).

Bulimia   **Bulimia** is an eating syndrome characterized by alternating cycles of binge eating and purging through such techniques as vomiting, laxative abuse, extreme dieting or fasting, and drug or alcohol abuse (Hamilton, Gelwick, & Meade, 1984). Binging appears to be caused at least in part by dieting. Dieting breaks down customary associations between physiological cues of hunger and eating, replacing them with a cognitively based regulatory system. Eating in response to cognitive cues is easily disrupted, as by stressful events or other distracting stimuli, and consequently leaves the dieter vulnerable to binging (Polivy & Herman, 1985a). The binge eating phase usually occurs when the individual is alone; it is experienced as aversive; and it is associated with feeling out of control. About half the individuals diagnosed with anorexia are also bulimic, although up to 10% of the normal population may also experience bulimia, especially girls with a history of being overweight. Thus, whereas anorectics typically lose at least 20% of their body weight, bulimics are often of normal weight or overweight. In fact, bulimia is significantly more prevalent the more obese a person is (Telch, Agras, & Rossiter, 1988) and is more common among women whose fat is distributed in their hips and buttocks than in their abdomens (Radke-Sharpe, Whitney-Saltiel, & Rodin, 1990), perhaps because excess weight in these areas more obviously violates the cultural norm of thinness. As with anorexia, bulimia is most common among girls between the ages of 12 and 20.

A number of different explanations have been offered for the disorder. Cultural explanations for the frequency of eating disorders center around the value placed on being thin and the difficulty many women have in achieving that value (see, for example, Orbach, 1978). The binge phase has been variously interpreted as an expression of rage against the value of thinness (Orbach, 1978) or as an extreme reaction to trauma, loneliness, or anger. The purge phase may follow in an effort to regain control. Families that place a high value on thinness and appearance are more likely to produce bulimic daughters (Boskind-White & White, 1983). There may also be familial clusterings of eating disorders, suggesting a possible genetic basis (see Rodin et al., in press, for a review). Bulimics may be also less likely than normal eaters to use food as a form of self-nurturance and thus may need to be trained in other ways of making themselves feel good (Lehman & Rodin, 1989).

Bulimics may differ from normal eaters in other ways. They are more likely to be depressed, to suffer from low self-esteem, and to exhibit impulsive and emotionally overreactive behavior than those not prone to bulimia (Hamilton et al., 1984). Stress, especially interpersonal stress, may be implicated in the onset of binge-purge cycles by reducing the salience of cues that would normally restrain eating (Cattanach & Rodin, 1988). In a study of disordered eating among college freshmen, Striegel-Moore, Silberstein, Frensch, and Rodin (1989) found that worsening of disordered eating was associated with upset feelings about one's weight, feeling that one was unattractive, experiencing a lot of stress, and feeling generally ineffective. Overall, disordered eating symptoms grew worse over the course of the school year.

Physiological accounts of the disorder include hormonal dysfunction, a hypothalamic dysfunction, food allergies, a disorder of the endogenous opioid system (Mitchell, Laine, Morley, & Levine, 1986), a neurological disorder, or a combination of these. There may also be subtypes of bulimia that fall into different categories (Rau & Green, 1984). The set point theory of weight control provides an explanation for the binging phenomenon as well. When people drop below their natural body weight, they react as if they may starve: Metabolism slows, and they begin to respond to external food cues instead of actual hunger. Food can become a constant thought. Restrained eating, then, can set the stage for a binge. Thus, a history of being overweight and thereby being prone to a higher weight set point may be a better predictor of bulimia than a particular psychological or emotional makeup (Polivy, Herman, & Olmstead, 1984).

A number of different therapies have been developed to treat bulimia. The particular combination of therapeutic techniques employed depends on the individual case. Cognitive-behavioral techniques have been used successfully in an attempt to alter the reinforcement contingencies associated with eating (e.g., Agras, Schneider, Arnow, Raeburn, & Telch, 1989). Typically, treatment begins by instructing the patient to keep a diary of eating habits, including time, place, type of food consumed, and emotions experienced. Simple self-monitoring can produce decreases in binge/purge behavior (Orleans & Barnett, 1984; Wilson, 1984), a point observed in other poor health habits as well. Most therapies combine monitoring with other behavioral treatments in an individualized effort to bring eating under control (Agras et al., 1989; Kirkley, Agras, & Weiss, 1985). Increased perceptions of self-efficacy with respect to eating facilitate the success of cognitive-behavioral interventions (Schneider, O'Leary, & Agras, 1987).

When bulimia is viewed as an addictive disorder, techniques such as Marlatt's and Gordon's (1980) relapse prevention model are often used. For example, the patient may be trained to identify situations that may trigger binge eating and develop coping skills to avoid it. She may also be taught relaxation and stress management skills (Goldfried & Davison, 1976; Suinn, 1977). When the disorder is viewed as a compulsive disorder, outright pre-

vention of the bulimic behavior may be required. The patient may be removed from situations in which binging or purging is possible or may be trained to lengthen the time before a binging or purging response is made. In addition, some kind of therapeutic intervention, whether individually or in a support group, is often included to help alleviate the emotional and self-esteem problems that may have precipitated the disorder (Orleans & Barnett, 1984). Antidepressant treatments have also been used to improve mood and have shown at least some success (Rossiter, Agras, & Losch, 1988). Directive intervention regarding eating behavior can also help bulimics make progress. Specifically, increasing the regularity of meals, eating a greater variety of foods, delaying the impulse to purge as long as possible, and eating favorite foods in new settings not previously associated with binges, can all help women break down patterns that help maintain bulimia and can also help instill better eating habits (Kirkley, Schneider, & Bachman, 1989).

DIET

Weight control is not the only eating-related problem that is tied to increased mortality and rates of chronic disease. Diet itself has also been a focus of concern. As we saw in Chapter 2, salt has been linked to hypertension and to cardiovascular disease, and high levels of fats and dietary cholesterol have been tied to atherosclerosis and, ultimately, to coronary heart disease (CHD). A poor diet, with its resulting high levels of LDLs (low-density lipoproteins), may also be aggravated by co-occurrence with other risk factors. There is some evidence for stress-induced lipid reactivity, such that the cholesterol response to physical and psychological stressors is greater than in the absence of stress (Dimsdale & Herd, 1982). There is increasing recognition that diet can play a role in the development of cancer.

Certain modifications in diet reduce the risk for atherosclerosis. For example, studies have found that reducing cholesterol through dietary interventions or a combination of drug intervention and a low-cholesterol, low-fat diet diminishes the incidence of CHD morbidity and mortality (Caggiula et al., 1981; Hjerman, Velve Byre, Holme, & Leren, 1981; Kornitzer et al., 1983; Kushi et al., 1985; Lewis et al., 1981; Lipid Research Clinics Program, 1984; Mann & Marr, 1981; May, Eberlein, Furberg, Passamani, & Demets, 1982; Multiple Risk Factor Intervention Trial Research Group, 1982; Oliver, 1981; Puska et al., 1979; Salonen, Heinonen, Kottke, & Puska, 1981; World Health Organization European Collective Group, 1982). Even when studies have been unable to assess the long-term impact on CHD morbidity and mortality, they provide convincing evidence that adherence to dietary restrictions can lower blood cholesterol level (see Carmody, Matarazzo, & Istvan, 1987, for a review).

However, it is often very difficult to induce people to modify their diet even when they are participating in a medical study, when they are at high risk for CHD, or when they are under the instruction of a physician (Hjerman et al., 1981; Rose, Tunstall-Pedoe, & Heller, 1983). Indeed, the desire to improve appearance is at least as often a motivating factor as health is to get people to consume a diet low in cholesterol, fats, calories, and additives and high in fiber, fruits, and vegetables (Hayes & Ross, 1987).

Prescribed dietary change is usually a lifetime recommendation, and although people may comply at first, over time their adherence may fall off. The fact that adherence to dietary recommendations can be monitored only indirectly both by patients themselves and by medical authorities, as through biomedical markers, may contribute to lapses or relapses in diet (Carmody et al., 1987). Some dietary recommendations are restrictive, monotonous,

expensive, hard to find and prepare, and otherwise a turn off for those expected to consume them. Drastic changes in shopping, meal planning, cooking methods, and eating habits may be required. Attitudes are also a barrier to positive dietary habits. A low sense of self-efficacy (that is, believing that one will be unable to change one's diet), a preference for meat, a low level of health consciousness, a low interest in exploring new foods, and low awareness of the link between eating habits and illness are all associated with poor dietary habits (Hollis, Carmody, Connor, Fey, & Matarazzo, 1986).

Controversies over dietary recommendations themselves may also undermine adherence. Current media debates over the strength of the relationship of blood level cholesterol to cardiovascular disease, over whether cholesterol can be successfully reduced through diet, and over whether or not asymptomatic individuals should make major changes in their diet may attenuate adherence to dietary recommendations (Becker, 1987). While there may be merit in some of these challenges, health experts still urge a reduction in cholesterol level for those with a total count over 200. Yet to the extent that debate undermines adherence, consequent reductions in risk status and potential declines in morbidity and mortality due to CHD are obviously attenuated. Therefore, psychologists have become involved in the design of interventions to help individuals modify their diet.

As we noted in the previous chapter, the most successful interventions are those that modify behavior for the largest number of individuals at once. Following this criterion, the effort to modify diet has frequently been implemented on a large-scale basis (e.g., Foreyt et al., 1979; Meyer, Nash et al., 1980). One study (Foreyt, Scott, Mitchell, & Gotto, 1979) exposed a target population in the Houston, Texas area to one of four interventions: a diet booklet explaining how individuals can alter their salt and cholesterol intake; formal education in nutrition; a behavioral intervention involving a group discussion; or a combination of all three. The results indicated that each approach significantly reduced cholesterol levels in the target population immediately after the intervention, but none maintained behavior change. After initial drops in cholesterol levels, a substantial number of participants reverted to their former behavior (see also Reeves et al., 1983). Similarly, a nutrition education campaign mounted in a number of supermarkets revealed no increase in diet knowledge and no changes in product sales, compared to control supermarkets (Jeffery, Pirie, Rosenthal, Gerber, & Murray, 1982). Box 5.3 describes a program designed to control hyperlipidemia by modifying diet.

The Three-Community Study developed by Meyer and his associates (Meyer, Nash et al., 1980) used a mass media approach to multiple risk factors for cardiovascular disease, including changing diet to reduce cholesterol. The target community received a mass media campaign involving television, radio, newspaper, billboards, bus cards, and direct-mail leaflets, as well as face-to-face interventions. The combination of media and personal instruction appears to have been successful in producing dietary change and lowering cholesterol levels (Farquhar et al., 1977; Maccoby, Farquhar, Wood, & Alexander, 1977), although some critics have questioned whether the magnitude of these changes had any real effect on risk (Kasl, 1980; Leventhal, Safer et al., 1980).

Although mass media campaigns have promise because they can easily reach large numbers of people, cognitive-behavioral interventions may be more successful in actually bringing about behavior change. When evaluated against media campaigns alone (Meyer, Nash et al., 1980) or against more traditional

---

Box 5.3
Dietary Intervention to Control Hyperlipidemia

Hyperlipidemia is an abnormally high plasma cholesterol level and/or triglyceride level (Carmody et al., 1982). People who are at risk for cardiovascular disease or those who have already been diagnosed as having CHD are often urged to initiate changes in their diets to avoid or to reduce hyperlipidemia. A representative diet developed by Connor and Connor (1977) targets the reduction of dietary cholesterol from an average of 500 to 700 mg for the typical American to only 100 mg per day. In addition, dietary fat intake is severely restricted.

In the first phase of the dietary plan, foods high in cholesterol and saturated fats, such as egg yolks, butterfat, lard, and most meats, are eliminated from the diet. In the second phase, the amount of meat the patient may eat is reduced from between 12 and 16 oz per day to between 6 and 8 oz per day; the patient is also urged to restrict the intake of high-fat cheeses. Meatless meals are gradually introduced. In the third phase of the diet, meat consumption is reduced still further (to 3 or 4 oz a day), and low-cholesterol cheeses are substituted. At this point, an individual's diet consists primarily of cereals, vegetables, fruits, legumes, and low-fat dairy products. Dietary plans like these have been successful in reducing hyperlipidemia.

nutrition training (Foreyt et al., 1979; Meyer & Henderson, 1974), cognitive-behavioral methods such as self-monitoring, stimulus control, and contingency contracting have shown better results (for a review, see Carmody, Fey, Pierce, Connor, & Matarazzo, 1982). Increasingly, cognitive-behavioral interventions to help people modify their diets have included relapse prevention components. As in other such programs, participants are urged to identify high-risk-for-relapse situations, such as holidays, banquets, or weddings, and to develop specific coping techniques to keep them from eating the wrong foods.

Recently, efforts to intervene in the dietary habits of high-risk individuals have focused on the family group (Carmody, Istvan, Matarazzo, Connor, & Connor, 1986). There are several good reasons for focusing intervention on the family. When all family members are committed to and participate in dietary change, it is easier for the target family member to do so as well. Moreover, different aspects of diet are influenced by different family members. Whereas wives still usually do the shopping and food preparation, husbands' food preferences are often a more powerful determinant of what the family eats (Weidner, Archer, Healy, & Matarazzo, 1985).

One program, called the Family Heart Study, intervenes with family members through group discussion and decision making to help them achieve family-based dietary change (Carmody et al., 1986). The first part of this intervention involves an educational effort to explain the need to reduce cholesterol and to provide specific information about how to do it. After the educational intervention, the family meets as a group to discuss specific ways in which they might change and to bring up any potential barriers to change, such as not liking particular foods. A dietary counselor then meets with the family, offering advice and suggestions as to how to overcome these barriers, and often family members themselves come up with alternatives to meet these problems. In addition to individual family counseling, target families are brought together with other families who are also attempting to make dietary changes. In these monthly meetings, participants share suggestions and problems that have developed in their attempts to modify their diet. The program also includes social activities in which people share recipes and bring food to potlucks that enable them to pool their knowledge. Finally, each family receives printed media, including a monthly newsletter, handouts containing recipes, consumer shopping guides to finding healthier foods, and new meal-planning ideas that can help the family maintain their dietary changes at home. Such family interventions appear to have considerable promise in modifying diet.

To summarize, then, cholesterol levels can be reduced by dietary interventions, which, in turn, can reduce mortality and morbidity associated with CHD. However, the modification of diet is not an easy matter. Media campaigns alone are typically unsuccessful; even in intensive studies with individualized instruction, compliance with dietary recommendations may fade over time. Consequently, this problem lends itself to cognitive-behavioral therapy, particularly at the family level. As the role of diet in the development of many chronic diseases is more clearly established, we will no doubt see increasing attention being paid to the question of how best to make diet healthier.

SUMMARY

1. Health-enhancing behaviors are those practiced by asymptomatic individuals to improve or enhance their current or future health and functioning. Chief among health-enhancing behaviors are exercise, accident prevention measures, breast and testicular self-examination, weight control, and a healthy diet.

2. Aerobic exercise is known to reduce risk for heart attack and improve other aspects of bodily functioning. Exercise also appears to improve mood and self-esteem and to reduce stress.

3. Few people are able to adhere regularly to the standard exercise prescription of aerobic exercise just short of maximal intensity for 15 minutes three times a week. People are more likely to exercise when the form of exercise is convenient and they like it. If their attitudes favor exercise and they come from families where exercise is practiced, they are also more likely to practice.

4. Cognitive-behavioral interventions including relapse prevention components have been at least somewhat successful in helping people adhere to regular exercise programs.

5. Accidents are a major cause of preventable death, especially among children. Among these, motorcycle and automobile accidents account for the most deaths.

6. Recent years have seen increases in the use of accident-prevention measures, especially car safety restraint devices for children. These changes have been credited to mass media intervention, the increasing availability of restraint devices, and the link between obstetrical and newborn care and promotion of safety restraint devices for children.

7. One out of every eleven American women will contract breast cancer. Yet breast self-examination is rarely practiced, because women have difficulty detecting change, are uncertain if they are doing it correctly, and fear what may happen if a lump is detected.

8. The personal practice of BSE improves confidence, and practice on a model improves the ability to detect lumps. Statistics promoting the value of early detection may reduce fear. Regular practice can also be enhanced by monthly prompts or more-than-monthly practice of BSE.

9. Testicular self-examination is important for men between the ages of 15 and 35, for whom testicular cancer is a leading cause of death.

10. Obesity is a health risk that has been linked to cardiovascular disease, kidney disease, and diabetes.

11. Factors associated with obesity include genetic predisposition, early diet, family history of obesity, low SES, little exercise, and cultural values. Ironically, dieting may contribute to the propensity for obesity by enhancing the efficiency of food use and lowering metabolic rate. Weight may also be regulated by an ideal set point and by prior caloric consumption. Individual differences such as externality do not seem to explain obesity very well. However, some individuals do eat in response to stress, and stress eating may exacerbate existing weight problems.

12. Obesity has been treated through diets, fasting, drugs, surgical procedures, and, more recently, cognitive-behavioral approaches. Most current interventions use a multimodal approach to maladaptive

eating behavior that includes monitoring eating behavior, modifying environmental stimuli that control eating, gaining control over the eating process, and reinforcing new eating habits. Relapse prevention skills training helps in long-term maintenance.

13. Weight-loss programs have been initiated with some success in the worksite using work group competition and in commercial weight-loss programs that employ cognitive-behavioral weight-loss techniques. Such programs can produce weight losses of nearly 2 pounds a week for up to 20 weeks, maintained over a 2-year period.

14. Increasingly, interventions are focusing on weight-gain prevention with children in obese families and with high-risk adults. At the same time, however, research and clinical practice are increasingly recognizing the problems that ap-

pear to result from an overemphasis on the thin physique, including yo-yo dieting, anorexia nervosa, and bulimia.

15. Dietary interventions involving reductions in cholesterol, fats, calories, and additives and increases in fiber, fruits, and vegetables are widely recommended. Yet adherence to such diets over time is low for many reasons: Recommended diets are often boring, relation of dietary change to improvement in health is uncertain, attitudes may not favor dietary change, and despite recommendations for lifetime change, behavior often falls off over time due to sheer inertia.

16. Dietary interventions through the mass media and existing community resources have promise as intervention techniques. Intervening with the family unit also appears to be useful for promoting and maintaining dietary change.

KEY TERMS

aerobic exercise
anorexia nervosa
breast self-examination (BSE)
bulimia
obesity

"set point" theory of weight
stress eating
testicular self-examination (TSE)
yo-yo dieting

6

HEALTH-COMPROMISING BEHAVIORS

In the previous chapter, we considered the practice of health-enhancing behaviors and their determinants. In this chapter, we turn our attention to health-compromising behaviors, behaviors practiced by people that undermine or harm their current or future health. In this context, we consider two of the most important health-compromising behaviors, alcohol abuse and smoking.

ALCOHOLISM AND PROBLEM DRINKING

Alcohol abuse accounts for thousands of deaths each year and billions of dollars in economic loss and treatment costs. Originally characterized as a social ill, alcoholism was officially recognized as a disease by the American Medical Association in 1957 (Jellinek, 1960). As a health issue, alcohol consumption has been linked to a number of disorders, including cirrhosis of the liver, some forms of cancer, and fetal alcohol syndrome, a condition of retardation and physiologic abnormalities that arises in the offspring of heavy-drinking mothers (Streisguth, Landesman-Dwyer, Martin, & Smith, 1980). Excessive drinking also accounts for substantial cognitive impairments, many of them irreversible (Goldman, 1983; McGuire, 1982). Drunk driving represents a particularly serious health problem. Approximately 50% of the 50,000 annual highway fatalities are attributed to drinking and driving (McGuire, 1982). It is estimated that one in every two Americans will be in an alcohol-related accident during his or her lifetime, and each of us has a one in nine chance of being involved in a serious alcohol-related accident. Economically, it is estimated that chronic alcoholism costs the economy as much as $42 billion a year in poor job performance and absenteeism. An estimated 15% of the national health bill goes to the treatment of alcoholism (Holden, 1987). Whether normal consumption of beverage alcohol is a health risk remains to be seen, although for some groups, even small amounts of alcohol may pose a health risk, as is the case for the offspring of pregnant women.

Defining the scope of the alcohol abuse problem has proven to be difficult. It is estimated that one out of every ten adult Americans is an alcoholic or problem drinker, which places the overall figure at approximately 10 million individuals (U.S. Department of Health and Human Services, 1981). The difficulty in defining the scope of the problem stems from at least two factors.

First, many problem drinkers keep their problem hidden, at least for a time. Individuals who have no employment outside the home, such as homemakers, may be able to drink without noticeable disruption of their daily activities. Other problem drinkers confine their drinking to particular times, so that it does not attract much attention. These individuals do not show up in the ranks of those seeking formal treatment, at least for a while.

Second, **problem drinking** and **alcoholism** encompass a variety of specific behavior patterns (Jellinek, 1960; Wanburg & Horn, 1983). The term "alcoholic" is usually reserved for someone who is physically addicted to alcohol. Alcoholics show withdrawal symptoms when they attempt to become abstinent, they have a high tolerance for alcohol, and they have little ability to control their drinking. Problem drinkers may not evidence these symptoms, but they may have substantial social, psychological, and biomedical problems resulting from alcohol.

Problem drinking and alcoholism have been defined by a variety of specific behaviors that range from the milder ones associated with problem drinking to the severe ones associated with alcoholism. These patterns include the need for daily use of alcohol, the inability to cut down on drinking, repeated efforts to control drinking through temporary abstinence or restriction of alcohol to certain times of the day, binge drinking, occasional con-

sumptions of large quantities of alcohol, loss of memory while intoxicated, continued drinking despite known health problems, and drinking of nonbeverage alcohol. Symptoms of alcohol abuse also include difficulty in performing one's job due to alcohol consumption, the inability to function well socially without alcohol, and legal difficulties encountered while drinking, such as drunk driving convictions (American Psychiatric Association, 1980).

From the above description, one can see that alcoholism and problem drinking have been defined largely in terms of behavior. There is increasing pressure, however, to characterize the alcohol-dependent syndrome in terms of the physiological and psychological needs experienced with respect to alcohol. These include increasingly stereotyped drinking, drinking that maintains blood alcohol at a particular level, the ability to function at a level that would incapacitate less tolerant drinkers, experiencing increased frequency and severity of withdrawal, drinking earlier in the day and in the middle of the night, a sense of loss of control over drinking, and a subjective craving for alcohol (Straus, 1988). These characteristics may lead to a revision of the American Psychiatric Association's guidelines concerning alcohol-related problems (Institute of Medicine, 1987). Yet, as Jellinek (1960) pointed out, much alcohol abuse can occur without any physical or psychological dependency. For example, if an individual is enmeshed in a social environment that promotes heavy drinking, that individual would not necessarily be identified as a problem drinker by physiological and psychological criteria. This debate underscores the difficulty of defining and identifying alcoholism and problem drinking.

Origins of Alcoholism and Problem Drinking

What leads to alcoholism and problem drinking? Several theories have been offered.

One approach maintains that biological and genetic factors, such as a predisposition to addiction, account for alcoholism. In support of this position, studies of families reveal high rates of alcoholism among relatives of alcoholics. Twin studies show higher rates of alcoholism and alcohol-related problems in identical twins than in fraternal twins. Sons of alcoholic fathers appear to be especially at risk (Cloninger, 1987), data which support the likelihood of a genetic factor in alcohol abuse (Institute of Medicine, 1987). Alcoholism has also been attributed to sociodemographic factors such as low income. Overall, however, factors such as demographic variables and genetic predisposition appear to explain relatively little—only about 20%—of the variance in alcoholic behavior (Moos, Cronkite, & Finney, 1982). Rather, the development of alcoholism might better be thought of as a longitudinal process that acknowledges the interdependent roles of physiological, behavioral, and sociocultural variables (Zucker & Gomberg, 1986).

Drinking, including problem drinking, clearly occurs in part as an effort to buffer the impact of stress (Baer, Garmezy, McLaughlin, Pokorny, & Wernick, 1987; Neff & Husaini, 1985; Seeman, Seeman, & Budros, 1988). For example, men who show the Type A behavior syndrome involving impatience, a chronic sense of time urgency, competitiveness, aggressive drive, and hostility drink more frequently (though not more alcohol per occasion) than Type B individuals, who do not show these same behavioral propensities. Alcohol may enable the Type A man to relax, since it is known that Type As have greater difficulty relaxing than Type Bs (Folsom et al., 1985). A general sense of powerlessness in one's life has also been related to alcohol use and abuse (Seeman et al., 1988; see also Seeman & Anderson, 1983).

There appears to be a window of vulnerability for alcohol use and abuse. Chemical dependence generally starts between the ages of 12 and 21 and peaks in the 18 to 25 age group (Dupont, 1988). One consequence of this fact has been the development of interventions in junior high and high school to keep children from starting chemical dependence problems, such as alcohol and drug use, and efforts to combat the problem directly among college students, among whom alcohol-related fatalities are the major cause of death.

For years, alcohol abuse was regarded as an intractable problem that was resistant to intervention. However, decades of research and treatment programs reveal that alcohol abuse can be modified. Some alcoholics are able to alternate long periods of moderate or abstinent drinking with heavy drinking. Between 10 and 20% of all alcoholics stop drinking on their own, and as many as 32% are able to stop with minimal help (Moos & Finney, 1983). A number of alcoholics "mature out" of alcoholism, cutting down or eliminating their alcohol intake in the later years of their lives (Stall & Biernacki, 1986). Research evidence from a variety of programs designed to help alcoholics, including behavior-modification programs, residential treatment programs, and self-help groups such as Alcoholics Anonymous, all show success in reducing alcoholism. Unhappily, despite some successes, alcohol abuse is also highly resistant to intervention. Many programs have high dropout rates, and long-term evaluations of program success demonstrate that as many as 60% of the individuals treated returned to alcohol abuse (Moos & Finney, 1983).

Treatment of Alcohol Abuse

Treatment approaches to problem drinking and alcoholism try to deal with the full complexity of alcohol abuse. In particular, alcohol abuse is now known to depend on the social and cultural environment of the drinker as well as on biological and genetic factors (Wanburg & Horn, 1983). Drinking occurs in particular environments, and those environments can elicit and maintain drinking behav-

Adolescence and young adulthood represent a window of vulnerability to problem drinking and alcoholism. Successful intervention with this age group may reduce the scope of the alcoholism problem.

ior. For example, associating with heavy-drinking friends or relatives, getting used to drinking at particular times of the day to reduce tension, and having a social life centered on drinking (such as going to bars), all create cues for drinking that can maintain the behavior independent of the underlying addiction. Perhaps the strongest evidence for this point is the differential recovery rate for alcoholics of high socioeconomic status (SES) and high social stability (that is, with a regular job and an intact family and circle of friends) versus those of low SES and lower social stability. Alcoholics of high SES and high social stability show a recovery rate between 33 and 68%, whereas alcoholics of low SES and low social stability have success rates of typically 18% or less (U.S. Department of Health and Human Services, 1981; Moos & Finney, 1983). Even the most intensive treatment program will be unsuccessful if the alcoholic returns to an en-

vironment with little social support, no employment, and no consideration of how he or she is to make ends meet (U.S. Department of Health and Human Services, 1981).

In view of these facts, current treatment programs for alcoholism and problem drinking typically use multimodal and broad-spectrum cognitive-behavioral therapy to treat biological and environmental factors simultaneously (Wanburg & Horn, 1983). The goals of this approach are to decrease the reinforcing properties of alcohol, to teach people new behaviors that are incompatible with alcohol abuse, and to modify the environment to include positive reinforcements for activities that do not involve alcohol (Miller & Eiser, 1976). Multimodal approaches combine various methods of cognitive-behavioral change to modify drinking behavior and the environments in which it occurs. Broad-spectrum approaches attempt to identify life problems that may be related to alcohol abuse and to deal with them by instilling a broad range of coping skills. Relapse prevention techniques are customarily built into these programs to enhance long-term maintenance.

Treatment Programs Specifically, what are treatment programs for alcohol abuse like? For hard-core alcoholics, the first phase of treatment may be **detoxification.** Since this can produce severe symptoms and health problems, it is typically conducted in a carefully supervised and medically monitored setting. Once the alcoholic has at least partly dried out, therapy begins. The typical program begins with a short-term, intensive, inpatient treatment followed by a period of continuing treatment on an outpatient basis (U.S. Department of Health and Human Services, 1981). Typically, inpatient programs last between 10 and 60 days, with an average of approximately 3 weeks (U.S. Department of Health and Human Services, 1981). After discharge, some patients attend follow-up sessions, whereas others are discharged to supervised living arrangements.

A variety of behavior-modification techniques have been incorporated into alcohol treatment programs. One approach is the classical conditioning technique of aversion therapy. In this technique, the drinking of alcohol is paired with an aversive agent, most commonly a chemical called Emetine. The ingestion of Emetine and alcohol produces nausea and vomiting. Some programs pair alcohol consumption with electric shock or other chemical agents such as Antabuse (U.S. Department of Health and Human Services, 1981).

How successful is aversion therapy? In clinical practice, aversion therapy is typically combined with other techniques; therefore its unique contribution to overall success is difficult to estimate (U.S. Department of Health and Human Services, 1981). However, experimental studies that disentangle the effects of aversion therapy suggest mixed effects. Electric shock has generally not been successful in reducing alcohol abuse (U.S. Department of Health and Human Services, 1981). However, experiments using aversion conditioning with Emetine or Antabuse have demonstrated some success (U.S. Department of Health and Human Services, 1981), and evaluations of programs employing these therapies suggest rates as high as 60% abstinence over a 1-year period (Wiens & Menustik, 1983). Unfortunately, there is a major difficulty with these aversion therapy procedures. Successful maintenance and behavior change often require patients to continue the conditioning procedure on their own outside of therapy. If patients choose not to take the chemical agent, they may, over time, reduce the effectiveness of the classical conditioning that was initially produced in the treatment program (see Mahoney, 1974a).

Other approaches are also used in these multimodal or broad-spectrum approaches to alcohol abuse. Many programs include a self-monitoring phase in which the alcoholic or problem drinker begins to understand the situations that give rise to and maintain drinking. Contingency contracting is frequently employed, in which the individual agrees to a psychologically or financially costly outcome in the event of failure. Many successful treatment programs have also attempted to provide alcoholics with responses that they can substitute for drinking. As noted earlier, alcohol is sometimes used as a method of coping with stress. For example, the occurrence of a major stressful event within the first 90 days after treatment is one of the best predictors of relapse among apparently recovered alcoholics (Marlatt & Gordon, 1980). Moreover, negative life events are reported to be more prevalent among relapsed than recovered alcoholics (Moos, Mehren, & Moos, 1978). All this information suggests that successful alcohol abuse programs should include skills training in stress management.

Consequently, various forms of relaxation training have been employed to teach alcoholics and problem drinkers methods of coping with stress that do not involve drinking. Assertiveness training and training in social skills help the alcoholic or problem drinker deal with problem situations without resorting to alcohol. In some cases, family therapy and group counseling are offered as well. The particular advantage of family counseling is to ease the alcoholic's or problem drinker's transition back into his or her family (Marlatt, 1982; U.S. Department of Health and Human Services, 1981).

Relapse Prevention   Relapse is a major difficulty in treatment for alcohol abuse. It is estimated that only 26% of alcoholics remain improved 1 year after treatment (Baker, Cooney, & Pomerleau, 1987). A substantial contributor to the relapse problem is the craving for alcohol that many alcoholics experience, expressed as nervousness, restlessness, fatigue, and depression. **Craving** appears to involve an interrelated set of psychological, physiological, behavioral, and biochemical responses. Alcoholics show conditioned responses to cues associated with alcohol, including higher skin conductance and greater salivation in the presence of alcohol (Kaplan et al., 1985; Pomerleau, Fertig, Baker, & Cooney, 1983). These cues are also associated with a self-reported increased desire to drink.

Extinction training is one helpful training in reducing these cravings. For example, the craving response may diminish over time if an alcoholic beverage is presented, but does not produce anticipated pharmacologic effects (Baker et al., 1987). This may happen either because the alcoholic beverage is not consumed or because a sham beverage is substituted which contains no alcohol. Aversive conditioning has also been employed, in which craving is paired with an aversive experience such as electric shocks or Antabuse. Finally, training in relapse prevention skills, in-

cluding the identification of situations likely to evoke craving and ways to deal with it other than drinking have been undertaken. Social-skills training, involving the refusal of a drink, and the substitution of nonalcoholic drinks, for example, and avoiding or leaving situations that evoke the experience of craving, have been employed to reduce this problem. Interventions for heavy-drinking college students using these kinds of approaches are described in Box 6.1.

Evaluation of Alcohol Treatment Programs
A review of alcohol abuse treatment programs suggested that several factors are consistently associated with favorable treatment outcomes (Costello, 1975a, 1975b): an active orientation that takes account of all the factors in the environment that might control drinking, a moderate length of participation (about 6 to 8 weeks), use of aversion therapy, outpatient aftercare, and active involvement of relatives and employers in the treatment process (see also Kite & Kogutek, 1979; Kogutek & Kite, 1978; Patton, 1979). When all these features were combined into an intensive inpatient alcoholism program, the program produced a 40% treatment success rate, which is comparable to some of the best outcomes found in other studies (Costello, Baillargeon, Biever, & Bennett, 1980; U.S. Department of Health and Human Services, 1981).

With the growing costs of health care generally and of residential treatment programs more specifically, treatment programs for alcoholism have come under close scrutiny to determine if they are cost-effective. A chief feature that has attracted critical attention is the lengthy inpatient stay that is a feature of most inpatient programs (Holden, 1987). In an assessment of alcohol treatment programs, Miller & Hester (1986) found that there was no particular advantage for residential over nonresidential settings, for longer or for shorter inpatient programs, or for more intensive or less intensive interventions. Only the severely deteriorated or less socially stable alcoholics

Box 6.1
The Drinking College Student

Between 70 and 96% of U.S. college students drink alcohol, and as many as 15 to 25% of them are heavy drinkers (Kivilan, Coppel, Fromme, Williams, & Marlatt, 1989). If anything, these statistics are increasing, as college women begin to drink as heavily as college men. Many colleges have tried to deal with the heavy drinking problem by providing educational materials about the harmful effects of alcohol (Kivilan et al., 1989). However, the information conflicts markedly with the personal experiences of many college students who find drinking in a party situation to be satisfying, even exhilarating behavior. Moreover, most college students do not see drinking as a problem (Baer, Kivilan, Fromme, & Marlatt, in press), but rather regard it as a natural outgrowth of their social environment. Consequently, motivating students even to attend alcohol abuse programs, much less to follow their recommendations, is difficult.

Therefore, some of the more successful efforts to modify college students' drinking have encouraged students to gain self-control over drinking, rather than explicitly trying to get them to reduce or eliminate alcohol altogether. A program developed by Lang and Marlatt (1982; Baer et al., in press; Marlatt & Gordon, 1985) incorporates techniques derived from attitude-change research and from cognitive-behavioral therapy in a total program to help college students gain such control. The program includes information about the risks of alcohol consumption, the acquisition of skills to moderate alcohol consumption, the use of drinking limits, relaxation training and lifestyle rebalancing, nutritional information, aerobic exercise, relapse prevention skills designed to help people cope with high-risk situations, assertiveness training, and drink refusal training.

Such programs typically begin by getting students to monitor their drinking and to under-stand what blood alcohol levels mean and what their effects are. Often, merely monitoring drink-ing and recording the circumstances in which it occurs actually leads to a reduction in drinking (Alden, 1988, cited in Baer et al., in press).

The consumption of alcohol among students is heavily under the control of peer influence and the need to relax in social situations (Collins & Marlatt, 1981; Murphy, Pagano, & Marlatt, 1986). Thus, many intervention programs include a social skills training component or stress management component designed to get students to find alternative ways to relax and have fun in social situations. Since alcohol use is also related to negative emotional states such as anxiety or depression (Marlatt, 1987), training in alternative ways to relax can sometimes improve mood overall.

To gain personal control over drinking, students are first taught to identify the circumstances in which they are most likely to drink and especially to drink to excess. Then students are taught specific coping skills so that they can moderate their alcohol consumption. For example, one technique for controlling alcohol consumption in high-risk situations such as a party is **placebo drinking.** This involves either the consumption of nonalcoholic beverages while others are drinking, or the alternation of an alcoholic with a nonalcoholic beverage to reduce the total volume of alcohol consumed.

Students are also encouraged to engage in **lifestyle rebalancing** (Marlatt & George, 1988). This involves developing a healthier diet, engaging in aerobic exercise, and making other positive health changes, such as stopping smoking. As the student comes to think of himself or herself as health-oriented, excessive alcohol consumption becomes incompatible with other aspects of the new lifestyle.

Evaluations of 8-week training programs with college students involving these components have shown a fair degree of success. Students reported significant reductions in their drinking, compared to a group that received only educational materials about the dire effects of excessive drinking. Moreover, these gains persisted over a year-long follow-up period.

(Baer et al., in press)

showed any particular benefit from intensive inpatient treatments (Miller & Hester, 1986). Similarly, lengthy inpatient programs do not appear to succeed any more often than brief hospitalization, partial hospitalization, or outpatient programs (Holden, 1987). Findings like these have put increased pressure on alcohol treatment centers to develop lower-cost outpatient programs that are still effective.

Overall, some have concluded that the best predictors of success involve the characteristics of the patients themselves. Alcoholics who have little abuse of other drugs, whose primary diagnosis is depression, who have a job, stable relationships, no history of previous treatment failures, and no indication of other psychopathology seem to have a very high success regardless of the specific details of the treatment program (Holden, 1987).

To summarize, then, an effective approach to alcohol abuse appears to be one in which biological and environmental factors are acknowledged and treated simultaneously. Combining aversion therapy with a supportive restructuring of the patient's environment as well as long-term monitoring and relapse prevention skills appears to be the most successful approach. When multimodal and or broad-spectrum approaches like these are evaluated against minimal interventions with alcoholics and problem drinkers, they demonstrate considerable success (U.S. Department of Health and Human Services, 1981).

Overall, statistics suggest that approximately 85% of all alcoholics and problem drinkers do not receive any formal treatment. Approximately 671,000 of the remaining 15% participate in Alcoholics Anonymous (Box 6.2). However, at least 8 million American alcoholics and problem drinkers are not receiving any formal services (U.S. Department of Health and Human Services, 1981). Moreover, dropout rates in alcoholism programs are estimated to be over 50% (Holden, 1987). Thus, despite treatment advances, alcohol abuse remains a substantial, largely untreated problem.

Can Recovered Alcoholics Ever Drink Again?

A controversial issue in the treatment of alcohol abuse is whether alcoholics and problem drinkers can learn to drink in moderation (Lang & Marlatt, 1982). For decades, research and self-help treatment programs for alcoholism have argued that the alcoholic is an alcoholic for life and must abstain from all drinking. The concept that a recovered alcoholic might be able to drink in moderation also flies in the face of Alcoholics Anonymous, one of the oldest and most active alcoholism treatment programs.

Research suggests that this belief is still largely true. Despite media-popularized programs that purportedly enable recovered alcoholics to drink in moderation (Sobell & Sobell, 1973), there is no convincing evidence that such programs have any long-term success (Armor, Polich, & Stambul, 1976; Vogler, Common, & Weissbach, 1975).

One study supporting this point (Foy, Nunn, & Rychtarik, 1984) enlisted chronic alcoholics in a multimodal behavioral treatment program. All participants received education about the effects of alcohol, group therapy, individual therapy, self-management skills, job-seeking and interpersonal skills training, drink-refusal skills training, and relaxation training. In addition, some participants were assigned to learn **controlled drinking skills;** they received 15 hours of training in which they learned to discriminate their blood alcohol level to control the extent of their drinking. They also received training in responsible drinking skills and social drinking practice sessions. Follow-up of these patients at 6 months indicated that the subjects in the controlled drinking group were significantly less successful in controlling their drinking. They had fewer abstinent days and more abuse-drinking days (e.g., drinking to excess, binge drinking) than subjects who were abstinent. Long-term follow-up of these study participants, however, suggested no long-term negative impact

Box 6.2
A Profile of Alcoholics Anonymous

No one knows exactly when Alcoholics Anonymous (A.A.) began, but it is believed that the organization was formed around 1935 in Akron, Ohio. The first meetings were attended by a few acquaintances who discovered that they could remain sober by attending services of a local religious group and sharing with other alcoholics their problems and efforts to remain sober. By 1936, weekly A.A. meetings were taking place around the country.

Who participates in A.A.? Currently, its membership is estimated to be well over 5 million individuals worldwide. The sole requirement for participation in A.A. is a desire to stop drinking. Originally the organization attracted hardened drinkers who turned to it as a last resort; more recently, however, it has attracted many people who are experiencing drinking problems but whose lives are otherwise intact. Members come from all walks of life, including all socioeconomic levels, races, cultures, sexual preferences, and ages.

The philosophy of Alcoholics Anonymous is a commitment to the concept of self-help. Members believe that the person who is best able to reach an alcoholic is a recovered alcoholic. In addition, members are encouraged to immerse themselves in the culture of A.A.— to attend "90 meetings in 90 days." At these meetings, A.A. members speak about the drinking experiences that prompted them to seek out A.A. and what sobriety has meant to them. Time is set aside for prospective members to talk informally with longtime members, so that they may learn and imitate the coping techniques recovered alcoholics have used. Some meetings include only regular A.A. members and cover issues of problem drinking.

A.A. has a firm policy regarding alcohol consumption. It maintains that alcoholism is a disease that can be managed but never cured. Recovery means that an individual must acknowledge that he or she has a disease, that it is incurable, and that alcohol can play no part in future life. Recovery depends completely upon staying sober.

Is Alcoholics Anonymous successful in getting people to stop drinking? A.A.'s dropout rate is unknown, and success over the long term has not been carefully chronicled. Moreover, because the organization keeps no membership lists (it is anonymous), it is difficult to evaluate its success. However, A.A. itself maintains that two out of three individuals who wish to stop drinking have been able to do so through its program, and one authorized study reported a 75% success rate for the New York A.A. chapter.

Researchers attempting to understand the effectiveness of A.A. programs have pointed to several important elements. A.A. is like a conversion experience in which an individual adopts a totally new way of life; such experiences can be powerful in bringing about behavior change. Also, a member who shares his or her experiences comes, through the sharing process, to develop a commitment to other members. The process of giving up alcohol contributes to a sense of emotional maturity and responsibility, forcing the alcoholic to accept responsibility for his or her life. A.A. may also provide a sense of meaning and purpose in the individual's life—most chapters have a strong spiritual or religious bent and urge members to commit themselves to a power greater than themselves. The group can also provide affection and satisfying personal relationships and thus help people overcome the isolation that many alcoholics experience. Too, the members provide social reinforcement for each other's abstinence.

A.A. is significant as an organization for several reasons. First, it was one of the earliest self-help programs for individuals suffering from a health problem; therefore, it has provided a model for self-help organizations whose members have other addictive problems, such as Overeaters Anonymous and Gamblers Anonymous, among many others. Second, in having successfully treated alcoholics for decades, A.A. demonstrated that the problem of alcoholism was not as intractable as had been widely assumed.

(Based on Robinson, 1979.)

of the controlled drinking training. Maintenance of stable remission was equally problematic for those in the controlled drinking skills program as in the comparison subjects trained to be totally abstinent (Rychtarik, Foy, Scott, Lokey, & Prue, 1987).

It does appear that a narrow group of problem drinkers may be able to drink in moderation. In particular, those who are young and employed, who have not been drinking long, and who live in supportive environments may be able to engage in moderate drinking (Miller, 1980; Oxford, Oppenheimer, & Edwards, 1976). Drinking in moderation has some particular advantages for the problem drinker (Pomerleau, Pertschuk, Adkins, & Brady, 1978). First, moderate drinking represents a more realistic social behavior for the environments that a recovered problem drinker may encounter. Second, traditional therapeutic programs that emphasize total abstinence often have high dropout rates. Programs for problem drinkers that emphasize moderation may be better able to hold onto these participants.

One example of a successful approach to controlled drinking was developed by Miller, Taylor, and West (1980). Their program, called Behavioral Self-Control Training (BSCT), focused directly on drinking behavior. It included setting specific goals for the amount of alcohol consumption, self-monitoring alcohol consumption, training in controlling the rate of alcohol ingestion, self-reinforcement for controlled drinking, functional analysis of drinking behavior, and instructions in alternatives to alcohol abuse. In one study (Miller et al., 1980), BSCT was evaluated against bibliotherapy, in which participants read self-help materials in an effort to control their drinking; the BSCT intervention plus 12 sessions of relaxation, communication, and assertiveness training; and BSCT plus 12 weekly sessions of individually tailored broad-spectrum approaches to problem drinking. Bibliotherapy participants showed more drinking problems than participants in the other three conditions;

the other three groups were equivalent in success.

The success of BSCT is significant for two reasons. First, it demonstrates that programs of controlled drinking can be successful with at least some problem drinkers. Second, it suggests that these programs need not be as complex, intensive, and expensive as the typical multimodal, or broad-spectrum, approach to alcohol abuse. The more focused treatment produced equivalent success rates to the multimodal approach and did so in a shorter period of time with less expense. Ultimately, then, these focused approaches to problem drinking may be as successful or nearly as successful as the more involved multimodal and broad-spectrum approaches (Miller et al., 1980).

Drinking and Driving

A final alcohol-related problem we will consider concerns vehicular fatalities that result from drunken driving. When drunken drivers are arrested and brought to court, they are typically referred out to drinking programs not unlike those we have just discussed. How successful are these referral programs? A review (McGuire, 1982) examining these programs suggested that light drinkers did well in most of them. Unfortunately, heavy drinkers typically did very poorly. As yet, it seems there is no good rehabilitation program for the heavy-drinking driver. Yet this aspect of alcohol consumption is probably the one that most mobilizes the general public against alcohol abuse. In the last few years, programs such as MADD (Mothers Against Drunk Driving) and SADD (Siblings Against Drunk Driving) were founded and staffed by the parents, brothers, and sisters of children and adults killed by drunk drivers. Increasingly, the political impact of these and related groups is being felt, as they pressure state and local governments for tougher alcohol control measures and stiffer penalties for convicted drunk drivers.

SMOKING

Smoking has been called the single greatest cause of preventable death (U.S. Department of Health, Education, and Welfare, 1979). In the United States, it accounts for approximately 125,000 deaths from cancer annually—about 30% of all cancer deaths (American Cancer Society, 1989)—and another 170,000 deaths from cardiovascular disease (*Oncology Times*, 1984). In addition to the obvious risks of heart disease and lung cancer, smoking increases the risk of chronic bronchitis, emphysema, peptic ulcers, respiratory disorders, damage and injuries due to fires and accidents, lower birth weight in offspring, and retarded fetal development (Centers for Disease Control, 1989). Cigarette smokers also appear to be less health-conscious more generally and are more likely to engage in other unhealthy behaviors than nonsmokers, including alcohol and coffee consumption (Carmody, Brischetto, Matarazzo, O'Donnell, & Connor, 1985; Castro, Newcomb, McCreary, & Baezconde-Garbanati, 1989; Istvan & Matarazzo, 1984). An additional concern is that smoking appears to serve as an entry-level drug for subsequent substance use and abuse. Trying cigarettes makes one significantly more likely to use other drugs in the future (Fleming, Leventhal, Glynn, & Ershler, 1989; see also Hanson, Henggeler, & Burghen, 1987).

The dangers of smoking are not confined to the smoker. Studies of second-hand smoke encountered by those in regular close contact with smokers demonstrate that spouses, family members of smokers, and co-workers are at risk for a variety of health disorders (Marshall, 1986). More recently, research has accumulated to suggest that family cigarette smoking may actually lower test performance among adolescents (e.g., Bauman, Koch, & Fisher, 1989). The likely mechanism whereby this occurs is that carboxyhemoglobin is increased by exposure to tobacco smoke, reducing the oxygen capacity of the blood and increasing car-

The risks of smoking are not confined to the smoker. Co-workers, spouses, and other family members of smokers are at continued risk for many smoking-related disorders.

bon monoxide levels, which adversely influence mental performance (Bauman, Koch, & Fisher, 1989).

Synergistic Effects of Smoking

Evidence is beginning to suggest that smoking may enhance the impact of other risk factors in compromising health (Dembroski & MacDougall, 1986; Pomerleau & Pomerleau, 1988). That is, smoking may have synergistic effects on other risk factors. For example, Perkins (1985) found that smoking and serum cholesterol interact to produce higher rates of morbidity and mortality than would be expected from simply adding together the risk of smoking and high cholesterol. Since nicotine stimulates the release of free fatty acids, it may increase the synthesis of triglycerides, which, in turn, decreases high-density lipoprotein (HDL) production (the so-called "good" cholesterol). Carbon monoxide from cigarettes also inhibits low-density lipoproteins (LDL), possibly by altering HDL levels. The blood of smokers also coagulates more easily than that of nonsmokers (Pomerleau & Pomerleau, 1989a). These points imply that efforts to reduce smoking and modify diet should be focused especially on the more than 25 million young and middle-aged Americans who both smoke and have elevated serum cholesterol.

Stress and smoking can also interact to produce a cardiac crisis in people already compromised by adverse changes in the heart tissue. Dembroski and his colleagues (Dembroski, MacDougall, Cardozo, & Krug-Fite, 1985) found that men who smoked a cigarette and then engaged in a mildly stressful event had increases in heart rate and blood pressure that were about equal to the sum of the effects produced by either smoking or stress alone (see also MacDougall, Musante, Castillo, & Acevedo, 1988; Perkins, Epstein, Jennings, & Stiller, 1986; Pomerleau & Pomerleau, 1988). However, in women, the combination of stress and cigarette smoking produced blood pressure and heart rate responses that were larger than the effects of smoking and stress added together (Dembroski, Macdougall, Cardozo et. al., 1985; but see MacDougall et al., 1988). Nicotine produces a variety of stimulating effects on the cardiovascular system. Although these changes may be tolerated in people who do not have cardiovascular damage, they may provoke a cardiac crisis in those who do. Sudden death in smokers, for example, may result from deficient blood flow due to constricted or obstructed blood vessels (ischemia) combined with arrhythmias in the heart's action produced by increased circulating catecholamines (Benowitz, 1988). Nicotine can also induce spasms in the coronary arteries (vasospasm) of people with atherosclerotic disease (see Pomerleau & Pomerleau, 1989b, for a review).

Possibly, smoking and other risk factors for CHD are related to each other. One study (MacDougall, Musante, Howard, Hanes, & Dembroski, 1986) found large stable individual differences in cardiovascular reactivity to both stress and smoking that were modestly correlated with each other. These results suggest the possibility that one or more common variables may explain blood pressure reactivity to both stress and cigarette smoking. Manuck & Krantz (1986) suggested that physiological hyperresponsivity to behavioral stimuli may contribute to the etiology of CHD. Responsivity to stressful events may, in turn, increase the propensity to smoke. Whether clinically significant and sustained irregularities in cardiovascular function and lipid activity occur as a result of stress and smoking, and whether or not such reactions may be exaggerated in at-risk individuals, remains to be seen. However, the evidence to date is consistent with such hypotheses.

Another set of potential synergistic factors concerns the relation of Type A behavior and smoking. We cover Type A behavior more fully in Chapter 14. To describe it briefly, Type A behavior refers to a personal style of coping with stress that is a risk factor for cardiovascular disease. It is characterized by easily-aroused hostility, a sense of time urgency, and competitive achievement striving. Type B individuals are less driven individuals who do not show these behavior patterns. Although Type A and Type B smokers do not appear to differ in the number of puffs taken or puff volume, Type A smokers' inhalation duration is longer than Type Bs'. As a result, their alveolar carbon monoxide level is higher. Thus, this difference in consummatory behavior of Type As may help explain the relation between Type A behavior and coronary heart disease for smokers. Type A smokers may actually be at greater risk for cancer and lung disease than Type B smokers by virtue of their smoking patterns (Lombardo & Carreno, 1987). Interestingly, in one study, in which smokers either smoked or did not smoke before being measured on Type A behaviors, those who smoked showed significantly higher levels of behaviors traditionally associated with Type A behavior, such as speaking loudly and in an explosive and rapid fashion, than did sham smokers (those who smoked nicotine-free cigarettes) or people who did not smoke. These results imply the possibility that in chronic smokers, Type A behavior is exacerbated (Dembroski & MacDougall, 1986).

Finally, weight and smoking may also interact to increase mortality. Specifically, Sidney, Friedman, and Siegalaub (1987) found that thin cigarette smokers were at increased risk of mortality compared with average-weight smokers. Thinness was not associated with increased mortality in those who had never smoked or among ex-smokers. The reasons for this relationship are at present unclear.

Whether smoking is simply another factor that contributes additively to the risk for cardiovascular disease or whether it operates synergistically with other factors enhancing risk over what would be expected from either risk factor alone remains unclear. Evidence suggests both types of effects at present. What remains evident is that smoking is a substantial risk factor, which may, in turn, increase the risks associated with other risk factors (e.g., Dembroski & MacDougall, 1986).

Can these problems be reversed? A number of interventions have now demonstrated that when middle-aged men are induced to quit smoking, their risk for CHD is substantially lowered (e.g., Hjermann et al., 1981; Kornitzer et al., 1983; Puska et al., 1979; Rose et al., 1983; Salonen, Puska, & Mustaniemi, 1979; World Health Organization European Collective Group, 1982). In addition, the risk of lung cancer is also reduced by stopping smoking. Despite these statistics, 55 million Americans continue to smoke (American Cancer Society, 1989).

A Brief History of the Smoking Problem

For years, smoking was considered to be a sophisticated and manly habit. Characterizations of eighteenth- and nineteenth-century gentry, for example, often depicted men retiring to the drawing room after dinner for cigars and brandy. Cigarette advertisements of the early

twentieth century built on this image and, by 1955, 53% of the adult male population in the United States was smoking. Women did not begin to smoke in large numbers until the 1940s. However, once smoking became an acceptable habit for women, advertisers began to bill cigarette smoking as a symbol of feminine sophistication as well (Blitzer, Rimm, & Geifer, 1977).

In 1964, the first Surgeon General's report on smoking came out (U.S. Department of Health, Education, and Welfare and U.S. Public Health Service, 1964), accompanied by an extensive publicity campaign to highlight the dangers of smoking. Although male smoking subsequently declined (to 39% by 1975), women's smoking actually increased during the same period, from 25% in 1955 to 29% by 1979. More frightening still, the percentage of teenage female smokers increased to 20.5% as of 1986, a figure that exceeds 16.0% for teenage boys (Cancer Information Service of California, 1989). Despite dawning awareness of the threat of smoking, then, smoking continued to be a formidable problem.

Moreover, counterarguments to the smoking threat, many fueled by the tobacco industry, were plentiful. Rumors persisted that the data linking smoking to cancer were based on studies of rats who smoked excessively in laboratories, and people familiar with the smoking data pointed out that the correlations between smoking and lung cancer were small and statistically significant only for males. Moreover, since lung cancer is a disease of older people, many smokers perceived the immediate threat to their health to be small. Newspapers and magazine articles heralded the likely appearance of a tarfree cigarette or a cigarette containing a noncarcinogen such as lettuce. On this basis, many smokers felt that by the time smoking became a health risk for them, there would be a tobacco alternative. Other smokers switched from heavy tar and nicotine cigarettes to less strong brands in the belief that they were taking a step toward

Smoking has been represented by the tobacco industry as a glamorous habit, and one task of interventions has been to change attitudes about smoking.

good health. Subsequent research has suggested that this effort was misguided. To make up for reduced nicotine, people often smoke more and harder, taking in as much or more tar and carbon monoxide as before (Benowitz, Hall, Herning, Jacob, & Mines, 1983).

Viable alternatives to tobacco never developed, and the statistics tying smoking to lung cancer and heart disease became more clear and evident for women as well as men. In fact, lung cancer is now projected to replace breast cancer as the major cause of cancer deaths among American women over the next decade (American Cancer Society, 1989). The magnitude of the smoking hazard has taken increasingly ominous shape with each decade that vast numbers of Americans continue to smoke. Table 6.1 presents current figures on the incidence of smoking.

TABLE 6.1   SMOKING PREVALENCE BY AGE AND SEX

	PERCENTAGE OF POPULATION	
AGE	MALES	FEMALES
20–24	31.3%	31.9
25–34	39.2	32.6
35–44	38.6	31.7
45–64	35.7	31.4
65+	19.8	13.5

(Source: Centers for Disease Control, 1989)

WHY DO PEOPLE SMOKE?

Smoking runs in families, and some twin and adoption studies suggest that there may be some genetic influences on smoking (see Epstein, Grunberg, Lichtenstein, & Evans, 1989, for a review; but see Swan, Carmelli, & Rosenman, 1988). It is possible that genetically based differences in reaction to nicotine moderate smoking. Some people are exposed to nicotine but do not become dependent. Some people are stimulated by nicotine, whereas others are calmed or even depressed by it (Pomerleau & Pomerleau, 1984). Some people smoke substantially but do not succumb to disease. There are also wide differences in the ability to stop smoking and not relapse, which may have a genetic component. Genetic factors may influence smoking via innate differences in personality or via innate sensitivity to the reinforcing, punishing, or dependence-producing properties of nicotine or tobacco.

Smoking begins early. The Centers for Disease Control (1989) indicate that more than 15% of the adolescent population between the ages of 12 and 18 already smoke cigarettes regularly and consider themselves to be smokers; if anything, these statistics probably underestimate the adolescent smoking rate (Mittelmark, Murray, Luepker, & Pechacek, 1982). However, smoking does not start all at once. There is a period of initial experimentation during which an individual tries out cigarettes, experiences peer pressure to smoke, and develops attitudes about what a smoker is like (Leventhal & Cleary, 1980; Pechacek et al., 1984). An understanding of this process may help solve the problem of adolescent smoking.

Factors Associated with Smoking in Adolescents

Considerable research effort has gone into identifying the factors associated with early smoking. Adolescents are more likely to start smoking if their parents smoke, if they have a favorable image of the smoker, if they are lower class, and if they feel social pressure to smoke (e.g., Biglan, McConnell, Severson, Bavry, & Ary, 1984; Leventhal & Cleary, 1980). Low self-esteem, dependency, and powerlessness all increase the tendency to imitate others' behavior (Bandura, 1977); consistent with these findings, low-achieving students, female students, and students with an external locus of control (Clark, MacPherson, & Holmes, 1982) are more likely to smoke than are male students with high self-esteem and an internal locus of control. Thus, some individual difference factors contribute to becoming a smoker.

Smoking, especially beginning smoking in young smokers, appears to be part of a syndrome of problem behavior generally, in that problem drinking, illicit drug use, delinquent-type behavior, and precocious sexual activity seem to comprise a single behavioral syndrome in adolescents (Donovan & Jessor, 1985). This factor may be more important in predisposing children to begin smoking in environments in which smoking has not yet taken hold, whereas other factors such as exposure to smoking peers may be more important for older smokers and for those for whom an environment conducive to smoking exists (Jessor & Jessor, 1977, 1984). Smoking also appears to be associated with enhanced testosterone functioning (Bauman, Koch, Bryan, Haley, Downtown, & Orlandi, 1989). Although the full implications have yet to be understood, the potential moderating role of testosterone production in initiating or maintaining adolescent cigarette smoking merits consideration.

Of the environmental factors associated with early smoking, two of the most significant are the image of the smoker and peer pressure. Early on, a substantial proportion of preadolescents develop the image of the smoker as a rebellious, tough, mature, iconoclastic individual. Smoking comes to be regarded as a habit that conveys this image. Thus, youngsters who may be suffering the insecurities often associated with adolescence may find that cigarettes enable them to communicate the image they would like to convey. Consistent with this point, research indicates that teenagers whose ideal self-image is close to that of a typical smoker are most likely to intend to smoke (Barton, Chassin, Presson, & Sherman, 1982).

A second factor that is influential in adolescent smoking is the peer group. From age 10 or 12 on, children are exposed to social influences to smoke, and one study estimated that 71% of all cigarettes smoked by adolescents were smoked in the presence of another person, often a peer (Biglan et al., 1984). Social conformity and peer influence may be especially important influences on smoking under conditions of stress. Castro and his colleagues (Castro, Maddahian, Newcomb, & Bentler, 1987)

found that social conformity and peer influence were mediators between stressful life events (perceived stress and disruptive family events) and the coping response of cigarette smoking. The complex set of variables associated with adolescent smoking is pictured in Figure 6.1.

The Nature of Addiction in Smoking

Smoking is clearly an addiction, reported to be harder to stop than drug addiction or alcoholism by many who suffer from multiple addictions (Kozlowski et al., 1989). Evidence for the importance of this addictive component is the fact that the probability of smoking is highly related to the time since the last cigarette and to current plasma nicotine level. Several theories of smoking addiction have been developed, all of them centering around nicotine.

FIGURE 6.1   Some Factors That Determine Whether or Not an Adolescent Begins to Smoke

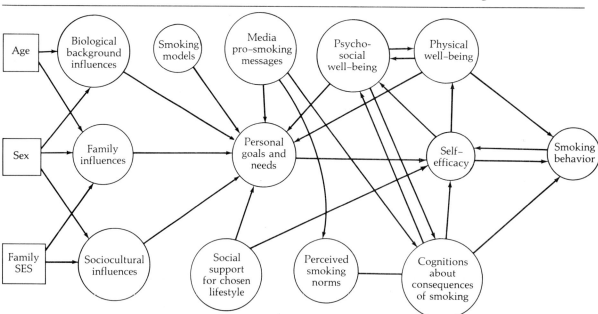

(Source: McCarthy, 1986)

The Nicotine Fixed-Effect Theory   The first of these, the **nicotine fixed-effect theory,** maintains that smoking is reinforcing because nicotine stimulates reward centers in the nervous system (Hall, Rappaport, Hopkins, & Griffin, 1973). Nicotine also speeds up the heart, causes relaxation of the skeletal muscles, and has an indirect effect on the level of circulating catecholamines. Subjectively, nicotine has the paradoxical capacity to produce feelings of mental alertness and relaxation simultaneously.

A factor arguing against the nicotine fixed-effect theory is that nicotine's effects on the body are short-lived and disappear when the drug is not present. Thus, although the effects of nicotine may prompt the repeated use of cigarettes, they cannot account for the fact that many people return to smoking weeks, months, or even years after they have stopped (Russell, 1971a, 1971b). If the effects of nicotine were the only reason for smoking, one would expect that any therapy that could induce people to stop smoking temporarily might be successful over the long term.

The Nicotine Regulation Theory   A second theory, called the **nicotine regulation theory,** maintains that smoking regulates the level of nicotine in the body. When plasma levels of nicotine depart from the ideal level, smoking occurs (Jarvik, 1973). An ingenious study that is consistent with this theory was conducted by Schachter, Kozlowski, and Silverstein (1977). This study's design was based on the fact that, since the excretion of nicotine depends partly on the pH (acidity-alkalinity) of the urine, nicotine (an alkaloid) is excreted when urinary pH is low (acidic). On the other hand, when urinary pH is high (alkaline), nicotine is retained. If smoking acts to regulate nicotine within the body, then smoking should increase when urinary pH drops below a given level.

To test this hypothesis, Schachter and his colleagues gave smokers either vitamin C, glutamic acid (Acidulin), bicarbonate, or a placebo pill over each of several successive weeks. Smokers did not know which kind of pill they had received. Since vitamin C and Acidulin are both acidic and thus decrease urinary pH, one would expect subjects receiving these substances to increase their smoking behavior to compensate for increased acidity. However, smokers ingesting either a placebo or bicarbonate should not excrete nicotine at high levels; thus, their smoking behavior should remain the same. Consistent with this hypothesis, subjects who received the vitamin C or Acidulin increased their smoking by about four cigarettes a day. These findings suggest that smoking does serve to regulate nicotine.

Critics of the nicotine-regulation model suggest that smoking also regulates stress, anxiety, boredom, and other emotional states. As evidence, they point out that smokers smoke more during stressful events such as seminar presentations or parties. Schachter and associates (Schachter, Silverstein, & Perlick, 1977) responded that when individuals are exposed to high stress, the urinary pH becomes more acidic, which, in turn, increases smoking. To test this point, they conducted another ingenious study. Half of a group of smokers were first given either three bicarbonate capsules (to make their pH more alkaline) or three placebo capsules. All subjects were then exposed either to a highly stressful or a less stressful task involving electric shock. Schachter and his colleagues predicted that high stress would produce more smoking than low stress, but only when subjects had been given placebo pills; subjects who had ingested bicarbonate pills and who were then exposed to high stress should not experience a drop in urinary pH because the bicarbonate would keep their pH more alkaline. Thus, they should not need to increase their smoking. The results were consistent with these predictions.

Despite evidence supporting the nicotine-regulation model, a number of factors argue against it (for a review, see Leventhal & Cleary, 1980). Some of the critical ones are as follows. First, smokers do not alter their smoking behavior enough to compensate for changes produced by manipulated pH level; second, smoking is responsive to rapidly changing forces in the environment before these forces can affect urinary pH; third, high rates of relapse among smokers can be observed long after urinary nicotine levels are at zero levels (Jacobs, Knapp, Rosenthal, & Haskell, 1970). In a review of the research on the alkaline effects on smoking, Grunberg and Kozlowski (1986) concluded that the research is still inconclusive. Alkaline probably does not influence smoking cessation, but it may help somewhat in smoking reduction and thereby may have some therapeutic potential.

The Multiple-Regulation Model   Leventhal and Cleary (1980) developed a **multiple-regulation model** of smoking. They argue that emotional factors are central to smoking and that nicotine simply becomes conditioned to these emotional states. How might this model work? Let us adopt a hypothetical example of a novice smoker, an adolescent who is socially anxious. Initially, he may smoke to develop feelings of security and maturity. Smoking, then, acts to reduce his social anxiety. Once he finishes a cigarette, however, the anxiety will reappear and urinary nicotine levels will begin to drop. Over time, then, anxiety will become conditioned to declines in nicotine level because of their continual pairing. The sensations produced by a decline in urinary nicotine level then will, in turn, become a craving for smoking, since smoking alters both nicotine level and social anxiety. This is not the only way in which the craving for smoking may develop, but it provides one possible explanation.

Like the other theories of smoking addiction, the multiple-regulation model does not account for all that is known about smoking. Its complexity may fit the complicated nature of smoking better than either the fixed-effect

model or the nicotine-regulation model. However, the model's very flexibility is also its current weakness. It has yet to be as clearly delineated as the other models are and, as a consequence, it is difficult to test.

Pomerleau and Pomerleau's Theory   Pomerleau and Pomerleau (1984, 1989a) developed an explanation of smoking as a neuroregulator, which, in conjunction with addiction to nicotine, may help explain why it is so difficult for people to stop smoking permanently. Specifically, they suggested that nicotine may be a way of regulating performance and affect. Nicotine alters the availability of active neuroregulators, including acetylcholine, norepinephrine, dopamine, endogenous opioids, and vasopressin. Nicotine may be used by smokers to engage these neuroregulators because they produce temporary improvements in performance or affect. Consequently, a large number of internal and external cues unrelated to the nicotine-dependence cycle may come to serve as discriminative stimuli for smoking, but they may have nothing to do with the addictive aspects of nicotine per se or the need to avoid withdrawal.

In support of this theory, memory appears to improve in response to acetylcholine, norepinephrine, and vasopressin. Reduction of anxiety and tension have been tied to acetylcholine and beta-endorphins. Enhancement of pleasure appears to be facilitated by dopamine, norepinephrine, and endogenous opioids. Facilitation of task performance appears to be improved by acetylcholine and norepinephrine. Consequently, smoking among habitual smokers increases concentration, recall, alertness, arousal, psychomotor performance, and the ability to screen out irrelevant stimuli. It also reduces anxiety and tension.

Moreover, not smoking in habitual smokers leads to reduced concentration and a decline in the ability to tune out irrelevant stimuli, impairment of memory and psychomotor performance, and dullness, as well as increases in anxiety, tension, irritability, craving, and dysphoria. Ex-smokers may return to smoking because they have learned that nicotine is at least a temporarily effective coping response to the demands of daily living. Of particular interest is the fact that smoking produces an initial pattern of arousal and alertness followed by a calming, tension-reduction pattern, which may result from the cholinergic/catecholaminergic activation followed by cholinergic blocking or the release of endogenous opioids. Smokers apparently can adjust their nicotine intake to selectively enhance these effects, which may add to its appeal as a coping mechanism.

In summary, then, people smoke for a number of reasons. There may be some genetic influences on smoking; smoking typically begins in early adolescence, when youngsters may have little idea of the problems they face in response to smoking; smoking clearly has an addictive component related to nicotine; and smoking also regulates moods and responses to stressful circumstances. As a consequence, it has been a very difficult problem to treat.

INTERVENTIONS TO REDUCE SMOKING

Changing Attitudes Toward Smoking

The release of the Surgeon General's report gave rise to a massive media campaign, launched by health agencies, warning of the hazards of smoking. In theory, a mass media approach to the smoking problem can be highly cost-effective. If antismoking messages are communicated to smokers in this way and decreases in smoking behavior result, then a large number of people can be influenced with minimal cost.

Studies have assessed reactions to antismoking messages both in laboratory settings and through the media, and the results are similar. When smokers are alerted to the risks of smoking, they typically develop attitudes that favor quitting, and they may intend to stop smoking (e.g., Chassin, Presson, Sherman, & McGrew, 1987; Leventhal & Cleary, 1980). Some smokers even succeed in giving up smoking temporarily (Leventhal & Cleary, 1980). Media interventions with adolescents have had similar effects. Although students exposed to these messages are more knowledgeable about the problems associated with smoking, their smoking behavior may be only slightly affected (for a review, see Leventhal & Cleary, 1980). Similar results were demonstrated in the Stanford Heart Disease Prevention Program (Meyer, Nash et al., 1980) described in Chapter 4.

Do these evaluations of attitude and media campaigns mean that the mass media can have little impact on the smoking problem? The answer is no. First, media campaigns can be extremely effective for providing information about health habits. National polls now indicate that the majority of the country's smokers know that smoking is a bad practice and want to stop (Damon, 1973; Gallup, 1981a, 1981b; Leventhal & Cleary, 1980). Media campaigns against smoking have helped instill an antismoking attitude in the general population. These attitudes have also been very effective in discouraging adults from beginning to smoke as well as persuading them to remain nonsmokers (Warner, 1977, 1981; Warner & Murt, 1982).

Moreover, particular types of mass media campaigns or mass media combined with other kinds of interventions may hold even more promise. In a review of forty mass media programs to reduce cigarette smoking, Flay (1987) found that mass media smoking-cessation clinics were effective when supplemented with a community-based intervention designed to enhance social support for the ex-smoker. Flay concluded that a large percentage of smokers who are not otherwise reached could be by television or radio programs designed to help people stop smoking. In particular, by encouraging a large number of people to quit simultaneously, the social milieu for the ex-smoker becomes a supportive one. Television programs may well be superior to written self-help materials, inasmuch as television provides opportunities to demonstrate skills more vividly than in written materials. An additional advantage of the mass media is that they are highly cost-effective for approaching the smoking problem.

The media have also been used to reinforce antismoking messages in populations exposed to behavioral intervention. For example, one study (Mogielnicki et al., 1986) found that study participants who were exposed to the media after their participation in the program smoked significantly less than those not exposed to the follow-up media intervention. Thus, the media may play an important supportive role in reinforcing and maintaining messages introduced by more focused behavioral programs.

In essence, then, antismoking messages in the media "set the stage" for efforts to quit smoking. Thus, the media are effective primarily in inculcating, enhancing, or maintaining people's motivation to quit. What the media have not been able to do by themselves is communicate specific instructions about how to quit smoking to specific individuals. As we saw in Chapter 4, without explicit instructions on how to deal with a habit, an attitudinal message may have little effect.

This is not to suggest, however, that attitudinal factors are irrelevant to success in stopping smoking. As we have already seen, attitudes toward stopping smoking must be favorable in order for the person to attempt to quit in the first place. Moreover, particular attitudes may predict the ability to profit from some behavioral intervention. One study, for example (Eiser et al., 1985) found that those attempting to stop smoking were more successful if they believed that the health benefits

of stopping smoking would be great and had confidence in their own ability to stop (see also Sutton & Eiser, 1984). Kaufert and his colleagues (Kaufert, Rabkin, Syrotuik, Boyko, & Shane, 1986) found that general health concern and perceived vulnerability to smoking-related disorders correlated significantly with successful reduction of smoking in conjunction with a smoking-cessation program. Self-efficacy beliefs also predict success in not smoking and particularly may help keep people from relapsing (Baer, Holt, & Lichtenstein, 1986). Different attitudes may also be significant for different kinds of smokers. Chassin, Presson, Sherman, Corty, and Olshavky (1984), for example, found that attitudes, normative beliefs, and behavioral intentions predicted whether students who had tried cigarettes continued to smoke (Ajzen & Fishbein, 1980). However, personality factors and the perceived supportiveness of the environment were more likely to predict whether those who had never smoked went on to try cigarettes (see Eysenck, 1981; Jessor & Jessor, 1977).

The Therapeutic Approach to Smoking

Because attitude-change campaigns often do not help smokers stop smoking, psychologists have increasingly adopted a therapeutic approach to the smoking problem. From this standpoint, the smoker is viewed as a patient requiring professional treatment. Some of the following therapeutic techniques have been used.

Nicotine Gum   Nicotine gum has been used to help motivated smokers initially with quitting. However, smokers do not enjoy chewing nicotine gum, possibly because nicotine is absorbed slowly through this method. There is some evidence that the fast-rise time of nicotine from cigarette smoking is important for producing the reinforcements peculiar to

---

Box 6.3
Is Smoking an Informed Choice?

Smoking is one of the most controversial health habits. The tobacco industry has argued that the decision to begin to smoke represents an informed choice, that people know what they are doing, and that by deciding to smoke, they assume responsibility for this habit and its repercussions.

Recently, however, psychologists have challenged this viewpoint (Leventhal, Glynn, & Fleming, 1987). The idea that people choose to smoke assumes that when they begin they have well-informed beliefs about smoking. However, 95% of regular smokers start to smoke before they are 20 years old, and the question arises whether these youngsters have accurate information. One factor that raises the question of the degree of choice experienced by adolescents concerns the fact that the tobacco industry systematically targets adolescents in their smoking advertising (Albright, Altman, Slater, & Maccoby, 1988). By appealing directly to this audience and playing upon their vulnerabilities and needs, these youngsters may be swayed in the direction of smoking before they are fully able to weigh the evidence concerning this habit.

Moreover, there is substantial evidence that adolescents are badly misinformed regarding the risks associated with smoking. A study of 895 urban adolescents assessed attitudes and beliefs about smoking and found that, generally, respondents were poorly informed about the prevalence and risks of this habit. They overestimated how many adults smoke and how many of their peers smoke. They also underestimated the extent to which other people hold negative attitudes toward smoking. A large proportion of the respondents believed that they were less likely than other people to contract a smoking-related illness. And, generally speaking, respondents showed a poor understanding of the unpleasant consequences people experience when they try to quit.

Perhaps, most significantly, these misperceptions were most common among those who had already begun to smoke, who had friends or family members who smoke, or who intended to begin smoking in the future. These points argue significantly against the tobacco industry's claim that smoking is an informed choice and, rather, suggest that it is based on considerable misinformation and poor assessments of personal risk.

---

smoking (Pomerleau, 1986). Some have suggested that an alternative is to develop nicotine-replacement therapies that mimic the sharp rise produced by inhaling tobacco smoke. Although this has some advantages for weaning people off cigarettes, nicotine is itself addictive and has substantial cardiovascular risks. Consequently, inasmuch as the goal of therapy should be to get people to avoid nicotine altogether, enthusiasm for developing nicotine-replacement therapies has been muted (Pomerleau & Pomerleau, 1988). Nicotine gum can lead to physical dependence, which may produce subsequent behavioral dependence on the gum beyond the period recommended for substitution (Hughes, Hatsukami, & Skoog, 1986).

Aversion Therapy Another common early step in cognitive-behavioral approaches to smoking is aversion therapy. Typically, the act of smoking is paired with some unpleasant stimulus so that smoking will take on negative associations. This stimulus might be electric shock or the imagination of an aversive scene such as the following:

> You are sitting at your desk in the office [preparing a paper for class]. There is a pack of cigarettes to your right. While you are writing, you put down your pencil and start to reach for the cigarettes. You get a nauseous feeling in your stomach. You begin to feel sick to your stomach, as if you are about to vomit. You touch the pack of cigarettes and bitter spit comes into your mouth. When you take the cigarette out of the pack, some pieces of food come into your throat. Now you feel sick and have stomach cramps. As you are about to put the cigarette into your mouth, you puke all over the pack of cigarettes. The cigarette in your hand is very soggy and full of green vomit. There is a stink coming from the vomit. Snots are coming from your nose. Your hands feel all slimy and full of vomit. The whole desk is a mess. Your clothes are all full of puke. You get up from your desk and turn away from the vomit and cigarettes. You immediately begin to feel better being away from the vomit and cigarettes. You go to the bathroom and wash up and feel great being away from the vomit and the cigarettes. (Cautela, 1971, p. 113)

The most commonly used form of aversion therapy is called **focused smoking** (Hackett & Horan, 1978). In this method, the smoker takes a puff on a cigarette at prescribed regular intervals. While smoking, he or she is urged to attend closely to all of its unpleasant elements: the smoke, the stinging burn in the throat, the smell. In a related technique, **rapid smoking** (Lichtenstein, Harris, Birchler, Wahl, & Schmahl, 1973), the smoker is placed in a room with warm, smoky air and inhales from a cigarette rapidly every few seconds while concentrating on the resulting negative effects. This technique is no longer used as much as it once was, because some health professionals believe that it might precipitate a heart attack in patients with latent cardiac problems (Hackett & Horan, 1978).

Some studies of focused and rapid smoking report initial quit rates between 60 and 90%, with as high as 45% abstinence over a 6-month or 1-year period (Lichtenstein et al., 1973; see also Leventhal & Cleary, 1980). However, other studies suggest that these methods have no advantages over behavioral techniques. In fact, some studies suggest a success rate no more than 20% at the 6-month follow-up (for a review, see Leventhal & Cleary, 1980). Therefore, focused and rapid smoking are now typically viewed as a means of inducing people to stop smoking initially, but they are not regarded as sufficient for convincing people to remain nonsmokers (Leventhal, Baker, Brandon, & Fleming, 1989).

Operant Conditioning   Operant conditioning procedures have also been employed in cognitive-behavioral interventions with smokers. As with all poor health habits, smoking is embedded in the environment, and there are stimuli that elicit and reinforce smoking behavior. Thus, some operant procedures are designed to extricate smoking from those environmental stimuli. For example, a smoker may carry around a buzzer that sounds at irregular intervals, indicating that it is time to smoke. When smoking becomes a response to the buzzer, it becomes independent of the environmental cues that usually evoke and maintain it, such as a cup of coffee, a drink, or a conversation with a friend. In theory, when the buzzer is eliminated, smoking may be as well. Shapiro and co-workers (Shapiro, Tursky, Schwartz, & Shnidman, 1971) indicated an initial success rate of 75% of smokers stopping with this method; however, this rate declined to 43% over 3½ months. Other operant procedures have also been used with smokers, including compiling external rewards for not smoking (e.g., Miller & Gimpl, 1971).

How successful have conditioning procedures been in getting people to stop smoking? Typically, they yield high initial quit rates but produce poor maintenance of nonsmoking over time. One reason may be that conditioning procedures undermine smokers' perceptions of their own self-efficacy; that is, when the smoker perceives that his behavior is under the control of external factors, he may come to doubt that he has the personal ability to control smoking behavior and so returns to it over the long term (Leventhal & Cleary, 1980).

Multimodal Intervention　As a consequence, smoking researchers have increasingly adopted a multimodal focus that incorporates elements of self-control therapies to increase the smoker's sense of participation in the therapeutic process (Leventhal & Cleary, 1980). As is true for other poor health practices, researchers are increasingly recognizing that the process of behavior change unfolds across many stages that may require different intervention strategies (Marlatt & Gordon, 1985; Prochaska & DiClemente, 1984a). Work by Leventhal and his colleagues has explicitly incorporated the stage model into planned interventions. Typically, these interventions focus on four stages in changing from the status of smoker to nonsmoker (Leventhal & Baker, 1986): (1) instilling the motivation to stop smoking, (2) making the decision and planning to stop, (3) behavioral management of quitting, and (4) maintenance of status as a nonsmoker through relapse prevention.

Motivation can be instilled by emphasizing the adverse health consequences of smoking and by bringing social pressures to bear on people not to smoke (e.g., playing on the fear that one's children will become smokers or be injured by one's smoking). The motivation to change smoking behavior may ebb and flow, and so taking advantage of teachable moments is important. For example, pregnant

women show very high smoking quit rates, but, unfortunately, they also show a high postpartum return to smoking. Better use of this window of opportunity could be made.

The next stage, *decision and planning*, includes a timeframe for quitting, a program of how to quit, and awareness of potential difficulties coupled with noting the benefits of quitting. *Behavioral management* in quitting smoking consists of many of the cognitive-behavioral techniques we have seen employed with other health habits. For example, the patient may be trained in self-observation and self-monitoring to keep a record of smoking, the circumstances under which it occurs, and the reactions that it prompts during the initial effort to understand the dimensions of the behavior. She may then also be actively involved in developing self-reward techniques to extricate smoking behavior from the environmental cues with which it has been associated. Aversive smoking or rapid smoking may be employed to aid in initial quitting, and nicotine gum also appears to be a useful quitting aid (Leventhal & Baker, 1986).

As is true for interventions involving many health habits, additional components have been added to many cognitive-behavioral programs. For example, those who would stop smoking have been trained to enlist social support from spouses, friends, and co-workers in their resolution to stop. People are more likely to stop smoking and to be successful over the short term if their partner is highly supportive and if they perceive themselves as having nonsmoking support resources more generally in their environment, such as friends who do not smoke. The presence of smokers in a person's social network is a hindrance to maintenance and significantly predicts relapse (Mermelstein, Cohen, Lichtenstein, Baer, & Kamarck, 1986).

Smoking develops in response to or serves to reduce social anxiety (Spielberger, 1986; Tomkins, 1968). In one study, for example, smokers reported that they felt less anxious and more successful in changing others' opinions and expressing their own points of view when they were smoking than when they were not. In addition, when participants were smoking, heart rate increases during social interactions were smaller than typically reported for smokers seated quietly in nonsocial situations. Thus, smoking appears to regulate emotional functioning in social situations (Gilbert & Spielberger, 1987). Consequently, relaxation training has been introduced to try to help smokers relax in situations in which they might have smoked instead (Grunberg, 1985). Exercise has been investigated as a possible disincentive to smoke. Although there appears to be a decreased desire for cigarettes right after vigorous exercise, it is unclear whether a long-term program of exercise can be used either to enable people to cut down on smoking or to maintain abstinence after quitting (Pomerleau et al., 1987).

Increasingly, too, researchers have tackled the problem of maintaining abstinence directly (see Schumaker & Grunberg, 1986, for a review). Relapse prevention is an important problem because quitting smoking shows a steady month-by-month decline, so that within 2 years after smoking intervention, even the best program does not exceed a 50% abstinence rate (Leventhal & Baker, 1986). Relapse prevention techniques often begin by preparing people for the management of withdrawal, including cardiovascular changes, increases in appetite, variations in the urge to smoke, increases in coughing and discharge of phlegm, and the like. These problems may occur intermittently during the first 7 to 11 days. In addition, relapse prevention focuses on the more long-term, high-risk situations that lead to a craving for cigarettes, such as drinking coffee or alcohol. As just noted, relapse prevention may especially need to focus on teaching people coping techniques for dealing with stressful interpersonal situations. In one study, those who were successfully able to quit smoking had better coping skills for dealing with such situations than those who ended up relapsing (Abrams et al., 1987).

Some relapse prevention approaches have included contingency contracting, in which the smoker pays a sum of money that is returned only on condition of cutting down or abstaining. Buddy systems, follow-up booster sessions (e.g., see Hunt & Matarazzo, 1973), and follow-up phone calls (McConnell, Biglan, & Severson, 1984) have also been used, but to date booster sessions have shown limited success as a maintenance technology (Lichtenstein, 1982; Wilson, 1985). Another approach to maintenance has involved self-hypnosis, in which the smoker repeats a simple message, such as "My body is a machine, I live in my body, I must take care of my body, I must not smoke" (Perry & Mullen, 1975; cited in Leventhal & Cleary, 1980).

Factors that predict short-term maintenance and long-term maintenance may differ. For example, Kamarck and Lichtenstein (1988) found that those trying to quit smoking were best able to do so on the short term if they had alternative methods of regulating their affect than those who did not. That is, smoking is known to produce feelings of arousal and/or relaxation, which can be controlled by experienced smokers. Those who were able spontaneously to develop alternative ways of producing these states were less likely to relapse on the short term. Over the long term, however, simply monitoring smoking predicted abstinence better than did affect regulation processes.

Evaluation of Multimodal Interventions

How successful have multimodal approaches to smoking been? One dilemma in evaluating smoking programs has been picking criteria for success. People's self-reports of abstinence are not grossly off-base, but are somewhat higher than the verifications offered by biochemical techniques. Consequently, biochemical measures such as alveolar carbon monoxide (amount of carbon monoxide in the alveoli) (Glynn, Gruder, & Jegerski, 1986; Lombardo & Carreno, 1987) and salivary thiocyanate (a sulfur-based salt in the saliva produced by smoking) (Fears, Gerkovich, O'Connell, & Cook, 1987) are often used to supplement self-reports. The latter technique, however, has been criticized as unreliable (Bliss & O'Connell, 1984). Measurement issues and the best way to validate smoking behavior will continue to be important in evaluating smoking programs.

Virtually every imaginable combination of therapies for getting people to stop has been tested. Typically, these programs show high initial success rates for quitting, followed by high rates of return to smoking (Leventhal & Cleary, 1980). Yet there is also considerable variability in outcomes. Some studies report that combinations of motivation training, skills training, and therapeutic approaches such as aversive smoking can show good outcomes (Delehunt & Curran, 1976; Elliott & Denny, 1978; Lando, 1977). However, in other cases, combined treatments produced no gain over single therapies (Danaher, 1977), and some studies demonstrated even poorer success rates for combined therapies over single techniques (Lamontagne, Gagnon, & Gaude, 1978; for a review, see Leventhal & Cleary, 1980). Lando (1981) suggested that combined treatments can create information overload and may consequently be less effective than less intensive efforts.

Summarizing the results of the therapeutic approach to smoking, Leventhal and Cleary (1980) offered four conclusions. First, most approaches to modifying smoking behavior show high initial rates of success, often as high as 90%. Second, programs to curb smoking also have dropout rates as high as 50%. Third, the rate of return to smoking is extraordinarily high. The success rate of most programs 6 months to 1 year after initial contact with clients is rarely better than 10 to 25% (Lando & McGovern, 1985; Ockene, Hymo-

witz, Sexton, & Broste, 1982), although occasional studies report rates as high as 35 to 40% (Glynn, Leventhal, & Hirschman, 1986; Lando & McGovern, 1985; Ockene et al., 1982). Fourth, no particular methods of behavior change, including multimodal approaches, emerge as especially successful.

Cognitive-behavioral interventions to help people quit smoking have been modestly successful, about as successful as other kinds of techniques (Glasgow & Lichtenstein, 1987). Programs combining behavioral skills training with nicotine gum seem to be more effective than either component alone. Intensive approaches, such as those that initially employ aversive smoking, have very high initial quit rates, but also show substantial relapse. Self-help programs, in contrast, often show lower relapse, but the initial quit rates can be quite low. Some of the best short-term and long-term abstinence rates are achieved by combining aversive or focused smoking as an initial quitting technique with coping response training as a relapse prevention method (Leventhal, Baker et al., 1989). At this point, no one model of relapse or maintenance appears superior to others in reducing the problem of returning to smoking (see Curry, Marlatt, Gordon, & Baer, 1988). Virtually all interventions are more effective with lighter than heavier smokers.

Is social support a critical element in smoking cessation? Research evaluating whether social support can enhance the effects of cognitive-behavioral programs suggests no improvement in quit or maintenance rates compared with a cognitive-behavioral intervention alone. Yet self-reports of social support in stopping smoking consistently predict success. Moreover, there is some evidence that women spontaneously use social support to help them maintain quitting more than men do and thus may be more susceptible to interventions focused on social support (Sorensen & Pechacek, 1987). As we will see shortly, deficits in social skills (Flay, 1985) and feelings of social incompetence (e.g., Botvin, 1985) distinguish young smokers from those who do not begin to smoke. Likewise, a number of researchers have maintained that social support is important in successful smoking cessation (Carmody et al., 1985; Mermelstein et al., 1986). For example, the presence of supportive nonsmokers in an ex-smoker's environment can help reduce recidivism. Earlier we also noted that social support can enhance the effects of a media intervention, in that when others are simultaneously attempting to modify a bad habit such as smoking, the efforts of any one person are likely to be successful. Consequently, our ability to enlist social support as one technique for helping people stop smoking and maintain quitting has yet to be realized from an intervention perspective (Cohen et al., 1988; Lichtenstein, Glasgow, & Abrams, 1986). It is possible, too, that different kinds of social support will be helpful at different stages or for different types of smokers during the effort to stop smoking, and that simple interventions designed to provide across-the-board social support do not tap or provide this more differentiated picture of the value of social support.

Health educators and psychologists have yet to discover the ideal program that produces a high rate of long-term abstinence. Most smokers who join formal cessation programs do not quit permanently. As a result, some have urged that we must develop interventions to help smokers smoke fewer cigarettes a day or to shift to very low-tar cigarettes. Switching to smoking one or two noninhaled pipes or cigars each day would also reduce health risks. These more modest goals assume that smokers will not compensate for reduced tar by blocking filter vents on cigarettes or inhaling tobacco products more deeply (Kozlowski, 1988–1989).

Before lapsing into pessimism, we may need to consider the cumulative effects of quit-smoking programs rather than the effects of individual programs in isolation (Schachter, 1982). Any given effort to stop smoking may yield only 20% long-term abstinence. However, given multiple attempts to quit and multiple techniques for quitting, eventually the effort may be successful. Indeed, at least 65% of all smokers can eventually quit, albeit not necessarily the first time they try. Formal smoking-cessation programs, then, may look less successful than they really are. Over time, the individual may amass enough successful techniques and enough motivation to persist.

Who Is Best Able to Induce People to Stop Smoking?

In addition to searching for the best technique to get people to stop smoking, researchers have examined whether any particular change agent is markedly more successful than others. For example, is a person more likely to stop if a *psychotherapist* or a *physician* urges him or her to do so? People who seek psychotherapy for stopping smoking do not appear to do any better than those who use other techniques; thus, evidence for the success of psychotherapy is limited (Leventhal & Cleary, 1980). Studies evaluating physicians' effectiveness in getting their patients to stop smoking suggests that the quit rates over 6 months are between 17 and 38%; this figure is equivalent to statistics found with other interventions (Leventhal & Cleary, 1980).

However, the physician may be effective in getting a patient to stop smoking at critical points in the patient's health (Pederson, 1982). For example, if pregnant smokers are told by their physicians to stop smoking, they are more likely to do so than at other times in their lives (Barec, MacArthur, & Sherwood, 1976). Likewise, patients with symptoms of heart disease or chest congestion or a history of myocardial infarction are more likely to stop smoking when told to do so by a physician or other health care professional than at other times (Grunberg & Bowen, 1985; Havik & Maeland, 1988). Thus, vulnerability coupled with a physician's advice to quit is conducive to quitting.

Increasingly, business organizations have sponsored smoking-cessation clinics for their employees. Such programs are regarded as potentially cost-effective due to the economic losses incurred from smoking-related illnesses. Moreover, in theory, the support provided by the employee peer group may increase the success of these programs. To date, interventions at the *worksite* do not appear to be substantially more effective than other types of interventions (Leventhal & Cleary, 1980); however, it may be that we have not yet made maximal use of the work environment (Danaher, 1980). One set of antismoking programs introduced at the worksite included a contest and a pool of reward money distributed to participants by employers. The majority of employees who smoked were successfully recruited to the intervention. At 6 months' follow-up, 80 to 91% of the original participants reported that they were still abstinent, and these high rates were cross-checked by questioning friends and relatives of the ex-smokers. Those most able to profit from the program were those with lighter rather than heavier smoking habits, a desire to stop smoking, confidence in the ability to quit, and a partner in the competition who was a close friend (Cummings, Hellmann, & Ermont, 1988; see also Klesges & Cigrans, 1988). Thus, by building on a sense of healthy competition and instilling motivation socially, these workplace cessation programs may achieve high rates of success (Stachnik & Stoffelmayr, 1983; see also Windsor, Lowe, & Bartlett, 1988).

A variety of commercial *stop-smoking clinics* have come into being. Often, these clinics require a substantial enrollment fee to induce commitment to the program. Typically, they use such techniques as providing health information, encouragement, group therapy, moral support, and social pressure to get clients to stop smoking (Leventhal & Cleary, 1980). Cognitive-behavioral techniques for changing smoking have also been adopted by the more sophisticated clinics. Although cure rates are often advertised to be very high, these assessments may be based only on short-term and therefore misleading statistics (Bernstein & McAlister, 1976).

Public health approaches to reducing smoking have involved *community intervention trials* combining media interventions with behavioral interventions directed at high-risk individuals. The Stanford Three-Community Study described earlier is an example. However, such studies are often extremely expensive ways of intervening with the general public. Consequently, community approaches to smoking have concentrated on developing low-cost interventions. Interventions that focus on mobilizing existing community resources rather than implementing organizational changes have the potential to reach large numbers of people while simultaneously being cost-effective and becoming well-integrated into the community.

Why Is Smoking So Hard to Change?

As we have seen, smoking is a highly resistant behavior pattern. Although people are initially able to stop, relapse rates are very high. What are some of the factors that make it so difficult for smokers to quit?

The difficulties people have in stopping smoking stem in part from our lack of understanding of smoking itself. As Leventhal and Cleary (1980) insightfully point out, efforts to curb smoking draw on models of intervention rather than on models of smoking. Thus, principles of learning theory have been applied to the smoking problem without an effective understanding of smoking itself. To change smoking behavior, one must understand the dimensions of the underlying behavior: its frequency, its association with external stimuli, its developmental course, its addictive component, and the psychological needs that it meets (Chassin, Presson, & Sherman, 1985).

In addition, several specific factors make smoking resistant to change. First, research reveals that there are a variety of reasons for smoking. People may smoke for stimulation, for pleasure and relaxation, to reduce tension, to reduce general anxiety, to reduce social anxiety, to reduce craving, to hold a cigarette, or because smoking is habitual (Ikard, Green, & Horn, 1969). All these motives appear to be largely independent of each other, and a single intervention cannot hope to address all of them. For example, smokers for whom addiction plays an important part may be well treated by nicotine-replacement therapies, whereas smokers who smoke because of coping deficits may do better with behaviorally oriented techniques (Jarvik & Schneider, 1984; Pomerleau, 1986).

Second, many interventions do not address the environmental context in which smoking occurs. There may be little analysis of the environmental stimuli that control the smoking behavior of a particular individual.

Third, interventions may fail to take account of the developmental course of smoking (Leventhal & Cleary, 1980). The smoking behavior of a light smoker who has not been smoking for very long is fundamentally different from that of a heavy smoker who may have been smoking for several years. Different factors influence different stages of smoking. In the preparatory stage, when young people are developing attitudes toward cigarettes, observation of adult smoking models and impressions formed from cigarette advertising are influential (Chassin et al., 1985). In the second stage, initiation, peer smoking and a lack of refusal skills for declining a cigarette are important. The third stage of becoming a smoker is heavily dependent on peer factors and the self-image associated with smoking. In the fourth stage, maintenance, which typically takes 2 years or more of smoking, a variety of more individualized factors support and maintain the habit. (Glynn, Leventhal et al., 1986).

Factors that influence relapse after quitting are completely different from those that influence the ability to return to abstinence (Swan & Denk, 1987).

Another set of factors influencing the difficulty of modifying smoking concerns attitudes. Smokers appear to hold attitudes that may make them resist persuasive communications. For example, they report being less knowledgeable and less concerned with the health consequences of smoking than are nonsmokers (Klesges et al., 1988). Gender may also influence receptivity to different kinds of quit-smoking programs. Overall, men appear to be more interested in stopping smoking than women are. Women may be less likely to perceive the health benefits of quitting and are more concerned about weight gain and coping with job pressures after quitting. In contrast, women appear to rely more on informal sources of social support, such as encouragement from co-workers in helping quitting. Thus, different interventions might be targeted toward women than toward men (Sorenson & Pechacek, 1987).

Smoking and Weight   Smoking keeps body weight down, and this factor contributes to difficulty in stopping smoking (Klesges, 1989; Klesges, Meyers, Klesges & LaVasque, 1989). Those who show weight gains in response to stopping smoking are more likely to have been moderate smokers and to have had a history of weight problems (Hall, Ginsberg, & Jones, 1986; Klesges et al., 1989). The fact that smoking successfully controls weight may be a particular deterrent to women smokers, since women are typically more concerned than men with their weight in Western society (Grunberg, Bowen, & Winders, 1986).

Several explanations have been offered for why smoking keeps weight down. One maintains that when people stop smoking, they ingest more food or they change their patterns of food consumption. In particular, those who have quit smoking show a shift in preference for sweet-tasting carbohydrates with a higher caloric value than their previous diet, which appears to be a major factor in weight gains. Carbohydrates may be used to modulate and improve mood after smoking stops, because mood declines when smoking stops and carbohydrates are known to improve mood. Also, nicotine is accompanied by significant decreases in circulating insulin levels and temporary increases in levels of catecholamines. Because nicotine may alter glucose availability in the body, a preference for sweets may result after smoking stops (Grunberg, 1986).

Another explanation is that stopping smoking may change energy-utilization or -expenditure patterns (Grunberg, 1986; see also Grunberg et al., 1988). Such changes are consistent with the idea that nicotine increases energy utilization (Grunberg et al., 1988). Changes in body weight do not appear to be explained by alterations in physical activity itself, although decreases in physical activity after stopping smoking may also contribute to post-smoking body weight gain (Grunberg & Bowen, 1985; Rodin, 1987). Stress-induced eating, namely eating in response to emotionally stressful situations, also appears to explain part of the weight gain seen in those who stop smoking (Hall et al., 1986).

Can weight gain after stopping smoking be avoided? Several points regarding the relation between smoking and body weight suggest directions for interventions (Gritz, Klesges, & Meyers, 1989). The use of nicotine gum is one possible technique because it appears to control the biochemical processes that, at least in part, regulate the weight gain that results from stopping smoking. Alerting people to the potential difficulty of weight gain after quitting and developing dietary and exercise interventions so that they will not put on any extra weight may also be helpful (Klesges et al., 1989).

Withdrawal   Among the physiological factors that contribute to the difficulty smokers have in quitting are symptoms of immediate withdrawal, such as decreases in heart rate and blood pressure, declines in body temperature, and drops in epinephrine and norepinephrine. These may be experienced as aversive and act as an impetus for resuming smoking. More long-term changes, such as weight gain, difficulty in performing customary activities, nausea, headache, constipation, drowsiness, fatigue, difficulty sleeping, and increases in anxiety, irritability, and hostility are also often reported by ex-smokers and may contribute to the high rate of return to the habit (Clavel, Benhamou, & Flamant, 1987; Leventhal & Cleary, 1980). Too, over time, smoking may come to be a conditioned response to changes in blood nicotine level. Increasingly, as an individual smokes, the addictive component of smoking may become at least as important as the underlying emotional needs that smoking initially regulated.

People Who Stop on Their Own

Between 1964 and 1982, 30 million Americans successfully quit smoking, 70 to 80% on their own (U.S. Public Health Service, 1982). Those who quit smoking on their own appear to be no more successful at maintaining abstinence than participants in stop-smoking programs (Cohen et al., 1989). However, many people try to stop smoking several times, and with each effort to stop, the likelihood increases that at least one such effort will be successful. Those who quit on their own appear to be able to do so because they have good self-control skills, self-confidence in their ability to stop, and a perception that the health benefits of not smoking are substantial (Katz & Singh, 1986). It is easier to stop smoking if one has a socially supportive network that does not smoke, and if one was a light rather than a heavy smoker previously (Cohen et al., 1989;

Katz & Singh, 1986). A list of guidelines for people who wish to stop on their own appears in Table 6.2.

SMOKING PREVENTION

Partly because smoking is resistant to interventions and partly because we now know a lot about why young people develop the smoking habit, emphasis on smoking reduction has shifted in recent years from getting smokers to stop smoking to keeping potential smokers from ever starting.

What does this background tell us about **smoking prevention programs?** First, such programs must catch potential smokers early.

TABLE 6.2   SUGGESTIONS FOR TAPERING OFF AND STOPPING SMOKING

Try to Taper Off

- Smoke every cigarette halfway.
- Don't inhale with every cigarette, try every other one.
- Only buy packs, never cartons.
- Try to cut your smoke intake by half.

Shrink Your Habit Step by Step

- Tape a piece of paper to your pack. Record each cigarette you smoke, the time of day, your activity at the moment (coffee break, etc.).
- Check the pattern that emerges after 2 or 3 days.
- Decide to eliminate cigarettes at certain times of the day.
- First try to eliminate the cigarettes that will be easiest to eliminate (at the end of the day, for instance).
- Then try to eliminate the most difficult ones (the ones you want most, after breakfast, perhaps).

(Source: Adapted from American Lung Association, 1986)

Second, programs designed to prevent smoking behavior in adolescents and preadolescents must deal with some of the underlying motivations to smoke, such as the positive image of the smoker and peer pressure (Chassin et al., 1985).

Social Influence Interventions

An early example of a program to keep adolescents from smoking was developed by Evans and his colleagues in the Houston School District (Evans et al., 1988). Two theoretical principles were central in the design of Evans's **social influence intervention.** First, the fact that parental smoking and peer pressure promote smoking in adolescents indicates that children acquire smoking at least partly through the modeling of others. By observing models who are apparently enjoying a behavior they know to be risky, the children's fears of negative consequences are reduced and their expectation of positive consequences is enhanced. Thus, Evans (1976) reasoned, a successful intervention program with adolescents must include the potential for modeling high-status nonsmokers.

A second theoretical principle on which Evans's intervention was based is the concept of behavioral inoculation developed by McGuire (1964, 1973). **Behavioral inoculation** is similar in rationale to inoculation against disease. If one can expose an individual to a weak dose of some germ, one may prevent infection because antibodies against that germ will develop. Likewise, if one can expose individuals to a weak version of a persuasive message, they may develop counterarguments against that message so that they can successfully resist it if they encounter it in a stronger form.

The elements of Evans's intervention program involve three key points: (1) information about the negative effects of smoking is carefully constructed so as to appeal to adolescents; (2) materials are developed to convey a positive image of the nonsmoker (rather than the smoker) as an independent, self-reliant individual; (3) the peer group is used to facilitate not smoking rather than smoking. Let us consider each component in turn.

Most adolescents know that smoking is a risky behavior (Evans, 1976). However, the fact that they continue to smoke suggests that they ignore much of what they know. Therefore, selection of appropriate antismoking materials for this group is critical. Typically, the adolescent's time frame does not include concern about health risks that are 20 to 30 years away. Therefore, Evans reasoned, antismoking materials must highlight the disadvantages of smoking now. The antismoking materials included in his intervention highlighted the negative effects of smoking on immediate health, the financial costs of smoking, and negative social consequences of smoking (such as rejection by others) rather than long-term health risks.

The image of the nonsmoker was also addressed in Evans's materials. Specifically, films and posters were developed to appeal to adolescents' need for independence, conveying such messages as, "You can decide for yourself" and "Here are the facts so you can make a decision." These media messages also showed how cigarette advertisers use subtle techniques to try to get people to smoke, in the hopes that the students would resist cigarette advertising when they encountered it. Simultaneously, these messages also conveyed an image of the smoker as someone who is vulnerable to advertising gimmicks.

Evans addressed the significance of the peer group in several ways. First, high-status, slightly older peer leaders were featured in the films and posters as the primary agents delivering the interventions. They demonstrated through role playing how to resist peer pressure and maintain the decision not to smoke. The films conveyed techniques that adolescents could use to combat pressure, such as stalling for time or using counterpressure (for

example, telling the smoker that she is a fool for ruining her health). In some cases, these messages were reinforced by actual contact with a peer leader in a small-group interaction after exposure to the filmed material.

Do these programs work? Addressing this question is more complex than it seems at first. We must assess smoking not only on the short term, but also over the long term. Smoking prevention programs could simply delay the start of smoking, but have no impact on overall rates of smoking or numbers of smokers. The question of how best to assess effectiveness is also important. Self-reports of smoking may be unreliable. Students know that they are not supposed to smoke and those in the intervention conditions (as compared to control conditions) may especially realize that they should not report smoking.

Some efforts to validate self-report measures via chemical measures of smoking have been attempted. Saliva thiocyanate and expired air carbon monoxide have been two of the most commonly employed measures in this literature. However, relations between self-reported smoking and these biochemical measures are weaker among younger students and early smokers than among more long-term smokers, making these measures unreliable and potentially invalid indicators of adolescent smoking. Consequently, how to measure how much an adolescent smokes has been a difficult question to answer (Pechacek et al., 1984).

Attrition (drop-out) in smoking-cessation studies must also be carefully assessed for the degree to which it may contribute to apparent but not real treatment effects. For example, studies suggest that heavier smokers are more likely to drop out of treatment programs than lighter smokers are. If attrition occurs differentially from the treatment group, this may make the treatment group look more successful than it really is (Biglan, Severson, Ary, Faller et al., 1987).

It has also been difficult to examine the processes involved in undertaking smoking or in successfully preventing its onset. Researchers, for example, have related certain descriptive factors, such as the number of smoking peers, to the likelihood that a person will begin smoking. But this does not necessarily mean that there is peer pressure to smoke, an assumption that has sometimes been made by researchers. A need to draw these kinds of distinctions and examine the processes of smoking or abstaining more closely is evident (Evans, Dratt, Raines, & Rosenberg, 1988).

Film and poster interventions, coupled with the use of peer leaders as primary intervention agents, have now been widely used in smoking prevention programs (Flay, 1985). Overall, results suggest that social influence programs can reduce smoking rates for as long as 4 years (Murray, Davis-Hearn, Goldman, Pirie, & Luepker, 1988; see also Flay, 1985; Murray, Richards, Leupker, & Johnson, 1987). Others (Kozlowski, Coambs, Ferrence, & Adlaf, in press), however, argue that the impact of social influence programs is small and brief, and that experimental smoking is affected more than regular smoking; experimental smokers, they suggest, would probably stop on their own (Biglan Severson, Ary, Faller et al., 1987; Flay et al., in press). What is needed are programs that will reach the child destined to become a regular smoker, and as yet we know little about the factors that may be most helpful in keeping these youngsters from starting to smoke (Kozlowski et al., in press) and in helping them successfully quit once experimental smoking has been undertaken (Ershler, Leventhal, Fleming, & Glynn, 1989). In social influence studies, it is still not clear what the most potent elements in these multifactor interventions may be, and, consequently, future research must help determine which program components are most effective for whom and under what conditions (Flay, 1985; McCaul & Glasgow, 1985).

Thus, research interest is now focusing on why these programs are successful when they are. We do know that public commitment to not smoke does not appear to be an important factor in adolescents' resistance to smoking pressures, at least on the basis of the evidence currently available (McCaul, Glasgow, Schafer, & O'Neill, 1983). Brief daily reminders via telephone are successful in getting adolescents to report on their smoking (McConnell et al., 1984).

Certain kinds of smoking interventions may be more successful with particular groups of smokers than others. Health education appears to be especially effective in preventing initial experimentation with cigarettes (Biglan et al., 1987; Flay, 1985; McCaul & Glasgow, 1985). Once students have begun smoking, however, health education has less effect than social influence techniques aimed at helping students develop refusal skills for dealing with peer pressure to smoke (Ary & Biglan, 1988; Johnson, Hansen, Collins, & Graham, 1986). Neither health education nor social influence intervention, however, appear to be especially successful for those who have gone beyond the stage of experimentation. This point underscores the importance of intervening early with these adolescent populations.

In light of this goal, recent interventions have tried to "bottle" the most useful components of social influence programs and administer them in relatively short-term, cost-effective interventions with young adolescents. Hirschman and Leventhal (1989), for example, developed a three-session smoking prevention program designed to keep children who had already tried smoking from moving to regular smoking status. The intervention detailed information associated with different stages of smoking, information about symptoms, and skills to resist influence to smoke. The results showed significantly lower rates of smoking over an 18-month period than in a control group that saw only smoking prevention films and participated in an unstructured discussion. The program thus had at least modest long-term effectiveness, and the fact that such results could be achieved in three sessions is promising.

The Life-Skills-Training Approach

Another effort to prevent smoking in the adolescent population has been called the **life-skills-training approach** (Botvin & Eng, 1982; Botvin, Eng, & Williams, 1980; Botvin, Renick, & Baker, 1983). Interestingly enough, this approach to smoking prevention deals with cigarette smoking per se in only a small way. Rather, the rationale for the intervention is that if adolescents are trained in self-esteem and coping enhancement as well as social skills, they will not feel as much need to smoke to bolster their self-image: The skills will enhance the adolescent's sense of being an efficacious person. The life-skills approach maintains that any intervention that brings the adolescent closer to conveying a desired image will have the beneficial side effect of reducing smoking onset. The results of these programs to date appear to be as encouraging as the smoking prevention programs based on social influence processes (Botvin & Eng, 1982; Botvin et al., 1980, 1983). These programs also show some success in the reduction of smoking onset over time (Flay, 1985) in minority as well as in white youngsters (Botvin, Dusenbury, Baker, James-Ortiz, & Kerner, 1989).

Advantages of Smoking Prevention Programs

What are the advantages of smoking prevention programs? Their chief advantage is their apparent success in inducing adolescents not to smoke. In addition, they have several other advantages. The programs can easily be implemented through the school system, which is the best method for gaining access to young adolescents: Little class time is needed, and no training of any school personnel is required. The programs build in methods for reiterating elements of the intervention, such as posters placed in key locations around the school. Consequently, students are reminded of the intervention at regular points during their school day. Overall, such programs have the potential to be highly cost-effective as well as effective in preventing adolescents from smoking.

Social Engineering and Smoking

Ultimately, smoking may be more successfully modified by social engineering than by techniques of behavioral change (Kozlowski, 1988–1989). It is unlikely that cigarettes will be outlawed altogether, since previous experience with the prohibition of alcohol has questioned its efficacy as an engineering strategy. However, there are a number of social engineering alternatives to banning cigarettes outright that may force people to reduce their smoking. Taxation is one possibility. Although increases in smoking taxes have not substantially reduced smoking to date, most smokers report that they would reduce their smoking behavior if smoking became prohibitively expensive (Leventhal & Cleary, 1980; Walsh & Gordon, 1986). Smoking can also be controlled by restricting smoking to particular places. The rationale for such interventions is the known harm that can be done to nonsmokers by second-hand smoke (Box 6.4). Thus, not permitting smoking in public buildings, requiring nonsmoking sections in restaurants and other public places, and otherwise protecting the rights of nonsmokers are social engineering alternatives that are being implemented through legislation. Increasingly, business organizations are also developing policies about smoking. Some organizations have developed smoking-cessation programs for their employees, others restrict on-the-job smoking to particular times or places, and still others have banned smoking. No doubt, social engineering interventions to restrict smoking will increase in the coming years.

Box 6.4
Can Nonsmokers Be Harmed by "Second-Hand Smoke"?

One reason why smoking has not been fully attacked on the legislative level is that, until recently, scientists and lawmakers assumed that smokers hurt only themselves. However, increasing evidence suggests that smokers harm not only themselves but also others who are exposed to their smoking. This so-called **passive smoking,** or **second-hand smoke,** which involves inhaling smoke and smoky air produced by others who smoke, has been tied to higher levels of carbon monoxide in the blood, reduced pulmonary functioning, and possibly also higher rates of lung cancer (Garfinkel, 1981; Greenberg, Haley, Etzel, & Loda, 1984; Hirayama, 1981; White & Froeb, 1980).

Two groups that may be at particular risk are the infant children and spouses of smokers. One study (Greenberg et al., 1984) found that infants exposed continually to parental smoking absorbed the constituents of tobacco smoke as measured by urinalysis. Although this study did not tie such exposure to ultimate illness, one might expect that higher rates of smoking-related disorders could be found over time. In fact, a study conducted in Japan (Hirayama, 1981) followed 540 nonsmoking wives of smoking or nonsmoking husbands for 14 years and examined mortality due to lung cancer. The wives of heavy smokers had a higher rate of lung cancer than did wives of husbands who smoked little or not at all. Moreover, these women's risk of dying from lung cancer was between one-third and one-half of what they would have faced, had they been smokers themselves. Even dogs whose owners smoke are at 50% greater risk of developing lung cancer than those whose owners are non-smokers (Riess, 1990).

The fact that passive smoking can be harmful to one's health adds teeth to the idea that nonsmokers have rights vis-à-vis smokers. Increasingly, we are likely to see the effects of passive smoking used as a basis for legislative action against smoking.

SUMMARY

1. Health-compromising behaviors are those in which a person engages that may threaten or undermine good health either in the present or in the future. Consequently, the goal of health psychologists is to eliminate these health-compromising behaviors.

2. Alcoholism accounts for thousands of deaths each year through cirrhosis, can-cer, fetal alcohol syndrome, and accidents connected with drunk driving.

3. Alcoholism and problem drinking encompass a wide range of specific behavior problems with associated physiological and psychological needs.

4. Alcoholism has a genetic component and is also tied to sociodemographic factors,

such as low SES. Drinking also arises in an effort to buffer the impact of stress and appears to peak between ages 18 and 25.

5. Most treatment programs for alcoholism use broad-spectrum cognitive-behavioral approaches. Many begin with an inpatient drying-out period, followed by the use of cognitive-behavioral change methods such as aversion therapy and relapse prevention techniques.

6. The best predictor of success is the patient. Alcoholics with mild drinking problems, little abuse of other drugs, and a supportive, financially secure environment do better than those without such supports.

7. Smoking accounts for over 300,000 deaths annually in the U.S. due to heart disease, cancer, and a variety of lung disorders. Smoking adds to and may even exacerbate other risk factors associated with CHD, including stress, cholesterol level, and Type A behavior.

8. Several theories have attempted to explain the addictive nature of smoking, including theories that involve nicotine regulation and others that argue that smoking and nicotine control neuroregulators.

9. In the last few decades, attitudes toward smoking have changed dramatically for the negative. Although antismoking media campaigns by themselves seem to have little effect, when combined with cognitive-behavioral interventions, they may reinforce and perpetuate elements in behavior-change programs.

10. Most programs for stopping smoking begin with nicotine gum or a form of aversion therapy such as rapid smoking. Operant conditioning techniques are then used to disembed smoking from the environmental cues with which it is usually associated. Many multimodal programs include social-skills training programs or relaxation therapies. Relapse prevention is an important component of these programs.

11. No particular venue for changing smoking behavior appears to be especially effective. However, physicians working directly with patients at risk may achieve greater success than other change agents working with patients at other times in their lives. Increasingly, community approaches and worksite interventions are being used to reduce smoking.

12. Smoking is highly resistant to change. Even after successfully stopping for a short period of time, most people relapse. Genetic factors may be responsible for some resistance to stopping smoking. Other factors include the fact that smoking is a highly idiosyncratic behavior that may change across the lifetime depending on whether the smoker is a novice smoker or an experienced one.

13. Stopping smoking is associated with weight gain, in that ex-smokers shift their food preferences and show altered patterns of energy utilization.

14. Withdrawal due to addiction is another factor making it difficult to give up smoking.

15. Smoking-prevention programs have developed to keep young adolescents from beginning to smoke. Many of these programs use a social influence approach and teach youngsters how to resist peer pressure to smoke. Others stress the need for adolescents to improve their life skills and self-image.

16. Social engineering approaches to control smoking have also been employed, the rationale being that second-hand smoke harms others in the smoker's environment.

KEY TERMS

alcoholism
behavioral inoculation
controlled drinking skills
craving
detoxification
extinction training
focused or rapid smoking
life-skills-training approach
lifestyle rebalancing

multiple-regulation model
nicotine fixed-effect theory
nicotine regulation theory
passive smoking, or second-hand smoke
placebo drinking
problem drinking
smoking prevention programs
social influence interventions

PART 3

STRESS AND COPING

7

STRESS AND THE DEVELOPMENT OF ILLNESS

WHAT IS STRESS?

Most of us have more first-hand experience with stress than we care to remember. **Stress** is being stopped by a traffic cop after running a red light. It is waiting to take an exam when you are not sure that you have prepared well enough or studied the right material. It is missing a bus on a rainy day full of important appointments.

Despite commonalities in experience, stress has proven to be an elusive concept to define and study. Some researchers have focused on the physiological changes produced by stress. Most of us know this experience intimately. Your body moves into a state of heightened arousal, your mouth goes dry, your heart beats faster, your hands may shake a little, and you perspire more heavily. Knowing what stress feels like does not, however, tell us what stress is and what causes it.

Other researchers have focused on stressful events—on what are called **stressors.** Such events might include noise, crowding, a bad relationship, a round of job interviews, or commuting to work. The study of stressors has helped to define some conditions that are more likely to produce stress than others, but a focus on stressful events cannot fully explain the experience of stress. Each one of the experiences mentioned above may be stressful to some people but not to others. If the "noise" is your radio playing the latest rock music, then it will probably not be stressful to you, although it may be to your neighbor. Whereas one person might find loss of a job highly stressful, another might see it as an opportunity to try a new field. Therefore, one person might see a job interview as threatening, while another might welcome it as a challenge. How one perceives a potential stressor, then, substantially determines whether or not one will experience stress.

Therefore most definitions of stress emphasize the relationship between the individual and the environment. Stress is the consequence of a person's appraisal processes: the assessment of whether personal resources are sufficient to meet the demands of the environment. Stress, then, is a function of the degree of **person-environment fit** (Lazarus & Folkman, 1984; Lazarus & Launier, 1978; Pervin, 1968). When a person's resources are more than adequate to deal with a difficult situation, he or she may feel little stress. When the individual perceives that his or her resources will probably be sufficient to deal with the event but only at the cost of great effort, he or she may feel a moderate amount of stress. When the individual perceives that his or her resources will probably not suffice to meet an environmental stressor, he or she may experience a great deal of stress. *Stress, then, is the process of appraising events (as harmful, threatening, or challenging), of assessing potential responses, and of responding to those events; responses may include physiological, cognitive, emotional, and behavioral changes.* To see how stress researchers have arrived at this definition of stress, it is useful to consider some of the early contributions to the field.

Early Contributions to the Study of Stress

One of the earliest contributions to stress research was Walter Cannon's (1932) description of the **fight-or-flight response.** Cannon proposed that when the organism perceives a threat, the body is rapidly aroused and motivated via the sympathetic nervous system and the endocrine system. As we saw in Chapter 2, this response to stress is marked by the secretion of catecholamines. Heart rate speeds up; blood pressure, blood sugar, and respiration increase; the circulation of blood to the skin is reduced; and circulation to the muscles is increased. This concerted physiological response mobilizes the organism to attack the threat or to flee; hence, it is called the fight-or-flight response.

Cannon reasoned that, on the one hand, the fight-or-flight response is adaptive because it enables the organism to respond quickly to threat. On the other hand, he concluded, stress can be harmful to the organism because it disrupts emotional and physiological functioning and can cause medical problems over time. In particular, when an organism is unable to either fight or flee and is exposed to prolonged stress, the state of physiological arousal may continue unabated, laying the groundwork for health problems. For example, early work with dogs and monkeys (Mahl, 1952) revealed that prolonged exposure to anxiety-producing conditions produced excessive secretion of hydrochloric acid, which can lead to the formation of ulcers.

In the 1940s, Wolf and Wolff (1947) continued this line of work with both animal and human subjects. In one classic study, they followed an ulcer patient, Tom, who had been fitted with a gastric fistula (an opening in the stomach to facilitate drainage of acid). The fistula enabled them to observe changes in the gastric mucosa and acid secretion arising from changes in emotion. When Tom was sad or withdrawn, the mucosa became pale and acid secretion was inhibited; when Tom was angry, on the other hand, the mucosa became engorged with blood and acid secretion increased. Intense anger or anxiety produced intense physiological reactions, including hemorrhaging, which encouraged the development of ulcers.

From this and other studies, Wolf and Wolff concluded that people develop distinct physiological responses that will manifest themselves across a wide variety of stressful events. Because this physiological pattern is overused, a particular disorder will eventually result. They hypothesized that there may be individual, inherited predispositions to respond to stress in particular ways, and that stress experiences initiate and maintain these responses. As a consequence, individuals exposed to the same source of stress may develop different disorders. One person may develop an ulcer, while another may develop high blood pressure.

To conclude, then, early stress research revealed conclusively that stimuli that threaten an organism produce physiological arousal. Although this arousal is protective because it mobilizes the organism to confront or flee the threatening stimulus, it may also produce health problems when an individual is exposed to repeated or prolonged stress. Repeated stress produces general wear and tear on the system and may also cause a specific illness when stress is coupled with a preexistent bodily weakness, such as a genetic predisposition toward a particular disorder.

Selye's General Adaptation Syndrome

Perhaps the most important of the early contributions to the field of stress is Hans Selye's (1956, 1976) work on the general adaptation syndrome. Although Selye initially explored the effects of sex hormones on physiological functioning, he became interested in the stressful impact his interventions seemed to have. Accordingly, he exposed rats to a variety of prolonged stressors—such as extreme cold and fatigue—and observed their physiological responses. To his surprise, all stressors, regardless of type, produced essentially the same pattern of physiological responding. In particular, they all led to an enlarged adrenal cortex, shrinking of the thymus and lymph glands, and ulceration of the stomach and duodenum. Thus, whereas Cannon's work explored adrenomedullary responses to stress, specifically catecholamine secretion, Selye's work more closely explored adrenocortical responses to stress and the secretion of corticosteroids.

From these observations, Selye (1956) developed his concept of the **general adaptation syndrome.** He argued that when an organism confronts a stressor, it mobilizes itself for action. This mobilization effort is directed by the adrenal glands, which promote sympathetic nervous system activity. The response itself is _nonspecific_ with respect to the stressor: That is, regardless of the cause of the threat, the individual will respond with the same physiological pattern of reactions. Over time, with repeated or prolonged exposure to stress, there will be wear and tear on the system.

The general adaptation syndrome consists of three phases. In the first phase, alarm, the organism becomes mobilized to meet the threat. In the second stage, resistance, the organism makes efforts to cope with the threat, as through confrontation. The third stage, exhaustion, occurs if the organism fails to over-

FIGURE 7.1   This figure illustrates the three phases of Selye's (1974) general adaptation syndrome. Phase A is the alarm response, in which the body first reacts to a stressor. At this time, resistance is diminished. Phase B, the stage of resistance, occurs with continued exposure to a stressor. The bodily signs associated with an alarm reaction disappear and resistance rises above normal. Phase C is the stage of exhaustion that results from long-term exposure to the same stressor. At this point resistance may again fall to below normal.

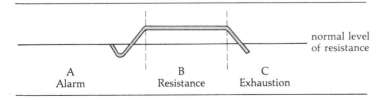

come the threat and depletes its physiological resources in the process of trying. These stages are pictured in Figure 7.1.

The substantial impact of Selye's model on the field of stress continues to be felt today. One reason is that it offers a general theory of reactions to a wide variety of stressors over time. As such, it provides a way of thinking about the interplay of physiological and environmental factors. Second, it posits a physiological mechanism for the stress-illness relationship. Specifically, Selye believed that repeated or prolonged exhaustion of resources, the third stage of the syndrome, was responsible for the physiological damage that laid the groundwork for disease. In fact, prolonged or repeated stress has been implicated in disorders such as cardiovascular disease, arthritis, hypertension, and immune-related deficiencies, as we shall see in Chapters 14 and 15.

Selye's model has also been criticized on several grounds. First, it assigns a very limited role to psychological factors, and researchers now believe that the psychological appraisal of events is important in the determination of stress (Lazarus & Folkman, 1984a). A second criticism concerns the assumption that responses to stress are uniform (Hobfoll, 1989). There is evidence that particular stressors produce distinct endocrinological responses (Appley & Trumbull, 1986; Mason, 1974, 1975). Moreover, how people respond to stress is substantially influenced by their personalities,

perceptions, and biological constitutions (Lazarus & Folkman, 1984b; Meichenbaum, 1977; Moos, 1984). A third criticism concerns the fact that Selye assessed stress as an outcome, such that stress was evident only when the general adaptation syndrome was in effect. In this respect, the model confounds the experience of stress with its outcomes (Hobfoll, 1989). Despite these limitations and reservations, Selye's model remains today a cornerstone of the field of stress.

Psychological Appraisal and the Experience of Stress

As just noted, an emphasis on psychological factors was substantially missing from early models of stress. This was in the large part due to the fact that early stress work was conducted on animals, with the goal of identifying the endocrinological concomitants of stress. However, as work on human populations progressed, the importance of psychological factors became evident.

Lazarus is a chief proponent of the psychological view of stress (Lazarus, 1968; Lazarus & Folkman, 1984a). He maintains that when individuals confront a new or changing environment, they engage in a process of **primary appraisal** to determine the meaning of the event (see Figure 7.2). Events may be perceived as positive, neutral, or negative in their consequences. Negative or potentially nega-

FIGURE 7.2   The Experience of Stress

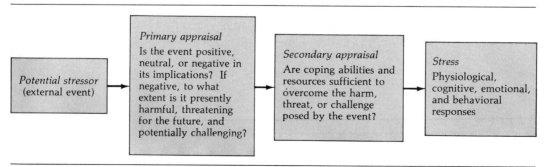

tive events are further appraised for their possible harm, threat, or challenge. "Harm" is the assessment of the amount of damage that has already been done by an event. Thus, for example, a man who has just been fired from his job may perceive present harm in terms of his own loss of self-esteem and his embarrassment as his co-workers silently watch him pack up his desk. "Threat" is the assessment of possible future damage that may be brought about by the event. Thus, the man who has lost his job may anticipate the problems that loss of income will create for him and his family in the future. Finally, events may be appraised in terms of their "challenge," the potential ultimately to overcome and profit from the event. For example, the man who has lost his job may perceive that a certain amount of harm and threat exists, but he may also see his unemployment as an opportunity to try something new.

The importance of primary appraisal in the experience of stress is illustrated in a classic study of stress by Speisman, Lazarus, Mordkoff, and Davidson (1964). College students viewed a gruesome film depicting unpleasant tribal initiation rites that included genital surgery. Before viewing the film, they were exposed to one of four experimental conditions. One group listened to an intellectual anthropological description of the rites. Another group heard a lecture that deemphasized the pain the initiates were experiencing and emphasized their excitement over the events. A third group heard a description that emphasized the pain and trauma that the initiates were undergoing. A fourth group heard no sound track. Measures of autonomic arousal (skin conductance, heart rate) and self-reports suggested that the first two groups experienced considerably less stress than did the group whose attention was focused on the trauma and pain. Thus, this study illustrated that stress was not only intrinsic to the gruesome film itself but also depended on the viewer's appraisal of it.

Once primary appraisals of potentially stressful events have occurred, secondary appraisal is initiated. **Secondary appraisal** is the assessment of one's coping abilities and resources and whether or not they will be sufficient to meet the harm, threat, and challenge of the event. Ultimately, the subjective experience of stress is a balance between primary and secondary appraisal. When harm and threat are high and coping ability is low, substantial stress is felt. When coping ability is high, stress may be minimal.

RESPONSES TO STRESS

Potential responses to stress are many and include physiological, cognitive, emotional, and behavioral consequences. Some of these responses can be thought of as involuntary reactions to stress, whereas others are voluntarily initiated in a conscious effort to cope.

Physiological Consequences   There are manifold physiological consequences of stress that involve the nervous system and the endocrine system. As noted in Chapter 2, a pattern of enhanced arousal is initiated in response to the appraisal of stress that involves sympathetic nervous system activity. Blood pressure, heart rate, pulse rate, skin conductivity, and respiration all increase. These responses are augmented by the sympathethic nervous system's impact on the endocrine system. It leads the adrenal medulla to produce epinephrine and norepinephrine, the catecholamines that travel throughout the body and augment physiological arousal.

Stress also exerts an effect on the body via the pituitary gland, which is located under and is controlled by the hypothalamus in the brain. The pitutary stimulates the adrenal cortex, which, in turn, releases corticosteroids, such as cortisol. The brain produces and secretes corticotropin-releasing factor, which, in turn, leads to the secretion of ACTH and beta-

Stressful events, like being stuck in traffic, produce agitation and physiological arousal.

lipotropin/beta-endorphin from the anterior pituitary (Meyerhoff, Mougey, & Kant, 1987). These peptides appear to be heavily responsible for activating the immune system in response to stress. Long-term physiologic stimulation of endogenous opioid release appears to inhibit the immune system (see Meyerhoff, Oleshansky, & Mougey, 1988). Stress also triggers the release of glucocorticoids, which in some respects act to protect the body against stress. As a late-developing response, they help to mute initial arousal in response to stress, thereby helping to restore homeostasis. Similarly, late-occurring parasympathetic nervous system activation helps to dampen the arousal initiated by sympathetic nervous system activity and secretion of the catecholamines.

While the above description represents the general patterns of nervous system and hormonal activities that occur in response to stress, physiological reactions to stress may show some degree of specificity as a function of the particular stressor and the individual's appraisal of it. For example, uncontrollable stressors may activate endogenous opioids more than controllable ones do (Natelson, Ottenweller, Pitman, & Tapp, 1988). This specificity of physiological reaction and its concomitant effects on the immune system will prove to be a useful direction for future research.

Cognitive Responses   Cognitive responses to stress include outcomes of the appraisal process such as specific beliefs about the harm or threat of an event and about its causes or controllability. Cognitive responses also include involuntary stress responses such as distractability and inability to concentrate; performance disruptions on cognitive tasks (e.g., Cohen, 1980; Zajonc, 1965); and intrusive, repetitive, or morbid thoughts (Horowitz, 1975). Cognitive responses are also involved in the initiation of coping activities, as we will see in the next chapter.

Emotional and Behavioral Responses   Potential emotional reactions to stressful events range widely; they include fear, anxiety, excitement, embarrassment, anger, depression, and even stoicism or denial. Potential behavioral responses are virtually limitless, depending on the nature of the stressful event. Confrontative action against the stressor ("fight") and withdrawal from the threatening event ("flight") constitute two general categories of behavioral responses. We will examine others in the course of our discussion.

The Measurement of Stress   Given that stress can produce various responses, what is the best way to measure it? Researchers have used a wide variety of indicators of stress. These include self-reports of perceived stress, life change, and emotional distress; behavioral measures, such as task performance under stress; physiological measures of arousal, such as skin conductivity, heart rate, and blood pressure; and biochemical markers, (or indicators), especially blood levels and urinary levels of 17-hydroxycorticosteroids (especially cortisol) and catecholamines (Baum, Grunberg, & Singer, 1982; Dimsdale, Young, Moore, & Strauss, 1987). In each case, these measures have proven to be useful indicators.

However, each type of measurement has its own associated problems. For example, catecholamine secretion is enhanced by a variety of factors other than stress. Both biochemical and psychophysiological techniques of measurement can be expensive and require equipment that may itself influence the stressful experience. Self-report measures are subject to a variety of biases, since individuals may want to present themselves in as desirable light as possible. Behavioral measures are subject to multiple interpretations. For example, performance declines can be due to declining motivation, fatigue, or cognitive strain, among other factors. Consequently, stress researchers have called for the use of multiple measures (Baum et al., 1982). With several measures, the possibility of obtaining a good model of the stress experience is increased.

To summarize, then, events are stressful to the extent that they are perceived as stressful. Responses to stress are manifold and include physiological changes, cognitive reactions, emotional reactions, and behavioral responses. These stress responses may create the possibility of a variety of **stress markers** that can be measured in an effort to assess directly the degree of stress a person experiences.

WHAT MAKES EVENTS STRESSFUL?

Dimensions of Stressful Events

As we have just noted, events themselves are not inherently stressful. Rather, whether or not they are stressful depends on how they are appraised by an individual. What are some

characteristics of potential stressors that make them more likely to be appraised as stressful?

Negative events are more likely to produce stress than are positive events. A wide variety of events, both positive and negative, have the potential to be stressful because they present people with extra work or special problems that may tax or exceed their resources. Shopping for Christmas, planning a party, coping with an unexpected job promotion, or getting married are all positive events that draw off substantial time and energy. Nonetheless, these positive experiences are less likely to be reported as stressful than are undesirable events such as getting a traffic ticket, trying to find a job, coping with a death in the family, or getting divorced.

Negative events show a stronger relationship to both psychological distress and physical symptoms than do positive ones (e.g., McFarland, Norman, Streiner, Roy, & Scott, 1980; Myers, Lindenthal, & Pepper, 1972; Sarason, Johnson, & Siegel, 1978; Stokols, Ohlig, & Resnick, 1978; Vinokur & Selzer, 1975). This may be because only stressful events that have negative implications for the self-concept produce potential or actual loss of self-esteem or erosion of a sense of mastery or identity (Thoits, 1986). There is one exception to this pattern. Among people who hold negative views of themselves, positive life events appear to have a detrimental effect on health, whereas for those with high self-esteem, positive life events are linked to better health (Brown & McGill, 1989).

Uncontrollable or unpredictable events are more stressful than controllable or predictable ones. Negative events like noise, crowding, or discomfort might seem to be inherently stressful, but stress research consistently demonstrates that uncontrollable events are perceived as more stressful than controllable ones. When people feel they can predict, modify, or terminate an aversive event or feel they have access to someone who can influence it, they experience it as less stressful, even if they actually do nothing about it (e.g., Frankenhaeuser, 1975; Glass & Singer, 1972; Suls & Mullen, 1981; Thompson, 1981). For example, unpredictable bursts of noise are experienced as more stressful than are predictable ones (Glass & Singer, 1972). Under some circumstances, feelings of control may augment stress, at least initially. One study found that being able to anticipate stressful events and feeling that one had control over them initially heightened perceived stress but also increased the ability to adjust to the stressful event (Vinokur & Caplan, 1986).

Feelings of control not only mute the subjective experience of stress but also influence biochemical reactivity to it. Believing that one can control stressors such as noise level (Lundberg & Frankenhaeuser, 1976) or crowding (Singer, Lundberg, & Frankenhaeuser, 1978) is associated with lower catecholamine levels than is believing that one has no control over it. Feelings of control appear to influence the endogenous opioid systems. People under stress who perceive that they cannot exercise control over the stressful events have increased the flow of endogenous opioids. Those who perceive that they will be efficacious in overcoming the stress do not show stress-activated release of endogenous opioids (Bandura, Cioffi, Taylor, & Brouillard, 1988).

Ambiguous events are often perceived as more stressful than clear-cut events. When a potential stressor is ambiguous, a person has no opportunity to take action. He or she must instead devote energy to trying to understand the stressor, which can be a time-consuming, resource-sapping task. Clear-cut stressors, on the other hand, let the person get on with the job of finding solutions and do not leave him or her stuck at the problem-definition stage. The ability to take confrontative action is usually associated with less distress and better coping (Billings & Moos, 1984; Gal & Lazarus, 1975; Kaloupek & Stoupakis, 1985).

The importance of clarity in coping with stress is particularly well illustrated in the oc-

cupational stress literature, as we will shortly see. A common problem reported by workers is role ambiguity: a feeling of unclarity or ambiguity about the requirements of one's role, in this case the work role. Role ambiguity can result from having no clear task guidelines, no clear standards of performance, or contradictory guidelines or standards, as when one supervisor directs an employee to do one thing while another supervisor demands another. Role ambiguity is uniformly reported as one of the major factors contributing to work-related stress (Cooper & Marshall, 1976).

Overloaded people are more stressed than people with fewer tasks to perform (e.g., Cohen, 1978; Cohen & Williamson, 1988). People who simply have too many tasks in their lives report higher levels of stress than those who have fewer tasks. Again, research on occupational stress is informative. One of the main sources of work-related stress that people experience is job overload, the perception that one is responsible for doing too much in too short a period of time.

To summarize, then, events that are negative, uncontrollable, ambiguous, or overwhelming are more likely to be perceived as stressful than events that are positive, controllable, clear-cut, or manageable.

Can People Adapt to Stress?

If a stressful event becomes a permanent or chronic part of their environment, will people eventually habituate to it or will they develop **chronic strain?** Will it no longer cause them distress, drain psychological resources, or lead to symptoms of illness? The answer to this question is equivocal and seems to depend on the type of stressor, the subjective experience of stress, and which indicator of stress is considered.

Animal models of stress suggest evidence for both habituation and chronic stress. For example, rats exposed to relatively low-level stressors tend to show initial physiological re-

Events like crowding are experienced as stressful only to the extent that they are appraised that way. Some situations of crowding make people feel happy, whereas others are experienced as aversive.

sponsiveness followed by habituation. When the stimuli employed to induce stress are intense, however, the animal may show no habituation at all (Pitman, Ottenweller, & Natelson, 1988; Thompson & Glanzman, 1976; Thompson & Spencer, 1966). Intensity of a stressor also seems to predict how quickly chronic stress will develop, as measured by basal plasma corticosteroids. Intense stressors produce chronic strain more quickly. One may see both habituation and signs of chronic stress in the same organism. For example, one study with rats found that intensely stressed rats showed some habituation of their corticosteroid response, but at the same time, their responses were elevated above baseline levels (Pitman et al., 1988).

Most people may be able to adapt to moderate or predictable stressors. At first, any novel, threatening situation can produce stress, but such reactions often subside over time (Frankenhaeuser, 1975; Stokols, Novaco, Stokols, & Campbell, 1978). Even monkeys exposed to a shock-avoidance task showed few signs of stress after the first few sessions (Mason, Brady, & Tolliver, 1968). However, some indicators of stress suggest more adaptation than others. Whereas corticosteroid reactions

to stressful events often subside over time, catecholamine reactions may not (Rose, 1980). The meaning of these differences is not yet clear.

Moreover, evidence on adaptation to particular stressors is also equivocal. One study of unemployed factory workers (Kasl & Cobb, 1970) found that short-term unemployment produced marked physiological and psychological signs of stress; over time, however, as unemployment continued, these responses declined, especially physiological signs of stress. These results suggest that the stress response to unemployment may be short-term, or acute, rather than long-term, or chronic. However, other research (e.g., Fleming, Baum, Reddy, & Gatchel, 1984) found no reduction in stress among long-term unemployed workers.

Research on the effects of environmental noise and crowding (Cohen, Glass, & Phillip, 1978) indicates few or no long-term adverse health or psychological effects, suggesting that most people simply adapt to these chronic stressors. For example, laboratory studies that expose people to noise while they are trying to complete some task find that people may simply change their task strategies or attentional focus to adapt to the noise experience. As a consequence, task performance may suffer little or not at all (Glass & Singer, 1972). However, particularly vulnerable populations, especially children, the elderly, and poor people, do seem to be adversely affected by these stressors (Cohen et al., 1978); they may show signs of helplessness and difficulty in performing tasks. One possible reason is that these groups already experience little control over their environments and may accordingly already be exposed to fairly high levels of stress; the addition of an environmental stressor like noise or crowding may push their resources to the limit, so that psychological and physical stress results.

Thus, the answer to the question of whether people can adapt to chronic stress might best be summarized as follows: People (and animals) show signs of both long-term strain and habituation to chronically stressful events. Most people can adapt moderately well to stressful events; however, it may be difficult or impossible for them to adapt to highly stressful events, and already-stressed populations may be unable to adapt to even moderate stressors. Box 7.1 examines this issue as it affects children.

Must a Stressor Be Ongoing to Be Stressful?

Does the stress response occur only while a stressful event is happening, or can stress result in anticipation of or as an aftereffect of exposure to a stressor? One of the wonders and curses of human beings' symbolic capacities is their ability to conceptualize things before they materialize. We owe our abilities to plan, invent, and reason abstractly to this skill, but we also get from it our ability to worry. Unlike lower animals, human beings do not have to be exposed to a stressor to suffer stress. The anticipation of a stressor can be at least as

stressful as its actual occurrence and often more so. Consider the strain of anticipating a confrontation with a boyfriend or girlfriend or worrying about a test that will occur the next day. Sleepless nights and days of distracting anxiety testify to the ability of the human being's capacity for anticipatory distress.

Adverse **aftereffects of stress,** such as decreases in performance and attention span, are also well documented. In fact, one of the reasons that stress presents both a health hazard and a challenge to the health psychology researcher is that the effects of stress often persist long after the stressful event itself is no longer present. The so-called aftereffects of stress can be even more devastating than the impact of stress while it is going on. Aftereffects of stress have been observed in response to a wide range of stressors, including noise, high task load, electric shock, bureaucratic stress, crowding, and laboratory-induced stress (Cohen, 1980).

In a series of studies, Glass and Singer (1972) put subjects to work on a simple task and also exposed them to an uncontrollable, unpredictable stressor in the form of random, intermittent bursts of noise over a 25-minute period. After the noise period was over, subjects were given additional tasks to perform, including solvable and unsolvable puzzles and a proofreading task. Subjects who had been exposed to the noise consistently performed more poorly on these tasks. These results have been confirmed by other investigators (Cohen et al., 1978).

The fact that stressful events produce aftereffects should not be surprising. As we saw in Selye's research on the general adaptation syndrome, exposure to a stressor may be cumulative, so that reserves may be drained and resistance may break down when a person has to cope with a stressful event over a long or intermittent period of time. Although many stressors produce aftereffects, unpredictable and uncontrollable stressful events are more

Box 7.1
Are Children Vulnerable to Noise?

Although studies of noise generally suggest few long-term negative effects, children do appear to be vulnerable to the stress of noise. Cohen, Glass, and Singer (1973) tested children living in apartment buildings built on bridges that spanned a busy expressway. Children who lived in the noisier apartments showed greater difficulty with auditory discrimination tasks and in reading than did children who lived in quieter apartments. These effects were stronger, the longer the children had lived there. A study of railroad noise found that children taught in classrooms on the side of an elementary school facing the railroad tracks read less well than children on the quieter side of the building (Bronzaft & McCarthy, 1975). A study of children exposed to aircraft noise (Cohen, Evans, Krantz, & Stokols, 1980) found that children who lived and attended school in the air corridor performed less well on both simple and difficult problem-solving tasks than did children not living or attending school in the air corridor. Moreover, children exposed to the aircraft noise were more likely to give up on difficult tasks than were children who lived in the quiet neighborhoods. Clearly, then, children can experience a number of problems as a consequence of sustained exposure to noise, including difficulty in learning, poor task performance, and giving up on tasks. What are some reasons for these effects?

Most people cope with noise by altering their attentional focus—that is, by tuning out extraneous noise and attempting to focus only on relevant information. However, children raised in noisy environments who attempt to use this attentional strategy may have difficulty distinguishing between appropriate and inappropriate cues. Because they are young, they may not be able to distinguish between speech-relevant and speech-irrelevant sounds as well as adults can. They may consequently lose potentially important verbal experience that would help them develop these skills. One reason that they may end up having more difficulty with verbal skills and reading, then, may be because they tune out verbal elements in their environment.

The fact that children exposed to long-term stressors give up on tasks more quickly than children not so exposed is particularly chilling. It suggests that these children may have learned to be helpless; they may have experienced repeated unsuccessful efforts to master tasks or make themselves understood. Over time, they may come to perceive a lack of relationship between their efforts and their outcomes; as a result, they experience helplessness. Consequently, even when they are placed in new environments where control is possible, they may not recognize this possibility and still give up more quickly (Cohen et al., 1980).

A reason that children may be more vulnerable than adults to the learned helplessness effects of noise is that children already experience a relatively lower level of control in their lives than adults do. It is possible that the additional lack of control that comes from a long-term stressor like noise may be the decisive factor that impairs their ability to perform well on tasks requiring concentration and the motivation to persist.

stressful than predictable or controllable ones; accordingly, they are particularly likely to produce deleterious aftereffects (Glass & Singer, 1972).

Both laboratory and field studies have found that when stressors are controllable or predictable, the aftereffects of stress are substantially reduced and may be eliminated altogether. For example, if subjects believe that they can terminate the aversive event, this belief in control can undermine the negative aftereffects of stress even if control is never exerted. Likewise, people who believe that they have access to someone who can reduce the stress obtain the same beneficial effects.

There is some evidence that stressors can produce deleterious aftereffects on social behavior as well as on cognitive tasks. Several studies have found that when subjects are exposed to unavoidable stressful events such as noise or crowding, they are less likely to help someone in distress when the stressor is over. For example, in one study (Cohen & Spacapan, 1978, experiment 2), subjects shopped in a shopping center that was either crowded or uncrowded and were required to purchase a large or a small number of items in a short period of time. Later, all subjects encountered a woman who pretended to have lost a contact lens and who requested help finding it. Subjects who had performed the high-load task or who were more crowded were less likely to help the woman than were subjects who performed their task under low-load or uncrowded conditions.

In summary, the effects of stress can persist long after the stressor has ended. Negative aftereffects of stress have been found on a variety of cognitive and social tasks. These effects appear to be most problematic when the stressor is uncontrollable or unpredictable. Stress aftereffects can be reduced or eliminated if people feel they can exert some control over the stressful event. A dramatic example of the aftereffects of stress appears in Box 7.2.

THEORIES OF STRESS: WHY IS STRESS STRESSFUL?

Several theories have been offered to explain why events perceived as stressful have negative effects on physiological, cognitive, emotional, and behavioral functioning. Each posits a different central process. One position emphasizes the centrality of the *cognitive disruption* in producing negative consequences of stress; another theory maintains that *physiological arousal* is central to the negative effects of stress; a third gives *emotional responses* to stress central status; and a fourth maintains that the experience of *helplessness* is central to stress. None of these theories tries to explain all that is known about stress, so none is a sufficient explanation. However, each provides a conceptual framework that may clarify the stress experience and ultimately point to interventions to reduce stress.

Theories of Cognitive Costs

One set of explanations maintains that stress taxes perceptual and cognitive resources by drawing off attention, overtaxing cognitive capabilities, or depleting cognitive resources for other tasks. This approach, called the **cognitive-costs hypothesis** (Glass & Singer, 1972), maintains that any stressful event requires an individual to expend cognitive resources in order to cope. One must understand what the stressful event is, how bad it is going to be, whether it will be ongoing, and the like. These efforts draw resources away from other aspects of life. Thus, there is less time and energy to focus on other tasks or potential problems, leading to arousal, performance decrements, and other symptoms of stress.

Similarly, Cohen (1978) argued that attention is overloaded during periods of stress because individuals must continually monitor the environment for threatening stimuli. Attention narrows and fatigue results, reducing

Box 7.2
Post-Traumatic Stress Disorder

Following the Vietnam War, a number of unnerving events were reported in the media regarding men who had been in Vietnam and who as civilians apparently relived some of the experiences they had undergone during battle. In one especially distressing case, a man took charge of a section of a shopping mall, believing that it was under attack by the North Vietnamese, and actually shot and wounded several policemen before he was shot in an effort to subdue him.

When a person has been the victim of a highly stressful event, symptoms of the stress experience may persist long after the event is over. In this context, we examined the aftereffects of stress, which can include physiological arousal, distractability, and other negative side effects that last for hours after a stressful event has occurred. In the case of major traumas, these stressful aftereffects may go on intermittently for months or years. Such long-term reactions have been especially documented in the wake of violent wars, such as occurred in Korea and Vietnam in the last few decades. The term **post-traumatic stress disorder (PTSD)** has been developed to explain these effects.

The person suffering from PTSD has typically undergone a stressor of extreme magnitude. One of the reactions to this stressful event is a numbing in responsiveness, such as diminished interest in activities,

detachment from friends, or constriction in emotions. In addition, the person often relives aspects of the trauma. Usually, those suffering from post-traumatic stress disorder also experience hyperalertness, sleep disturbances, guilt, impaired memory or concentration, avoidance of the experience, and intensification of adverse symptoms associated with other stressful events (American Psychiatric Association, 1980). Any major stressor can produce PTSD, although war experiences seem to evoke it most fully (Wilson, Smith, & Johnson, 1985).

Who is most likely to develop post-traumatic stress disorder? In several studies, researchers have found that men who had more combat experience, who observed atrocities, and who actually participated in atrocities were most likely to experience PTSD (Breslau & Davis, 1987; Laufer, Gallops, & Frey-Wouters, 1984; Wilson, Smith, & Johnson, 1985). Those who develop the symptoms of PTSD may also be more vulnerable generally to emotional disorder, inasmuch as they sometimes suffer from other psychological problems as well (Keane, 1988). Finally, those with an external sense of control who have little social support and use primarily emotion-focused coping show more symptoms of PTSD; with increases in social support and a shift toward problem-focused coping, symptoms of PTSD decline (Solomon, Mikulincer, & Avitzur, 1988)

the reserve of attention for other tasks. For example, when people must perform a task after they have already been exposed to a stressor like noise, they perform less well on tasks demanding close attention than on those calling for relatively little attention.

Supporting the cognitive-costs analysis is

the fact that unpredictable or uncontrollable events are more stressful than predictable or controllable ones. Presumably, less cognitive work is required when a stressor is predictable or controllable than when it is not, because when a predictable stressor is present, a person does not have to be constantly vigilant to the possibility of threat. However, this position does not resolve the question of why stress creates adverse aftereffects.

Arousal and Stress

Another viewpoint maintains that the effects of stress follow from physiological arousal (see Cohen, 1978). High levels of arousal are known to narrow and focus attention. On simple tasks, moderate arousal can improve performance because it concentrates attention on task demands. On complex tasks, however, arousal can interfere with performance because important cues may escape attention. Thus, as arousal increases with stress, task performance should improve or decline depending on the complexity of the task.

Unfortunately, definitive tests of this idea are hard to conduct because arousal is so hard to measure. Although there are a number of physiological measures of arousal such as heart rate, respiration rate, and skin conductivity, they do not relate to each other very well and may not be reliable indicators of arousal.

The arousal interpretation may explain some of the cognitive consequences of stress and its aftereffects on performance. It also points to the physiological processes through which stress may erode health. However, it is hard to see why arousal per se would necessarily produce the psychological distress that can be associated with stress. Thus, the arousal position contributes to the biopsychosocial understanding of stress and illness, but it also does not explain the stress experience in its entirety.

Theories of Emotional Functioning

Another approach to understanding the effects of stress gives emotional responses central status. Stress can produce frustration, which is known to cause annoyance and irritation. These mood changes may, in turn, lead to reduced interest in and performance on subsequent tasks. Frustration can also produce aggression (Dollard & Miller, 1950), which may explain why people under stress help others less and are less likely to engage in other positive social behaviors (Cohen, 1980).

However, the explanation based on emotional functioning may apply only to certain kinds of stress. First, not all stress produces a negative mood, yet reduced motivation and performance may still be observed. Second, stress does not always produce annoyance. It can also produce fear, depression, and other moods that need not lower motivation or reduce performance. Thus, as in the case of the explanation based on physiological arousal, this is only a partial explanation of the effects of stress.

Helplessness and Stress

Another theory of the effects of stress maintains that stress produces feelings of helplessness. The centrality of **helplessness** to stress has already been noted. The definition of stress offered at the beginning of this chapter emphasized that stress results when the demands of the environment exceed the individual's resources. Likewise, the fact that uncontrollable events produce more stress than controllable ones clearly implicates control or loss of it in the experience of stress.

Seligman's Theory of Learned Helplessness. The helplessness model has been most clearly delineated by Martin Seligman (1975) in his theory of **learned helplessness;** hence it is useful to begin by detailing that theory. Everyone has had the experience of trying to bring about some event and not succeeding. One calls up an acquaintance for a date and is turned down, or one tries to explain an idea to a teacher and is misunderstood. For people under chronic stress, these kinds of experiences can occur over and over again, at least in certain areas of their lives. The crux of learned helplessness is that when one's efforts at control repeatedly come to naught, one not only ceases to strive for that particular outcome (helplessness) but also may fail to exert control in some new situation in which control is possible. In other words, people can learn to be helpless by experiencing repeated instances of lack of control. For example, in one experiment (Hiroto & Seligman, 1975), students were assigned to one of three initial training groups. One group heard a loud noise, which they could terminate by pressing a button; the second group heard a loud noise, but they had no control over its termination; the third group experienced no noise. In the second session of the experiment, _all_ subjects were exposed to noise that, unknown to them, could be terminated by moving a shuttle in front of them. Although the "controllable-noise" and the "no-noise" groups quickly learned this fact, subjects in the initial uncontrollable-noise condition failed to discover it and instead listened passively to the noise. They had "learned," erroneously, that the noise situation was something they could not control.

Seligman and his colleagues (e.g., Maier & Seligman, 1976) maintained that learned helplessness creates three deficits. The first is _motivational_, in that the helpless person makes no effort to take the steps necessary to change the outcome. The second is _cognitive_, in that helpless people fail to learn new responses that could help them avoid the aversive outcomes. The third is _emotional_, in that learned helplessness can produce mild or severe depression.

Causal attributions are important determinants of how chronic and pervasive feelings of helplessness will be (Abramson, Garber, & Seligman, 1980). Three attributional dimensions are important in producing helplessness. The first dimension is _internality-externality_. One can attribute helplessness externally ("No one could do anything about this problem") or internally ("I couldn't do anything about this problem"). Internal attributions may produce greater helplessness. For example, a job loss due to layoffs might produce fewer feelings of helplessness than a job loss due to personal incompetence. The second dimension is _stability_. Stable attributions (e.g., "There's just no market for my kind of skills") will produce more helplessness than unstable ones ("This just isn't the job for me"). The third dimension is _globality_, the extent to which the helplessness is confined to one sphere of life or extends to many spheres of life. Global attributions (e.g., "I'm just an incompetent person") may produce more pervasive helplessness than nonglobal ones (e.g., "I'm not very talented in this line of work"). By implication, then, internal, stable, and global perceived causes of helplessness produce the most pervasive adverse emotional, motivational, cognitive, and behavioral consequences.

How might the learned helplessness model fit some common situations of stress? Consider, for example, trying to cope with a romantic relationship in which you are continually disappointed. Every time you think a problem is solved, it arises again or a new one takes its place. Eventually, you will lose interest in the relationship, think about it less, and make fewer efforts to keep it afloat. With repeated unsuccessful efforts, you may conclude that internal, stable, global factors are responsible. Consequently, you may give up trying in the expectation that future relationships will be as disappointing as those in the past. Jaded lovers who flee from all but the most casual romantic encounter fit this pattern well. Or, consider trying to do well in a new course area (such as chemistry), where a good grade is continually elusive. After a few efforts to write different kinds of papers or study the material in a different way, you may decide to write the course off altogether. You may study little for the final and swear off chemistry courses for the future, in the belief that your talents clearly lie elsewhere. Box 7.3 describes a research project in college dormitories that involves learned helplessness.

Box 7.3
Dormitory Crowding: An Example of Learned Helplessness

Many students have had the experience of arriving at college and finding that the college admitted too many students for the academic year. Rooms designed as singles suddenly become doubles, doubles become triples, and dormitory television rooms are turned into makeshift homes for the overflow. Clearly, these kinds of experiences are stressful, but do they have any impact beyond the trivial annoyances they may produce? Research by Baum and his associates suggests that they do (Baum, Aiello, & Calesnick, 1978; Baum & Valins, 1977).

Baum and Valins studied residents of college dormitories who lived in one of two situations. One group of students lived on long corridors and therefore had prolonged and repeated encounters with the large number of other individuals on their floor. The second group of students lived in either short corridors or suites and had relatively few forced encounters with other individuals. Subjects in these two groups were brought into the laboratory and exposed to a variety of interpersonal and task situations.

In a series of studies, Baum and Valins found that students who lived on the long corridors showed behavior that could be interpreted as helplessness. They initiated fewer conversations with a stranger, spent less time looking at the stranger, and sat farther away from him or her. They were less able to reach a group consensus after a discussion, were more likely to give up in a competitive game situation, and were less likely to assert themselves by asking questions in an ambiguous situation. Responses to questionnaire items confirmed that the students felt helpless.

Baum and Valins argued that, because of repeated uncontrollable personal interactions with others, the students had learned to be helpless. The level of stress they experienced in their natural living situation led them to shy away from interpersonal contact with strangers. It also made them less likely to act assertively in ambiguous situations, perhaps because they had learned that they had little control over their environment. Results like these make it clear how stress produced by something as simple as a living situation can affect many other aspects of life.

How does the helplessness model explain these stressful experiences? Specifically, the helplessness phase, in which one's efforts repeatedly come to naught, is analogous to ongoing stress. Learned helplessness, when the individual gives up responding in both the old and new environments, is analogous to exhaustion: Resources are depleted, and activity is minimal. The helplessness perspective on stress can also explain the aftereffects of stress—the fact that performance on many other tasks declines after prolonged exposure to stress. These aftereffects can be explained as learned helplessness.

The attributional analysis of learned helplessness helps explain why uncontrollable events are more stressful than controllable ones. If a person attributes her lack of impact to stable, unmodifiable factors, she will believe that no personal effort can remedy the situation. Accordingly, she will perceive her resources to be inadequate to meet stressful circumstances, a condition that will produce a greater subjective feeling of stress. The attribution model is also useful for understanding the beneficial effects of control-enhancing interventions in times of stress. That is, as noted earlier, stress effects are less pronounced when individuals are given some response that enables them to control or believe they can control the stressor (e.g., Glass & Singer, 1972; Thompson, 1981). The helplessness argument would maintain that when a person is encouraged to feel that he has control over a stressful event, he will change his attributions for the cause of the stress. His belief that he can bring about desired outcomes is restored; therefore, the cognitive, motivational, and behavioral deficits associated with helplessness should be reversed.

Considerable support for the attributional model of learned helplessness, particularly its ability to explain depression, has emerged (Peterson & Seligman, 1984). However, the model as applied to the experience of stress is not without criticisms. Research does not uniformly support its predictions (Brewin, 1985; Cochran & Hammen, 1985), and it has also been applied inappropriately to stressful situations that do not meet the conditions thought to evoke learned helplessness (Abramson, Metalsky, & Alloy, 1988; Peterson, 1982). Nonetheless, it provides an intriguing perspective on stress that may be helpful for guiding future research and interventions.

To summarize, no one theory can account for all the negative consequences of stress. Each may explain part of the stress response or reactions to particular kinds of stressors. Other theories of stress also exist, and no doubt new ones will be developed. The usefulness of these theoretical approaches lies in their ability to highlight certain aspects of the stress response, to suggest new ways of looking at stress and its effects, and to suggest ways of managing it, a point we will cover in Chapter 8. Box 7.4 examines stress in relation to man-made disasters.

STRESS AND ILLNESS

Having defined stress, examined some of its manifestations, and probed its dimensions, we now consider directly the question: Does stress cause illness? There is no simple answer. The stress-illness relationship can be very complex, since it is influenced by a number of preexisting and intervening factors.

Models of the Relationship Between Stress and Illness

The Direct Route   Stress may have a direct route to illness. Stress can produce physiological and psychological changes conducive to the development of illness; precursors (forewarnings) of illness such as fatigue and achiness then develop, which, if untreated, can lead to illness. However, not everyone exposed to the same source of stress will develop an illness. This is because individual or environmental factors can intervene to disrupt the path between stress and illness. Some people may take action against the stressor early on, before any psychological and physiological damage is done. For example, a student may decide to put the anxiety of a forthcoming exam out of her mind, or a dissatisfied worker may quit his job. Some people may intervene when they experience early symptoms. Thus, one person who finds herself rundown may be sure to eat well, exercise, and get extra sleep and so prevent an actual illness, whereas another person may ignore the same symptoms, attending to them only when he has actually become ill. It is clear that the direct route from stress to illness is subject to considerable variability as people react differently to the same stressors and the same symptoms.

The Personality Route   A second approach to understanding the process by which stress affects illness argues that certain people are predisposed by virtue of their personalities to

Box 7.4
Stress and Man-Made Disasters

Increasingly, stress researchers are turning their attention to how people cope with man-made disasters such as the threats posed by nuclear contamination or toxic wastes. Although in many ways reactions to man-made disasters are similar to reactions to natural disasters such as fire, tornado, or flood, there are important differences. Natural catastrophes are usually time-limited, and they dissipate over time. Also, governments have programs ready to move in almost immediately to ameliorate the effects of natural disasters. In contrast, the threat posed by toxic waste dumps or leaks from nuclear power plants may be ongoing, and solutions for them have yet to be developed.

In a study of the Love Canal, a toxic waste dump adjacent to a neighborhood in the Niagara Falls area, researchers report that the psychological damage from this disaster may ultimately turn out to rival or even exceed the physical damage. Like other man-made disasters, such as the nuclear accident at Three Mile Island, the problems at Love Canal have forced residents to cope with several stressors simultaneously. First, they must face the possibility of serious, life-threatening illness. Residents have highlighted cases of miscarriage, stillbirth, birth defects, respiratory problems, urinary problems, and cancer in an effort to convince scientists and government officials that the threat to their health is real. Second, residents do not yet know the extent of damage. Unlike flood victims who can quickly see the extent of their loss, Love Canal residents may spend most of their lives wondering what effects the poisons will have on their systems and worrying about whether these poisons will have effects on their children and grandchildren for generations to come. Third, the residents must cope with their feelings of helplessness and betrayal because the government has done so little to help them. The result has been panic, deep distress, and hostility, resulting in mass demonstrations and the taking of government hostages in a vain effort to get action.

Most of the former residents have suffered a variety of vague psychophysiological problems including depression, irritability, dizziness, nausea, weakness, fatigue, insomnia, and numbness in the extremities. In addition to these symptoms, family strain is prevalent. More than 40% of the couples evacuated from the area have separated or divorced in the 2 years after their departure. Typically, the husband wanted to remain in the neighborhood and salvage what he could of the family's home and possessions, whereas the wife chose to leave for the sake of the children and their health.

Although the Niagara Falls Community Health Center put together a program on coping with stress and publicized available counseling programs, few Love Canal residents used the opportunity. In trying to explain the reasons for this, researchers have suggested two possibilities. First, within this working-class population, counseling may still be viewed as a stigma, an option to be used only by those who are mentally disturbed and not by normal people coping with a "real" stress. Second, the practice of stress management may be perceived as indicating that the problem is "all in one's head" rather than objectively "out there" in the dump site itself. Instead of using available mental health services, residents have been getting psychological aid through self-help—that is, talking with one another informally or through organized groups.

The type of stress observed at Love Canal raises an unnerving specter for stress researchers in the future. There are hundreds of chemical dump sites around the country, physical and psychological disasters waiting to be discovered. As researchers increasingly uncover other toxic substances (such as, for example, those posed by herbicides and nuclear accidents), this kind of stress—the stress of not knowing what the damage is and not being able to find ways of overcoming it because of government indecision—will undoubtedly increase.

(Holden, 1980)

experience stress and distress in their lives, which, in turn, affects their rates of illness. This line of research has focused on a variable called **negative affectivity** (Watson & Clark, 1984), a pervasive negative mood marked by anxiety, depression, and hostility. According to this approach, specific events are less important in the psychological experiences of stress and distress than the general predisposition to view things negatively. Individuals high in negative affectivity express distress, discomfort, and dissatisfaction across a wide range of situations (Watson & Clark, 1984). Negative affectivity has been related to alcoholism (Beck, 1986; Frances, Franklin, & Flavin, 1986), depression (Francis, Fyer, & Clarkin, 1986), and suicidal behavior (Cross & Hirschfeld, 1986; Paykel & Dienelt, 1971).

To examine the role of negative affectivity in the experience of stress, Watson and Pennebaker (1989) had subjects complete a battery of tests assessing negative affectivity. They found that negative affectivity was substantially correlated with self-reported stress; however, negative affectivity was not related to health complaints, biological dysfunction and pathology, fitness and lifestyle variables, health-related visits for illness, or overall mortality. Although people with high degrees of negative affectivity expressed a large number of health complaints and symptoms of stress, they did not appear to be more likely to visit physicians or to have documented signs of illness. The authors concluded that negative affectivity should be treated largely as a nuisance variable that complicates assessments of the stress-illness relationship, rather than as a psychological factor that increases the likelihood of illness.

Other research, however, suggests that this conclusion may need to be tempered. In a review of literature relating personality factors to five diseases—asthma, arthritis, ulcers, headaches, and coronary artery disease—Friedman and Booth-Kewley (1987) found weak but consistent evidence of a relationship between these disorders and negative emotions. They tentatively suggested that negative affectivity involving depression, anger, hostility, and anxiety may constitute the basis of a generic "disease-prone" personality that predisposes people to these disorders (e.g., Aneshensel, Frerichs, & Huba, 1984).

In related investigations, Seligman and his colleagues (Burns & Seligman, 1989; Peterson, Seligman, & Vaillant, 1988) found evidence for a **pessimistic explanatory style** that may relate to illness. Recall from our discussion of learned helplessness that explanations for stressful events that refer to internal, stable, global qualities seem to produce the greatest emotional, motivational, cognitive, and behavioral deficits. Seligman and his associates have argued that some people characteristically explain events with reference to these factors, and that doing so may lay the groundwork for poor health. In one study (Peterson et al., 1988), interviews completed by graduates of the Harvard University classes of 1942 to 1944 when they were 25 years old, were analyzed to see how the men habitually explained the negative events in their lives. Specifically, they were asked about difficult experiences they had encountered during World War II, such as combat situations, relations with superiors, and battles in which they were actively involved, and they were asked whether or not they felt they had dealt successfully or unsuccessfully with these wartime situations. Some of the men also talked about difficulties they were having getting established in careers and relationships. Their answers were then coded as reflecting an optimistic or pessimistic style.

An example of explaining a negative event in terms of a pessimistic explanatory style is provided by one man who died before age 55: "I cannot seem to decide firmly on a career....this may be an unwillingness to face reality." Another man, who also died before age 55, stated that he disliked work because he had "a fear of getting in a rut, doing the same thing day after day, year after year." In contrast, one of the healthy men referred to his army career as follows: "My career in the army has been checkered, but on the whole, characteristic of the army." Another referred to his effort to deal with a difficult situation. "I tried to bluff my way through a situation....I didn't know the facts, a situation common to all green junior officers when they are first put in charge of men." The differences between the two sets of responses is that the first two men referred to negative events in terms of their own stable qualities, with no apparent hope of escape. In contrast, the two healthy men also described negative experiences, but with reference to external factors ("That's the army") or by maintaining that a less-than-capable response was one that "any green junior officer" would have done. Those men who explained bad events by referring to their own internal, stable, global negative qualities had significantly poorer health between ages 45 through 60, some 20 to 35 years later. This was true, even when physical and mental health at age 25 were taken into account. Thus, pessimism in early adulthood seems to be a risk factor for poor health in middle and late adulthood.

The possibility of direct links among personality, distress, and illness are important for several reasons. First, they suggest a propensity for certain individuals to be distress-prone, with a resulting toll on their physical health. Second, they suggest important factors that must be examined and controlled for in assessing other routes through which stress may cause illness. For example, stressful circumstances may appear to yield high rates of illness falsely if the experience of stress is confounded with a personality predisposition to experience negative affect. The links between personality and illness clearly require additional explication, focusing especially on the biological pathways through which this predisposition may exert adverse effects on the body. Moreover, the effects of negative affectivity on symptom reporting, psychological distress, and possibly also the propensity to seek help require further examination.

The Interactive Route   A third model of the stress-illness relationship, one that is receiving increasing attention, might best be termed the *interactive route*. This model emphasizes the importance of preexisting psychological or physical vulnerabilities in the stress-illness relationship, suggesting that stress leads to illness only among people who have an initial vulnerability; stress alone or vulnerability alone is not sufficient to produce illness. Stress may have different effects on the body and be more or less likely to produce illness depending on these preexisting states.

Using an animal model, Tapp and Natelson (1988) examined the impact of stress on hamsters suffering from inherited heart disease. If the animal was stressed early on in the disease process, heart failure did not develop. However, after cardiac changes had developed, stress precipitated heart failure. When the animal was in overt heart failure, administered stress increased the likelihood that it would die. Moreover, the pattern of results suggests that the stress was not merely an additional burden for an animal with a vulnerability, but that the pathological effects of stress were multiplied by the existence of the prior illness or organic vulnerability. The model implies not only that organisms may be more susceptible to the impact of stress when they have preexisting vulnerabilities, but that already-weakened populations may be especially susceptible to the adverse health effects of stress.

We have also seen an example of the interactive model in studies of the effects of crowding and noise. Generally, crowding and noise produce few deleterious health effects. However, among vulnerable populations such as children, the elderly, and the poor, these stressors have greater negative effects. The role of stress in the development of hypertension may follow a similar pattern, as we will see in Chapter 14. That is, stress may have little chronic impact on blood pressure levels except among individuals who already have elevated blood pressure.

The Health Behavior Route   A fourth model of the stress-illness relationship maintains that stress can indirectly affect illness by altering a person's behavior patterns—the *health behavior route.* Consider, for example, the hypothetical case of a man who is separated from his wife. Separation and divorce are known to be major stressful events that produce substantial lifestyle and emotional disruption (Bloom, Asher, & White, 1978). If the couple had a traditional marriage, the husband may be used to having his meals prepared for him; left to his own devices, he may eat poorly or not at all. If he is used to sharing the bed with her, he may have difficulty sleeping without his wife. Because of his distress, he may increase his alcohol consumption or smoking. Using a measure of perceived stress, Cohen and Williamson (1988) found exactly this kind of relationship between stress and health behaviors. In their study, people who reported they were under more stress reported getting less sleep, being less likely to eat breakfast, consuming more alcohol, and using more drugs more frequently (see also Cohen and Williamson, 1988). To the extent that health habits are altered by stress, then, illness may be a consequence (Conway, Vickers, Ward, & Rahe, 1981).

The Illness Behavior Route   A fifth model of the stress-illness relationship maintains that stress can affect illness behavior directly without causing illness—the *illness behavior route.* In fact, research evidence indicates that people under stress are more likely to use health services than people who are not under stress (Gortmaker, Eckenrode, & Gore, 1982). Stress produces a variety of symptoms, including

anxiety, depression, fatigue, insomnia, shaking, distractibility, sweating, and jumpiness. Some people mistake these symptoms for signs of illness and seek medical treatment (e.g., Eastman & McPherson, 1982). In other cases, individuals may play the role of a sick person by staying home in bed to avoid the stressful events they encounter in their daily lives (Mechanic, 1972, 1978b; Mechanic & Volkhart, 1961; Roghmann & Haggerty, 1973). Illness behavior brings *secondary gains* in the form of attention, sympathy, and freedom from unwanted responsibilities and thus may itself be a way of coping with illness. Although we cover these issues more thoroughly in Chapter 9, it is important to raise them here for a particular reason: In conducting research on the stress-illness relationship, one must know that one is measuring illness and not just illness behavior. Figure 7.3 presents a diagram of the stress-illness relationship.

The Stress-Illness Relationship

With these different models of the relationships among stress, illness, and illness behavior in mind, we now turn to the evidence for a stress-illness relationship. It is, of course, difficult to see the relationship directly. One cannot bring subjects into the laboratory, expose them to a short-term stressor, and expect to see illness consequences immediately. Therefore, the evidence for a stress-illness relationship is inferential. We will look at several types of studies examining it. Research on life events, sudden death, daily hassles, and chronic strain all attempt to tie illness to life change. Studies of societal-level stressors relate attributes of populations or environments (such as the unemployment rate) to illness rates. Studies of occupational stress explore relationships between job characteristics, symptoms of stress, and the development of particular disorders.

FIGURE 7.3   The Stress-Illness Relationship

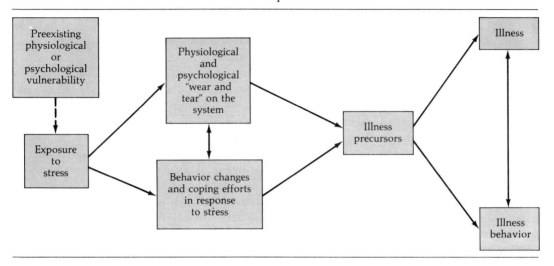

Measurement of Stressful Life Events   One line of research that has explored the stress-illness relationship has examined the illness-producing role of **stressful life events.** These range from cataclysmic events, such as the death of a spouse or being fired from a job, to more mundane but still problematic events, such as moving to a new home. On the basis of the work of Cannon, Selye, and others, one can speculate that major life events are stressful because of the adaptations they force people to make. When an organism must make a substantial adjustment to the environment, the likelihood of depleting reserves and laying the groundwork for illness is greater. Drawing on these assumptions, two stress researchers, Holmes and Rahe (1967), tested this reasoning. They developed the Social Readjustment Rating Scale (SRRS), which lists a variety of potentially stressful events (Table 7.1). As can be seen, many of these events are fairly serious, and each is given a point value.

How were the events selected and the point values determined? Through extensive testing, these events were determined to be the ones that, on the average, force people to make the most changes in their lives. The point values reflect the relative amount of

change that must be made. Thus, for example, if one's spouse dies, virtually every aspect of life is disrupted; accordingly, this event has the highest number of "life-change units." On the other hand, getting a traffic ticket may be upsetting and annoying, but, in and of itself, it is unlikely to produce much change in one's life.

Once stressful life events and their point values were established through the SRRS, the Schedule of Recent Experiences (SRE) was developed. This self-administered questionnaire asks the person to look through the list of events from the SRRS and check off every event that has occurred within the past year. To obtain a final score, one simply totals up the point values associated with those events. Although all people experience at least some stressful events over the course of a year, some will experience a lot. It is this group, according to Holmes and Rahe, that is most vulnerable to illness.

A look at the items reveals that positive events, such as "getting married" and "Christmas," are included along with negative events. As noted earlier, negative events seem to be stressful, whereas positive events are a source of joy and satisfaction. The ratio-

TABLE 7.1   THE SOCIAL READJUSTMENT RATING SCALE

Rank	Life Event	Mean Value
1.	Death of spouse	100
2.	Divorce	73
3.	Marital separation from mate	65
4.	Detention in jail or other institution	63
5.	Death of a close family member	63
6.	Major personal injury or illness	53
7.	Marriage	50
8.	Being fired at work	47
9.	Marital reconciliation with mate	45
10.	Retirement from work	45
11.	Major change in the health or behavior of a family member	44
12.	Pregnancy	40
13.	Sexual difficulties	39
14.	Gaining a new family member (e.g., through birth, adoption, oldster moving in, etc.)	39
15.	Major business readjustment (e.g., merger, reorganization, bankruptcy, etc.)	39
16.	Major change in financial state (e.g., a lot worse off or a lot better off than usual)	38
17.	Death of a close friend	37
18.	Changing to a different line of work	36
19.	Major change in the number of arguments with spouse (e.g., either a lot more or a lot less than usual regarding child-rearing, personal habits, etc.)	35
20.	Taking out a mortgage or loan for a major purchase (e.g., for a home, business, etc.)	31
21.	Foreclosure on a mortgage or loan	30
22.	Major change in responsibilities at work (e.g., promotion, demotion, lateral transfer)	29
23.	Son or daughter leaving home (e.g., marriage, attending college, etc.)	29
24.	Trouble with in-laws	29
25.	Outstanding personal achievement	28
26.	Wife beginning or ceasing work outside the home	26
27.	Beginning or ceasing formal schooling	26
28.	Major change in living conditions (e.g., building a new home, remodeling, deterioration of home or neighborhood)	25
29.	Revision of personal habits (dress, manners, associations, etc.)	24
30.	Trouble with the boss	23
31.	Major change in working hours or conditions	20
32.	Change in residence	20
33.	Changing to a new school	20
34.	Major change in usual type and/or amount of recreation	19
35.	Major change in church activities (e.g., a lot more or a lot less than usual)	19
36.	Major change in social activities (e.g., clubs, dancing, movies, visiting, etc.)	18
37.	Taking out a mortgage or loan for a lesser purchase (e.g., for a car, TV, freezer, etc.)	17
38.	Major change in sleeping habits (a lot more or a lot less sleep, or change in part of day when asleep)	16
39.	Major change in number of family get-togethers (e.g., a lot more or a lot less than usual)	15
40.	Major change in eating habits (a lot more or a lot less food intake, or very different meal hours or surroundings)	15
41.	Vacation	13
42.	Christmas	12
43.	Minor violations of the law (e.g., traffic tickets, jaywalking, disturbing the peace, etc.)	11

(From Holmes & Rahe, 1967)

nale for the inclusion of positive events is that these also require an individual to make changes. Anyone who has ever had to plan a wedding or a birth can testify to this. Positive events, like negative ones, can cause wear and tear on the system, which leads to illness. However, the types of events included on the scale have been a source of some controversy, and we will return to this shortly.

Because the SRE provides a badly needed and relatively objective measure of stress, it has frequently been used to examine the stress-illness relationship. Typically, either the number of life events or the total point values of those life events are summed over the course of a year and the score is correlated with illness experienced within the previous 6 months. Alternatively, life-event scores for the previous 6 months may be tallied and used prospectively to predict illness over the next 6 months. Rahe, Mahan, and Arthur (1970), for example, obtained SRE scores on sailors who were about to depart on 6-month cruises, and they were able to predict with some success who got sick and for how long. Theorell (1974) found that men who died of sudden heart attacks had had a higher number of stressful life events (as reported by their widows) in the previous 6 months than did a control population. The SRE has also predicted psychopathological disorders such as depression and schizophrenia (Paykel, 1974). Life events also influence health behaviors: Negative life events led to increased smoking and sleeping for women and to increased smoking and alcohol use for men. Men also responded to life events with more physical activity, suggesting that it might be a coping mechanism for them (Gottlieb & Green, 1984).

To summarize the results of a large number of studies, the ability of the SRE to predict illness is exceedingly modest. For the statistically minded, the correlations are rarely greater than .3, and are typically lower, accounting for no more than between 2 and 9% of the variance. For those who are not statisti-cally minded, those figures mean that the SRE does predict illness, but not very well.

Criticisms of the Schedule of Recent Experiences   As a measure of stress, the SRE has come under considerable criticism (e.g., Hough, Fairbank, & Garcia, 1976; Kasl, 1983; Tausig, 1982). First, some of the items on the list are vague; for example, "personal injury or illness" could mean anything from a cold to a heart attack. Second, since events have preassigned point values, individual differences in the way events are experienced are not taken into account (Redfield & Stone, 1979; Schroeder & Costa, 1984). For example, a divorce may mean welcome freedom to one partner but a collapse in living standard or self-esteem to the other. Consequently, some researchers feel that people's perceptions of their stress level is a better indication of stress than objective measurement of life events (Cohen, Kamarck, & Mermelstein, 1983).

Some criticisms concern the nature of the events themselves. As noted earlier, the SRE includes both positive and negative events. It also includes events that individuals choose, such as getting married, as well as events that simply happen, like the death of a close friend. Some researchers (e.g., Billings & Moos, 1982; McFarland, Norman, Streiner, & Roy, 1983; Sarason et al., 1978; Suls & Mullen, 1981) have argued that these differences matter and that events should not be treated the same regardless of valence or choice. Research suggests that sudden, negative, unexpected, and uncontrollable events predict illness better than events that are positive, expected, gradual in onset, or under personal control (Glass, 1977). Consequently, researchers have suggested that by adding up undesirable events or by having people weight items according to the subjective distress they experience, one obtains better measures of stress and predictors of illness than by combining numbers of positive and negative events (Ross & Mirowsky, 1979).

Others argue that the measurement of life events may confound the relationship between stress and illness or psychological distress because many of the items on these inventories measure health-related events, events related to neuroticism or negative affectivity, and events that are only stressful in their interpretation (Schroeder & Costa, 1984). Schroeder and Costa attempted to unconfound the measurement of life events by removing items that seemed to measure the outcome variables (those related to health, neuroticism, and subjectivity). They found that the relationship between life events and physical illness disappeared when these statistical cautions were undertaken (see also Brett, Brief, Burke, George, & Webster, 1990). Similarly, in an an investigation of psychiatric distress, Grant, Patterson, Olshen, and Yager (1987) found that when initial symptom levels of distress were controlled for, there was no relationship between life events and subsequent psychiatric symptoms. The results suggest that life-event inventories may be contaminated in these ways and thus artificially inflate the relationship between stress and physical or mental illness (see also Brett et al., 1990).

Another potential source of confounding in life-event inventories is the possibility that the measurement of specific stressful events may also tap ongoing life strain—that is, the chronic stress that is a part of everyday life (e.g., Avison & Turner, 1988). The life events that people experience show some degree of continuity over time (Billings & Moos, 1982; Norris & Murrell, 1987), consistent with the idea that event inventories may reflect chronic life strain and not only isolated discrete events. Poor people, young people, the unmarried, and well-educated people are more likely to experience stressful life events than those who are more well-to-do, older, married, or poorly educated (Goldberg & Comstock, 1980). These demographic differences would seem to reflect a pre-existing vulnerability to life events as a result of chronic strain. However, in one study in which researchers controlled for individuals' initial symptom levels and propensity to experience stressful life events, an increase in negative life events was still related to an increase in reported physical symptoms (Avison & Turner, 1988). Thus, removing the contribution of chronic life strain to the measurement of stressful life events may reduce but not eliminate the relationship between life events and illness.

Another source of confounding in assessing the relationship between stressful life events and illness concerns whether people who report experiencing a large number of life events are simply more reactive to events in general. One study examining this possibility had people respond to two discomforting stimuli in the laboratory—a cold pressor test involving the immersion of one's hand into ice water, and reaction to loud noise (Harney & Brigham, 1985). The results suggested that people who report a high amount of life change tolerate these discomforting stimuli significantly less well than people reporting less life change. These results are consistent with the possibility that life events may be experienced as more stressful by people with a propensity to react strongly to adverse events.

There are also problems in trying to use the SRE to predict illness. Many people believe that stress causes illness. Therefore, when they are asked to report how much stress and illness they have experienced in a given time period, they may distort the two to correspond with each other. There are other possible biases as well. For example, in Theorell's study of men who had died of heart attacks, widows reported a high number of work-related stressors just prior to the event, but few home-related stressors; by doing so, they may have tried to avoid guilt or blame in their husbands' deaths.

Another source of problems stems from the fact that people often forget what life events they have experienced (Hurst, Jenkins, &

Rose, 1976). Forgetting seems to be a particular problem for middle- and low-level stressful events, whereas highly salient stressful events are less frequently forgotten (Klein & Rubovits, 1987). Overall, the amount of forgetting that occurs in attempting to record life events contributes to unreliability in their measurement (Funch & Marshall, 1984).

A general difficulty in trying to estimate the stress-illness relationship concerns the time period between the two that is examined. As noted earlier, usually stress over a 1-year period is correlated with the most recent 6 months of illness bouts. Yet, is it reasonable to assume that January's crisis caused June's cold? Or that last month's financial problems produced a malignancy detected this month? After all, malignancies can grow undetected for 10 or 20 years. Obviously, these are extreme cases, but they illustrate some of the problems in studying the stress-illness relationship over time.

The method of relating life events to number of illnesses may also ignore certain important features of illnesses that need to be taken into account. The sheer number of illnesses an individual experiences in a given time period may not matter as much as their severity and duration, points which many of these investigations do not take into account. Clearly, a protracted flu that hangs on for weeks is a more important illness experience than a cold that lasts 2 days. Thus, it is possible that stress exerts effects on illness in ways other than increasing vulnerability to it. For example, one study (Melick, 1978) compared individuals whose homes had been flooded with a matched control group whose homes had not been flooded. There were no differences in the number and nature of illnesses experienced by the flood and non-flood individuals. However, those whose homes had been flooded experienced longer illnesses (see also Phifer, Kaniasty, & Norris, 1988).

It may seem from the severity and diversity of criticisms of the SRE that we should not use it at all. In fact, a number of similar instruments that correct many of these problems are now more commonly used than the SRE (see Cohen & Williamson, 1988; Ross & Mirowsky, 1979; Sarason et al., 1978). Nonetheless, the SRE has been one of the methodological breakthroughs in studying stress; if its limitations are increasingly becoming evident, it is primarily because it has been a badly needed research tool that has enjoyed wide use. Box 7.5 presents an alternative way of measuring stress.

Major Life Events and Sudden Death   An understanding of the relationship between serious life events and health would not be complete without a consideration of the **sudden death syndrome.** Like the research on life change, sudden death syndrome also illustrates the relationship between cataclysmic stressful events and illness, but in extreme and rapid form.

> A dramatic example is the death of the 27-year-old army captain who had commanded the ceremonial troops at the funeral of President Kennedy. He died 10 days after the President of a "cardiac irregularity and acute congestion," according to the newspaper report of the medical findings.
>
> A 39-year-old pair of twins who had been inseparable died within a week of each other; no cause of death was mentioned.
>
> A 64-year-old woman who was said never to have recovered from the death of her son in an auto accident 14 years earlier died 4 days after her husband was murdered in a holdup. (Engel, 1971, p. 774)

Sudden death seems to depend on at least two factors. The first is a preexisting somatic weakness of some sort, such as a heart weakness or an infection. The second is the presence of some unexpected, uncontrollable, and severe shock to the individual, such as the death of a spouse, child, or friend (Cottington,

Box 7.5
A Measure of Perceived Stress

Because people vary so much in what they consider to be stressful, many researchers feel that **perceived stress** is a better measure of stress than are instruments that measure whether people have been exposed to particular events. To address this issue, Cohen et al. (1983) developed a measure of perceived stress, some items of which are provided below. Note the differences between this measure of stress and the items on the Social Readjustment Rating Scale in Table 7.1.

Items and Instructions for the Perceived Stress Scale

The questions in this scale ask you about your feelings and thoughts during the last month. In each case, you will be asked to indicate how often you felt or thought a certain way. Although some of the questions are similar, there are differences between them, and you should treat each one as a separate question. The best approach is to answer each question fairly quickly. That is, don't try to count up the number of times you felt a particular way, but, rather, indicate the alternative that seems like a reasonable estimate.

For each question, choose from the following alternatives:

0   never
1   almost never
2   sometimes
3   fairly often
4   very often

1. In the last month, how often have you been upset because of something that happened unexpectedly?
2. In the last month, how often have you felt nervous and "stressed"?
3. In the last month, how often have you found that you could not cope with all the things that you had to do?
4. In the last month, how often have you been angered because of things that happened that were outside your control?
5. In the last month, how often have you found yourself thinking about things that you had to accomplish?
6. In the last month, how often have you felt difficulties were piling up so high that you could not overcome them?

Matthews, Talbott, & Kuller, 1980), a loss in work status, or the end of a marriage. Engel (1971) has suggested that the incident produces a sense of complete loss of control due to intense feelings of helplessness and hopelessness. A "giving up–given up" syndrome results, such that the person loses all desire to carry on. This state, coupled with the somatic weakness, can produce a dramatic and rapid change in the individual's physical status. Box

7.6 describes a striking form of this phenomenon.

It is easy to overestimate and exaggerate the frequency and clinical significance of this kind of death, because the incidents, however rare, are so colorful. However, their etiology is often identical to that of other stress-related illnesses; the process of disease development may simply occur faster than in the usual case of a stress-related illness.

Box 7.6
"Nightmare Death": Sudden Death Among Southeast Asian Refugees

Since July 1977, the federal government's Centers for Disease Control (CDC) in Atlanta have been investigating the strange phenomenon of sudden, unexpected nocturnal death among male Southeast Asian refugees to the United States. Between July 1977 and October 1982, sixty such cases were reported to the CDC. They occurred primarily among Hmong refugees from Laos, but Mien-Yao, Khmer, Lao, and Vietnamese refugees were also involved. Apparently, death often occurs within the first few hours of sleep. The victim begins to gurgle and to move about in bed. He cannot be awakened, and he dies shortly thereafter. To date, autopsies have revealed no specific cause of death.

Several hypotheses have been offered to account for the deaths. All propose an interaction among psychological, cultural, and physiological factors. One possible physiological factor is a rare malfunction of the heart's pacemaker that is genetically transmitted only to males. The genetic theory has credence because the sudden death pattern is found only in males of particular ethnicity, and it seems to cluster in particular families. But how and why would such a defect be manifested or triggered during sleep?

The deaths appear to have occurred among two groups of refugees: those who have recently arrived and those who have been in the United States for a few months or years. Among the recent arrivals, death often occurs within a few days or weeks of arrival. Interviews with several of the victims' families suggested that frequently the victim or a close relative experienced a dream foretelling the death. Among the Hmong, dreams are taken seriously. Thus, although ritualistic measures were taken to avert the death, anxiety from the dreams may have played a contributory role. Interviews with survivors who were resuscitated in time indicate that they may have experienced a severe night terror—an intensely frightening dream that occurs during deep sleep, and which often produces abrupt and dramatic physiological changes. Interviews also suggested that the night terrors may have been evoked by watching television.

Among the earlier arrivals, the deaths were not associated with any identifiable trauma or psychological trigger. However, there was often evidence that the victims had been exhausted, having combined full-time jobs with demanding night school classes or other enterprises. In some cases, the fatal sleep occurred immediately after a family argument, late television watching, or interrupted sleep.

Overall, it appears that the pressures of adjusting to American life have had some role in the deaths. The victims may have been overwhelmed by cultural differences, the language barrier, difficulties finding jobs, and dependency on welfare, a humiliating experience for proud, hardworking people.

In sum, while it is still uncertain exactly why the sudden deaths occur, one possible explanation is that cultural and psychological factors produce extreme stress. This stress, in turn, interacts with a congenital weakness to produce sudden death.

(Lemoine & Mougne, 1983).

Chronic Strain Earlier, we posed the question, Can people adapt to chronically stressful events? The answer provided by somewhat incomplete data was that people can adapt to a degree, but may continue to show signs of stress in response to severe chronic strains in their lives. **Chronic strain** can come from a number of sources: a long-term but basically unsatisfying relationship, a work situation that is stressful, long-term financial concerns, and the like.

Compared to research on stressful life events, little work has addressed the role of chronic strain on psychological and physical health outcomes. However, chronic strain also appears to be important in physical and psychological distress. In an early study, Pearlin and Schooler (1978) found that chronic strain in marriage, parenting, household functioning, or occupation predicted psychological distress in a community sample of 2,300 persons. Brown and Harris (1978) also found that chronic strains that lasted more than 2 years were implicated in the development of depression. Gannon and Pardie (1989) reported that psychosomatic symptoms in women were predicted not only by the number of stressors reported in their lives but also by their controllability and chronicity; uncontrollable and long-term stressors were associated with more symptoms.

The importance of chronic strain has also been implicated in studies of occupational stress. As House and Smith (1989) noted, chronic exposure to hazardous or stressful work situations are most likely to affect health adversely, as opposed to extreme but isolated stress-related work events. In a study of hardship and depression, Ross and Huber (1985) found that ongoing economic hardship, as evidenced by low income, low education, being young, and having young children, increased the propensity for depression. Husbands' depression was directly related to their earnings, whereas the wives' depression was influenced more by education and the number of children they had. In a study examining the impact of chronic strain and stressful life events on psychological dysfunction, chronic strains were more strongly and consistently related to the severity of psychological dysfunction than were acute life events (Eckenrode, 1984; see also Cronkite & Moos, 1984).

The preceding studies suggest that chronic strain may have an adverse effect on psychological and health outcomes. Chronic strain may also influence the relationship between specific stressful life events and outcome variables such as depression. In a study of 1,000 adults that examined both life events and chronic strains, Pearlin, Meaghan, Lieberman, and Mullan (1981) found that both chronic stressors and negative life events predicted changes in depression over time; in particular, the impact of a negative life event appeared to be mediated by the increase in the chronic strain that it produced. For example, a sudden loss of income affected psychological well-being largely because it exacerbated preexisting financial problems. Chronic strain may also predispose people to react more severely to stressful events when they occur. In one study that examined the effects of chronic strain on reactions to an acute stressor, people from crowded or uncrowded neighborhoods worked on a challenging task while their blood pressure and heart rate were measured. People experiencing the chronic strain of crowding showed increased cardiovascular reactivity to the challenging event, whereas those from uncrowded neighborhoods did not react as strongly (Fleming, Baum, Davidson, Rectanus, & McArdle, 1987).

Chronic strain may also *produce* life events. Brown and Harris (1978) suggest that ongoing stress can exacerbate the impact of life events by straining the person's coping capacities when he or she is confronted with yet another problem to manage. For example, the loss of a spouse creates hardship in a number of areas of life. To the extent that chronic strain mediates the impact of stressful life events on distress and health, an assessment of life events alone is likely to underestimate the impact of these events.

Research on the relationship between chronic strain and psychological distress and illness has been difficult to conduct effectively for several reasons (Kessler, Price, & Wortman, 1985). First, chronic strain is assessed largely subjectively on the basis of self-reports. Unlike life events, which can often be objectively assessed, it can be more difficult to determine objectively whether particular chronic strains are actually going on. Second, as in the measurement of life events, inventories that attempt to assess chronic strain may also tap psychological distress, neuroticism, and negative affectivity, rather than the objective existence of stressful conditions. Finally, as noted in the section on the measurement of stressful life events, life-event inventories may confound assessments of chronic strain with assessment of stressful life events so that the impact of chronic strain on psychological and physical health is underestimated (Avison & Turner, 1988).

Minor Life Events and Stress   In contrast to the work on major stressful life events and illnesses, researchers are now exploring the role of minor stressful events, or **daily hassles,** and their cumulative impact on health and illness. Such hassles might include being stuck in a traffic jam, waiting in line, doing household chores, or having difficulty making a small decision. Minor stressful life events can conceivably exert an impact on illness and health outcomes via one of several routes. First, the cumulative impact of small stressors may themselves predispose an individual to become ill. Second, such events may moderate the relationship between major life events and illnesses. For example, if a major life event is experienced at a time when minor life events

are at a minimum, the stress may not be as great as it would otherwise be (Holmes & Holmes, 1970; Lewinsohn & Talkington, 1979; McLean, 1976; Monroe, 1983).

Lazarus and his associates (Kanner, Coyne, Schaeffer, & Lazarus, 1981; Lazarus, 1980; Lazarus & Cohen, 1977; Lazarus, Cohen, Folkman, Kanner, & Schaefer, 1980) developed a measure of minor stressful life events termed the "hassles" scale. In one study (Kanner et al., 1981), 100 middle-aged adults completed the hassles scale for 9 consecutive months and reported psychological symptoms, including depression and anxiety. Hassles proved to be a better predictor of symptoms than were more major life events (see also Monroe, 1983; Weinberger, Hiner, & Tierney, 1987). Kanner and associates and Monroe found no evidence that the impact of major life events on subsequent psychological symptoms was influenced by the presence of daily hassles. However, in a study of arthritis patients, Weinberger et al. (1987) did find that life events increased hassles, which, in turn, negatively affected health status. Research has also tied the presence of daily hassles to declines in physical health (DeLongis, Coyne, Dakof, Folkman, & Lazarus, 1982). Examples of items from the hassles scale are shown in Box 7.7.

Although the initial response to the measurement of daily hassles was a positive one, subsequent research has suggested that the measurement of hassles may be confounded with psychiatric and physical symptoms in some of the same ways that inventories of major life events are. Specifically, the Dohrenwends and their associates (Dohrenwend & Shrout, 1985; Dohrenwend, Dohrenwend, Dodson, & Shrout, 1984) found that the hassles scale overlaps substantially with psychological symptom checklists. This kind of research implies that rather than being an objective measure of stress, the hassles scale may simply reflect subjective reactions to it, and thus measure rather than predict psychological distress.

Box 7.7
The Measurement of Hassles

Recently, psychologists have examined the role of minor stresses and strains in the development of illness. Some sample items from the "hassles" scale (Kanner et al., 1981) are included below as an early example of how these stresses and strains are measured.

Instructions

Hassles are irritants that can range from minor annoyances to fairly major pressures, problems, or difficulties. They can occur few or many times. Listed below are a number of ways in which a person can feel hassled. First, circle the hassles that have happened to you in the past month. Then, look at the numbers on the right of the items you circled. Indicate by circling a 1, 2, or 3 how *severe* each of the circled hassles has been for you in the past month. If a hassle did not occur in the last month do *not* circle it.

Severity

1   somewhat severe

2   moderately severe

3   extremely severe

Hassles

1. Misplacing or losing things	1	2	3
2. Troublesome neighbors	1	2	3
3. Social obligations	1	2	3
4. Inconsiderate smokers	1	2	3
5. Thoughts about death	1	2	3
6. Health of a family member	1	2	3
7. Not enough money for clothing	1	2	3
8. Concerns about owing money	1	2	3

In an effort to address this problem, Reich and his colleagues (Reich, Parrella, & Filstead, 1988) assessed external stressors and the strength of internal responses to them separately. They found evidence that both measures were independently and jointly associated with psychological distress, suggesting that hassles have both a subjective and an objective component. Lazarus and his associates (Lazarus, DeLongis, Folkman, & Gruen, 1985) identified each of the hassles on their scale as unconfounded, neutral, or potentially confounded with physical or psychological distress. They found evidence that all three groups of hassles were correlated with psychological symptoms in similar ways. They also conducted a factor analysis of the hassles scale and identified eight factors, some of which were primarily judged to be external (e.g., financial responsibilities), others of which were judged to be internal (e.g., inner concerns). Both sets of factors predicted psychological symptoms in similar ways. Although more research will undoubtedly be undertaken on this issue, the conclusion to be drawn at present is similar to the conclusion characterizing major life event inventories. While some confounding of psychological distress, physical symptoms, and stress appears to occur in these measures, the confounding does not explain away the relations among hassles, psychological distress, and physical symptoms.

To summarize, research relating life change caused by major and minor life events to illness has suggested a small but consistent relationship. Difficulties in measuring both life change and illness may have partially obscured the strength of this relationship. However, it is also likely that the small degree of relationship stems from the fact that the links between stress and illness are moderated by many other factors. Although we explore some of these factors in Chapter 8, others currently remain unknown.

Societal-Level Stress and Illness   Thus far, we have examined individuals' personal experiences with stress and the propensity to develop illness. Another way in which researchers have examined the links between stress and illness is by relating societal-level measures of stress to illness rates in the population. How can stress be measured at the societal level? Any variable that indicates how much upheaval a society is experiencing can potentially be used as a measure of the stress of that society's population. An example is the unemployment rate. Areas with high levels of unemployment should be under greater stress than areas with low levels of unemployment. Consequently, we might expect to find higher levels of illness (as measured by hospital admissions or physician visits, for example) in such areas than in areas with low unemployment rates. Another example is the rate at which dwelling units change hands. If people within a given geographic region move frequently, we would expect them to be under greater stress than if their residences remained stable. Consequently, we might expect to find higher illness rates in areas with high rates of geographic mobility. A voluminous literature in sociology has explored these and similar issues; we can only scratch the surface here.

However, it is important to realize that this is another method for studying the stress-illness relationship.

High geographic mobility and migration have generally been viewed as stressful circumstances that lead to higher illness rates. Reviews of this research, however (Kasl & Berkman, 1983; Lindheim & Syme, 1983; Micklin & Leon, 1978), suggest that the relationship may not be as strong as was once believed (Kasl & Berkman, 1983). It appears that mobility and migration per se are not associated with higher illness rates. For example, some immigrants are able to move to a new country and remain in an ethnic enclave that insulates them from the psychological distress of the new society and many of the detrimental effects of being uprooted from their home community (Kuo & Tsai, 1986). Moreover, at least certain immigrants may possess personality resources that enable them to cope with the stress of moving more successfully than others who do not (Kuo & Tsai, 1986). There is some reason to believe that immigrant cohorts may actually include more people with a sense of internal control and mastery that may buffer against stress (Kuo & Tsai, 1986). However, some of the changes that migration and geographic mobility produce may well be associated with greater illness. For example, migration and geographic mobility are often associated with a disruption in personal ties among people. When these supportive ties are broken, illness may be more likely. Likewise, when people are removed from their biological, personal, and historical past circumstances, they appear to show higher rates of illness. The uprootedness and lack of social ties that may result from geographic mobility and immigration may also produce greater psychological distress (Lindheim & Syme, 1983).

Economic stress can have a similar effect. Research (Brenner, 1976) suggests that, with each 1% increase in the national unemployment rate, there are approximately 2% more deaths from heart disease and cirrhosis, 4% more suicides, and a 2 to 4% increase in first-time mental hospital admissions. Unemployment, then, does produce stress, which is manifested in higher psychological distress and illness rates (see also Catalano, Dooley, & Jackson, 1985; Dooley & Catalano, 1984).

Cultures that are experiencing rapid social and technical change may be more vulnerable to certain illnesses and psychological disorders. Intensive studies of ethnic enclaves that are disrupted by the intrusion of another culture show higher death rates, higher illness rates, and higher rates of accidents. For example, the Papago Indians, a southwestern tribe, have been increasingly exposed to the dominant American culture in recent years. As contact has increased, so have accident rates, physical illness, and behavioral disturbances such as alcoholism (Patrick & Tyroler, 1972).

Social status has also been tied to illness and to psychological distress (Kessler, 1979; Lindheim & Syme, 1983). As we shall see in Chapter 9, people in the lowest socioeconomic positions in society have the highest rates of psychological distress, illness, and mortality, a condition that may be further aggravated by racial status or discrimination (Kessler & Neighbors, 1986). Similarly, people lower in an organizational hierarchy have higher rates of cardiovascular disorders (Lindheim & Syme, 1983). For example, lower-ranking civil servants are more likely to have cardiovascular health problems than are those in the upper levels of the civil service. Low social status has also been correlated with psychological distress (Kessler, 1979).

These are a few examples of a growing body of evidence relating social change, upheaval, or stress to psychological distress and illness. It should be noted that these studies cannot illustrate exactly the routes by which stress may produce illness. Do these stressful events change health habits, reduce social support, or increase life change? Further research will clarify these relationships. At present, they clearly indicate that not only do individual experiences of stress lead to illness, but the stress level of a population can also predict its level of illness.

Stress in the Workplace

A voluminous literature has examined the causes and consequences of occupational stress. Occupational stress has been related to psychological distress (e.g., Revicki & May, 1985) and to adverse health outcomes (see Mackay & Cooper, 1987). Studies of occupational stress are important for several reasons. First, they help identify some of the most common stressors of everyday life. Second, they provide additional evidence for the stress-illness relationship. Third, work stress may be one of our preventable stressors and thereby provide possibilities for intervention. Although not all occupational stress can be avoided, knowledge of job factors that are stressful raises the possibility of redesigning jobs and implementing stress-management interventions.

Stressful Job Factors One source of occupational stress is the erosion of physical state that can result. Many workers are exposed as a matter of course to *physical, chemical, and biological hazards*. These risks can be associated with many adverse health outcomes, including injuries, cancers, and respiratory and cardiovascular disease (House & Smith, 1989). In addition, the changing patterns of work may erode certain health benefits of work that used to occur as a matter of course. For example, the most common work that people undertook before the Industrial Revolution involved agricultural production, in which people engaged in physical exercise as they were going about their work tasks. As people have moved into office jobs or other work contexts that require very little output of physical energy, the amount of exercise that they normally get in their work life has declined substantially (House & Smith, 1989). Since there is evidence that work-related and leisure-activity levels may be tied to health, this change in the nature of work creates the possibility of vulnerability to illness (Eichner, 1983; Rigotti, Thomas, & Leaf, 1983).

Work overload is a chief factor producing high levels of occupational stress. Workers who feel required to work too long and too hard at too many tasks feel more stressed (e.g., Caplan & Jones, 1975), practice poorer health habits (Sorensen et al., 1985), and sustain more health risks than do workers not suffering from overload. A study of industrial workers under age 45, for example, found that those who worked 48 hours or more a week had twice the death rate from coronary artery disease than did workers holding similar jobs who worked 40 hours a week or less (Breslow & Buell, 1960).

Overload may stem not only from too many job demands but also from attempting to combine too many demanding roles. Working women with young children may be especially vulnerable to the adverse effects of overload. Some studies find employment to be beneficial for women, while others find either no increase in distress or some symptoms of stress (see Warr & Parry, 1982, for a review; Parry, 1986). Quality of the home and work environments appears to mediate these results. For example, in one study (Krause & Markides, 1985), Mexican-American women who worked outside the home were benefitted psychologically by work status if they were divorced or separated. The impact of work outside the home for married women was mediated by whether or not there was help with housework and whether or not they regarded work outside the home as congruent with their sex-role expectations. Similarly, Ross and Mirowsky (1988) found that employed women who had no difficulty finding child care or whose husbands shared child care had very low depression levels, but employed women who

had difficulty arranging child care or who had sole responsibility for child care had very high depression levels. Whether work is beneficial to women in terms of protecting them against psychological distress depends also on the rewards obtained from work (Downey & Moen, 1987) and the nature of the job (Lennon, 1987). Full-time work and low levels of job complexity are associated with greater distress (Lennon, 1987).

Overall, the psychological impacts of having multiple roles are mixed. On the one hand, the more roles one has, the more one is at risk for overload and for specific role-related events. As Thoits put it: "One must have, to lose" (Thoits, 1987, p. 18). On the other hand, having multiple roles can buffer one against setbacks in one area of life (Linville, 1985, 1987). At least under some circumstances, depression in response to setbacks in one domain of life can be lessened or buffered by the presence of rewarding activities in other domains of life. Research suggests, however, that there may be limits to the ability of different life domains to buffer setbacks in other domains. Kandel, Davies, and Raveis (1985), for example, found that being employed buffered women against the stresses associated with marriage and family roles, but being a parent actually exacerbated stress associated with one's occupation. The beneficial and detrimental ways in which multiple roles interact with each other in producing or guarding against stress, distress, and physical illness will no doubt continue to occupy research attention.

Work pressure also leads to stress. For example, one study of university faculty found that the more professors felt pressured to achieve, the higher was their serum uric acid level, a stress indicator. Perceived work pressure, in turn, produced work overload, because these faculty members felt they had to work longer and harder than their colleagues (Brooks & Mueller, 1966; French, Tupper, & Mueller, 1965). In a longitudinal study of community

dence to suggest that it does. It is easiest to document the relationship by looking at acute disorders. Research attempting to link occupational stress to chronic disease may underestimate the relationship by failing to take into account the complex etiology and temporal course of chronic disease. Only by following respondents suffering from chronic occupational stress at multiple points in time is it possible to properly estimate this relationship (House, 1987).

Stress shows up in other ways than illness that may be extremely costly to an organization. Many of these factors may represent workers' efforts to control or to offset stress before it ever gets to the point of causing illness. For example, workers who cannot participate actively in decisions about their jobs show higher rates of absenteeism, job turnover, tardiness, job dissatisfaction, and sabotage and lower levels of performance on the job (Cooper & Marshall, 1976). In essence, these workers have taken stress into their own hands and reduced it by refusing passively to work as long, as hard, or as well as their employers apparently expect. Substance abuse is another potential way of coping with occupational stress. However, research suggests that such abuse may be more related to general feelings of powerlessness, alienation, and lack of commitment than to specific job characteristics (Mensch & Kandel, 1988; Seeman, Seeman, & Budros, 1988).

Reducing Occupational Stress   What are some solutions to these workplace stresses? A blueprint for change has been offered by several organizational stress researchers (e.g., Kahn, 1981; McGregor, 1967). First, physical work stressors such as noise, harsh lighting, crowding, or temperature extremes should be reduced as much as possible.

Second, an effort to minimize unpredictability and ambiguity in expected tasks and standards of performance reduces stress.

When workers know what they are expected to do and at what level, they are less distressed.

Third, involving workers as much as possible in the decisions that affect their work life reduces stress. A number of corporations have now given workers at least some control over facets of their jobs, including working hours, the rate at which a task is performed, and the order in which tasks are performed, with corresponding increases in productivity and drops in absenteeism and tardiness (McGregor, 1967). Using the primary work group as the decision-making body, rather than more removed authorities in the company, also reduces stress (Kahn, 1981; Sutton & Kahn, 1986).

Fourth, making jobs as interesting as possible may contribute to the reduction of stress. In some plants, workers who previously worked on an assembly line and were responsible for assembling a small part of a product were retrained to perform several tasks or even to assemble the entire product. These "job enlargement" or "job enrichment" programs have produced increases in productivity and product quality and decreases in job dissatisfaction (McGregor, 1967).

Fifth, providing workers with opportunities to develop or promote meaningful social relationships potentially can reduce stress or buffer its impact (Buunk, 1989; Moos, 1985). Developing worker teams on the job and providing social and recreational facilities for break times, lunch time, and after-hours free time can improve social relations on the job. Extending facilities to workers' families for after-hours and weekend events have all been used to try to bring families into corporations (Cooper & Marshall, 1976), inasmuch as family support can buffer the impact of work-related stress (Revicki & May, 1985). Some interventions are directed at improving social relations at work, since these relationships can reduce occupational stress and buffer a person against its adverse health affects. Studies show that both good relations with co-workers and good relations with supervisors have these beneficial effects; under some circumstances, supervisor support may be even more important than co-worker support (Eaker & Feinleib, 1983; Haynes & Feinleib, 1980; Larocco et al., 1980). However, the effects may be fairly weak or limited to certain kinds of settings (Buunk, Janssen, & VanYperen, in press).

Sixth, rewarding workers for good work, rather than focusing on punishment for poor work, improves morale and provides incentives for better future work. Avoidance learning through punishment of poor performance is, in itself, a poor method for changing behavior (Hilgard & Bower, 1966; Kahn, 1981).

Finally, those who are in a supervisory position in workplace settings can look for signs of stress before stress has an opportunity to do significant damage. For example, supervisors can watch for negative affect such as boredom, apathy, and hostility among workers, since these affective reactions often precede more severe somatic and behavioral reactions to stress. Likewise, pockets of absenteeism or tardiness may point to particular types of jobs that may require redesign or enlargement.

Overall, then, the stress-illness relationship has been clearly documented in the workplace and has been tied to a number of specific job-related factors. This knowledge has, in turn, provided the basis for a number of important workplace interventions to reduce stress. In this sense, the occupational stress literature provides a good model for stress prevention. If one can identify stressors early through signs of psychological distress or illness precursors such as catecholamine excretion, one can intervene in the stress-illness relationship before illness occurs.

SUMMARY

1. Events are perceived as stressful when people believe that their resources (such as time, money, and energy) may not be sufficient to meet the harm, threat, or challenge in the environment. Stress produces many changes, including adverse emotional reactions, cognitive responses, physiological changes, and performance decrements.

2. Early research on stress examined how the organism mobilizes its resources to fight or flee from threatening stimuli (the fight-or-flight response). Building on this model, Selye proposed the general adaptation syndrome, arguing that reactions to stress go through three phases: alarm, resistance, and exhaustion.

3. More recent research on stress demonstrates the importance of psychological appraisal. Events are not inherently stressful, but their impact depends on how they are interpreted. Events that are negative, uncontrollable or unpredictable, ambiguous, or overwhelming are likely to be perceived as stressful.

4. Although people can adapt to stress to a degree, highly stressful events remain so over time. Stress can have disruptive aftereffects, including persistent physiological arousal, psychological distress, reduced task performance, and, over time, declines in cognitive capabilities. Vulnerable populations such as children, the elderly, or the poor may be particularly adversely affected by stress.

5. Stress can increase the likelihood of illness

and illness behavior in several ways. It can alter health habits, increase the likelihood that one will seek medical attention, increase wear and tear on the physiological system, or interact with preexisting vulnerabilities to illness, both psychological and physical.

6. Life-event researchers maintain that any event that forces a person to make change increases stress and the likelihood of illness. Cataclysmic life events, such as the loss of a spouse, can produce sudden death. Chronic exposure to stressful situations can also affect health adversely, as can the daily hassles of life.

7. Studies of social indicators suggest that cultures under chronic stress (highly mobile cultures or cultures undergoing rapid change) experience higher illness, death, and accident rates.

8. Studies of occupational stress suggest that work hazards, work overload, work pressure, role conflict and ambiguity, inability to develop satisfying job relationships, inadequate career development, inability to exert control in one's job, and unemployment can produce increased illness, job dissatisfaction, absenteeism, tardiness, and turnover. Many of these job stresses can be prevented or offset through intervention.

KEY TERMS

aftereffects of stress
chronic strain
cognitive-costs hypothesis
daily hassles
fight-or-flight response
general adaptation syndrome
helplessness
learned helplessness
negative affectivity
perceived stress
person-environment fit

pessimistic explanatory style
post-traumatic stress disorder (PTSD)
primary appraisal
role conflict
secondary appraisal
stress
stressful life events
stress markers
stressors
sudden death syndrome

8

COPING WITH STRESS

People respond very differently to stress. We all know people who throw up their hands in despair when the slightest thing goes wrong with their plans, and yet we know others who seem to meet setbacks and challenges with equanimity, bringing their personal and social resources to bear on the problem at hand. This chapter examines the ways in which people cope with stressful events and whether or not their coping efforts are successful in reducing stress.

In Chapter 7, we examined the phenomenon of stress and reviewed the evidence relating stress to psychological distress, physical symptoms, illness behavior, and, ultimately, illness itself. Yet, as the above examples indicate, everyone who is exposed to the same potentially stressful event does not experience stress, and those who experience stress may do so to different degrees. This variability in the stress experience is due to the many factors that moderate the impact of stress and its relationship to illness.

In this chapter, we review these moderating factors. First, we examine the coping efforts people use to try to reduce the impact of stressful events. Next, we consider the resources that people bring to any stressful experience that may influence its impact. These include coping style, personality variables, social support, social class, and other life stressors, among others. Finally, we consider stress-management techniques that people can be taught to use in order to cope with stressful events.

WHAT IS COPING?

The impact of any potentially stressful event is substantially influenced by how a person copes with it. According to Lazarus's view of stress, any new event or change in the environment prompts the individual to make *primary appraisals* of the significance of the event. An event may be judged to be positive, neutral, or negative in its implications for the self. If an event is judged to be negative, it will be further judged in terms of the *harm or loss* that has already been done, the future *threat* associated with the event, and the potential *challenge* of the event—that is, the perception that gain, growth, or mastery may result from dealing with the event. Once these primary appraisals are made, the individual makes a *secondary appraisal*. Secondary appraisal is the evaluation of one's coping resources and options to determine whether they will be sufficient to overcome the harm and threat that the event represents (Lazarus & Folkman, 1984a).

Coping is the process of managing demands (external or internal) that are appraised as taxing or exceeding the resources of the person (Lazarus & Folkman, 1984b). "Coping consists of efforts, both action-oriented and intrapsychic, to manage (i.e., master, tolerate, reduce, minimize) environmental and internal demands and conflicts among them" (Lazarus & Launier, 1978, p. 311).

This definition of coping has several important aspects. First, the relationship between coping and a stressful event represents a dynamic process. Coping is a series of transactions between a person who has a set of resources, values, and commitments and a particular environment with its own resources, demands, and constraints (Lazarus & Launier, 1978). Thus, coping is not a one-time action that someone takes; rather, it is a set of reciprocal responses, occurring over time, by which the environment and the person influence each other. For example, the impending breakup of a romantic relationship can produce a variety of reactions, ranging from emotional responses, such as sadness or indignation, to actions, such as efforts at reconciliation or attempts to find engrossing, distracting activities. These coping efforts will, in turn, be influenced by the way the partner in the relationship responds. With encouragement from the partner, the person may make renewed efforts at reconciliation, whereas an-

ger or rejection may drive the person farther away.

A second important aspect of the definition of coping is its breadth. The definition clearly encompasses a great many actions and reactions to stressful circumstances. Viewed within this definition, then, emotional reactions, including anger or depression, can be thought of as part of the coping process just as are actions that are voluntarily undertaken to confront the event. In turn, coping efforts are moderated by the resources that the individual has available. An illustration may help to explain this. Figure 8.1 presents a diagram of the coping process; we will cover each of these aspects of coping in turn.

Generally, two types of coping efforts can be distinguished: problem-solving efforts and emotion-focused coping (cf. Folkman, Schaefer, & Lazarus, 1979; Leventhal & Nerenz, 1982; Pearlin & Schooler, 1978). *Problem-solving efforts* are attempts to do something constructive about the stressful conditions that are harming, threatening, or challenging an individual. *Emotion-focused coping* involves efforts to regulate the emotional consequences of the stressful event. Sometimes problem-solving efforts and emotional regulation work together. For example, a person who takes action to reduce industrial noise in his community may both reduce his anger and simultaneously have an effect on the stressor. Problem-solving efforts and emotional regulation may also work at cross purposes, however. For example, in denying that stressors on the job are causing her distress, a worker may keep her daily anger low but fail to deal with the cumulative damage these stressors may cause.

An individual will use a wide variety of specific coping strategies in managing a single stressful event. Some will be problem-focused and others will be oriented toward emotional regulation. Which coping responses will be used and what their effects are depends in a large part on the nature of the stressor itself

FIGURE 8.1   The Coping Process

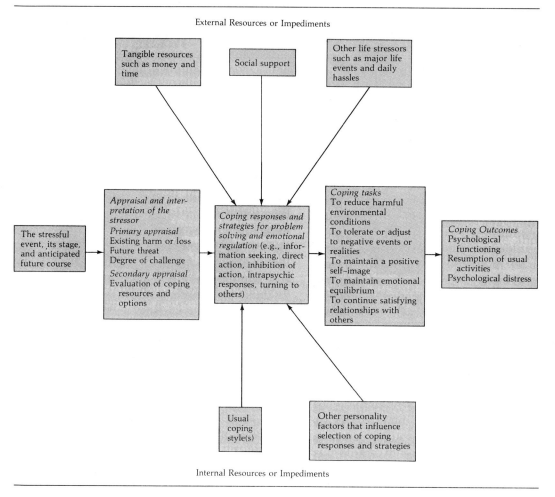

(Sources: Cohen & Lazarus, 1979; Hamburg & Adams, 1967; Lazarus & Folkman, 1984; Moos, 1988; Taylor, 1983)

and the problems that are imposed by the particular setting within which the event has arisen.

In an early effort to examine coping strategies comprehensively, Folkman and Lazarus (1980) enrolled 100 adult men and women in a 12-month study of stress, coping, and emotions. Respondents were interviewed monthly about their most stressful experiences, and they completed a 68-item checklist called the

Ways of Coping instrument to indicate the thoughts and actions that they had used in dealing with these stressful encounters. Respondents reported using both problem-focused and emotion-focused coping in 98% of their stressful attitudes, suggesting that both types of coping are useful for most types of stressful events. Work-related problems most commonly led people to attempt problem-focused coping efforts, such as taking direct action or seeking help from others. Health problems, in contrast, led to more emotion-focused coping, perhaps because a threat to one's health is an event that must be tolerated but which is not necessarily amenable to direct action. These findings suggest that situations in which something constructive can be done will favor problem-focused coping, whereas those that simply must be accepted favor emotion-focused coping (see also Forsythe & Compas, 1987; McCrae, 1984).

Subsequent research has suggested that coping strategies may be more varied than the simple distinction between problem-focused coping and emotion-focused coping suggests (e.g., Fleishman, 1984). A study by Folkman, Lazarus, and their colleagues (Folkman, Lazarus, Dunkel-Schetter, DeLongis, & Gruen, 1986) explored this possibility in a study with eighty-five married California couples. The respondents were interviewed once a month for 6 months about their most stressful event of the previous week, and coping was assessed using the Ways of Coping instrument. Eight distinct coping strategies emerged in this study. *Confrontative coping* characterized aggressive efforts to change the situation (e.g., "I stood my ground and fought for what I wanted"). *Seeking social support* characterized efforts to obtain emotional comfort and information from others (e.g., "I talked to someone to find out more about the situation"). *Planful problem-solving* described deliberate problem-focused efforts to solve the situation (e.g., "I made a plan of action and followed it"). These three factors most clearly relate to the problem-focused coping dimension identified earlier.

Other specific coping strategies were more focused on the regulation of emotion. *Self-control* described efforts to regulate one's feelings (e.g., "I tried to keep my feelings to myself"). *Distancing* described efforts to detach oneself from the stressful situation (e.g., "I didn't let it get to me. I refused to think about it too much"). *Positive reappraisal* characterized efforts to find positive meaning in the experience by focusing on personal growth (e.g., "I came out of the experience better than I went in"). *Accepting responsibility* acknowledged one's role in the problem (e.g., "I criticized or lectured myself"). And finally, *Escape/avoidance* described wishful thinking (e.g., "I wished that the situation would go away") or efforts to escape or avoid the situation by eating, drinking, smoking, using drugs, or taking medications. Many subsequent studies have used the Ways of Coping instrument and, in general, a similar set of strategies emerges (e.g., Dunkel-Schetter & Marshall, 1987; Pearlin & Schooler, 1978). A sample of items from the Ways of Coping instrument that draws from all eight of the specific coping strategies appears in Box 8.1.

Although the Ways of Coping instrument currently enjoys wide use among coping researchers, other measures of coping are also available. For example, Stone and Neale (1984) developed a measure of daily coping designed for use in longitudinal studies to see how coping changes on a day-to-day basis over time (see also the Cope measure developed by Carver, Scheier, & Weintraub, 1989). The patterns identified by these instruments produce dimensions of coping that are similar to those identified by the Ways of Coping measure.

While general coping measures have particular advantages for researchers because they enable them to look at commonalities in coping strategies across a wide range of stressors, it is also clear that to get an in-depth sense of how people cope with specific events, sometimes coping measures tailored to those specific events can be more informative. For example, the kinds of stressful events that adolescents typically experience are not necessarily the same as those of adults in work situations and marriages. Wills (1986) designed a coping measure that is specifically tailored to the kinds of problems that adolescents encounter and the kinds of strategies they might use to mute those stressful events.

There are a variety of internal and external **coping resources** and constraints that influ-

Box 8.1
Ways of Coping

Until recently, the measurement of coping has been elusive. However, a number of standardized measures, including the popular Ways of Coping instrument, developed by Lazarus and his associates, are now available to understand the many ways in which people deal with stressful events.

In using the Ways of Coping instrument, the person is asked to name a specific stressor (such as beginning college freshman year) and then rate on a 5-point scale how stressful the experience has been. After rating the stressfulness of the experience, subjects are asked to rate each of a large number of coping strategies to indicate the extent to which they had used it in dealing with this problem. Instructions for the Ways of Coping instrument, using the example of beginning college, follow, as well as some of the specific items from the Ways of Coping instrument that assess how people cope with this event.

How stressful has college been for you in the past few weeks?

1. Extremely stressful
2. Stressful
3. Somewhat stressful
4. Slightly stressful
5. Not stressful

When we experience stress in our lives, we usually try to manage it by trying out different ways of thinking or behaving. These can be called ways of "coping." Sometimes our attempts are successful in helping us solve a problem or feel better and other times they are not. The next set of items is on the ways of coping you may have used in trying to manage the stress of beginning college. Please read each item below and indicate *how often you have tried this in the past few weeks* in attempting to cope with college. It is important that you answer every item as best you can.
(Box continues on next page.)

(Folkman & Lazarus, 1988)

---

ence the selection or use of particular coping strategies. These factors are called "moderators" of the stress experience because they influence how stressful an experience will be and what coping strategies an individual will bring to bear on the stressful experience. Internal resources or impediments consist of coping styles and other personality factors. External resources or impediments include money and time, social support, and other life stressors that may be occurring simultaneously with the stressful event, including both major life events and daily hassles. To get a true picture of the coping process, one must understand how these various forces interact (e.g., Cohen & Edwards, 1989; Pearlin, Meaghan, Lieberman, & Mullan, 1981).

MODERATORS OF THE STRESS EXPERIENCE

Coping Style

One internal moderator of the stress experience is a person's coping style. **Coping style** is a general propensity to deal with stressful events in a particular way. As an example, we all know people who deal with stress by tell-

	RARELY	SOME-TIMES	OFTEN	VERY OFTEN	DOES NOT APPLY/ NEVER
1. Talked to someone who could do something concrete about the situation	1	2	3	4	0
2. Hoped a miracle would happen	1	2	3	4	0
3. Just concentrated on what I had to do next, the next step	1	2	3	4	0
4. Tried to analyze the situation in order to understand it better	1	2	3	4	0
5. Tried to maintain a positive attitude about the problem	1	2	3	4	0
6. Tried to keep my feelings about the problem to myself	1	2	3	4	0
7. Believed I changed or grew as a person in a good way	1	2	3	4	0
8. Made a plan of action and tried to follow it	1	2	3	4	0
9. Realized I brought the problem on myself	1	2	3	4	0
10. Prepared myself for the worst	1	2	3	4	0
11. Daydreamed or imagined a better time or place than the one I was in	1	2	3	4	0
12. Asked a relative or friend I respected for advice	1	2	3	4	0
13. Tried to make myself feel better by overeating, drinking, smoking, or using drugs or medication	1	2	3	4	0

ing other people about it, whereas other people keep their problems to themselves. Although a variety of coping styles exist, only a few have received systematic study.

Avoidance vs. Confrontation Researchers have extensively studied individuals who cope with a threatening event by using an **avoidant (minimizing) coping style,** comparing them with people who are more likely to use a **confrontative (vigilant) coping style,** by gathering information or taking direct action (Holahan & Moos, 1987a). Neither style is necessarily more effective in managing stress; each seems to have its advantages and liabili-

ties, depending on the situation in which it is employed. Vigilant strategies may be more successful than avoidance in coping with stressful events, if one can focus on the information (such as sensory details) present in the situation, rather than on one's emotions (Suls & Fletcher, 1985).

Whether avoidant or vigilant strategies are more successful also depends on the temporal course of the stressor. People who cope with stress by minimizing or avoiding threatening events seem to cope effectively with short-term threats (e.g., Kaloupek & Stoupakis, 1985; Kaloupek, White, & Wong, 1984; Kiyak, Vitaliano, & Crinean, 1988; Wong & Kalou-

Coping researchers have found that direct action often leads to better adjustment to a stressful event than coping efforts aimed at avoidance of the issue or denial.

pek, 1986). However, if the threat is repeated or persists over time, a strategy of avoidance may not be so successful. People who cope by using avoidance seem unable to deal with the possibility of future threat; hence, they may not make enough cognitive and emotional efforts to anticipate and manage subsequent problems (Suls & Fletcher, 1985; Taylor & Clark, 1986). In contrast, individuals who cope with threatening events through confrontation or vigilance may well engage in the cognitive and emotional efforts needed to deal with long-term threats. In the short term, however, they may pay a price in anxiety (Goldstein, 1973; Miller & Mangan, 1983). Thus, the "avoider" or "minimizer" may cope well with a trip to the dentist but cope poorly with ongoing job stress. In contrast, the "vigilant" coper may fret over the visit to the dentist but make efforts to reduce stress on the job.

Research by Holahan and Moos (1987b; see also Holahan & Moos, 1986) suggests that the risks of avoidant coping may be underesti-

mated by short-term studies. In a 1-year longitudinal study of negative life events and emotional and physical distress in 400 adults and their children, avoidance coping predicted distress even when initial levels of distress were controlled for. Holahan and Moos concluded that the chronic use of avoidance as a coping style constitutes a psychological risk factor for adverse responses to stressful life circumstances (see also Cronkite & Moos, 1984; Felton, Revenson, & Hinrichsen, 1984; Quinn, Fontana, & Reznikoff, 1987).

The emphasis on coping style might seem to be in conflict with the idea that people use a variety of coping strategies to solve most stressful events. However, both points appear to be true. That is, while most people have a number of coping strategies available to deal with a stressful event, they may also characteristically favor certain kinds of coping strategies over others. For example, people who have more personal and environmental resources, such as higher income, more friends, a confident interpersonal style, or a good job, seem to rely more on active coping efforts and less on avoidance coping (Holahan & Moos, 1987a).

Catharsis   Recently, research has begun to explore the value of venting—or **catharsis**—as a coping strategy for dealing with traumatic events. For many years, researchers have suspected that when people undergo traumatic events about which they cannot communicate, those events may fester inside them, producing obsessive thoughts for years and even decades (see, for example, Silver, Boon, & Stones, 1983). This inhibition of traumatic events involves physiological work, and the more people are forced to inhibit their thoughts, emotions, and behaviors, the more their physiological activity may increase (Pennebaker, 1985; Pennebaker & Susman, 1988). Consequently, the ability to confide in others or to consciously confront these feelings and perceptions may eliminate the need to obsess about and inhibit the event, and it may also reduce the physiological activity associated with it. Consistent with this point, Pennebaker, Hughes, and O'Heeron (1987) found that when people talk about traumatic events, their skin conductance, heart rate, and systolic and diastolic blood pressure all decrease. Reasoning that these changes may have long-term positive effects on health outcomes, Pennebaker and his associates initiated a set of studies to examine the short- and long-term effects of venting about traumatic events.

Pennebaker and O'Heeron (1984), for example, found that individuals whose spouses had died the previous year either by suicide or in an automobile accident were less likely to become ill during the subsequent year the more they talked about the death with others. It is possible, of course, that adjusting well to an event and talking about it are part of some underlying personality variable, such as personal control, and so longitudinal studies are needed to address the direction of causality. In a longitudinal study, Pennebaker and Beall (1986) had forty-six undergraduates write about either the most traumatic and stressful event of their life or about trivial topics. Although the individuals writing about traumas were more upset after they wrote their essays (see also Pennebaker, Colder, & Sharp, in press), they were less likely to visit the student health center for illness in the next 6 months (see also Greenberg and Stone, 1990; Pennebaker, 1988; Pennebaker, Kiecolt-Glaser, & Glaser, 1988).

There are many reasons to think that talking about a stressful event or confiding in others should be useful for coping. Talking with others allows one to gain information about the event or about effective coping; it may also elicit positive reinforcement and emotional support from others. In addition, there may be reliable cognitive effects associated with talking about or writing about a traumatic event, such as organizing one's thoughts and being able to find meaning in the experience. Additional research can help identify the pathways by which catharsis improves coping with a trauma.

Multiple Coping Strategies   Successful coping may depend more on matching available coping strategies to the features of a stressful event than on finding the particular coping strategy that is more successful. Most stressful events involve a variety of smaller problems, each of which may be conducive to different coping strategies. For example, a person going through a divorce must deal with his or her emotions, disentangle finances from those of the ex-spouse, help arrange for sharing custody of the children, and the like. Each of these aspects of the divorce will require different strategies. Consistent with this point, research suggests that multiple coping strategies may be most adaptive in managing at least some stressful events (Collins, Taylor, & Skokan, in press; Pearlin & Schooler, 1978).

Costs of Coping   Although coping efforts may successfully mute the impact of a stressful event, they are not without their costs. Coping takes effort, concentration, and attention, thereby reducing the availability of these resources for other tasks. For example, while a student is attempting to cope with the aftermath of a romantic breakup, his or her attention to schoolwork may decline because current energies are focused on managing the stressful event. Similarly, other stressful events, such as an automobile accident, require commitments of time and funds that reduce their availability for meeting other goals and pursuing more desirable activities. To date, these **costs of coping** have received relatively little attention, but they are clearly important (Cohen, Evans, Stokols, & Krantz, 1986).

Personality Factors

In addition to coping styles, other personality factors have been studied that appear to affect stress and the coping process in positive or negative ways. One can make a crude distinction between those personality variables that affect the amount of stress a person experiences and those that promote effective coping (Betz & Thomas, 1979; Wheaton, 1983).

Sensation Seeking   A variable that influences how much stress a person experiences is **sensation seeking.** People vary in their need for and tolerance of stimulation. Some people actively seek the thrills of auto racing, hang gliding, and traveling to exotic places, whereas others become distressed when their familiar routine is even mildly disturbed. Preference for sensation seeking is measured by the Sensation-Seeking Scale, which includes such items as, "I would like a job that would require a lot of travel" and "I sometimes like to do things that are a little frightening" (Zuckerman, 1971). Research suggests that people who have a low need for stimulation

experience more distress when they encounter stressful life events than people who are high in sensation seeking (Johnson, Sarason, & Siegel, 1979). Other personality factors that influence the amount of stress a person experiences may be identified by future research.

In contrast to personality variables that directly affect the experience of stress, there are also personality variables that may promote positive coping (Betz & Thomas, 1979; Wheaton, 1983). As examples, we will look at two personality variables—hardiness and optimism—that moderate the impact of stress on illness.

Hardiness   In an early investigation of "hardiness," Kobasa (1979) studied middle- and upper-level business executives to see which ones developed illness as a consequence of their stressful lifestyle and which ones did not. First, using the Schedule of Recent Life Events, she divided the group into executives who had experienced a lot of stress during the previous 3 years and those who had experienced less stress. Then, looking only at the high-stress executives, she compared those who had had a lot of illnesses with those who had had relatively few illnesses to see what distinguished them. She found that the highly stressed but healthy executives had a multifaceted personality style she termed hardiness.

Hardiness is composed of several characteristics. The first is a sense of *commitment,* or the tendency to involve oneself in whatever one encounters. The second factor is a belief in *control,* the sense that one causes the events that happen in one's life and that one can influence one's environment. The third component is *challenge,* a willingness to undertake change and confront new activities that represent opportunities for growth. As a result of their sense of commitment, control, and challenge, hardy individuals may appraise potentially stressful life events more favorably than would individuals who are not so hardy.

Therefore they may take more direct action to find out about these events, to incorporate them into their lives, and to learn from them what may be of value for the future. Consequently, an important way by which the hardy individual may avoid the illness that potentially stressful events can cause is by transforming these events into less stressful ones.

Many research investigations have found that hardiness relates to both good physical and good mental health (Kobasa, Maddi, & Courington, 1981; Kobasa, Maddi, & Puccetti, 1982; Kobasa & Puccetti, 1983; Nowack, 1989; Wiebe & McCallum, 1986). In one study (Kobasa, Maddi, Puccetti, & Zola, 1985), male business executives who had reported experiencing a high level of stress in the preceding year filled out questionnaires to measure their illness over the past year, their hardiness, the degree of social support they experienced, and the extent to which they exercised. A year later, they completed the survey on illness again for the intervening year. The results indicated that hardiness, social support, and exercise, were all protective. Men who had high levels of hardiness, experienced high levels of social support, and exercised more were less likely to develop illness.

The hardiness concept has been criticized on a number of grounds. Some have argued that hardiness is a response style, rather than a set of personality resources for transforming stressful events. That is, it may be that hardy people focus on the positive aspects of their lives and therefore do not report as much stress as non-hardy individuals. Thus, those who score low on the hardiness scale may simply be people with a propensity for negative affect (depression, anxiety, and hostility), which, in turn, influences how they appraise and interpret their life experiences (Allred & Smith, 1989; Rhodewalt & Zone, 1989). Others have argued that hardiness is not a unitary construct; the subcomponents of commitment,

control, and challenge may be relatively poorly related to each other and related in different ways to health outcomes (Hull, Van Treuren, & Virnelli, 1987; see also Funk & Houston, 1987). In particular, only the commitment and control variables appear to be systematically related to health outcomes. A sense of personal control, of course, has been independently related to the ability to combat stress, and some have argued that this may be the most important component of the hardiness construct (Cohen & Edwards, 1989). Lack of commitment and lack of control may be associated with illness because they are psychologically stressful states, as opposed to resources that moderate the stress-illness relationship (Hull et al., 1987).

Finally, research has questioned whether those exhibiting hardiness actually combat stress better or whether hardiness influences the stress-illness relation via health practices (Allred & Smith, 1989; Wiebe & McCallum, 1986). Those high in hardiness take better care of themselves when they encounter stress than do individuals low in hardiness. As such, hardiness may have little impact on physiological reactivity with respect to the development of disease but may, rather, affect health behaviors associated with the likelihood of disease.

Despite these questions about the status of the hardiness construct, the work has been important for several reasons. It helps focus research attention on the positive psychological states that people may bring to bear on stressful events that may help them cope more effectively. As such, it is an illustration of an important method of studying stress—namely, focusing attention on the people who do not succumb to stress rather than on the ones who do. This emphasis was echoed by stress researcher Aron Antonovsky (1979), who urged health psychologists to examine the causes of good health and not merely those factors that lead people to be stressed or ill.

Optimism   Recently, the idea has been proposed that an optimistic nature can lead people to cope more effectively with stress and, consequently, reduce their risk for illness (Horowitz, Adler, & Kegeles, 1988; Scheier & Carver, 1985). Scheier and Carver began their research by developing a measure of dispositional **optimism** aimed at identifying generalized expectations that outcomes will be positive. Box 8.2 lists the items on this measure, the Life Orientation Test (LOT). In a study with undergraduates, respondents were asked to complete several questionnaires, including the LOT, 4 weeks before the end of the semester. Students who reported being highly optimistic were less likely to be bothered by physical symptoms at the end of the semester than those scoring lower on the optimism scale.

Moreover, this relationship persisted, even when the investigators controlled statistically for the initial numbers of physical symptoms reported by the students.

Exactly how might optimism exert a positive impact on symptom expression, psychological adjustment, and health outcomes? Scheier, Weintraub, and Carver (1986) examined the kind of coping strategies typically associated with dispositional optimism and pessimism. In studies conducted with undergraduates given both the LOT and the Ways of Coping Inventory, they found that optimism was associated with more use of problem-focused coping, seeking of social support, and emphasizing the positive aspects of a stressful situation. Pessimism, in contrast, was associated with denial and distancing

---

Box 8.2
The Measurement of Optimism

People vary in whether they are fundamentally optimistic or pessimistic about life. Scheier and Carver (1985) developed a scale of dispositional optimism to measure this pervasive individual difference. Items from the Life Orientation Test (LOT) are as follows. (For each item, answer "true" or "false.")

1. In uncertain times, I usually expect the best.
2. It's easy for me to relax.
3. If something can go wrong for me, it will.
4. I always look on the bright side of things.
5. I'm always optimistic about my future.
6. I enjoy my friends a lot.

7. It's important for me to keep busy.
8. I hardly ever expect things to go my way.
9. Things never work out the way I want them to.
10. I don't get upset too easily.
11. I'm a believer in the idea that "every cloud has a silver lining."
12. I rarely count on good things happening to me.

Items 2, 6, 7, and 10 are filler items. This means that they are not assumed to measure optimism. Items 1, 4, 5, and 11 are optimistically worded items. Items 3, 8, 9, and 12 are reversed prior to scoring, since they are phrased in the pessimistic direction. Total your score and see how optimistic you are.

from the event, focusing directly on stressful feelings, and disengagement from the goal with which the stressor was interfering.

In a study with coronary artery bypass patients (Scheier et al., 1989), optimism was also an important predictor of coping efforts and of recovery from surgery. Specifically, optimists used more problem-focused coping and made less use of denial. They had a faster rate of recovery during hospitalization and a faster rate of returning to normal life activities after discharge. There was also a strong relationship between optimism and postsurgical quality of life 6 months later, with optimists doing better. It may be, then, that optimism reduces symptoms and improves adjustment to illness, because it is associated with the use of effective coping strategies. However, just as the hardiness construct has been criticized for its overlap with other constructs, the LOT may also be confounded with neuroticism (Smith, Pope, Rhodewalt, & Poulton, 1989) and with mastery (Marshall & Lang, 1990).

Additional Coping Resources   In addition to hardiness and optimism, other variables have been suggested that may facilitate coping. These include a sense of self-efficacy, that is, the belief that one is the sort of person who can accomplish one's goals (Bandura, 1977; Cohen & Edwards, 1989; McClelland, 1989), high self-esteem (Leventhal & Nerenz, 1982), self-confidence (Holahan & Moos, 1987a), an easygoing disposition (Holahan & Moos, 1987a), affiliative trust in others (McClelland, 1989), intelligence (e.g., Krasnoff, 1959), and ego strength (Worden & Sobel, 1978), a measure of an individual's capacity to adapt to threat. In addition, having a sense of coherence about one's life (Antonovsky, 1979), having a sense of purpose or meaning in one's life (Visotsky, Hamburg, Goss, & Lebovitz, 1961), and having a sense of humor (Cousins, 1979; Moody, 1978) have all been suggested as internal resources that may promote effective coping.

Unfortunately, relatively few investigations have examined these factors systematically as potential moderators of the stress experience. Cohen and Edwards (1989) argued that there is evidence that a sense of personal control effectively buffers the experience of stress. The ability to positively reevaluate a stressful experience may also buffer people against the adverse effects of stressful experiences, as may coping flexibility and sensation-seeking. The evidence is not sufficiently plentiful to address other variables definitively at the present time (Cohen & Edwards, 1989). Box 8.3 illustrates how some AIDS patients cope with the stress of having the disease.

Despite cautions and insufficient evidence, the preceding conjectures raise the possibility that there is a health-prone personality, characterized by a sense of control, optimism, and resilience. This is an important counterpoint to the research considered in Chapter 7, which examines the possibility of an illness-prone personality, characterized by a pessimistic explanatory style and negative affectivity (Friedman & Booth-Kewley, 1987; Peterson et al., 1988; see Taylor, 1989).

COPING AND EXTERNAL RESOURCES

Coping is influenced not only by the internal resources an individual has but also by external resources. These include time, money, education, and standard of living; social support; and the absence of other life stressors. Researchers have questioned whether resources affect coping directly by improving a person's ability to cope with both low and high levels of stress, or whether resources act primarily as a buffer against stress. In this latter view, resources may have little effect on a person's coping success at low levels of stress, but may become important at high levels of stress (the buffering hypothesis).

One study explored the buffering hypothesis and examined the personal resources of

Box 8.3
Coping with AIDS

AIDS has killed many thousands of people, and thousands more live, sometimes for years, with the knowledge that they have the disease. Such a threat requires and elicits many forms of coping, some of which are illustrated in the excerpts from these interviews with AIDS patients.

Social Support or Seeking Information

A key point in my program is that I have a really good support network of people who are willing to take the time, who will go the extra mile for me. I have spent years cultivating these friendships.

My family has been extremely supportive, and my lover has been extremely supportive, but it really wasn't quite enough. They weren't helping me in the right ways. That's when I went and got a therapist. Basically, she is the one who has helped me cope with [AIDS] and understand it.

I try to find people that have manifested long-term living with AIDS or have been healed. There are a few people out there, and I try to listen to them. There are also a lot of people who are angry and bitter and more than willing to give advice. I have learned a lot from them about what not to do, which is just as important as learning what to do.

Direct Action

My main concern is making it through another day without getting any disorder. I would really like to completely beat it.

My first concern was that, as promiscuous as I have been, I could not accept giving this to anyone. So I have been changing my lifestyle completely, putting everything else on the back burner.

The main thing I did was to get all my paperwork in order. I was good at it before, but when AIDS hit, I made sure everything was spelled out perfectly, and I figure that makes it easier for my lover left behind. He will go through grief, but he will not have to be sorting through all my junk.

Strategies of Distraction, Escape, or Avoidance

I used to depend on drugs a lot to change my mood. Once in a while, I still find that if I can't feel better any other way, I will take a puff of grass or have a glass of wine, or I use music. There are certain recordings that can really change my mood drastically. I play it loud and I dance around and try to clear my head.

I do exactly what I want to do, as much as possible, things that amuse me, entertain me, and pamper me.

There's an old disco song that says, "Keep out of my mind what's out of my hands." I try to do that, to not fret over things I really don't have control over.

It was important to me to focus on something besides AIDS, and my job is the most logical thing. I'm very good at what I do. I have a supervisory position, so I deal with other people's problems, which is good for me, because I take their problems and solve them and I forget about mine. I think that's a real constructive distraction for me.

I drive. I feel so much more at peace when I am driving down the road in a car, listening to music, having my dog next to me. It is wonderful.
(Box continues on next page.)

Emotional Regulation/Ventilation

When you're sad, you cry. That's what I've done a lot lately, over silly, well, not silly things, but over small things, and over reminders of a life that's probably cut short, the expectations of things that you were going to do and planned on doing and don't seem possible now.

I try to be like Spock on "Star Trek." So this is an emotion. So that's what it makes you feel like. I try to analyze it and look as a third party would, like I am an observer from the fiftieth century.

Sometimes I will allow myself to have darker feelings, and then I grab myself by the bootstraps and say, okay, that is fine, you are allowed to have these feelings but they are not going to run your life.

Personal Growth

In the beginning, AIDS made me feel like a poisoned dart, like I was a diseased person and I had no self-esteem and no self-confidence. That's what I have been really working on, is to get the self-confidence and the self-esteem back. I don't know if I will ever be there, but I feel very close to being there, to feeling like my old self.

I've made sure everybody knows how I feel about them. I have given away some of my precious things, some back to the people who gave them to me. I make sure that everyone has something from my past, everyone who's been important in my life, and for the most part, I've sent them all letters too. Not that it was always received well. . . .

When something like this happens to you, you can either melt and disappear or you can come out stronger than you did before.

It has made me a much stronger person. I literally feel like I can cope with anything. Nothing scares me, nothing. If I was on a 747 and they said we were going down, I would probably reach for a magazine.

I really have an advantage in a sense over other people. I know there is a possibility that my life may not go on for as many years as other people's. I have the opportunity to look at my life, to make changes, and to deeply appreciate the time that I have.

Positive Thinking and Restructuring

Everyone dies sooner or later. I have been appreciating how beautiful the Earth is, flowers, and the things I like. I used to go around ignoring all those things. Now I stop to try and smell the roses more often, and just do pleasurable things.

I have been spending a lot of time lately on having a more positive attitude. I force myself to become aware every time I say something negative during a day, and I go, "Oops," and I change it and I rephrase it. So I say, "Wonderful," about 42,000 times a day. Sometimes I don't mean it, but I am convincing myself that I do.

I made a list of all the other diseases I would rather not have than AIDS. Lou Gehrig's disease, being in a wheelchair; rheumatoid arthritis, when you are in knots and in terrible pain. So I said, you've got to get some perspective on this, and where you are on the Great Nasty Disease List.

The last chapter has not been written. The fat lady has not sung. I'm still here.

(Reed, 1989)

health, self-esteem, social support, education, and living in an urban environment (Norris & Murrell, 1984). The researchers found that although these resources did not reduce the likelihood of experiencing a stressful event, they did mute the impact of such events and protected against depression. However, as the amount of stress increased, the advantage of people with strong resources shrank, suggesting that at a certain point stress may overwhelm even the best of resources. This study provides intriguing evidence against the buffering hypothesis by suggesting that resources are primarily helpful at low to moderate levels of stress, but not necessarily at high levels of stress. As we shall see, this is not always the case with social support, although it may characterize external resources more generally. More research is needed about the impact of external resources on the likelihood of experiencing stress and on the ability to combat stress effectively at both high and low levels. In this section, we consider specific external coping resources, beginning with social support.

Social Support

Social ties and relationships with others have long been regarded as emotionally satisfying aspects of life. Recently, the possibility that they may also mute the effects of stress and help an individual cope has been explored by stress researchers with promising results. People undergoing stressful events may turn to others to help them deal with stressful events or to provide them with solace (Bachrach & Zautra, 1985; Ferraro, Mutran, & Barresi, 1984). **Social support** has been defined as information from others that one is loved and cared for, esteemed and valued, and part of a network of communication and mutual obligations (Cobb, 1976). Such information can come from a spouse or lover; other relatives, friends, social and community contacts such as churches or clubs, or even a devoted pet (Culliton, 1987). People with high levels of so-

cial support may experience less stress when they confront a stressful experience, and they may cope with it more successfully.

Benefits of Social Support   What, exactly, are the benefits that social support provides? Researchers have typically grouped potential benefits into three categories: tangible assistance, information, and emotional support (House, 1981; Pinneau, 1975; Schaefer, Coyne, & Lazarus, 1981). Family and friends may provide tangible assistance in the form of actual goods and services during times of stress. For example, the gifts of food that often arrive after a death in a family mean that the bereaved family members will not have to cook for themselves and for visiting relatives at a time when their energy and enthusiasm for such tasks is low. Second, family and friends can provide *information* by suggesting specific actions an individual can take to combat a stressor. The person under stress can try out his or her definition of the problem and potential solutions, and supportive friends and family can provide feedback. For example, if an individual is having problems with work overload, discussions with friends or co-workers may provide helpful feedback and advice on how to manage time or delegate tasks appropriately.

During times of stress, people often suffer emotionally and may experience bouts of depression, sadness, anxiety, and loss of self-esteem. Supportive friends and family can provide *emotional support* by reassuring the person that he or she is a valuable individual who is cared for by others. The warmth and nurturance provided by others can enable a person under stress to approach it with greater assurance.

Research demonstrates that social support effectively reduces distress during times of stress (see Cohen & Wills, 1985; Kessler & McLeod, 1985; Wallston, Alagna, DeVellis, & DeVellis, 1983, for reviews). For example, a number of studies of soldiers in combat suggest that the camaraderie within the combat team (such as a bomber crew or a gunnery team) reduces the distress of battle (e.g., Mandelbaum, 1952; Rose, 1980). A study of residents near the site of the Three Mile Island nuclear accident in 1979 revealed that people with high levels of social support felt less distressed than those with low levels of social support (Fleming, Baum, Gisriel, & Gatchel, 1982). Moreover, the lack of social support during times of need can itself be very stressful, especially for people with high needs for social support but insufficient opportunities to obtain it. These may include the elderly, the recently widowed (Dunkel-Schetter & Wortman, 1981; Glick, Weiss, & Parkes, 1974) and other victims of sudden, severe, uncontrollable life events.

Effect of Social Support on Illness and Health Habits   Social support also appears to lower the likelihood of illness, to speed recovery from illness when it does occur (e.g., Kulik & Mahler, 1989), and to reduce the risk of mortality due to serious disease (House, Umberson, & Landis, 1988). In-depth studies that control for initial health status showed that people with a high quantity and sometimes a high quality of social relationships had lower mortality rates (Berkman, 1985; House et al., 1988). Social isolation also appears to be a major risk factor for death from a number of causes for both humans and animals (House et al., 1988). Thus, the evidence linking social support to a reduced risk of mortality is substantial.

As an example, some impressive evidence for the role of social support in combating the threat of illness comes from a survey of adults in Alameda County, California (Berkman & Syme, 1979). Almost 7,000 people were asked about their social and community ties, and their death rate was tracked over a 9-year period. The results showed that people who had

few social and community ties were more likely to die during this period than were people with many such ties. Having social contacts enabled women to live an average of 2.8 years longer and men an average of 2.3 years longer. These effects were not caused by differences in socioeconomic status, health status at the beginning of the study, or the practice of health habits.

People with high levels of social support have fewer complications during pregnancy (Nuckolls, Cassell, & Kaplan, 1972), less susceptibility to herpes attacks (VanderPlate, Aral, & Magder, 1988), lower rates of myocardial infarction (Bruhn, 1965), and lower rates of psychological distress (Billings & Moos, 1982; Eaton, 1978; Kaplan, Robbins, & Martin, 1983; Lin, Simeone, Ensel, & Kuo, 1979; Williams, Ware, & Donald, 1981). Those with high levels of social support are also less likely to suffer psychological or physical adverse health consequences of highly stressful events, such as residential crowding (e.g., Evans, Palsane, Lepore, & Martin, 1989). However, studies investigating differences in illness rates among people with high versus low levels of social support have found mixed results (Holahan & Moos 1986; Sarason & Sarason, 1984; Wallston et al., 1983; Wortman, 1984). It may be that social support is more effective in reducing stress and distress than in actually preventing illness.

Social support does seem to enhance the prospects for recovery among people who are already ill (Wallston et al., 1983). Social support has been associated with better or faster recoveries from congestive heart failure (Chambers & Reiser, 1953), kidney disease (Dimond, 1979), childhood leukemia (Magni, Silvestro, Tamiello, Zanesco, & Carl, 1988), and stroke (Robertson & Suinn, 1968) and with a reduced likelihood of mortality from myocardial infarction (Wiklund et al., 1988), better diabetes control (Marteau, Bloch, & Baum, 1987; Schwartz, Springer, Flaherty, & Kiani, 1986; but see Kaplan & Hartwell,

In addition to being an enjoyable aspect of life, social support from family and friends helps keep people healthy and may help them recover faster when they are ill.

1987), and less pain among arthritis patients (DeVellis, DeVellis, Sauter, & Cohen, 1986). Social support also appears to reduce the distress that may accompany illness. For example, studies of patients with AIDS and AIDS-related complex (ARC) found that the more available social support was perceived to be, the less depression and hopelessness these patients experienced (Zich & Temoshok, 1987).

Although social support has an impact on health independent of any influence on health habits, it also appears to affect health habits directly (Umberson, 1987). People with high levels of social support are more compliant with their medication regimens (Cobb, 1976; Wallston et al., 1983), and they are more likely to use health services, especially when the support network is positively inclined toward those services (Geersten, Klauber, Rindflesh, Kane, & Gray, 1975; Wallston et al., 1983). Some social influences may adversely affect some health habits, however, as when one's peer group smokes, drinks heavily, or takes

drugs, (Caplan, Cobb, & French, 1975; Wills & Vaughan, 1989).

Moderation of Stress by Social Support
What, exactly, is the role of social support in moderating the effects of stress? Two possibilities have been extensively explored. One hypothesis maintains that social support is generally beneficial during nonstressful times as well as during highly stressful times (the **direct effects hypothesis**). The other hypothesis, known as the **buffering hypothesis,** maintains that the health and mental health benefits of social support are chiefly evident during periods of high stress; when there is little stress, social support may have few physical or mental health benefits. According to this hypothesis, what social support does is act as a reserve and resource that blunts the effects of stress or enables the individual to cope with stress more effectively when it is at high levels.

Evidence suggesting both direct effects and buffering effects of social support has amassed (Cohen & Hoberman, 1983; Cohen & McKay, 1983; Gore, 1978; Pilisuk, Boylan, & Acredolo, 1987; Thoits, 1982; Turner, 1981; Wills, 1984). Generally, when researchers have looked at social support in social integration terms, such as the numbers of people one identifies as friends or the number of organizations one belongs to, direct effects of social support on health have been found. When social support has been assessed more qualitatively, such as the degree to which a person feels that there are others available to him in the environment to help him if he needs it, then buffering effects of social support have been found (Cohen & Wills, 1985; House et al., 1988; Kessler & McLeod, 1985; Wortman & Dunkel-Schetter, 1979). Whether the perceived availability of support buffers stress because it reflects actual support that may promote health and adjustment or because it enables people to appraise stressful events differently remains unknown (Wethington & Kessler, 1986; see also Wheaton, 1985).

Not all aspects of social support are equally protective against stress (for a review, see Lieberman, 1982). For example, having a confidante (such as a spouse or partner) may be the most effective social support (Lin, Woelfel, & Light, 1985; Umberson, 1987), especially for men (see House, Robbins, & Metzner, 1982). The beneficial effects of social support are also not necessarily cumulative. For example, with respect to friends, the critical factor for effective social support is having at least one close friend. Having a dozen close friends may be no more beneficial than having two or three (Langner & Michael, 1960). Thus, it is not necessarily the case that more social support is better. Rather, the important factor is having at least some close social support. In fact, there is some evidence that too much or overly intrusive social support may actually exacerbate stress (Lieberman, 1982). People who belong to "dense" social networks (friendship or family groups that are highly interactive and in which everyone knows everyone else) may find themselves besieged by advice and interference in times of stress.

The effectiveness of social support further depends on how an individual uses a social support network. Some people may be ineffective in extracting the support they need from others, prompting researchers to wonder if the effective use of social support is more of a personality difference than a resource. For example, Dunkel-Schetter, Folkman, and Lazarus (1987) found evidence that person predispositions relate strongly to emotional support, but not as strongly to aid or information support. These findings tentatively suggest that the ability to extract emotional support from others may be a personality factor (such as sociability or likeability), at least more so than is true for other kinds of social support (see also Connell & D'Augelli, 1990).

To examine this hypothesis further, Cohen, Sherrod, and Clark (1986) assessed incoming college freshmen as to their social competence, social anxiety, and self-disclosure skills.

Their purposes were to see if these skills related to whether or not the students were able to develop and use social support effectively, and to identify if these same skills could account for the positive effects of social support in combating stress. Their results only partially confirmed the idea that the effective use of social support depends on personality. Those with greater social competence, lower social anxiety, and better self-disclosure skills did develop more effective social support and were more likely to form friendships. However, social support exerted a buffering effect against stress independent of these personality variables. Individual differences in personality, then, may promote the development of effective social support networks, but do not in themselves appear to account for the effectiveness of social support in buffering stress (House et al., 1988).

Providing Effective Social Support   Providing effective social support is not always easy for the support network. It requires substantial skill. When it is provided by the wrong person, support may be unhelpful or even rejected, as, for example, when a stranger tries to comfort a lost child. Social support may also be ineffective if the type of support provided is not exactly the kind that is needed. In this context, Thoits (1986) reconceptualized social support as coping assistance, arguing that different stressful events create different needs, which, in turn, elicit coping efforts. She argued that social support may be constructively viewed as assisting those coping efforts. Thus, social support should be most effective when support providers suggest or participate in the kinds of coping strategies that will be most effective in reducing the problems associated with that particular stressor. Thoits argued that empathetic understanding is a critical skill for providers to have, so that they can sense what kinds of support will be most helpful to a person undergoing a particular stressor. Consistent with this viewpoint, Dunkel-Schetter et al. (1987) found that individuals' ways of coping were strongly associated with the types of support they received. These findings imply that the coping strategies people use when they are under stress communicate that support is needed and what particular kind of support may be needed.

The conceptualization of social support as coping assistance, in turn, has fostered the idea that effective social support may depend on a match between one's needs and what one receives from others in one's social network (the **matching hypothesis**) (cf. Jacobson, 1986). In a preliminary effort to address this hypothesis, Cutrona and Russell (in press) identified qualities of stressful events and then made predictions about the kinds of social support that might best meet the needs of people suffering from those types of stressors. The dimensions they identified were controllability of the stressor, valence (positive, negative), and domain; domain referred to stressors in the areas of tangible assets (e.g., lack of money), achievement (e.g., loss of a job), relationships (e.g., a romantic breakup), and social role (e.g., being retired). They argued that uncontrollable stressors should require greater levels of emotional support, whereas controllable stressors should require a greater preponderance of problem-solving activity, such as information and advice. In terms of valence, they predicted that positive events would require support that aided in the reduction of anxiety and that negative events would require support that aided in the reduction of depression. In terms of domain, they predicted that support that helped replace or offset the specific kind of loss entailed would be most valued. Thus, tangible aid should help when there is a threat to personal assets, and reassurance of capabilities and self-worth should help when there is a threat to achievement.

Generally, the results supported the predictions, particularly for the controllability/uncontrollability dimension. Results were less consistent in terms of the domain-specific predictions. It appears that a stressful event in a particular domain (such as loss of finances) has so many repercussions for one's life more generally that many types of support become valuable, not just support designed to replenish the area that was threatened initially by the stressful event (see also Stroebe & Stroebe, 1983). Timing of particular forms of coping assistance to the temporal cause of a stressor may further refine these matching approaches (Jacobson, 1986).

Studies with cancer patients (Dakof & Taylor, 1990; Dunkel-Schetter, 1984) suggested a somewhat different version of the matching hypothesis. They suggest that different kinds of support may be valued from different members of one's social support network, in that each member may have unique abilities to be helpful along particular dimensions. These studies suggest that emotional support is most important from intimate others, whereas information and advice may be more valuable from experts, in this case physicians and nurses. Thus, a person who desires solace from a family member but receives advice instead may find that, rather than being supportive, the family member actually makes the stressful situation worse (Brownell & Dooley, 1981; Cohen & McKay, 1983; Dakof & Taylor, 1990; Schaefer et al., 1981).

Stressful events themselves can interfere with the ability to use potential social support effectively. People who are under extreme stress may continually express distress to others and drive those others away, thus making a bad situation even worse. For example, there is evidence that severely depressed people tend to repel their friends and family instead of using them effectively for social support (Coyne, 1976; Coyne et al., 1987; see also Mitchell & Moos, 1984).

Support providers may also react adversely to the stressful event. For example, Wortman and Dunkel-Schetter (1979) suggested that the stressful event of cancer in a loved one or friend creates fear and aversion to the cancer, but a simultaneous awareness of the need to provide support. These tensions may produce a variety of negative outcomes, such as physically avoiding the patient, avoiding open communication about the cancer, minimizing its impact, or demonstrating forced cheerfulness that does little to actually raise the patient's spirit (see also Dakof & Taylor, 1990). Other stressful events such as AIDS (Zich & Temoshok, 1987), unemployment (Atkinson, Liem, & Liem, 1986), Alzheimer's disease (Kiecolt-Glaser, Dyar, & Shuttleworth, 1988), or mental illness (Fisher & Tessler, 1986) may similarly alarm and create conflict for a person's social support network.

Researchers are also increasingly turning their attention to the problems that providers experience in their attempts to provide social support, as in attempting to care for an ill family member (Coyne et al., 1987; Kessler, McLeod, & Wethington, 1985; Kiecolt-Glaser, Dyar, & Shuttleworth, 1987; Schulz, Tompkins, Wood, & Decker, 1987). For example, the stress involved for a family member in taking care of a patient with Alzheimer's disease is enormous, aggravated in part by the fact that the recipient of the support may be unaware of those efforts and consequently unappreciative. When a close friend, family member, or partner is going through a stressful event, often the event also has an impact on close family members who may themselves have resulting needs for social support that may go unmet (e.g., Cassileth et al., 1988; Ell, Nishimoto, Mantell, & Hamovitch, 1988; Wellisch, Jamison, & Pasnau, 1978; Zarski, West, DePompei, & Hall, 1988). The brunt of caring for family members may fall particularly heavily on women's shoulders. Women report more stressful life events involving loved ones

and are more responsive to them than men (Kessler, McLeod, & Wethington, 1985). To the extent that family members and friends are adversely affected by the stressful event, they may be less able to provide social support to the person in greatest need.

Remaining Issues   Research on social support itself contains problems that make the relationships among stress, social support, and psychological and health outcomes unclear. How to measure social support has been a major question, and researchers are not agreed on the best way to do so (House & Kahn, 1985; Wortman, 1984). The amount of support that is available, desired, and actually received may be very different. As noted earlier, different measures (such as social network measures versus more qualitative measures of perceived support) suggest different kinds of relations between social support and psychological and health outcomes. Of concern, too, is the methodology employed for demonstrating the effects of social support (Heitzmann & Kaplan, 1988). Relatively few studies have collected the best kind of evidence for the effects of social support, namely longitudinal investigations that relate the availability and use of support to psychological and health outcomes at a later point in time. Finally, stress itself often produces loss of social support, and thus the two variables are often confounded (see Thoits, 1982; Wortman, 1984).

One of the most important tasks facing social support researchers at the present time is attempting to identify the psychological and biological pathways by which different aspects of social support exert their effects on health (Cohen, 1988; House et al., 1988). The fact that social support alters health behaviors may account for its impact on disease. Alternatively, support may directly affect the biological response a person has to stress and thereby reduce disease. Support may have an impact on both behavior and biological response (Cohen, 1988). In terms of its impact on stress, social support may enable people to appraise stressful events more favorably and to damp down their endocrine responses to a stressful event after reappraisal. In an analysis of the possible relations among social support, stress, and illness and psychological outcomes, Cohen outlined more than twenty possible models that may characterize these relationships and which merit consideration (Cohen, 1988).

Another important issue that merits increased research attention is what constitutes unsupportive interactions in times of stress and how such unsupportive actions may make things worse. There is some evidence that negative aspects of social interaction may have a more adverse effect on well-being than positive social interactions have on improving well-being. In a study of 120 widowed women, Rook (1984) found that negative social interactions were consistently and more strongly related to well-being than were positive social outcomes. Dilemmas such as having one's privacy invaded by family and friends, being taken advantage of, having promises of help broken, and being involved with people who provoked conflict or anger were among the events that worsened psychological adjustment. Such findings are an important corrective to the general emphasis on the positive effects of social interaction and suggest that research must focus not merely on how to enhance effective social support but also on how to help people avoid social relationships or social situations that actually tax their well-being.

Overall, qualifications about the effects of social support on stress show that the relationships are complex and require further research. On balance, however, social support is advantageous. It reduces the experience of stress, enhances the ability to cope, can reduce the prospect of mental and physical distress or illness, and speeds recovery when illness does occur.

Health psychologists, then, should view social support as an important resource in primary prevention (Gottlieb, 1983; Pilisuk, 1982). Finding ways to increase the effectiveness of existing or potential naturally occurring support from patients' family and friends should be a high research priority. People need to be encouraged to recognize the potential sources of social support in their own environment and to be taught how to draw on these resources more effectively. People might also be taught how to develop social support resources, as by joining community groups, interest groups, or informal social groups that meet regularly. In addition, the family members and significant others of those who are undergoing extremely stressful events, such as a life-threatening illness, can receive guidance in the most effective ways to provide social support and in the well-intended actions they should nonetheless avoid because they actually make the stressful situation worse (e.g., Dakof & Taylor, 1990). Psychologists can contribute to the development of social support mechanisms, explore ways of creating social ties, and develop means of identifying and aiding socially marginal individuals who cannot avail themselves of this valuable resource.

Other External Factors That Moderate Stress

A variety of other external factors also moderate the experience of stress. Money is one obvious example. When a wealthy person rear-ends a car, his stress will be lower and his ability to cope higher than those of a poor person with no insurance. Time is another coping resource. If you are the unfortunate person who got rear-ended, it will be easier for you to get your car repaired if you are on summer vacation than if you are in the middle of final exams.

The presence of other life stressors also moderates coping responses. People who must simultaneously deal with several other sources of stress in their lives—such as a failing marriage, financial difficulties, or other health problems—will have fewer resources left to use in coping with a new stressor than will people who do not have to deal with other life stressors (Cohen & Lazarus, 1979).

COPING OUTCOMES

Coping must be thought of not only as a set of processes that occur in reaction to the problems posed by a particular stressor but also as efforts aimed at the achievement of certain goals. These goals may be thought of as the tasks of coping. A large number of researchers have attempted to identify the tasks of coping (Cohen & Lazarus, 1979; Hamburg & Adams, 1967; Hamburg, Hamburg, & DeGoza, 1953; Taylor, 1983; Visotsky et al., 1961). Summarizing this large literature, Cohen and Lazarus (1979) suggested that coping efforts center on five main tasks: (1) to reduce harmful environmental conditions and enhance the prospects of recovery, (2) to tolerate or adjust to negative events or realities, (3) to maintain a positive self image, (4) to maintain emotional equilibrium, and (5) to continue satisfying relationships with others (p. 232).

To elaborate, the individual must first deal with the immediate demands of the stressor itself. He or she must come to terms with any negative and irreversible problems that the stressor has produced. For example, a newly widowed woman must acknowledge the fact that her husband is no longer with her. Next, one must anticipate future threats and take actions that can reduce further risk: The widow must take stock of her financial situation and must pull herself together so that she can continue to perform the tasks of daily living. The person under stress must also attempt to reduce emotional distress, both that caused by already existing harm and that occasioned by anticipated future stress: The widow must

keep her grieving within manageable bounds so that it does not interfere with her ability to go on with her life. Similarly, she must maintain enough emotional control so that subsequent setbacks, such as the discovery that a life insurance policy had expired, do not become devastating experiences. In the face of severe blows and setbacks, the person under stress must try to maintain self-esteem: The widow must remind herself that she is a person of value and worth, even though the person most likely to encourage that self-image is now deceased. Finally, the person under stress must revive and maintain social relationships as a source of ongoing sustenance. The widow should turn to her social network of relatives and friends so that they can ease her loneliness and unhappiness.

Throughout our discussion we have referred several times to successful coping. It is now appropriate to address the very important question: What constitutes successful coping? First, however, the relationship between coping tasks and **coping outcomes** should be clarified. Figure 8.1 implies that successful coping depends on successful resolution of coping tasks. However, the relationship between coping tasks and coping outcomes is not this direct. There is no research, for example, demonstrating that people must solve every one of these tasks in order to cope well with a stressor. Rather, coping tasks should be thought of as issues around which coping efforts are structured— issues that may or may not be resolved and may continue on a long-term basis. To the extent that coping tasks are solved, one would expect successful coping to occur, but one can undoubtedly cope successfully while still attempting to manage uncompleted coping tasks.

Researchers attempting to define successful coping have evaluated coping with respect to a variety of outcomes. A primary set of coping outcomes has included measures of physiological and biochemical functioning. Coping efforts are generally judged to be more successful if they reduce arousal and its indicators, such as heart rate, pulse, and skin conductivity. If blood or urine levels of catecholamines and corticosteroids are reduced, coping is judged to be more successful.

A second criterion of successful coping is whether and how quickly people can return to their pre-stress activities. Many stressors, especially severe ones like the death of a spouse or chronic ones like excessive noise, interfere with the conduct of daily life activities. To the extent that people's coping efforts enable them to resume usual activities, coping may be judged to be successful. However, there is an implicit bias in this criterion, to the effect that the person's prior living situation was in some sense an ideal one. This is not always true. In fact, substantial life change may follow a stressful event, and this may be a sign of successful rather than unsuccessful coping (Taylor, 1983). For example, a sick person who is overworked and hates his job may not be showing successful adjustment if he returns to the same work situation; revising the work situation would be a more successful form of coping. Finally, and most commonly, researchers judge coping according to its effectiveness in reducing psychological distress. When a person's anxiety or depression is reduced, the coping response is judged to be successful.

Some have argued that coping efficacy can be measured in terms of how successful coping is in reducing the relationship between role strains and emotional distress. By this criterion, someone who copes effectively is a person who continues to experience severe strain but less distress (Pearlin & Schooler, 1978). Unfortunately, however, this criterion may underestimate the impact of coping strategies. If coping strategies are successful in directly reducing stress and not just in terms of reducing the psychological outcomes of stress, then coping efficacy would be underestimated

by the relationship between role strain and emotional stress. Thus, in order to get a full assessment of coping efficacy with respect to stress, it is necessary to look at both the ability of coping efforts to modify the stressful event itself and the degree to which psychological distress and other adverse outcomes are reduced (cf. Pearlin & Schooler, 1978).

In summary, then, there are a number of ways to infer that coping has been successful. It is important to realize, however, that whether or not coping is judged to be successful can depend on the measure of the outcome used (e.g., Stone, 1985). A particular coping response may be judged successful in terms of one coping outcome but not on the basis of another. Thus, a coping effort, such as denial, may reduce psychological distress but also interfere with an individual's ability to take action against the stressor. Or a direct coping effort, such as initiating a legislative action to reduce aircraft noise, may ultimately achieve results, but only at the expense of long-term psychological distress. Coping is a complex process that must be judged according to a number of different criteria, some of which may be affected positively by the effort and others negatively.

Great strides in coping research have been made in the last decade. Researchers have identified many of the common coping strategies that people bring to bear on stressful events. These conceptual developments have been paralleled by advances in the measurement of coping. The field now has several available measures that enjoy wide use and consequently make it possible to compare across studies to identify how people cope with different kinds of stressful events and what commonalities exist in their coping strategies across different classes of stressful events. There remain, however, many conceptual and methodological issues to be examined (e.g., Stone, Kennedy-Moore, Newman, Greenberg, & Neale, in press). In particular, the next frontier of coping research may be to identify the biopsychosocial pathways through which coping efforts and the resources that are brought to bear on the coping process influence psychological and health outcomes. Recent research has begun to explore these avenues and chief among the candidates is the immune system (e.g., Stone et al., in press). More research of this type is clearly needed.

THE MANAGEMENT OF STRESS

Individuals' coping responses are often spontaneous; that is, people do whatever comes naturally to them and what has worked in the past. But sometimes these efforts will not be enough. The stressor may be so novel, so chronic, or so elusive that people's own efforts may be unsuccessful in reducing stress.

Moreover, as we have seen, individual efforts to control stress are not always adaptive, especially in the long term. Coping with chronic stress through excessive alcohol or drug use, for example, may bring relief in the short run, but often the person is worse off for these efforts; the source of stress itself remains unchanged, and the individual may have an addiction to combat on top of all the other sources of stress.

Because people so obviously have difficulty managing stress themselves, health psychologists have increasingly turned their attention to developing techniques of **stress management** that can be taught. Who participates in stress management programs? Some people obtain help in stress management through private therapists in a one-to-one psychotherapeutic experience. More commonly, stress management is taught through workshops. For example, increasingly, stress management courses are offered in the workplace. Stress-related disorders account for as much as $17 billion a year in lost productivity, and one estimate places the annual cost of stress-related illness at $69 billion (Adams, 1978). Conse-

quently, organizations have been motivated to help their workers identify and cope with the variety of stressful events that they experience on the job (e.g., Cooper & Marshall, 1976; Ganster, Mayes, Sime, & Tharp, 1982; Peters, Benson, & Porter, 1977).

Stress-management programs have also been employed extensively with people who suffer from or are at risk for stress-related illnesses. Stress management programs have been used successfully to treat muscle contraction headaches (Holroyd, Andrasik, & Westbrook, 1977), and elements of stress management have been incorporated into treatment programs for migraine headache sufferers (see Turk, Meichenbaum, & Berman, 1979). As we note in Chapter 5, the treatment of alcohol abuse and obesity also frequently incorporates stress management skills (U.S. Department of Health and Human Services, 1981). As we see in Chapter 14, individuals with symptoms of cardiovascular disease or a history of angina or myocardial infarction are often trained in techniques for coping with stress differently to help them control their Type A behavior (e.g., Chesney, Eagleston, & Rosenman, 1981; Roskies, 1980; Roskies et al., 1978); moreover, stress management programs have helped individuals suffering from chronically high blood pressure learn to control it (see Shapiro, Schwartz, Ferguson, Redmond, & Weiss, 1977). Effective stress management has clear health benefits in controlling stress-related disorders and in reducing not only risk factors associated with CHD but also CHD morbidity itself (Carver & Humphries, 1982; Chesney et al., 1981; Roskies, 1980).

Finally, stress management courses are increasingly being offered to groups experiencing particular kinds of problems. In the next section, we describe stress management with reference to a program that has recently been developed at a large U.S. university to help students cope with the stress of college life.

Basic Techniques of Stress Management

Stress management programs typically involve three phases. In the first stage, participants learn what stress is and how to identify the stressors in their own lives. In the second phase, they acquire and practice skills in coping with stress. In the final phase, they practice these stress management techniques in the targeted stressful situations and monitor their effectiveness (Meichenbaum & Jaremko, 1983). To illustrate these phases, let us take the example of a program developed for college students who are having difficulty coping with the stresses of academic life.

College can be an extremely stressful experience for many students. For some, it is the first time away from home, and they must cope with the problems of living in a dormitory surrounded by strangers. They may have to share a room with another person of a very different background with very different personal habits. High noise levels, communal bathrooms, institutional food, and rigorous academic schedules may all be trying experiences to new students. In addition, academic life may prove to be more rigorous than they had expected. Whereas each student may have been a star in high school, there is heavier competition at college, where the students are more similar in intellectual caliber. Consequently, course loads are heavier and grades are typically lower. Because the student was able to do well in high school with relatively little effort, he or she may never have developed the concentration, study skills, or motivation required to excel in the college environment. Coping with a first C, D, or F can be a deflating and anxiety-arousing experience. If the student sees little prospect for improvement, he or she may become increasingly anxious, find that the college environment is too stressful, and drop out. Recognizing that these pressures exist, college administrators have increasingly made stress management programs available to their students.

One university responded to these problems by developing a stress management program that reaches troubled students before the stresses of academic life lead them to flunk out or drop out. The program, called Combat Stress Now (CSN), makes use of the three phases of education, skill acquisition, and practice described above. In the first phase of the CSN program, participants learn what stress is and how it creates physical wear and tear. In sharing their personal experiences of stress, many students find reassurance in the fact that so many other students have experiences similar to their own. Students then learn that stress is a process of psychological appraisal rather than a factor inherent in events themselves. Thus, college life is not inherently stressful, but, rather, a consequence of the individual's perceptions of it. Through these messages, the students begin to see that if they are armed with appropriate stress management techniques, they will come to experience currently stressful events as less stressful.

In the self-monitoring phase of the CSN program, students are trained to observe their own behavior closely and to record the circumstances that they find most stressful. In addition, they record their physiological, emotional, and behavioral reactions to those stresses as they experience them. They also record their own maladaptive efforts to cope with these stressful events, including excessive sleeping or eating, watching television, consuming alcohol, and other such responses.

Once they learn to chart stress responses, they are encouraged to examine the antecedents of these experiences. In particular, they learn to focus on what events happened just before they experience subjective feelings of stress. For example, one student may feel overwhelmed with academic life only when she contemplates speaking out in class; another student may experience stress primarily

There are many stressful aspects of college life, such as speaking in front of large groups. Stress management programs can help students master these experiences.

when he thinks about having to use the computer in a particularly demanding course. Thus, by pinpointing exactly those circumstances that initiate feelings of stress, the students can more precisely identify their own trouble spots.

As in many stress management courses, students in the CSN course are trained to recognize the negative self-talk they go through when they face stressful events. Negative self-talk can contribute to irrational feelings that perpetuate stress (Meichenbaum, 1975). For example, the student who fears speaking out in class may recognize how her own self-statements contribute to this process: "I hate asking questions", "I always get tongue-tied," "I'll probably forget what I want to say."

In addition to the exercises that students perform in class, they also have take-home assignments. In particular, students keep a

stress diary in which they record the events they find stressful and how they responded to them. As they become proficient in identifying stressful incidents, they are encouraged to record the negative self-statements or irrational thoughts that accompany the stressful experience (see Ellis, 1962).

As in most stress management training programs, the second stage of CSN involves skill acquisition and practice. The skills of stress management vary widely and include cognitive-behavioral management techniques, time management skills, behavioral regulation techniques, and other behaviors such as diet or exercise. Some of these techniques are designed to eliminate the stressful event, whereas others are geared toward reducing the experience of stress without necessarily modifying the event itself.

For example, in the CSN program, students

begin to attack their stressful events by setting new goals, engaging in positive self-talk, and using self-instruction. Specifically, first, each student sets several specific goals that he or she wants to meet to reduce the experience of college stress. For one student, the goal may be learning to speak in class without suffering overwhelming anxiety. For another, the goal may be going to see a particular professor about a problem.

Once the goals have been set, the next challenge is to identify specific behaviors that will meet those goals. In some cases, an appropriate response may be leaving the stressful event altogether. For example, the student who is having substantial difficulty in a rigorous physics course may need to modify his goal of becoming a physicist. Alternatively, the student may be encouraged to turn a stressor into a challenge. Thus, the student who fears speaking up in class may come to realize that she must not only master this fearful event, but actually come to enjoy it if she is to realize her long-term goal of becoming a trial lawyer. In other cases, the student may have to put up with a stressful event but simply learn to manage it more effectively. If a particular English course is highly stressful but is required for graduation, the student must learn to cope with the course as best he can. Thus, goal setting is important in effective stress management, first, because it forces a person to distinguish among stressful events to be avoided, tolerated, or overcome. Second, it forces the individual to be specific and concrete about exactly which events need to be tackled and what is to be done.

Once students have set some realistic goals and identified some target behaviors for reaching those goals, they learn how to engage in self-instruction and positive self-talk, two skills that can help in achieving those goals. Positive self-talk involves providing the self with specific encouragements. For example, the student desiring to overcome a fear of oral presentation might remind herself of all the occasions when she has spoken successfully in public. Once some proficiency in public speaking is achieved, the student might encourage herself by highlighting the positive aspects of the experience (for example, holding the attention of the audience, making some points, winning over a few converts, and the like.) As a skill, self-instruction involves reminding oneself of the specific steps that are required to achieve the particular goal. Thus, the would-be trial lawyer should try to create opportunities for public speaking and plan to reward herself when the speaking goes successfully. Each time the student speaks, she may need to rehearse carefully the steps that go into an effective presentation, composing her thoughts before speaking, making notes, rehearsing, and the like. By outlining precisely what she wants to say, the student may make a more effective public presentation.

In some stress-management programs, contingency contracting (Chapter 4) is encouraged. For example, in the CSN program, students whose problems are motivational are encouraged to make a contract with the self. Thus, the student who fears making oral presentations may define a specific goal, such as asking three questions in class in a week, which is to be followed by a particular reward, such as tickets to a rock concert.

These techniques to control stress present a wide array of cognitive-behavioral therapy techniques that an individual can use to combat stress: self-monitoring, the modification of internal dialogues, goal setting, homework assignments, positive self-talk, self-instruction, and contingency contracting. Most stress management programs include this cafeteria-like array of techniques, so that the individual has a broad set of skills from which to choose. In this way, each individual can discover the skills that work best for him or her. Thus, individuals can "inoculate" themselves against stress (Meichenbaum & Turk, 1982). This **stress inoculation** training, as Meichenbaum and Turk called it, enables people to confront stressful events with a clear plan in mind and an array of potential measures that they can take before the stressful event becomes overwhelming.

Relaxation Training and Stress Management

Whereas most of the techniques we have discussed so far are designed to give an individual cognitive insights into the nature and control of stress, another set of techniques—relaxation training techniques—is designed to affect the physiological experience of stress by reducing arousal. Relaxation training therapies include progressive muscle relaxation training, guided imagery, Transcendental Meditation, and other forms of meditation including yoga and hypnosis (Benson, Greenwood & Klemchuk, 1975; English & Baker, 1983; Ragland, 1977). These techniques can reduce heart rate, skin conductance, muscle tension, blood pressure, energy utilization, self-reports of anxiety, and tension (see English & Baker, 1983). Recently, however, research has challenged the efficacy of some of these techniques. Meditation does not appear to reduce somatic arousal beyond the resting state, and there is little evidence that it controls arousal in situations of threat (Holmes, 1984). However, the ability to relax in times of stress is helpful in coping even if meditation does not consistently induce that state.

Because of the value of relaxation, students in the CSN program are trained in relaxation therapy. First, they learn how to control their breathing, taking no more than six to eight breaths per minute. They are trained to relax the muscles in each part of the body progressively, until they experience no tension (progressive muscle relaxation). They are urged to identify the particular spots that tense up during times of stress, such as a jaw that clamps shut or fists that tighten up. By becoming especially aware of these reactions, they can relax these parts of the body as well. Thus, for example, when students find that the stress of college life is catching up with them, they can take a 5- or 10-minute break in which they breathe deeply and relax completely. They can return to their tasks, free of some of their previous tensions.

Ancillary Skills of Stress Management

In addition to the basic cognitive and relaxation skills of stress management, many programs also include training in supplementary skills. In many cases, the experience of stress depends heavily on feeling that one has too much to do in too little time. Consequently, many stress management programs include training in **time management** and planning. CSN helps students set specific work goals for each day, establish priorities, avoid timewasters, and learn what to ignore altogether. Thus, a student may learn to set aside 2 hours for a particularly important task, such as studying for a test. In this way, the student has a particular goal and particular time period in which to pursue it and therefore is less subject to interruption. Several simple "how to" manuals effectively illustrate the time management approach to stress management (e.g., Lakein, 1973; Mackenzie, 1972).

Many stress management programs, such as the CSN program, emphasize good health habits and social skills as adjunct techniques for the control of stress (e.g. Adams, 1978). These include appropriate eating habits, good exercise habits, assertiveness in social situations, and utilization of social support. Stress often affects eating habits adversely: People under stress consume too many stimulants such as coffee, too much sugar, and too much junk food. By learning to control dietary habits effectively and by eating three balanced meals a day, the student can ameliorate physiological reactions to stress. Likewise, regular exercise reduces stress. At least 15 minutes of sustained exercise three times a week is widely encouraged for all participants in the CSN program.

Assertiveness training is sometimes incorporated into stress management. Often, people experience stress because they are unable to confront those who contribute to their stress. For example, in the CSN program, students who have identified other individuals in their environment as causing them special stress (called **stress carriers**) help one another practice dealing with these individuals. One student may practice approaching a professor with whom he is having difficulty communicating, or another student may practice dealing tactfully with a roommate who constantly brags about how well she is doing in her classes.

As we have already seen, social support can buffer the adverse effects of stress. Unfortunately, people under stress sometimes alienate those who might provide social support rather than using them effectively. The harried executive snaps at his wife and children, or the student facing a threatening exam angrily rejects a friend's well-intentioned advice. Students in the CSN program are trained to recognize the important functions that social support can serve in helping them combat stress. They are urged to confide in close friends, to seek advice from people who can help them, and to use their relationships with others as sources of positive reinforcement after successfully meeting their goals.

In the final stage of the CSN program, stress management techniques are put into effect. Trainees practice the stress management techniques they have learned and monitor their effectiveness in daily situations. If some techniques fail to work, the trainees are urged to figure out why. Students bring their experiences of stress management back to the group situation where successes and failures can be analyzed. If initial efforts to cope with a stressful event are unsuccessful, the student may need to practice use of the particular technique or shift to a different type of stress management technique.

SUMMARY

1. Coping is the process of managing demands that tax or exceed a person's resources. Coping is influenced by primary appraisals (is the event harmful, threatening, or challenging?) and by secondary appraisals (what are my coping resources and how adequate are they?)

2. Coping efforts may be directed at solving problems or at regulating emotions. Most stressful events evoke both types of coping.

3. Coping styles consist of predispositions to cope with stressful situations in particular ways. Avoidance versus confrontation is one prominently studied coping style. Recent research has begun to explore the value of catharsis.

4. Selection of coping efforts is guided by internal and external resources. Internal resources include preferred coping style and other personality traits, such as sensation-seeking, hardiness, and optimism. External resources include time, money, the presence of other simultaneous life stressors, and social support.

5. Social support can be an effective resource in times of stress. It reduces psychological distress and the likelihood of illness by providing tangible aid, giving information, and providing emotional support. However, some events can undermine or

threaten social support resources.

6. The tasks toward which coping efforts are typically directed include reducing harmful environmental conditions and enhancing the adjustment process, tolerating and adjusting to negative events and realities, maintaining a positive self-image, maintaining emotional equilibrium, and continuing satisfying relations with others.

7. Coping efforts are judged to be successful when they reduce physiological indicators of arousal, enable the person to return to pre-stress activities, and free the individual from psychological distress.

8. Stress management programs exist for those who need aid in developing their coping skills. These programs teach people to identify sources of stress in their lives, to develop coping skills to deal with those stressors, and to practice employing stress management skills and monitoring their effectiveness.

KEY TERMS

assertiveness training
avoidant (minimizing) coping style
buffering hypothesis
catharsis
confrontative (vigilant) coping style
coping
coping outcomes
coping resources
coping style
costs of coping

direct effects hypothesis
hardiness
matching hypothesis
optimism
sensation seeking
social support
stress carriers
stress inoculation
stress management
time management

PART 4

THE PATIENT IN THE TREATMENT SETTING

9

THE USE OF HEALTH SERVICES

On the surface, the question of who uses health services and why would seem to be a medical issue, not a psychological one. The obvious answer is that people use services when they are sick. But when and how does a person decide that he or she is sick? When is a symptom labeled as serious and when is it dismissed as inconsequential? When does a person decide that a symptom requires treatment by professionals and when do chicken soup, fluids, and bed rest seem to be all that is needed?

At any given time, between 70 and 90% of the population has a medical condition that is diagnosable and potentially treatable by a health practitioner, but between two-thirds and three-quarters of those people do not consult a health practitioner for treatment. Of those people who report that they feel "ill," only about 40% actually seek medical aid (Kosa & Robertson, 1975). Some of these people stay out of the health care system because they cannot afford it; others do not seek services because they believe their symptoms are not serious enough to warrant formal care; and others may doubt the ability of the health care system to treat their disorder effectively.

Accordingly, there are several ways in which psychological factors enter into the decision to use health services. First, psychological factors influence how people recognize symptoms and interpret their meaning (Mechanic, 1972; Pennebaker, 1983); second, psychological factors influence whether those symptoms are interpreted as illness; and, third, psychological factors influence whether the health care system is perceived as the best place to obtain treatment for those symptoms (Safer, Tharps, Jackson, & Leventhal, 1979). We will consider each of these psychological factors in turn.

RECOGNITION AND INTERPRETATION OF SYMPTOMS

Although people certainly have some awareness of what is going on in their bodies, that awareness may be fairly limited. People's abilities to report heart rate, finger temperature, nasal congestion, breathing rate, and other internal processes are fairly poor (Pennebaker, 1983). Thus, access to and awareness of one's internal states is by no means direct. This limitation leaves a great deal of room for social and psychological factors to operate in the recognition of symptoms and the interpretation of illness. Thus, instead of a straightforward relationship between the perception of symptoms and a visit to the physician, symptom recognition and interpretation and consequent illness behavior represent components of a complex self-regulatory system involving both internal and social feedback about the meaning of sensations (Carver & Scheier, 1982; Leventhal & Diefenbach, in press).

Recognition of a Symptom

Common observation reveals that some individuals maintain their normal activities in the face of what would seem to be overwhelming symptoms, whereas others take to their beds the moment they detect any minor bodily disturbance. Some of these *individual differences* are stable. That is, some people are consistently more likely to notice a symptom than others (Mandler & Kahn, 1960). For example, as we see in Chapter 11, there are large and reliable differences in pain threshold—that is, how intense a stimulus must be before it is perceived as painful. Some individuals feel pain at relatively low levels of sensation, whereas for others a sensation can be very intense before it is perceived as painful. For example, people who cope with aversive events by using the defense mechanism of **repression** are less likely to experience symptoms and side effects (Ward, Leventhal, & Love, 1988).

People vary along the dimension of **monitoring/blunting,** which may also relate to how quickly they recognize symptoms and what they make of them. The monitoring/ blunting dimension (Miller, Brody, & Summerton, 1988) refers to whether people deal with threat by monitoring the environment for threat-relevant information or by ignoring threat-relevant information, that is, by "blunting." Miller and her colleagues (Miller et al., 1988) found that monitors came to the physician with less severe medical problems than did blunters, but with equivalent levels of discomfort, dysfunction, and distress. In the week after their visit, monitors experienced less symptom improvement than blunters.

There also appear to be reliable *cultural differences* in how quickly and what kind of symptoms are recognized. For example, Burnam, Timbers, and Hough (1984) found differences between Mexicans and Anglos, such that Anglos reported a greater number of infrequent symptoms but Mexicans reported symptoms that occurred more frequently. Cultural differences in symptom experience and reporting have been known about for decades (Zola, 1966), but, as yet, the reasons underlying cultural differences are not fully understood.

Attentional differences among people also influence their experience of symptoms. People who are focused on themselves (their bodies, their emotions, and their reactions in general) are quicker to notice symptoms than people who are externally focused on their environment and activities (Pennebaker, 1983). Thus, people who hold boring jobs, are socially isolated, keep house for a living, or live alone report more physical symptoms than do people who have interesting jobs, who have active social lives, who work outside the home, or who live with others. One possible reason is that these latter people experience more distractions and attend less to themselves than do those who have little activity in their lives (Pennebaker, 1983). In Chapter 14, we consider Type A individuals, who are highly competitive people with a strong sense of time urgency. Type A people seem to suppress the fatigue they feel when they are working hard, and they generally persist at a task when the Type B individual would already have decided it was time to pack up and go home (Carver, Coleman, & Glass, 1976; Weidner & Matthews, 1978). Outside the work situation, however, Type As may be more likely than Type Bs to report symptoms (Skelton & Pennebaker, 1978), perhaps because they have relaxed their vigilance and can now be attentive to internal symptoms or perhaps because they have worked so hard, they now experience more symptoms. The blunting/monitoring distinction may also apply to attentional differences in symptom recognition, in that monitors may be chronically more vigilant to the experience of physical change in their bodies.

Situational factors also influence whether or not a person will recognize a symptom. A boring situation makes people more attentive to symptoms than an interesting one. For example, people are more likely to notice itching or tickling in their throats and to cough in response to the sensations during boring parts of movies than during interesting parts (Pennebaker, 1980). Any experience that causes a person to direct attention inward increases the likelihood that a symptom will be perceived, whereas any factor that directs attention outward reduces the chance that a symptom will be perceived (Fillingim & Fine, 1986; Pennebaker, 1983; Scheier, Carver, & Gibbons, 1979). For example, a symptom is more likely to be perceived on a day when a person is at home resting than on a day full of frenzied activity. Intense physical activity takes attention away from symptoms, whereas quiescence increases the likelihood of their recognition.

Stress can also precipitate or aggravate the experience of symptoms. When people are under stress, they may believe they are more vulnerable to illness and so attend more closely to their bodies. They may also experience stress-related physiological changes, such as accelerated heart beat or breathing, and interpret these as symptoms of illness (Gortmaker, Eckenrode, & Gore, 1982; Mechanic, 1980).

Mood also influences self-appraised health (Salovey & Birnbaum, 1989). When people are in a positive mood, they rate themselves as more healthy, report fewer illness-related memories, and report fewer symptoms. People in a bad mood, however, are more likely to perceive their health negatively, whether they are already sick or currently healthy (Salovey & Birnbaum, 1989). The effect appears to be due to the fact that people in a bad mood are able to recall illness-related memories, whereas those in a positive mood are less likely to access such memories (Croyle & Uretsky, 1987). These findings may tie in with the research we examined in Chapter 7 on negative affectivity, the individual difference variable that predisposes people to experience symptoms and that may also lead them to seek medical help (Pennebaker & Watson, 1989; Zonderman, Heft, & Costa, 1985). Perhaps negative affectivity also leads people to remember illness better and thus experience more symptoms. Mood may also be an important cue for care-seeking behavior, adherence, and recovery from illness (Salovey & Birnbaum, 1989).

Any situational factor that makes illness or symptoms especially *salient* promotes their likely recognition. For example, a common phenomenon in medical school is **medical student's disease.** As they study each illness, a substantial portion of the class is certain to imagine that they have it. The fact of studying the symptoms leads students to focus on their own fatigue; as a consequence, symptoms consistent with the illness under study seem to emerge (Mechanic, 1972; Woods, Natterson, & Silverman, 1966).

In summary, then, symptom recognition is determined both by individual differences in attention to one's body and by transitory situational factors that influence the direction of one's attention. When attention is directed outward, as by vigorous physical activity or a highly distracting environment, symptoms are less likely to be noticed. When attention is directed toward the body, on the other hand, as by cues that suggest illness, symptoms are more likely to be detected.

Recent research suggests that people may actually be experiencing more symptoms and disability than was true as recently as 30 years ago (Barsky, 1988). People report greater numbers of disturbing somatic symptoms, more disability, and more feelings of general illness than was true then. To what can we attribute this trend? First, advances in medical care have lowered the mortality rate from acute infectious diseases, resulting in an increased prevalence of chronic and degenerative disorders, thus heightening the experience of symptoms and disability. Second, a heightened consciousness about health may prompt greater self-scrutiny, leading people to amplify bodily symptoms and feelings of illness generally. Third, the increasing focus on health issues in the media may have created a climate of apprehension or concern about illness that manifests itself in greater awareness of symptoms. And, finally, increasing developments in medical technology may lead people to have unrealistic expectations for cure that may make their untreatable infirmities or unavoidable ailments seem worse. Thus, while health care has undeniably improved over the last years, paradoxically its effects may be in part to diminish perceptions of good health (Barsky, 1988).

Interpretation of Symptoms

The interpretation of symptoms is also a heavily psychological process. Consider the following incident. During medical intake interviews at a large metropolitan hospital, a man in his late 20s came to the emergency room with the sole symptom of a sore throat. He brought with him six of his relatives, including his mother, father, sister, aunt, and two cousins. Since patients usually come to an emergency room with only one other person and since a sore throat is virtually never seen in the emergency room, the staff were understandably curious about the reason for his visit. There was much chuckling about how Italian families stick together and how they panic at any sign of a disturbance in health. But one particularly sensitive medical student reasoned that something more must have caused the man to come to the emergency room with his entire family in tow, so he probed cautiously but persistently during the intake interview with the patient. Gradually, it emerged that the young man's brother had died a year earlier of Hodgkin's disease, a form of cancer that involves the progressive infection and enlargement of the lymph nodes. The brother's first symptom had been a sore throat that he and the family had allowed to go untreated.

This poignant incident illustrates how important psychological factors can be in understanding people's interpretations of their symptoms. To this family, the symptom "sore throat" had special significance. It had a history for them that overrode its usual association with the beginnings of a cold (what the young man, in fact, turned out to have) (cf. Turk, Litt, Salovey, & Walker, 1985). Moreover, it symbolized for them a past failure of the family to respond adequately to an emergency, a failure that they were determined not to repeat. What this incident also illustrates, albeit in a less direct way, is that individual, historical, cultural, and social factors all conspire to produce an interpretation of the symptom experience.

Prior Experience   The interpretation of symptoms is heavily influenced by prior experience. A long personal history with a particular symptom can lead people to make assumptions about its meaning. For example, a person whose colds are always accompanied by swollen glands may pay little attention when these glands swell up, whereas a person who has never had swollen glands before may conclude that the symptom is serious and merits attention (e.g., Safer et al., 1979). Prior history with a symptom may also alert the sufferer to possible danger; when a symptom is similar to one experienced with a prior serious health problem, it may produce the same alarm on the repeat occasion (Leventhal, Nerenz, & Strauss, 1980).

A symptom's meaning will also be heavily influenced by how common it is within a person's range of acquaintances or culture.

> When [an] aberration is fairly widespread, this, in itself, might constitute a reason for its not being considered "symptomatic" or unusual. Among many Mexican-Americans in the Southwestern United States, diarrhea, sweating, and coughing are everyday experiences, while among certain groups of Greeks, trachoma [an inflammation of the eyes] is almost universal. Lower back pain is a quite common condition among lower class women, and so it is not considered symptomatic of any disease or disorder but part of their expected everyday existence. (Zola, 1966, cited in Cox & Mead, 1975, pp. 25–26)

Any time a symptom is very widespread, this fact in itself may be seen as a reason for attaching little significance to it (see also Burnam et al., 1984). In a related vein, people who have a history of a medical condition estimate its prevalence to be greater and regard the condition as less likely to be life-threatening than people with no history of the condition (Jemmott, Croyle, & Ditto, 1988).

Expectations   Expectations also influence the interpretation of symptoms. People may ignore "symptoms" they are not expecting and amplify "symptoms" that they do expect (Leventhal, Nerenz, & Strauss, 1980). For example, women who believe they are close to their menstrual periods may interpret otherwise vague sources of discomfort as premenstrual symptoms; women who believe that their periods are several days away may ignore the same "symptoms" (McFarland, Ross, & DeCourville, 1989; Ruble, 1977); see Box 9.1.

"Seriousness" of the Symptoms   The meaning attached to a symptom also depends substantially on what that symptom is. Symptoms that affect highly valued parts of the body may be interpreted as more serious and as more likely to require attention than symptoms that affect less valued organs. For example, people are more anxious when their eyes or face are affected than if the symptom involves part of the trunk. A symptom will cause more concern if it limits mobility than if it does not. Above all, if a symptom causes pain, it will be interpreted as more serious and as more likely to require treatment than if it does not cause pain (e.g., Safer et al., 1979; Turk, Litt, Salovey, & Walker, 1985).

Acknowledging the existence of a symptom does not necessarily lead to speedy treatment for it. In one study (Ditto, Jemmott, & Darley, 1988), undergraduates were led to believe that they tested positive or negative on a saliva test for a risk factor for a fictitious disease. In addition, half the subjects were told that there was a simple preventive treatment for the disease, whereas the other half were not led to believe there was a treatment. Those who tested positive for the risk factor, especially those uniformed about treatment, minimized threat by decreasing their estimates of the reliability of the test, decreasing their beliefs in the seriousness of the risk factor, and decreasing their estimations of how serious the disease was.

Box 9.1
Can Expectations Influence Sensations?
The Case of Premenstrual Symptoms

Many women experience a variety of unpleasant physical and psychological symptoms just before the onset of menstruation, including swollen breasts, cramping, irritability, and depression. Generally, physicians and psychologists have assumed that these symptoms have a physiological basis. However, recent research by Ruble (1972) suggests a possible psychological basis. Specifically, it may be that women experience these symptoms partly because they expect to experience them (McFarland et al., 1989).

To test this idea, Ruble recruited a number of women to participate in a study. She told them she was using a new scientific technique that would predict their date of menstruation. She then randomly told subjects the technique indicated either that their period was due within the next day or two (premenstrual group) or that their period was not due for a week to 10 days (intermenstrual group). In fact, all the women were approximately a week from their periods. All the women were then asked to complete a questionnaire indicating the extent to which they were experiencing symptoms typically associated with the premenstrual state.

The results strongly supported Ruble's hypothesis. The women who were led to believe that their period was due within the next day or two reported more of the psychological and physiological symptoms of premenstruation than did women who were told their periods were not due for a week to 10 days. Of course, the results of this study do not mean that no women experience any actual premenstrual symptoms. Indeed, the prevalence and seriousness of premenstrual syndrome (PMS) bears testimony to the debilitating effect that premenstrual bodily changes can have on physiological functioning and behavior. Rather, the results suggest that women tend to overstate or exaggerate naturally fluctuating bodily states when they believe they are premenstrual. Research findings like these demonstrate the significance of psychological factors in the experience of symptoms (see also McFarland et al., 1989).

Cognitive Representations of Illness

A number of researchers have suggested that people hold organized, cognitive representations of health and illness that influence how they react to symptoms and illness (e.g., Bishop, 1990; Garrity, 1975; Lau & Hartman, 1983; Lau, Bernard, & Hartman, 1989; Leventhal, Nerenz, & Steele, 1984; Millstein & Irwin, 1987; Nerenz & Leventhal, 1983; see also Turk, Rudy, & Salovey, 1986).

Illness representations (or schemas) include such factors as the identity, conse-quences, cause, duration, and cure of the disease (Lau & Hartman, 1983; Nerenz & Leventhal, 1983). The *identity* or label for an illness is its name; its *consequences* are the symptoms and treatments that result, as well as the extent to which the person believes the illness has ramifications for his or her life; *causes* are the factors that the person believes gave rise to the illness; *duration* refers to the expected length of time the illness will last; and *cure* identifies whether or not the person believes the illness can be cured through appropriate treatment. People have at least three dominant models of illness (Nerenz & Leventhal, 1983):

- *Acute* illness is believed to be caused by specific viral or bacterial agents and is short in duration, with no long-term consequences.
- *Chronic* illness is caused by manifold factors, including poor health habits, and is long in duration, with often severe consequences.
- *Cyclic* illness is marked by alternating periods when there are no symptoms and others when there are many.

Bishop and his colleagues (Bishop, Briede, Cavazos, Grotzinger, & McMahon, 1987) argued that these elements of illness schemas provide the basis for **disease prototypes,** which are abstract representations of particular diseases. Thus, a person may have a prototype for cardiac disease—a chronic illness that involves smoking, being overweight, and poor exercise as causes; chest pain and risk of heart attack as consequences; a long time duration; and the possibility of the disorder being fatal.

Disease prototypes may help people organize and evaluate information about physical sensations that might otherwise not be interpretable. Thus, for example, a cancer patient's belief that he has a metastatic disease may lead him to interpret ambiguous symptoms of fatigue and pain as indicating a progression of the disease. To a person who believes himself to be cured of cancer, however, the same symptoms could easily be dismissed as the aches and pains that result from exercise or sleeping in a bad position. Disease prototypes, then, not only represent the abstracted knowledge that people have about their own disorders, but lead them to interpret new information in such a way that may lead them to seek treatment, alter their medication regimen, and engage in other illness- and health-related behaviors (Bishop & Converse, 1986).

Illness schemas and disease prototypes are important because people use these concepts to give meaning to the symptom experiences they have (Millstein & Irwin, 1987) and as a basis for deciding what to do about them (Leventhal et al., in press). In a study of community residents' perceptions of medical situations, Prohaska, Keller, Leventhal, and Leventhal (1987) found that when people perceived their symptoms to be severe, they were more upset, they engaged in more self-care, and they were more likely to seek treatment than when they perceived the symptoms to be less severe. Similarly, when the symptoms had lasted a long time, people reported that they would be much more likely to seek medical care. In a similar vein, Bishop (1987) found that disruptive symptoms that interfered with daily activities led to a reduction of those activities and more self-care. When symptoms were perceived to be due to psychological factors (such as stress or depression), people were less likely to report seeking professional care than when they had symptoms perceived as physically based. People with strong identity (a clear label) and cure components (belief that cure is possible) in their common-sense representations of illness report being more likely to visit a physician when they are feeling ill than are people who have weak identity and cure components in their representations (Lau, Bernard, & Hartman, 1989). In contrast, when people attribute their symptoms to aging, they are more likely to see them as uncontrollable and with a lowered potential for cure. As a consequence, they may be less likely to seek out medical attention (Prohaska et al., 1987).

The meaning of a symptom ultimately blends into diagnosis, a process that begins not in the physician's office but in an individual's conversations with friends and relatives. Sociologists have written at length about the **lay referral network,** an informal network of family and friends who offer their own interpretations of symptoms well before any medical treatment is sought (Freidson, 1960). The patient may mention the symptoms to a family member or co-worker, who may then respond with personal views of what the symptom is likely to mean ("George had that, and it turned out to be nothing at all"). The friend or relative may offer advice about the advisability of seeking medical treatment ("All he got for going to see the doctor was a big bill") and recommendations for various home remedies ("Honey, lemon juice, and a little brandy will clear that right up") (e.g., Stoller, 1984).

Despite the apparent informality of the lay referral system, it can be highly systematic. First, symptomatic individuals are likely to consult close family and friends with whom they regularly come into contact. They may then consult someone who is known to have had a similar problem (Hayes-Bautista, 1976). For example, among the elderly, same-age peers appear to be an important reference group for assessing personal health and making decisions about how to treat any problems (Stoller, 1984). In many communities, a powerful lay figure—such as an older woman who has had many children—may act as a lay practitioner, because years of experience are assumed to have given the person wisdom in medical matters (Freidson, 1960).

The advice given to patients by such a figure is often as extensive as any formal medical regimen, including instructions to return, should the disorder not clear up. Freidson refers to this process as the "casual exploration of diagnoses," and its result may be that the patient who finally sees a physician presents symptoms that are weeks or even months old, that have already been "treated" in a variety of confusing and even contradictory ways, and that may have gotten worse as a result of the delay in seeking professional help. However, use of the lay referral network need not always result in exacerbated symptoms and useless treatments. Some home remedies do, in fact, work, and sometimes simple rest allows an illness to run its course. These actual and apparent cures can perpetuate use of the lay referral network. At other times, the lay referral network can act as a go-between for a patient and a medical care system, coaching the patient on how to make use of institutions and have their complaints heard (Hayes-Bautista, 1976).

THE USE OF HEALTH SERVICES

Just as illness is not evenly distributed across the population, neither is the use of health services. Although differences in disease patterns can explain much about patterns of use and nonuse of health services, they cannot do so entirely. Rather, to understand the use of health services, one must understand not only how people interpret their symptoms but also how they perceive the medical system and whether or not they have access to it. Demographic, sociocultural, social-psychological, and individual difference characteristics all influence the decision to use health services.

A Portrait of the User of Health Services: Demographic Factors

Those who study health services have drawn a clear portrait of who uses services and who does not. Age is an important factor. The very young and the elderly use health services most frequently (Aday & Andersen, 1974). Young children develop a number of infectious "childhood" diseases as they are acquiring their immunities; therefore they frequently require the care of a pediatrician. Both illness frequency and the use of services decline in adolescence and throughout young adulthood. Use of health services increases again in late adulthood, when people begin to develop chronic conditions and diseases. The elderly use services most for a variety of disorders related to the aging process (Wolinsky, Mosely, & Coe, 1986).

Gender also determines use of services, with women using medical services more than

Women use medical services more than men. They appear to be sick more than men, it is often easier for them to use services, and they require services for such gender-related needs as maternity care.

men (Mechanic, 1976, 1978b; Nathanson, 1975, 1977; Verbrugge, 1979, 1980). Much of the gender difference in health services use can be explained by pregnancy and childbirth, but not all (Cleary, Mechanic, & Greenley, 1982). Even when childbirth visits are not counted, women still seek care more than men do, and this is true in most countries. Various explanations have been offered. For example, women have better homeostatic mechanisms than men do: They report pain earlier, experience temperature changes more rapidly, and detect new smells faster. Thus, they may also be more sensitive to bodily dysfunctions, especially minor ones (e.g., Leventhal et al., 1980). Another possible explanation for the gender difference stems from the fact that there are different social norms regarding the expression of pain and discomfort for men and women. Men are expected to project a tough, macho image that includes being able to ignore pain and not "give in" to illness, whereas

women are not subject to these same pressures (Lewis & Lewis, 1977; Mechanic, 1964; Verbrugge, 1980). Another possibility is that the economic costs of being ill may be greater for the average man than for the average woman. Although more women are working outside the home than ever, there are still a great many female part-time workers and nonworkers who do not have to take time off from work to seek treatment and who do not lose pay if they are ill. Thus, women may use health services more because seeking treatment for illness disrupts their lives less and costs them less (Marcus & Siegel, 1982).

The lower social classes use medical services less than do the upper classes (Herman, 1972). One obvious reason for this fact is that the lower classes have less money to spend on health services. However, with Medicare for the elderly, Medicaid for the poor, and other inexpensive health services, the gap between medical service use by the rich and by the poor has narrowed somewhat. The disadvantaged financial position of the lower classes may not, however, be the main reason for their low use of services (Crandall & Duncan, 1981; Rundall & Wheeler, 1979). There simply are not as many medical services for the poor as for the well-to-do, and what services there are are often inadequate and understaffed. Physicians are among the most economically privileged people in our country, and they may prefer to focus on a clientele that resembles themselves: well-to-do people who are articulate in describing their complaints and able to pay their bills. Accordingly, it is often difficult to attract physicians to poor areas, especially rural areas. As a consequence, poor people are more likely than the well-to-do to see a physician on an emergency basis and to receive any regular medical care through a clinic. The poor are also less likely to have a regular physician than are middle- and upper-class people, who are more likely to get their medical treatment in a private office from the same physician on a regular basis (Kronenfeld, 1978; Rundall & Wheeler, 1979). Having a source of regular medical care is a significant determinant of use of health services (Kronenfeld, 1978; Wan & Gray, 1978).

The social-class difference in use of health services is particularly problematic, because the poor are also less healthy than the rich (Herman, 1972). They tend to be sick more often and for longer periods of time than are the well-to-do. Moreover, the biggest gap in use of services due to income differences is for preventive health services, such as inoculations against diseases and screening for treatable disorders. This contributes still further to the higher illness rate among the poor.

Health services, then, are used by those who have time, money, and access to them. Those who use services most are disproportionately likely to be married females and people with high education, income, and occupation.

The Sociocultural Approach to the Use of Health Services

Although demographic factors help uncover why some people use services and others do not, this is not a sufficient basis for understanding the use of services (McKinlay, 1972; Wolinsky, 1978). Obviously, not every upper-middle-class female uses services when she is ill, and not every working-class elderly man fails to use health services when he is ill. The demographic analysis of use of services can be augmented by a sociocultural approach, which examines how the values, lifestyle, norms, cultural interpretations, and mythologies of a particular culture influence the way individual members of that culture come to recognize, interpret, and act on particular symptoms they experience (McKinlay, 1972). We have already noted one way in which culture contributes to the understanding of symptoms by defining what is a normal body state and what is unusual. Thus, some "symptoms" are not recognized as such because they are so widely experienced in a given culture (Zola, 1973).

Cultural factors also influence whether or not a person seeks formal treatment and how he or she responds to it (Burnam et al., 1984; Langlie, 1977; Suchman, 1964). People who live in insular ethnic neighborhoods often develop folk health beliefs that may not correspond to the values of the medical profession and which, accordingly, keep them from seeking formal treatment. Instead, they may utilize a lay system of care. More cosmopolitan people with a broader array of social contacts are more likely to be exposed to norms that favor professional health care; therefore, they make use of it for a variety of illnesses and preventive measures (Rosenstock & Kirscht, 1979). These points underscore the importance of normative factors in seeking treatment, which, it will be recalled, are heavily implicated in the theory of planned behavior (Ajzen & Fishbein, 1980).

Cultural factors also influence how a symptom is presented to a practitioner. For example, Stoeckle, Zola, and Davidson (1963) found that Irish patients typically presented very specific, limited physical complaints ("an upset stomach") in a stoic, accepting manner, whereas Italian patients tended to describe more diffuse complaints ("generally feeling achy") to which they reacted with greater emotionality. Zborowski (1952) noted that different cultures reacted to different aspects of their complaints and were therefore reassured by different kinds of information. Italian patients were likely to react to the pain or discomfort they were experiencing and to be most comforted by anything that made the pain go away, whereas Jews tended to react to the potential significance of the pain and to be comforted when they received an adequate explanation for the pain or discomfort.

In summary, then, the sociocultural approach to health and illness tries to identify which symptoms are perceived as normal and which are not; why some groups use medical services and others do not; how ethnic groups differ in the style in which symptoms are presented; and how ethnic differences influence reactions to treatment.

Social-Psychological Determinants of the Use of Health Services

Social-psychological factors also influence who uses health services (McKinlay, 1972). Social-psychological approaches examine how an individual's attitudes, beliefs about symptoms and health services, and knowledge about health contribute to the decision to use services. This approach particularly sheds light on the psychological factors that influence use of health services and aids in the development of interventions to get people to use services promptly.

The Health Belief Model   The most influential social-psychological model of the use of health services is the health belief model (Rosenstock, 1966). As we saw in Chapter 3 and 4, this model states that whether or not a person seeks treatment for a symptom can be predicted from two factors: the extent to which the person perceives a threat to his or her health and the degree to which he or she believes that a particular health measure will be effective in reducing that threat. The perception of a threat is itself influenced by general health values, specific beliefs about vulnerability to a particular disorder, and beliefs about the seriousness of the consequences of that disorder. Belief in the efficacy of treatment consists of whether or not the individual thinks a specific measure will be effective against the disorder in question and whether or not the barriers to undertaking that measure exceed the benefits of the measure (Rosenstock, 1974b).

A large number of studies suggest that the health belief model explains people's use of services quite well (for reviews, see Becker, 1974; Kirscht, 1983; Rosenstock & Kirscht, 1979). For example, people who believe they are susceptible to polio, who believe polio has severe consequences, and who believe that vaccination is effective against polio are more likely to go to a health service to be vaccinated (Rosenstock, Derryberry, & Carriger, 1959). As we noted in Chapter 3, the health belief model helps explain who practices health behaviors that require access to the health care system, such as health examinations, yearly medical checkups, vaccinations, and disease-specific screening programs (Kasl, 1975; Rosenstock et al., 1959).

Not all research supports the health belief model (e.g., Haefner et al., 1967). The health belief model does a better job of explaining the behavior of people who have funds and access to health services than that of people who do not (Anderson & Bartkus, 1973; Gochman, 1972; Wolinsky, 1978). It may also predict the health service use of people who are already familiar with a disorder and with the services available to treat it. The health behavior of individuals who do not know the meaning of a particular symptom or do not know how to go about obtaining treatment for it is not very well explained by the health belief model.

Zola's Five "Triggers"   Although the health belief model explains a lot about the use of health services, it does ignore important other social determinants of seeking treatment (e.g., Langlie, 1977; Turk, Litt et al., 1985). Zola (1964, 1973) identified five "triggers" that may prompt an individual to seek treatment for a disorder. His first trigger, *the degree to which an individual is frightened by the symptoms,* corresponds to the health belief model's "perceived threat" variable. The second trigger, *the nature and quality of the symptoms,* we have already discussed: That is, symptoms have different meanings for different patients depending on their prior experiences with symptoms or beliefs about them.

Zola's other three triggers are interpersonal in nature. The third trigger, an *interpersonal crisis,* may be set off when a symptom threatens a relationship between the patient and some other individual. For example, if one member of a couple is "always tired," eventually the partner will become annoyed and insist that the other do something about the constant fatigue. *Social interference* is the fourth trigger: When valued activities or social demands such as a job or vacation are threatened by the presence of a symptom, an individual is more likely to seek prompt treatment than if no such threat is posed. The fifth trigger is the presence of *social sanctioning,* as when an employer applies pressure on the symptomatic individual to seek treatment or return to work.

The Influence of Social Position   Other research indicates that the social position of an individual in a culture or community influences the use of health services (see Suchman,

1964). In particular, isolates in a community are less likely to use health services than are people who are well integrated. For example, people may be less likely to use a cardiovascular screening program if they are not integrated into their communities or if they are members of a minority group. Those who take advantage of such a screening program are more likely to have lived in the community longer, to have close friends in the community, to be active members of the community's social organizations, and to work in the community.

Social position may influence the use of health services in several ways. First, it may affect the likelihood that one will hear about a program in the first place; marginal individuals in a community may be less likely to hear about health opportunities by word of mouth, and they may be less likely to be in places where relevant notices are posted. Second, social position may influence use of services directly. One may be less inclined to use a service like a cardiovascular screening program if one does not have a friend to go with or if one will not know many people when one gets there.

Health services that are offered through the community can be social activities and be responded to as such by potential participants. In support of this point, one study that attempted to enroll eligible women in a breast self-examination training program found that a large proportion of the eligible participants failed to participate because they had come with friends who were ineligible for the program; on finding that the friend could not participate, the eligible woman did not want to participate either (Berkanovic, Gerber, Brown, & Breslow, 1983).

Individual Preferences for Involvement in Health Care

Researchers have also considered individual differences that may influence use of health services. Preference for involvement in health care is one such factor. Specifically, some people want a very strong role in their own health care, whereas others do not. To measure this variable, Krantz and his associates (Krantz, Baum, & Wideman, 1980) developed the Krantz Health Opinion Survey, which assesses two factors: preference for *behavioral involvement* in health care and preference for *information* about one's care.

The first scale, behavioral involvement, measures attitudes toward self-care and the active involvement of patients in their medical care. High scorers on this scale endorse such statements as "Except for serious illness, it's generally better to take care of your own health than to seek professional help" and "It is better to rely less on physicians and more on your common sense when it comes to caring for your body." Believers in self-care, then, prefer treating themselves to putting themselves in the hands of health care practitioners.

The second scale, information, also measures active involvement in health care, but from a different perspective. High scorers on the information scale ask questions and want to be informed about medical procedures, but they do not necessarily engage in self-care. High scorers on the information scale endorse such items as, "I usually ask the doctor or nurse lots of questions about the procedures during a medical exam" and "I'd rather be given many choices about what's best for my health than to have the doctor make the decisions for me."

Preference for behavioral involvement and preference for information do predict different health behaviors, as one might expect. Studies of college students show that high-scoring individuals on the behavioral-involvement scale were more likely to enroll in a health self-care course than were low scorers. Those high in behavioral involvement also made fewer visits to the health service than low scorers; when they did seek treatment from health care prac-

titioners, they were more likely than low scorers to offer their own diagnoses for their disorders and to take a role in choosing their own medications. High scorers on the information scale, in contrast, asked more questions during a health exam but did not engage in self-care (Krantz et al., 1980).

The research conducted so far on preference for involvement in one's health care suggests that such factors as behavioral involvement and desire for information do predict health behaviors generally and use of health services in particular.

THE MISUSE OF HEALTH SERVICES

Health services may be abused as well as used. In this section, we consider two types of abuse. The first occurs when individuals seek out health services for problems that are not medically significant. The second type of abuse involves delay behavior, when individuals should seek health care for a problem but do not.

Using Health Services for Emotional Disturbances

Physicians estimate that as much as two-thirds of their time is taken up by patients whose complaints are psychological rather than medical in nature (Shapiro, 1978). This problem is more common for general practitioners than for specialists, although no branch of medicine is immune. (College health services periodically experience a particular version of this phenomenon; see Box 9.2.) Most commonly, these nonmedical complaints stem from anxiety and depression, both of which, unfortunately, are widespread.

Why do people seek a physician's care when their complaints should be addressed by a mental health specialist? There are several reasons. Anxiety, depression, and other psy-

---

Box 9.2
College Student's Disease

Visit the health service of any college or university just before exams begin and you will see a unit bracing itself for an onslaught. Admissions to health services can double or even triple as papers become due and examinations begin. Why does this occur?

Some of the increase in health service visits is due to an actual increase in illness. Students who are under pressure to do well work long hours and eat and sleep poorly. As they run themselves down, their vulnerability to many common disorders can increase. Moreover, any one individual who develops an infectious disorder can give it to others who live in close proximity.

Some students may not actually be sick, but they think they are. Stressors like exams can produce a variety of symptoms—such as inability to concentrate, sleeplessness, and upset stomach—that may be mistaken for illness. Moreover, exam time may preclude other activities that would provide distraction, so students may be more aware of these symptoms than they would otherwise be. In addition, the "symptoms" may make it hard for students to study, and disruption in important activities often acts as an impetus for seeking treatment.

Finally, there is the chronic procrastinator with four papers due but enough time to complete only two of them. What better excuse than illness for failure to meet one's obligations? Illness legitimizes procrastination, lack of motivation, lack of activity, and a host of other personal failures.

---

chological disorders are accompanied by a number of physical symptoms (e.g., Pennebaker, Burnam, Schaeffer, & Harper, 1977). Anxiety can produce diarrhea, upset stomach, sweaty hands, shortness of breath, difficulty in sleeping, poor concentration, and general agitation. Depression can lead to fatigue, difficulty in performing everyday activities, listlessness, loss of appetite, and sleep disturbances. People may mistake the symptoms associated with their mood disorder for legitimate medical problems and thus seek a physician's care because they think it is appropriate to do so (Costa & McCrae, 1980; Mechanic, 1972; Tessler & Mechanic, 1978). In a study of the **worried well,** those who frequently and inappropriately use medical services, Wagner and Curran (1984) found this group to be more concerned about their physical and mental health, to perceive minor symptoms as more serious than appropriate users, and to believe that they should take care of their own health; paradoxically, this belief in self-care actually led them to use health services more.

Another reason people use health services for psychological complaints is that medical disorders are perceived as more legitimate than psychological ones. As a consequence, use of health services is more likely to be approved of by others than is the use of mental health services. For example, a man who hates his job and who stays home to avoid it will find that his behavior is more acceptable to both his boss and his wife if he says he is ill than if he admits he is simply depressed. Many people are even unwilling to admit to themselves that they have a psychological problem, believing that it is shameful to see a mental health specialist or to have mental problems. Thus, they convince themselves that they are physically ill and that a physician's treatment will make them better.

Illness also brings many benefits, termed **secondary gains,** including the ability to rest, to be freed from unpleasant tasks, and to be cared for by others. In fact, there are so many reinforcements for being ill that it can be difficult to induce some people to become well again (Gordon, 1966; Parsons, 1951). Illness may also be a means of coping with failure (Parsons, 1951; Shuval, Antonovsky, & Davies, 1973). It may be hard for some people to admit failure both to themselves and to others; therefore, if they can maintain that they are ill instead, they can avoid the shame of failure. (Some of these factors may have played a role in one famous case of hysterical contagion; see Box 9.3).

Finally, the inappropriate use of health services can represent true malingering. A person who does not want to go to work may know all too well that the only acceptable excuse that will prevent dismissal for absenteeism is illness. Moreover, workers may be required to document their absences in order to collect wages or disability payments and may thus have to keep looking until they find a physician who is willing to "treat" the "disorder."

Delay Behavior

A very different kind of misuse of health services occurs when an individual should seek treatment for a symptom but puts off doing so. Serious symptoms such as a lump, chronic shortness of breath, blackouts, skin discoloration, irradiating chest pain, seizures, and severe stomach pains are among those for which people should seek treatment promptly, and yet they are frequently ignored. An individual may live with one or more potentially serious symptoms for months and not seek help. This

is called **delay behavior.** For example, one study found that, on average, patients waited 1 year from the time they first noticed a skin lesion to receiving a diagnosis of malignant melanoma. Similarly, a major problem contributing to the high rate of death and disability from heart attacks is the fact that patients so often delay seeking treatment for its symptoms, instead normalizing them as gastric distress, muscle pain, and other, less severe disorders.

Delay is defined as the time between when a person recognizes the existence of a symptom and when the person seeks treatment. Delay is actually composed of three time periods, diagrammed in Figure 9.1: **appraisal delay,** which is the time it takes an individual to decide that a symptom is serious; **illness delay,** which is the time between the recognition that a symptom implies an illness and the decision to seek treatment; and **utilization delay,** which is the time between deciding to seek treatment and actually doing so (Safer et al., 1979).

How long should one delay? Obviously, some symptoms merit a little delay. A runny nose or a mild sore throat may indicate little more than a cold, and a short period of waiting to see if the symptoms will clear up on their own is appropriate. When serious, often highly debilitating symptoms persist for weeks or even months, however, one must wonder what causes the person to wait when something is so clearly wrong.

The reasons for delay behavior have been extensively explored (e.g., Antonovsky & Hartman, 1974). Not surprisingly, the portrait of the delayer bears strong similarities to the portrait of the nonuser of services generally. A major factor in delay is the perceived expense of treatment, especially for poor people. When money is not readily available, people may persuade themselves that the symptoms are not serious enough to justify the expense (Safer et al., 1979). The delayer is more likely to be poorly educated and lower-class. Older

Box 9.3
The June Bug Epidemic: A Case of Hysterical Contagion

In June of 1962, a mysterious epidemic broke out in the dressmaking department of a southern textile plant. Sixty-two employees were afflicted. The symptoms reported by the workers varied but usually included nausea, numbness, dizziness, and, occasionally, vomiting. Some of the ill required hospitalization, but most were simply excused from work for several days.

Almost all the affected workers reported having been bitten by some kind of gnat or mite immediately before they experienced the symptoms. Several employees who were not afflicted said they saw their fellow workers bitten before they came down with the disease. However, local, state, and federal health officials who were called in to investigate the incident could obtain no reliable description of the suspected insect. Furthermore, careful inspection of the textile plant by entomologists and exterminators turned up only a small variety of insects—beetles, gnats, flies, an ant, and a mite—none of which could have caused the reported symptoms.

Company physicians and experts from the U.S. Public Health Service Communicable Disease Center began to suspect that the epidemic might be a case of mass hysteria. They hypothesized that, although some of the afflicted individuals may have been bitten by some insect, anxiety or nervousness was more likely responsible for the onset of the symptoms. On hearing this conclusion, employees insisted that the "disease" was caused by a bite from an insect that was in a shipment of material recently received from England.

In shifting from a medical to a social explanation, health experts highlighted several points. First, the entire incident, from the first to the last reported case, lasted a period of 11 days, and fifty of the sixty-two cases (80%) occurred on two consecutive days after the news media had sensationalized earlier incidents. Second, most of the afflicted individuals worked at the same time and place in the plant. Fifty-nine of the sixty-two afflicted employees worked on the first shift, and fifty-eight worked in one large work area. Third, the fifty-eight working at the same time and place were all women; one other woman worked on a different shift, two male victims worked on a different shift, and one man worked in a different department. Moreover, most of these women were married and had children; they were accordingly trying to combine a job and motherhood—often an exhausting arrangement.

The "epidemic" occurred at a busy time in the plant—June being a crucial month in the production of fall fashions—and there were strong incentives for employees to put in overtime and to work at a high pace. The plant was relatively new, and personnel and production management were not well organized. Thus, the climate was ripe for the development of severely anxious feelings among the employees.

Who, then, got "bitten" by the "June bug," and why? Most vulnerable were workers with the most stress in their lives (married women with children) who were trying to cope with the further demands of increased productivity and overtime. Job anxieties, coupled with the physical manifestations of fatigue (such as dizziness), created a set of symptoms that, given appropriate circumstances, could be labeled as "illness." The rumor of a suspicious bug and the presence of ill co-workers apparently provided the appropriate circumstances, legitimatizing the "illness" and leading to the "epidemic" that resulted.

(Kerckhoff & Back, 1968; see Colligan et al., 1979).

FIGURE 9.1   Stages of Delay in Seeking Treatment for Symptoms

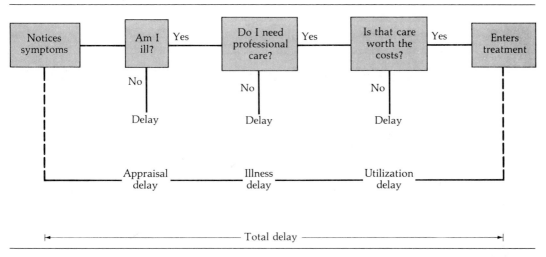

(From Safer et al., 1979)

people delay longer than younger people, as do people with no regular contact with a physician. Delay, like nonuse of services in general, is more common among people who seek treatment primarily in respose to pain or social pressure (King & Leach, 1950). People who are fearful of doctors, examinations, surgery, and medical facilities generally delay longer than do people who are not fearful. People with generally good medical habits are less likely to delay, and they will seek attention quickly for a condition that is unusual or potentially serious. (See Box 9.4 for a discussion of delay behavior as a factor in cancer.)

Since the delayer looks so much like the nonuser of services, one might expect the health belief model to predict delay behavior as well as use of services. In fact, it does explain some delay behavior (Rosenstock & Kirscht, 1979). For example, people who fail to seek treatment for symptoms that may indicate cancer are more likely to believe that treatments will be extremely painful (high perceived barriers or "costs" of treatment) and to believe that nothing can be done to cure cancer (low perceived efficacy of treatment)

(Antonovsky & Hartman, 1974; Kirscht, Haefner, Kegeles, & Rosenstock, 1966; Safer et al., 1979).

Another factor that predicts delay is the nature of the symptoms. When a symptom is similar to one that previously turned out to be minor, the individual will seek treatment less quickly than if the symptom is new (see, for example, Safer et al., 1979). For example, women with a history of benign breast lumps may be less likely to have a new suspicious lump checked out than are women with no such history. Highly visible symptoms, symptoms that do not hurt, symptoms that do not change quickly, and symptoms that are not incapacitating are less likely than their opposites to prompt a person to seek medical treatment (Safer et al., 1979). Any time a symptom is easily accommodated to and does not provoke alarm, treatment may be delayed. For example, in the case of melanoma (Cassileth et al., 1988), patients have difficulty distinguishing between moles and melanomas and therefore delay seeking treatment.

Delay behavior is also predicted by attitudes. In an examination of Ajzen and Fish-

Box 9.4
Delay Behavior and Cancer

Delay in seeking treatment for cancer is one of the most problematic kinds of delay behavior. The reason is that many cancers can be cured if they are treated promptly, but with each day of delay the chance that the cancer will spread increases. The American Cancer Society lists seven danger signs of cancer that should lead people to seek treatment: change in bowel or bladder habits, a sore that does not heal, unusual bleeding or discharge, a thickening or lump in the breast or elsewhere, indigestion or difficulty in swallowing, obvious change in a wart or mole, and nagging cough or hoarseness. Yet it is clear that the majority of patients wait at least a month after first noticing one of these suspicious symptoms, and between 35 and 50% delay for over 3 months (Antonovsky and Hartman, 1974).

One reason for delay among subsequently identified cancer patients is ignorance of the meaning of symptoms. If their symptom does not hurt, does not change quickly, and is not incapacitating, as is true for many of the early symptoms of cancer, then people may not seek treatment. They simply get used to the symptom.

Feelings of invulnerability may also predict delay in seeking treatment for cancer (Weinstein, 1979). Highly secure, independent, self-confident people who believe that they are generally invulnerable to illness are less threatened by symptoms and so may ignore them (Fisher, 1967; Hammerschlag, Fisher, DeCosse, & Kaplan, 1964). Yet another group

of patients fails to seek treatment because they are convinced they have cancer and they believe nothing can be done to cure them (Cameron & Hinton, 1968; Greer, 1974; Safer et al., 1979). This sense of fatalism is particularly tragic, since prompt treatment can improve the chance of a cure.

Finally, fear of treatment can also act as a deterrent to seeking treatment. For example, some women who mistakenly believe that all breast cancer is treated by mastectomy (removal of the breast) may delay seeking treatment for a lump because they believe the cure is worse than the disease. Or, some individuals who are familiar with the debilitating side effects of radiation or chemotherapy for advanced cancers will mistakenly assume that they will automatically have to go through these treatments; therefore, their fear prevents them from seeking treatment (see Wurtele, Galanos, & Roberts, 1980).

Unfortunately, knowing what causes subsequently identified cancer patients to delay seeking treatment does not point unambiguously to solutions. Although educating the public about cancer symptoms may bring some people in for early treatment, it may intensify the fears of others (Antonovsky & Hartman, 1974). The enlargement of general screening programs and facilities for early detection as well as better education of physicians may remain the best strategies for this difficult and perplexing problem (Antonovsky & Hartman, 1974).

bein's theory of reasoned action, Timko (1987) found that women's intentions to delay seeking treatment for a suspicious breast symptom was related to favorable attitudes toward delay and perceived social pressure that favored delay. Apparently, these women be-

lieved that delaying seeking treatment would allow them to retain control over and avoid the disruption to their own and others' lives without necessarily resulting in negative health outcomes.

Surprisingly enough, delay behavior does

not end with the first treatment visit. Even after a consultation, up to 25% of patients delay taking recommended treatments, put off getting tests, or postpone acting on referrals. In some cases, patients have had their curiosity satisfied by the first visit and no longer feel any urgency about their condition. In other cases, precisely the opposite occurs: Patients become truly alarmed by the symptoms and, to avoid thinking about them, take no further action.

Delay on the part of the health care practitioner is also a significant factor, accounting for at least 15% of all delay behavior (Cassileth et al., 1988; Greer, 1974). Medical delay occurs when an appropriate test or treatment is not undertaken with a patient until some time after it has become warranted. In most cases, practitioners delay as a result of honest mistakes. A condition is misdiagnosed and treated as something else either until treatments produce no improvement or until new symptoms appear. For example, a symptom like blackouts can indicate any of many disorders ranging from heat prostration or overzealous dieting to diabetes or a brain tumor. A practitioner may choose to rule out the more common causes of the symptom before proceeding to the more invasive or expensive tests needed to rule out a less probable cause. Thus, when the more serious diagnosis is found to apply, the appearance of unwarranted delay exists. In other cases, medical delay may be caused by malpractice—for example, failing to do the appropriate tests, misreading test results, or failing to prescribe appropriate medications.

What factors contribute to medical delay? **Medical delay** is more likely when a patient deviates from the profile of the average person with a given disease. For example, since breast cancer is most common among women aged 45 or older, a 25-year-old with a breast lump might be sent home with a diagnosis of fibrocystic disease (a noncancerous condition) without being given a biopsy to test for possible malignancy. When a patient's symptom

departs from the standard profile for a particular disorder, medical delay is more likely. Continuing the breast cancer example, a woman whose primary symptom is a breast lump may receive appropriate care faster than a woman whose primary symptom is an irregularity in the nipple. When a symptom indicates more than one possible diagnosis, the time before a proper diagnosis is reached may be increased. And, finally, symptoms that are highly representative of a disorder may prompt faster diagnosis than symptoms that are less typical. For example, a woman who reports pain on urination may be more quickly diagnosed as having a urinary tract infection that one whose primary symptom is diffuse abdominal pain.

THE PATIENT IN THE HOSPITAL SETTING

About 33 million people are admitted yearly to the country's more than 7,000 hospitals (American Hospital Association, 1987). These figures represent an increase in use since the 1950s, largely because the role of the hospital has changed substantially over the last few decades. As recently as 60 or 70 years ago, hospitals were thought of primarily as places where people went to die. Our grandparents may still think of hospitals in terms of dying. Now, however, as we will see, the hospital has assumed many treatment functions. As a consequence, the average length of a hospital stay has decreased to its current level of 6.6 days (American Hospital Association, 1989), as shown in Figure 9.2.

The hospital of today is an extremely complex organization, incorporating both historical trends and current innovations. The hospital has always fascinated social scientists because its functions are so many and varied. It is a custodial unit, a treatment center, a teaching institution, a research center, and a laboratory (Wilson, 1963). Because of the diversity of treatment needs, many different

FIGURE 9.2   Hospital Admissions Have Leveled Off, Whereas Average
Length of Stay Has Declined

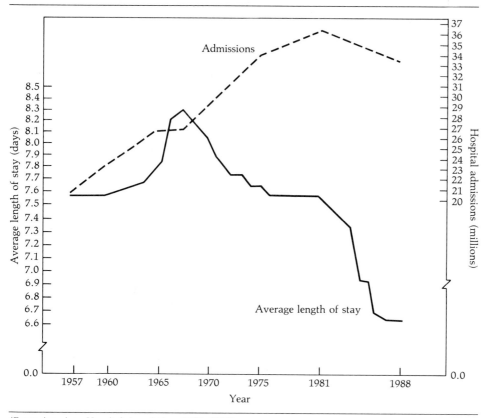

(From American Hospital Association, 1982, 1989)

kinds of skills are needed in hospitals, and the number of different kinds of personnel needed by hospitals is staggering (Wilson, 1963).

Structure of the Hospital

To understand the psychological impact of hospitalization, it is useful to have a working knowledge of its structure and functions (Shumaker & Pequegnat, 1989). The structure of hospitals depends on the health program under which care is delivered. For example, some health maintenance organizations (HMOs) and other prepaid health care systems have their own hospitals and employ their own physicians. Consequently, the hos-

pital structure is organized very much like any other hierarchically organized bureaucracy, with administration at the top and physicians, nurses, and technicians as employees.

In the case of the private hospital, a more unusual structure typically dominates. There are two lines of authority—a medical line, which is based on technical skill and expertise, and an administrative line, which runs the business of the hospital. Physicians are at the top of the medical line of authority and are accorded high status because they are chiefly responsible for the treatment of patients. Typically, however, they are not directly employed by the hospital, but, rather, act as invited guests, bringing their patients into the hospital in exchange for laboratories, custodial services, equipment, and teaching facilities that the hospital can provide. Because physicians are not directly under the administrative line of authority, the two lines of authority can sometimes be at odds. For example, a teaching physician who brings a class of medical students in to see patients can disrupt the hospital's custodial procedures. Thus, the relationship between the two lines of authority can be uneasy.

The nurse is part of both lines of authority. Employed by the hospital, she or he is also considered an assistant by the physician and is thus subject to both lines of authority, which can create conflicting requirements and needs (Coser, 1962). For example, if a doctor asks a particular nurse to get a piece of equipment, which requires her to leave the ward, should she follow the directive? Multiple responsibilities to these two lines of authorities often produce role ambiguity and role overload, which, coupled with poor pay, have led to a high degree of dissatisfaction and turnover in the nursing profession.

The implicit conflict among different groups in the hospital setting relates directly to the different goals to which the different professional groups may devote themselves. The goal of *cure* is typically the physician's responsibility: He or she is charged with performing any treatment action that has the potential to restore patients to good health, that is, to cure them. Patient *care,* in contrast, is the orientation of the nursing staff, and it involves the humanistic side of medicine. The goal of care is not only to restore the patient to good health, but to do so as much as possible by keeping the patient's emotional state and physical comfort in mind. In contrast, the administration of the hospital is concerned with maintaining the *core* of the hospital: ensuring the smooth functioning of the system and the flow of resources, services, and personnel (Mauksch, 1973).

These goals are not always compatible. For example, a clash between the cure and care orientations might occur in the decision of whether or not to administer chemotherapy to an advanced cancer patient. The cure orientation would maintain that chemotherapy should be initiated even if the chance for survivial is slim, whereas the care orientation might argue against the chemotherapy on the grounds that it causes patients great physical and emotional distress. In short, then, the different professional goals that exist within a hospital treatment setting produce orientations toward different goals. Although these goals are often compatible, they do at times make for conflicting demands on the resources and personnel of the hospital.

Functioning of the Hospital

Ambiguities and inconsistencies in the structure and goals of the hospital are mirrored in its functioning. As the complexity of the hospital system increases, the likelihood of decentralized decision-making also increases (Alexander & Fennell, 1986). Moreover, the hospital setting is constantly changing in response to changing realities. New patients are brought in who pose unexpected problems, other patients are discharged, and others show sudden changes in their condition that require immediate attention. Because of the changing demands of the hospital setting, the social order in which patient care is delivered is continually negotiated by the participants (Strauss, Schatzman, Bucher, Erlich, & Sarshim, 1963). Although each person involved in patient care, whether nurse, physician, or orderly, has general ideas about his or her functions, it is understood that under conditions of emergency, each must perform the tasks that he or she knows best, while remaining flexible to respond effectively to the changing situation. An analogy can be drawn to an improvisational theatrical production that is constantly changing, in which the actors have roles that they act out as the drama unfolds, sometimes in unpredictable ways (Goffman, 1961). Patient care, then, is a loosely structured process that is negotiated by the hospital staff on the basis of their skills, formal duties, positions in the hierarchy, and formal obligations and rights (Mauksch, 1973). It is a continually changing reality, so much that one cannot know what the hospital is at any given time without a grasp of these factors (Strauss et al., 1963).

The different goals of different professionals in the hospital setting are reflected in hospital workers' communication patterns. Occupational segregation in the hospital is high: Nurses talk to other nurses, physicians to other physicians, and administrators to other administrators (Wesson, 1972). Lack of communication across professional boundaries can create problems. Physicians have access to some information that nurses may not see, while nurses interact with patients daily and know a great deal about their day-to-day progress. Yet often their notes on charts may go unread by physicians. Few other opportunities to communicate may present themselves.

An example of the problems associated with lack of communication was provided by a study on nosocomial infection—that is, infection that results from exposure to disease in the hospital setting (Raven, Freeman, & Haley, 1982). It is well established that hospital workers often break the seemingly endless rules designed to control infection. Of all hospital workers, physicians seem to be the most likely to commit such infractions. As the highest eschelon in the treatment hierarchy, they may act as bad role models for others. Moreover, they appear to be rarely corrected by those under them. Nurses, for example, report that they would feel free to correct other nurses or orderlies, but they would probably not correct physicians (Raven et al., 1982). Administrators who say they would correct physicians in fact would be unlikely to observe them committing the infractions (Raven & Haley, 1980). Improved communication, then, could clearly have some role in reducing infection. If staff members felt free to communicate across the different levels of the hospital hier-

archy and felt free to point out violations to others in a constructive way, better infection control might result.

The preceding discussion has emphasized potential sources of conflict, ambiguity, and confusion in the hospital structure. Burnout, a problem that can result, in part, from these ambiguities is described in Box 9.5. However, this presents an incomplete picture. In many respects, hospital functioning is remarkably effective, given the changing realities to which it must accommodate at any given time. Thus, the ambiguities in structure, potential conflicts in goals, and problems of communication occur within a system that generally functions quite well.

Recent Changes in Hospitalization

In recent years, a variety of alternatives to traditional inpatient treatment have emerged that patients use for many disorders. Walk-in clinics in ambulatory medical centers, for example, can deal with less serious complaints such as minor surgeries that used to require hospitalization. Emergency clinics can handle a large proportion of the smaller emergencies that historically have filled the hospital emergency room. Home help services and hospices provide services for the chronically and terminally ill who require primarily palliative and custodial care, rather than active medical intervention. A consequence of removing these bread-and-butter cases from acute care hospitals has been to increase the proportion of resources devoted to the severely ill. Their care tends to be expensive and labor-intensive. With these pressures toward increasing costs, many hospitals may find themselves unable to survive (Boudewyns & Nolen, 1985).

Recent changes in health policies have had major effects on hospital utilization. Since the early 1970s, there have been increasing pressures to contain spiraling health care costs. One cost-containment effort has been the creation of **diagnostic-related groups (DRGs)**,

Box 9.5
Burnout Among Health Care Professionals

Burnout is an occupational risk for anyone who works with needy people. It is a particular problem for physicians, nurses, and other medical personnel who work with sick and dying people. As a syndrome, burnout is marked by three components: emotional exhaustion, depersonalization of the client, and a reduced sense of accomplishment in one's job. Staff members suffering from burnout show a cynical and apparently callous attitude toward those whom they serve. Their view of clients is more negative than that of other staff members, and they treat clients in more detached ways (Maslach, 1979; Shinn, Rosario, Morch, & Chestnut, 1984).

The effects of burnout are manifold. Burnout has been linked to absenteeism, high job turnover, and lengthy breaks during working hours. When burned out workers go home, they are often irritable and experience more discord within their families. They are more likely to suffer from insomnia as well as drug and alcohol abuse, and they have a higher rate of psychosomatic disorders. Thus, burnout has substantial costs for both the institution and the individual (Maslach, 1979).

Why does burnout develop? It is often the outcome of a social relationship in which a staff member is required to provide services for a highly needy individual who may not be helped by those services: The problems may be just too severe. Moreover, such jobs often require the staff member to be consistently empathic; this demand is unrealistic, as it is hard for anyone to maintain an empathic orientation indefinitely. Substantial amounts of time spent with clients, little feedback, little sense of control or autonomy, little sense of success, role conflict, and role ambiguity are job factors that all aggravate burnout (see Chapter 7) (Maslach, 1979).

High rates of burnout have been found in nurses who work in stressful environments such as intensive care, emergency, or terminal care (Francis, 1980; Moos & Schaefer, 1987). These nurses are expected to be sympathetic to patients and maintain interest, concern, warmth, and caring. Yet, they are also supposed to be objective. Many nurses find it difficult to protect themselves from the pain they feel from watching their patients suffer and die. To deal with these emotions, they become removed and distant. The stress of the work environment including the hectic pace of the hospital and the hurried, anxious behavior of co-workers also contributes to burnout (Francis, 1980; Moos & Schaefer, 1987).

How can burnout be avoided? Studies have suggested that individual coping efforts do not relieve job stresses very well (Shinn et al., 1984). Rather, people who show few symptoms of burnout habitually turn to others for help. They are more likely to talk to their clients and to their co-workers to help solve problems. Institutionalizing this kind of natural buffer against burnout may be a possible way to control the incidence of the syndrome (Maslach, 1979; Moos & Schaefer, 1987; Shinn et al., 1984).

One way of doing this is by developing support groups. Such groups can provide workers such as nurses with an opportunity to meet informally with other nurses to deal with the problems they face and to discuss the emerging signs of burnout. These support groups can give them the opportunity to obtain emotional support, reduce their feelings of being alone, share feelings of emotional pain about death and dying, and vent emotions in a supportive atmosphere. In so doing, the groups can promote feelings of togetherness, ultimately also improving client care (Duxbery, Armstrong, Dren, & Henley, 1984; Francis, 1980). The benefits of support groups are clear. Simply knowing that others share one's feelings can be very valuable (Francis, 1980). In addition, hearing other people talk about their own experiences of burnout and how they have attempted to deal with them can give others in the group possible strategies and clues as to how they can solve their own problems as well.

a patient classification scheme developed by the federal government and increasingly adopted by state Medicaid programs and private insurance companies. DRGs specify the nature and length of treatment for particular disorders. Patients in a DRG category (e.g., hernia surgery candidates) are assumed to represent a homogeneous group that is clinically similar and that should require approximately the same types and amounts of treatments, length of stay of hospitalization, and ultimate cost. DRGs define trim points, which indicate unusually long or short lengths of stay. If patient care falls within the classification scheme, reimbursement for care will be forthcoming from the third party, whether the federal or state government or an insurance company. In the case of an outlier (e.g., a patient who stays in the hospital longer than the DRG specifies), the case is typically subject to review and the extra costs may not be paid. This puts pressure on hospitals to cut patient stays and treatment costs. Consequently, with the institution of DRGs, hospitals have gone from being overcrowded to being underused, and vacancy rates may be as high as 70%.

Another cost containment strategy that has affected the functioning of hospitals is the **preferred provider organization (PPO).** Increasingly, insurance companies and other third-party providers designate the particular hospital or treatment facility that a patient must use in order to be reimbursed for services. Patients are directed to these services because they are judged to provide the least expensive appropriate care. Patients who wish to go elsewhere have to pay the additional fees themselves. The consequence has been to keep treatment costs lower than they might otherwise be.

Hospitals are experiencing a variety of other changes as well. Nearly 45% of U.S. hospitals are currently part of a multihospital system (American Hospital Association, 1987). This means that hospitals are no longer as independent as they once were, and instead

may be subject to rules and regulations established by a higher level of authority (Weil & Stam, 1986). Another recent development is that approximately 50% of U.S. hospitals currently have collective bargaining contracts for resolving conflicts between groups such as nurses and administrators or physicians and administrators (Alexander & Bloom, 1987). The potential for conflict in hospitals and the likelihood that collective bargaining agreements will be created increases with organizational complexity (Alexander & Bloom, 1987). Changes in the structure and functioning of hospitals involving outside regulation, physician competition, and the corporatization of health services have also altered the traditional separation of power between hospital administration and physicians. Administrators are increasingly involved in some of the decisions previously left to physicians, and the reverse is true as well (Alexander, Morrisey, & Shortell, 1986). The full effect of these changes on patient care and its costs is not yet evident.

The Impact of Hospitalization on the Patient

> The patient comes unbidden to a large organization which awes and irritates him, even as it also nurtures and cares. As he strips off his clothing so he strips off, too, his favored costume of social roles, his favored style, his customary identity in the world. He becomes subject to a time schedule and a pattern of activity not of his own making. (Wilson, 1963, p. 70)

Patients arrive at the hospital with anxiety over their illness or disorder, confusion and anxiety over the prospect of hospitalization, and concern over all the role obligations they must leave behind unfulfilled. The hospital does little, if anything, to calm anxiety, and, in many cases, it exacerbates it (Mason, Sachar, Fishman, Hamburg, & Handlon, 1965). The admission is often conducted by a clerk who asks about scheduling, insurance, and money.

The patient is then ushered into a strange room, given strange clothes, provided with an unfamiliar roommate, and subjected to peculiar tests. The patient may entrust him- or herself completely to strangers in a peculiar uncertain environment in which all procedures are new. The patient is expected to be cooperative, dependent, and helpful without demanding excessive attention. The patient quickly learns that the hospital is organized for the convenience of staff rather than patients. He or she is also physically confined, making adjustment to the new situation that much more difficult.

Hospital patients may show a variety of problematic psychological symptoms, especially anxiety and depression. Nervousness over tests or surgery and their results can produce insomnia, terrifying nightmares, and a general inability to concentrate. Procedures that isolate a patient from social contact or render him or her immobile in a changeless environment are particularly likely to have adverse

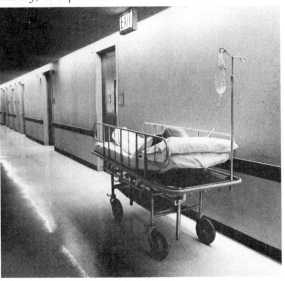

The hospital can be a lonely and frightening place for many patients, leading to feelings of helplessness, anxiety, or depression.

effects (e.g., Benoliel, 1977). Hospital care can be highly fragmented. As many as thirty different staff people may pass through a patient's room each day, making tests, taking blood, bringing food, or cleaning up. Often the staff members have little time to spend with the patient beyond exchanging greetings.

The lack of communication between staff and patients is one of the most universal complaints of hospital patients (Skipper & Leonard, 1965). In some cases, staff members may deliberately withhold information because they fear the patient will misinterpret it or be alarmed by it.

> Giving information to patients about their illness may seem as something which patients do not need to know, would probably not understand anyway, might cause an emotional reaction which would interfere with their instrumental care and cure, and at the very least, takes the time of nurses and physicians away from more important tasks. (Skipper, Tagliacozzo, & Mauksch, 1964, pp. 35–36)

The disorienting consequences of illness and hospitalization and lack of communication make the patient very likely to adopt the **hospital patient role,** one into which patients are socialized by hospital staff on their arrival. Patients are expected to be cooperative, pleasant, and quiet unless there is an emergency. They are expected to turn themselves over to medical authorities who accept responsibility for making them well (Parsons, 1951). The major task of patients becomes following instructions to reduce the chances of becoming sicker and to increase those of recovering. Patients believe that physicians expect cooperation, trust, and confidence, and they perceive nurses as expecting them to be undemanding, respectful, and considerate. Thus, the hospitalized patient regards one of his or her chief role obligations as that of pleasing the physician and nurse by behaving properly (Tagliacozzo and Mauksch, 1972).

Despite the fact that the ''good'' patient is

Box 9.6
The Land of Hospital

A month ago, in the course of having a test in a hospital lab, I incurred a severe injury to my hand—loss of feeling and motion, three bedridden weeks in the hospital strung up on i.v.'s and other contraptions... the works. I am not telling you this to try to break your heart; my hand is still there and intact, and with a couple of months of therapy and medicine it should be workable again. Nor am I trying to establish a case here; the precise reason for my injury is still under discussion and review. But I do feel as though I have just come back from a foreign place worth reporting on and one visited in the course of any year by many more *Newsweek* readers that fetch up in Manila or Riyadh or any of the other spots from which I have felt compelled to record my observations.

This foreign place is, of course, the land of Hospital, a nation—a universe, really—of its own, within which one quickly and progressively sinks into the role of patient, analogous in the way it transforms your personality and gnaws at both your assurance and sense of self to being a tourist in an unfathomable, dangerous land.

According to the best figures I can get, not counting psychiatric care, more than 35 million of us spend some time in the hospital every year. I am sure my treatment was atypical, since once a hospital—any hospital—perceives that it has an inmate from the dread Daily Bugle in room 604, certain amenities and extra solicitude follows; and I know that even without that I would have been better off than patients with less means than I of looking out for themselves. But even with these advantages there was no escaping the distinctive, essential hospital experience of our times: a maddening combination of individual excellence and systemic incompetence, the one tirelessly and heroically saving life and limb, the other forever putting both at mindless risk.

Total trust: The hospital is, in this sense, I think, the paradigm of our newly demystified high-tech institutions—NASA, the agencies concerned with our air-traffic safety, you name it. Our inclination has previously been toward awe, submission, marvel at the wonder of it all and total, uncritical trust in the stewardship of others. The esoteric science and dazzling machinery involved have reinforced a disposition to yield up all authority, independence and judgment of one's own.

Only fairly recently have we been forced to acknowledge that this isn't good enough. In the same building with the state-of-the-art machine that can see your brain and hear your blood are the crumpled Kleenexes and old dressings that should have been disposed of, all lying there under the unconcerned eye of the technical assistant who is thinking mainly of lunch. Beside the sensitive electronic scanner of your transatlantic luggage stands the so-called inspector gazing into the middle distance or diverted by the chitchat of a buddy. Behind the towering Oz-like wonder of space travel nest the tight little bureaucratic substructures that impose their motives and values on people who should know better

What we know now is not that these institutions are bad but that they are presided over and manned by human beings and that they are at a minimum fallible because the good guys and the good instincts don't always prevail. And we have to help them prevail. In other words, we have to assume responsibility for ourselves in relation to such institutions. We can't just lie back and let the old magic take over. There is no magic.

Cumulative disaster: This is a lot harder for a very sick hospital patient to accomplish than it is, say, for a layman congressman or business manager who is suddenly called on to assume oversight of a higly technical program. The patient is relentlessly reduced, by both external circumstance (his ailment, traditional hospital procedure) and his own powerful impetus toward passivity in such a situation. The sick person is in fact sort of re-created as a baby. We brighten and decorate his room to cheer him up. We wave gaily colored artifacts before him to make him smile. We send him gewgaws and toys and tricks.

I treasured each one of these offerings as it came in, along with the beloved sprays of flowers. Each attested to a friend "out there" and a continuing existence independent of my strange hospital life. So I had everything stashed conspicuously on windowsills and tabletops. But what was individually gratifying was cumulatively disastrous. By the end of ten days my quarters looked like the scene of a five-year-old's birthday party. In one of my increasingly infrequent adult moments I noticed this. I noticed that, as with a child who needs to be patronized and humored, we had all taken to talking and thinking of me as "she"—as if I weren't there: "She is doing better with her exercises now...she didn't eat her dinner..." etc. I rose up as best I could, being attached to a number of tubes and other fixtures, and commanded the artifacts out of my room. I was in search of my identity and the duty to care for my own fate that it implied.

I had wonderful doctors and nurses and therapists who rescued me, along with some superior hospital staff and administrators. They and their technological equipment operate against a background of remorseless human shortcoming, bureaucratic inefficiency and indifference. That, not some need to understand the exotic equipment or science, is the problem. What is required is a fundamental, painstaking re-education process on the part of a whole institution—a relearning of attentiveness, individual accountability, care. And something similar will be required to salvage and repair all our ailing technological enterprises. It will be protracted, painful and very slow to show results if it is to succeed—a little, I am afraid, like the hurting-healing therapist's drill. "Stretch," she says to me. "Ouch," I say to her. "Again," she insists. "You're kidding," I protest. She is adamant—and she is right: "Harder."

(Greenfield, 1986).

---

the type most appreciated by staff, the patient who fully takes on the patient role is not necessarily well-adjusted or satisfied. Two-thirds of the patients in one study (Tagliacozzo & Mauksch, 1972) indicated that they had needs and criticisms of the hospital system that they had not felt free to express. "Being on good terms" was seen by these patients not merely as convenient, but as essential to their welfare. Patients felt that needed services could be withheld unless they made themselves acceptable.

One hospital watcher (Taylor, 1979) suggested that the hospital environment may actually encourage patients to become helpless (see Box 9.6). Finding that their questions go unanswered or that their desires for attention will not be fulfilled, patients may develop learned helplessness, an inability to exert control when control is possible (Raps et al., 1982; Seligman, 1979). Thus, "good" patient behavior may actually be detrimental to recovery by keeping patients from taking an active role in their own care (Brown, 1963; Taylor, 1979).

What percentage of patients actually play out the good patient role? Lorber (1975) divided patients into three types: the good patient (25%), the average patient (50%), and the problem patient (25%). Good patients have simple medical problems, they are uncomplaining and docile, they take up little time, and they have uncomplicated recoveries. Average patients are like good patients except that they have some minor complaints that can usually be handled routinely. The third group, "bad" patients, fall into two subtypes: those who are seriously ill and complain and those who are not seriously ill but complain anyway (see Table 9.1). While the seriously ill are often forgiven their complaints, those

TABLE 9.1   LOSS OF CONTROL, GOOD PATIENT BEHAVIOR, AND BAD PATIENT BEHAVIOR IN
HOSPITAL PATIENTS: CHARACTERISTICS AND CONSEQUENCES

STATE	BEHAVIORS	COGNITIONS	AFFECT	PHYSICAL STATE	RESPONSES FROM STAFF
Loss of control (depersonalization)	Nondiscriminant information seeking and use; complaints to staff	Inadequate expectations; confusion	Anxiety	Heightened physical reactions to symptoms and unpleasant medical procedures; possible increased need for medication; lengthened hospital stay	Depersonalizing treatment
Good patient behavior (helplessness)	Compliance, passivity, learned helplessness, inability to take in information, failure to provide condition-relevant information	Feelings of helplessness, powerlessness, possible denial or fatalism	Anxiety and depression	Possible norepinephrine depletion; helplessness also related to sudden death and gradual erosion of health	Responsiveness to emergencies but routine failure to solicit information from patient
Bad patient behavior (reactance)	Complaints to staff, demands for attention, mutinous behavior, possible self-sabotage	Commitment to a right to know; suspicion (or paranoia) regarding condition, treatment, and staff behavior	Anger	Heightened catecholamine secretion and hydrocortisone production; possible aggravation of blood pressure, hypertension, tachycardia, angina; eventual epinephrine depletion	Condescension; ignoring patients' complaints; medication given only to placate; psychiatric referrals; possible premature discharge

(Source: Based on Taylor, 1979)

complainers who are not seriously ill arouse considerable irritation in staff (see Leiderman & Grisso, 1985). Why do these patients cause so much trouble?

Many freedoms are withdrawn when the medical patient enters the hospital. Some of these are medically based, such as the requirement that a patient with a broken leg not stand on it or that a patient receiving intravenous medication stay in bed. Other freedoms are withdrawn to protect the freedoms of other patients, the ability of the staff to go about their work, and the hospital's ability to function, such as the fact that visitors are restricted to particular visiting times. This threat to freedom rarely counts for much in itself, but when combined with the patient's distress over being ill, it can create a management problem.

Hospitalization can induce **reactance**, an angry reaction against the abrupt and seemingly arbitrary withdrawal of freedoms (Brehm & Brehm, 1981). At its least problematic level, reactance in the hospital can be manifested as petty acts of mutiny, making passes at nurses, drinking in one's room, smoking against medical advice, wandering up and down the halls—incidents that irritate nursing and custodial staff but rarely do any real damage. However, reactance can also take the form of self-sabotage, such as failure to take essential medications or behavior that could actually be fatal. Hospitals and medical staff can inadvertently contribute to reactance by failing to treat patients as adults, to take their demands seriously, and to explain seemingly arbitrary directives and regulations. In fairness, it is often difficult for staff members to find time for such individualized care.

At its most benign, the staff treats the irascible patient with good-humored condescension or ignores him or her altogether. But one study (Lorber, 1975) revealed that "problem patients" actually ran health risks at the hands of staff. Staff were most likely to deal with these patients by medicating them, ignoring them, referring them to a psychiatrist, and, in some cases, actually discharging them prematurely. These steps were most likely to occur if the patient's complaints were perceived as out of proportion to the ailment.

Some of the potential adverse effects of problematic reactions to hospitalization are summarized in Table 9.1. As can be seen in that table, the loss of control instituted by the hospital setting can itself have adverse cognitive and physiological effects. Moreover, how the patient responds to that loss of control, whether with good patient behavior or bad patient behavior, can also adversely affect care (Baltes & Skinner, 1983; Raps et al., 1982). Thus, the psychological responses of patients to hospitalization clearly merit additional research attention designed primarily toward identifying the kinds of interventions that can be used to help patients adjust to their hospitalization more successfully.

INTERVENTIONS TO INCREASE CONTROL IN HOSPITAL SETTINGS

Largely in response to both informal observation and research evidence suggesting that people experience adverse effects of loss of control in hospitals, many hospitals have provided interventions that help prepare patients generally for hospitalization and more specifically for the procedures that they will undergo.

Coping with Surgery Through Control-Enhancing Interventions

In 1958, psychologist Irving Janis conducted a landmark study that would forever change the preparation of patients for surgery. Janis was asked by a hospital to study its surgery patients to see if something could be done to reduce the stress that many of them experienced both before and after operations. One of Janis's earliest observations was that, without some anticipatory worry, patients were not able to cope well with surgery. He termed this the "work of worrying," reasoning that patients must work through the fear and loss of control that are raised by surgery before they are able to adjust to it.

To get a clearer idea of the relationship between worry and adjustment, Janis first grouped the patients according to the level of fear they experienced before the operation (high, medium, and low). Then he studied how well they understood and used the information that the hospital staff gave them to help them cope with the aftereffects of surgery. High-fear patients generally remained fearful and anxious after surgery and showed many negative side effects, such as vomiting, pain, urinary retention, and inability to eat. Patients who had initially been low in fear also showed unfavorable reactions after surgery, becoming angry or upset or complaining. Of the three groups, the moderately fearful patients coped with postoperative stress most effectively as determined by both interviews and staff reports.

In interpreting these results, Janis reasoned that high-fear patients had been too absorbed with their own fears preoperatively to process the preparatory information adequately and low-fear patients were insufficiently vigilant to understand and process the information effectively. Patients with moderate levels of fear, in contrast, were vigilant enough but not overwhelmed by their fears, so they were able to develop realistic expectations of what their postsurgery reactions would be; when they later encountered these sensations and reactions, they expected them and were ready to deal with them.

Subsequent studies have borne out some but not all of Janis's observations (e.g., Kiyak et al., 1988). Whereas Janis believed that fear and the work of worrying are essential ingredients in processing information about surgery (see also Salmon et al., 1988), most researchers now believe that the effect is primarily determined by the informational value of the preparatory communication itself (Anderson & Masur, 1983; Johnson, Lauver, & Nail, 1989). That is, patients who are carefully prepared for surgery and its aftereffects will show good postoperative adjustment; patients who are not well prepared for the aftereffects of surgery will show poor postoperative adjustment.

Janis's initial work sparked a large number of intervention studies. An example of this kind of research is the work of Egbert and his colleagues with patients facing intra-abdominal surgery (Egbert, Battit, Welch, & Barlett, 1964). In this study, half the patients were alerted to the likelihood of postoperative pain and were given information about its normality, duration, and severity. They were also taught breathing exercises that would reduce the pain. The other half of the patients received no such instructions. When examined postoperatively, patients in the instruction group showed better postoperative adjust-

ment: They required fewer narcotics and were able to leave the hospital sooner than the patients who had not received the preparatory instructions.

A large number of studies have now examined the role of preparatory information in adjustment to surgery, and the conclusion is overwhelmingly that such preparation has a beneficial effect on patients. Patients who are given information about the sensations they can expect after surgery are less emotional postoperatively (Johnson, 1984) and are able to leave the hospital sooner than are patients who do not receive such information (Johnson, 1984). Patients who are taught to perform physical activities (such as walking around, doing leg exercises, doing deep breathing exercises) after their surgery that will help them to become mobile again are also less distressed after surgery (Fortin & Kirouac, 1976; Johnson, Fuller, Endress, & Rice, 1978; Johnson, Rice, Fuller, Endress, 1978); in some cases, they are also able to leave the hospital sooner (Johnson, Fuller et al., 1978; Schmitt & Wooldridge, 1973). Information that orients patients to the events of surgery and their order of occurrence also consistently reduces postsurgical distress (Felton, Huss, Payne, & Srsic, 1976; Fortin & Kirouac, 1976; Johnson, Rice et al., 1978; Schmitt & Wooldridge, 1973) and may also shorten hospital stay. Adequate preoperative preparation can reduce the need for narcotics (Egbert et al., 1964), the amount of postoperative vomiting (Dumas & Leonard, 1963), and psychological distress (Vernon & Bigelow, 1974). One study (Kulik & Mahler, 1989) even found that preoperative roommate assignment could provide information that influenced how patients coped with the aftermath of surgery (see Box 9.7).

Most surgical preparation communications provide information about sensations and procedures designed to increase ambulation to improve postsurgical adjustment. However, there is some evidence that in-

Box 9.7
Social Support and Distress from Surgery

Patients who are hospitalized for serious illnesses or surgery often experience anxiety. From our discussion of social support, we know that emotional support from others can often reduce emotional distress when people are undergoing stressful events. Recently, researchers have made use of these observations in developing interventions for hospitalized patients.

Kulik and Mahler (1989) developed a social support intervention for patients about to undergo cardiac surgery. Some of the patients were assigned a roommate who was also waiting for surgery (preoperative condition), whereas others were assigned a roommate who had already had surgery (postoperative condition). In addition, patients were placed with a roommate undergoing surgery that was either similar or dissimilar to their own.

The results suggested that patients who had a postoperative roommate profited from this contact. Patients with a postoperative roommate were less anxious preoperatively, were more ambulatory postoperatively, and were released more quickly from the hospital than patients who had been paired with a roommate who was also awaiting surgery.

Similarity versus dissimilarity of the type of surgery made no difference, only whether or not the roommate's surgery had already taken place.

Why exactly did rooming with a postoperative surgical patient improve the adjustment of those awaiting surgery? It may be that postoperative patients were able to provide relevant information to patients about the postoperative period by telling them how they felt and what the patient might expect. Postoperative roommates may also have acted as role models for how one might feel and react postoperatively. Alternatively, those awaiting surgery may simply have been relieved to see somebody who had undergone surgery and come out all right. Whatever the specific explanation, the social contact produced by the presence of the postoperative roommate clearly had a positive impact on the preoperative and postoperative adjustment of these surgery patients. These results have intriguing implications and may well be used to design future interventions to improve the adjustment of those awaiting unpleasant medical procedures such as surgery.

---

structing patients how to think about postoperative sensations differently can improve adjustment as well. Langer, Janis, and Wolfer (1975) gave patients awaiting surgery cognitive reappraisal training in which patients were instructed to distract themselves from the unpleasant aspects of surgery and attend only to its favorable aspects (such as the benefits the procedure would produce). As compared with a group that got no cognitive reappraisal training, these patients

showed a reduced need for pain-relieving medications postoperatively.

To summarize, it is clear that **control-enhancing interventions** with patients awaiting surgery can have a marked effect on postoperative adjustment, as evidenced both by patients' emotional reactions and by objective indicators, such as amount of medication required and length of hospitalization. Moreover, a variety of control-based interventions successfully affect postsurgical adjustment including information, behavioral, and cognitive interventions. These demonstrations of the value of psychological control have led to important changes in how patients are prepared for surgery.

Coping with Stressful Medical Procedures Through Control-Enhancing Interventions

Although control-enhancing interventions were first used in hospitals to help patients cope with surgery, they are also being used increasingly to help patients cope with a variety of other stressful medical procedures. Anticipating an invasive medical procedure is often a crisis situation for patients who have extreme anxiety about such procedures (Auerbach & Kilmann, 1977; Janis, 1958). Accordingly, any intervention that can reduce anxiety both before the procedure and during it will achieve welcome benefits for both patients and the medical staff.

Control-enhancing interventions have now been used with a variety of these procedures, including gastroendoscopic examinations (Johnson & Leventhal, 1974), childbirth (Leventhal, Leventhal, Shacham, & Easterling, 1989), the management of peptic ulcers (Putt, 1970), chemotherapy (Burish & Lyles, 1979), hysterectomy (Johnson, Christman, & Stitt, 1985), radiation therapy (Johnson, Laurer, & Nail, 1989), cardiac catheterization (Kendall et al., 1979), and sigmoidoscopy (examination of the sigmoid colon via a small scope inserted through the anus) (Kaplan, Atkins, & Lenhard, 1982). An example follows.

Cardiac catheterization is an exploratory diagnostic procedure that is used with people who are suspected of having irregularities in coronary circulation. A catheter (a hollow tube) is inserted into the base of the aorta, next to the heart, and dye is injected, which makes it possible to visualize the entire coronary area. A practitioner can then see such circulatory abnormalities as valve defects or holes in the wall of the aorta and can use this information to recommend treatment, such as coronary bypass surgery. Patients are fully conscious during the procedure and receive only a local anesthetic and a tranquilizing agent such as Valium. Although the procedure is not particularly painful, it does arouse a lot of anxiety in many patients.

In a study designed to reduce the stressfulness of this procedure (Kendall et al., 1979), patients who were scheduled for cardiac catheterization were assigned to one of four intervention groups. In the first group (cognitive intervention), patients were first taught to recognize the signs of their own anxiety. They were then instructed to use these internal signals to initiate cognitive coping skills of their own. The intervention trainer provided a model by confessing her own fears about a stressful event in her own life and by describing the techniques she used to overcome her fears. Patients were then encouraged to discuss their fears and the coping techniques they typically used to overcome anxiety. The goal of this intervention, then, was to help patients recognize their anxiety and initiate personal coping techniques to achieve relaxation.

In the second group (information intervention), patients received individual instruction, using a model of the heart to illustrate points about heart disease and the catheterization procedure. They were also given reading materials about the procedure, and their questions were answered. In the third group (social support), patients were told that a therapist would talk to them before and during the procedure to help them relax and cope. The therapist engaged the patient in general conversation, which lasted as long as the orientation interventions with the first two groups. This condition is a control condition because there is no reason to think that merely talking to a patient during a stressful medical procedure will necessarily reduce anxiety. Inclusion of this group enabled the researchers to see if the intervention groups experienced benefits over and above the effect that mere talking has. Finally, a fourth group of patients received the hospital's standard preparatory information, which consisted of a brief description of the procedure. All patients then went through the cardiac catheterization procedure.

Patients were asked to report their anxiety before the procedure; to say, in retrospect, how much anxiety they felt during the procedure; and to indicate their level of anxiety after the procedure was over. In addition, physicians and technicians made ratings of patient adjustment. Results clearly showed that the cognitive intervention and the information intervention had significant roles in reducing anxiety during the procedure. Of the two interventions, the cognitive intervention was the more successful. These effects persisted after the procedure, thus ameliorating post-procedural anxiety as well.

An important aspect of the cardiac catheterization procedure is that there is little that a patient can do behaviorally to make it easier. Many other unpleasant medical procedures, including chemotherapy and bone marrow transplants for cancer, also force the patient to be passive. For such tests, information and cognitive-control techniques would seem to be the interventions of choice, in that the main goal of the intervention is the reduction of anxiety.

Reviewing a large number of studies, Ludwick-Rosenthal and Neufeld (1988) concluded that information, relaxation, and cognitive-behavioral interventions have all been quite successful in reducing anxiety, improving coping, and enabling people to overcome the adverse effects of medical procedures more quickly. Exactly why these effects occur is still unknown. It may be that these interventions enhance a patient's sense of predictability and control over an aversive situation. Alternatively, the interventions may provide patients with coping strategies that enable

them to manage the stressful events more successfully. There may be side effects of interventions, such as emotional supportiveness, that improve mood and enhance physical and psychological functioning. Research will continue to evaluate the mechanisms by which these interventions so clearly have positive effects.

The evidence on the beneficial effects of psychological control should not be taken to suggest that control is a panacea for all aversive situations (Schultheis, Peterson, & Selby, 1987). People differ reliably in their desire for control (Burger & Cooper, 1979), and those who desire control may cope more successfully with it than those who do not. Control may be aversive if it gives people more responsibility than they feel able to tolerate or if it gives them the responsibility to achieve some outcome (such as reduced distress) which they feel they are unlikely to attain (see, for example, Burger, 1989; Thompson, Cheek, & Graham, 1988). Sometimes patients need to know that physicians and other medical authorities are in charge, and being instilled with a sense that they have personal control over their reactions to a medical procedure may be aversive (Thompson et al., 1988). Efforts to exert control in a medical situation may fail, leaving patients more poorly off than if they had not tried to exert control in the first place (Thompson et al., 1988). And too much control, such as being instructed to focus on too much information or to make too many choices, may be stressful, exacerbating distress over the medical procedure (see, for example, Mills & Krantz, 1979; Thompson et al., 1988). There are limits, then, to the success of control-based interventions with medical patients.

THE HOSPITALIZED CHILD

While it is generally acknowledged that people should be hospitalized only when it is absolutely necessary, this caution is particularly important in the care of the ill child. Some hospitalized children show adverse reactions to hospitalization, ranging from regressive, dependent behavior such as social withdrawal, bed-wetting, and extreme fear to rebelliousness and temper tantrums. Although many of these reactions can be observed while the child is in the hospital, problematic responses to hospitalization often do not become evident until the child returns home, and these effects can last for months.

Anxiety is the most common adverse response to hospitalization. At young ages (2 to 4), children's anxiety may arise from their wish to be with the family as much as possible and more than may be practical. Children between ages 3 and 6 may become upset because they feel they are being rejected, deserted, or punished by their family. Between 4 and 6, children may act out their anxiety by developing new fears, such as a fear of darkness or of hospital staff. Sometimes, too, anxiety will be converted into bodily symptoms such as headaches or stomachaches. In somewhat older children (ages 6 to 10), anxiety may be more free floating: It may make the child more irritable and distractible without being tied to any particular issue.

When children do react badly to the hospital environment, there are many possible reasons that may be hard to untangle. They may be frightened by illness, may feel ignored and unloved because they cannot receive the regular parenting that is available at home, may experience the hospital environment itself as strange and frightening, or may be experiencing **separation anxiety.**

Until recent years, psychologists usually attributed adverse reactions to hospitalization entirely to separation anxiety. Bowlby (1969, 1973) suggested that long-term separation of a child from the mother can produce extreme upset, even grief and mourning reactions under some circumstances. However, as children's attachments to both parents have become more widely acknowledged and as researchers have learned that effective mothering can come from caregivers other than the mother, the value of the concept of separation anxiety has been questioned.

One study (Branstetter, 1969) divided hospitalized children into three groups: One-third of the children saw their mothers only during visiting hours, the hospital's standard custom; one-third had their mothers with them for extended periods during their hospitalization; and one-third were assigned a "substitute mother," a student nurse or graduate student who talked with and played with them for extended periods. The results indicated that the children with mothers present for extended periods or with mother substitutes showed less emotional disturbance than the group that saw their mothers only during visiting hours. These results suggest that a warm, nurturant relationship with a caregiver can offset some of the adverse effects of hospitalization and that the mother need not be the person who provides that relationship.

The fact remains, however, that it is hard for a child to be separated from family and home. Some children may not understand why they have been taken away from their families. They may mistakenly infer that the family does not want them any more or that they are being punished for some misdeed. If most of the family members work or go to school and cannot visit the child as often as would be desirable, this may exacerbate the child's feelings of abandonment. The hospital environment itself can be lonely and isolating. Physical confinement in bed or confinement due to casts or traction keeps children from discharging energy through physical activity. The dependency that is fostered by bedrest and reliance on staff can lead to regression. Children, especially children just entering puberty, can be embarrassed or ashamed by having to expose themselves to strangers. The child may also be subject to confusing or painful tests and procedures.

Preparing Children for Medical Interventions

In the previous section, we considered how principles of **psychological control** have been used to create interventions for adult patients undergoing stressful medical procedures such as surgery. The principles of psychological control have also been generalized to children's hospital experiences. A number of studies have experimentally varied aspects of hospital preparation for children and found that certain kinds of interventions can reduce distress.

In one study (Melamed & Siegel, 1975), children about to undergo elective surgery were shown either a film of a peer being hospitalized and receiving surgery or an unrelated control film. Results suggested that those exposed to the relevant film showed less preoperative and postoperative distress than those exposed to the control film. Moreover, parents of the children exposed to the modeling film reported fewer problem behaviors after hospitalization than did parents of children who saw the control film. Other studies have confirmed the beneficial effects of videotaped modeling interventions to prepare children psychologically for surgery (Pinto & Hollandsworth, 1989). Additional research has suggested that whereas older children may be well served by seeing a film several days before hospitalization, younger children may need exposure to information immediately before the relevant events (Melamed, Meyer, Gee, & Soule, 1976; see also Ferguson, 1979; Peterson & Shigetomi, 1981).

Recently, research has attempted to identify the components of interventions with children that may be most successful in reducing their anxiety and distress over aversive medical procedures. For example, Zastowny, Kirschenbaum, and Meng (1986) gave children and their parents information describing typical hospitalization and surgery experiences, relaxation training to reduce anxiety, or a coping skills intervention to teach children constructive self-talk. Both the anxiety-reduction and the coping skills interventions reduced fearfulness and parents' distress. Overall, the children exposed to the coping skills intervention exhibited the fewest maladaptive behaviors during hospitalization, less problematic behavior in the week before admission, and fewer problems after discharge (Peterson & Shigetomi, 1981).

With some exceptions, the studies that have exposed children to preparatory information before hospitalization or before undergoing unpleasant medical procedures have found beneficial effects. How much preparation interacts with prior experience with a procedure, however, is one unresolved issue (Murray, Liddell, & Donohue, 1989). In one study (Melamed, Yurcheson, Fleece, Hutcherson, & Hawes, 1978), children awaiting one of three dental procedures profited most from a film showing a peer model if they had had prior experience with the procedure; children with no prior experience appeared to be sensitized by the procedure, showing more behavior problems after viewing the film. However, prior experience with a procedure can also remind children exactly how unpleasant the procedure can be, and, consequently, preparation for it may simply bring back those unpleasant memories rather than soothe the child with adaptive coping strategies and emotional support (Jay, Ozolins, Elliott, & Caldwell, 1983). For example, Faust and Melamed (1984) found that children who had had previous surgical experience showed greater sweat increase after exposure to a relevant preparatory film than children without previous experience. Moreover, showing the film the same day of surgery produced no reduction in distress. Rather, a distracting film was more effective. It may be, then, that children are best prepared for in-hospital experiences if they see preparation films in conjunction with admission procedures, but not just before more stressful procedures such as surgery.

Dahlquist et al. (1986) attempted to identify if children with previous positive or negative experiences with medical examinations would profit from different kinds of interventions. Children were randomly assigned to one of six conditions before undergoing a medical examination and throat culture: sensory information about the exam; training in coping skills; deep breathing and positive self-talk; a combination of sensory information and coping skills training; attention control (distraction); and a no-treatment control. The results indicated that children who had previously had negative experiences showed more distress going through the procedures than did children who had previously had positive or neutral medical experiences. The attention (distraction) condition appeared to increase the distress of these children more than did the other conditions. Thus, the quality of the prior experience clearly moderates its role in influencing how children react to subsequent medical procedures.

Whether children prefer to cope with stress using avoidant rather than vigilant coping strategies may also influence their responsiveness to preparation. Field and her associates (Field, Alpert, Vega-Lahr, Goldstein, & Perry, 1988) observed that children who coped using a vigilant coping style were more talkative, expressive, and active during their hospitalization, observed the procedures more, sought out information about the procedures, and protested more than children who coped through repression. However, these vigilant copers also required fewer hours of intensive care. Similar results have been reported by Peterson and Toler (1986). Another individual difference factor that may influence how children react to stressful medical procedures is chronic level of anxiety. Chronically anxious children may be more likely to develop anxiety around specific medical procedures, which may interfere with adjusting successfully to those procedures (Brown, Wright, & McMurray, 1986).

Despite these qualifications, the benefits of at least some preparation of children for hospitalization are now so widely acknowledged that preparation is more the rule than the exception. As of 1980, over 75% of pediatric hospitals provided some kind of psychological preparation for children (Peterson & Ridley-Johnson, 1980). Preparation of the child should focus not only on the need for hospitalization and the nature of the hospital experience but also on the illness and its treatment (Johnson, Kirchoff, & Endress, 1975; Melamed & Siegel, 1975). If the child understands what the illness is, what it feels like, and how soon he or she will get better, anxiety due to illness can be reduced. If the child is given information about each medical procedure, what it will feel like, and how long it will last, he or she may adjust to it more successfully (e.g., Roberts, Wurtele, Boone, Ginther, & Elkins, 1981). Even very young children should be told something about their treatment; they should have procedures explained to them, and they should be encouraged to express emotions and ask questions.

Much preparation can be undertaken by parents. If a parent prepares a child for admission several days before hospitalization—explaining the reason for it, what it will be like, who will be there, how often the parent will visit—this may ease the transition. During admission procedures, a parent or other familiar adult can remain with the child until the child is settled into the new room and engaged in some activity. Parents who remain with the child in the hospital can be partially responsible for explaining procedures and tests, knowing what the child will best understand.

It should be noted that the presence of parents during stressful medical procedures is not an unmitigated benefit. Parents do not always help to reduce children's fears, pain, and discomfort (Bush, Melamed, Sheras, & Greenbaum, 1986; Melamed & Bush, 1985). While the provision of information can sometimes help a child understand and explore a situation more fully, reassurance can sometimes backfire, producing more distress for the child; moreover, parents who show distress over a procedure, may communicate this to the child, exacerbating the child's own anxiety (Bush et al., 1986).

If a parent cannot stay with the child or if the hospital has no rooming-in arrangement, then it is up to the hospital and its staff to make the experience as unthreatening to the child as possible. Continuity in the staff who interact with the child makes it possible for the child to develop relationships and trust with particular people who can carry the child through unfamiliar and strange procedures.

The area of working with hospitalized children has been a story with something like a happy ending. Initial concern that these procedures would lead to high rates of infection proved to be unfounded. There was also some fear that children would actually be made more upset by frequent arrivals and departures of parents, but this fear also proved to be groundless. Rather, the presence of a diverse and diffuse social support system seems to offset potential upset over any particular person's visiting schedule. The majority of hospitals now also provide opportunities for extended parental visits, including 24-hour parent visitation. Some hospitals make it possible for parents to "room in" with the child so

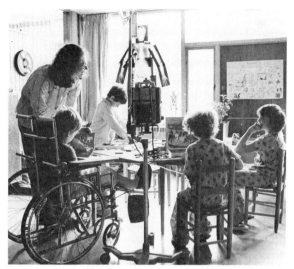

Recent changes in hospitalization procedures for children have made hospitals less frightening places to be. Increasingly, medical personnel have recognized children's need for play and provided opportunities for play in hospital settings.

that the child will feel less lonely, anxious, and threatened. Truly substantial changes have been made in a fairly short time, and children's adverse reactions to hospitalization have declined as a result. Hospitals now have many more busy, active children with things to do and people to play with than they had 25 years ago.

SUMMARY

1. The detection of symptoms, their interpretation, and the perception and use of health services are all heavily influenced by psychological processes.

2. Whether a symptom is noticed is influenced by pain threshold, focus of attention, the presence of distracting or involving activities, the salience of illness or symptoms, and individual differences in the tendency to monitor threat.

3. The interpretation of symptoms is influenced by prior experience and expectations about their likelihood and meaning.

4. Illness schemas (that identify the type of

disease, its cause, duration, and consequences) and disease prototypes (conceptions of specific diseases) influence how people interpret their symptoms and whether or not they act on them by seeking medical attention.

5. Social factors, such as the lay referral network, can act as a go-between for the patient and the medical care system.

6. Health services are used disproportionately by the very young or very old, by women, and by middle- to upper-class people.

7. The health belief model, which ascertains whether or not a person perceives a threat to health and whether or not a person believes that a particular health measure can overcome the disorder, influences use of health services. Other social-psychological factors include an individual's social location in a community and social pressures to seek treatment.

8. Health services may also be abused. A large percentage of patients who seek medical attention have depression or anxiety.

9. People commonly ignore symptoms that are serious, resulting in dangerous delay behavior.

10. The hospital is a complex organizational system buffeted by the changing medical, organizational, and financial climates in which it exists. Different groups in the hospital develop different goals, such as cure, care, or core, that may clash. Such problems are exacerbated by communication barriers.

11. Hospitalization can be a frightening and depersonalizing experience for patients. It may lead them to act as "good patients" or "bad patients," in either case, sustaining physiological, emotional, and behavioral risks to health. The adverse reactions of children in hospitals have received particular attention.

12. Control-restoring and control-enhancing interventions improve adjustment to hospitalization and to stressful medical procedures in both adults and children. The benefits of information, relaxation training, and coping skills training have all been documented.

KEY TERMS

appraisal delay
control-enhancing interventions
delay behavior
diagnostic-related groups (DRGs)
disease prototypes
hospital patient role
illness delay
illness representations (or schemas)
lay referral network
medical delay

medical student's disease
monitoring/blunting
preferred provider organization (PPO)
psychological control
reactance
repression
secondary gains
separation anxiety
utilization delay
worried well

10

PATIENT-PRACTITIONER INTERACTION

Nearly everyone has a horror story about a visit to a physician. Long waits, insensitivity, apparently faulty diagnoses, and treatments that have no effect are the stuff of indignant cocktail party stories. Yet in the same breath, the storyteller may expound on the virtues of his or her latest physician with an enthusiasm bordering on worship. To what do we attribute this seemingly contradictory attitude toward health care practitioners?

Health ranks among the values Americans hold most dear. Good health is a prerequisite to nearly every other activity, and poor health can block nearly all one's goals. Moreover, illness is usually uncomfortable, so people want to be treated quickly and successfully. Perhaps, then, it is no wonder that physicians and other health care professionals are alternately praised and vilified: Their craft is fundamental to the enjoyment of life.

In this chapter, we take up the complex issue of patient-practitioner interaction. First, we consider why patient-practitioner communication is important. Next, we look at the nature of patient-practitioner communication and the factors that erode it. Then, we consider some of the consequences of poor communication, including noncompliance with treatment regimens and malpractice litigation. Finally, we consider some efforts to improve patient-practitioner communication and to reduce noncompliance through communication training, behavioral interventions, and expansion of the practitioner role.

In the following pages, we refer to the "practitioner" rather than to the "physician." Although physicians continue to be the main agents of health care, Americans are increasingly receiving much of their primary care from individuals other than physicians. Most notable among these individuals are **nurse-practitioners.** Trained in traditional nursing, nurse-practitioners also receive special training in primary care. Many nurse-practitioners are affiliated with physicians in private practice; they see their own patients, provide all routine medical care, prescribe for treatment, monitor the progress of chronically ill patients, and see walk-in patients with a variety of disorders. As a consequence, they interact with patients just as physicians do and, in the course of their practice, must explain disorders as well as their origins, diagnosis, prognosis, and treatment. Even in medical practices that do not employ nurse-practitioners, much patient education falls to nurses. Nurses frequently give treatment instructions or screen patients before they are seen by a physician. **Physicians' assistants,** graduates of 2-year programs in health care, also perform some routine health care functions such as taking down medical information or explaining some treatment regimens to patients.

As medical practice has become increasingly complex, other professions have also become involved in specialized care. For example, patients who are learning to control stress-related disorders may work with a biofeedback technician or a psychologist. Obstetrical patients may work with a nurse-midwife. Thus, the term "practitioner" acknowledges that a variety of individuals operating in different professional capacities work with medical patients. Consequently, issues of communication—especially poor communication—that arise in medical settings are by no means the exclusive province of the physician.

NATURE OF PATIENT-PRACTITIONER COMMUNICATION

The medical stories one hears at parties rarely praise practitioners for their ability to communicate effectively; rather, people usually tell about volumes of jargon, little feedback, and depersonalized care. Clearly, the quality of communication with a practitioner is important to patients, but the question is whether it does more than produce a vague sense of sat-

isfaction or dissatisfaction in the patient's mind. The answer is yes. As just noted, poor patient-practitioner communication has been tied to outcomes as problematic as patient noncompliance with treatment recommendations and the initiation of malpractice litigation.

Moreover, people often judge the adequacy of their care by criteria that are irrelevant to the technical quality of the care (Ben-Sira, 1976; Ware, Davies-Avery, & Steward, 1978). Although we might be able to discern a case of blatant incompetence, most of us are insufficiently knowledgeable about medicine and standards of practice to know if we have been treated well or not. Most of the time, we judge success by whether the symptoms of the disease have improved—a criterion that may be only somewhat related to good treatment. What people do know is whether or not they liked the practitioner: whether he or she was warm and friendly or cool and uncommunicative. When people are asked what is important to them in their medical care, they rate the manner in which their care is delivered at least as high as or higher than technical quality of care (Feletti, Firman, & Sanson-Fisher, 1986; Scarpaci, 1988; Ware et al., 1978).

Even more significant, since people are poor judges of technical quality of care, they often judge technical quality on the basis of the manner in which care is delivered (Ben-Sira, 1976, 1980). For example, if a physician expresses uncertainty about the nature of the patient's condition, patient satisfaction declines (Johnson, Levenkron, Suchman, & Manchester, 1988). A warm, confident, friendly practitioner is often judged to be both nice and competent, whereas a cool, aloof practitioner may be judged less favorably, as both unfriendly and incompetent (see Buller & Buller, 1987; DiMatteo, Linn, Chang, & Cope, 1985). In fact, technical quality of care and the manner in which care is delivered are unrelated (e.g., Gough, 1967; Gough, Hall, & Harris, 1963, 1964). Communication between patient and practitioner is critical if patients are to be satisfied with their care. Yet one study found that the relationship between patients' reports of satisfaction with a physician visit and the physicians' perceptions of the patients' satisfaction were virtually unrelated (see DiMatteo, Hays, & Prince, 1986).

What are some of the factors that erode communication? They include aspects of the office setting itself, the changing nature of the health care delivery system, practitioner behaviors, patient behaviors, and qualities of their interaction. We will consider each in turn.

The Setting

On the surface of it, the medical office is an unlikely setting for effective communication. A person who has defined the self as ill must communicate that fact to another person, often a stranger; he or she must respond to often specific and difficult questions and then be content to be poked and prodded while the diagnostic process goes on. At the very least, it is difficult to present one's complaints effectively when one is in pain or has a fever, and the patient's ability to be articulate may be reduced further by any anxiety or embarrassment he or she feels about the symptoms.

The practitioner, on the other hand, has the task of extracting significant information as quickly as possible from the unhappy body that is before him or her. The practitioner is often on a tight schedule, with other patients backing up in the waiting room. The difficulties presented by the patient may have been made more complex by the use of various home remedies, so that symptoms may now be masked and distorted. The patient's idea of which symptoms are important may not correspond to the practitioner's knowledge, so important signs may be overlooked. With the patient seeking solace and the practitioner trying to maximize the effective use of time, it is clear that there are many potential sources of strain and miscommunication.

The Structure of the Health Care Delivery System

Until a few decades ago, the majority of Americans received their health care from private physicians whom they paid directly on a visit-by-visit basis (termed **private, fee-for-service care**). Each individual visit was followed by a bill, which the patient typically paid out of pocket. Under this kind of system, a practice was directly dependent on the amount of business that could be generated, and keeping an active practice meant keeping satisfied customers (Mechanic, 1975). Since, as we have seen, patients judge the quality of their care heavily on the manner in which it is dispensed, the most successful practitioners were typically those who did a good job of satisfying their patients' emotional needs.

Economic pressures toward pleasing the patient no doubt produce a high quality of emotional care. Patients who have private-practice physicians believe that their doctors care about them as people (Freidson, 1961). The private practitioner is likely to have ties to the community and to share interests with the patient. However, private, fee-for-service care can often be less technically competent for the same reasons that it is emotionally satisfying. As noted in Chapter 9, as many as two-thirds of all medical complaints may be primarily psychological in nature, yet patients believe that their problems are medical and want treatment. Thus, the private practitioner is pushed into a more active stance (for example, prescribing medications) toward an illness than might otherwise be advisable, simply in order to satisfy the patient (see Scarpaci, 1988). A general pattern of overmedication of private-practice patients can result (Freidson, 1961; see also Gill & Horobin, 1972). Moreover, private, fee-for-service care discourages the use of specialists. If a practitioner refers a patient out for specialized care, he or she loses the case and the income. Thus, there are economic pressures to continue to see a patient for as long as possible, and this can mean that a patient who needs specialized care may not receive it at the right time (Freidson, 1961).

That picture has changed. An estimated 33 million Americans now receive their health care through a prepaid financing and delivery system termed a **health maintenance organization (HMO).** By this arrangement, an employer or employee pays an agreed-on monthly rate, and the employee is then entitled to use services at no additional (or a greatly reduced) cost. In some cases, HMOs have their own staff from which enrollees must seek treatment. In other preferred-provider organizations (PPOs), there is a network of affiliated practitioners who have agreed to charge preestablished rates for particular services. Enrollees in the PPO must choose from these practitioners when seeking treatment.

The changing structure of the health care delivery system contributes to dissatisfaction with health services by altering the nature of patient-practitioner interactions (Freidson, 1961; Mechanic, 1975; Ross, Mirowsky, & Duff, 1982; Ross, Wheaton, & Duff, 1981). Prepaid plans often operate on a referral basis, so that the practitioner who first sees the patient determines what is wrong and then recommends any number of specialists to follow up with treatment. Since practitioners are often paid according to the number of cases they see, referrals are desirable. Therefore a **colleague orientation,** rather than a client or **patient orientation,** usually develops (Barr, 1983; Mechanic, 1975). Since the patient no longer pays directly for service and since the practitioner's income is not directly affected by whether or not the patient is pleased by the service, the practitioner may not be as concerned with patient satisfaction. The practitioner is, however, concerned with what his or her colleagues think, because it is on their recommendations that he or she receives additional cases. Thus, such a system can produce high technical quality of care, since practitioners who make errors receive fewer referrals;

however, there is less incentive to offer emotionally satisfying care (Barr, 1983; Freidson, 1961).

Indeed, quite the contrary is true. If practitioners are trying to see or are pressured to see as many patients as possible, the consequences can be long waits and short visits. These problems are compounded when the patient is referred to several specialists, since each such referral may lead to another long wait and short visit. Patients can come to feel that they are being shunted from practitioner to practitioner with no continuity in their care and no opportunity to build up a personal relationship with any one individual.

Increasingly, as Figure 10.1 suggests, third-party payment systems adopt cost-saving strategies that may inadvertently restrict clients' choices over when and how they can receive medical services. One study (Curbow, 1986) found in a simulated choice experiment that people who could not choose their health plan, who had fewer choices about their care than they expected, and who did not accept restricted choice had more negative perceptions of the health care program.

In fairness, not all prepaid group plans create such a dismal situation (Greenley & Schoenherr, 1981; Ross et al., 1981). Although some studies (Davies, Ware, Brook, Peterson, & Newhouse, 1986) have found that people prefer fee-for-service health care over prepaid health care, people self-select into HMOs on the basis of personal preference, financial needs, and the like (see also Allen, 1984). Consequently, those who elect this type of coverage may be those more likely to be satisfied with it (Polich, Iversen, & Parker, 1985), although the response is by no means universally positive (Allen, 1984). Moreover, precisely because problems have developed, some HMOs have taken steps to reduce long waits, to allow for personal choice, and to make sure a patient sees the same practitioner at each visit. But it is clear that the changing structure of medical practice generally, although likely to produce more tech-

FIGURE 10.1   Types of Group Health Plans (Based on Employers Surveyed). A 1984 employer survey reported that 96% of insured workers were enrolled in traditional health plans. As of 1988, only 28% were.

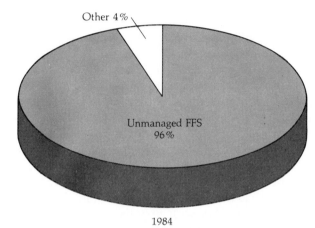

1984

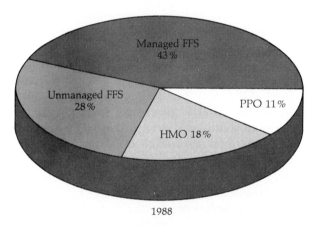

1988

Unmanaged Fee for Service: Old–fashioned coverage that allows workers to choose their own doctors and get reimbursed for all or part of whatever physicians and hospitals charge
Managed Fee for Service: Like the old plans, but keeps tabs on utilization by, for example, requiring prior approval for some hospital admissions
Health Maintenance Organization (HMO): Companies hired for a fixed overall fee to provide medical care for employees. Workers are covered only for treatment approved by the HMO.
Preferred Provider Organization (PPO): A group of medical personnel who contract to furnish services at discounted prices in return for prompt payment and a certain number of patients. Employees must choose doctors from the list.

nically competent care, may also tend to undermine emotional satisfaction (Friedson, 1961).

In the last chapter we discussed DRGs (diagnostic related groups), which are guidelines for patient care in particular disease or disorder categories. The argument is that DRGs can produce efficient patient care, thereby producing reductions in costs. The impact of DRGs on medical care are several. First, because the DRG system implicitly rewards institutions for the detection and treatment of complications or co-occurring medically problematic conditions, the system provides an impetus for diagnostic vigilance. It is to the practitioner's advantage to find everything that is wrong with the patient before treatment. Another consequence of DRGs is that they implicitly adopt very biomedically oriented criteria for how and how long a disease should be treated. In fact, DRGs are quite poor predictors of patients' need for services and length of stay. Finally, DRGs can potentially undermine effective treatment, in that they may create a tendency to discharge patients before they exceed the DRGs' boundaries for length of stay. Thus, while the presence of DRGs can have some positive effects on quality of care (such as attentiveness to the diagnostic process), they may also compromise care as well.

In summary, then, the changing structure of the health care delivery service from private, fee-for-service practice to third-party arrangements can inadvertently exert adverse effects on patient-practitioner communication and on patient choice. The colleague orientation of the third-party system makes it less necessary for physicians to please patients; and, while it may increase quality of care, a colleague orientation may undermine the quality of interactions with patients. In addition, cost-saving strategies may restrict patient choices of treatment options and overly constrain the length of care and kind of treatments they receive.

Changes in the Philosophy of Health Care Delivery

A number of changes underlying the philosophy of health care delivery are affecting how patients and practitioners relate to each other. The physician's role is changing. The development of new organizational systems for delivering services, such as HMOs, and the rising numbers of women in the medical profession have added variability to what was once a very clear physician role, characterized by dominance and authority (Goldstein, Jaffe, Sutherland, & Wilson, 1987). In apparent response to an increase in consumerist attitudes among patients, there are signs that medical students become more egalitarian in their relationships with patients as medical school progresses (Lavin, Haug, Belgrave, & Breslau, 1987).

In addition, the movement toward holistic health and holistic medicine has led to a very different type of patient orientation among practitioners who subscribe to this orientation, and the presence of the holistic movement itself has made inroads in traditional medicine. The concept of **holistic health** is characterized by a belief that health is a positive state to be actively achieved, not merely the absence of disease. The viewpoint acknowledges psychological and spiritual influences on the development of illness and the achievement of health, and it gives the patient substantial responsibility for both health and illness through his or her behaviors, attitudes, and spiritual beliefs. Holistic health emphasizes health education, self-help, and self-healing. There is an emphasis on using natural, low-technology interventions and non-Western techniques of medical practice when possible. Most important for the present argument is the fact that the holistic movement characterizes the relationship between practitioner and patient as open, equal, and reciprocal, involving emotional contact (Goldstein, Jaffe, Garell, & Berk, 1986). This, of course, is in sharp opposition to the traditional physician role, characterized as dominant and autonomous, based on a relative monopoly over the knowledge, training, and technology required to cure patients (see Freidson, 1960; Parsons, 1954).

In their interactions with patients, holistic physicians try to structure an egalitarian relationship in which they help the patient assume responsibility for his or her state of health. Although willing to use medical technology when necessary, they recognize that there are other, less intrusive ways of achieving the same outcomes, which they will often employ in their treatments (Goldstein et al., 1986). In a study that attempted to identify the attributes associated with a holistic orientation among physicians, Goldstein et al. (1987) compared members of the American Holistic Medical Association with members of the California Family Practice physician organization. Although the groups were similar on demographic characteristics, personal experiences with religion, spirituality, or psychotherapy and a personal orientation toward health distinguished the holistically oriented physicians from the family practice physicians. Holistic physicians were somewhat more likely to endorse particular nontraditional treatment methods, such as herbal medicine, acupuncture, acupressure, massage, psychic diagnosis, spiritual healing, the laying on of hands, and dance therapy than were the more traditionally oriented physicians.

The impact of holistic attitudes toward health and the concomitant consumerism that has developed is felt more in some segments of society than in others. Lower-class people still are more or less passive recipients of medical services (Cockerham, Lueschen, Kunz, & Spaeth, 1986). Although medicine and the mass media have promoted the idea of a healthy lifestyle, the corresponding need to encourage consumerism in the patient-practitioner relationship has not occurred to the same degree. Consequently, consumerism is more likely to be seen in institutions that have positive sanctions for consumerism but not in their absence (Cockerham et al., 1986).

Practitioners' Behaviors that Contribute to Faulty Communication

Communication between the patient and physician can be eroded by certain practitioner behaviors. One problematic practitioner behavior is *not listening*. In a study of the physician's initial response to patient-initiated visits, Beckman and Frankel (1984) studied seventy-four office visits. In only 23% of the cases did the patient have the opportunity to finish his or her explanation of concerns. In 69% of the visits, the physician interrupted, directing the patient toward a particular disorder. Moreover, on an average, physicians interrupted after their patients had spoken for only 18 seconds. The authors argue that the consequence of this controlling effort to manage the interaction not only prevents patients from discussing their concerns but may also lead to potential loss of important information. Since physicians knew their behavior was being recorded during the office visits, the study may actually underestimate the extent of this problem.

The use of jargon and technical language is another important factor in poor communication. Studies reveal that patients understand relatively few of the complex terms practitioners often use (e.g., Samora, Saunders, & Larson, 1961; Seligmann, McGrath, & Pratt, 1957).

An example is provided by a patient:

> I'll tell you something, a good one on me. When my first child was born, the doctor kept coming in every day and asking, "Have you voided?" So I'd say, "No." So in comes the nurse with some paraphernalia that was scary. So I said, "What the devil are you going to do?" And she said, "I'm going to catheterize you, you haven't voided." Well, of course, I knew what catheterization was. I said, "You are going to play hell. I've peed every day

since I've been here." [The nurse explained that the doctor had told her the patient hadn't voided.] I said, "Is that what he said?" And she said, "Of course, Rusty, didn't you know?" And I said, "Well, of course, why didn't he just ask me if I'd peed? I'd have told him." (Samora et al., 1961)

Why do practitioners use complex, hard to understand language? In some cases, jargon-filled explanations may be used to keep the patient from asking too many questions or from discovering that the practitioner is not certain what the patient's problem is.

> Physicians have long used medical jargon to impress gullible laymen. As far back as the thirteenth century, the medieval physician, Arnold of Villanova, urged colleagues to seek refuge behind impressive-sounding language when they could not explain a patient's ailment. "Say that he has an obstruction of the liver," Arnold wrote, "and particularly use the word obstruction because patients do not understand what it means." (*Time*, November 2, 1970, p. 35)

One physician explained to the author, with great amusement, that if the term "itis" (meaning "inflammation of") was connected to whatever organ was troubled (for example, "stomachitis"), this would usually forestall any additional questions from the patient (see Waitzkin, 1985).

More commonly, however, practitioners' use of jargon may be a carryover from their technical training. Practitioners learn a complex vocabulary for understanding illnesses and communicating about them to other professionals; they often find it hard to remember that the patient does not share this expertise. Thus, much use of jargon stems from simple forgetting. The use of jargon may also stem from an inability to gauge what the patient will understand and to figure out the appropriate nontechnical explanation. How much should one tell a patient? Does the patient need to know how the disorder developed? If so, how should that explanation be provided?

Having misjudged a patient's ability to understand aspects of the illness and treatment, a practitioner may go to the opposite extreme and resort to the use of *baby talk and simplistic explanations.*

> "Nurse, would you just pop off her things for me? I want to examine her." In the hospital, everything is "popped" on or off, slipped in or out. I don't think I met a single doctor who, in dealing with patients, didn't resort to this sort of nursery talk. I once heard one saying to patient, an elderly man, "We're just going to pop you into the operating theater to have a little peep into your tummy." Nurses, too, had people "popping" all over the place—in and out of lavatories, dressing gowns, beds, scales, wheelchairs, bandages. (Toynbee, 1977)

As these remarks indicate, overly simple explanations coupled with infantilizing baby talk are likely to make the patient feel like a helpless child. Moreover, such behavior can forestall questions. Having received a useless explanation, the patient may not know how to begin to ask for solid information. The tendency to lapse into simple explanations with a patient may become almost automatic. One woman, who is both a cancer researcher and a cancer patient, reports that when she goes to see her cancer specialist, he talks to her in a very complex and technical manner until the examination starts. Once she is on the examining table, he shifts to very simple sentences and explanations. She is now a patient and no longer a colleague.

The truth about what patients can understand lies somewhere between the extremes of technical jargon and infantilizing baby talk. Typically, practitioners underestimate the ability of patients to understand information about the origins, diagnosis, prognosis, and treatment of their disorders (McKinlay, 1975; Waitzkin, 1985). In one ingenious study, McKinlay (1975) followed physicians around the maternity ward as they made their hospital visits, noting what medical terms they used most frequently in discussing patient disor-

ders either with or in front of patients. After he had catalogued the most frequently used terms, he tested the patients' knowledge of those terms and compared patients' actual information level with that attributed to them by physicians. What he found was that patients' knowledge of the relevant medical terms was quite high and, more importantly, much higher than that attributed to them by their doctors. McKinley's interpretation of these results is that practitioners "blame the victim," attributing to patients stupidity and fear, which are presumed to make it impossible for them to learn about their illnesses. The fact is that patients can be motivated to learn and do a reasonably creditable job of it despite the frequent absence of adequate explanations from the practitioner.

Depersonalization of the patient is another problem that impairs the quality of the patient-practitioner relationship (Chafetz, 1970; Kaufman, 1970). This nonperson treatment may be employed intentionally to try to keep the patient quiet while an examination, procedure, or test is being conducted, or it may be employed unintentionally because the patient (as object) has become the focus of the practitioner's attention.

> Recently, when I was being given emergency treatment for an eye laceration, the resident surgeon abruptly terminated his conversation with me as soon as I lay down on the operating table. Although I had had no sedative, or anesthesia, he acted as if I were no longer conscious, directing all his questions to a friend of mine—questions such as, "What's his name? What occupation is he in? Is he a real doctor?" etc. As I lay there, these two men were speaking about me as if I were not there at all. The moment I got off the table and was no longer a cut to be stitched, the surgeon resumed his conversation with me, and existence was conferred upon me again. (Zimbardo, 1969, p. 298).

To understand this phenomenon of nonperson treatment, consider what a nuisance it can be for a practitioner to have the patient actually there during a treatment—fussing, giving unhelpful suggestions, and asking questions. If patients could drop their bodies off, as they do their cars, and pick them up later, it would save both the practitioner and the patients a lot of trouble and anxiety. As it is, the practitioner is like an auto mechanic who has the misfortune of having the car's owner following him or her around, creating trouble, while he or she is trying to fix the car (Goffman, 1961). Goffman suggests that practitioners cope with their bad luck by pretending that the patient is not there: "The patient is greeted with what passes for civility, and said farewell to in the same fashion, with everything in between going on as if the patient weren't there as a social person at all, but only as a possession someone has left behind" (pp. 341–342).

Nonperson treatment may be employed at particularly stressful moments to keep the patient quiet and enable the practitioner to concentrate. In that way, it may serve a valuable medical function. But patient depersonalization can also have adverse medical effects. Medical staff making hospital rounds often use either highly technical or euphemistic terms when discussing cases with their colleagues. Unfortunately, these terms may confuse or alarm the nonparticipating but physically present patient, an effect to which the practitioner may be oblivious. In fact, one study found that the number of heart disease complications increased among patients after physicians' rounds (Jarvinen, 1955).

There is another function of patient depersonalization that should not be ignored, and that is the emotional protection it provides for the practitioner. It is difficult for a practitioner to work in a continual state of awareness that his or her every action influences someone's state of health and happiness. The responsibility can be crushing. Moreover, every practitioner has tragedies—as when a patient dies or is left incapacitated by a treatment—but the practitioner must find a way to continue to practice. Depersonalization helps provide such a way.

Communication may especially be eroded when physicians encounter patients or diseases that they would prefer not to treat (Morgan, 1985; Schmelkin, Wachtel, Schneiderman, & Hecht, 1988). For example, many physicians have negative perceptions of the elderly (Ford & Sbordone, 1980; Najman, Klein, & Munro, 1982; see Haug & Ory, 1987, for a review). There is some evidence that this group is less likely to be resuscitated in emergency rooms or given active treatment protocols for life-threatening diseases (Roth, 1977). These problems may be exacerbated by any communication difficulties the elderly person has (Haug & Ory, 1987; Morgan, 1985). The negative attitudes of physicians seem to be reciprocated in the elderly, in that among those 65 and over, only 54% expressed high confidence in physicians.

Patients who are regarded as seeking treatment largely for depression, anxiety, or other forms of psychological disorder also evoke negative reactions from physicians. With these groups of patients, physician attention may be especially cursory and communication problems may be especially acute. Physicians prefer acutely ill to chronically ill patients, in that chronic illness poses uncertainties and questions about prognosis that acute disease does not (Butler, 1978). Male physicians and female patients do not always communicate well with each other. The matching of gender between patient and practitioner appears to foster more rapport and disclosure, which may enhance communication (Levinson, McCollum, & Kutner, 1984; Weisman & Teitelbaum, 1985).

Patients' Contributions to Faulty Communication

Within a few minutes of having discussed their illness with a practitioner, many patients—as many as one-third—cannot repeat their diagnosis; up to one-half do not understand important details about the illness or treatment (Golden & Johnston, 1970; Reader, Pratt, & Mudd, 1957). Some of this inability to repeat illness- and treatment-related information stems from the problems just discussed, namely, jargon-filled explanations that patients do not understand (Ley & Spelman, 1967). But some of it also stems from factors having to do with patients. Thus, whereas dissatisfied patients complain about the incomplete or overly technical explanations they receive from practitioners, dissatisfied practitioners complain that even when they give clear, careful explanations to patients, the explanation goes in one ear and out the other.

There are several factors on the patient's part that contribute to poor patient-practitioner communications. One of the chief of these is *patient anxiety* (Bush & Osterweis, 1978; Davis, 1966). When people are anxious, their learning can be impaired. Anxiety makes it difficult to concentrate attention and process incoming information. Even when information is learned, the distracting effects of anxiety may make it hard to retain it. Since anxiety is often a concomitant part of a visit to a physician, it is not surprising that patients retain so little information.

Other factors that influence patients' ability to understand and retain information about their condition include *intelligence* and *experience with the disorder*. Some patients are not intelligent enough to understand even simple information about their case, and so even the clearest explanation falls on deaf ears (Davis, 1966). Physicians are usually upper-middle class white males, whereas their patients may be of a lower social class, a different race, and a different sex. Consequently, there may also be class-based, sociolinguistic factors that contribute to poor communication (Waitzkin, 1985). In contrast, patients who have had an illness before, who have received a clear explanation of their disorder and treatment, or

who know that their illness is not serious show relatively little distortion of information. Those for whom the illness is new and who have little prior information about the disorder show the greatest distortion in their explanations (DiMatteo & DiNicola, 1982).

Recall, too, that *patients respond to different cues* about their illness than do practitioners. Patients place considerable emphasis on pain and on symptoms that interfere with their activities. But practitioners are more concerned with the underlying illness—its severity and treatment. Patients may misunderstand the practitioner's emphasis on factors that they consider to be incidental, so they may pay little attention when vital information is being communicated. Alternatively, they may dismiss the practitioner's advice because they believe he or she has made an incorrect diagnosis (Korsch & Negrete, 1972; see also Young, 1980).

Finally, patients may give practitioners *faulty cues* about their true concerns. A number of patients, perhaps as many as two-thirds in some settings (Reader et al., 1957), make medical appointments because they fear they have a truly serious disease such as cancer or heart disease. Particularly among older people, there may still be the belief that when symptoms signify a serious disorder, physicians do not tell the patient. Anticipating evasiveness or fearing that the worst will be confirmed, patients will sometimes present the symptom that is actually the most distressing to them as something of little concern—for example, "It's probably nothing, but...," or "Oh, by the way..." (Greer, 1974). Patients may fear asking questions because they do not think they will receive straight answers, and practitioners may erroneously assume that because no questions have been asked, the patient does not want any information. The practitioner may accordingly give the fear-arousing symptoms little attention, not realizing that the patient is truly upset about them. But lack of concern may be interpreted by the patient as secrecy and confirmation of his or her worst fears. Following a polite but relatively uninformative conversation with a practitioner, the patient's belief that the disorder is serious may be even stronger. The following episode illustrates the lengths to which such misconceptions can be carried.

At the age of 59, [Mr. Tischler] suffered progressive discomfort from a growing lump in his groin. He did not discuss it with his wife or anyone else until six weeks prior to his admission to the hospital, when he began to fear that it was cancer. When Mrs. Tischler heard about it, she, too, was fearful of cancer, but she did not mention this to her husband. She did, however, discuss his condition with a close friend who was the secretary of a local surgeon. Through this friend, Mr. Tischler was introduced to the surgeon who examined him, made a diagnosis of a hernia, and recommended hospitalization for repair of the hernia. Both Mr. and Mrs. Tischler thought the surgeon was trying to be kind to them since Mr. Tischler, in their fearful fantasies, was afflicted with cancer. The surgeon scheduled admission to the hospital for elective repair of the hernia. After the surgery, the hernia disappeared, the incision healed normally, and there were no complications. Mr. Tischler then realized that the surgeon had been accurate in his diagnosis and prognosis. He returned to work in three weeks, free from pain and all disability. (Duff & Hollingshead, 1968, p. 300)

Interactive Aspects of the Communication Problem

Qualities of the interaction between practitioner and patient also perpetuate faulty communication. A major problem is that patient-practitioner interaction does not provide the opportunity for feedback to the practitioner. Practitioners rarely know whether or not information was communicated effectively because they rarely learn about the results of the communications.

Specifically, the practitioner sees the patient, the patient is diagnosed, treatment is recommended, and the patient leaves. When the patient does not return, any number of things may have happened: The treatment may have cured the disorder; the patient may have gotten worse and decided either to seek additional treatment or to seek it from someone else; the treatment may have failed, but the disorder may have cleared up anyway; or the patient may have died. Not knowing which of these alternatives has actually occurred, the practitioner does not know the impact and success rate of the advice given. Obviously, it is to the practitioner's psychological advantage to believe that the diagnosis was correct, that the patient followed the advice, and that the patient's disorder was cured; but the practitioner may never find out for certain.

The practitioner may also find it hard to know when a satisfactory personal relationship has been established with a patient. Many patients are relatively cautious with practitioners; if they are dissatisfied, rather than complain about it directly, they may simply change practitioners. The practitioner who finds that a patient has stopped coming does not know if the patient has moved out of the area or switched to another practice. When practitioners do get feedback, it is more likely to be negative than positive: patients whose treatments have failed are more likely to come back than patients whose treatments are successful (Rachman & Phillips, 1978).

Two points are important here. First, learning is fostered more by positive than by negative feedback; positive feedback tells one what one is doing right, whereas negative feedback may tell one what to stop doing but not necessarily what to do instead. Since practitioners get more negative than positive feedback, this situation is not conducive to learning. Second, learning occurs only with feedback, but, in the practitioner's case, lack of feedback is the rule. Clearly, it is extremely difficult for the practitioner to know if communication is adequate and, if not, how to change it. It is no wonder, then, that when social scientists display their statistics on poor patient-practitioner communication, each practitioner can say with confidence, "Not me," because he or she indeed has no basis for self-recrimination (Davis, 1966). Since the best persuader may be personal experience rather than objective statistics (Nisbett & Borgida, 1975), this issue of feedback between patient and practitioner is no small problem; unfortunately, there is no easy solution to it.

To summarize, qualities of the interaction that exacerbate the communication problem include the facts that the practitioner receives little feedback concerning the effectiveness of treatment (unless the treatment does not work), and patients may give little feedback about the effectiveness of the practitioner's communication.

Overall, then, a substantial number of factors make it unlikely that patient and practitioner will communicate effectively. These include the nature of the setting, the structure of the health care delivery system, practitioner behaviors, patient behaviors, and qualities of the interaction itself. What are the consequences of the ineffective interactions that result?

RESULTS OF POOR PATIENT-PRACTITIONER COMMUNICATION

The communication problems just described would be little more than an unfortunate casualty of medical treatment were it not for the toll they take on health. Dissatisfied patients are less likely to use medical services in the future (Ross & Duff, 1982; Ware et al., 1978). They are more likely to turn to services that satisfy emotional needs rather than medical needs (Ben-Sira, 1976; Ware et al., 1978), services that may sacrifice technically competent care for satisfying emotional interactions. Dissatisfied patients are less likely to obtain med-

ical checkups and are more likely to change doctors and to file formal complaints (Hayes-Bautista, 1976; Ware et al., 1978). Thus, it appears that patient dissatisfaction with patient-practitioner interaction not only fosters health risks by leading patients to avoid using services in the future but also poses costly and time-consuming dilemmas for the health care agencies themselves. In this section, we focus on perhaps the best-documented and most medically problematic consequence of all: patient nonadherence with medical regimens. We also discuss the rise of malpractice litigation.

Nonadherence to Treatment Regimens

In Chapters 5 and 6, we examined the topic of **adherence** to treatment regimen in the context of health behaviors. In that context, we looked at the difficulties that people often encounter when trying to modify or eliminate a poor health habit, such as smoking or excessive alcohol consumption, or in trying to achieve a healthy lifestyle through weight loss, dietary modification, and other healthy behaviors. Here, too, we identified long-term maintenance and relapse prevention as the most important steps involved in health behavior change. In this context, we examine more specifically the role of health institutions, and particularly the role of the practitioner, in promoting adherence. We raise the issue again here because nonadherence has been so clearly tied to communication issues.

The seventeenth-century French playwright, Molière, aptly described the relationship that physicians and patients often have with respect to treatment recommendations:

> THE KING: You have a physician. What does he do?
> MOLIÈRE: Sire, we converse. He gives me advice which I do not follow and I get better.
> (Treue, 1958, p. 41, cited in Koltun & Stone, 1986)

When patients do not adopt the behaviors and treatments their practitioners recommend, the result is termed "nonadherence." **Nonadherence** is a formidable medical problem (Haynes, Taylor, & Sackett, 1979; Kirscht & Rosenstock, 1979). Depending on the disorder and recommended treatment, estimates of nonadherence vary from a low of 15% to a staggering high of 93% (Alpert, 1964; Baekeland & Lundwall, 1975; Davis, 1968a; Rapoff & Christophersen, 1982). For short-term antibiotic regimens, one of the most common prescriptions, it is estimated that at least one-third of all patients fail to comply adequately (see Rapoff & Christopherson, 1982). Between 50 and 60% of patients do not keep appointments for modifying preventive health behaviors (DiMatteo & DiNicola, 1982). Between 20 and 80% of patients drop out of lifestyle change programs designed to treat such health problems as smoking or obesity (Dunbar & Agras, 1980; Turk & Meichenbaum, 1989). Of 750 million new prescriptions written each year, approximately 520 million are responded to with partial or total nonadherence (Buckalew & Sallis, 1986). In a study of children treated for ear infection, it was estimated that 5% of the parents fully adhered to the medication regimen (Mattar, Markello, & Yaffe, 1975).

Obtaining reliable indications of nonadherence is not an easy matter (Turk & Meichenbaum, 1989). One study that attempted to assess use of the drug, theophylline, for patients suffering from chronic obstructive pulmonary disease (COPD) found that physicians reported that 78% of their COPD patients were on the medication, chart audit revealed 62% of the patients were on the medication, videotaped observation of patient visits produced an estimate of 69%, and only 59% of the patients reported they were on theophylline (Gerbert, Stone, Stulbarg, Gullion, & Greenfield, 1988). And the study did not even assess whether theophylline was administered correctly, only if it was prescribed at all!

Pill counts, that is, the amount of medication left over in a bottle when the course of medication is completed, provides an objective assessment of nonadherence, but it too is subject to several forms of bias. Patients may remove some pills from the bottle, for example, or they may have pills left over from a previous treatment that they take instead. Moreover, even if one knew reliably how many pills had been taken, one would not know if they had been taken in the correct amount or at the correct times (Turk & Meichenbaum, 1989).

Asking physicians about their patients' adherence yields unreliable and artificially high estimates (e.g., Turk & Meichenbaum, 1989; Witenberg, Blanchard, McCoy, Suls, & McGoldrick, 1983). Since most patients know they are supposed to adhere, they may bias their answers to appear more compliant than they really are (Roth, 1987; Turk & Meichenbaum, 1989). It is simply not feasible to follow each and every patient around to see if he or she is taking medicine or adhering to the prescribed medical regimen. As a consequence, researchers draw on indirect measures of adherence, such as the number of follow-up or referral appointments kept, but even these measures can be biased. Some of the more reliable assessments of adherence, such as urine tests and assays, are expensive and impractical for monitoring compliance (Dubbert et al., 1985; Rapoff & Christophersen, 1982).

Treatment outcome is another potential way to assess nonadherence, but there is little evidence of a clear relationship between extent of adherence and health outcomes. Improvement may occur with a minimal dose of the medication, for example. Alternatively, patients may get better in spite of low rates of adherence, or they may not improve even if they have adhered closely to the treatment. Consequently, many factors obscure the relationship between adherence and recovery (Turk & Meichenbaum, 1989). The unnerving conclusion is that, if anything, the research statistics on nonadherence underestimate the amount that is actually going on.

When physicians are shown these statistics and asked to explain the reasons for it, they usually attribute nonadherence to patients' uncooperative personalities, to their ignorance, to lack of motivation, or to their forgetfulness (Davis, 1968a; House, Pendelton, & Parker, 1986). In fact, personality theorists' efforts to identify the types of patients that are most likely to be nonadherent have been relatively unsuccessful (Meichenbaum & Turk, 1987). Although, as we shall shortly see, there are some factors in a patient's situation that can contribute to nonadherence, the greatest cause is poor communication.

Causes of Nonadherence

A variety of communication factors are responsible for nonadherence. These include whether or not the patient has made a decision to adhere to the treatment regimen, whether or not the patient understands the treatment regimen, emotional satisfaction with the relationship, what the qualities of the treatment regimen are, and reactions of the patient to the regimen, including creative nonadherence, reactance, and self-labeling.

The first step in adherence, one that is frequently overlooked, involves *the patient's decision to adhere to a prescribed medical regimen.* Many practitioners may simply assume that patients will follow their advice, without realizing that the patients must first decide to do so. The health belief model (Rosenstock, 1966) described in Chapters 3 and 4 predicts adherence and may do so in part through its impact on decision making. Belief in vulnerability to a disorder, belief that the disorder is serious, belief in the efficacy of recommended treatment (Becker & Maiman, 1975; Kirscht & Rosenstock, 1979), and belief that one will be able to discharge the recommendation (self-efficacy) (Stanton, 1987) all promote higher levels of adherence.

The second step in adherence is *understanding the treatment regimen.* Expecting that a patient will comply with a medical recommendation presupposes that the patient knows what to do (e.g., Svarstad, 1976). But much nonadherence can be traced to the fact that the patient simply does not understand what the treatment regimen is (Hauenstein, Schiller, & Hurley, 1987; Stanton, 1987). Accordingly, as one might expect, adherence is highest when a patient receives a clear, jargon-free explanation of the etiology, diagnosis, and treatment recommendations associated with the disorder. It is also enhanced by factors that promote good learning: Adherence is higher if the patient has been asked to repeat the instructions, if the instructions are written down, if unclear recommendations are pointed out and clarified, and if the instructions are repeated more than once (DiMatteo & DiNicola, 1982).

Satisfaction with the emotional side of the relationship with the practitioner also predicts adherence. When patients perceive the practitioner to be warm and caring, they are more compliant, and practitioners who show anger or impatience toward their patients have more nonadherent patients (Davis, 1968b; Korsch, Gozzi, & Francis, 1968). Practitioners who answer patients' questions and give them information about their symptoms have more compliant patients, perhaps because, by such actions, patients are convinced that practitioners know what they are doing (Korsch et al., 1968).

Qualities of the treatment regimen also influence the degree of adherence a patient will exhibit (Haynes, 1979a). Treatment regimens that must be followed over a long period of time, that are highly complex, and that interfere with other desirable behaviors in a person's life all show low levels of adherence (Turk & Meichenbaum, 1989). Keeping first appointments and obtaining medical tests (Alpert, 1964; for a review, see DiMatteo & DiNicola, 1982), in contrast, show high adherence rates. Adherence is high (about 90%)

when the advice is perceived as "medical" (for example, taking medication), but lower (76%) if the advice is vocational (for example, taking time off from work) and lower still (66%) if the advice is social or psychological (for example, avoiding stressful social situations) (Turk & Meichenbaum, 1989). Adherence is higher for treatment recommendations that seem like medicine (taking pills), but it is much lower when the treatment seems nonmedical (resting). Adherence is very poor (20 to 50%) when people are asked to change personal habits such as smoking or drinking (DiMatteo & DiNicola, 1982).

Complex self-care regimens show the lowest level of overall adherence. Often these treatment regimens require patients to perform a number of different and complex activities that must be carried out on a daily basis over the long term, but bear unknown relationship to treatment outcomes (Blumenthal & Emery, 1988; Siegel, Grady, Browner, & Hulley, 1988; Stegman, Miller, Hageman, & Irby, 1987). Diabetic patients, for example, must often take injections of insulin, monitor their blood glucose fluctuations, strictly control their dietary intake, and, in some programs, engage in prescribed exercise programs and efforts at stress management. Even with the best of intentions, it is difficult to engage in all the required behaviors that take up several hours a day (Turk & Meichenbaum, 1989).

Some *health care delivery* systems can inadvertently undermine at least certain aspects of adherence. A consequence of many prepaid services is that on a visit-by-visit basis they are free. One of the problems that can plague such facilities is high no-show rates—that is, the failure by patients to keep appointments they have made because they do not have to pay for them. One study found that by introducing a nominal fee of $3.00, they were able to substantially reduce this no-show rate (Wesch, Lutzker, Frisch, & Dillon, 1987).

Some *demographic factors* also predict non-adherence. Women, whites, and older people are more likely to follow prescriptions, and the perception that health care is available improves adherence (Bush & Osterweis, 1978). Nonadherence has also been tied to social class and language or cultural barriers (Samora et al., 1961). As we pointed out earlier, most United States physicians are white, upper-class, English-speaking males who may be intimidating or foreign to those of lower status or non-U.S. origins. Moreover, if physicians are uncomfortable dealing with people unlike themselves, they may adopt a more formal manner than usual, creating an atmosphere that keeps patients from asking questions (Davis, 1968b).

Other patient factors that influence adherence include the presence of life stressors, both major and minor. Nonadherent patients cite lack of time, no money, or distracting problems at home, such as instability and conflict (Davis, 1968a; Davis & Eichhorn, 1963) as impediments to adherence (Davis, 1967; MacDonald, Hagberg, & Grossman, 1963; Riffenbaugh, 1966).

Creative Nonadherence One especially interesting form of nonadherence is termed **creative nonadherence,** or intelligent nonadherence (Weintraub, 1976), because it involves modifying and supplementing a prescribed treatment regimen. For example, a poor patient may change the dosage level of required medication to make the medicine last as long as possible or may keep some medication in reserve in case another family member comes down with the same disorder. Creative nonadherence may also be a response to concerns or confusion over the treatment regimen. Not understanding the dosage level may lead some people not to take any at all, in the fear that they will overmedicate. Others may stop a medication because of unpleasant side effects that disrupt the quality of their lives. One study of nonadherence among the elderly estimated that 73% of nonadherence was intentional rather than accidental (Cooper, Love, & Raffoul, 1982).

In some cases, the patient may be right. Diabetics who are well-versed in different types of insulin and their effects, for example, may have a better sense of how to control their blood glucose level than a physician unfamiliar with the particular case. A study of pediatric asthma patients (Deaton, 1985) found that parental modification of the asthma regimen on the basis of the child's severity of disease, seasonable variability, and symptoms and side effects, actually led to better asthma control than more strict adherence to the medical regimen.

Creative nonadherence can also result from private theories about a disorder and its treatment. For example, in looking over what the practitioner has prescribed, the patient may decide that particular symptoms that merit treatment were ignored by the practitioner; he or she may then supplement the treatment regimen with over-the-counter preparations or home remedies that interact with prescribed drugs in unpredictable, even dangerous ways. Alternatively, the patient may alter the dosage requirement, reasoning, for example, that if four pills a day for 10 days will clear up the problem, eight pills a day for 5 days will do it twice as quickly. One motive for this sometimes risky behavior may be to overcome the sense of loss of control that illness brings with it (Turk & Meichenbaum, 1989). Indeed, some researchers now suspect that nonadherence generally is a response to reassert control in the patient-practitioner relationship in particular as well as over illness more generally (e.g., Hayes-Bautista, 1976). Patients may be rebelling against the seemingly arbitrary, authoritarian manner of the practitioner and the passive patient role that the practitioner and illness have forced on them.

Reactance, Self-Labeling, and Nonadherence
Reactance is a psychological state that results when people feel that their freedoms have been arbitrarily restricted by some external factor or agent (Brehm, 1966; Brehm & Brehm, 1981). This state is characterized by anger, and it may be accompanied by efforts to regain the threatened freedoms. For some patients, illness itself or the practitioner may have this psychological effect; therefore, nonadherence may be partly an effort to restore lost freedoms. Let us explore this argument more fully.

The withdrawal of freedom can be very threatening, particularly when highly valued and far-reaching activities are involved (Brehm, 1966; Wortman & Brehm, 1975). Obviously, many illnesses and treatments have precisely this impact. For the acutely ill person, virtually all activities will be at least temporarily threatened. Many treatment regimens force patients to abandon highly valued activities such as overeating, smoking, and drinking. Illness and treatment-related restrictions may make patients feel that they have lost all control over their environment.

Reactance can be enhanced by the threat engendered by labeling oneself as sick. This is a particular problem with chronically ill patients, especially those with heart ailments. Consider the threat posed to an ostensibly healthy businessman in his mid-40s who has been told he is at high risk for a heart attack. His treatment regimen may exclude not only valued vices (such as smoking) and valued activities (such as certain high-pressure situations) but also his whole fast-paced, highly stimulating, exciting lifestyle. This may be the only method he knows for relating to people and situations. He is being told, in effect, not merely to curtail his activities but to change his personality as well, from that of a healthy man to that of an illness-conscious semi-invalid. Each time he declines a cigar or takes a pill, he reminds himself that he is sick, and the self-label of "ill person" may be intolerable to him.

According to reactance theory, the greater the threats to freedom, the more reactance will be aroused; and the more reactance, the greater the attractiveness of the forbidden activities and the greater the desire to resume them (Brehm, 1966; Brehm & Brehm, 1981). In this context, then, it may be easier to understand why some patients who are told what they cannot do not only fail to adhere to the advice but actually violate it flagrantly. Rhodewalt and Strube (1985) argue that reactance may characterize certain Type A individuals and their concomitant low adherence to treatment regimen. As noted in Chapter 4, Type A behavior refers to an individual difference marked by easily aroused hostility, a sense of time urgency, and competitive achievement strivings. These behaviors are especially in evidence under conditions of stress or threat. Typically, Type As, more than Type Bs, value their behavioral freedom and see it as under their personal control. Consequently, when their behavioral freedom is reduced, Type As are more likely to demonstrate reactance. Moreover, Type As and Bs seem to differ in the causal attributions they make for what happens to them. Type As are more likely to attribute their problems to their own ability and effort (internal attributions), whereas Type Bs are more likely to cite external factors.

In a study of thirty-two patients who were being treated for running-related injuries, Type A behavior, preference for control over and involvement in treatment, and attributions for and reactions to injury were related to subsequent recovery. Specifically, Type As made poorer progress than Type Bs. Moreover, those Type As who attributed the problems to themselves were more angry about their injuries than were the patients judged to have made good progress. In a related study, Type A diabetic individuals showed poorer blood glucose control, which as in the case of Type A runners was related to more extreme self-attributions about the causes of diabetes and increased anger about the disorder (Rhodewalt & Marcroft, 1988). The results confirm that at least some Type As may be prone to nonadherence and that this pattern may be produced by the reactance induced by threats to freedom.

Obviously, not all patients react to the restrictions of illness and treatment with reactance. Reactance is most likely to occur if the restriction on freedom is perceived as arbitrary (Brehm, 1966). Practitioners who hand down directives to their patients without adequately explaining the reasons for them or the relationship of the restrictions to treatment goals may inadvertently contribute to the behavior.

Nonadherence, then, is a widespread and complex behavior. Some of the contributing factors are listed in Table 10.1. As the table shows, nonadherence can result from poor communication between patient and practitioner, qualities of the treatment regimen (such as how "medical" a treatment seems to be), and patient factors such as social class or beliefs about health. Unfortunately, nonadherence can also represent a creative—if foolhardy—reaction to loss of control. As a consequence, efforts to reduce nonadherence, a problem we will address shortly, must focus on the full range of its causes. There is no simple way to reduce it.

Patient-Practitioner Communication and Malpractice Litigation

Dissatisfaction and nonadherence are not the only problematic outcomes of poor patient-practitioner communication. Malpractice suits are another. Malpractice litigation is currently close to epidemic levels. Statistics from the American Medical Association indicate that the number of claims per 100 physicians went from 2.5 in 1976 to 10.6 by 1989 (Gonzalez & Emmons, 1989). The average award size has also increased, averaging nearly $1,117,000 per suit in 1989 (Jury Verdict Research Inc., 1990).

Much of the increase in malpractice litigation has been attributed to the increasing complexity of medicine. New technology tends to

TABLE 10.1   SOME DETERMINANTS OF
ADHERENCE TO TREATMENT REGIMENS
AND CARE

	FOLLOWING PRESCRIBED REGIMEN	STAYING IN TREATMENT
Social characteristics		
Age	0	+
Sex	0	0
Education	0	0
Income	0	0
Psychological dispositions		
Beliefs about threat to health	+	+
Beliefs about efficacy of action	+	+
Knowledge of recommendation and purpose	+	+
General attitudes toward medical care	0	0
General knowledge about health and illness	0	0
Intelligence	0	0
Anxiety	−?	−
Internal control	0?	0
Psychic disturbance	−	−
Social context		
Social support	+	+
Social isolation	−	−
Primary group stability	+	+
Situational demands		
Symptoms	+	+
Complexity of action	−	−
Duration of action	−	−
Interference with other actions	−	−
Interactions with health care system		
Convenience factors	+	+
Continuity of care	+	+
Personal source of care	+	+
General satisfaction	0	0
Supportive interaction	+	+

*Table entries indicate whether a factor encourages compliance (+), works against it (−), has no impact (0), or has uncertain impact (?).

(*Source: Adapted from Kirscht & Rosenstock, 1979, p. 215*)

be overused at first, because practitioners are enthusiastic about its promise and want to try it out (Illich, 1976). However, the overuse of new and complex machinery can lead to patient harm, either because the treatment is not necessary or because the side effects of the technology are not known. As medicine becomes more specialized and complex, and treatments become more numerous, **iatrogenesis** (injury or illness caused by medical treatment) becomes more common (see Halberstam, 1971; Illich, 1976). Malpractice litigation has also been tied to the administrative complexity of the health care system. Patients may be unwilling to sue an individual physician, but if they can sue an institution and convince themselves that the settlement money will never be missed because the insurance company pays it, they are more likely to sue (Halberstam, 1971).

Some of the increase in malpractice litigation can be traced to human factors—the depersonalization of patients in general, and poor patient-practitioner communication in particular. Depersonalization may create an environment conducive to malpractice. For example, a series of articles on abuses at a large metropolitan hospital some years ago (deMaehl & Thurston, 1977) accused the hospital of conducting dangerous or unnecessary surgery primarily for the purpose of teaching medical students rather than because the patients needed the treatments. The articles maintained that far simpler procedures were medically warranted and safer for the patients, but because the patients were poor and inarticulate, they were unable to assert their rights.

Although the most common grounds for a malpractice suit continue to be incompetence and negligence, patients are increasingly citing factors related to poor communication as a basis for their suits, such as not being fully informed about a treatment. An early, classic study designed to unearth the causes of discretionary malpractice litigation confirmed the importance of communication factors (Blum,

1957, 1960). In the study, physicians who had a greater than average number of suits brought against them were compared with physicians who were less likely than average to have a suit brought against them. The research found that more suits were initiated against physicians who were fearful of patients, insecure with them, or derogatory in their manner toward them. When patients felt their medical complaints had been ignored or rudely dismissed, they were more likely to file suit, perhaps as retaliation against the rude treatment. The study further suggested that physicians who were unable to accept their own limitations or who were indifferent to and rejecting of patients were more suit-prone. In support of this interpretation, researchers are increasingly viewing medical malpractice suits as a way that the patient can get back at impersonal medical care (Halberstam, 1971).

To summarize, although many factors contribute to the high rate of malpractice problems, one of the chief contributors is clearly poor communication. Any efforts that improve the interaction process, then, may have the welcome side effect of reducing this problem.

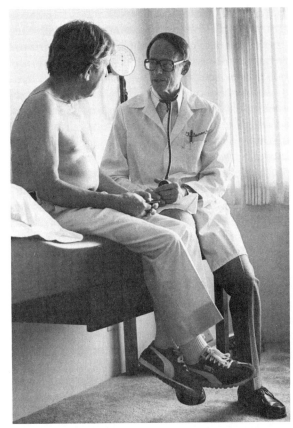

When physicians make lifestyle change advice concrete, patients are more likely to adhere.

IMPROVING PATIENT-PRACTITIONER COMMUNICATION AND REDUCING NONADHERENCE

The fact that poor patient-practitioner communication appears to be so widespread and the fact that it is clearly tied to problematic outcomes such as dissatisfaction with health care, nonadherence with treatment regimen, and malpractice litigation suggest that improving the communication process should be a high priority for psychologists and practitioners. One potential attack on the problem is to teach practitioners how to communicate more effectively.

Teaching Practitioners How to Communicate

Practitioners have known for some time that the course of medical treatment can be affected by communication (see, for example, Shattuck, 1907). Yet they habitually underestimate their role in patients' nonadherence (Stone, 1979). For the most part, efforts to improve communication have consisted of little more than chatty advice or directives such as "communicate effectively" or "be more attentive to the patient's needs" (e.g., Kaufman, 1970). Perhaps the reason for the absence of more concrete advice is that the "bedside manner'' or so-called ''art of medicine'' was assumed to be just that—an art or knack that one either had or did not have. Good, effective communicators were assumed to be born, not made.

As a consequence of this belief, considerable research efforts went into finding the personality traits that discriminate sensitive from insensitive physicians. The goal was to employ these factors as additional criteria in the medical school admissions decision-making process. Accordingly, great numbers of medical students were tested at length and their interactions with patients were observed some time later (for a review, see Gough et al., 1963). The results of such investigations revealed only one reliable predictor of physician sensitivity: the would-be physician's indication of interest in people. What these results seem to suggest is that physician sensitivity is more a matter of motivation than of skill; hence, anyone, given the desire, has the potential to be an effective communicator. The notion that communication is a knack, not a skill, seems to be incorrect and therefore not a basis for rejecting communication training.

A second reason for the lack of focus on communication training stemmed from a belief that effective communication may actually interfere with the ability to be a competent physician by making a person too sensitive and not tough enough to deal with the problems faced by physicians every day. Indeed, there is some evidence that the traditional medical curriculum not only does not instill good communication skills and humanistic concerns but may actually interfere with their development (e.g., Eisenberg, Kitz, & Webber, 1983).

When medical students begin their education, they often do so with idealistic goals and humanitarian motivations, but studies show that students become increasingly cynical the longer they have been in training. This increasing cynicism appears to be due to several factors, including little contact with patients during the early years of school and the strong emphasis on mastery of technical skills. Later, when students do have patient contact, their cynicism may serve a protective function, allowing them to continue to function following tragedy and death (Bloom, 1965; Gray, Newman, & Reinhardt, 1966; Kimball, 1973).

In the face of such pressures against communication skills, how can one justify including them in the medical curriculum? One can directly counter the criticism that effective communication and a humanitarian orientation interfere with the practice of good technical medicine. Studies consistently reveal that the two sets of skills are unrelated (Gough et al., 1964). A sensitive physician is as likely as an insensitive one to be technically competent.

However, the most vocal and persistent criticism of communication training has stemmed from the feeling that physicians have enough difficulty just staying on top of the technical side of medical care without becoming socioemotional specialists as well. Critics have noted that, were every physician to attempt to draw the patient into a warm and open relationship, the time costs would be prohibitive. Clearly, then, any systematic communication training of medical practitioners must take into account the time pressures under which medicine must often be practiced.

With these points in mind, what constitutes realistic training in communication skills? Any communication program should emphasize the development of skills that can be learned easily, that can be incorporated in medical routines easily, and that, over time, come to be automatic. For example, many communication failures in medical settings stem from violation of simple rules of courtesy. These rules can be incorporated into the practitioner's behavior with a minimum of effort: greeting patients, addressing them by name, telling them where they can hang up their clothes if an examination is necessary, explaining the purpose of a procedure while it is going on, saying goodbye, and, again, using the patient's name. Such simple behaviors add a few seconds at most to a visit, and yet they are seen as warm and supportive (DiMatteo & DiNicola, 1982).

Communication courses should also be taught as much as possible in settings that mirror the situations in which the skills will later be used. Training that has worked well for both medical and nursing students has used direct, supervised contact with patients in which the student is given feedback immediately after an interview with a patient (e.g., Leigh & Reiser, 1986). Many courses include videotaping the student's interactions with patients, so that the tapes can be played back and good and bad points in the interview can be pointed out (e.g., Levenkron, Greenland, & Bowlby, 1987). Some programs use specially made tapes that illustrate particular problems that commonly arise in medical settings, so that students can see both the right and the wrong ways to handle them (see, for example, Jason, Kagan, Werner, Elstein, & Thomas, 1971; Kagan, 1974).

Fledgling practitioners are taught not only how to deal with patients on a verbal level but also how nonverbal communication can create an atmosphere of warmth or coldness. A forward lean and direct eye contact, for example, can reinforce an atmosphere of supportiveness, whereas a backward lean, little eye contact, and a postural orientation away from the patient can undercut verbal efforts at warmth by suggesting distance or discomfort (Blondis & Jackson, 1977; DiMatteo, Friedman, & Taranta, 1979). The ability to understand what patients' nonverbal behaviors mean may also be associated with better communication and adherence (DiMatteo et al., 1986).

Once these basic skills are learned, they should be practiced so that they come automatically to the practitioner. At this point, too, more complex material may be introduced, such as how to draw out a reticent patient, how to deal with a patient's guilt or shame

over particular symptoms, and how to learn what the symptom means to the patient so as to better understand the patient's reaction to it (see, for example, Lederere, 1952).

Increasingly, those who would improve the patient-practitioner interaction are turning to patients in the expectation that by teaching them skills designed to elicit good information from physicians, the communication process more generally will improve. For example, Greenfield, Kaplan, Ware, Yano, & Frank (1988) developed a simple intervention for increasing diabetic patients' involvement in their health care. The patient and a research assistant met just prior to a doctor's appointment to review the patient's medical record, to identify issues likely to arise during the visit, and to rehearse communication skills. Compared to standard patient education, the intervention group had the same knowledge of diabetes, but had better blood sugar control some weeks later, fewer days lost from work, and more success obtaining information from their physician. The authors suggested that involvement in the medical process improved adherence, resulting in better blood sugar control.

Increasingly, then, improving patient-practitioner communication may involve not only intervening with physicians to teach them better communication skills, but also intervening with patients to teach them methods of communicating their needs and extracting the information they desire during visits to the practitioner.

Reducing Nonadherence

In this section, we discuss some of the strategies that have been developed for improving adherence. It is important, however, to set these strategies into context. As the role of lifestyle factors has become increasingly clear, both in the maintenance of a healthy lifestyle and in the development of the most prevalent illnesses, the role of the practitioner has gradually but clearly been forced to change. Increasingly, the physician's role must involve some counseling for health promotion and health-habit modification. This is a foreign concept to many physicians, who have defined their role primarily as involving the diagnosis and treatment of disorder. Dramatic testimony to the physician's disinclination to provide effective health promotion is provided by analyses of time spent on these issues during office visits. One study (Reisinger & Bires, 1980) found that physicians spent an average of 97 seconds talking with parents of infants about health-promotion issues likely to arise in pediatric care and an average of 7 seconds on health-promotion issues with adolescents.

Several barriers to changing this role exist. Physicians may have little training in effective health promotion and health-habit modification. Depending on the health care system under which they operate, time spent on health-habit modification and health promotion may not be reimbursable. No immediately visible results derive from health-promotion efforts relative to diagnosing and treating disease. Disorders may be effectively treated and cleared up within days or even hours, whereas the impact of health promotion may never be detectable, nor indeed may bad habits even be successfully modified. Many physicians also doubt the underlying value of preventive care, feeling more comfortable with the biomedical, disease-oriented model. A survey of primary care physicians, for example, found that less than 50% believed that moderating or eliminating alcohol use, decreasing sodium consumption, avoiding saturated fats, engaging in regular exercise, avoiding cholesterol, and minimizing sugar intake were important for health promotion (Wechsler, Levine, Idelson, Rothman, & Taylor, 1983). And, inasmuch as effective prevention often involves knowledge, resources, and ties to community organizations that the physician may not have, the physician may feel incapable of providing effective health promotion (Demak & Becker, 1987; Eriksen, Green, & Fultz, 1988).

Without corresponding changes in medical school education, as well as materials designed to educate physicians further in these efforts, many physicians may feel confused about their role in health promotion and health-habit modification. They may feel, for example, that although they should tell a patient to stop smoking, their responsibility ends at this point and it is the patient's responsibility to figure out exactly how to do it. Yet, as we saw in Chapters 3, 4, 5, and 6, it is often extremely difficult for patients to change these deeply ingrained health habits, and, consequently, they may need more effective guidance than the physician feels able to provide. With this background in mind, we now examine the strategies for reducing nonadherence.

Strategies for reducing nonadherence are many and varied. Some involve institutional interventions. Others involve modifing the presentation of the treatment regimen. A third approach involves improving patient-practitioner communication. A fourth approach draws on social support. Finally, behavioral technologies have increasingly been employed to improve compliance. We will consider each in turn.

Some *institutional innovations* can foster compliance. As we noted earlier, prepaid health care plans often produce emotionally unsatisfying care by inadvertently treating patients in a depersonalizing manner or by making them wait long periods of time. As a consequence, patients may be disinclined to use the service in the future. Rates of compliance with appointments can be improved if the institution sends out postcard reminders or telephones patients to remind them to come back in (Friman et al., 1986). If the facility has a chronic problem of low attendance, any method that can reduce the amount of time the patient must wait before receiving service will improve the rate of keeping appointments (Haynes, 1979b; Mullen & Green, 1985).

The presentation of the treatment regimen can also influence adherence. Treatment recommendations should be written down whenever possible, and the patient should be tested for understanding and recall. Giving the patient a medication information sheet that describes the treatment, the dosage level of medication, and possible side effects can also improve compliance (Peck & King, 1982). Instructions that include take-home pill calendars, special pill packaging designed to aid recall, and pill containers with time-alarm buzzers are helpful devices (Haynes, 1979b).

Since nonadherence is also tied to *practitioner communication skills,* one method for improving adherence involves courses in communication skills for practitioners. To begin with, practitioners overestimate how much time they spend communicating and giving advice to their patients. One study found that during an average office visit of 20 minutes, approximately one minute was spent by the physician giving advice and information, but when physicians were asked to estimate how much time had been spent in this regard, they estimated closer to 8 to 10 minutes (Waitzkin & Stoeckle, 1976). Through courses, practitioners can be trained to avoid jargon whenever possible; to provide a clear explanation of what the patient's problem is and what the treatment will be; to pay attention to what is distressing the patient, not merely to clinically meaningful symptoms; and to provide feedback on the patient's questions. In addition, the practitioner can be encouraged to communicate an atmosphere of warmth and caring, using some of the verbal and nonverbal skills described above. Box 10.1 suggests specific steps that should be incorporated into communication efforts to help patients comply with medical advice.

But, if the practitioner is willing to invest just a little more time, even greater levels of communication and compliance can potentially be achieved. There are a great many ways in which the practitioner's *personal authority* can be used to instill compliance once the foundations for effective communication have been laid (Raven, 1988; Rodin & Janis, 1979). The health practitioner, especially the physician, is a high-status figure for most patients, and what he or she says is generally accepted as valid. Accordingly, the practitioner's information about the disorder and recommendations for treatment will have high credibility. The practitioner is in a position to underscore the patient's personal vulnerability to the disorder: He or she has intimate personal knowledge of the patient. The practitioner can help the patient decide to adhere to a medical treatment regimen by highlighting its advantages, downplaying attendant disadvantages, and stressing the disadvantages of nonadherence (Becker et al., 1979; Janis, 1983a; Janis & Mann, 1977).

Practitioners can also draw on what is called their "referent" power. That is, by becoming a significant individual in the patient's life, one whose approval and acceptance is rewarding, the practitioner is best able to influence those attitudes, values, and decisions of the patient that relate to adherence. When the practitioner is able to draw on referent power as well as the legitimate power of medical authority, adherence is substantially increased (Janis, 1983a; Rodin & Janis, 1979).

The practitioner can also probe for potential barriers to adherence. The face-to-face contact of the medical interview setting provides an opportunity for the patient and the practitioner to explore together any problems that the patient may face in implementing the treatment regimen. For example, if the patient has been told to avoid stressful situations but anticipates several high-pressure meetings the following week at work, the patient and physician together might consider how to resolve this dilemma, as by having a co-worker take the patient's place at some of the meetings, with the patient attending only the critical ones.

For the vocational and social advice on

Box 10.1
Improving Adherence to Treatment

Nonadherence to treatment is a formidable medical problem, and many of the reasons can be traced directly to poor communication between the practitioner and the patient. Following are some guidelines generated by research findings that can help improve adherence. This list can be given to health care providers to enable them to gear their conversations with patients toward improving adherence.

1. Listen to the patient.
2. Ask the patient to repeat what has to be done.
3. Keep the prescription as simple as possible.
4. Give clear instructions on the exact treatment regimen, preferably in writing.
5. Make use of special reminder pill containers and calendars.
6. Call the patient if an appointment is missed.
7. Prescribe a self-care regimen in concert with the patient's daily schedule.
8. Emphasize the importance of adherence at each visit.
9. Gear the frequency of visits to adherence needs.
10. Acknowledge the patient's efforts to adhere at each visit.
11. Involve the patient's spouse or other partner.
12. Whenever possible, provide patients with instructions and advice at the start of the information to be presented.
13. When providing patients with instructions and advice, stress how important they are.
14. Use short words and short sentences.
15. Use explicit categorization where possible. (For example, divide information clearly into categories of etiology, treatment, or prognosis.)
16. Repeat things where feasible.
17. When giving advice, make it as specific, detailed, and concrete as possible.
18. Find out what the patient's worries are. Do not confine yourself merely to gathering objective medical information.
19. Find out what the patient's expectations are. If they cannot be met, explain why.
20. Provide information about the diagnosis and the cause of the illness.
21. Adopt a friendly rather than a businesslike attitude.
22. Avoid medical jargon.
23. Spend some time in conversation about nonmedical topics.

(Based on Haynes, Wang, & da-Mota-Gomes, 1987; Ley, 1977)

which nonadherence rates are known to be high, special measures are needed. The practitioner can begin by explaining why these seemingly nonmedical aspects of the treatment regimen are, in fact, important to health. For example, the benefits of regular exercise can be concretely explained, or the necessity for avoiding stress can be illustrated by providing concrete examples of the stress-illness relationship. Social and vocational advice usually has the disadvantage of being more vague than is "medical" advice, such as dosage level. In a face-to-face setting, the practitioner can ensure that the patient is interpreting the advice correctly. For example, to improve compliance with the advice to avoid stressful situations, the patient and practitioner might list common stressful situations of everyday life and develop some practical techniques for avoiding such situations. Or the practitioner might check to see if the patient's interpretation of the phrase "plenty of bed rest" concurs with the practitioner's interpretation of the same phrase. Finally, because of the face-to-face nature of patient-practitioner interaction, the practitioner may be in a good position to extract a commitment from the patient—that is, a promise that the recommendations will be undertaken and followed through. Such verbal commitments are associated with increased adherence (Kulik & Carlino, 1987).

Breaking advice down into manageable subgoals that can be monitored by the practitioner is another way of increasing adherence. For example, if the patient has been told to alter his diet and lose weight, intermediate weight-loss goals that can be checked at successive appointments might be established (for example, "Try to lose 3 pounds this week").

In the privacy of the office setting, the practitioner can probe for potential sources of resistance to advice. For example, the patient with fibrocystic breast disease (chronically lumpy breasts) who has been trained in breast self-examination may decide not to do it because she feels it is morally wrong to touch her breasts. Discussion with the practitioner at least allows these concerns to be aired.

So far, our discussion has assumed that the physician and patient together are working out the treatment plan. However, increasingly, there are programs available through the community, hospital, or clinics that can help people undertake health behavior change on their own. Thus, for example, a stress management program may be available to help patients cope with stress, or a rehabilitation program involving exercise for cardiac patients may be sponsored by the hospital. In these cases, the physician's responsibility may be primarily to make the recommendation, rather than to work out the development of the program with the patient.

The importance of the physician's recommendation should not be underestimated. When lifestyle change programs are "prescribed" for patients by physicians, patients show higher rates of adherence than if they are simply urged to make use of them. For example, one stress management program to which patients were referred by practitioners found that 90% agreed to enroll initially and that 76% completed the stress program in its entirety. Although the high completion rate is no doubt due to certain intrinsically attractive features of the program, the initial high agreement rate is likely due to the liaison between practitioner and the program (Kabat-Zinn & Chapman-Waldrop, 1988).

It should be clear from this discussion that the practitioner's role in producing adherence goes far beyond giving the patient a few quick instructions. A summary of some of the reasons why the health practitioner can effectively change health behaviors is presented in Table 10.2. It is the practitioner's responsibility to see that the patient hears the instructions and understands them. Moreover, adherence will clearly be improved if the practitioner is willing to help the patient overcome resistance to the treatment regimen by anticipating problems with it and help the patient integrate the program into his or her life.

TABLE 10.2   WHY THE HEALTH PRACTITIONER CAN BE AN EFFECTIVE AGENT OF BEHAVIOR CHANGE

- The health practitioner is a highly credible source with knowledge of medical issues.
- The health practitioner can make health messages simple and tailor them to the individual needs and vulnerabilities of each patient.
- The practitioner can help the patient decide to adhere by highlighting the advantages of treatment and the disadvantages of nonadherence.
- The private, face-to-face nature of the interaction provides an effective setting for holding attention, repeating and clarifying instructions, extracting commitments from a patient, and assessing sources of resistance to adherence.
- The personal nature of the interaction enables a practitioner to establish referent power by communicating warmth and caring.
- The health practitioner can enlist the cooperation of other family members in promoting adherence.
- The health practitioner has the patient under at least partial surveillance and can monitor progress during subsequent visits.

When all family members are enlisted in treatment efforts, the patient's level of adherence is usually higher.

Social Support and Adherence   If the practitioner can gain access to the patient's family, nonadherence can be further reduced. Research has demonstrated that when family members' cooperation is enlisted, adherence is higher (e.g., Davis & Eichhorn, 1963; Wallston et al., 1983). Family involvement improves the chances that at least one family member will remember what to do. Family members can help the patient stick to a regimen by reminding the patient of this responsibility. Patients are more likely to comply with a recommendation the easier it is to do, the more concretely it is tied to already existing activities, and the more habitual it is. Accordingly, family members can help the patient and practitioner integrate the regimen

into daily activities by tying adherence to the patient's ongoing activities.

As we noted in previous chapters (3 through 6), sources of social support other than the family and the practitioner can also bolster adherence. For example, having parents meet in groups to discuss well-child care can increase attendance at well-child appointments (Osborn & Woolley, 1981; see also Christophersen, Finney, & Friman, 1986). If patients enter self-help programs with other individuals like themselves to change troublesome behaviors like smoking or overeating, they may show higher levels of adherence for several reasons. First, they must commit themselves to change their behavior in front of other individuals. Commitment to a decisional course can frequently improve adherence (Cummings, Becker, Kirscht, & Levin, 1981; Janis, 1983a; Wurtele, Galanos, & Roberts, 1980). In the course of interacting with others, the patient may also learn techniques that others have used successfully to maintain adherence and adopt them to combat his or her own problem. Finally, the emotional support and encouragement that others with similar problems provide can also encourage adherence.

Investigations across a wide variety of health issues (for a review, see Janis, 1983b) indicate that as long as individuals attempting to combat health problems are in treatment, they maintain fairly high levels of compliance; most backsliding occurs after visits stop (Marlatt & Gordon, 1985). One source of help is social support via a buddy system, in which one individual who previously had a problem similar to that of the patient can be influential in reducing this backsliding. Phone calls or visits of encouragement can keep the patient on a charted course.

Behavioral Approaches to Adherence Another source of help is behavioral technologies that emphasize long-term maintenance. There are many *behavioral technologies for improving adherence* to treatment regimens (Davidson, 1982; Epstein & Cluss, 1982; Haynes, 1982). Many of these were covered in Chapter 4, but the basic principles bear repeating here. Many behavioral interventions can be employed by a patient alone or with the aid of the practitioner and family. Self-observation and self-monitoring may be used by an individual to chart the target behavior so that there will be an ongoing record of adherence. In some cases, self-monitoring alone can increase the practice of the desired behavior (e.g., McFall, 1970). Reinforcement procedures can also improve adherence. For example, the patient, family, and practitioner can develop a reinforcement program in which adherence is rewarded with a desired activity (such as a game of golf) and nonadherence is not rewarded or is punished (for example, no television).

As we have already noted, tying treatment regimens to ongoing activities improves adherence, and building on this practice by incorporating discriminative stimuli into the process—such as strategic signs posted around the house, a timer set to go off at the time a medication is to be taken, or a calendar on which medication requirements are indicated to be crossed out once taken—can improve ad-

herence still further (Christophersen et al., 1986). For behaviors that require a direct attack on the patient's motivation, as may be necessary for the modification of desirable but unhealthy behaviors like smoking or overeating, modifying internal dialogues through standard techniques of reinforcement can help. If the patient can continually be reminded of all the good reasons for engaging in the desired behavior and the bad reasons for not complying, adherence may be higher. Contingency contracting, in which an individual pledges to do an aversive activity if he or she is nonadherent, can improve adherence rates as well (Thoresen & Mahoney, 1974). Biofeedback can improve adherence by showing an individual that he or she is successfully altering a physical process such as heart rate or blood pressure (see Chapter 11) (e.g., Reeves & Shapiro, 1978; Waggoner & LeLieuvre, 1981).

As we saw in Chapter 4, for some health habits, a multimodal, or broad-spectrum, cognitive-behavioral therapy program may be required to bring adherence up to necessary levels. Such a program may go well beyond the current expertise of many health practitioners. Two solutions to this problem are possible. First, health practitioners can be given training in some of the simpler methods of cognitive-behavioral change so that they can use them effectively with their patients. Alternatively, individuals such as psychologists, who are explicitly trained in the modification of behavior, may be needed to help individuals adhere fully to a complex or difficult treatment regimen.

In short, then, nonadherence is a formidable problem that can be attacked on several fronts simultaneously. Modifying institutional procedures for following patients, presenting the treatment regimen clearly, increasing the skill of the practitioner in communicating with the patient, enlisting social support, and employing cognitive-behavioral change methodologies all have potential for addressing this issue.

SUMMARY

1. Evaluations of health care are based as much on the quality of an interaction with a practitioner as on the technical quality of care.

2. Many factors impede effective patient-practitioner communication. For example, the office setting and the structure of the health care delivery system are often designed for efficient rather than warm and supportive health care. Pressures toward more humane health care treatment are fueled by movements toward holism and wellness.

3. Practitioners contribute to poor communication by not listening, by using jargon-filled explanation, by alternating between overly technical explanations and infantilizing baby talk, and by depersonalizing the patient.

4. Patients contribute to poor communication by failing to learn and remember details of their disorder and treatment, by failing to give practitioners correct cues about their complaints, and by failing to follow through on treatment recommendations. Patient anxiety, lack of intelligence, lack of experience with the disorder, and incomplete information or faulty cues about the meaning of symptoms interfere with effective communication as well.

5. Because the practitioner usually receives little feedback about whether the patient followed instructions or if the treatments were successful, it is difficult to identify and correct these problems in communication.

6. Communication is one of the main factors leading to high rates of nonadherence to treatment.

7. Adherence is lower when recommendations do not seem "medical," when lifestyle modification is needed, when complex self-care regimens are required, and when patients have private and conflicting theories about the nature of their illness or treatment.

8. Adherence is increased when patients have decided to adhere, when they feel the practitioner cares about them, when they understand what to do, and when they have received clear, written instructions.

9. Poor communication has also been related to the initiation of malpractice litigation.

10. Efforts to improve communication have included training in communication skills and taking full advantage of the practitioner's potent professional role. Face-to-face communication with a physician can enhance adherence to treatment because of the personalized relationship that exists. Social support from family and cognitive-behavioral interventions can also improve adherence.

KEY TERMS

adherence
colleague orientation
creative nonadherence
health maintenance organization (HMO)
holistic health
iatrogenesis

nonadherence
nurse-practitioners
patient orientation
physicians' assistants
private, fee-for-service care
reactance

11

PAIN AND ITS MANAGEMENT

One of the most significant aspects of illness is the pain it can produce. Pain is the symptom of chief concern to patients. As such, knowledge of the pain experience is critical for understanding how patients react to symptoms, how they interact with caregivers, and how they respond to treatment. In this chapter, we consider the pain experience and the research and treatment interventions of the last two decades that have led to new insights about the neural and chemical foundations of pain. We then consider the management of acute and chronic pain. Finally, we consider the placebo effect, one of the mainstays of pain control.

SIGNIFICANCE OF PAIN

On the surface, the significance of pain would seem to be obvious. Pain hurts, and it can be so insistent that it can overwhelm other very basic needs. But the significance of pain goes far beyond this. Pain is significant for managing daily activities. Although we normally think of pain as an unusual occurrence, we actively live with minor pains all the time. These pains are critical for survival because they provide low-level feedback about the functioning of our bodily systems, feedback that we then use, often unconsciously, as a basis for making minor adjustments, such as shifting our posture, rolling over while asleep, or crossing and uncrossing our legs.

Pain also has important medical consequences. It is the symptom most likely to lead an individual to seek treatment (see Chapter 9). Unfortunately, though, the relationship between pain and severity of a symptom can be weak. For example, a cancerous lump rarely produces pain, at least in its early stages, yet it is of great medical importance. Pain is also medically significant because it can be a source of misunderstandings between the patient and the medical practitioner. From the patient's standpoint, pain may be the problem. To the practitioner, in contrast, pain is a by-product of a disorder. In fact, pain is often considered by practitioners to be so unimportant that many medical schools have virtually no systematic coverage of pain management in their curriculum. One student, reporting on his medical school experience, stated that pain had been mentioned exactly four times in the entire 4-year curriculum, and that only one lecture had even a portion of its content devoted to pain management. Although the practitioner focuses attention on symptoms, which, from a medical standpoint, may be more meaningful, the patient may feel that an important problem is not getting sufficient attention. As we saw in Chapter 10, patients may choose not to comply with physician's recommendations if they feel they have been misdiagnosed or if their chief symptoms have been ignored (Korsch & Negrete, 1972).

Pain has psychological as well as medical significance. When patients are asked what they fear most about illness and its treatment, the common response is pain (Melzack, 1973). The dread of not being able to reduce one's own suffering arouses more anxiety than the prospect of surgery, the loss of a limb, or even death.

No discussion of the significance of pain would be complete without a consideration of its prevalence and cost. At least $100 billion is spent annually in the United States on over-the-counter pain remedies to reduce the temporary pain of colds, headaches, and other minor disorders. Twenty million tons of aspirin are consumed annually by headache sufferers alone. In addition, there are an estimated 7 million sufferers of chronic pain in this country who spend close to $50 billion annually to control their pain. The pain business is big business, reflecting the chronic and temporary suffering that many millions of people experience.

At least $100 billion is spent annually in the United States on over-the-counter remedies to reduce the temporary pain of minor disorders.

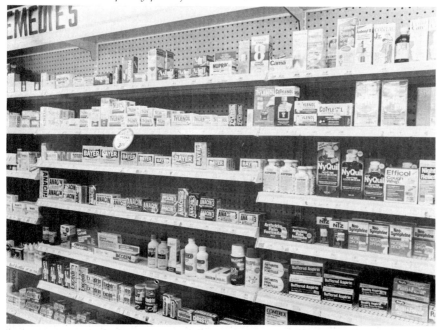

ELUSIVE NATURE OF PAIN

Pain has been one of the more mysterious and elusive aspects of illness and its treatment. It is fundamentally a psychological experience, and the degree to which it is felt and how incapacitating it is depends in large part on how it is interpreted. Howard Beecher, a physician, was one of the first to recognize this (Beecher, 1959).

During World War II, Beecher served in the medical corps, where he observed many wartime injuries. In treating the soldiers, he noticed a curious fact: Only one-quarter of them requested morphine (a widely used painkiller) for what were often severe and very likely to be painful wounds. When Beecher returned to his Boston civilian practice, he often treated patients who sustained comparable injuries from surgery. However, in contrast to the soldiers, 80% of the civilians appeared to be in substantial pain and demanded painkillers. To make sense of this apparent discrepancy, Beecher concluded that the meaning attached to pain substantially determines how it is experienced. For the soldier, an injury meant that he was alive and was likely to be sent home. For the civilian, the injury represented an unwelcome interruption of valued activities.

Pain is also heavily influenced by the context in which it is experienced. Sports lore is full of accounts of athletes who have injured themselves on the playing field but stayed in the game, apparently oblivious to their pain. In contrast, shut-ins who have little to occupy their time other than minding their aches and pains may feel each one acutely (Pennebaker, 1983). Pain has a substantial cultural component, such that members of some cultures report pain sooner and react more intensely to it than individuals in other cultures (Zborowski, 1958). An example of these kinds of cultural differences appears in Box 11.1.

Even more mysterious are pains that have no apparent physiological basis. These pains are called **clinical pains,** because they have clinical significance (that is, people suffer from them and seek treatment for them), but there may be no underlying disorder that can be treated (Melzack, 1973). The common clinical pains are **causalgia** (a burning pain that appears after a wound is healed), **neuralgia** (a sudden sharp pain along a nerve pathway for which no basis can be found), and **phantom limb pain** (pain experienced in the place where an amputated limb used to be, see Box 11.2). Clinical pains present a puzzle to the practitioner because there seems to be no organic basis for their occurrence. Yet neither do they seem to be purely "psychological," that is, all in the head. Clinical pain, then, cannot be dismissed as being entirely psychological. It clearly involves the interplay of both physiological and psychological factors, although its causes and treatments have often remained elusive.

Measuring Pain

One barrier to the treatment of pain is the difficulty people have describing it objectively. If you have a lump, you can point to it, or if a bone is broken, it can be seen in an x-ray. Pain does not have these objective references. We do have a large informal vocabulary for describing pain (see Melzack & Torgerson, 1971), and this can be of some help to practitioners. But recently researchers and clinicians have developed a variety of alternative methods for measuring and recording pain.

One early effort to get at the multiple aspects of pain was developed by Melzack and Torgersen (1971); they had subjects sort words describing pain into piles to differentiate aspects of the pain experience. Three general classes emerged. Some words described the sensory aspects of pain in terms of temporal, spatial, pressure, thermal, and other qualities of the experience; such terms include pulsing, shooting, gnawing, and burning. The second class of words described affective qualities as-

Box 11.1
A Cross-Cultural Perspective on Pain:
The Childbirth Experience

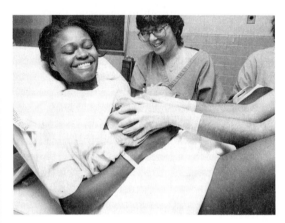

The meaning attached to an experience substantially determines whether or not it is perceived as painful. For many women, the joy of childbirth can mute the pain associated with the experience.

Although babies are born in every society, the childbirth experience varies dramatically from culture to culture, and so does the experience of pain associated with it (Jordan, 1983). Among Mexican women, for example, the word for labor (*dolor*) means sorrow or pain, and the expectation of giving birth can produce a great deal of fear. Most interesting is the fact that this fear and anticipation of pain often translate into a more painful experience with more complications than is true for women who do not bring these fears and expectations to the birthing experience (Scrimshaw, Engle, & Zambrana, 1983).

In stark contrast is the culture of Yap in the South Pacific, where childbirth is treated as an everyday occurrence. Women in Yap perform their normal activities until they begin labor, at which time they retire to a childbirth hut to give birth with the aid of perhaps one or two other women. Following the birth, there is a brief period of rest, after which the woman again resumes her activities. Problematic labors and complications during pregnancy are reported to be low (Kroeber, 1948).

There is no simple and direct relationship between expectations about pain and the actual childbirth experience, but expectations do play an important role in how labor is experienced. Cultural lore and customs are a significant source of these expectations.

sociated with pain, including terms such as annoying, terrifying, or sickening. Finally, words reflecting the evaluative experience of pain represented its perceived intensity; examples are terms like mild, distressing, and excruciating. From this descriptive terminology, Melzack (1975) developed the McGill Pain Questionnaire (Figure 11.1), a tool that enables clinicians and researchers to objectify the pain experience. The questionnaire groups words within each category—sensory, affective, and evaluative—and ranks them according to intensity. The pain patient indicates his or her experience of pain within each of the categories listed on the questionnaire. The questionnaire yields two main measures. The first is a pain rating scale, which is the summed rank value of the words chosen in each of the three categories. The second score is the present pain intensity score, which measures overall intensity on a scale from 0 to 5. Although adapted by others, this measure and

Box 11.2
Phantom Limb Pain: A Case History

Nerve injury of the shoulder is becoming increasingly common because motorcycles are widely accessible and, all too often, their power is greater than the skill of their riders. On hitting an obstruction, the rider is catapulted forward and hits the road at about the speed the bike was traveling. In the most severe of these injuries, the spinal roots are avulsed—that is, ripped out of the spinal cord—and no repair is possible. In 1979, well over 100 brachial plexus avulsions occurred in England alone.

C. A., aged 25, an air force pilot, suffered such an accident. After 8 months, he had completely recovered from the cuts, bruises, and fractures of his accident. There had been no head injury and he was alert, intelligent, and busy as a student shaping a new career for himself. His right arm was completely

paralyzed from the shoulder down, and the muscles of his arm were thin. In addition, the limp arm was totally anesthetic, so that he had no sensation of any stimuli applied to it. On being questioned, he stated that he could sense very clearly an entire arm, but it had no relationship to his real arm. This "phantom" arm seemed to him to be placed across his chest while the real, paralyzed arm hung at his side. The phantom never moved and the fingers were tightly clenched in a cramped fist with the nails digging into the palm. The entire arm felt "as though it was on fire." Nothing has helped his condition, and he finds that he can control the pain only by absorbing himself in his work.

(From Melzack & Wall, 1982, pp. 21–22.)

measures like it continue to enjoy wide use in the pain literature (e.g., Corson & Schneider, 1984). These kinds of instruments make it possible to develop profiles of different pains and to assess their intensity.

Another set of pain assessment techniques often used in the laboratory involve **pain threshold** measures (Sternbach & Tursky, 1965). Typically, in this procedure, an individual is exposed to some unpleasant stimuli, such as an electric shock, beginning at very low levels and progressively increasing. The individual is asked first to indicate the sensation threshold, or the lowest value at which a sensation is experienced. The next step is to indicate the lowest value at which pain is felt, termed the pain perception threshold. The pain tolerance level is the level at which the person asks to have the stimulation stopped,

and the encouraged pain tolerance level is the highest level that a person will accept after being encouraged to go on (Melzack, 1983). Research indicates that sensation thresholds are relatively uniform, but that individuals vary widely in their pain threshold and their encouraged pain tolerance level.

Tourniquet techniques developed by Sternbach (1983) have also been used to measure clinical pain. In this procedure, a patient or laboratory subject wears a blood pressure cuff and squeezes a hand exerciser as the blood pressure cuff is tightened. The patient indicates when the pain produced by this method matches the intensity of the clinical pain experienced. This rating is then divided by the person's tourniquet pain tolerance threshold, which is the point at which the person maintains that he or she cannot stand the

FIGURE 11.1   The McGill Pain Questionnaire

Patient's name _____ Date _____ Time _____ am/pm

1 Flickering ___ Quivering ___ Pulsing ___ Throbbing ___ Beating ___ Pounding ___	11 Tiring ___ Exhausting ___ 12 Sickening ___ Suffocating ___ 13 Fearful ___ Frightful ___ Terrifying ___	
2 Jumping ___ Flashing ___ Shooting ___		
3 Pricking ___ Boring ___ Drilling ___ Stabbing ___ Lancinating ___	14 Punishing ___ Gruelling ___ Cruel ___ Vicious ___ Killing ___ 15 Wretched ___ Blinding ___	

Brief ___	Rhythmic ___	Continuous ___
Momentary ___	Periodic ___	Steady ___
Transient ___	Intermittent ___	Constant ___

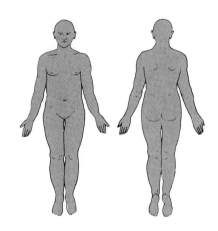

E = External
I = Internal

PPI

0 No pain ___	
1 Mild ___	
2 Discomforting ___	
3 Distressing ___	
4 Horrible ___	
5 Excruciating ___	

4 Sharp ___
 Cutting ___
 Lacerating ___

5 Pinching ___
 Pressing ___
 Gnawing ___
 Cramping ___
 Crushing ___

6 Tugging ___
 Pulling ___
 Wrenching ___

7 Hot ___
 Burning ___
 Scalding ___
 Searing ___

8 Tingling ___
 Itchy ___
 Smarting ___
 Stinging ___

9 Dull ___
 Sore ___
 Hurting ___
 Aching ___
 Heavy ___

10 Tender ___
 Taut ___
 Rasping ___
 Splitting ___

16 Annoying ___
 Troublesome ___
 Miserable ___
 Intense ___
 Unbearable ___

17 Spreading ___
 Radiating ___
 Penetrating ___
 Piercing ___

18 Tight ___
 Numb ___
 Drawing ___
 Squeezing ___
 Tearing ___

19 Cool ___
 Cold ___
 Freezing ___

20 Nagging ___
 Nauseating ___
 Agonizing ___
 Dreadful ___
 Torturing ___

Comments:

(From Melzack, 1975)

tourniquet being tightened any further. This and similar methods have proven to be valid and reliable ways of describing the intensity of clinical pain.

A number of recent efforts to assess pain have focused on **pain behaviors.** Some approaches have been developed to assess behaviors associated with varying types and degrees of pain reliably. In one such study (Turk, Wack, & Kerns, 1985), four clusters of pain behavior were identified: distorted ambulation or posture, negative affect, facial and audible expressions of distress, and avoidance of activity. Such descriptive analysis helps provide a basis for the assessment of degree of pain behavior. Similar efforts have focused on pain behaviors within particular pain groups, such as chronic low back pain patients (Follick, Ahern, & Aberger, 1985). Such syndrome-specific profiles have focused on both pain behaviors and pain descriptions and have proven useful in identifying the dynamics of different pain syndromes (Jamner & Tursky, 1987). A method used in the assessment of headache pain measures patients' responses to external stimuli experienced as aversive. For example, a patient may be exposed to varying degrees of noise or bright light and asked to indicate his or her response to the stimulus on a scale ranging from "comfortable" to "definitely unpleasant" (Philips & Hunter, 1982). In these and other ways, pain researchers and clinicians are better able to objectify experiences that are otherwise subjective.

Physiology of Pain

The view of pain as having sensory, affective, and evaluative components is useful for making sense of the manifold pathways and receptors involved in the pain experience. The pain experience is complex. Although there are nerve fibers whose specific function it is to conduct pain, other nerve fibers may also give rise to pain if they are stimulated beyond a certain threshold. Thus, pain has a certain

number of specific pathways, but it can involve other pathways as well. Moreover, patterns of stimulation are important in the experience of pain. The receptors, fibers, and nervous system pathways involved in the transmission of pain respond to patterned information rather than to pain-specific impulses.

At least two different kinds of fibers are associated with different kinds of pain. So-called A-delta fibers are responsible for the conduct of fast, sharp, well-localized pain, or pain that is experienced quickly. C-fibers appear to conduct slow, aching, burning, long-lasting, and poorly localized pain (Mountcastle, 1980). The difference between these two sets of fibers relates to the sensory, affective, and evaluative distinctions raised earlier. In particular, the sensory aspect of pain appears to be determined primarily by activity in the A-delta fibers, which project onto particular areas of the thalamus and the sensory areas of the cerebral cortex. The motivational and affective elements of pain are influenced more strongly by the C-fibers, which project onto different thalamic, hypothalamic, and cortical areas. The limbic system and the reticular formation are implicated in motivational and affective responses to pain. Finally, processes in the cerebral cortex are involved in cognitive judgments about pain, including the evaluation of its meaning. The overall experience of pain, then, is a complex outcome of the interaction of these elements of the pain experience.

Gate Theory of Pain

Any theory of pain must account for the specificity of pain, different types of pain, and the important role of psychological factors. Such a theoretical context is provided by the gate theory of pain developed by Melzack and Wall (1965), diagrammed in Figure 11.2.

The central assumption of **gate theory** is that a number of structures in the central nervous system are involved in the pain experi-

FIGURE 11.2   Gate Theory and the Physiology of Pain
A schematic diagram of the gate-control theory of pain.
L indicates the large-diameter A-beta fibers; S indicates
the small-diameter A-delta and C fibers. The fibers
project to the substantia gelatinosa (SG) and the
transmission (T) cells in the spinal column. Excitatory
effects are indicated by white circles and inhibitory
effects are indicated by black circles. The central control
trigger is represented by a line running from the large
fiber system to the central control mechanism; this
mechanism, in turn, projects back to the gate-control
system. In addition, there is descending inhibitory
control from the brain-stem system.

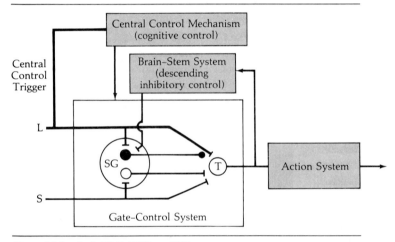

(From Melzack & Wall, 1982, p. 130)

ence; these affect the operation of a gatelike
mechanism in the dorsal horns of the spinal
column that controls the flow of pain stimulation to the brain. According to the theory,
pain is not merely a sensation that is transmitted directly from the peripheral nerve endings
to the brain. Rather, sensations are modified
as they are conducted to the brain by way of
the spinal cord, and they are also influenced
by downward pathways from the brain that
interpret the experience.

Let us look at this theory more closely. In
the absence of pain, the peripheral nerve endings pick up sensations from our physical actions, such as walking or touching. These sensations are transmitted via multiple neural
pathways to the spinal column; they are then
carried up the spinal column to the brain. At
this point, the spinal gating mechanism is
closed. When the peripheral nerve endings
are exposed to injurious stimuli, multiple
pathways are again activated and sensations
are transmitted to the spinal column. If the
patterning of stimulation is sufficiently intense
to make the sensations reach a certain threshold and if the upper centers of the brain interpret the event as painful, then the gate will
open and sensations of pain will be transmitted up the spinal column to the brain.

The experience of pain is affected by the
balance of activity in large and small nerve fibers, which determine the patterning and intensity of stimulation. Activity in the large fibers (called A-beta fibers) tends to close the

gate, whereas activity in the small fibers (A-delta and C fibers) tends to open the gate, facilitating the transmission of pain.

In addition, fibers descending from the brain continually influence the stimulus input at the spinal cord, facilitating the flow of some patterns and inhibiting others. This mechanism is called the **central control mechanism.** Information about the painful experience is interpreted in the higher centers of the nervous system, transmitted to the limbic system and the reticular formation, and transmitted down the spinal cord to modulate the experience of pain. Through this mechanism, affective reactions such as anxiety or fear can exacerbate the experience of pain, and intense involvement in other activities or positive experiences such as laughter can mute the pain experience (Cogan, Cogan, Waltz, & McCue, 1987). In addition, there is a system in the brain stem that responds to stimulation from the gate and exerts an inhibitory effect, thus tending to close it.

The gating mechanism itself appears to involve the interaction of two types of cells in the dorsal horns of the spinal column, the substantia gelatinosa and the transmission (T) cells. The substantia gelatinosa modulates the stimulation from the periphery and the feedback from the fibers descending from the brain, causing the transmission (T) cells either to conduct (excitatory influence) or not conduct (inhibitory influence) pain sensations to the brain.

There are several important points to gate control theory. First, it acknowledges some degree of specificity in the pain transmission system. However, it builds in the importance of overall patterning in the experience of pain. It also allows for a substantial role of psychological processes in the pain experience by positing the central control mechanism. It helps explain the different kinds of pain that individuals experience and integrates the importance of sensory, affective, and evaluative components into the model. As we shall see, gate theory has also been of substantial clinical value in suggesting techniques of pain control

and explaining the way in which pain control methods work.

Neurochemical Bases of Pain and Its Inhibition

Melzack and Wall (1965, 1982) maintained that the brain can control the amount of pain an individual experiences by transmitting messages down the spinal cord to block the transmission of pain signals. One landmark study that confirmed this hypothesis was conducted by Reynolds (1969). He demonstrated that by electrically stimulating a portion of the rat brain, one could produce such a high level of analgesia that the animal would not feel the pain of abdominal surgery. This phenomenon has been termed stimulation-produced analgesia (SPA). Reynolds' findings prompted researchers to look for the neurochemical basis of this effect and in 1972, Akil, Mayer, and Liebeskind (1972; 1976) uncovered the existence of endogenous opioids.

What are **endogenous opioids?** Opiates, including heroin and morphine, are drugs manufactured from plants that help control pain. Opioids—opiatelike substances produced within the body—constitute a neurochemically based, internal pain-regulation system. Opioids are produced in many parts of the brain and glands of the body; they project onto specific selective receptor sites in various parts of the body.

The endogenous opioids constitute three general families: beta-endorphins, which produce peptides that project to the limbic system and brain stem, among other places; proenkephalin (peptides that have widespread neuronal, endocrine, and central nervous system distributions); and prodynorphin, in the gut, the posterior pituitary, and the brain (Akil et al., 1984). Each of these families of opioids has a variety of forms, with widely differing potencies, pharmacological profiles, and receptor selectivities (Akil et al., 1984). For example, one opioid receptor may be receptive to beta-endorphins but not to proenkephalin or prodynorphin. Thus, the system of endogenous opioids in the body is highly complex.

Endogenous opioids, then, are considered to be neurochemicals important in the natural pain suppressing system of the body. Clearly, however, this pain suppression system is not always in operation. Particular factors must trigger its arousal. Research on animals suggests that stress is one such factor. Acute stress, such as that caused by administration of shock to the foot of a rat, produces reliable insensitivity to pain. This phenomenon is called stress-induced analgesia (SIA), and research demonstrates that SIA can be accompanied by an increase in brain endogenous opioids (Lewis, Terman, Shavit, Nelson, & Liebeskind, 1984; Madden, Akil, Patrick, & Barchas, 1977). Research on humans also suggests that endogenous opioids may be secreted in response to stress.

Researchers do not yet know all the functions of endogenous opioids. They are one method of inhibiting pain, particularly under stressful circumstances. Since the endogenous opioids can be found in the adrenal glands, the pituitary gland, and the hypothalamus, they are clearly involved in bodily responses to stress. Opioids have been implicated in immune functioning and cardiovascular control as well (Akil et al., 1984; Holaday, 1983), and thus, release of opioids may represent one route by which stress depresses immune functioning (see Chapter 15). Whether the endogenous opioids will make direct contributions to the management of clinical pain remains to be seen. However, the release of endogenous opioids may be one of the mechanisms underlying various techniques of pain control (Bolles & Fanselow, 1982).

CLINICAL MANAGEMENT OF PAIN

Historically, pain has been managed by physicians and other health care workers. Tradi-tional pain-management techniques include pharmacological, surgical, and sensory techniques. Increasingly, because of the important role that psychological factors play in the experience of pain, psychologists have become involved in pain management. As a result, techniques that include a heavily psychological component have been used to combat pain. These include biofeedback, relaxation, hypnosis, acupuncture, distraction, guided imagery, and other cognitive techniques.

Acute Versus Chronic Pain

As noted in the last chapter, pain is the symptom for which patients most frequently seek treatment. There are two main kinds of clinical pain: acute and chronic. **Acute pain** typically results from some specific injury that produces tissue damage, such as a wound or broken limb. While it is going on, acute pain produces substantial anxiety and prompts its sufferer to engage in an urgent search for relief. Once painkillers are administered or the injury begins to heal, the pain decreases and anxiety dissipates (Bond, 1979).

Chronic pain typically begins with an acute episode, but, unlike acute pain, it does not decrease with treatment and the passage of time. Most commonly, the patient with chronic pain is suffering from one of the following: muscle or joint pain (especially back pain but also pain due to inflammation of the joints, muscles, or tendons; bursitis; or tendinitis); one of the clinical pain syndromes (causalgia, neuralgia, or phantom limb pain); vascular pain (pain due to engorgement of the blood vessels, especially migraine headaches); or pain caused by destruction of tissue, as in terminal cancer (Melzack & Wall, 1982).

It is estimated that 65 million Americans suffer from chronic pain at any given time. Such pain is not necessarily present every moment, but the fact that it is chronic virtually forces sufferers to organize their lives around it (Fordyce, 1976; Sternbach, 1974). The following case history suggests the disruption and agony that can be experienced by the chronic pain sufferer.

> A little over a year ago, George Zessi, 54, a New York furrier, suddenly began to have excruciating migraine headaches. The attacks occurred every day and quickly turned Zessi into a pain cripple. "I felt like I was suffering a hangover each morning without even having touched a drop. I was seasick without going near a boat," he says. Because of the nausea that often accompanies migraines, Zessi lost fifty pounds.
>
> At his workshop, Zessi found himself so sensitive that he could not bear the ringing of a telephone. "I was incapacitated. It was difficult to talk to anyone. On weekends, I couldn't get out of bed," he says. A neurologist conducted a thorough examination and told Zessi he was suffering from tension. He took several kinds of drugs, but they did not dull his daily headaches. (Clark, 1977, p. 58)

As this case history suggests, chronic pain can entirely disrupt a person's life. Many such sufferers have left their jobs, abandoned their leisure activities, withdrawn from their families and friends, and evolved an entire lifestyle around pain (Clark, 1977; Fordyce, 1976). Typically, they have little social or recreational life and may even have difficulty performing simple tasks of self-care. Because their income is often reduced, their standard of living may be low and they may need public assistance. Therefore, the loss of self-esteem that is experienced by these patients can be substantial. Reduced social contact contributes to the fact that many of these people turn inward and become self-absorbed. Neurotic behavior, including preoccupation with physical and emotional symptoms, can result (Bond, 1979; see also Chibnall & Tait, 1989). As a consequence, many chronic pain patients are clinically depressed; a large number have also contemplated or attempted suicide.

Frequently, patients with chronic pain have amassed huge medical bills and experienced a number of radical treatments, such as surgery (Fordyce, 1976). Often, these treatments make

the pain worse rather than better. These patients also consume large quantities of painkillers; these drugs may be only partially effective, and they have a variety of undesirable side effects, including inability to concentrate and addiction. Nerve-blocking agents may be administered to reduce pain, but these can also produce side effects, including anesthesia, limb paralysis, and loss of bladder control; moreover, even when they are successful, the pain will usually return within a short time. In addition, pain is often aggravated by the symptoms of the disorder that produced it, such as the vomiting and loss of bladder control that can accompany advancing cancer (Bond, 1979).

Why is the distinction between acute and chronic pain important in clinical management? There are several reasons. First, acute and chronic pain present different psychological profiles, since the latter type of pain often carries an overlay of psychological distress that complicates diagnosis and treatment. Second, most of the pain control techniques we will consider work well to control acute pain but are relatively unsuccessful with chronic pain, which requires individualized multiple techniques for its management. Third, chronic pain is often a mixture of an acute disorder and a psychological overlay. For example, chronic pain may be more responsive to anxiety or threat than acute pain. Although chronic pain patients do not seem to experience a higher baseline level of pain, they appear to be more sensitive to the experience of pain under conditions of threat and return to baseline levels more slowly (Flor & Turk, 1989b).

Chronic pain also has a component of functional or **operant pain,** that is, pain that is experienced by having been paired with reinforcement and that consequently fulfills certain functions in the pain patient's life (Fordyce, 1976). As we saw in Chapter 4, a basic principle of psychology is that when a response is followed by reinforcement, it is likely to be repeated. Pain can be unintentionally conditioned in this way. When people are in pain, they may receive some rewards: attention from family and friends; freedom from certain activities, such as job or chores; financial compensation, such as disability payments; and pain-relieving drugs that may have pleasant side effects. Through the repeated pairing of pain with these reinforcements, pain can be maintained because it is functional. A functional overlay on organic pain can make pain a more difficult experience to treat, because the patient has been unintentionally reinforced for being in pain.

In addition, chronic pain leads to a variety of pain-related behaviors that can also maintain the pain experience. For example, chronic pain patients typically make major changes in their environment and activities. They may

avoid loud noises and bright lights, reduce physical activity, and avoid social contacts. These alterations in lifestyle then become part of the pain problem (e.g., Fordyce, 1988; Philips, 1983). At the same time that these patients are trying to overcome pain, they are expected to resume a normal life; this prospect may be both burdensome and threatening. Thus, pain-related behaviors may persist and interfere with successful treatment (Philips, 1983). Understanding what pain behaviors an individual engages in, whether or not they persist after the treatment of pain, and how they can be extinguished are important factors in treating the total pain experience.

Pain and Personality

Since psychological factors are so clearly implicated in the experience of pain and since at least some pain is clearly functional for the chronic pain sufferer, researchers have examined whether there might not be a **pain-prone personality:** a constellation of personality traits that predispose a person to experience chronic pain. Research suggests that this hypothesis is too simplistic. First, pain itself can produce at least temporary alterations in personality. Therefore, personality variables that are consistently associated with pain can be consequences of the pain experience, not necessarily causes. Second, individual experiences of pain are far too varied and complex to be explained by a single personality profile. Rather, different personality factors may be implicated in different kinds of pain (see Bradley, 1983, Cox, Chapman, & Black, 1978). Third, although particular individuals may be more inclined than others to experience pain, these individuals make up a relatively small portion of the pain population. Consequently, personality researchers have tried to find ways of identifying these subgroups rather than to develop a profile that will explain all pain behavior. It is now clear that personality factors can be involved either as predisposing factors

More than 65 million Americans, many of them elderly, suffer from chronic pain.

or as consequents of the pain experience (Weisenberg, 1977).

To examine these issues, researchers have drawn on a variety of personality instruments, especially the Minnesota Multiphasic Personality Inventory (MMPI). This lengthy questionnaire measures patients' self-reports of physical and emotional symptoms and provides scores on fourteen different scales. The MMPI reliably distinguishes acute pain patients from chronic pain patients (Bond, 1979; Cox et al., 1978). The acute pain patient shows elevated scores on two particular scales of the MMPI: hypochondriasis (the tendency to be overly concerned about one's physical health and to experience or report a high number of symptoms) and hysteria (the manifestation of extreme emotional behavior and a tendency to exaggerate symptoms). In some cases, acute pain patients also show elevations on the mania subscale, a reflection of the agitation and anxiety that are involved in the experience of acute pain.

Chronic pain patients typically show elevated scores on three MMPI subscales: hypochondriasis, hysteria, and depression (Bond, 1979). This constellation of three factors is commonly referred to as the "neurotic triad" because it so frequently shows up in the personality profiles of patients with neurotic disorders. Depression reflects the feelings of despair or hopelessness that can often accompany long-term experience with unsuccessfully treated pain. Pain does not appear to be a sufficient condition for the development of depression but, rather, leads to a reduction in activity level, perceptions of control, and feelings of personal mastery, which, in turn, lead to depression (Rudy, Kerns, & Turk, 1988). This profile has implications for the treatment of pain because it indicates that the treatment regimen must take into account chronic mood changes that have arisen in response to pain.

MMPI profiles may also prove to be useful in identifying some individuals for whom pain serves particular functions. For example, research has suggested that patients who show elevations on the neurotic triad accompanied by an elevation on another subscale—such as schizophrenia, psychopathic deviance, or paranoia—may be suffering from pain that has been prompted at least in part by pre-pain characterological disturbances (for a review, see Bradley, 1983). These patients may actually be suffering less intense pain than they report, and they may show adaptation to the chronic invalid lifestyle (see Bradley & Van der Heide, 1984). In contrast, chronic pain patients who show only the neurotic triad and no other elevations in the MMPI profile may be suffering more intense pain or at least more emotionally arousing pain.

The MMPI has also been used to develop subprofiles within categories of particular pain, such as low back pain (Bradley & Van der Heide, 1984; Guck, Meilman, Skultety, & Poloni, 1988; Moore, Armentrout, Parker, & Kivlahan, 1986; Rappaport, McAnulty, Waggoner, & Brantley, 1987; Rosen, Grubman, Bevins, & Frymoyer, 1987). Although other instruments have been used to evaluate pain, such as the Milan Behavioral Health Inventory (Sweet, Breuer, Hazlewood, Toye, & Pawl, 1985), the SCL-90 (Jamison, Rock, & Parris, 1988), and self-monitored pain intensity (Kerns, Finn, & Haythornthwaite, 1988), the MMPI remains the major assessment tool in this arena at present.

PAIN CONTROL TECHNIQUES

With this background in mind, we now turn to pain control techniques, examining individual techniques that have been used to reduce pain. Evidence for the success of these techniques comes from both experimental studies with laboratory subjects and studies of patients suffering from clinical pain. However, the success of most of these techniques is most evident with the patient suffering from acute pain. A subsequent section deals more fully with efforts to treat chronic pain.

Some pain control techniques achieve their

effects primarily by chemical or physical means. Such techniques have until recently been the mainstay of pain control. They include pharmacological, surgical, and sensory stimulation techniques. In addition, newer techniques that include a heavily psychological component have come into increasing use. They include biofeedback, relaxation, hypnosis, distraction, guided imagery, and other cognitive techniques. It should be noted, however, that the distinction between chemical/physical and psychological techniques is to some extent artificial. Each of the techniques that we will consider almost certainly has both psychological as well as physiological and neurochemical consequences.

What exactly is pain control? **Pain control** refers to a variety of different factors. It can mean that a patient no longer feels anything in an area that once hurt. It can mean that the person feels sensation but not pain. It can mean that he or she feels pain but is no longer concerned about it. Or it can mean that he or she is still hurting but is now able to stand it. Unfortunately, evaluations of pain control techniques typically ask only whether or not pain has been reduced as indicated by verbal reports, medications, and pain-related behaviors. Consequently, the distinctions among these four responses are usually blurred. Nonetheless, it is clear that some pain control techniques (for example, spinal blocking agents) work because they eliminate feeling altogether, while others (such as sensory control techniques) may succeed because they reduce pain to sensation, and still others (such as many of the more psychological approaches) succeed because they enable patients to tolerate pain more successfully. It will be useful to bear these distinctions in mind as we evaluate the success of individual techniques in the control of pain.

Pharmacological Control of Pain

The traditional and most common method of controlling pain is through the administration of drugs. In particular, morphine (named after Morpheus, the Greek god of sleep) has been the most popular painkiller for decades (Melzack & Wall, 1982). A derivative of opium, morphine has a strong disadvantage: It is highly addictive and patients may require progressively larger doses to provide the same relief. As a consequence, researchers and physicians have sought other possibilities that do not have this side effect.

In addition to morphine, any drug that can influence neural transmission is a candidate for pain relief. Some drugs, such as local anesthetics, can influence transmission of pain impulses from the peripheral receptors to the spinal cord. The application of an analgesic to a wounded area is an example of this approach. The injection of drugs, such as spinal blocking agents that block the transmission of pain impulses up the spinal cord, is another method. Pharmacological relief from pain may also be provided by drugs that influence the central control mechanism in the brain. For example, antidepressants may combat pain by reducing anxiety and improving mood.

Surgical Control of Pain

The surgical control of pain also has an extensive history. Surgical treatment involves cutting or creating lesions in the so-called pain fibers at various points in the body, so that pain sensations can no longer be conducted. Some surgical techniques attempt to disrupt the conduct of pain from the periphery to the spinal cord, whereas others are designed to interrupt the flow of pain sensations from the spinal cord upward to the brain.

Although these surgical techniques are sometimes successful in reducing pain temporarily, the effects are often short-lived. Therefore many sufferers who have submitted to one or more operations to reduce pain may find that only short-term benefits were gained at substantial cost: the risks, possible side effects, and tremendous expense of surgery (Melzack & Wall, 1982). It is now believed that the nervous system has substantial regenerative powers and that blocked pain impulses find their way to the brain via different neural pathways (Zimmerman, 1979). Moreover, there is some indication that surgery can ultimately worsen the problem because it damages the nervous system, and this damage can itself be a chief cause of chronic pain. Hence, whereas surgical treatment for pain was once relatively common, researchers and practitioners are increasingly doubtful of its value even as a treatment of last resort.

Sensory Control of Pain

One of the oldest known techniques of pain control is counterirritation, a sensory method. **Counterirritation** involves inhibiting pain in one part of the body by stimulating or mildly irritating another area. The next time you hurt yourself, you can demonstrate this technique on your own (and may have done so already) by pinching or scratching an area of your body near the part that hurts. Typically, the counterirritation produced when you do this will suppress the pain to some extent. This common observation has been increasingly incorporated into the pain treatment process (Zimmerman, 1979). An example of a pain control technique that uses this principle is dorsal column stimulation (Nashold & Friedman, 1972). A set of small electrodes is placed or implanted near the point where the nerve fibers from the painful area enter the spinal cord. When the patient experiences pain, he or she activates a radio signal that delivers a mild electrical stimulus to that area of the spine, thus inhibiting pain.

Although counterirritation has been used for centuries, how it achieved its effects was unknown until recently. Gate theory provides an explanation. Specifically, counterirritation provided by methods like electrical stimulation may activate the large-diameter fibers that close the gate. In particular, the stimulation of these fibers may activate the cells of the substantia gelatinosa, which, in turn, inhibit

the conduct of pain sensations by the T cells (Melzack & Wall, 1982).

Overall, sensory control techniques have had some success in reducing the experience of pain. However, their effects are often only short-lived, and they may therefore be appropriate primarily for temporary relief from acute pain or as part of a general regimen for chronic pain.

The techniques of pain control discussed so far involve primarily physical, electrical, or chemical interventions to reduce pain. The techniques we are about to describe rely more clearly on the pain sufferer's inner psychological resources. Basically, these techniques—including biofeedback, relaxation, hypnosis, distraction, guided imagery, and other cognitive techniques—act in several ways. First, they act on the pain experience by reducing anxiety, redirecting attention, and providing direct suggestion regarding how to interpret pain. Second, they can enable a patient to achieve some degree of control over the muscles, blood vessels, and other physical processes that play a role in pain.

Unlike the pharmacological, surgical, and sensory pain-management techniques considered so far, these more psychological techniques require active participation and learning on the part of the patient. Therefore they can be somewhat more effective for managing slow-rising pains, which can be anticipated and prepared for, than sudden, intense, or unexpected pains.

Biofeedback

Biofeedback, a method of achieving control over a bodily process, has been used to treat a variety of pains and other health problems (Basmajian, 1989). We introduce it in the context of pain primarily because it has been widely touted as a successful pain therapy. As noted in previous chapters, biofeedback has also been employed to induce relaxation in stress-management programs and to reduce blood pressure in hypertension.

Biofeedback comprises a wide variety of techniques that provide biophysiological feedback to a patient about some bodily process of which the patient is usually unaware. Biofeedback training can be thought of as an operant learning process. First, a target body function to be brought under control, such as blood pressure or heart rate, is identified. This function is then tracked by a machine and information about the function is passed on to the patient. For example, heart rate might be converted into a tone, so the patient can hear how fast or slowly his or her heart is beating. The patient then makes efforts to change the bodily process. Through trial and error and continuous feedback, he or she learns what factors will modify the bodily function. Thus, for example, a patient might learn that blocking out all sounds, concentrating, and breathing slowly help reduce heart rate. In some cases, the particular steps the patient undertakes to change the process may not be clear, merely the fact that they are successful. Through this learning process, the patient often becomes highly proficient at controlling a bodily function that was once automatic. Advocates of biofeedback assume that once patients are able to bring a process under bodily control with feedback from the machine, they will be able to bring about these changes on their own in natural settings without benefit of the machine (Turk, Meichenbaum, & Berman, 1979).

Biofeedback has been employed with several chronic or intermittent pain conditions. Chief among these are muscle-contraction headaches and migraine headaches. Muscle-contraction headaches appear to result from excessive long-term contraction of the forehead or neck muscles, often in conjunction with stress (Bakal, 1975; Gannon, Haynes, Cuevas, & Chavez, 1987). Because the muscle activity of the forehead can easily be monitored using an electromyograph (EMG), a number of studies have provided this kind of EMG feedback to sufferers of this type of headache (e.g., Budzynsky, Stoyva, Adler, &

Biofeedback has been used successfully to treat muscle-tension headaches, migraine headaches, and Raynaud's disease. However, evidence to date suggests that other less expensive relaxation techniques may be equally successful.

Mullaney, 1973). Results have generally indicated that EMG biofeedback successfully reduces the incidence of the headaches. However, other recent evidence (Sargent, Solbach, Coyne, Spohn, & Segerson, 1986 for a review; see Turk et al., 1979) suggests that EMG biofeedback may be no more successful at reducing muscle-tension headaches than other, more easily implemented and less expensive techniques, such as relaxation training or other stress management techniques (e.g., Holroyd, Andrasik, & Westbrook, 1977), and may work better with younger than with older clients (Holroyd & Penzien, 1986). Moreover, at least some of these studies using alternative methods found improvement in headaches without changes in EMG activity, raising the possibility that EMG activity is not a central element in the intensity of muscle-tension headaches.

Has biofeedback training worked for migraine headache sufferers? Between 5 and 10% of all Americans suffer from migraines, a disorder characterized by severe periodic headaches ranging from a few minutes to several days' duration. (Box 11.3 offers a description of migraine from the patient's viewpoint.) The headaches are often associated with nausea, aversion to light of any kind, irritability, constipation, diarrhea, or vomiting (Beeson & McDermott, 1967, as cited in Birk, 1973). They appear to be caused primarily by pressure on major arteries induced by extreme and prolonged dilation of veins and arteries (Beeson & McDermott, 1967), and they may occur in response to stress (Rojan & Gerhards, 1986). Frequently, migraine headaches are treated by administering vasoconstrictors (drugs designed to constrict the dilated arteries), but such treatments may be unsuccessful or produce unpleasant side effects for a majority of patients (Beeson & McDermott, 1967).

How can biofeedback be used to reduce the pain of migraine headaches? It is difficult to control dilation of the arteries in the head directly. However, if one can increase blood flow to the body's periphery, a decrease in blood flow to the cranium should result. Hence, migraine patients may be hooked up to a machine that gives them a temperature reading of both a finger and their forehead. Often, such patients are then taught to relax fully and note the effect that relaxation has on these temperatures. Next, the patient may be instructed to increase the temperature of the finger, using the feedback of the machine as an aid. Once the instruction phase is complete, patients are urged to practice at home, noting whether or not they are able to increase relaxation and warmth in the finger and how long it takes. Once the patient has mastered the technique, he or she is urged to use it to control headaches. When the patient feels a headache coming on, he or she attempts to warm up the fingers; in theory, blood flow is diverted from the arteries in the head to the periphery, vascular pressure in the cranium is reduced, and the migraine headache is eliminated or reduced in intensity (Sargent & Walters, 1972; Sargent, Walters, & Green, 1973; for a review, see Turk et al., 1979).

Evaluations of efforts to control migraine headaches by biofeedback yield results similar to those of studies with muscle-tension headaches. Biofeedback techniques do appear to reduce the severity of migraine headaches. However, muscular relaxation produces similar results. Moreover, evidence relating changes in temperature control directly to reduction in headaches is equivocal (e.g., Gauthier, Bois, Allaire, & Drolet, 1981; for a review, see Turk et al., 1979). Again, then, less expensive and more easily utilized treatment methods may be appropriate for migraine headaches.

Biofeedback has also been used to treat Raynaud's disease. Raynaud's is a disorder of the cardiovascular system in which the small arteries in a person's extremities constrict, limiting blood flow to the periphery. The symptoms are a cold, numb aching of the peripheral limbs, especially the hands or feet. In extreme cases, gangrene can result, and amputation of the extremities may be required. Although it is not caused by stress, Raynaud's disease can be aggravated by it.

An extended evaluation of behavioral treatments for Raynaud's disease concludes that temperature biofeedback enables patients to voluntarily control their capillary blood flow and that improvements may extend up to 3 years. The effects appear to be mediated by a beta andrenergic vasodilating mechanism rather than via physiological relaxation. Relaxation-based procedures appear to produce smaller symptom reduction with little retention of physiological effects over time (Freedman, 1987; see also Friedman et al., 1988).

What must we conclude about the efficacy of biofeedback in treating pain patients? Despite widely touted claims for the efficacy of biofeedback, there is only modest evidence that it is effective in reducing pain. This is partly because the research reports on biofeedback training have not been methodologically sound. It is relatively rare to find a study that examines biofeedback training with

Box 11.3
On Migraine Headaches

To someone unfamiliar with chronic pain, the experience may seem foreign, hard to imagine. Joan Didion, the prominent novelist and essayist and herself a victim of migraine headaches, may make it easier for those fortunate enough not to suffer from chronic pain to understand the agony of those who do.

Three, four, sometimes five times a month, I spend the day in bed with a migraine headache, insensible to the world around me. Almost every day of every month, between these attacks, I feel the sudden irrational irritation and the flush of blood into the cerebral arteries which tell me that migraine is on its way, and I take certain drugs to avert its arrival. If I did not take the drugs, I would be able to function perhaps one day in four. . . .

When I was 15, 16, even 25, I used to think that I could rid myself of this error by simply denying it, character over chemistry. "Do you have headaches sometimes? frequently? never?" the application forms would demand. "Check one." Wary of the trap . . . I would check one. "Sometimes," I would lie. That in fact I spent one or two days a week almost unconscious with pain seemed a shameful secret, evidence not merely of some chemical inferiority but of all my bad attitudes, unpleasant tempers, wrongthink.

I fought migraine then, ignored the warnings it sent, went to school and later to work in spite of it, sat through lectures in Middle English and presentations to advertisers with involuntary tears running down the right side of my face, threw up in washrooms, stumbled home by instinct, emptied ice trays onto my bed and tried to freeze the pain in my right temple, wished only for a neurosurgeon who would do a lobotomy on house call, and cursed my imagination.

Once an attack is under way, no drug touches it. When I am in a migraine aura (for some people the aura lasts fifteen minutes, for others several hours), I will drive through red lights, lose the house keys, spill whatever I am holding, lose the ability to focus my eyes or frame coherent sentences, and generally give the appearance of being on drugs, or drunk. The actual headache, when it comes, brings with it chills, sweating, nausea, a debility that seems to stretch the very limits of endurance. That no one dies of migraine seems, to someone deep into an attack, an ambiguous blessing.

I have learned now to live with it, learned when to expect it, how to outwit it, even how to regard it, when it does come, as more friend than lodger. We have reached a certain understanding, my migraine and I. It never comes when I am in real trouble. Tell me that my house is burned down, my husband has left me, that there is gunfighting in the streets and panic in the banks, and I will not respond by getting a headache. It comes instead when I am fighting not an open but a guerrilla war with my own life, during weeks of small household confusions, lost laundry, unhappy help, canceled appointments, on days when the telephone rings too much and I get no work done and the wind is coming up. On days like that my friend comes uninvited. And when the pain recedes, ten or twelve hours later, everything goes with it, all the hidden resentments, all the vain anxieties. The migraine has acted as a circuit breaker, and the fuses have emerged intact. There is a pleasant convalescent euphoria. I open the windows and feel the air, eat gratefully, sleep well. I notice the particular nature of a flower in a glass on the stair landing. I count my blessings.

(From "In Bed," an essay by Joan Didion from *The White Album*, 1979, pp. 168–172.)

appropriate control groups. Thus, one important change that is required in this area is the use of better research techniques (Shapiro & Surwit, 1979; Turk et al., 1979; White & Tursky, 1982).

However, even when biofeedback is effective, the research evidence suggests that it may be no more so than less expensive, more easily used techniques like relaxation (e.g., Belar, 1979; Blanchard, Andrasik, & Silver, 1980; Bush, Ditto, & Feuerstein, 1985; Silver & Blanchard, 1978). In addition, when biofeedback training is successful, it is not clear exactly why. There is little evidence that success at controlling a target process and corresponding reduction of pain are related. This raises the possibility that something other than modification of the target process is producing the beneficial effects of biofeedback. For example, relaxation, suggestion, an enhanced sense of control, or even a placebo effect may be responsible for the efficacy of the technique (e.g., Turk et al., 1979). When biofeedback does succeed in controlling pain, it may do so through a variety of relatively independent physiological mechanisms rather than through some unitary physiological/psychological event (DeGood & Redgate, 1982).

The mixed results to date, then, suggest that we must begin to look for more complex models of biofeedback use. For example, the combination of biofeedback training with other cognitive or behavioral interventions may prove to be more useful for particular patient groups with particular disorders than biofeedback alone (Shapiro & Surwit, 1979; Turk et al., 1979). Alternatively, we may find that the expense of biofeedback training does not justify its continued use when less expensive techniques are equally effective (Turk et al., 1979). In view of these results, Melzack's (1975) warning about biofeedback is still justified: "Don't hold the party yet" (for reviews, see Holmes, 1981; Shapiro & Surwit, 1979; Turk et al., 1979; White & Tursky, 1982; see also Roberts, 1985). Overall, we know that

biofeedback can be an effective treatment for certain kinds of chronic pains. What we do not yet know is if and when biofeedback is an essential or a specific treatment for chronic pain that produces effects over and above those that would be expected from relaxation training or similar interventions alone (Roberts, in press).

Relaxation Techniques

Various types of relaxation training have been employed with pain patients, either alone or in concert with other pain control techniques (Davidson & Schwartz, 1976; Kabat-Zinn, Lipworth, & Burney, 1985). Originally, relaxation techniques were developed to deal with anxiety-related emotional disorders (Jacobson, 1938; Wolpe, 1958). For example, individuals with phobias about snakes, heights, closed-in places, or other fears can be trained through formal relaxation methods to become calm in the presence of these once-threatening stimuli. Consequently, one rationale for including relaxation training in pain management is that it can reduce anxiety. As we noted in the last chapter, anxiety can increase pain; consequently, anxiety reduction should ameliorate pain. A second way in which relaxation can reduce pain is by directly affecting a physical process that is responsible for pain. For example, the reduction of muscle tension or the diversion of blood flow induced by relaxation may reduce pains that are tied to these physiological processes.

Relaxation begins when an individual is induced to shift the body into a state of low arousal (Davidson & Schwartz, 1976). One way of accomplishing this is through the progressive relaxation of different parts of the body. An instructor might say: "Shake out your arms. Let them flop by your sides. (Pause) Now relax your shoulders. Roll them up. Drop them down. (Pause) Now relax your neck. Get rid of any tension." This process would continue until every part of the body was relaxed.

Controlled breathing is another component of relaxation (Davidson & Schwartz, 1976). As the body slows down, breathing changes from relatively short, shallow breaths to deeper, longer breaths. Relaxation can be induced sooner when an individual intentionally strives to create this breathing pattern. Deep breathing usually begins with a cleansing breath in which the air in the lungs is blown out through the mouth. Long, deep breaths lasting as long as 10 seconds then replace earlier shorter, shallower breaths. Anyone who has been trained in prepared childbirth will recognize that this technique is used to induce relaxation in early labor.

An alternative method of inducing relaxation is through meditation. In this process, a person attempts to focus attention fully on some very simple and usually unchanging stimulus. For example, one may repeat a very simple syllable (such as ''Om'') slowly over and over again; this process is used in Transcendental Meditation, and the syllable is called a mantra. More recently, some researchers have used a flotation tank (flotation REST), in an environment with restricted stimulation, to successfully induce relaxation (Jacobs, Heilbronner, & Stanley, 1984). Box 11.4 gives two examples of the use of relaxation in pain control.

How successful have relaxation strategies been in the management of pain? Meditation per se does not appear to be successful, primarily because it does not reliably achieve the tar-

---

Box 11.4
Using Relaxation to Combat Pain

The following are case histories of patients treated with relaxation to reduce pain that, in some instances, proved resistant to other pain-control methods.

Case 1

A 65-year-old ex-steeplejack was hospitalized for evaluation of increasingly severe intermittent chest pain which had been present for over 10 years. An extensive work-up revealed esophagitis (inflammation of the esophagus). The patient used relaxation exercises frequently both for general relaxation and for relief of moderate pain. ''I get into it and just sort of forget all about the pain.'' Over a period of six months, he found the method very useful. ''If I catch the pain early enough, I can stop it before it gets too bad.'' He typically used the method for 10 to 15 minutes, following which he went directly to sleep.

Case 2

A dramatic response was seen in a 22-year-old man who was hospitalized following extensive bullet wounds in the abdomen and hip. During the three months of hospitalization, he suffered severe pain, which responded partially to surgery. He was anxious, depressed, irritable, and occasionally panicky due to the continual pain. He ate poorly and steadily lost weight. Using relaxation, he was able to sleep if the pain was not severe. He stated, ''I stay there as long as I can—maybe 30 minutes. The trouble is, I go to sleep.'' There was a marked improvement in his general mood and he began eating well.

(From French & Tupin, 1974, pp. 283, 285)

get state of relaxation (Holmes, 1981). Generally, results suggest modestly positive effects of relaxation with some acute pains (Turk et al., 1979; Weisenberg, 1977). Studies in experimental contexts (Weisenberg, 1977) as well as with patients suffering from headache and pain in the facial muscles (Turk et al., 1979; Weisenberg, 1977) suggest that relaxation can effectively reduce some pains. However, in and of itself, relaxation training may not be a sufficient therapy, and its value, particularly with chronic pain patients, may be evident primarily when it is combined with other methods of pain control (Weisenberg, 1977).

Hypnosis

Hypnosis is one of our oldest techniques for managing pain, and it is also one of the most misunderstood. Its mere mention conjures up visions of Svengali-like power-seekers forcing others to do their bidding by inducing a hypnotic trance. In one of his most troublesome cases, Sherlock Holmes was nearly assassinated by a young man ordered to kill him while under the hypnotic control of a bewitching woman. In fact, there are strict limitations on what a hypnotized subject will do while in a trance. Although such subjects may perform some minor feats that they do not customarily perform, they typically cannot be induced to do injury to themselves or others (Hilgard, 1965, 1971). So much for mythology.

The fact that hypnosis can help control pain has been noted for centuries. Old medical textbooks and anthropological accounts of cultural healing rituals provide anecdotes of such extreme interventions as surgery conducted with no apparent pain while the patient was under an hypnotic trance. For example:

> In 1829, prior to the discovery of anesthetic drugs, a French surgeon, Dr. Cloquet, performed a remarkable operation on a sixty-four-year-old woman who suffered from cancer of the right breast. After making an incision from the armpit to the inner side of the breast, he re-

moved both the malignant tumor and also several enlarged glands in the armpit. What makes this operation remarkable is that, during the surgical procedure, the patient, who had not received any drugs, conversed quietly with the physician and showed no signs of experiencing pain. During the surgery, her respiration and pulse rate appeared stable and there were no noticeable changes in her facial expression. The ability of this patient to tolerate the painful procedures was attributed to the fact that she had been mesmerized immediately prior to the operation. (Kroger, 1957; cited in Chaves & Barber, 1976, p. 443)

Cloquet's case is one of the first reports of painless surgery with mesmerism or, as it was later called, hypnosis.

As an intervention, hypnosis relies on several pain-reduction techniques (Barber, 1965; Hilgard, 1978). First, a state of relaxation is engendered, so that the trance can be induced; relaxation alone can, of course, help reduce pain. Next, patients are explicitly told that the hypnosis will reduce pain; the suggestion that pain will decline is also sufficient to reduce pain (Weisenberg, 1977). Hypnosis is itself a distraction from the pain experience, and distraction can reduce the experience of pain (Melzack & Wall, 1982). In the hypnotic trance, the patient is usually instructed to think about the pain differently; as noted earlier in this chapter, the meaning attached to pain influences its occurrence. And, finally, patients undergoing painful procedures with hypnosis are also often given painkillers. The beneficial effects of hypnosis in reducing pain are due at least in part to the composite effects of relaxation, reinterpretation, distraction, and drugs.

Debate has raged over whether hypnosis is something more than the composite of these methods (see especially Chaves & Barber, 1976; Hilgard, 1975). Some (e.g., Chaves & Barber, 1976) say not, maintaining that the pain-reducing effects of hypnosis are no more than a composite of the pain-reducing techniques with which it is associated. Others, especially Hilgard (1975), maintain that hypnosis is an altered state of consciousness and point to evidence that hypnotized people experience certain effects under hypnosis that subjects pretending to be under hypnosis do not experience. At present, the balance of evidence seems to favor Hilgard's position (e.g., Orne, 1977, 1980).

Regardless of the exact mechanism by which it works, the efficacy of hypnosis for the management of some acute pains now appears to be established (Hilgard, 1975, 1978). It has been used successfully to control acute pain due to surgery, childbirth, dental procedures, burns, and headaches as well as pain due to a variety of laboratory procedures (Hilgard, 1978). It has also been used with some success in the treatment of chronic pain, such as that due to cancer (Hilgard, 1978). When hypnosis is used clinically to manage acute pain, it is typically combined with other pain-reducing techniques. Although controlled clinical trials of its effectiveness are still few in number, overall, hypnosis has one of the better records in the clinical management of pain.

Acupuncture

Acupuncture has been in existence in China for over 2,000 years. In acupuncture treatment, long thin needles are inserted into specially designated areas of the body that theoretically influence the areas where a patient is experiencing a disorder. Although the main goal of acupuncture is to cure illness, it is also used in pain management because it appears to have an analgesic effect. In fact, in China, a substantial percentage of patients are able to undergo surgery with only the analgesia of acupuncture. During surgery, these patients are typically conscious, fully alert, and able to converse while the procedures are going on (Melzack, 1973).

How does acupuncture control pain? This is not fully known. It is possible that acupuncture functions partly as a sensory method of controlling pain (Andersson, 1979). The stimulation of the needles may activate the large fibers that help to close the spinal gating mechanism (Andersson, 1979). Researchers also believe that acupuncture may work because it is associated with other psychologically based techniques for pain control. In particular, patients believe that acupuncture will work, and their expectations may help reduce pain. The belief that acupuncture will reduce pain can reduce anxiety, inducing a state of relaxation; relaxation itself can reduce the experience of pain. Before the acupuncture process begins, patients are usually fully prepared for it and are told what the sensations of the needles will be and how to tolerate them. Such informed preparation often reduces fear and increases tolerance of pain (see Chapter 9). Acupuncture needles and the process of inserting them are distracting; accordingly, attention may be directed away from pain. Distraction itself can be an effective method of pain control (Melzack & Wall, 1982). Patients undergoing acupuncture often receive analgesic drugs of various kinds that also reduce the pain experience. Finally, it is possible that acupuncture triggers the release of endorphins, thus reducing the experience of pain. When naloxone (an opiate antagonist that suppresses the effects of endorphins) is administered to acupuncture patients, the success of acupuncture in reducing pain is reduced (Mayer, Price, Barber, & Rafii, 1976; for a review, see Andersson, 1979).

Overall, is acupuncture an effective method of pain control? Apparently it can help reduce some kinds of short-term pain, but it may not be as effective for chronic pain (e.g., Bakal, 1979; Murphy, 1976). Indeed, it may be less effective than hypnosis or other successful pain-control techniques, but at present there are not enough data to evaluate its comparative effectiveness. Acupuncture may be well-suited to the management of some pains, but not others.

Distraction

Earlier, we noted how individuals who are involved in intense activities like sports or military maneuvers can be oblivious to painful injuries. These are extreme examples of a commonly employed pain technique: **distraction.** By focusing attention on some irrelevant and attention-getting stimulus or by distracting oneself with a high level of activity, one can turn attention away from pain. There are two quite different mental strategies for controlling discomfort. One is to distract oneself by focusing on some other activity. Some examples of control techniques that rely on distraction are provided by children describing how they deal with stressful or painful events (Bandura, in press). For instance, an 11-year-old boy described how he reduced pain by distracting himself while in the dentist's chair:

> When the dentist says, 'Open,' I have to say the Pledge of Allegiance to the flag backwards three times before I am even allowed to think about the drill. Once he got all finished before I did.

The other kind of mental strategy for controlling stressful events is to focus directly on the events but to reinterpret the experience. The following is a description from an 8-year-old boy who confronted a painful event directly:

> As soon as I get in the dentist's chair, I pretend he's the enemy and I'm a secret agent, and he's torturing me to get secrets, and if I make one sound, I'm telling him secret information, so I never do. I'm going to be a secret agent when I grow up, so this is good practice.

According to Albert Bandura, who reported these stories, occasionally the boy "got carried away with his fantasy role-playing. One time the dentist asked him to rinse his mouth. Much to the child's own surprise, he snarled, 'I won't tell you a damned thing,' which momentarily stunned the dentist."

Distraction appears to be a successful technique of pain control. One method of distraction that has been evaluated experimentally is audioanalgesia, which literally means the use of sound to reduce pain. In one study illustrating this technique, Melzack, Weisz, and Sprague (1963) worked with three groups of subjects exposed to the experimentally induced pain of a cold pressor test (placing one's hand in ice water for a prolonged time). The first group of subjects was told that while they were engaged in the task, they would hear either music or noise (a low level of static). They were told that the sound would increase their tolerance for pain and that they could control the volume of the sound by turning a knob next to them. A second group was also told that they would hear music or noise and that they could control its volume; however, they were not explicitly told that the sound would help them cope with the pain more effectively. A third group of patients heard a monotone (rather than music or static) but were told that the tone would help them cope better with pain. Subjects were asked to indicate when they could no longer tolerate the pain.

Only patients in the first group—who were exposed to the sound, believed it would help them tolerate pain, and could control it—showed increased tolerance for pain. This result indicates that sound alone is not sufficient to reduce pain; rather, the sound must be intense and one must also believe that the sound is going to reduce pain. Furthermore, observations of subjects during the experiment indicated that the first group of subjects actively employed the sound as a distractor. When they felt pain, they turned the sound up or down or varied the volume in an apparent effort to distract themselves from the discomfort.

Somewhat surprisingly, the practical lessons of this important study (and those that followed it) have gone largely unheeded. For example, although music is usually present in dentists' offices, patients are rarely told that it will help them cope with pain, and they are rarely given control over its volume. Rather, the music alone is mistakenly thought to be sufficient to reduce pain.

A review of the distraction literature for reducing pain revealed several general principles about when it is most effective. The more attention was drawn to alternative tasks, the more successful distraction was in reducing pain. Distraction had stronger effects on pains of low intensity than on pains of high intensity. For mild pain stimuli, distraction proved to be a more effective method of controlling pain than redefinition of sensations, but at more intense levels of pain stimuli, the reverse was true. Overall, distraction appears to be an effective way of coping with low-level pain (McCaul & Malott, 1984).

Although distraction can relieve the experience of pain, its practical significance is somewhat limited. Chronic pain patients cannot distract themselves indefinitely, so distraction is not successful in the treatment of chronic pain. Even acute pain can be managed by distraction only if it is of short duration and of relatively low intensity. Thus, distraction techniques for the control of pain may be best used for managing short-term pain, such as that due to painful medical procedures. Distraction may also be effective when used in conjunction with other pain-control techniques, such as relaxation.

Guided Imagery

Guided imagery has also been used to control some acute pain and discomfort (e.g., Lyles, Burish, Krozely, & Oldham, 1982). In **guided imagery,** a patient is instructed to conjure up a picture which he or she holds in mind during the painful experience. Some practitioners of guided imagery use it primarily to induce relaxation (e.g., Horan, Layng, & Pursell, 1976). The patient is encouraged to visualize a peaceful, relatively unchanging scene, to hold it in mind, and to focus on it fully. This process brings on a relaxed state, concentrates attention, and distracts the patient from the pain or discomfort—all techniques that have been shown to reduce pain.

The use of guided imagery to induce relaxation can control slow-rising pains that can be anticipated and prepared for, or it can be used to control the discomfort of a painful medical procedure. As an example of the former use, advocates of prepared childbirth encourage the woman in labor to develop a focal point—a real or imagined picture that she can focus on fully when labor pains begin. An example of using guided imagery to control the discomfort of a medical procedure is provided by a patient undergoing radiation therapy.

> When I was taking the radiation treatment, I imagined I was looking out my window and watching the trees and seeing the leaves go back and forth in the wind. Or, I would think of the ocean and watch the waves come in over and over again, and I would hope, "Maybe this will take it all away."

A very different kind of visualization technique may be used by patients trying to take a more personally aggressive stance toward pain. Instead of using imagery to calm and soothe themselves, these patients may use it to rouse themselves into a confrontive stance by imagining a combative, action-filled scene. The following examples are from patients who used aggressive imagery in conjunction with their chemotherapy treatment.

> I happened to see something my husband was watching on T.V. It was on World War II and the Nazis were in it. They were ruthless. They killed everything. I visualized my white blood cells were the German Army, and that helped me get through chemotherapy.

> I imagined that the cancer was this large dragon and the chemotherapy was a cannon, and when I was taking the chemotherapy, I would imagine it blasting the dragon, piece by piece.

Although one purpose of such aggressive imagery may be to improve the efficacy of the therapy itself (e.g., Simonton & Simonton, 1975)—a highly controversial use of imaging—the use of aggressive imagery may also improve coping with the uncomfortable effects of illness or treatment. When the body is in a state of excitement or arousal, pain can be inhibited (Melzack & Wall, 1982). Moreover, aggressive imagery can serve as a distraction to pain, and it gives the patient something to focus on.

Although relaxation imagery is more often used to combat pain than is aggressive imagery, aggressive imagery may work, too. In fact, one chemotherapy patient apparently profited from the use of both:

> It was kind of a game with me, depending on my mood. If I was peaceful and wanted to be peaceful, I would image a beautiful scene, or if I wanted to do battle with the enemy, I would mock up a battle and have my defenses ready.

It is interesting to note that these two virtually opposite forms of imagery may actually achieve some beneficial effects in controlling pain through the same means. Both may induce a positive mood state (relaxation or excitement) that contributes to the reduction of pain, and both focus attention and provide a distraction from pain, one by concentrating attention on a single, unchanging or repetitive stimulus, the other by diverting attention to the drama of an active scene.

How effective is guided imagery in controlling pain? Guided imagery is typically used in conjunction with other pain control techniques, so its unique contribution to pain reduction, if any, is as yet unknown. If it does prove to add something to the control of pain, it will likely be in the treatment of acute, slow-rising pain.

Additional Cognitive Techniques to Control Pain

Distraction and guided imagery both represent time-tested cognitive approaches to control pain. Recently, psychologists have focused on developing and refining additional cognitive and cognitive-behavioral interventions that may be useful in the management of at least some clinical pains, either alone or in concert with other treatments. Typically, cognitive-behavioral interventions to control pain have several objectives (Flor & Turk, 1989a). First, they encourage patients to reconceptualize the problem from overwhelming to manageable. The rationale is that the pain problem must be seen as modifiable for cognitive and behavioral methods to have any impact. Second, clients must be convinced that the skills necessary to control the pain can and will be taught to them, thereby enhancing their expectations that the outcome of this training will be successful. Third, clients are encouraged to reconceptualize their own role in the pain management process, from being passive recipients of pain to being active, resourceful, and competent individuals who can aid in the control of pain. These cognitions are important in the pain experience and may promote feelings of self-efficacy. Indeed, in one study, self-efficacy beliefs accounted for the degree of pain and disability experienced better than disease-related variables (Flor & Turk, 1989a).

Fourth, clients learn how to monitor their thoughts, feelings, and behaviors to break up maladaptive cognitions that may have resulted in response to pain. As we noted in Chapter 4, patients often inadvertently undermine behavior change by engaging in discouraging self-talk. By modifying this behavior and instilling internal monologues that favor a successful outcome, the probability that the outcome can be achieved may be increased. Fifth, patients are also taught how and when to employ overt and covert behaviors in order to make adaptive responses to the pain problem. This skills training component of the intervention may include biofeedback training or relaxation, for example. Sixth and finally, clients are encouraged to attribute their success to their own efforts. By making internal attributions for success, they promote a view of themselves as efficacious agents of change and may be in a better position to monitor subsequent changes in the pain and bring about successful pain modification. In the relapse prevention part of cognitive-behaviorally-based pain management programs, clients are led to anticipate the problems that may develop and to discuss ways of dealing with these potential problems (Turk & Rudy, 1988).

There is some evidence that such cognitive-behavioral packages for dealing with pain can be successful. For example, Turner (1982) assigned patients with orthopedic pain to a cognitive-behavioral treatment package, to a progressive relaxation training intervention, or to a control condition that placed patients on a wait list for the intervention but did not provide them with any treatment during the study. Both active interventions were superior to the waiting list control at post-treatment, as measured by daily pain ratings, although the two active conditions did not differ from each other. Over an 18-month follow-up, patients in the active intervention conditions also used health care services less. The cognitive-behavioral approach appeared to be superior to relaxation training in that patients were more likely to report greater pain tolerance and had the ability to maintain normal activities (see also Fordyce, Brockway, Bergman, & Spengler, 1986; Heinrich, Cohen, Naliboff, Collins, & Bonebakker, 1985). In addition, compared to the physical management of pain, behavioral treatments may have an advantage in maintaining pain behavior change over the long term (Fordyce et al., 1986).

Of the various cognitively oriented efforts that have been undertaken to control pain, those designed to increase self-efficacy may be especially helpful. Self-efficacy expectations are important primarily because patients must believe they have the ability to undertake the required responses in order to bring about any change. Self-efficacy may also be important

because declines in perceptions of personal efficacy and mastery appear to be heavily responsible for the development of depression among chronic pain patients and for some of the marital stress and strain that may result from chronic pain (e.g., Elliott, Trief, & Stein, 1986). One of many studies demonstrating the importance of self-efficacy in the perception of pain (Litt, 1988) put female undergraduates through a cold pressor task in which they either did or did not receive prior self-efficacy expectations. That is, half the subjects were led to believe that they would be able to deal successfully with the discomfort, whereas the other half were not. The results indicated that self-efficacy expectations reduced the impact of the aversive stimulus on subjects' persistence at the task. Recent evidence suggests that the impact of self-efficacy expectations on the pain experience may be mediated at least in part by opioid activation (Bandura et al., 1988; Bandura, O'Leary, Gauthier, & Gossard, 1987). It should be noted that feelings of control or self-efficacy need not be actually exercised in order to have beneficial effects on pain and discomfort. The simple belief that one has perceived but never-used control can also have beneficial effects (e.g., Staub, Tursky, & Schwartz, 1971).

So far, our discussion of cognitive techniques to control pain has focused largely on interventions. However, patients also spontaneously employ cognitive strategies in an effort to manage pain (Chaves & Brown, 1987). While there are anecdotal reports that such methods can be successful pain control techniques (see, for example, Taylor, Lichtman, & Wood, 1984b), full evaluation of such spontaneous efforts has not yet been undertaken.

MANAGEMENT OF CHRONIC PAIN

But what of the chronic pain patient? As we noted in our previous discussion, no pain control technique has been identified that is clearly effective in modifying chronic pain. Thus, typically, the chronic pain patient runs the gamut of techniques and finds them all to be unsuccessful.

Until 30 years ago, the patient who suffered from chronic pain had few treatment avenues available, save the tragedy of addiction to morphine or other painkillers and rounds of only temporarily successful operations. Now, however, an institutional form of treatment has developed to treat chronic pain. These institutions are termed **pain centers,** and they concentrate all that is known about pain control so that all potential technologies can be made available to patients (Fordyce, 1976). The first pain center was founded in Seattle at the University of Washington by John Bonica, M.D., in 1960. At present, there are numerous such clinics around the country.

Types of Pain-Clinic Programs

There are two main types of pain-clinic programs (Fordyce & Steger, 1979). One type, the "pure" or **operant pain-treatment program,** is oriented primarily toward extinguishing pain behavior, and it is based on principles of reinforcement. The pure or operant pain-management program maintains that pain behavior becomes chronic for reasons other than organic pain. Chronic pain can be understood in terms of the conditioning of factors in the environment that provide reinforcement for pain behavior. Intrapsychic factors, such as personality or motivation, are typically not treated in this approach. Consequently, counterconditioning or behavior-change principles are the focal approaches to reduce the association between pain behavior and the factors that maintain it.

The second type of pain-management program is termed "mixed," because it treats both pain behavior and pain itself through a variety of medical management techniques. The **mixed pain-treatment program** maintains that the pain experience is a combination of or-

ganic pain, operant pain, and an overlay of psychological distress that may have resulted from coping with long-term pain. Consequently, according to this approach, it is important to understand the personality and motivational factors involved in the experience of pain as well as factors in the environment that may maintain pain behavior. This viewpoint contends that counterconditioning or behavior-change principles are only one of many strategies that may be brought to bear on the management of pain. It holds that, although treatment must focus on pain behavior, it must also treat the pain itself and deal with any personality changes that may have occurred in response to pain.

Pure or Operant Pain-Treatment Programs An example of a pure or operant pain-treatment program is that at the University of Washington (Fordyce, 1976). It is a 4- to 8-week inpatient program designed to increase activity level and sociability and to decrease the use of pain medication. In this program, reinforcements such as attention, rest, or medication are contingent on adaptive rather than pain-related behaviors. Thus, the program attempts to extinguish pain behavior such as complaining, social withdrawal, limitation of physical activity, or requesting pain medication and to reinforce such behaviors as social interaction, physical activity, and expressions that pain has been relieved. To eliminate the addictive component of pain, painkillers are often administered on a noncontingent basis. That is, instead of being administered when the patient complains of pain, thus constituting a reinforcement for pain, the painkillers may instead be given at regular time intervals regardless of the patient's reports of pain. In this way, the positive reinforcer of narcotics becomes independent of pain.

In order to attack the patient's dependence on painkillers, several measures are taken. First, the time intervals between administration of painkillers are gradually increased, so that the patient must go for longer periods of time without medication. Second, the strength of pain medications may be gradually reduced over the duration of treatment. One way of so doing is by using the "pain cocktail," a mixture of pain medications and a cherry-flavored syrup, in which the dosage of pain medication is gradually reduced. Ideally, the patient is drinking only the syrup by the end of treatment (Fordyce, 1976).

Operant programs are not appropriate for all chronic pain patients; consequently, these programs often carefully screen participants before accepting them. For example, patients who stand to benefit financially from their pain, as though settlement of a lawsuit, would be poor candidates for such a program. Moreover, patients who do not seem to have a substantial amount of operant pain, such as a stoic cancer patient with advancing disease, would also probably receive little benefit from an operant program. However, for the right kinds of patients, operant programs can be highly successful (Fordyce, 1976; Fordyce, Shelton, & Dundore, 1982).

Mixed Pain-Treatment Programs   How is a mixed program similar to and different from a pure or operant program of pain management? Like the operant program, the first phase of a mixed pain-treatment program involves developing a profile of the chronic pain patient's pain and pain behavior. According to this approach, the practitioner must first know the history of the pain (when it started and how it has changed) and how it has been treated in the past (with what painkillers, surgeries, and individual therapies). Techniques like the McGill Pain Questionnaire may be used to develop a profile of the pain's sensory and affective qualities as well as its intensity. In the mixed program, personality tests like the MMPI may also be employed to develop a profile of the patient and thus to help under-

stand the pain more clearly. For example, is the pain complicated by pre-pain characterological disorders? Is it a mixed pain that includes some functional or operant pain as well? The nature of the patient's pain behaviors is also explored. As we noted at the beginning of this chapter, it can be useful for the practitioner to understand what changes pain patients have had to make in their lives. For example, the depression and humiliation that can result from loss of a job may require treatment. If patients have withdrawn from physical and social activities, efforts to revive their involvement in these activities may be required along with the primary therapies to treat the pain.

Once the diagnosis phase is completed, a program of intervention is developed that is individually tailored for each patient. If deemed appropriate, efforts to extinguish operant pain are undertaken, similar to those used in operant programs. Measures to reduce the patient's reliance on painkillers are also introduced. Unlike the operant program, the mixed program typically introduces a combination of techniques to attack the organic pain itself. Biofeedback or some other kind of relaxation technique is commonly employed. Nerve-blocking agents may be used. Some kind of sensory therapy involving counter-irritation may also be used, as well as physical therapy including exercise, massages, and baths. Sometimes individual or group psychotherapy is also made available to deal with the depression that chronic pain can cause and to help deal with social issues, such as family problems or unemployment, that may have resulted from prolonged pain. Once a patient's pain control regimen has been developed, it is monitored closely. Therapies that work are maintained; those that seem not to work are modified or eliminated.

At this point, treatment enters a new phase. The goal of this phase is to shift the control over the patient's regimen from medical personnel to the patient (Fordyce, 1976).

Whatever therapies are employed must now be implemented by the patient. Biofeedback training should now be to the point where the machine is no longer needed. A sensory control technique that requires medical management may be replaced by a self-administered technique such as a dorsal column stimulator. And, most important, the patient learns psychological self-control techniques such as relaxation, distraction, or rethinking the meaning of the pain.

A relatively new consideration in the development of pain programs involves attempting to match individual difference characteristics of the pain patient with particular kinds of techniques. For example, Kleinke and Spangler (1988) found that whether or not a pain regimen's outcome was successful depended on the patients' coping styles and whether or not their pain treatments matched their coping styles. For example, patients experiencing high levels of pain preferred treatments involving ice or heat, whereas patients experiencing somewhat lower levels of pain had a preference for physical therapy, social work, lectures, or relaxation. By matching treatments to patients' particular coping styles, one may maximize the benefits of treatment.

Pain center programs appear to be successful in helping to control chronic pain. For example, one program evaluated patients with low back or head and neck pain in a four-weekend program consisting of medication reduction, physical therapy, behavioral group therapy, self-monitoring, contingency contracting, and biofeedback/relaxation training. As long as a year later, the patients showed reduced need for medication; improvement in physical functioning, employment status, and health behaviors; and fewer reports of pain (Cinciripini & Floreen, 1982; see also Fordyce, Roberts, & Sternbach, 1985). Pain clinics extend a promise of relief to thousands of sufferers who previously had little to aid them. They offer not only the possibility of a pain-free existence but also the dignity that comes from self-control of pain management and freedom from a life of addiction and depression.

Pain: A Postscript

The management of pain represents a major medical and psychological advance of the last several decades. For many years, pain was managed exclusively through drugs when it was managed at all. Indeed, in some cases, pain was considered to be something that must be withstood as an unpleasant but necessary side effect of disease or treatment. Until recently, myths persisted that infants and animals do not experience pain, and so both infants and animals were often subjected to severe physical trauma through surgery and other interventions without benefit of pain management techniques.

Some maintain that acute pain remains chronically undertreated (Angell, 1982; Liebeskind & Melzack, 1987; Marks & Sachar, 1973). Health care professionals have become so concerned with the possibility of addiction to opiates and their potential side effects, such as the depression of respiration, that they may underrecommend pain medication for patients (Morgan & Puder, 1989). Even when pain medication is made available, as to those recovering from surgery, usually the administration of medication remains under medical personnel's rather than patients' control, in the fear that patients may overmedicate. Yet one study has found that when patients were able to control their own analgesia postsurgically, they actually used less medication than when health care personnel administered pain medication (Morgan & Puder, 1989).

In many respects, the gradually changing climate that favors effective pain management is a manifestation of increased concern with quality of life, and, as such, pain management represents one of the better examples of the impact of a biopsychosocial model on medical practice. That is, increasingly, practitioners are realizing that pain is a problem that must be managed and treated appropriately in its own right if patients are to achieve a high quality of life.

THE PLACEBO AS HEALER

A Historical Perspective

In the early days of medicine, there were few drugs or treatments that gave any real physical benefit (Shapiro, 1960). As a consequence, patients were treated with a variety of bizarre, largely ineffective therapies. Egyptian patients were medicated with "lizard's blood, crocodile dung, the teeth of a swine, the hoof of an ass, putrid meat, and fly specks" (Findley, 1953), concoctions that were not only ineffective but dangerous. If the patient did not succumb to the disease, he or she had a good chance of dying from the treatment. Medical treatments of the Middle Ages were somewhat less lethal, but not much more effective. These European patients were treated with ground-up "unicorn's horn" (actually ground ivory), bezoor stones (supposedly a "crystallized tear from the eye of a deer bitten by a snake" but actually an animal gallstone or other intestinal piece), theriac (made from ground-up snake and between thirty-seven and sixty-three equally exotic ingredients), and, for healing wounds, powdered Egyptian mummy (Shapiro, 1960).

In some cases, a clear, if somewhat naive logic was present in these treatments. For example, consumption (tuberculosis of the lung, which is marked by short-windedness) was treated with ground-up fox lung, because the fox is a long-winded animal. As late as the seventeenth and eighteenth centuries, patients were subject to bloodletting, freezing, and repeatedly induced vomiting to bring about a cure (Shapiro, 1960).

Such accounts make it seem miraculous that anyone survived these early medical treat-

This sixteenth-century woodcut shows the preparation of theriac, a supposed antidote to poison. If theriac was a successful treatment, it was entirely due to the placebo effect.

ments. But people did; moreover, they often seemed to get relief from these peculiar and largely ineffective remedies. Physicians have, for centuries, been objects of great veneration and respect, and this was no less true when few remedies were actually effective. To what can one attribute the fair level of success that these treatments provided and the widespread faith in the effectiveness of physicians? The most likely answer is that these are examples of the tremendous power of the **placebo effect**. Moreover, placebo effects continue to be powerful today, even though medicine now boasts a large number of truly effective treatments.

What Is a Placebo?

A **placebo** is "any medical procedure that produces an effect in a patient because of its therapeutic intent and not its specific nature, whether chemical or physical" (Liberman,

1962, p. 761). Any medical procedure, ranging from drugs to surgery or psychotherapy, can have a placebo effect. The role of placebos in reducing pain and discomfort is substantial. Many patients who ingest useless substances or who undergo useless procedures find that, as a result, their symptoms disappear and their health improves.

Moreover, placebo effects extend well beyond the beneficial results of ineffective substances. Much of the effectiveness of active treatments that produce real cures on their own can be attributed to a placebo component. For example, in one study (Beecher, 1959), patients complaining of pain were injected with either morphine or a placebo. Although morphine was substantially more effective in reducing pain than was the placebo, the placebo was a successful painkiller in 35% of the cases. Another study demonstrated that morphine loses as much as 25% of its effectiveness in reducing pain when patients do not know they have been injected with a painkiller and are therefore not preset to show the drug's effects. In summarizing placebo effects, Shapiro (1964) stated:

> Placebos can be more powerful than, and reverse the action of, potent active drugs.... The incidence of placebo reactions approaches 100% in some studies. Placebos can have profound effects on organic illnesses, including incurable malignancies.... Placebos can mimic the effects usually thought to be the exclusive property of active drugs. (p. 74)

How does a placebo work? The placebo effect is not necessarily psychological, as stereotypes would have us believe. That is, people do not get better simply because they *think* they are going to get better. The placebo response is a complex, psychologically mediated chain of events that often has physiological effects. For example, if the placebo reduces anxiety, bodily resources like epinephrine have a chance to replenish themselves. In addition, there is now some evidence that placebos may

work in part by stimulating the release of endorphins (Levine, Gordon, & Fields, 1978). However, the evidence on this point is still mixed. Box 11.5 describes a case of a successful placebo effect with a cancer patient.

Placebos can be more or less successful. In some cases a placebo may produce an apparently successful recovery, whereas in other cases it may have no effect. What factors determine when placebos will be most effective? Placebos achieve their effects for a variety of reasons, each of which merits consideration: practitioner behavior and beliefs, patient characteristics, aspects of the patient-practitioner relationship, situational factors, characteristics of the placebo itself, and social norms. We will discuss each in turn.

Practitioner Behavior and Placebo Effects

The effectiveness of a placebo varies depending on how a practitioner interacts with the patient and how much he or she seems to believe in the curative powers of the treatment being offered. Practitioners who exude warmth, confidence, and empathy get stronger placebo effects than do more remote and formal practitioners. When the practitioner radiates competence and provides reassurance to the patient that the condition will improve, placebo effects are also strengthened. Taking time with patients and not rushing them strengthens placebo effects (Liberman, 1962; Shapiro, 1964).

The practitioner's faith in the treatment is another influence on the effectiveness of placebos. Signs of doubt or skepticism may be communicated subtly, even nonverbally, to a patient, and these signs will reduce the placebo effect. Even clearly effective drugs lose much of their effectiveness when practitioners express doubt over their effectiveness. In one study, for example, patients were given chlorpromazine (a tranquilizer commonly used with psychiatric patients) by a practitio-

---

Box 11.5
Cancer and the Placebo Effect

A dramatic example of the efficacy of the placebo effect is provided by description of a cancer patient, Mr. Wright. The patient thought he was being given injections of a controversial drug, Krebiozen, about which his physician was highly enthusiastic. In fact, knowing that Krebiozen was not an effective treatment, the physician gave Mr. Wright daily injections of nothing but fresh water. The effects were astonishing.

> Tumor masses melted. Chest fluid vanished. He became ambulatory and even went back to flying again. At this time he was certainly the picture of health. The water injections were continued since they worked such

wonders. He then remained symptom-free for over two months. At this time the final AMA announcement appeared in the press—"Nationwide Tests Show Krebiozen to Be a Worthless Drug in Treatment of Cancer."

Within a few days of this report, Mr. Wright was readmitted to the hospital in extremis; his faith was now gone, his last hope vanished, and he succumbed in less than two days.

(Klopfer, 1959, p. 339)

---

ner who either expressed great confidence in its effectiveness or who voiced some doubt as to its ability to reduce symptoms. This usually effective drug's actual effectiveness dropped from 77 to 10% when the practitioner was doubtful regarding its effectiveness (Feldman, 1956; see also Volgyesi, 1954).

Patient Characteristics and Placebo Effects

Although there is no **placebo-prone personality,** some types of patients show stronger placebo effects than others. People who have a high need for approval (Liberman, 1962), who have low self-esteem, who are externally oriented toward their environment, and who are persuasible in other contexts show somewhat stronger placebo effects. People who are high in self-esteem, low in need for approval, and internally oriented show less strong placebo effects (Shapiro, 1964).

Anxiety also seems to facilitate the placebo effect. The reason for this fact, however, seems to lie less in the significance of anxiety as a personality factor than in the fact that anxiety produces a large number of physical symptoms; these include distractibility, racing heart, sweaty palms, nervousness, and difficulty sleeping. When a placebo is administered, anxiety may well be reduced and this overlay of anxiety-related symptoms may disappear (Shapiro, 1964; see also Sharpe, Smith, & Barbre, 1985).

Despite the fact that some personality differences do predict placebo effects, these findings must be set in the context of many dozens of studies that have failed to show effects. Sex, age, hypochondriasis (the tendency to report physical symptoms), dependency, and general neuroticism do not discriminate those who show placebo effects from those who do not. Likewise, results on personality tests such as the MMPI or the Rorschach (inkblot) test do not predict who will show a placebo response (for reviews, see Liberman, 1962; Shapiro, 1964).

Patient-Practitioner Communication and Placebo Effects

As noted in Chapter 10, good communication between practitioner and patient is essential if patients are to follow through successfully on their prescribed treatment regimens. This point is no less true for placebo responses. For patients to show a placebo response, they must understand what the treatment is supposed to do and what they need to do. Hence, in predicting the strength of a placebo response, one must ask: Does the physician have the patient's undivided attention? Does the patient know what to do and when to do it? Does the patient know what the medication is supposed to do, and does he or she believe it? When the practitioner-patient relationship is based on effective communication, placebo effects will be stronger.

Another aspect of the patient-practitioner relationship that enhances the placebo effect is the symbolic value the placebo may have for the patient. When patients seek medical treatment, it is because they want someone, an expert, to tell them what is wrong and what to do about it. When a disorder is diagnosed and a treatment regimen is prescribed, however vacuous or ineffective, the patient has tangible evidence for the belief that the practitioner knows what is wrong and that he or she has done something about it (Shapiro, 1964).

Situational Determinants of Placebo Effects

Particular aspects of the placebo itself and the setting in which it is administered all influence the strength of the placebo response. A setting that has all the trappings of medical formality (medications, machines, uniformed personnel) will induce stronger placebo effects than will a less formal setting. If all the attendants radiate as much faith in the treatment as the physician, placebo effects will be heightened. The shape, size, color, taste, and quantity of the placebo influences its effectiveness: The more a drug seems like medicine, the more effective it will be (Shapiro, 1964). Thus, for example, foul-tasting, peculiar-looking little pills that are taken in precise dosage ("take two" as opposed to "take two or three") and that are taken at prescribed intervals will show stronger placebo effects than will good-tasting, candylike pills with dosage levels and intervals that are only roughly indicated ("take one any time you feel discomfort"). Similarly, treatment regimens that seem "medical" and include precise instructions, medications, and the like will produce stronger placebo effects than will regimens that do not seem very "medical"; for example, exercise prescriptions or dietary restrictions show weaker placebo effects than do pills and other medications.

Social Norms and Placebo Effects

The placebo effect is facilitated by norms that surround treatment regimens—that is, the expected way in which treatment will be enacted. Drug taking is clearly a normative behavior (see Sharpe et al., 1985). Americans spend more than $100 billion each year on drugs. One study of a random sample of nonhospitalized adults found that 55% of them had taken some medication within the previous 24 hours and 40% of them took some form of medicine on a regular basis (Dunnell & Cartwright, 1972). Another study of hospitalized patients found that the average patient was receiving fourteen drugs simultaneously; one patient had received thirty-two drugs, and no patient had had less than six (Dunlop, 1970, cited in Rachman & Phillips, 1978).

Moreover, a large number of people are killed or seriously injured by overzealous drug taking. It has been estimated that between 30,000 and 160,000 deaths and as many as

300,000 serious side effects result each year from improperly prescribed and unnecessary drugs (Brody, 1976). Yet the drug-taking epidemic continues unabated. Clearly, there is enormous faith in medications, and the psychological if not the physical benefits can be quite substantial. Thus, placebos have their effects in part because people believe that drugs work and because they have a great deal of experience in drug taking.

Equally important is the fact that most people have no experience that disconfirms their drug taking. If one is ill, takes a drug, and subsequently gets better, as most of us do most of the time, one does not in reality know exactly what caused this result: A drug may be responsible; the disease may have run its course; one's mood may have picked up, altering the body's physiological balance and making it no longer receptive to an invader. Probably a combination of factors is at work. Regardless of the actual cause of success, the patient acting as his own naive physician will probably attribute success to whatever drug he or she took, however erroneous that conclusion may be. Thus, the drug will appear to be effective even if it is not. In most cases, then, people are not aware that drug-taking behavior is ineffective. If a person takes vitamins and stays healthy, he or she attributes it to the vitamins. If a person falls ill, takes a useless drug, and gets better, he or she will likely attribute it to the drug. If a person takes a drug and fails to get better immediately, he or she may assume that it is the wrong one and switch medications until the "right one" is found. Thus, drug taking continues, based on personal experience that often suggests, erroneously, that it has been successful.

Generalizability of Placebo Effects

How general are placebo effects? They may achieve their greatest success in the absence of tissue damage. It is estimated that about 65% or more of symptoms presented to physicians are emotional in origin (Shapiro, 1978). For example, anxiety may produce diarrhea, sleeplessness, upset stomach, and shaking. Depression may produce loss of energy and fatigue. Any sign of action and caring by the physician can have a direct impact on the emotional state of a patient, thereby clearing up emotionally caused symptoms.

However, placebo effects are not reserved to inert drugs and pills. As noted earlier, virtually any medical procedure can have placebo effects (Miller, 1989). For example, many surgical patients show improvement simply as a function of having had surgery and not as a result of the actual procedure employed (Beecher, 1959). Psychiatry and clinical psychology also show placebo effects; some patients feel better simply knowing that a psychiatrist or psychologist has found a cause for their problems, even if this cause is not the real one. The knowledge that someone is analyzing the problem and coming up with interpretations may be as helpful or more helpful than the therapeutic procedure itself or the content of a therapist's interpretations. Every specialty within medicine has placebo effects (Shapiro, 1964).

In summary, the efficacy of the placebo should not be thought of as either a medical trick or a purely psychological response on the part of the patient. Placebo effects merit respect. The placebo achieves success in the absence of truly effective therapy. It increases the efficacy of a therapy that has only modest effects of its own. It reduces substantial pain and discomfort. It is the foundation of most of early medicine's effectiveness, and it continues to account for many of medicine's effects today. Its continued success should be encouraged (Miller, 1989).

The Placebo as a Methodological Tool

The placebo response is so powerful that no drug can be marketed in the United States unless it has been evaluated against a placebo.

The standard method for so doing is termed a **double-blind experiment.** In such a test, a researcher gives half a group of patients a real drug that is supposed to cure a disease or alleviate symptoms; the other half receives a placebo. The procedure is called double-blind because neither the researcher nor the patient knows whether the patient received the drug or the placebo; both are "blind" to the procedure. Once the effectiveness of the treatment has been measured, the researcher looks in the coded records to see which treatment the patient got. The difference between the effectiveness of the drug and the effectiveness of the placebo is considered to be a measure of the drug's actual effectiveness. Comparison of a drug against a placebo is essential for accurate measurement of a drug's actual success. Drugs may look four or five times more successful than they really are if there is no effort to evaluate them against a placebo (Miller, 1989; Shapiro, 1964).

SUMMARY

1. Pain is a significant aspect of illness because it is the symptom of chief concern to patients and leads them to seek medical attention. Yet pain is often considered of secondary importance to practitioners, producing the potential for miscommunication.

2. Pain is intensely subjective and, consequently, has been difficult to study. There are several "clinical" pains (causalgia, neuralgia, phantom limb) for which no underlying neurological basis can be found. Pain is heavily influenced by the context in which it is experienced and by the cultural origins of its sufferer.

3. To objectify the experience of pain, pain researchers have developed questionnaires that assess its dimensions, as well as pain threshold techniques, tourniquet techniques, and methods to assess pain behaviors.

4. The gate theory of pain was an important advance in specifying the physiology of pain. A-delta fibers conduct fast, sharp, localized pain; C-fibers conduct slow, aching, burning, and long-lasting pain; and higher-order brain processes influence the experience of pain through the central control mechanism.

5. Recent neurochemical advances in the understanding of pain center around the discovery of endogenous opioids that regulate the pain experience.

6. Acute pain is short-term and specific to a particular injury or disease, whereas chronic pain does not decrease with treatment and time. More than 65 million Americans suffer from chronic pain, which may lead them to disrupt their entire lives in an effort to cure it. Chronic pain is complicated to treat, because it has a functional and psychological overlay, in that the patient has often been unintentionally reinforced for being in pain.

7. Efforts to find a pain-prone personality have been largely unsuccessful. Nonetheless, personality profiles based on the MMPI do suggest that chronic pain patients have elevated scores on the so-called neurotic triad.

8. Pharmacological (e.g., morphine), surgical, and sensory stimulation techniques (e.g., dorsal column stimulator) have been the mainstays of pain control. Increas-

ingly, treatments with psychological components, including biofeedback, relaxation, hypnosis, distraction, and guided imagery, have been added to the pain control arsenal. Although all these techniques show at least some success, the exact mechanisms by which they do so are often still elusive. Most recently, cognitive-behavioral techniques, involving the addition of self-control technologies to biofeedback or relaxation, have been used successfully in the treatment of pain.

9. Chronic pain is often now managed in pain clinics oriented toward managing the pain, extinguishing pain behavior, and reestablishing a viable lifestyle. These programs employ a mix of technologies in an effort to develop an individualized treatment program for each patient.

10. A placebo is any medical procedure that produces an effect in a patient because of its therapeutic intent and not its actual nature. Virtually every medical treatment shows some degree of placebo effect.

11. Placebo effects are enhanced when the physician shows faith in a treatment, the patient is pre-set to believe it will work, these expectations are successfully communicated, and the trappings of medical treatment are in place.

12. Placebos are also a useful methodological tool in evaluating drugs and other treatments.

KEY TERMS

acupuncture
acute pain
biofeedback
causalgia
central control mechanism
chronic pain
clinical pains
counterirritation
distraction
double-blind experiment
endogenous opioids
gate theory
guided imagery
hypnosis

mixed pain-treatment program
neuralgia
operant pain
operant pain-treatment program
pain behaviors
pain centers
pain control
pain-prone personality
pain threshold
phantom limb pain
placebo
placebo effect
placebo-prone personality

PART 5

MANAGEMENT OF CHRONIC AND TERMINAL ILLNESS

12

MANAGEMENT OF CHRONIC ILLNESS

At any given time, 50% of the population has some chronic condition that requires medical management. These conditions range from relatively mild ones, such as partial hearing losses, to severe and life-threatening disorders, such as cancer, coronary artery disease, and diabetes. For example, arthritis in its various forms afflicts 37 million Americans (Lawrence et al., 1989); 5 million Americans have had cancer (American Cancer Society, 1989); diabetes afflicts 11 million people (American Diabetes Association, 1986); more than 2 million have sustained a stroke (American Heart Association, 1988); and almost 5 million people have a history of heart attack and/or chest pain (American Heart Association, 1988). Nearly 29 million people have hypertension (U.S. Bureau of the Census, 1987), and estimates of the prevalence of high blood pressure run as high as 60 million (American Heart Association, 1988).

A perhaps more startling statistic is that most of us will eventually develop at least one chronic disability or disease that may ultimately be the cause of our death. Thus, there is every probability that, at some time, each of us will hear a physician tell us that our condition is chronic and cannot be cured; it can only be managed. We may be told, for instance, that loss of a sense, such as sight or hearing, is permanent; that a limb will be permanently disabled; that our activities must be curtailed because of risk of a heart attack; or that we must have immediate treatment for cancer.

In this chapter, we consider some of the problems posed by chronic illness. We begin with a consideration of quality of life and how it may be assessed. Next, we consider patients' psychological reactions to chronic illness, including denial, anxiety, and depression. We next consider patients' spontaneous efforts to deal with the problems and emotional reactions posed by illness, their individual coping efforts, and their illness-related cognitions. We then turn to the specific issues of rehabilitation posed by chronic illness, including physical management, vocational problems, and problems in social functioning, and suggest some general strategies for comprehensive rehabilitation programs. Individual efforts are not always successful in solving the problems associated with chronic illness, and therefore they can usefully be supplemented with interventions effectively targeted to particular problems experienced by the chronically ill. The last section focuses on some of the interventions that have been developed or that might be developed for dealing with the stress of chronic illness.

QUALITY OF LIFE

Until relatively recently, **quality of life** was not considered an issue of psychological importance for the chronically ill. For many years, it was measured solely in terms of length of survival and signs of presence of disease, with virtually no consideration of the psychosocial consequences of illness and treatments (Aaronson, Calais de Silva et al., 1986; Aaronson, van Dam, Polak, & Zittoun, 1986; Gore, 1988; Hollandsworth, 1988). In fact, an examination of the research literature on quality of life reveals that medical citations to works that assess morbidity and mortality outnumber psychological citations more than ten to one (Taylor & Aspinwall, 1990).

Until the last decade, quality of life was assessed mainly by physicians and drew primarily on the medical criteria just described. However, physician ratings are only weakly related to patients' or to relatives' assessments of quality of life. In fact, one notable study of hypertension (Jachuck, Brierley, Jachuck, & Willcox, 1982) found that although 100% of the physicians reported their patients' quality of life had improved following hypertensive medication, only half the patients agreed and virtually none of the relatives did. Thus, quality of life can be a heavily subjective experience.

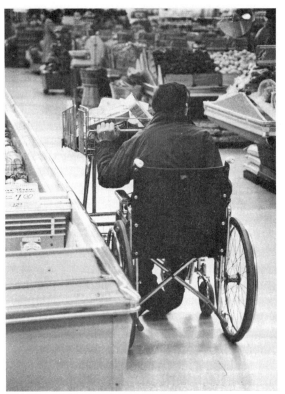

In the last decade, researchers have begun to consider psychosocial functioning as an important aspect of quality of life among the chronically ill.

In recent years, the measurement of quality of life has shifted away from objective indicators of physical functioning to a consideration of psychological, social, and economic factors. There is increasing recognition that quality of life is a subjective experience that can best be rated by the patient. Unfortunately, agreement on the need to assess subjective quality of life has not produced conceptual or methodological agreement on how to do so. Recently, research has produced a few reliable and valid measures. One that enjoys wide use, the Sickness Impact Profile (SIP) (Bergner, Bobbitt, Carter, & Gilson, 1981), assesses functioning in three categories: physical, psychosocial, and other (sleep, eating, work, recreation). SIP scores appear to be responsive to changes in chronic diseases and treatments. Another widely used measure, the Index of Activities of Daily Living (ADL) (Katz, Ford, Moscowitz, Jackson, & Jaffee, 1983), yields independent scores for six functions (bathing, dressing, toileting, mobility, continence, and feeding). In addition, there are quality of life measures that have been developed for specific diseases, such as cancer (e.g., the Cancer Inventory of Problem Situations [Schag, Heinrich, Aadland, & Ganz, 1990] and the Karnovsky Performance Scale [see Grieco & Long, 1984]).

Why do we need to study quality of life among the chronically ill? There are several reasons. First, quality of life measures can help pinpoint which particular problems are likely to emerge for patients with particular diseases. Such a measure, for example, might indicate that sexual functioning is a problem for patients with certain kinds of cancer but that depression is a more common problem for patients with other kinds. Such information would be helpful in anticipating the kinds of interventions that might be required (Schag & Heinrich, 1986). Second, it is important to assess the impact of treatments on quality of life. For example, in the cancer literature, one needs to assess whether treatment is more harmful than the disease itself if it has disappointing survival rates and produces adverse side effects (Aaronson, Calais de Silva et al., 1986). Quality of life measures have made it possible to assess the impact of unpleasant therapies such as antihypertensive regimens and to identify some of the determinants of poor adherence. Quality of life information can also be used to compare therapies. For example, if two therapies produce approximately equivalent survival rates but one lowers quality of life substantially, this information can be integrated into decisions about what treatments to use with patients (see Taylor & Aspinwall, 1990, for a review). Finally, quality of life information is useful

for policy-level decision making. It can be important to treatment decisions to maximize the likelihood of long-term survival with the highest quality of life possible. Quality of life information can also enable health policymakers to compare the impact of different chronic diseases on health care costs and to assess the cost-effectiveness of different interventions, given quality of life information (Kaplan, 1985; Kaplan & Bush, 1982; Lubeck & Yelin, 1988).

Despite the fact that there is still ambiguity over how best to assess quality of life, such measures have been useful in pinpointing some of the areas that require particular attention and rehabilitation efforts following the diagnosis of a chronic disease.

EMOTIONAL RESPONSES TO CHRONIC ILLNESS

Many chronic diseases affect all aspects of a patient's life (Burish & Bradley, 1983; Taylor & Aspinwall, 1990). As in acute diseases, there is a temporary first phase when all life activities are disrupted. Chronic disease, however, also carries the need to make intermittent or permanent changes in physical, vocational, and social activities. In addition, sufferers from chronic illnesses must integrate the patient role into their lives psychologically if they are to adapt to their disorders.

Immediately after a chronic disease is diagnosed, patients are often in a state of crisis marked by physical, social, and psychological disequilibrium (Moos, 1977). They find that their habitual ways of coping with problems do not work, at least temporarily; therefore, they may experience intense feelings of disorganization, anxiety, fear, and other emotions (Taylor & Aspinwall, 1990).

Eventually the crisis phase of chronic illness passes, and patients begin to develop a sense of how the chronic illness will alter their lives and can be integrated into them. At this point, more long-term difficulties that require ongoing rehabilitative attention may set in. These problems and issues fall into the general categories of physical rehabilitation, vocational rehabilitation, social rehabilitation, and psychological issues. In the next sections, we first consider emotional issues and coping with chronic illness, and then turn to more general issues of rehabilitation.

Denial

The diagnosis of a chronic illness often comes as a tremendous shock to a patient. Within a few minutes, everything suddenly changes. A life course that had rolled out into the indefinite future may now seem to disappear. Every plan—ranging from what to do tomorrow to what to do for the rest of one's life—may have to change. The initial diagnosis may be so disorienting and uprooting that it is impossible for the patient to fathom immediately the depth of change that will be required. The patient may be as likely to wonder who will stop at the dry cleaner's tomorrow as to wonder whether or not there is any point in returning to school, moving to a new home, having another child, or going on a long-planned trip. It may be days or even weeks before these questions fall into place, arranging themselves in a proper hierarchy. Each moment may bring to mind another plan that must now be modified. The sheer quantity of issues to be considered may make the patient appear unresponsive, preoccupied by the wrong problems, and unable to understand the scope and limits of the treatments that will be required. The emotions most likely to accompany these initial feelings of disorientation are denial and anxiety. Later, depression may become more prominent.

Denial is a defense mechanism by which people avoid the implications of an illness. They may act as if the illness were not severe, that it will shortly go away, or that it will have few long-term implications. In extreme cases, the patient may even deny that he or she has the illness, despite having been given clear information about the diagnosis. Denial, then, is the subconscious blocking out of the full realization of the reality and implications of the disorder. Denial is a common reaction to chronic illness that has been observed among heart patients (Krantz & Deckel, 1983), stroke patients (Diller, 1976), and cancer patients (Katz, Weiner, Gallagher, & Hellman, 1970; Levine & Zigler, 1975; Meyerowitz, 1983).

At one time, denial was thought to be a primitive and ultimately unsuccessful defense mechanism that only temporarily masked anxiety. Now, however, researchers are recognizing its potential benefits as well as its liabilities. When is denial beneficial and when is it not? The answer appears to depend on the phase of illness in which the patient exhibits denial and the criterion the researcher is using to measure adjustment (Meyerowitz, 1983).

Denial of the implications of symptoms may act as a deterrent to seeking proper treatment (Hackett & Cassem, 1973; Katz et al., 1970; Matt, Sementilli, & Burish, 1988; Meyerowitz, 1983; Wool & Greenberg, 1986). The role of denial in delay behavior has been well documented for both cancer and coronary heart disease. However, immediately after the diagnosis of illness, during the acute phase when the patient is often in the hospital, denial can serve a protective function. It can keep the patient from having to come to terms with the full range of problems posed by the illness at a time when he or she may be least able to do so (Hackett & Cassem, 1973; Lazarus, 1983; Mastrovito, 1974; Polivy, 1977). One study of patients with myocardial infarction (MI) found that high initial denial was associated with fewer days in intensive care and fewer signs of cardiac dysfunction (Levine et al., 1988). As testimony to its stress-reducing value, denial can be associated with lower levels of corticosteroids (Katz et al., 1970). Denial can also reduce the experience of unpleasant symptoms and side effects of treatment (Ward, Leventhal, & Love, 1988). Denial can mask the terror associated with a chronic disease, until the patient is more accustomed to the diagnosis and better able to sort out realistically the restrictions that it will pose.

During the rehabilitative phase of illness, denial may have adverse effects if it interferes with the ability to take in necessary information that will be part of the patient's treatment or self-management program. For example, in the study that found initial benefits of denial among MI patients (Levine et al., 1988) in the year after discharge, high deniers showed poorer adaptation to disease. The high deniers were less adherent to their treatment regimen and required more days of rehospitalization, suggesting that denial was interfering with successful monitoring of the long-term nature of their condition. When patients must be actively involved with a treatment regimen— that is, when they must be able to assess their activities realistically and comply with medications and other changes in their lifestyle—denial can be an impediment (Garrity et al., 1976). However, among patients who do not have to follow prescribed treatment regimens, denial can help protect them psychologically, making it possible for them to resume their normal lives quickly (e.g., Hackett & Cassem, 1973; Meyerowitz, 1983; O'Malley, Koocher, Foster, & Slavin, 1979).

Overall, then, denial may be useful in helping patients control their emotional reactions to illness, but it may interfere with their ability to monitor their conditions, to take the initiative in seeking treatment, or to follow through when they must act as responsible co-managers of their illness.

Anxiety

Immediately after the diagnosis of a chronic illness, **anxiety** is also a common response. Many patients become overwhelmed by the specter of potential changes in their lives and by the prospect of death. Anxiety may also arise intermittently throughout the disease process (Derogatis, 1983; Hughes, 1987; Popkin, Callies, Lentz, Colon, & Sutherland, 1988). For example, every twinge of chest pain will likely raise concern over another heart attack for the patient recuperating from a myocardial infarction. Many cancer patients are constantly vigilant to changes in their physical condition, and each minor ache or pain may prompt fear, being seen as a possible sign of a recurrence.

Anxiety is a problem not only because it is intrinsically distressing, but because it can interfere with good functioning. Highly anxious patients cope poorly with radiotherapy for cancer (Graydon, 1988) and may benefit less from behavioral treatments designed to reduce distress associated with chemotherapy (Carey & Burish, 1985); anxious diabetic patients report poor glucose control and increased symptoms (Lustman, 1988); and anxious MI patients are less likely to return to work on schedule (Maeland & Havick, 1987b).

Several kinds of events reliably increase anxiety. Anxiety is highest when people are waiting for test results, receiving diagnoses, awaiting invasive medical procedures, experiencing adverse side effects of treatment (e.g., Anderson, Karlsson, Anderson, & Tewfik, 1984), anticipating substantial lifestyle alterations, feeling dependent on health professionals, and experiencing concern over recurrence (Scott, 1983; Welch-McCaffrey, 1985; see Taylor & Aspinwall, 1990, for a review). As these findings imply, uncertainty about one's situation and treatments explains a substantial amount of the emotional distress and anxiety that patients experience (Christman et al., 1988). Scheduled visits to the physician to check the course of a chronic illness such as cancer or coronary artery disease often produce intense fear just before the visit, as the patient wonders whether the diagnostic procedures will reveal a worsening course. While anxiety directly attributable to the disease may decrease over time, anxiety about possible complications, its implications for the future, and its impact on work and leisure time activities may actually increase with time (Christman et al., 1988; Thompson, Webster, Cordle, & Sutton, 1987). Thus, both assessment and treatment of anxiety may be needed, an issue we will turn to later in this chapter.

Depression

Depression is a common and often debilitating reaction to chronic illness. Up to one-third of all medical inpatients with chronic disease report at least moderate symptoms of depression, while up to one-quarter suffer from severe depression (Rodin & Voshart, 1986; see also Massie & Holland, 1987; Popkin, Callies et al., 1988; Primeau, 1988, for stroke). Although there is evidence that depression may occur somewhat later in the adjustment process than denial or severe anxiety, it can also occur intermittently throughout adjustment to chronic disease. It has been documented for stroke patients, cancer patients, and heart patients, as well as those suffering from many other chronic diseases (Taylor & Aspinwall, 1990, for a review).

Depression may be a delayed reaction to chronic illness because it often takes time for patients to understand the full implications of their condition. During the acute phase and immediately after diagnosis, the patient may be hospitalized, be awaiting treatments, and have other immediate decisions to make. There may be little time to reflect fully on the implications of the illness. Once the acute phase of chronic illness has ended and patients have been discharged from the hospital and returned home, the full implications of the disorder may begin to sink in. For example, a stroke patient comments on his discharge from the hospital:

> That was a glorious day. I started planning all the things I could do with the incredible amount of free time I was going to have, chores I had put off, museums and galleries to

visit, friends I had wanted to meet for lunch. It was not until several days later that I realized I simply couldn't do them. I didn't have the mental or physical strength, and I sank into a depression. (Dahlberg, 1977, p. 121)

Similarly, the full meaning of the term "cancer" may now hit the cancer patient. Cardiac patients who were instructed to change their daily activities may find that it was easy to agree in principle but less easy to change their behavior.

Depression is important not only for the distress it produces but also because it may have an impact on long-term rehabilitation and recovery (Primeau, 1988). Depressed stroke patients have longer hospital stays and are more often discharged from the hospital to nursing homes than other patients (Cushman, 1986). They show less motivation to undergo rehabilitation (Thompson, Sobolew-Shubin, Graham, & Janigian, 1989), they are less likely to maintain gains during rehabilitation (Sinyor et al., 1986), and they are less likely to restore their quality of life to pre-stroke levels (Niemi, Laaksonen, Kotila, & Waltimo, 1988). Rheumatoid arthritis patients with high levels of depression are more likely to catastrophize, overgeneralize, and negatively interpret their situation (Smith, Peck, Milano, & Ward, 1988). MI patients who were depressed while in the hospital are less likely to return to work one year later and are more likely to be rehospitalized (Stern, Pascale, & Ackerman, 1977). Depression over illness and treatment has also been linked to suicide among the chronically ill and the elderly. For example, one out of every six long-term dialysis patients over the age of 60 stops treatment, resulting in death (Neu & Kjellstrand, 1986). The rate of suicide among cancer patients is approximately one-and-a-half times greater than that among non-ill adults (Louhivouri & Hakama, 1979; Marshall, Burnett, & Brasure, 1983), and the rate of suicide among men with AIDS has been estimated at more than thirty-six times the national rate for their age group (Mazurk et al., 1988). Unlike anxiety, which ebbs and flows during the course of a chronic illness, depression can be a long-term reaction. For many illnesses, it may last a year or more following onset of the disorder (Lustman, Griffith, & Clouse, 1988; Meyerowitz, 1980; Robinson & Price, 1982; Stern et al., 1977).

Assessment of depression in the chronically ill can be problematic. Many of the physical signs of depression, such as fatigue, sleeplessness, or weight loss, may also be symptoms of disease or side effects of a treatment. If depressive symptoms are attributed to aspects of illness or treatment, their significance may be less apparent and, consequently, depression may go untreated (Hughes, 1987; Massie & Holland, 1987; Rodin & Voshart, 1986). For example, one study of depressed stroke patients found that only one-third had been referred for treatment of the depression (Lustman & Harper, 1987; Sinyor et al., 1986). These issues are especially problematic for illnesses such as cancer, stroke, diabetes, AIDS, and epilepsy that can affect brain functioning (House, 1987; Massie & Holland, 1987; Primeau, 1988).

Another barrier to properly diagnosing and treating depression among the chronically ill is that there are no standards for diagnosing depression in these populations (Rodin & Voshart, 1986). Depression often goes untreated because many people believe that one is *supposed* to feel depressed after a diagnosis of chronic illness (Greer, 1987; Koenig, Meador, Cohen, & Blazer, 1988; Robinson, 1986). If those caring for the chronically ill believe that depression is to be expected as an understandable result of the disease, patients may be denied useful psychological interventions.

What are the factors that predict depression among the chronically ill? While this issue will no doubt receive further research attention, several factors have already been identified. In general, depression increases with the severity of the illness (e.g., Cassileth et al., 1985; Dakof & Mendelsohn, 1986; Koenig et al., 1988). Extent of pain and disability, in particular, predict depression (e.g., Hawley & Wolfe, 1988; Turner & Noh, 1988). There may be a reciprocal sustaining relationship between physical impairment and depression. That is, being disabled contributes to high levels of depression, which, in turn, increases the extent of disability experienced. Some suggest that depression is most severe shortly after diagnosis, whereas others suggest that it becomes worse once chronically ill patients recognize the full extent of their disabilities (Baum, 1982; Hughes & Lee, 1987).

Depression is also associated with factors other than those specifically related to the disease. Chronically ill patients who are experiencing other negative life events, social stress, and lack of social support experience higher levels of depression (Bukberg, Penman, & Holland, 1984; Murphy, Creed, & Jayson, 1988; Thompson, Sobolew-Shubin et al., 1989). There is some evidence that physical factors may predict depression somewhat better earlier in chronic illness, whereas psychological factors may better explain depression later on. For example, one study of stroke patients found that the location of stroke damage predicted depression in the first 6 months, whereas later on, cognitive impairment, physical disability, social support, changes in body image and self-esteem, and the adverse mood effects of therapeutic drugs were stronger determinants of depression (Morris & Raphael, 1987).

The fact that so many patients go through intense emotional responses to chronic illness, coupled with the fact that some responses appear to be more common early on while others occur later, has led some researchers to hypothesize that there may be a series of stages through which patients pass in adjusting to chronic illness (e.g., Falek & Britton, 1974; for a review, see Silver & Wortman, 1980). However, efforts to delineate a set of stages have proven unsuccessful (Silver & Wortman, 1980). For example, although denial appears to be common early, it may also be intermittent throughout the adjustment process. Likewise, although depression often does not appear until after the acute phase of illness is over, some acutely ill patients are depressed as well. Emotional reactions do not occur in any predetermined sequence, and they may recur throughout the adjustment process.

Thus, a more useful approach to studying emotional reactions to chronic illness is to try to understand what emotions occur, when they are most likely to occur, what factors are most likely to give rise to them, and whether or not they impede or promote the goals of recovery and treatment management. Moreover, preliminary work suggesting that certain positive emotions, such as joy (Levy, Lee, Bagley, & Lippman, 1988) and optimism (Scheier, Weintraub, & Carver, 1986) serve a beneficial function in recovery from illness, imply that we should attend to the potential protective effects of positive emotions, as we are attempting to understand the factors that lead to adverse emotional reactions. With such understanding, appropriate psychological interventions can be developed to enable patients to manage their emotional responses.

To summarize, patients exhibit a wide variety of emotional reactions to chronic illness. Common responses are denial, anxiety, and depression. These emotional reactions are entirely normal; indeed, lack of emotional response to a severe threat can be associated with poor recovery (Cohen & Lazarus, 1979). On the other hand, although emotional responses to chronic illness are expected, they are not always beneficial to treatment goals. Denial can protect a patient from anxiety, but it can also interfere with seeking treatment for symptoms and complying with treatment goals. Although some depression is expected, long-term depression can be associated with poor recovery. Thus, emotional adjustments to chronic illness merit careful monitoring during the recovery and adjustment process.

COPING WITH CHRONIC DISEASE

Despite the fact that most patients with chronic disease suffer at least some adverse psychological reactions as a result of the disease, most do not seek formal or informal psychological treatment for these symptoms. Instead, they draw on their internal and social resources for solving problems and alleviating psychological distress.

Coping Strategies and Chronic Illness

In many ways, coping with a diagnosis of a chronic illness is like coping with any other severely stressful event. The appraisal of a chronic disease as threatening or challenging leads to the initiation of coping efforts (see Chapter 8; Lazarus & Folkman, 1984a, 1984b). Relatively few investigations have looked systematically at coping strategies among chronically ill patient groups. In one of the few such studies (Dunkel-Schetter et al., 1988), cancer patients were asked to identify the aspect of their cancer they found to be the most stressful. The results indicated that fear and uncertainty about the future was most common (41%), followed by limitations in physical abilities, appearance, and lifestyle (24%), followed by pain management (12%). Patients were then asked to indicate the coping strategies they had used to deal with these problems. The five identified strategies were *Social Support/Direct Problem-Solving* (e.g., ''I talked to someone to find out more about the situation''), *Distancing* (e.g., ''I didn't let it get to me''), *Positive Focus* (e.g., ''I came out of the experience better than I went in''), *Cognitive Escape/Avoidance* (e.g., ''I wished that the situation would go away''), and *Behavioral Escape/ Avoidance* (e.g., efforts to avoid the situation by eating, drinking, or sleeping) (cf. Felton & Revenson, 1984; Felton, Revenson, & Hinrichsen, 1984; Moos & Tsu, 1977).

The strategies identified in this investigation are not substantially different from those employed to deal with other stressful events (see Chapter 8). One notable point is that the coping strategies identified have few direct action factors like planful problem-solving or confrontative coping. This may be because certain chronic illnesses, in this case, cancer, raise so many uncontrollable concerns that coping strategies employed favor distraction, avoidance, and emotional regulation. One might find that in coping with the aftermath of myocardial infarction, for example, confrontative coping and planful problem-solving would emerge, as people attempt to modify their health habits and lifestyle with the hope of reducing subsequent risk.

A logical next step in the analysis of coping strategies employed by patients managing the stresses of chronic disease is to identify which strategies facilitate psychological adjustment. There is some evidence that, like coping with other stressful events, the use of avoidant coping is associated with increased psychological distress, and thereby may be a risk factor for adverse responses to illness (e.g., Felton et al., 1984). Similarly, Weisman & Worden (1976–77) found poor adjustment to be associated with efforts to forget the disease, fatalism, passive acceptance, withdrawal from others, blaming of others, and self-blame. Avoidant coping has also been related to poor glycemic control among insulin-dependent diabetics (Frenzel, McCaul, Glasgow, & Schafer, 1988). Correspondingly, research has found lower psychological distress to be associated with positive, confrontative responses to stress; with a high internal locus of control (Burgess, Morris, & Pettingale, 1988); and with beliefs that one can personally direct control over an illness (Affleck, Tennen, Pfeiffer, & Fifield, 1987; Jenkins & Pargament, 1988; Taylor, Lichtman, & Wood, 1984a; see also Hilton, 1989).

There is also some evidence that those who employ multiple coping strategies may cope better with the stress of chronic disease than those who engage in a predominant coping style. A rationale for this finding is that coping strategies may be most effective when they are matched to the particular problem for which they are most useful. If people have available to them multiple coping strategies, they may be more able to engage in this matching process than those who have a predominant coping style (see Collins, Taylor, & Skokan, in press). However, this point requires further research (see Chapter 8).

An answer to the question, which coping strategies work best for managing chronic illness?, then, is complex, depending on which aspects of the stressful event an individual is coping with at a particular point in time in the adjustment process. Despite this caution, a general conclusion is that active coping efforts seem to be more consistently associated with good adjustment than avoidant strategies, so long as there are aspects of the illness amenable to active coping efforts.

Patients' Beliefs About Chronic Illness

If patients are to adjust to chronic illness satisfactorily, they must somehow integrate their illness into their lives. Virtually all chronic illnesses require some alteration in activities and some degree of management. For example, diabetic patients must control their diet and perhaps take daily injections of insulin. Cancer patients, even those whose cancer is not currently active, must remain vigilant to possible signs of recurrence. Both stroke and heart patients must make substantial alterations in their daily activities as a consequence of their physical and psychological impairments. Patients who are unable to incorporate chronic illness into their lives may be poor patients. They may fail to follow their treatment regimen and be nonadherent. They may engage in denial and thus be improperly attuned to possible signs of recurrent or worsening disease. They may engage in foolhardy behaviors that pose a risk to their health, or they may fail to practice important health behaviors that could reduce the possibility of recurrence or other complicating illnesses. Thus, developing a realistic sense of one's illness, the restrictions it imposes, and the regimen that is required is an important process of coping with chronic illness.

Beliefs About the Nature of the Illness

One of the problems that often arises in adjustment to chronic illness is that patients adopt an inappropriate model for their disorder, most notably, the acute model (see Chapter 9). For example, hypertensive patients may believe incorrectly that if they feel all right it is no longer necessary to take medication since their hypertension must be under control. Breast cancer patients may believe incorrectly that their vulnerability to subsequent episodes of breast cancer is not very high; accordingly, they may fail to monitor their condition closely (Nerenz, 1979; Ringler, 1981). Thus, it is often important for practitioners and others involved in health care to probe patients' comprehension of their illness to check for significant gaps and misunderstandings in their knowledge that may interfere with self-management.

Beliefs About the Cause of the Illness

Of the many beliefs that patients hold about their illness, two may relate to long-term adjustment: perceptions of the cause of their illness and beliefs about whether or not the illness can be controlled. A large number of researchers have noted that people suffering from both acute and chronic illness develop theories about where their illnesses came from (Affleck, Tennen, Croog, & Levine, 1987; Bard & Dyk, 1956; Lowery, Jacobsen, & McCauley, 1987; Meyerowitz, 1980; Schain, 1976). Patients' theories about the origins of chronic illness include stress, physical injury, disease-causing bacteria, and God's will. Of perhaps greater significance is where patients ultimately place the blame for their illness. Do they blame themselves, another person, the environment, or a quirk of fate?

Self-blame for chronic illness is widespread. Patients frequently perceive themselves as having brought on their illnesses through their own actions. In some cases, these perceptions are to some extent correct. Poor health habits such as smoking, improper diet, or lack of exercise can produce heart disease, stroke, and cancer. In other cases, the patient's self-blame may be ill placed, as when a disease is caused by a genetically based defect. What are the consequences of self-blame?

Unfortunately, a definitive answer to this question is not available. Some researchers (Abrams & Finesinger, 1953; Kiecolt-Glaser & Williams, 1987; see also Krantz & Deckel, 1983) suggest that self-blame can lead to guilt, self-recrimination, or depression. Self-blaming patients may be poorly adjusted to their illness because they focus on things they could have or should have done to prevent it. On the other hand, other research suggests that self-blame may be adaptive. One study (Bulman & Wortman, 1977) found that patients with spinal cord injuries (paraplegics and quadriplegics) who took responsibility for the circumstances that produced their injuries were better adjusted. Perceiving the cause as self-generated may represent an effort to assume control over the disorder; such feelings can be adaptive in coping with and coming to terms with the disorder (Bulman & Wortman, 1977). However, still other research suggests that self-blame may be neither maladaptive nor adaptive (Miller & Porter, 1983; Schulz & Decker, 1985; Silver, 1982; Taylor, Lichtman, & Wood, 1984a; Turnquist, Harvey, & Anderson, 1988; see also Timko & Janoff-Bulman, 1985). It may be that self-blame may be adaptive under certain conditions but not others.

What are the effects of other attributions for illness? So far, no relationships have been found between attributions to luck and adjustment or between attributions to environmental factors and adjustment (Affleck, Tennen, Pfeiffer, & Fifield, 1987; Bulman & Wortman, 1977; Taylor, Lichtman, & Wood, 1984a;

Turnquist et al., 1988). However, research suggests that blaming another person for one's disorder is maladaptive (Affleck, Tennen, Pfeiffer, and Fifield, 1987; Bulman & Wortman, 1977; Taylor, Lichtman, & Wood, 1984a). For example, some patients believe that their disorders were brought about by stress caused by family members, ex-spouses, or colleagues at work. Blame of this other person or persons may be tied to unresolved hostility, which can interfere with efforts to adapt to the disease.

Beliefs About the Controllability of the Illness Researchers have also examined whether patients who believe they can control their illness are better off than those who do not see their illness as under their control. Patients develop a number of control-related beliefs with respect to chronic illness. They may believe, as do many cancer patients, that they can prevent a recurrence of the disease through good health habits or even sheer force of will. They may believe that by complying with treatments and physicians' recommendations, they achieve vicarious control over their illness. They may believe that they personally have direct control over the illness through self-administration of a treatment regimen. These control-related beliefs may or may not be accurate. For example, if patients do maintain a treatment regimen, they may very well be exercising real control over the possibility of recurrence or exacerbation of their illness. On the other hand, the belief that one's illness can be controlled through a positive attitude may or may not be correct.

Recall from earlier chapters that feelings of psychological control may be beneficial for good mental functioning. Individuals who feel they have at least some control over their lives may be better adjusted than those who feel they have no control in their lives. As noted in Chapter 9, interventions that attempt to instill feelings of control are often highly successful in promoting good adjustment to illness and treatment and in reducing physiological and emotional distress caused by illness and its treatment. Do feelings of control have the same beneficial effects when they are self-generated by patients attempting to deal with chronic illness?

What evidence there is suggests that belief in control is generally adaptive. For example, cancer patients who believed that they had control over their illness were better adjusted to their cancer than patients without such beliefs (Taylor, Lichtman, & Wood, 1984a; see also Marks, Richardson, Graham, & Levine, 1986). Similar results have been reported for patients suffering from rheumatoid arthritis (Affleck, Tennen, Pfeiffer, and Fifield, 1987), patients with AIDS (Taylor, Helgeson, Reed, & Skokan, in press), spinal cord–injured patients (Schulz & Decker, 1985), and post–myocardial infarction patients (Michela, 1982). Several studies that have attempted to enhance feelings of control in cardiac patients also suggest beneficial effects (Cromwell, Butterfield, Brayfield, & Curry, 1977; Klein, Kliner, Zipes, Troyer, & Wallace, 1968; see also Krantz & Schulz, 1980). However, one study (Burish et al., 1984) found that, among chemotherapy patients, those with a high external locus of control orientation had lower levels of physiological arousal and reported less negative affect in response to chemotherapy. The authors interpreted these findings to suggest that in medical situations in which little personal control is possible, an external health locus of control may be more helpful. Thus, the benefits and liabilities of control and the circumstances under which control is advantageous or not requires additional research. Box 12.1 describes a study dealing with these issues.

In summary, then, patients' beliefs about their illnesses represent an exciting new avenue for research investigation. These cognitions can lead to better health behavior, higher rates of compliance, and ultimately better quality of life. Yet it is clear, too, that some

Box 12.1
Causal Attributions, Feelings of Control, and Recovery from Myocardial Infarction

Studies of patients recovering from myocardial infarction (MI) illustrate the importance of both causal attributions for illness and feelings of control (Bar-On, 1986, 1987). In one study, patients were asked (1) why they thought they had a heart attack and (2) what health measures they planned to take as a result of the attack. Several months later, their work and social functioning were measured.

Patients who attributed the cause of their MI to modifiable factors under their personal control (such as stress or smoking) were more likely to have initiated active plans for their recovery (for example, changing jobs or starting exercise) and to have returned to work and resumed other activities. In contrast, patients who attributed the MI to external factors beyond their personal control (bad luck or fate, for instance) were less likely to have generated active plans for recovery or to have returned to work; they were also less likely to have resumed other activities (cf. Affleck, Tennen, Croog, & Levine, 1987).

Bar-On (Bar-On & Dreman, 1987) also looked at the attributions that spouses made for the heart attack. Under most circumstances,

when spouses made the same attributions for the heart attack as their mates, short-term rehabilitation progressed well. However, if the patient's attributions were to external, uncontrollable factors or if the patient denied the infarct, long-term rehabilitation progressed better when spouses' attributions were incongruent with patients' attributions. In this case, the spouse's attribution to internal and controllable factors may have counteracted the patient's tendency toward denial, nudging him in the direction of becoming more aware of the things he could do to reduce his risk for a second heart attack.

These results strongly suggest that when illness conditions are perceived as being modifiable and under one's personal control, the process of recovery from chronic disease is enhanced (cf. Affleck, Tennen, Croog, & Levine 1987). Moreover, these kinds of perceptions may be even more important predictors of successful rehabilitation than more traditional physical cues employed by physicians in predicting rehabilitation (Bar-On, 1986, 1987).

cognitions may be maladaptive, and these require continued research investigation.

REHABILITATION AND CHRONIC ILLNESS

In the previous section, we saw how patients often make spontaneous efforts to cope with their illness and develop the cognitions that

will enable them to address the problems illness raises. However, chronic illness also raises a number of highly specific problem-solving tasks that patients encounter on the road to recovery. These include physical problems associated with the illness, vocational problems, problems with social relationships, and personal issues concerned with chronic illness. We next turn to these issues.

Physical Problems Associated with Chronic Illness

Physical rehabilitation of chronically ill or disabled patients typically involves several goals: to help them use their bodies as much as possible; to enable them to sense changes in the environment and within themselves so that they can make the appropriate physical accommodations; to learn new physical and management skills; to pursue a necessary treatment regimen; and to learn how to control the expenditure of energy. Patients must develop the capacity to read bodily signs that signal the onset of a crisis, know how to respond to that crisis, and maintain whatever treatment regimen is required (Gartner & Reissman, 1976).

Physical problems associated with chronic illness may be divided into two general types. First, problems arise as a result of the illness itself, and, second, problems emerge as a consequence of the treatment. Physical problems produced by the disease itself range widely. They may include physical pain, such as the chest pain experienced by heart patients or the discomfort associated with cancer. Breathlessness associated with respiratory disorders, metabolic changes associated with diabetes and cancer, and motor difficulties produced by spinal cord injuries also represent important physical problems. Cognitive impairments may occur, such as the language, memory, and learning deficits associated with stroke. In many cases, then, the physical consequences of a chronic disorder place severe restrictions on an individual's life.

Treatment of primary symptoms and the underlying disease also produce difficulties in physical functioning. Cancer patients receiving chemotherapy must often face nausea, vomiting, hair loss, skin discoloration, and other unattractive and uncomfortable bodily changes. Those cancer patients who receive radiation therapy must cope with burning of the skin, gastrointestinal problems, and other

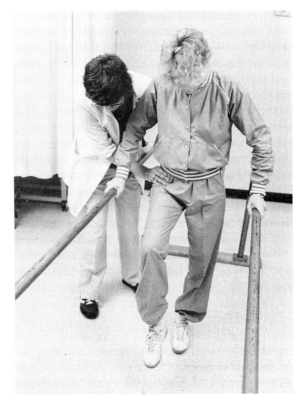

Physical rehabilitation of the chronically ill concentrates on enabling them to use their bodies as much as possible, to learn new physical management skills if necessary, and to pursue an integrated treatment regimen.

temporary disturbances (Nail, King, & Johnson, 1986). Chemotherapy can produce changes in taste acuity and taste aversions, sometimes leading to anorexia (Grunberg, 1985). Medications for hypertension can produce a variety of unpleasant side effects including drowsiness, weight gain, and impotence. Sexual dysfunction as a result of illness and/or treatment may occur for those with hypertension, myocardial infarction, and cancer (e.g., Andersen, Andersen, & deProsse, 1989a, 1989b). Restrictions on the activities of patients who have had a heart attack—including dietary changes, elimination of smoking, and exercise requirements—may pervade their entire way of life. In many cases, patients may feel that, in terms of the discomfort and restrictions they impose, the treatments are as bad as the disease.

Comprehensive physical rehabilitation must take into account all these illness- and treatment-related factors. Patients may need a pain management program for the alleviation of discomfort. They may require prosthetic devices, such as an artificial limb after amputation related to diabetes. They may need training in the use of adaptive devices; for example, the patient with multiple sclerosis or a spinal cord injury may need to learn how to use crutches or a wheelchair. Certain cancer patients may elect cosmetic surgery, such as the implantation of a synthetic breast after a mastectomy or the insertion of a synthetic jaw after head and neck surgery.

In addition, a program for identifying and controlling factors that may contribute to recurrence or that may exacerbate the disease may be required. For example, stress has been increasingly implicated in the downward course of such diseases as diabetes (see Turk & Speers, 1983), heart disease (see Krantz, 1980), hypertension (Harrell, 1980), multiple sclerosis (Mei-Tal, Meyerowitz, & Engel, 1970), and cancer (Visintainer, Volpicelli, & Seligman, 1982). As a consequence, stress management programs are increasingly incorporated into the physical treatment regimens of many chronically ill patients.

Physical rehabilitation must also tackle the very complex and serious problem of adherence to a long-term medical regimen. Cognitive and behavioral interventions may be needed to help a patient comply with a medication regimen. For example, diabetic patients may be trained in how to recognize and treat symptoms as they change. Unfortunately, the features that characterize the treatment regimens of chronically ill patients are those typically associated with high levels of nonadherence. As will be recalled from Chapter 10, treatment regimens that must be followed

over a long time period, that are complex, that interfere with other desirable life activities, and that involve lifestyle change show very low levels of adherence (Turk & Meichenbaum, 1989). Often these treatment regimens require patients to perform many different and complex activities carried out on a daily basis over the long term that bear uncertain relationships to treatment outcomes. Many diabetic patients, for example, must take daily injections of insulin, monitor their blood glucose fluctuations, strictly control their diet, engage in prescribed exercise, and attempt to manage stress effectively. Similarly, patients diagnosed with coronary artery disease must often stop smoking, lose weight, exercise, lower their cholesterol, and modify their volume of food intake simultaneously. Yet the relation of these changes to risk once a diagnosis of coronary heart disease has already been made may be weak (e.g., Blumenthal & Emery, 1988; Siegel, Grady, Browner, & Hulley, 1988; Stegman, Miller, Hageman, & Irby, 1987). Moreover, adherence to one aspect of a complex regimen does not necessarily predict adherence to other aspects of the regimen (Orme & Binik, 1989), underscoring the fact that health behaviors are often only minimally related to each other even in chronic illness.

One factor that contributes heavily to high rates of nonadherence among chronically ill patients is the side effects of treatment that adversely affect quality of life (Love, Leventhal, Easterling, & Nerenz, 1989; Williams, Croog, Levine, Testa, & Sudilovsky, 1987). This is a particular problem in the management of hypertension. However, other treatments show high rates of adherence despite attendant negative side effects such as adherence to chemotherapy (Taylor, Lichtman, & Wood, 1984b; see also Richardson et al., 1987). Factors that favor high rates of adherence to these treatments include the fact that they are regarded as critical to ongoing health and potentially life-saving. The features of chemotherapy, for instance, match treatments that show high rates of adherence more generally: It is administered in the physician's office by a nurse using a syringe, and adherence is actively monitored—patients are called, and appointments are rescheduled when they are missed. Treatments that seem medical and that can be easily monitored may, then, be adhered to, despite their adverse side effects.

Creative nonadherence is also high in chronically ill patients, as discussed in Chapter 10. Creative nonadherence is not always problematic. Because chronically ill patients know their disease extremely well, often their intuitions about how to adhere to treatment are correct. Diabetics who are well-versed in types of insulin and their effects, for example, may better control their blood glucose level than a physician less familiar with a particular case. Nonetheless, creative nonadherence can also lead to mistakes, as well as to the use of questionable or unorthodox treatments that are not only useless but physically taxing, expensive, or even harmful (Cassileth, 1989).

At least half of all patients with chronic disorders do not adhere as fully as possible to their treatment regimens (Taylor & Aspinwall, 1990). In Chapter 4, we discussed a variety of behavioral methods of improving compliance, and in Chapter 10, we considered many of the psychosocial determinants of nonadherence. The methodologies suggested in these two chapters can be employed in physical rehabilitation programs to provide some guidelines for improving adherence. For example, by tailoring medical treatment programs to the individual patient (for example, by tying the medication schedule to habitual events in a patient's life), one can increase adherence (Epstein & Cluss, 1982). Reinforcement techniques have proven somewhat successful, although self-monitoring of medication and symptoms have not always been effective (Epstein & Cluss, 1982). Relapse prevention techniques are especially important with the chronically ill, given the long-term nature of

necessary behavior change and the multiple behaviors that must often be altered simultaneously (Brownell, Marlatt et al. 1986; Marlatt & Gordon, 1985). Further research will elucidate other successful and unsuccessful techniques.

Self-efficacy beliefs are also an important determinant of adherence among the chronically ill (Strecher, DeVellis, Becker, & Rosenstock, 1986). In a study of hypertension (Stanton, 1987), high expectations for controlling one's health and knowledge of the treatment regimen were significant predictors of adherence, along with social support. In a study of adherence among insulin-dependent diabetics, self-efficacy expectations were also a strong predictor of adherence (Grossman, Brink, & Hauser, 1987; McCaul, Glasgow, & Schafer, 1987).

As is true of adherence generally, lack of knowledge can predict nonadherence among the chronically ill. Insufficient information about glucose utilization, energy metabolism, and the metabolic control of insulin and diabetes has been related to poor adherence among diabetic patients (Hauenstein, Schiller, & Hurley, 1987). Interventions that more fully explain the rationale for and details of complex treatment regimens may improve adherence (Wilson & Pratt, 1987; Wood, 1989). These kinds of educational efforts have improved adherence among cancer patients' compliance with pain medication (Rimer et al., 1987) and reporting of chest pain in patients at risk for myocardial infarction (Rawles & Haite, 1988). For a more extended discussion of factors that promote adherence to treatment regimens, the reader is referred back to Chapters 4 and 10. Overall, tackling the adherence issue early on in treatment and building in methods for improving adherence may help combat this formidable problem.

To summarize, then, effective physical rehabilitation requires consideration of all of the illness- and treatment-related factors that may influence a patient's level of functioning. It requires pooling the skills of many specialists, including physical therapists and health psychologists, to make sure that the most effective methods of meeting treatment goals are employed. An eclectic collection of physical, behavioral, and cognitive interventions may be needed to develop the ideal physical management program that is individually tailored to each patient to control disabilities and treatment-related side effects, as well as to promote adherence. Such a program should be initiated early in the patient's recovery, with provision for alterations in training as illness and treatment goals change. A crucial element in all such programs is the patient's active role as a co-manager in rehabilitation. That is, rehabilitation is not something that is done to a patient. It is done with his or her full cooperation and participation.

Unfortunately, this programmatic approach to physical rehabilitation is currently the exception rather than the rule. Although patients' physical rehabilitative needs do receive attention in the recovery process, the kind of organized, concerted effort proposed here is rare. Perhaps more important is the fact that the crucial educational, behavioral, and cognitive training efforts that enlist the patient's cooperative co-management are even more rare. Rather, patients may be given medications and rehabilitation aids without sufficient consideration of motivational problems or educational gaps that can prevent them from profiting maximally from these rehabilitative efforts. Comprehensive physical rehabilitation, including the use of demonstrably effective behavioral and cognitive technologies, is a goal toward which we are currently striving. The health psychologist is a key figure in this emerging effort.

Vocational Issues in Chronic Illness

Many chronic illnesses create problems for patients' vocational activities and work status. Some patients may need to restrict or change their work activities. The stroke patient may

be unable to resume work activities because he or she has difficulty with language. The cardiac patient may be required to reduce stress at work because his or her high-pressure work environment may have contributed to the development of the disorder. The cancer patient may have difficulty managing interactions with others who have unrealistic fears about cancer.

Some of these changes will require vocational retraining. For example, a salesman who previously conducted his work from his car but is now newly diagnosed as an epileptic may need to switch to a job where he can use the telephone instead. Patients with spinal cord injuries who previously held positions that required physical activity will need to acquire skills that will let them work from a seated position. This kind of creative job change is illustrated in Box 12.2.

Many chronically ill patients, such as heart patients, cancer patients, and AIDS patients face job discrimination (e.g., Davidson, 1983). When these patients return to their jobs, they may be moved into less demanding positions and they may be promoted less quickly because the organization believes that they have a poor prognosis and are not worth the investment of time and resources required to train them for more advanced work.

Because of these potential problems, potential job difficulties that the patient may encounter should be assessed early in the recovery process. Job counseling, retraining programs, and advice on how to avoid or combat discrimination can then be initiated promptly. Box 12.3 focuses on some health care professionals who deal with such problems.

Finally, a difficulty related to the vocational problems of chronic illness concerns the enormous financial impact that chronic illness can often take on the patient and the family. Many people are not covered by insurance sufficient to meet their needs. In other cases, patients who must cut back on their work or stop working altogether will lose their insurance

---

Box 12.2
Epilepsy and the Need for a Job Redesign

In infancy, Colin S. developed spinal meningitis, and, although he survived, the physician expressed some concern that permanent brain damage might have occurred. Colin was a normal student in school until approximately age 11, when he began to have spells of blanking out. At first, his parents interpreted these as a form of acting out, the beginnings of adolescence. However, as it became clear that Colin had no recollection of these periods and became angry when questioned about them, they took him to a physician for evaluation. After a lengthy workup, the doctor concluded that Colin was suffering from epilepsy.

Shortly thereafter, Colin's blackouts (known as petit mal seizures) became more severe and frequent; then, soon after that, he began to have grand mal seizures, involving severe and frightening convulsions. The doctors tried several medications and eventually were able to control the seizures successfully. Indeed, so successful was the medication that Colin eventually was able to obtain a driver's license, having gone 5 years without a seizure. After he completed high school and college, Colin chose social work as his career and became a caseworker. His livelihood depended on his ability to drive because his schedule involved visiting many clients for in-home evaluations. Moreover, Colin had married, and he and his wife together were supporting two young children.

In his early 30s, Colin began to experience seizures again. At first, he and his wife tried to pretend that nothing was wrong and that it soon would be better, but quite quickly they knew that the epilepsy was no longer under successful control. This represented a major threat to the family's income because Colin would no longer be able to keep his job as a caseworker. Moreover, his ability to find reemployment could also become compromised by the revocation of his driver's license. With considerable anxiety, Colin went to see his employer, the director of the social service unit.

After considerable consultation, the higher-ups in Colin's unit determined that he had been a valuable worker and they did not want to lose him. They therefore redesigned his position so that he could have a desk job that did not require the use of a car. By shifting his responsibilities away from monitoring cases to the initial evaluation of cases, and by giving him an office instead of a set of addresses to visit, Colin was able to use the skills he had worked so hard to develop in very similar ways. In this case, then, Colin's employer responded sympathetically and effectively to the compromises that needed to be made in his job responsibilities. Unfortunately, not all victims of epilepsy or other chronic diseases are as fortunate as Colin turned out to be.

---

coverage, adding enormous financial costs to the burden of their care. In this sense, then, the threat to vocation that chronic illness sometimes raises can be a double whammy: The chronically ill patient's capacity to earn income may be reduced and, simultaneously, the benefits that would have helped shoulder the costs of care may be cut back.

Social Interaction Problems in Chronic Illness

The development of a chronic illness can create problems of social interaction for the patient. After diagnosis, patients may have trouble reestablishing normal social relations. They may complain of others' pity or rejection

Box 12.3
Who Works with the Chronically Ill?

A variety of professionals are involved in the rehabilitation of the chronically ill. Many of these are physicians, nurses, and psychologists. However, a number of other individuals with technical training in particular aspects of rehabilitation also work with the chronically ill. Some of them are profiled here.

Physical Therapists

About 61,000 people work as licensed physical therapists in hospitals, nursing homes, rehabilitation centers, and schools for disabled children (U.S. Department of Labor, 1988–1989). **Physical therapists** help people with muscle, nerve, joint, or bone diseases or injuries to overcome their disabilities. They work primarily with accident victims, disabled children, and older people.

Physical therapists are responsible for the administration and interpretation of tests of muscle strength, motor development, functional capacity, and respiratory and circulatory efficiency. On the basis of these tests, they then develop individualized treatment programs. They are responsible for the ongoing evaluation and modification of these programs in light of treatment goals.

The purpose of physical rehabilitation is to increase strength, endurance, coordination, and range of motion. In addition, physical therapists help patients learn to use adaptive devices and become accustomed to new ways of performing old tasks. Physical therapists also use heat, cold, light, water, electricity, or massage to relieve pain and improve muscle function. Physical therapists typically receive their training at the college undergraduate level or in a graduate master's program, both of which lead to required licensure.

Occupational Therapists

Occupational therapists work with emotionally and physically handicapped individuals to determine skills, abilities, and limitations. They evaluate the existing capacities of patients, help them set goals, and plan a therapy program with other members of a rehabilitation team to try to build on and expand these skills. They help patients to regain physical, mental, or emotional stability; to relearn daily routines such as eating, dressing, writing, or using a telephone; and to prepare for employment. They plan and direct educational, vocational, and recreational activities to help patients become more self-sufficient.

Patients who are seen by occupational therapists range from children involved in craft programs to adults who must learn new skills such as typing or the use of power tools. In addition, occupational therapists teach creative tasks such as painting, weaving, leather working, and other craft activities that help relax patients, provide a creative outlet, and offer some variety to those who are institutionalized. Occupational therapists usually obtain their training through one of the occupational therapy training programs located in universities and colleges around the country and, like physical therapists, they must be formally licensed.

Dietitians

Dietitians are also involved in management of the chronically ill. Although many **dietitians** are employed as administrators and apply the principles of nutrition and food management to meal planning for hospitals, universities, schools, and other institutions, others work directly with the chronically ill to help plan and manage special diets. In particular, these clinical dietitians assess the dietetic needs of patients, supervise the service of meals, instruct patients in the requirements and importance of their diets, and suggest ways of maintaining adherence to diets after discharge. Thus, dietitians work particularly with diabetics and with patients who have disorders related to obesity, since both groups need to control their caloric intake and types of foods. Dieticians are also formally licensed and must complete a 4-year degree program and clinically supervised training to be registered with the American Dietetic Association.

Social Workers

Social workers help individuals and families deal with their problems by providing therapy, making referrals to other services, and engaging in more general social planning. Medical social workers are trained to help patients and their families with the many social problems that can develop during illness and recovery. These social workers work in hospitals, clinics, community mental health centers, rehabilitation centers, and nursing homes. A medical social worker might help a patient understand illness more fully and deal with emotional responses to illness, such as depression or anxiety, through therapy. A

social worker can also help a desperate patient and family find the resources they need to solve their problems. For example, if the patient has been a homemaker—responsible for cooking, cleaning, and coordinating family activities—the social worker can help the family get temporary help to fulfill these tasks. If the patient will need vocational retraining after a chronic illness, the social worker can help find or even develop the facilities to make this possible. If the patient needs to transfer from the hospital into a special facility such as a nursing home or rehabilitation center, the social worker is often the one who will make these arrangements.

In 1986, approximately 365,000 individuals were employed as social workers; two-thirds of them worked for the local, state, or federal government. The minimum qualification for social work is a bachelor's degree, but for many positions a master's degree (M.S.W.) is required. About 370 colleges nationwide offer accredited undergraduate programs in social work and about 100 colleges and universities offer graduate programs (U.S. Department of Labor, 1988–1989).

---

but behave in ways that inadvertently elicit these behaviors. They may withdraw from other people altogether or may thrust themselves into social activities before they are ready.

Patients are not solely responsible for whatever difficulties and awkwardness arise in interaction with others. Friends and relatives may have problems of their own adjusting to the patients' altered condition. Extensive studies of reactions to the disabled reveal that they tend to elicit ambivalence. Acquaintances may

give verbal signs of warmth and affection while nonverbally conveying revulsion or rejection through their gestures, contacts, and body postures (Kleck, Ono, & Hastorf, 1966; Wortman & Dunkel-Schetter, 1979). The newly disabled patient has difficulty interpreting and reacting to these behaviors.

In attempting to understand the adverse changes in social relationships after chronic disease, Wortman and Dunkel-Schetter (1979) offered the following account. They suggested that the stressful event of a chronic disease, such as cancer, creates fear and aversion in family and friends but a simultaneous awareness of the need to provide social support. These tensions may produce a variety of adverse outcomes, such as physically avoiding the patient, avoiding open communication about the disease, minimizing its impact, or demonstrating forced cheerfulness. Under such conditions, effective social support may be reduced (Chrvala & Weiner, 1989; Stephens, Kinney, Norris, & Ritchie, 1987). Distant relationships with friends and acquaintances appear to be more adversely affected in these ways than intimate relations (Dakof & Taylor, 1990; Fitzpatrick, Newman, Lamb, & Shipley, 1988). However, intimate others may themselves be distressed by the loved one's condition (e.g., Tompkins, Schulz, & Rau, 1988) and be ineffective in providing support because their own support needs are unmet (e.g., Cassileth et al., 1985; Ell, Nishimoto, Mantell, & Hamovitch, 1988; Hobfoll & Lerman, 1989; Michela, 1987; Zarski, West, DePompei, & Hall, 1989). Additional research identifying some of the factors that may interfere with the availability or use of social support is clearly needed.

Working through problems with family members often helps patients lay the groundwork for reestablishing other social contacts. As the first social group with whom the patient interacts, the family can be a social microcosm on whom the patient tries out his coping efforts and who react to him in turn. By developing effective ways of dealing with family members and friends in various contexts, the patient simultaneously builds skills for dealing with other people in a variety of social situations (see Adams & Lindemann, 1974).

It has been said that individuals do not develop chronic diseases, families do. The reason for this belief is that the family is a social system (Minuchen, 1977), and disruption in the life of one family member invariably affects the lives of others (Leventhal, Leventhal, & Nguyen, 1985). One of the chief changes

brought about by chronic illness is an increased dependency of the chronically ill individual on other family members. If the patient is married, the illness inevitably places increased responsibilities on the spouse. Simultaneously, other responsibilities may fall to children and other family members living at home. Consequently, one of the major changes that occurs when a family member develops chronic illness is that the chores and responsibilities of all other family members increase.

Increased responsibilities may be difficult to handle. If family members' resources are already stretched to the limit, accommodating new tasks is very difficult. The wife of a stroke patient suggests some of the burdens such patients can create for their families.

> In the first few weeks, Clay not only needed meals brought to him, but countless items he wanted to use, to look at, and so forth. He was not aware of how Jim [the patient's son] and I developed our leg muscles in fetching and carrying. When he was on the third floor I would say "I am going downstairs. Is there anything you want?" No, he couldn't think of a thing. When I returned he remembered something, but only one thing at a time. There are advantages to a home with stairs, but not with a stroke victim in the family. (Dahlberg, 1977, p. 124)

Young children who are suddenly forced into taking on more responsibilities than would normally be expected for their age group may react by rebelling or acting out (e.g., Wellisch, 1979). Disturbances may include regression (such as bed-wetting), problems at school, truancy, sexual acting out, drug use, and antagonism toward other family members.

Many chronic illnesses—including heart disease, stroke, and cancer—lead to a decrease in sexual activity. In some cases, the condition itself prompts temporary restrictions on sexual activity; more commonly, however, the decline can be traced to conditions that have psychological origins (such as loss of desire, fears about aggravating the chronic condition, or impotence). Sexual problems may compound existing strains in the marital relationship produced by the chronically ill patient's increased dependency. Moreover, chronically ill patients often experience alterations in mood, such as increases in anxiety or depression, which, in turn, may affect the other family members adversely.

Despite the clear sources of strain that develop when a member of a family has a chronic illness, there is no evidence that such strains are catastrophic. There is no higher divorce rate among families with a chronic illness, nor do such families show less cohesion (Litman, 1974). Moreover, some families are actually drawn closer as a consequence of chronic illness (Masters, Cerreto, & Mendlowitz, 1983).

As noted earlier, social relationships other than those in the immediate family may also be strained. Chronically ill patients may need to think through whether they want to disclose the fact of their illness to those outside their immediate family. If they decide to do so, they may need to consider the best approach, since certain illnesses, particularly cancer, AIDS, and epilepsy, may elicit negative responses from others. Friends may be unable to talk openly about the disorder and may withdraw from the patient and be unable to provide the social support they would normally be able to give (e.g., Lichtman, Taylor, & Wood, 1983; Wortman & Dunkel-Schetter, 1979). The question of disclosure is moot in cases where a patient is left physically disabled or scarred. In these cases, proper guidance can help patients anticipate and deal with the avoidance, ambivalence, and oversolicitousness they may encounter from others.

There is some evidence that chronically ill women may experience more deficits in social support than chronically ill men. One study found disabled women experienced less social support because they were less likely to be married or get married than disabled men (Kutner, 1987; see also Bramwell, 1986). Being married appears to protect men but not women from being institutionalized after a stroke (Kelly-Hayes et al., 1988). Stern et al. (1977) found that women post-MI were less likely to get married, and if they were married, they were more likely to die shortly after the myocardial infarction. Since ill and/or elderly women may experience reduced quality of life for other reasons as well, such as poor income and high levels of disability (Haug & Folmar, 1986), problems in social support may exacerbate these already-existing differences. Gender differences in the availability and effects of social support among the chronically ill clearly merit additional study.

The social issues created by chronic illness require attention in the rehabilitative process. Some of these issues are crises that call for immediate, intensive action over a short period of time (crisis intervention). For example, immediately after the diagnosis of a chronic disorder, family members' schedules may be disrupted by the need to provide care for the sick person. A counselor can help the patient and family arrange for outside help that can ease this burden. Alternatively, patients or individual family members may seek individual long-term counseling to help solve and overcome some of the issues. A third fruitful approach is family therapy, in which patients and family members can work through their difficulties together in conjunction with a therapist. We will return to the issue of therapeutic intervention later in this chapter.

Personal Issues in Chronic Illness

At the beginning of this chapter, we considered the question of quality of life and the need to assess potential adverse effects of chronic diseases and their treatments. Throughout the chapter, we have focused on many of these adverse changes and what can be done to ameliorate them. This focus tends to obscure an important point, however—namely, that chronic illness can confer positive outcomes as well as negative ones. In one study of cancer patients (Collins et al., in press), over 90% of the respondents reported at least some beneficial changes in their lives as a result of the cancer. They reported an increased ability to appreciate each day and the inspiration to do things now in life rather than postponing them. In terms of relationships, these patients reported that they were putting more effort into their relationships and believed they had acquired more awareness of others' feelings and more sympathy and compassion for others. They reported feeling stronger, more self-assured, and more compassionate toward the unfortunate. Similarly, a study of myocardial infarction patients found that 46% reported that their lives were unchanged by the disease, 21% reported that it had worsened, but 33% felt that their lives had improved overall. Moreover, half the patients reported increased joy in life and increased value in families, hobbies, and health (Laerum, Johnsen, Smith, & Larsen, 1987; Waltz, 1986). Two studies have compared the quality of life experienced by cancer patients with a normal sample free of chronic disease, and both found the quality of life experienced by the cancer sample to be higher than that of the non-ill sample (Danoff, Kramer, Irwin, & Gottlieb, 1983; Tempelaar et al., 1989; see also Cassileth et al., 1984).

How do patients suffering from chronic illness with its often-severe consequences and emotional trauma nonetheless manage to achieve such a high quality of survival? When people experience an adverse event like a chronic disease, they often strive to actively minimize its negative impact (Taylor, 1983, 1989; see Taylor & Brown, 1988). When they encounter damaging information and circumstances, they try to reduce the negative implications for themselves or think of it in as unthreatening a manner as possible. When

negative consequences are difficult to deny, a person may attempt to offset them with perceived gains incurred from the event, such as finding meaning through the experience or believing that the self is a better person for having withstood the event. In short, people rearrange their priorities and their beliefs in such a way that they are able to extract some benefit and meaning from the event. Box 12.4 describes such a case. To fully understand these issues requires a consideration of the self, its sources of resilience, and its vulnerabilities.

The self is one of the central concepts in psychology (Wylie, 1961, 1979). Psychologists refer to the **self-concept** as a stable set of beliefs about one's qualities and attributes. **Self-esteem** refers to the evaluation of the self-concept—namely, whether one feels good or bad generally about one's qualities and attributes. People have a stable self-concept and a stable level of self-esteem. Nonetheless, particular events, such as a chronic illness, can produce drastic changes in self-concept and self-esteem. Many of these will be temporary and some will be permanent. Likewise, although researchers typically measure global self-esteem, it is important to realize that the self-concept is a composite of self-evaluations regarding many aspects of one's life. Some of these aspects are involved in the disease process and include body image, achievement, social functioning, and self-identification (Gates, 1974).

The Physical Self   **Body image** is the perception and evaluation of one's physical functioning and appearance (Fisher & Cleveland, 1958). The body-image component of self-concept is obviously affected by illness. Studies of hospitalized patients show that body image plummets during illness. Not only is the affected part of the body evaluated negatively, but also the whole body image may take on a negative aura (Schwab & Hameling, 1968). For acutely ill patients, changes in body image are

---

Box 12.4
"Intoxicated by My Illness": A Patient Describes His Experience

When you learn that your life is threatened, you can turn toward this knowledge or away from it. I turned toward it. It was not a choice, but an automatic shifting of gears, a tacit agreement between my body and my brain. I thought that time had tapped me on the shoulder, that I had been given a real deadline at last. It wasn't that I believed the cancer was going to kill me, even though it had spread beyond the prostate—it could probably be controlled, either by radiation or hormonal manipulation. No, what struck me was the startled awareness that one day something, whatever it might be, was going to interrupt my leisurely progress. It sounds trite, yet I can only say that I realized for the first time that I don't have forever.

When my friends heard I had cancer, they found me surprisingly cheerful and talked about my courage. But it has nothing to do with courage, at least not for me. As far as I can tell, it's a question of desire. I'm filled with desire—to live, to write, to do everything. Desire itself is a kind of immortality. While I've always had trouble concentrating, I now feel as concentrated as a diamond or a microchip.

In the first stages of my illness, I couldn't sleep, urinate, or defecate—the word ordeal comes to mind. Then when my doctor changed all this and everything worked again, what a voluptuous pleasure it was. With a cry of joy I realized how marvelous it is simply to function. My body, which in the last decade or two had become a familiar, no longer thrilling old flame, was reborn as a brand-new infatuation.

As I look ahead, I feel like a man who has awakened from a long afternoon nap to find the evening stretched out before me. I'm reminded of D'Annunzio, the Italian poet, who said to a duchess he had just met at a party in Paris, "Come, we will have a profound evening." Why not? I see the balance of my life—everything comes in images now—as a beautiful paisley shawl thrown over a grand piano.

(Broyard, 1989).

---

short-lived; but for the chronically ill, negative evaluations may last longer. Patients who must adjust to a permanent alteration in their physical appearance may take some time to do so. Most researchers exploring body image believe, however, that such changes are eventually made, although the process may take a year or more.

The sole exception seems to be facial disfigurement. Patients whose faces have been scarred or disfigured may never truly accept their altered appearance. The reasons why facial disfigurements produce chronic alterations in body image appear to be two. First, the face is often associated with personality, and when the face is deformed, both patients themselves and others reacting to them may see the individual's whole nature as tainted (Richardson, Goodman, Hastorf, & Dornbusch, 1961). Second, facial disfigurements cannot be masked: They are apparent to all passersby, who may act with involuntary disgust or withdrawal. An example of the potent impact of facial disfigurement is the case of Mrs. Dover:

> Before her disfigurement (amputation of half of her nose), Mrs. Dover, who lived with one of her two married daughters, had been an independent, warm and friendly woman who enjoyed travelling, shopping, and visiting her many relatives. The disfigurement of her face, however, resulted in a definite alteration in her way of living. The first two or three years she seldom left her daughter's home, preferring to remain in her room or to sit in the backyard. "I was heartsick," she said; "the door had been shut on my life." (Goffman, 1963, p. 12)

The degree of threat to body image that is posed by a chronic illness depends on a variety of factors. These include the patient's previous body image, the amount of body damage or scarring, and the level of activity possible following the illness or injury. For example, it may be particularly difficult to cope with deterioration of appearance or loss of physical mobility if these have been regarded as valued assets. A particularly attractive person or an athlete, for example, may have more difficulty coping with chronic illness that interferes with body image than would someone whose self-worth depended less critically on body image. Treatments that leave substantial scars and alter body appearance appear to be more difficult to adjust to than procedures that are less scarring and mutilating. For example, in the treatment of breast cancer, the literature has, with some exceptions, found that women are better adjusted psychologically after lumpectomy than after mastectomy (see Taylor et al., 1985, for a review; but see Levy, Herberman, Lee et al., 1989). When illness threatens sexual functioning—as it does for stroke, paralysis, and some cancers and heart conditions—body image may be affected. The body image of a person with a permanent disfigurement or a severe or an advancing disability can be improved by stressing other aspects of appearance and health. Researchers have sometimes noted spontaneous increases in physical exercise and improvement of other aspects of physical appearance as a reaction to illness (Taylor, Wood, & Lichtman, 1983).

The Achieving Self   Achievement through vocational and avocational activities is also an important aspect of self-esteem and self-concept. Many people derive their primary satisfaction from their job or career; others take great pleasure in their hobbies and leisure activities (Kahn, 1981). To the extent that chronic illness threatens these valued aspects of the self, self-concept may be damaged. In particular, it is common to find this problem among heart patients, who must alter their lifestyles by reducing the number of stressful activities in which they participate.

Although threats to work and leisure activities can create problems for self-concept and self-esteem after chronic illness, the ability to find meaning through personal achievement can also offset the stress that arises from chronic illness. When work-related activities are not threatened or curtailed by illness, the patient has these sources of satisfaction from which to derive self-esteem. Work and hobbies can come to take on new meaning. In some cases, chronic illness may prompt people to reevaluate their lives, place priority on the activities that are most meaningful to them, and, consequently, allocate more of their time to those activities; as a result, both their morale and self-satisfaction are improved. Patients whose work activities and hobbies are threatened by illness may develop new interests that provide new sources of satisfaction. Thus, work and leisure activities can serve protective and creative functions by adding balance to life. To the extent, however, that they too are threatened by the disease process, they can exacerbate an already problematic recovery or readjustment.

The Social Self   As we have already seen, rebuilding the social self is an important aspect of readjustment after chronic illness. Interactions with family and friends can be a critical source of self-esteem. Social resources provide chronically ill patients with badly needed information, goods and services, and emotional support. A breakdown in the support system has implications for logistical functioning, emotional functioning, and long-term recovery. Perhaps for these reasons, fears about withdrawal of support are among the most common worries of chronically ill patients (Lichtman, 1982). It is for this reason that family participation in the rehabilitation process is so widely encouraged.

The Private Self   The residual core of a patient's identity—his or her ambitions, goals, and desires for the future—will also predict adjustment to chronic illness. It is important to know what plans and dreams are now impossible as a consequence of the restrictions of the illness or treatment. Occasionally, adjustment to chronic illness may be impeded because the patient has an unrealized secret dream that has now been shattered, or at least appears to be. Encouraging the patient to discuss this difficulty may reveal alternative paths to fulfillment and awaken the ability to establish new ambitions, goals, and plans for the future.

It is clear, then, that the self-concept and its various facets are all affected by chronic illness. Nonetheless, many of these effects will be only temporary. To the extent that a patient is able to derive satisfaction from aspects of life that are not threatened by illness, these compensations may offset some of the losses and blows that are experienced in other areas. Thus, for example, a patient who receives support from family and friends may find it easier to return to work. Returning to work, in turn, may make it easier to see how future plans can be realized. Unfortunately, the opposite can also occur. For example, if a patient places faith in social support, which is abruptly withdrawn, work, social relation-ships, and body image may also decline. Or the threat that a disease poses to the patient's continuing work life may lower mood, driving family and friends away. Fortunately, however, this kind of occurrence appears to be relatively uncommon. What is most striking about the self-concept is how robust it is. Although patients usually have some difficulty incorporating a sudden change in health status into the self-concept, their ultimate ability to adjust to altered life circumstances is remarkable.

It should be noted that this section has focused on research on the major chronic diseases, such as heart disease, cancer, and, to a lesser extent, diabetes and hypertension. Extensive analyses of the psychosocial issues of patients facing epilepsy (Bleck, 1987), Parkinson's disease (Dakof & Mendelsohn, 1986), and other diseases have also been conducted. These and other in-depth analyses of particular chronic diseases raise many of the problems just discussed in this chapter, as well as many problems that develop with respect to particular disorders. Consequently, a full understanding of the impact of chronic disease requires not only a general picture, as provided by this chapter, but also the more specific view that can come into focus only with an in-depth investigation of particular disorders.

When the Chronically Ill Patient Is a Child

Chronic illness can be especially problematic when the chronically ill patient is a child. First, children may not fully understand the nature of their diagnosis and treatment and thus experience confusion as they are trying to cope with illness and treatment. Second, because chronically ill children often cannot follow their treatment regimen by themselves, the family must participate in the illness and treatment process even more than is the case with a chronically ill adult (e.g., Gross, Eudy,

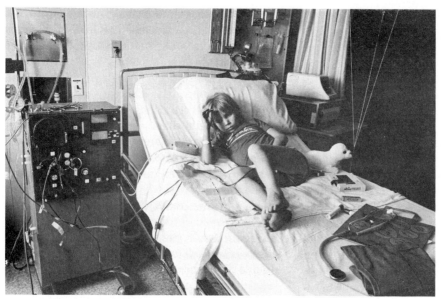

Children's needs to be informed about their illness and their need to exert control over illness-related activities and their lives more generally have prompted interventions to involve children more in their own care.

& Drabman, 1982). Frequently, children must be exposed to isolating and terrifying procedures to treat their condition (Kellerman, Rigler, & Siegel, 1979), which can also present adjustment problems.

Although many children adjust to these radical changes in their lives quite successfully, others do not. Children suffering from chronic illness exhibit a variety of behavioral problems, including rebellion and withdrawal from others. They may suffer low self-esteem either because they believe that the chronic illness is a punishment for bad behavior or because they feel less than whole as a consequence of being ill. Underachievement in school and other types of regressive behavior such as bed-wetting or throwing temper tantrums are not uncommon. These problems can be aggravated if families do not have adequate styles of communicating with each other and of resolving conflict (e.g., Mattsson, 1977; Minuchin, Rosman, & Baker, 1978).

Several factors can improve a chronically ill child's ability to cope. Realistic parental attitudes toward the disorder and its treatment can soothe the child emotionally and provide an informed basis for care. If children are encouraged to engage in self-care as much as possible and only realistic restrictions are placed on their lives, adjustment will be better. Encouraging regular school attendance and reasonable physical activities is particularly beneficial. If the parent can learn to remain calm in crisis situations, maintain emotional control, and become familiar with the child's illness, these factors can contribute positively to the child's functioning (Mattsson, 1977). When families are unable to provide help for their chronically ill child and develop ineffective communication patterns, interventions may be needed. In particular, family therapy and training the family in the treatment regimen can improve family functioning.

INTERVENTIONS FOR PSYCHOLOGICAL ISSUES AFTER CHRONIC ILLNESS

As we have seen, the majority of chronically ill patients appear to achieve a relatively high quality of life after diagnosis and treatment for their illness. In fact, many who are free from pain or advancing disease achieve at least as high, if not higher, quality of life than before the illness, by their self-reports. However, as we have also seen, there are reliable adverse effects of chronic disease, such as anxiety, depression, and disturbances in interpersonal relations. Consequently, health psychologists have increasingly focused on ways to ameliorate these problems.

The fact that anxiety and depression are intermittently high among chronically ill patients suggests that evaluation for these particular problems should be a standard part of chronic care. Patients' early reactions to and perceptions of their illness clearly play a role in their recovery. Thus, researchers and clinicians should develop ways to identify people who are at high risk for emotional disorders (e.g., Maeland & Havick, 1987b; Marks et al., 1986). Patients who have a history of depression prior to their illness or other mental illness are at particular risk and therefore should be evaluated early for potential interventions (Goldberg, 1981; Morris & Raphael, 1987). A variety of interventions have been developed to deal with these and other problems associated with chronic illness.

Pharmacological Interventions

Pharmacological treatment of depression in chronically ill patients has yet to be extensively researched, but antidepressants may be appropriate for patients suffering from major depression associated with chronic illness (Massie & Holland, 1987; Primeau, 1988; Robinson, 1986; Rodin & Voshart, 1986). In what was reported to be the first such study,

Evans, Dratt, Raines, and Rosenberg (1988) presented evidence showing improvement in depression among cancer patients after antidepressant treatment. There are, however, several risks associated with such interventions. For example, there are contraindications of the use of antidepressants in elderly patients, and many patients simply may not take the drugs as prescribed (Evans et al., 1988; Lustman et al., 1988).

Individual Therapy

Individual therapy is one of the most common psychological interventions for chronic illness, and some guidelines regarding its practice are useful. There are important differences between psychotherapy with medical patients and psychotherapy that is conducted with patients who have primarily psychological complaints (Wellisch, 1979). First, therapy with medical patients is more likely to be episodic rather than continuous. Chronic illness raises crises and issues intermittently that may require help. For example, problems with an adolescent daughter after her mother has been treated for breast cancer may not occur immediately but may develop over the next few months (Lichtman, Taylor, Wood et al., 1984). Recurrence or worsening of a condition will present a crisis that may need to be addressed with a therapist, as for a heart patient who has had a second heart attack or a patient who has developed a new malignancy.

Second, collaboration with the patient's physician and family members is critical in therapy with medical patients. The physician is in an important position to appraise the psychologist or other counselor of a patient's current physical status. Problems experienced by the medical patient will likely have implications for other family members' activities; accordingly, family members are almost inevitably involved in the problems created by illness.

Third, therapy with medical patients more

frequently requires respect for patients' defenses than does traditional psychotherapy. In traditional psychotherapy, one of the therapist's goals may be to challenge a patient's defenses that may interfere with an adequate understanding of his or her problems. However, in the case of medical patients, these same defenses may serve a benign function in protecting them from the full realization of the ramifications of their disease.

Fourth and finally, the therapist working with a medical patient must have a comprehensive understanding of the patient's illness and its modes of treatment. Since many of the issues are centered around particular aspects of illness and treatment, the therapist who is uninformed about the illness will not be able to provide adequate help. Moreover, illness and treatments themselves produce psychological problems (for example, depression due to chemotherapy), and a therapist who is ignorant of this fact may make incorrect interpretations.

Brief Psychotherapeutic Interventions

A variety of short-term interventions ranging from informal communication with a health care professional to brief psychotherapy have been proposed to alleviate emotional distress in chronically ill patients. Many brief informational interventions can be accomplished on a preventive basis within the medical setting. For example, telling patients and their families what they may expect during the course of diagnosis and treatment can substantially alleviate or even forestall anxiety (e.g., Egbert et al., 1964; Maguire, 1975). Simply telling patients that anxiety is a normal response to the stress of chronic illness (Welch-McCaffrey, 1985) or that depression is a common consequence of certain disorders such as stroke (Goodstein, 1983; Robinson, 1986) may alleviate patients' and family members' concerns over whether the patient is reacting normally to his or her illness. This kind of patient-staff communica-

tion can improve the detection of mood disorders and also improve the flow of information (Holland & Massie, 1987).

Increasingly, psychologists have turned to short-term structured interventions in an attempt to develop standardized approaches that may help the most people in the shortest period of time. Preliminary evidence suggests that such interventions can be successful. For example, Telch and Telch (1986) compared group coping skills training to supportive group therapy for highly distressed cancer patients. After 6 weeks, the coping skills patients showed less emotional stress and more vigor than did the group therapy or no-treatment patients. Patients in the coping skills training group also reported heightened feelings of self-efficacy and fewer problems. The success of the coping skills instruction appears to be due to its highly specific nature directed toward enhancing perceptions of control.

Similar **patient education** programs that include coping skills training have been found to increase knowledge about the disease, to reduce anxiety, to increase patients' feelings of purpose and meaning in life (Johnson, 1982), to reduce pain and depression (Lorig, Chastain, Ung, Shoor, & Holman, 1989), to improve coping (Maeland & Havick, 1987a), to increase adherence to treatment (Greenfield, Kaplan, Ware, Yano, & Frank, 1988), and to increase confidence in the ability to manage pain and other side effects (Parker et al., 1988), relative to wait-list patients who have not yet participated in the program or to patients who did not participate at all. Research is needed to identify if there are particular patients who do not profit from such interventions, such as those who choose to cope through denial (Welch-McCaffrey, 1985) or whose prognosis is unfavorable (Telch & Telch, 1986).

Relaxation and Exercise

Relaxation training is now a widely used and promising intervention with the chronically ill. It appears to decrease anxiety and nausea from chemotherapy and to decrease pain for cancer patients (Bridge, Benson, Pietroni, & Priest, 1986; Carey & Burish, 1988; Sims, 1987). Combinations of relaxation training with stress management and blood pressure monitoring have proven useful in the treatment of essential hypertension (Agras, Taylor, Kraemer, Southam, & Schneider, 1987; Chesney, Black, Swan, & Ward, 1987; Patel & Marmot, 1987; Wittrock, Blanchard, & McCoy, 1988). Exercise interventions have been most commonly undertaken with myocardial infarction patients. It is unclear whether exercise has a direct impact on mood in these patients. However, physical fitness is reliably improved, and exercise can also improve quality of life (Blumenthal & Emery, 1988; Greenland & Chu, 1988; Taylor, Houston-Miller, Ahn, Haskell, & DeBusk, 1986).

Social Support Interventions

As we noted in Chapter 8, social support appears to be an important resource for those suffering from chronic disease. Chronically ill patients who report good social relationships are also more likely to be positively adjusted to their illness. This relationship has been found for cancer patients (Fitzpatrick et al., 1988; Neuling & Winefield, 1988), arthritis patients (Fitzpatrick et al., 1988), patients suffering from end-stage renal disease (Siegel, Mesagno, Chen, & Christ, 1987), and patients with spinal cord injuries (Schulz & Decker, 1985), among others. But, as also noted, social support resources can be threatened by a chronic illness. Consequently, many interventions around chronic illness may need to deal with issues of social support. Finding ways to increase the effectiveness of existing or potentially naturally occurring support from patients, family, and friends should be a high research and intervention priority. Patients need to recognize the potential sources of support

in their environment and to be taught how to draw on these resources effectively. For example, they might be urged to join community groups, interest groups, informal social groups, and self-help groups.

In addition, family members and significant others who are going through stressful events with the patient could receive guidance in the most effective ways to provide social support and in the well-intended actions they should avoid because they may actually make a stressful situation worse (e.g., Dakof & Taylor, 1990). At different times during the course of an illness, a patient may be best served by different kinds of social support. Tangible aid may be helpful at some points, such as being driven to and from medical appointments or having errands and housekeeping done during times of infirmity. At other times, however, emotional support may be more valuable. Emotional support appears to be the most important and most valued type of support from intimate others, whereas information and advice may be more valuable from experts and actually experienced as aversive when received from intimate others (Dakof & Taylor, 1990; Dunkel-Schetter, 1984).

As noted earlier, friends and relatives may themselves require interventions. Even the simple provision of information may be helpful to those attempting to provide social support to the chronically ill. In one study of wives of MI patients, the majority reported feeling poorly informed about myocardial infarction, they reported few opportunities to ask experts questions, and they consequently experienced a high degree of stress (Thompson & Cordle, 1988). Even a short intervention designed to acquaint them with myocardial infarction could have ameliorated this situation. Enlisting the cooperation of "community linking individuals," such as teachers or clergy, who can communicate helpful information to the families and friends of the chronically ill is another potential intervention prospect (Bramwell, 1986; Kutner, 1987).

Support Groups

Social **support groups** represent another social support resource for the chronically ill. Such groups are available for many patients with chronic illnesses, including stroke patients, patients recovering from myocardial infarction, and cancer patients. Some of these groups are initiated by a therapist, and in some cases they are patient-led. These support groups discuss issues of mutual concern that arise as a consequence of illness. They often provide specific information about how others have successfully dealt with the problems raised by the illness and provide people with an opportunity to share their emotional responses with others facing the same problems (Gottlieb, 1983, 1988; Lieberman, Borman et al., 1979).

There are also formal support services for particular disorders that help patient groups deal with specific problems. For example, the American Cancer Society sponsors Reach-to-Recovery, a program to help mastectomy pa-tients cope with physical and emotional difficulties after surgery. The American Cancer Society runs groups for ostomy patients (those who have had a portion of their intestine removed and replaced by an external bag for elimination), a group that experiences many difficulties in physical, emotional, social, and sexual adjustment (Follick, Smith, & Turk, 1984). In some cases, these socially supportive ties may evolve from rehabiliation programs, as for myocardial infarction patients, and in other cases, linkages between the primary health care setting and established groups (such as I Can Cope for cancer patients) may facilitate entry into such programs.

Potentially, social support groups can satisfy unmet needs for social support from family and caregivers. Alternatively, such support groups may act as an additional source of support provided by those going through the same event. Chronically ill patients report a variety of positive as well as negative experiences from such contacts. On the positive side, among cancer patients, fellow patients

Social support groups can satisfy unmet needs for social support from family and friends and can also enable people to share their personal experiences with others like themselves.

were reported to be especially helpful when they acted as good role models on whom the patients could pattern their own coping efforts, or when they functioned as role models simply by surviving over the long term (e.g., Taylor, Falke, Shoptaw, & Lichtman, 1986). Patients who practiced poor health behaviors or who expressed substantial psychological distress were unhelpful (Dakof & Taylor, 1990).

Generally, studies that have evaluated the efficacy of social support groups vis-à-vis people waiting to participate or nonparticipants have found beneficial results. This has been true for rheumatoid arthritis patients (e.g., Bradley et al., 1987), cancer patients (e.g., Telch & Telch, 1986), and MI patients (e.g., Dracup, 1985). Self-help groups may help victims especially cope with the stigma associated with certain disorders, such as cancer or epilepsy (Droge, Arntson, & Norton, 1986), and it may help patients develop the motivation and techniques to adhere to complicated treatment regimens (Storer, Frate, Johnson, & Greenberg, 1987). There is even some beginning evidence that participation in social support groups may promote better health and long-term survival. One study of patients in a weekly cancer support group found that par-

ticipants survived longer than nonparticipants (Spiegel, Bloom, & Gottheil, 1983).

Although widely heralded as a low-cost, convenient treatment option for people to deal with a wide variety of personal problems, self-help groups currently reach only a small proportion of chronically ill patients (e.g., Andersen, 1988; Taylor et al., 1986). Moreover, they appear to appeal disproportionately to well-educated, middle-class white women. Not only is this the segment of the population that is already served by traditional treatment services, but those who participate in self-help groups may actually be the same individuals. There is some evidence that people who participate in self-help groups are significantly more likely to use helping services of all kinds (Taylor et al., 1986). The potential for self-help groups to be a general resource for the chronically ill, then, has yet to be fully realized.

To summarize, several psychotherapeutic interventions are available to chronically ill patients who are trying to cope with complex problems. Each possibility including crisis intervention, family therapy, individual therapy, group therapy, and support groups has distinctive features and benefits, and different options may be better suited to some problems than others.

SUMMARY

1. At any given time, 50% of the population has a chronic condition that requires medical management. Yet only recently has research attention turned to the psychosocial aspects of quality of life. Quality of life measures pinpoint problems associated with diseases and treatments and help in policy decision making about the effectiveness and cost-effectiveness of interventions.

2. Chronically ill patients often suffer from denial, intermittent anxiety, and long-term

depression. Yet too often, these reactions, especially anxiety and depression, are underdiagnosed, confused with symptoms of disease or treatment, or presumed to be normal and therefore not worthy of intervention.

3. Anxiety is reliably tied to illness events, such as awaiting test results or obtaining regular checkups. Depression increases with the severity of disease, pain, and disability.

4. Despite problems, most patients cope with chronic illness as they cope with other stressful events in life. Active coping and multiple coping efforts may be more successful than avoidance, passive coping, or using one predominant coping strategy.

5. Patients also develop concepts of their illness, its cause, and its controllability that relate to their coping. Perceived control is associated with good adjustment.

6. Rehabilitation centers around: physical problems, especially recovering functioning and adherence to treatment; vocational retraining, job discrimination, and financial loss and loss of insurance; gaps and problems in social support; and personal losses, such as the threat that disease poses for long-term goals. Yet the majority of patients appear to achieve some positive outcomes of chronic illness as well as negative ones. This may occur because patients compensate for losses in some areas of their lives with value placed on other aspects of life.

7. Interventions with the chronically ill include pharmacological interventions; individual therapy; brief psychotherapeutic interventions oriented toward solving crises or providing information; relaxation and exercise; social support interventions; and support groups. Support groups appear to be an especially underused but potentially helpful resource for the chronically ill.

KEY TERMS

anxiety
body image
denial
depression
dietitian
occupational therapist
patient education

physical rehabilitation
physical therapist
quality of life
self-concept
self-esteem
social worker
support group

13

PSYCHOLOGICAL ISSUES IN ADVANCING AND TERMINAL ILLNESS

Comedian Woody Allen is said to have remarked on his 40th birthday, "I shall gain immortality not through my work but by not dying" (quoted in Feifel, 1977). Many of us would echo this desire to live forever, but life inevitably ends in death. A mere 100 years ago, people died primarily from infectious diseases like tuberculosis, influenza, or pneumonia. Now those illnesses are much less widespread because of substantial advances in public health and preventive medical technologies that have developed in the twentieth century. The average American can now expect to live 74.9 years (Hoffman, 1988). When death does come, it will probably stem from a chronic illness such as heart disease or cancer, rather than from an acute disorder. This fact means that instead of facing a rapid, unanticipated death, the average American may know what he or she will probably die of for 5, 10, or even more years.

To understand the psychological issues associated with death and dying first requires a tour, a rather grim tour, of death itself. What is the most likely cause of death for a person of any given age and what kind of death will it be? We next consider some of the psychological and social issues raised by terminal disease. These include changes in the self-concept, communication patterns, social interaction, and physical management. Some researchers have suggested that people go through a predictable series of stages in adjusting to the prospect of death, and we next consider the viability of this idea, drawing on Kübler-Ross's influential and controversial stage theory. Following that discussion, we look at the role of medical staff in the psychological management of the terminally ill patient and consider how psychological therapists can play a role, through either individual or family therapy, to help the patient achieve an "appropriate death." Next, we look briefly at two alternatives to hospital care for the terminally ill, home care and hospice care, which have very different psychological effects on patients and their families than does more traditional care. Finally, we consider the survivors: How do they adjust? What is the best way to prepare people for the deaths of their family and friends?

DEATH ACROSS THE LIFE SPAN

Death in Infancy and Childhood

Despite the fact that the United States is one of the most technologically developed countries in the world, our **infant mortality rate** is twentieth in the world (10.0 per 1,000; U.S. Bureau of the Census, 1987), higher than is true for most Western European nations. Moreover, both the overall rate and the gap between the white and black infant mortality rates have gotten worse. While the infant mortality rate for white infants is 9 deaths per 1,000, it is 18 deaths per 1,000 among blacks. To what do we attribute such upsetting statistics? The countries that have a lower infant mortality rate than the United States all have national medical programs that provide free or low-cost maternal care during pregnancy. We are one of the few technologically developed nations without such a program. When infants are born prematurely or die at birth, the problems can frequently be traced to poor prenatal care for the mother.

During the first year of life, the main causes of death are congenital abnormalities and **sudden infant death syndrome (SIDS).** The causes of SIDS are unknown—the infant simply stops breathing—but epidemiological studies reveal that it is more likely to occur in lower-class urban environments and when the mother smoked during her pregnancy (SIDS, 1974). Mercifully, it appears to be a gentle death for the child, although not for at least some of the parents: The confusion, self-blame, and suspicion of others who do not understand this phenomenon can take an enormous psychological toll on the parents (Downey, Silver, & Wortman, 1990). Adjust-

ment seems to be better for mothers who already have children, if they do not blame themselves for the death, and if they have some contact with the infant, as by seeing the infant or receiving a picture of it (Graham, Thompson, Estrada, & Yonekura, 1987).

After the first year, the main cause of death among children under age 15 is accidents, which account for 40% of all deaths in this group (National Center for Health Statistics, 1986). In early childhood, accidents are most frequently due to accidental poisoning, injuries, or falls in the home. In later years, automobile accidents take over as the chief cause of accidental death (Hoffman, 1988).

Cancer, especially leukemia, is the second leading cause of death in youngsters between ages 1 and 15. Leukemia is a form of cancer that strikes the bone marrow, which produces the white blood cells that combat disease. In leukemia, an excessive number of white blood cells is produced, leading to severe anemia and other complications. As recently as 30 years ago, a diagnosis of leukemia was a virtual death sentence for a child. Now, because of advances in treatment, including chemotherapy and bone marrow transplants, as many as 70% of its victims survive the disease (National Cancer Institute, 1989). These procedures, especially bone marrow transplants, can be very painful and produce a variety of unpleasant side effects. But they have given leukemia sufferers and their families hope when there used to be none. Box 13.1 outlines some of the issues faced by victims of childhood leukemia.

A discussion of death in childhood and infancy is incomplete without some mention of how children develop a concept of death. The child's idea of death appears to develop quite slowly. Up to age 5, most children think of death as a great sleep. Children at this age are often curious about death rather than frightened or saddened by it, partly because they may not understand that death is final and irreversible. Rather, the dead person is thought

Box 13.1
Mainstreaming the Leukemic Child

At one time, a diagnosis of leukemia inevitably meant death for a child. Now, however, many children who have had leukemia are living long, full lives, some with intermittent periods of disease and treatment, others with no sign of disease at all. Because so many leukemic children have periods of remission (the symptom-free state), many are being "mainstreamed" back into their communities, instead of being cared for in separate treatment facilities, as was once the case (see Michael & Copeland, 1987).

Although there are many advantages to mainstreaming, there are some difficulties as well. Leukemic children may look different from others. They may be thin, pale, and even bald from rigorous treatments like chemotherapy. They may have little energy for physical activities and may need to go back to the hospital from time to time for treatments. Because leukemia is a form of cancer, it has the stigma of cancer associated with it, and its earlier association with death makes it upsetting to many people who do not understand it. Therefore, mainstreaming the leukemic child can require careful, sensitive preparation.

One large metropolitan children's hospital has developed several programs for such mainstreaming. The primary goal of the program is to work with the entire family (the ill child, parents, and siblings) and the child's total environment (home and school) to make the transition as smooth as possible, Several of the programs begin while the child is still in the acute phase of illness. The hospital provides a residential hotel for families of children undergoing radiation therapy. In this way, the parents can be near the child throughout treatment. A community kitchen, dining room, and living room enable parents to meet and share information and concerns.

Special recreational programs developed by trained patient activity specialists enable sick children to play and, at the same time, to work out conflicts about illness and treatment. Doctor-patient games and body-image games, for example, can reveal adjustment problems.

Games like these help the child begin to make the transition back to normal life. Siblings who are having trouble adjusting to their brother's or sister's illness can also participate in the playrooms and work on their own confusion and adjustment difficulties.

Other programs help the family understand the leukemic child's situation. Parents can participate in 2-month-long educational programs that are designed to allay fears, teach the parents to provide daily home care, and help the parents help the child adjust to the disease. A special telephone line encourages parents to network by putting them in contact with other families of leukemic children.

Patient activity specialists also work with the schools to ease the child's transition back into the school environment. Following interviews with the child and family to identify potential problems and strains, the specialist will meet with the child's principal, teachers, school nurse, and other staff both to educate them about the child's disease and needs and to help them make the child feel comfortable in the school setting. The specialist may also meet with the other children in the child's class to inform them about the disease and allay any fears. Alternatively, the specialist may help the child prepare a talk for the class about leukemia and its treatments. These steps help the peers of leukemic children relate to them normally.

Ironically, some programs help children ease into a normal life by exposing them to other children who have leukemia. For example, the hospital runs a summer camp for leukemic and other children with cancer or blood disorders. The primary goal is the development of a positive self-image. Many of the counselors have themselves been leukemia patients, so they act as living, positive role models for the younger children.

This kind of comprehensive rehabilitation is an impressive example of what can be done when a conscientious effort is made to address all of the chronically ill patient's social and psychological needs.

to be still around, breathing and eating, but in an altered state, like Snow White or Sleeping Beauty waiting for the prince (Bluebond-Langner, 1977; Kastenbaum, 1977; Nagy, 1948).

Between ages 5 and 9, the idea that death is final may develop, although most children of this age do not have a biological understanding of death. For some of these children, death is personified into a shadowy figure such as a ghost or the devil. They may, for example, believe that death occurs because a supernatural being came to take the person away. The idea that death is universal and inevitable may not develop until age 9 or 10. At this point, the child typically has some understanding of the processes involved in death (such as burial and cremation), knows that the body decomposes, and realizes that the person who has died will not return (Bluebond-Langner, 1977; Kastenbaum, 1977; Nagy, 1948).

Death in Young Adulthood

When asked their view of death, the majority of young adults envision a trauma or fiery accident of some kind. This perception is realistic. Although the death rate in adolescence is low (about 1.1 per 1,000 from ages 15 to 19 and about 1.4 per 1,000 from ages 19 to 25), about 60% of deaths in this age group can be accounted for by accidents, mainly involving automobiles. Homicide, suicide, cancer, and AIDS account for most of the rest (U.S. Bureau of the Census, 1987).

Next to the death of a child, the death of a young adult is considered the most tragic. Young adults are products of years of socialization and education and are on the verge of starting their own families and careers. Their deaths are tragic both because of the seeming waste of life and because they are robbed of the chance to develop and mature (Kalish, 1977; Kastenbaum, 1977).

Not surprisingly, when young adults do receive a diagnosis of a terminal illness like cancer, they may feel shock, outrage, and an acute sense of injustice. Partly for these rea-

sons, medical staff often find it difficult to work with these patients. They are likely to be angry much of the time and, precisely because they are otherwise in good health, may face a long and drawn-out period of dying. For them, unlike older people, there are simply fewer biological competitors for death, so they do not quickly succumb to complications like pneumonia or kidney failure (Schneidman, 1977). Most difficult to deal with emotionally is the terminally ill parent of young children. Not surprisingly, these parents feel cheated of the chance to see their children grow up and develop, and they feel special concern over what will happen to their children without them.

Death in Middle Age

In middle age, death begins to assume more realistic and, in some cases, fearful proportions, both because it is more common and because people develop the chronic health problems that may ultimately kill them. The much popularized **midlife crisis** (Conway, 1978; Gould, 1972; Sheehy, 1974) that occurs around age 40 is believed to stem partly from the gradual realization of impending death. It may be touched off by the death of a parent, acquaintance, or friend or by clear bodily signs that one is aging (Kastenbaum, 1977). The fear of death may be symbolically acted out as a fear of loss of physical appearance, sexual prowess, or athletic ability. Or it may be focused on one's work: the realization that it may be meaningless and that many youthful ambitions will never be realized. The abrupt life changes that are sometimes made in response to this crisis—such as a divorce, remarriage to a much younger person, or radical job change—may be viewed partly as an effort to postpone death (Gould, 1972). Box 13.2 offers a poignant example of such an experience.

The main cause of **premature death** in adulthood—that is, death that occurs before the projected age of 75—is sudden death due to heart attack or stroke. Members of a cancer

---

Box 13.2
The Midlife Crisis: A Confrontation with Mortality

Direct experiences with death can prompt a person to reevaluate the course of his or her life and, sometimes, to make radical life changes. In this excerpt from her book *Passages* (1974, pp. 2–3, 5), writer Gail Sheehy describes the circumstances that led to her own midlife crisis.

Without warning, in the middle of my thirties, I had a breakdown of nerve. It never occurred to me that while winging along in my happiest and most productive stage, all of a sudden simply staying afloat would require a massive exertion of will. Or of some power greater than will.

I was talking to a young boy in Northern Ireland where I was on assignment for a magazine when a bullet blew his face off. That was how fast it all changed. We were standing side by side in the sun, relaxed and triumphant after a civil rights march by the Catholics of Derry. We had been met by soldiers at the barricade; we had vomited tear gas and dragged those dented by rubber bullets back to safety. Now we were surveying the crowd from a balcony. "How do the paratroopers fire those gas canisters so far?" I asked.

"See them jammin' their rifle butts against the ground?" the boy was saying when the steel slug tore into his mouth and ripped up the bridge of his nose and left of his face nothing but ground bone meal.

"My God," I said dumbly, "they're real bullets." I tried to think how to put his face back together again. Up to that moment in my life I thought everything could be mended.... When I flew home from Ireland, I couldn't write the story, could not confront the fact of my own mortality....

Some intruder shook me by the psyche and shouted: Take stock! Half your life has been spent. What about the part of you that wants a home and talks about a second child? Before I could answer, the intruder pointed to something else I had postponed: What about the side of you that wants to contribute to the world? Words, books, demonstrations, donations—is this enough? You have been a performer, not a full participant. And now you are 35.

To be confronted for the first time with the arithmetic of life was, quite simply, terrifying.

---

conference some years ago were startled to hear the keynote speaker say that he wished everyone would die of a heart attack. What he meant is that, compared to a slow and painful death like that caused by cancer, sudden death is quick and relatively painless. When asked how they would die if they could choose their death, most people reply that they would prefer a sudden, painless, and nonmutilating death. Although sudden death has the disadvantage of not allowing people to prepare their exit, in some ways it facilitates a

more graceful departure, since the dying person does not have to cope with physical deterioration, discomfort, pain, and loss of mental faculties.

Sudden death is, in some ways, kinder to family members as well. The family does not have to go through the emotional torment of watching the patient's worsening condition, and finances and other resources are not as severely taxed. The risk of sudden death is that one cannot choose one's moment, so it may come at an especially bad time. When death

Box 13.3
Why Do Women Live Longer Than Men?

Women live an average of 7 years longer than men in the United States. This difference in average age of death also exists in most other industrialized countries. (The only places where women do not live longer than men are underdeveloped countries in which many women die during childbirth. In countries where maternal and prenatal care are high priorities and the technology surrounding childbirth is well developed, this type of mortality declines substantially and women therefore live longer than men.) A number of possible reasons have been offered for this surprising statistic.

One theory maintains that women are biologically more fit than men. Although more male than female fetuses are conceived, more males are stillborn or miscarried than are females. This trend persists in infancy, during which the male death rate remains higher. In fact, the male death rate is higher at all ages of life. Thus, although more males than females are born, there will be more females than males left alive by the time young people reach their 20s. Exactly what biological mechanisms might make females more fit are still unknown. Some factors may be genetic, others may be hormonal. For example, women's buffered X-chromosome may protect them against certain disorders to which men are more vulnerable (Holden, 1987). Estrogen and prolactin may protect against some major diseases, including heart disease. Women may also have stronger immune response. At present, all these hypotheses are reasonable (Holden, 1987; Wingard, 1982).

Another reason why men may die in greater numbers at all ages than do women is that men engage in more risky behaviors. Chief among these is smoking, which may account for as much as 40% of the mortality difference between men and women. Smoking, of course, is a risk factor for such major disorders as coronary heart disease, cancer, and emphysema, which directly cause death. In addition, the Type A behavior syndrome,

discussed in Chapter 7, is more prevalent among men than women, adding to men's risk for coronary heart disease (Wingard, 1982).

Men also participate in other risky behaviors. For example, they are typically exposed to more occupational stress than women and more often hold hazardous jobs, as in construction work, police work, or firefighting. Men's alcohol consumption is greater than women's, exposing them to liver damage, and they consume more drugs than do women. Men are more likely to participate in hazardous sports and to use firearms recreationally. Men's greater access to firearms, in turn, makes them more likely to use guns to commit suicide—a method that is more effective than the methods (such as poison) typically favored by women. Men also use motor vehicles, including automobiles and motorcycles, more than women, contributing to their high death rate from accidents (Waldron & Johnston, 1976; Wingard, 1982).

A third theory maintains that social support may serve more of a protective function for women than for men. On the one hand, it is clear that being married benefits men, in terms of mortality, more than women. In fact, marriage for women seems to serve little or no protective function, whereas married men live substantially longer than unmarried men. However, women report having more close friends and participating in more group activities, such as church, that may offer support. Whether these factors contribute to women's longer life span remains to be seen (Wingard, 1982).

Which of these theories is correct? All may be correct to some extent. Clearly, smoking and Type A behavior account for some part of the sex difference in mortality (40%), and another 33% appears to be due to men's higher rates of suicide, accidents, cirrhosis of the liver due to alcohol consumption, respiratory cancers, and emphysema. However, such factors as women's social support or women's biological fitness may play an indirect role in the occurs and family members are not reconciled with the one who has died, they may feel guilt over possibly having contributed to the death, upset over having failed to make peace with the victim, and pained at having been deprived of the chance to make amends. As a consequence, the psychologist or other counselor may sometimes have a role in helping the survivors come to terms with the death and work through their guilt and self-blame (Kastenbaum, 1979).

Death in Old Age

> In olden times, as was the custom, an elderly woman went out of sight of others to become young again. She swam off a little way and discarded her aged skin, but on her return she was not recognized by her granddaughter, who became frightened and drove her away. The aged woman recovered her old skin from the water and resumed it. From then on, this power was lost to man; aging and death was inevitable. (Melanesian folk tale, Hinton, 1967, p. 36)

Dying is not easy at any time during the life cycle, but it may be easier at some times than others. Old age is one of those times. The elderly are generally more prepared to face death than are the young. They are more likely than young people to have thought about their death and to have made some initial prepara-

tions. The elderly have seen friends and relatives die and often express greater readiness to die themselves. They are more likely than younger people to have been through some of the issues associated with death, such as loss of appearance and failure to meet all the goals they once had for themselves (Kalish, 1977). They may have already experienced a shrinking of their social world through the death of a spouse or friends, and they may have withdrawn from other activities because of their now limited energy (Cumming, 1964; Cumming, Dean, Newell, & McCafferty, 1960; Kalish, 1977).

Typically, the elderly die of degenerative diseases such as cancer, stroke, heart failure, or just general physical decline that predisposes them to infectious disease or organ failure. Although degenerative diseases are not themselves easy to cope with, the actual death experienced by the elderly may be easier. The terminal phase of illness is generally shorter for them because there is often more than one biological competitor for death. As an age group, the elderly may have a greater chance to achieve death with dignity.

One curious fact about the elderly is that typically women live longer than men. Box 13.3 explores some of the reasons for this difference in mortality rates between men and women. Table 13.1 provides a formula for roughly calculating personal longevity.

TABLE 13.1   How Long Will You Live?

This is a rough guide for calculating your personal longevity. The basic life expectancy for males is age 67 and for females it is age 75. Write down your basic life expectancy. If you are in your 50s or 60s, you should add 10 years to the basic figure because you have already proven yourself to be quite durable. If you are over age 60 and active, add another 2 years.

Basic Life Expectancy   _____
Describe how each item below applies to you and add or subtract the appropriate number of years from your basic life expectancy.

1. Family history
   Add 5 years if 2 or more of your grandparents lived to 80 or beyond.   _____
   Subtract 4 years if any parent, grandparent, sister, or brother died of a heart attack or   _____
   stroke before 50. Subtract 2 years if anyone died from these diseases before 60.
   Subtract 3 years for each case of diabetes, thyroid disorders, breast cancer, cancer of   _____
   the digestive system, asthma, or chronic bronchitis among parents or grandparents.

2. Marital status
   If you are married and male, add 10 years; if married and female, add 4 years.   _____
   If you are over 25 and not married, subtract 1 year for every unwedded decade.   _____

3. Economic status
   Subtract 2 years if your family income is over $400,000 per year.   _____
   Subtract 3 years if you have been poor for greater part of life.   _____

4. Physique
   Subtract 1 year for every 10 pounds you are overweight.   _____
   For each inch your girth measurement exceeds your chest measurement deduct 2   _____
   years.
   Add 3 years if you are over 40 and not overweight.   _____

5. Exercise
   Regular and moderate (jogging 3 times a week), add 3 years.   _____
   Regular and vigorous (long-distance running 3 times a week), add 5 years   _____
   Subtract 3 years if your job is sedentary. Add 3 years if it is active.   _____

6. Alcohol*
   Add 2 years if you are a light drinker (1–3 drinks a day).   _____
   Subtract 5 to 10 years if you are a heavy drinker (more than 4 drinks a day).   _____
   Subtract 1 year if you are a teetotaler.   _____

7. Smoking
   Two or more packs of cigarettes per day, subtract 8 years.   _____
   One to two packs per day, subtract 4 years.   _____
   Less than one pack, subtract 2 years.   _____
   Subtract 2 years if you regularly smoke a pipe or cigars.   _____

8. Disposition
   Add 2 years if you are a reasoned, practical person.   _____
   Subtract 2 years if you are aggressive, intense and competitive.   _____
   Add 1–5 years if you are basically happy and content with life.   _____

TABLE 13.1   How Long Will You Live? **(Continued)**

 9. Education
    Less than high school, subtract 2 years.   _____
    Four years of school beyond high school, add 1 year.   _____
    Five or more years beyond high school, add 3 years.   _____

10. Environment
    If you have lived most of your life in a rural environment, add 4 years.   _____
    Subtract 2 years if you have lived most of your life in an urban environment. _____

11. Sleep
    More than 9 hours a day, subtract 5 years.   _____

12. Temperature
    Add 2 years if your home's thermostat is set at no more than 68°F.   _____

13. Health care
    Regular medical checkups and regular dental care, add 3 years.   _____
    Frequently ill, subtract 2 years.   _____

(Source: Schulz, 1978, pp. 97–98)

*It should be noted that these calculations for alcohol consumption are controversial and require additional evidence. It is not clear that moderate drinking is healthful relative to teetotaling, and indeed the reverse may be true.

PSYCHOLOGICAL ISSUES IN ADVANCING ILLNESS

Although many people die very suddenly, particularly in adolescence or middle adulthood, most of the terminally ill know that they are going to die and what they will die of for some time before their death. Advancing illness brings with it the gradual awareness of death; as a consequence, a variety of medical and psychological issues arise for the patient (Levy, 1983).

Continued Treatment and Advancing Illness

Advancing and terminal illness frequently bring the need for continued treatments with debilitating and unpleasant side effects (e.g., Levy, 1983). For example, radiation therapy and chemotherapy for cancer may produce discomfort, nausea and vomiting, chronic diarrhea, hair loss, skin discoloration, fatigue, and loss of energy (Edelstyn, 1969). Surgical intervention is also commonly required. The patient with advancing diabetes may require amputation of extremities such as fingers or toes because poor circulation has made them gangrenous. The patient with advancing cancer may require removal of an organ to which the illness has now spread, such as a lung or part of the liver. The patient with degenerative kidney disease may be given a transplant in the hope that it will forestall further deterioration.

Many patients find themselves repeated objects of surgical or chemical therapy in a desperate effort to save their lives; after several such efforts, the patient may resist any further intervention. Patients who have undergone repeated surgery may feel that they are being disassembled bit by bit. Or, the person who has had several rounds of chemotherapy may feel despair over the apparent uselessness of any new treatment. Each procedure raises anew the threat of death and underscores the fact that the disease has not been arrested. Frequently, too, these procedures may lead to permanent disabilities or loss of functioning. For example, the young woman who has had a hysterectomy because her estrogen production is promoting the growth of a cancer will have to come to terms with the finality of her lost childbearing ability. And in many cases, the sheer number of treatments can lead to exhaustion, discomfort, and depression (McCorkle, 1973).

Thus, there comes a time when the question of whether or not to accept any new treatments becomes an issue (e.g., Hunt & Arras, 1977; McCorkle, 1973). When a patient refuses to accept any more treatments, it can indicate any of several psychological states. On the one hand, if the patient feels robbed of self-

Many terminally ill patients who find themselves repeated objects of intervention become worn out and eventually refuse additional treatment

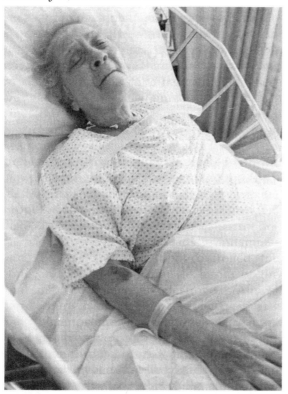

control by the disease, medical interventions, or both, he or she may refuse treatment as an expression of anger and an effort to regain mastery over the environment (see Brehm, 1966; Brehm & Brehm, 1981). Alternatively, refusal of treatment may indicate depression and a feeling of hopelessness. In other cases, if a patient recognizes that therapy will not improve the situation and, furthermore, realizes that the therapy is at least partially responsible for resultant physical discomfort, refusing treatment may represent a carefully thought-out decision (McCorkle, 1973). These different reasons for refusing therapy suggest different psychological approaches. When anger is involved, the patient may need a more involving role in treatment decisions, or at least in the small decisions of everyday life (for example, regarding what to eat or wear) to offset the feelings of loss of control or hopelessness; once some sense of control is restored, the decision as to whether or not to continue treatment can be evaluated in its own right. When the patient's decision to refuse therapy is supported by a thoughtful choice, the patient's wishes should be respected.

As the courts have become increasingly concerned with when treatment should be discontinued, the issue has become increasingly thorny. A recent California case involved a paraplegic woman who desired to end her own life by refusing to have any more food. The hospital took the case to court to get permission to force-feed the patient to keep her alive. A controversial Massachusetts case involved parents of a child with cancer who refused to permit chemotherapy on religious grounds, despite the fact that the chemotherapy could potentially save the boy's life. These issues become especially problematic, of course, when it is agents other than the patient making the decision. For example, in the Karen Ann Quinlan case, involving a young girl who had been in a coma for many months, the parents went to the courts to get permission to withdraw the life-support system. Initially, the courts refused to permit it, a decision that was later reversed. Issues like these will no doubt continue to arise and unless the medical community is prepared to develop more standardized and formal guidelines for making these difficult decisions, the courts will impose solutions.

Related to the question of when and if to terminate treatments is the concept of a **living will.** In 1977, California enacted a law enabling people with terminal diseases to write a "living will" requesting that extraordinary life-sustaining procedures not be used in the event that they were unable to make this decision on their own. The will, which is signed in front of witnesses, is usually developed when the person is diagnosed as having a terminal illness. It provides instructions and legal protection for the physician, so that life-prolonging interventions such as respirators will not be indefinitely undertaken in an ulti-

mately vain effort to keep the patient alive. The concept of living wills has been a controversial one. It is not always 100% clear that an illness is terminal in that remission may sometimes occur. It is also not clear how long or painful the ending of an illness may be. Although it might be desirable to resolve these issues on a case-by-case basis with physicians using their own judgment with input and help from the family members and patient, at present physicians may need the protection of the living will to justify termination of life-support systems and other controversial actions that may hasten death. Box 13.4 presents a daughter's perspective on some of these issues with regard to her dying father.

Eventually, our culture will have to struggle with the issue of **euthanasia,** that is, ending the life of a person who is suffering from a painful terminal illness through such methods as drug injections. Although illegal in the United States, euthanasia is condoned in The Netherlands under certain restricted conditions, and similar laws are under consideration in other countries. In cases of euthanasia, the courts have so far been irregular in their rulings. While some cases of euthanasia have gone unprosecuted, others have resulted in convictions for those who chose to help a severely ill spouse or other family member end his or her life.

Increasingly, the courts have arbitrated issues of life and death. The photograph below shows the parents of Karen Ann Quinlan (a young girl who was in a coma for many months as a result of an accident), who petitioned the courts to withdraw the life-support system, because they knew she would never recover.

Changes in the Patient's Self-Concept

Just as chronically ill patients must engage in new health-related activities and continued monitoring of their physical condition, so must patients with advancing illness adjust their expectations and activities according to the stage of their disorder. The difference is that for patients with progressive diseases such as cancer or severe diabetes, life is a constant act of readjusting expectations and activities to accommodate an ever-expanding patient role.

Box 13.4
Death: A Daughter's Perspective

My father sleeps, I sit writing...trying to get something on paper I know is there, but which is as elusive and slippery as the life that's ending before me.

My father has cancer. Cancer of the sinuses, and as the autopsy will show later, of the left occipital lobe, mastoid, cerebellum.

I have not seen my father for nine months, when the lump was still a secret below his ear. A few months later I heard about it and headaches, and then from time to time all the diagnoses of arthritis, a cyst, sinusitis...even senility. Then finally—the lump now a painful burden to be carried— he was subjected to nine days of tests of bowels, bladder, blood. And on the last day a hollow needle was inserted into the growth; the cells gathered, magnified, interpreted and pronounced cancer. Immediate surgery and/or cobalt treatment indicated.

And after the trauma of no dentures, no hearing aid and one unexpected cobalt treatment, triumphant that his mind functioned and his voice was firm, he stated unfalteringly: "Let me alone. No more

treatments. I am 75. I have had an excellent life. It is time for me to die in my own way." His decision was not to be met with approval.

Death is not easy under any circumstances, but at least he did not suffer tubes and IV's and false hope, and we did not suffer the play-acting, the helpless agonies of watching a loved one suffer to no purpose, finally growing inured to it all or even becoming irritated with a dying vegetable that one cannot relate to any longer. In the end, I have learned, death is a very personal matter between parents and offspring, husbands and wives, loving neighbors and friends, and between God or symbols of belief and the dying ones and all who care about them.

There comes a point where it is no longer the business of the courts, the American Medical Association, the government. It is private business. And I write now publicly only because it needs to be said again, and my father would have agreed.

(Gross, 1976)

The problems of incorporating the patient role into one's life are exacerbated by the difficulties such accommodations create for the existing self-concept. As the disease progresses, patients are increasingly less able to present themselves effectively (Liegner, 1986–1987). It may become difficult for them to maintain control of biological and social functioning. They may be incontinent (unable to control urination or bowel movements); they may drool, have distorted facial expressions, or shake uncontrollably. None of this is attractive either to the patient or others. These patients may also be in intermittent pain, may suffer from uncontrollable retching or vomiting, and may experience a shocking deterioration in appearance due to weight loss, the stress of treatments, or the sheer drain of illness. Even more threatening to some patients is mental regression and inability to concentrate. Such losses may be due either to the progressive nature of the disease itself or to the tranquilizing and disorienting effects of painkillers. Mental regression may be the most threatening loss of all, since it undermines the patient's very identity.

Issues of Social Interaction

The threats to the self-concept that stem from loss of mental and physical functioning spill over into threats to social interaction. Although terminally ill patients often want and need visitors, they may be afraid that their obvious mental and physical deterioration will upset visitors (Carey, 1975). Moreover, a single visit from someone who has not been warned of the changes in the patient and who inadvertently expresses revulsion or alarm can disturb the patient. One consequence of these unsatisfying social interactions is that patients may begin a process of social withdrawal, whereby they gradually restrict visits to only a few family members (Hinton, 1967). Family and friends can help make this withdrawal less extreme: They can prepare prospective visitors in advance for the patient's state so that the visitor's reaction can be controlled; they can also screen out some visitors who cannot keep their emotions in check.

There are reasons for a patient's withdrawal other than concern over mental and physical deterioration. Some disengagement from the social world is normal and may represent a grieving process through which the final loss of family and friends is anticipated (Abrams, 1966). This period of anticipatory grieving may exacerbate communication difficulties because it is hard for the patient to express affection for others while simultaneously preparing to leave them.

In other cases, withdrawal may be caused by fear of depressing others and becoming an emotional burden. The patient may feel guilty for taking up so much of the family's time, energy, and money and may therefore withdraw so as not to be even more of a burden (Carey, 1975). In such cases, it is easy for misunderstandings to arise. The family may mistakenly

believe that the patient wishes to be left alone and may therefore respect these wishes. Instead, family and friends may need to make a strong and concerted effort to draw the patient out to forestall a potential severe depression (Abrams, 1966; Hinton, 1967). Yet another cause of withdrawal may be the patient's bitterness over impending death and resentment of the living. In such cases, the family may need to understand that such bitterness is normal and that it usually passes.

Social interactions during the terminal phase of illness, then, are complex and often marked by the patient's gradual or intermittent withdrawal. In determining how to respond to this withdrawal, one must try to understand which of several reasons may be producing the behavior (Hinton, 1967).

Communication Issues

As long as a patient's prognosis is favorable, communication is usually open; however, as the prognosis worsens and therapy becomes more drastic, communication may start to break down (Kastenbaum & Aisenberg, 1972; Kübler-Ross, 1969; Livingston & Zimet, 1965; Payne & Krant, 1969). Medical staff may become evasive when questioned about the patient's status. Family members may be cheerfully optimistic with the patient, but confused and frightened when they try to elicit information from medical staff. The potential for a breakdown in communications as illness advances can be traced to several factors.

First, death itself is still very much a taboo topic in our society (Schoenberg, Carr, Peretz, & Kutscher, 1970, 1977). The issue is generally avoided in polite conversation, little research is conducted on death (Schulz, 1978), and even when death strikes within a family, the survivors often try to bear their grief alone. The proper thing to do, many people feel, is not to bring it up.

A second reason why communication breaks down in advancing illness is because of assumptions, possibly faulty ones, about what others want to hear. Each of the parties—medical staff, patient, and family—believes that the others do not want to talk about death. Patients fear upsetting their families or the medical staff by asking questions about death. Family members may not bring up the issue because they fear that the patient does not know that the prognosis is poor and they believe that any discussion of the point will stress the patient, making the medical condition worse (Schoenberg et al., 1977). Physicians and other medical staff do not bring up the issue of death for fear of stressing the patient and family (White, 1977).

But a third reason for the breakdown in communication is that each of the principals in the communication process has strong personal reasons for not wanting to discuss death. Many patients do not really want to hear the answers to their unasked questions. In reality, they already know the answers and fear having to cope with the finality of having them verbally confirmed by a medical authority (Peck, 1972). As long as no one has actually said anything concrete, terminally ill patients can continue to treasure those moments when they convince themselves that everything will be fine and they will soon be well; in more lucid moments, these patients are all too aware that this is not the case.

Families may wish to avoid acknowledging the prospective death of the family member because they would be forced to confront their own guilt and lingering questions: "If we had urged him to see a doctor earlier, would he be cured now?" "Did we do anything to bring this on?" "Did our complacency aggravate the condition?" "Why is it him and not me?" "Have I treated her as well as I should have all these years?" "Should we have spared no expense and tried every possible clinic and treatment?"

Finally, medical staff have strong reasons for not wanting to confront the patient's death directly (Liegner, 1986–1987). They may fear having to cope with the upset of the family or

with angry reproaches from the family and the patient over the apparent failure of treatment (White, 1977). Perhaps as a consequence of these fears and the wishful thinking that can evolve from them, it was once thought best not to tell patients that they had a terminal illness; cheerful optimism and secrecy were felt to be the preferred approach. In some cases, family members might be told, but the patient was believed to be unaware of the truth and better off in this ignorance (e.g., Litin, 1960). However, it has become clear that patients not only know that they have a terminal illness but also want to know the truth (e.g., Cappon, 1969; Dempsey, 1975; Kelly & Friesen, 1950; Peck, 1972). Patients can read the cues on the faces around them, and when openness and honesty in communication change to half-hearted reassurances and hasty exits, the message is clear (Hackett & Weisman, 1969).

The Issue of Nontraditional Treatment

As both health and communication deteriorate, some terminally ill patients turn away from traditional medical care in desperation or anger. Many such patients fall victim to the alternative and dubious remedies offered outside the formal health care system. Frantic family members, friends who are trying to be helpful, and patients themselves may scour fringe publications for seemingly effective remedies or cures; they may invest thousands of dollars in their generally unsuccessful search.

What prompts people to take these often uncomfortable, inconvenient, and useless measures? Some are so frantic and unable to face the prospect of death that they will use up both their own savings and those of the family in the hope of a miracle cure. In other cases, the turn to nontraditional medicine may be a symptom of a deteriorating relationship with the health care system. Seemingly abandoned by physicians who have no more time or inclination to work with them or who have not given them straightforward information about their physical care, patients may turn to quacks who seem to be providing more information, more optimism, and more humanistic care. This is not to suggest that a solid patient-practitioner relationship can prevent every patient from turning to quackery. However, when the patient is well-informed and feels cared for by others, he or she is less likely to look for alternative remedies.

Strong criticism of nontraditional medicine frequently prompts strenuous objections coupled with loudly touted case histories of dramatic improvement due to some unlikely treatment. Such criticism should not be taken to mean that no patient ever survives nontraditional treatments or that some will not be found eventually to be effective treatments. Indeed, as Chapter 11 clearly indicates, placebo effects alone effect miracle cures in some cases. However, these are relatively rare, and the small chance of being among them may not justify the great expense and hardship involved in undergoing these dubious therapies.

Although nontraditional "cures" do hold out a promise of health to some, most dying patients eventually come to accept their situation. How do patients cope with such knowledge?

ARE THERE STAGES IN ADJUSTMENT TO DYING?

The idea that people pass through a predictable series of **stages of dying** in coming to terms with the prospect of death has appeared commonly in the research literature on death and dying (e.g., Falek & Britton, 1974; Glaser, 1972; Kübler-Ross, 1969; Pattison, 1967). Of the different formulations that have developed, Elisabeth Kübler-Ross's has had the most impact; it is accordingly to her work that we turn. Kübler-Ross's contributions are striking for several reasons. Death has often been a taboo topic, both in research literature and in the popular media (Schulz, 1978). In stark contrast to this general pattern of evasion and silence, Kübler-Ross's book, *On Death and Dying,* a popularized account of her observations and her theory about how people die, maintained a top position on many best-seller lists for nearly 2 years. Few books achieve such remarkable success. That a book on death should do so is astonishing. This fact indicates that although there is a general taboo on talking about death, there is an enormous need to do so. Kübler-Ross's work filled this need for many millions of people.

Kübler-Ross's Five-Stage Theory

With this general information, let us turn to her theory. Kübler-Ross suggested that people pass through five predictable stages as they adjust to the prospect of death: denial, anger, bargaining, depression, and acceptance.

Denial   The first stage, denial, is thought to be a person's initial reaction on learning of the diagnosis of terminal illness. The immediate response may be that some mistake has been made, that the test results or x-rays have been mixed up with those of someone else, and that the diagnosis will shortly be reversed. For most people, this shock and the denial that anything is wrong lasts only a few days.

Most of us have probably experienced a similar reaction when something we had counted on fails to occur. Being rejected by a school to which we had expected to be admitted or being abandoned by a lover when we thought all was well can produce a similar response. The shocked reaction of denial may occur because, in assuming that all would progress as we expected, we made plans for the future and envisioned how things would be; as a consequence of the bad news, these cognitive and emotional commitments to the future must now be withdrawn and a new future must be constructed. Doing so takes some time. While these things are sorting themselves through, denial serves a protective function. Thus, denial early on in adjustment to life-threatening illness is both normal and useful (Lazarus, 1983).

Sometimes denial lasts longer than a few days. When it does, it may require psychological intervention. Extreme denial ("this is not happening to me, it is happening to someone else") may be manifested by terrified patients who are unable to confront the fact of their illness or the likelihood of their eventual death. But is it not helpful to a patient to be able to deny death? Denial may give the appearance of being a successful psychological shelter from reality; as such, one might be tempted to encourage it. However, denial is thought to be a primitive and ultimately unsuccessful defense (Weisman, 1972). It may mask anxiety without making it go away. The patient who is denying the implications of illness often appears rigidly overcontrolled, as if a crack in the defense would cause the entire facade to crumble. In fact, reality can break through for a few minutes or hours at a time, leaving the patient vulnerable, frightened, and possibly even hysterical. Long-term denial of one's illness, then, is a defensive pattern from which a patient should be coaxed through therapeutic intervention.

Anger   Denial usually gives way after a few days because the illness itself creates circumstances that must be met. Decisions must be made regarding future treatments, if any, where the patient will be cared for, and by whom. At this point, according to Kübler-Ross, the second stage, anger, may set in. The angry patient is asking the question "Why me?" Considering all the other people who could have gotten the illness, all the people who had the same symptoms but got a favorable diagnosis, and all the people who are older, dumber, more bad-tempered, less productive, or just plain evil, why should the patient be the one who is dying? Kübler-Ross quotes one of her dying patients:

I suppose most anybody in my position would look at somebody else and say, "Well, why couldn't it have been him?" and this has crossed my mind several times. An old man whom I have known ever since I was a little kid came down the street. He was eighty-two years old, and he is of no earthly use as far as we mortals can tell. He's rheumatic, he's a cripple, he's dirty, just not the type of person you would like to be. And the thought hit me strongly, now why couldn't it have been old George instead of me? (Quoted in Kübler-Ross, 1969, p. 50)

The angry patient may show resentment toward anyone who is healthy, such as hospital staff, family members, or friends. Angry patients who cannot express their anger directly by shouting or being irritable may do so indirectly by becoming embittered. Bitter patients show resentment through death jokes, cracks about their deteriorating appearance and capacities, or pointed remarks about all the exciting things that they will not be able to do because those events will happen after their death. Anger is one of the harder responses for family and friends to manage. They are, in effect, being blamed by the patient for being well. The family may need to work together with a therapist to understand that the patient is not really angry with them but at fate; they need to see that this anger will be directed at anyone who is nearby, especially toward people with whom the patient feels no obligation to be polite and well-behaved. Unhappily, family members often fall into this category.

Bargaining   Bargaining is the third stage of Kübler-Ross's formulation. At this point, the patient abandons anger in favor of a different strategy: trading good behavior for good health. Bargaining frequently takes the form of a pact with God in which the patient agrees to engage in good works or at least to abandon selfish ways in exchange for health or more time. A sudden rush of charitable activity or uncharacteristically pleasant behavior may be a sign that the patient is trying to strike such a bargain.

Let us step back for a moment to try to understand exactly what may motivate the responses of anger and bargaining in reaction to death. Basically, both are manifestations of principles of social exchange or equity. People have a deep-seated need to believe that the world is just: that good things happen to good people and that evil befalls evildoers (Lerner, 1970). When a threatening event like terminal illness occurs, it seems to violate the natural order. Accordingly, people make efforts to preserve their sense that the world is just, first by becoming angry at the violation and later by attempting to restore justice through a bargain. That is, with the response of anger, the patient is essentially saying, "I behaved well, or certainly no worse than anyone else, so why is this happening to me?" Bargaining is likewise an appeal to the principles of equity, in that the patient seems to think that good works can be the basis of an exchange in which the disease will be taken away.

Depression   Once it becomes apparent that illness does not conform to the laws of justice, that it may strike at random and be unresponsive to efforts to drive it away, depression may set in. Depression, the fourth stage in Kübler-Ross's model, may be viewed as coming to terms with lack of control. The patient acknowledges that little can now be done to stay the course of illness. This realization may be coincident with a worsening of symptoms, tangible evidence that the illness is not going to be cured. At this stage patients may feel nauseated, breathless, and tired. They may find it hard to eat, to control elimination, to focus attention, and to escape pain or discomfort. If treatment regimens have been continued, the associated side effects can further aggravate these reactions.

Kübler-Ross refers to the stage of depression as a time for "anticipatory grief," when patients mourn the prospect of their own deaths. This grieving process seems to occur in two stages, as the patient first comes to terms with the loss of past valued activities and friends and later begins to anticipate the future loss of activities and relationships. Patients must also deal with their deteriorating appearance and, in some cases, deteriorating mental functioning as well. The stage of depression, though far from pleasant, can be very functional in that patients begin to prepare for what will come in the future. As a consequence, it may sometimes be wise not to intervene immediately with depression but rather to let it run its course, at least for a brief time (Kübler-Ross, 1969).

The difficulties of dealing with the depression of terminal illness are well illustrated by the following comments of a particularly articulate terminally ill patient:

> I've just experienced several days of deep depression, full of morbid thoughts of death and illness. The thing that disturbs me about such depression is my uncertainty as to their generation and cause. If they are psychochemical or endocrinological in origin, then I can dismiss them more easily than if I believe they are the upwelling of some great hidden angst. Are they the maudlin, morbid reflections of a chemically unbalanced brain? This is somewhat of an alienating idea, those thoughts aren't me, they're just my body acting up. Having read more deeply into existentialist ideas lately, it's intellectually somewhat emotionally repugnant to me to alienate my "inner self." But with such thoughts of death, decay, the aging in my body and mind, my love for Bob [the patient's husband] and my pain at eventually leaving him—all inevitably true—(I can't dismiss them as fantasies), I can't live happily. Solomon says life isn't meant to be happy, but I'm thinking that I prefer the delusion if such feelings as I have are the alternative. (Schneidman, 1977, p. 78)

The advice to let depression run its course obviously does not extend to clear cases of pathological depression, in which the patient is continually morose, unresponsive to social stimuli, unable to eat, and basically uninterested in activity. In these cases, a therapist may have to intervene. In so doing, however, it is important that depression be distinguished from further physical deterioration. In advanced illness, patients often have so little energy that they cannot discharge activities on their own. What such patients may need—rather than a therapist—is a quiet companion, someone to spoonfeed them, and someone to sponge them off from time to time.

Acceptance   The fifth stage in Kübler-Ross's theory is acceptance. At this point, the patient may be too weak to be angry and too accustomed to the idea of dying to be depressed. Instead, a tired, peaceful, though not necessarily pleasant calm may descend. The patient is resigned to the prospect of death. He or she may spend much time sleeping and, when awake, have little energy. Conversation may be slow and marked by long quiet periods. Some patients use this time to make preparations, deciding how to divide up their last personal possessions and saying goodbye or writing notes to old friends and family members.

Evaluation of Kübler-Ross's Theory

How good an account of the process of dying is Kübler-Ross's stage theory? As a description of the reactions of dying patients, her work has been invaluable. She has chronicled nearly the full array of reactions to death, as those who work with the dying will be quick to acknowledge. Her work is also of inestimable value in pointing out the counseling needs of the dying, both the existence of such needs and the forms counseling might take. Finally, along with other researchers, she has broken through the silence and taboos surrounding death, making them objects of both scientific study and sensitive concern.

What her work has not done is to identify stages of dying. "Stage" is a technical term, and a stage theory should be able to demonstrate that each patient goes through every

stage and no patient progresses to a later stage without having gone through the ones on which it is thought to be built. Kübler-Ross's theory does not meet these criteria. Patients do not go through five stages in a predetermined order. Some patients never go through a particular stage. Others will go through a stage more than once. All the feelings associated with the five stages may be experienced by some patients on an alternating basis. The resigned patient has moments of anger or depression. The angry patient may also experience denial. The depressed patient may still be hoping for a last-minute reprieve (see Schulz & Aderman, 1974; Weisman, 1972).

In particular, periods of intermittent denial often occur throughout the process of dying. That is, the patient is likely to have occasional periods when he or she simply wants to avoid the thought of death. The patient will not talk about it, may deny that it is imminent if the subject is brought up, and may become cross and insistent that recovery is on the horizon if the topic is pursued. Alternating with this denial, however, may be long periods in which this same patient will speak openly of death, of plans for the burial and memorial service, or of what others will be doing after he or she dies (Kastenbaum & Aisenberg, 1972).

Kübler-Ross's stage theory also does not fully acknowledge the importance of anxiety, which can be present throughout the dying process. Indeed, other researchers have suggested that, next to depression, anxiety is one of the most commonly observed responses (Hinton, 1967; Schulz & Aderman, 1974). Often, however, anxiety is less tied to dying itself than to the symptoms experienced during terminal illness. What patients fear most is not being able to control pain; they may welcome or even seek death to avoid it (Hinton, 1967). Other symptoms, such as difficulty breathing or uncontrollable vomiting, likewise produce anxiety, which may exacerbate the patient's already deteriorating physical and mental condition.

In all fairness to Kübler-Ross, it should be noted that she readily acknowledges that her "stages" can occur in varying, intermittent order. Unfortunately, this point is sometimes missed by her audience. Some researchers have reported that those who work with the dying—such as nurses, physicians, and social workers—may expect a dying person to go through these stages in order, and that they become upset when a patient does not "die right" (Liss-Levinson, 1982; Pattison, 1967; Silver & Wortman, 1980).

Is Kübler-Ross's stage theory wrong and some other stage theory correct, or is it simply inappropriate to talk about stages of dying? The answer is that no stage model can be infallibly applied to the process of dying (Schulz & Aderman, 1974). Although depression commonly occurs just before death, this is the only consistency found in temporal analyses of the dying process (Schulz & Aderman, 1974). Dying is a complex and individual process, subject to no rules and few regularities.

PSYCHOLOGICAL MANAGEMENT OF THE TERMINALLY ILL

Medical Staff and the Terminally Ill Patient

Most people—some 70%—die in a medical institution rather than at home; in urban areas, the figure can be closer to 90% (Raether & Slater, 1977). Unfortunately, death in the institutional environment can be very depersonalized and fragmented. Often the reason for keeping the patient in the hospital is to continue treatments in hope of a last-minute cure; thus, patients may be subject to painful medical procedures at the time when they are least able to withstand them. Although these procedures do, in some cases, restore people to health, they often simply prolong the dying process. Wards may be understaffed, so the staff may be unable to provide the kind of emotional support the patient needs. Hospital regulations may restrict the number of visitors

Medical staff can be very significant to a dying patient, because they see the patient on a regular basis, provide realistic information, and are privy to the patient's last personal thoughts and wishes.

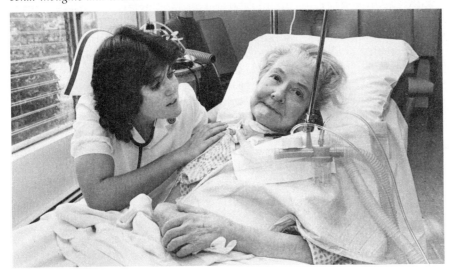

or the length of time that they can stay, thereby reducing the availability of support from family and friends. Thus, death in an institution can be a long, lonely, mechanized, and dehumanizing experience.

The Significance of Medical Staff to the Patient   For these reasons, medical staff can come to be very significant to a patient. Physical dependence on medical staff is great, since the patient may need help for even the smallest thing, such as brushing teeth or turning over in bed. Frequently, staff are the only people to see the patient on a regular basis if he or she has no friends or family who can visit regularly. Moreover, staff can also be the only people who know the patient's actual physical state; hence, they are the patient's only source of realistic information. They may also know the patient's true feelings when others do not; often patients put up a cheerful front for family and friends so as not to upset them, or the patient may find that his or her need to talk is actively discouraged by family and friends who cannot absorb the additional pain of communicating directly about death (e.g., Abrams, 1966). The patient, then, may welcome communication with staff because he or she can be fully candid with them. Finally, staff are important because they are privy to one of the patient's most personal and private acts, the act of dying. By virtue of this shared intimacy, patients often feel especially close to staff.

Terminal care is very hard on medical staff, however. It is the least interesting physical care because it is so often **palliative,** or designed to make the patient feel comfortable, rather than curative, or designed to cure the patient's disease (Benoliel, 1977). It involves a lot of unpleasant custodial work, such as feeding, changing, and bathing the patient. Even more important is the emotional strain terminal care places on staff. The staff may "burn

out" from watching patient after patient die despite their efforts (Maslach, 1977).

The temptation to withdraw into a crisply efficient manner, rather than a warm and supportive one, so as to avoid continued personal pain, is great (e.g., Maslach, 1979; Payne & Krant, 1969).

The Physician's Role in Terminal Care   What are the roles staff can assume that help them as well as patients manage the intense experience that has been thrust on them? Certain roles fall to the primary physician, who typically has the responsibility for explaining the diagnosis and prognosis to the patient initially and on whom patients continue to rely heavily for information and support (Holland, 1973; White, 1977). Unfortunately, as noted earlier, researchers have found that communication between physician and patient is likely to remain open only as long as the prognosis is good. As therapy becomes more drastic and the prognosis looks less favorable, communication can break down, and this happens for several reasons. As care becomes palliative, there is often little that a physician can actively do to help the patient that some other staff member could not do at least as well. Understandably, physicians want to reserve their time for the patients who can most profit from it. A second reason is that a dying patient often means failure to the physician, both of medical procedures generally and of his or her efforts to effect a cure. Time spent with such a patient brings reminders that the treatment did not work and that death will be the outcome. Some physicians cannot easily face a patient's grief, anger, or hysteria on learning that death is imminent; they may not have been trained to cope with such an outburst. In fact, Kübler-Ross (1969) noted an instance where a patient confronted her physician with the remark, "I wish it were you down here, instead of me."

Although physicians have understandable reasons for withdrawing from a patient who is not expected to live, terminally ill patients interpret such behavior as abandonment and take it very hard. Accordingly, a continued role for the physician in the patient's terminal care in the form of brief but frequent visits is desirable. The physician continues to be the person who knows the most about the patient's changing condition. Therefore he or she can provide important information that may be unavailable from others (Holland, 1973). The physician can alert the patient to ways in which his or her condition will change, explain the probable meaning of new and perhaps frightening symptoms, and help allay the patient's anxiety by providing correct information and a realistic timetable of events (Dempsey, 1975; Glaser & Strauss, 1965; Holland, 1973). This is not to say that the patient should be told when death will come; neither the physician nor anyone else can know that exactly. Rather, the physician can provide a rough indication of how much time remains and how active the patient can be during that time. The patient can then plan accordingly, knowing when to arrange last visits with friends, when to make final arrangements, and so on.

Death is a "status passage," a dramatic change from one situation to another, much like birth, marriage, or divorce (Glaser & Strauss, 1965). All status changes involve personal upheaval that can be reduced by adequate financial, social, and psychological preparation (Kalish, 1977). Patients who are uninformed about the course of their illness do not have the basic information needed to make these preparations. Thus, the physician who provides well-timed communications about changes in the patient's medical situation can enable the status passage to progress smoothly.

The patient and physician may also use their time together to make decisions about medical interventions. Some patients want to have every possible chance and are prepared to be sustained indefinitely on life-support systems. Others may refuse such treatment, wishing to be allowed to end their lives without such measures. Ultimately, the physician may have to decide when to withdraw a life-support system, and—knowing the patient's and family members' wishes—can provide guidance in this difficult matter (see Levy, 1983).

The Role of Other Medical Staff in Terminal Care Although physicians can and should continue to have an active role in the care of the dying patient, their visits will be brief. Thus, most of the care and social interaction the patient receives will be provided by other hospital staff (Benoliel, 1977). As noted in our discussion of hospitalization (Chapter 9), in a given day, any single patient may have contact with as many as thirty or forty different staff members with whom he or she may at least exchange a few words. Therefore, one important issue is consistency of communications (Holland, 1973). As the prognosis worsens, there will be shifts in the amount and type of attention a patient receives from staff—changes to which the patient is sensitive. Moreover, as patients become more anxious about their condition, they may attempt to elicit information from every person with whom they interact. If everyone is closed-mouth or, worse, if the information given by one person contradicts that obtained from another, an already problematic psychological state may be worsened. Alternatively, a well-meaning staff member may touch off false optimism if a patient seizes on a piece of information and attaches too much significance to it; when the optimism proves to be baseless, the resulting depression, anxiety, disappointment, and suspiciousness may create a serious management problem (Pearlman, Stotsky, & Dominick, 1969).

Medical staff who work with the terminally ill should have an agreed-upon communication policy, preferably one that emphasizes tactful openness (Liegner, 1986–1987). One method of avoiding potential contradictions is to add to the patient's chart information about exactly what the patient has been told, what conclusions he or she seems to have reached, what the family has been told, what their reactions were, and whether or not counseling is advisable (Payne & Krant, 1969). In this way, the staff always has a constant and consistent set of guidelines and up-to-date information.

The attitudes that staff display toward terminal patients' symptoms are also important. Such patients exhibit a variety of symptoms that are frightening to both themselves and others, including pain, difficulty in breathing, and persistent vomiting. Responding to these symptoms in a calm, confident, unhurried, matter-of-fact, and supportive manner can reduce the fear these symptoms produce and can possibly reduce their severity. Patients may suffer loss of self-esteem when they exhibit such symptoms and fear that the staff will now find them repulsive. Continuing to maintain a respectful and personal manner toward the patient can alleviate these fears (Payne & Krant, 1969).

Another aspect of terminal illness to which sensitive staff can make a difference is feelings of loss of control. Control over one's body, one's social interactions, one's ability to concentrate, and the future, are all threatened or lost in terminal illness. This can lead to depression and feelings of helplessness, which may, in turn, aggravate the patient's physical condition. One possible way of offsetting such feelings is to make patients feel like informed participants in their own care. Thus, for example, prompt attentiveness to each new symptom and an adequate explanation of its meaning can instill some feelings of predictability if not control. Fully informing the patient about procedures and possible treatment side effects

(so as to reduce confusion over which symptoms are related to treatment and which are related to the illness) can also make the patient feel more in control. If the terminally ill patient can also be involved in decisions about care, even in small ways, this too can help.

A physician recounted the following incident, which illustrates the importance of even small degrees of control:

> I had been assisting in the management of a cancer patient for several months, and it was clear to me that she was going downhill. Her oncologist decided to try one last kind of chemotherapy before stopping treatment. She told him that she would do it as long as she had twenty-four hours in which to steel herself for it. The oncologist agreed, but through a misunderstanding and over the patient's protestations, chemotherapy was started immediately. When I saw her two days later, she had been hospitalized for uncontrollable vomiting. She told me, "I could have done it if they'd just listened to me and given me my twenty-four hours."

To the extent that hospital regimen allows, the patient should be allowed to make decisions such as what to eat, whether to eat in bed or move to a chair, what to watch on television, and when to visit the solarium, so that some degree of control can be maintained.

Some patients will not want control; in that case, control should not be thrust upon them. They may feel that they are in the hospital partly so that they will not have to take responsibility to make decisions; accordingly, they may wish to have even the least thing done for them. Moreover, after a certain point in illness, even small bits of control may be impossible. The patient may lack the will or energy to make a decision (Morris & Sherwood, 1987). A simple question like "Do you want soup or crackers?" may prompt the response, "You decide. I'm too tired."

To summarize, then, hospital staff often have an important role in the life of the dying patient, one that can be rewarding but which is also highly stressful. Psychiatrist Avery Weisman (1972, 1977), who has worked with dying patients for many years, outlined a very useful set of goals for medical staff in their work with the dying:

1. Informed consent—Patients should be told the nature of their condition and treatment and, to some extent, be involved in their own treatment.

2. Safe conduct—The physician and other staff should act as helpful guides for the patient through this new and frightening stage of life.

3. Significant survival—The physician and other medical staff should help the patient use his or her remaining time as well as possible.

4. Anticipatory grief—Both the patient and his or her family members should be aided in working through their anticipatory sense of loss and depression.

5. Timely and appropriate death—The patient should be allowed to die when and how he or she wants to, as much as possible. The patient should be allowed to achieve death with dignity.

Individual Counseling with the Terminally Ill

However much medical staff might wish to devote time to each terminally ill patient and however much each patient might want and need such nurturance, such personalized care is often not possible, given the demands on medical institutions. But patients obviously need more than just physical management, straightforward information, and at least some small role in decisions about their care. Many patients need the chance to talk with someone about how they feel about themselves, their lives, their families, and death, and they need

the opportunity to regain a sense of control over their lives (Sobel, 1981). Accordingly, therapy for dying patients is becoming an increasingly available and utilized option (Golston, 1977; LeShan & LeShan, 1961; Sobel, 1981).

Therapy with the dying is different from more usual psychotherapy in several respects. First, for obvious reasons, it is likely to be short-term. Second, it is unlikely to be initiated by the patient, but may rather be suggested by the primary physician (Golston, 1977); as a consequence, the purpose of the therapy may sometimes be misunderstood by the patient. The patient may feel that he or she is being singled out for "dying badly" or for having particular problems of adjustment. The therapist will need to emphasize that therapy can be a good experience for all who are facing imminent death, and that the patient is not a problem case.

As already noted, patients are especially sensitive to their effect on others. Feeling that they have already burdened medical staff, family, and friends, they may wonder why they should burden yet another well-intentioned person. Accordingly, patients may have to be reminded repeatedly of the availability of therapy, and the therapist may actively have to seek out the patient rather than waiting for the patient to take the initiative. The therapist—whether a psychiatrist, clinical psychologist, or social worker—should show an active interest in the patient, a clear desire to stay and visit, and a willingness to listen and to talk about whatever is on the patient's mind. Even one visit can uncover important areas of strain in the dying person's life, and regular visits at least break up the monotony of dying and offer the patient a willing ear.

The format of therapy with the dying also varies from that of traditional psychotherapy (Pattison, 1967). The nature and timing of visits must depend on the inclination and energy level of the patient rather than on a fixed schedule of appointments. The agenda of the meeting should be set at least partly by the patient. If an issue arises that the patient clearly does not wish to discuss, this wish should be respected. Often, this aspect of therapy goes against the training of therapists who have been taught to probe areas of resistance. But the terminally ill patient is entitled to resistance. What good will exposure do, particularly when it can create stress for which the patient has little energy? Moreover, it may be these very sources of resistance that enable the patient to deal with oncoming death. Their elimination can unleash terror (Pattison, 1967; Sobel, 1981).

Terminally ill patients may need help in coming to terms with the course of their lives. Has it been a useful life, or should it have been lived differently? Unfinished activities and tasks may prey on the patient's mind, as will goals that will never be met. Dependent children may shortly be left alone with insufficient resources and an uncertain future. The therapist can help the patient make whatever arrangements are possible and come to terms with the fact that some things will remain undone (Abrams, 1966).

Some **thanatologists** (that is, those who study death and dying) have suggested that behavioral and cognitive-behavioral therapies can be constructively employed with dying patients (Sobel, 1981). For example, progressive muscle relaxation can ameliorate discomfort and also instill a renewed sense of control. Positive self-talk such as focusing on one's life achievements can undermine the depression that often accompanies dying.

From the therapist's perspective, therapy with the dying is challenging but difficult for a number of reasons (Sobel, 1981). First, and most obvious, is the fact that it is emotionally exhausting to become involved repeatedly with people who have only a short time to live. Second, in some important ways, therapy with the dying seems to contradict implicitly some of the basic reasons for doing therapy.

One helps people solve their difficulties so that they can live more satisfying lives, unfettered by their problems—not so they can die. Just as physicians may avoid the terminally ill because they feel their time is better spent on those with a good prognosis, so psychological therapists would also rather spend their time with people who are going to live.

A third difficulty in doing therapy with the dying is that there are few available guidelines. Few programs in social work, psychiatry, or clinical psychology include courses covering therapy with the dying (**clinical thanatology**), and virtually none of the traditional psychotherapies provides clear guidelines. Finally, and perhaps most challenging, is the fact that therapists working with the terminally ill must have their own feelings toward death at least partially worked out, which is no small accomplishment in itself. Yet one study (Razavi, Delvaux, Farvacques, & Robaye, 1988) found that a short-term training program for professionals in dealing with terminally ill patients was successful in changing attitudes toward death and dying and toward dying patients, suggesting that these skills can be taught without extensive retraining.

Therapy with the terminally ill may be conducted individually or with the family. In individual therapy, the goals may be very similar to those espoused by Weisman (1977) for medical staff working with the terminally ill. In particular, the therapist can help patients achieve an appropriate death, one that they would choose if they were able to plan it themselves. This may mean helping patients place their lives in perspective. Many people find meaning in **symbolic immortality,** a sense that one is leaving behind a legacy through one's children or one's work, or that one is joining the afterlife and becoming one with God (Lifton, 1977). Thus, the last weeks can crystallize the meaning of a lifetime. Accomplishments are set into relief against the irrelevant details, and love is exposed in a more personal and direct manner than ever before. People make explicit things they have only felt before. As one patient put it, "I can die in peace now, knowing why I have lived, what I have meant to other people, and what I have left behind me."

Family Therapy with the Terminally Ill

For several reasons, some therapists who work with the dying prefer to do family therapy. First, dying rarely happens in a vacuum; it is generally a group experience, shared by those who are closest to the patient—usually family members. Second, family members usually experience a variety of adverse effects in coping with terminal illness, including a deterioration in their health, disturbed thought processes, and adverse emotional reactions, such as depression (Howell, 1986). Family therapy has the potential to ameliorate at least some of these difficulties. Third, the needs of the living and the dying are inherently in conflict, thus setting the stage for difficulties in adjustment and communication. The living need to maintain their resources and perform their daily activities, while the dying sap these same resources and pull family members away from their other roles (Kalish, 1977). Fourth, many of the issues that arise with terminally ill patients concern their relationships with family members. They may need to say goodbye but be unable to find the right words. A fifth reason for doing therapy in families is that the most lasting effects of the therapy will be on family members, not the one who is dying. Thus, the therapist can have a long-term impact by helping survivors go on living relatively free of guilt and unresolved issues.

Chief among the tasks of family therapy is dealing with issues of communication. Often, problems in communication are as simple as not understanding what is happening to a patient, such as why a particular symptom has appeared or why a medication has been changed. In these cases, the therapist can act as an interpreter for medical staff, explaining the meaning of daily events to the patient and family members.

Sometimes, family difficulties may stem from long-standing personal conflicts over issues or events that happened years ago. The therapist can help the family put such issues behind them—or, at least, aside—so that they do not interfere with the positive outcomes that can come from family therapy. Other times, difficulties in communication may be tied specifically to the dying process. Patients may feel guilty tying up the finances, time, and emotional energies of the family, yet they may not know how to express these concerns. Family members, in turn, may feel that they are not spending enough time with the patient or responding in the right ways to the patient's worries. Often, just getting these problems aired is helpful, even if they cannot be solved.

A therapist can also help if the family and patient are mismatched in their adjustment to the illness. As Kübler-Ross (1969) noted, families can go through many of the same reactions patients themselves experience (denial, anger, bargaining, depression, and acceptance), but at different times. Family members may hold out hope for a cure or seek additional treatments when the patient may already be resigned to dying. Or, the family may need to share their feelings with the patient just when the patient is most hostile and rejecting. Emotions run strong in families with a terminally ill member. If the therapist can help each person see that these problems are normal and that emotions like anger and depression are usually short-lived, then family members can adjust to each other's emotional reactions.

As noted earlier, over the course of illness, patients may narrow the circle of people they are willing to see. They may not have enough energy for lots of visitors, and some people are too noisy, intrusive, or demanding to be with. Too, as physical and mental deterioration progresses, patients may be too embarrassed to let any but a few special people see them in this condition. But the patient's withdrawal can be very threatening to the friends and family who have been rejected. They may feel jealousy or suspicion toward those who are still in the patient's circle of visitors. A therapist can anticipate these problems and prepare the family for them, so that the patient's withdrawal is not misunderstood and seen as a basis for conflict.

Perhaps the most important function that family therapy can fill is to create an atmosphere in which everyone can communicate mutual love and respect. Family members should feel free to tell the dying member how much he or she has meant to them. In this way, the patient can see the beneficial effects he or she has had on others, gain a sense of the importance of his or her existence, and come to terms with the fact of leaving the family, knowing that much of benefit will be left behind. In turn, the patient needs to be able to say goodbye to family members in a way that communicates to them how important they have been (Pattison, 1967). For many families, terminal illness can be a time of great closeness and sharing. It may be the only time when the family sets aside time to interact as a family and to say what their lives within the family have meant.

The Management of Terminal Illness in Children

Working with terminally ill children, whether in terms of physical care or psychological care, is perhaps the most stressful of all terminal care. First, it is often the hardest kind of death to accept. Medical staff typically serve only limited rotations in units with terminally ill children because they find the work so psychologically painful. Moreover, one must work not only with a confused and often frightened child but usually also with unhappy, frightened, and confused parents

(Barbarin & Chesler, 1986). The prospective death of a child is wrenching for parents, who may blame themselves for the illness even if there is no possible way that the illness could have been foreseen or avoided (Steinhauser, Mushin, & Rae-Grant, 1974).

Death in childhood can often be painful, which adds to the distress it causes to others. A common cause of childhood death is leukemia, which is not only painful in itself but is treated through a variety of stressful medical procedures such as bone marrow transplants. Thus, one must deal not only with the child's confusion and fear about death but also with the upset produced by the procedures. Finally, the child's concept of death is often undeveloped. Accordingly, whereas terminally ill adults have a fair idea of what will happen to them, terminally ill children often do not and may ask many questions that are difficult to answer.

For these reasons, terminally ill children often receive even less straightforward information about their condition than do terminally ill adults (Spinetta, 1974). Their questions may go unanswered or they and their parents may be led to falsely optimistic conclusions, so that medical staff can avoid painful confrontations. To what extent is this a defensible policy? Precisely because they are children, it is easy to rationalize not giving children true information about their treatments and condition on the grounds that they will not understand it or that it will make them fearful.

Yet it is clear that, just as is true for terminally ill adults, terminally ill children know more about their situation than they are given credit for (Spinetta, 1974, 1982). As Bluebond-Langner's (1977) work with leukemic children demonstrates, children use cues from their treatments and from the people around them to infer what their condition must be. At first, they may believe that, although they have a serious illness, they will soon recover and go home. As relapses occur and as treatments continue or become more frequent or invasive, they begin to realize that they may not re-cover. Later, as they observe children around them dying of the same illness that they have, they may come to realize that they themselves are likely to die. As their own physical condition deteriorates, they develop a conception of their own death and the realization that it may not be far off.

> TOM: Jennifer died last night. I have the same thing. Don't I?
> NURSE: But they are going to give you different medicines.
> TOM: What happens when they run out?
> (Bluebond-Langner, 1977, p. 55)

Attempting to shield a child from death and avoiding discussion of death may do a child a disservice, because it does not give the child a chance to get upsetting fantasies into the open (Bluebond-Langner, 1977; Spinetta, 1974).

It may often be difficult to know what to tell a child. Unlike adults, children may not express their knowledge, concerns, or questions directly. They may communicate the knowledge that they will die only indirectly, as by wanting to have Christmas early so that they will be around for it. Or they may suddenly stop talking about their future plans.

> One child, who when first diagnosed said he wanted to be a doctor, became quite angry with his doctor when she tried to get him to submit to a procedure by explaining the procedure and telling him, "I thought you would understand, Sandy. You told me once you wanted to be a doctor." He screamed back at her, "I'm not going to be anything," and then threw an empty syringe at her. She said, "OK, Sandy." The nurse standing nearby said, "What are you going to be?" "A ghost," said Sandy, and turned over. (Bluebond-Langner, 1977, p. 59)

In some cases, death fantasies may be acted out by burying a doll or by holding a funeral for a toy (Bluebond-Langner, 1977; Spinetta, 1974; Spinetta, Spinetta, Kung, & Schwartz, 1976).

Moreover, because terminally ill children have so little information of their own and because they are accordingly highly dependent on the information they pick up from their parents and medical staff, those working with the terminally ill child must be attentive to what messages the child has already received. What is the nature of the child-parent relationship? Is the child receiving warmth and affection? Are his or her questions being answered? Is the family withdrawn or distant? Are they avoiding the child's questions about death (Korsch, Fraad, & Barnett, 1954)? What emotions and attitudes are the medical staff persons manifesting? Are they anxious? Are they withdrawing from a particularly appealing child to protect their own emotions? What is the impact of this on the child? Furthermore, as we noted in Chapter 9, hospitalization itself can be frightening for children; in some cases, what may seem to be a reaction to illness or impending death may actually be a fearful response to the hospital environment (Bluebond-Langner, 1977). Knowledge of the answers to these questions is extremely important to understanding why a child is expressing particular emotions or asking particular questions (Bluebond-Langner, 1977; Spinetta, 1974).

How, then, does the parent, medical caregiver, or psychological counselor approach the task of counseling the terminally ill child? As is true in counseling terminally ill adults, one can take one's cues of what to say directly from the child, talking only when the child feels like talking and only about what the child wants to talk about. Sometimes it is easiest to broach the topic of death if some other child in the same treatment facility has recently died (Bluebond-Langner, 1977; Spinetta, 1974). Listening very carefully to what the child says about death and observing any acted-out fantasies can help give a consoling nurse, social worker, or parent an idea of how the child conceives of death and how disturbing this concept is. Researchers who have worked with dying children recommend counseling guidelines very similar to those for adults: Medical staff should try to answer a child's questions about death, illness, or treatment as simply but honestly as possible, without making up fantasies or providing more information than the child has requested.

In many cases, it is not just the terminally ill child who requires some kind of counseling intervention, but the family as well. Family dynamics are often severely disrupted by the terminal illness of a child. The needs of other children may go relatively ignored, and they may come to feel confused and resentful about their own position in the family. The resources of the family are focused heavily on one member, diverting energies that would otherwise go to provision for the family's basic physical and psychological needs. Thus, to understand adaptation and coping in childhood chronic and terminal illness, it is important to understand the interactive coping strategies of the family and not just the needs of the terminally ill child (Kazak, 1989). Parents themselves have substantial coping needs that are influenced by the medical context in which care is received. In one study, parents of children with cancer who had poor relationships with medical staff had to make use of information-seeking, problem-solving, and help-seeking methods in a sheer effort to find out what was going on with their child, whereas parents with good relationships with medical staff were able to concentrate more on the management of their emotional state (Barbarin & Chesler, 1986).

To summarize, then, management of the terminally ill child is not substantially different from working with terminally ill adults, but it is substantially harder. As with adults, one takes one's cues from the patient and provides honest and straightforward information and answers to questions. What makes this process hard is the fact that the child's level of information and questions are often a jumble of reactions to the hospital, to the emotional responses of parents and staff, and to vague or incomplete ideas about what death and illness are. Often, these concepts only peep out through painful and heart-wrenching fantasies. Yet children can often show a startling maturity, finding meaning for both themselves and their families through the difficult process of dying.

ALTERNATIVES TO HOSPITAL CARE FOR THE TERMINALLY ILL

We have already considered some of the problems with hospital care for the terminally ill. The fact that care is palliative, emotionally wrenching, and demanding of personalized attention in ways that may go beyond the resources of the hospital has led to the development of treatment alternatives (Cassileth & Donovan, 1983). As a result, two types of care have become increasingly popular: home care and hospice care.

Home Care

In recent years, we have witnessed renewed interest in **home care** for dying patients. Home care appears to be the care of choice for a substantial percentage of terminally ill patients, 50% in one study (Mor & Hiris, 1983; see also Brescia, Sadof, & Barstow, 1984). Because hospital costs have escalated so markedly, many people cannot afford hospitalization for terminal illness, particularly if the death is long and drawn out. Moreover, resources in hospitals—in terms of bed space as well as personnel—can be in short supply. Drawing on such resources for patients who require primarily custodial care means depriving patients who are in need of acute or intensive care.

Although home care would solve many of these logistical difficulties, the very real question of quality of care arises. Can patients receive as competent care at home as in the hospital? Researchers who have examined this issue believe that they can, provided that there is regular contact between medical personnel and family members and that the family is adequately trained (Aitken-Swan, 1959; Malkin, 1976; Wilkes, 1965).

Psychological factors are increasingly raised as legitimate reasons for home care. In contrast to the mechanized and depersonalized environment of the hospital, the home environment is familiar and comfortable. In the home, the patient is surrounded by personal items. Scrapbooks or chests full of old things can all be sorted through at leisure, and the patient can derive pleasure from the memories these things bring back. In the home, the patient can make more decisions, such as what to wear, what to eat, when to have visitors, and what to watch on television. Usually, the patient is surrounded by family, rather than by medical staff, who care about and love the patient in ways that even the most sensitive medical attendant cannot. The strongest psychological advantages of home care, then, are the patient's opportunity to have more control as well as more opportunities for social support and interaction (see Aitken-Swan, 1959; Malkin, 1976; Wilkes, 1965).

Although home care is often easier on the patient psychologically, it can be very stressful for the family (Young & Kahana, 1987). Even if the family is able to afford around-the-clock nursing, often at least one family member's energies must be devoted to the patient on an almost full-time basis. Given work schedules and other daily tasks, it may be difficult for any family member to do this. Such constant contact with the dying person is also stressful, and the family member may need to be relieved by others whose schedules may, unfortunately, be less flexible. Strains within the family over who is doing what can result. Moreover, the process of having someone die in the home is stressful in itself (Hinton, 1967). Family members may be torn between wanting to keep the patient alive and wanting the patient to die, so as to relieve suffering all around. On the other hand, home care gives the family an opportunity to share their feelings and to be together at this important time. These benefits may well offset the stresses, and studies often find that families prefer home to hospital care (see Aitken-Swan, 1959; Malkin, 1976; Wilkes, 1965).

In summary, then, although home care can provide clear psychological advantages for the patient, it can have mixed effects on the family. It can be expensive and time-consuming, and it drains emotional reserves. On the other hand, it can permit personal sharing and closeness at this most critical time.

Hospice Care

In the last few years, **hospice care,** an alternative to hospital and home care, has developed (Buckingham, 1983; Kastenbaum, 1979; Saunders, 1977). In medieval Europe, a **hospice** was a place that provided care and comfort for travelers. In keeping with this original goal, the idea behind hospice care is to provide personal, warm comfort for terminally ill patients, similar to what would be provided in the home but without the strains that home care can produce. Medical care in the hospice is custodial and palliative, designed to make the patient comfortable and to achieve a high quality of life. Thus, typically, painful or invasive therapies are discontinued. Instead, care is aimed toward managing symptoms such as reducing pain and controlling nausea. Most important, the patient's psychological comfort is stressed (Dush, 1985; Kastenbaum, 1979; Saunders, 1977).

How is psychological comfort achieved in the hospice? Hospice programs vary, but most contain some of the following features. First, patients may be encouraged to personalize their living areas as much as possible by bringing in their own familiar things. Thus, each room may look very different, reflecting the personality and interests of its occupant. Patients also wear their own clothes and determine their own activities in an effort to establish the kind of routine they might develop on their own at home. Second, hospice care is particularly oriented toward improving a patient's social support system. Restrictions on visits from family or friends are removed as much as possible. Family may be encouraged to spend days with the patient, to stay over in the hospice if possible, to eat together with the patient. Staff are especially trained to interact with patients in a warm, emotionally caring way. Usually, therapists are made available—either on an individual basis or through family therapy—to deal with such problems as communication difficulties or depression. Some programs also make discussion groups available to patients who wish to discuss their thoughts with others who are also facing

death (Kastenbaum, 1979; Saunders, 1977). Open and honest communication, thus, is one of the most important goals of the hospice (Aiken & Marx, 1982; Young-Brockopp, 1982).

When hospice care was first initiated, there was some concern that moving a patient to a facility that specialized in death, as hospices in essence do, would depress and upset both patients and family members. Such fears have largely proved groundless. One study (Parkes, 1977, cited in Saunders, 1977) that evaluated patients who participated in the hospice program with comparable patients who remained in a hospital setting for their terminal care found a number of positive benefits of the hospice experience: Hospice patients were more mobile, reported having less pain, and were able to spend more time with their families. Family members, in turn, re-

Hospice care, an alternative to hospital and home care for the terminally ill, is designed to provide personalized palliative treatment without the strains that home care can produce. This photograph shows a 73-year-old woman in a hospice, surrounded by photos of her family.

ported that they felt they had more access to staff, and they reported being less anxious. Overall, the death of the patient was perceived as less stressful for the family in the hospice than in the hospital environment (see also Adkins, 1984; Tehan, 1982). Many family members perceived the hospice and staff as an extension of their home, and some hospices are partially staffed by family volunteers who provide care to others after their own family member has died.

While hospices were originally instituted as facilities separate from hospitals, their success as a treatment model has led to them increasingly being incorporated into traditional hospitals. Approximately half of the more than 1500 hospices in the United States are currently affiliated with hospitals, the remaining ones being privately- or community-based (Paradis, 1984). With this incorporation of hospices into traditional treatment, however, has come increasing standardization and less flexibility in patient services (Paradis & Cummings, 1986). As a result, the individualized care that the original hospices were able to provide has decreased somewhat, and the quality of psychosocial care may be somewhat less than was true in the early years (Paradis, 1984; Paradis & Cummings, 1986).

Not all hospice care is residential (Parkes, 1977). Many hospice programs have a home-care component. Hospice staff visit homes on a regular basis, teaching family members how to provide the patients with palliative care and helping both the patient and family cope with whatever stresses may have arisen. Residential hospice care is usually a backup option. In many ways, this flexible program can meet all needs: patients can remain in the home as long as the family members are able to manage it (Buckingham, 1983). If home care becomes too difficult, there is a residential treatment facility that is oriented toward personalized care to fall back on (Kastenbaum, 1979; Saunders, 1977). However, one study found that, compared with residential treat-

ment, the surviving relatives who had made use of home hospice care for their dying relatives were less satisfied. They indicated that there were problems in communication with the physician, the patient had experienced more pain, and there was less availability of care. Consequently, for home hospice care to be a viable option for large numbers of terminally ill patients, family members need to be assured of the availability of care, adequate pain control, and measures to provide them with temporary relief from the burden of home care (McCusker, 1985).

The hospice is in some way analogous to the pain center, discussed in Chapter 11. Just as pain is complex to manage, so is death, and just as pain has a heavily psychological component, so does dying. Traditional treatment facilities often do not have the time or the expertise to provide ideal care for either problem. Just as the pain center concentrates all the physical and psychological technology that is needed to manage pain, so the hospice concentrates the physical and psychological expertise that goes into helping a patient achieve an appropriate death. Therefore, a good hospice program can go a long way toward making the last, often loneliest, experience of life a fitting one.

Formally evaluating hospice care has been difficult. Rarely is the kind of research that makes for a fair evaluation conducted. Patients are not randomly assigned to hospice care, hospital care, or home care, but rather select the type of care they want. In one study (Kane, Klein, Bernstein, Rothenberg, & Wales, 1985; Kane, Wales, Bernstein, Leibowitz, & Kaplan, 1984), however, 247 patients and their relatives were randomly assigned to receive either hospice care or traditional terminal care. There were no significant differences in length of mortality, in number of invasive diagnostic procedures and treatments, or in numbers of days spent in the hospital. There were also no differences in pain, symptoms reported, depression, or anxiety. Patients in both groups were equally satisfied with their environment. However, hospice patients were significantly more satisfied with their interpersonal care and their involvement in that care. Their relatives showed less anxiety and greater satisfaction with their involvement in the care as well. Thus, some benefits of hospice care over traditional care were observed. A second major study, known as the National Hospice Study (Holden, 1983), randomly assigned patients to traditional care, hospital-based hospice care, and home-based hospice care. Although no significant differences in quality of life were found, the hospice patients were less likely to receive invasive terminal care and the costs were substantially lower than for traditional care. Number of days spent in the hospital in this case varied substantially, with those receiving conventional care spending three times as much time in the hospital as those at home. Thus far, then, it is difficult to infer regularities in whether hospice care is superior to traditional terminal care, and, if so, in what ways.

PROBLEMS OF SURVIVORS

The death of a family member may be the most upsetting and dreaded event in a person's life. For many people, the death of someone close is a more terrifying prospect than their own death or illness (Diggory & Rothman, 1961; Geer, 1965; Kalish & Reynolds, 1976). Even when a death is anticipated and on some level actually wished for, it may be very hard for survivors to cope successfully.

We have already discussed several methods of helping families prepare for the death of one of their members. Family therapy, participation in a hospice program, and contact with sensitive medical staff members all help prepare the family for the death. But few such programs can really help the family to prepare for life after the death. Such preparations might be thought premature, insensitive, or

tasteless. Nonetheless, it is often at this point that family members need the most help, and it can be when they are least likely to get it (Feifel, 1977).

The weeks just before the patient's death are often a period of frenzied activity. Visits to the hospital are increased, preliminary legal or funeral preparations may be made, last-minute therapies may be initiated, or the patient may be moved to another facility. Family members are kept busy by the sheer amount of work that must be done. Even after the patient dies, there is typically a great deal of work (Raether & Slater, 1977): Funeral arrangements must be made; burial and tombstone details must be worked out; family members who have arrived for the services must be housed and fed; and well-intentioned friends who drop by to express their condolences must be talked to. (Box 13.5 explores various approaches to these activities.) Then, very abruptly, the activities cease. Visitors return home, the patient has been cremated or buried, and the survivor is left alone, perhaps wondering what to do next (Feifel, 1977).

The Adult Survivor

During the period of terminal illness, the survivor's regular routine was probably replaced by illness-related activities. Because of these activities and preoccupation with the patient's illness, the survivor may have withdrawn from customary social activities. It may be hard to remember what one used to do before the illness began; even if one can remember, one may not feel much like doing it.

The survivor, then, is often left with lots of time and little to do but grieve. Moreover, the typical survivor is a widow in her 60s or older who may have physical problems of her own (Kastenbaum, 1977). If she has lived in a traditional marriage, she may find herself with tasks to do, such as preparing her income tax return and making household repairs, that she has never had to do before. Survivors may be

Box 13.5
Cultural Attitudes Toward Death and Death-Related Ceremonies

Cultural attitudes toward death vary widely. Whereas some cultures fear death, others see it as a normal part of life. Each culture, accordingly, has developed death-related ceremonies that reflect these cultural beliefs. A few examples are as follows.

Within traditional Japanese culture, death is regarded as a process of traveling from one world to another. When someone dies, that person goes to a purer country, a place often described as beautifully decorated with silver, gold, and other precious metals. The function of death rituals is to help the spirit make the journey. Thus, a series of rites and ceremonies take place, aided by a minister, to achieve this end. The funeral events begin with a bedside service in which the minister consoles the family. The next service is the *Yukan*, the bathing of the dead. An appreciation service follows the funeral, with food for all who have traveled long distances to attend. When the mourning period is over, a final party is given for friends and relatives as a way of bringing the mourners back into the community (Kübler-Ross, 1975).

The Andaman Islanders, located in the Bay of Bengal, are an example of many societies that respond to death with ritual weeping. Friends and relatives gather together with the mourners during the funeral to weep and show other signs of grief. This ritual of weeping is an expression of the bonds among individuals within the society and serves to reaffirm these bonds when they are broken arbitrarily by death. Mourners are separated from the rest of society for a short time after the death; during this time, they become associated with the world of the dead. At the end of the mourning period, they are reunited with the rest of the community (Radcliffe-Brown, 1964).

In Hinduism, which is the main religion of India, death is not viewed as separate from life or as an ending. Rather, it is considered a continuous, integral part of life. Because Hindus believe in reincarnation, they believe that birth is followed by death and death by rebirth; every moment one is born and dies again. Thus, death is like any transition in life. The Hindus teach that one should meet death with tranquility and meditation. Death is regarded as the chief fact of life and a sign that all earthly desires are in vain. Only when an individual neither longs for nor fears death is that person capable of transcending both life and death and achieving "nirvana"—merging into unity with the Absolute. In so doing, the individual is freed from the fear of death, and death comes to be seen as a companion to life (Kübler-Ross, 1975).

What would people from another culture think about American attitudes toward death if they witnessed our death practices? First, they would see that in the United States, the majority of deaths take place in the hospital without the presence of close relatives. Once death has occurred, the corpse is promptly removed without the help of the bereaved, who see it again only after morticians have made it acceptable for viewing. In some cases, the corpse is cremated shortly after death and is never again seen by the family. A paid organizer, often a director of a funeral home, next takes over much of the direction of the viewing and burial rituals, deciding matters of protocol and the timing of services. In most subcultures within the United States, a time is set aside when the bereaved family accepts condolences from visiting sympathizers. A brief memorial service is then held, after which the bereaved and their friends may travel to the cemetery where the corpse or ashes are buried. Typically, there are strong social pressures on the friends and relatives of the deceased to show little sign of emotion. The family is expected to establish this pattern and other visitors are expected to follow suit. A friend or relative who is out of control emotionally will usually withdraw from the death ceremony or will be urged to do so by others. Following the ceremony, there may be a brief get-together at the home of the bereaved, after which the mourners return home (Huntington & Metcalf, 1979).

left with few resources to turn to for aid (Kastenbaum, 1977).

Grief, which is the psychological response to bereavement, involves a feeling of hollowness, often marked by preoccupation with the image of the deceased person, expressions of hostility toward others, and guilt over the death. Bereaved people often show a restlessness and inability to concentrate on activities (Glick, Weiss, & Parkes, 1974; Parkes & Weiss, 1983; see also Stroebe & Stroebe, 1987), and they also experience adverse physical symptoms (Lindemann, 1944; see Stroebe & Stroebe, 1987).

Grief involves a feeling of hollowness, a preoccupation with the deceased person, and guilt over the death. Often, outsiders fail to appreciate the depth of a survivor's grief or the length of time it takes to get over the bereavement.

It may be difficult for outsiders to appreciate the degree of a survivor's grief. They may feel that, because the death was a long time in coming, the survivor should be ready for it and thus show signs of recovery shortly after the death. Widows report that often, within a few weeks of their spouse's death, friends are urging them to pull out of their melancholy and get on with life. In some cases, the topic of remarriage is brought up within weeks after the death (Glick et al., 1974). Yet normal grieving may go on for months, and a large percentage of widows and widowers are still deeply troubled by their spouse's death several years later (Silver & Wortman, 1980; Stroebe & Stroebe, 1987). The grief response appears to be aggravated in men and in those whose loss was sudden and unexpected (Stroebe & Stroebe, 1987). As we will see in Chapter 15, the experience of bereavement can lead to adverse changes in immunologic functioning, increasing the risk of disease and even death (Janson, 1986; Osterweis, 1985; Stroebe & Stroebe, 1987). In addition, increases in alcohol and drug abuse, depression, and inability to work are common among survivors (Aiken & Marx, 1982). Programs designed to provide counseling to the bereaved have the potential to offset these adverse reactions (Aiken & Marx, 1982).

The Child Survivor

Surviving spouses are not the only people who need help adjusting to death. Explaining the death of a parent or sibling to a surviving child can be particularly difficult (Corr & Corr, 1985; Ross, 1985). As noted earlier, the child's understanding of death may be incomplete, so the child may not understand that death is final and irreversible. As a consequence, the child may keep expecting the dead person to return, and this becomes troubling both to the child and to other family members. When the child does understand that the dead person is not going to return, he or she may not understand why. The child may believe either that the parent intended to leave or that the parent left because the child was "bad." It may take several counseling sessions to make a child see that this is not true.

The death of a sibling raises particular complications, because many children have fervently wished, at one time or another, that a sibling were dead. When the sibling actually does die, the child may feel that he or she somehow caused it. The likelihood that this will be a problem may be enhanced if the sibling was ill for some time before death. Very possibly, the surviving child did not get much attention during that time and may thus feel some temporary elation when the sibling is no longer around as a source of competition (Lindsay & McCarthy, 1974). As one child remarked on learning of his sibling's death, "Good. Now I can have all his toys" (Bluebond-Langner, 1977, p. 63). Such reactions are typically only temporary and may exacerbate the sorrow or guilt the child feels later on (Binger, 1973; Gogan, Koocher, Foster, & O'Malley, 1977; Sourkes, 1980).

> Lars was seven when his sister died of leukemia. He was never told that she was sick and when she did die, he was sent away to a relative. After the funeral he returned home to find his sister gone and his parents in a state of grief. No explanation was offered and Lars was convinced he had done something that caused his sister's death. He carried this burden of guilt with him until he was fifteen. Academically, he had many problems. His math and reading remained at about the second-grade level. His parents were concerned and cooperative, but it was impossible for them to identify the problem. After leukemia was discussed in a health science class, Lars hesitantly told the teacher his story. Lars wanted to believe that he was not responsible for his sister's death, but he needed to hear it directly from his parents. A conference was set up, and with the support of his teacher, Lars told his parents his feelings of guilt. The parents were astonished. They had no idea their son felt any responsibil-

ity. Through many tears, they told him the entire story and tried to reassure him that in no way was he responsible. In fact, he had been a source of comfort and support to both his sister and his parents. (Spinetta et al., 1976, p. 21)

In leading a child to cope with the death of a parent or a sibling, it is best not to wait until the death has actually occurred. Rather, the child should be prepared for the death, perhaps by drawing on the death of a pet or a flower to aid understanding (Bluebond-Langner, 1977). The child's questions about death should be answered as honestly as possible, but without unwanted detail. Sometimes a parent will wait until a child asks one question and use that as an occasion for extensive discussion. But the topic of death is anxiety-arousing even to a child who does not fully understand its implications, so providing only what is asked for when the timing is right is the better course.

Death Education

Some educators and researchers have maintained that one way to make surviving easier is to educate people about death earlier in their lives, before they have had much personal experience with it (Leviton, 1977). Because death has been a taboo topic, many people have misconceptions about it, including the idea that the dying wish to be left alone, without talking about their situation. Because of these concerns, some courses on dying, which may include volunteer work with dying patients, have been developed for college students. This approach is believed to eliminate myths and to promote realistic perceptions about what can be done to help the dying (Schulz, 1978). A potential problem with such courses is that they may attract the occasional suicidal student and provide unintended credibility and encouragement for self-destructive leanings. Accordingly, some instructors have recommended confronting such problems head-on, in the hopes that they can be forestalled.

Whether or not college students are the best and the only population that should receive death education is another concern. Unfortunately, organized means of educating people outside the university system are few, so college courses remain one of the more viable vehicles for death education. Through death education, it may be possible to develop realistic expectations, both about what modern medicine can achieve and about the kind of care the dying want and need. Courses on death and dying, then, constitute a potential means for breaking through the silence that has surrounded the dying process for so long (Leviton, 1977).

SUMMARY

1. Causes of death vary over the life cycle. In infancy, congenital abnormalities and sudden infant death syndrome account for most deaths. From ages 1 to 15, the causes shift to accidents and childhood leukemia. In young adulthood, death is often due to auto accidents, homicide, suicide, cancer, and AIDS. In adulthood, sudden death due to heart attack is the most common cause of death. Death in old age is usually due to heart attacks, stroke, cancer, and physical degeneration.

2. Concepts of death also change over the life cycle. In childhood, death is conceived of first as a great sleep, and later as a ghostlike figure that takes a person away. Finally, death is seen as an irreversible biological stage. Many believe that adulthood is the time when people first begin to come to terms with their own death, sometimes resulting in mid-life crises.

3. Advancing disease raises many psychological issues, including treatment-related discomfort and decisions of whether or not to continue treatment. Increasingly, issues concerning living wills (the patient's directive to withhold extreme life-prolonging measures) and euthanasia have been topics of concern in both medicine and law.

4. Patients' self-concepts must continually change in response to the progression of illness, change in appearance, energy level, control over physical processes, and degree of mental alertness. The patient may withdraw from family and friends as a result. Thus, issues of communication are a focal point for intervention.

5. Kübler-Ross's theory of dying suggests that people go through a series of predictable stages, progressing through denial, anger, bargaining, depression, and finally acceptance. Research shows, however, that patients do not go through these stages in sequence, but that all of these phenomena describe reactions of dying people to a degree.

6. Much of the responsibility for psychological management of terminal illness falls on medical staff. Medical staff become very important to terminal patients, providing information, reassurance, and care when others in the environment cannot. Medical staff can help a patient achieve a dignified and appropriate death by finding small ways of restoring the patient's lost sense of control and by permitting the patient to openly communicate his or her needs and desires.

7. Psychological counseling needs to be made available to terminally ill patients because many need a chance to develop a perspective on their lives. Developing methods for training therapists in psychiatric and psychological thanatology, then, is an educational priority. Family therapy may be needed to soothe the problems of the family and to help the patient and family say goodbye to each other.

8. Counseling terminally ill children is especially important, because both parents and children may be confused and frightened. Families of dying children may need help in developing effective coping, which can be influenced by the medical environment.

9. Home care and hospice care are alternatives to hospital care for the dying. Palliative care in a homelike environment can have beneficial psychological effects on dying patients and their survivors.

10. Grief is marked by a feeling of hollowness, preoccupation with an image of the deceased person, guilt over the death, expressions of hostility toward others, and restlessness and inability to concentrate. Many people do not realize how long normal grieving takes.

KEY TERMS

clinical thanatology
death education
euthanasia
grief
home care
hospice
hospice care
infant mortality rate
living will

midlife crisis
palliative care
premature death
stages of dying
sudden infant death syndrome (SIDS)
symbolic immortality
terminal care
thanatology

14

HEART DISEASE, HYPERTENSION, STROKE, AND DIABETES

In this chapter, we take up four major chronic disorders, namely heart disease, hypertension, stroke, and diabetes. The first three are disorders involving the circulatory system, and the fourth, diabetes, is often a complicating factor in adult heart disease. As such, the problems created by these disorders share some commonalities. Moreover, due to their frequency, they affect large numbers of people, including the increasing number of older people who suffer from more than one chronic disease simultaneously.

CORONARY HEART DISEASE

Cardiovascular disease is the number one killer in the United States, accounting for 40% of all deaths. It was not a major cause of illness and death until the twentieth century because, before that, most people died of infectious diseases. Around the turn of the century, however, coronary heart disease (CHD) began to increase, although it has recently begun to level off. Nonetheless, it is estimated that a million new cases are identified annually. One of the most significant aspects of CHD is that many of the over 600,000 deaths each year are premature deaths; that is, they occur well before age 75 (American Heart Association, 1984). In addition to the high death rate associated with it, CHD is also a major chronic disease. Millions of Americans live with its symptoms. Because of its great frequency and the toll it takes on relatively young people, finding the causes and cures of heart disease has been a high priority of health research.

Coronary heart disease is a general term that refers to illnesses caused by atherosclerosis, the narrowing of the coronary arteries, the vessels that supply the heart with blood. As we saw in Chapter 2, when these vessels become narrowed or closed, the flow of oxygen and nourishment to the heart is partially or completely obstructed. Temporary shortages of oxygen and nourishment frequently cause pain, called angina pectoris, that radiates across the chest and arm. When severe deprivation occurs, a heart attack (**myocardial infarction**) can result.

Heart disease is particularly common among males and the elderly. It also has a family history component, being more common among the offspring of individuals who have had heart disease. Risk factors include high blood pressure, diabetes, cigarette smoking, obesity, high serum cholesterol level, and low levels of physical activity (American Heart Association, 1988; Criqui, 1986). Recent research has focused on the contribution that stress and an individual's particular methods of coping with it may make in the development of heart disease. These coping methods may interact with other risk factors, such as elevated cholesterol level, in enhancing overall risk (e.g., Lombardo & Carreno, 1987). However, taking all known risk factors together accounts for less than half of all newly diagnosed cases of CHD; accordingly, a number of risk factors remain to be identified, which may help in early identification of people who are at high risk for CHD.

CHD is, to a degree, a disease of modernization and industrialization. As we saw in Chapter 7, occupational stress has been related to its incidence (Cooper & Marshall, 1976). So has general stress, as measured by social mobility, status incongruity, dissatisfaction with one's life plan or activities, chronic anxiety, and amount of life change (Jenkins, 1971). Urban and industrialized countries have a higher incidence of CHD than do underdeveloped countries. Migrants have a higher incidence of CHD than do geographically stable individuals. People who are occupationally, residentially, or socially mobile in a given culture have a higher frequency of coronary heart disease than do those who are less mobile (Kasl & Berkman, 1983). Men married to more highly educated women or to women in white-collar jobs appear to be at increased risk

for cardiovascular disease (Kannel & Eaker, 1986).

Less research has focused on women than on men, largely because premature death from cardiovascular disease does not occur as often for women as for men. Overall, working women do not show higher rates of CHD than nonworking women. However, working women show higher CHD rates after age 55 if they have been married, had raised three or more children, and have held clerical jobs. Among working women, clerical workers with children and married to blue-collar workers are at the highest risk of developing CHD, presumably because their multiple roles put excessive demands on their functioning (Haynes & Feinleib, 1980).

Modifying risk factors may help prevent further damage and subsequent heart attacks in individuals already diagnosed with coronary heart disease. Stopping smoking reduces the incidence of CHD, although switching to low tar and nicotine cigarettes does not. The benefits of treating substantially elevated blood pressure are indisputable, although the benefits of treating milder hypertension are inconclusive. Reducing cholesterol has beneficial effects, with approximately a 2% reduction in disease for every 1% reduction in total cholesterol (Criqui, 1986). Modifying behavioral methods of coping with stress also appears to reduce the risk of a repeat infarct (Friedman et al., 1986). Given the likelihood of being able to reduce further damage with interventions, the role of the health psychologist in research about and interventions for heart disease is indisputably important.

Type A Behavior

A particular behavior pattern called the **Type A behavior syndrome** has been identified as a risk factor for CHD (e.g., Cooper, Detre, & Weiss, 1981; Dembroski, MacDougall, Shields, Petitto, & Lushene, 1978). It is estimated that Type A men have a twofold increase in risk for

CHD, relative to Type Bs (Haynes, Feinlieb, & Kannel, 1980). Type A behavior appears to be a particular risk factor for coronary artery disease among younger people (Williams et al., 1988).

The Type A behavior syndrome was originally formulated by two physicians (Friedman & Rosenman, 1974) as a behavioral and emotional style marked by an aggressive, unceasing struggle to achieve more and more in less time, often in competition with other individuals or forces. In particular, the Type A syndrome was characterized by three components: easily aroused hostility, a sense of time urgency, and competitive achievement strivings (Rosenman, 1978). So-called Type Bs, with whom Type As are frequently compared, are less driven individuals who do not show these behavior patterns.

Type A individuals lead fast-paced lives. For example, they work longer weeks and more discretionary work hours than do Type Bs. They have little tolerance for what they perceive as others' "slow" behavior, completing other people's sentences for them or showing other signs of impatience. They often concentrate on several activities simultaneously, a behavior that is called polyphasic thought. For example, a Type A may work on a report, talk on the telephone, and eat supper all at the same time. Type As are often preoccupied with their own concerns and are relatively insensitive to others, at least during times of stress. Despite often substantial accomplishments, they may evaluate their achievements in terms of quantity instead of quality and be dissatisfied with their output. They are likely to challenge and compete with others, especially in moderately competitive situations. And in response to successful competition, they maintain high blood pressure longer, suggesting that they experience continued stimulation from successful competition (Jones, 1985). They may also suffer from free-floating (or unfocused) hostility (Rosenman, 1978).

The Type A's sense of time urgency has been demonstrated in several ways. For example, people designated as Type A estimate that a minute has passed more quickly than do Type Bs (Bortner & Rosenman, 1967). They also have more trouble with tasks that require delayed responses than do Type Bs (Glass, Snyder, & Hollis, 1974). The greater hostility and aggressiveness of Type A individuals has also been demonstrated in research. For example, Type As are more likely to aggress against someone else after they have been frustrated than are Type Bs (Carver & Glass, 1978; Van Egeren, Sniderman, & Roggelin, 1982).

The greater achievement strivings of Type As have also been demonstrated in a variety of circumstances. For example, Type As are more likely to go on to graduate school after college than are Type Bs (Glass, 1977). They take on more work than do Type Bs without any deadline hanging over them (Burnam, Pennebaker, & Glass, 1975). Both men and women Type As work longer hours, have higher occupational mobility, and are less likely to have supportive interactions with co-workers (Sorensen et al., 1987).

Type As and Type Bs deal with stress differently. Laboratory studies have exposed Type As and Bs to arithmetic tests, the cold pressor test, stressful interviews (e.g., Dimsdale, Stern, & Dillon, 1988), and, more recently, social stressors, such as instructions to persuade another individual (e.g., Smith, Allred, Morrison, & Carlson, 1989). Type A individuals are more reactive to difficult tasks, threats to self-esteem, threats to control, and negative interpersonal interactions, but they are not more reactive in situations that involve minimal levels of psychological challenge or demand (Contrada, Wright, & Glass, 1985; Ward et al., 1986). Overall, differences in the responses of Type A and Type B individuals are most likely to emerge in situations that are moderately competitive and uncontrollable, that require endurance, that require slow, careful work, and that call for a broad focus of attention (Matthews, 1982).

One area of controversy in the Type A literature has been whether Type As suppress physical symptoms. While they are engaged in a task, Type As may suppress symptoms of fatigue, enabling them to work longer and harder. For example, Type As report experiencing fewer symptoms when they are under stress than do Type Bs (Carver, DeGregorio, & Gillis, 1981; Schlegel, Wellwood, Copps, Gruchow, & Sharratt, 1980), and they work more effectively under distracting conditions like noise (Weidner & Matthews, 1978). However, in laboratory stressful events, Type As are not necessarily less aware of their arousal than Type Bs (Essau & Jamieson, 1987). Moreover, when asked to complete symptom checklists under nonstressful conditions, Type As actually report more physical symptoms than Type Bs. This difference seems to be a reporting difference, however, inasmuch as Type As do not show higher rates of physical illness generally (Suls & Wan, 1989). Thus, the relationship of Type A to the experience and report of physical symptoms is complex (see Offutt & Lacroix, 1988).

Control appears to be more important to Type As than to Type Bs. For example, Type As try harder than Type Bs to assert control in situations where control is threatened (for a review, see Carver & Humphries, 1982). Consequently, they may also be more vulnerable to helplessness and learned helplessness (see Glass, 1977; see Chapter 7), particularly when the events to which they are exposed are undesirable, unexpected, and of uncertain controllability (see Carver & Humphries, 1982).

How does the Type A fare in marriage? One study (Blaney, Brown, & Blaney, 1986) suggested that Type A husbands with Type B wives show poor marital adjustment, perhaps because the work orientation of the husband cannot be overcome by a traditional Type B wife. Type A women, in contrast, appear to be better off when married to Type B than Type A men.

Most of the early work on the assessment and behavioral correlates of Type A behavior was conducted on men. However, research on women suggests similar effects. Type A women tend to show greater autonomic arousal to laboratory stressors as well as greater time urgency and speed, more goal-directedness, a preference to work alone under stressful conditions, and more competitiveness/aggressiveness than Type B women. The Type A behavior syndrome in women correlates positively with anger, hostility, and a masculine sex role orientation (Baker, Dearborn, Hastings, & Hamberger, 1984).

Does the Type A individual's enhanced striving and greater success ultimately pay off by providing him or her with a more satisfying life? Although this is a complex and difficult question, it appears the answer may be no. Type As experience more dissatisfaction with their careers. They may also jeopardize their home lives by failing to spend sufficient time with their families. In fact, generally, Type As may sacrifice their social skills to their achievement orientation (see Carver & Humphries, 1982). Moreover, the association of Type A with CHD means that the Type A individual may ultimately have more health problems.

Measurement of Type A Behavior

Type A behavior is typically measured either by a structured interview or through questionnaires. The structured interview (Rosenman, 1978) asks people about their usual way of responding to situations that typically elicit impatience, hostility, or competitiveness from Type A individuals, such as working with slow individuals or waiting in lines. Although the answers to these questions constitute part of the measure of Type A, more important is the style of interaction that the interviewer elicits from the interviewee. Specifically, some of the questions are intentionally posed in a way designed to elicit Type A speech patterns. The interviewer may speak very slowly in asking a question or challenge the interviewee's answer to a particular question. Type A individuals are more likely to complete the interviewer's sentence or to show annoyance at being challenged. The interviewer's scores are then used to categorize individuals as full Type As, partially developed Type As, balanced between Type A and Type B, or full Type Bs.

Other techniques for measuring Type A behavior use questionnaire methodology. One commonly used measure is the Jenkins Activity Survey (JAS), a self-report questionnaire of approximately fifty items (Jenkins, Zyzanski, & Rosenman, 1979). Box 14.1 gives examples of these items. A third method of measuring Type A behavior is the ten-item Framingham Type A Scale (FTA) (Haynes et al., 1980), which is similar to the JAS, but shorter.

The structured interview, JAS, and FTA measures do not relate well to one another and differ from one another in some important ways (Matthews, 1988; Siegel, 1984). The structured interview predicts physiological and psychological reactions to events that are frustrating, difficult, and moderately competitive. These reactions include rapid, loud, and explosive speech; elevations in catecholamines, systolic blood pressure, and (to a lesser

---

Box 14.1
The Jenkins Activity Survey:
A Measure of Type A Behavior

The Jenkins Activity Survey measures Type A behavior by asking people about their typical responses to frustrating, difficult, and competitive situations. The following are a few examples of items that appear on that survey.

1. When you listen to someone talking and this person takes too long to come to the point, how often do you feel like hurrying the person along?
____ Frequently
____ Occasionally
____ Never

2. Do you ever set deadlines or quotas for yourself at work or at home?
____ No
____ Yes, but only occasionally
____ Yes, once a week or more

3. Would people you know well agree that you tend to get irritated easily?
____ Definitely yes
____ Probably yes
____ Probably no
____ Definitely no

4. Would people who know you well agree that you tend to do most things in a hurry?
____ Definitely yes
____ Probably yes
____ Probably no
____ Definitely no

If you answered these questions by giving the high-frequency answers, you show at least some characteristics of the Type A individual.

(From Jenkins, Zyzanski, & Rosenman, 1979)

extent) diastolic blood pressure and heart rate; and slower return to baseline than Type Bs (Allen, Lawler, Matthews, Rakaczky, & Jamison, 1987; Contrada, 1989; Jamieson & Lavoie, 1987; Matthews, 1982; Ward et al., 1986). As such, the structured interview appears to be a better predictor of physiological changes that have been associated with the development of coronary heart disease than are questionnaire measures (see Booth-Kewley & Friedman, 1987; Contrada et al., 1985; Friedman & Booth-Kewley, 1988; Matthews, 1988). The relation between cardiovascular reactivity and Type A behavior appears to be stronger for men than for women (Contrada & Krantz, 1988).

The JAS appears to measure the vigorous achievement and competitive orientation of aggressive individuals. It predicts some cardiovascular changes (such as systolic blood pressure) during difficult and moderately competitive events (Matthews, 1982), but it typically does so less well than does the structured interview (Dembroski et al., 1978). The FTA appears to measure discomfort and dissatisfaction with job pressures and competition (Matthews, 1982). Lately, there has been some suspicion that self-report measures of Type A behavior may, in part, assess chronic emotional distress or neuroticism; thus, the structured interview may be a more pure measure of Type A behavior (Smith, O'Keefe, & Allred, 1989; Suls & Wan, 1989).

Because of the large number of measures of Type A and because the most popular measures appear to tap different aspects of the Type A behavior syndrome, accuracy of measurement continues to be an ongoing issue (e.g., Kittel, Kornitzer, DeBacker, & Dramaix, 1982; Mayes, Sime, & Ganster, 1984). Overall, researchers have concluded that, at present, the structured interview is the best way of measuring Type A when one is concerned about coronary heart disease and its precursors (Friedman & Booth-Kewley, 1988; Matthews, 1988).

Hostility, Type A Behavior, and CHD

Recently, investigators have suggested that not all aspects of Type A behavior are equally likely to increase the risk of CHD. Hostility is more strongly implicated as a risk factor for CHD than the other dimensions of Type A behavior (Dembroski & Costa, 1988; Dembroski, MacDougall, Williams, Haney, & Blumenthal, 1985; Glass, Lake, Contrada, Kehoe, & Erlanger, 1983; MacDougall, Dembroski, Dimsdale, & Hackett, 1985; Williams & Barefoot, 1988; Williams, Barefoot, & Shekelle, 1985). A particular type of hostility may be especially implicated, namely cynical hostility, characterized by suspiciousness, resentment, frequent anger, antagonism, and distrust of others (Barefoot, Dodge, Peterson, Dahlstrom, & Williams, 1989; Dembroski & Costa, 1988; Siegman, Dembroski, & Ringel, 1987; Smith & Frohm, 1985; Williams & Barefoot, 1988). Interestingly, among Type Bs with cardiac damage, hostile cognitions are also greater. Thus, hostility may be a risk factor for cardiac damage independent of its relation to the Type A behavior syndrome (Weinstein, Davison, DeQuattro, & Allen, 1987). As yet, however, the measurement of hostility has itself proved controversial (Spielberger et al., 1985). Moreover, while most studies have found an association between hostility and CHD, not all studies have (McCranie, Watkins, Brandsma, & Sisson, 1986).

Other negative emotional states in addition to hostility may be implicated in the development of CHD. Dembroski et al. (1985) found that hostility and anger were interactive in producing increased risk for CHD. In a large-scale review of the literature, Booth-Kewley and Friedman (1987) concluded that coronary proneness may be characterized more by negative emotional states than by the hurried, impatient workaholic that had previously been thought to epitomize the disorder. They found strong associations between CHD and depression, as well as relations between anger, hostility, aggression, and anxiety and CHD (see also MacDougall et al., 1985). A case history that illustrates the relation of negative emotions to symptoms of CHD appears in Box 14.2

Although still a matter of ongoing research, these developments in refining the Type A construct and identifying its lethal components are important for several reasons. First, they enable researchers and clinicians to see exactly which components of the behavior may need to be modified to reduce risk for CHD. If hostility is the chief culprit in the Type A complex, then more refined interventions specifically directed at hostility may be more successful in reducing CHD risk than interventions directed more generally to Type A behavior. For example, such interventions as relaxation therapy, exercise, and modification of stereotypic male behaviors may be called

for (Helgeson, in press; Rosenman, 1986). In addition, these results imply that other aspects of what have previously been regarded as integral aspects of the Type A behavior pattern may be either non-CHD-related or actually healthy (see Wright, 1988).

Mechanisms Linking Type A Behavior and CHD

The Type A behavior pattern is associated with enhanced physiological reactivity to stress, which may be the mechanism that initiates and hastens the development of CHD (Contrada et al., 1985; Krantz & Manuck, 1984; McKinney, Hofshire, Buell, & Eliot, 1984). As just noted, Type As typically show a hyper-responsiveness in anticipation of (Contrada et al., 1985) and in the early stages of adjusting

Box 14.2
Negative Emotions and Coronary Heart Disease

Negative emotions in conjunction with stressful events can exacerbate symptoms associated with coronary heart disease, as the following case history illustrates.

A 45-year-old housewife came to the hospital with complaints of palpitations both at rest and upon exertion, which she had had for four years.... for almost 20 years prior to the onset of her symptoms the patient had wavered in her attachment to two men. One she had loved, but feeling unsure of him, she had married the other one who appeared to be stronger but proved to be also unkind. As her husband increasingly maltreated her she finally resolved to divorce him. In the setting of this decision she became aware of marked tension and anxiety and noted the onset of

her symptoms. These continued as her conflict was prolonged by her inability to detach herself from her husband (following the divorce) and marry the second man. Anxiety was joined by resentment when she blamed both men for her unhappiness. [An exercise intolerance test at the height of her anxiety showed a marked inability of the heart to tolerate standard exercise tests in the laboratory].... Following this the patient came to the clinic over a seven-month period during which she ventilated and discussed her conflicts and the origins of her emotional disturbance. During this period she gradually became more relaxed and all her symptoms greatly improved.

(Stevenson, Duncan, Wolf, Ripley, & Wolff, 1949, p. 1540).

to stress: They have more sympathetic nervous system activity and more catecholamine secretion in response to stressful events than do Type Bs (e.g., Dembroski et al., 1978; DeQuattro, Loo, Yamada, & Foti, 1985; Manuck, Craft, & Gold, 1978). Typically, Type As also show a slower return to baseline levels of sympathetic nervous system activity following a stressful event. If the stressful event continues, Type As eventually show a hyporesponsiveness to the event over time: Sympathetic activity decreases dramatically. Considerable research has provided evidence that these individual differences in reactivity exist (Krantz & Manuck, 1984), are stable (Glass et al., 1983; McKinney et al., 1984), generalize to nonlaboratory situations (McKinney et al., 1984), and may have a genetic component (Carmelli, Chesney, Ward, & Rosenman, 1985; Carmelli, Rosenman, & Chesney, 1987; Carmelli et al., 1988; Smith et al., 1987). There is also some evidence that Type Bs show higher levels of parasympathetic antagonism of sympathetic effects, which may exert a protective effect on their risk for cardiovascular disease (Muranaka, Lane et al., 1988; Muranaka, Monou et al., 1988).

There are basically two theories on how the Type A tendency toward greater reactivity to stress may lead to the development of coronary heart disease. The "mechanical" theory (Eliot & Buell, 1983) suggests that in some individuals, stress causes vasorestriction in peripheral areas of the heart and at the same time accelerates heart rate. Thus, Type A individuals attempt to transfer more and more blood through ever-shrinking vessels. Presumably, this process produces wear and tear on the coronary arteries, which, in turn, produces atherosclerotic lesions. An alternative theory proposes a hormone-based reaction (Dembroski & Williams, in press; Haft, 1974; Wright, 1984). Catecholamines may exert a direct chemical effect on blood vessels. The rise and fall of catecholamine levels may prompt continual changes in blood pressure that un-

dermine the resilience of the vessels (Glass, 1977; Herd, 1978). Sympathetic activation also causes lipids to be shunted into the bloodstream, another possible contributor to atherosclerosis. Currently, there is some basis for preferring the hormone theory, although both theories are viable.

Thus, exaggerated cardiovascular responses under conditions of stress may be the mechanism that links hostility and style of anger expression with a risk of hypertension and coronary artery disease (Krantz & Manuck, 1984). Anger and hostility are significantly associated with magnitude of increases in blood pressure and heart rate during laboratory-based stressful events (Houston, 1988). However, the relation of style of anger expression to reactivity is unclear: Some studies suggest greater blood pressure increases and heart rate reactivity to outward expression of anger (Dembroski et al., 1978; Diamond et al., 1984), while others suggest that holding anger in is associated with greater reactivity (Holroyd and Gorkin, 1983; MacDougall, Dembroski, & Krantz, 1981). In partial resolution of this issue, Engebretsen, Matthews, & Scheier (1989) found that the influence of anger on physiological responses depends first on whether anger is actually instigated by the task and second on whether people are able to use their preferred or nonpreferred methods of anger expression in response to the instigation.

One implication of the idea that Type As may be genetically disposed to enhanced sympathetic nervous system responsivity to stress is that Type A behavior may, in part, be a *result* as well as a cause of excessive neuroendocrine reactions to environmental stressors (Krantz & Deckel, 1983). One study (Kahn, Kornfeld, Frank, Heller, & Hoar, 1980), for example, found that Type A individuals undergoing bypass surgery showed greater blood pressure increases than Type Bs. Since all patients were unconscious, the results suggest that Type As may be physiologically aroused by stressful events generally. If this is true, then Type A behavior may represent a method of coping with a propensity for greater physiological reactivity, rather than a cause of that activity (Krantz & Durel, 1983). That is, the overt Type A behavior pattern may itself be a reflection of excess sympathetic response to environmental stressors (Krantz, Arabian, Davis, & Parker, 1982).

These observations also suggest that Type As may not simply react to stressful events with enhanced reactivity, but may also create physiologically taxing situations through their behavior and thoughts (Byrne & Rosenman, 1986). In responding psychologically to their enhanced physiological reactivity, Type As may take situations that others would experience as less stressful and make them more so. In achievement tasks, for example, they may raise the standards or increase the pressure to complete work. In interpersonal situations, they may attempt to be more persuasive or competitive. Their marriages appear to be marked by more discord (Kelly & Houston, 1985). They respond to interpersonal provocation with greater aggression (Holmes & Will, 1985; Strube, Turner, Cerro, Stevens, & Hinchey, 1984; see Smith, 1989, for a review). In other words, the Type A pattern may represent an ongoing process of creating challenge and responding with demand-engendering behavior that produces pathogenic physiological results (Smith, 1989). Thus, while the original view that Type A behavior becomes lethal primarily in the context of events that require active coping remains true, the role of Type As in creating such situations is increasingly being recognized and argued to be of significance in understanding the relationship between this behavior pattern and CHD risk.

The propensity for Type As to get themselves into stressful situations has also been regarded as a potential general risk factor for physical disorder (Suls & Sanders, 1989). While Type A behavior does not appear to be associated with illness generally, Type As are

more likely to have accidents, to die from accidents or violence, or to have cerebrovascular and peripheral atherosclerosis. Type As appear to be more prone to both migraine and muscle-contraction headaches as well (Woods, Morgan, Day, Jefferson, & Harris, 1984). The propensity for hostility may be linked to other risk factors for cardiovascular disease, such as smoking. Type As drink more than Type Bs (Folsom et al., 1985). Hostility has also been linked to a propensity to drink, at least among white males (Johnson, Hunter, Amos, Elder, & Berenson, 1989). Type As tend to have higher levels of cholesterol than do Type Bs, and so they may suffer more arterial damage (Weidner, Sexton, McLellarn, Connor, & Matarazzo, 1987). There is some evidence that, in addition to their greatly enhanced risk for CHD, Type As may have a slightly increased risk of dying from cancer (Fox, Ragland, Brand, & Rosenman, 1987). However, this evidence is still somewhat preliminary. When self-report measures of Type A behavior are used, there is a small relationship between Type A behavior and minor illnesses and symptoms. This link, however, may be due to a self-report bias rather than to an actual propensity for Type As to become more ill (Suls & Sanders, 1989). Suls and Sanders (1989) proposed a "dangerous situations" hypothesis, suggesting that Type As are at greater risk for a variety of disorders because they are chronically exposed to inherently more risky circumstances than Type Bs. Thus, Type As may more often be in abnormally stressful situations. This may occur because Type As are not responsive to symptoms, engage in strenuous exercise, show certain patterns of risky eating and drinking activity, and may create deficient social support networks (Cohen & Matthews, 1987).

Modification of Type A Behavior

Efforts to modify Type A behavior have recently been undertaken, with promising results (Levenkron & Moore, 1988). Many programs designed to help Type As change their reactions to stress have included training in relaxation and deep breathing (e.g., Roskies et al., 1978). In one study, thirty-six subjects were trained in progressive relaxation training, transcendental meditation, or a control condition. Relaxation training did not reduce cardiovascular responses during stress, but it did result in more rapid blood pressure reductions in the stress recovery period (English & Baker, 1983). Another study (Roskies et al., 1986) exposed Type A men to one of three short-term treatments (aerobic exercise, cognitive-behavioral stress management, and weight training) to modify behavioral and cardiovascular reactivity to laboratory stressors. The stress management group showed significant reduction in behavioral reactivity, although none of the groups showed any reduction in physiological reactivity.

As just implied, exercise has been recommended for the modification of Type A behavior, and it can achieve positive effects of both physiological and psychological functioning. In one study (Blumenthal et al., 1988), healthy Type A men were assigned to either an aerobic exercise training group or a strength-and-flexibility training group. After 12 weeks, both groups showed declines in the behavioral manifestations of Type A. In addition, the aerobic exercise group showed attenuation of heart rate, systolic and diastolic blood pressure, and estimated myocardial oxygen consumption during a behavioral challenge, and they had lower blood pressure, heart rate, and myocardial oxygen consumption during recovery. Thus, aerobic exercise may be an appropriate method for reducing cardiovascular risk among healthy Type A men. Psychotherapy has also been used to attempt to change the Type A's perceptions of the importance of success and the need to use a hard-driving, competitive strategy to attain it (Friedman & Rosenman, 1974). Some programs train Type As to modify their Type A habits, such as explosive speech or the tendency to show hostility, by monitoring both the environment and

their own behavior closely and by substituting different responses (e.g., Friedman & Rosenman, 1974).

Levenkron and Moore (1988) reviewed eighteen studies that evaluated interventions for the Type A behavior pattern. The majority of the studies examined short-term behavior change in small groups of subjects employing behavioral therapies composed largely of cognitive, educational, and relaxation techniques to promote the development and use of skills for coping with stress. Short-term success in reducing certain of the characteristics associated with the Type A syndrome have typically been found. One study (Roskies et al., 1986) found a reduction in physiological reactivity to stress, a particularly important result and objective for future research. While more assessment of ways in which to modify Type A behavior is clearly needed, results to date are promising. Particularly needed are studies with longer term treatments and follow-ups and larger samples in order to examine the long-term impact on morbidity and mortality due to CHD.

One important such research program examined the impact of interventions designed to modify Type A behavior and found clinically significant reductions in cardiac recurrences among CHD patients who have successfully modified the behavior pattern (Friedman et al., 1984, 1986). In this study, 1,013 post-MI patients were followed for 4½ years to see if their Type A behavior could be altered and what effect such alteration might have on cardiac disease morbidity and mortality. Eight-hundred-sixty-two of the participants were randomly assigned either to a control condition that received group cardiac counseling or to an experimental condition that received cardiac counseling and Type A behavior counseling. The remaining patients served as an untreated comparison group. At the end of 4½ years, 35% of the patients exposed to Type A counseling, compared with 9.8% of the participants given only cardiac counseling, showed a decrease in Type A behavior. This also translated into significantly fewer recurrences and deaths (Friedman et al., 1986). In a similar study employing 118 senior U.S. Army officers, behavioral counseling for Type A not only reduced Type A behavior but also reduced serum cholesterol (Gill et al., 1985).

Thus, efforts to modify Type A behavior show considerable promise not only for changing behavior but also for having an impact on CHD morbidity and mortality. However, the modification of Type A behavior is incomplete without a consideration of the interpersonal, institutional, and cultural environments in which it is embedded and which maintain its existence (Margolis, McLeroy, Runyan, & Kaplan, 1983). For example, Type A behavior is valued generally in western culture and particularly in certain environments, such as the business world, in which it thrives. Consequently, modification of the syndrome must take into account the cultural, institutional, and interpersonal supports for it, rather than simply focusing on the individual's expression of it.

Development of Type A Behavior

In recent years, researchers have tried to identify the antecedents of Type A behavior in children (e.g., Matthews, 1977; Matthews & Woodall, 1988). The rationale for identifying and examining the phenomenon early is that atherosclerosis begins early in life, as shown by autopsy data on children and on young men killed in battle (Enos, Holmes, & Beyer, 1953; McNamara, Molot, Stremple, & Cutting, 1971). If the behavior syndrome can be identified and modified early, potentially many people whose lifestyles would be severely compromised by heart disease in middle age will be able to avoid these problems by developing a healthy lifestyle.

Type A behavior can be reliably assessed in children and adolescents (Jackson & Levine, 1987; Matthews & Woodall, 1988). The most common measure used is the Matthews Youth Test for Health (MYTH). Children identified on the MYTH measure as Type A are more outgoing, talkative, and physically active than Type B children. They are also more aggressive in their interactions with others and more likely to experience a greater number of aversive life events. Like Type A adults, Type A children report significantly more physical symptoms than Type B children, and their self-ratings of stress and tension are high. However, they miss no more school, nor do they use physician services more often than Type Bs, suggesting that, as is the case with adults, this may be a reporting difference rather than an actual difference in illness rates (Eagleston et al., 1986). The relation of Type A behavior to physiological reactivity in children has been inconclusive. Some studies comparing Type A and Type B children have found no differences in resting heart rate or in diastolic or systolic blood pressure (Murray, Matthews, Blake, Prineas, & Gillum, 1986). Others have found that children with the Type A behavior pattern resemble Type A adults on measures of physiological responses to stress (Lawler, Allen, Critcher, & Standard, 1981).

Childhood Type A behavior does appear to be associated with the development of components of adult Type A behavior, especially in males (e.g., Keltikangas-Jarvinen, 1989). In one study, competitive boys and girls and Type A girls had significantly higher achievement scores and classroom grades in one study than did noncompetitive children or Type B girls, suggesting that the competitive aspect of Type A behavior can promote early achievement independent of ability. Type A children were also more likely to attribute their performance to effort, although when performance standards were unclear, they perceived themselves as having more difficulty and attributed performance to luck and task difficulty (Murray, Blake, Prineas, & Gillum, 1985). In a study of adolescent anger, anger predicted physical and psychological measures of cardiovascular risk (Siegel, 1984).

What are the antecedents of Type A behavior in children? Evidence that parental Type A scores are correlated with children's Type A scores (Weidner, Sexton, Matarazzo, Pereira, & Friend, 1988) suggests that Type A and B children experience differences in upbringing or have a genetic predisposition to Type A behavior. (It should be noted that these correlations have been demonstrated for father-son pairs only [Weidner et al., 1988].) Relations between blood pressure, heart rate, and blood volume pulse in parents and their offspring tend to be higher than between members of married couples, suggesting that early environment or genetic factors may be more important in cardiovascular reactivity than ongoing environmental factors (Ditto, France, & Miller, 1989). Modeling of parental behavior may also be involved in young children's development of the Type A syndrome. For example, MacEvoy and associates (MacEvoy et al., 1988) found that lively and sociable children were more likely to develop the adult Type A irritability and hurried behavior clusters, and that this was related to the mother's liveliness, orderliness, and intelligence. Young Type A boys but not girls were more likely to have Type A mothers and fathers, suggesting the possible modeling of their behavior. Another study found no relation between fathers' Type A scores and children's, but maternal behavior was found to have an effect on children's Type A behavior (Sweda, Sines, Lauer, & Clarke, 1986).

Matthews and her colleagues (Matthews, Stoney, Rakaczky, & Jamison, 1986) found that Type A children were not more likely to have families with a history of cardiovascular disease, but that their behavior evoked different patterns of responses from others than is true of Type Bs. Type A children elicit more encouragement to try harder, whether from their own mothers or from strangers. Mothers of Type A children, however, made infrequent positive remarks about their children's performance (see Matthews & Woodall, 1988, for a review). Taken together, the results suggest that Type A children are repeatedly urged to do better, but are not necessarily given criteria to determine when they have been successful, and thus they may not learn internal standards by which to evaluate achievement.

Thus, Type As may have been exposed to different childrearing behaviors than Type Bs. Matthews (1977) and Price (1982) suggest that Type As may have upbringings characterized by continually escalating performance standards, constant disapproval, and punitive or harsh methods of control. Consistent with such predictions, male college students asked to retrospect about their own upbringing recalled parents as significantly more likely to place a high emphasis on achievement, to expect competence in a wide variety of areas, and to constantly demand better performance. They also remembered the parents as being strict and using physical punishment or other hostile methods of control, and frequently expressing disapproval (McCranie & Simpson, 1987).

Has knowledge of Type A behavior in children and adolescents led to interventions? The answer is, not yet. It is important to remember that not all children who show incipient Type A behavior will become Type A adults, and many Type A adults will not develop CHD. Moreover, although related to the adult syndrome, Type A behavior in children also departs in important ways from the syndrome in adulthood. For example, Type A is positively associated with psychological adjustment in children, is unrelated to adjustment in adolescence, and is negatively correlated with adjustment in adulthood (Steinberger, 1986). To what extent, then, is one justified in labeling someone as "at risk" and intervening in their behavior, particularly in childhood? To what extent are Type A intervention programs justifiable, in terms of their costs, if only a few individuals are likely to develop CHD? These thorny issues have yet to be fully resolved. As a consequence, Type A modification programs with children or adolescents are implemented only with individuals who show other risk factors or who already have signs of CHD (see Siegel, 1984).

RECOVERY FROM MYOCARDIAL INFARCTION

Approximately 1.5 million individuals suffer a heart attack each year in the United States. About one-quarter of them die within a few hours of the attack and one-third die within the first few weeks. Nonetheless, about half of all heart attack victims return home after hospitalization. Therefore a number of long- and short-term issues of rehabilitation arise.

The process of adjusting emotionally to the experience of a heart attack begins almost immediately. A number of heart attack patients experience cardiac arrest during their myocardial infarction (MI) and have to be resuscitated through artificial means. Being a victim of cardiac arrest can produce a number of psychological difficulties, including nightmares, chronic anxiety, depression, and low expectations of regaining health and vigor (Druss & Kornfeld, 1967). During the acute phase of illness, the MI patient is typically hospitalized in a coronary care unit in which cardiac functioning is continually monitored. Some MI patients experience anxiety at this time, as they cope with the possibility of recurrence and see their cardiac responses vividly illustrated on the machines before them (Doehrman, 1977; Froese, Hackett, Cassem, & Silverberg, 1974). Commonly, however, MI patients in the acute phase of the disease cope by using denial and thus may be relatively anxiety-free during this period.

Cardiac Rehabilitation

Once the acute phase of illness has passed, patients are encouraged to become more active. At this point, a program of education and intervention—covering such topics as medical regimen, health risks, exercise, work, and emotional stress—prepares the patient for discharge. **Cardiac rehabilitation** is defined as the active and progressive process by which individuals with heart disease attain their optimal physical, medical, psychological, social, emotional, vocational, and economic status (Dracup, 1985). The goals of rehabilitation are to produce relief from symptoms, to reduce the severity of the disease, to limit further progression of disease, and to promote psychological and social adjustment. The components of the typical cardiac rehabilitation program include exercise therapy with some psychological counseling as through support groups, nutritional counseling, and education about coronary artery disease (Dracup et al., 1984).

Preparation for the rehabilitation regimen typically begins by familiarizing the patient with the medications to be taken for the control of blood pressure and heart pain. Physical rehabilitation often involves the administration of beta-blockers on a regular basis to block sympathetic nervous system activity in response to stressful events. Beta-blockers not only appear to reduce the risk for heart attack but also seem to reduce Type A behavior, a point consistent with the suggestion that Type A behavior may represent, in part, a response to an overactive sympathetic nervous system. Beta-blockers, however, may have a variety of unpleasant side effects, including fatigue and impotence, which may lead people to take them only intermittently. Digitalis, the customary drug treatment for patients with the potential for heart failure, is problematic, because there is a narrow zone between the drug's therapeutic effectiveness and the development of potentially life-threatening arrhythmias. Stress may aggravate that process, producing arrhythmias at quite low levels of digitalis administration (Natelson, 1988). As a result, some have suggested that behavioral stress management procedures might be used when beta-blocker therapy is not desired, is not practical, or is medically contraindicated for some reason. In a study evaluating this possibility (Gatchel, Gaffney, & Smith, 1986), post-myocardial infarction patients were either administered the beta-blocker propranolol or were trained in stress management techniques. The behavioral stress management intervention reduced psychophysiological reactivity to a stressful event to the same level as the propranolol, thus suggesting that it may be useful when beta-blockers are contraindicated.

Dietary restrictions may be imposed on the recovering MI patient in an attempt to lower the patient's cholesterol level. Instructions to

reduce smoking, lose weight, and control alcohol consumption are also frequently given. Most patients are put on an exercise program involving medically supervised walking, jogging, bicycling, or calisthenics three times a week for 30 to 45 minutes (DeBusk, Haskell, Miller, Berra, & Taylor, 1985). The effectiveness of exercise programs is well documented from a physiological standpoint (Naughton, Hellerstein, & Mohler, 1973; Roviaro, Holmes, & Holmsten, 1984). Psychological responses to illness may also be positively affected by participation in physical activity programs (e.g., Hackett & Cassem, 1973; McPherson et al., 1967; Naughton, Bruhn, & Lategola, 1968; Roviaro et al., 1984). Adherence to this aspect of the treatment regimen is best ensured by seeing to it that the exercise is regularly supervised. If the patient must come to an exercise facility and be monitored, adherence is likely to be high. When patients are left to exercise on their own, however, adherence drops off.

Patients also receive instructions about resumption of their previous activities. Most are urged to return to their prior employment as soon as possible. However, patients in high-stress jobs may be advised to cut back, to work part-time, or to take a position with fewer responsibilities. Unfortunately, adherence is not high in this area of life, typically ranging from 50 to 80% (Croog & Levine, 1977). One reason for this low rate of adherence is that advice to cut back on work activities is often phrased in very vague terms, and patients may not understand exactly how they should implement these goals.

Another important step in recovery from myocardial infarction is the management of stress. For example, patients may be urged to avoid stressful situations at work and to minimize family tensions. This is often a very difficult treatment goal to meet, because the patient is merely given the general admonition to avoid stressful situations. What constitutes a stressful situation and how to avoid it are often difficult questions for the patient to an-

The treadmill test provides a useful indicator of the functional capacity of recovering myocardial infarction patients.

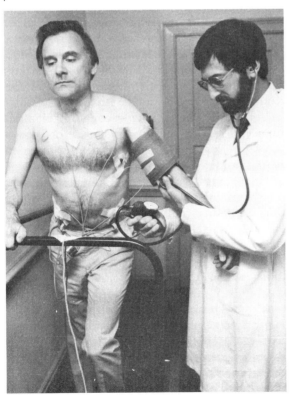

swer. As many as 40 to 50% of patients (Croog & Levine, 1977) report that they are unable to control the degree of stress in their lives, and a minority of MI patients find that their personal lives are even more stressful than they were before the MI.

Aid in stress management can be provided in at least two ways. First, patients may be trained in specific techniques such as relaxation therapy or modification of Type A behavior, as noted earlier. Second, the general advice to avoid stressful situations can be made more concrete by talking through with the patient what constitutes a stressful situations in his or her own life. The practitioner and patient together can develop means of recognizing when stress is likely to occur, how to avoid it, and what to do about it if it is unavoidable. Making this general treatment goal as concrete for the patient as possible will aid in adherence.

Implementation of Lifestyle Changes

One of the complicating issues in recovery from MI is that many patients must be trained to modify several health habits simultaneously. For example, a patient may have to start exercising, arrange for a change of diet, and stop smoking all at the same time. As already noted, adherence with lifestyle change is often low and may be lower still if a number of health habits must be changed at the same time.

Several approaches to the modification of multiple health habits have been mounted. One approach is a residential treatment program of several weeks' duration. Here treatment goals are established with each patient at the outset, and an organized program of daily activities involving each of the health habits is initiated. Patients are trained in menu planning and taught a variety of maintenance techniques for not smoking and for adhering to exercise and diet regimens. Unfortunately, this kind of residential program is extremely ex-

pensive and may not be effective over the long term. Less expensive ways of modifying multiple health habits must be found. Outpatient programs that are structured similarly to residential treatment programs are one possibility, but these, too, call for a large staff and are very expensive; moreover, it is not yet clear that they are effective. Nonetheless, with no alternative solution in sight, it appears that this kind of intensive effort targeted to multiple health behaviors is currently the best way to achieve these treatment goals.

Problems of Social Support

As we have seen in previous chapters, social support can help people recover more quickly from disorders once they are ill. This also appears to be true for patients suffering from coronary heart disease. In a longitudinal study of recovery from CHD, evidence suggested that social support from family and friends reduced the experiences of stress and distress, thereby improving cardiac symptoms. It appeared to be more influential during the 6 months just following hospitalization for CHD than in the second half of the year (Fontana, Kerns, Rosenberg, & Colonese, 1989).

Yet many factors may erode the potential for social support. In the home setting, one of the MI patient's chief complaints is loss of independence. Myocardial infarction sharply reduces an individual's physical stamina, and many patients are surprised by the extent of their disability (Finlayson & McEwen, 1977). Feelings of shame, helplessness, and low self-esteem may result. Conflict over changes in lifestyle can result in marital strife (Croog & Fitzgerald, 1978; Michela, 1987). The patient may find it difficult to adhere to dietary restrictions and exercise, whereas the spouse may be highly motivated to induce the patient to comply. Stressful interactions over the need to modify daily activities can aggravate the patient's perceptions of dependence and exacerbate already existing depression.

Spouses of heart attack victims themselves often show severe psychological responses to the MI, including nightmares and chronic anxiety over the patient's survival (Skelton & Dominian, 1973). One study (Michela, 1987) suggested a mismatch in patients' and spouses' adjustment to the myocardial infarction. Whereas patients' adverse reactions to the MI showed a steady decrease over time, wives' adverse responses and corresponding marital dissatisfaction often peaked some time after the MI and then declined. As a consequence of problematic interactions in the home, wives of heart attack victims tend to see their recovering husbands as dependent and irritable (Skelton & Dominian, 1973), whereas recovering husbands regard their wives as meddling and overprotective (Adsett & Brohn, 1968; Croog & Levine, 1977). Wives may find themselves in untenable situations, wanting on the one hand to help the patient adhere to his treatment regimen and, on the other hand, eliciting the patient's hostility.

In his studies of couple functioning after a husband's heart attack, Michela (1987) found that husbands needed extra services, which wives often provided, but that husbands did not always express the appreciation that was needed to keep wives from reacting adversely to their enhanced efforts. In addition, expressions of displeasure about the lifestyle changes recommended for recovery reduced marital satisfaction. Despite these sources of marital tension, there is no evidence that heart attacks drive married couples apart; neither, however, does it necessarily bring them closer together (Croog & Levine, 1977).

Cardiac invalidism can be one consequence of an MI, such that patients and their spouses both see the patient's abilities as lower than they actually are. In a study designed to reduce this problem, Taylor, Bandura, Ewart, Miller, and DeBusk (1985) either provided wives of recovering MI patients with information about their husbands' cardiovascular capabilities, had them observe their husbands' performance on a treadmill task, or had them actually take part in the treadmill activity personally. Wives who personally experienced the treadmill task increased their perceptions of their husbands' physical and cardiac efficacy after observing their husbands' treadmill attainments and receiving information. Wives who were simply informed or who observed treadmill activity continued to regard their husbands as impaired.

Additional research is needed to identify exactly what the social support gaps may be for patients adjusting to myocardial infarction (Ell & Dunkel-Schetter, in press). What kinds of social support interventions might be most successful also merits attention, inasmuch as research with cancer patients has found that some kinds of efforts at social support, such as emotional support, achieve their intended effects, whereas other efforts to express support, such as advice, may not (Dunkel-Schetter & Wortman, 1981; Ell & Dunkel-Schetter, in press).

Psychosocial Responses to MI

Over time, as patients begin to come to terms with the threat posed by the disease and the restrictions that it will impose on their lives, they may become increasingly anxious or depressed (Cay, Vetter, Philip, & Dugard, 1972; Hackett & Cassem, 1973). Thus, interventions that deal with these adverse psychological and social consequences of MI may also be needed. As noted earlier, one of the recovering patient's most extreme fears is the possibility of another attack. To best prepare the patient for this possibility in a relatively unthreatening manner, two actions are possible. First, patients often deny that the symptoms they are experiencing are indicative of a heart attack. Accordingly, they may delay for long periods of time before they get the necessary medical help (Matthews, Siegel, Kuller, Thompson, & Varat, 1983). Both patients and family members should be taught how to recognize the symptoms of an impending heart attack, how to differentiate them from more minor physical complaints such as heartburn, and how to activate the emergency system. In this way, delay behavior can be reduced and treatment can be improved in the event of a repeat event. Family members of the MI patient should also be trained in **cardiopulmonary resuscitation (CPR)**. Approximately 70% of potential sudden deaths from heart attacks occur in the home rather than the workplace, but relatively few programs have been initiated to train family members in CPR. More programs should be available for MI families (Dracup, Guzy, Taylor, & Barry, in press).

As noted in Chapter 12, patients experience a variety of unpleasant and possibly long-term psychological symptoms as a consequence of MI. For example, a year after a heart attack, as many as one-quarter of all MI patients are still severely depressed (Croog & Levine, 1977). Moreover, this depression can have deleterious effects on both physical and social indices of recovery (Davidson, 1983; Mumford, Schlesinger, & Glass, 1982). In some cases, depression may stem from an unrealistic assessment of current and future risk, although in other cases it may stem from the realistic threat of a repeat event and the restrictions that have been placed on the patient as a consequence of the treatment regimen. Such patients may benefit from individual or group psychotherapy.

Interventions that help the patient solve social and vocational problems created by MI may also be required. Marital counseling or family therapy may be required to deal with marital strain. As employment is sometimes affected by heart disease, economic problems may result that require counseling. Since 20% of myocardial infarction patients do not return to their previous jobs, they often suffer a loss of income. These families may require financial counseling or retraining to help them offset their losses. The problems experienced by

one man in returning to work after a myocardial infarction are described in Box 14.3.

As noted in Chapters 9 and 12, patients' specific beliefs about illness, treatment, and recovery can be important determinants of their adjustment, and this message bears repeating in the context of MI. Some researchers believe that no intervention program can be successfully mounted with MI patients unless they have developed the proper cognitions about illness (Garrity, 1973, 1975). For example, whether or not patients understand their clinical status correctly and whether or not they understand restrictions on their physical abilities will substantially determine the extent to which they are able and willing to return to work and full social involvement as well as their ability to meet other treatment goals. Krantz (1980) suggests that chief among the health perceptions that influence recovery are feelings of helplessness produced by the illness and its restrictions. Helplessness can reduce feelings of competence and lead to depression. Interventions that enable MI patients to see their lives as controllable, that present them with choices they can make in their recovery process, and that offer them opportunities to exert actual control may help break down these feelings of helplessness, instill feelings of competence, and enable patients to make greater gains in their recovery (Krantz, 1980).

Many of these interventions, however, may be time-consuming and costly, and many recovering MI patients are not in a position financially to afford the individual and group counseling that may be needed. Are there short-term, cost-effective interventions that can alleviate some of these psychosocial difficulties? One study designed to improve the physical, psychological, and lifestyle status of patients after myocardial infarction randomized patients into an educational intervention consisting of relaxation procedures and information about heart disease and its treatment; a counseling intervention consisting of the education intervention plus six to ten sessions of counseling; or standard medical/nursing care.

Box 14.3
The Heart Patient Returns to Work

People who have gone through a heart attack often experience difficulties when they try to return to work. They may be warned against certain activities, particularly those that are stress-related or that may tax sympathetic nervous system activity. The following shows how one man attempted to cope with this advice, and the repercussions that followed.

> The physician instructed the patient that he could carry out all usual activities, except, "Avoid lifting." "Don't pick up heavy boxes at the office." In the first weeks of work return, he finds a sympathetic attitude among co-workers and pleasant relationships. As the occasion arises, he calls upon one or another to lift heavy boxes for him. Co-workers assist him, most willingly, in the first days after his return to work. Eventually, the tone in the office changes, and resentment stirs among those who are called upon to interrupt their own work and lift the occasional heavy boxes. The character of his informal associations alters, and he begins to have the feeling of becoming an outsider. Yet he has received doctor's orders on lifting, and he is unwilling to risk his health or his life by picking up boxes.

> Occasional mild chest pain and shortness of breath remind him that he is not the man he used to be. One day he asks a fellow worker to lift a box for him. The response comes, "Why don't you go ahead and drop dead, you lazy son-of-a-bitch!"

> The solutions are limited for this 55-year-old man. Transferring to another department is not possible, as the company is a small one. Leaving for another job is not possible for many reasons: limited employment opportunities in the marketplace during a recession; a record of years of personal attachment to the company; the strains of job hunting, relocating, and adjusting to a new work situation. Trying to win understanding and cooperation from fellow workers is a fruitless task, since the intermesh of personalities, resentments, and personal rivalries common to many offices continue to interfere.

> So picking up the heavy boxes seems the easiest solution—but for how long can he continue? What will be the eventual effects on his heart? Anxiety about health, death, and his family colors his life.

(Croog, 1983, pp. 300–301)

Follow-ups over a 1-year period showed that the intervention groups did better on psychological and lifestyle functioning, reported fewer symptoms of heart disease, and were not as dependent on treatment as those in the standard care condition. This type of intervention compares favorably with routine outpatient cardiac rehabilitation (Oldenburg, Perkins, & Andrews, 1985). In that the two intervention groups showed equivalent rates of success, the less expensive educational intervention may be sufficient. This search for cost-effective interventions for this population will, no doubt, continue.

HYPERTENSION

Overview

Hypertension, or high blood pressure, occurs when the supply of blood through the vessels is excessive, putting pressure on the vessel walls. When high blood pressure is a recurring pattern, it can cause hardening of the arterial walls and deterioration of the cell tissue. Hypertension is a serious medical problem for several reasons. There are approximately 60 million hypertensives in the United States, and each year there are about 16,000 deaths due to hypertensive heart disease. Moreover, hypertension is a risk factor for other disorders, such as coronary artery disease, kidney failure, and stroke. It may also produce some cognitive impairments (Madden & Blumenthal, 1989).

Hypertension is determined by the levels of systolic and diastolic blood pressure as measured by a sphygmomanometer. As noted in Chapter 2, systolic blood pressure is the greatest force developed during contraction of the heart's ventricles. It is sensitive both to the volume of blood leaving the heart and to the arteries' ability to stretch to accommodate blood (their elasticity). Diastolic pressure is the pressure in the arteries when the heart is relaxed; it is related to resistance of the blood

Hypertension is a symptomless disease. As a result, unless they obtain regular physical checkups or participate in hypertension screening programs, many adults are unaware that they have this disorder.

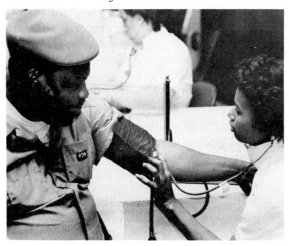

vessels to blood flow. Of the two, diastolic pressure has somewhat greater value in diagnosing hypertension. Mild hypertension is defined by a diastolic pressure consistently between 90 and 104; moderate hypertension involves a pressure consistently between 105 and 119; and severe hypertension means a diastolic pressure consistently above 119. In the past, only moderate and severe hypertensives received treatment, but there is now evidence that mild hypertensives can also profit from early therapy (Kolata, 1979). Increasingly, left ventricular hypertrophy (abnormal enlargement of the heart's left ventricle) is being recognized as a significant prognostic indicator of essential hypertension that can be identified relatively early by an echocardiogram (Devereux, 1988). Inasmuch as left ventricular hypertrophy may be directly related to hypertension-related deaths due to coronary artery disease, it may be a particularly useful indicator (Yurenev et al., 1988).

Approximately 5% of hypertension is caused by failure of the kidneys to regulate blood pressure. However, almost 90% of all hypertension is *essential*—that is, of unknown origin. Some risk factors have been identified. Males are at greater risk for hypertension than females. Genetic factors clearly also play a role (see also Smith et al., 1987): If one parent has high blood pressure, the offspring have a 45% chance of developing it; if two parents have high blood pressure, the probability increases to 95%. Blood pressure hyperreactivity in children predicts later development of hypertension, consistent with the possibility of a genetic mechanism (Sallis, Dimsdale, & Caine, 1988). The genetic factor may be a hereditary predisposition to be physiologically reactive to stressful events. Obesity is another risk factor for hypertension. Dietary factors such as salt intake may play a causal role, but as yet the nature of diet-hypertension relationships has not been fully explored (Galton, 1973; Shapiro & Goldstein, 1982). There may also be personality factors implicated in this constellation of risk factors, such as a tendency toward anger (Harburg et al., 1973; Johnson, Schork, & Spielberger, 1987), cynical distrust (Williams, 1984), or excessive striving in the face of significant odds (James, Hartnett, & Kalsbeek, 1983). As yet, the evidence relating anger expression and active coping to hypertension remains inconclusive (James, 1987).

Hypertension is especially prevalent among lower-income blacks. Part of this risk appears to be associated with such factors as parental history of hypertension. There are also racial differences in neuropeptide and cardiovascular responses to stressors that may influence the development of hypertension (Anderson, Lane, Taguchi, & Williams, 1989; Durel et al., 1989; Light & Sherwood, 1989; McNeilly & Zeichner, 1989; Tischenkel et al., 1989). Low-income blacks are also more likely to live in stressful neighborhoods, conditions associated with the development of hypertension, and they may also be constitutionally predisposed to greater cardiovascular reactivity to stress (Fleming, Baum, Davidson, Rectanus, & McArdle, 1987; Harburg et al., 1973). Low-income blacks report more psychological distress than do higher-income whites and blacks, and chronic life stress may interfere with sympathetic nervous system recovery in response to specific stressors (Pardine & Napoli, 1983). Exposure to racism may aggravate blood pressure among blacks (Armstead, Lawler, Gordon, Cross, & Gibbons, 1989).

Relationship Between Stress and Hypertension

Stress has been suspected as a contributor to hypertension for many years (Henry & Cassel, 1969). Substantial evidence relates increases in blood pressure to stressful events (for a review, see Harrell, 1980; Shapiro & Goldstein, 1982). A large body of experimental literature indicates that laboratory-induced stressors including breath-holding, bright lights, emotionally disturbing questions, arithmetic tests,

injections, and electric shock all produce rises in blood pressure (for a review, see Shapiro & Goldstein, 1982). These effects have been found for both blacks and whites (Anderson et al., 1986). Increased blood pressure responses to natural and unnatural disasters have been observed in populations as varied as soldiers engaged in desert warfare (Graham, 1945) and residents adjusting to a chemical explosion (Ruskin, Beard, & Schaeffer, 1948). Crowded, high-stress, and noisy locales all produce higher rates of hypertension, and abundant research demonstrates that populations that have migrated from rural to urban areas have higher rates of hypertension (James, 1987). As we noted in Chapter 7, job stress and unemployment have also been tied to higher blood pressure.

In a well-controlled reanalysis of all available case-control studies of blood pressure and heart rate response to stress, Fredrickson and Matthews (in press) compared the reactions of three groups to stressful events: essential hypertensives, borderline hypertensives, and normotensive (normal) offspring of hypertensives. Essential hypertensives showed large blood pressure responses to all stressors. The effects were somewhat stronger for passive stressors, which do not require a behavioral response, than for active stressors, which do require a behavioral response. In contrast, borderline hypertensives showed moderately large and more reliable blood pressure and heart rate responses primarily to stressors that required an active behavioral response. The normotensive offspring also exhibited moderately large and reliable blood pressure increases to stressors, predominantly to those that required an active behavioral response.

The results provide some evidence that excessive sympathetic nervous system activity during stressful times can have a pathophysiologic role in the development of hypertension, at least in some individuals. The results are also consistent with the conclusion that stressful events that require active adaptation may have a greater role in the development of hypertension than do stressful events that require only passive acceptance. However, in those already diagnosed with hypertension, all stressful events may be implicated in elevated blood pressure responses.

The results also suggested that factors that reduce cardiovascular reactivity to stress in normotensives may not do so in hypertensives. For example, feelings of personal control often enable people to cope more successfully with stressful events. However, these effects do not appear to show up in those diagnosed with essential hypertension. That is, personal control has no buffering effect over the impact of stressful events on elevated blood pressure.

Chronically hypertensive individuals may be **stress-sensitive.** Many hypertensives show a stronger blood pressure response than do normotensives to a wide variety of stressors, including mental tasks (such as arithmetic) and painful activities (such as immersing one's hand in ice water for several minutes). Typically, hypertensives also take longer to return to normal once their blood pressure has been raised in response to stress (Harrell, 1980). It is possible that this heightened responsivity to stress is genetically based. One study examined responses to stress among thirty subjects with a family history of hypertension but who did not have hypertension themselves. These individuals showed reliably greater cardiovascular reactivity during stress tasks and in anticipation of stressful events. Thus, it is possible that a genetically based excess reactivity of the sympathetic nervous system is implicated in at least some essential hypertension (Jorgensen & Houston, 1981).

Animal models involving studies with dogs have demonstrated that genetically normotensive animals exposed to stimulus deprivation or to intermittent aversive stimulation, particularly under conditions of high sodium and low potassium intake, can develop and sustain hypertension. The behavioral and physiological adaptations observed in these animals support the idea that activation of the hypothalamic-pituitary-adrenocortical system could also be involved in hypertension, potentially clarifying the role of behavioral factors for at least some forms of human hypertension (Anderson, 1987).

With recurring or prolonged exposure to stress, the physiological changes produced by heightened reactivity may cause permanent damage, laying the groundwork for chronic hypertension. Specifically, with recurring elevated blood pressure, there is more hardening and narrowing of the arteries. Psychological factors may also produce changes in the body's regulation of salt excretion over time and in the mechanism that adjusts blood volume (Harrell, 1980).

Recently, evidence has emerged for a possible role of endogenous opioid peptides in blood pressure responses to stressful situations. Endogenous opioid peptides regulate neuroendocrine and circulatory responses to behavioral stress. Thus, with the administration of an opiate antagonist, such as naloxone, one would expect to see increased blood pressure responses to stress. However, in a study that compared young adults with high, medium, or low blood pressure, naloxone increased blood pressure responses to stress in subjects with low blood pressure, but had no effect on subjects with high pressure. These results tentatively suggest that the opioid-energic inhibition of sympathetic nervous activity may be deficient in at least some people at risk for hypertension (McCubbin, Surwit, & Williams, 1985). Possibly this deficiency is mediated by a lesion at the adrenal medulla or it may exist at levels of central autonomic control (McCubbin, Surwit, & Williams, 1988).

Overall, it is unlikely that one single stress–hypertension link will be found that explains all hypertension. There are several different types of hypertension that may be caused by the failure of different physiologic mechanisms to function effectively (Laragh, 1988a;

Parfyonova, Korichneva, Suvorov, & Krasnikova, 1988). And, just as the physiologic profile of hypertension is heterogeneous, it is likely that the psychological profile will turn out to be heterogeneous as well (Harrell, 1980).

Personality Factors and Hypertension

Originally, hypertension was thought to be marked by a constellation of personality factors, dominated by suppressed anger (Alexander, 1950; Dunbar, 1943). Research now clearly indicates that personality factors alone are not sufficient for the development of hypertension (Harrell, 1980). However, certain personality traits may be important in conjunction with other risk factors. A large amount of research has focused on suppressed hostility as a predictor of hypertension (Dimsdale et al., 1986; James, 1987; Sommers-Flanagan & Greenberg, 1989). One of the main problems in establishing such a link is finding reliable and valid measures of suppressed rage. It is also possible that suppressed rage alone is not sufficient to lead to hypertension, but that its effects may be evident only in the presence of other risk factors.

The relation of rage to hypertension has led some to suggest that Type A behavior may be implicated in the development of hypertension as well as in coronary artery disease. However, Type A individuals do not exhibit chronically higher blood pressure or a greater prevalence of hypertension than Type Bs. On the other hand, borderline and established hypertensives do show greater cardiovascular reactivity to mental stressors in the laboratory and often have difficulty managing hostility and anger. It is possible, then, that increased cardiovascular reactivity may be a marker for elevated blood pressure in some people at increased risk for hypertension, but it may not be a causal factor in its development (Rosenman, 1987). Accordingly, more sophisticated models of the relationship between suppressed rage and hypertension need to be tested (James, 1987).

An example of such an approach is provided by Harburg and his associates' study of hypertension in black males (Harburg et al., 1973). They developed and tested a model of the causes of hypertension, which included several factors: high stress, suppressed hostility, minority status, and skin color. The research was conducted on a population of blacks and whites in the Detroit area. First, the researchers identified high- and low-stress locales in the city of Detroit. High-stress locales were defined as areas characterized by low socioeconomic status, high population density, high geographical mobility, high rates of marital breakup, and high crime; low-stress areas had more favorable ratings on all these variables. Suppressed rage was measured as guilt and inwardly directed anger; these variables were coded from each individual's responses to a series of vignettes about injustices (such as an arbitrary rent hike) frequently faced by residents of the inner city.

The results indicated that several factors were related to hypertension. First, higher rates of hypertension were found in high-stress than in low-stress locales. Second, black men had higher blood pressure than white men, especially dark-skinned black men who lived in the high-stress areas. Overall, the highest blood pressure ratings were found among dark-skinned black men in high-stress locales who dealt with their anger by suppressing it. It does indeed appear, then, that high day-to-day stress—as measured by characteristics of one's immediate environment, the suppression of anger, and minority status—can combine to produce a high rate of hypertension (see also Gentry, Chesney, Gary, Hall, & Harburg, 1982).

In this context, recent research has examined the phenomenon known as **John Henryism.** John Henry, the "steel-driving" man, was an uneducated black laborer who allegedly defeated a mechanical steam drill in a contest to see which could complete the most work in the shortest period of time. However, after winning the battle, John Henry reportedly dropped dead from exhaustion. James et al. (1983) coined the term "John Henryism" to stand for the person-environment interaction that Harburg et al. (1973) suggested might be related to understanding hypertension risk in black Americans of low SES (James, LaCroix, Kleinbaum, & Strogatz, 1984). John Henryism is a personality predisposition to cope actively with psychosocial stressors. It becomes a lethal predisposition when active coping efforts are likely to be unsuccessful. The person scoring high on John Henryism would try harder and harder against ultimately insurmountable odds. Consequently, one would expect to find John Henryism to be especially lethal among the disadvantaged, especially low-income and poorly educated blacks. Recent studies confirm these characteristics. One study found that low-SES blacks who scored high on a measure of John Henryism were almost three times as likely to be hypertensive as higher-status blacks who scored high on John Henryism. There was no relationship between John Henryism and SES among whites (James, Strogatz, Wing, & Ramsey, 1987). In another study, men with low levels of education and high levels of John Henryism had significantly higher diastolic blood pressure than men who were high on education and John Henryism (James et al., 1983). This pattern of managing stress, then, appears to be useful in understanding the high rates of hypertension that have been documented in blacks, especially low-SES blacks.

Since social support and exercise appear to buffer stress, are they effective buffers against hypertension? In the case of social support, this issue has not been fully evaluated. However, there is some evidence to suggest that, especially in blacks, social ties may buffer individuals against hypertension-related mortality (Strogatz & James, 1986). Exercise has been identified as a buffer against stress (Brown &

Siegel, 1988), and it may be a buffer against stress-induced hypertension as well. In a study of genetically normotensive rats, the group that had access to exercise showed no increase in hypertension in response to stress, whereas rats not able to exercise did (Mills & Ward, 1986). Stress buffers in hypertension represent a useful line of research for the future.

Treatment of Hypertension

Overview   Hypertension has been controlled in a variety of ways. Commonly, patients are put on low-sodium diets to restrict their sodium intake to approximately 2 grams a day. Recently, however, the use of sodium-restricted diets has been controversial because sodium depletion can adversely affect sympathetic nervous system activity. We will return to this issue shortly. Reduction of alcohol is also recommended for hypertension patients. Weight reduction in overweight patients is strongly urged, and exercise is recommended for all hypertensive patients. Although the role of caffeine in the aggravation of blood pressure has yet to be conclusively determined (Goldstein & Shapiro, 1987), caffeine restriction is often included as part of the dietary treatment of hypertension. Caffeine does increase systolic blood pressure (Greenberg & Shapiro, 1987). It may be implicated as an aggravating or interactive factor with stress that increases blood pressure response, primarily in those with a family history of hypertension (Greenstadt, Yang, & Shapiro, 1988; Shapiro, Lane, & Henry, 1988).

Drug Treatments   Most commonly, hypertension is treated pharmacologically. Such techniques include diuretics, which reduce blood volume by promoting the excretion of sodium. Another common treatment is beta-adrenergic blockers, which exert their antihypertensive effects by decreasing cardiac output and decreasing plasma renin activity.

Central adrenergic inhibitors are also used to reduce blood pressure by decreasing the sympathetic outflow from the central nervous system. Although these drugs can be tolerated in small doses, in large doses they have many unfavorable side effects, such as depression and impotence, thereby promoting nonadherence. Peripheral adrenergic inhibitors are also used to deplete catecholamines from the brain and the adrenal medulla. The major side effects are depression and indifference to the environment, and, thus, they too create adherence problems. Alpha-adrenergic blockers, vasodilators, angiotensin-converting enzyme inhibitors, and calcium channel blockers have also been used in the treatment of hypertension. These techniques show some success in reducing blood pressure, but the adverse side effects are often so great that nonadherence with recommended treatments is very high (Rosen & Kostis, 1985).

Recently, drug treatments for hypertension have become controversial. Hypertension is only one of a cluster of factors that lead to the development of coronary artery disease. Certain of the drug treatments may have positive effects in reducing blood pressure but ultimately increase the likelihood of coronary artery disease by augmenting sympathetic nervous system activity overall. Diuretics and beta-blockers, for example, have potentially adverse metabolic effects, whereas alpha adrenoreceptor inhibitors may beneficially affect the metabolic factors that influence risk for coronary artery disease.

A recent review of nineteen antihypertensive treatment trials, which spanned 20 years of research, showed that although drug treatment significantly reduced blood pressure-related complications of hypertension, it did not prevent coronary artery disease, morbidity, or mortality. In fact, the antihypertensive drugs used in most of the clinical trials were associated with enhanced sympathetic activity. Most risk factors for coronary artery disease involve enhanced sympa-

thetic nervous system activity, which may be a final common pathway for their adverse affects; thus, changing the risk factor without considering the impact on sympathetic nervous system activity is unwise. Hypertension may be managed more effectively by therapy that neutralizes sympathetic tone (Lee et al., 1988). Thus, it makes sense to emphasize drugs that do not increase the metabolic prediliction to coronary artery disease.

Cognitive-Behavioral Treatments The fact that antihypertensive medications can actually aggravate sympathetic nervous system activity, coupled with the success of cognitive-behavioral therapy in other areas of health psychology, has led to an increasing use of cognitive-behavioral modification techniques in the treatment of hypertension. The hope is that if they are successful, somewhat lower levels of drugs may be required (Glasgow, Engel, & D'Lugoff, 1989). A variety of behavioral and cognitive-behavioral methods have been evaluated for their potential success in lowering blood pressure (for a review, see Glasgow & Engel, 1987). Methods that draw on relaxation include biofeedback, progressive muscle relaxation, hypnosis, and meditation, all of which are thought to reduce blood pressure via the induction of a state of low arousal. Deep breathing and imagery are often added to accomplish this task. Generally, the results evaluating biofeedback and relaxation therapy for hypertension suggest positive effects (Aivazyan, Zaitsev, Salenko, Yurenev, & Patrusheva, 1988; Blanchard, Khramelashvili et al., 1988; Blanchard, McCoy et al., 1988; Ewart et al., 1987; Glasgow & Engel, 1987; Hoelscher, Lichstein, & Rosenthal, 1986; Richter-Heinrich, Enderlein, Knust, Schmidt, & Wiedemann, 1989; Vinck, Arickx, & Hongenaert, 1987), although patients do not always practice relaxation as much as they should or claim to (Hoelscher et al., 1986). Relaxation therapy may be especially effective with patients who have elevated sympathetic tone and low left ventricular mass (as noted earlier, left ventricular hypertrophy is a risk factor for sudden death in hypertensive patients) (Lee et al., 1987). Training in relaxation does seem to be essential to its positive effects in reducing blood pressure. When people are simply urged to try to keep their blood pressure down, the effort can actually be counterproductive, leading to increases rather than decreases in blood pressure (Suls, Sanders, & Lebrecque, 1986).

Other stress management techniques have also been employed in the treatment of hypertension (Horan & Roccella, 1988; McEntee & Peddicord, 1987; Oakley & Shapiro, 1989; Weiss, 1988). Such techniques train people to identify their particular stressors and to develop plans for dealing with them. The programs include training in self-reinforcement, self-calming talk, goal setting, and time management. These cognitive-behavioral techniques are thought to reduce blood pressure by helping people avert the anxiety they would otherwise develop in response to environmental stressors. In one study that evaluated stress management training, forty-one mild to moderately hypertensive black men were assigned to one of three groups: cognitive self-management, an attention placebo control, or an irrelevant control condition. Those receiving the cognitive self-management training reported significant increases in the use of cognitive coping strategies in their lives, demonstrated significant decreases in anxiety and systolic blood pressure, and showed some reduction in diastolic blood pressure as well (Bosley & Allen, 1989).

Exercise may also help in blood pressure control. One study (Perkins, Dubbert, Martin, Faulstich, & Harris, 1986) found that aerobically trained mild hypertensives reacted to mildly stressful situations with smaller blood pressure increases than untrained mild hypertensives. Thus, aerobic training, which itself may reduce blood pressure in mild hyper-

tensives, may also exert a favorable effect in some stressful situations by reducing cardiovascular reactivity among hypertensives.

The suggestion of the relationship between suppressed anger and hypertension tentatively implies that teaching people to express their anger might be useful. However, research has suggested (Johnson & Broman, 1987) that the direct expression of anger may also be associated with health problems. In a study with black adults, those who expressed anger outwardly had a higher number of health problems than those who expressed low or moderate amounts of anger (Johnson & Broman, 1987). Thus, direct interventions to control expressions of anger have yet to be undertaken as an intervention tool against hypertension.

How do behavioral techniques fare comparatively in the treatment of hypertension? Behavioral methods appear to be more successful than no treatment, blood pressure self-monitoring, and attention control conditions (e.g., Agras, Taylor et al., 1987). No particular behavioral treatment emerges as better than any other (Hoelscher et al. 1986). Biofeedback, relaxation, drug treatment, and stress management can all reduce blood pressure. Preliminary evidence suggests that in certain patients with mild hypertension, behavioral treatments may actually substitute for pharmacological approaches (Richter-Heinrich et al., 1988). However, with the severely hypertensive, behavioral treatment is clearly less effective than drug treatments (Wadden, Luborsky, Greer, & Crits-Christoph, 1984). Moreover, evidence to date suggests that noncompliance with cognitive-behavioral approaches is roughly the same as nonadherence with drug treatments (see Hoelscher et al., 1986). The chief advantages of behavioral methodologies are that they are relatively easy to implement, people can use them without supervision, and there are no side effects. Theoretically, successful behavioral treatments might also make it possible to reduce drug dosages in hypertensives. At present, both approaches are still typically combined to produce the best outcomes.

As we have seen, hypertension is a complex disease that varies widely from individual to individual. Consequently, the best treatment for any person often involves a uniquely tailored combination of drug and behavioral interventions that seems to work in that particular case. The primary goal of current treatment for hypertension is to give each patient the fewest drugs in the smallest amount with the lowest frequency possible for the often lifetime commitment that treatment for hypertension may involve (Laragh, 1988b). Behavioral methods appear to be an important weapon in the arsenal to bring about this goal.

Problems in Treating Hypertension   The biggest problems related to the control of hypertension concern high rates of nondiagnosis and nonadherence to therapy. Indeed, adherence to hypertension regimen has been one of the most widely studied examples of high rates of nonadherence (Koltun & Stone, 1986). What are the reasons for these problems? A first difficulty is that hypertension is largely a symptomless disease. People typically do not know they have high blood pressure, so they do not come to a practitioner for treatment; rather, the condition is often diagnosed during a standard physical examination. Many thousands of people who suffer from hypertension receive no treatment, and many who might benefit from early detection are not screened. National campaigns to educate the public about hypertension have been successful in improving the knowledge base about this common disease (Horan & Roccella, 1988). Worksite-based screening and care programs may also be successful in identifying those with hypertension and in providing care on an ongoing basis (Alderman & Lamport, 1988). What kind of message would be most likely to appeal to someone at risk for hyper-

tension? In a study by Gintner, Rectanus, Achord, & Parker (1987), undergraduates with and without a hypertensive parent were given printed information about hypertension and the importance of early detection. The message was framed either in terms of wellness or in terms of the threat of illness. The results indicated that these students were twice as likely to attend the screening when given a wellness message than when given a threatening message.

Adherence is also adversely affected by the symptomless nature of the disease. Because hypertensive patients ''feel fine,'' it can be difficult to induce them to practice sick-role behaviors by taking medications on a regular basis. Many patients erroneously believe they can tell when their blood pressure is high, and they treat it accordingly. Many of us believe that when we are ''cranked up,'' under stress, or annoyed, our blood pressure is high. In fact, the correlation between beliefs about level of blood pressure and actual blood pressure is low. Unfortunately, hypertensives tend to have such theories and may choose to medicate themselves on the basis of them, thus showing nonadherence with their prescribed regimen and sustaining substantial health risks as well (Meyer, Leventhal, & Gutmann, 1985).

Another basis for the adherence problem among hypertensives is that, as just noted, most of the available medications have unpleasant side effects, such as dizziness, inability to concentrate, and impotence. Many hypertensive patients are unwilling to trade the apparent benefits of the drugs for their noxious side effects, particularly when their disease is symptomless. Yet in some cases, these drugs may help restore performance capacity that may have been lost to hypertensive disease (Streufert, DePadova, McGlynn, Piasecki, & Pogash, 1989).

What can be done to reduce the nonadherence problem? Clearly, one solution is to educate patients fully about the largely symptomless nature of the disease and the critical importance of treatment for controlling it. Information can help people practice appropriate follow-up of screening results, at least on the short term (Zimmerman, Safer, Leventhal, & Baumann, 1986). It may be necessary, too, to demonstrate to patients that their theories about their blood pressure are often wrong: When they think their blood pressure is high, it may not be. Although some individuals appear to be able to detect their blood pressure at better than chance level, these findings are not yet to a point where they have therapeutic implications (Barr, Pennebaker, & Watson, 1988; Pennebaker, Gonder-Frederick, Stewart, Elfman, & Skelton, 1982). Unfortunately, research to date suggests that hypertensives and borderline hypertensives are only moderately responsive to information indicating that they are unable to control their blood pressure (Baumann, Zimmerman, & Leventhal, 1989).

Compliance with hypertension regimen is also influenced by factors that predict adherence more generally. When patients expect greater control over health and hypertension, have greater knowledge of the treatment regimen, and have stronger social support, they are more likely to adhere to their hypertension regimen (Stanton, 1987). Interventions may be able to draw on these findings as well.

In summary, it is evident that essential hypertension can have many causal factors. These include a genetic link, behavioral risk factors such as obesity, a possible kidney malfunction, and possible sensitivity to salt. Stress also appears to be implicated in several ways. Some hypertensives may be stress-sensitive. Stress may produce physiologic damage that, over time, can lay the groundwork for chronic hypertension. Particular methods of coping with stress or particular personality variables (such as the suppression of anger) may be more characteristic of hypertensives than of others. Although medication and diet have been the major treatment methods to date, cognitive-behavioral tech-

niques that include relaxation and stress management are increasingly being added to treatment regimens.

RECOVERY FROM STROKE

Stroke, the third major cause of death in the United States, results from a disturbance in blood flow to the brain. Some strokes occur when blood flow to localized areas of the brain is interrupted, a condition that can be due to arteriosclerosis or hypertension. For example, when arteriosclerotic plaques damage the cerebral blood vessels, the damaged area may trap blood clots (thrombi) or produce circulating blood clots (emboli) that block the flow of blood. Stroke can also be caused by cerebral hemorrhage (caused by the rupture of a blood vessel in the brain). When blood leaks into the brain, large areas of nervous tissue may be compressed against the skull, producing widespread or fatal damage. Strokes cause approximately 10% of all deaths. The mortality rate is around 30% during the first month after a stroke, and those who survive may suffer some degree of permanent physical and cognitive impairment.

Consequences of Stroke

Stroke affects all aspects of one's life: personal, social, vocational, and physical (Thompson, Sobolew-Shubin et al., 1989). Although many victims have already reached retirement age, stroke can also attack younger people. Patients who have sustained a minimal handicap following stroke may return to work after a few months, but many patients are unable to return to work even part-time (for reviews see Gordon & Diller, 1983; Krantz & Deckel, 1983). Stroke almost inevitably leads to increased dependence on others, at least for a while; as a consequence, family or other social relationships may be profoundly affected.

Immediately after a stroke, motor difficulties are common. Because the right side of the brain controls movement in the left half of the body and the left side of the brain controls movement in the right side of the body, motoric impairments occur on the side opposite to the side of the brain that was damaged in the stroke. It is usually difficult or impossible for the patient to move the arm and leg on the affected side; therefore, he or she usually requires help walking, dressing, and performing other physical activities. With physical therapy, some of these problems are greatly diminished (Gordon & Diller, 1983).

The cognitive difficulties that the stroke victim faces depend on which side of the brain was damaged. Patients with left-brain damage may have communication disorders such as aphasia, which involves difficulty in understanding others and expressing oneself. A stroke patient describes a relevant incident:

> One of my first shopping expeditions was to a hardware store, but when I got there I couldn't think of the words, "electric plug," and it took me a while to get the message across. Naturally, I was humiliated and frustrated. I was close to tears at the store, and let them out to Jane [the patient's wife] at home. I was learning day by day the frustrations of a body and mind I could not command. (Dahlberg, 1977, p. 124)

Other problems of left-brain dysfunction include cognitive disturbances, an apparent reduction in intellect, and difficulty in learning new tasks. In particular, cognitive tasks that require the use of short-term memory seem to be particularly affected after a stroke that causes left-brain damage.

> Everyone repeats some stories, but within 15 minutes I told three stories that Jane had just heard—from me. Such experiences have not brought me humility, but I have lost some confidence, and I have developed patience with people. In the past, I have sometimes been arrogant. But since the stroke I have learned to say, "excuse me" and "I don't know." (Dahlberg, 1977, p. 126)

Patients with right-brain damage may experience visual disturbances. As a result, such a patient may shave only one side of his face or put makeup on only half her face. The patient may eat only the food on the right-hand side of the plate and ignore the food on the left. He or she may have trouble reading a clock, dialing a phone, or making change. These patients sometimes have difficulty perceiving distances accurately and may bump into objects or walls. Patients with right-brain damage may also feel that they are going crazy because they cannot understand the words they read or seem to be able to perceive only the last part of each word. They may also think they are hearing voices if a speaker is physically positioned on the patient's impaired side and can thus be heard but not seen (Gordon & Diller, 1983).

Emotional problems after a stroke are common. Patients with left-brain damage may react to their disorder with extreme anxiety and depression; patients with right-brain damage more commonly appear indifferent to their situation, although they, too, may be depressed. Although these findings have prompted considerable debate, a number of researchers now believe that differences in emotionality are due to neurological damage (e.g., Robinson & Benson, 1981). Left anterior infarcts typically produce more depression. Right-brain-damaged patients who appear depressed may be manifesting aprosodia, a brain disorder that leads to difficulty in expressing and comprehending affect (Ross, 1981, 1982). The fact that right-brain-damaged patients sometimes show difficulties with other emotions such as humor is consistent with this interpretation.

As we have seen, depression is a serious problem for stroke patients, and its degree depends on the site of the stroke and its severity. However, psychosocial factors also predict the degree of depression. In an interview study of stroke patients, Thompson and her colleagues (Thompson, Sobolew-Shubin et al., 1989) found that overprotection by a caregiver, a less recent stroke, and lack of meaningfulness in life independently predicted depression after severity and site of the stroke were controlled for. Stroke patients are more depressed if they are in worse circumstances after the stroke, if they interpret their situation negatively, if they have a poor relationship with their caregiver, and if they have a caregiver who sees the situation more negatively (Thompson, Sobolew-Shubin et al., 1989).

The stroke patient may face problems connected with social interaction. In many cases, the stroke produces effects that interfere with effective communication or that drive others away. The facial muscles of the stroke patient may fail to work properly, thus producing some disfigurement. There is often cognitive impairment, involving apparent memory loss, difficulties in concentration, and other cognitive impairments that may impede social communication. A condition known as multi-infarct dementia, which results from the accumulating effects of small strokes, may produce Alzheimer's-like symptoms. As previously noted, emotional responses may be inappropriate after a stroke, and depression is especially common. Thus, the consequences of stroke can be socially stigmatizing, and patients may find they are avoided or rejected by their colleagues and friends (Newman, 1984).

Not only patients recovering from stroke, but also their caregivers can show adverse reactions to the stroke. Tompkins et al. (1988) found that caregivers most at risk for depression were those with an earlier history of depression, less optimism, more concern about future care for the patient, lower household income, and a closer relationship (i.e., marriage) to the patient. In addition, these people typically named fewer people in their social network and were less satisfied with their social networks (Tompkins et al., 1988). Thus, changes in the patient's personality and behavior that may occur after a stroke may have adverse effects on those who live with the patient, especially if they are already at risk for

distress and have few other social contacts and few resources, such as finances, to help them. Interventions are needed for caregivers.

Types of Rehabilitative Interventions

Interventions with stroke patients have typically taken three approaches: group psychotherapy; cognitive remedial training to restore intellectual functioning; and use of structured, stimulating environments to challenge the stroke patient's capabilities (Krantz & Deckel, 1983).

Counseling has long been advocated for stroke patients. Although individual counseling is employed with some, group therapy is more common (for a review, see Krantz & Deckel, 1983). In addition, some programs have sent teams of lay volunteers to stroke patients in an effort to encourage them to return to their full capacities. Presumably, these interventions are effective because they both provide badly needed support for the confused and frightened stroke patient and offer specific encouragement and suggestions so that the stroke patient can regain the use of some faculties.

Interventions designed to deal with cognitive deficits after stroke involve a series of complex goals (Gordon & Diller, 1983). First, patients must be made aware that they have problems. Often, the stroke patient thinks he or she is performing adequately when this is simply not so. A risk of making patients aware of these problems is the sense of discouragement or failure that may arise. Thus, it is important to induce patients to see that these deficits are correctable.

Gordon and his associates (e.g., Gordon & Diller, 1983; Weinberg et al., 1977) have used a variety of techniques to help right-brain-damaged stroke patients regain a full visual field. One method is to spread an array of money out before a patient and ask him or her to pick all of it up. The right-brain-damaged patient will pick up only the money on the right-hand side, ignoring that on the left. When the patient is induced to turn his or her head toward the impaired side, he or she will see the remaining money and can then pick it up as well.

A scanning machine can improve this process further. Patients are first instructed to follow a moving stimulus with their eyes. When the stimulus moves to the left side of the stimulus array, it is out of sight of right-brain-damaged patients unless they turn their heads. Thus, patients quickly learn to turn their heads so they can pick up all information when the scanner moves into the left side of the visual field. Various tasks that require scanning, such as number canceling, are then introduced, so the patient can get a concrete sense of progress dealing with the entire visual field. Gradually, the patient is induced to maintain performance on the task without benefit of the artificial scanner. Through these kinds of retraining efforts, many stroke patients are able to regain many of their lost capabilities. Eventually, they can negotiate the world much as they did before the stroke (Gordon & Diller, 1983).

MANAGEMENT OF DIABETES

Diabetes is the third most common chronic illness in this country and one of the leading causes of death. It directly causes approximately 38,000 deaths per year and may contribute to as many as 300,000 deaths annually, including many from heart disease and kidney failure. Currently there are approximately 5 million diagnosed diabetics and a suspected 5 million who are as yet undiagnosed. Moreover, the number of cases is increasing at approximately 6% a year, making diabetes an increasingly important and formidable health problem (American Diabetes Association, 1986).

Diabetes is a chronic disorder in which the body is not able to manufacture or properly utilize insulin. Insulin is the hormone secreted by the pancreas that controls the movement of glucose into cells and glucose metabolism. When there is an insulin dysfunction, there is an excess of glucose in the blood, and this is discharged into the urine (American Diabetes Association, 1986).

Types of Diabetes

There are two major types of diabetes, insulin-dependent (or Type I) diabetes and non-insulin-dependent (or Type II) diabetes. Type I diabetes usually develops relatively early in life, earlier for girls than for boys. It may first arise between the ages of 5 and 6 or later between 10 and 13. The most common early symptoms are frequent urination, unusual thirst, excessive drinking of fluids, weight loss, fatigue, weakness, irritability, nausea, uncontrollable craving for food (especially sweets), and fainting. These symptoms are due to the body's attempt to find sources of energy, which prompts it to feed off its own fats and proteins. By-products of these fats then build up in the body, producing symptoms; if the condition is untreated, a coma can result. Type I diabetes is by far the more serious of the two; fortunately, it accounts for only 10% of all diabetes. It is managed primarily through direct injections of insulin; hence the name insulin-dependent diabetes (American Diabetes Association, 1986).

Type II (or non-insulin-dependent) diabetes typically occurs after age 40 and is milder than the insulin-dependent type. The symptoms include frequent urination; fatigue; dryness of the mouth; impotence; irregular menstruation; loss of sensation; frequent infection of the skin, gums, or urinary system; pain or cramps in legs, feet, or fingers; slow healing of cuts and bruises; and intense itching and drowsiness. In Type II diabetes, insulin may be produced by the body, but there may not be enough of it or the body may not be sensitive to it. The majority of Type II diabetics are obese (60%), and Type II diabetes is more common in women, whites, and individuals of low socioeconomic status (American Diabetes Association, 1986).

Implications of Diabetes

The diabetic is vulnerable to two blood sugar problems, hypoglycemia (a blood sugar level that is too low) and hyperglycemia (a blood sugar level that is too high). Hypoglycemia results when there is too much insulin, causing an excessive decline in blood sugar. This reaction is typically sudden. The skin turns pale and moist and the individual feels excited, nervous, irritable, and confused. Breathing can be rapid and shallow, and the tongue may have a moist, numb, tingling sensation. The person will be hungry and may be in pain, and there will be little or no sugar in the urine. When signs of possible insulin reaction occur, something containing sugar must be eaten immediately.

The reaction of hyperglycemia is more gradual. The skin is flushed and dry, and the individual feels drowsy and has deep labored breathing. Vomiting may be present, and the tongue will be dry; feelings of hunger are rare but thirst is common. Abdominal pain may occur, and large amounts of sugar will be detectable in the urine. Hyperglycemia may require medical intervention since coma may result, requiring hospitalization.

Despite these potential problems, the reason why diabetes is such a major public health problem stems less from the consequences of insufficient insulin production per se than from complications that may develop. Diabetes is associated with a thickening of the arteries due to the buildup of wastes in the blood. As a consequence, diabetic patients show high rates of coronary heart disease. Diabetes is also the leading cause of blindness among adults, and it accounts for 50% of all the patients who require renal dialysis for kidney failure. Diabetes may also be associated with

nervous system damage, including pain and loss of sensation. In severe cases, amputations of the extremities, such as toes and feet, are required. As a consequence of these manifold complications, diabetics have a considerably shorter life expectancy than do nondiabetic individuals (American Diabetes Association, 1986). Diabetes may also exacerbate other difficulties in functioning, such as eating disorders (Wing, Nowalk, Marcus, Koeske, & Finegold, 1986) and sexual dysfunction in both men and women (Schreiner-Engel, Schiavi, Vietorisz, & Smith, 1987). Diabetes may also produce central nervous system impairment that interferes with memory (Taylor & Rachman, 1988), especially among the elderly (Mooradian, Perryman, Fitten, Kavonian, & Morley, 1988).

Causes of Diabetes

What causes diabetes? It can be caused by viral or bacterial damage to the pancreas and the insulin-producing cells and may result from an autoimmune dysfunction. It also has a substantial hereditary component. However, it is clear that other factors must be implicated in the onset of diabetes, and many of these are not yet known. It is possible, for example, that dietary factors themselves figure in the onset of diabetes, but this is not yet well established.

Since the early days of psychosomatic medicine, there has been a suspicion that psychological factors predispose people to develop diabetes. In particular, prolonged depression or anxiety were thought to play a role. The diabetic personality was said to be characterized by diminished alertness, apathy, hypochondriacal tendencies, and vulnerability to depression; these, in turn, were believed to be caused by immaturity, passivity, masochism, sexual identity conflicts, and oral dependency (Dunbar, Wolfe, & Riosh, 1936; Menninger, 1935). Research now indicates that the causal role of these factors in the onset of diabetes is doubtful (Johnson, 1980; see Taylor & Aspinwall, 1990, for a review). Rather, it is more likely that some behavioral disturbances can accompany diabetes and are consequences, not causes, of the disease (Feinglos, & Surwit, 1988; Johnson, 1980).

Diabetics appear to be sensitive to the effects of stress. Although the effects of stress on Type I diabetes are still uncertain, it is evident that stress can precipitate hyperglycemia, at least in animal studies, and that it is important in glycemic control in Type II diabetes (Surwit & Feinglos, 1988). At least fourteen studies have reported direct links between stress and poor diabetic control (see Brand, Johnson, & Johnson, 1986; Hanson & Pichert, 1986), and this relationship is not mediated by differences in adherence (Hanson, Henggeler, & Burghen, 1987), coping efforts (Frenzel, McCaul, Glasgow, & Schafer, 1988), insulin regimen, diet, or exercise (Hanson & Pichert, 1986). Type A diabetics experiencing high levels of stress show poorer blood glucose control than Type B diabetics under stress. This may occur because Type A individuals react more strongly to threats to personal control, which elicits active and often stressful efforts to cope, thereby elevating sympathetic nervous system activity and, correspondingly, glucose levels (Rhodewalt & Marcroft, 1988).

Recent research on sympathetic nervous system activity among diabetics has begun to suggest some mechanisms through which stress may aggravate the disease. It is becoming increasingly clear that sympathetic nervous system activity is involved in the pathophysiology of Type II diabetes. This group appears to be characterized by a hyperresponsivity to epinephrine, higher levels of circulating catecholamines, and elevated levels of endogenous opioid peptides that may also be an indication of abnormal sympathetic nervous system activity. Thus, theoretically, as is the case with heart disease and hypertension, interventions to reduce sympathetic nervous system activity may, in theory, be useful in modulating hyperglycemia.

Problems in Self-Management of Diabetes

The treatment goal for diabetes is to keep blood sugar at normal levels. Although stress management represents one possible method for achieving this goal, it is more commonly accomplished through regular insulin injections, dietary control, weight control, and exercise. Insulin injections are most often recommended on a regular basis for Type I diabetes, whereas diet, weight control, and exercise figure more prominently in the management of Type II diabetes. Dietary intervention involves drastically reducing the sugar and carbohydrate intake of diabetic patients. In addition, the number of calories taken in each day must be relatively constant. Food intake must be controlled by a meal plan and not by temptation or appetite. Obesity seems to tax the insulin system especially, so patients are encouraged to achieve a normal weight. Exercise is encouraged, since it helps use up glucose in the blood (Feinglos & Surwit, 1988).

Unfortunately, adherence to such programs appears to be low. For example, one set of investigations found that 80% of diabetic patients administered insulin incorrectly, 58% administered the wrong dosage, 77% tested their urine for sugar content inaccurately, 75% were not eating at sufficiently regular intervals, and 75% were not eating prescribed foods (Watkins, Roberts, Williams, Martin, & Coyle, 1967; Watkins, Williams, Martin, Hogan, & Anderson, 1967; see Wing, Nowalk et al., 1986). Overall, only about 15% of patients appear to adhere to all their treatment recommendations.

What are the reasons for this low rate of adherence? There appear to be several. First, the chief factors that require self-control, namely diet and exercise, are lifestyle factors, and, as we noted in Chapters 3 and 10, adherence to recommendations to alter lifestyle is very low. One reason for this fact is that such advice is often not seen as medical but as advisory and

The management of Type I diabetes critically depends on proper monitoring of blood glucose level and regular injections of insulin, yet many adolescents and adults fail to adhere properly to their treatment regimen.

discretionary, and patients often fail to follow their regimen or modify it according to their own theories and desires. Another reason is that dietary control and exercise are very difficult health habits to follow regularly. The person attempting to exert rigorous dietary control is constantly besieged by temptations to depart from a preset course, and the person trying to fit exercise into an already busy day may find it easy to forget this activity when other demands seem more pressing or necessary. Voluntarily restricting calories, avoiding desired foods, and engaging in an exercise program may seem like self-punishment, something that many patients are unwilling to

do. Moreover, many of the severe complications that arise from diabetes are not evident for 15 or 20 years after its onset. Therefore, complications do not frighten people into being adherent. They may feel no symptoms and, because the disease does not seem insistent on a day-to-day basis, fail to adhere to their treatment regimen. It appears that many of the errors made by diabetics in adhering to their treatment regimen, then, are errors of omission rather than errors of comission. That is, it is relatively unusual for diabetics to intentionally relapse but common for them to forget to undertake particular behaviors they are supposed to do regularly (Kirkley & Fisher, 1988).

One of the dilemmas involved in adequate adherence is that diabetes patients often fail to self-monitor their blood glucose level. Instead, like hypertension patients, they rely on what their blood glucose level "feels like," and appear to rely strongly on their mood for making this judgment (Gonder-Frederick, Cox, Bobbitt, & Pennebaker, 1986). In one study, diabetic patients were trained in glucose level awareness to see if they could learn to discriminate when their blood glucose level needed to be modified. Some increase in accuracy was found as a result of this training, resulting in a 31% reduction in dangerous blood glucose estimate errors. However, even after training, subjective estimates were significantly less accurate than actual monitoring of blood glucose level, suggesting that this type of training is not currently to a point where it has treatment implications (Diamond, Massey, & Covey, 1989; Gonder-Frederick et al., 1986).

Does social support improve adherence to diabetes regimen? We know that, generally speaking, social support improves adherence. However, it does not necessarily do so for diabetics. Satisfaction with social support helped women diabetics maintain their complex behavioral regimen of diet and exercise. However, size of one's social network was related to increased weight, cholesterol, and triglycerides, especially in men. The authors concluded that when one is part of a dense social network, the network norms may be dissimilar to the desired behavior and that, as a result, people may experience more norm conflicts than if their social network were smaller (Kaplan & Hartwell, 1987). Under such circumstances, social support may actually undermine rather than promote adherence.

A number of health beliefs are important determinants of adherence to diabetes regimen (Brownlee-Duffeck et al., 1987). A first factor is the goal to which treatment may be directed. One study documenting high levels of nonadherence to treatment among parents regulating their children's juvenile diabetes found that parents' and physicians' efforts were aimed toward different goals. The parents' goals were determined by the desire to avoid hypoglycemia, a short-term threat, whereas the physicians' goals were based more around the long-term threat of diabetic complications and the need to keep blood glucose levels steady. These differences in goals appeared to be responsible for the low adherence to the diabetes medication (Marteau, Johnston, Baum, & Bloch, 1987; see also Pendleton, House, & Parker, 1987).

Lack of knowledge is also related to adherence. Insufficient information about glucose utilization, energy metabolism, and metabolic control of insulin in diabetes is associated with poor adherence. Since until recently this information was rarely incorporated into explanations of the treatment program, some diabetic patients have little understanding of the underpinnings of their treatments (Hauenstein et al., 1987). One intervention designed to address this issue found that an in-hospital education program for diabetics about their diabetes produced better adherence for all self-care behaviors than did nonparticipation in the program (Wood, 1989). In a study with elderly non-insulin-dependent diabetics, diabetes education in conjunction with a peer-support intervention improved weight loss and reduc-

tion in glycemic control (Wilson & Pratt, 1987). Self-efficacy beliefs also appear to be important predictors of adherence to diabetes regimen. Those who believe themselves able to adhere to the complex treatment regimen are more able to do so (Grossman, Brink, & Hauser, 1987; McCaul et al., 1987).

Interventions with Diabetics

A variety of behaviorally oriented interventions have been undertaken with diabetics to improve adherence to different aspects of their regimen. Some programs have focused on helping diabetics engage in appropriate self-injection (see Wing, Nowalk et al., 1986). Others have focused more on training patients to monitor blood sugar levels effectively (Wing, Epstein, Nowalk, Scott et al., 1986). As a result of ties between stress and diabetes, behavioral investigators have examined the effect of various stress management programs on diabetic control. One such program, which trained diabetic patients in relaxation, found better glucose tolerance after training compared with a control group that did not receive the intervention (Surwit & Feinglos, 1983). Similar findings have been reported by other investigators. Relaxation therapy appears to be more effective in helping Type II diabetics achieve glucose control than Type I diabetics (Feinglos & Surwit, 1988). An example of combating stress to control diabetes appears in Box 14.4.

Weight loss also appears to improve glycemic control and reduce the need for medication (Wing, Epstein, Nowalk, Koeske, & Hagg, 1985; Wing et al., 1987; Wing, Nowalk et al., 1986), and so behavioral interventions designed to help diabetic patients reduce weight have been undertaken and appear to show at least some success (Wing, Epstein, Nowalk, Scott et al., 1986). Training in self-monitoring of blood glucose, however, does not appear to improve weight, eating, exercise, or blood glucose control (Wing, Epstein

---

Box 14.4
Stress Management and the Control of Diabetes

Mrs. Goldberg had had Type II diabetes for some time. Her doctor had made the diagnosis 10 years earlier, just after her 40th birthday. She watched her diet, got sufficient exercise, and was able to control her blood glucose with oral medication. During the past several months, however, Mrs. Goldberg's diabetes control had begun to deteriorate. Despite the fact that she continued to follow her diet and exercise regimen, her blood glucose levels became elevated more frequently.

Mrs. Goldberg consulted her physician, who asked her if her lifestyle had changed in any way over the past several months. She told him that her boss had added several new responsibilities to her job and that they made her workday much more stressful. Things were so bad that she was having trouble sleeping at night and dreaded going to work in the morning. Mrs. Goldberg's physician told her that this additional stress might be responsible for her poor diabetes control. Rather than

initially changing her medications, he suggested that she first speak with her boss to see if some of the stress of her job might be relieved. Fortunately, her boss was understanding and allowed Mrs. Goldberg to share her responsibilities with another employee. Within several weeks, she no longer dreaded going to work, and her diabetes control improved significantly.

This case illustrates how a relatively simple manipulation of the patient's environment may have a clinically significant impact on blood glucose control. It underscores the need for the physician to be aware of what is happening in the patient's life in order to determine requirements for treatment. Under the circumstances described, it would have been inappropriate to have altered this patient's medication.

(From Feinglos & Surwit, 1988, p. 29).

---

et al., 1986). This may occur because some patients who make the necessary changes in eating and exercise are still unable to achieve target blood glucose values (Wing, Epstein, Nowalk, & Scott, 1988).

Wing, Epstein, Nowalk, and Lamparski (1986) have suggested that multiple interventions for diabetics might best be combined into a single treatment program that teaches patients appropriate self-regulation: monitoring blood sugar accurately, using the information as a basis for making changes in behavior as through self-injection, reinforcing themselves for efforts to improve blood sugar control, managing stress, controlling diet, and exercising. By seeing the relations among these com-

ponents in an organized program of self-regulation, adherence to the separate aspects of the regimen may be improved.

Special Problems of Adolescent Diabetics

The management of diabetes is a particular problem with adolescents (Johnson, 1980). These patients are entangled in issues of independence and developing self-concept; diabetes and the restrictions that it imposes are inconsistent with these developmental tasks. Adolescents may see their parents' limitations on food as efforts to control them and may regard the need to monitor diet or to be conscientious about injections as rules and regulations imposed from the outside. Moreover, within the adolescent peer culture, those who are different are often stigmatized. Thus, the adolescent diabetic may neglect proper care to avoid rejection (Turk & Speers, 1983).

Problems of managing Type I diabetes among adolescents are not confined to the diabetic's own difficulties of accepting the limitations imposed by the disease. Other family members, including the parents, may also react in ways that defeat management efforts. Parents, for example, may treat their newly diagnosed adolescent diabetic as a child and restrict activities beyond what is necessary, infantilizing the adolescent and increasing dependence. Alternatively, the parents and family members may attempt to convince the child that he or she is normal, like everyone else; yet the adolescent quickly learns that this is not true. The family environment can be important to diabetic control and adherence (for a review, see Hanson, Henggeler, Harris, Burghen, & Moore, 1989; Johnson, 1980; Marteau, Bloch, & Baum, 1987). One study (Minuchin et al., 1978) found that diabetic children with poor control improved substantially after family therapy that attempted to break down faulty methods of communication and conflict resolution. Individual therapy failed to achieve the same outcomes.

The health psychologist, then, has an important role to play in the management of diabetes. With the young diabetic, problems of clinical interest may arise that may require psychotherapeutic intervention, both individually with the diabetic and in family therapy, where all family members can be encouraged to take a supportive role vis-à-vis the patient's situation. The juvenile also experiences behavioral management problems, which can be addressed by behavioral technologies to instill good health habits (e.g., Schafer, Glasgow, & McCaul, 1982). Similarly, with adults, behavioral technologies can increase adherence to dietary restrictions, weight-control measures, and exercise regimens, greatly improving what is a currently poor compliance rate. Behavioral interventions, such as relaxation therapy, may also improve the Type II diabetic's ability to tolerate glucose. Finally, the role of stress in the course of diabetes requires additional exploration. As we learn more about the stress response and how individuals can control their reactions to stress, these findings may also have implications for the control of diabetes in the future. These are all promising avenues for future research and intervention.

SUMMARY

1. Coronary heart disease is the number one killer in the United States. It is a disease of lifestyle, and risk factors include cigarette smoking, obesity, elevated serum cholesterol, low levels of physical activity, and particular methods of coping with stress known as Type A behavior.

2. Type A behavior is characterized by easily aroused hostility, a sense of time urgency, and competitive achievement strivings.

Recent research suggests that the propensity for hostility may be the most lethal component of Type A behavior and the only one reliably associated with coronary heart disease morbidity and mortality.

3. Type A behavior is associated with hyperreactivity to stressful situations, including a slow return to baseline. Some have suggested that these exaggerated cardiovascular responses to stress may be

genetically based and that Type A behavior may be, in part, a result of excessive neuroendocrine reactivity to environmental stressors.

4. Efforts to modify Type A behavior through training in relaxation and stress management show promise in reducing not only cardiovascular reactivity to stressful situations but also morbidity and mortality due to CHD.

5. Type A behavior can be identified early in childhood and may be related to a parental style involving escalating performance standards, disapproval, and punitive or harsh methods of control. Research with children has not typically translated into interventions because not all children who show Type A behavior will become Type A adults, nor will all Type A adults develop CHD.

6. Cardiac rehabilitation is a program designed to help post-MI patients obtain their optimal physical, medical, psychological, social, emotional, vocational, and economic status. Components of these programs typically include education in CHD, nutritional counseling, supervised exercise, stress management, and, under some circumstances, psychological counseling and/or social support group participation.

7. MI patients typically have difficulty managing the stress-reduction aspects of their regimens, and sometimes marital relations can be strained as a result of the changes forced on the patient and the spouse by the post-MI rehabilitative regimen.

8. Hypertension, or high blood pressure, affects approximately 60 million Americans. Most hypertension is of unknown origin, although risk factors include a family history of hypertension. Low-SES blacks are particularly vulnerable to the disorder.

9. Hypertensives show heightened reactivity to stressful events. Certain personality factors or ways of coping with stress may also be implicated, such as suppressed rage or "John Henryism," which is vigorous efforts to achieve against ultimately insurmountable odds.

10. Hypertension is typically treated by diuretics or beta-blocking drugs that often have adverse side effects. Recently, cognitive-behavioral treatments including stress management have been used in an effort to control the disorder and to reduce drug dosages.

11. The biggest problems related to the control of hypertension concern high rates of nondiagnosis and nonadherence to therapy. The fact that the disease is symptomless helps explain both problems. Low rates of adherence are also explained by adverse side effects of drugs.

12. Stroke results from a disturbance in blood flow to the brain. It may disrupt all aspects of life. Motor difficulties, cognitive impairments, and depression are particular problems associated with stroke.

13. Interventions for stroke patients have typically involved group psychotherapy, cognitive remedial training to restore intellectual functioning, and structured, stimulating environments to challenge the stroke patient's capabilities.

14. Diabetes is the third most common chronic disease in the United States. Insulin-dependent, or Type I, diabetes typically develops in childhood and is more severe than non-insulin-dependent, or Type II, diabetes, which develops typically after age 40. Stress is known to exacerbate glycemic control in Type II diabetes, but as yet the relationship between stress and Type I diabetes is unclear.

15. The diabetes self-care regimen is complex,

involving testing urine for sugar content, administering insulin, eating prescribed foods, eating at regular intervals, and exercising regularly. Adherence to this regimen is very poor. Interventions can improve adherence, especially if the different components of the regimen are logically linked to each other in a programatic effort toward effective self-care.

KEY TERMS

cardiac invalidism
cardiac rehabiliation
cardiopulmonary resuscitation (CPR)
coronary heart disease (CHD)
diabetes
hypertension

John Henryism
myocardial infarction
stress-sensitive
stroke
Type A behavior syndrome

15

PSYCHO-
IMMUNOLOGY,
AIDS, CANCER,
AND
ARTHRITIS

For many years, the immune system was one of the most poorly understood systems of the human body. However, in the last two decades, research advances in this area have been enormous, leading to the burgeoning field of psychoimmunology. In this chapter, we consider many of these recent developments and then turn in more detail to three disorders believed to be related to immunologic functioning: AIDS, cancer, and arthritis.

PSYCHOIMMUNOLOGY

The Immune System

As noted in Chapter 2, the immune system is the surveillance system of the body. It guards against infection, allergies, cancer, and autoimmune disorders. (**Autoimmune disorders** are those in which the immune system turns on itself and attacks healthy tissue in the body.) The primary function of the immune system is to distinguish between what is the "self" and what is foreign and then to attack and rid the body of foreign invaders.

The primary organs of the immune system involved in this response are known as lymphoid organs, and they include the thymus, lymph nodes, spleen, tonsils, appendix, Peyer's patches (clumps of lymphoid tissue in the small intestine), and bone marrow. The bone marrow produces three types of white blood cells (leukocytes): polymorphonuclear granulocytes (PMN), mononuclear phagocytes (MN), and lymphocytes (T, B, and natural killer [NK] cells). The PMN phagocytes are circulating cells that recognize, ingest, and destroy antigens. Termed granulocytes because they contain granules filled with enzymes that enable them to digest microorganisms, they contribute to inflammatory and allergic reactions (Calabrese, Kling, & Gold, 1987). The MN phagocytes include both monocytes and macrophages. These phagocytes recognize, ingest, and destroy foreign organisms. Macrophages also assist in the activation of T cells through the secretion of cytokine. Natural killer cells are a type of granular lymphocyte that attacks and destroys cells infected by a virus. Natural killer cells also secrete interferon, which inhibits viral reproduction in uninfected cells.

As noted in Chapter 2, there are two basic immunologic reactions—humoral and cell-mediated. Humoral immunity is mediated by B lymphocytes. The functions of B lymphocytes include providing protection against bacteria, neutralizing toxins produced by bacteria, and preventing viral reinfection. B cells confer immunity by the production and secretion of antibodies. When they are activated, they differentiate into two types of cells: (1) mature, antibody-secreting plasma cells and (2) resting, nondividing, memory B cells, which differentiate into antigen-specific plasma cells only when reexposed to the same antigen. Plasma cells produce antibodies or immunoglobulins, which are the basis of the antigen-specific reactions.

Cell-mediated immunity, involving T lymphocytes from the thymus gland, is a slower-acting response. Rather than releasing antibodies into the blood, as humoral immunity does, cell-mediated immunity operates at the cellular level. When stimulated by the appropriate antigen, T cells secrete chemicals that kill invading organisms and infected cells. T lymphocytes confer protection against viral and fungal infections, reject grafts of foreign tissues, and cause delayed hypersensitivity reactions. There are three major types of T lymphocytes: cytotoxic T (T_C cells), helper T (T_H cells), and suppressor T (T_S cells). T_C cells respond to specific antigens and kill by producing toxic substances that destroy virally infected cells. T_H cells enhance the functioning of T_C cells, B cells, and macrophages by producing various lymphokines, including interleukin-2. T_S cells serve a counterregulatory immune function, producing lymphokines that suppress immune activity. A defect in the T_S

cells' functioning is believed to be involved in autoimmune disease (Calabrese et al., 1987).

What, then, does the integrated immune response look like? When a foreign antigen enters the body, the first line of defense involves mechanistic maneuvers, such as coughing or sneezing. Once the invader has penetrated the body's surface, the phagocytes attempt to eliminate it by **phagocytosis.** If this process is unsuccessful, more complex immune responses come into play. Macrophages engulf and digest the antigen, release interleukin-1, and display part of the antigen material on their surface as a signal to the T_H cells. These, in turn, secrete interleukin-2, which promotes the growth and differentiation of the T_C and T_S cells. As is true for T_H cells, T_C and T_S cells secrete substances that promote the development of antigen-specific B cells into antibody-producing plasma cells, which then assist in destroying the antigen. T_H cells also secrete gamma-interferon, which enhances the cytotoxicity of the macrophages around the site of the invasion and promotes the differentiation of T_C cells. Macrophages and NK cells also secrete various types of interferon, which enhances the killing potential of the NK cells and inhibits viral reproduction in uninfected cells. In addition, macrophages, NK cells, and T_C cells directly kill infected cells. During this process, the T_S cells down regulate and eventually turn off the immune response.

Assessing Immunocompetence

As must be obvious, there are many potential indicators of immune functioning. Typically, two general approaches have been used: measuring the amount of various components of the immune system in the blood, and assessing the functioning of immune cells. Examples of the first approach involve counting the numbers of T, T_C, T_H, T_S, B, and NK cells, and assessing the amount of circulating lymphokine or antibody levels in the blood. Assessing the functioning of cells involves exam- ining the activation, proliferation, transfor- mation, and cytotoxicity of cells. Common measures include the ability of lymphocytes to kill invading cells (lymphocyte cytotoxicity), the ability of lymphocytes to reproduce when artificially stimulated by a chemical (mitogen), the ability of lymphocytes to produce antibod- ies, and the ability of certain white blood cells to ingest foreign particles (phagocytotic activ- ity). For example, in the mitogenic stimulation technique, it is assumed that the more prolifer- ation that occurs in response to the mitogen, the better the cells are functioning. When indi- cators suggest that the immune system is work- ing effectively, a state of **immunocompetence** is said to exist. When these indicators suggest that immune functioning may have been dis- rupted or reduced below optimal level, a state of **immunocompromise** is said to exist.

Because the immune system is so complex and involves so many different components, there are many measures of its functioning, not all of which will relate well to each other. One indicator of immunologic functioning may show an effect of a stressful event, for ex- ample, whereas another may not. Moreover, many activities and events in people's lives have an impact on the immune system that can obscure or falsely enhance the apparent relationship between stressful events and im- mune functioning. For example, alcohol and other drugs, nutrition, general health status, smoking, caffeine intake, physical activity, sleep patterns, and medication use can all influence the immune system, and, if uncon- trolled, these factors may enhance the appar- ent relationship between stress and immu- nocompromise, inasmuch as all of these behaviors may increase in response to stress (Kiecolt-Glaser & Glaser, 1988). In addition, timing of blood samples and the particular lab- oratory in which analyses are conducted can exert influences on results. Thus, good re- search on psychoimmunology is extremely hard to do; it involves rigor and care.

Stress and Immune Functioning

Despite these difficulties, a number of studies suggest that many commonplace stressors can adversely affect the immune system. Research on animals conclusively demonstrates that ex- perimentally manipulated stressors can alter immunologic functioning and susceptibility to disorders that are under immunologic regula- tion (e.g., Borysenko & Borysenko, 1982). For example, **lymphocyte suppression** in animals has been tied to exposure to loud noise (Monjan & Collector, 1977), electric shock (Keller, Weiss, Schleifer, Miller, & Stein, 1981), infant-mother separation (Laudenslager, Reite, & Harbeck, 1982), and separation from peers (Reite, Harbeck, & Hoffman, 1981).

Research on humans shows similar effects. In a classic study, Ishigami (1919) observed decreases in phagocytic activity of tuberculosis patients' white blood cells when they were emotionally excited; this result suggested to him that immunologic functioning was sup- pressed during times of excitement. A large volume of literature now confirms these early observations. Research with children shows an increase in rates of infectious disease when the family is under stress (Boyce et al., 1977; Meyer & Haggerty, 1962). Research on adults has tied stressful events to infectious diseases such as the common cold and trench mouth (for a review, see Jemmott & Locke, 1984; O'Leary, in press). Stress is also a risk factor for the development of herpes virus infec- tions, including cold sores, genital lesions, chicken pox, mononucleosis, Epstein-Barr, and other clinical manifestations of the five ba- sic human herpes viruses. Stress can enhance susceptibility to primary herpes virus infec- tions and can also increase the severity of the initial infection (see Kiecolt-Glaser & Glaser, 1987; VanderPlate, Aral, & Magder, 1988). These lines of work are suggestive of an ad- verse effect of stress on the immune system, but do not provide direct evidence.

Stress has been related directly to various

indicators of immunocompetence as well. Some of the earliest evidence came from studies of the Apollo and Skylab astronauts. Both groups showed immunologic deficiencies after splashdown, a period of high stress. Specifically, Apollo astronauts showed higher lymphocyte counts after splashdown (Fischer et al., 1972), and Skylab astronauts showed higher white blood cell counts at recovery as compared with preflight levels (Kimzey, 1975; Leach & Rambaut, 1974). Considering that the pilots in the space program had been carefully trained to withstand the adverse effects of stressful circumstances, these changes in immune functioning associated with splashdown were especially notable.

Several studies have examined whether daily hassles are associated with reduced immunocompetence. One study focused especially on a group of people who are chronically low in natural killer cell activity. They found that the two factors that best predicted this group were age and severity of daily hassles. The authors concluded that younger people who perceived the events that occurred to them as especially serious were likely to exhibit chronically low NK cell cytotoxic activity (Levy, Herberman, Simons et al., 1989; see also Moss, Moss, and Peterson, 1989).

Anticipatory stress may also compromise immune functioning. In a longitudinal study of patients vulnerable to genital herpes recurrences, Kemeny and colleagues (Kemeny, Cohen, Zegans, & Conant, 1989) found that over a 6-month period, the number of stressful events experienced was associated with a decreased percentage of T_H and T_S cells. More interesting is the fact that anticipated stressors, those that had not yet occurred but which were expected, also related to decreased percent of T_H cells. In addition, daily hassles were related to an increase in T_S cells.

Other research has focused on adjustment to long-term stressors. Two investigations, for example, have studied people living near the Three Mile Island nuclear power station after the nuclear accident (McKinnon, Weisse, Reynolds, Bowles, & Baum, 1989; Schaeffer et al., 1985). Schaeffer et al. (1985) found significantly lower levels of saliva IgA and lower percentages of B cells, total T cells, and T_H and T_S cells among the residents, suggesting that the stress of living near the site had adversely compromised their immune functioning. McKinnon et al. (1989) found fewer B cells, a lower T_S to T_C ratio, a lower level of natural killer cells, and higher antibody titers to several viruses among the residents. Both studies are notable for having compared residents with a matched control sample from a demographically similar area, and for controlling for diet, smoking history, and health. It is important to take these factors into account, in that diet, smoking, and health can themselves be associated with changes in immunologic status.

Academic Stress and Immune Functioning

Largely because students are a captive population that is often willing and able to participate in research, much of the groundbreaking work on stress and the immune system has involved students coping with the stress of school. Students may take grim satisfaction from studies indicating that, indeed, examinations and other stressful events of academic life can lead to immunosuppression (e.g., Dorian et al. 1982; Dorian, Keystone, Garfinkel, & Brown, 1981; Glaser, Kiecolt-Glaser, Stout et al., 1985; Glaser et al., 1987; Glaser, Rice, Speicher, Stout, & Kiecolt-Glaser, 1986; Jemmott et al., 1983; Kiecolt-Glaser et al., 1986). For example, one study followed West Point cadets who were EBV seropositive (positive for the Epstein-Barr virus) for 4 years. Those who had a high level of motivation for military career, poor academic performance, and fathers who were "overachievers" were more likely to develop mononucleosis and were hospitalized longer than individuals who did not show these risk factors (Kasl, Evans, & Niederman, 1979).

Studies show that exams and other stressful aspects of academic life can adversely compromise immune functioning.

More direct evidence for the mediating role of immune functioning was found by Glaser and his colleagues (Glaser, Kiecolt-Glaser, Stout, et al., 1985; Glaser et al., 1986). They assessed immune parameters in a sample of 40 second-year medical students at 6 weeks before finals and then again during final exams. Subjects showed an increase in distress from the first to the second time period, and the percentages of total T, T_H, and T_S lymphocytes were significantly lower during exams. There was also a decrease in natural killer cells and a significant depression in natural killer cell cytotoxic activity. Lymphocyte responsivity was lower during the exam period than at baseline, as was the quantity of interferon produced by stimulated leukocytes. A number of follow-up studies by these investigators support and extend their initial findings, indicating a variety of immune alterations at the time of exams. Academic stress, then, does appear to compromise immune functioning.

Stress, Immune Functioning, and Interpersonal Relationships

Both human and animal research suggests the importance of personal relationships to im-

mune functioning. In one animal study, premature separation of rat pups from their mothers revealed immunocompromise on several indicators. The mechanism through which these effects occurred is not entirely clear. Early maternal separation may lead to adverse effects on nutrition, disturbed hypothalamic functioning, or poor maturation of the immune system (Ackerman et al., 1988).

Disruptions in interpersonal relationships also appear to affect the human immune system adversely. One of the earliest set of investigations examined bereavement. In a prospective study, Bartrop and associates (Bartrop, Lockhurst, Lazarus, Kiloh, & Penny, 1977) looked at twenty-six bereaved individuals and twenty-six comparison subjects matched for age, sex, and race. A number of immunologic parameters were examined 3 weeks after bereavement and again 6 weeks later. At the second time point, the bereaved group showed less responsiveness to mitogenic challenge than the comparison group (see also Schleifer, Keller, Camerino, Thornton, & Stein, 1983). In another study, recently bereaved women showed lower natural killer cell activity than age-matched nonbereaved women (Irwin, Daniels, Smith, Bloom, & Weiner, 1987).

Marital disruption has also been tied to high rates of physical and emotional illness (Stein, 1985). In a study by Kiecolt-Glaser, Fisher et al. (1987), women who had been separated 1 year or less showed poorer functioning on some immune parameters than their matched married counterparts. Among separated and divorced women, recent separation and continued attachment or preoccupation with the ex-husband were associated with poorer immune functioning and with more depression and loneliness. Similar results have been found for men facing separation or divorce (Kiecolt-Glaser et al., 1988). Compared with age-matched married men, separated and divorced men were more distressed and lonelier, they reported having significantly more recent illnesses, and they had poorer values on two functional indices of immunity (antibody titers to two herpes viruses). They did not, however, differ in the percentage of helper and suppressor T cells or their ratio (Kiecolt-Glaser et al., 1988). Among separated and divorced men, those separated within the last year who had initiated the separation were less distressed, had better health, and had better EBV antibody titers than did the noninitiators (Kiecolt-Glaser et al., 1988).

Other studies have looked at the relation between marital satisfaction and immune functioning in couples that remained together. Unhappily married people have poorer health generally than happily married people (Levenson & Gottman, 1985). In one study of married men (Kiecolt-Glaser et al., 1988), poor marital quality was associated with greater distress, a poorer antibody titer to Epstein-Barr virus, and a lower T_H to T_S ratio.

Recently, stressful interpersonal relationships other than marital ones have been examined for their potential to exert adverse effects on immune functioning. One of the most stressful interpersonal roles is caregiving, that is, providing for a friend or family member with a long-term illness, such as AIDS or Alzheimer's disease. Recent research has found that this role can act as a chronic

stressor and compromise immune functioning (Kiecolt-Glaser, Glaser et al., 1987). In one study, Alzheimer's patients' caregivers were more depressed and showed lower life satisfaction than a comparison sample. They had higher EBV antibody titers (an indication of poor immune control of latent virus reactivation), lower percentages of total T cells and T_H cells, and a lower T_H to T_S ratio. These differences did not appear to be related to nutrition, alcohol use, or caffeine consumption. In addition, although caregivers reported getting less sleep than a comparison sample, their apparent sleep deprivation was not correlated with these immune parameter changes.

Loneliness also appears to adversely affect immune functioning. Lonely people have poorer health and show more immunocompromise on certain indicators than do people who are not lonely (Glaser, Kiecolt-Glaser, Speicher, & Holliday, 1985; Kiecolt-Glaser, Garner et al., 1984; Kiecolt-Glaser, Speicher, Holliday, & Glaser, 1984).

Negative Affect and Immune Functioning

A question that arises is whether stress directly compromises immune functioning or whether it is mediated by other adverse changes, such as depression or other negative moods that occur in response to stressful events. A number of studies have examined this possibility (e.g., Cohen, Kearney et al., 1989; Kemeny et al., 1989). Evidence relating anxiety to immunocompromise is inconclusive. Very few studies have been conducted (Greene, Betts, Ochitill, Iker, & Douglas, 1978; Linn, Linn, & Jensen, 1981; Locke & Heisel, 1977), and most have not found very strong effects. Only one study has attempted to assess the potential role of hostility in immunocompromise and, again, the results are only suggestive (Pettingale, Greer, & Tee, 1977).

By far, depression has been most heavily researched as the potential culprit in the stress-immunocompromise relationship. In studies of bereaved samples, several investigators found evidence that responding to bereavement with depression predicts adverse immunologic changes, not simply the fact of bereavement (Irwin, Daniels, Bloom, Smith, & Weiner, 1987; Irwin, Daniels, Bloom, & Weiner, 1986; Irwin, Daniels, Weiner, & Bloom, 1986; Linn, Linn, & Jensen, 1984). However, studies of clinically depressed individuals have been inconsistent. Research by Kronfol and his colleagues suggests a possible impairment in cell-mediated immunity in patients with primary depressive illness (Kronfol & House, 1984; Kronfol et al., 1983; Kronfol, Turner, Nasrallah, & Winokur, 1984). Calabrese and colleagues (Calabrese et al., 1986) and Schleifer et al. (1984) found reductions in lymphocyte responsivity to mitogenic stimulation in psychiatrically depressed patients (see also Schleifer, Keller, Siris, Davis, & Stein, 1985; Kiecolt-Glaser, Stephens, Lipetz, Speicher, & Glaser, 1985). Depressed mood has been associated with lower T_S cells and more herpes recurrences as well (Kemeny et al., 1989). Other studies, however, have found no differences between depressed and nondepressed patients (e.g., Albrecht, Helderman, Schlesser, & Rush, 1985; Darko et al., 1989). In a recent large-scale study, Schleifer, Keller, Bond, Cohen, and Stein (1989) concluded that altered immunity need not be related to a major depressive disorder, but that quantitative and functional measures of immune functioning may be adversely affected in some subgroups of depressed patients.

Coping and Coping Resources as Moderators of the Stress–Immune Functioning Relationship

In Chapter 8, we saw that the impact of stressful events on distress and adverse health outcomes can sometimes be muted by coping methods such as problem-solving, stress management, and relaxation and by coping re-

sources such as social support. Is there any evidence that these factors can influence the impact that stress has on the immune system? Research on social support is inconclusive. One study of medical students facing final exams (Kiecolt-Glaser, Garner et al., 1984) found that adverse changes in immune functioning were greater for those students high in loneliness than for those who were less lonely. Similar effects have been found in other studies (Glaser, Kiecolt-Glaser, Speicher, & Holiday, 1985; Jemmott & Magloire, 1988; Kiecolt-Glaser, Speicher et al., 1984; Levy, Herberman, Maluish, Schlien, & Lippman, 1985; Levy, Herberman, Lee et al., 1987). However, in most of these studies, it is not clear whether adverse social relations, as might be reflected in loneliness, were simply another stressful event to which subjects were responding simultaneously or whether positive support actually muted the stressful impact of the exams. Thus, whether social support can buffer the adverse impact of stressful events on the immune system remains to be determined.

Do particular coping techniques mute the impact of stress on immune functioning? A study of female rheumatoid arthritis patients (Zautra, Okun, Roth, & Emmanual, 1989) found that those who perceived themselves as able to cope with stressful events and who felt satisfied with their ability to cope showed higher levels of circulating B cells. A study by Cohen and colleagues (Cohen et al., 1989) examined whether optimism as a coping strategy could mute the impact of stressful events on immune functioning. For optimists, a negative relation was found between chronic stressors and percentage of T_C cells, while for pessimists, a negative relationship existed between acute stressors and percentage of T_S cells (Cohen, Kearney et al., 1989). Thus, the impact of optimism depended on whether the stressful event was chronic or short-term.

There is some evidence that feelings of self-efficacy and the ability to exercise control over stressful events are associated with less immunocompromise under stress. Such changes could conceivably come about in any of three ways (Bandura, 1989): Perceived self-efficacy may reduce the experience of stress itself; it may reduce the tendency to develop depression in response to stressful events; or it may create some expectancy-based central nervous system modulation of immunologic reactivity.

Other coping styles may also be related to the stress-immune functioning relationship (Locke, Hurst, & Heisel, 1979). One study with hamsters found that those that responded to social stress with agitation had poorer tumor outcomes than did those that responded to extensive social contact with a pattern of inactivity and dominance-related behavior (Temoshok, Peeke, & Mehard, 1988). Among humans, ego strength may be an adaptive coping resource. For example, in one study, antibody reactions to vaccination were stronger among patients high in ego strength (feelings of self-worth and competence) than among those low in ego strength (Roessler, Cate, Lester, & Couch, 1979). A number of studies suggest that people who have high power needs but attempt to restrain those needs may have greater vulnerability to infectious disorders and show reduced immunocompetence on some indicators (e.g., Jemmott et al., 1983; McClelland, Alexander, & Marks, 1982). Hardiness (see Chapter 8) correlates with beta-endorphin secretion and natural killer cell activity. Thus, hardiness may be a coping style that moderates physical health (Solomon, Fiatarone et al., 1988). Exercise activates beta-endorphins, which stimulate natural killer cell activity (Fiatarone et al., 1988). Thus, the potential role of exercise as a stress buffer merits additional attention. As yet, then, evidence suggesting that coping techniques and coping resources may mute the relation between stress and adverse immunologic outcomes remains suggestive, though not conclusive, and thus it is a ripe area for additional research.

Interventions to Enhance Immunocompetence

On the assumption that effective coping with stress can reduce its adverse effects, a number of investigators have examined whether stress management interventions can mute the impact of stressful events on the immune system. In Chapter 8, we saw that catharsis appears to enhance health and mood in individuals who have suffered a traumatic event. These results may be immunologically mediated. In one study (Pennebaker, Kiecolt-Glaser, & Glaser, 1988), fifty undergraduates wrote about either traumatic experiences or superficial topics for 20 minutes on each of four consecutive days. Those who wrote about traumatic or upsetting events demonstrated a higher mitogenic response compared to baseline than the control subjects.

Relaxation may mute the effects of stress on the immune system. In a study with elderly adults (a group at risk because of age-related declines in immune functioning generally), subjects were assigned to relaxation training,

Training in relaxation may help people learn how to mute the adverse effects of stress on the immune system.

social contact, or no intervention (Kiecolt-Glaser, Glaser, Williger et al., 1985). Participants in the relaxation condition had significantly higher levels of natural killer cell activity after the intervention than at baseline and significantly lower antibody titers to herpes simplex virus I, suggesting some enhancement of cellular immunity associated with the relaxation intervention. In a study of medical students facing examinations, half of the sample was randomly assigned to a relaxation group and half to a no-treatment group. Frequent practice of relaxation was related to more helper T lymphocytes after controlling for baseline, although no impact on natural killer cell activity was found (Kiecolt-Glaser et al., 1986). In a study of malignant melanoma patients, Fawzy et al. (in press) found that those patients assigned to a group intervention program that involved relaxation, problem-solving skills, and effective coping strategies showed higher NK activity, higher percentages of NK cells, lower percentages of T_H cells, and higher interferon-augmented NK cell cytotoxic activity than did the comparison subjects 6 months after the intervention was completed.

However, some studies have found no effect of stress management interventions on immune functioning. In one study (Arnetz et al., 1987), unemployed women receiving standard economic benefits were assigned either to a control condition or to a self-help psychosocial intervention, and their immune functioning was compared with that of an employed group of age-matched controls. Lymphocyte functioning was greater in the employed than the unemployed women, but the psychosocial intervention had no effect on any immune parameters. A study with men testing positive for the AIDS virus evaluated an intervention involving systematic relaxation, health-habit change, and stress management skills; no impact on immune parameters was found (Coates, McKusick, Kuno, & Stites,

1989). At present, then, it may be possible to enhance immunocompetence in certain populations with certain techniques, although considerably greater research is needed to establish these relations conclusively.

The Conditioning of Immunity

Recent evidence suggests that immune responses can be classically conditioned (Ader, 1987; Ader & Cohen, 1985; Bovbjerg, Cohen, & Ader, 1987; Grota, Ader, & Cohen, 1987). In the first such study to examine this phenomenon, Ader and Cohen (1985) paired a novel taste (saccharine) with an injection of cyclophosphamide, a powerful immunosuppressive drug in mice, in a single-condition trial experiment. Conditioned mice that were reexposed to saccharine at the later time showed signs of **immunosuppression** relative to control animals that were conditioned and not reexposed to saccharine, nonconditioned animals provided with saccharine, or animals exposed to a placebo.

What are the implications of the fact that immunity can be conditioned? One possibility is that stimuli or events paired with immunosuppression would prompt an avoidance response in animals or people in the future. For example, one study found that pairing a neutral solution with an immunosuppressive drug produced subsequent taste aversion (Grota, Ader, & Cohen, 1987). However, substantial doses of immunosuppressive drugs appear to be required to demonstrate this kind of avoidance learning. Nonetheless, the implications are that it might be possible to use conditioned immunoenhancing responses to prolong good health and life. For example, if one can create a conditioned immunoenhancing response to a neutral substance, it may be possible to obtain significant drug effects with lower drug dosages by administering the conditioned substance in conjunction with the drug.

Pathways from Stress to Immunocompromise

As we have seen, there is now considerable evidence that stressful events can exert an adverse effect on immune functioning. The question arises as to exactly how such links may occur. While this is one of the major avenues for future research, there are several possibilities. First, it is clear that there are links between the neuroendocrine system and the immune system. Corticosteroids, for example, have an immunosuppressive effect. Increases in cortisol have been related both to decreased lymphocyte responsivitiy to mitogens and to decreased lymphocyte cytotoxicity (Cunningham, 1981). The catecholamines (epinephrine and norephinephrine) and other hormones (androgens, estrogens, and progesterone) also appear to have both immunosuppressive and immunoenhancing effects under different conditions, while other hormones such as prolactin and the growth hormone may have some immunoenhancing effects (Cunningham, 1981).

Increasingly, it is clear that the immune system and the brain influence each other. Many of the substances involved in this communication appear to be neuropeptides (Morley, Kay, Solomon, & Plotnikoff, 1987). In particular, the release of beta-endorphins from the pituitary in response to stress may represent a pathway by which the central nervous system modulates the immune system (Morley, Kay, & Solomon, 1988). Neuropeptides appear to have a structure similar to certain lymphokines, thus producing potential functional interchangeability between neuropeptides and lymphokines. Lymphocytes appear to produce neuropeptides, and brain cells produce lymphokines and monokines (Morley et al., 1987). Thus, circulating lymphocytes may act as sensory organs, converting information from contact with pathogens to endocrine signals for the brain. Finally, there appear to be direct anatomical links between the autonomic nervous system and immune organs. It appears that fibers from the autonomic nervous system extend to the immune organs, allowing direct neurotransmission to the lymphocytes (e.g., Felten et al., 1987).

Other factors that merit extended study include the impact of stress in early life on immune functioning over the lifetime. There is some suggestion that the developing immune system may be more vulnerable to effects of adverse psychological states such as stress or depression; moreover, these experiences may permanently affect the immune system in ways that persist into adulthood (Schleifer, Scott, Stein, & Keller, 1986). In particular, early loss experiences, such as premature maternal separation, may be implicated as problematic both in early life and in adulthood, at least on the basis of animal research conducted to date (Schleifer et al., 1986).

Stress-induced modulation of immunity is highly complex, involving a wide range of enhancing and inhibitory mechanisms. This will no doubt continue to be an important line of work in the future.

AIDS

Exactly when AIDS first appeared is unknown. It appears to have begun in Central Africa, perhaps some time in the early 1970s. It spread rapidly throughout Zaire, Uganda, and other central African nations, largely because its origins were not understood. A high rate of extramarital sex, little condom use, and a high rate of gonorrhea also facilitated the spread of the AIDS virus in the heterosexual population. Medical clinics may have inadvertently promoted the spread of AIDS because, in attempting to vaccinate as many people as possible against the common diseases in the area, needles were used over and over again, promoting the exchange of fluids. From

Africa, the disease appears to have made its way slowly to Europe and to Haiti, and from Haiti into the United States, as Americans vacationing in Haiti may have brought the virus back.

The first case of **AIDS (Acquired Immune Deficiency Syndrome)** in the United States was diagnosed in 1981. It now appears, however, that there may have been isolated cases of AIDS before that date. The viral agent is a retrovirus, the **human immunodeficiency virus (HIV),** and it attacks the immune system, most notably the helper T cells (Solomon & Temoshok, 1987). The virus appears to be transmitted exclusively by the exchange of cell-containing bodily fluids, especially semen and blood. The period between contracting the virus and developing symptoms of AIDS is highly variable, with some individuals developing symptoms quite quickly and others free of symptoms for as long as 8 or 9 years or more. Usually, AIDS is diagnosed through the presence of an unusual opportunistic infection that results from the impairment of the immune system, such as pneumocystis carinii pneumonia or an unusual neoplasm (cancer) such as Kaposi's sarcoma or non-Hodgkins' lymphoma. A lesser clinical syndrome also results from the HIV virus, which is called the **AIDS-Related Complex (ARC).** At one time believed to be a separate disease, most researchers now believe that ARC patients will eventually go on to develop AIDS.

In many cases of HIV infection, the virus grows very rapidly within the first few weeks of infection and spreads throughout the body. At this point, the virus affects primarily two types of immune cells, the helper T cells and the macrophages. Early symptoms experienced at this time are mild, with swollen glands and mild flulike symptoms predominating. After 3 to 6 weeks, the infection may abate, leading to a long asymptomatic period, during which viral growth is slow and controlled. At this time the infection is likely to be transmitted to others. The amount of virus

typically rises gradually, eventually severely compromising the immune system by killing the helper T cells and producing a vulnerability to opportunistic infections that leads to the diagnosis of AIDS. Whether the course of HIV infection inevitably follows this course remains to be seen.

The rate at which these changes take place can differ widely. Low-income blacks and Hispanics who test positive for the AIDS virus go on to develop AIDS twice as fast as whites (NBC News, Los Angeles, April 3, 1990). Drug users who live on the streets often succumb to the complications from the disease in less than a year, due to lifestyle factors and generally poor health. Individuals from higher SES groups have a much greater chance of long-term survivorship. Such individuals are more likely to take care of their health in the first place and have greater access to experimental drug treatment programs, such as the use of AZT, through private physicians who are participating in studies. Consequently, socioeconomic factors have a major impact on both the time between progression from HIV+ status to a diagnosis of AIDS and how quickly an individual dies after a diagnosis of AIDS.

Primary Prevention of AIDS

In the United States at present, the two major at-risk groups are homosexual men and intravenous needle–sharing drug abusers. Among drug users, needle-sharing leads to the exchange of bodily fluids, thereby spreading the virus. Among homosexual men, exchange of the virus has been tied to a number of sexual practices, especially anal-receptive sex involving the exchange of semen without a condom. As the disease spreads more widely into the heterosexual population, other modes of transmission, including vaginal intercourse, will come to be more closely associated with the transmission of AIDS. The likelihood of developing AIDS also increases with the number of sexual partners a person has had and

The overwhelming majority of early AIDS cases occurred among gay men. The gay community responded with dramatic and impressive efforts to reduce risk-related behaviors.

with the number of anonymous sexual partners, and thus these behaviors are also considered to be risk-related. The United States has been quite slow to develop programs to reduce risk practices for AIDS, a problem that has been attributed to a mix of disbelief, confusion, inefficiency, **homophobia,** and politics (Shilts, 1987). A number of specific obstacles have thwarted effective education. These have included disagreement about the appropriateness of providing educational messages to prevent AIDS, uncertainty about the extent of risk to the general population, conflicting responses of the government alternating between reassurance and alarm, and the sheer complexity of the behavior change that must be undertaken (Fineberg, 1988). As a result, the United States has not yet developed a nationwide educational program to prevent the spread of AIDS. However, within the gay

community, a population that accounted for the overwhelming majority of the early victims of AIDS, AIDS education spread fairly rapidly with corresponding behavior change. As the significance of anal-receptive sex without a condom became known, many of the country's gay communities responded impressively with efforts to reduce the behavior. For example, a San Francisco study (Doll et al., 1987) found that the rate of engaging in unprotected receptive-anal intercourse with nonregular partners was twenty-seven times higher in 1978 than in 1985, and other studies have also found major declines in this practice (Martin, 1987; McKusick, Horstman, & Coates, 1985; Winkelstein et al., 1987). The sharp decline in new HIV+ cases and in rectal gonorrhea also suggests that behavior change must have occurred.

However, not all studies report such opti-

Box 15.1
A Profile of Patient Zero

In the 1970s, a number of seemingly isolated cases of Kaposi's sarcoma and other rare opportunistic infections broke out in the gay community. By the early 1980s, the Centers for Disease Control (CDC) were able to put together these anomalous and seemingly unrelated disorders into a pattern defined as Acquired Immune Deficiency. As the cluster of disorders associated with this syndrome became more clear, agents from the CDC began to track the cases in an effort to identify common links. They soon became aware that one name was turning up repeatedly as a sexual partner of those now suffering from Acquired Immune Deficiency, the name of Gaetan Dugas.

Gaetan Dugas was an attractive, sexually active French-Canadian airline flight attendant. His job and sexual proclivities made him an effective and deadly carrier for spreading the AIDS virus as far and wide as possible.

Gaetan was the man everybody wanted, the ideal for this community, at this time and in this place. His sandy hair fell boyishly over his forehead, his mouth easily curled into an inviting smile, and his laugh could flood color into a room of black and white. He bought his clothes in the trendiest shops of Paris and London. He vacationed in Mexico and on the Caribbean beaches. Americans tumbled for his soft, Quebecois accent and sexual magnetism....

There was no place that the 28-year-old airline steward would rather have the boys fall for him than in San Francisco. Here, Gaetan could satisfy his voracious sexual appetite with the beautiful California men he liked so much. He returned from every stroll down Castro Street with a pocketful of match covers and napkins that were crowded with addresses and phone numbers. He recorded names of his most passionate admirers in his fabric-covered address book. But lovers were like suntans to him: they would be so wonderful, so sexy for a few days, and then fade. At times, Gaetan would study his address book with genuine curiosity, trying to recall who this or that person was....

He didn't feel like he had cancer at all. That was what the doctor had said after cutting that bump from his face. Gaetan had wanted the small purplish spot removed to satisfy his vanity. The doctor had wanted it for a biopsy. Weeks later, the report came back that he had Kaposi's sarcoma, a bizarre skin cancer that hardly anyone got.... He was terrified at first, but he consoled himself with the knowledge that you can beat cancer. He had created a life in which he could have everything and everyone he wanted. He'd figure a way around this cancer, too. (Shilts, 1987, pp. 21–22)

When he was finally tracked down by the CDC in 1982, Dugas readily and happily acknowledged his sexual activities, apparently unaware that he had infected dozens of homosexual men. "Including his nights at the baths, he figured he had 250 sexual contacts a year. He'd been involved in gay life for about 10 years, and easily had had 2500 sexual partners" (p. 83). By the time he learned he was contagious, he had had the disease for almost 2 years and it had progressed only minimally. Although Dugas was urged to stop having sex by the CDC, he responded: "Of course I'm going to have sex. Nobody's proven to me that you can spread cancer. Somebody gave this to me; I'm not going to give up sex" (p. 138).

Nonetheless, he cooperated by providing as many names and phone numbers of his previous lovers as he could locate. Time after time, these connections led back to small enclaves of AIDS in the San Francisco, New York, and other gay communities. "By April, 1982, epidemiologists found that 40 of the first 248 gay men diagnosed could be tied directly to Gaetan Dugas. All had either had sex with him or sex with someone who had. In fact, from just one tryst with Gaetan, 11 early cases could be connected. He was connected to nine of the first 19 cases in L.A., 22 in New York City, and nine in eight other American cities" (p. 147). The odds that this could be a coincidence were calculated to be zero.

CDC officials started talking to the San Francisco city attorneys to see if any laws existed to enable them to take formal action against Dugas. There weren't. "It was around this time that rumors began on Castro Street about a strange guy at the 8th and Howard bathhouse, a blonde with a French accent. He would have sex with you, turn up the lights in the cubicle, and point out his Kaposi's sarcoma lesions. 'I've got gay cancer,' he'd say. 'I'm going to die and so are you'" (p. 165). Eventually he became well enough known in the San Francisco gay community that other gay men tried to stop him from having anonymous sex at the bathhouses. Finally, after having AIDS for 4 years, Gaetan Dugas died in March 1984.

Originally the CDC speculated that Dugas was *the* person who brought AIDS to North America. It now appears that he may have been one of several, but it is evident that he "played a key role in spreading the virus from end of the United States to the other" (p. 439). Author Randy Shilts summarized the legacy of Gaetan Dugas: "At one time, Gaetan had been what every man wanted from gay life; by the time he died, he had become what every man feared" (p. 439).

mistic figures. It appears that the San Francisco community has been particularly successful in reducing this behavior, while estimates of unprotected anal intercourse in New York, Chicago, and other cities have been somewhat higher (see Stall, Coates, & Hoff, 1988, for a review). Unfortunately, too, the amount of risk-reducing behavior may not be enough to protect an individual from contracting AIDS. In a 1987 study, Joseph et al. found that, among gay men who were sexually active, 7% reported no change in their behavior in response to AIDS, 40% still had anonymous sexual partners, 49% practiced receptive intercourse, and of those engaged in the practice, 73% had not modified their behavior by using condoms or withdrawing before ejaculation (see also Martin, 1987). The most frequently reported changes are a decrease in the number of sexual partners, a reduction in the number of anonymous sexual partners, and a decreased use of bathhouses for sex. Although extent and type of sex with a primary sex partner has not changed dramatically, men with a primary sex partner have made more changes in reducing the numbers of partners than single men (Klein et al., 1987; McKusick et al., 1985). However, of those men who typically meet their sexual partners at bathhouses or bars, only 65% report that they have made any changes in their lives to adapt to AIDS.

What, then, are effective ways to modify behavior further? Generally speaking, knowledge about AIDS has shown relatively little relationship to risk-reduction behavior (Joseph et al., 1987; McKusick et al., 1985). However, this may be because among gay men the level of knowledge is extremely high. Educational efforts, then, may still be important in populations in which the level of information about AIDS is lower (Emmons et al., 1986; see also Joseph et al., 1987).

Perceived self-efficacy should be important in predicting the ability to control sexual practices related to AIDS (Bandura, 1989), and research to date suggests that it is. Compulsive sexual behavior is a problem for some gay men, and, consequently, the perception that they can actually modify their behavior may be low (Emmons et al., 1986). Perceived personal efficacy thus appears to be an important factor in reducing behaviors leading to high risk for AIDS (Communication Technologies, 1984; Doll et al. 1987; Joseph et al., 1987).

For many men, too, being gay is associated with the belief that they should be free to do what they want sexually, and, consequently, modifying sex practices can represent a major threat to identity and preferred lifestyle (McKusick et al., 1985). One study (McKusick et al., 1985) found that men who used sex to release tension or to express their gay identity were less likely to engage in protected anal sex, whereas personal knowledge of one or more men with AIDS in the advanced stages of the disease reduced the frequency of high-risk sexual behavior.

Efforts to change behavior may need to target not only high-risk sexual practices themselves, but other practices that facilitate high-risk sex, for example, drug and alcohol use. That is, people who are otherwise aware that they should not engage in particular practices may be less inhibited about so doing when under the influence of drugs or alcohol (Communication Technologies, 1987; Siegel et al., 1987; Stall, Wiley, McKusick, Coates, & Ostrow, 1986).

In a review of the literature on health behavior change in response to AIDS, Becker and Joseph (1988) concluded that the changes

The possibility that the AIDS virus may move into the adolescent population is substantial, but as yet there are few signs that adolescents have changed their sexual practices in response to the threat of AIDS.

in behavior among homosexual and bisexual men in response to the threat of AIDS may constitute the most rapid and profound response to a health threat that has ever been documented. Longitudinal studies, however, suggest a fair degree of instability in individual behavior, with fairly high rates of at least temporary return to prior behavior. For the most part, people have modified rather than eliminated risky behavior.

We know, then, that gay men have been very responsive to the need to make behavior changes. But what of other populations at risk? Considerably less behavior change has been found in the drug-using community (Friedman, de Jong, & Des Jarlais, 1988). Sharing needles is still a common practice. Urban minorities also do not appear to have changed their risk-reduction behaviors very much (Becker & Joseph, 1988). Adolescents and young adults are a population at potential risk for AIDS and any other sexually transmitted disease, because they are the most sexually active element in the population. However, as Box 15.2 shows, there is little reason to believe that college students and other young adults have made major changes in their sexual behavior, even as the statistics documenting increasing rates of HIV infection in this population are emerging (Becker & Joseph, 1988).

Interventions to Reduce Risk Behaviors for AIDS

Some intervention efforts have drawn on theory and research about health behaviors in an effort to induce people to modify their sexual behaviors. For example, in a cognitive-behavioral intervention (Kelly, Lawrence, Hood, & Brasfield, 1989), gay men were taught how to exercise self-control in sexual relationships and to resist pressure to engage in high-risk sexual behavior through modeling, role playing, and corrective feedback. With this training, the men became somewhat more skillful in handling sexual relationships and were able to reduce their risky sexual behaviors and use condoms.

Whether these kinds of interventions will be successful with teenagers or with IV drug users to reduce sharing of infected needles remains to be seen, inasmuch as these populations may not have as good impulse control. However, provision of information about AIDS transmission, needle exchange programs, and instruction on how to sterilize needles can reduce risky injection practices among IV drug users (Des Jarlais, 1988; Watters, 1987). Methadone maintenance treatments may help to reduce the spread of AIDS by reducing the frequency of injections and shared needle contacts (Ball, Lange, Myers, & Friedman, 1988).

In Britain, the government has now begun to use the press in an effort to fight AIDS among teenagers and young adults. Such efforts were initially begun in 1986, but an evaluation of this national campaign strategy, which consisted largely of full-page advertisements about AIDS, suggested that the health education campaign had little or no impact on attitudes, desire for information, behavioral intentions, or anxiety (Sher, 1987). However, in January 1987, a multimillion dollar campaign against AIDS began on the BBC radio and through other educational methods, and, according to recent polls, these campaigns may finally be paying off. Young single people report more use of condoms, and married people report fewer extramarital affairs (Moseley, 1987). These results, then, suggest that the press can be used successfully to increase concern about AIDS, which provides a basis for changing attitudes and behaviors (Temoshok, Grade, & Zich, 1988).

One of the problems with intervening effectively to reduce the spread of AIDS is that certain important elements of the population have been largely ignored. For example, although blacks make up only about 12% of the American population, approximately 25% of those diagnosed with AIDS have been black. In addition, there appears to be a greater incursion of the virus into the heterosexual black population than is true for whites (Mays & Cochran, 1987). To date, the particular cultural and community factors that may imply the need for different sorts of education and prevention programs for the black community have been largely ignored.

Interventions have also not been systematically targeted to women at risk for AIDS and may need to concentrate especially on the dynamics of pressure to engage in sexual activity that may compromise their ability to practice

Box 15.2
Young Adults and Safe Sex

Young adults are the most sexually active element of the population, having more sex with more different partners than people at other times in their lives. The potential for any sexually transmitted disease, including AIDS, to strike this population with major force is therefore enormous. Despite this fact, young adults in the United States appear to be relatively unconcerned about their risk for AIDS and to have made relatively few changes in their lifestyle in response to the threat.

One of the largest barriers to the prevention of the spread of AIDS concerns the knowledge of relevant health practices. A 1986 survey of over 1,000 adolescents in San Francisco (DiClemente, Zorn, & Temoshok, 1986) found marked variability in knowledge about AIDS, particularly the need to use condoms and to take other precautionary measures to reduce the risk of infection during sexual intercourse. Despite calls for the development and implementation of education programs in the schools to provide better information, as of 1989, such massive education has not yet occurred.

Effective interventions with this group will be difficult. Most communications directed to young adults begin with the statement, "If you are at risk for AIDS...." Yet little information is provided to help young adults judge if they are at risk for AIDS. Moreover, most researchers now consider that *all* sexually active young adults are at risk for AIDS. Other barriers to successful intervention involve communication. Pamphlets often urge young adults to discuss the risk for AIDS with their partners, yet typically the exchange of information relevant to risk, such as how many partners one has previously had and whether or not one is bisexual, occurs after, not before, intimacy. Thus, the advice contained in interventions designed to get adolescents and young adults to change their behavior may be impractical, given the dynamics of sexual

encounters (Cochran & Mays, in press). The adolescent population regards condom use as something done by people who are not cool (Collins & Aspinwall, 1989). As long as safe sex is regarded as the province of undesirable partners, the likelihood that the adolescent population will change its behavior is small.

Another barrier to effective risk-reduction behavior is that young adults appear to believe that they can accurately tell whether a partner has been infected or not (Cochran & Mays, in press). There is a common perception that those infected with the AIDS virus are slovenly vagrants and that clean-cut, attractive people with money and other resources are probably okay. Yet, as AIDS researchers point out, it is the latter person who is probably having more sex than the former, inasmuch as most people willingly reject the advances of the slovenly vagrant in favor of those made by the more attractive person. The cues that people use to decide if a potential partner might be HIV+ probably bear very little relationship to reality.

Lying also represents a barrier to the exchange of useful information about the risk of developing AIDS. In an anonymous investigation, college students were asked if they would be willing to lie to a sexual partner about their past sexual history in order to obtain sex. A large proportion of both men and women indicated that they would readily lie in order to obtain sex, with the numbers substantially higher for men than for women (Cochran & Mays, in press).

In short, a number of myths appear to contribute to the young adult's unwillingness to change sexual behavior in the face of the threat of AIDS. These include false perceptions of low risk, false beliefs that one can tell whether a partner has been infected or not, little knowledge about AIDS and the modes of transmission, and the belief that condom use is just not cool.

safe sex (Cochran & Mays, 1989). Interventions are needed to help women recognize the threat of AIDS and develop skills to achieve the goal of safe sex in high-pressure, high-risk situations (Cochran & Mays, 1989). Poor and ethnic-minority women who identify AIDS as a gay white disease may fail to perceive themselves at risk and thus not develop the skills to take precautionary behavior (Mays & Cochran, 1988).

Community-based interventions are clearly one of the best ways of changing AIDS-related behaviors, inasmuch as AIDS is so heavily concentrated within particular communities, such as gay men, urban minorities, and those who engage in IV drug use (Coates & Greenblatt, 1989). The coming years will no doubt bring additional evidence of what constitutes an effective community-based intervention.

Testing for the AIDS Virus

One of the most controversial issues surrounding the prevention of AIDS has been the role of **AIDS antibody testing** and whether it should be mandatory for particular groups. Some have suggested that testing will help stop the spread of the disease, yet evidence to date suggests that testing positive is by no means a guarantee of safe sex and other AIDS-related health behaviors (Coates et al., 1988). Some individuals testing positive may choose not to tell their partners, thus leaving their potentially infected partners free to infect others through ignorance (Kegeles, Catania, & Coates, 1988). Moreover, AIDS antibody testing itself can have both positive and negative effects. On the one hand, knowing that one is seropositive could lead one to seek prophylactic treatments. For example, AZT has been shown to be effective with HIV+ individuals who are asymptomatic for AIDS. But testing positive may also create adverse effects, such as depression. As one report suggests, widespread testing for the AIDS virus needs to be accompanied by assurances of confidentiality,

acceptable test standards, assurances of nondiscrimination, and availability of effective physical and, if necessary, psychological treatment (McKusick, 1988).

More drastic and controversial measures for AIDS control have not yet become popular. Although there have been some calls for quarantining those with AIDS and imposing other restrictions on civil liberties, for the most part, such measures have not been taken too seriously. However, if the risk of AIDS to the general population increases, the willingness to impose such severe social restrictions could well increase, leading to a dangerous threat to civil liberties for AIDS patients (Hogan, 1989).

Coping with HIV+ Status

Thousands of people currently test positive for the AIDS virus but have not yet developed AIDS. Although most health experts believe that the majority will go on to develop AIDS, the extent of this risk is not yet entirely clear. Thus, this group of people lives with a major threatening event (HIV+ status) coupled with substantial uncertainty, confusion, and fear. How do these people cope? One might expect that being infected with the AIDS virus would lead to considerable agitation, depression, and other adverse psychological responses. While HIV infection is undeniably a stressor, there is evidence to suggest that people cope better than might be expected. For example, Kessler and his colleagues (Kessler, O'Brien et al., 1988) found that seropositivity for HIV was not associated with elevated levels of social or emotional impairment. Similarly, Kemeny and her colleagues (Taylor, Kemeny, Reed, & Aspinwall, in press) found that HIV+ gay and bisexual men were actually slightly better adjusted on certain dimensions than HIV– men. To explain these paradoxical results, they suggested that contracting the AIDS virus is a major stressor that prompts coping activity which then reduces stress. Being HIV- leaves individuals in a state of threat but without a specific stressor to combat, and coping efforts may therefore not be fully initiated. These results do not suggest that men react with equanimity to the stressor of AIDS. Indeed, being HIV+ is a major stressful event that can produce many adverse psychosocial responses. Yet coping efforts appear generally to be successful in muting the impact of this stress.

One of the major issues that faces gay men with HIV infection and all people with AIDS is the negative attitudes of the general public (Triplet & Sugarman, 1987; Weiner, Perry, & Magnusson, 1988). Gay men have grown up as a minority in a majority that is often actively hostile to them and, as a result, have often suffered discrimination, hatred, and even violence. The AIDS crisis has exacerbated this climate. Pryor and his colleagues (Pryor, Reeder, & Vinacco, 1989) suggest that negative attitudes toward persons with HIV infection or AIDS stem from both the fear that one may contract AIDS and symbolic factors, such as attitudes toward homosexuality. As such, HIV+ individuals and AIDS patients may experience substantial secondary victimization, namely social discrimination and aversion, in conjunction with their primary victimization, namely having contracted the HIV virus (Taylor et al., 1983). These negative attitudes can be very powerful and spill over into irrelevant circumstances. Pryor and his colleagues (Pryor, Reeder, & McManus, in press) found that persuasive messages designed to reassure coworkers that they could not become infected with the AIDS virus as a result of interacting with an AIDS-infected co-worker produced positive attitudes only in individuals who did not hold negative attitudes toward homosexuality. Thus, the fact that AIDS may symbolize for some people the homosexual lifestyle may act as a factor that increases feelings of aversion and fear over and above that experienced in response to AIDS. Moreover, these feelings of aversion may generalize to targets that are not homosexual, simply by virtue of their having a disease that has been associated with homosexuality.

At present, we know relatively little about the sources of stress and the coping efficacy of people who are HIV+ but are not yet diagnosed with AIDS. A number of studies are currently being conducted to examine these issues. Hopefully, we will know more about this limbo status and interventions which may make it easier to adjust in the coming years.

Coping with AIDS

A number of adverse psychosocial responses can occur in response to a diagnosis of AIDS. Immediately after diagnosis, patients may regard AIDS as an imminent death sentence and may respond by becoming depressed and isolating themselves from others (Reed, 1989). As the fact that they will not die immediately becomes evident, such people may reintegrate into their social networks, at least to a degree. Intermittent anxiety and depression are very common. Expecting that the disease will eventually kill them, many AIDS patients commit suicide to avoid the painful, lingering death associated with the disease. Mazurk and his colleagues (Mazurk et al., 1988) reported a thirty-six-fold increase in the rate of suicide among men with AIDS.

AIDS also eventually leads to neurological involvement. Early symptoms of central nervous symptom impairment are similar to those of depression and include forgetfulness, inability to concentrate, psychomotor retardation, decreased alertness, apathy, withdrawal, diminished interest in work, and loss of sexual desire. In more advanced stages, patients experience confusion, disorientation, seizures, profound dementia, coma, and even death. CNS disturbance is variable, not appearing until the late stages in some patients, but developing early among others (U.S. Department of Health and Human Services, 1986).

Several studies have examined attributions that AIDS patients make for the cause of their disease and how this affects their psychosocial adjustment to it. As we noted in Chapter 13, causal attributions for a disease can have an impact on psychosocial adjustment and health behaviors. One study found that attributing the cause of AIDS to oneself was associated with depression, anxiety, and general mood disturbance (Moulton, Sweet, Temoshok, & Mandel, 1987). Another study, however (Reed, 1989), found very little self-blame among gay men with AIDS, despite the fact that most regarded their own promiscuous sexual behavior as the cause of AIDS. In Reed's study, causal attributions were not associated with adjustment. Thus, the relations of causal attributions, as well as attributions of personal responsibility and self-blame to adjustment, remain at issue.

Previously we noted that the perception that one can exert personal control over a stressor is usually associated with better adjustment to that stressor. Consistent with this point, Moulton and his colleagues (Moulton et al., 1987) found that attributing the possibility of improvement to themselves was associated with better mood among ARC patients. Reed and his colleagues (Taylor, Helgesen, Reed, & Shokan, in press) asked AIDS patients about their ability to exert control over the disease itself, their daily symptoms, and their treatment. He also inquired about their perception that others, such as medical personnel, were able to exert control over the disease, symptoms, and treatment. Consistent with previous research, he found that perceptions of personal control were associated with better adjustment to AIDS. However, somewhat surprisingly, he found that perceptions that others could exert control over one's disease was strongly negatively associated with adjustment. That is, men who perceived that health care personnel could influence their symptoms, disease, or treatment were more poorly adjusted. This surprising finding could be accounted for by any of several factors. For example, previous research reporting positive effects of control by others has been based heavily on women subjects (e.g., Taylor, Lichtman, & Wood, 1984a). It may be that men benefit from the perception that they per-

sonally have control but not from the perception that others have control. Alternatively, as Reed et al. argued, the gay community has often experienced discrimination and prejudice from the larger heterosexual community. Moreover, the initial response of health care institutions to the AIDS crisis was to ignore it and hope that it would go away. In addition, many health care professionals fear and avoid those with AIDS (Gerbert, Maguire, Badner, Altman, & Stone, 1988). Given this legacy of neglect, prejudice, and homophobia, it may be difficult for gay men to profit emotionally from the belief that others can exert control over their disease.

Interventions to Cope with the Threat of AIDS

Counseling programs have grown up in response to the AIDS crisis and to date have been directed largely toward the gay male population. Some of these involve small group discussions with other gay men. Generally, these appear to be helpful, although there is the risk that constant contact with a population that is also highly at risk for developing AIDS may actually fuel rather than soothe fears (Wayment, 1989). Inasmuch as the experience of loneliness and the absence of a confidante appear to be associated with psychological distress among many men at risk for AIDS, interventions should focus strongly around issues of social support and ways of improving it.

Psychosocial Factors that Affect the Course of AIDS

In recent years, health psychologists have explored psychosocial factors that may influence the clinical course of AIDS or the likelihood that an HIV+ individual will develop symptoms of AIDS. As we saw in the last section, there is substantial evidence from psychoimmunology that some psychosocial variables may suppress immunity, and these variables are chief candidates for influencing the course of AIDS. From that literature, the variables that emerge as the strongest candidates for adverse effects on the immune systems of those already exposed to the HIV virus are bereavement, relationship strain, the need to provide for others, depression, and stress (Kiecolt-Glaser & Glaser, 1988). Research is currently being undertaken to determine whether or not these variables indeed predict who will develop AIDS among HIV+ individuals and whether the clinical course of AIDS will be rapid or slow.

Among the potential implications of such findings are possibilities for intervention. As we noted in the last section, stress management interventions have been undertaken in efforts to augment the immune systems of those already compromised by stress or testing positive for particular viruses. A beginning effort has been made in this regard with individuals who test HIV+. One study examined the impact of stress management training on the sexual behavior and immune functioning of sixty-four gay men infected with the HIV virus. Half the group was randomized to a stress management condition that met for eight 2-hour sessions and one all-day session to learn relaxation techniques and stress management skills. Compared to those in the control group, subjects in the relaxation condition reported fewer sexual partners in the months right after the post-test. However, there were no differences in lymphocyte numbers and functioning (Coates et al., 1989). Although this intervention was not successful in enhancing selected immune parameters, given some history of success with other populations, this remains a promising area for continued research and intervention.

CANCER

Cancer is a set of more than 100 diseases that have several factors in common. All cancers result from a dysfunction in DNA—that part of the cellular programming that controls cell growth and reproduction. Instead of ensuring the regular, slow production of new cells, this malfunctioning DNA causes excessively rapid cell growth and proliferation. Unlike other cells, cancerous cells provide no benefit to the body. They merely sap it of resources.

A number of factors make cancer very difficult to study; therefore its causes are still poorly understood (Fox, 1978). Many cancers are species-specific, and some species are more vulnerable to cancer than others. For example, mice typically contract a lot of cancers, whereas monkeys get very few. Moreover, even a cancer that develops in more than one species may develop in different ways. For example, breast cancer in dogs is very different from breast cancer in humans. As a consequence, it is difficult to use animal models to understand factors that influence the development and course of some human cancers. Many cancers have long or irregular growth cycles that contribute to difficulties in studying them. Tumors are measured in terms of their doubling time—that is, the time it takes a tumor to double in size. Doubling time ranges from 23 to 209 days; thus, a tumor may take anywhere from 2 to 17 years to reach a size that can be detected (Fox, 1978). There is also high within-species variability, such that some subgroups within a species are susceptible to certain cancers while other subgroups are susceptible to different ones. Thus, for example, three individuals all exposed to the same carcinogen may develop different tumors at different times, or one individual may develop a tumor while the others remain tumor-free.

Who Gets Cancer? A Complex Profile

The distribution of malignancies in the population adds to the complexity of the cancer profile. Many cancers run in families. However, this does not necessarily imply that there is a genetically inherited predisposition to cancer. Many things run in families besides genes, including diet and other lifestyle factors that may influence the incidence of an illness. Some cancers are ethnically linked. For example, breast cancer is extremely common among northern Europeans and is relatively rare among Asians (World Health Organization, 1968–1969). Some cancers are also culturally linked through lifestyle. For example, Japanese-American women are more susceptible to breast cancer the longer they have lived in the United States and the more they have adopted the American culture (Wynder et al., 1963). The probability of developing some cancers changes with socioeconomic status. For example, white women are more likely than black women to develop breast cancer, but among black women who have moved up the socioeconomic ladder, the breast cancer rate is the same as for white women at the same economic level (Leffall, White, & Ewing, 1963). These kinds of statistics clearly link lifestyle factors to the development of cancer (American Cancer Society, 1989).

Married people, especially married men, develop fewer cancers than single people. The sole exception to this pattern is sexually related cancers, such as prostate or cervical cancer, to which married people are somewhat more vulnerable than single people. The protective function of being married is at present poorly understood. Health benefits may derive from having a regular source of social support, regularity in health habits, or some other as-yet-unidentified factors (Fraumeni, Lloyd, & Smith, 1969). Dietary factors are also implicated in cancer development. Cancers are more common among people who are chronically malnourished and among those who consume high levels of fats, certain food additives such as nitrates, and alcohol (American Cancer Society, 1989).

Psychosocial Factors and Cancer

As may be obvious from the above description, there are a number of ways in which

psychosocial factors can affect cancer. In terms of initiation of the disease, behavioral factors are involved in people's exposures to **carcinogens,** such as tobacco and occupational carcinogens. Psychosocial variables may also indirectly affect the initiation of cancer through such factors as consumption of a fatty diet or exposure to stress (Levy, 1983). Psychosocial factors may also be involved in the progression of a cancer after it is initiated. For example, one's emotional response or willingness to fight may predict the progression of cancer. Behavioral factors are also involved indirectly in the progression of a cancer, through such variables as failing to adhere to a low-cancer diet, nonadherence with treatment, and failure to use screening or early detection methods (Levy, 1983).

We have already considered many of the factors that initiate and lead to a progression of cancer, including such risk factors as smoking, alcohol consumption, or fatty diet (Chapters 3 through 6), and variables that promote delay behavior and nonadherence (Chapters 9 and 10). In this chapter, we focus more heavily on the evidence for the roles of stress and personality in the initiation and progression of cancer. As must be evident from the problems just identified in studying the causes of cancer, these are very difficult problems to address (Fox, 1978; Fox & Temoshok, 1988). Several lines of research have explored the issues from different vantage points (for a review, see Baltrusch & Waltz, in press; Fox & Temoshok, 1988; Levy, 1983).

The role of personality factors in the development of cancer has been suspected for centuries (see LeShan & Worthington, 1956). Early research attempted to tie specific cancers to particular personality structures. For example, breast cancer was attributed to conflicts surrounding motherhood and femininity and to masochistic tendencies involving an inability to discharge negative emotions and unresolved hostility toward the mother (Renneker & Cutler, 1952). As in the case of other personality-specific models of illness, there is little evidence for such speculation.

Another line of investigation explored the idea of a cancer-prone personality. For decades, there has been a stereotype of a cancer-prone personality as an individual who is easygoing and acquiescent, repressing emotions that might interfere with smooth social and emotional functioning. As Woody Allen remarked in *Manhattan,* "I can't express anger, that's one of the problems I have. I grow a tumor instead." The cancer-prone person is described as inhibited, oversocialized, conforming, compulsive, and depressive. He or she is said to have particular trouble expressing tension, anger, or anxiety, instead presenting the self as pleasant, calm, compliant, and passive (Bahnson, 1981; Renneker, 1981). Bahnson (1981) proposed that cancer patients use particular defense mechanisms, such as denial and repression, and express their emotions abnormally (see Greer & Morris, 1975; Scherg, 1987). The so-called Type C, or cancer-prone, personality has been characterized as responding to stress with depression and hopelessness, the muting of negative emotions, and the potential for learned helplessness (Temoshok, 1987).

Some studies of cancer-prone personality traits have suffered from methodological problems that make it impossible to determine whether cancer patients develop cancer because they have these particular personality factors or whether these personality factors develop as a consequence of cancer (see Scherg, 1987). However, longitudinal studies on the role of individual predispositions avoid some of these methodological problems. Using scores from the Minnesota Multiphasic Personality Inventory (MMPI) that had been collected some years earlier, Dattore, Shontz, and Coyne (1980) compared the profiles of patients who subsequently developed cancer with the profiles of those who did not. The results indicated that the cancer group was significantly different from the noncancer group

on two scales: They showed a greater tendency to repress their emotions and reported less depression. However, other research has found a positive association between depression and cancer, albeit a small and inconsistent one (Dattore et al., 1980; Persky Kempthorne-Rawson, & Shekelle, 1987; Shekelle et al., 1981; see Fox, 1988, for a review). Yet a third set of longitudinal studies have failed to identify any psychosocial predictors of cancer (Helsing, Comstock, & Szklo, 1982; Joffres, Reed, & Nomura, 1985; Keehn, 1980; Thomas, 1976). Thus, the relation of personality traits to cancer as assessed by the best available longitudinal studies to date is inconclusive.

Another effort to examine the stress-cancer link has focused on major life events and their relationship to cancer development. Generally, studies on both animals and humans suggest such a link. Animals exposed to stressors such as crowding show higher malignant tumor rates (e.g., Amkraut & Solomon, 1977; Kavetskii, 1958). Retrospective studies with cancer patients suggest that these individuals experienced a higher rate of stressful life events before the onset of cancer (Sklar & Anisman, 1981). More convincing evidence comes from the few prospective studies that have also found evidence of such a link (Sklar & Anisman, 1981).

As we noted in the last chapter, uncontrollable events produce more stress than controllable ones. Consistent with this analysis, cancer onset has been tied more to uncontrollable than to controllable events. For example, in one study, rats were implanted with a cancerous tumor preparation and were then exposed to inescapable electric shock, escapable electric shock, or no shock. Significantly fewer of the rats that received an inescapable shock were able to reject the tumor than were rats in the other two groups (Visintainer, Seligman, & Volpicelli, 1983).

Research on humans suggests a similar effect. Experiences in helplessness are hypothesized to produce hopelessness, which, in turn, may contribute to development of cancer. Individuals high in hopelessness are defined as having a long-standing history of little activity, devotion to causes with little or no feeling of success or pleasure, low sense of responsibility for achievement, and high susceptibility to failure. A feeling of hopelessness is expressed through feelings of being doomed or finished, experienced in connection with a loss for which the person assumes personal responsibility, such as the death of a spouse (Schmale & Iker, 1971). Research suggests that individuals fitting this profile of hopelessness are more susceptible to cancer. In one study of patients awaiting biopsies for cervical cancer (Schmale & Iker, 1971), those with high degrees of hopelessness were more likely to have a diagnosis of malignancy than were those low in hopelessness. Since evidence from both human and animal studies links cancer to uncontrollable stressful events, this research avenue is promising.

However, on the whole, research with animals has seemed more convincing than research with people, but drawing inferences from these data are difficult. Rodent strains, for example, are highly inbred, often for cancer susceptibility, whereas the human population is outbred. Stress experiments with animals often involve very heavy doses of carcinogens that do not mimic exposure to carcinogens in humans. Rats are more responsive to corticosteroids than are humans, hormones that are implicated in stress-induced immune suppression (Fox, 1988). These and other cautions make inferences from the animal data to the human situation inconclusive.

Lack or loss of social support has also been proposed to affect the onset and course of cancer (Sklar & Anisman, 1981). The absence of close family ties in childhood appears to predict cancer better than it predicts other chronic diseases such as hypertension or coronary heart disease (Grassi & Molinari, 1986; Shaffer, Duszynski, & Thomas, 1982). The absence of a current social support network has

been tied to both a higher incidence of cancer (Thomas & Duszynski, 1974) and to a more rapid course of illness (Reynolds & Kaplan, 1986; Worden & Weisman, 1975). A long-term study of factors related to cancer incidence, mortality, and prognosis in Alameda County, California, found that women who were socially isolated were at significantly elevated risk of dying from cancer of all sites (Kaplan & Reynolds, 1988). However, other studies have found no relationship between social support problems and cancer (see Joffres et al., 1985). Keehn (1980), for example, found no increased cancer risk among prisoners of war, a group exposed to stress and often socially isolated for long periods of time. There also does not appear to be a higher rate of cancer deaths among the bereaved, which might be expected if absence or loss of social support relates to cancer (see Fox, 1988, for a review). Consequently, evidence relating cancer to gaps in social support remains inconclusive.

Psychosocial Factors and the Course of Cancer

Researchers have also attempted to relate personality factors to the course of cancer—that is, to whether it progresses rapidly or slowly (see Levy, 1983). In particular, a rapid course of illness terminating in an early death has been found among polite, unaggressive, acquiescent individuals, whereas a longer course of illness and/or better immune functioning is associated with a more combative, angry stance toward illness and toward medical practitioners (Derogatis, Abeloff, & Melasaratos, 1979; Levy et al., 1985; Pettingale et al., 1977; Rogentine et al., 1979). But the data are not consistent regarding the relationship between personality and progression, either. Temoshok (1987), for example, found dysphoric emotion and distress to be predictive of a poorer outcome in melanoma patients (see also Temoshok et al., 1985). Currently, the relationship of specific emotions and their expression to cancer course remains intriguing but unclear.

Recently, models to address the role of emotions in cancer progression have focused on the possibility of interactions among risk factors. For example, Linkins and Comstock (1988) found that depressed mood had no general effect on cancer risk. However, among those who were smokers, the risk of cancer was substantially elevated in those who were depressed. Compared with the risk in those who had never smoked and did not have depressed mood, depressed mood at the highest level of smoking was associated with a 4.5 increase in risk for total cancer, a 2.9 increase for nonsmoking-associated cancer, and an 18.5 increase for smoking-associated cancer. These results are consistent with a model of carcinogenesis that maintains that carcinogens such as smoking initiate cancer, which is promoted by depressed mood. If this model is correct, it can help explain why the relation between depression and cancer is weak and inconsistent. One would expect cancer in depressed people only if they had previously been exposed to a carcinogen.

To summarize, then, a substantial body of research suggests links among stress, coping, and cancer. Individuals who cope with stress by being acquiescent and pleasant and by repressing negative emotions *may* be more likely to develop malignancies. Malignancies *may* be more likely to develop or may develop more rapidly in individuals who feel helpless, hopeless, depressed, or out of control. Cancer has been tentatively tied more specifically to problems with social support and to stressful life events.

Despite promising evidence in undercovering the potential contributory role of psychological and social factors to the onset or course of cancer, a caution that frequently appears in the literature bears repeating here: There is little firm evidence of a causal relationship between any psychosocial factor and cancer incidence, mortality, or progression.

There are, rather, intriguing hypotheses that require additional research (Fox, 1988).

Mechanisms Linking Stress and Cancer

How, exactly, might stressful events and cancer be linked? A number of researchers have implicated the immune system (see Levy, 1983). As we saw in Chapter 2, cellular immunity may serve a surveillance function in the body, customarily guarding against the proliferation of cancerous or precancerous cells. Prolonged or severe stress may reduce immunologic competence at some critical time, allowing mutant cells to grow. Consistent with this analysis is the fact that cancer patients show reduced immunologic competence and are sometimes successfully treated with therapies designed to enhance immune functioning (Solomon, Amkraut, & Kasper, 1974). The role of humoral immunity in moderating these effects is currently less clear (Solomon et al., 1974).

Stress may also impair DNA repair (Glaser, Thorn, Tarr, Kiecolt-Glaser, & D'Ambrosio, 1985). When lymphocytes are confronted with an antigen, they typically respond with increases in cellular DNA and subsequent proliferation. This fact suggests the importance of the DNA link in the development of cancer. One study that exposed rats to acute stress after they consumed a carcinogen found that methyltranspherase, a DNA-repair enzyme, was significantly lower in animals that had been stressed. To examine a link between psychological stress and carcinogenesis in humans, twenty-eight newly admitted, nonpsychotic, nonmedicated psychiatric patients were divided into those demonstrating high versus low depression. Some lymphocytes were isolated and exposed to irradiation in order to damage cellular DNA. High-distress subjects showed poorer DNA repair, whereas low-distress subjects showed better DNA repair (Kiecolt-Glaser et al., 1985).

Natural killer cell activity is also believed to

be involved in the extent to which a carcinogen takes hold after exposure. As noted earlier, natural killer cells are those cells whose primary function appears to be the surveillance and destruction of tumor cells and virally infected cells, and, therefore, they are believed to have a role in tumor surveillance in the body. Psychological stress appears to adversely affect the ability of natural killer cells to destroy tumors (e.g., Glaser et al., 1986; Locke, Kraus, & Leserman, 1984). The pathways by which stress may have an impact on the initiation and cause of cancer will continue to be a fruitful avenue for research over the next decades.

ADJUSTING TO CANCER

Cancer is the second leading cause of death in the United States. One out of every four people will eventually develop cancer, and each year cancer causes approximately 600,000 deaths. The psychosocial toll taken by cancer is enormous. Two out of every three families will have a family member that develops cancer, and virtually every member of these families will be affected by the disease. However, more than one-third of cancer's victims live at least 5 years after their diagnosis, thus creating many rehabilitation issues (Cohen, Cullen, & Martin, 1982; Cullen, Fox, & Isom, 1976).

Physical Problems

Cancer takes a substantial toll, both physically and psychologically. The physical difficulties usually stem from the pain and discomfort cancer can produce, particularly in the advancing and terminal phases of illness. Difficulties also arise as a consequence of treatment. Some cancers are treated surgically. Removal of organs can create cosmetic problems, as for patients with breast cancer who may have a breast removed (mastectomy) or for patients with head-and-neck cancer who

may have a portion of this area removed. In other cases, organs that are vital to bodily functions must be taken over by a prosthesis. For example, a urinary ostomy patient must be fitted with a special apparatus that makes it possible to excrete urine. A patient whose larynx has been removed must learn to speak with the help of a prosthetic speech device. Side effects due to surgery are also common. For example, treatment of breast cancer through mastectomy and removal of adjacent lymph nodes can produce chronic weakness and edema (swelling) of the area as well as limit the arm's mobility. A colostomy (prosthetic replacement of the lower colon) produces a loss of bowel control. Many cancer patients also receive debilitating follow-up treatments, such as radiation therapy and **chemotherapy,** that have a variety of unpleasant side effects, including nausea, vomiting, and loss of appetite (anorexia).

Psychological Problems

Psychological problems also arise as a consequence of cancer, which is perhaps the most frightening and poorly understood disease in our country. Its victims are often terrified beyond the proportions of their illness, and family and friends may likewise be severely distressed when someone close to them develops cancer. Some researchers have maintained that cancer patients are "victimized" by family members and friends. They may be avoided and even isolated by others, whose terror about the disease and mistaken conceptions (such as the belief that it is contagious) make them unable to provide badly needed social support (Wortman & Dunkel-Schetter, 1979). Even in the best of cases, strains can arise with both family and friends (Lichtman, 1982)

Disturbances in marital relationships after diagnosis of cancer are common, with sexual functioning showing particular vulnerability. Sexual functioning can be directly affected by

Box 15.3
Controlling the Side Effects of Chemotherapy

Many cancer patients who receive intravenously administered chemotherapy experience intense nausea and vomiting. Interventions using relaxation and guided imagery can substantially improve these problems.

Cancer patients who must undergo chemotherapy face an aversive and debilitating experience that can produce a variety of unpleasant side effects, including loss of appetite, nausea, vomiting, anxiety, and depression. Some of these problems are side effects of the drugs that are used. However, they are often made worse by psychologically conditioned reactions to the treatment experience. For example, in anticipation of unpleasant sensations associated with chemotherapy, patients may actually begin to vomit or feel nauseated without having had any chemical treatment at all. Therefore, behavioral interventions to reduce these side effects are a high research priority.

Nausea associated with chemotherapy is also a serious problem for some cancer patients. Patients who experience **anticipatory nausea** have more post-treatment nausea and vomiting, are more depressed, and are

characteristically more anxious than other patients (van Komen & Redd, 1985). Anticipatory nausea may develop from a conditioned response to aspects of the environment associated with chemotherapy (Andrykowski, 1987, 1988).

Relaxation training and guided imagery provide one possible behavioral technique for reducing the side effects of chemotherapy. A program developed by Burish and his associates (Burish & Lyles, 1979; Lyles et al., 1982) is representative of this approach. Approximately an hour before the first chemotherapy session will begin, patients are given training in relaxation and guided imagery. They are first told that the aim of relaxation training is to enable them to become as calm and relaxed as possible while receiving treatment, thereby making the experience of chemotherapy less unpleasant and reducing the likelihood and severity of side effects. The patient is told that the ability to relax is a learned skill, requiring active participation and frequent practice. It is further noted that relaxation is a general coping strategy that the patient may find helpful in dealing with a variety of stressful situations in addition to chemotherapy. The therapist then demonstrates and discusses progressive muscle relaxation training procedures.

Once a patient has become relatively skillful at muscle relaxation, he or she is told that relaxation will be more successful if it is coupled with an effort to focus attention on very relaxing scenes. The therapist asks the patient to describe one or two scenes that the patient finds very pleasant and relaxing to imagine (for example, scenes of distant snow-capped mountains, gentle waves rolling onto a beach, or flowers softly swaying in a breeze). When necessary, the therapist helps the patient embellish the scenes with detail.

Once the patient is able to use relaxation

and guided imagery reasonably well, the chemotherapy session is begun. The nurse enters the room and begins to administer the drugs intravenously. The therapist continues guided imagery instructions throughout treatment. At the close of the session, the patient is told to practice relaxation procedures daily at home and is given a brief set of written relaxation training instructions to follow as an aid. At the next visit, the patient is told that the therapist will no longer be present during chemotherapy, and that he or she should use the relaxation and guided imagery procedures on his or her own.

In an evaluation of this procedure, patients who received relaxation training with guided imagery reported feeling significantly less anxious and less nauseated during chemotherapy. They showed significantly less physiological arousal and reported less anxiety and depression immediately after chemotherapy, and they also reported significantly less severe and protracted nausea later on at home. Nurses who administered the chemotherapy protocol also reported that the patients who had had relaxation training and guided imagery seemed better adjusted to the procedure (Lyles et al., 1982).

---

treatments (Andersen & Hacker, 1983) such as surgery or chemotherapy and indirectly affected by anxiety or depression, which often reduce sexual desire. Problems among a cancer patient's children are relatively common. Young children may show extreme fear or distress over the parent's prognosis. Older children may find new responsibilities thrust on them and may respond by rebelling. Problems with children may be especially severe if the cancer is one with a hereditary component, since children may blame the parent for putting them at increased risk (Lichtman et al., 1984).

Vocational disruption may occur for patients who have chronic discomfort from cancer or its treatments, and job discrimination against cancer patients has been documented. Difficulties in managing social interactions can result from alterations in physical appearance, disrupting social and recreational activity. An ostomy patient, for example, describes his fear of revolting others:

When I smelled an odor on the bus or subway before the colostomy, I used to feel very annoyed. I'd think that the people were awful, that they didn't take a bath or that they should have gone to the bathroom before traveling. I used to think that they might have odors from what they ate. I used to be terribly annoyed; to me it seemed that they were filthy, dirty. Of course, at the least opportunity I used to change my seat and if I couldn't, it used to go against my grain. So naturally, I believe that the young people feel the same way about me if I smell. (Goffman, 1963, p. 34)

To summarize, then, cancer creates a wide variety of rehabilitative problems, including physical disability, family and marital disruptions, sexual difficulties, self-esteem problems, social and recreational disruptions, and general psychological distress. Therefore a wide variety of rehabilitative services have developed for the cancer patient.

Types of Rehabilitative Interventions

Rehabilitative interventions for cancer patients generally fall into three categories: pharmacologic interventions, behavioral interventions, and psychotherapeutic interventions.

Pharmacologic Interventions   Pharmacologic management of the cancer patient typically centers on one of four issues: nausea and vomiting induced by chemotherapy; anorexia and other eating difficulties; emotional disorders such as depression and anxiety; and pain. Nausea and vomiting are usually treated by the use of drugs. Marijuana has proven to be particularly successful in combating the nausea and vomiting associated with chemotherapy, and drugs such as Thorazine, Valium, and Compazine also help. Anorexia is treated most successfully through dietary supplements, since appetite stimulants do not seem to work very well. Depression and anxiety may be managed pharmacologically with the help of such drugs as Valium, and pain may be managed by using morphine, methadone, or antianxiety drugs and antidepressants (Holland & Rowland, 1981).

Behavioral Interventions   Behavioral and cognitive-behavioral approaches to the management of cancer patients have focused on pain, appetite control, side effects associated with chemotherapy and radiation therapy, and treatment of cancer itself (Holland & Rowland, 1981; Spiegel & Bloom, in press). Relaxation therapy, hypnosis, cognitive-reappraisal techniques, visual imaging, and self-hypnosis have all proven to be at least somewhat useful in the management of pain due to cancer and discomfort caused by chemotherapy and radiation. An example of one such approach is presented in Box 15.3. Cognitive-behavioral techniques that urge cancer patients to try to control the cancer itself are somewhat more controversial. Simonton and Simonton (1975), for example, sug-

gested that cancer patients can help prevent a recurrence of cancer by using imagery. They maintained that such techniques as visualizing the white cells engulfing and destroying the diseased cancer cells can have a direct effect on the spread of cancer. There is currently no evidence to support this claim.

Pain is a relatively common problem among cancer patients and often provokes anxiety or depression, which, as we saw in Chapter 11, may exacerbate its severity. Although painkillers remain the primary method of treating cancer-related pains, increasingly, behavioral interventions are being adopted in an effort to reduce pain and its associated adverse psychological side effects (Davis, Vasterling, Bransfield, & Burish, 1987). Behavioral intervention appears to be more appropriate for chronic pain associated with cancer than for acute pain.

Psychotherapeutic Interventions   In contrast to pharmacological and behavioral interventions, which are directed primarily toward reducing the physical discomfort and other side effects associated with cancer and its treatment, psychotherapeutic interventions—including individual psychotherapy, group therapy, family therapy, and cancer support groups—attempt to meet the psychosocial and informational needs of cancer patients. Patients seeking individual therapy after a diagnosis of cancer are most likely to have one of four problems: (1) significant anxiety, depression, or suicidal thoughts; (2) central nervous system dysfunctions produced by the illness and treatment, such as the inability to concentrate; (3) specific problems that have arisen as a consequence of the illness, its management, or family dynamics; or (4) previously existing psychological problems that have been exacerbated by cancer (Holland, 1973).

Individual therapy with cancer patients typically follows a crisis-intervention format rather than an intensive psychotherapy model. That is, therapists working with cancer patients try to focus on the specific issues faced by the patient rather than attempting a more general, probing, long-term analysis of the patient's psyche. The most common issues arising in individual therapy are fear of recurrence, pain, or death; fear of loss of organs as a consequence of additional surgeries; interference with valued activities; practical difficulties, such as job discrimination and problems with dating and social relationships; and communication problems with families.

Family therapy represents another commonly used option for cancer patients. As previously noted, cancers almost always have an impact on other family members; therefore, the family therapy experience provides an opportunity for all family members to share their problems and difficulties in communicating. Additional reasons for the inclusion of family members in therapy is that families can either help or hinder an individual cancer patient's adjustment to illness. By providing social support, the family can smooth the patient's adjustment, whereas a reaction of terror and withdrawal can make the patient's problems more difficult. Issues that commonly arise in family therapy are problems with children, especially adolescents; role changes and increased dependency; and problems of sexual functioning (Wellisch, 1981).

A number of cancer service programs have developed to help the patient adjust to problems posed by a particular cancer. Several of these are sponsored by the American Cancer Society; they include Reach to Recovery for breast cancer patients and groups for patients who have ostomies. These programs provide either a one-on-one or a group experience in which individuals can discuss some of their common problems. Reach to Recovery is run on what is termed a peer counseling approach, in which a well-adjusted breast cancer patient acts as an adviser to a newly diagnosed patient. Ostomy groups constitute one of a growing number of self-help organiza-

tions in which groups of patients with the same disorder discuss the problems and issues they face. Although the self-help experience currently appeals to a fairly limited portion of the cancer population, it appears to be beneficial for those who try it. A possible reason is that the self-help format presents patients with an array of potential coping techniques from which they can draw skills that fit in with their particular styles and problems (Taylor, Falke et al., 1986; Wortman & Dunkel-Schetter, 1979).

ARTHRITIS

As noted in Chapter 2, there is a set of diseases known as autoimmune diseases, in which the body falsely identifies its own tissue as foreign matter and attacks it. The most prevalent of these autoimmune diseases is arthritis, and we will consider it both because of its relationship to immune functioning and because it is one of the most common of the chronic diseases.

Arthritis means inflammation of a joint; it refers to more than eighty diseases that attack the joints or other connective tissues. About 37 million people in the United States (about one in every seven people) are afflicted with arthritis severe enough to require medical care. Although it is rarely fatal, arthritis ranks second only to heart disease as the most widespread chronic disease in the United States today.

The severity of and prognosis for arthritis depend on the type; the disease ranges from a barely noticeable and occasional problem to a crippling, chronic condition. The three major forms of arthritis are rheumatoid arthritis, osteoarthritis, and gout.

Rheumatoid Arthritis

Rheumatoid arthritis affects approximately 5 million people in the United States and is the

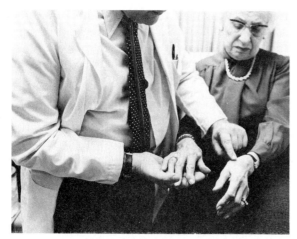

More than 5 million people in the United States have rheumatoid arthritis, and it is especially common among older women. The frustration of being unable to do things that one used to do and the need to be dependent on others are problems for this group.

most crippling form. The disease strikes primarily the 40-to-60 age group, although it can attack people of any age. It usually affects the small joints of the hands and feet and also the wrists, knees, ankles, and neck. In mild cases, only one or two joints are involved, but sometimes the disease becomes widespread. In severe cases, there may be inflammation of the heart muscle, blood vessels, and tissues that are just beneath the skin. Rheumatoid arthritis may be brought on by an autoimmune process: Agents of the immune system that are supposed to protect the body against invaders instead attack the thin membranes surrounding the joints. This attack leads to inflammation, stiffness, and pain. If not controlled, the bone and surrounding muscle tissue of the joint may be completely destroyed. Almost half of the victims recover completely, nearly half remain somewhat arthritic, and about 10% are severely disabled.

The exact cause of rheumatoid arthritis is unknown. At one time, psychologists speculated that there might be a "rheumatoid arthritis personality." This personality type was characterized as perfectionistic, depressed, and restricted in emotional expression, especially the expression of anger. Though a number of studies investigated these possible antecedents of rheumatoid arthritis, most contained methodological flaws. Studies that have related personality characteristics to arthritis are more reasonably explained as reactions to the disease, rather than causes of it (Anderson, Bradley, Young, McDaniel, & Wise, 1985; see Taylor & Aspinwall, 1990).

Efforts to relate stress to the onset or course of rheumatoid arthritis have also been inconclusive. The literature has, however, consistently identified disturbed interpersonal relationships as major stressful events among rheumatoid arthritis patients, and it is possible that these events figure into the development of the disease (Anderson et al., 1985). In a careful review of the literature, Anderson et al. (1985) concluded that the role of psychological factors in the development of rheumatoid arthritis remains unclear, although psychological factors do appear to play an important role in its course. Rheumatoid arthritis patients have higher levels of electrical activity in the muscle tissue near their affected joints. They show greater increases and slower returns to baseline EMG (electromyograph) levels in response to stress, and they show increases in electrodermal activity in response to stress. It is likely that future research will focus on the potential of psychoimmunologic mediation of these effects (Anderson et al., 1985). For example, one study examined the relationship between life stress among rheumatoid arthritis patients and lymphocyte alterations and found that minor stressful events were related to the proportion of circulating B cells, that psychological distress was inversely related to the proportion of circulating T cells, and that major life events were associated with lowered T helper/T suppressor cell ratios (Zautra et al., 1989). Such results suggest that stressful events of various kinds can exert disruptive effects on the immune system, which may, in turn, exacerbate the disease.

Treatments to arrest or control rheumatoid arthritis include aspirin (which relieves both pain and inflammation), rest, and supervised exercise. Surgery is rarely needed, and hospitalization is necessary only in extreme cases or for extreme pain or flare-ups. More recently, psychologists have explored the possibility of cognitive-behavioral treatments for rheumatoid arthritis. In one study (O'Leary, Shoor, Lorig, & Holman, 1988), rheumatoid arthritis patients were randomized into a cognitive-behavioral treatment that taught skills in managing stress, pain, and symptoms of the disease, or they received an arthritis self-help book containing useful information about arthritis self-management. The cognitive-behavioral treatment was designed to increase perceptions of self-efficacy with respect to the disease. Results indicated that those in the cognitive-behavioral treatment experienced reduced pain and joint inflammation and improved psychosocial functioning. The degree to which people improved was correlated with the degree of self-efficacy enhancement, suggesting that the enhancement of perceived self-efficacy to manage the disease was responsible for the positive effects. There was no difference in the number or function of T-cell subsets, however.

As just noted, one way of controlling rheumatoid arthritis is through exercise. Yet, as is the case with all forms of exercise, adherence to exercise recommendations among arthritic patients is low. To enhance adherence to exercise for arthritic hands and fingers, Waggoner and LeLieuvre (1981) developed a hand exerciser with an electronic counter and visual display to provide feedback on the number of exercises completed. Although the method was examined in only a small number of patients, results were promising. The number of nonadherent patients was reduced and the amount of nonadherence exhibited was also reduced substantially. Apparently, just seeing their accomplishments visually displayed was an incentive for these patients to continue. Thus, the use of specific feedback through a visual display may improve adherence to exercise regimens, at least in this population, perhaps also by increasing perceptions of self-efficacy.

Self-efficacy may be important more generally to rheumatoid arthritis patients. The frustration of being unable to do things that one used to do and the need to be dependent on others are the main problems reported by patients. Consequently, interventions that have the potential to increase self-sufficiency are promising not only for improving functional status but also for improving psychosocial adjustment (Cornelissen, Rasker, & Valkenburg, 1988). As one patient in such an intervention put it, "I went from thinking about arthritis as a terrible burden that had been thrust upon me to something I could control and manage. I redefined it for myself. It's no longer a tragedy, it's an inconvenience."

Another form of rheumatoid arthritis is juvenile rheumatoid arthritis. Its causes and symptoms are similar to those of the adult form, but the victims are children between the ages of 2 and 5. Among them, the disease flares up periodically until puberty. The disease is rare and affects girls four times as often as boys. With treatment, most children recover. However, there is a juvenile form of rheumatoid disease that can be severely crippling and can lead to extensive psychological and physical problems for its sufferers, including missed school and participation in few social activities (Billings, Moos, Miller, & Gottlieb, 1987). Social support from family members is also important in helping the juvenile rheumatoid arthritis patient adjust successfully to the disorder.

Osteoarthritis

Osteoarthritis afflicts at least 10 million Americans. It develops when the smooth lining of a joint, known as the articular cartilage, begins to crack or wear away due to overuse, injury, or other causes. Thus, the disease tends to affect the weight-bearing joints: the hips, knees, and spine. As the cartilage deteriorates, the joint may become inflamed, stiff, and painful. The disease afflicts many elderly people and some athletes.

With proper treatment, osteoarthritis can be managed through self-care. Treatment includes keeping one's weight down, obtaining proper exercise, and taking aspirin. Occasionally, use of more potent pain relievers, anti-inflammatory drugs, or steroids is needed. Those who cope with the pain of osteoarthritis through active coping efforts, spontaneous pain control efforts, and "rational thinking" appear to cope better with the disease (Keefe et al., 1987).

Gout

A third form of arthritis is **gout.** About 1 million Americans suffer from gout, and it is ten times more prevalent in males than in females. This condition is caused by a buildup of uric acid in the body due to the kidneys' inability to excrete the acid in the urine. Consequently, the uric acid forms crystals, which may become lodged in the joints. The area most likely to be affected is the big toe (because the blood supply there is too small to carry away the uric acid crystals). The joint then becomes inflamed, causing severe pain. Occasionally, the uric acid crystals can become lodged in the kidney itself, causing kidney failure. The exact cause of the buildup of uric acid is unknown. A genetic component is believed to play a role, and the condition can be triggered by stress as well as by certain foods. Other causal factors include infections and some antibiotics and diuretics.

Gout can be managed by limiting the intake of alcohol and certain foods and by maintaining proper weight, exercise, and fluid intake. Aspirin is not used, as it slows the removal of uric acid. For severe cases, anti-inflammatory drugs or drugs that control uric acid metabolism may be used. Gout can usually be controlled; when left untreated, however, it can lead to death from kidney disease, high blood pressure, coronary artery disease, or stroke (Kunz, 1982; National Health Education Committee, 1976; Rubenstein & Federman, 1983).

To summarize, arthritis is our second most prevalent chronic disease. Although it rarely kills its victims, it causes substantial pain and discomfort, creating problems of management. The self-care regimen of arthritis patients centers largely around pain control, dietary control, and exercise; therefore the health habits and issues of adherence that we have discussed throughout this book are clearly important in the effective management of arthritis.

Summary

1. The immune system is the surveillance system of the body that guards against foreign invaders. It involves a number of complex processes, comprising humoral immunity and cell-mediated immunity.

2. Studies suggest that stressors, such as academic exams and stressful interpersonal relationships, including bereavement, divorce, separation, and caregiving, can compromise immune functioning.

3. Negative emotions such as depression or anxiety may also compromise immune functioning. Particular coping methods may help buffer the immune system against adverse changes due to stress.

4. Studies have evaluated the potential of conditioned immune responses and interventions such as relaxation and stress management as clinical efforts to augment immune functioning in the face of stress.

5. Acquired Immune Deficiency Syndrome (AIDS) was first diagnosed in the United States in 1981. It results from the human immunodeficiency virus (HIV) and is marked by the presence of unusual opportunistic infectious diseases that result when the immune system, especially the helper T cells, have been compromised in their functioning.

6. Gay men and intravenous needle–sharing drug abusers are at primary risk for AIDS in the United States. Although substantial changes in risk behaviors have been seen in the gay community, behavior change may prove to be insufficient to stop the spread of the virus. Even fewer changes have been noted in the drug-abusing community and in adolescents and young adults. The need for effective education and intervention with at-risk populations is paramount.

7. Thousands of people live with HIV+ infection or AIDS for months or years. Consequently, studies are currently being undertaken to assess the psychosocial problems that these individuals face and to develop interventions that may ameliorate these problems.

8. Cancer is a set of more than 100 diseases marked by malfunctioning DNA and rapid cell growth and proliferation. Research investigations have attempted to relate psychosocial factors to the onset and progression of cancer. To date, results suggest a potential role for helplessness, depression, and repression of emotions, especially in the progression of cancer, but as yet results are not definitive.

9. Cancer can produce a range of physical and psychosocial problems, including surgical scarring, the need for prostheses, avoidance or rejection by the social network, vocational disruption, and adverse psychological responses such as depression. Increasingly, behavioral and psychotherapeutic interventions are being used successfully to manage these problems.

10. Arthritis, involving inflammation of the joints, affects about 37 million people in the United States. Rheumatoid arthritis is the most crippling form. Stress appears to exacerbate the disease.

11. Interventions involving cognitive-behavioral techniques designed to help people manage pain effectively and increase perceptions of self-efficacy have proven helpful in alleviating some of the discomfort and psychosocial difficulties associated with arthritis.

KEY TERMS

AIDS (Acquired Immune Deficiency Syndrome)
AIDS antibody testing
AIDS-Related Complex (ARC)
anticipatory nausea
arthritis
autoimmune disorders
carcinogens
chemotherapy
gout

homophobia
human immunodeficiency virus (HIV)
immunocompetence
immunocompromise
immunosuppression
lymphocyte suppression
osteoarthritis
phagocytosis
rheumatoid arthritis

PART 6

TOWARD THE FUTURE

16

HEALTH PSYCHOLOGY: CHALLENGES FOR THE FUTURE

In the last two decades, health psychology has made dramatic and impressive advances. The last chapter first highlights some of the research accomplishments and future directions in which the field is likely to move, with reference to health promotion, stress and its management, use of health services, patient-practitioner communication, management of pain, management of chronic and terminal illness, and causes and consequences of specific health disorders.

We then turn to general issues facing the field of health psychology. Some of these will be posed by medicine. As the practice of medicine changes, as patterns of disease and disorders shift, and as new methods of treatment develop, so inevitably must health psychology change. Other challenges are internal to the discipline and represent coming trends in the research and practice of health psychology.

THE RESEARCH AGENDA OF HEALTH PSYCHOLOGY

Each of the subareas of health psychology described in this volume has already made important contributions to the field. Most of these developments have occurred within the last 15 to 20 years. In building on these advantages, each area has also highlighted a likely agenda for the future.

Health Promotion

In a large part, because of the media attention that has been focused on risk factors such as smoking, diet, and exercise, Americans have made substantial gains in altering their poor health habits. Many people have successfully stopped smoking, and many have reduced their consumption of high-cholesterol and high-fat foods. Although alcohol consumption patterns remain largely unchanged, exercise has increased (Matarazzo, 1984). Clearly, most people know that they need to practice good health behaviors and many have tried to develop or change them on their own. Not everyone is successful, however, and therein lies the potential for health psychology to make a contribution.

Because of changing patterns of disease and disorder, preventive health behavior has become one of the critical ways to combat disease and disorder in the twentieth century. Our research efforts have delineated when people are most likely to practice preventive health behaviors and which people are most likely to do so. Correspondingly, research has clearly demonstrated how complex health behaviors are. They are relatively autonomous and unstable, making intervention a difficult and complex process.

An array of cognitive and behavioral techniques have been applied to health-habit change. Alcoholism, smoking, obesity, poor diet, lack of exercise, and accident prevention have all been attacked by health psychologists with varying degrees of intensity and with modest amounts of success. In the last decade, the clearest problem to come into view is behavior change maintenance—the need to help people stick with their better health practices. Perhaps the most important development in the modification of preventive health behaviors has been the articulation of relapse prevention technologies to help people avoid going back to their health-compromising ways.

What can we expect to see in the future in the area of health promotion? Increasingly, we will see efforts to identify the most potent and effective elements of behavior change programs and to incorporate them into cost-effective, efficient interventions that reach the largest number of people simultaneously. In particular, we can expect to see the design of interventions for mass consumption at the community level, the workplace level, and the schools. By reaching people through the institutions in which they live and work, and by integrating health behavior change materials

into existing resources, we may approximate the goal of modifying the most people's behavior in the most efficient and cost-effective manner.

By integrating health behavior change programs in existing community resources, we may also deal with another problem of health behavior change: Most people know they should practice good health habits, but they do not seek help in changing their health behavior. They use whatever intuitive strategies for behavior change they hold, which may not be as systematically related to positive outcomes as those developed by health psychologists. Accordingly, bringing interventions to people through the places where they live and work may attract those who are motivated to change their behavior but are unable to do so on their own. Demonstrating to the public that health psychologists can achieve behavior change may increase the use of our programs and techniques.

As medicine increasingly pays attention to risk factors for chronic illness, the at-risk role will be increasingly important. Individuals who are identified early as at risk for particular disorders may need to learn how to cope psychologically with their risk status and how to change their modifiable risk-relevant behaviors. Psychologists can aid substantially in both these tasks. Moreover, a conscientious examination of populations at risk for developing particular disorders can be useful in identifying additional risk or promoting factors for these disorders. Not everyone who is at risk for an illness will develop it. By identifying those individuals who do and do not, further precipitating or promoting factors of illness can be identified.

Preventing poor health habits from ever developing will continue to be an important priority for health psychology. **Behavioral immunization** programs are already in existence for smoking, drug abuse, and, in some cases, diet. As we have seen, preadolescent children can be exposed to antismoking campaigns before they ever start smoking, and these programs appear to be at least somewhat successful in keeping some adolescents from undertaking the habit. Behavioral immunization for other health habits—including safe sex and condom use, diet, seat belt use, and alcohol consumption—may also be successful. In such ventures, we must reach the captive populations in the elementary schools if we are to make a dent many years later when problems often develop. For some health habits, we may need to start even earlier and initiate behavioral pediatric programs to teach parents how to reduce the risks of accidents in the home, how to practice good safety habits in automobiles, and how to practice good health habits such as exercise, proper diet, regular immunization and medical checkups, and regular dental care.

Our efforts to concentrate on the young, however, must not blind us to the importance of the health promotion needs of older people as well, including the elderly. The rapid aging of the population means that within the next 20 years, we will have the largest elderly cohort ever seen in this and other Western countries. This cohort can be an ill one, placing a drain on medical and psychological services, or it can be a healthy, active one. Through appropriate planning and the development of necessary interventions, we may help the elderly achieve the highest level of functioning possible, through programs that emphasize diet, exercise, and other health habits (Ory & Williams, 1989; Riley, Matarazzo, & Baum, 1987; Rowe & Kahn, 1987).

The importance of health promotion is evident, yet in recent years it has taken on the status of an ideology, with exaggerated claims of the importance of certain health habits far out of proportion to their actual impact on health. Health habits can come to be a tyrannical aspect of life (Becker, 1986). As Mark Twain once grumbled, "The only way to keep your health is to eat what you don't want, drink what you don't like, and do what you'd

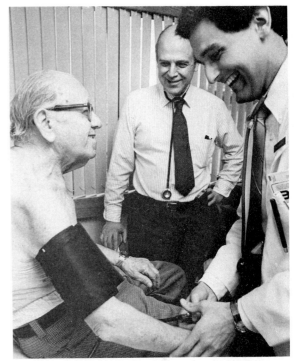

The health needs of the elderly will take on increasing importance with the aging of the population. Helping the elderly achieve a high level of functioning through interventions that emphasize diet, exercise, and other health habits is a high priority for the future.

rather not." Clearly, as we make the case for the importance of health behavior, we must also recognize that healthy habits are but one part of a full and meaningful life, an important part surely, but not an aspect of life that should govern activities beyond reason.

Keeping this goal in mind suggests the need for some reorientation of our health-promotion strategies. First, mortality is currently overemphasized relative to morbidity. As McGuire (1984) notes, morbidity may ultimately be more important, inasmuch as those who are disabled or who live diminished lives through compromising health problems such as alcoholism or chronic illness can make their own and others' lives miserable for long periods of time. Reorienting the focus of health promotion toward reducing the period of morbidity, rather than delaying mortality, may ultimately do more for quality of life (Fries, Green, & Levine, 1989). In a similar vein, we need to consider the age at which most chronic health problems begin. Although cardiovascular disease and cancer are the major causes of death in this country, they strike primarily older people. In contrast, accidents, suicides, and homocides are more common among younger people. Perhaps we should put greater weight on understanding and solving the problems associated with early mortality.

Second, we may need to reorient our thinking about risk factors for illness. As Becker (1986) has noted, going after all risk factors tends to trivialize health promotion by setting an impossible agenda both for health policymakers and for individuals. What we need to do is identify and focus attention on the major risk factors, such as smoking, that account for the majority of deaths and disabilities. Finally, we may need to give greater weight to the positive factors that may reduce the period of morbidity or delay mortality due to serious illness. For example, although eliminating heart disease and cancer would lengthen lives by several years, marriage is estimated to add 10 years to a man's life and 4 years to a woman's life. McGuire (1984) suggests facetiously that health psychologists could make a giant leap forward by going after this health-related factor and opening a marriage bureau. The point is well-taken. Focusing on early causes of mortality and morbidity, major risk factors, and health-promoting factors that exert the strongest reductions on morbidity and mortality may ultimately prove to be the cornerstones of a more practical health promotion philosophy developed on the basis of health psychology's data.

The problems of preventive health behavior and a true philosophy of health promotion can never be adequately addressed until a focus on health promotion becomes an integral part of medicine and medical practice as well. Although some progress in this direction has been made, we are still far away from having a health care system that is oriented toward health promotion. As noted in Chapter 3, there is as yet no formal diagnostic process for identifying and targeting preventive health behaviors on an individual basis. In the future, we may begin to see practicing physicians integrate prevention into their daily practice with asymptomatic individuals.

If this badly needed step occurs, it will have important ramifications for health psychologists' interventions directed to preventive health behavior. First, medicine's acknowledgment of the importance of prevention will lend weight to the value of psychological interventions designed to modify health behaviors. Second, physicians' offices or clinics may come to be settings in which effective programs for health behavior change can be initiated. Third, medicine's acknowledgment of the importance of health promotion and primary prevention can lay the groundwork for a cooperative enterprise between medicine and psychology at a level heretofore unseen. As partners, psychologists and physicians can develop the media interventions, community interventions, and individual interventions necessary to get people to modify their health behaviors. Health psychologists can serve medicine even further by developing programs to ensure that people never form problematic health habits in the first place. In this way, the future of health psychology will be not only shaped by the future of medicine, but health psychology may shape the future of medicine as well.

In developing a program of health promotion, we must not lose sight of the fact that individual health behavior changes alone may not substantially improve the health of the general population. What is needed is individual change coupled with social change (Slater & Carlton, 1985). Although the United States spends more on health care than any other country in the world, we have neither the longest life expectancy nor the lowest infant mortality rate. As many as 37 million working Americans have no health insurance at all. Although Medicaid, instituted in 1965, was designed to help the poor achieve high-quality health care, in many states it has eroded to the point where families with poverty-level incomes are not eligible for benefits. These surprising points are best accounted for by the fact that we have a two-tiered medical system and are increasingly moving in the direction of strengthening and maintaining two tiers. Disproportionately, high-quality and high-technology care go to the well-to-do and not to the poor. As long as socioeconomic differences influence the ability to get health care, the situation will not change appreciably. A true philosophy of health promotion involves not

only reorienting medical practice to the issues of health promotion and primary prevention but also making preventive, as well as treatment-based, health care readily available to all members of the society.

Stress and Its Management

Substantial advances in stress research have been made in the last two decades. Physiological, cognitive, motivational, and behavioral consequences of stress have been clearly identified. Moreover, the controversy over whether stress is "out there" or "in the head" has virtually been resolved. On the one hand, stress is clearly the result of the psychological appraisal of an event or situation. On the other hand, certain events and situations are more likely to be stressful, such as those that

Stressful living situations with noise, crowding, and crime take a particular toll on vulnerable populations, such as children, the elderly, and the poor. Increasingly, research must focus on interventions to alleviate the impact of these events.

are uncontrollable, overwhelming, ambiguous, unexpected, and negative.

Particular advances have been made in research on environmental and occupational stress. Stressors like noise or crowding do not show consistently adverse effects but do appear to adversely affect vulnerable populations. Thus, the health needs of children, the elderly, and the poor have taken special priority in the study of stress and its reduction. Occupational stress researchers have clearly identified many of the job characteristics that are tied to stress. As a consequence, promising workplace interventions have been developed to redesign jobs or reduce on-the-job stressors.

Nonetheless, the demographics of stress may be offsetting whatever concessions can or might be made in the workplace. The majority of American families find that both parents must work in order to make ends meet. Yet, like all families, the two-career family must absorb an extra month a year of housework, home activities, and child care. Typically, this extra month a year is taken on by women (Hochschild, 1989; see Scarr, Phillips, & McCartney, 1989). Moreover, increasing numbers of adult children have responsibility for their aging parents, and these responsibilities, too, more frequently fall to women than men. These trends put the adult American female population under unprecedented degrees of stress, patterns that may be increasingly reflected in other countries as well. One consequence is that women are sick more than men (Verbrugge, 1985, 1990). Additional health and mental health consequences, as well as effective solutions to these dilemmas, have yet to fully emerge (see Repetti, Matthews, & Waldrun, 1989).

What can we expect to see in the future? Research should continue to be focused on those populations at particular risk for stress-related disorders in an attempt to reduce or offset their stressful circumstances. The adverse effects of major stressful events, such as earthquakes, hurricanes, and other disasters, will continue to occupy attention. In theory, knowledge of how people adjust successfully to stressful events can be translated into interventions to help those coping unsuccessfully to cope more successfully (Taylor, 1983, 1989).

Perhaps the greatest advances in stress research will come from research on the psychophysiology of stress, particularly the links between stress and corticosteroid functioning, temperamental differences in sympathetic nervous system activity, and factors influencing the release of endogenous opioid peptides and their links to the immune system. Through these studies, we may begin to identify the conditions under which and the pathways by which stress exerts adverse effects on health.

One of the most significant advances in stress research is the discovery that social support can buffer stress. For example, intervention studies with disabled, chronically ill, and recovering populations show that social support can have positive effects on both physical and psychological outcomes. These findings suggest that we need to do more to help people draw effectively on this important resource. First, we should think of social support as a resource in primary prevention. Socializing people to build on their social ties is critical at this time in our social history. The two-job family has less time for meeting social support needs, and the increasing mobility of the population leaves fewer opportunities to build long-term ties and friendships. Families have fewer children and are less likely to live in extended families, and they may belong to fewer clubs or have fewer long-term opportunities for social contact. Even children, who historically spent many hours with at least one parent, may now see parents less than children once did, instead developing ties with childcare workers (cf. Scarr et al., 1989). Fostering social support systems to offset the trends that isolate individuals should be a high priority for prevention.

In addition, through education and what we already know of the benefits of social support, it may be possible to teach people to better provide support for others. We know that difficult and stressful relationships can adversely affect health and mental health, just as positive social relations can protect against those outcomes. Teaching what constitutes effective social support may, then, be an educational opportunity for the future.

Self-help groups are one possible way of providing social support for those who otherwise might lack it. At least 6 million people are currently attempting to deal with some specific problem through self-help groups. Through this format, people can discuss a common problem with each other and try to help each other work it out. Once oriented primarily around particular illnesses such as cancer or particular health problems such as obesity, these groups are becoming increasingly available for those going through divorce, the loss of a child, and other specific stressful events. Despite growing participation, self-help groups continue to appeal disproportionately to only a small fraction of the population, most notably relatively well-educated, white, middle-class women. If self-help groups are to be a vehicle for social support in the future, ways must be developed to broaden their appeal more generally for the population.

Use of Health Services

Decades of research have indicated that people who are ill and those who are treated for illness are frequently not the same individuals. For financial or cultural reasons, many ill people do not find their way into the health care delivery system, and a substantial portion of people who seek and receive treatment have complaints that are of largely psychological interest.

Increasingly, we are understanding when and how well people detect changes in their body. This knowledge may ultimately be useful for teaching people how to discriminate important symptoms and/or to monitor their chronic conditions, such as hypertension or diabetes. It should be noted, however, that symptom detection requires considerably more research before such applications are warranted. In addition, psychological models of health services that stress health beliefs and social barriers to seeking treatment may provide a basis for interventions to promote the appropriate use of health services.

The appropriate use of health services assumes increasing urgency in the context of current changes in its technology and costs. Medicine increasingly is high technology, and high technology is expensive. At over $500 billion a year, the annual bill for health care services is large and growing. The potent factors affecting the use of health services in the future may well be the solutions imposed on the health care system by the government and third-party providers to contain costs. Such solutions as preferred provider systems and strict guidelines regarding treatment such as DRGs (see Chapter 10) will set the standards for care and costs. Whether this leads to more appropriate use of services and promotes satisfaction with health care services remains to be seen.

Patient-Practitioner Communication

Historically, medicine has been concerned with the arts of diagnosis and treatment. Partly due to the efforts of health psychologists, the art of communication is increasingly coming to be recognized as important. It does little good to diagnose a disorder correctly and prescribe appropriate treatment if the patient cannot or will not follow through on treatment recommendations. Communication issues are critical in this process. Research has shown that people judge the quality of their medical care heavily on the quality of communication they have with their practitioner, and the probability that they will bring suit against the practitioner is also affected by the communication process. Perhaps most important is the fact that communication influences the degree of adherence to prescribed treatment. Increasingly, we are realizing that medical problems ranging from drug errors in the chronically ill and the elderly (e.g., Green, Mullen, & Stainbrook, 1986; Green & Simons-Morton, 1988) to inability to control diabetes or hypertension effectively can be traced directly to the patient's willingness and ability to adhere to the treatment regimen. Moreover, as preventive health behaviors become increasingly important in the achievement of good health and in secondary prevention with the chronically ill, the fact that 97% of patients fail to adhere properly to lifestyle recommendations takes on added significance. Finding effective treatments to improve adherence is only half the battle. Communicating it effectively and persuasively is the other half.

Trends within medical care suggest that the problem of patient-practitioner communication is likely to get worse, not better. Increasingly, patients are receiving their medical care through prepaid colleague-centered services rather than through private, fee-for-service, client-centered practices. As noted in Chapters 9 and 10, these structural changes can improve the quality of medical care but sacrifice the quality of communication. The probability that communication suffers in these settings is strengthened by the fact that the clientele served by prepaid plans is disproportionately poor, poorly educated, and non-English-speaking. Although the well-to-do can pay for emotionally satisfying care, the poor increasingly cannot. Health settings that rob patients of feelings of control can breed anger or depression, motivate people not to return for care, and possibly even contribute to a physiological state conducive to illness or its exacerbation. Thus, there is an expanding role for psychologists in the development and the design of future health services. In particular, the beneficial changes that have been intro-

duced into children's wards of hospitals may provide a model for adult care as well.

A main agenda for the area of patient-practitioner communication over the next decade is to develop training programs to teach health practitioners to communicate more effectively. At a minimum, such programs should include the basic qualities of communication and courtesy that can be easily incorporated into interactions with patients without being time-consuming. The effective communication of information about treatment regimen and self-management goals requires special consideration in this training. The health psychologist's role as health educator and the integration of health psychology into the curricula of medical schools as well as schools of nursing, social work, and public health will help in the achievement of this goal (cf. Eisenberg, 1988).

Perhaps more important, budgeting roles and time for more extensive patient education will become increasingly critical. The current high level of chronic illness, coupled with projected increases over the next 50 years due to the aging of the population, makes it essential that people understand the importance of appropriate health behaviors, particularly those that reduce their risk. Nurses and patient educators are among those whose jobs will be substantially devoted to this type of effort. The integration of this educational effort into standard medical practice will be an important advance in helping to bring about an orientation toward health promotion in traditional medicine.

Management of Pain

Working in concert with a variety of other disciplines, health psychology has made remarkable breakthroughs in the last decade in understanding pain and its treatment. After lying dormant for many years, two critical research discoveries, the development of the gate theory of pain and the discovery of endorphins, led to an explosion in basic research.

Partly because of these breakthroughs, the technology of pain control has also made substantial advances over the last decade. Three trends are especially significant. First, there has been a shift away from dependence on expensive pharmacological and invasive surgical pain control techniques that create side effects, including addiction or loss of sensation, respectively. Instead, practitioners are increasingly using behavioral techniques such as cognitive-behavioral methods, relaxation, and biofeedback that do not have these unfortunate consequences. Second, the responsibility for pain control has shifted from the practitioner to co-management between patient and practitioner. This is an important psychological shift in that it gives patients a sense of participation in and control over their situation. It is also an important treatment shift in that it makes some patients able to reduce their pain without the extreme dependence on the medical system that traditional pain management techniques required and fostered. Third, the development of pain centers has been critical in bringing together all that is known about pain management techniques. Chronic pain patients are no longer dependent on the particular technologies that happen to be available at their local clinic or hospital. Rather, they can use pain clinics, knowing that all technologies potentially useful in treating their disorders will be available.

As just noted, beliefs in self-efficacy are clearly crucial to the success of pain management techniques. Similarly, control-based interventions have been particularly useful in the management of treatment-induced discomfort. It is becoming a matter of course in most hospitals to prepare patients thoroughly prior to their operations for the aftereffects of surgery. Increasingly, the same procedures are being adopted for other unpleasant medical procedures. These developments are very important, not only because they represent in-

creasingly widespread use of psychological techniques in combating discomfort, but also because they tacitly underscore the patient's role as co-manager in the illness and treatment process.

Management of Chronic Illness

As chronic illness has become our major health problem, its physical, vocational, social, and psychological consequences have been increasingly recognized. Although a number of specific programs have been initiated to deal with particular problems posed by chronic illness, these efforts are as yet not systematically coordinated or widely available to the majority of chronically ill patients.

A chief goal for health psychologists in the coming years, then, should be to help develop programs to assess quality of life in the chronically ill and to develop cost-effective interventions to improve quality of life. Initial assessment of needs in all domains of life during the acute period is an important step. In addition, supplementing initial assessment with regular needs assessment over the long term can help identify potential problems, such as anxiety or depression, before they fully disrupt the patient's life. More systematic assessment, in turn, can help define further the needs of the chronically ill, pointing to new services that may need to be developed. In the short run, the coordination of existing services within a community can identify and mobilize services to which chronically ill patients can be referred when appropriate.

In the management of specific chronic disorders, there are both accomplishments and gaps in knowledge. As implied earlier, one of the chief remaining tasks is to identify the best ways to gain adherence to multiple treatment goals simultaneously. That is, how does one induce a patient to control diet, alter smoking, manage stress, and get exercise all at the same time? How does one maximize compliance with the often aversive or complex regimens used to treat such diseases as hypertension or diabetes? This will be one of the chief challenges of the future.

Advances in Management of Terminal Illness

The last 20 years have witnessed substantial changes in attitudes toward death and dying. Once taboo topics, death and dying are now more openly discussed in college courses, best-selling books, and social conversation. Health psychology research has been both the cause and an effect of these changing attitudes. Clinicians and researchers have increasingly turned their attention to the needs of the terminally ill, chronicaling both the experience of the dying and the gaps in psychological care that still exist.

In the last decade, the appearance of AIDS as a major health problem has fueled these efforts. The AIDS population is unique, being a large, predominantly male population in the prime of life, that would otherwise be facing the challenges of forming careers and lasting relationships. For this group, dying may be particularly frightening and unexpected, requiring special counseling needs. Moreover, the face of AIDS is quickly changing. New treatments are being developed that keep AIDS patients alive for years. Patients and practitioners now face psychological issues posed by a disease that is intermittently life-threatening, alternating with periods of relatively good health. The disease is also marked by many of the signs of aging, such as loss of sight, deterioration of mental capacity, and loss of energy, creating unique challenges for health psychologists and others in the helping professions to provide effective aid and counseling.

One of the most important developments in terminal care has been the institution of hospices, homelike residential or outpatient programs for the care of the terminally ill. These programs concentrate what is known about the palliative and psychological management of dying people so that individualized care can be developed to serve the particular needs of each patient. A benefit of these programs is that they often constitute a solution midway between hospital care and home care, and, in the best of cases, they can provide the best of both worlds.

Ethical issues surrounding death and dying will increasingly assume importance, including living wills, the patient's right to die, family decision making in death and dying, and euthanasia. If a beginning resolution to these complex issues cannot be found by medical agencies and its allied fields, including health psychology, then the solutions will undoubtedly be imposed externally by the courts.

Specific Health Disorders: Causes and Consequences

In Chapters 14 and 15, we considered several specific disorders and what we know about their causes and management. These disorders illustrate an important point about the directions health psychology research has increasingly assumed over the last decade. We have now identified some of the important factors involved in the development of coronary heart disease, hypertension, stroke, diabetes, AIDS, cancer, and arthritis. In the case of Type A behavior as a risk for coronary heart disease, the potential for hostility is now thought to be the lethal component of the behavior syndrome. It may interact with or be a manifestation of a chronic and potentially genetically based predisposition to respond to stressful events with enhanced sympathetic nervous system activity. In the case of cancer, a number of carcinogens have been identified, as well as psychosocial variables that may promote the development of cancer, once exposure to a carcinogen has already occurred. In the case of AIDS, we know the specific risk behaviors associated with infection and are increasingly recognizing that psychosocial factors may be important in the progression from HIV+ status to a diagnosis of AIDS. Stress has been implicated as an exacerbating factor for hypertension, diabetes, and arthritis.

An important task of future research is to identify the specific psychophysiologic pathways through which psychological and social factors, in conjunction with other risk factors, may lead to the development of these disorders. As these pathways are more precisely delineated, the potential for developing interventions specifically directed to the lethal components of behavioral risk factors will improve. For example, in theory, interventions designed to modify Type A behavior should be most successful if they are targeted toward reducing the potential for hostility rather than other, less lethal components of the Type A behavior syndrome. Similarly, if depression and bereavement continue to be identified as factors that compromise immune functioning, then interventions directed to the adverse effects of those states may reduce the likelihood of illness in the recently bereaved or chronically depressed.

The substantial shift in the population toward the older years poses a challenge for health psychologists to identify now what the important lifestyle problems will be for this population and how they will influence the health of the elderly (Riley et al., 1987). What kinds of living situations will these increasing numbers of elderly people have and what kinds of economic resources will they have available to them? How will this influence their health habits, their level of health, and their ability to seek treatment? How can we evaluate and monitor care in residential treatment settings, such as nursing homes, to guard against the risks of maltreatment (Pillemer, 1988)? As our population ages, we can also expect to see a higher incidence of chronic but not life-threatening conditions like arthritis, osteoporosis, hearing losses, blindness, and fecal and urinary incontinence (Solomon, Judd, Sier, Rubenstein, & Morley,

1988). Some effort to control these disorders must necessarily focus on prevention. For example, the incidence of deafness is rising and not all of the causes of this increase are known. Monitoring sound levels in the workplace and other environments and finding ways to reduce them are two priorities. In the case of arthritis, health psychologists can develop behavioral management techniques that may reduce pain, which may be preferable to current forms of management including drug use, with its consequent side effects.

TRENDS FOR THE FUTURE

The Changing Nature of Medical Practice

Health psychology is, of necessity, responsive to changes in medical practice. A recent and dramatic example is the rising incidence of AIDS, with the corresponding need to monitor and change risk behaviors such as sexual practices and condom use. Basic research that identifies potential psychosocial cofactors in the development of AIDS, such as depression or bereavement, also constitutes a contribution that health psychology can make to the effort to deal with the formidable problem. Developing interventions to help those who test positive for the AIDS virus but who have not yet developed AIDS and those who have AIDS and are facing the possibility of death is another undertaking in which the talents of health psychologists will be very useful. Thus, the nature both of the basic science and of the clinical practice of health psychology must remain responsive to changing features of medicine.

The practice of medicine is also affected by cultural trends, and health psychologists can be useful by anticipating these trends and their implications for medical practice. A recent example is posed by the current enthusiasm for jogging and other "weekend" sports. Although sports medicine has been a subarea of medicine for some time, for many years it was confined largely to the problems of the professional athlete. In recent years, with numerous individuals participating erratically or regularly in sports, the number of sports-related injuries has increased overwhelmingly, necessitating a more detailed and widely used set of technologies for dealing with these injuries.

Another way in which the changing culture will affect the practice of health psychology is through the changing technology of medicine. As medicine has become more technologically complex, it has also become more awesome to many patients. Explaining the purposes of these technologies and using control-enhancing interventions to enable people to feel like active participants in their treatment can help reduce fear. As medical technology grows, it raises complex questions about how it should be used. In the case of a transplant, for example, issues include how to increase the supply of transplantable organs, how to determine appropriate transplant-recipient selection criteria, how to develop commitment across transplant centers to quality of life issues, and how to evaluate the cost-effectiveness of transplantation (Kutner, 1987). Health psychologists will also be involved in the ethical implications of using these technologies. What adverse psychological effects may occur from transplantation, if any? What are the ethics of the donor-recipient relationship? How are a patient's attitudes toward a transplant affected, if at all, by knowledge of the source of a transplant? Will those attitudes have implications for the success of the transplant (Parisi & Katz, 1986)? These kinds of issues have yet to be systematically addressed by health psychologists.

Another trend within medicine that affects health psychology is the movement toward **comprehensive intervention models.** There are already several models that concentrate and coordinate medical and psychological expertise in well-defined areas of medical prac-

tice. One is the pain center, in which all available treatments for pain have been brought together so that individual regimens can be developed for each patient who arrives at the pain center. The hospice is a second model in which palliative management technologies and psychotherapeutic technologies are available to the dying patient. Coordinated residential and outpatient rehabilitation programs for coronary heart disease patients, in which multiple health habits are dealt with simultaneously, constitute a third example. Similar interventions for other chronic diseases such as cancer and AIDS may be developed in the coming years. Coordinated health promotion interventions that make use of multiple communication channels simultaneously and multiple community resources represent a potential though not yet fully realized coordinated intervention for the future. Moving toward coordinated intervention models should provide better care and enhance the credibility of health psychology as a profession, as it increasingly plays a co-management role in these efforts.

Patient Consumerism

Increasing **patient consumerism** among medical patients has implications for health psychology. This trend began in the 1960s and continues to the present day. In part, the trend is due to the increasing incidence of chronic disease. Patients with chronic disease are, almost of necessity, more sophisticated about their illnesses than individuals with acute disorders. Because individuals with chronic diseases have had their diseases longer, they have more familiarity with the vagaries of their own case and they have more experience with treatments. Pressures toward consumerism are also prompted by alterations in informed consent procedures, inspired partly by increases in malpractice litigation. Increasingly, patients must be even more fully informed about the potential side effects and

Patient consumerism has increased over the last few decades. While many patients welcome an increased role in their health care, other patients find the consumer role confusing and burdensome. Health psychologists can help patients learn how to ask questions and get more information, so that they can be informed participants in their own care.

problems associated with treatments. Of necessity, therefore, they are pushed into a more active stance vis-à-vis their illness than they may desire. Moreover, as medical technology has become more complex, there are more treatment options for more diseases. As a consequence, patients are often called on to assume responsibility in the decision-making process (see Levy, Herberman, Lee, Lippman, & d'Angelo, 1989; Wagener & Taylor, 1986). All these changes that produce consumer behavior strongly challenge the traditional patient and practitioner roles.

Consumerism undermines the absolute authority of the physician in the decision-making process. It may also put patients in a role they are unprepared to accept. Some patients may feel uncomfortable adopting an active stance vis-à-vis their illness and others who may be willing to adopt the consumer role may not know how to do so effectively. Thus, one role the health psychologist can increasingly play is acting as a specialist in this communication process. Health psychologists can train patients to ask questions and get more information about their illness (Greenfield, Kaplan, & Ware, 1984). Health psychologists can help physicians present information effectively to patients and enhance patients' feelings of control in the decision-making process (DiMatteo & DiNicola, 1982).

Systematic Documentation of Treatment Effectiveness

An important professional goal of health psychology for the future is the continued documentation of the **treatment effectiveness** of health psychology's technologies. We know that our behavioral, cognitive, and psychotherapeutic technologies work, but we must increasingly find ways to communicate this success to others. A beginning way to address this issue is to develop and standardize measures of evaluation. A wide range of health status measures is currently available. Assessing their appropriateness and outlining standards for use should be a high priority for the field. This issue assumes greater importance when psychological variables are the outcome measures. Some psychological outcome measures used in health studies were initially developed on psychopathological populations and, consequently, may have minimal appropriateness for psychologically normal but physical ill samples. Measures developed specifically to assess psychosocial status as a function of illness may be more appropriate. The urgency of this issue is illustrated by a recent review of the literature on quality of life (Hollandsworth, 1988). This review found that sixty-nine clinical trials of quality of life after chronic illness conducted between 1980 and 1984 used eighty-three different measures of quality of life. Clearly, this is not a trend that health psychology can afford to continue.

Systematic Documentation of Cost-Effectiveness

One of the major forces facing health psychology, as well as every other disciplinary contributor to behavioral medicine, is the growing cost of health care services and the accompanying mounting pressure to contain costs. Fueled by the spiraling expense of high-tech medicine and the increasing costs of malpractice insurance, health care draws off 11% of the gross national product. The growing spectre of the AIDS crisis threatens to push costs even further, simultaneously putting affordable health care and insurance out of the reach of increasing numbers of people.

This unhappy reality is relevant to health psychologists in several respects. It nudges the field to keep an eye on the bottom line in research and intervention. While effective health care interventions are an important goal of the field, their likelihood of being integrated into medical practice will be influenced by their **cost-effectiveness.** Moreover, one of the effects that DRGs may come to have on health psychology is to restrict the behavioral treatment of medical disorders. The kinds of long-term behavior change that may be essential to treatment success, such as dietary modification, smoking cessation, and exercise prescriptions for cardiac patients, may fall outside the time period in the DRG treatment guidelines (see Chapter 10). Moreover, since DRGs require nonphysician expenses to be bundled together, psychologists are not able to bill separately for services. Consequently, any long-term behavior change programs must be initiated and followed through on only within the time period of the DRG. The incentive to include psychologists in care, then, exists only to the extent that such services can reduce length of stay and increase profitability (Boudewyns & Nolan, 1985).

Subtly, the pressures of **cost containment** push the field in the direction of research questions designed to keep people out of the health care system altogether. On the clinical practice side, interventions increasingly examine the benefits and liabilities of such interventions as self-help groups, peer counseling, self-management programs (e.g., Kirschenbaum, Sherman, & Penrod, 1987), and other inexpensive ways to provide services to those who might otherwise not receive care. Research suggesting that the stress reduction and pain amelioration benefits of expensive biofeedback interventions can be achieved by simple, less expensive techniques of relaxation and other cognitive-behavioral interventions (Blanchard, McCoy et al., 1988) also underscores this viewpoint.

On the research side, the emphasis on cost

containment draws researchers into health promotion activities designed to keep people healthy, over expensive and often individualized rehabilitation activities designed to aid those who are already ill. Although the theory underlying the emphasis on health promotion is laudable, this implicit goal may prove to be a pipe dream. Research examining the efficacy of health behavior interventions in reducing the incidence of disease and lowering health care costs has so far not been very encouraging (Kaplan, 1984; Slater & Carlton, 1985).

There are benefits and risks to the formidable role that economic factors play in the field of health psychology. On the one hand, the field cannot afford to pursue its scientific and clinical mission without regard to cost. On the other hand, cost containment issues can compromise scientific and intervention missions of the field by prematurely choking off areas of inquiry that do not immediately appear to be cost-effective. The relative lack of attention to issues of rehabilitation in contrast to the heavy preponderance of research in primary prevention activities can be regarded as one casualty of these pressures.

Many of our interventions have the potential to save substantial funds and other resources, and documenting this fact should increasingly be a high priority. What are some of these potential savings? Interventions designed to enhance feelings of control among patients awaiting unpleasant medical procedures have clear cost-saving benefits. As noted in Chapter 9, these interventions can lead patients to require less medication, make fewer complaints, demand less staff time, and leave the hospital early. The trade-off of these costs saved with the minimal costs incurred (the time and personnel necessary to provide patients with information) can be substantial. Similarly, training practitioners in effective communication improves patient satisfaction with medical care, can enhance adherence,

and may possibly reduce malpractice litigation. The savings to health institutions that could be gained by this training have yet to be systematically documented. The management of chronic pain represents another documentable cost saving. Prior to the implementation of behavioral technology to control pain, the typical chronic pain patient underwent several surgeries, took numerous and expensive medications, sought frequent consultations and multiple opinions from practitioners, and stayed in the health care system without successful treatment for many years. The concentration of technology in the pain center and the use of behavioral methods in the effective management of pain have rendered some of these costs unnecessary. Similar documentation of the cost-effectiveness of other health psychology interventions can and should be developed in other areas so that these interventions may be judged as successful not only on their own merits but also on cost-saving grounds. In addition, health psychology could be more oriented toward developing interventions that save costs. For example, finding ways of identifying and drawing off the two-thirds of patients whose medical complaints are believed to be primarily of psychological origin would save the health care delivery system billions of dollars yearly and would direct these people more appropriately into psychological services.

Foretelling the future is never an easy task. Some trends, such as the aging of the population, are obvious and have relatively clear implications for the field. Others are not so easily anticipated and thus their implications for health psychology are still elusive. The foregoing set of issues represents an estimate of some of the ways in which health psychology will be shaped and molded by the changing dimensions of medicine and psychology over the next decades.

SUMMARY

1. We have made substantial gains in altering faulty health practices. Yet health psychology research continues to document how complex these behaviors are. Cognitive and behavioral technologies have been modestly successful in changing behavior, and relapse prevention techniques hold promise for managing the formidable problem of maintenance.

2. A priority for the future is to identify the most potent and effective elements of behavior change programs and to incorporate them into cost-effective interventions that reach the largest number of people simultaneously at the community level, the workplace, and schools.

3. Health psychology interventions should continue to focus on those at risk for particular disorders, toward preventing poor health habits from ever developing, and toward developing effective health promotion interventions with the elderly.

4. The goal of health promotion must, however, be tempered by the recognition that we may make only a modest dent in disease and that good health habits are only one aspect of a full and meaningful life.

5. As medicine develops a health promotion orientation, the potential for collaborative interventions between psychologists and medical practitioners through the media, the community, and the physician's office may come to be fully realized.

6. Yet an effective health promotion program must involve not only health behavior change but also social change that makes high-quality health care available to all elements of the population.

7. Research on stress should continue to focus on vulnerable populations and on trends in the economy and culture that increase the stress on particular subpopulations, such as children, the elderly, the poor, and women.

8. In the future, the greatest advances in stress research will likely come from research examining the pathways by which stress exerts adverse effects on health. In addition, increasing knowledge of stress buffers, such as social support and the development of ways to improve such coping aids, will be a target of research.

9. The appropriate use of health services will be an important target for the future. It may come about through interventions to draw off the patients who currently make inappropriate use of health services for psychological complaints, and by such interventions as teaching patients to better discriminate and monitor their symptoms and conditions.

10. Communication issues will be increasingly important in reducing health costs that relate to improper use of services, initiation of malpractice litigation, and failure to adhere appropriately to medication and lifestyle recommendations.

11. Trends in the management of pain have increasingly moved away from dependence on pharmacological and surgical interventions toward less expensive cognitive-behavioral methods and relaxation therapies. In addition, the control of pain has shifted from the practitioner to co-management between patient and practitioner. The development of pain centers has been critical in pooling pain management technology.

12. The management of chronic illness must

increasingly focus on quality of life and appropriate ways to measure it. The management of terminal illness must increasingly focus on ways of enabling people to die physically and psychologically comfortable deaths, as much as possible. In addition, ethical issues involving living wills, the patient's right to die, family decision making in death and dying, and euthanasia will continue to be important.

13. An important target for future work is identification of the health and lifestyle issues that will be created by the aging of the population. Anticipating medical disorders and developing interventions to offset their potential adverse effects should be targets for research now.

14. Health psychology needs to be responsive to changes in medical practice, including changes in disease demographics (such as age) and cultural trends with medical implications (such as sports injuries). The changing face of medicine creates challenges for health psychologists in anticipating the impact of technologically complex interventions and helping to prepare patients for them.

15. Patient consumerism and the need for patients to become involved in medical decision making also create communication roles for health psychologists.

16. Important goals for health psychology for the future are systematic documentation of treatment effectiveness, systematic documentation of the cost-effectiveness of interventions, and continued efforts to find ways to reduce health costs.

KEY TERMS

behavioral immunization
comprehensive intervention models
cost containment

cost-effectiveness
patient consumerism
treatment effectiveness

References

Aaronson, N. K., Calais de Silva, F., Yoshida, O., van Dam, F. S. A. M., Fossa, S. D., Miyakawa, M., Raghavan, D., Riedl, H., Robinson, M. R. G., & Worden, J. W. (1986). Quality of life assessment in bladder cancer clinical trials: Conceptual, methodological and practical issues. *Progress in Clinical and Biological Research, 22,* 149–170.

Aaronson, N. K., van Dam, F. S. A. M., Polak, C. E., & Zittoun, R. (1986). Prospects and problems in European psychosocial oncology: A survey of the EORTC Study Group on Quality of Life. *Journal of Psychosocial Oncology, 4,* 43–53.

Abel, G. G., Rouleau, J-L., & Coyne, B. J. (1987). Behavioral medicine strategies in medical patients. In A. Stoudemire & B. S. Fogel (Eds.), *Principles of medical psychiatry* (pp. 329–345). Orlando, FL: Grune & Stratton.

Abraham, S., Collins, G., & Nordsieck, M. (1971). Relationship of childhood weight status to morbidity in adults. *Public Health Reports, 86,* 273–284.

Abrams, D. B., Monti, P. M., Pinto, R. P., Elder, J. P., Brown, R. A., & Jacobus, S. I. (1987). Psychosocial stress and coping in smokers who relapse or quit. *Health Psychology, 6,* 289–303.

Abrams, R. D. (1966). The patient with cancer: His changing patterns of communication. *New England Journal of Medicine, 274,* 317–322.

Abrams, R. D., & Finesinger, E. (1953). Guilt reactions in patients with cancer. *Cancer, 6,* 474–482.

Abramson, L. Y., Garber, J., & Seligman, M. E. P. (1980). *Learned helplessness in humans: An attributional analysis.* In J. Garber & M. E. P. Seligman (Eds.), *Human helplessness: Theory and applications.* New York: Academic Press.

Abramson, L. Y., Metalsky, G. I., & Alloy, L. B. (1988). The hopelessness theory of depression: Does the research test the theory? In L. Y. Anderson (Ed.), *Social cognition and clinical psychology: A synthesis* (pp. 33–65). New York: Guilford Press.

Ackerman, S. H., Keller, S. E., Schleifer, S. J., Schindledecker, R. D., Camerino, M., Hofer, M. A., Weiner, H., & Stein, M. (1988). Premature maternal separation and lymphocyte function. *Brain, Behavior, and Immunity, 2,* 161–165.

Adams, J. D. (1978). Improving stress management: An action-research based OD intervention. In W. W. Burke (Ed.), *The cutting edge.* La Jolla, CA: University Associates.

Adams, J. E., & Lindemann, E. (1974). Coping with long term disability. In G. V. Coelho, D. A. Hamburg, & J. E. Adams (Eds.), *Coping and adaptation* (pp. 127–138). New York: Basic Books.

Aday, L. A., & Andersen, R. (1974). A framework for the study of access to medical care. *Health Services Research, 9,* 208–220.

Ader, R. (1987). Conditioned immune responses: Adrenocortical influences. In E. R. de Kloet, V. M. Wiegant, & D. de Wied (Eds.), *Progress in brain research* (Vol. 72, pp. 79–90). North Holland: Elsevier.

Ader, R., & Cohen, N. (1985). CNS-immune system interactions: Conditioning phenomena. *Behavioral and Brain Sciences, 8,* 379–394.

Ader, R., Grota, L. J., & Cohen, N. (1987). Conditioning phenomena and immune function. *Annals of the New York Academy of Sciences, 496,* 532–544.

Adkins, L. (1984). Hospice care for terminally ill children. *Child Welfare, 63,* 559–562.

Adsett, C. A., and Brohn, J. G. (1968). Short-term group psychotherapy for post-myocardial infarction patients and their wives. *Canadian Medical Association Journal, 99,* 577.

Affleck, G., Tennen, H., Croog, S., & Levine, S. (1987). Causal attribution, perceived control, and recovery from a heart attack. *Journal of Social and Clinical Psychology, 5,* 339–355.

Affleck, G., Tennen, H., Pfeiffer, C., & Fifield, C. (1987). Appraisals of control and predictability in adapting to a chronic disease. *Journal of Personality and Social Psychology, 53,* 273–279.

Agras, W. S., Kraemer, H. C., Berkowitz, R. I., Korner, A. F., & Hammer, L. D. (1987). Does a vigorous feeding style influence early development? *Journal of Pediatrics, 110,* 799–804.

Agras, W. S., Schneider, J. A., Arnow, B., Raeburn, S. D., & Telch, C. F. (1989). Cognitive-behavioral and response-prevention treatments for bulimia nervosa. *Journal of Consulting and Clinical Psychology, 57,* 215–221.

Agras, W. S. Taylor, C. B., Kraemer, H. C., Southam, M. A., & Schneider, J. A. (1987). Relaxation training for essential hypertension at the worksite: II. The poorly controlled hypertensive. *Psychosomatic Medicine, 49,* 264–273.

Aiken, L. H., & Marx, M. M. (1982). Hospices: Perspectives on the public policy debate. *American Psychologist, 37,* 1271–1279.

Aitken-Swan, J. (1959). Nursing the late cancer patient at home. *Practitioner, 183,* 64–69.

Aivazyan, T. A., Zaitsev, V. P., Salenko, B. B., Yurenev, A. P., & Patrusheva, I. F. (1988). Efficacy of relaxation techniques in hypertensive patients. *Health Psychology, 7*(Suppl.), 193–200.

Ajzen, I. (1985). From intentions to actions: A theory of planned action. In J. Kuhl & J. Beckman (Eds.), *Action control: From cognition to behavior* (pp. 11–39). New York: Springer.

Ajzen, I., & Fishbein, M. (1977). Attitude-behavior relations: A theoretical analysis and review of empirical research. *Psychological Bulletin, 84,* 888–918.

Ajzen, I., & Fishbein, M. (1980). *Understanding attitudes and predicting social behavior.* Englewood Cliffs, NJ: Prentice-Hall.

Ajzen, I., & Madden, T. J. (1986). Prediction of goal-directed behavior: Attitudes, intentions, and perceived behavioral control. *Journal of Experimental Social Psychology, 22,* 453–474.

Akil, H., Mayer, D. J., & Liebeskind, J. C. (1972). Comparaison chez le Rat entre l'analgesie induite par stimulation de la substance grise periaqueducale et l'analgesie morphinique. *C. R. Academy of Science, 274,* 3603–3605.

Akil, H., Mayer, D. J., & Liebeskind, J. C. (1976). Antagonism of stimulation-produced analgesia by naloxone, a narcotic antagonist. *Science, 191,* 961–962.

Akil, H., Watson, S. J., Young, E., Lewis, M. E., Khachaturian, H., & Walker, J. M. (1984). Endogenous opioids: Biology and function. *Annual Review of Neuroscience, 7,* 223–255.

Alagna, S. W., & Reddy, D. M. (1984). Predictors of proficient technique and successful lesion detection in breast self-examination. *Health Psychology, 3,* 113–127.

Albrecht, J., Helderman, J. H., Schlesser, M. A., & Rush, A. J. (1985). A controlled study of cellular immune function in affective disorders before and during somatic therapy. *Psychiatry Research, 15,* 185–193.

Albright, C. L., Altman, D. G., Slater, M. D., & Maccoby, N. (1988). Cigarette advertisements in magazines: Evidence for a differential focus on women's and youth magazines. *Health Education Quarterly, 15,* 225–233.

Alderman, M. H., & Lamport, B. (1988). Treatment of hypertension at the workplace: An opportunity to link service and research. *Health Psychology, 7*(Suppl.), 283–295.

Alderman, M. H., & Schoenbaum, B. A. (1975). Detection and treatment of hypertension at the work site. *New England Journal of Medicine, 2,* 65–68.

Alexander, F. (1950) *Psychosomatic medicine.* New York: Norton.

Alexander, J. A., & Bloom, J. R. (1987). Collective bargaining in hospitals: An organizational and environmental analysis. *Journal of Health and Social Behavior, 28,* 60–73.

Alexander, J. A., & Fennell, M. L. (1986). Patterns of decision making in multihospital systems. *Journal of Health and Social Behavior, 27,* 14–27.

Alexander, J. A., Morrissey, M. A., & Shortell, S. M. (1986). Effects of competition, regulation, and corporatization on hospital-physician relationships. *Journal of Health and Social Behavior, 27,* 220–235.

Alexandrov, A., Isakova, G., Maslennikova, G., Shugaeva, E., Prokhorov, A., Olferiev, A., & Kulikov, S. (1988). Prevention of atherosclerosis among 11-year-old schoolchildren in two Moscow administrative districts. *Health Psychology, 7*(Suppl.), 247–252.

Allen, H. M., Jr. (1984). Consumers and choice: Cost containment strategies for health care provision. *Health Psychology, 3,* 411–430.

Allen, M. T., Lawler, K. A., Matthews, K. A., Rakaczky, C. J., & Jamison, W. (1987). Type A behavior pattern, parental history of hypertension, and cardiovascular reactivity in college males. *Health Psychology, 6,* 113–130.

Allred, K. D., & Smith, T. W. (1989). The hardy personality: Cognitive and physiological responses to evaluative threat. *Journal of Personality and Social Psychology, 56,* 257–266.

Alpert, B., Field, T., Goldstein, S., & Perry, S. (1990). Aerobics enhances cardiovascular fitness and agility in preschoolers. *Health Psychology, 9,* 48–56.

Alpert, J. J. (1964). Broken appointments. *Pediatrics, 34,* 127–132.

American Cancer Society. (1989). *Cancer facts and figures—1989.* Atlanta, GA: Author.

American Diabetes Association. (1976). *What you need to know about diabetes.* New York: Author.

American Diabetes Association. (1986). *Diabetes: Facts you need to know.* Alexandria, VA: Author.

American Heart Association. (1984). *Heart facts, 1984.* Dallas, TX: Author.

American Heart Association. (1988). *1989 heart facts.* Dallas, TX: Author.

American Hospital Association. (1982). *Hospital Statistics.* Chicago: Author.

American Hospital Association. (1987). *Hospital statistics.* Chicago: Author.

American Hospital Association. (1989). *Hospital statistics.* Chicago: Author.

American Lung Association. (1986). *Freedom from smoking in 20 days.* New York: Author.

American Psychiatric Association. (1980). *Diagnostic and statistical manual of mental disorders* (3rd ed.). Washington, DC: Author.

American Running and Fitness Association. (1981). *Statistical report.* Washington, DC: Author.

Amkraut, A., & Solomon, G. F. (1977). From the symbolic stimulus to the pathophysiologic response: Immune mechanisms. In Z. P. Lipowski, D. R. Lipsitt, & P. C. Whybrow (Eds.), *Psychosomatic medicine: Current trends and clinical applications* (pp. 228–252). New York: Oxford University Press.

Andersen, B. L., Anderson, B., & deProsse, C. (1989a). Controlled perspective longitudinal study of women with cancer: I. Sexual functioning outcomes. *Journal of Consulting and Clinical Psychology, 57,* 683–691.

Andersen, B. L., Anderson, B., & deProsse, C. (1989b). Controlled perspective longitudinal study of women with cancer: II. Psychological outcomes. *Journal of Consulting and Clinical Psychology, 57,* 692–697.

Andersen, B. L., & Hacker, N. F. (1983). Treatment for gynecologic cancer: A review of the effects on female sexuality. *Health Psychology, 2,* 203–221.

Andersen, B. L., Karlsson, J. A., Anderson, B., & Tewfik, H. H. (1984). Anxiety and cancer treatment: Response to stressful radiotherapy. *Health Psychology, 3,* 535–551.

Andersen, R. (1988). The contribution of informal care to the management of stroke. *International Disability Studies, 10,* 107–112.

Anderson, D. E. (1987). Experimental behavioral hypertension in laboratory animals. In S. Julius & D. R. Bassett (Eds.), *Handbook of hypertension: Vol 9. Behavioral factors in hypertension* (pp. 226–245). North Holland: Elsevier.

Anderson, J. C., & Bartkus, D. (1973). Choice of medical care: A behavioral model of health and illness behavior. *Journal of Health and Social Behavior, 14,* 348–362.

Anderson, K. O., Bradley, L. A., Young, L. D., McDaniel, L. K., & Wise, C. M. (1985). Rheumatoid arthritis: Review of psychological factors related to etiology, effects, and treatment. *Psychological Bulletin, 98,* 358–387.

Anderson, K. O., & Masur, F. T. III. (1983). Psychological preparation for invasive medical and dental procedures. *Journal of Behavioral Medicine, 6,* 1–40.

Anderson, N. B., Lane, J. D., Taguchi, F., & Williams, R. B., Jr. (1989). Patterns of cardiovascular responses to stress as a function of race and parental hypertension in men. *Health Psychology, 8,* 525–540.

Anderson, N. B., Williams, R. B., Jr., Lane, J. D., Haney, T., Simpson, S., & Houseworth, S. J. (1986). Type A behavior, family history of hypertension, and cardiovascular responsivity among black women. *Health Psychology, 5,* 393–406.

Andersson, S. A. (1979). Pain control by sensory stimulation. In J. J. Bonica, J. C. Liebeskind, and D. G. Albe-Fessard (Eds.), *Proceedings of the Second World Congress on Pain: Vol. 3. Advances in pain research and therapy* (pp. 569–586). New York: Raven Press.

Andrykowski, M. A. (1987). Do infusion-related tastes and odors facilitate the development of anticipatory nausea? A failure to support the hypothesis. *Health Psychology, 6,* 329–341.

Andrykowski, M. A. (1988). Defining anticipatory nausea and vomiting: Differences among cancer chemotherapy patients who report pretreatment nausea. *Journal of Behavioral Medicine, 11,* 59–70.

Aneshensel, C. S., Frerichs, R. R., & Huba, G. J. (1984). Depression and physical illness: A multiwave, nonrecursive causal model. *Journal of Health and Social Behavior, 25,* 350–371.

Angell, M. (1982). The quality of mercy. *New England Journal of Medicine, 306,* 98–99.

Antonovsky, A. (1979). *Health, stress, and coping.* San Francisco: Jossey-Bass.

Antonovsky, A., & Hartman, H. (1974). Delay in the detection of cancer: A review of the literature. *Health Education Monographs, 2,* 98–128.

Appley, M. H., & Trumbull, R. (Eds.). (1986). *Dynamics of stress: Physiological, psychological, and social perspectives.* New York: Plenum.

Armor, D. I., Polich, I. M., & Stambul, H. B. (1976). *Alcoholism and treatment.* Santa Monica, CA: Rand Corporation.

Armstead, C. A., Lawler, K. A., Gordon, G., Cross, J., & Gibbons, J. (1989). Relationship of racial stressors to blood pressure responses and anger expression in black college students. *Health Psychology, 8,* 541–557.

Arnetz, B. B., Wasserman, J., Petrini, B., Brenner, S. O., Levi, L., Eneroth, P., Salovaara, H., Hjelm, R., Salovaara, L., Theorell, T., & Petterson, I. L. (1987). Immune function in unemployed women. *Psychosomatic Medicine, 49,* 3–12.

Ary, D. V., & Biglan, A. (1988). Longitudinal changes in adolescent cigarette smoking behavior: Onset and cessation. *Journal of Behavioral Medicine, 11,* 361–382.

Atkin, C. (1979). Research evidence on mass mediated health communication campaigns. In D. Nimmo (Ed.), *Communication yearbook 3.* New Brunswick, NJ: Transaction Books.

Atkinson, T., Liem, R., & Liem, J. H. (1986). The social costs of unemployment: Implications for social support. *Journal of Health and Social Behavior, 27,* 317–331.

Auerbach, S. M., & Kilmann, P. R. (1977). Crisis intervention: A review of outcome research. *Psychological Bulletin, 84,* 1189–1217.

Averill, J. R. (1973). Personal control over aversive stimuli and its relationship to stress. *Psychological Bulletin, 80,* 286–303.

Avison, W. R., & Turner, R. J. (1988). Stressful life events and depressive symptoms: Disaggregating the effects of acute stressors and chronic strains. *Journal of Health and Social Behavior, 29,* 253–264.

Axelrod, S., Hall, R. V., Weis, L., & Rohrer, S. (1974). Use of self-imposed contingencies to reduce the frequency of smoking behavior. In M. J. Mahoney & C. E. Thoresen (Eds.), *Self-control: Power to the person* (pp. 77–85). Monterey, CA: Brooks-Cole.

Bachrach, K. M., & Zautra, A. J. (1985). Coping with a community stressor: The threat of a hazardous waste facility. *Journal of Health and Social Behavior, 26,* 127–141.

Baekeland, F., & Lundwall, L. (1975). Dropping out

of treatment: A critical review. *Psychological Bulletin, 82*, 738–783.

Baer, J. D., Kivilan, D. R., Fromme, K., & Marlatt, G. A. (in press). Secondary prevention of alcohol abuse with college student populations: A skills-training approach. In N. Heather, W. R. Miller, & J. Greeley (Eds.), *Self-control and the addictive behaviors*. Notre Dame, IN: Notre Dame University.

Baer, J. S., Holt, C. S., & Lichtenstein, E. (1986). Self-efficacy and smoking reexamined: Construct validity and clinical utility. *Journal of Consulting and Clinical Psychology, 54*, 846–852.

Baer, P. E., Garmezy, L. B., McLaughlin, R. J., Pokorny, A. D., & Wernick, M. J. (1987). Stress, coping, family conflict, and adolescent alcohol use. *Journal of Behavioral Medicine, 10*, 449–466.

Bahnson, C. B. (1981). Stress and cancer: The state of the art. *Psychosomatics, 22*, 207–220.

Bakal, D. A. (1975). Headache: A biopsychological perspective. *Psychological Bulletin, 82*, 369–382.

Bakal, D. A. (1979). *Psychology and medicine: Psychobiological dimensions of health and illness*. New York: Springer.

Baker, L. H., Cooney, N. L., & Pomerleau, O. F. (1987). Craving for alcohol: Theoretical processes and treatment procedures. In *Treatment and prevention of alcohol problems: A resource manual* (pp. 183–202). New York: Academic Press.

Baker, L. J., Dearborn, M., Hastings, J. E., & Hamberger, K. (1984). Type A behavior in women: A review. *Health Psychology, 3*, 477–497.

Ball, J. C., Lange, W. R., Myers, C. P., & Friedman, S. R. (1988). Reducing the risk of AIDS through methadone maintenance treatment. *Journal of Health and Social Behavior, 29*, 214–226.

Baltes, M. M., & Skinner, E. A. (1983). Cognitive performance deficits and hospitalization: Learned helplessness, instrumental passivity, or what? Comment on Raps, Peterson, Jonas, and Seligman. *Journal of Personality and Social Psychology, 45*, 1013–1016.

Baltrusch, H. I., & Waltz, E. M. (in press). Cancer from a biobehavioral and social epidemiological perspective. *Social Science and Medicine*.

Bandura, A. (1969). *Principles of behavior modification*. New York: Holt, Rinehart, & Winston.

Bandura, A. (1977). Self-efficacy: Toward a unifying theory of behavioral change. *Psychological Review, 84*, 191–215.

Bandura, A. (1986). *Social foundations of thought and action: A social cognitive theory*. Englewood Cliffs, NJ: Prentice-Hall.

Bandura, A. (1989). Perceived self-efficacy in the exercise of control over AIDS infection. In S. J. Blumenthal, A. Eichler, & G. Weissman (Eds.), *Women and AIDS*. Washington, DC: American Psychiatric Press.

Bandura, A. (in press). Self-efficacy mechanism in physiological activation and health-promotion behavior. In J. Madden IV, S. Matthysse, & J. Barchas (Eds.), *Adaptation, learning, and affect*. New York: Raven Press.

Bandura, A., Blanchard, E. B., & Ritter, B. (1969). The relative efficacy of desensitization and modeling approaches for inducing behavioral, affective and longitudinal changes. *Journal of Personality and Social Psychology, 13*, 173–199.

Bandura, A., Cioffi, D., Taylor, C. B., & Brouillard, M. E. (1988). Perceived self-efficacy in coping with cognitive stressors and opioid activation. *Journal of Personality and Social Psychology, 55*, 479–488.

Bandura, A., O'Leary, A., Taylor, C. B., Gauthier, J., & Gossard, D. (1987). Perceived self-efficacy and pain control: Opioid and nonopioid mechanisms. *Journal of Personality and Social Psychology, 53*, 563–571.

Barbarin, O. A., & Chesler, M. (1986). The medical context of parental coping with childhood cancer. *American Journal of Community Psychology, 14*, 221–235.

Barber, T. X. (1965). Physiological effects of "hypnotic suggestions": A critical review of recent research (1960–64). *Psychological Bulletin, 63*, 201–222.

Bard, M., & Dyk, R. B. (1956). The psychodynamic significance of beliefs regarding the cause of serious illness. *Psychoanalytic Review, 43*, 146–162.

Barec, L., MacArthur, C., & Sherwood, M. (1976). A study of health education aspects of smoking in pregnancy. *International Journal of Health Education, 19*(Suppl. 1), 1–17.

Barefoot, J. C., Dodge, K. A., Peterson, B. L., Dahlstrom, W. G., & Williams, R. B. (1989). The Cook-Medley hostility scale: Item content and ability to predict survival. *Psychosomatic Medicine, 51*, 46–57.

Bar-On, D. (1986). Professional models vs. patient models in rehabilitation after heart attack. *Human Relations, 39*, 917–932.

Bar-On, D. (1987). Causal attributions and the rehabilitation of myocardial infarction victims. *Journal of Social and Clinical Psychology, 5,* 114–122.

Bar-On, D., & Dreman, S. (1987). When spouses disagree: A predictor of cardiac rehabilitation. *Family Systems Medicine, 5,* 228–237.

Barr, I. K. (1983). Physicians' views of patients in prepaid group practice: Reasons for visits to HMOs. *Journal of Health and Social Behavior, 24,* 244–255.

Barr, M., Pennebaker, J. W., & Watson, D. (1988). Improving blood pressure estimation through internal and environmental feedback. *Psychosomatic Medicine, 50,* 37–45.

Barsky, A. J. (1988). The paradox of health. *New England Journal of Medicine, 318,* 414–418.

Barton, J., Chassin, L., Presson, C. C., & Sherman, S. J. (1982). Social image factors as motivators of smoking initiation in early and middle adolescence. *Child Development, 53,* 1499–1511.

Bartrop, R. W., Lockhurst, E., Lazarus, L., Kiloh, L. G., & Penny, R. (1977). Depressed lymphocyte function after bereavement. *Lancet, 1,* 834–836.

Basmajian, J. V. (1989). Combined behavioral therapy for the hemiplegic arm and hand. In J. V. Basmajian (Ed.), *Biofeedback: Principles and practice for clinicians* (3rd ed., pp. 119–122). Baltimore, MD: Williams & Wilkins.

Baum, A., Aiello, J. R., & Calesnick, L. E. (1978). Crowding and personal control: Social density and the development of learned helplessness. *Journal of Personality and Social Psychology, 36,* 1000–1011.

Baum, A., Grunberg, N. E., & Singer, J. E. (1982). The use of psychological and neuroendocrinological measurements in the study of stress. *Health Psychology, 1,* 217–236.

Baum, A., & Valins, S. (1977). *Architecture and social behavior: Psychological studies of social density.* Hillsdale, NJ: Erlbaum.

Baum, J. (1982). A review of the psychological aspects of neumatic diseases. *Seminars in Arthritis and Rheumatism, 11,* 352–361.

Bauman, K. E., Koch, G. G., Bryan, E. S., Haley, N. J., Downtown, M. I., & Orlandi, M. A. (1989). On the measurement of tobacco use by adolescents: Validity of self-reports of smokeless tobacco use and validity of nicotine as an indicator of cigarette smoking. *American Journal of Epidemiology, 130,* 327–337.

Bauman, K. E., Koch, G. G., & Fisher, L. A. (1989).

Family cigarette smoking and test performance by adolescents. *Health Psychology, 8,* 97–105.

Baumann, L. J., Zimmerman, R. S., & Leventhal, H. (1989). An experiment in common sense: Education at blood pressure screening. *Patient Education and Counseling, 14,* 53–67.

Beck, A. T. (1986). Hopelessness as a predictor of eventual suicide. *Annals of the New York Academy of Sciences, 487,* 90–96.

Becker, M. H. (1974). The health belief model and sick role behavior. *Health Education Monographs, 2,* 409–419.

Becker, M. H. (1986). The tyranny of health promotion. *Public Health Review, 14,* 15–25.

Becker, M. H. (1987). The cholesterol saga: Whither health promotion? *Annals of Internal Medicine, 106,* 623–626.

Becker, M. H., & Janz, N. K. (1987). On the effectiveness and utility of health hazard/health risk appraisal in clinical and nonclinical settings. *Health Services Research, 22,* 537–551.

Becker, M. H., & Joseph, J. G. (1988). AIDS and behavioral change to reduce risk: A review. *American Journal of Public Health, 78,* 394–410.

Becker, M. H., Kaback, M., Rosenstock, I., & Ruth, M. (1975). Some influences on public participation in a genetic screening program. *Journal of Community Health, 1,* 3–14.

Becker, M. H., & Maiman, L. A. (1975). Sociobehavioral determinants of compliance with health and medical care recommendations. *Medical Care, 13,* 10–24.

Becker, M. H., Maiman, L. A., Kirscht, J. P., Haefner, D. P., & Drachman, R. H. (1977). The health belief model and dietary compliance: A field experiment. *Journal of Health and Social Behavior, 18,* 348–366.

Becker, M. H., Maiman, L. A., Kirscht, J. P., Haefner, D. P., Drachman, R. H., & Taylor, D. W. (1979). Patient perceptions and compliance: Recent studies of the health belief model. In R. B. Haynes, D. W. Taylor, & D. L. Sackett (Eds.), *Compliance in health care* (pp. 78–112). Baltimore, MD: Johns Hopkins University Press.

Beckman, H. B., & Frankel, R. M. (1984). The effect of physician behavior on the collection of data. *Annals of Internal Medicine, 101,* 692–696.

Beecher, H. K. (1959). *Measurement of subjective responses.* New York: Oxford University Press.

Beeson, P. B., & McDermott, W. (Eds.). (1967).

Cecil-Loeb textbook of medicine (12th ed.). Philadelphia: Saunders. As quoted in Birk, L. (1973). *Biofeedback: Behavioral medicine*. New York: Grune & Stratton.

Belar, C. (1979). A comment on Silver and Blanchard's (1978) review of the treatment of tension headaches via EMG feedback and relaxation training. *Journal of Behavioral Medicine, 2,* 215–220.

Belisle, M., Roskies, E., & Levesque, J-M. (1987). Improving adherence to physical activity. *Health Psychology, 6,* 159–172.

Belloc, N. D., & Breslow, L. (1972). Relationship of physical health status and family practices. *Preventive Medicine, 1,* 409–421.

Benoliel, J. Q. (1977). Nurses and the human experience of dying. In H. Feifel (Ed.), *New meanings of death* (pp. 123–142). New York: McGraw-Hill.

Benowitz, N. L. (1988). Toxicity of nicotine: Implications with regard to nicotine replacement theory. In O. F. Pomerleau & C. S. Pomerleau (Eds.), *Nicotine replacement: A critical evaluation* (pp. 187–217). New York: Liss.

Benowitz, N. L., Hall, S. M., Herning, R. I., Jacob, P., & Mines, A. H. (1983). Smokers of low yield cigarettes do not consume less nicotine. *New England Journal of Medicine, 309,* 139–142.

Ben-Sira, Z. (1976). The function of the professional's affective behavior in client satisfaction: A revised approach to social interaction theory. *Journal of Health and Social Behavior, 17,* 3–11.

Ben-Sira, Z. (1980). Affective and instrumental components in the physician-patient relationship: An additional dimension of interaction theory. *Journal of Health and Social Behavior, 21,* 170–180.

Benson, H., Greenwood, M. M., & Klemchuk, H. (1975). The relaxation response: Psychophysiological aspects and clinical applications. *International Journal of Psychiatry in Medicine, 6,* 87–98.

Bentler, P. M., & Speckart, G. (1979). Models of attitude-behavior relations. *Psychological Review, 86,* 451–464.

Berger, L. R. (1981). Childhood injuries: Recognition and prevention. *Current Problems in Pediatrics, 12,* 1–59.

Bergner, M., Bobbitt, R. A., Carter, W. B., & Gilson, B. S. (1981). The sickness impact profile: Development and final revision of a health status measure. *Medical Care, 19,* 787–805.

Berkanovic, E., Gerber, B., Brown, H. G., & Breslow, L. (1983). Some issues concerning community-based chronic disease control programs. In C. Mettlin & G. P. Murphy (Eds.), *Progress in cancer control* (Vol. 4, pp. 271–282). New York: Liss.

Berkman, L. F. (1985). The relationship of social networks and social support to morbidity and mortality. In S. Cohen & S. L. Syme (Eds.), *Social support and health* (pp. 241–262). Orlando, FL: Academic Press.

Berkman, L. F., & Syme, S. L. (1979). Social networks, host resistance, and mortality: A nine-year followup study of Alameda County residents. *American Journal of Epidemiology, 109,* 186–204.

Berkowitz, R. I., Agras, W. S., Korner, A. F., Kraemer, H. C., & Zeanah, C. H. (1985). Physical activity and adiposity: A longitudinal study from birth to childhood. *Journal of Pediatrics, 106,* 734–738.

Bernstein, D. A., & McAlister, A. (1976). The modification of smoking behavior: Progress and problems. *Addictive Behaviors, 1,* 89–102.

Betz, B. J., & Thomas, C. B. (1979). Individual temperament as a predictor of health or premature death. *Johns Hopkins Medical Journal, 144,* 81–89.

Biglan, A., Glasgow, R., Ary, D., Thompson, R., Severson, H., Lichtenstein, E., Weissman, W., Faller, C., & Gallison, C. (1987). How generalizable are the effects of smoking prevention programs? Refusal skills training and parent messages in a teacher-administered program. *Journal of Behavioral Medicine, 10,* 613–628.

Biglan, A., McConnell, S., Severson, H. H., Bavry, J., & Ary, D. (1984). A situational analysis of adolescent smoking. *Journal of Behavioral Medicine, 7,* 109–114.

Biglan, A., Severson, H., Ary, D., Faller, C., Gallison C., Thompson R., Glasgow R., & Lichtenstein, E. (1987). Do smoking prevention programs really work? Attrition and the internal and external validity of an evaluation of a refusal skills training program. *Journal of Behavioral Medicine, 10,* 159–171.

Billings, A. C., & Moos, R. H. (1982). Social support and functioning among community and clinical groups: A panel model. *Journal of Behavioral Medicine, 5,* 295–312.

Billings, A. C., & Moos, R. H. (1984). Coping, stress, and social resources among adults with unipolar depression. *Journal of Personality and Social Psychology, 46,* 877–891.

Billings, A. C., Moos, R. H., Miller, J. J. III, & Gottlieb, J. E. (1987). Psychosocial adaptation in juvenile rheumatoid disease: A controlled evaluation. *Health Psychology, 6,* 343–359.

Binger, C. (1973). Childhood leukemia—emotional impact on siblings. In E. J. Anthony & C. Koupernik (Eds.), *The child and his family: The impact of disease and death.* New York: Wiley.

Birk, L. (1979). *Biofeedback: Behavioral medicine.* New York: Grune & Stratton.

Bishop, G. D. (1987). Lay conceptions of physical symptoms. *Journal of Applied Social Psychology, 17,* 127–146.

Bishop, G. D. (1990). Understanding the understanding of illness: Lay disease representations. In J. A. Skelton & R. T. Croyle (Eds.), *Mental representation in health and illness* (pp. 373–394). New York: Springer.

Bishop, G. D., Briede, C., Cavazos, L., Grotzinger, R., & McMahon, S. (1987). Processing illness information: The role of disease prototypes. *Basic and Applied Social Psychology, 8,* 21–43.

Bishop, G. D., & Converse, S. A. (1986). Illness representations: A prototype approach. *Health Psychology, 5,* 95–114.

Blackburn, H. (1983a). Physical activity and coronary heart disease: A brief update and popular view: Part I. *Journal of Cardiac Rehabilitation, 3,* 101–111.

Blackburn, H. (1983b). Physical activity and coronary heart disease: A brief update and popular view: Part II. *Journal of Cardiac Rehabilitation, 3,* 171–174.

Blair, S. N., Jacobs, D. R., & Powell, K. E. (1985). Relationships between exercise or physical activity and other health behaviors. *Public Health Reports, 100,* 172–180.

Blanchard, E. B., Andrasik, F., & Silver, B. V. (1980). Biofeedback and relaxation in the treatment of tension headaches: A reply to Belar. *Journal of Behavioral Medicine, 3,* 227–232.

Blanchard, E. B., Khramelashvili, V. V., McCoy, G. C., Aivazyan, T. A., McCaffrey, R. J., Salenko, B. B., Musso, A., Wittrock, D. A., Berger, M., Gerardi, M., & Pangburn, L. (1988). The USA-USSR collaborative cross-cultural comparison of autogenic training and thermal biofeedback in the treatment of mild hypertension. *Health Psychology, 7* (Suppl.), 175–192.

Blanchard, E. B., McCoy, G. C., Wittrock, D.,

Musso, A., Gerardi, R. J., & Pangburn, L. (1988). A controlled comparison of thermal biofeedback and relaxation training in the treatment of essential hypertension: II. Effects on cardiovascular reactivity. *Health Psychology, 7,* 19–33.

Blaney, N. T., Brown, P., & Blaney, P. H. (1986). Type A, marital adjustment, and life stress. *Journal of Behavioral Medicine, 9,* 491–502.

Bleck, T. P. (1987). Epilepsy. *Disease-a-Month, 33,* 604–679.

Bliss, R. E., & O'Connell, K. A. (1984). Problems with thiocyanate as an index of smoking status: A critical review with suggestions for improving the usefulness of biochemical measures in smoking cessation research. *Health Psychology, 3,* 563–581.

Blitzer, P. H., Rimm, A. A., and Geifer, E. E. (1977). The effect of cessation of smoking on body weight in 57,032 women: Cross-sectional and longitudinal analyses. *Journal of Chronic Diseases, 30,* 415–429.

Blondis, M. N., and Jackson, B. E. (1977). *Nonverbal communication with patients.* New York: Wiley.

Bloom, B. L., Asher, S. J., & White, S. W. (1978). Marital disruption as a stressor: A review and analysis. *Psychological Bulletin, 85,* 867–894.

Bloom, S. (1965). The sociology of medical education: Some comments on the state of a field. *Milbank Memorial Fund Quarterly, 43,* 143–184.

Bloom, S. W. (1986). Institutional trends in medical sociology. *Journal of Health and Social Behavior, 27,* 265–276.

Bluebond-Langner, M. (1977). Meanings of death to children. In H. Feifel (Ed.), *New meanings of death* (pp. 47–66). New York: McGraw-Hill.

Blum, R. H. (1957). *The psychology of malpractice suits.* San Francisco: California Medical Association.

Blum, R. H. (1960). *The management of the doctor-patient relationship.* New York: McGraw-Hill.

Blumenthal, J. A., & Emery, C. F. (1988). Rehabilitation of patients following myocardial infarction. *Journal of Consulting and Clinical Psychology, 56,* 374–381.

Blumenthal, J. A., Emery, C. F., Walsh, M. A., Cox, D. R., Kuhn, C. M., Williams, R. B., & Williams, R. S. (1988). Exercise training in health Type A middle-aged men: Effects of behavioral and cardiovascular responses. *Psychosomatic Medicine, 50,* 418–433.

Bolles, R. C., & Fanselow, M. S. (1982). Endorphins and behavior. *Annual Review of Psychology, 33,* 87–101.

Bond, M. R. (1979). *Pain: Its nature, analysis and treatment.* New York: Longman.

Booth, C. S., Safer, M. A., & Leventhal, H. (1986). Use of physician services following participation in a cardiac screening program. *Public Health Reports, 101,* 315–319.

Booth-Kewley, S., & Friedman, H. S. (1987). Psychological predictors of heart disease: A quantitative review. *Psychological Bulletin, 101,* 343–362.

Bootzin, R. R. (1975). *Behavior modification and therapy: An introduction.* Cambridge, MA: Winthrop.

Bortner, R. W., & Rosenman, R. H. (1967). The measurement of pattern A behavior. *Journal of Chronic Diseases, 20,* 466–475.

Borysenko, M., & Borysenko, J. (1982). Stress, behavior, and immunity: Animal models and mediating mechanisms. *General Hospital Psychiatry, 4,* 59–67.

Boskind-White, M., & White, W. C. (1983). *Bulimarexia: The binge/purge cycle.* New York: Norton.

Bosley, F., & Allen, T. W. (1989). Stress management training for hypertensives: Cognitive and physiological effects. *Journal of Behavioral Medicine, 12,* 77–90.

Botvin, G. J. (1985). The Life-Skills Training Program as a health-promotion strategy: Theoretical issues and empirical findings. *Special Services in the Schools, 1,* 9–25.

Botvin, G. J., Dusenbury, L., Baker, E., James-Ortiz, S., & Kerner, J. (1989). A skills training approach to smoking prevention among Hispanic youth. *Journal of Behavioral Medicine, 12,* 279–296.

Botvin, G. J., & Eng, A. (1982). The efficacy of a multicomponent approach to the prevention of cigarette smoking. *Preventive Medicine, 11,* 199–211.

Botvin, G. J., Eng, A., & Williams, C. L. (1980). Preventing the onset of cigarette smoking through life skills training. *Preventive Medicine, 9,* 135–143.

Botvin, G. J., Renick, N. L., & Baker, E. (1983). The effects of scheduling format and booster sessions on a broad-spectrum psychosocial approach to smoking prevention. *Journal of Behavioral Medicine, 6,* 359–380.

Boudewyns, P. A., & Nolan, W. P. (1985). Prospective payment: Its impact on psychology's role in health care. *Health Psychology, 4,* 489–498.

Bovbjerg, D., Cohen, N., & Ader, R. (1987). Behaviorally conditioned enhancement of delayed-type hypersensitivity in the mouse. *Brain, Behavior, and Immunity, 1,* 64–71.

Bowlby, J. (1969). *Attachment and loss: Vol. 1 Attachment.* New York: Basic Books.

Bowlby, J. (1973). *Attachment and loss: Vol. 2. Separation.* New York: Basic Books.

Boyce, W. T., Jensen, E. W., Cassel, J. C., Collier, A. M., Smith, A. H., & Ramey, C. T. (1977). Influence of life events and family routines on childhood respiratory tract illness. *Pediatrics, 60,* 609–615.

Bradley, L. A. (1983). Relationships between the MMPI and the McGill Pain Questionnaire. In R. Melzack (Ed.), *Pain measurement and assessment.* New York: Raven Press.

Bradley, L. A., & Van der Heide, L. H. (1984). Pain-related correlates of MMPI profile subgroups among back pain patients. *Health Psychology, 3,* 157–174.

Bradley, L. A., Young, L. D., Anderson, K. O., Turner, R. A., Agudelo, C. A., McDaniel, L. K., Pisko, E. J., Semble, E. L., & Morgan, T. M. (1987). Effects of psychological therapy on pain behavior of rheumatoid arthritis patients: Treatment outcome and six-month followup. *Arthritis and Rheumatism, 30,* 1105–1114.

Bramwell, L. (1986). Wives' experiences in the support role after husbands' first myocardial infarction. *Heart and Lung, 15,* 578–584.

Brand, A. H., Johnson, J. H., & Johnson, S. B. (1986). Life stress and diabetic control in children and adolescents with insulin-dependent diabetes. *Journal of Pediatric Psychology, 11,* 481–495.

Branstetter, E. (1969). The young child's response to hospitalization: Separation anxiety or lack of mothering care? *American Journal of Public Health, 59,* 92–97.

Bray, G. A. (1976). *The obese patient.* Philadelphia: Saunders.

Brehm, J. W. (1966). *A theory of psychological reactance.* New York: Academic Press.

Brehm, S. S., and Brehm, J. W. (1981). *Psychological reactance: A theory of freedom and control.* New York: Academic Press.

Brenner, M. H. (1976). *Estimating the social costs of national economic policy: Implications for mental and physical health, and criminal violence.* Report prepared for the Joint Economic Committee of Congress. Washington, DC: U.S. Government Printing Office.

Brescia, F. J., Sadof, M., & Barstow, J. (1984). Retrospective analysis of a home care hospice program. *Omega, 15,* 37–44.

Breslau, N., & Davis, G. C. (1987). Posttraumatic stress disorder: The stressor criterion. *Journal of Nervous and Mental Disease, 175,* 255–264.

Breslow, L., & Buell, P. (1960). Mortality from coronary heart disease and physical activity of work in California. *Journal of Chronic Disease, 11,* 615–626.

Breslow, L., & Enstrom, J. E. (1980). Persistence of health habits and their relationship to mortality. *Preventive Medicine, 9,* 469–483.

Breslow, L., & Somers, A. R. (1977). The lifetime health-monitoring program. *New England Journal of Medicine, 296,* 601–608.

Brett, J. F., Brief, A. P., Burke, M. J., George, J. M., & Webster, J. (1990). Negative affectivity and the reporting of stressful life events. *Health Psychology, 9,* 57–68.

Brewin, C. (1985). Depression and causal attributions: What is their relation? *Psychological Bulletin, 2,* 297–309.

Bridge, L. R., Benson, P., Pietroni, P. C., & Priest, R. G. (1986). Relaxation and imagery in the treatment of breast cancer. *British Medical Journal, 297,* 1169–1172.

Brody, J. E. (1976, January 28). Prescriptions killing thousands. *The New York Times.*

Bronzaft, A. L., & McCarthy, D. P. (1975). The effects of elevated train noise on reading ability. *Environment and Behavior, 7,* 517–527.

Brooks, G. W., & Mueller, E. F. (1966). The relationship of serum urate levels to drive, achievement, and leadership in university professors. *Journal of the American Medical Association, 195,* 1476–1481.

Brown, D. F., Wright, F. A. C., & McMurray, N. E. (1986). Psychological and behavioral factors associated with dental anxiety in children. *Journal of Behavioral Medicine, 9,* 213–218.

Brown, E. (1963). Meeting patients' psychosocial needs in the general hospital. *Annals of the American Academy of Political and Social Science, 346,* 117–122.

Brown, G. W., & Harris, T. (1978). *Social origins of depression: A study of psychiatric disorder in women.* New York: Free Press.

Brown, J. D., & McGill, K. L. (1989). The cost of good fortune: When positive life events produce negative health consequences. *Journal of Personality and Social Psychology, 57,* 1103–1110.

Brown, J. D., & Siegel, J. M. (1988). Exercise as a buffer of life stress: A prospective study of adolescent health. *Health Psychology, 7,* 341–353.

Brownell, A., & Dooley, D. (1981). *Perceived social support: A moderator of health-related stress.* Unpublished manuscript, University of California, Irvine.

Brownell, K. D. (1982). Obesity: Understanding and treating a serious, prevalent and refractory disorder. *Journal of Consulting and Clinical Psychology, 50,* 820–840.

Brownell, K. D. (1986). Public health approaches to obesity and its management. *Annual Review of Public Health, 7,* 521–533.

Brownell, K. D. (1988, January). Yo-yo dieting. *Psychology Today,* pp. 20, 22–23.

Brownell, K. D. (1990). *The Learn Program for weight control.* Dallas, TX: Brownell & Hager.

Brownell, K. D., Cohen, R. Y., Stunkard, A. J., Felix, M. R. J., & Cooley, B. (1984). Weight loss competitions at the work site: Impact on weight, morale, and cost-effectiveness. *American Journal of Public Health, 74,* 1283–1285.

Brownell, K. D., & Felix, M. R. J. (1987). Competitions to facilitate health promotion: Review and conceptual analysis. *American Journal of Health Promotion, Summer,* 28–36.

Brownell, K. D., Greenwood, M. R. C., Stellar, E., & Shrager, E. E. (1986). The effects of repeated cycles of weight loss and regain in rats. *Physiology and Behavior, 38,* 459–464.

Brownell, K. D., & Jeffrey, R. W. (1987). Improving long-term weight loss: Pushing the limits of treatment. *Behavior Therapy, 18,* 353–374.

Brownell, K. D., Kelman, M. S., & Stunkard, A. J. (1983). Treatment of obese children with and without their mothers: Changes in weight and blood pressure. *Pediatrics, 71,* 515–523.

Brownell, K. D., & Kramer, F. M. (1989). Behavioral management of obesity. *Medical Clinics of North America, 73,* 185–201.

Brownell, K. D., Marlatt, G. A., Lichtenstein, E., & Wilson, G. T. (1986). Understanding and preventing relapse. *American Psychologist, 41*, 765–782.

Brownell, K. D., Steen, S. N., & Wilmore, J. H. (1987). Weight regulation practices in athletes: Analysis of metabolic and health effects. *Medicine and Science in Sports and Exercise, 19*, 546–556.

Brownell, K. D., & Stunkard, A. J. (1981). Couples training, pharmacotherapy and behavior therapy in the treatment of obesity. *Archives of General Psychiatry, 38*, 1224–1229.

Brownell, K. D., Stunkard, A. J., & McKeon, P. E. (1985). Weight reduction at the work site: A promise partially fulfilled. *American Journal of Psychiatry, 142*, 47–52.

Brownlee-Duffeck, M., Peterson, L., Simonds, J. F., Goldstein, D., Kilo, C., & Hoette, S. (1987). The role of health beliefs in the regimen adherence and metabolic control of adolescents and adults with diabetes mellitus. *Journal of Consulting and Clinical Psychology, 55*, 139–144.

Broyard, A. (1989, November 12). Intoxicated by my illness. *New York Times Magazine*, pp. 10, 12.

Brubaker, R. G., & Wickersham, D. (1990). Encouraging the practice of testicular self-examination: A field application of the theory of reasoned action. *Health Psychology, 9*, 154–163.

Bruch, H. (1973). *Eating disorders*. New York: Basic Books.

Bruhn, J. G. (1965). An epidemiological study of myocardial infarction in an Italian-American community. *Journal of Chronic Diseases, 18*, 326–338.

Buckalew, L. W., & Sallis, R. E. (1986). Patient compliance and medication perception. *Journal of Clinical Psychology, 42*, 49–53.

Buckingham, R. W. (1983). Hospice care in the United States: The process begins. *Omega, 13*, 159–171.

Budzynsky, J., Stoyva, J., Adler, C., & Mullaney, D. (1973). EMG biofeedback and tension headache: A controlled outcome study. In L. Birk (Ed.), *Biofeedback: Behavioral medicine*. New York: Grune & Stratton.

Bukberg, J., Penman, D., & Holland, J. C. (1984). Depression in hospitalized cancer patients. *Psychosomatic Medicine, 46*, 199–212.

Buller, M. K., & Buller, D. B. (1987). Physicians' communication style and patient satisfaction. *Journal of Health and Social Behavior, 28*, 375–388.

Bulman, J. R., and Wortman, C. B. (1977). Attributions of blame and coping in the "real world": Severe accident victims react to their lot. *Journal of Personality and Social Psychology, 35*, 351–363.

Burger, J. M. (1989). Negative reactions to increases in perceived personal control. *Journal of Personality and Social Psychology, 56*, 246–256.

Burger, J. M., & Cooper, H. M. (1979). The desirability of control. *Motivation and Emotion, 3*, 381–393.

Burgess, C., Morris, T., & Pettingale, K. W. (1988). Psychological response to cancer diagnosis: II. Evidence for coping styles. *Journal of Psychosomatic Research, 32*, 263–272.

Burish, T. C., & Bradley, L. A. (1983). *Coping with chronic disease: Research and applications*. New York: Academic Press.

Burish, T. C., Carey, M. P., Wallston, K. A., Stein, M. J., Jamison, R. N., & Lyles, J. N. (1984). Health locus of control and chronic disease: An external orientation may be advantageous. *Journal of Social and Clinical Psychology, 2*, 326–332.

Burish, T. C., & Lyles, J. N. (1979). Effectiveness of relaxation training in reducing the aversiveness of chemotherapy in the treatment of cancer. *Journal of Behavior Therapy and Experimental Psychiatry, 10*, 357–361.

Burnam, M. A., Pennebaker, J. W., & Glass, D. C. (1975). Time consciousness, achievement-striving and the Type A coronary-prone behavior pattern. *Journal of Abnormal Psychology, 84*, 76–79.

Burnam, M. A., Timbers, D. M., & Hough, R. L. (1984). Two measures of psychological distress among Mexican Americans, Mexicans and Anglos. *Journal of Health and Social Behavior, 25*, 24–33.

Burnett, K. F., Taylor C. B., & Agras, W. S. (1985). Ambulatory computer-assisted therapy for obesity: A new frontier for behavior therapy. *Journal of Consulting and Clinical Psychology, 53*, 698–703.

Burns, M. O., & Seligman, M. E. P. (1989). Explanatory style across the life span: Evidence for stability over 52 years. *Journal of Personality and Social Psychology, 56*, 471–477.

Bush, C., Ditto, B., & Feuerstein, M. (1985). A controlled evaluation of paraspinal EMG biofeedback in the treatment of chronic low back pain. *Health Psychology, 4*, 307–321.

Bush, J. P., Melamed, B. G., Sheras, P. L., &

Greenbaum, P. E. (1986). Mother-child patterns of coping with anticipatory medical stress. *Health Psychology, 5*, 137–157.

Bush, P. J., & Osterweis, M. (1978). Pathways to medicine use. *Journal of Health and Social Behavior, 19*, 179–189.

Butler, R. N. (1978). The doctor and the aged patient. In W. Reichel (Ed.), *The geriatric patient* (pp. 199–206). New York: HP.

Buunk, B. (1989). Affiliation and helping within organizations: A critical analysis of the role of social support with regard to occupational stress. In W. Stroebe & M. Hewstone (Eds.), *European review of social psychology* (Vol. 1). Chichester, England: Wiley.

Buunk, B., Janssen, P. P. M., & VanYperen, N. W. (in press). Stress and affiliation reconsidered: The effects of social support in stressful and non-stressful work units. *Social Behaviour.*

Byrne, D. G., & Rosenman, R. H. (1986). The Type A behavior pattern as a precursor to stressful life-events: A confluence of coronary risks. *British Journal of Medical Psychology, 59*, 75–82.

Caggiula, A. W., Christakis, G., Farrand, M., Hulley, S. B., Johnson, R., Lasser, N. L., Stamler, J., & Widdowson, G. (1981). The Multiple Risk Factor Intervention Trial (MRFIT): IV. Intervention on blood lipids. *Preventive Medicine, 10*, 443–475.

Calabrese, J. R., Kling, M. A., & Gold, P. W. (1987). Alterations in immunocompetence during stress, bereavement, and depression: Focus on neuroendocrine regulation. *American Journal of Psychiatry, 144*, 1123–1134.

Calabrese, J. R., Skwerer, R. G., Barna, B., Gulledge, A. D., Valenzuela, R., Butkus, A., Subichin, S., & Krupp, N. E. (1986). Depression, immunocompetence, and prostaglandins of the E series. *Psychiatry Research, 17*, 41–47.

Califano, J. A., Jr. (1979a). *Healthy people: Background papers.* Washington, DC: U.S. Government Printing Office.

Califano, J. A., Jr. (1979b). *Healthy people: The Surgeon General's report on health promotion and disease prevention.* Washington, DC: U.S. Government Printing Office.

Calnan, M. W., & Moss, S. (1984). The health belief model and compliance with education given at a class in breast self-examination. *Journal of Health and Social Behavior, 25*, 198–210.

Cameron, A., & Hinton, J. (1968). Delay in seeking treatment for mammary tumors. *Cancer, 21*, 1121–1126.

Cameron, N. (1963). *Personality development and psychology: A dynamic approach.* Boston: Houghton-Mifflin.

Campbell, B. M., Hunter, W. W., & Stutts, J. C. (1984). The use of economic incentives and education to modify safety belt use behavior of high school students. *Health Education, 15*, 30–33.

Cancer Information Service of California. (1989). *Cancer information service smoking and health fact sheet: Smoking demographics.* San Diego, CA: Author.

Cannon, W. B. (1932). *The wisdom of the body.* New York: Norton.

Caplan, R. D., Cobb, S., & French, J. R. P. (1975). Relationships of cessation of smoking with job stress, personality, and social support. *Journal of Applied Psychology, 60*, 211–219.

Caplan, R. D., & Jones, K. W. (1975). Effects of work load, role ambiguity, and Type A personality on anxiety, depression and heart rate. *Journal of Applied Psychology, 60*, 713–719.

Cappon, D. (1969). Attitudes of and toward the dying. *Journal of the Canadian Medical Association, 87*, 693–700.

Carey, M. P., & Burish, T. G. (1985). Anxiety as a predictor of behavioral therapy outcome for cancer chemotherapy patients. *Journal of Consulting and Clinical Psychology, 53*, 860–865.

Carey, M. P., & Burish, T. G. (1988). Etiology and treatment of the psychological side effects associated with cancer chemotherapy: A critical review and discussion. *Psychological Bulletin, 104*, 307–325.

Carey, R. G. (1975). Living with death: A program of service and research for the terminally ill. In E. Kübler-Ross (Ed.), *Death: The final stage of growth.* Englewood Cliffs, NJ: Prentice-Hall.

Carmelli, D., Chesney, M. A., Ward, M. W., & Rosenman, R. H. (1985). Twin similarity in cardiovascular stress response. *Health Psychology, 4*, 413–423.

Carmelli, D., Rosenman, R., & Chesney, M. (1987). Stability of the Type A structured interview and related questionnaires in a 10-year follow-up of an adult cohort of twins. *Journal of Behavioral Medicine, 10*, 513–525.

Carmelli, D., Rosenman, R., Chesney, M., Fabsitz,

R., Lee, M., & Borhani, N. (1988). Genetic heritability and shared environmental influences of Type A measures in the NHLBI twin study. *American Journal of Epidemiology, 127,* 1041–1052.

Carmody, T. P., Brischetto, C. S., Matarazzo, J. D., O'Donnell, R. P., & Connor, W. E. (1985). Co-occurrent use of cigarettes, alcohol, and coffee in healthy, community-living men and women. *Health Psychology, 4,* 323–335.

Carmody, T. P., Fey, S. G., Pierce, D. K., Connor, W. E., & Matarazzo, J. D. (1982). Behavioral treatment of hyperlipidemia: Techniques, results, and future directions. *Journal of Behavioral Medicine, 5,* 91–116.

Carmody, T. P., Istvan, J., Matarazzo, J. D., Connor, S. L., & Connor, W. E. (1986). Applications of social learning theory in the promotion of heart-healthy diets: The Family Heart Study dietary intervention model. *Health Education Research, 1,* 13–27.

Carmody, T. P., Matarazzo, J. D., & Istvan, J. A. (1987). Promoting adherence to heart-healthy diets: A review of the literature. *Journal of Compliance in Health Care, 2,* 105–124.

Carver, C. S., Coleman, A. E., & Glass, D. C. (1976). The coronary-prone behavior pattern and the suppression of fatigue on a treadmill test. *Journal of Personality and Social Behavior, 33,* 460–466.

Carver, C. S., DeGregorio, E., & Gillis, R. (1981). Challenge and Type A behavior among intercollegiate football players. *Journal of Sport Psychology, 3,* 140–148.

Carver, C. S., & Glass, D. C. (1978). Coronary-prone behavior pattern and interpersonal aggression. *Journal of Personality and Social Psychology, 36,* 361–366.

Carver, C. S., & Humphries, C. (1982). Social psychology of the Type A coronary-prone behavior pattern. In G. S. Saunders & J. Suls (Eds.), *Social psychology of health and illness* (pp. 33–64). Hillsdale, NJ: Erlbaum.

Carver, C. S., & Scheier, M. F. (1982). Control theory: A useful conceptual framework for personality—social, clinical, and health psychology. *Psychological Bulletin, 92,* 111–135.

Carver, C. S., Scheier, M. F., & Weintraub, J. K. (1989). Assessing coping strategies: A theoretically based approach. *Journal of Personality and Social Psychology, 56,* 267–283.

Cassileth, B. R. (1989). The social implications of questionable cancer therapies. *Cancer, 63,* 1247–1250.

Cassileth, B. R., & Donovan, J. A. (1983). Hospice: History and implications of the new legislation. *Journal of Psychosocial Oncology, 1,* 59–69.

Cassileth, B. R., Lusk, E. J., Strouse, T. B., Miller, D. S., Brown, L. L., Cross, P. A. (1985). A psychological analysis of cancer patients and their next-of-kin. *Cancer, 55,* 72–76.

Cassileth, B. R., Lusk, E. J., Strouse, T. B., Miller, D. S., Brown, L. L., Cross, P. A., & Tenaglia, A. N. (1984). Psychosocial status in chronic illness: A comparative analysis of six diagnostic groups. *New England Journal of Medicine, 311,* 506–511.

Cassileth, B. R., Temoshok, L. Frederick, B. E., Walsh, W. P., Hurwitz, S., Guerry, D., Clark, W. H., DiClemente, R. J., Sweet, D. M., Blois, M. S., & Sagebiel, R. W. (1988). Patient and physician delay in melanoma diagnosis. *Journal of the American Academy of Dermatology, 18,* 591–598.

Castro, F. G., Maddahian, E., Newcomb, M. D., & Bentler, P. M. (1987). A multivariate model of the determinants of cigarette smoking among adolescents. *Journal of Health and Social Behavior, 28,* 273–289.

Castro, F. G., Newcomb, M. D., McCreary, C., & Baezconde-Garbanati, L. (1989). Cigarette smokers do more than just smoke cigarettes. *Health Psychology, 8,* 107–129.

Catalano, R. A., Dooley, D., & Jackson, R. L. (1985). Economic antecedents of help seeking: Reformulation of time-series tests. *Journal of Health and Social Behavior, 26,* 141–152.

Catalano, R. A., Rook, K., & Dooley, D. (1986). Labor markets and help-seeking: A test of the employment security hypothesis. *Journal of Health and Social Behavior, 27,* 277–287.

Cataldo, M. F., Green, L. W., Herd, J. A., Parkinson, R. S., & Goldbeck, W. B. (1986). Preventive medicine and the corporate environment: Challenge to behavioral medicine. In M. F. Cataldo & T. J. Coates (Eds.), *Health and industry: A behavioral medicine perspective* (pp. 399–419). New York: Wiley.

Cattanach, L., & Rodin, J. (1988). Psychosocial components of the stress process in bulimia. *International Journal of Eating Disorders, 7,* 75–88.

Cautela, J. R. (1971). Covert conditioning. In A. Jacobs & L. B. Sachs (Eds.), *The psychology of pri-*

vate events: Perspective on covert response systems (pp. 112–130). New York: Academic Press.

Cay, E. L., Vetter, N. J., Philip, A. E., & Dugard, P. (1972). Psychological status during recovery from an acute heart attack. *Journal of Psychosomatic Research, 16,* 425–435.

Centers for Disease Control. (1980). *Risk factor update.* Atlanta, GA: U.S. Department of Health and Human Services.

Centers for Disease Control. (1989). *Surgeon General's report on smoking: Reducing health consequences of smoking: 25 years of progress, 1964–1989.* Washington, DC: Central Office for Health Promotion and Education on Smoking and Health, U.S. Government Printing Office.

Chafetz, M. E. (1970). No patient deserves to be patronized. *Medical Insight, 2,* 68–75.

Chambers, W. N., & Reiser, M. F. (1953). Emotional stress in the precipitation of congestive heart failure. *Medicine, 15,* 38–60.

Chaney, E. F., O'Leary, M. R., & Marlatt, G. A. (1978). Skill training with alcoholics. *Journal of Consulting and Clinical Psychology, 46,* 1092–1104.

Chassin, L., Presson, C. C., & Sherman, S. J. (1985). Stepping backward in order to step forward: An acquisition-oriented approach to primary prevention. *Journal of Consulting and Clinical Psychology, 53,* 612–622.

Chassin, L., Presson, C. C., Sherman, S. J., Corty, E., & Olshavsky, R. W. (1984). Predicting the onset of cigarette smoking in adolescents: A longitudinal study. *Journal of Applied Social Psychology, 14,* 224–243.

Chassin, L., Presson, C. C., Sherman, S. J., & McGrew, J. (1987). The changing smoking environment for middle and high school students 1980–1983. *Journal of Behavioral Medicine, 10,* 581–594.

Chaves, I. F., & Barber, T. X. (1976). Hypnotism and surgical pain. In D. Mostofsky (Ed.), *Behavioral control and modification of physiological activity.* Englewood Cliffs, NJ: Prentice-Hall.

Chaves, J. F., & Brown, J. M. (1987). Spontaneous cognitive strategies for the control of clinical pain and stress. *Journal of Behavioral Medicine, 10,* 263–276.

Chesney, M. A., Black, G. W., Swan, G. E., & Ward, M. M. (1987). Relaxation training for essential hypertension at the worksite: I. The untreated mild hypertensive. *Psychosomatic Medicine, 49,* 250–263.

Chesney, M. A., Eagleston, J. R., & Rosenman, R. H. (1981). Type A behavior: Assessment and intervention. In C. K. Prokop & L. A. Bradley (Eds.), *Medical psychology: Contributions to behavioral medicine* (pp. 485–497). New York: Academic Press.

Chibnall, J. T., & Tait, R. C. (1989). The psychosomatic symptom checklist revisited: Reliability and validity in a chronic pain population. *Journal of Behavioral Medicine, 12,* 297–308.

Christman, N. J., McConnell, E. A., Pfeiffer, C., Webster, K. K., Schmitt, M., & Ries, J. (1988). Uncertainty, coping, and distress following myocardial infarction: Transition from hospital to home. *Research in Nursing and Health, 11,* 71–82.

Christophersen, E. R., Finney, J. W., & Friman, P. C. (1986). Medical compliance in pediatric practice. In N. A. Krasnegor, J. Arasteh, & M. F. Cataldo (Eds.), *Child health behavior: A behavioral pediatrics perspective* (pp. 435–452). New York: Wiley.

Christophersen, E. R., Sosland-Edelman, D., & LeClaire, S. (1985). Evaluation of two comprehensive infant car seat loaner programs with 1-year follow-up. *Pediatrics, 76,* 36–42.

Chrvala, C. A., & Weiner, A. W. (1989, April). *Need and availability of social support for the cancer patient.* Paper presented at the annual meeting of the Western Psychological Association, Reno, NV.

Cinciripini, P. M., & Floreen, A. (1982). An evaluation of a behavioral program for chronic pain. *Journal of Behavioral Medicine, 5,* 375–390.

Clark, J. H., MacPherson, B. V., & Holmes, D. R. (1982). Cigarette smoking and the external locus of control among young adolescents. *Journal of Health and Social Behavior, 23,* 253–259.

Clark, M. (1977). The new war on pain. *Newsweek, 89*(17), 48–58.

Clavel, F., Benhamou, S., & Flamant, R. (1987). Nicotine dependence and secondary effects of smoking cessation. *Journal of Behavioral Medicine, 10,* 555–558.

Cleary, P. D., Mechanic, D., & Greenley, J. R. (1982). Sex differences in medical care utilization: An empirical investigation. *Journal of Health and Social Behavior, 23,* 106–119.

Cloninger, C. R. (1987). Neurogenetic adaptive mechanisms in alcoholism. *Science, 236,* 410–416.

Coates, T. J., & Greenblatt, R. M. (1989). Behavioral change using interventions at the community level. In K. G. Holmes, P. A. Mardh, P. F. Sparling, & P. J. Weisner (Eds.), *Sexually transmitted diseases* (2nd ed., pp. 1075–1080). New York: McGraw-Hill.

Coates, T. J., McKusick, L., Kuno, R., & Stites, D. P. (1989). Stress reduction training changed number of sexual partners but not immune function in men with HIV. *American Journal of Public Health, 79*, 885–887.

Coates, T. J., Morin, S. F., & McKusick, L. (1987). Behavioral consequences of AIDS antibody testing among gay men. *Journal of the American Medical Association, 258*, 1889.

Coates, T. J., Stall, R. D., Kegeles, S. M., Lo, B., Morin, S. F., & McKusick, L. (1988). AIDS antibody testing: Will it stop the AIDS epidemic? Will it help people infected with HIV? *American Psychologist, 43*, 859–864.

Cobb, S. (1976). Social support as a moderator of life stress. *Psychosomatic Medicine, 38*, 300–314.

Cochran, S. D., & Hammen, C. L. (1985). Perceptions of stressful life events and depression: A test of attributional moods. *Journal of Personality and Social Psychology, 48*, 1562–1571.

Cochran, S. D., & Mays, V. M. (1989). Women and AIDS-related concerns: Roles for psychologists in helping the worried well. *American Psychologist, 44*, 529–535.

Cochran, S. D., & Mays, V. M. (1990). AIDS-related sexual behavior and disclosure: Is it safe if you ask? *New England Journal of Medicine, 322*, 774–775.

Cockerham, W. C., Lueschen, G., Kunz, G., & Spaeth, J. L. (1986). Social stratification and self-management of health. *Journal of Health and Social Behavior, 27*, 1–14.

Cogan, R., Cogan, D., Waltz, W., & McCue, M. (1987). Effects of laughter and relaxation on discomfort thresholds. *Journal of Behavioral Medicine, 10*, 139.

Cohen, F., Kearney, K. A., Zegans, L. S., Kemeny, M. E., Neuhaus, J. M., & Stites, D. P. (1989). *Acute stressors, chronic stressors, and immunity and the role of optimism as a moderator.* Manuscript submitted for publication.

Cohen, F., & Lazarus, R. (1979). Coping with the stresses of illness. In G. C. Stone, F. Cohen, & N. E. Adler (Eds.), *Health psychology: A handbook* (pp. 77–112). San Francisco: Jossey-Bass.

Cohen, J., Cullen, J. W., & Martin, J. R. (Eds.). (1982). *Psychosocial aspects of cancer.* New York: Raven Press.

Cohen, R. Y., Stunkard, A., & Felix, M. R. J. (1986). Measuring community change in disease prevention and health promotion. *Preventive Medicine, 15*, 411–421.

Cohen, S. (1978). Environmental load and allocation of attention. In A. Baum, J. E. Singer, & S. Valins (Eds.), *Advances in environmental psychology* (Vol. I, pp. 1–29). Hillsdale, NJ: Erlbaum.

Cohen, S. (1980). Aftereffects of stress on human performance and social behavior: A review of research and theory. *Psychological Bulletin, 88*, 82–108.

Cohen, S. (1988). Psychosocial models of the role of social support in the etiology of physical disease. *Health Psychology, 7*, 269–297.

Cohen, S., & Edwards, J. R. (1989). Personality characteristics as moderators of the relationship between stress and disorder. In R. W. J. Neufeld (Ed.), *Advances in the investigation of psychological stress* (pp. 235–283). New York: Wiley.

Cohen, S., Evans, G. W., Krantz, D. S., & Stokols, D. (1980). Physiological, motivational, and cognitive effects of aircraft noise on children. *American Psychologist, March*, 231–243.

Cohen, S., Evans, G. W., Stokols, D., & Krantz, D. S. (1986). *Behavior, health, and environmental stress.* New York: Plenum.

Cohen, S., Glass, D. C., & Phillip, S. (1978). Environment and health. In H. E. Freeman, S. Levine, & L. G. Reeder (Eds.), *Handbook of medical sociology* (pp. 134–149). Englewood Cliffs, NJ: Prentice-Hall.

Cohen, S., Glass, D. C., & Singer, J. E. (1973). Apartment noise, auditory discrimination, and reading ability in children. *Journal of Experimental Social Psychology, 9*, 407–422.

Cohen, S., & Hoberman, H. M. (1983). Positive events and social supports as buffers of life change stress. *Journal of Applied Social Psychology, 13*, 99–125.

Cohen, S., Kamarck, T., & Mermelstein, R. (1983). A global measure of perceived stress. *Journal of Health and Social Behavior, 24*, 385–396.

Cohen, S., Lichtenstein, E., Mermelstein, R., Kingsolver, K., Baer, J. S., & Kamarck, T. W. (1988). Social support interventions for smoking cessation. In B. H. Gottlieb (Ed.), *Marshalling social support: Formats, processes, and effects* (pp. 211–240). Newbury Park, CA: Sage.

Cohen, S., Lichtenstein, E., Prochaska, J. O., Rossi, J. S., Gritz, E. R., Carr, C. R., Orleans, C. T., Schoenbach, V. J., Biener, L., Abrams, D., DiClemente, C., Curry, S., Marlatt, G. A., Cummings, K. M., Emont, S. L., Giovino, G., & Ossip-Klein, D. (1989). Debunking myths about self-quitting: Evidence from ten prospective studies of persons quitting smoking by themselves. *American Psychologist, 44,* 1355–1365.

Cohen, S., & Matthews, K. A. (1987). Social support, Type A behavior, and coronary artery disease. *Psychosomatic Medicine, 49,* 325–330.

Cohen, S., & McKay, G. (1983). Social support, stress, and the buffering hypothesis: A theoretical analysis. In A. Baum, S. E. Taylor, & J. Singer (Eds.), *Handbook of psychology and health* (Vol. 4, pp. 253–268). Hillsdale, NJ: Erlbaum.

Cohen, S., Sherrod, D. R., & Clark, M. S. (1986). Social skills and the stress-protective role of social support. *Journal of Personality and Social Psychology, 50,* 963–973.

Cohen, S., & Spacapan, S. (1978). The aftereffects of stress: An attentional interpretation. *Environmental Psychology and Nonverbal Behavior, 3,* 43–57.

Cohen, S., & Williamson, G. M. (1988). Perceived stress in a probability sample of the United States. In S. Spacapan & S. Oskamp (Eds.), *The social psychology of health* (pp. 31–67). Newbury Park, CA: Sage.

Cohen, S., & Wills, T. A. (1985). Stress, social support, and the buffering hypothesis. *Psychological Bulletin, 98,* 310–357.

Colletti, R. B. (1984). A statewide hospital-based program to improve child passenger safety. *Health Education Quarterly, 11,* 207–213.

Colligan, M. J., Urtes, M. A., Wisseman, C., Rosensteel, R. E., Anania, T. L., & Hornung, R. W. (1979). An investigation of apparent mass psychogenic illness in an electronics plant. *Journal of Behavioral Medicine, 2,* 297–309.

Collins, B. E., & Aspinwall, L. G. (1989, May). Impression management in negotiations for safer sex. Paper presented at the Second Iowa Conference on Interpersonal Relationships, Iowa City, IA.

Collins, R. L., & Marlatt, G. A. (1981). Social modeling as a determinant of drinking behavior: Implications for prevention and treatment. *Addictive Behaviors, 6,* 233–240.

Collins, R. L., Taylor, S. E., & Skokan, L. A. (in press). A better world or a shattered vision?: Changes in perspectives following victimization. *Social cognition.*

Communication Technologies, Inc. (1984). *Designing an effective AIDS prevention campaign strategy for San Francisco: Results from the first probability sample of an urban gay male community.* Unpublished report. (Available from the San Francisco AIDS Foundation, San Francisco, CA.)

Communication Technologies, Inc. (1987). *A report on designing an effective AIDS prevention campaign strategy for San Francisco: Results from the fourth probability sample of an urban gay male community.* Unpublished report. (Available from the San Francisco AIDS Foundation, San Francisco, CA.)

Connell, C. M., & D'Augelli, A. R. (1990). The contribution of personality characteristics to the relationship between social support and perceived physical health. *Health Psychology, 9,* 192–207.

Connor, W. E., & Connor, S. L. (1977). Dietary treatment of hyperlipidemia. In B. M. Rifkind & R. I. Levy (Eds.), *Hyperlipidemia: Diagnosis and therapy.* New York: Grune & Stratton.

Contrada, R. J. (1989). Type A behavior, personality hardiness, and cardiovascular responses to stress, *Journal of Personality and Social Psychology, 57,* 895–903.

Contrada, R. J., & Kantz, D. S. (1988). Stress, reactivity, and Type A behavior: Current status and future directions. *Annals of Behavioral Medicine, 10,* 64–70.

Contrada, R. J., Wright, R. A., & Glass, D. C. (1985). Psychophysiological correlates of Type A behavior: Comments on Houston (1983) and Holmes (1983). *Journal of Research in Personality, 19,* 12–30.

Conway, J. (1978). *Men in mid-life crisis.* Elgin, IL: Cook.

Conway, T. L., Vickers, R. R., Ward, H. W., & Rahe, R. H. (1981). Occupational stress and variation in cigarette, coffee, and alcohol consumption. *Journal of Health and Social Behavior, 22,* 155–165.

Cooper, C. J., & Marshall, J. (1976). Occupational sources of stress: A review of the literature relating to coronary heart disease and mental ill health. *Journal of Occupational Psychology, 49,* 11–28.

Cooper, J. K., Love, D. W., & Raffoul, P. R. (1982). Intentional prescription nonadherence (noncompliance) by the elderly. *Journal of the American Geriatric Society, 30,* 329–333.

Cooper, R., Soltero, I., & Stamler, J. (1982). Smoking cessation in the Chicago Coronary Prevention Evaluation. *Journal of the American Medical Association, 74,* 349–355.

Cooper, T., Detre, T., & Weiss, S. M. (1981). Coronary prone behavior and coronary heart disease: A critical review. *Circulation, 63* 1199–1215.

Cornelissen, P. G. J., Rasker, J. J., & Valkenburg, H. A. (1988). The arthritis sufferer and the community: A comparison of arthritis sufferers in rural and urban areas. *Annals of the Rheumatic Diseases, 47,* 150–156.

Corr, C. A., & Corr, D. M. (1985). Situations involving children: A challenge for the hospice movement. *The Hospice Journal, 1,* 63–77.

Corson, J. A., & Schneider, M. J. (1984). The Dartmouth pain questionnaire: An adjunct to the McGill pain questionnaire. *Pain, 19,* 59–69.

Coser, R. L. (1962). *Life in the ward.* East Lansing: Michigan State University Press.

Costa P. T., Jr., & McCrae, R. R. (1980). Somatic complaints in males as a function of age and neuroticism: A longitudinal analysis. *Journal of Behavioral Medicine, 3,* 245–258.

Costello, R. M. (1975a). Alcoholism treatment and evaluation: In search of methods. *International Journal of the Addictions, 10,* 251–275.

Costello, R. M. (1975b). Alcoholism treatment and evaluation: Collation of two-year followup studies. *International Journal of the Addictions, 10,* 276–291.

Costello, R. M., Baillargeon, J. G., Biever, P., & Bennett, R. (1980). Therapeutic community treatment for alcohol abusers: A one-year multivariate outcome evaluation. *International Journal of the Addictions, 15,* 215–232.

Cottington, E. M., Matthews, K. A., Talbott, E., & Kuller, L. H. (1980). Environmental events preceding sudden death in women. *Psychosomatic Medicine, 42,* 567–574.

Cousins, N. (1979). *Anatomy of an illness.* New York: Norton.

Cox, C., & Mead, A. (Eds.) (1975). *A sociology of medical practice.* London: Collier-Macmillan.

Cox, D. J., Tisdelle, D. A., & Culbert, J. P. (1988). Increasing adherence to behavioral homework assignments. *Journal of Behavioral Medicine, 11,* 519–522.

Cox, G. B., Chapman, C. R., & Black, R. G. (1978). The MMPI and chronic pain: The diagnosis of psychogenic pain. *Journal of Behavioral Medicine, 1* 437–444.

Coyne, J. C. (1976). Toward an interactional description of depression. *Psychiatry, 39,* 28–40.

Coyne, J. C., Kessler, R. C., Tal, M., Turnbull, J., Wortman, C. B., & Greden, J. F. (1987). Living with a depressed person. *Journal of Consulting and Clinical Psychology, 55* 347–352.

Crandall, L. A., & Duncan, R. P. (1981). Attitudinal and situational factors in the use of physician services by low-income persons. *Journal of Health and Social Behavior, 22,* 64–77.

Craun, A. M., & Deffenbacher, J. L. (1987). The effects of information, behavioral rehearsal, and prompting on breast self-exam. *Journal of Behavioral Medicine, 10,* 351–366.

Criqui, M. H. (1986). Epidemiology of atherosclerosis: An updated overview. *American Journal of Cardiology, 57,* 18C–23C.

Cromwell, R. L., Butterfield, E. C., Brayfield, F. M., & Curry, J. J. (1977). *Acute myocardial infarction: Reaction and recovery.* St. Louis, MO: Mosby.

Cronkite, R. C., & Moos, R. H. (1984). The role of predisposing and moderating factors in the stress-illness relationship. *Journal of Health and Social Behavior, 25,* 372–393.

Croog, S. H. (1983). Recovery and rehabilitation of heart patients: Psychosocial aspects. In D. S. Krantz & J. S. Singer (Eds.), *Handbook of psychology and health* (Vol. III, pp. 295–334). Hillsdale, NJ: Erlbaum.

Croog, S. H., & Fitzgerald, E. F. (1978). Subjective stress and serious illness of a spouse: Wives of heart patients. *Journal of Health and Social Behavior, 9,* 166–178.

Croog, S. H., & Levine, S. (1977). *The heart patient recovers.* New York: Human Sciences Press.

Cross, C. K., & Hirschfeld, M. A. (1986). Psychosocial factors and suicidal behavior. *Annals of the New York Academy of Sciences, 487,* 77–89.

Croyle, R. T., & Jemmott, J. B. III. (in press). Psychological reactions to risk factor testing. In J. A. Skelton & R. T. Croyle (Eds.), *The mental representation of health and illness.* New York: Springer.

Croyle, R. T., & Uretsky, M. B. (1987). Effects of mood on self-appraisal of health status. *Health Psychology, 6,* 239–253.

Cullen, J. W., Fox, B. H., & Isom, R. N. (Eds.).

(1976). *Cancer: The behavioral dimension.* New York: Raven Press.

Culliton, B. J. (1987). Take two pets and call me in the morning. *Science, 237,* 1560–1561.

Cumming, E. M. (1964). New thoughts on the theory of disengagement. In R. Kastenbaum (Ed.), *New thoughts on old age.* New York: Springer.

Cumming, E. M., Dean, L., Newell, D., & McCafferty, P. (1960). Disengagement: A tentative theory of aging. *Sociometry, 23,* 23–35.

Cummings, K. M., Becker, M. H., Kirscht, J. P., & Levin, N. W., (1981). Intervention strategies to improve compliance with medical regimens by ambulatory hemodialysis patients. *Journal of Behavioral Medicine, 4,* 111–128.

Cummings, K. M., Hellmann, R., & Ermont, S. L. (1988). Correlates of participation in a worksite stop-smoking contest. *Journal of Behavioral Medicine, 11,* 267–278.

Cummings, K. M., Jette, A. M., & Rosenstock, I. M. (1978). Construct validation of the health belief model. *Health Education Monographs, 6,* 394–405.

Cunningham, A. J. (1981). Mind, body, and immune response. In R. Ader (Ed.), *Psychoneuroimmunology* (pp. 609–617). New York: Academic Press.

Curbow, B. (1986). Health care and the poor: Psychological implications of restrictive policies. *Health Psychology, 5,* 375–391.

Curry, S. J., Marlatt, G. A., Gordon, J., & Baer, J. S. (1988). A comparison to alternative theoretical approaches to smoking cessation and relapse. *Health Psychology, 7,* 545–556.

Cushman, L. A. (1986). Secondary neuropsychiatric complications in stroke: Implications for acute care. *Archives of Physical Medicine and Rehabilitation, 69,* 877–879.

Cutrona, C. E., & Russell, D. W. (in press). Type of social support and specific stress: Toward a theory of optimal matching. In G. Sarason, B. R. Sarason, & G. R. Pierce (Eds.), *Social support: An interactional view.* New York: Wiley.

Dahlberg, C. C. (1977, June). Stroke. *Psychology Today,* pp. 121–128.

Dahlquist, L. M., Gil, K. M., Armstrong, F. D., DeLawyer, D. D., Greene, P., & Wuori, D. (1986). Preparing children for medical examinations: The importance of previous medical experience. *Health Psychology, 5,* 249–259.

Dakof, G. A., & Mendelsohn, G. A. (1986). Parkinson's disease: The psychological aspects of a chronic illness. *Psychological Bulletin, 99,* 375–387.

Dakof, G. A., & Taylor, S. E. (1990). Victims' perceptions of social support: What is helpful from whom? *Journal of Personality and Social Psychology, 58,* 80–89.

Damon, A. (1973). Smoking attitudes and practices in seven preliterate societies. In W. I. Dunn, Jr. (Ed.), *Smoking behavior: Motives and incentives* (pp. 219–230). Washington, DC: Winston.

Danaher, B. G. (1977). Research on rapid smoking: Interim summary and recommendations. *Addictive Behaviors, 2,* 151–166.

Danaher, B. G. (1980). Smoking cessation programs in occupational settings. *Public Health Reports, 95,* 149–157.

Danoff, B., Kramer, S., Irwin, P., & Gottlieb, A. (1983). Assessment of the quality of life in long-term survivors after definitive radiotherapy. *American Journal of Clinical Oncology, 6,* 339–345.

Darko, D. F., Gillin, C., Risch, S. C., Bulloch, K., Golshan, S., Tasevska, Z., & Hamburger, R. N. (1989). Mitogen-stimulated lymphocyte proliferation and pituitary hormones in major depression. *Biological Psychiatry, 26,* 145–155.

Dattore, P. I., Shontz, F. C., & Coyne, L. (1980). Premorbid personality differentiation of cancer and noncancer groups: A test of the hypothesis of cancer proneness. *Journal of Consulting and Clinical Psychology, 48,* 388–394.

Davidson, A. R., & Jaccard, J. J. (1975). Population psychology: A new look at an old problem. *Journal of Personality and Social Psychology, 31,* 1073–1082.

Davidson, D. M. (1983). Return to work after cardiac events: A review. *Journal of Cardiac Rehabilitation, 3,* 60–69.

Davidson, P. O. (1982). Issues in patient compliance. In T. Millon, C. Green, & R. Meagher (Eds.), *Handbook of clinical health psychology.* New York: Plenum.

Davidson, R. J., & Schwartz, G. E. (1976). Psychobiology of relaxation and related states: A multiprocess theory. In D. Mostofsky (Ed.), *Behavior modification and control of physiologic activity.* Englewood Cliffs, NJ: Prentice-Hall.

Davies, A., Ware, J., Jr., Brook, R., Peterson, J., & Newhouse, J. (1986). Consumer acceptance of prepaid and fee-for-service medical care: Results from a randomized controlled trial. *Health Services Research, 21,* 429–452.

Davis, M., Vasterling, J., Bransfield, D., & Burish, T. G. (1987). Behavioural interventions in coping with cancer-related pain. *British Journal of Guidance and Counselling, 15,* 17–28.

Davis, M. S. (1966). Variations in patients' compliance with doctors' orders: Analysis of congruence between survey responses and results of empirical investigations. *Journal of Medical Education, 41,* 1037–1048.

Davis, M. S. (1967). Predicting non-compliant behavior. *Journal of Health and Social Behavior, 8,* 265–271.

Davis, M. S. (1968a). Physiologic, psychological, and demographic factors in patient compliance with doctors' orders. *Medical Care, 6,* 115–122.

Davis, M. S. (1968b). Variations in patients' compliance with doctors' advice: An empirical analysis of patterns of communication. *American Journal of Public Health, 58,* 274–288.

Davis, M. S., & Eichhorn, R. L. (1963). Compliance with medical regimen: A panel study. *Journal of Health and Social Behavior, 4,* 240–250.

Dawber, T. R. (1980). *The Framingham Study: The epidemiology of atherosclerotic disease.* Cambridge, MA: Harvard University Press.

Deaton, A. V. (1985). Adaptive noncompliance in pediatric asthma: The parent as expert. *Journal of Pediatric Psychology, 10,* 1–14.

DeBusk, R. F., Haskell, W. L., Miller, N. H., Berra, K., & Taylor, C. B. (1985). Medically directed at-home rehabilitation soon after clinically uncomplicated acute myocardial infarction: A new model for patient care. *American Journal of Cardiology, 55,* 251–257.

DeGood, D. E., & Redgate, E. S. (1982). Interrelationship of plasma cortisol and other activation indices during EMG biofeedback training. *Journal of Behavioral Medicine, 5,* 213–224.

Delahunt, J., & Curran, J. P. (1976). Effectiveness of negative practice and self-control techniques in the reduction of smoking behavior. *Journal of Consulting and Clinical Psychology, 44,* 1002–1007.

DeLongis, A., Coyne, J. C., Dakof, G., Folkman, S., & Lazarus, R. S. (1982). Relationship of daily hassles, uplifts, and major life events to health status. *Health Psychology, 1,* 119–136.

deMaehl, S., & Thurston, L. (1977). Crimes in the clinic: A report on Boston City Hospital. *The Second Wave, 7,* 17–20.

Demak, M. M., & Becker, M. H. (1987). Current perspectives: The changing patient-provider relationship: Charting the future of health care. *Patient Education and Counseling, 9,* 5–24.

Dembroski, T. M., & Costa, P. T. (1988). Assessment of coronary-prone behavior: A current overview. *Annals of Behavioral Medicine, 10,* 60–63.

Dembroski, T. M., & MacDougall, J. M. (1986). Stress and cigarette smoking: Implications for cardiovascular risk. In T. H. Schmidt, T. M. Dembroski, & G. Blumchen (Eds.), *Biological and psychological factors in cardiovascular disease* (pp. 246–257). Berlin, Federal Republic of Germany: Springer-Verlag.

Dembroski, T. M., MacDougall, J. M., Cardozo, S. R., & Krug-Fite, J. (1985). Selective cardiovascular effects of stress and cigarette smoking in young women. *Health Psychology, 4,* 153–167.

Dembroski, T. M., MacDougall, J. M., Shields, J. L., Petitto, J., & Lushene, R. (1978). Components of the Type A coronary-prone behavior pattern and cardiovascular responses to psychomotor performance challenge. *Journal of Behavioral Medicine, 1,* 159–176.

Dembroski, T. M., MacDougall, J. M., Williams, R. B., Haney, T. L., & Blumenthal, J. A. (1985). Components of type A, hostility, and anger-in: Relationship to angiographic findings. *Psychosomatic Medicine, 47,* 219–233.

Dembroski, T. M., & Williams, R. B. (in press). Definition and assessment of coronary-prone behavior. In N. Schneiderman, P. Kaufmann, & S. M. Weiss (Eds.), *Handbook of research methods in cardiovascular behavioral medicine.* New York: Plenum.

Dempsey, D. (1975). *The way we die.* New York: McGraw-Hill.

DeMuth, N. M., Fielding, J. E., Stunkard, A., & Hollander, R. B. (1986). Evaluation of industrial health promotion programs: Return-on-investment and survival of the fittest. In M. F. Cataldo & T. J. Coates (Eds.), *Health and industry* (pp. 433–453). New York: Wiley.

DeQuattro, V., Loo, R., Yamada, D., & Foti, F. (1985). Blood pressure and sympathoadrenal tone in Type A behavior: A review of the stress responsiveness studies. In A. Zanchetti & P. Turner (Eds.), *Towards preventative treatment of coronary-prone behavior* (pp. 25–34). New York: Hans Huber.

Derogatis, L. R., Abeloff, M., & Melasaratos, N. (1979). Psychological coping mechanisms and survival time in metastatic breast cancer. *Journal of the American Medical Association, 242,* 1504–1508.

Des Jarlais, D. C. (1988). *Effectiveness of AIDS educational programs for intravenous drug users.* Unpublished manuscript, State of New York Division of Substance Abuse Services, New York.

DeVellis, R. F., DeVellis, B. M., Sauter, S. V. H., & Cohen, J. L. (1986). Predictors of pain and functioning in arthritis. *Health Education Research, 1,* 61–67.

Devereux, R. B. (1988). Echocardiography, hypertension, and left ventricular mass. *Health Psychology, 7*(Suppl.), 89–104.

Diamond, E. L., Schneiderman, N., Schwartz, D., Smith, J. C., Vorp, R., & Pasin, R. D. (1984). Harassment, hostility, and Type A as determinants of cardiovascular reactivity during competition. *Journal of Behavioral Medicine, 7,* 171–189.

Diamond, J. (1989). Blood, genes, and malaria. *Natural History, February,* 8, 10, 12, 14, 16, 18.

Diamond, J., Massey, K. L., & Covey, D. (1989). Symptom awareness and blood glucose estimation in diabetic adults. *Health Psychology, 8,* 15–26.

DiClemente, R. J., Zorn, J., & Temoshok, L. (1986). Adolescents and AIDS: A survey of knowledge, attitudes and beliefs about AIDS in San Francisco. *American Journal of Public Health, 87,* 1443–1445.

Didion, J. (1979). *The white album.* New York: Simon & Schuster.

Diggory, J. C., & Rothman, D. Z. (1961). Values destroyed by death. *Journal of Abnormal and Social Psychology, 30,* 11–17.

Diller, L. (1976). A model of cognitive retraining in rehabilitation. *Journal of Clinical Psychology, 29,* 74–79.

DiMatteo, M. R., & DiNicola, D. D. (1982). *Achieving patient compliance: The psychology of the medical practitioner's role.* New York: Pergamon.

DiMatteo, M. R., Friedman, H. S., & Taranta, A. (1979). Sensitivity to bodily nonverbal communication as a factor in practitioner-patient rapport. *Journal of Nonverbal Behavior, 4,* 18–26.

DiMatteo, M. R., Hays, R. D., & Prince, L. M. (1986). Relationship of physicians' nonverbal communication skill to patient satisfaction, appointment noncompliance, and physician workload. *Health Psychology, 5,* 581–594.

DiMatteo, M. R., Linn, L. S., Chang, B. L., & Cope, D. W. (1985). Affect and neutrality in physician behavior: A study of patients' values and satisfaction. *Journal of Behavioral Medicine, 8,* 397–410.

Dimond, M. (1979). Social support and adaptation to chronic illness: The case of maintenance hemodialysis. *Research in Nursing and Health, 2,* 101–108.

Dimsdale, J. E., & Herd, J. A. (1982). Variability of plasma lipids in response to emotional arousal. *Psychosomatic Medicine, 44,* 413–430.

Dimsdale, J. E., Pierce, C., Schoenfeld, D., Brown, A., Zusman, R., & Graham, R. (1986). Suppressed anger and blood pressure: The effects of race, sex, social class, obesity, and age. *Psychosomatic Medicine, 48,* 430–436.

Dimsdale, J. E., Stern, M. J., & Dillon, E. (1988). The stress interview as a tool for examining physiological reactivity. *Psychosomatic Medicine, 50,* 64–71.

Dimsdale, J. E., Young, D., Moore, R., & Strauss, H. W. (1987). Do plasma norepinephrine levels reflect behavioral stress? *Psychosomatic Medicine, 49,* 375–382.

Dishman, R. K. (1981). Biologic influences on exercise adherence. *Research Quarterly for Exercise and Sport, 52,* 143–159.

Dishman, R. K. (1982). Compliance/adherence in health-related exercise. *Health Psychology, 1,* 237–267.

Ditto, B., France, C., & Miller, S. (1989). Spouse and parent-offspring similarities in cardiovascular response to mental arithmetic and isometric hand-grip. *Health Psychology, 8,* 159–173.

Ditto, P. H., Jemmott, J. B. III, & Darley, J. M. (1988). Appraising the threat of illness: A mental representational approach. *Health Psychology, 7,* 183–201.

Doehrman, S. R. (1977). Psychosocial aspects of recovery from coronary heart disease: A review. *Social Science and Medicine, 11,* 199–218.

Dohrenwend, B. P., & Shrout, P. E. (1985). "Hassles" in the conceptualization and measurement of life stress variables. *American Psychologist, 40,* 780–785.

Dohrenwend, B. S., Dohrenwend, B. P., Dodson, M. & Shrout, P. E. (1984). Symptoms, hassles, social supports, and life events: Problem of confounded measures. *Journal of Abnormal Psychology, 93,* 222–230.

Doll, L., Darrow, W. W., Jaffe, H., Curran, L., O'Malley, P., Bodecker, T., Campbell, J., &

Franks, D. (1987, June). *Self-reported changes in sexual behaviors in gay and bisexual men from the San Francisco City Clinic Cohort.* Paper presented at the Third International Conference on AIDS, Washington, DC.

Dollard, J., & Miller, N. E. (1950). *Personality and psychotherapy.* New York: McGraw-Hill.

Donovan, J. E., & Jessor, R. (1985). Structure of problem behavior in adolescence and young adulthood. *Journal of Consulting and Clinical Psychology, 53,* 890–904.

Dooley, D., & Catalano, R. (1984). Why the economy predicts help-seeking: A test of competing explanations. *Journal of Health and Social Behavior, 25,* 160–176.

Dorian, B. J., Garfinkel, P. E., Brown, G. M., Shore, A., Gladman, D., & Keystone, E. (1982). Aberrations in lymphocyte subpopulations and function during psychological stress. *Clinical and Experimental Immunology, 50,* 132–138.

Dorian, B. J., Keystone, E., Garfinkel, P. E., & Brown, G. M. (1981). Immune mechanisms in acute psychological stress. *Psychosomatic Medicine, 43,* 84 (abstract).

Downey, G., & Moen, P. (1987). Personal efficacy, income, and family transitions: A longitudinal study of women heading households. *Journal of Health and Social Behavior, 28,* 320–333.

Downey, G., Silver, R. C., & Wortman, C. B. (1990). Reconsidering the attribution-adjustment relation following a major negative event: Coping with the loss of a child. *Journal of Personality and Social Psychology, 59.*

Dracup, K. (1985). A controlled trial of couples' group counseling in cardiac rehabilitation. *Journal of Cardiopulmonary Rehabilitation, 5,* 436–442.

Dracup, K., Guzy, P. M., Taylor, S. E., & Barry, J. (in press). Consequences of cardiopulmonary resuscitation training for family members of high-risk cardiac patients. *Archives of Internal Medicine.*

Dracup, K., Meleis, A., Clark, S., Clyburn, A., Shields, L., & Staley, M. (1984). Group counseling in cardiac rehabilitation: Effect on patient compliance. *Patient Education and Counseling, 6,* 169–177.

Droge, D., Arntson, P., & Norton, R. (1986). The social support function in epilepsy self-help groups. *Small Group Behavior, 17,* 139–163.

Druss, R. G., & Kornfeld, D. S. (1967). Survivors of cardiac arrest: Psychiatric study. *Journal of the American Medical Association, 201,* 291–296.

Dubbert, P. M., King, A., Rapp, S. R., Brief, D., Martin, J. E., & Lake, M. (1985). Riboflavin as a tracer of medical compliance. *Journal of Behavioral Medicine, 8,* 287–300.

Duff, R. S., & Hollingshead, A. B. (1968). *Sickness and society.* New York: Harper & Row.

Dumas, H., & Leonard, L. (1963). The effect of nursing on the incidence of post-operative vomiting. *Nursing Research, 12,* 12–15.

Dunbar, F. (1943). *Psychosomatic diagnosis.* New York: Hoeber.

Dunbar, H. F., Wolfe, T. P., & Riosh, J. McK. (1936). Psychiatric aspects of medical problems: The psychic component of the disease process (including convalescence) in cardiac, diabetic and fracture patients. *American Journal of Psychiatry, 93,* 646–679.

Dunbar, J. M., & Agras, W. S. (1980). Compliance with medical instructions. In J. M. Ferguson & C. B. Taylor (Eds.), *Comprehensive handbook of behavioral medicine* (Vol. 3). New York: Spectrum.

Dunkel-Schetter, C. (1984). Social support and cancer: Findings based on patient interviews and their implications. *Journal of Social Issues, 40,* 77–98.

Dunkel-Schetter, C., Feinstein, L., Taylor, S. E., & Falke, R. (1988). *Patterns of coping with cancer and their correlates.* Manuscript submitted for publication.

Dunkel-Schetter, C., Folkman, S., & Lazarus, R. S. (1987). Correlates of social support receipt. *Journal of Personality and Social Psychology, 53,* 71–80.

Dunkel-Schetter, C., & Marshall, G. (1987, August). *Current findings and issues in the study of coping.* Paper presented at Symposium in the 95th annual meeting of the American Psychological Association, New York.

Dunkel-Schetter, C., & Wortman, C. B. (1981). Dilemmas of social support: Parallels between victimization and aging. In S. B. Kiesler, J. N. Morgan, & V. K. Oppenheimer (Eds.), *Aging: Social change* (pp. 349–381). New York: Academic Press.

Dunlop, D. (1970). Abuse of drugs by the public and by doctors. *British Medical Bulletin, 6,* 236–239.

Dunnell, K., & Cartwright, A. (1972). *Medicine takers, prescribers, and hoarders.* Boston: Routledge & Kegan Paul.

Dupont, R. L. (1988). The counselor's dilemma:

Treating chemical dependence at college. In T. M. Rivinus (Ed.), *Alcoholism/chemical dependency and the college student* (pp. 41–61). New York: Haworth Press.

Durel, L. A., Carver, C. S., Spitzer, S. B., Llabre, M. M., Weintraub, J. K., Saab, P. G., & Schneiderman, N. (1989). Associations of blood pressure with self-report measures of anger and hostility among black and white men and women. *Health Psychology, 8,* 557–576.

Dush, D. (1985). Psychosocial care of the terminally ill: Research and clinical issues. In K. Gardner (Ed.), *Quality of care for the terminally ill: An examination of the issues* (pp. 113–123). Chicago: Joint Commission on Accreditation of Hospitals.

Duxbury, M. L., Armstrong, G. D., Dren, D. J., & Henley, S. J. (1984). Head nurse leadership style with staff nurse burnout and job satisfaction in neonatal intensive care units. *Nursing Research, 33,* 97–101.

Dworkin, B. (1982). Instrumental learning for the treatment of disease. *Health Psychology, 1,* 45–59.

Eagleston, J. R., Kirmil-Gray, K., Thoresen, C. E., Weidenfeld, S. A., Bracke, P., Heft, L., & Arnow, B. (1986). Physical health correlates of Type A behavior in children and adolescents. *Journal of Behavioral Medicine, 9,* 341–362.

Eaker, E. D., & Feinleib, M. (1983). Psychosocial factors and the ten-year incidence of cerebrovascular accident in the Framingham Heart Study. *Psychosomatic Medicine, 45* (1), 84 (Abstract).

Eastman, C., & McPherson, I. (1982). General practitioners' perceptions of psychological problems and the relevance of clinical psychology. *British Journal of Clinical Psychology, 21,* 85–92.

Eaton, W. W. (1978). Life events, social supports, and psychiatric symptoms: A re-analysis of the New Haven data. *Journal of Health and Social Behavior, 19,* 230–234.

Eckenrode, J. (1984). Impact of chronic and acute stressors on daily reports of mood. *Journal of Personality and Social Psychology, 46,* 907–918.

Edelstyn, G. (1969). Surgery and radiotherapy for breast cancer. *British Journal of Hospital Medicine, 2,* 1861–1871.

Egbert, L. D., Battit, G. E., Welch, C. E., & Bartlett, M. K. (1964). Reduction of postoperative pain by encouragement and instruction of patients: A study of doctor-patient rapport. *New England Journal of Medicine, 270,* 825–827.

Eichner, E. R. (1983). Exercise and heart disease. *American Journal of Medicine, 75,* 1008–1023.

Eisenberg, J. M., Kitz, D. S., & Webber, R. A. (1983). Development of attitudes about sharing decision-making: A comparison of medical and surgical residents. *Journal of Health and Social Behavior, 24,* 85–90.

Eisenberg, L. (1988). Science in medicine: Too much or too little and too limited in scope? *American Journal of Medicine, 84,* 483–491.

Eiser, J. R., & Gentle, P. (1988). Health behavior as goal-directed action. *Journal of Behavioral Medicine, 11,* 523–536.

Eiser, J. R., van der Pligt, J., Raw, M., & Sutton, S. R. (1985). Trying to stop smoking: Effects of perceived addiction, attributions for failure, and expectancy of success. *Journal of Behavioral Medicine, 8,* 321–342.

Eliot. R. S., & Buell, J. C. (1983). The role of the central nervous system in sudden cardiac death. In T. M. Dembroski, T. Schmidt, & G. Blunchen (Eds.), *Biobehavioral bases of coronary-prone behavior.* New York: Plenum.

Ell, K. O., & Dunkel-Schetter, C. (in press) Social support and adjustment to myocardial infarction, angioplasty and coronary artery bypass surgery. In S. A. Shumaker & S. M. Czajkowski (Eds.), *Social support and cardiovascular disease.* New York: Plenum.

Ell, K. O., Nishimoto, R. H., Mantell, J. E., & Hamovitch, M. B. (1988). Psychological adaptation to cancer: A comparison among patients, spouses and nonspouses. *Family Systems Medicine, 6,* 335–348.

Elliott, C. H., & Denny, D. R. (1978). A multiple-component treatment approach to smoking reduction. *Journal of Consulting and Clinical Psychology, 46,* 1330–1339.

Elliott, D. J., Trief, P. M., & Stein, N. (1986). Mastery, stress, and coping in marriage among chronic pain patients. *Journal of Behavioral Medicine, 9,* 549–558.

Ellis, A. (1962). *Reason and emotion in psychotherapy.* New York: Lyle Stuart.

Emmons, C-A., Joseph, J. G., Kessler, R. C., Wortman, C. B., Montgomery, S. B., & Ostrow, D. G. (1986). Psychosocial predictors of reported behavior change in homosexual men at risk for AIDS. *Health Education Quarterly, 13,* 331–345.

Engebretson, T. O., Matthews, K. A., & Scheier,

M. F. (1989). Relations between anger expression and cardiovascular reactivity: Reconciling inconsistent findings through a matching hypothesis. *Journal of Personality and Social Psychology, 57,* 513–521.

Engel, B. T. (1986). Psychosomatic medicine, behavioral medicine, just plain medicine. *Psychosomatic Medicine, 48,* 466–479.

Engel, G. L. (1971). Sudden and rapid death during psychological stress. *Annals of Internal Medicine, 74,* 771–782.

Engel, G. L. (1977). The need for a new medical model: A challenge for biomedicine. *Science, 196,* 129–136.

Engel, G. L. (1980). The clinical application of the biopsychosocial model. *American Journal of Psychiatry, 137,* 535–544.

English, E. H., & Baker, T. B. (1983). Relaxation training and cardiovascular response to experimental stressors. *Health Psychology, 2,* 239–259.

Enos, W. F., Holmes, R. H., & Beyer, J. (1953). Coronary disease among U.S. soldiers killed in action in Korea. *Journal of the American Medical Association, 152,* 1090–1093.

Epstein, L. H., & Cluss, P. A. (1982). A behavioral medicine perspective on adherence to longterm medical regimens. *Journal of Consulting and Clinical Psychology, 50,* 950–971.

Epstein, L. H., Grunberg, N. E., Lichtenstein, E. & Evans, R. I. (1989). Smoking research: Basic research, intervention, prevention, and new trends. *Health Psychology, 8,* 705–721.

Epstein, L. H., Koeske, R., Wing, R. R., & Valoski, A. (1986). The effect of family variables on child weight change. *Health Psychology, 5,* 1–11.

Eriksen, M. P., Green, L. W., & Fultz, F. G. (1988). Principles of changing health behavior. *Cancer, 62*(Suppl.), 1768–1775.

Ershler, J., Leventhal, H., Fleming, R., & Glynn, K. (1989). The quitting experience for smokers in sixth through twelfth grades. *Addictive Behaviors, 14,* 365–378.

Essau, C. A., & Jamieson, J. L. (1987). Heart rate perception in the Type A personality. *Health Psychology, 6,* 43–54.

Evans, A. M., Love, R. R., Meyerowitz, B. E., Leventhal, H., & Nerenz, D. R. (1985). Factors associated with active participation in a cancer prevention clinic. *Preventive Medicine, 14,* 358–371.

Evans, G. M., Palsane, M. N., Lepore, S. J., & Martin, J. (1989). Residential density and psychological health: The mediating effects of social support. *Journal of Personality and Social Psychology, 57,* 994–999.

Evans, R. I. (1976). Smoking in children: Developing a social-psychological strategy of deterrence. *Journal of Preventive Medicine, 5,* 122–127.

Evans, R. I. (1988). Health promotion—science or ideology? *Health Psychology, 7,* 203–219.

Evans, R. I., Dratt, L. M., Raines, B. E., & Rosenberg, S. S. (1988). Social influences on smoking initiation: Importance of distinguishing descriptive versus mediating process variables. *Journal of Applied Social Psychology, 18,* 925–943.

Evans, R. I., Rozelle, R. M., Lasater, T. M., Dembroski, I. M., & Allen, B. P. (1970). Fear arousal, persuasion, and actual versus implied behavioral change: New perspectives utilizing a real-life dental hygiene program. *Journal of Personality and Social Psychology, 16,* 220–227.

Ewart, C. K., Harris, W. L., Iwata, M. M., Coates, T. J., Bullock, R., & Simon, B. (1987). Feasibility and effectiveness of school-based relaxation in lowering blood pressure. *Health Psychology, 6,* 399–416.

Eysenck, H. J. (Ed.). (1981). *A model for personality.* New York: Springer.

Falek, A., & Britton, S. (1974). Phases in coping: The hypothesis and its implications. *Social Biology, 21,* 1–7.

Farquhar, J. W., Maccoby, N., Wood, P. D., Alexander, J. K., Breitrose, H., Brown, W. B., Jr., Haskell, W. L., McAlister, A. L., Meyer, A. J., Nash, J. D., & Stern, M. P. (1977). Community education for cardiovascular health. *Lancet, 1,* 1192–1195.

Faust, J., & Melamed, B. G. (1984). Influence of arousal, previous experience, and age on surgery preparation of same day surgery and in-hospital pediatric patients. *Journal of Consulting and Clinical Psychology, 52,* 359–365.

Fawzy, F. I., Cousins, N., Kemeny, M. E., Fawzy, N. W., Elashoff, R., Morton, D., & Fahey, H. L. (in press). A structured psychiatric intervention for cancer patients: II. Changes over time in immunological parameters. *Archives of General Psychiatry.*

Fears, B. A., Gerkovich, M. M., O'Connell, K. A., & Cook, M. R. (1987). Evaluation of salivary thiocyanate as an indicator of smoking behavior. *Health Psychology, 6,* 561–568.

Federspiel, J. F. (1983). *The ballad of Typhoid Mary*. New York: Dutton.

Feifel, H. (Ed.). (1977). *New meanings of death*. New York: McGraw-Hill.

Feinglos, M. N., & Surwit, R. S. (1988). *Behavior and diabetes mellitus*. Kalamazoo, MI: The Upjohn Company.

Feldman, P. E. (1956). The personal element in psychiatric research. *American Journal of Psychiatry, 113*, 52–54.

Feletti, G., Firman, D., & Sanson-Fisher, R. (1986). Patient satisfaction with primary-care consultations. *Journal of Behavioral Medicine, 9*, 389–400.

Felix, M. R. J., Stunkard, A. J., Cohen. R. Y., & Cooley, R. B. (1985). Health promotion at the worksite: I. A process for establishing programs. *Preventive Medicine, 14*, 99–108.

Felten, D. L., Felten, S. Y., Bellinger, D. L., Carlson, S. L., Ackerman, K. D., Madden, K. S., Olschowski, J. A., & Livnat, S. (1987). Noradrenergic sympathetic neural interactions with the immune system: Structure and function. *Immunological Review, 100*, 225–260.

Felton, B. J., & Revenson, T. A. (1984). Coping with chronic illness: A study of illness controllability and the influence of coping strategies on psychological adjustment. *Journal of Consulting and Clinical Psychology, 52*, 343–353.

Felton, B. J., Revenson, T. A., & Hinrichsen, G. A. (1984). Stress and coping in the explanation of psychological adjustment among chronically ill adults. *Social Science and Medicine, 18*, 889–898.

Felton, G., Huss, K., Payne, E. A., & Srsic, K. (1976). Postoperative nursing intervention with the patient for surgery: Outcomes of three alternative approaches. *International Journal of Nursing Studies, 13*, 83–96.

Ferguson, B. F. (1979). Preparing young children for hospitalization: A comparison of two methods. *Pediatrics, 64*, 656–664.

Ferraro, K. F., Mutran, E., & Barresi, C. M. (1984). Widowhood, health, and friendship support in later life. *Journal of Health and Social Behavior, 25*, 245–259.

Fiatarone, M. A., Morley, J. E., Bloom, E. T., Benton, D., Makinodan, T., & Solomon, G. F. (1988). Endogenous opioids and the exercise-induced augmentation of natural killer cell activity. *Journal of Laboratory and Clinical Medicine, 112*, 544–552.

Field, T., Alpert, B., Vega-Lahr, N., Goldstein, S.,

& Perry, S. (1988). Hospitalization stress in children: Sensitizer and repressor coping styles. *Health Psychology, 7*, 433–445.

Fielding, J. E. (1978). Successes of prevention. *Milbank Memorial Fund Quarterly, 56*, 274–302.

Fielding, J. E. (1982). Effectiveness of employee health improvement programs. *Journal of Occupational Medicine, 24*, 907–916.

Fillingim, R. B., & Fine, M. A. (1986). The effects of internal versus external information processing on symptom perception in an exercise setting. *Health Psychology, 5*, 115–123.

Findley, T. (1953). The placebo and the physician. *Medical Clinics of North America, 37*, 1821–1826.

Fineberg, H. V. (1988). Education to prevent AIDS: Prospects and obstacles. *Science, 239*, 592–596.

Finlayson, A., & McEwen, J. (1977). *Coronary heart disease and patterns of living*. New York: Watson.

Fischer, C. L., Daniels, J. C., Levin, S. L., Kimzey, S. L., Cobb, E. K., & Ritzman, W. E. (1972). Effects of the spaceflight environment on man's immune system: II. Lymphocyte counts and reactivity. *Aerospace Medicine, 43*, 1122–1125.

Fishbein, M. (1965). A consideration of beliefs, attitudes, and their relationships. In J. D. Steiner & M. A. Fishbein (Eds.), *Current studies in social psychology* (pp. 107–120). New York: Holt, Rinehart & Winston.

Fishbein, M. (1972). Toward an understanding of family planning behavior. *Journal of Applied Social Psychology, 2*, 214–227.

Fishbein, M. (1980). A theory of reasoned action: Some applications and implications. In M. M. Page (Ed.), *1979 Nebraska Symposium on Motivation*. Lincoln: University of Nebraska Press.

Fisher, G. A., & Tessler, R. C. (1986). Family bonding of the mentally ill: An analysis of family visits with residents of board and care homes. *Journal of Health and Social Behavior, 27*, 236–249.

Fisher, S. (1967). Motivation for patient delay. *Archives of General Psychiatry, 16*, 676–678.

Fisher, S., & Cleveland, S. E. (1958). *Body image and personality*. Princeton, NJ: Van Nostrand.

Fitzpatrick, R., Newman, S., Lamb, R., & Shipley, M. (1988). Social relationships and psychological well-being in rheumatoid arthritis. *Social Science and Medicine, 27*, 399–403.

Flay, B. R. (1985). Psychosocial approaches to smoking prevention: A review of findings. *Health Psychology, 4*, 448–488.

Flay, B. R. (1987). Mass media and smoking cessation: A critical review. *American Journal of Public Health, 77*, 153–160.

Flay, B. R., Koepke, D., Thomson, S. J., Santi, S., Best, J. A., & Brown, K. S. (in press). Six year follow-up of the first Waterloo school smoking prevention trial. *American Journal of Public Health.*

Fleishman, J. A. (1984). Personality characteristics and coping patterns. *Journal of Health and Social Behavior, 25*, 229–244.

Fleming, R., Baum, A., Davidson, L. M., Rectanus, E., & McArdle, S. (1987). Chronic stress as a factor in physiologic reactivity to challenge. *Health Psychology, 6*, 221–237.

Fleming, R., Baum, A., Gisriel, M. M., & Gatchel, R. J. (1982). Mediating influences of social support on stress at Three Mile Island. *Journal of Human Stress, September*, 14–23.

Fleming, R., Baum, A., Reddy, B. M., & Gatchel, R. J. (1984). Behavioral and biochemical effects of job loss and unemployment stress. *Journal of Human Stress, Spring*, 12–17.

Fleming, R., Leventhal, H., Glynn, K., & Ershler, J. (1989). The role of cigarettes in the initiation and progression of early substance use. *Addictive Behaviors, 14*, 261–272.

Flor, H., & Turk, D. C. (1989a). Chronic back pain and rheumatoid arthritis: Predicting pain and disability from cognitive variables. *Journal of Behavioral Medicine, 11*, 251–265.

Flor, H., & Turk, D. C. (1989b). Psychophysiology of chronic pain: Do chronic pain patients exhibit symptom-specific psychophysiological responses? *Psychological Bulletin, 105*, 215–259.

Folkman, S., & Lazarus, R. S. (1980). An analysis of coping in a middle-aged community sample. *Journal of Health and Social Behavior, 21*, 219–239.

Folkman, S., & Lazarus, R. S. (1988). *Manual for the Ways of Coping Questionnaire.* Palo Alto, CA: Consulting Psychologist Press.

Folkman, S., Lazarus, R. S., Dunkel-Schetter, C., DeLongis, A., & Gruen, R. J. (1986). Dynamics of a stressful encounter: Cognitive appraisal, coping, and encounter outcomes. *Journal of Personality and Social Psychology, 50*, 992–1003.

Folkman, S., Schaefer, C., & Lazarus, R. S. (1979). Cognitive processes as mediators of stress and coping. In V. Hamilton & D. M. Warburton (Eds.), *Human stress and cognition: An information processing approach* (pp. 265–298). London, England: Wiley.

Follick, M. J., Ahern, D. K., & Aberger, E. W. (1985). Development of an audiovisual taxonomy of pain behavior: Reliability and discriminant validity. *Health Psychology, 4*, 555–568.

Follick, M. J., Smith, T. W., & Turk, D. C. (1984). Psychosocial adjustment following ostomy. *Health Psychology, 3*, 505–517.

Folsom, A. R., Hughes, J. R., Buehler, J. F., Mittelmark, M. B., Jacobs, D. R., Jr., & Grimm, R. H., Jr. (1985). Do Type A men drink more frequently than Type B men? Findings in the Multiple Risk Factor Intervention Trial (MRFIT). *Journal of Behavioral Medicine, 8*, 227–235.

Fontana, A. F., Kerns, R. D., Rosenberg, R. L., & Colonese, K. L. (1989). Support, stress, and recovery from coronary heart disease: A longitudinal causal model. *Health Psychology, 8*, 175–193.

Ford, C. V., & Sbordone, R. J. (1980). Attitudes of psychiatrists toward elderly patients. *American Journal of Psychiatry, 137*, 571–575.

Fordyce, W. E. (1976). *Behavioral methods in chronic pain and illness.* St. Louis, MO: Mosby.

Fordyce, W. E. (1988). Pain and suffering: A reappraisal. *American Psychologist, 43*, 276–283.

Fordyce, W. E., Brockway, J. A., Bergman, J. A. & Spengler, D. (1986). Acute back pain: A control-group comparison of behavioral vs. traditional management methods. *Journal of Behavioral Medicine, 9*, 127–140.

Fordyce, W. E., Roberts, A. H., & Sternbach, R. A. (1985). The behavioral management of chronic pain: A response to critics. *Pain, 22*, 113–125.

Fordyce, W. E., Shelton, J. L., & Dundore, D. E. (1982). The modification of avoidance learning pain behaviors. *Journal of Behavioral Medicine, 5*, 405–414.

Fordyce, W. E., & Steger, J. C. (1979). Chronic pain. In O. F. Pomerleau & J. P. Brady (Eds.), *Behavioral medicine: Theory and practice.* Baltimore, MD: Williams & Wilkins.

Foreyt, J. P. (1987). Issues in the assessment and treatment of obesity. *Journal of Consulting and Clinical Psychology, 55*, 677–684.

Foreyt, J. P., Scott, L. W., Mitchell, R. E., & Gotto, A. M. (1979). Plasma lipid changes in the normal population following behavioral treatment. *Journal of Consulting and Clinical Psychology, 47*, 440–452.

Forster, J. L., Jeffrey, R. W., Schmid, T. L., & Kramer, L. M. (1988). Preventing weight gain in adults: A pound of prevention. *Health Psychology, 7,* 515–525.

Forsythe, C. J., & Compas, B. E. (1987). Interaction of cognitive appraisals of stressful events and coping: Testing the goodness of fit hypothesis. *Cognitive Therapy and Research, 11,* 473–485.

Fortin, F., & Kirouac, S. (1976). A randomized trial of preoperative education. *International Journal of Nursing Studies, 13,* 11–24.

Foster, G. M., & Anderson, B. G. (1978). *Medical anthropology.* New York: Wiley.

Fox, B. H. (1978). Premorbid psychological factors as related to cancer incidence. *Journal of Behavioral Medicine, 1,* 45–134.

Fox, B. H. (1988). Psychogenic factors in cancer, especially its incidence. In S. Maes, D. Spielberger, P. B. Defares, & I. G. Sarason (Eds.), *Topics in health psychology* (pp. 37–55). New York: Wiley.

Fox, B. H., Ragland, D. R., Brand, R. J., & Rosenman, R. H. (1987). Type A behavior and cancer mortality. *Annals of the New York Academy of Sciences, 496,* 620–627.

Fox, B. H., & Temoshok, L. (1988). Mind-body and behavior in cancer incidence. *Advances, Institute for the Advancement of Health, 5,* 41–50.

Foy, D. W., Nunn, L. B., & Rychtarik, R. G. (1984). Broad-spectrum behavioral treatment for chronic alcoholics: Effects of training in controlled drinking skills. *Journal of Consulting and Clinical Psychology, 52,* 218–230.

Frances, R. J., Franklin, J., & Flavin, D. (1986). Suicide and alcoholism. *Annals of the New York Academy of Sciences, 487,* 316–326.

Francis, A., Fyer, M., & Clarkin, J. (1986). Personality and suicide. *Annals of the New York Academy of Sciences, 487,* 281–293.

Francis, B. (1980). A nursing network to battle burnout. *Journal of Practical Nursing, 30,* 25–27.

Frankenhaeuser, M. (1975). Sympathetic-adrenomedullary activity behavior and the psychosocial environment. In P. H. Venables & M. J. Christie (Eds.), *Research in psychophysiology* (pp. 71–94). New York: Wiley.

Fraumeni, J. F., Jr., Lloyd, J. W., & Smith, E. M. (1969). Cancer mortality among nuns: Role of marital status in etiology of neoplastic disease in women. *Journal of the National Cancer Institute, 42,* 455–468.

Fredrickson, M., & Matthews, K. A. (in press). Cardiovascular responses to behavioral stress and hypertension: A meta-analytic review. *Annals of Behavioral Medicine.*

Freedman, R. R. (1987). Long-term effectiveness of behavioral treatments for Raynaud's disease. *Behavior Therapy, 18,* 387–399.

Freidson, E. (1960). Client control and medical practice. *American Journal of Sociology, 65,* 374–382.

Freidson, E. (1961). *Patients' views of medical practice.* New York: Russell Sage.

French, A. P., & Tupin, J. P. (1974). Therapeutic application of a simple relaxation method. *American Journal of Psychotherapy, 28,* 282–287.

French, J. R. P., Jr. (1974). Person role fit. In A. McLean (Ed.), *Occupational stress* (pp. 70–79). Springfield, IL: Thomas.

French, J. R. P., Jr., & Caplan, R. D. (1973). Organizational stress and the individual strain. In A. J. Marrow (Ed.), *The failure of success.* New York: AMACON.

French, J. R. P., Jr., Tupper, C. J., & Mueller, E. I. (1965). *Workload of university professors.* Unpublished manuscript, University of Michigan, Ann Arbor.

Frenzel, M. P., McCaul, K. D., Glasgow, R. E., & Schafer, L. C. (1988). The relationship of stress and coping to regimen adherence and glycemic control of diabetes. *Journal of Social and Clinical Psychology, 6,* 77–87.

Friedman, H. S., & Booth-Kewley, S. (1987). The "disease-prone" personality: A meta-analytic view of the construct. *American Psychologist, 42,* 539–555.

Friedman, H. S., & Booth-Kewley, S. (1988). Validity of the Type A construct: A reprise. *Psychological Bulletin, 104,* 381–384.

Friedman, M., & Rosenman, R. H. (1974). *Type A behavior and your heart.* New York: Knopf.

Friedman, M., Thoresen, C. E., Gill, J. J., Powell, L. H., Ulmer, D., Thompson, L., Price, V. A., Rabin, D. D., Breall, W. S., Dixon, T., Levy, R., & Bourg, E. (1984). Alteration of Type A behavior and reduction in cardiac recurrences in myocardial infarction patients. *American Heart Journal, 108,* 237–248.

Friedman, M., Thoresen, C. E., Gill, J. J., Powell, L. H., Ulmer, D., Thompson, L., Price, V. A., Rabin, D. D., Breall, W. S., Dixon, T., Levy, R., & Bourg, E. (1986). Alteration of Type A behavior and its effect on cardiac recurrences in post myocardial infarction patients: Summary results of the recurrent coronary prevention project. *American Heart Journal, 112,* 653–665.

Friedman, S. R., de Jong, W. M., & Des Jarlais, D. C. (1988). Problems and dynamics of organizing intravenous drug users for AIDS prevention. *Health Education Research, 3,* 49–57.

Fries, H. (1977). Studies on secondary amenorrhea, anorectic behavior and body image perception: Importance for the early recognition of anorexia nervosa. In R. Vigersky (Ed.), *Anorexia nervosa.* New York: Raven Press.

Fries, J. F., Green, L. W., & Levine, S. (1989). Health promotion and the compression of morbidity. *Lancet, 1,* 481–483.

Friman, P. C., & Christophersen, E. R. (1986). Biobehavioral prevention in primary care. In N. A. Krasnegor, J. Arasteh, & M. F. Cataldo (Eds.), *Child health behavior: A behavioral pediatrics perspective* (pp. 254–280). New York: Wiley.

Friman, P. C., Finney, J. W., Glasscock, S. G., Weigel, J. W., & Christophersen, E. R. (1986). Testicular self-examination: Validation of a training strategy for early cancer detection. *Journal of Applied Behavior Analysis, 19,* 87–92.

Froese, A., Hackett, T. P., Cassem, N. H., & Silverberg, E. L. (1974). Trajectories of anxiety and depression in denying and nondenying acute myocardial infarction patients during hospitalization. *Journal of Psychosomatic Research, 18,* 413–420.

Funch, D. P., & Marshall, J. R. (1984). Measuring life stress: Factors affecting fall-off in the reporting of life events. *Journal of Health and Social Behavior, 25,* 453–464.

Funk, S. C., & Houston, B. K. (1987). A critical analysis of the Hardiness Scale's validity and utility. *Journal of Personality and Social Psychology, 53,* 572–578.

Gal, R., & Lazarus, R. S. (1975). The role of activity in anticipating and confronting stressful situations. *Journal of Human Stress, 1*(December), 4–20.

Gallup, G. (1981a). Percentage of smokers lowest in 37 years. Part One. Abstracted in *Bibliography on smoking and health—1982.* Washington, DC: Superintendent of Documents.

Gallup, G. (1981b). Smoking level declines as more perceive health hazard. Part Two. Abstracted in *Bibliography of smoking and health—1982.* Washington, DC: Superintendent of Documents.

Gallup Organization, Inc. (1979). *Women's attitudes regarding breast cancer.* Survey conducted for the American Cancer Society. New York: Author.

Galton, L. (1973). *The silent disease: Hypertension.* New York: Crown.

Gannon, L. R., Haynes, S. N., Cuevas, J., & Chavez, R. (1987). Psychophysiological correlates of induced headaches. *Journal of Behavioral Medicine, 10,* 411–423.

Gannon, L. R., & Pardie, L. (1989). The importance of chronicity and controllability of stress in the context of stress-illness relationships. *Journal of Behavioral Medicine, 12,* 357–372.

Ganster, D. C., Mayes, B. T., Sime, W. E., & Tharp, G. D. (1982). Managing organizational stress: A field experiment. *Journal of Applied Psychology, 67,* 533–542.

Garfinkel, L. (1981). Time trends in lung cancer mortality among nonsmokers and a note on passive smoking. *Journal of the National Cancer Institute, 66,* 1061–1066.

Garfinkel, P. E., & Garner, D. M. (1982). *Anorexia nervosa: A multidimensional perspective.* New York: Brunner/Mazel.

Garfinkel, P. E., & Garner, D. M. (1983). The multidetermined nature of anorexia nervosa. In P. L. Darby, P. E. Garfinkel, D. M. Garner, & D. V. Coscina (Eds.), *Anorexia nervosa: Recent developments in research.* New York: Liss.

Garrity, T. F. (1973). Social involvement and activeness as predictors of morale six months after myocardial infarction. *Social Science and Medicine, 7,* 199–207.

Garrity, T. F. (1975). Morbidity, mortality, and rehabilitation. In W. D. Gentry & R. B. Williams, Jr. (Eds.), *Psychological aspects of myocardial infarction and coronary care.* St. Louis, MO: Mosby.

Garrity, T. F., McGill, A., Becker, M., Blanchard, E., Crews, J., Cullen, J., Hackett, T., Taylor, J., & Valins, S. (1976). Report of the task group on cardiac rehabilitation. In S. M. Weiss (Ed.), *Proceedings of the National Heart and Lung Institute Working Conference on Health Behavior* (DHEW Publication No. 76–868). Washington, DC: U.S. Government Printing Office.

Gartner, A., & Reissman, F. (1976). Health care in a technological age. In *Self help and health: A report.* New York: New Human Services Institute.

Gatchel, R. J., Gaffney, F. A., & Smith, J. E. (1986).

Comparative efficacy of behavioral stress management versus propranolol in reducing psychophysiological reactivity in post-myocardial infarction patients. _Journal of Behavioral Medicine, 9,_ 503–513.

Gates, C. C. (1974). _The emotional impact of mastectomy—the self-esteem process._ Unpublished manuscript, Peter Bent Brigham Hospital, Salt Lake City, UT.

Gauthier, J., Bois, R., Allaire, D., & Drolet, M. (1981). Evaluation of skin temperature biofeedback training at two different sites for migraine. _Journal of Behavioral Medicine, 4,_ 407–420.

Geer, J. H. (1965). The development of a scale to measure fear. _Behavior Research and Therapy, 3,_ 45–53.

Geersten, R., Klauber, M. R., Rindflesh, M., Kane, R. L., & Gray, R. (1975). A re-examination of Suchman's reviews of social factors in health care utilization. _Journal of Health and Social Behavior, 16,_ 426–437.

Gemming, M. G., Runyan, C. W., Hunter, W. W., & Campbell, B. J. (1984). A community health education approach to occupant protection. _Health Education Quarterly, 11,_ 147–158.

Gentry, W. D., Chesney, A. P., Gary, H. E., Hall, R. P., & Harburg, E. (1982). Habitual anger-coping styles: I. Affect on mean blood pressure and risk for essential hypertension. _Psychosomatic Medicine, 44,_ 195–202.

Gerbert, B., Maguire, B., Badner, V., Altman, D., & Stone, G. (1988). Why fear persists: Health care professionals and AIDS. _Journal of the American Medical Association, 260,_ 3481–3483.

Gerbert, B., Stone, G., Stulbarg, M., Gullion, D. S., & Greenfield, S. (1988). Agreement among physician assessment methods: Searching for the truth among fallible methods. _Medical Care, 26,_ 519–535.

Gibson, R., & Waldo, D. (1982). National health expenditures, 1981. _Health Care Financing Review,_ 4(1):1–36. HCFA Pub. No. 03146. Office of Research and Demonstrations, Health Care Financing Administrations. Washington, DC: U.S. Government Printing Office.

Gielen, A. C., Eriksen, M. P., Daltroy, L. H., & Rost, K. (1984). Factors associated with the use of child restraint devices. _Health Education Quarterly, 11,_ 195–206.

Gilbert, D. G., & Spielberger, C. D. (1987). Effects

of smoking on heart rate, anxiety, and feelings of success during social interaction. _Journal of Behavioral Medicine, 10,_ 629–638.

Gill, D. G., & Horobin, G. W. (1972). Doctors, patients, and the state: Relationships and decision-making. _Sociological Review, 20,_ 505–520.

Gill, J. J., Price, V. A., Friedman, M., Thoresen, C. E., Powell, L. H., Ulmer, D., Brown, B., & Drews, F. R. (1985). Reduction in Type A behavior in healthy middle-aged American military officers. _American Heart Journal, 110,_ 503–514.

Gintner, G. G., Rectanus, E. F., Achord, K., & Parker, B. (1987). Parental history of hypertension and screening attendance: Effects of wellness appeal versus threat appeal. _Health Psychology, 6,_ 431–444.

Glaser, B. G. (1972). Disclosure of terminal illness. In E. G. Jaco (Ed.), _Patients, physicians, and illness_ (pp. 204–213). New York: Free Press.

Glaser, B. G., & Strauss, A. L. (1965). Temporal aspects of dying as a nonscheduled status passage. _American Journal of Sociology, 71,_ 48–59.

Glaser, R., Kiecolt-Glaser, J. K., Speicher, C. E., & Holliday, J. E. (1985). Stress, loneliness, and changes in herpesvirus latency. _Journal of Behavioral Medicine, 8,_ 249–260.

Glaser, R., Kiecolt-Glaser, J. K., Stout, J. C., Tarr, K. L., Speicher, C. E., & Holliday, J. E. (1985). Stress-related impairments in cellular immunity. _Psychiatry Research, 16,_ 233–239.

Glaser, R., Rice, J., Sheridan, J., Fertel, R., Stout, J., Speicher, C., Pinsky, D., Kotur, M., Post, A., Beck, M., & Kiecolt-Glaser, J. (1987). Stress-related immune suppression: Health implications. _Brain, Behavior, and Immunity, 1,_ 7–20.

Glaser, R., Rice, J., Speicher, C. E., Stout, J. C., & Kiecolt-Glaser, J. K. (1986). Stress depresses interferon production by leukocytes concomitant with a decrease in natural killer cell activity. _Behavioral Neuroscience, 100,_ 675–678.

Glaser, R., Thorn, B. E., Tarr, K. L., Kiecolt-Glaser, J. K., & D'Ambrosio, S. M. (1985). Effects of stress on methyltransferase synthesis: An important DNA repair enzyme. _Health Psychology, 4,_ 403–412.

Glasgow, M. S., & Engel, B. T. (1987). Clinical issues in biofeedback and relaxation therapy for hypertension. In J. P. Hatch, J. G. Fisher, & J. D. Rugh (Eds.), _Biofeedback_ (pp. 81–121). New York: Plenum.

Glasgow, M. S., Engel, B. T., & D'Lugoff, B. C. (1989). A controlled study of a standardized behavioral stepped treatment for hypertension. *Psychosomatic Medicine, 51,* 10–26.

Glasgow, R. E., & Lichtenstein, E. (1987). Long-term effects of behavioral smoking cessation interventions. *Behavior Therapy, 18,* 297–324.

Glass, D. C. (1977). *Behavior patterns, stress, and coronary disease.* Hillsdale, NJ: Erlbaum.

Glass, D. C., Lake, C. R., Contrada, R. J., Kehoe, K., & Erlanger, L. R. (1983). Stability of individual differences in physiological responses to stress. *Health Psychology, 2,* 317–341.

Glass, D. C., & Singer, J. E. (1972). *Urban stress.* New York: Academic Press.

Glass, D. C., Snyder, M. L., & Hollis, J. (1974). Time urgency and the Type A coronary-prone behavior pattern. *Journal of Applied Social Psychology, 4,* 125–140.

Glick, I. O., Weiss, R. S., & Parkes, C. M. (1974). *The first year of bereavement.* New York: Wiley.

Glynn, K., Leventhal, H., & Hirschman, R. (1986). A cognitive developmental approach to smoking prevention. *Prevention research: Deterring drug abuse among school children and adolescents, National Institute on Drug Abuse Prevention Monograph Series* (pp. 130–152, DHHS Publication No. ADM 86–1334). Washington, DC: U.S. Department of Health and Human Services, Alcohol, Drug Abuse, and Mental Health Administration.

Glynn, S. M., Gruder, C. L., & Jegerski, J. A. (1986). Effects of biochemical validation of self-reported cigarette smoking on treatment success and on misreporting abstinence. *Health Psychology, 5,* 125–136.

Gochman, D. (1972). Development of health beliefs. *Psychological Reports, 31,* 259–266.

Godin, G., Desharnais, R., Jobin, J., & Cook, J. (1987). The impact of physical fitness and health-age appraisal upon exercise intentions and behavior. *Journal of Behavioral Medicine, 10,* 241–250.

Goffman, E. (1961). *Asylums.* Garden City, NY: Doubleday.

Goffman, E. (1963). *Stigma: Notes on the management of spoiled identity.* Englewood Cliffs, NJ: Prentice-Hall.

Gogan, J. L., Koocher, G. P., Foster, D. J., & O'Malley, J. E. (1977). Impact of childhood cancer on siblings. *Health and Social Work, 2,* 41–57.

Goldberg, E. L., & Comstock, G. W. (1980). Epidemiology of life events: Frequency in general populations. *American Journal of Epidemiology, 111,* 736–752.

Goldberg, R. J. (1981). Management of depression in the patient with advanced cancer. *Journal of the American Medical Association, 246,* 373–376.

Golden, J. S., & Johnston, G. D. (1970). Problems of distortion in doctor-patient communications. *Psychiatry in Medicine, 1,* 127–149.

Goldfried, M. R., & Davison, G. C. (1976). *Clinical behavior therapy.* New York: Holt, Rinehart & Winston.

Goldman, M. S. (1983). Cognitive impairment in chronic alcoholics: Some cause for optimism. *American Psychologist, 38,* 1045–1054.

Goldstein, I. B., & Shapiro, D. (1987). The effects of stress and caffeine on hypertensives. *Psychosomatic Medicine, 49,* 226–235.

Goldstein, M. J. (1973). Individual differences in response to stress. *American Journal of Community Psychology, 1,* 113–137.

Goldstein, M. S., Jaffe, D. T., Garell, D., & Berk, R. E. (1986). Holistic doctors: Becoming a nontraditional medical practitioner. *Urban Life, 14,* 317–344.

Goldstein, M. S., Jaffe, D. T., Sutherland, C., & Wilson, J. (1987). Holistic physicians: Implications for the study of the medical profession. *Journal of Health and Social Behavior, 28,* 103–119.

Golston, S. E. (1977, August). *The life crisis of death as an opportunity for primary preventive interventions with families having young children: The way things are and the way things could be.* Paper presented at the Symposium on Death and Dying: Innovations in Training and Service Delivery, American Psychological Association annual meetings, San Francisco.

Gonder-Frederick, L. A., Cox, D. J., Bobbitt, S. A., & Pennebaker, J. W. (1986). Blood glucose symptom beliefs of diabetic patients: Accuracy and implications. *Health Psychology, 5,* 327–341.

Gonzalez, M. L., & Emmons, D. W. (Eds.). (1989). *Socioeconomic characteristics of medical practice.* Chicago, IL: American Medical Association Center for Health Policy Research.

Goodstein, R. (1983). Overview: Cerebrovascular accident and the hospitalized elderly—A multidimensional clinical problem. *American Journal of Psychiatry, 140,* 141–147.

Gordon, G. (1966). *Role theory and illness: A sociolog-*

ical perspective. New Haven, CT: College and University Press.

Gordon, J. R., & Marlatt, G. A. (1981). Addictive behaviors. In J. L. Shelton & R. L. Levy (Eds.), _Behavioral assignments and treatment compliance_ (pp. 167–186). Champaign, IL: Research Press.

Gordon, W. A., & Diller, L. (1983). Stroke: Coping with a cognitive deficit. In T. G. Burish & L. A. Bradley (Eds.), _Coping with chronic disease: Research and applications_. New York: Academic Press.

Gordus, J. P., & McAlinden, S. (1984). _Economic change, mental illness, physical illness and social deviance_. Washington, DC: U.S. Government Printing Office.

Gore, S. (1978). The effect of social support in moderating the health consequences of unemployment. _Journal of Health and Social Behavior, 19_, 157–165.

Gore, S. M. (1988). Integrating reporting of quality and length of life—A statistician's perspective. _European Heart Journal, 9_, 228–234.

Gortmaker, S. L., Eckenrode, J., & Gore, S. (1982). Stress and the utilization of health services: A time series and cross-sectional analysis. _Journal of Health and Social Behavior, 23_, 25–38.

Gottlieb, B. H. (1983). _Social support strategies: Guidelines for mental health practice_. Beverly Hills, CA: Sage.

Gottlieb, B. H. (Ed.). (1988). _Marshalling social support: Formats, processes, and effects_. Newbury Park, CA: Sage.

Gottlieb, N. H., & Green, L. W. (1984). Life events, social network, life-style, and health: An analysis of the 1979 national survey on personal health practices and consequences. _Health Education Quarterly, 11_, 91–105.

Gottlieb, N. H., & Green, L. W. (1988). Ethnicity and lifestyle health risk: Some possible mechanisms. _American Journal of Health Promotion, 2_, 37–45, 51.

Gough, H. G. (1967). Nonintellectual factors in the selection and evaluation of medical students. _Journal of Medical Education, 42_, 642–650.

Gough, H. G., Hall, W. B., & Harris, R. E. (1963). Admissions procedures as forecasters of performance in medical training. _Journal of Medical Education, 38_, 983–998.

Gough, H. G., Hall, W. B., & Harris, R. E. (1964). Evaluation of performance in medical training. _Journal of Medical Education, 39_, 679–692.

Gould, R. (1972). The phases of adult life: A study in developmental psychology. _American Journal of Psychiatry, 129_, 521–531.

Grady, K. E., Goodenow, C., & Borkin, J. R. (1988). The effect of reward on compliance with breast self-examination. _Journal of Behavioral Medicine, 11_, 43–58.

Graham, J. D. P. (1945). High blood pressure after battle. _Lancet, 1_, 239–240.

Graham, M. A., Thompson, S. C., Estrada, M., & Yonekura, M. L. (1987). Factors affecting psychological adjustment to a fetal death. _American Journal of Obstetrics and Gynecology, 157_, 254–257.

Grant, I., Patterson, T., Olshen, R., & Yager, J. (1987). Life events do not predict symptoms: Symptoms predict symptoms. _Journal of Behavioral Medicine, 10_, 231–240.

Grassi, L., & Molinari, S. (1986). Intrafamilial dynamics and neoplasia: Prospects for a multidisciplinary analysis. _Rivista di Psichiatria, 21_, 329–341.

Gray, R. M., Newman, W. R. E., & Reinhardt, A. M. (1966). The effect of medical specialization on physicians' attitudes. _Journal of Health and Human Behavior, 7_, 128–133.

Graydon, J. E. (1988). Factors that predict patients functioning following treatment for cancer. _International Journal of Nursing Studies, 25_, 117–124.

Green, J. H. (1978). _Basic clinical physiology_ (3rd ed.). New York: Oxford University Press.

Green, L. (1970). Status, identity and preventive health behavior. _Pacific Health Education Reports, 1_(1).

Green, L. W. (1986). Health promotion and the elderly: Why do it and where does it lead? A national policy perspective. In K. G. Andreoli, L. A. Musser, & S. J. Reiser (Eds.), _Health care for the elderly: Regional responses to national issues_ (pp. 271–276). New York: Haworth Press.

Green, L. W., & McAlister, A. L. (1984). Macrointervention to support health behavior: Some theoretical perspectives and practical reflections. _Health Education Quarterly, 11_, 322–339.

Green, L. W., Mullen, P. D., & Stainbrook, G. L. (1986). Programs to reduce drug errors in the elderly: Direct and indirect evidence from patient education. _Journal of Geriatric Drug Therapy, 1_, 3–18.

Green, L. W., & Raeburn, J. M. (1988). Health promotion. What is it? What will it become? _Health Promotion, 3_, 151–159.

Green, L. W., & Simons-Morton, D. G. (1988). Denial, delay and disappointment: Discovering and overcoming the causes of drug errors and missed appointments. In D. Schmidt & I. E. Leppik (Eds.), *Compliance in epilepsy (Epilepsy research, suppl. 1)* (pp. 7–21). North Holland: Elsevier.

Greenberg, M. A., & Stone, A. A. (1990). Writing about disclosed versus undisclosed traumas: Health and mood effects. *Health Psychology, 9,* 114–115.

Greenberg, R. A., Haley, N. J., Etzel, R. A., & Loda, F. A. (1984). Measuring the exposure of infants to tobacco smoke. *New England Journal of Medicine, 310,* 1075–1078.

Greenberg, W., & Shapiro, D. (1987). The effects of caffeine and stress on blood pressure in individuals with and without a family history of hypertension. *Psychophysiology, 24,* 151–156.

Greene, W. A., Betts, R. F., Ochitill, H. N., Iker, H. P., & Douglas, R. G. (1978). Psychosocial factors and immunity: Preliminary report. *Psychosomatic Medicine, 40,* 87 (abstract).

Greenfield, M. (1986, June 30). The land of hospital. *Newsweek,* p. 74.

Greenfield, S., Kaplan, S. H., & Ware, J. E., Jr. (1984). *Expanding patient involvement and care: Effects on patient outcome.* Manuscript submitted for publication.

Greenfield, S., Kaplan, S. H., Ware, J. E., Jr., Yano, E. M., & Frank, H. J. L. (1988). Patients' participation in medical care: Effects on blood sugar control and quality of life in diabetes. *Journal of General Internal Medicine, 3,* 448–457.

Greenland, P., & Chu, J. S. (1988). Efficacy of cardiac rehabilitation services with emphasis on patients after myocardial infarction. *Annals of Internal Medicine, 109,* 650–663.

Greenley, J. R., & Schoenherr, R. A. (1981). Organization effects on client satisfaction with humaneness of service. *Journal of Health and Social Behavior, 22,* 2–18.

Greenstadt, L., Yang, L., & Shapiro, D. (1988). Caffeine, mental stress, and risk for hypertension: A cross-cultural replication. *Psychosomatic Medicine, 50,* 15–22.

Greer, S. (1974). Psychological aspects: Delay in the treatment of breast cancer. *Proceedings of the Royal Society of Medicine, 64,* 470–473.

Greer, S. (1987). Psychotherapy for the cancer patient. *Psychiatric Medicine, 5,* 267–279.

Greer, S., & Morris, T. (1975). Psychological attributes of women who develop breast cancer: A controlled study. *Journal of Psychosomatic Research, 19,* 147–153.

Grieco, A., & Long, C. J. (1984). Investigation of the Karnofsky Performance Status as a measure of quality of life. *Health Psychology, 3,* 129–142.

Gritz, E. R., Klesges, R. C., & Meyers, A. W. (1989). The smoking and body weight relationship: Implications for intervention and postcessation weight control. *Annals of Behavioral Medicine, 11,* 144–153.

Gross, A. M., Eudy, C., & Drabman, R. S. (1982). Training parents to be physical therapists with their physically handicapped child. *Journal of Behavioral Medicine, 5,* 321–328.

Gross, C. K. (1976, January 12). Death is a personal matter. *Newsweek,* p. 9.

Grossman, H. Y., Brink, S., & Hauser, S. T. (1987). Self-efficacy in adolescent girls and boys with insulin-dependent diabetes mellitus. *Diabetes Care, 10,* 324–329.

Grota, L. J., Ader, R., & Cohen, N. (1987). Taste aversion learning in autoimmune Mrl − lpr/lpr and Mrl +/ + mice. *Brain, Behavior and Immunity, 1,* 238–250.

Grunberg, N. E. (1985). Specific taste preferences: An alternative explanation for eating changes in cancer patients. In T. G. Burish, S. M. Levy, & B. E. Meyerowitz (Eds.), *Cancer, nutrition, and eating behavior: A biobehavioral perspective* (pp. 43–61). Hillsdale, NJ: Erlbaum.

Grunberg, N. E. (1986). Nicotine as a psychoactive drug: Appetite regulation. *Psychopharmacology Bulletin, 22,* 875–881.

Grunberg, N. E., & Bowen, D. J. (1985). Coping with the sequelae of smoking cessation. *Journal of Cardiopulmonary Rehabilitation, 5,* 285–289.

Grunberg, N. E., Bowen, D. J., & Winders, S. E. (1986). Effects of nicotine on body weight and food consumption in female rats. *Psychopharmacology, 90,* 101–105.

Grunberg, N. E., & Kozlowski, L. T. (1986). Alkaline therapy as an adjunct to smoking cessation programs. *International Journal of Biosocial Research, 8,* 43–52.

Grunberg, N. E., Popp, K. A., Bowen, D. J.,

Nespor, S. M., Winders, S. E., & Eury, S. E. (1988). Effects of chronic nicotine administration on insulin, glucose, epinephrine, and norepinephrine. *Life Sciences, 42,* 161–170.

Guck, T. P., Meilman, P. W., Skultety, F. M., & Poloni, L. D. (1988). Pain-patient Minnesota Multiphasic Personality Inventory (MMPI) subgroups: Evaluation of long-term treatment outcome. *Journal of Behavioral Medicine, 11,* 159–170.

Hackett, G. F., & Horan, J. J. (1978). Focused smoking: An unequivocally safe alternative to rapid smoking. *Journal of Drug Education, 8,* 261–265.

Hackett, T. P., & Cassem, N. H. (1973). Psychological adaptation to convalescence in myocardial infarction patients. In J. P Naughton, H. K. Hellerstein, & I. C. Mohler (Eds.), *Exercise testing and exercise training in coronary heart disease.* New York: Academic Press.

Hackett, T. P., & Weisman, A. D. (1969). Denial as a factor in patients with heart disease and cancer. *Annals of the New York Academy of Sciences, 164,* 802–817.

Haefner, D., Kegeles, S., Kirscht, J., & Rosenstock, I. (1967). Preventive actions in dental disease, tuberculosis, and cancer. *Public Health Reports, 82,* 451–459.

Haefner, D., & Kirscht, J. (1970). Motivational and behavioral effects of modifying health beliefs. *Public Health Reports, 85,* 478–484.

Haft, J. I. (1974). Cardiovascular injury induced by sympathetic catecholamines. *Progress in Cardiovascular Disease, 17,* 73.

Halberstam, M. J. (1971, February 14). The doctor's new dilemma: Will I be sued? *New York Times Magazine,* pp. 8–9, 33–39.

Hall, A., & Crisp, A. H. (1983). Brief psychotherapy in the treatment of anorexia nervosa: Preliminary findings. In P. L. Darby, P. E. Garfinkel, D. M. Garner, & D. V. Coscina (Eds.), *Anorexia nervosa: Recent developments in research* (pp. 41–56). New York: Liss.

Hall, R. A., Rappaport, M., Hopkins, H. K., & Griffin, R. (1973). Tobacco and evoked potential. *Science, 180,* 212–214.

Hall, S. C., Adams, C. K., Stein, C. H., Stephenson, H. S., Goldstein, M. K., & Pennypacker, H. S. (1980). Improved detection of human breast lesions following experimental training. *Cancer, 46,* 408–414.

Hall, S. M., Ginsberg, D., & Jones, R. T. (1986). Smoking cessation and weight gain. *Journal of Consulting and Clinical Psychology, 54,* 342–346.

Hall, S. M., & Hall, R. G. (1982). Clinical series in the behavioral treatment of obesity. *Health Psychology, 1,* 359–372.

Hamburg, D. A., & Adams, J. E. (1967). A perspective on coping behavior: Seeking and utilizing information in major transitions. *Archives of General Psychiatry, 19,* 277–284.

Hamburg, D. A., Hamburg, B., & DeGoza, S. (1953). Adaptive problems and mechanisms in severely burned patients. *Psychiatry, 16,* 1–20.

Hamilton, M. K., Gelwick, B. P., & Meade, C. J. (1984). The definition and prevalence of bulimia. In R. C. Hawkins, W. J. Fremouw, & P. F. Clement (Eds.), *The binge-purge syndrome* (pp. 3–26). New York: Springer.

Hammerschlag, C. A., Fisher, S., DeCosse, J., & Kaplan, E. (1964). Breast symptoms and patient delay: Psychological variables involved. *Cancer, 17,* 1480–1485.

Hanson, C. L., Henggeler, S. W., & Burghen, G. A. (1987). Models of associations between psychosocial variables and health-outcome measures of adolescents with IDDM. *Diabetes Care, 10,* 752–758.

Hanson, C. L., Henggeler, S. W., Harris, M. A., Burghen, G. A., & Moore, M. (1989). Family system variables and the health status of adolescents with insulin-dependent diabetes mellitus. *Health Psychology, 8,* 239–253.

Hanson, C. L., & Pichert, J. W. (1986). Perceived stress and diabetes control in adolescents. *Health Psychology, 5,* 439–452.

Harburg, E., Erfurt, J. C., Havenstein, L. S., Chape, C., Schull, W. J., & Schork, M. A. (1973). Socio-ecological stress, suppressed hostility, skin color, and black-white male blood pressure: Detroit. *Psychosomatic Medicine, 35,* 276–296.

Harney, M. K., & Brigham, T. A. (1985). Tolerance of aversive stimuli in relation to life change. *Journal of Behavioral Medicine, 8,* 21–36.

Harrell, J. P. (1980). Psychological factors and hypertension: A status report. *Psychological Bulletin, 87,* 482–501.

Harris, D. M., & Guten, G. (1979). Health-protective behavior: An exploratory study. *Journal of Health and Social Behavior, 20,* 17–29.

Harris, P. R. (1980). *Promoting health preventing disease: Objectives for the nation.* Washington, DC: U.S. Government Printing Office.

Hastrup, J. L. (1985). Inaccuracy of family health information: Implications for prevention. *Health Psychology, 4,* 389–397.

Hauenstein, M. S., Schiller, M. R., & Hurley, R. S. (1987). Motivational techniques of dieticians counseling individuals with Type II diabetes. *Journal of the American Diabetic Association, 87,* 37–42.

Haug, M. R., & Folmar, S. J. (1986). Longevity, gender, and life quality. *Journal of Health and Social Behavior, 27,* 332–345.

Haug, M. R., & Ory, M. G. (1987). Issues in elderly patient-provider interactions. *Research on Aging, 9,* 3–44.

Havik, O. E., & Maeland, J. G. (1988). Changes in smoking behavior after a myocardial infarction. *Health Psychology, 7,* 403–420.

Hawley, D. J., & Wolfe, F. (1988). Anxiety and depression in patients with rheumatoid arthritis: A prospective study of 400 patients. *Journal of Rheumatology, 15,* 932–941.

Hayes, D., & Ross, C. E. (1986). Body and mind: The effect of exercise, overweight, and physical health on psychological well-being. *Journal of Health and Social Behavior, 27,* 387–400.

Hayes, D., & Ross, C. E. (1987). Concern with appearance, health beliefs, and eating habits. *Journal of Health and Social Behavior, 28,* 120–130.

Hayes-Bautista, D. E. (1976). Modifying the treatment: Patient compliance, patient control, and medical care. *Social Science and Medicine, 10,* 233–238.

Haynes, R. B. (1979a). Determinants of compliance: The disease and the mechanics of treatment. In R. B. Haynes, D. W. Taylor, & D. L. Sackett (Eds.), *Compliance in health care* (pp. 49–62). Baltimore, MD: John Hopkins University Press.

Haynes, R. B. (1979b). Strategies to improve compliance with referrals, appointments, and prescribed medical regimens. In R. B. Haynes, D. W. Taylor, & D. L. Sackett (Eds.), *Compliance in health care* (pp. 121–143). Baltimore, MD: John Hopkins University Press.

Haynes, R. B. (1982). Improving patient compliance. In R. B. Stuart (Ed.), *Adherence, compliance, and generalization in behavioral medicine* (pp. 56–78). New York: Brunner/Mazel.

Haynes, R. B., Taylor, D. W., & Sackett, D. L. (Eds.). (1979). *Compliance in health care.* Baltimore, MD: Johns Hopkins University Press.

Haynes, R. B., Wang, B., & da-Mota-Gomes, M. (1987). A critical review of intentions to improve compliance with prescribed medications. *Patient Education and Counseling, 10,* 155–166.

Haynes, S. G., & Feinleib, M. (1980). Women, work and coronary heart disease: Prospective findings from the Framingham Heart Study. *American Journal of Public Health, 70,* 133–141.

Haynes, S. G., & Feinleib, M., & Kannel, W. B. (1980). The relationship of psychosocial factors to coronary heart disease in the Framingham Study: I. Methods and risk factors. *American Journal of Epidemiology, 107,* 362–383.

Heinrich, R. L., Cohen, M. J., Naliboff, B. D., Collins, G. A., & Bonebakker, A. D. (1985). Comparing physical and behavior therapy for chronic low back pain on physical abilities, psychological distress, and patients' perceptions. *Journal of Behavioral Medicine, 8,* 61–78.

Heitzmann, C. A., & Kaplan, R. M. (1988). Assessment of methods for measuring social support. *Health Psychology, 7,* 75–109.

Helgeson, V. S. (in press). The role of masculinity as a prognostic predictor of heart attack severity. *Sex Roles.*

Helsing, K. J., Comstock, G. W., & Szklo, M. (1982). Causes of death in a widowed population. *American Journal of Epidemiology, 116,* 524–532.

Henry, J. P. & Cassel, J. C. (1969). Psychosocial factors in essential hypertension: Recent epidemiologic and animal experimental evidence. *American Journal of Epidemiology, 90,* 171–200.

Herd, J. A. (1978). Physiological correlates of coronary-prone behavior. In T. Dembroski, S. Weiss, J. Sheilds, S. Haynes, & M. Feinleib (Eds.), *Coronary-prone behavior.* New York: Springer.

Herman, C. P. (1987). Social and pychological factors in obesity: What we don't know. In H. Weiner & A. Baum (Eds.), *Perspectives in behavioral medicine: Eating regulation and discontrol* (pp. 175–187). Hillsdale, NJ: Erlbaum.

Herman, M. (1972). The poor: Their medical needs and the health services available to them. *Annals of the American Academy of Political and Social Science, 399,* 12–21.

Hershey, D. (1974). *Life-span and factors affecting it.* Springfield, MA: Thomas.

Higbee, K. (1969). Fifteen years of fear arousal: Research on threat appeals, 1953–1968. *Psychological Bulletin, 72,* 426–444.

Hilgard, E. R. (1965). *Hypnotic susceptibility.* New York: Harcourt, Brace & World.

Hilgard, E. R. (1971). Hypnotic phenomena: The struggle for scientific acceptance. *American Scientist, 59,* 567–577.

Hilgard, E. R. (1975). The alleviation of pain by hypnosis. *Pain, 1,* 213–231.

Hilgard, E. R. (1978). Hypnosis and pain. In R. A. Sternbach (Ed.), *The psychology of pain.* New York: Raven Press.

Hilgard, E. R., & Bower, G. H. (1966). *Theories of learning.* New York: Appleton-Century Crofts.

Hilton, B. (1989). The relationship of uncertainty, control, commitment, and threat of recurrence to coping strategies used by women diagnosed with breast cancer. *Journal of Behavioral Medicine, 12,* 39–54.

Hinton, J. M. (1967). *Dying.* Baltimore, MD: Penguin.

Hirayama, T. (1981). Non-smoking wives of heavy smokers have a higher risk of lung cancer: A study from Japan. *British Medical Journal, 282,* 183–185.

Hiroto, D. S., & Seligman, M. E. P. (1975). Generality of learned helplessness in man. *Journal of Personality and Social Psychology, 31,* 311–327.

Hirsch, J., Fried, S. K., Edens, N. K., & Leibel, R. L. (1989). The fat cell. *Medical Clinics of North America, 73,* 83–95.

Hirschman, R. S., & Leventhal, H. (1989). Preventing smoking behavior in school children: An initial test of a cognitive-development program. *Journal of Applied Social Psychology, 19,* 559–583.

Hjermann, I., Velve Byre, K., Holme, I., & Leren, P. (1981). Effect of diet and smoking intervention on the incidence of coronary heart disease. *Lancet, 2,* 1303–1310.

Hobfoll, S. E. (1989). Conservation of resources: A new attempt at conceptualizing stress. *American Psychologist, 44,* 513–524.

Hobfoll, S. E., & Lerman, M. (1989). Predicting receipt of social support: A longitudinal study of parents' reactions to their child's illness. *Health Psychology, 8,* 61–77.

Hochbaum, G. (1958). *Public participation in medical screening programs* (DHEW Publication No. 572, Public Health Service). Washington, DC: U.S. Government Printing Office.

Hochschild, A. (1989). *The second shift: Working parents and the revolution at home.* New York: Viking Penguin.

Hoelscher, T. J., Lichstein, K. L., & Rosenthal, T. L. (1986). Home relaxation practice in hypertension treatment: Objective assessment and compliance induction. *Journal of Consulting and Clinical Psychology, 54,* 217–221.

Hoffman, M. (Ed.). (1988). *The world almanac and book of facts.* Washington, DC: Newspaper Enterprises Association, Inc.

Hogan, T. (1989). Psychophysical relation between perceived threat of AIDS and willingness to impose social restrictions. *Health Psychology, 8,* 255–266.

Holaday, J. W. (1983). Cardiovascular effects of endogenous opiate systems. *Annual Review of Pharmacology and Toxicology, 23,* 541–594.

Holahan, C. J., & Moos, R. H. (1986). Personality, coping, and family resources in stress resistance: A longitudinal analysis. *Journal of Personality and Social Psychology, 51,* 389–395.

Holahan, C. J., & Moos, R. H. (1987a). Personal and contextual determinants of coping strategies. *Journal of Personality and Social Psychology, 52,* 946–955.

Holahan, C. J., & Moos, R. H. (1987b). Risk, resistance, and psychological distress: A longitudinal analysis with adults and children. *Journal of Abnormal Psychology, 96,* 3–13.

Holahan, C. K., Holahan, C. J., & Belk, S. S. (1984). Adjustment in aging: The roles of life stress, hassles, and self-efficacy. *Health Psychology, 3,* 315–328.

Holden, C. (1980). Love Canal residents under stress. *Science, 208,* 1242–1244.

Holden, C. (1983). Hospices compared with conventional care. *Science, 222,* 601.

Holden, C. (1987). Is alcoholism treatment effective? *Science, 236,* 20–22.

Holland, J. C. (1973). Psychological aspects of cancer. In I. F. Holland & E. Frei III (Eds.), *Cancer medicine.* Philadelphia: Lea & Febiger.

Holland, J. C., & Massie, M. J. (1987). Psychosocial aspects of cancer in the elderly. *Clinics in Geriatric Medicine, 3,* 533–539.

Holland, J. C., & Rowland, J. H. (1981). Psychiatric,

psychosocial, and behavioral interventions in the treatment of cancer: A historical overview. In S. M. Weiss, J. A. Herd, & B. H. Fox (Eds.), *Perspectives on behavioral medicine.* New York: Academic Press.

Hollandsworth, J. G., Jr. (1988). Evaluating the impact of medical treatment on the quality of life: A 5-year update. *Social Science and Medicine, 26,* 425–434.

Hollis, J. F., Carmody, T. P., Connor, S. L., Fey, S. G., & Matarazzo, J. D. (1986). The nutrition attitude survey: Associations with dietary habits, psychological and physical well-being, and coronary risk factors. *Health Psychology, 5,* 359–374.

Hollon, S. D., & Beck, A. T. (1986). Cognitive and cognitive-behavioral therapies. In S. L. Garfield & A. E. Bergin (Eds.), *Handbook of psychotherapy and behavior change* (3rd ed., pp. 443–482). New York: Wiley.

Holmes, D., & Will, M. (1985). Expression of interpersonal aggression by angered and nonangered persons with Type A and Type B behavior patterns. *Journal of Personality and Social Psychology, 48,* 723–727.

Holmes, D. S. (1981). The use of biofeedback for treating patients with migraine headaches, Raynaud's disease, and hypertension: A critical evaluation. In C. K. Prokop & L. A. Bradley (Eds.), *Medical psychology: Contributions to behavioral medicine* (pp. 423–441). New York: Academic Press.

Holmes, D. S. (1984). Meditation and somatic arousal reduction: A review of the experimental evidence. *American Psychologist, 39,* 1–10.

Holmes, T. H., & Rahe, R. H. (1967). The social readjustment rating scale. *Journal of Psychosomatic Research, 11,* 213–218.

Holmes, T. S., & Holmes, T. H. (1970). Short-term intrusions into the life style routine. *Journal of Psychosomatic Research, 14,* 121–132.

Holroyd, K. A., Andrasik, F., & Westbrook, T. (1977). Cognitive control of tension headache. *Cognitive Therapy and Research, 1,* 121–133.

Holroyd, K. A., & Gorkin, L. (1983). Young adults at risk for hypertension: Effects of family history and anger management in determining responses to interpersonal conflict. *Journal of Psychosomatic Research, 27,* 131–138.

Holroyd, K. A., & Penzien, D. B. (1986). Client variables and the behavioral treatment of recurrent tension headache: A meta-analytic review. *Journal of Behavioral Medicine, 9,* 515–536.

Homme, L. E. (1965). Perspectives in psychology, XXIV: Control of coverants, the operants of the mind. *Psychological Record, 15,* 501–511.

Hongladrom, T., & Hongladrom, G. C. (1982). The problem of testicular cancer: How health professionals in the armed services can help. *Military Medicine, 147,* 211–213.

Horan, J. J., Layng, F. C., & Pursell, C. H. (1976). Preliminary study of effects of "in vivo" emotive imagery on dental discomfort. *Perceptual and Motor Skills, 42,* 105–106.

Horan, M. J., & Roccella, E. J. (1988). Nonpharmacologic treatment of hypertension in the United States. *Health Psychology, 7*(Suppl.), 267–282.

Horowitz, M., Adler, N., & Kegeles, S. (1988). A scale for measuring the occurrence of positive states of mind: A preliminary report. *Psychosomatic Medicine, 50,* 477–483.

Horowitz, M. J. (1975). Sliding meanings: A defense against threat in narcissistic personalities. *International Journal of Psychoanalysis and Psychotherapy, 4,* 167–180.

Hough, R. L., Fairbank, D. T., & Garcia, A. M. (1976). Problems in the ratio measurement of life stress. *Journal of Health and Social Behavior, 17,* 70–82.

House, J. A. (1981). *Work stress and social support.* Reading, MA: Addison-Wesley.

House, J. A., McMichael, A. J., Wells, J. A., Kaplan, B. H., & Landerman, L. R. (1979). Occupational stress and health among factory workers. *Journal of Health and Social Behavior, 20,* 139–160.

House, J. A., Robbins, C., & Metzner, H. L. (1982). The association of social relationships and activities with mortality: Prospective evidence from the Tecumseh Community Health Study. *American Journal of Epidemiology, 116,* 123–140.

House, J. S. (1987). Chronic stress and chronic disease in life and work: Conceptual and methodological issues. *Work and Stress, 1,* 129–134.

House, J. S., & Kahn, R. L. (1985). Measures and concepts of social support. In S. Cohen & S. L. Syme (Eds.), *Social support and health* (pp. 83–108). New York: Academic Press.

House, J. S., & Smith, D. A. (1985). Evaluating the health effects of demanding work on and off the job. In T. F. Drury (Ed.), *Assessing physical fitness and physical activity in population-base surveys.* (pp. 481–508). Hyattsville, MD: National Center for Health Statistics.

House, J. S., Strecher, V., Meltzner, H. L., & Robbins, C. A. (1986). Occupational stress and health among men and women in the Tecumseh Community health study. *Journal of Health and Social Behavior, 27,* 62–77.

House, J. S., Umberson, D., & Landis, K. R. (1988). Structures and processes of social support. *American Review of Sociology, 14,* 293–318.

House, W. C., Pendelton, L., & Parker, L. (1986). Patients' versus physicians' attributions of reasons for diabetic patients' noncompliance with diet. *Diabetes Care, 9,* 434.

Houston, B. K. (1988). Division 38 survey: Synopsis of results. *Health Psychologist, 10,* 2–3.

Howell, D. (1986). The impact of terminal illness on the spouse. *Journal of Palliative Care, 2,* 22–30.

Hubert, H. B., Feinleib, M., McNamara, P. M., & Castelli, W. P. (1983). Obesity as an independent risk factor for cardiovascular disease: A 26-year follow-up of participants in the Framingham Heart Study. *Circulation, 67,* 968–977.

Hughes, J. E. (1987). Psychological and social consequences of cancer. *Cancer Surveys, 6,* 455–475.

Hughes, J. E., & Lee, D. (1987). Depressive symptoms in patients with terminal cancer. In M. Watson & S. Greer (Eds.), *Psychosocial issues in malignant disease.* Oxford, England: Pergamon.

Hughes, J. R. (1984). Psychological effects of habitual aerobic exercise: A critical review. *Preventive Medicine, 13,* 66–78.

Hughes, J. R., Casal, D. C., & Leon, A. S. (1986). Psychological effects of exercise: A randomized cross-over trial. *Journal of Psychosomatic Research, 30,* 355–360.

Hughes, J. R., Hatsukami, D. K., & Skoog, K. P. (1986). Physical dependence on nicotine in gum: A placebo substitution trial. *Journal of the American Medical Association, 255,* 3277–3279.

Hull, J. G., Van Treuren, R. R., & Virnelli, S. (1987). Hardiness and health: A critique and alternative approach. *Journal of Personality and Social Psychology, 53,* 1–13.

Hunt, R., & Arras, I. (1977). *Ethical issues in modern medicine.* Palo Alto, CA: Mayfield.

Hunt, W. A., & Matarazzo, J. D. (1973). Three years later: Recent developments in the experimental modification of smoking behavior. *Journal of Abnormal Psychology, 81,* 107–114.

Huntington, R., & Metcalf, P. (1979). *Celebrations of death: The anthropology of mortuary ritual.* New York: Cambridge University Press.

Hurst, M., Jenkins, D., & Rose, R. (1976). The relation of psychological stress to onset of medical illness. *Annual Review of Medicine, 27,* 301–312.

Ikard, F. F., Green, D. E., & Horn, D. A. (1969). A scale to differentiate between types of smoking as related to management of affect. *International Journal of the Addictions, 4,* 649–659.

Illich, I. (1976). *Medical nemesis.* New York: Pantheon.

Institute of Medicine. (1987). *Causes and consequences of alcohol related problems: An agenda for research.* Washington, DC: National Academy Press.

Irwin, M., Daniels, M., Bloom, E., Smith, T. L., & Weiner, H. (1987). Life events, depressive symptoms, and immune function. *American Journal of Psychiatry, 144,* 437–441.

Irwin, M., Daniels, M., Bloom, E., & Weiner, H. (1986). Life events, depression, and natural killer cell activity. *Psychopharmacology Bulletin, 22,* 1093–1096.

Irwin, M., Daniels, M., Smith, T. L., Bloom, E., & Weiner, H. (1987). Impaired natural killer cell activity during bereavement. *Brain, Behavior, and Immunity, 1,* 98–104.

Irwin, M., Daniels, M., Weiner, H., & Bloom, E. (1986). Depression and changes in T-cell subpopulations. *Psychosomatic Medicine, 48,* 303–304 (abstract).

Ishigami, T. (1919). The influence of psychic acts on the progress of pulmonary tuberculosis. *American Review of Tuberculosis, 2,* 470–484.

Istvan, J., & Matarazzo, J. D. (1984). Tobacco, alcohol, and caffeine use: A review of their interrelationships. *Psychological Bulletin, 95,* 301–326.

Jachuck, S. J., Brierley, H., Jachuck, S., & Willcox, P. M. (1982). The effect of hypotensive drugs on the quality of life. *Journal of the Royal College of General Practitioners, 32,* 103–105.

Jackson, C., & Levine, D. W. (1987). Comparison of the Matthews Youth Test for Health and the Hunter-Wolf A-B Rating Scale: Measures of Type A behavior in children. *Health Psychology, 6,* 255–267.

Jacobs, G. D., Heilbronner, R. L., & Stanley, J. M. (1984). The effects of short term flotation REST on relaxation: A controlled study. *Health Psychology, 3*, 99–112.

Jacobs, M. A., Knapp, P. H., Rosenthal, S., & Haskell, D. (1970). Psychological aspects of cigarette smoking in men—clinical evaluation. *Psychosomatic Medicine, 32*, 469–485.

Jacobs, M. L., & Lau, R. R. (1989). *Health promotion, health locus of control, and health behavior: Two field experiments.* Manuscript submitted for publication.

Jacobson, D. E. (1986). Types and timing of social support. *Journal of Health and Social Behavior, 27*, 250–264.

Jacobson, E. (1938). *Progressive relaxation* (2nd ed.). Chicago: University of Chicago Press.

Jacoby, D. B. (1986). Letter to the Editor. *New England Journal of Medicine, 315*, 399.

James, S. A. (1987). Psychosocial precursors of hypertension: A review of the epidemiologic evidence. *Circulation, 76*(Suppl. I), I-60–I-66.

James, S. A., Hartnett, S. A., & Kalsbeek, W. D. (1983). John Henryism and blood pressure differences among black men. *Journal of Behavioral Medicine, 6*, 259–278.

James, S. A., LaCroix, A. Z., Kleinbaum, D. G., & Strogatz, D. S. (1984). John Henryism and blood pressure differences among black men: II. The role of occupational stressors. *Journal of Behavioral Medicine, 7*, 259–310.

James, S. A., Strogatz, D. S., Wing, S. B., & Ramsey, D. L. (1987). Socioeconomic status, John Henryism, and hypertension in blacks and whites. *American Journal of Epidemiology, 126*, 664–673.

Jamieson, J. L., & Lavoie, N. F. (1987). Type A behavior, aerobic power, and cardiovascular recovery from a psychosocial stressor. *Health Psychology, 6*, 361–371.

Jamison, R. N., Rock, D. L., & Parris, W. C. V. (1988). Empirically derived symptom checklist for 90 subgroups of chronic pain patients: A cluster analysis. *Journal of Behavioral Medicine, 11*, 147–158.

Jamner, L. D., & Tursky, B. (1987). Syndrome-specific descriptor profiling: A psychophysiological and psychophysical approach. *Health Psychology, 6*, 417–430.

Janis, I. L. (1958). *Psychological stress.* New York: Wiley.

Janis, I. L. (1967). Effects of fear arousal on attitude change: Recent developments in theory and experimental research. In L. Berkowitz (Ed.), *Advances in experimental social psychology* (Vol. 3, pp. 167–225). New York: Academic Press.

Janis, I. L. (1983a). Improving adherence to medical recommendations: Prescriptive hypotheses derived from recent research in social psychology. In A. Baum, S. E. Taylor, & J. Singer (Eds.), *Handbook of psychology and health* (Vol. 4, pp. 113–148). Hillsdale, NJ: Erlbaum.

Janis, I. L. (1983b). The role of social support in adherence to stressful decisions. *American Psychologist, 38*, 143–160.

Janis, I. L., & Mann, I. (1977). *Decision making: A psychological analysis of conflict, choice, and commitment.* New York: Free Press.

Janson, M. A. H. (1986). A comprehensive bereavement program. *Quality Review Bulletin, 12*, 130–135.

Janz, N. K., & Becker, M. H. (1984). The health belief model: A decade later. *Health Education Quarterly, 11*, 1–47.

Jarvik, M. E., & Schneider, N. (1984). Degree of addiction and effectiveness of nicotine gum therapy for smoking. *American Journal of Psychiatry, 141*, 790–791.

Jarvik, M. E. (1973). Further observations on nicotine as the reinforcing agent in smoking. In W. L. Dunn, Jr. (Ed.), *Smoking behavior: Motives and incentives* (pp. 33–50). Washington, DC: Winston.

Jarvinen, K. A. J. (1955). Can ward rounds be dangerous to patients with myocardial infarction? *British Medical Journal, 1*, 318–320.

Jason, H., Kagan, N., Werner, A., Elstein, A. S., & Thomas, J. B. (1971). New approaches to teaching basic interview skills to medical students. *American Journal of Psychiatry, 127*, 140–143.

Jay, S. M., Ozolins, M., Elliott, C. H., & Caldwell, S. (1983). Assessment of children's distress during painful medical procedures. *Health Psychology, 2*, 133–147.

Jeffery, R. W., Pirie, P. L., Rosenthal, B. S., Gerber, W. M., & Murray, D. M. (1982). Nutritional education in supermarkets: An unsuccessful attempt to influence knowledge and produce sales. *Journal of Behavioral Medicine, 5*, 189–200.

Jellinek, E. M. (1960). *The disease concept of alcoholism.* Highland Park, NJ: Hillhouse Press.

Jemmott, J. B. III, Borysenko, J. Z., Borysenko, M.,

McClelland, D. C., Chapman, R., Meyer, D., & Benson, H. (1983). Academic stress, power motivation, and decrease in salivary secretory immunoglobulin A secretion rate. *Lancet, 1,* 1400–1402.

Jemmott, J. B. III, Croyle, R. T., & Ditto, P. H. (1988). Commonsense epidemiology: Self-based judgments from laypersons and physicians. *Health Psychology, 7,* 55–73.

Jemmott, J. B. III, & Locke, S. E. (1984). Psychosocial factors, immunologic mediation, and human susceptibility to infectious diseases: How much do we know? *Psychological Bulletin, 95,* 78–108.

Jemmott, J. B. III, & Magloire, K. (1988). Academic stress, social support, and secretory immunoglobulin A. *Journal of Personality and Social Psychology, 55,* 803–810.

Jenkins, C. D. (1971). Psychologic and social precursors of coronary disease. *New England Journal of Medicine, 284,* 244–255, 307–317.

Jenkins, C. D. Zyzanski, S. J., & Rosenman, R. H. (1979). *Jenkins Activity Survey.* Cleveland, OH: Psychological Corp.

Jenkins, R. A., & Pargament, K. I. (1988). Cognitive appraisals in cancer patients. *Social Science and Medicine, 26,* 625–633.

Jessor, R., & Jessor, S. L. (1977). *Problem behavior and psychosocial development: A longitudinal study of youth.* New York: Academic Press.

Jessor, R., & Jessor, S. L. (1984). Adolescence to young adulthood: A twelve-year prospective study of problem behavior and psychosocial development. In S. A. Mednick, M. Harway, & K. M. Finello (Eds.), *Handbook of longitudinal research in the United States* (Vol. 2, pp. 34–61). New York: Praeger.

Joffres, M., Reed, D. M., & Nomura, A. M. Y. (1985). Psychosocial processes and cancer incidence among Japanese men in Hawaii. *American Journal of Epidemiology, 121,* 488–500.

Johnson, C. A., Hansen, W. B., Collins, L. M., & Graham, J. W. (1986). High-school smoking prevention: Results of a three-year longitudinal study. *Journal of Behavioral Medicine, 9,* 439–452.

Johnson, C. C., Hunter, S. MacD., Amos, C. I., Elder, S. T., & Berenson, G. S. (1989). Cigarette smoking, alcohol, and oral contraceptive use by Type A adolescent—the Bogalusa Heart Study. *Journal of Behavioral Medicine, 12,* 13–24.

Johnson, C. G., Levenkron, J. C., Suchman, A. L.,

& Manchester, R. (1988). Does physician uncertainty affect patient satisfaction? *Journal of General Internal Medicine, 3,* 144–149.

Johnson, E. H., & Broman, C. L. (1987). The relationship of anger expression to health problems among black Americans in a national survey. *Journal of Behavioral Medicine, 10,* 103–116.

Johnson, E. H., Schork, N. J., & Spielberger, C. D. (1987). Emotional and familial determinants of elevated blood pressure in black and white adolescent females. *Journal of Psychosomatic Research, 31,* 731–741.

Johnson, J. (1982). The effects of a patient education course on persons with a chronic illness. *Cancer Nursing, 5,* 117–123.

Johnson, J. E. (1984). Psychological interventions and coping with surgery. In A. Baum, S. E. Taylor, & J. E. Singer (Eds.), *Handbook of psychology and health* (Vol. 4, pp. 167–188). Hillsdale, NJ: Erlbaum.

Johnson, J. E., Christman, N., & Stitt, C. (1985). Personal control interventions: Short- and long-term effects on surgical patients. *Research in Nursing and Health, 8,* 131–145.

Johnson, J. E., Fuller, S. S., Endress, M. P., & Rice, V. H. (1978). Altering patients' responses to surgery: An extension and replication. *Research in Nursing and Health, 1,* 111–121.

Johnson, J. E., Kirchoff, K., & Endress, M. P. (1975). Altering children's distress behavior during orthopedic cast removal. *Nursing Research, 75,* 404–410.

Johnson, J. E., Lauver, D. R., & Nail, L. M. (1989). Process of coping with radiation therapy. *Journal of Consulting and Clinical Psychology, 57,* 358–364.

Johnson, J. E., & Leventhal, H. (1974). Effects of accurate expectations and behavioral instructions on reactions during a noxious medical examination. *Journal of Personality and Social Psychology, 29,* 710–718.

Johnson, J. E., Rice, V. H., Fuller, S. S., & Endress, M. P. (1978). Sensory information, instruction in a coping strategy, and recovery from surgery. *Research in Nursing and Health, 1,* 4–17.

Johnson, I. H., Sarason, I. G., & Siegel, J. M. (1979). Arousal seeking as a moderator of life stress. *Perceptual and Motor Skills, 49,* 665–666.

Johnson, S. B. (1980). Psychosocial factors in juvenile diabetes: A review. *Journal of Behavioral Medicine, 3,* 95–116.

Jones, K. V. (1985). The thrill of victory: Blood-pressure variability and the Type A behavior pattern. *Journal of Behavioral Medicine, 8,* 277–286.

Jordan, B. (1983). *Birth in four cultures.* Montreal, Quebec, Canada: Eden Press.

Jorgensen, R. S., & Houston, B. K. (1981). Family history of hypertension, gender and cardiovascular reactivity and stereotypy during stress. *Journal of Behavioral Medicine, 4,* 175–190.

Joseph, J. G., Montgomery, S., Kirscht, J., Kessler, R. C., Ostrow, D. G., Emmons, C. A., & Phair, J. P. (1987, June). *Behavioral risk reduction in a cohort of homosexual men: Two year follow-up.* Paper presented at the Third International Conference on AIDS, Washington, DC.

Jury Verdict Research, Inc. (1990). *Current award trends.* Cleveland, OH: Jury Verdict Research, Inc.

Kabat-Zinn, J., & Chapman-Waldrop, A. (1988). Compliance with an outpatient stress reduction program: Rates and predictors of program completion. *Journal of Behavioral Medicine, 11,* 333–352.

Kabat-Zinn, J., Lipworth, L., & Burney, R. (1985). The clinical use of mindfulness meditation for the self-regulation of chronic pain. *Journal of Behavioral Medicine, 8,* 163–190.

Kagan, N. I. (1974). Teaching interpersonal relations for the practice of medicine. *Lakartidningen, 71,* 4758–4760.

Kahn, J. P., Kornfeld, D. S., Frank, K. A., Heller, S. S., & Hoar, P. F. (1980). Type A behavior and blood pressure during coronary artery bypass surgery. *Psychosomatic Medicine, 42,* 407–414.

Kahn, M., & Baker, B. (1968). Desensitization with minimal therapist contact. *Journal of Abnormal Psychology, 73,* 198–200.

Kahn, R. L. (1981). *Work and health.* New York: Wiley.

Kahn, R. L., Wolfe, D. M., Quinn, R. P., Snoek, J. D., & Rosenthal, R. A. (1964). *Organizational stress.* New York: Wiley.

Kalish, R. A. (1977). *Dying and preparing for death: A view of families.* In H. Feifel (Ed.), *New meanings of death.* New York: McGraw-Hill.

Kalish, R. A., & Reynolds, D. K. (1976). *Death and ethnicity: A psychocultural investigation.* Los Angeles: University of Southern California Press.

Kaloupek, D. G., & Stoupakis, T. (1985). Coping with a stressful medical procedure: Further investigation with volunteer blood donors. *Journal of Behavioral Medicine, 8,* 131–148.

Kaloupek, D. G., White, H., & Wong, M. (1984). Multiple assessment of coping strategies used by volunteer blood donors: Implications for preparatory training. *Journal of Behavioral Medicine, 7,* 35–60.

Kamarck, T. W., & Lichtenstein, E. (1988). Program adherence and coping strategies as predictors of success in a smoking treatment program. *Health Psychology, 7,* 557–574.

Kandel, D. B., Davies, M., & Raveis, V. H. (1985). The stressfulness of daily social roles for women: Marital, occupational and household roles. *Journal of Health and Social Behavior, 26,* 64–78.

Kane, R. L., Klein, S. J., Bernstein, L., Rothenberg, R., & Wales, J. (1985). Hospice role in alleviating the emotional stress of terminal patients and their families. *Medical Care, 23,* 189–197.

Kane, R. L., Wales, J., Bernstein, L., Liebowitz, A., & Kaplan, S. (1984). A randomized controlled trial of hospice care. *Lancet, 1,* 890–894.

Kannel, W. B., & Eaker, E. D. (1986). Psychosocial and other features of coronary heart disease: Insights from the Framingham Study. *American Heart Journal, 112,* 1066–1073.

Kannel, W. B., & Gordon, T. (1979). Physiological and medical concomitants of obesity: The Framingham Study. In G. A. Bray (Ed.), *Obesity in America* (NIH Publication No. 79–359). Washington, DC: U.S. Government Printing Office.

Kanner, A. D., Coyne, J. C., Schaeffer, C., & Lazarus, R. S. (1981). Comparison of two modes of stress measurement: Daily hassles and uplifts versus major life events. *Journal of Behavioral Medicine, 4,* 1–39.

Kaplan, G. A., & Reynolds, P. (1988). Depression and cancer mortality and morbidity: Prospective evidence from the Alameda County study. *Journal of Behavioral Medicine, 11,* 1–13.

Kaplan, G. A., Seeman, T. E., Cohen, R. D., Knudsen, L. P., & Guralnik, J. (1987). Mortality among the elderly in the Alameda County study: Behavioral and demographic risk factors. *American Journal of Public Health, 77,* 307–312.

Kaplan, H. B., Robbins, C., & Martin, S. S. (1983). Antecedents of psychological distress in young adults: Self-rejection, deprivation of social support, and life events. *Journal of Health and Social Behavior, 24,* 230–244.

Kaplan, H. I. (1975). Current psychodynamic concepts in psychosomatic medicine. In R. O.

Pasnau (Ed.), *Consultation-liaison psychiatry*. New York: Grune & Stratton.

Kaplan, R. F., Cooney, N. L., Baker, L. H., Gillespie, R. A., Meyer, R. E., & Pomerleau, O. F. (1985). Reactivity to alcohol-related cues: Physiological and subjective responses in alcoholics and nonproblem drinkers. *Journal of Studies on Alcohol, 46*, 267–272.

Kaplan, R. M. (1984). The connection between clinical health promotion and health status: A critical overview. *American Psychologist, 39*, 755–765.

Kaplan, R. M. (1985). Quality of life measurement. In P. Karoly (Ed.), *Measurement strategies in health psychology* (pp. 115–146). New York: Wiley.

Kaplan, R. M., Atkins, C. I., & Lenhard, L. (1982). Coping with a stressful sigmoidoscopy: Evaluation of cognitive and relaxation preparations. *Journal of Behavioral Medicine, 5*, 67–82.

Kaplan, R. M., & Bush, J. W. (1982). Health-related quality of life measurement for evaluation research and policy analysis. *Health Psychology, 1*, 61–80.

Kaplan, R. M., & Hartwell, S. L. (1987). Differential effects of social support and social network on physiological and social outcomes in men and women with Type II diabetes mellitus. *Health Psychology, 6*, 387–398.

Kasl, S. V. (1975). Issues in patient adherence to health care regimens. *Journal of Human Stress, 1*, 5–17.

Kasl, S. V. (1980). Cardiovascular risk reduction in a community setting: Some comments. *Journal of Consulting and Clinical Psychology, 48*, 143–149.

Kasl, S. V. (1983). Pursuing the link between stressful life experiences and disease: A time for reappraisal. In C. I. Cooper (Ed.), *Stress research* (pp. 79–102). New York: Wiley.

Kasl, S. V., & Berkman, L. (1983). Health consequences of the experience of migration. *Annual Review of Public Health, 4*, 69–90.

Kasl, S. V., & Cobb, S. (1966). Health behavior, illness behavior, and sick role behavior. *Archives of Environmental Health, 12*, 246–266.

Kasl, S. V., & Cobb, S. (1970). Blood pressure changes in men undergoing job loss: A preliminary report. *Psychosomatic Medicine, 32*, 19–38.

Kasl, S. V., Evans, A. S., & Niederman, J. C. (1979). Psychosocial risk factors in the development of infectious mononucleosis. *Psychosomatic Medicine, 41*, 445–466.

Kastenbaum, R. (1977). Death and development through the lifespan. In H. Feifel (Ed.), *New meanings of death* (pp. 17–46). New York: McGraw-Hill.

Kastenbaum, R. (1979). "Healthy dying": A paradoxical quest continues. *Journal of Social Issues, 35*, 185–206.

Kastenbaum, R., & Aisenberg, R. B. (1972). *The psychology of death*. New York: Springer.

Katz, J. L., Weiner, H., Gallagher, T. F., & Hellman, I. (1970). Stress, distress, and ego defenses: Psychoendocrine response to impending breast tumor biopsy. *Archives of General Psychiatry, 23*, 131–142.

Katz, R. C., & Singh, N. N. (1986). Reflections on the ex-smoker: Some findings on successful quitters. *Journal of Behavioral Medicine, 9*, 191–202.

Katz, S. T., Ford, A. B., Moskowitz, R. W., Jackson, B. A., & Jaffee, M. W. (1983). Studies of illness in the aged: The index of ADL. *Journal of the American Medical Association, 185*, 914–919.

Kaufert, J. M., Rabkin, S. W., Syrotuik, J., Boyko, E., & Shane, F. (1986). Health beliefs as predictors of success of alternate modalities of smoking cessation: Results of a controlled trial. *Journal of Behavioral Medicine, 9*, 475–490.

Kaufman, M. R. (1970). Practicing good manners and compassion. *Medical Insight, 2*, 56–61.

Kavetskii, R. E. (1958). *The neoplastic process and the nervous system*. Kiev, USSR: State Medical Publishing House. (Translated from Russian and available from the National Technical Information Service, Springfield, VA 22151, Publication No. 60-21860.)

Kazak, A. E. (1989). Families of chronically ill children: A systems and social-ecological model of adaptation and challenge. *Journal of Consulting and Clinical Psychology, 57*, 25–30.

Kazdin, A. E. (1974). Self-monitoring behavior change. In M. J. Mahoney & C. E. Thoresen (Eds.), *Self-control: Power to the person* (pp. 218–246). Monterey, CA: Brooks-Cole.

Keane, T. M. (1988, November). *Comorbidity in posttraumatic stress disorder*. Paper presented at the NIMH-Sponsored Workshop on Traumatic Stress: Defining Terms and Instruments, Rockville, MD.

Kearns, D. (1976). *Lyndon Johnson and the American dream*. New York: Harper & Row.

Keefe, F. J., Caldwell, D. S., Queen, K. T., Gil, K. M., Martinez, S., Crisson, J. E., Ogden, N., &

Nunley, J. (1987). Pain coping strategies in osteoarthritis patients. *Journal of Consulting and Clinical Psychology, 55,* 208–212.

Keene, R. J. (1980). Follow-up studies of World War II and Korean conflict prisoners. *American Journal of Epidemiology, 111,* 194–200.

Kegeles, S. (1963). Why people seek dental care: A test of a conceptual formulation. *Journal of Health and Human Behavior, 4,* 166–173.

Kegeles, S. M., Catania, J. A., & Coates, T. J. (1988). Intentions to communicate positive HIV-antibody status to sex partners. *Journal of the American Medical Association, 259,* 218–219.

Kegeles, S. S. (1985). Education for breast self-examination: Why, who, what, and how? *Preventive Medicine, 14,* 702–720.

Keller, S. E., Weiss, J. M., Schleifer, S. J., Miller, N. E., & Stein, M. (1981). Suppression of immunity by stress: Effect of a graded series of stressors on lymphocyte stimulation in the rat. *Science, 213,* 1397–1400.

Kellerman, J., Rigler, D., & Siegel, S. E. (1979). Psychological responses of children to isolation in a protected environment. *Journal of Behavioral Medicine, 2,* 263–274.

Kelly, J. A., Lawrence, J. S., Hood, H. V., & Brasfield, T. L. (1989). Behavioral intention to reduce aids risk activities. *Journal of Consulting and Clinical Psychology, 57,* 60–67.

Kelly, K. E., & Houston, B. K. (1985). Type A behavior in employed women: Relation to work, marital and leisure variables, social support, stress, tension, and health. *Journal of Personality and Social Psychology, 48,* 1067–1079.

Kelly, W. D., & Friesen, S. (1950). Do cancer patients want to be told? *Surgery, 27,* 822–826.

Kelly-Hayes, M., Wolf, P. A., Kannel, W. B., Sytkowski, D., D'Agostino, R. B., & Gresham, G. E. (1988). Factors influencing survival and need for institutionalization following stroke: The Framingham Study. *Archives of Physical and Medical Rehabilitation, 69,* 415–418.

Keltikangas-Jarvinen, L. (1989). Stability of Type A behavior during adolescence, young adulthood, and adulthood. *Journal of Behavioral Medicine, 12,* 387–396.

Kemeny, E., Hovell, M. F., Mewborn, C. R., Dockter, B., & Chin, L. (1988). Breast self-examination: The effects of prescribed frequency on adherence, accuracy, and detection ability.

American Journal of Preventive Medicine, 4, 140–145.

Kemeny, M. E., Cohen, R., Zegans, L. S., & Conant, M. A. (1989). Psychological and immunological predictors of genital herpes recurrence. *Psychosomatic Medicine, 51,* 195–208.

Kendall, P. C., Williams, L., Pechacek, T. F., Graham, L. E., Shisslak, C., & Herzoff, N. (1979). Cognitive-behavioral and patient education interventions in cardiac catheterization procedures: The Palo Alto Medical Psychology Project. *Journal of Consulting and Clinical Psychology, 47,* 49–58.

Kendzierski, D. (1990). Exercise self-schemata: Cognitive and behavioral correlates. *Health Psychology, 9,* 69–82.

Kerckhoff, A. C., & Back, K. W. (1986). *The June bug: A study of hysterical contagion.* New York: Appleton-Century-Crofts.

Kerns, R. D., Finn, P., & Haythornthwaite, J. (1988). Self-monitored pain intensity: Psychometric properties and clinical utility. *Journal of Behavioral Medicine, 11,* 71–82.

Kessler, R. C. (1979). Stress, social status, and psychological distress. *Journal of Health and Social Behavior, 20,* 259–272.

Kessler, R. C., & McLeod, J. D. (1985). Social support and mental health in community samples. In S. Cohen & S. L. Syme (Eds.), *Social support and health* (pp. 219–240). Orlando, FL: Academic Press.

Kessler, R. C., McLeod, J. D., & Wethington, E. (1985). The costs of caring: A perspective on the relationship between sex and psychological distress. In I. C. Sarason & B. R. Sarason (Eds.), *Social support: Theory, research, and applications* (pp. 491–506). Dordrecht, The Netherlands: Martinus Nijhoff.

Kessler, R. C., & Neighbors, H. W. (1986). A new perspective on the relationship among race, social class, and psychological distress. *Journal of Health and Social Behavior, 27,* 107–115.

Kessler, R. C., O'Brien, K., Joseph, J. G., Ostrow, D. G., Phair, J. P., Chmiel, J. S., Wortman, C. B., & Emmons, C-A. (1988). Effects of HIV infection, perceived health and clinical status on a cohort at risk for AIDS. *Social Science and Medicine, 6,* 569–578.

Kessler, R. C., Price, R. H., & Wortman, C. B. (1985). Social factors in psychopathology: Stress, social support, and coping processes. *Annual Review of Psychology, 36,* 531–572.

Kessler, R. C., Turner, J. B., & House, J. S. (1987). Intervening processes in the relationship between unemployment and health. *Psychological Medicine, 17,* 949–961.

Kessler, R. C., Turner, J. B., & House, J. S. (1988). Effects of unemployment on health in a community survey: Main, modifying, and mediating effects. *Journal of Social Issues, 44,* 69–85.

Kiecolt-Glaser, J. K., Dyer, C. S., & Shuttleworth, E. C. (1988). Upsetting social interactions and distress among Alzheimer's disease family caregivers: A replication and extension. *American Journal of Community Psychology, 116,* 825–837.

Kiecolt-Glaser, J. K., Fisher, L., Ogrocki, P., Stout, J. C., Speicher, C. E., & Glaser, R. (1987). Marital quality, marital disruption, and immune function. *Psychosomatic Medicine, 49,* 13–34.

Kiecolt-Glaser, J. K., Garner, W., Speicher, C., Penn, G. M., Holliday, J., & Glaser, R. (1984). Psychosocial modifiers of immunocompetence in medical students. *Psychosomatic Medicine, 46,* 7–14.

Kiecolt-Glaser, J. K., & Glaser, R. (1987). Psychosocial influences on herpesvirus latency. In E. Kurstak, Z. J. Lipowski, & P. V. Morozov (Eds.), *Viruses, immunity, and mental disorders* (pp. 403–412). New York: Plenum.

Kiecolt-Glaser, J. K., & Glaser, R. (1988). Methodological issues in behavioral immunology research with humans. *Brain, Behavior, and Immunity, 2,* 67–78.

Kiecolt-Glaser, J. K., Glaser, R., Shuttleworth, E., Dyer, C. S., Ogrocki, P., & Speicher, C. E. (1987). Chronic stress and immunity in family caregivers of Alzheimer's disease victims. *Psychosomatic Medicine, 49,* 523–535.

Kiecolt-Glaser, J. K., Glaser, R., Strain, E., Stout, J., Tarr, K., Holliday, J., & Speicher, C. (1986). Modulation of cellular immunity in medical students. *Journal of Behavioral Medicine, 9,* 5–21.

Kiecolt-Glaser, J. K., Glaser, R., Williger, D., Stout, J., Messick, G., Sheppard, S., Ricker, D., Romisher, S. C., Briner, W., Bonnell, G., & Donnerberg, R. (1985). Psychosocial enhancement of immunocompetence in a geriatric population. *Health Psychology, 4,* 25–41.

Kiecolt-Glaser, J. K., Kennedy, S., Malkoff, S., Fisher, L., Speicher, C. E., & Glaser, R. (1988). Marital discord and immunity in males. *Psychosomatic Medicine, 50,* 213–229.

Kiecolt-Glaser, J. K., Speicher, C. E., Holliday, J. E., & Glaser, R. (1984). Stress and the transformation of lymphocytes by Epstein-Barr virus. *Journal of Behavioral Medicine, 7,* 1–12.

Kiecolt-Glaser, J. K., Stephens, R. E., Lipetz, P. D., Speicher, C. E., & Glaser, R. (1985). Distress and DNA repair in human lymphocytes. *Journal of Behavioral Medicine, 8,* 311–320.

Kiecolt-Glaser, J. K., & Williams, D. A. (1987). Self-blame, compliance, and distress among burn patients. *Journal of Personality and Social Psychology, 53,* 187–193.

Kimball, C. P. (1973). Medical education as a humanizing process. *Journal of Medical Education, 48,* 71–77.

Kimzey, S. L. (1975). The effects of extended spaceflight on hematologic and immunologic systems. *Journal of the American Medical Women's Association, 30,* 218–232.

King, R. A., & Leach, J. E. (1950). Factors contributing to delay by patients seeking medical care. *Cancer, 3,* 571–579.

Kirkley, B. G., Agras, W. S., & Weiss, J. J. (1985). Nutritional inadequacy in the diets of treated bulimics. *Behavior Therapy, 16,* 287–291.

Kirkley, B. G., & Fisher, E. B., Jr. (1988). Relapse as a model of nonadherence to dietary treatment of diabetes. *Health Psychology, 7,* 221–230.

Kirkley, B. G., Schneider, J. A., Agras, W. J., & Bachman, J. A. (1985). Comparison of two group treatments for bulimia. *Journal of Consulting and Clinical Psychology, 53,* 43–48.

Kirschenbaum, D. S., Sherman, J., & Penrod, J. D. (1987). Promoting self-directed hemodialysis: Measurement and cognitive-behavioral intervention. *Health Psychology, 6,* 373–385.

Kirscht, J. P. (1983). Preventive health behavior: A review of research and issues. *Health Psychology, 2,* 277–301.

Kirscht, J. P., Becker, M., Haefner, D., & Maiman, L. (1978). Effects of threatening communications and mothers' health beliefs on weight change in obese children. *Journal of Behavioral Medicine, 1,* 147–157.

Kirscht, J. P., Haefner, D., Kegeles, S., & Rosenstock, I. M. (1966). A national study of health beliefs. *Journal of Health and Human Behavior, 7,* 248–254.

Kirscht, J. P., & Rosenstock, I. M. (1979). Patients' problems in following recommendations of health experts. In G. C. Stone, F. Cohen, & N. E. Adler (Eds.), *Health psychology—A handbook* (pp. 573–590). San Francisco: Jossey-Bass.

Kite, W. R., & Kogutek, M. D. (1979). *Care unit program evaluation study: A summary.* Newport Beach, CA: Comprehensive Care Corporation.

Kittel, F., Kornitzer, M., DeBacker, G., & Dramaix, M. (1982). Metrological study of psychological questionnaires with reference to social variables: The Belgian Heart Disease Prevention Project (BHDPP). *Journal of Behavioral Medicine, 5,* 9–36.

Kivilan, D. R., Coppel, D. B., Fromme, K., Williams, E., & Marlatt, G. A. (1989). Secondary prevention of alcohol-related problems in young adults at risk. In K. D. Craig & S. M. Weiss (Eds.), *Prevention and early intervention: Biobehavioral perspectives.* New York: Springer.

Kiyak, H. A., Vitaliano, P. P., & Crinean, J. (1988). Patients' expectations as predictors of orthognathic surgery outcomes. *Health Psychology, 7,* 251–268.

Kleck, R., Ono, M., & Hastorf, A. M. (1966). The effects of physical deviance upon face-to-face interaction. *Human Relations, 19,* 425–436.

Klein, D. C., Sullivan, G., Wolcott, D. L., Landsverk, J., Nemir, S., & Fawzy, F. I. (1987). AIDS risk behaviors (ARB): Changes in homosexual male physicians and university students. *American Journal of Psychiatry, 144,* 742–747.

Klein, D. N., & Rubovits, D. R. (1987). The reliability of subjects' reports on stressful life events inventories: A longitudinal study. *Journal of Behavioral Medicine, 10,* 501–512.

Klein, R. F., Kliner, V. A., Zipes, D. F., Troyer, W. G., & Wallace, A. G. (1968). Transfer from a coronary care unit. *Archives of Internal Medicine, 122,* 104–108.

Kleinke, C. L., & Spangler, A. S., Jr. (1988). Psychometric analysis of the audiovisual taxonomy for assessing pain behavior in chronic back-pain patients. *Journal of Behavioral Medicine, 11,* 83–94.

Klesges, R. C. (Ed.). (1989). *Annals of Behavioral Medicine, 11* (whole volume).

Klesges, R. C., & Cigrans, J. A. (1988). Worksite smoking cessation programs: Clinical and methodological issues. *Progress in Behavior Modification, 23,* 36–61.

Klesges, R. C., Meyers, A. W., Klesges, L. M., & LaVasque, M. E. (1989). Smoking, body weight, and their effects on smoking behavior: A com-prehensive review of the literature. *Psychological Bulletin, 106,* 204–230.

Klesges, R. C., Somes, G., Pascale, R. W., Klesges, L. M., Murphy, M., Brown, K., & Williams, E. (1988). Knowledge and beliefs regarding the consequences of cigarette smoking and their relationships to smoking status in a biracial sample. *Health Psychology, 7,* 387–401.

Kobasa, S. C. (1979). Stressful life events and health: An inquiry into hardiness. *Journal of Personality and Social Psychology, 37,* 1–11.

Kobasa, S. C., Maddi, S. R., & Courington, S. (1981). Personality and constitution as mediators in the stress-illness relationship. *Journal of Health and Social Behavior, 22,* 368–378.

Kobasa, S. C., Maddi, S. R., & Puccetti, M. C. (1982). Personality and exercise as buffers in the stress-illness relationship. *Journal of Behavioral Medicine, 5,* 391–404.

Kobasa, S. C., Maddi, S. R., Puccetti, M. C., & Zola, M. A. (1985). Effectiveness of hardiness, exercise, and social support as resources against illness. *Journal of Psychosomatic Medicine, 29,* 525–533.

Kobasa, S. C., & Puccetti, M. C. (1983). Personality and social resources in stress resistance. *Journal of Personality and Social Psychology, 45,* 839–850.

Koenig, H. G., Meador, K. G., Cohen, H. J., & Blazer, D. G. (1988). Depression in elderly hospitalized patients with medical illness. *Archives of Internal Medicine, 148,* 1929–1936.

Kogutek, M. D., & Kite, W. R. (1978). *Care unit program evaluation study: A summary.* Newport Beach, CA: Comprehensive Care Corporation.

Kolata, G. B. (1979). Is labile hypertension a myth? *Science, 204,* 489.

Koltun, A., & Stone, G. A. (1986). Past and current trends in patient noncompliance research: Focus on diseases, regimens-programs, and provider-disciplines. *Journal of Compliance in Health Care, 1,* 21–32.

Kornitzer, M., DeBacker, G., Dramaix, M., Kittel, F., Thilly, C., Graffar, M., & Vuylsteek, K. (1983). Belgian Heart Disease Prevention Project: Incidence and mortality results. *Lancet, 1,* 1066–1070.

Korsch, B. M., Fraad, L. E., & Barnett, H. L. (1954). Pediatric discussions with parent groups. *Journal of Pediatrics, 44,* 703–717.

Korsch, B. M., Gozzi, E. K., & Francis, V. (1968).

Gaps in doctor-patient communication: I. Doctor-patient interaction and patient satisfaction. *Journal of Pediatrics, 42,* 855–871.

Korsch, B. M., & Negrete, V. F. (1972). Doctor-patient communication. *Scientific American, 227,* 66–74.

Kosa, J., & Robertson, L. (1975). The social aspects of health and illness. In J. Kosa & I. Zola (Eds.), *Poverty and health: A sociological analysis.* Cambridge, MA: Harvard University Press.

Kozlowski, L. T. (1988–1989). Reduction of tobacco health hazards in continuing users: Individual behavioral and public health approaches. *Journal of Substance Abuse, 1,* 345–355.

Kozlowski, L. T., Coambs, R. B., Ferrence, R. G., & Adlaf, E. M. (1989). Preventing smoking and other drug use: Let the buyers beware and the interventions be apt. *Canadian Journal of Public Health, 80,* 452–456.

Kozlowski, L. T., Wilkinson, D. A., Skinner, W., Kent, C., Franklin, T., & Pope, M. (1989). Comparing tobacco cigarette dependence with other drug dependencies: Greater or equal "difficulty quitting" and "urges to use," but less "pleasure" from cigarettes. *Journal of the American Medical Association, 261,* 898–901.

Krantz, D. S. (1980). Cognitive processes and recovery from heart attack: A review and theoretical analysis. *Journal of Human Stress, 6,* 27–38.

Krantz, D. S., Arabian, J. M., Davis, J. E., & Parker, J. S. (1982). Type A behavior and coronary artery bypass surgery: Intraoperative blood pressure and perioperative complication. *Psychosomatic Medicine, 44,* 273–284.

Krantz, D. S., Baum, A., & Wideman, M. V. (1980). Assessment of preferences for self-treatment and information in health care. *Journal of Personality and Social Psychology, 39,* 977–990.

Krantz, D. S., & Deckel, A. W. (1983). Coping with coronary heart disease and stroke. In T. G. Burish & L. A. Bradley (Eds.), *Coping with chronic disease: Research and applications.* New York: Academic Press.

Krantz, D. S., & Durel, L. A. (1983). Psychobiological substrates of the Type A behavior pattern. *Health Psychology, 2,* 393–412.

Krantz, D. S., & Manuck, S. B. (1984). Acute psychophysiologic reactivity and risk of cardiovascular disease: A review and methodological critique. *Psychological Bulletin, 96,* 435–464.

Krantz, D. S., & Schulz, R. (1980). A model of life crisis, control and health outcomes: Cardiac rehabilitation and relocation of the elderly. In A. Baum & J. E. Singer (Eds.), *Advances in environmental psychology* (Vol. 2). Hillsdale, NJ: Erlbaum.

Krasnoff, A. (1959). Psychological variables and human cancer: A cross-validation study. *Psychosomatic Medicine, 21,* 291–295.

Krause, N., & Markides, K. S. (1985). Employment and psychological well-being in Mexican American women. *Journal of Health and Social Behavior, 26,* 15–26.

Kroeber, A. L. (1948). *Anthropology.* New York: Harcourt.

Kronenfeld, J. J. (1978). Provider variables and the utilization of ambulatory care services. *Journal of Health and Social Behavior, 19,* 68–76.

Kronfol, Z., & House, J. D. (1984). Depression, cortisol, and immune function. *Lancet, 1,* 1026–1027.

Kronfol, Z., Silva, J., Greden, J., Dembinski, S., Gardner, R., & Carroll, B. (1983). Impaired lymphocyte function in depressive illness. *Life Sciences, 33,* 241–247.

Kronfol, Z., Turner, R., Nasrallah, H., & Winokur, G. (1984). Leukocyte regulation in depression and schizophrenia. *Psychiatry Research, 13,* 13–18.

Kübler-Ross, E. (1969). *On death and dying.* New York: Macmillan.

Kübler-Ross, E. (1975). *Death: The final stage of growth.* Englewood Cliffs, NJ: Prentice-Hall.

Kulik, J. A., & Carlino, P. (1987). The effect of verbal communication and treatment choice on medication compliance in a pediatric setting. *Journal of Behavioral Medicine, 10,* 367–376.

Kulik, J. A., & Mahler, H. I. M. (1987). Health status, perceptions of risk, and prevention interest for health and nonhealth problems. *Health Psychology, 6,* 15–27.

Kulik, J. A., & Mahler, H. I. M. (1989). Social support and recovery from surgery. *Health Psychology, 8,* 221–238.

Kunz, J. R. M. (Ed.). (1982). *The American Medical Association family medical guide.* New York: Random House.

Kuo, W. H., & Tsai, Y-M. (1986). Social networking, hardiness and immigrant's mental health. *Journal of Health and Social Behavior, 27,* 133–149.

Kushi, L. H., Lew, R. W., Sture, F. J., Ellison, C. R., Lozy, M. E., Bourke, G., Daly, L., Graham, I., Hicky, N., Mulcuhy, R., & Kevaney, J. (1985). Diet and 20-year mortality from coronary heart disease: The Ireland-Boston Diet Heart Study. *New England Journal of Medicine, 312,* 811–818.

Kutner, N. G. (1987). Issues in the application of high cost medical technology: The case of organ transplantation. *Journal of Health and Social Behavior, 28,* 23–36.

Laerum, E., Johnsen, N., Smith, P., & Larsen, S. (1987). Can myocardial infarction induce positive changes in family relationships? *Family Practice, 4,* 302–305.

Lakein, A. (1973). *How to get control of your time and your life.* New York: Signet.

Lamontagne, Y., Gagnon, M. A., & Gaude, G. (1978). Thought-stopping, pocket timers and their combination in the modification of smoking behavior. *British Journal of Addiction, 73,* 220–224.

Lando, H. A. (1977). Successful treatment of smokers with a broad-spectrum behavioral approach. *Journal of Consulting and Clinical Psychology, 45,* 361–366.

Lando, H. A. (1981). Effects of preparation, experimenter contact, and a maintained reduction alternative on a broad-spectrum program for eliminating smoking. *Addictive Behaviors, 6,* 107–114.

Lando, H. A., & McGovern, P. G. (1985). Nicotine fading as a nonaversive alternative in a broad spectrum test. *Addictive Behaviors, 10,* 153–161.

Lang, A. R., & Marlatt, G. A. (1982). Problem drinking: A social learning perspective. In R. J. Gatchel, A., Baum, & J. E. Singer (Eds.), *Handbook of psychology and health: Vol 1. Clinical psychology and behavioral medicine: Overlapping disciplines* (pp. 121–169). Hillsdale, NJ: Erlbaum.

Langer, E. J., Janis, I. L., & Wolfer, J. A. (1975). Reduction of psychological stress in surgical patients. *Journal of Experimental Social Psychology, 11,* 155–165.

Langlie, J. K. (1977). Social networks, health beliefs, and preventive behavior. *Journal of Health and Social Behavior, 18,* 244–259.

Langner, T., & Michael, S. (1960). *Life stress and mental health.* New York: Free Press.

Lankford, T. R. (1979). *Integrated science for health students* (2nd ed.). Reston, VA: Reston Publishing.

Laragh, J. H. (1988a). Pathophysiology of diastolic hypertension. *Health Psychology, 7*(Suppl.), 15–31.

Laragh, J. H. (1988b). A modern plan for treating hypertension. *Health Psychology, 7*(Suppl.), 253–265.

Larocco, J. M., House, J. S., & French, J. R. P., Jr. (1980). Social support, occupational stress, and health. *Journal of Health and Social Behavior, 21,* 202–218.

Lau, R. R. (1988). Beliefs about control and health behavior. In D. Gochman (Ed.), *Health behavior: Emerging research perspectives* (pp. 43–63). New York: Plenum.

Lau, R. R., Bernard, T. M., & Hartman, K. A. (1989). Further explorations of common-sense representations of common illness. *Health Psychology, 8,* 195–219.

Lau, R. R., & Hartman, K. A. (1983). Common-sense representations of common illnesses. *Health Psychology, 2,* 167–185.

Lau, R. R., Hartman, K. A., & Ware, J. E., Jr. (1986). Health as a value: Methodological and theoretical considerations. *Health Psychology, 5,* 25–43.

Lau, R. R., Kane, R., Berry, S., Ware, J. E., Jr. & Roy, D. (1980). Channeling health: A review of televised health campaigns. *Health Education Quarterly, 7,* 56–89.

Lau, R. R., & Klepper, S. (1988). The development of illness orientations in children aged 6 through 12. *Journal of Health and Social Behavior, 29,* 149–168.

Lau, R. R., Quadrel, M. J., & Hartman, K. A. (in press). Development and change of young adults' preventive health beliefs and behaviors: Influence from parents and peers. *Journal of Health and Social Behavior.*

Lau, R. R., & Ware, J. E., Jr. (1981). Refinements in the measurement of health-specific locus-of-control beliefs. *Medical Care, 19,* 1147–1158.

Laudenslager, M. L., Reite, M., & Harbeck, R. J. (1982). Suppressed immune response in infant monkeys associated with maternal separation. *Behavior and Neural Biology, 36,* 40–48.

Laufer, R. S., Gallops, M. S., & Frey-Wouters, E. (1984). War stress and trauma: The Vietnam veteran experience. *Journal of Health and Social Behavior, 25,* 65–85.

Lavin, B., Haug, M., Belgrave, L. L., & Breslau, N. (1987). Change in student physicians' views on authority relationships with patients. *Journal of Health and Social Behavior, 28,* 258–272.

Lawler, K. A., Allen, M. T., Critcher, E. C., & Standard, B. A. (1981). The relationship of physiological responses to the coronary-prone behavior pattern in children. *Journal of Behavioral Medicine, 4,* 203–216.

Lawrence, R. C., Hochberg, M. C., Kelsey, J. L., McDuffie, F. C., Medsger, T. A., Felts, W. R., & Schulman, L. E. (1989). Estimates of the prevalence of selected arthritic and musculo-skeleto diseases in the U.S. *Journal of Rheumatology, 16,* 327–441.

Lazarus, A. A. (1971). *Behavior therapy and beyond.* New York: McGraw-Hill.

Lazarus, R. S. (1968). Emotions and adaptation: Conceptual and empirical relations. In W. Arnold (Ed.), *Nebraska symposium on motivation* (pp. 175–266). Lincoln: University of Nebraska Press.

Lazarus, R. S. (1981). The stress and coping paradigm. In C. Eisdorfer, D. Cohen, & A. Kleinman (Eds.), *Conceptual models for psychopathology* (pp. 177–214). New York: Spectrum.

Lazarus, R. S. (1983). The costs and benefits of denial. In S. Bresnitz (Ed.), *Denial of stress* (pp. 1–30). New York: International Universities Press.

Lazarus, R. S., & Cohen, J. B. (1977). Environmental stress. In I. Attman & J. F. Wohlwill (Eds.), *Human behavior and the environment: Current theory and research* (Vol. 2). New York: Plenum.

Lazarus, R. S., Cohen, J. B., Folkman, S., Kanner, S., & Schaefer, C. (1980). Psychological stress and adaptation: Some unresolved issues. In H. Selye (Ed.), *Selye's guide to stress research* (Vol. 1). New York: Van Nostrand, Reinhold.

Lazarus, R. S., Delongis, A., Folkman, S., & Gruen, R. (1985). Stress and adaptational outcomes: The problem of confounded measures. *American Psychologist, 40,* 770–779.

Lazarus, R. S., & Folkman, S. (1984a). *Stress, appraisal, and coping.* New York: Springer.

Lazarus, R. S., & Folkman, S. (1984b). Coping and adaptation. In W. D. Gentry (Ed.), *The handbook of behavioral medicine* (pp. 282–325). New York: Guilford Press.

Lazarus, R. S., & Launier, R. (1978). Stress-related transactions between person and environment. In L. A. Pervin & M. Lewis (Eds.), *Internal and external determinants of behavior* (pp. 287–327). New York: Plenum.

Leach, C. S., & Rambaut, P. C. (1974). Biochemical responses of the Skylab crewmen. *Proceedings of the Skylab Life Sciences Symposium, 2,* 427–454.

Lederere, H. D. (1952). How the sick view their world. *Journal of Social Issues, 8,* 4–16.

Lee, C. (1989). Perceptions of immunity to disease in adult smokers. *Journal of Behavioral Medicine, 12,* 267–278.

Lee, D. D-P., DeQuattro, V., Allen, J., Kimura, S., Aleman, E., Konugres, G., & Davison, G. (1988). Behavioral versus beta-blocker therapy in patients with primary hypertension: Effects on blood pressure, left ventricular function and mass, and the pressor surge of social stress anger. *American Heart Journal, 116,* 637–644.

Lee, D. D-P., DeQuattro, V., Cox, T., Pyter, L. Foti, A., Allen, J., Barndt, R., Azen, S., & Davison, G. (1987). Neurohumoral mechanisms and left ventricular hypertrophy: Effects of hygenic therapy. *Journal of Human Hypertension, 1,* 147–151.

Leffall, L. D., Jr., White, J. E., & Ewing, J. (1963). Cancer of the breast in Negroes. *Surgery, Gynecology, Obstetrics, 117,* 97–104.

Lehman, A. K., & Rodin, J. (1989). Styles of self-nurturance and disordered eating. *Journal of Consulting and Clinical Psychology, 57,* 117–122.

Leiderman, D. B., & Grisso, J-A. (1985). The Gomer phenomenon. *Journal of Health and Social Behavior, 25,* 222–232.

Leigh, H., & Reiser, M. F. (1986). Comparison of theoretically oriented and patient-oriented behavioral science courses. *Journal of Medical Education, 61,* 169–174.

Lemoine, J., & Mougne, C. (1983). Why has death stalked the refugees? *Natural History, 92,* 6–19.

Lennon, M. C. (1987). Sex differences in distress: The impact of gender and work roles. *Journal of Health and Social Behavior, 28,* 290–305.

Leon, A. S. (1983). Exercise and coronary heart disease. *Hospital Medicine, 19,* 38–59.

Leon, A. S., & Fox, S. M. III (1981). Physical fitness. In E. L Wynder (Ed.), *The book of health* (pp. 283–341). New York: Franklin Watts.

Lerner, M. (1970). The desire for justice and reactions to victims. In J. Macaulay & L. Berkowitz (Eds.), *Altruism and helping behavior* (pp. 205–230). New York: Academic Press.

LeShan, L. L., & LeShan, E. (1961). Psychotherapy and the patient with a limited life span. *Psychiatry, 24,* 281–324.

LeShan, L. L., & Worthington, R. E. (1956). Personality as a factor in the pathogenesis of cancer: Review of literature. *British Journal of Medical Psychology, 29,* 49.

Levenkron, J. C., Greenland, P., & Bowlby, N. (1987). Using patient instructors to teach behavioral counseling skills. *Journal of Medical Education, 62,* 665–672.

Levenkron, J. C., & Moore, L. G. (1988). The Type A behavior pattern: Issues for intervention research. *Annals of Behavioral Medicine, 10,* 78–83.

Levenson, R. W., & Gottman, J. M. (1985). Physiological and affective predictors of change in relationship satisfaction. *Journal of Personality and Social Psychology, 49,* 85–94.

Leventhal, E. A., Leventhal, H., Schacham, S., & Easterling, D. V. (1989). Active coping reduces reports of pain from childbirth. *Journal of Consulting and Clinical Psychology, 57,* 365–371.

Leventhal, H. (1970). Findings and theory in the study of fear communications. In L. Berkowitz (Ed.), *Advances in experimental social psychology* (Vol. 5, 120–186). New York: Academic Press.

Leventhal, H., & Baker, T. B. (1986). Strategies for smoking withdrawal. *Wisconsin Medical Journal, 85,* 11–13.

Leventhal, H., Baker, T. B., Brandon, T., & Fleming, R. (1989). Intervening and preventing cigarette smoking. In T. Ney & A. Gale (Eds.), *Smoking and human behavior* (pp. 313–336). New York: Wiley.

Leventhal, H., & Cleary, P. D. (1980). The smoking problem: A review of the research and theory in behavioral risk modification. *Psychological Bulletin, 88,* 370–405.

Leventhal, H., & Diefenbach, M. (in press). The active side of illness cognition. In J. A. Skelton & R. T. Croyle (Eds.), *Mental representation in health and illness.* New York: Springer.

Leventhal, H., Glynn, K., & Fleming, R. (1987). Is the smoking decision an "informed choice"?: Effect of smoking risk factors on smoking beliefs. *Journal of the American Medical Association, 257,* 3373–3376.

Leventhal, H., Leventhal, E. A., & Nguyen, T. V. (1985). Reactions of families to illness: Theoretical models and perspectives. In D. C. Turk & R. D. Kerns (Eds.), *Health, illness, and families: A lifespan perspective* (pp. 108–145). New York: Wiley.

Leventhal, H., & Nerenz, D. R. (1982). A model for

stress research and some implications for the control of stress disorders. In D. Meichenbaum & M. Jaremko (Eds.), *Stress prevention and management: A cognitive behavioral approach.* New York: Plenum.

Leventhal, H., & Nerenz, D. R., & Steele, D. J. (1984). Illness representations and coping with health threats. In A. Baum & J. Singer (Eds.), *A handbook of psychology and health* (vol. 4, pp. 219–252). Hillsdale, NJ: Erlbaum.

Leventhal, H., Nerenz, D., & Strauss, A. (1982). Self-regulation and the mechanisms for symptom appraisal. In D. Mechanic (Ed.), *Monograph series in psychosocial epidemiology 3: Symptoms, illness behavior, and help-seeking* (pp. 55–86). New York: Neale Watson.

Leventhal, H., Prohaska, T. R., & Hirschman, R. S. (1985). Preventive health behavior across the life span. In J. C. Rosen & L. J. Solomon (Eds.), *Prevention in health psychology* (Vol. 8, pp. 190–235). Hanover, NH: University Press of New England.

Leventhal, H., Safer, M. A., Cleary, P. D., & Gutmann, M. (1980). Cardiovascular risk modification by community-based programs for lifestyle change: Comments on the Stanford study. *Journal of Consulting and Clinical Psychology, 48,* 150–158.

Leventhal, H., Singer, R., & Jones, S. (1965). Effects of fear and specificity of recommendation upon attitudes and behavior. *Journal of Personality and Social Psychology, 2,* 20–29.

Leventhal, H., & Watts, J. C. (1966). Sources of resistance to fear-arousing communications on smoking and lung cancer. *Journal of Personality, 34,* 155–175.

Leventhal, H., Zimmerman, R., & Gutmann, M. (1984). Compliance: A self-regulation perspective. In W. D. Gentry (Ed.), *Handbook of behavioral medicine* (pp. 369–436). New York: Guilford Press.

Levine, J. D., Gordon, N. C., & Fields, H. L. (1978). The mechanism of placebo analgesia. *Lancet, 2,* 654–657.

Levine, J. D., & Zigler, E. (1975). Denial and self-image in stroke, lung cancer and heart disease patients. *Journal of Consulting and Clinical Psychology, 43,* 751–757.

Levine, M. N., Guyatt, G. H., Gent, M., De Pauw, S., Goodyear, M. D., Hryniuk, W. M., Arnold, A., Findlay, B., Skillings, J. R., Bramwell, V. H., Levin, L., Bush, H., Abu-Zahra, H., & Kotalik,

J. (1988). Quality of life in Stage II breast cancer: An instrument for clinical trials. *Journal of Clinical Oncology, 6,* 1798–1810.

Levinson, R. M., McCollum, K. T., & Kutner, N. G. (1984). Gender homophily in preferences for physicians. *Sex Roles, 10,* 315–325.

Leviton, D. (1977). Death education. In H. Feifel (Ed.), *New meanings of death.* New York: McGraw-Hill.

Levitz, L., & Stunkard, A. J. (1974). A therapeutic coalition for obesity: Behavior modification and patient self-help. *American Journal of Psychiatry, 131,* 423–427.

Levy, S. M. (1983). Host differences in neoplastic risk: Behavioral and social contributors to disease. *Health Psychology, 2,* 21–44.

Levy, S. M., Herberman, R. B., Lee, J. K., Lippman, M. E., & d'Angelo, T. (1989). Breast conservation versus mastectomy: Distress sequelae as a function of choice. *Journal of Clinical Oncology, 7,* 367–375.

Levy, S. M., Herberman, R. B., Maluish, A. M., Schlien, B., & Lippman, M. (1985). Prognostic risk assessment in primary breast cancer by behavioral and immunological parameters. *Health Psychology, 4,* 99–113.

Levy, S. M., Herberman, R. B., Simons, A., Whiteside, T., Lee, J., McDonald, R., & Beadle, M. (1989). Persistently low natural killer cell activity in normal adults: Immunological, hormonal and mood correlates. *Natural Immune Cell Growth Regulation, 8,* 173–186.

Levy, S. M., Lee, J. K., Bagley, C., & Lippman, M. (1988). Survival hazards analysis in first recurrent breast cancer patients: Seven-year follow-up. *Psychosomatic Medicine, 50,* 520–528.

Lewinsohn, P. M., & Talkington, J. (1979). Studies of the measurement of unpleasant events and relations with depression. *Applied Psychological Measurement, 3,* 83–101.

Lewis, B., Hammett, F., Katan, M., Kay, R. M., Merkx, I., Nobels, A., Miller, N. E., & Swan, A. V. (1981). Towards an improved lipid-lowering diet: Additive effects of changes in nutrient intake. *Lancet, 2,* 1310–1313.

Lewis, C. E., & Lewis, M. A. (1977). The impact of sexual equality on health. *New England Journal of Medicine, 297,* 863–869.

Lewis, J. W., Terman, S. W., Shavit, Y., Nelson, L. R., & Liebeskind, J. C. (1984). Neural,

neurochemical, and hormonal bases of stress-induced analgesia. In L. Kruger & J. C. Liebeskind (Eds.), *Advances in pain research and therapy* (Vol. 6, 277–288). New York: Raven Press.

Ley, P. (1977). Psychological studies of doctor-patient communication. In S. Richman (Ed.), *Contributions to medical psychology* (Vol. 1). Oxford, England: Pergamon.

Ley, P., & Spelman, M. S. (1967). *Communicating with the patient* (pp. 277–288). London, England: Staples.

Liberman, R. (1962). An analysis of the placebo phenomenon. *Journal of Chronic Diseases, 15,* 761–783.

Lichtenstein, E. (1982). The smoking problem: A behavioral perspective. *Journal of Consulting and Clinical Psychology, 50,* 804–819.

Lichtenstein, E., & Danaher, B. G. (1975). Modification of smoking behavior: A critical analysis of theory, research, and practice. In M. Hersen, R. M. Eisler, & P. M. Millers (Eds.), *Progress in behavior modification* (Vol. 3, pp. 79–132). New York: Academic Press.

Lichtenstein, E., Glasgow, R. E., & Abrams, D. B. (1986). Social support in smoking cessation: In search of effective interventions. *Behavior Therapy, 17,* 607–619.

Lichtenstein, E., Harris, D. E., Birchler, G. R., Wahl, J. M., & Schmahl, D. P. (1973). Comparison of rapid smoking, warm, smoky air, and attention placebo in the modification of smoking behavior. *Journal of Consulting and Clinical Psychology, 40,* 92–98.

Lichtman, R. R. (1982). *Close relationships after breast cancer.* Unpublished doctoral dissertation, University of California, Los Angeles.

Lichtman, R. R., Taylor, S. E., Wood, J. V. (1983). *Reactions to breast cancer: A test of the victimization perspective.* Unpublished manuscript, University of California, Los Angeles.

Lichtman, R. R., Taylor, S. E., Wood, J. V., Bluming, A. Z., Dosik, G. M., & Leibowitz, R. L. (1984). Relations with children after breast cancer: The mother-daughter relationship at risk. *Journal of Psychosocial Oncology, 2,* 1–19.

Lieberman, M. A. (1982). The effects of social supports on responses to stress. In L. Goldberger & L. Breznitz (Eds.), *Handbook of stress.* New York: Free Press.

Lieberman, M. A., Borman, L. D., & Associates. (1979). *Self-help groups for coping with crisis: Ori-*

gins, members, processes, and impact. San Francisco: Jossey-Bass.

Liebeskind, J. C., & Melzack, R. (1987). The International Pain Foundation: Meeting a need for education in pain management. *Pain, 30,* 1–2.

Liegner, L. M. (1986–1987). Suffering. *Loss, Grief, and Care, 1,* 93–96.

Lifton, R. J. (1977). The sense of immortality: On death and the continuity of life. In H. Feifel (Ed.), *New meanings of death.* New York: McGraw-Hill.

Light, K. C., & Sherwood, A. (1989). Race, borderline hypertension, and hemodynamic responses to behavioral stress before and after beta-adrenergic blockade. *Health Psychology, 8,* 577–596.

Lin, N., Simeone, R. S., Ensel, W. M., & Kuo, W. (1979). Social support, stressful life events, and illness: A model and an empirical test. *Journal of Health and Social Behavior, 20,* 108–119.

Lin, N., Woelfel, M. W., & Light, S. C. (1985). The buffering effect of social support subsequent to an important life event. *Journal of Health and Social Behavior, 26,* 247–263.

Lindemann, E. (1944). Symptomatology and management of acute grief. *American Journal of Psychiatry, 101,* 141–148.

Lindheim, R., & Syme, S. L. (1983). Environments, people, and health. *Annual Review of Public Health, 4,* 335–359.

Lindner, P. G., & Blackburn, G. I. (1976). Multidisciplinary approach to obesity using fasting modified by protein-sparing therapy. *Obesity and Bariatric Medicine, 5,* 198–216.

Lindsay, M., & McCarthy, D. (1974). Caring for the brothers and sisters of a dying child. In T. Burton (Ed.), *Care of the child facing death* (pp. 189–206). Boston: Routledge & Kegan Paul.

Lingsweiler, V. M., Crowther, J. H., & Stephens, M. A. P. (1987). Emotional reactivity and eating in binge eating and obesity. *Journal of Behavioral Medicine, 10,* 287–300.

Linkins, R. W., & Comstock, G. W. (1988). Depressed mood and development of cancer. *American Journal of Epidemiology, 128* (Abstract), 894.

Linn, B. S., Linn, M. W., & Jensen, J. (1981). Anxiety and immune responsiveness. *Psychological Reports, 49,* 969–970.

Linn, M. W., Linn, B. S., & Jensen, J. (1984). Stressful events, dysphoric mood, and immune responsiveness. *Psychological Reports, 54,* 219–222.

Linville, P. W. (1985). Self-complexity and affective extremity: Don't put all your eggs in one cognitive basket. *Social Cognition, 3,* 94–120.

Linville, P. W. (1987). Self-complexity as a cognitive buffer against stress-related depression and illness. *Journal of Personality and Social Psychology, 52,* 663–676.

Lipid Research Clinics Program. (1984). The Lipid Research Clinics coronary primary prevention trial results: I. Reduction in incidence of coronary heart disease. *Journal of the American Medical Association, 251,* 351–374.

Liss-Levinson, W. S. (1982). Reality perspectives for psychological services in a hospice program. *American Psychologist, 37,* 1266–1270.

Litin, E. M. (1960). Should cancer patients be told? *Postgraduate Medicine, 28,* 470–475.

Litman, A. (1980). Relapse in alcoholism: Traditional and current approaches. In G. Edwards & M. Grant (Eds.), *Alcoholism treatment in transition* (pp. 294–303). Baltimore, MD: University Park Press.

Litman, T. J. (1974). The family as the basic unit in health and medical care: A social behavioral overview. *Social Science and Medicine, 8,* 495–519.

Litt, M. D. (1988). Self-efficacy and perceived control: Cognitive mediators of pain tolerance. *Journal of Personality and Social Psychology, 54,* 149–160.

Livingston, P. B., & Zimet, C. N. (1965). Death anxiety, authoritarianism, and choice of specialty in medical students. *Journal of Nervous and Medical Disease, 140,* 222–230.

Locke, S. E., & Heisel, J. S. (1977). The influence of stress and emotions on the human immune response. *Biofeedback and Self-Regulation, 2,* 320 (abstract).

Locke, S. E., Hurst, M. W., & Heisel, S. J. (1979, April). *The influence of stress on the immune response.* Paper presented at the annual meeting of the American Psychosomatic Society, Washington, DC.

Locke, S. E., Kraus, L., & Leserman, J. (1984). Life change, stress, psychiatric symptoms, and natural killer cell activity. *Psychosomatic Medicine, 46,* 441–453.

Lombardo, T., & Carreno, L. (1987). Relationship of Type A behavior pattern in smokers to carbon monoxide exposure and smoking topography. *Health Psychology, 6,* 445–452.

Lorber, J. (1975). Good patients and problem patients: Conformity and deviance in a general hospital. *Journal of Health and Social Behavior, 16*, 213–225.

Lorig, K., Chastain, R. L., Ung, E., Shoor, S., & Holman, H. (1989). Development and evaluation of a scale to measure perceived self-efficacy in people with arthritis. *Arthritis and Rheumatism, 32*, 37–44.

Los Angeles Times. (1984, April 13). Illness, disability costs.

Louhivouri, K. S., & Hakama, M. (1979). Risk of suicide among cancer patients. *American Journal of Epidemiology, 109*, 57–65.

Love, R. R., Leventhal, H., Easterling, D. V., & Nerenz, D. R. (1989). Side effects and emotional distress during cancer chemotherapy. *Cancer, 63*, 604–612.

Lovitt, T. C., & Curtiss, K. (1969). Academic response rate as a function of teacher- and self-imposed contingencies. *Journal of Applied Behavior Analysis, 2*, 49–53.

Lowery, B. J., Jacobsen, B. S., & McCauley, K. (1987). On the prevalence of causal search in illness situations. *Nursing Research, 36*, 88–93.

Lubeck, D. P., & Yelin, E. H. (1988). A question of value: Measuring the impact of chronic disease. *The Millbank Quarterly, 66*, 444–464.

Ludwick-Rosenthal, R., & Neufeld, R. W. J. (1988). Stress management during noxious medical procedures: An evaluative review of outcome studies. *Psychological Bulletin, 104*, 326–342.

Lund, K. A., & Kegeles, S. S. (1982). Increasing adolescents' acceptance of long-term personal health behavior. *Health Psychology, 1*, 27–43.

Lundberg, U., & Frankenhaeuser, M. (1976). *Adjustment to noise stress*. Reports from the Department of Psychology, University of Stockholm, Sweden.

Lustman, P. J. (1988). Anxiety disorders in adults with diabetes mellitus. *Psychiatric Clinics of North America, 11*, 419–432.

Lustman, P. J., Griffith, L. S., & Clouse, R. E. (1988). Depression in adults with diabetes: Results of a 5-year follow-up study. *Diabetes Care, 11*, 605–612.

Lustman, P. J., & Harper, G. W. (1987). Nonpsychiatric physicians' identification and treatment of depression in patients with diabetes. *Comprehensive Psychiatry, 28*, 22–27.

Lyles, J. N., Burish, T. G., Krozely, M. G., & Oldham, R. K. (1982). Efficacy of relaxation training and guided imagery in reducing the aversiveness of cancer chemotherapy. *Journal of Consulting and Clinical Psychology, 50*, 509–524.

Maccoby, N., Farquhar, J. W., Wood, P. D., & Alexander, J. K. (1977). Reducing the risk of cardiovascular disease: Effects of a community-based campaign on knowledge and behavior. *Journal of Community Health, 3*, 100–114.

MacDonald, M. E., Hagberg, K. L., & Grossman, B. J. (1963). Social factors in relation to participation in follow-up care of rheumatic fever. *Journal of Pediatrics, 62*, 503–513.

MacDougall, J. M., Dembroski, T. M., Dimsdale, J. E., & Hackett, T. P. (1985). Components of Type A hostility, and anger-in: Further relationships to angiographic findings. *Health Psychology, 4*, 137–152.

MacDougall, J. M., Musante, L., Castillo, S., & Acevedo, M. C. (1988). Smoking, caffeine, and stress: Effects on blood pressure and heart rate in male and female college students. *Health Psychology, 7*, 461–478.

MacDougall, J. M., Musante, L., Howard, J. A., Hanes, R. L., & Dembroski, T. M. (1986). Individual differences in cardiovascular reactions to stress and cigarette smoking. *Health Psychology, 5*, 531–544.

MacEvoy, B., Lambert, W. W., Karlberg, P., Karlberg, J., Klackenberg-Larsson, I., & Klackenberg, G. (1988). Early affective antecedents of adult Type A behavior. *Journal of Personality and Social Psychology, 54*, 108–116.

Mackay, C. J., & Cooper, C. L. (1987). Occupational stress and health: Some current issues. In C. L. Cooper & I. T. Robertson (Eds.), *International review of industrial and organizational psychology* (pp. 167–199). Chichester, England: Wiley.

Mackenzie, R. A. (1972). *The time trap: Managing your way out*. New York: AMACON.

MacLean, P. D. (1970). The limbic brain in relation to the psychoses. In P. Black (Ed.), *Physiological correlates of emotion* (pp. 130–146). New York: Academic Press.

Madden, D. J., & Blumenthal, J. A. (1989). Slowing of memory-search performance in men with mild hypertension. *Health Psychology, 8*, 131–142.

Madden, J., Akil, H., Patrick, R. L., & Barchas, J. D. (1977). Stress-induced parallel changes in central opioid levels and pain responsiveness in the rat. *Nature, 265*, 358–360.

Maddux, J. E., Roberts, M. C., Sledden, E. A., & Wright, L. (1986). Developmental issues in child health psychology. *American Psychologist, 41*, 25–34.

Maddux, J. E., & Rogers, R. W. (1983). Protection motivation and self-efficacy: A revised theory of fear appeals and attitude change. *Journal of Experimental Social Psychology, 19*, 469–479.

Maeland, J. G., & Havik, O. E. (1987a). The effects of an in-hospital education programme for myocardial infarction patients. *Scandinavian Journal of Rehabilitation and Medicine, 19*, 57–65.

Maeland, J. G., & Havik, O. E. (1987b). Psychological predictors for return to work after a myocardial infarction. *Journal of Psychosomatic Research, 31*, 471–481.

Magni, G., Silvestro, A., Tamiello, M., Zanesco, L., & Carl, M. (1988). An integrated approach to the assessment of family adjustment to acute lymphocytic leukemia in children. *Acta Psychiatrica Scandinavia, 78*, 639–642.

Maguire, P. (1975). The psychological and social consequences of breast cancer. *Nursing Minor, 140*, 54–57.

Mahl, G. F. (1952). Relationship between acute and chronic fear and the gastric acidity and blood sugar levels in *Macaca mulatto* monkeys. *Psychosomatic Medicine, 14*, 182–210.

Mahoney, M. J. (1970). Toward an experimental analysis of covariant control. *Behavior Therapy, 1*, 510–521.

Mahoney, M. J. (1974a). *Cognition and behavior modification*. Cambridge, MA: Ballinger.

Mahoney, M. J. (1974b). Self-reward and self-monitoring techniques for weight control. *Behavior Therapy, 5*, 48–57.

Mahoney, M. J., Thoresen, C. E., & Danaher, B. G. (1972). Covert behavior modification: An experimental analysis. *Journal of Behavior Therapy and Experimental Psychiatry, 3*, 7–14.

Maier, S. F., & Seligman, M. E. P. (1976). Learned helplessness: Theory and evidence. *Journal of Experimental Psychology: General, 195*, 3–46.

Malkin, S. (1976). Care of the terminally ill at home. *Canadian Medical Journal, 115*, 129–130.

Mandelbaum, D. G. (1952). *Soldier groups and Negro soldiers*. Berkeley: University of California Press.

Mandler, G., & Kahn, M. (1960). Discrimination of changes in heart rate: Two unsuccessful attempts. *Journal of the Experimental Analysis of Behavior, 3*, 21–25.

Mann, J. J., & Marr, J. W. (1981). Coronary heart disease prevention: Trials of diets to control hyperlipidemia. In N. E. Miller & B. Lewis (Eds.), *Lipoproteins, atherosclerosis, and coronary heart disease*. North Holland: Elsevier.

Manson, J. E., Colditz, G. A., Stampfer, M. J., Willett, W. C., Rosner, B., Monson, R. R., Speizer, F. E., & Hennekens, C. H. (1990). A prospective study of obesity and risk of coronary heart disease in women. *New England Journal of Medicine, 322*, 882–888.

Manuck, S. B., Craft, S., & Gold, K. J. (1978). Coronary-prone behavior pattern and cardiovascular response. *Psychophysiology, 15*, 403–411.

Manuck, S. B., & Krantz, D. S. (1986). Psychophysiological reactivity in coronary heart disease and essential hypertension. In K. A. Matthews, S. M. Weiss, T. Detre, T. M. Dembroski, B. Falkner, S. B. Manuck, & R. B. Williams, Jr. (Eds.), *Handbook of stress, reactivity, and cardiovascular disease* (pp. 11–34). New York: Wiley.

Marcus, A. C., & Siegel, J. M. (1982). Sex differences in the use of physician services: A preliminary test of the fixed role hypothesis. *Journal of Health and Social Behavior, 23*, 186–197.

Marcus, M. D., Wing, R. R., & Hopkins, J. (1988). Obese binge eaters: Affect, cognitions, and response to behavioral weight control. *Journal of Consulting and Clinical Psychology, 56*, 433–439.

Margolis, L. H., McLeroy, K. R., Runyan, C. W., & Kaplan, B. H. (1983). Type A behavior: An ecological approach. *Journal of Behavioral Medicine, 6*, 245–258.

Marks, G., Richardson, J. L., Graham, J. W., & Levine, A. (1986). Role of health locus of control beliefs and expectations of treatment efficacy in adjustment to cancer. *Journal of Personality and Social Psychology, 51*, 443–450.

Marks, R. M., & Sachar, E. J. (1973). Undertreatment of medical inpatients with narcotic analgesics. *Annals of Internal Medicine, 78*, 173–181.

Marlatt, G. A. (1982). Relapse prevention: A self-control program for the treatment of addictive behaviors. In R. B. Stuart (Ed.), *Adherence, compliance, and generalization in behavioral medicine* (pp. 329–378). New York: Brunner/Mazel.

Marlatt, G. A. (1987). Alcohol, the magic elixir: Stress, expectancy, and the transformation of emotional states. In E. Gottheil, K. A. Druly, S. Pashko, & S. P. Weinstein, (Eds.), *Stress and addiction* (pp. 302–322). New York: Brunner/Mazel.

Marlatt, G. A., & George, W. H. (1988). Relapse prevention and the maintenance of optimal health. In S. Shumaker, E. Schron, & J. K. Ockene (Eds.), *The adoption and maintenance of behaviors for optimal health.* New York: Springer.

Marlatt, G. A., & Gordon, J. R. (1980). Determinants of relapse: Implications for the maintenance of behavior change. In P. O. Davidson & S. M. Davidson (Eds.), *Behavioral medicine: Changing health life-styles.* New York: Brunner/Mazel.

Marlatt, G. A., & Gordon, J. R. (1985). *Relapse prevention: Maintenance strategies in addictive behavior change.* New York: Guilford Press.

Marlotte, C. K., Fielding, J. F., & Danaher, B. G. (1981). Description and evaluation of the smoking cessation component of a multiple risk factor intervention program. *American Journal of Public Health, 71,* 844–847.

Marshall, E. (1986). Involuntary smokers face health risks. *Science, 234,* 1066–1067.

Marshall, G. N., & Lang, E. L. (1990). Optimism, self-mastery, and symptoms of depression in women professionals. *Journal of Personality and Social Psychology, 59,* 132–139.

Marshall, J., Burnett, W., & Brasure, J. (1983). On precipitating factors: Cancer as a cause of suicide. *Suicide and Life-Threatening Behavior, 13,* 15–27.

Marteau, T. M., Bloch, S., & Baum, J. D. (1987). Family life and diabetic control. *Journal of Child Psychology and Psychiatry, 28,* 823–833.

Marteau, T. M., Johnston, M., Baum, J. D., & Bloch, S. (1987). Goals of treatment in diabetes: A comparison of doctors and parents of children with diabetes. *Journal of Behavioral Medicine, 10,* 33–48.

Martin, J. E., & Dubbert, P. M. (1982). Exercise applications and promotion in behavioral medicine: Current status and future directions. *Journal of Consulting and Clinical Psychology, 50,* 1004–1017.

Martin, J. L. (1987). The impact of AIDS on gay male sexual behavior patterns in New York City. *American Journal of Public Health, 77,* 578–581.

Maslach, C. (1977, August). *Burn-out: A social psychological analysis.* Paper presented at the annual meeting of the American Psychological Association, San Francisco, CA.

Maslach, C. (1979). The burn-out syndrome and patient care. In C. Garfield (Ed.), *The emotional realities of life-threatening illness* (pp. 111–120). St. Louis, MO: Mosby.

Mason, E. (1970). Obesity in pet dogs. *Veterinary Record, 86,* 612–616.

Mason, J. W. (1974). Specificity in the organization of neuroendocrine response profiles. In P. Seeman & G. M. Brown (Eds.), *Frontiers in neurology and neuroscience research. First International Symposium of the Neuroscience Institute.* Toronto, Canada: University of Toronto.

Mason, J. W. (1975). A historical view of the stress field. *Journal of Human Stress, 1,* 22–36.

Mason, J. W., Brady, J. V., & Tolliver, G. A. (1968). Plasma and urinary 17-hydroxycortico-steroid responses to 72-hour avoidance sessions in the monkey. *Psychosomatic Medicine, 30,* 608–630.

Mason, J. W., Sachar, E. J., Fishman, J. R., Hamburg, D. A., & Handlon, J. H. (1965). Corticosteroid responses to hospital admission. *Archives of General Psychiatry, 13,* 1–8.

Massie, M. J., & Holland, J. C. (1987). Consultation and liaison issues in cancer care. *Psychiatric Medicine, 5,* 343–359.

Masters, J. C., Cerreto, M. C., & Mendlowitz, D. R. (1983). The role of the family in coping with childhood chronic illness. In T. G. Burish & L. A. Bradley (Eds.), *Coping with chronic disease: Research and applications* (pp. 381–408). New York: Academic Press.

Mastrovito, R. C. (1974). Cancer: Awareness and denial. *Clinical Bulletin, 4,* 142–146.

Matarazzo, J. D. (1980). Behavioral health and behavioral medicine: Frontiers for a new health psychology. *American Psychologist, 35,* 807–817.

Matarazzo, J. D. (1982). Behavioral health's challenge to academic, scientific, and professional psychology. *American Psychologist, 37,* 1–14.

Matarazzo, J. D. (1984). Behavioral health: A 1990 challenge for the health services professions. In. J. D. Matarazzo, S. M. Weiss, J. A. Herd, N. E. Miller, & S. M. Weiss (Eds.), *Behavioral health: A handbook of health enhancement and disease prevention* (pp. 3–40). New York: Wiley.

Matt, D. A., Sementilli, M. E., & Burish, T. G. (1988). Denial as a strategy for coping with cancer. *Journal of Mental Health Counseling, 10,* 136–144.

Mattar, M. E., Markello, J., & Yaffe, S. J. (1975). Inadequacies in the pharmacologic management of ambulatory children. *Journal of Pediatrics, 87,* 137–141.

Matthews, J. R., Friman, P. C., Barone, V. J., Ross, L. V., & Christophersen, E. R. (1987). Decreasing dangerous infant behaviors through parent instruction. *Journal of Applied Behavior Analysis, 20,* 165–169.

Matthews, K. A. (1977). Caregiver–child interactions and the Type A coronary-prone behavior pattern. *Child Development, 48,* 1752–1756.

Matthews, K. A. (1982). Psychological perspectives on the Type A behavior pattern. *Psychological Bulletin, 91,* 293–323.

Matthews, K. A. (1988). Coronary heart disease and Type A behaviors: Update on and alternative to the Booth-Kewley and Friedman (1987) quantitative review. *Psychological Bulletin, 104,* 373–380.

Matthews, K. A., Siegel, J. M., Kuller, L. H., Thompson, M., & Varat, M. (1983). Determinants of decisions to seek medical treatment by patients with acute myocardial infarction syndromes. *Journal of Personality and Social Psychology, 44,* 1144–1156.

Matthews, K. A., Stoney, C. M., Rakaczky, C. J., & Jamison, W. (1986). Family characteristics and school achievements of Type A children. *Health Psychology, 5,* 453–467.

Matthews, K. A., & Woodall, K. L. (1988). Childhood origins of overt Type A behaviors and cardiovascular reactivity to behavioral stressors. *Annals of Behavioral Medicine, 10,* 71–77.

Mattsson, A. (1977). Long term physical illness in childhood: A challenge to psychosocial adaptation. In R. H. Moos (Ed.), *Coping with physical illness* (pp. 183–200). New York: Plenum.

Mauksch, H. O. (1973). Ideology, interaction, and patient care in hospitals. *Social Science and Medicine, 7,* 817–830.

May, G. S., Eberlein, K. A., Furberg, C. D., Passamani, E. R., & Demets, D. L. (1982). Secondary prevention after myocardial infarction: A review of long-term trials. *Prognoses of Cardiovascular Disease, 24,* 331–352.

Mayer, D. J., Price, D. D., Barber, J., & Rafii, A. (1976). Acupuncture analgesia: Evidence for activation of a pain inhibitor system as a mechanism of action. In J. J. Bonica & D. Albe-Fessard (Eds.), *Advances in pain research and therapy* (Vol. 1, pp. 751–754). New York: Raven Press.

Mayer, J. A., & Frederiksen, L. W. (1986). Encouraging long-term compliance with breast self-examination: The evaluation of prompting strategies. *Journal of Behavioral Medicine, 9,* 179–190.

Mayes, B. T., Sime, W. E., & Ganster, D. C. (1984). Convergent validity of Type A behavior pattern scales and their ability to predict physiological responsiveness in a sample of female public employees. *Journal of Behavioral Medicine, 7,* 83–108.

Mays, V. M., & Cochran, S. D. (1987). Acquired immunodeficiency syndrome and black Americans: Special psychosocial issues. *Public Health Reports, 102,* 224–231.

Mays, V. M., & Cochran, S. D. (1988). Issues in the perception of AIDS risk and risk reduction activities by black and Hispanic/Latina women. *American Psychologist, 43,* 949–957.

Mazurk, P. M., Tierney, H., Tarfidd, K., Gross, E. M., Morgan, E. B., Hsu, M. A., & Mann, J. G. (1988). Increased risk of suicide in persons with AIDS. *Journal of the American Medical Association, 259,* 1332–1333.

McArdle, W. D., Katch, F. I., & Katch, V. L. (1981). *Exercise physiology: Energy, nutrition, and human performance.* Philadelphia: Lea & Febiger.

McBride, A. B. (1990). Mental health effects of women's multiple roles. *American Psychologist, 45,* 381–384.

McCann, I. L., & Holmes, D. S. (1984). Influence of aerobic exercise on depression. *Journal of Personality and Social Psychology, 46,* 1142–1147.

McCarthy, W. (1986). The cognitive developmental model and other alternatives to the social deficit model of smoking onset. In C. Bell & R. J. Battjes (Eds.), *Prevention research: Deterring drug abuse among children and adolescents* (NIDA Research Monograph No. 63). Washington, DC: U.S. Government Printing Office.

McCaul, K. D., & Glasgow, R. E. (1985). Preventing adolescent smoking: What have we learned about treatment construct validity? *Health Psychology, 4,* 361–387.

McCaul, K. D., Glasgow, R. E., & Schafer, L. C. (1987). Diabetes regimen behaviors: Predicting adherence. *Medical Care, 25,* 868–881.

McCaul, K. D., Glasgow, R. E., Schafer, L. C., & O'Neill, H. K. (1983). Commitment and the prevention of adolescent cigarette smoking. *Health Psychology, 2,* 353–365.

McCaul, K. D., & Malott, J. M. (1984). Distraction and coping with pain. *Psychological Bulletin, 95,* 516–533.

McClearn, G. (1981). Genetic studies in animals. *Alcoholism: Clinical and Experimental Research, 5,* 447–448.

McClelland, D. C. (1989). Motivational factors in health and disease. *American Psychologist, 44,* 675–688.

McClelland, D. C., Alexander, C., & Marks, E. (1982). The need for power, stress, immune function, and illness among male prisoners. *Journal of Abnormal Psychology, 91,* 61–70.

McConnell, S., Biglan, A., & Severson, H. H. (1984). Adolescents' compliance with self-monitoring and physiological assessment of smoking in natural environments. *Journal of Behavioral Medicine, 7,* 115–122.

McCorkle, M. R. (1973). Coping with physical symptoms in metastatic breast cancer. *American Journal of Nursing, 73,* 1034–1038.

McCrae, R. R. (1984). Situational determinants of coping responses: Loss, threat and challenge. *Journal of Personality and Social Psychology, 46,* 919–928.

McCranie, E. W., & Simpson, M. E. (1987). Parental child-rearing antecedents of Type A behavior. *Personality and Social Psychology Bulletin, 12,* 493–501.

McCranie, E. W., Watkins, L. O., Brandsma, J. M., & Sisson, B. D. (1986). Hostility, coronary heart disease (CHD) incidence, and total mortality: Lack of association in a 25-year follow-up study of 478 physicians. *Journal of Behavioral Medicine, 9,* 119–126.

McCubbin, J. A., Surwit, R. S., & Williams, R. B., Jr. (1985). Endogenous opiate peptides, stress reactivity, and risk for hypertension. *Hypertension, 7,* 808–811.

McCubbin, J. A., Surwit, R. S., & Williams, R. B., Jr. (1988). Opioid dysfunction and risk for hypertension: Naloxone and blood pressure responses during different types of stress. *Psychosomatic Medicine, 50,* 8–14.

McCusker, J. (1985). The use of home care in terminal cancer. *American Journal of Preventive Medicine, 1,* 42–52.

McEntee, M. A., & Peddicord, K. (1987). Coping with hypertension. *Nursing Clinics of North America, 22,* 583–592.

McFall, R. M. (1970). The effects of self-monitoring on normal smoking behavior. *Journal of Consulting and Clinical Psychology, 35,* 135–142.

McFarland, A. H., Norman, G. R., Streiner, D. L., & Roy, R. G. (1983). The process of social stress: Stable, reciprocal, and mediating relationships. *Journal of Health and Social Behavior, 24,* 160–173.

McFarland, A. H., Norman, G. R., Streiner, D. L., Roy, R. G., & Scott, D. J. (1980). A longitudinal study of the influence of the psychosocial environment on health status: A preliminary report. *Journal of Health and Social Behavior, 21,* 124–133.

McFarland, C., Ross, M., & DeCourville, N. (1989). Women's theories of menstruation and biases in recall of menstrual symptoms. *Journal of Personality and Social Psychology, 57,* 522–531.

McGinnis, J. M. (1984). Occupant protection as a priority in national efforts to promote health. *Health Education Quarterly, 11,* 127–131.

McGregor, D. (1967). *The professional manager.* New York: McGraw-Hill.

McGuire, F. L. (1982). Treatment of the drinking driver. *Health Psychology, 1,* 137–152.

McGuire, W. J. (1964). Inducing resistance to persuasion: Some contemporary approaches. In L. Berkowitz (Ed.), *Advances in experimental social psychology* (Vol. 1, pp. 192–231). New York: Academic Press.

McGuire, W. J. (1969). The nature of attitude and attitude change. In G. Lindzey & E. Aronson (Eds.), *The handbook of social psychology* (2nd ed., Vol. 3, pp. 136–314). Reading, MA: Addison-Wesley.

McGuire, W. J. (1973). Persuasion, resistance and attitude change. In I. de Sola Pool, F. W. Frey, W. Schramm, N. Maccoby, & E. B. Parker (Eds.), *Handbook of communication* (pp. 216–252). Chicago: Rand-McNally.

McGuire, W. J. (1984). Public communication as a strategy for inducing health-promoting behavioral change. *Preventive Medicine, 13,* 299–319.

McKennell, A. C. (1973). Is addictive smoking an independent trait? *International Journal of the Addictions, 8,* 505–509.

McKinlay, J. B. (1972). Some approaches and problems in the study of the use of services: An overview. *Journal of Health and Social Behavior, 13,* 115–152.

McKinlay, J. B. (1975). Who is really ignorant—physician or patient? *Journal of Health and Social Behavior, 16,* 3–11.

McKinney, M. E., Hofshire, P. J., Buell, J. C., & Eliot, R. S. (1984). Hemodynamic and biochemical responses to stress: The necessary link between Type A behavior and cardiovascular disease. *Behavioral Medicine Update, 6,* 16–21.

McKinnon, W., Weisse, C. S., Reynolds, C. P., Bowles, C. A., & Baum, A. (1989). Chronic stress, leukocyte subpopulations, and humoral response to latent viruses. *Health Psychology, 8,* 389–402.

McKusick, L. (1988). The impact of AIDS on practitioner and client: Notes for the therapeutic relationship. *American Psychologist, 43,* 935–940.

McKusick, L., Horstman, W., & Coates, T. (1985). AIDS and sexual behavior reported by gay men in San Francisco. *American Journal of Public Health, 75,* 493–496.

McLean, P. D. (1976). Depression as a specific response to stress. In I. G. Sarason & C. D. Spielberger (Eds.), *Stress and anxiety* (Vol. 3, pp. 297–324). New York: Halsted.

McNamara, S. S., Molot, M. A., Stremple, J. F., & Cutting, R. T. (1971). Coronary artery disease in combat casualties in Vietnam. *Journal of the American Medical Association, 216,* 1185.

McNeilly, M., & Zeichner, A. (1989). Neuropeptide and cardiovascular responses in intravenous catheterization in normotensive and hypertensive blacks and whites. *Health Psychology, 8,* 483–488.

McPherson, B. D., Paivio, A., Yuhasz, M. S., Rechnitzer, P. A., Pickard, H. A., & Lefcoe, N. M. (1967). Psychological effects of an exercise program for post-infarct and normal adult men. *Journal of Sports Medicine and Physical Fitness, 7,* 95–102.

McReynolds, W. T., Green, L., & Fisher, E. B., Jr. (1983). Self-control as choice management with reference to the behavioral treatment of obesity. *Health Psychology, 2,* 261–276.

Mechanic, D. (1964). The influence of mothers on their children's health attitudes and behavior. *Journal of Pediatrics, 33,* 444–453.

Mechanic, D. (1972). Social psychologic factors affecting the presentation of bodily complaints. *New England Journal of Medicine, 286,* 1132–1139.

Mechanic, D. (1975). The organization of medical practice and practice orientation among physicians in prepaid and nonprepaid primary care settings. *Medical Care, 13,* 189–204.

Mechanic, D. (1976). *The growth of bureaucratic medicine: An inquiry into the dynamics of patient behavior and the organization of medical care.* New York: Wiley.

Mechanic, D. (1978a). Effects of psychological distress on perceptions of physical health and use of medical and psychiatric facilities. *Journal of Human Stress, 4,* 26–32.

Mechanic, D. (1978b). *Medical sociology* (2nd ed.). New York: Free Press.

Mechanic, D. (1979). The stability of health and illness behavior: Results from a 16-year followup. *American Journal of Public Health, 69,* 1142–1145.

Mechanic, D. (1980). The experience and reporting of common physical complaints. *Journal of Health and Social Behavior, 21,* 146–155.

Mechanic, D., & Cleary, P. D. (1980). Factors associated with the maintenance of positive health behavior. *Preventive Medicine, 9,* 805–814.

Mechanic, D., & Volkhart, E. H. (1961). Stress, illness behavior, and the sick role. *American Sociological Review, 26,* 51–58.

Meichenbaum, D. H. (1971, September). *Cognitive factors in behavior modification: Modifying what clients say to themselves.* Paper presented at the annual meeting of the Association for Advancement of Behavior Therapy, Washington, DC.

Meichenbaum, D. H. (1975). A self-instructional approach to stress management: A proposal for stress inoculation training. In C. D. Spielberger & I. Sarason (Eds.), *Stress and anxiety* (Vol. 2, 237–264). New York: Wiley.

Meichenbaum, D. H. (1977). *Cognitive-behavior modification.* New York: Plenum.

Meichenbaum, D. H., & Cameron, R. (1974). The clinical potential and pitfalls of modifying what clients say to themselves. In M. J. Mahoney & C. E. Thoresen (Eds.), *Self-control: Power to the person* (pp. 263–290). Monterey, CA: Brooks-Cole.

Meichenbaum, D. H., & Jaremko, M. E. (Eds.). (1983). *Stress reduction and prevention.* New York: Plenum.

Meichenbaum, D. H., & Turk, D. (1982). Stress, coping, and disease: A cognitive-behavioral perspective. In R. W. J. Neufield (Ed.), *Psychological stress and psychopathology* (pp. 289–306). New York: McGraw-Hill.

Meichenbaum, D., & Turk, D. C. (1987). *Facilitating treatment adherence: A practitioner's guidebook.* New York: Plenum.

Mei-Tal, V., Meyerowitz, S., & Engel, G. I. (1970). The role of psychological process in a somatic disorder: M.S. 1. The emotional setting of illness onset and exacerbation. *Psychosomatic Medicine, 32,* 67–85.

Melamed, B. G., & Bush, J. P. (1985). The role of the family in acute illness. In D. Turk & R. Kerns (Eds.), *Health, illness, and families: A life-span perspective* (pp. 183–219). New York: Wiley.

Melamed, B. G., Meyer, R., Gee, C., & Soule, L. (1976). The influence of time and type of preparation on children's adjustment to hospitalization. *Journal of Pediatric Psychology, 1,* 31–37.

Melamed, B. G., & Siegel, L. (1975). Reduction of anxiety in children facing hospitalization and surgery by use of filmed modeling. *Journal of Consulting and Clinical Psychology, 43,* 511–521.

Melamed, B. G., Yurcheson, R., Fleece, L., Hutcherson, S., & Hawes, R. (1978). Effects of film modeling on the reduction of anxiety-related behaviors in individuals varying in level of previous experience in the stress situation. *Journal of Consulting and Clinical Psychology, 46,* 1357–1367.

Melick, M. E. (1978). Life change and illness. Illness behavior of males in the recovery period of a natural disaster. *Journal of Health and Social Behavior, 19,* 335–342.

Melzack, R. (1973). *The puzzle of pain.* New York: Basic Books.

Melzack, R. (1975). The McGill Pain Questionnaire: Major properties and scoring methods. *Pain, 1,* 277–299.

Melzack, R. (Ed.). (1983). *Pain measurement and assessment.* New York: Raven Press.

Melzack, R., & Torgerson, W. S. (1971). On the language of pain. *Anesthesiology, 34,* 50.

Melzack, R., & Wall, P. D. (1965). Pain mechanisms: A new theory. *Science, 150,* 971–979.

Melzack, R., & Wall, P. D. (1982). *The challenge of pain.* New York: Basic Books.

Melzack, R., Weisz, A. A., & Sprague, L. T. (1963). Stratagems for controlling pain: Contributions of auditory stimulation and suggestion. *Experimental Neurology, 8,* 239.

Menninger, W. C. (1935). The inter-relation of mental disorders and diabetes mellitus. *Journal of Mental Science, 81,* 332–357.

Mensch, B. S., & Kandel, D. B. (1988). Do job conditions influence the use of drugs? *Journal of Health and Social Behavior, 29,* 169–184.

Mermelstein, R., Cohen, S., Lichtenstein, E., Baer, J. S., & Kamarck, T. (1986). Social support and smoking cessation and maintenance. *Journal of Consulting and Clinical Psychology, 54,* 447–453.

Metropolitan Life Insurance Company. (1983). *Statistical bulletin.* New York: Metropolitan Life Insurance Company.

Meyer, A. J., & Henderson, I. B. (1974). Multiple risk factor reduction in the prevention of cardiovascular disease. *Preventive Medicine, 3,* 225–236.

Meyer, A. J., Maccoby, N., & Farquhar, J. W. (1980). Reply to Kasl and Leventhal et al. *Journal of Consulting and Clinical Psychology, 48,* 159–163.

Meyer, A. J., Nash, J. D., McAlister, A. L., Maccoby, N., & Farquhar, J. W. (1980). Skills training in a cardiovascular health education campaign. *Journal of Consulting and Clinical Psychology, 48,* 129–142.

Meyer, D., Leventhal, H., & Gutmann, M. (1985). Common-sense models of illness: The example of hypertension. *Health Psychology, 4,* 115–135.

Meyer, R. J., & Haggerty, R. J. (1962). Streptococcal infections in families. *Journal of Pediatrics, 29,* 539–549.

Meyerhoff, J. L., Mougey, E. H., & Kant, G. J. (1987). Paraventricular lesions abolish the stress-induced rise in pituitary cyclic adenosine monophosphate and attenuate the increases in plasma levels of proopiomelanocortin-derived peptides and prolactin. *Neuroendocrinology, 46,* 222–230.

Meyerhoff, J. L., Oleshansky, M. A., & Mougey, M. S. (1988). Psychologic stress increases plasma levels of prolactin, cortisol, and POMC-derived peptides in man. *Psychosomatic Medicine, 50,* 295–303.

Meyerowitz, B. E. (1980). Psychosocial correlates of breast cancer and its treatments. *Psychological Bulletin, 87,* 108–131.

Meyerowitz, B. E. (1983). Postmastectomy coping strategies and quality of life. *Health Psychology, 2,* 117–132.

Michael, B. E., & Copeland, D. R. (1987). Psychosocial issues in childhood cancer: An ecological framework for research. *American Journal of Pediatric Hematology and Oncology, 9,* 73–83.

Michela, J. L. (1982). Perceived changes in **marital**

relationships following myocardial infarction. *Dissertation Abstracts International, 48,* 4245-B.

Michela, J. L. (1987). Interpersonal and individual impacts of a husband's heart attack. In A. Baum & J. E. Singer (Eds.), *Handbook of psychology and health* (Vol. 5, pp. 255–301). Hillsdale, NJ: Erlbaum.

Micklin, M., & Leon, C. A. (1978). Life change and psychiatric disturbance in a South American city: The effects of geographic and social mobility. *Journal of Health and Social Behavior, 19,* 92–107.

Migler, B., & Wolpe, J. (1967). Automated self-desensitization: A case report. *Behaviour Research and Therapy, 5,* 133–135.

Miller, A. (1989). Can you afford to get sick? *Newsweek, January 30,* 47.

Miller, A., & Gimpl, M. (1971). Operant conditioning and self-control of smoking and studying. *Journal of Genetic Psychology, 119,* 181–186.

Miller, D. M., & Eisler, R. M. (1976). Alcohol and drug abuse. In W. E. Craighead, A. E. Kayden, & M. J. Mahoney (Eds.), *Behavior modification principles, issues and application.* Boston: Houghton-Mifflin.

Miller, D. T., & Porter, C. A. (1983). Self-blame in victims of violence. In R. Janoff-Bulman & I. H. Frieze (Eds.), *Journal of Social Issues, 39,* 139–152.

Miller, M. M. (1959). Treatment of chronic alcoholism by hypnotic aversion. *Journal of the American Medical Association, 171,* 1492–1495.

Miller, N. E. (1983). Behavioral medicine: Symbiosis between laboratory and clinic. *Annual Review of Psychology, 34,* 1–31.

Miller, N. E. (1989). Placebo factors in types of treatment: Views of a psychologist. In M. Shepherd & N. Sartorius (Eds.), *Non-specific aspects of treatment* (pp. 39–56). Lewiston, NY: Hans Huber.

Miller, S. M., Brody, D. S., & Summerton, J. (1988). Styles of coping with threat: Implications for health. *Journal of Personality and Social Psychology, 54,* 142–148.

Miller, S. M., & Mangan, C. E. (1983). Inter-acting effects of information and coping style in adapting to gynecologic stress: Should the doctor tell all? *Journal of Personality and Social Psychology, 45,* 223–236.

Miller, W. R. (1980). *The addictive behaviors.* London, England: Pergamon.

Miller, W. R., & Hester, R. K. (1986). Inpatient alcoholism treatment: Who benefits? *American Psychologist, 41,* 794–805.

Miller, W. R., Taylor, C. A., & West, I. C. (1980). Focused versus broad-spectrum behavior therapy for problem drinkers. *Journal of Consulting and Clinical Psychology, 48,* 590–601.

Millman, M. (1980). *Such a pretty face: Being fat in America.* New York: Norton.

Mills, D. E., & Ward, R. P. (1986). Attenuation of stress-induced hypertension by exercise independent of training effects: An animal model. *Journal of Behavioral Medicine, 9,* 599–606.

Mills, R. T., & Krantz, D. S. (1979). Information, choice, and reactions to stress: A field experiment in a blood bank with laboratory analogue. *Journal of Personality and Social Psychology, 4,* 608–620.

Millstein, S. G., & Irwin, C. E., Jr. (1987). Concepts of health and illness: Different constructs or variations on a theme? *Health Psychology, 6,* 515–524.

Minuchin, S., Rosman, B. L., & Baker, L. (1978). *Psychosomatic families.* Cambridge, MA: Harvard University Press.

Mitchell, J. E., Laine, D. E., Morley, J. E., & Levine, A. S. (1986). Naloxone but not CCK-8 may attenuate binge-eating behavior in patients with the bulimia syndrome. *Biological Psychiatry, 21,* 1399–1406.

Mitchell, J. E., & Moos, R. H. (1984). Deficiencies in social support among depressed patients: Antecedents or consequences of stress? *Journal of Health and Social Behavior, 25,* 438–452.

Mittelmark, M. B., Murray, D. M., Luepker, R. V., & Pechacek, T. F. (1982). Cigarette smoking among adolescents: Is the rate declining? *Preventive Medicine, 11,* 708–712.

Mogielnicki, R. P., Neslin, S., Dulac, J., Balestra, D., Gillie, E., & Corson, J. (1986). Tailored media can enhance the success of smoking cessation clinics. *Journal of Behavioral Medicine, 9,* 141–162.

Monjan, A. A., & Collector, M. I. (1977). Stress-induced modulation of the immune response. *Science, 196,* 307–308.

Monroe, S. (1983). Major and minor life events as predictors of psychological distress: Further issues and findings. *Journal of Behavioral Medicine, 6,* 189–205.

Moody, R. A. (1978). *Laugh after laugh: The healing power of humor.* Jacksonville, FL: Headwaters Press.

Mooradian, A. D., Perryman, K., Fitten, J., Kavonian, G. D., & Morley, J. E. (1988). Cortical function in elderly non-insulin dependent diabetic patients. *Archives of Internal Medicine, 148,* 2369–2372.

Moore, J. E., Armentrout, D. P., Parker, J. C., & Kivlahan, D. R. (1986). Empirically derived pain-patient MMPI subgroups: Prediction of treatment outcome. *Journal of Behavioral Medicine, 9,* 51–64.

Moos, R. H. (1977). *Coping with physical illness.* New York: Plenum.

Moos, R. H. (1984). Context and coping: Toward a unifying conceptual framework. *American Journal of Community Psychology, 12,* 5–25.

Moos, R. H. (1985). Creating health in human contexts: Environmental and individual strategies. In J. C. Rosen & L. J. Solomon (Eds.), *Prevention in health psychology* (pp. 366–389). Hanover, NH: University Press of New England.

Moos, R. H. (1988). Life stressors and coping resources influence health and well-being. *Psychological Assessment, 4,* 133–158.

Moos, R. H., Cronkite, R. C., & Finney, J. W. (1982). A conceptual framework for alcoholism treatment evaluation. In E. M. Pattison & E. Kaufman (Eds.), *Encyclopedic handbook of alcoholism.* New York: Gardner.

Moos, R. H., & Finney, J. W. (1983). The expanding scope of alcoholism treatment evaluation. *American Psychologist, 38,* 1036–1044.

Moos, R. H., Mehren, B., & Moos, B. J. (1978). Evaluation of a Salvation Army alcoholism treatment program. *Journal of Studies on Alcoholism, 39,* 1267–1275.

Moos, R. H., & Schaefer, J. A. (1987). Evaluating health care work settings: A holistic conceptual framework. *Psychology and Health, 1,* 97–122.

Moos, R. H., & Tsu, V. D. (1977). The crisis of physical illness: An overview. In R. H. Moos (Ed.), *Coping with physical illness* (pp. 3–22). New York: Plenum.

Mor, V., & Hiris, J. (1983). Determinants of site of death among hospice cancer patients. *Journal of Health and Social Behavior, 24,* 375–385.

Morehouse, L. E., & Miller, A. T. (1976). *Physiology of exercise.* St. Louis, MO: Mosby.

Morgan, D. L. (1985). Nurses' perceptions of mental confusion in the elderly: Influence of resident and setting characteristics. *Journal of Health and Social Behavior, 26,* 102–112.

Morgan, J. P., & Puder, K. S. (1989). Postoperative analgesia: Variations in prescribed and adminis-

tered opioid dosages. In C. S. Hill, Jr., & W. S. Fields (Eds.), *Advances in pain research and therapy* (Vol. 11, pp. 175–350). New York: Raven Press.

Morimoto, Y., Dishi, T., Hanasaki, N., Miyatake, A., Sato, B., Noma, K., Kakto, H., Yano, S., & Yamamura, Y. (1980). Interrelations among amenorrhea, serum gonadotropins and body weight in anorexia nervosa. *Endocrinology in Japan, 27,* 191–200.

Morley, J. E. (1987). Neuropeptide regulation of appetite and weight. *Endocrine Reviews, 8,* 256–287.

Morley, J. E., Flood, J. F., Cherkin, A., & Mitchell, J. E. (1989). Parallels in neurotransmitter control of feeding and memory. In A. J. Stunkard & A. Baum (Eds.), *Perspectives in behavioral medicine: Eating, sleeping, and sex* (pp. 54–71). Hillsdale, NJ: Erlbaum.

Morley, J. E., Kay, N. E., & Solomon, G. P. (1988). Opioid peptides, stress, and immune function. In Y. Tache, J. E. Morley, & M. R. Brown (Eds.), *Neuropeptides and stress* (pp. 222–234). New York: Springer.

Morley, J. E., Kay, N. E., Solomon, G. P., & Plotnikoff, N. P. (1987). Neuropeptides: Conductors of the immune orchestra. *Life Sciences, 41,* 527–544.

Morokoff, P. J., Baum, A., McKinnon, W. R., & Gilliland, R. (1987). Effects of chronic unemployment and acute psychological stress on sexual arousal in men. *Health Psychology, 6,* 545–560.

Morris, J. N., & Sherwood, S. (1987). Quality of life of cancer patients at different stages in the disease trajectory. *Journal of Chronic Diseases, 40,* 545–553.

Morris, P. L. P., & Raphael, B. (1987). Depressive disorder associated with physical illness: The impact of stroke. *General Hospital Psychiatry, 9,* 324–330.

Moseley, R. (1987, January 11). British now fight AIDS with ads. *San Francisco Sunday Examiner and Chronicle* (orig. *Chicago Tribune*), pp. A13–A18.

Moses, H. (producer) (1984). Helen. *Segment of 60 Minutes, XVI.* New York: CBS Television Network, February 18.

Moss, R. B., Moss, H. B., & Peterson, R. (1989). Microstress, mood, and natural killer-cell activity. *Psychosomatics, 30,* 279–283.

Moulton, J. M., Sweet, D. M., Temoshok, L., & Mandel, J. S. (1987). Attributions of blame and responsibility in relation to distress and health behavior change in people with AIDS and AIDS-related complex. *Journal of Applied Social Psychology, 17,* 493–506.

Mountcastle, V. B. (1980). *Medical physiology.* St. Louis, MO: Mosby.

Mullen, P. D., & Green, L. W. (1985). Meta-analysis points way toward more effective medication teaching. *Promoting Health, November–December,* 6–8.

Multiple Risk Factor Intervention Trial Research Group. (1982). Multiple Risk Factor Intervention Trial: Risk factor changes and mortality results. *Journal of the American Medical Association, 248,* 1465–1477.

Mumford, E., Schlesinger, H. J., & Glass, G. V. (1982). The effects of psychological intervention on recovery from surgery and heart attacks: An analysis of the literature. *American Journal of Public Health, 72,* 141–151.

Muranaka, M., Lane, J. D., Suarez, E. C., Anderson, N. B., Suzuki, J., & Williams, R. B., Jr. (1988). Stimulus-specific patterns of cardiovascular reactivity in Type A and B subjects: Evidence for enhanced vagal reactivity in Type B. *Psychophysiology, 25,* 330–338.

Muranaka, M., Monou, H., Suzuki, J., Lane, J. D., Anderson, N. B., Kuhn, C. M., Schanberg, S. M., McCown, N., & Williams, R. B., Jr. (1988). Physiological responses to catecholamine infusions in Type A and Type B men. *Health Psychology, 7*(Suppl.), 145–163.

Murphy, S., Creed, F., & Jayson, M. I. (1988). Psychiatric disorder and illness behavior in rheumatoid arthritis. *British Journal of Rheumatology, 27,* 357–363.

Murphy, T. J., Pagano, R. R., & Marlatt, G. A. (1986). Lifestyle modification with heavy alcohol drinkers: Effects of aerobic exercise and meditation. *Addictive Behaviors, 11,* 175–186.

Murphy, T. M. (1976). Subjective and objective follow-up assessment of acupuncture therapy without suggestion in 100 chronic pain patients. In J. J. Bonica & D. Albe-Fessard (Eds.), *Advances in pain research and therapy* (Vol. 1, pp. 811–816). New York: Raven Press.

Murray, D. M., Blake, S. M., Prineas, R., & Gillum, R. F. (1985). Cardiovascular responses in Type A children during a cognitive challenge. *Journal of Behavioral Medicine, 8,* 377–396.

Murray, D. M., Davis-Hearn, M., Goldman, A. I., Pirie, P., & Luepker, R. V. (1988). Four- and five-year follow-up results from four seventh-grade smoking prevention strategies. *Journal of Behavioral Medicine, 11,* 395–406.

Murray, D. M., Matthews, K. A., Blake, S. M., Prineas, R. J., & Gillum, R. F. (1986). Type A behavior in children: Demographic, behavioral, and physiological correlates. *Health Psychology, 5,* 159–169.

Murray, D. M., Richards, P. S., Luepker, R. V., & Johnson, C. A. (1987). The prevention of cigarette smoking in children: Two- and three-year follow-up comparisons of four prevention strategies. *Journal of Behavioral Medicine, 10,* 595–612.

Murray, P., Liddell, A., & Donohue, J. (1989). A longitudinal study of the contribution of dental experience to dental anxiety in children between 9 and 12 years of age. *Journal of Behavioral Medicine, 12,* 309–320.

Myers, J. K., Lindenthal, J. J., & Pepper, M. P. (1972). Life events and mental status: A longitudinal study. *Journal of Health and Social Behavior, 13,* 398–406.

Nagy, M. (1948). The child's view of death. In H. Feifel (Ed.), *The meaning of death.* New York: McGraw-Hill.

Nail, L. M., King, K. B., & Johnson, J. E. (1986). Coping with radiation treatment for gynecologic cancer: Mood and disruption in usual function. *Journal of Psychosomatic Obstetrics and Gynaecology, 5,* 271–281.

Najman, J. M., Klein, D., & Munro, C. (1982). Patient characteristics negative stereotyped by doctors. *Social Sciences and Medicine, 16,* 1781–1789.

Nashold, B. S., & Friedman, H. (1972). Dorsal column stimulation for pain: A preliminary report on thirty patients. *Journal of Neurosurgery, 36,* 590–597.

Natelson, B. H. (1988). Stress and digitalis toxicity. In H. E. Kulbertus & G. Franck (Eds.), *Neurocardiology* (pp. 301–311). Mount Kisco, NY: Futura Publishing.

Natelson, B. H., Ottenweller, J. E., Pitman, D., & Tapp, W. N. (1988). An assessment of prolactin's value as an index of stress. *Life Sciences, 42,* 1597–1602.

Nathanson, C. (1975). Illness and the feminine role: A theoretical review. *Social Science and Medicine, 9,* 57–62.

Nathanson, C. (1977). Sex, illness, and medical care. *Social Science and Medicine, 11,* 13–25.

National Cancer Institute. (1980). *Breast cancer: A measure of progress in public understanding* (DHHS/ NIH Publication No. 81-2291). Washington, DC: U.S. Government Printing Office.

National Cancer Institute. (1989). *Cancer statistics review.* Rockville, MD: National Cancer Institute.

National Center for Health Statistics. (1986). *Vital statistics of the United States, 1986: Vol. II. Mortality, part A* (DHHS Publication No. PHS-88-1122, Public Health Service). Washington, DC: U.S. Government Printing Office.

National Health Education Committee. (1976). *The killers and cripplers: Facts on major diseases in the United States today.* New York: David McKay.

Naughton, J. P., Bruhn, J. G., & Lategola, M. T. (1968). Effects of physical training on physiologic and behavioral characteristics of cardiac patients. *Archives of Physical Medicine and Rehabilitation, 49,* 131–137.

Naughton, J. P., Hellerstein, H. K., & Mohler, I. C. (Eds.). (1973). *Exercise testing and exercise training in coronary heart disease.* New York: Academic Press.

Neff, J. A., & Husaini, B. A. (1985). Stress-buffer properties of alcohol consumption: The role of urbanicity and religious identification. *Journal of Health and Social Behavior, 26,* 207–222.

Nerenz, D. R. (1979). *Control of emotional distress in cancer chemotherapy.* Unpublished doctoral dissertation, University of Wisconsin, Madison.

Nerenz, D. R., & Leventhal, H. (1983). Self-regulation theory in chronic illness. In T. G. Burish & L. A. Bradley (Eds.), *Coping with chronic disease: Research and applications* (pp. 13–38). New York: Academic Press.

Nethercut, G., & Piccione, A. (1984). The physician perspective of health psychologists in medical settings. *Health Psychology, 3,* 175–184.

Neu, S., & Kjellstrand, C. M. (1986). Stopping long-term dialysis: An empirical study of withdrawal of life-supporting treatment. *New England Journal of Medicine, 314,* 14–19.

Neuling, S. J., & Winefield, H. R. (1988). Social support and recovery after surgery for breast cancer: Frequency and correlates of supportive behaviors by family, friends, and surgeon. *Social Science and Medicine, 27,* 385–392.

Newman, S. (1984). The psychological conse-

quences of cerebrovascular accident and head injury. In R. Fitzpatrick et al. (Eds.), *The experience of illness.* London, England: Tavistock.

Niemi, M. L., Laaksonen, R., Kotila, M., & Waltimo, O. (1988). Quality of life 4 years after stroke. *Stroke, 19,* 1101–1107.

Nisbett, R. E., & Borgida, E. (1975). Attribution and the psychology of prediction. *Journal of Personality and Social Psychology, 32,* 932–943.

Norris, F. H., & Murrell, S. A. (1984). Protective function of resources related to life events, global stress, and depression in older adults. *Journal of Health and Social Behavior, 25,* 424–437.

Norris, F. H., & Murrell, S. A. (1987). Transitory impact of life-event stress on psychological symptoms in older adults. *Journal of Health and Social Behavior, 28,* 197–211.

Nowack, K. M. (1989). Coping style, cognitive hardiness, and health status. *Journal of Behavioral Medicine, 12,* 145–158.

Nuckolls, K. B., Cassell, J. C., & Kaplan, B. H. (1972). Psychosocial assets, life crisis, and the prognosis of pregnancy. *American Journal of Epidemiology, 95,* 431.

Oakley, M. E., & Shapiro, D. (1989). Editorial review: Methodological issues in the evaluation of drug-behavioral interactions in the treatment of hypertension. *Psychosomatic Medicine, 51,* 269–276.

Ockene, J. K., Hymowitz, N., Sexton, M., & Broste, S. K. (1982). Comparison of patterns of smoking behavior change among smokers in the Multiple Risk Factor Intervention Trial (MRFIT). *Preventive Medicine, 11,* 621–638.

O'Day, J., & Scott, R. E. (1984). Safety belt use, ejection and entrapment. *Health Education Quarterly, 11,* 141–146.

Offutt, C., & LaCroix, J. M. (1988). Type A behavior pattern and symptom reports: A prospective investigation. *Journal of Behavioral Medicine, 11,* 227.

Oldenburg, B., Perkins, R. J., & Andrews, G. (1985). Controlled trial of psychological intervention in myocardial infarction. *Journal of Consulting and Clinical Psychology, 53,* 852–859.

Oldridge, N. B. (1979). Compliance of post-myocardial infarction patients to exercise programs. *Medicine and Science in Sports, 11,* 373–375.

O'Leary, A. (in press). Stress, emotion, and human immune function. *Psychological Bulletin.*

O'Leary, A., Shoor, S., Lorig, K., & Holman, H. R. (1988). A cognitive-behavioral treatment for rheumatoid arthritis. *Health Psychology, 7,* 527–544.

Oliver, M. F. (1981). Coronary heart disease prevention: Trials using drugs to control hyperlipidemia. In N. E. Miller & B. Lewis (Eds.), *Lipoproteins, atherosclerosis, and coronary heart disease.* Amsterdam, The Netherlands: Elsevier North Holland Biomedical Press.

O'Malley, J. E., Koocher, G., Foster, D., & Slavin, L. (1979). Psychiatric sequelae of surviving childhood cancer. *American Journal of Orthopsychiatry, 49,* 608–616.

Oncology Times. (1984). Smoking-related deaths higher for heart disease than cancer. *Oncology Times, 6*(2), 3, 35.

Orbach, S. (1978). *Fat is a feminist issue: The anti-diet guide to permanent weight loss.* New York: Paddington Press.

Orleans, C. T., & Barnett, L. R. (1984). Bulimarexia: Guidelines for behavioral assessment and treatment. In R. C. Hawkins, W. J. Fremouw, & P. F. Clement (Eds.), *The binge-purge syndrome* (pp. 144–182). New York: Springer.

Orleans, C. T., & Shipley, R. H. (1982). Work-site smoking cessation initiatives: Review and recommendations. *Addictive Behaviors, 7,* 1–16.

Orme, C. M., & Binik, Y. M. (1987). Recidivism and self-cure of obesity: A test of Schachter's hypothesis in diabetic patients. *Health Psychology, 6,* 467–475.

Orme, C. M., & Binik, Y. M. (1989). Consistency of adherence across regimen demands. *Health Psychology, 8,* 27–43.

Orne, M. T. (1977). Mechanisms of hypnotic pain control. In J. J. Bonica & D. Albe-Fessard (Eds.), *Advances in pain research and therapy* (Vol. 1, pp. 717–726). New York: Raven Press.

Orne, M. T. (1980). Hypnotic control of pain: Toward a clarification of the different psychological processes involved. In J. J. Bonica (Ed.), *Pain* (pp. 155–172). New York: Raven Press.

Ory, M. G. (1988). Considerations in the development of age-sensitive indicators for assessing health promotion. *Health Promotion, 3,* 139–150.

Ory, M. G., & Williams, T. F. (1989). Rehabilitation: Small goals, sustained interventions. *Annals of American Political and Social Science, 503,* 60–71.

Osborn, L. M., & Woolley, F. R. (1981). Use of groups in well child care. *Pediatrics, 67,* 701–706.

Osterweis, M. (1985). Bereavement care: Special opportunities for hospice. In K. Gardner (Ed.), *Quality of care for the terminally ill: An examination of the issues* (pp. 131–135). Chicago: Joint Commission on Accreditation of Hospitals.

Ottawa Charter for Health Promotion. (1986). *Health Promotion, 1,* iii–v.

Oxford, J., Oppenheimer, E., & Edwards, G. (1976). Abstinence or control: The outcome for excessive drinkers two years after consultation. *Behavior Research and Therapy, 14,* 409–418.

Paffenbarger, R. S., Jr., Hyde, R. T., Wing, A. L., & Hsieh, C-C. (1986). Physical activity, all-cause mortality, and longevity of college alumni. *New England Journal of Medicine, 314,* 605–613.

Paffenbarger, R. S., Jr., Hyde, R. T., Wing, A. L., & Steinmetz, C. H. (1984). A natural history of athleticism and cardiovascular health. *Journal of the American Medical Association, 222,* 491–495.

Palinkas, L. A., & Hoiberg, A. (1982). An epidemiology primer: Bridging the gap between epidemiology and psychology. *Health Psychology, 1,* 269–287.

Palmore, E. (1970). Health practices and illness among the aged. *The Gerontologist, 1,* 313–316.

Paradis, L. F. (1984). Hospice program integration: An issue for policymakers. *Death Education, 8,* 383–398.

Paradis, L. F., & Cummings, S. B. (1986). The evolution of hospice in America toward organizational homogeneity. *Journal of Health and Social Behavior, 27,* 370–386.

Pardine, P., & Napoli, A. (1983). Physiological reactivity and recent life-stress experience. *Journal of Consulting and Clinical Psychology, 51,* 467–469.

Parfyonova, E. V., Korichneva, I. L., Suvorov, Y. I., & Krasnikova, T. L. (1988). Characteristics of lymphocyte b-adrenoceptors in essential hypertension: Effects of propranolol treatment and dynamic exercise. *Health Psychology, 7*(Suppl.), 33–52.

Parisi, N., & Katz, I. (1986). Attitudes toward posthumous organ donation and commitment to donate. *Health Psychology, 5,* 565–580.

Parker, J. C., Frank, R. G., Beck, N. C., Smarr, K. L., Buescher, K. L., Phillips, L. R., Smith, E. I., Anderson, S. K., & Walker, S. E. (1988). Pain management in rheumatoid arthritis patients: A cognitive-behavioral approach. *Arthritis and Rheumatism, 31,* 593–601.

Parkes, C. M. P. (1977). *Evaluation of family care in terminal illness.* Alexander Ming Fisher lecture, Columbia University, New York, 1975. Cited in Saunders, C., Dying they live: St. Christopher's Hospice. In H. Feifel (Ed.), *New meanings of death.* New York: McGraw-Hill.

Parkes, C. M. P., & Weiss, R. S. (1983). *Recovery from bereavement.* New York: Basic Books.

Parry, G. (1986). Paid employment, life events, social support, and mental health in working-class mothers. *Journal of Health and Social Behavior, 27,* 193–208.

Parsons, T. (1951). *The social system.* Glencoe, IL: Free Press.

Parsons, T. (1954). The professions and the social structure. In T. Parsons, *Essays in sociological theory* (pp. 34–49). New York: Free Press.

Patel, C., & Marmot, M. G. (1987). Stress management, blood pressure and quality of life. *Journal of Hypertension, 5*(Suppl. 1), S21–S28.

Patrick, R., & Tyroler, H. A. (1972). Papago Indian modernization: A community scale for health research. *Human Organization, 31,* 127–136.

Patterson, T. L., Sallis, J. F., Nader, P. R., Rupp, J. W., McKenzie, T. L., Roppe, B., & Bartok, P. W. (1988). Direct observation of physical activity and dietary behaviors in a structured environment: Effects of a family-based health promotion program. *Journal of Behavioral Medicine, 11,* 447–458.

Pattison, E. M. (1967). The experience of dying. *American Journal of Psychotherapy, 21,* 32–43.

Patton, M. (1979). *Validity and reliability of Hazelden treatment follow-up data.* Center City, MN: Hazelden Educational Services.

Pavlov, I. P. (1927). *Conditioned reflexes.* New York: Dover.

Paykel, E. S. (1974). Recent life events and clinical depression. In E. K. Gunderson & R. H. Rahe (Eds.), *Life stress and illness* (pp. 134–163). Springfield, IL: Thomas.

Paykel, E. S., & Dienelt, M. (1971). Suicide attempts following acute depression. *Journal of Nervous and Mental Disease, 153,* 234–243.

Payne, E. D., & Krant, M. J. (1969). The psychosocial aspects of advanced cancer. *Journal of the American Medical Association, 210,* 1238–1242.

Pearlin, L. I., Meaghan, E. G., Lieberman, M. A., & Mullan, J. T. (1981). The stress process. *Journal of Health and Social Behavior, 22,* 337–356.

Pearlin, L. I., & Schooler, C. (1978). The structure of coping. *Journal of Health and Social Behavior, 19,* 2–21.

Pearlman, J., Stotsky, B. A., & Dominick, J. R. (1969). Attitudes toward death among nursing home personnel. *Journal of Geriatic Psychology, 114,* 63–75.

Pechacek, T. F. (1979). Modification of smoking behavior. In N. A. Krasneger (Ed.), *The behavioral aspects of smoking* (Research Monograph Series, No. 26). Rockville, MD: National Institute on Drug Abuse.

Pechacek, T. F., Murray, D. M., Luepker, R. V., Mittelmark, M. B., Johnson, C. A., & Shutz, J. M. (1984). Measurement of adolescent smoking behavior: Rationale and methods. *Journal of Behavioral Medicine, 7,* 123–140.

Peck, A. (1972). Emotional reactions to having cancer. *American Journal of Roentgenology, Radium Therapy, and Nuclear Medicine, 114,* 591–599.

Peck, C. L., & King, N. J. (1982). Increasing patient compliance with prescriptions. *Journal of the American Medical Association, 248,* 2874–2877.

Pederson, L. L. (1982). Compliance with physician advice to quit smoking: A review of the literature. *Preventive Medicine, 11,* 71–84.

Pendleton, L., House, W. C., & Parker, L. E. (1987). Physicians' and patients' views of problems of compliance with diabetes regimens. *Public Health Reports, 102,* 21–26.

Penick, S. B., Filion, R., Fox, S., & Stunkard, A. J. (1971). Behavior modification in the treatment of obesity. *Psychosomatic Medicine, 33,* 49–55.

Pennebaker, J. W. (1980). Perceptual and environmental determinants of coughing. *Basic and Applied Social Psychology, 1,* 83–91.

Pennebaker, J. W. (1983). Accuracy of symptom perception. In A. Baum, S. E. Taylor, & J. Singer (Eds.), *Handbook of psychology and health* (Vol. 4, pp. 189–218). Hillsdale, NJ: Erlbaum.

Pennebaker, J. W. (1985). Traumatic experience and psychosomatic disease: Exploring the roles of behavioral inhibition, obsession, and confiding. *Canadian Psychology, 26,* 82–95.

Pennebaker, J. W. (1988). Confiding traumatic experiences and health. In S. Fisher & J. Reason (Eds.), *Handbook of life stress, cognition and health* (pp. 671–684). New York: Wiley.

Pennebaker, J. W., & Beall, S. (1986). Confronting a traumatic event: Toward an understanding of inhibition and disease. *Journal of Abnormal Psychology, 95,* 274–281.

Pennebaker, J. W., Burnam, M. A., Schaeffer, M. A., & Harper, D. C. (1977). Lack of control as a determinant of perceived physical symptoms. *Journal of Personality and Social Psychology, 35,* 167–174.

Pennebaker, J. W., Colder, M., & Sharp, L. K. (in press). Accelerating the coping process. *Journal of Personality and Social Psychology.*

Pennebaker, J. W., Gonder-Frederick, L., Stewart, H., Elfman, L., & Skelton, J. A. (1982). Physical symptoms associated with blood pressure. *Psychophysiology, 19,* 201–210.

Pennebaker, J. W., Hughes, C., & O'Heeron, R. C. (1987). The psychophysiology of confession: Linking inhibitory and psychosomatic processes. *Journal of Personality and Social Psychology, 52,* 781–793.

Pennebaker. J. W., Kiecolt-Glaser, J., & Glaser, R. (1988). Disclosure of traumas and immune function: Health implications for psychotherapy. *Journal of Consulting and Clinical Psychology, 56,* 239–245.

Pennebaker, J. W., & O'Heeron, R. C. (1984). Confiding in others and illness rate among spouses of suicide and accidental death victims. *Journal of Abnormal Psychology, 93,* 473–476.

Pennebaker, J. W., & Susman, J. R. (1988). Disclosure of traumas and psychosomatic processes. *Social Science and Medicine, 26,* 327–332.

Pennebaker, J. W., & Watson, D. (1988). Blood pressure estimation and beliefs among normotensives and hypertensives. *Health Psychology, 7,* 309–328.

Perkins, K. A. (1985). The synergistic effect of smoking and serum cholesterol on coronary heart disease. *Health Psychology, 4,* 337–360.

Perkins, K. A., Dubbert, P. M., Martin, J. E., Faulstich, M. E., & Harris, J. K. (1986). Cardiovascular reactivity to psychological stress in aerobically trained versus untrained mild hypertensives and normotensives. *Health Psychology, 5,* 407–421.

Perkins, K. A., Epstein, L. H., Jennings, J. R., & Stiller, R. (1986). The cardiovascular effects of nicotine during stress. *Psychopharmacology, 90,* 373–378.

Perry, C. L., & Mullen, G. (1975). The effect of hypnotic susceptibility on reducing smoking behav-

ior treated by a hypnotic technique. *Journal of Clinical Psychology, 31,* 387–390.

Persky, V. W., Kempthorne-Rawson, J., & Shekelle, R. B. (1987). Personality and risk of cancer: 20-year follow-up of the Western Electric Study. *Psychosomatic Medicine, 49,* 435–449.

Pervin, L. A. (1968). Performance and satisfaction as a function of individual-environment fit. *Psychological Bulletin, 69,* 56–68.

Peters, R. K., Benson, H., & Porter, D. (1977). Daily relaxation response breaks in a working population. I. Effects on self-reported measures of health, performance, and well-being. *American Journal of Public Health, 67*(10), 946–959.

Peterson, C. (1982). Learned helplessness and health psychology. *Health Psychology, 1,* 153–168.

Peterson, C., & Seligman, M. E. P. (1984). Causal explanations as a risk factor for depression: Theory and evidence. *Psychological Review, 91,* 347–374.

Peterson, C., Seligman, M. E. P., & Vaillant, G. E. (1988). Pessimistic explanatory style is a risk factor for physical illness: A thirty-five-year longitudinal study. *Journal of Personality and Social Psychology, 55,* 23–27.

Peterson, L. (1984). A brief methodological comment on possible inaccuracies induced by multimodal measurement analysis and reporting. *Journal of Behavioral Medicine, 7,* 307–314.

Peterson, L., Farmer, J., & Kashani, J. H. (1990). Parental injury prevention endeavors: A function of health beliefs? *Health Psychology, 9,* 177–191.

Peterson, L., & Ridley-Johnson, R. (1980). Pediatric hospital response to survey on prehospital preparation for children. *Journal of Pediatric Psychology, 5,* 1–7.

Peterson, L., & Shigetomi, C. (1981). The use of coping techniques to minimize anxiety in hospitalized children. *Behavior Therapy, 12,* 1–14.

Peterson, L., & Toler, S. M. (1986). An information seeking disposition in child surgery patients. *Health Psychology, 5,* 343–358.

Pettingale, K., Greer, S., & Tee, D. (1977). Serum IgA and emotional expression in breast cancer patients. *Journal of Psychosomatic Research, 21,* 395–399.

Phifer, J. F., Kaniasty, K. Z., & Norris, F. H. (1988). The impact of natural disaster on the health of older adults: A multiwave prospective study. *Journal of Health and Social Behavior, 29,* 65–78.

Philips, H. C. (1983). Assessment of chronic head-ache behavior. In R. Melzack (Ed.), *Pain measurement and assessment* (pp. 97–104). New York: Raven Press.

Philips, H. C., & Hunter, M. (1982). A laboratory technique for the assessment of pain behavior. *Journal of Behavioral Medicine, 5,* 283–294.

Phillips, R. E., Johnson, G. D., & Geyer, A. (1972). Self-administered systematic desensitization. *Behaviour Research and Therapy, 10,* 93–96.

Pilisuk, M. (1982). Delivery of social support: The social inoculation. *American Journal of Orthopsychiatry, 52,* 20–31.

Pilisuk, M., Boylan, R., & Acredolo, C. (1987). Social support, life stress, and subsequent medical care utilization. *Health Psychology, 6,* 273–288.

Pillemer, K. (1988). Maltreatment of patients in nursing homes: Overview and research agenda. *Journal of Health and Social Behavior, 29,* 227–238.

Pinneau, S. R., Jr. (1975). *Effects of social support on psychological and physiological stress.* Unpublished doctoral dissertation, University of Michigan, Ann Arbor.

Pinto, R. P., & Hollandsworth, J. G., Jr. (1989). Using videotape modeling to prepare children psychologically for surgery: Influence of parents and costs versus benefits of providing preparation services. *Health Psychology, 8,* 79–95.

Pitman, D. L., Ottenweller, J. E., & Natelson, B. H. (1988). Plasma corticosterone levels during repeated presentation of two intensities of restraint stress: Chronic stress and habituation. *Physiology and Behavior, 43,* 47–55.

Pliner, P. (1974). Effects of liquid and solid preloads in the eating behavior of obese and normal persons. In S. Schachter & J. Rodin (Eds.), *Obese humans and rats* (pp. 25–34). Washington, DC: Erlbaum/Wiley.

Polich, C. L., Iversen, L. H., & Parker, M. K. (1985, June). *Health maintenance organizations: The Medicare experience in the 1980s.* Paper presented at the annual meeting of the Gerontological Society of America, New Orleans, LA.

Polivy, J. (1977). Psychological effects of mastectomy on a woman's feminine self-concept. *Journal of Nervous and Mental Disease, 164,* 77–87.

Polivy, J., & Herman, C. P. (1985a). Dieting and binging: A causal analysis. *American Psychologist, 40,* 193–201.

Polivy, J., & Herman, C. P. (1985b). Dieting as a problem in behavioral medicine. In E. S. Katkin & S. B. Manuck (Eds.), *Advances in behavioral medicine* (Vol. 1, pp. 1–37). Greenwich, CT: JAI Press.

Polivy, J., & Herman, C. P. (1987). Diagnosis and treatment of normal eating. *Journal of Consulting and Clinical Psychology, 55,* 635–644.

Polivy, J., Herman, C. P., & Olmstead, M. P. (1984). Restraint and binge eating. In R. C. Hawkins, W. J. Fremouw, & P. F. Clement (Eds.), *The binge-purge syndrome* (pp. 104–122). New York: Springer.

Pomerleau, O. F. (1984). Reinforcing properties of nicotine: Smoking and induced vasopressin and beta-endorphin release, antioception and anxiety reduction. *Pavlovian Journal of Biological Science, 19,* 107.

Pomerleau, O. F. (1986). The "why" of tobacco dependence: Underlying reinforcing mechanisms in nicotine self-administration. In J. K. Ockene (Ed.), *Pharmacologic treatment of tobacco dependence: Proceedings of the World Congress* (pp. 32–47). Cambridge, MA: Institute for the Study of Smoking Behavior and Policy.

Pomerleau, O. F., & Brady, J. P. (1979). Introduction: The scope and promise of behavioral medicine. In O. F. Pomerleau & J. P. Brady (Eds.), *Behavioral medicine: Theory and practice.* Baltimore, MD: Williams & Wilkins.

Pomerleau, O. F., Fertig, J., Baker, L., & Cooney, N. (1983). Reactivity to alcohol cues in alcoholics and nonalcoholics: Implications for a stimulus control analysis of drinking. *Addictive Behaviors, 8,* 1–10.

Pomerleau, O. F., Pertschuk, M., Adkins, D., & Brady, J. A. (1978). A comparison of behavioral and traditional treatment of middle-income problem drinkers. *Journal of Behavioral Medicine, 1,* 187–200.

Pomerleau, O. F., & Pomerleau, C. S. (1984). Neuroregulators and the reinforcement of smoking: Towards a biobehavioral explanation. *Neuroscience and Biobehavioral Reviews, 8,* 503–513.

Pomerleau, O. F., & Pomerleau, C. S. (Eds.). (1988). *Nicotine replacement: A critical evaluation.* New York: Liss.

Pomerleau, O. F., & Pomerleau, C. S. (1989a). A biobehavioral perspective on smoking. In T. Ney & A. Gale (Eds.), *Smoking and human behavior* (pp. 69–93). New York: Wiley.

Pomerleau, O. F., & Pomerleau, C. S. (1989b). Stress, smoking, and the cardiovascular system. *Journal of Substance Abuse, 1,* 331–343.

Pomerleau, O. F., Scherzer, H. H., Grunberg, N. E.., Pomerleau, C. S., Judge, J., Fertig, J. B., & Burleson, J. (1987). The effects of acute exercise on subsequent cigarette smoking. *Journal of Behavioral Medicine, 10,* 117–127.

Popkin, M. K., Callies, A. L., Lentz, R. D., Colon, E. A., & Sutherland, D. E. (1988). Prevalence of major depression, simple phobia, and other psychiatric disorders in patients with long-standing Type I diabetes mellitus. *Archives of General Psychiatry, 45,* 64–68.

Price, V. A. (1982). *Type A behavior pattern: A model for research and practice.* New York: Academic Press.

Primeau, F. (1988). Post-stroke depression: A critical review of the literature. *Canadian Journal of Psychiatry, 33,* 757–765.

Prohaska, J. O., & DiClemente, C. C. (1984a). Self change processes, self-efficacy, and decisional balance across five stages of smoking cessation. In A. R. Liss (Ed.), *Advances in cancer control: Epidemiology and research.* New York: Liss.

Prohaska, J. O., & DiClemente, C. C. (1984b). *The transtheoretical approach: Crossing traditional boundaries of therapy.* Chicago: Dow Jones/Irwin.

Prohaska, T. R., Keller, M. L., Leventhal, E. A., & Leventhal, H. (1987). Impact of symptoms and aging attribution on emotions and coping. *Health Psychology, 6,* 495–514.

Pryor, J. B., Reeder, G. D., & McManus, J. A. (in press). Fear and loathing in the workplace: Reactions to AIDS-infected co-workers. *Personality and Social Psychology Bulletin.*

Pryor, J. B., Reeder, G. D., & Vinacco, R., Jr. (1989). The instrumental and symbolic functions of attitudes toward persons with AIDS. *Journal of Applied Social Psychology, 19,* 377–404.

Puska, P., Tuomilehto, J., Salonen, J., Neittaanmaki, L., Maki, J., Virtamo, J., Nissinen, A., Koskela, K., & Takalo, T. (1979). Changes in coronary risk factors during a comprehensive five-year community programme to control cardiovascular diseases (North Karelia project). *British Medical Journal, 2,* 1173–1178.

Putt, A. M. (1970). One experiment in nursing adults with peptic ulcers. *Nursing Research, 19,* 484–494.

Quinn, M. E., Fontana, A. F., & Reznikoff, M.

(1987). Psychological distress in reaction to lung cancer as a function of spousal support and coping strategy. *Journal of Psychosocial Oncology, 4,* 79–90.

Rachman, S. J., & Phillips, C. (1978). *Psychology and medicine.* Baltimore, MD: Penguin.

Radcliffe-Brown, A. R. (1964). *The Andaman Islanders.* New York: Free Press.

Radke-Sharpe, N., Whitney-Saltiel, D., & Rodin, J. (1990). Fat distribution as a risk factor for weight and eating concerns. *International Journal of Eating Disorders, 9,* 27–36.

Raether, H. C., & Slater, R. C. (1977). Immediate postdeath activities in the United States. In H. Feifel (Ed.), *New meanings of death* (pp. 233–250). New York: McGraw-Hill.

Ragland, D. R. (1977). *Behavioral approaches to the treatment of hypertension: A bibliography* (Publication No. NIH 77-1219m). Washington, DC: U.S. Government Printing Office.

Rahe, R. H., Mahan, J. L., & Arthur, R. J. (1970). Prediction of near-future health change from subjects' preceding life changes. *Journal of Psychosomatic Research, 14,* 401–406.

Rakoff, V. (1983). Multiple determinants of family dynamics in anorexia nervosa. In P. L. Darby, P. E. Garfinkel, D. M. Garner, & D. V. Coscina (Eds.), *Anorexia nervosa: Recent developments in research* (pp. 29–40). New York: Liss.

Rapoff, M. A., & Christophersen, E. R. (1982). Improving compliance in pediatric practice. *Pediatric Clinics of North America, 29,* 339–357.

Rappaport, N. B., McAnulty, D. P., Waggoner, C. D., & Brantley, P. J. (1987). Cluster analysis of Minnesota Multiphasic Personality Inventory (MMPI) profiles in a chronic headache population. *Journal of Behavioral Medicine, 10,* 49–60.

Raps, C. S., Peterson, C., Jonas, M., & Seligman, M. E. P. (1982). Patient behavior in hospitals: Helplessness, reactance, or both? *Journal of Personality and Social Psychology, 42,* 1036–1041.

Rau, J. H., & Green, R. S. (1984). Neurological factors affecting binge eating: Body over mind. In R. C. Hawkins, W. J. Fremouw, & P. F. Clement (Eds.), *The binge-purge syndrome* (pp. 123–143). New York: Springer.

Raven, B. H. (1988). Social power and compliance in health care. In. S. Maes, C. D. Spielberger, P. B. Defares, & I. G. Sarason (Eds.), *Topics in health psychology* (pp. 229–244). New York: Wiley.

Raven, B. H., Freeman, H. E., & Haley, R. W. (1982). Social science perspectives in hospital infection control. In A. W. Johnson, O. Grusky, & B. Raven (Eds.), *Contemporary health services: Social science perspectives* (pp. 139–176). Boston, MA: Auburn House.

Raven, B. H., & Haley, R. W. (1980). Social influence in a medical context: Hospital-acquired infections as a problem in medical social psychology. In L. Bickman (Ed.), *Applied social psychology annual* (Vol. 1, pp. 255–278). Beverly Hills, CA: Sage.

Rawles, J. M., & Haite, N. E. (1988). Patient and general practitioner delays in acute myocardial infarction. *British Medical Journal, 296,* 882–884.

Razavi, D., Delvaux, N., Farvacques, C., & Robaye, E. (1988). Immediate effectiveness of brief psychological training for health professionals dealing with terminally ill cancer patients: A controlled study. *Social Science and Medicine, 27,* 369–375.

Reader, G. C., Pratt, L., & Mudd, M. C. (1957). What patients expect from their doctors. *Modern Hospital, 89,* 88–94.

Redfield, J., & Stone, A. (1979). Individual viewpoints of stressful life events. *Journal of Consulting and Clinical Psychology, 47,* 147–154.

Reed, D. R., Contreras, R. J., Maggio, C., Greenwoods, M. R. C., & Rodin, J. (1988). Weight cycling in female rats increases dietary fat selection and adiposity. *Physiology and Behavior, 42,* 389–395.

Reed, G. M. (1989). *Stress, coping, and psychological adaptation in a sample of gay and bisexual men with AIDS.* Unpublished doctoral dissertation, University of California, Los Angeles.

Reed, G. M., Taylor, S. E., & Kemeny, M. E. (1990). *Perceived control and psychological adjustment in gay men with AIDS.* Manuscript submitted for publication.

Reeves, J. C., & Shapiro, D. (1978). Biofeedback and relaxation in essential hypertension. *International Review of Applied Psychology, 26,* 121–135.

Reeves, R. S., Foreyt, J. P., Scott, L. W., Mitchell, R. E., Wohlleb, M. S., & Gotto, A. M. (1983). Effects of a low-cholesterol eating plan on plasma lipids: Results of a three-year community study. *American Journal of Public Health, 73,* 873–877.

Reich, W. P., Parrella, D. P., & Filstead, W. J. (1988). Unconfounding the hassles scale: External sources versus internal responses to stress. *Journal of Behavioral Medicine, 11,* 239–250.

Reif, J. (1990). If dogs could talk. *East West, 20,* 13.

Reisinger, K. S., & Bires, J. A. (1980). Anticipatory guidance in pediatric practice. *Pediatrics, 66,* 889–892.

Reisinger, K. S., & Williams, A. F. (1978). Evaluation of programs designed to increase the protection of infants in cars. *Journal of Pediatrics, 62,* 280–287.

Reite, M., Harbeck, R., & Hoffman, A. (1981). Altered cellular immune response following peer separation. *Life Sciences, 29,* 1133–1136.

Renneker, R. (1981). Cancer and psychotherapy. In J. G. Goldberg (Ed.), *Psychotherapeutic treatment of cancer patients* (pp. 131–166). New York: Free Press.

Renneker, R., & Cutler, M. (1952). Psychological problems of adjustment to cancer of the breast. *Journal of the American Medical Association, 148,* 833–838.

Repetti, R. L., Matthews, K. A., & Waldrun, I. (1989). Employment and women's health. *American Psychologist, 44,* 1394–1401.

Revicki, D. A., & May, H. J. (1985). Occupational stress, social support, and depression. *Health Psychology, 4,* 61–77.

Reynolds, D. V. (1969). Surgery in the rat during electrical analgesia induced by focal brain stimulation. *Science, 164,* 444–445.

Reynolds, P., & Kaplan, G. (1986, March). *Social connections and cancer: A prospective study of Alameda County residents.* Paper presented at the annual meeting of the Society of Behavioral Medicine, San Francisco, CA.

Rhodewalt, F., & Marcroft, M. (1988). Type A behavior and diabetic control: Implications of psychological reactance for health outcomes. *Journal of Applied Social Psychology, 18,* 139–159.

Rhodewalt, F., & Strube, M. J. (1985). A self-attribution-reactance model of recovery from injury in Type A individuals. *Journal of Applied Social Psychology, 15,* 330–344.

Rhodewalt, F., & Zone, J. B. (1989) Appraisal of life change, depression, and illness in hardy and nonhardy women. *Journal of Personality and Social Psychology, 56,* 81–88.

Richardson, J. L., Marks, G., Johnson, C. A., Graham, J. W., Chan, K. K., Selser, J. N., Kishbaugh, C., Barranday, Y., & Levine, A. M. (1987). Path model of multidimensional compliance with cancer therapy. *Health Psychology, 6,* 183–207.

Richardson, S. A., Goodman, N., Hastorf, A. H., & Dornbusch, S. M. (1961). Cultural uniformity in reaction to physical disabilities. *American Sociological Review, 26,* 241–247.

Richter-Heinrich, E., Enderlein, J., Knust, U., Schmidt, K. H., & Wiedemann, R. (1989). Effects of a breath relaxation training. *Systems Research in Physiology* (Vol. 3, pp. 239–249). Amsterdam, The Netherlands: Gordon & Breach.

Richter-Heinrich, E., Homuth, B., Heinrich, B., Knust, U., Schmidt, K. H., Wiedemann, R., & Gohlke, H. R. (1988). Behavioral therapies in essential hypertensives: A controlled study. In T. Elbert, W. Langosch, A. Steptoe, & D. Vaitl (Eds.), *Behavioural medicine in cardiovascular disorders* (pp. 113–127). London, England: Wiley.

Riffenbaugh, R. S. (1966). The doctor-patient relationship in glaucoma therapy. *Archives of Opthamology, 75,* 204–206.

Rigotti, N. A., Thomas, G. S., & Leaf, A. (1983). Exercise and coronary heart disease. *Annual Review of Medicine, 34,* 391–412.

Riley, M. W., Matarazzo, J. D., & Baum, A. (Eds.) (1987). *Perspectives in behavioral medicine: The aging dimension.* Hillsdale, NJ: Erlbaum.

Rimer, B., Levy, M. H., Keintz, M. K., Fox, L., Engstrom, P. F., & MacElwee, N. (1987). Enhancing cancer pain control regimens through patient education. *Patient Education and Counseling, 10,* 267–277.

Rimm, D. C., & Masters, J. C. (1974). *Behavior therapy: Techniques and empirical findings.* New York: Academic Press.

Ringler, K. E. (1981). *Processes of coping with cancer chemotherapy.* Unpublished doctoral dissertation, University of Wisconsin, Madison.

Rippetoe, P. A., & Rogers, R. W. (1987). Effects of components of protection-motivation theory on adaptive & maladaptive coping with a health threat. *Journal of Personality and Social Psychology, 52,* 596–604.

Ritter, B. (1968). The group treatment of children's snake phobias using vicarious and contact desensitization procedures. *Behavior Research and Therapy, 6,* 1–6.

Roberts, A. H. (1985). Biofeedback: Research, training, and clinical roles. *American Psychologist, 40,* 938–941.

Roberts, A. H. (in press). Biofeedback and chronic pain: An update. *Journal of Pain and Symptom Management.*

Roberts, M. C., & Turner, D. S. (1984). Preventing death and injury in childhood: A synthesis of child safety seat efforts. *Health Education Quarterly, 11,* 181–193.

Roberts, W. C., Wurtele, S. K., Boone, R. R., Ginther, L. H., & Elkins, P. D. (1981). Reduction of medical fears by use of modeling: A preventive application in a general population of children. *Journal of Pediatric Psychology, 6,* 293–300.

Robertson, E. K., & Suinn, R. M. (1968). The determination of rate of progress of stroke patients through empathy measures of patient and family. *Journal of Psychosomatic Research, 12,* 189–191.

Robertson, K., Kelley, A., O'Neill, B., Wixom, C., Eisworth, R., & Haddon, W., Jr. (1974). A controlled study of the effect of television messages on safety belt use. *American Journal of Public Health, 64,* 1071–1080.

Robertson, L. S. (1975). Factors associated with safety-belt use in 1974 starter-interlock equipped cars. *Journal of Health and Social Behavior, 16,* 173–177.

Robinson, D. (1979). *Talking out of alcoholism: The self-help process of Alcoholics Anonymous.* London, England: Croom, Helm.

Robinson, R. G. (1986). Post-stroke mood disorder. *Hospital Practice, 21,* 83–89.

Robinson, R. G., & Benson, D. F. (1981). Depression in aphasia patients: Frequency, severity, and clinical-pathological correlations. *Brain and Language, 14,* 282–291.

Robinson, R. G., & Price, T. R. (1982). Post-stroke depressive disorders: A follow-up study of 103 patients. *Stroke, 13,* 635–640.

Robinson, R. R., (Ed.). (1974). *Proceedings of the Francis E. Camp international symposium on sudden and unexpected deaths in infancy.* Toronto, Canada: Canadian Foundation for the Study of Infant Deaths.

Roccella, E. J., & Horan, M. J. (1988). The National High Blood Pressure Education Program: Measuring progress and assessing its impact. *Health Psychology, 7*(Suppl.), 297–303.

Rodin, G., & Voshart, K. (1986). Depression in the medically ill: An overview. *American Journal of Psychiatry, 143,* 696–705.

Rodin, J. (1981). Current status of the internal-external hypothesis for obesity: What went wrong? *American Psychologist, 36,* 361–372.

Rodin, J. (1987). Weight change following smoking cessation: The role of food intake and exercise. *Addictive Behaviors, 12,* 303–317.

Rodin, J., & Plante, T. (1989). The psychological effects of exercise. In R. S. Williams and A. Wellece (Eds.), *Biological effects of physical activity* (pp. 127–137). Champaign, IL: Human Kinetics.

Rodin, J., Elias, M., Silberstein, L. R., & Wagner, A. (1988). Combined behavioral and pharmacologic treatment for obesity: Predictors of successful weight maintenance. *Journal of Consulting and Clinical Psychology, 56,* 399–404.

Rodin, J., & Janis, I. L. (1979). The social power of health-care practitioners as agents of change. *Journal of Social Issues, 35,* 60–81.

Rodin, J., Reed, D., & Jamner, L. (1988). Metabolic effects of fructose and glucose: Implications for food intake. *American Journal of Clinical Nursing, 47,* 683–689.

Rodin, J., Schank, D., & Striegel-Moore, R. (1989). Psychological features of obesity. *Medical Clinics of North America, 73,* 247–346.

Rodin, J., Silberstein, L. R., & Striegel-Moore, R. H. (1990). Vulnerability and resilience in the age of eating disorders: Risk and protective factors for bulimia. In J. E. Rolf, A. Masten, D. Cicchetti, K. Neuchterlein, & S. Weintraub (Eds.), *Risk and protective factors in the development of psychopathology* (pp. 361–383). Cambridge, England: Cambridge University Press.

Roessler, R., Cate, T. R., Lester, J. W., & Couch, R. B. (1979, March). *Ego strength, life events, and antibody titer.* Paper presented at the annual meeting of the American Psychosomatic Society, Dallas, TX.

Rogentine, G. N., Van Kammen, D., Fox, B., Docherty, J., Rosenblatt, J., Boyd, S., & Bunney, W. (1979). Psychological factors in the prognosis of malignant melanoma: A prospective study. *Psychosomatic Medicine, 41,* 647–655.

Rogers, W. (1984). Changing health-related attitudes and behavior: The role of preventive health psychology. In J. H. Harvey, E. Maddux, R. P., McGlynn, & C. D. Stoltenberg (Eds.), *Social perception in clinical and counseling psychology* (Vol. 2, pp. 91–112). Lubbock, TX: Texas Tech University Press.

Roghmann, K. J., & Haggerty, R. J. (1973). Daily stress, illness, and use of health services in young families. *Pediatric Research, 7,* 520–526.

Rojan, J., & Gerhards, F. (1986). Subjective stress sensitivity and physiological responses to an aversive auditory stimulus in migraine and control subjects. *Journal of Behavioral Medicine, 9,* 203–212.

Rook, K. S. (1984). The negative side of social interaction: Impact on psychological well-being. *Journal of Personality and Social Psychology, 46,* 1097–1108.

Rose, G., Tunstall-Pedoe, H. D., & Heller, R. F. (1983). U.K. heart disease prevention project: Incidence and mortality results. *Lancet, 2,* 1062–1065.

Rose, R. M. (1980). Endocrine responses to stressful psychological events. *Psychiatric Clinics of North America, 3,* 251–276.

Rosen, J. C., & Gross, J. (1987). Prevalence of weight reducing and weight gaining in adolescent girls and boys. *Health Psychology, 6,* 131–147.

Rosen, J. C., Grubman, J. A., Bevins, T., & Frymoyer, J. W. (1987). Musculoskeletal status and disability of MMPI profile subgroups among patients with low back pain. *Health Psychology, 6,* 581–598.

Rosen, R. C., & Kostis, J. B. (1985). Biobehavioral sequellae associated with adrenergic-inhibiting antihypertensive agents: A critical review. *Health Psychology, 4,* 579–604.

Rosenman, R. H. (1978). The interview method of assessment of the coronary-prone behavior pattern. In T. Dembroski, S. Weiss, J. Shields, S. Haynes, & M. Feinleib (Eds.), *Coronary-prone behavior.* New York: Springer.

Rosenman, R. H. (1986). Health consequences of anger and implications for treatment. *Activitas Nervosa Superior, 28,* 1–23.

Rosenman, R. H. (1987). Type A behavior and hypertension. In S. Julius & D. R. Bassett (Eds.), *Handbook of hypertension: Vol. 9. Behavioral factors in hypertension* (pp. 141–149). North Holland: Elsevier.

Rosenstock, I. M. (1966). Why people use health services. *Milbank Memorial Fund Quarterly, 44,* 94ff.

Rosenstock, I. M. (1974a). Historical origins of the health belief model. *Health Education Monographs, 2,* 328–335.

Rosenstock, I. M. (1974b). The health belief model and preventive health behavior. *Health Education Monographs, 2,* 354–386.

Rosenstock, I. M., Derryberry, M., & Carriger, B. (1959). Why people fail to seek poliomyelitis vaccination. *Public Health Reports, 74,* 98–103.

Rosenstock, I. M., & Kirscht, J. (1979). Why people use health services. In A. Stone, F. Cohen, & N. E. Adler (Eds.), *Health psychology* (pp. 189–206). San Francisco: Jossey-Bass.

Roskies, E. (1980). Considerations in developing a treatment program for the coronary-prone (Type A) behavior pattern. In P. O. Davidson & S. M. Davidson (Eds.), *Behavioral medicine: Changing health lifestyles* (pp. 38–69). New York: Brunner/Mazel.

Roskies, E., Seraganian, R., Hanley, J. A., Collu, R., Martin, N., & Smilga, C. (1986). The Montreal Type A intervention project: Major findings. *Health Psychology, 5,* 45–69.

Roskies, E., Spevack, M., Surkis, A., Cohen, C., & Gilman, S. (1978). Changing the coronary-prone (Type A) behavior pattern in a nonclinical population. *Journal of Behavioral Medicine, 1,* 201–216.

Ross, C. E., & Duff, R. S. (1982). Returning to the doctor: The effect of client characteristics, type of practice, and experiences with care. *Journal of Health and Social Behavior, 23,* 119–131.

Ross, C. E., & Huber, J. (1985). Hardship and depression. *Journal of Health and Social Behavior, 26,* 312–327.

Ross, C. E., & Mirowsky, J. (1979). A comparison of life-event-weighing schemes: Change, undesirability, and effect-proportional indices. *Journal of Health and Social Behavior, 20,* 166–177.

Ross, C. E., & Mirowsky, J. (1988). Child care and emotional adjustment to wives' employment. *Journal of Health and Social Behavior, 29,* 127–138.

Ross, C. E., Mirowsky, J., & Duff, R. S. (1982). Physician status characteristics and client satisfaction in two types of medical practice. *Journal of Health and Social Behavior, 23,* 317–329.

Ross, C. E., Wheaton, B., & Duff, R. S. (1981). Client satisfaction and the organization of medical practice: Why time counts. *Journal of Health and Social Behavior, 22,* 243–255.

Ross, E. D. (1981). The aprosodias. *Archives of Neurology, 38,* 561–569.

Ross, E. D. (1982). The divided self. *The Sciences, 22,* 8–12.

Ross, J. W. (1985). Hospice care for children: Psychosocial considerations. In K. Gardner (Ed.), *Quality of care for the terminally ill: An examination of the issues* (pp. 124–130). Chicago: Joint Commission on Accreditation of Hospitals.

Rossiter, E. M., Agras, W. S., & Losch, M. (1988). Changes in self-reported food intake in bulimics as a consequence of antidepressant treatment. *International Journal of Eating Disorders, 7,* 779–783.

Roth, H. P. (1987). Measurement of compliance. *Patient Education and Counseling, 10,* 107–116.

Roth, J. (1977). Some contingencies of the moral evaluation and control of clientele: The case of the hospital emergency service. *American Journal of Sociology, 1972,* 836–839.

Rotter, J. B. (1954). *Social learning and clinical psychology.* Englewood Cliffs, NJ: Prentice-Hall.

Rotter, J. B. (1966). Generalized expectancies for internal versus external control of reinforcement. *Psychological Monographs, 80* (whole No. 609, 1).

Roviaro, S., Holmes, D. S., & Holmsten, R. D. (1984). Influence of a cardiac rehabilitation program on the cardiovascular, psychological, and social functioning of cardiac patients. *Journal of Behavioral Medicine, 7,* 61–75.

Rowe, J. W., & Kahn, R. L. (1987). Human aging: Usual and successful. *Science, 237,* 143–149.

Rubenstein, E., & Federman, D. D. (Eds.). (1983). *Medicine.* New York: Scientific American, Inc.

Ruble, D. N. (1972). Premenstrual symptoms: A reinterpretation. *Science, 197,* 291–292.

Rudy, T. E., Kerns, R. D., & Turk, D. C. (1988). Chronic pain and depression: Toward a cognitive-behavioral mediation model. *Pain, 35,* 129–140.

Rundall, T. G., & Wheeler, J. R. C. (1979). The effect of income on use of preventive care: An evaluation of alternative explanations. *Journal of Health and Social Behavior, 20,* 397–406.

Ruskin, A., Beard, O. W., & Schaeffer, R. L. (1948). "Blast hypertension": Elevated arterial pressures in the victims of the Texas City disaster. *American Journal of Medicine, 4,* 228–236.

Russell, M. A. H. (1971a). Cigarette dependence: 1. Nature and classification. *British Medical Journal, 2,* 330–331.

Russell, M. A. H. (1971b). Cigarette smoking: Natural history of a dependence disorder. *British Journal of Medical Psychology, 44,* 1–16.

Rychtarik, R. G., Foy, D. W., Scott, T., Lokey, L., & Prue, D. M. (1987). Five–six-year follow-up of broad-spectrum behavioral treatment of alcoholism: Effects of training controlled drinking skills. *Journal of Consulting and Clinical Psychology, 55,* 106–108.

Safer, M. A., Tharps, Q. J., Jackson, T. C., & Leventhal, H. (1979). Determinants of three stages of delay in seeking care at a medical care clinic. *Medical Care, 17,* 11–29.

Sallis, J. F., Dimsdale, J. E., & Caine, C. (1988). Blood pressure reactivity in children. *Journal of Psychosomatic Research, 32,* 1–12.

Sallis, J. F., Patterson, T. L., Buono, M. J., Atkins, C. J., & Nader, P. R. (1988). Aggregation of physical activity habits in Mexican-American and Anglo families. *Journal of Behavioral Medicine, 11,* 31–42.

Salmon, P., Pearce, S., Smith, C. C. T., Heys, A., Manyande, A., Peters, N., & Rashid, J. (1988). The relationship of preoperative distress to endocrine and subjective responses to surgery: Support for Janis' theory. *Journal of Behavioral Medicine, 11,* 599–614.

Salonen, J. T., Heinonen, O. P., Kottke, T. E., & Puska, P. (1981). Change in health behavior in relation to estimated coronary heart disease risk during a community-based cardiovascular disease prevention program. *International Journal of Epidemiology, 10,* 343–354.

Salonen, J. T., Puska, P., & Mustaniemi, H. (1979). Changes in morbidity and mortality during a comprehensive community programme to control cardiovascular disease during 1972–77 in North Karelia. *British Medical Journal, 2,* 1178–1183.

Salovey, P., & Birnbaum, D. (1989). Influence of mood on health-relevant cognitions. *Journal of Personality and Social and Psychology, 57,* 539–551.

Salovey, P., Rudy, T. E., & Turk, D. C. (1987). Preaching and practicing: The structure and consistency of health-protective attitudes and behaviors. *Health Education Research, 2,* 195–205.

Saltzer, E. B. (1978). Locus of control and the intention to lose weight. *Health Education Monographs, 6,* 118–128.

Samora, J., Saunders, L., & Larson, R. F. (1961). Medical vocabulary knowledge among hospital patients. *Journal of Health and Social Behavior, 2,* 83–89.

Sarason, I. G., Johnson, J. H., & Siegel, J. M. (1978). Assessing the impact of life changes: Development of the Life Experiences Survey. *Journal of Consulting and Clinical Psychology, 46,* 932–946.

Sarason, I. G., & Sarason, B. R. (1984). Life changes, moderators of stress, and health. In A. Baum, S. E. Taylor, & J. E. Singer (Eds.), *Handbook of psychology and health: Vol 4. Social psychological aspects of health* (pp. 279–300). Hillsdale, NJ: Erlbaum.

Sargent, J. D., Solbach, P., Coyne, L., Spohn, H., & Segerson, J. (1986). Results of a controlled, experimental, outcome study of nondrug treatments for the control of migraine headaches. *Journal of Behavioral Medicine, 9,* 291–323.

Sargent, J. D., & Walters, E. D. (1972). The use of autogenic feedback training in a pilot study of migraine and tension headaches. *Headache, 12,* 120–124.

Sargent, J. D., Walters, E. D., & Green, E. E. (1973). Psychosomatic self-regulation of migraine headaches. *Seminars in Psychiatry, 5,* 415–428.

Saunders, C. (1977). Dying they live: St. Christopher's Hospice. In H. Feifel (Ed.), *New meanings of death* (pp. 153–180). New York: McGraw-Hill.

Scarpaci, J. L. (1988). Help-seeking behavior, use, and satisfaction among frequent primary care users in Santiago de Chile. *Journal of Health and Social Behavior, 29,* 199–213.

Scarr, S., Phillips, D., & McCartney, K. (1989). Working mothers and their families. *American Psychologist, 44,* 1402–1409.

Schachter, S. (1968). Obesity and eating. *Science, 161,* 751–756.

Schachter, S. (1971). *Emotion, obesity and crime.* New York: Academic Press.

Schachter, S. (1982). Recidivism and self-cure of smoking and obesity. *American Psychologist, 37,* 436–444.

Schachter, S., Goldman, R., & Gordon, A. (1968). Effects of fear, food deprivation, and obesity on eating. *Journal of Personality and Social Psychology, 10,* 91–97.

Schachter, S., Kozlowski, L. T., & Silverstein, B. (1977) 2. Effects of urinary pH on cigarette smoking. *Journal of Experimental Psychology: General, 106,* 13–19.

Schachter, S., Silverstein, B., & Perlick, D. (1977).

5. Psychological and pharmacological explanations of smoking under stress. *Journal of Experimental Psychology: General, 106,* 31–40.

Schaefer, C., Coyne, J. C., & Lazarus, R. S. (1981). The health-related functions of social support. *Journal of Behavioral Medicine, 4,* 381–406.

Schaeffer, M. A., McKinnon, W., Baum, A., Reynolds, C. P., Rikli, P., Davidson, L. M., & Fleming, I. (1985). Immune status as a function of chronic stress at Three Mile Island. *Psychosomatic Medicine, 47,* 85 (abstract).

Schafer, L. C., Glasgow, R. E., & McCaul, K. D. (1982). Increasing the adherence of diabetic adolescents. *Journal of Behavioral Medicine, 5,* 353–362.

Schag, C. A. C., & Heinrich, R. L. (1986). The impact of cancer on daily living: A comparison with cardiac patients and healthy controls. *Rehabilitation Psychology, 31,* 157–167.

Schag, C. A. C., Heinrich, R. L., Aadland, R. L., & Ganz, P. A. (1990). Assessing problems of cancer patients: Psychometric properties of the cancer inventory of problem situations. *Health Psychology, 9,* 83–102.

Schain, W. S. (1976). Psychological issues in counseling mastectomy patients. *Counseling Psychologist, 6,* 45–49.

Scheier, M. F., & Carver, C. S. (1985). Optimism, coping, and health: Assessment and implications of generalized outcome expectancies. *Health Psychology, 4,* 219–247.

Scheier, M. F., Carver, C. S., & Gibbons, F. X. (1979). Self-directed attention, awareness of bodily states, and suggestibility. *Journal of Personality and Social Psychology, 37,* 1576–1588.

Scheier, M. F., Matthews, K. A., Owens, J., Magovern, G. J., Sr., Lefebvre, R. C., Abbott, R. A., & Carver, C. S. (1989). Dispositional optimism and recovery from coronary artery bypass surgery: The beneficial effects on physical and psychological well-being. *Journal of Personality and Social Psychology, 57,* 1024–1040.

Scheier, M. F., Weintraub, J. K., & Carver, C. S. (1986). Coping with stress: Divergent strategies of optimists and pessimists. *Journal of Personality and Social Psychology, 51,* 1257–1264.

Scherg, H. (1987). Psychosocial factors and disease bias in breast cancer patients. *Psychosomatic Medicine, 49,* 302–312.

Schieken, R. M. (1988). Preventive cardiology: An overview. *Journal of the American College of Cardiology, 12,* 1090–1091.

Schlegel, R. P., Wellwood, J. K., Copps, B. E., Gruchow, W. H., & Sharratt, M. T. (1980). The relationship between perceived challenge and daily symptom reporting in Type A vs. Type B postinfarct subjects. *Journal of Behavioral Medicine, 3,* 191–204.

Schleifer, S. J., Keller, S. E., Bond, R. N., Cohen, J., & Stein, M. (1989). Major depressive disorder and immunity: Role of age, sex, severity, and hospitalization. *Archives of General Psychiatry, 46,* 81–87.

Schleifer, S. J., Keller, S. E., Camerino, M., Thornton, J. C., & Stein, M. (1983). Suppression of lymphocyte stimulation following bereavement. *Journal of the American Medical Association, 250,* 374–377.

Schleifer, S. J., Keller, S. E., Meyerson, A. T., Raskin, M. J., Davis, K. L., & Stein, M. (1984). Lymphocyte function in major depressive disorder. *Archives of General Psychiatry, 41,* 484–486.

Schleifer, S. J., Keller, S. E., Siris, S. G., Davis, K. L., & Stein, M. (1985). Depression and immunity: Lymphocyte function in ambulatory depressed patients, hospitalized schizophrenic patients, and patients hospitalized for herniorraphy. *Archives of General Psychiatry, 42,* 129–133.

Schleifer, S. J., Scott, B., Stein, M., & Keller, S. E. (1986). Behavioral and developmental aspects of immunity. *Journal of the American Academy of Child Psychiatry, 26,* 751–763.

Schmale, A. H., & Iker, H. (1971). Hopelessness as a predictor of cervical cancer. *Social Science and Medicine, 5,* 95–100.

Schmelkin, L. P., Wachtel, A. B., Schneiderman, B. E., & Hecht, D. (1988). The dimensional structure of medical students' perceptions of diseases. *Journal of Behavioral Medicine, 11,* 171–184.

Schmitt, E., & Wooldridge, J. (1973). Psychological preparation of surgical patients. *Nursing Research, 22,* 108–116.

Schneider, J. A., O'Leary, A., & Agras, W. S. (1987). The role of perceived self-efficacy in recovery from bulimia: A preliminary examination. *Behavioral Research and Therapy, 25,* 429–432.

Schneidman, E. S. (1977). The college student and death. In H. Feifel (Ed.), *New meanings of death.* New York: McGraw-Hill.

Schoenberg, B., Carr, A. C., Peretz, D., &

Kutscher, A. H. (Eds.). (1970). *Loss and grief* (pp. 67–88). New York: Columbia University Press.

Schoenberg, B., Carr, A. C., Peretz, D., & Kutscher, A. H. (1977). *Psychological aspects of terminal care.* New York: Columbia University Press.

Schreiner-Engel, P., Schiavi, R. C., Vietorisz, D., & Smith, H. (1987). The differential impact of diabetes type on female sexuality. *Journal of Psychosomatic Research, 31,* 23–33.

Schroeder, D. H., & Costa, P. T., Jr. (1984). Influence of life event stress on physical illness: Substantive effects or methodological flaws? *Journal of Personality and Social Psychology, 46,* 853–863.

Schuckitt, M. A. (1981). The genetics of alcoholism. *Alcoholism: Clinical and Experimental Research, 5,* 439–440.

Schultheis, K., Peterson, L., & Selby, V. (1987). Preparation for stressful medical procedures and person × treatment interactions. *Clinical Psychology Review, 7,* 329–352.

Schulz, R. (1978). *The psychology of death, dying, and bereavement.* Reading, MA: Addison-Wesley.

Schulz, R., & Aderman, D. (1974). Clinical research and the stages of dying. *Omega, 5,* 137–143.

Schulz, R., & Decker, S. (1985). Long-term adjustment to physical disability: The role of social support, perceived control, and self-blame. *Journal of Personality and Social Psychology, 48,* 1162–1172.

Schulz, R., Tompkins, C., Wood, D., & Decker, S. (1987). The social psychology of caregiving: The physical and psychological costs of providing support to the disabled. *Journal of Applied Social Psychology, 17,* 401–428.

Schumaker, S. A., & Grunberg, N. E. (Eds.). (1986). Proceedings of the National Working Conference on Smoking Relapse. *Health Psychology, 5* (whole Suppl.), 1–99.

Schwab, J. J. & Hameling, J. (1968). Body image and medical illness. *Psychosomatic Medicine, 30,* 51–71.

Schwartz, G. E. (1982). Testing the biopsychosocial model: The ultimate challenge facing behavioral medicine? *Journal of Consulting and Clinical Psychology, 50,* 1040–1053.

Schwartz, L. S., Springer, J., Flaherty, J. A., & Kiani, R. (1986). The role of recent life events and social support in the control of diabetes mellitus. *General Hospital Psychiatry, 8,* 212–216.

Scott, D. W. (1983). Anxiety, critical thinking, and information processing during and after breast biopsy. *Nursing Research, 32,* 24–28.

Scrimshaw, S. M., Engle, P. L., & Zambrana, R. E. (1983, August). *Prenatal anxiety and birth outcome in U.S. Latinas: Implications for psychosocial interventions.* Paper presented at the annual meeting of the American Psychological Association, Anaheim, CA.

Seeman, M., & Anderson, C. S. (1983). Alienation and alcohol: The role of work, mastery, and community in drinking behavior. *American Sociological Review, 48,* 60–77.

Seeman, M., Seeman, A. Z., & Budros, A. (1988). Powerlessness, work, and community: A longitudinal study of alienation and alcohol use. *Journal of Health and Social Behavior, 29,* 185–198.

Seligman, M. E. P. (1975). *Helplessness: On depression, development and death.* San Francisco: Freeman.

Seligman, M. E. P. (1979). *Helplessness.* San Francisco: Freeman.

Seligman, A. W., McGrath, N. E., & Pratt, L. (1957). Level of medical information among clinic patients. *Journal of Chronic Diseases, 6,* 497–509.

Selye, H. (1956). *The stress of life.* New York: McGraw-Hill.

Selye, H. (1974). *Stress without distress.* Philadelphia: Lippincott.

Selye, H. (1976). *Stress in health and disease.* Woburn, MA: Butterworth.

Serfass, R. C., & Gerberich, S. G. (1984). Exercise for optimal health: Strategies and motivational considerations. *Preventive Medicine, 13,* 79–99.

Sexton, M. M. (1979). Behavioral epidemiology. In O. F. Pomerleau & J. P. Brady (Eds.), *Behavioral medicine: Theory and practice* (pp. 3–22). Baltimore, MD: Williams & Wilkins.

Shaffer, W. J., Duszynski, K. R., & Thomas, C. B. (1982). Family attitudes in youth as a possible precursor of cancer among physicians: A search for explanatory mechanisms. *Journal of Behavioral Medicine, 5,* 143–164.

Shapiro, A. K. (1960). A contribution to a history of the placebo effect. *Behavioral Science, 5,* 109–135.

Shapiro, A. K. (1964). Factors contributing to the placebo effect: Their implications for psychotherapy. *American Journal of Psychotherapy, 18,* 73–88.

Shapiro, A. K. (1978). Placebo effects in medical and psychological therapies. In S. L. Garfield & A. E. Bergen (Eds.), *Handbook of psychotherapy and behavior change: An empirical analysis.* New York: Wiley.

Shapiro, A. P., Schwartz, G. E., Ferguson, D. C. E., Redmond, D. P., & Weiss, S. M. (1977). Behavioral methods in the treatment of hypertension: A review of their clinical status. *Annals of Internal Medicine, 86,* 626–636.

Shapiro, D., & Goldstein, I. B. (1982). Biobehavioral perspectives on hypertension. *Journal of Consulting and Clinical Psychology, 50,* 841–858.

Shapiro, D., Lane, J. D., & Henry, J. P. (1988). Caffeine, cardiovascular reactivity, and cardiovascular disease. In K. A. Matthews, S. M. Weiss, T. Detre, T. M. Dembroski, B. Falkner, S. B. Manuck, & R. M. Williams, Jr. (Eds.), *Handbook of stress, reactivity, and cardiovascular disease: Status and prospects* (pp. 311–327). New York: Wiley.

Shapiro, D., & Surwit, R. S. (1979). Biofeedback. In O. F. Pomerleau & J. P. Brady (Eds.), *Behavioral medicine: Theory and practice* (pp. 45–74). Baltimore, MD: Williams & Wilkins.

Shapiro, D., Tursky, B., Schwartz, G. E., & Shnidman, S. R. (1971). Smoking on cue: A behavioral approach to smoking reduction. *Journal of Health and Social Behavior, 12,* 108–113.

Sharpe, T. R., Smith, M. C., & Barbre, A. R. (1985). Medicine use among the rural elderly. *Journal of Health and Social Behavior, 26,* 113–127.

Shattuck, F. C. (1907). The science and art of medicine in some of their aspects. *Boston Medical and Surgical Journal, 157,* 63–67.

Sheehy, G. (1974). *Passages.* New York: Dutton.

Shekelle, R. B., Raynor, W. J., Ostfeld, A. M., Garron, D. C., Bieliauskas, L. A., Liu, S. C., Maliza, C., & Oglesby, P. (1981). Psychological depression and 17-year risk of death from cancer. *Psychosomatic Medicine, 43,* 117–125.

Shelton, J. L., & Levy, R. L. (1981). *Behavioral assignments and treatment compliance: A handbook of clinical strategies.* Champaign, IL: Research Press.

Shepard, R. J. (1986). Exercise in coronary heart disease. *Sports Medicine, 3,* 26–49.

Sher, L. (1987). An evaluation of the U.K. government health education campaign on AIDS. *Psychology and Health: An International Journal, 1,* 61–72.

Shiffman, S., Read, L., Maltese, J., Rapkin, D., & Jarvik, M. E. (1985). Preventing relapse in ex-smokers: A self-management approach. In G. A. Marlatt & J. R. Gordon (Eds.), *Relapse prevention: Maintenance strategies in the treatment of addictive*

behaviors (pp. 472–520). New York: Guilford Press.

Shilts, R. (1987). *And the band played on: Politics, people, and the AIDS epidemic.* New York: St. Martin's Press.

Shinn, M., Rosario, M., Morch, H., & Chestnut, D. E. (1984). Coping with job stress and burnout in the human services. *Journal of Personality and Social Psychology, 46,* 864–876.

Shipley, R. H., Butt, J. H., Horwitz, B., & Farbry, J. E. (1978). Preparation for a stressful medical procedure: Effect of amount of stimulus preexposure and coping style. *Journal of Consulting and Clinical Psychology, 46,* 499–507.

Shirom, A., Eden, D., Silberwasser, S., & Kellerman, J. J. (1973). Job stresses and risk factors in coronary heart disease among occupational categories in kibbutzim. *Social Science and Medicine, 7,* 875–892.

Shumaker, S. A., & Pequegnat, W. (1989). Hospital design, health providers, and the delivery of effective health care. In E. H. Zube & G. T. Moore (Eds.), *Advances in environment, behavior, and design* (Vol. 2, pp. 161–199). New York: Plenum.

Shuval, J. T., Antonovsky, A., & Davies, A. M. (1973). Illness: A mechanism for coping with failure. *Social Science and Medicine, 7,* 259–265.

Sidney, S., Friedman, G. D., & Siegelaub, A. B. (1987). Thinness and mortality. *American Journal of Public Health, 77,* 317–322.

Siegel, B. S. (1986). *Love, medicine, and miracles.* New York: Harper & Row.

Siegel, D., Grady, D., Browner, W. S., & Hulley, S. B. (1988). Risk factor modification after myocardial infarction. *Annals of Internal Medicine, 109,* 213–218.

Siegel, J. M. (1984). Anger and cardiovascular risk in adolescents. *Health Psychology, 3,* 293–313.

Siegel, K., Mesagno, F. P., Chen, J. Y., & Christ, G. (1987, June). *Factors distinguishing homosexual males practicing safe and risky sex.* Paper presented at the Third International Conference on AIDS, Washington, DC.

Siegman, A. W., Dembroski, T. M., & Ringel, N. (1987). Components of hostility and the severity of coronary artery disease. *Psychosomatic Medicine, 49,* 127–135.

Silberstein, L. R., Striegel-Moore, R. H., & Rodin, J. (1987). Feeling fat: A woman's shame. In H. B.

Lewis (Ed.), *The role of shame in symptom formation.* Hillsdale, NJ: Erlbaum.

Silver, B. V., & Blanchard, E. B. (1978). Biofeedback and relaxation training in the treatment of psychophysiological disorders: Or are the machines really necessary? *Journal of Behavioral Medicine, 1,* 217–240.

Silver, R. L. (1982). *Coping with an undesirable life event: A study of early reactions to physical disability.* Unpublished doctoral dissertation, Northwestern University, Evanston, IL.

Silver, R. L., Boon, C., & Stones, M. (1983). Searching for meaning in misfortune: Making sense of incest. *Journal of Social Issues, 39,* 81–102.

Silver, R. L., & Wortman, C. B. (1980). Coping with undesirable life events. In J. Garber & M. E. P. Seligman (Eds.), *Human helplessness: Theory and applications.* New York: Academic Press.

Simonton, O. C., & Simonton, S. (1975). Belief systems and management of the emotional aspects of malignancy. *Journal of Transpersonal Psychology, 7,* 29–48.

Sims, S. E. R. (1987). Relaxation training as a technique for helping patients cope with the experience of cancer: A selective review of the literature. *Journal of Advanced Nursing, 12,* 583–591.

Singer, J. E., Lundberg, U., & Frankenhaeuser, M. (1978). Stress on the train: A study of urban commuting. In A. Baum, J. E. Singer, & S. Valins (Eds.), *Advances in environmental psychology* (Vol. 1). Hillsdale, NJ: Erlbaum.

Sinyor, D., Amato, P., Kaloupek, D. G., Becker, R., Goldenberg, M., & Coopersmith, H. (1986). Post-stroke depression: Relationships to functional impairment, coping strategies, and rehabilitation outcomes. *Stroke, 17,* 1102–1107.

Skelton, J. A., & Pennebaker, J. (1978, August). *Dispositional determinants of symptom reporting: Correlational evidence.* Paper presented at the annual meeting of the American Psychological Association, Toronto, Canada.

Skelton, M., & Dominian, J. (1973). Psychological stress in wives of patients with myocardial infarction. *British Medical Journal, 2,* 101.

Skinner, B. F. (1938). *The behavior of organisms.* New York: Appleton.

Skipper, J., & Leonard, R. (Eds.). (1965). *Social interaction and patient care.* Philadelphia: Lippincott.

Skipper, J., Tagliacozzo, D., & Manksch, H. (1964). Some possible consequences of limited communication between patients and hospital functionaries. *Journal of Health and Social Behavior, 5,* 34–39.

Sklar, L. S., & Anisman, H. (1981). Stress and cancer. *Psychological Bulletin, 89,* 369–406.

Slater, C., & Carlton, B. (1985). Behavior, lifestyle, and socioeconomic variables as determinants of health status: Implications for health policy development. *American Journal of Preventive Medicine, 1,* 25–33.

Sleet, D. A. (1984). Reducing motor vehicle trauma through health promotion programming. *Health Education Quarterly, 11,* 113–125.

Slesinger, D. (1976). The utilization of preventive medical services by urban black mothers. In D. Mechanic (Ed.), *The growth of bureaucratic medicine.* New York: Wiley.

Smith, T. W. (1989). Interactions, transactions, and the Type A pattern: Additional avenues in the search for coronary-prone behavior. In A. W. Siegman & T. M. Dembroski (Eds.), *In search of coronary-prone behavior: Beyond Type A* (pp. 91–116). Hillsdale, NJ: Erlbaum.

Smith, T. W., Allred, K. D., Morrison, C. A., & Carlson, S. D. (1989). Cardiovascular reactivity and interpersonal influence: Active coping in a social context. *Journal of Personality and Social Psychology, 56,* 209–218.

Smith, T. W., & Frohm, K. D. (1985). What's so unhealthy about hostility? Construct validity and psychosocial correlates of the Cook and Medley HO scale. *Health Psychology, 4,* 503–520.

Smith, T. W., O'Keefe, J. L., & Allred, K. D. (1989). Neuroticism, symptom reports, and Type A behavior: Interpretive cautions for the Framingham scale. *Journal of Behavioral Medicine, 12,* 1–12.

Smith, T. W., Peck, J. R., Milano, R. A., & Ward, J. R. (1988). Cognitive distortion in rheumatoid arthritis: Relation to depression and disability. *Journal of Consulting and Clinical Psychology, 56,* 412–416.

Smith, T. W., Pope, M. K., Rhodewalt, F., & Poulton, J. L. (1989). Optimism, neuroticism, coping, and symptom reports: An alternative interpretation of the life orientation test. *Journal of Personality and Social Psychology, 56,* 640–648.

Smith, T. W., Turner, C. W., Ford, M. H., Hunt, S. C., Barlow, G. K., Stults, B. M., & Williams, R. R. (1987). Blood pressure reactivity in adult male twins. *Health Psychology, 6,* 209–220.

Sobal, J., & Stunkard, A. J. (1989). Socioeconomic status and obesity: A review of the literature. *Psychological Bulletin, 105,* 260–275.

Sobel, H. (1981). Toward a behavioral thanatology in clinical care. In H. Sobel (Ed.), *Behavioral therapy in terminal care: A humanistic approach* (pp. 3–38). Cambridge, MA: Ballinger.

Sobell, M. B., & Sobell, L. C. (1973). Individualized behavior therapy for alcoholics. *Behavior Therapy, 4,* 49–72.

Solomon, D. H., Judd, H. L., Sier, H. C., Rubenstein, L. Z., & Morley, J. E. (1988). New issues in geriatric care. *Annals of Internal Medicine, 108,* 718–732.

Solomon, G. F., Amkraut, A. A., & Kasper, P. (1974). Immunity, emotions, and stress (with special reference to the mechanism of stress effects on the immunity system). *Annals of Clinical Research, 6,* 313–322.

Solomon, G. F., Fiatarone, M. A., Benton, D., Morley, J. E., Bloom, E., & Makinodan, T. (1988). Psychoimmunologic and endorphin function in the aged. *Annals of the New York Academy of Science, 521,* 43–58.

Solomon, G. F., & Temoshok, L. (1987). A psychoneuroimmunologic perspective on AIDS research: Questions, preliminary findings, and suggestions. *Journal of Applied Social Psychology, 17,* 286–308.

Solomon, Z., Mikulincer, M., & Avitzur, E. (1988). Coping, locus of control, social support, and combat-related posttraumatic stress disorder: A prospective study. *Journal of Personality and Social Psychology, 55,* 279–285.

Sommers-Flanagan, J., & Greenberg, R. P. (1989). Psychosocial variables and hypertension: A new look at an old controversy. *Journal of Nervous and Mental Disease, 177,* 15–24.

Sorensen, G., Jacobs, D. R., Pirie, P., Folsom, A., Luepker, R., & Gillum, R. (1987). Relationships among Type A behavior, employment experiences, and gender: The Minnesota Heart Survey. *Journal of Behavioral Medicine, 10,* 323–336.

Sorenson, G., & Pechacek, T. F. (1987). Attitudes toward smoking cessation among men and women. *Journal of Behavioral Medicine, 10,* 129–138.

Sorensen, G., Pirie, P., Folson, A., Luepker, R., Jacobs, D., & Gillum, R. (1985). Sex differences in the relationship between work and health:

The Minnesota heart survey. *Journal of Health and Social Behavior, 26,* 379–394.

Sorlie, P., Gordon, T., & Kannel, W. B. (1980). Body build and mortality—the Framingham study. *Journal of the American Medical Association, 243,* 1828–1831.

Sourkes, B. M. (1980). Siblings of the pediatric cancer patient. In J. Kellerman (Ed.), *Psychological aspects of childhood cancer.* Springfield, IL: Thomas.

Speisman, J., Lazarus, R. S., Mordkoff, A., & Davidson, L. (1964). Experimental reduction of stress based on ego defense theory. *Journal of Abnormal and Social Psychology, 68,* 367–380.

Spiegel, D., & Bloom, J. R. (in press). Group therapy and hypnosis reduce metastatic breast carcinoma pain. *Psychosomatic Medicine.*

Spiegel, D., Bloom, J. R., & Gottheil, E. (1983). Family environment as a predictor of adjustment to metastatic breast carcinoma. *Journal of Psychosocial Oncology, 1,* 33–44.

Spielberger, C. D. (1986). Psychological determinants of smoking behavior. In R. D. Tollison (Ed.), *Smoking and society: Toward a more balanced assessment* (pp. 89–134). Lexington, MA: Heath.

Spielberger, C. D., Johnson, E. H., Russell, S. F., Crane, R. J., Jacobs, G. A., & Worden, T. J. (1985). In M. A. Chesney & R. H. Rosenman (Eds.), *Anger and hostility in cardiovascular and behavioral disorders* (pp. 5–30). New York: Hemisphere/McGraw-Hill.

Spinetta, J. J. (1974). The dying child's awareness of death: A review. *Psychological Bulletin, 81,* 256–260.

Spinetta, J. J. (1982). Behavioral and psychological research in childhood cancer: An overview. *Cancer, 50*(Suppl.), 1939–1943.

Spinetta, J. J., Spinetta, P. D., Kung, F., & Schwartz, D. B. (1976). *Emotional aspects of childhood cancer and leukemia: A handbook for parents.* San Diego, CA: Leukemia Society of America.

Spitzer, L., & Rodin, J. (1987). Effects of fructose and glucose preloads on subsequent food intake. *Appetite, 8,* 135–145.

Stachnik, T. J., & Stoffelmayr, B. E. (1982). Is there a future for smoking cessation programs? *Journal of Health Education, 7,* 47–56

Stachnik, T. J., & Stoffelmayr, B. E. (1983). Worksite smoking cessation programs: A potential for national impact. *American Journal of Public Health, 73,* 1395–1396.

Stachnik, T. J., Stoffelmayr, B. E., & Hoppe, R. B. (1983). Prevention, behavior change, and chronic disease. In T. G. Burish & L. A. Bradley (Eds.), *Coping with chronic disease: Research and applications* (pp. 447–474). New York: Academic Press.

Stall, R., & Biernacki, P. (1986). Spontaneous remission from the problematic use of substances: An inductive model derived from a comparative analysis of the alcohol, opiate, tobacco, and food/obesity literatures. *International Journal of the Addictions, 21,* 1–23.

Stall, R. D., Coates, T. J., & Hoff, C. (1988). Behavioral risk reduction for HIV infection among gay and bisexual men: A review of results from the United States. *American Psychologist, 43,* 878–885.

Stall, R. D., Wiley, J. A., McKusick, L., Coates, T. J., & Ostrow, D. (1986). Alcohol and drug use during sexual activity and compliance with safe sex guidelines for AIDS: The AIDS Behavioral Research Project. *Health Education Quarterly, 13,* 359–371.

Stanton, A. L. (1987). Determinants of adherence to medical regimens by hypertensive patients. *Journal of Behavioral Medicine, 10,* 377–394.

Staub, E., Tursky, B., & Schwartz, G. E. (1971). Self-control and predictability: Their effects on reactions to averse stimulation. *Journal of Personality and Social Psychology, 18,* 157–162.

Steele, D. V., Gotmann, M., Leventhal, H., & Easterling, D. (1983). *Symptoms and attributions as determinants of health behavior.* Unpublished manuscript. University of Wisconsin Madison.

Steen, S. N., Oppliger, R. A., & Brownell, K. D. (1988). Metabolic effects of repeated weight loss and regain in adolescent wrestlers. *Journal of the American Medical Association, 260,* 47–50.

Stegman, M. R., Miller, P. J., Hageman, R. K., & Irby, D. E. (1987). Myocardial infarction survival: How important are patients' attitudes and adherence behaviors? *American Journal of Preventive Medicine, 3,* 147–151.

Stein, M. (1985). Bereavement, depression, stress, and immunity. In R. Guillemin, M. Cohen, & T. Meinechuk, (Eds.), *Neural modulation of immunity* (pp. 29–44). New York: Raven Press.

Steinberger, L. (1986). Stability (and instability) of Type A behavior from childhood to young adulthood. *Developmental Psychology, 22,* 393–402.

Steinhauser, P. D., Mushin, D. N., & Rae-Grant, A. (1974). Psychological aspects of chronic illness. *Pediatric Clinics of North America, 21,* 825–840.

Stephens, M. A., Kinney, J. M., Norris, V. K., & Ritchie, S. W. (1987). Social networks as assets and liabilities in recovery from stroke by geriatric patients. *Psychology and Aging, 2,* 125–129.

Stephenson, H. S., Adams, C. K., Hall, D. C., & Pennypacker, H. S. (1979). Effects of certain training parameters on detection of simulated breast cancer. *Journal of Behavioral Medicine, 2,* 239–250.

Stern, M. J., Pascale, L., & Ackerman, A. (1977). Life adjustment postmyocardial infarction: Determining predictive variables. *Archives of Internal Medicine, 137,* 1680–1685.

Sternbach, R. A. (1974). *Pain patients: Traits and treatment.* New York: Academic Press.

Sternbach, R. A. (1983). The tourniquet pain test. In R. Melzack (Ed.), *Pain measurement and assessment* (pp. 27–32). New York: Raven Press.

Sternbach, R. A., & Tursky, B. (1965). Ethnic differences among housewives in psychophysical and skin potential responses to electric shock. *Psychophysiology, 1,* 241–246.

Stevenson, I. P., Duncan, L., Wolf, P. O., Ripley, H., & Wolff, G. (1949). Life situations, emotions and extrasystoles. *Psychosomatic Medicine, 11,* 257–269.

Stoeckle, J. D., Zola, I. K., & Davidson, G. E. (1963). On going to see the doctor: The contributions of the patient to the decision to seek medical aid. *Journal of Chronic Diseases, 16,* 975–989.

Stokols, D., Novaco, R. W., Stokols, J., & Campbell, J. (1978). Traffic congestion, Type A behavior, and stress. *Journal of Applied Psychology, 63,* 467–480.

Stokols, D., Ohlig, W., & Resnick, S. M. (1978). Perception of residential crowding, classroom experiences, and student health. *Human Ecology, 6,* 33–57.

Stoller, E. P. (1984). Self-assessments of health by the elderly: The impact of informal assistance. *Journal of Health and Social Behavior, 25,* 260–270.

Stone, A. A. (1985). Assessment of coping efficacy: A comment. *Journal of Behavioral Medicine, 8,* 115–117.

Stone, A. A., Kennedy-Moore, E., Newman, M. G., Greenberg, M., & Neale, J. M. (in press). Conceptual and methodological issues in current coping assessments. In B. N. Carpenter (Ed.), *Personal coping theory, research, and application.*

Stone, A. A., & Neale, J. M. (1984). New measure of daily coping: Development and preliminary results. *Journal of Personality and Social Psychology, 46,* 892–906.

Stone, G. C. (1979). Psychology and the health system. In G. C. Stone, F. Cohen, & N. E. Adler (Eds.), *Health psychology.* San Francisco: Jossey-Bass.

Storer, J. H., Frate, D. M., Johnson, S. A., & Greenberg, A. M. (1987). When the cure seems worse than the disease: Helping families adapt to hypertension treatment. *Family Relations, 36,* 311–315.

Straus, R. (1988). Interdisciplinary biobehavioral research on alcohol problems: A concept whose time has come. *Drugs and Society, 2,* 33–48.

Strauss, A., Schatzman, L., Bucher, R., Erlich, D., & Sarshim, M. (1963). The hospital and its negotiated social order. In E. Freidson (Ed.), *The hospital in modern society* (pp. 147–169). New York: Free Press.

Strauss, L. M., Solomon, L. J., Costanza, M. C., Worden, J. K., & Foster, R. S., Jr. (1987). Breast self-examination practices and attitudes of women with and without a history of breast cancer. *Journal of Behavioral Medicine, 10,* 337–350.

Straw, M. K. (1983). Coping with obesity. In T. G. Burish & L. A. Bradley (Eds.), *Coping with chronic disease: Research and applications* (pp. 219–258). New York: Academic Press.

Strecher, V. J., DeVellis, B. M., Becker, M. H., & Rosenstock, I. M. (1986). The role of self-efficacy in achieving health behavior change. *Health Education Quarterly, 13,* 73–92.

Streissguth, A. P., Landesman-Dwyer, S., Martin, J. C., & Smith, D. W. (1980). Teratogenic effects of alcohol in humans and laboratory animals. *Science, 209,* 353–361.

Streufert, S., DePadova, A., McGlynn, T., Piasecki, M., & Pogash, R. (1989). Effects of beta blockage with metoprolol on simple and complex task performance. *Health Psychology, 8,* 373–385.

Strickland, B. R. (1978). Internal-external expectancies and health-related behaviors. *Journal of Consulting and Clinical Psychology, 46,* 1192–1211.

Striegel-Moore, R. H., Silberstein, L. R., Frensch, P., & Rodin, J. (1989). A prospective study of disordered eating among college students. *International Journal of Eating Disorders, 8,* 499–511.

Stroebe, M. S., & Stroebe, W. (1983). Who suffers more? Sex differences in health risks of the widowed. *Psychological Bulletin, 93,* 279–301.

Stroebe, W., & Stroebe, M. S. (1987). *Bereavement and health: The psychological and physical consequences of partner loss.* New York: Cambridge University Press.

Strogatz, D. S., & James, S. A. (1986). Social support and hypertension among blacks and whites in a rural, Southern community. *American Journal of Epidemiology, 124,* 949–956.

Strube, M., Turner, C., Cerro, D., Stevens, J., & Hinchey, F. (1984). Interpersonal aggression and the Type A coronary-prone behavior pattern: A theoretical distinction and practical implications. *Journal of Personality and Social Psychology, 47,* 839–847.

Stuart, R. B. (1967). Behavioral control of overeating. *Behavioral Research and Therapy, 5,* 357–365.

Stunkard, A. J. (1975). From explanation to action in psychosomatic medicine: The case of obesity. *Psychosomatic Medicine, 37,* 195–236.

Stunkard, A. J. (1979). Behavioral medicine and beyond: The example of obesity. In O. F. Pomerleau & J. P. Brady (Eds.), *Behavioral medicine: Theory and practice* (pp. 279–298). Baltimore, MD: Williams & Wilkins.

Stunkard, A. J. (1986). The control of obesity: Social and community perspectives. In K. D. Brownell & J. P. Foreyt (Eds.), *The physiology, psychology, and treatment of the eating disorders.* New York: Basic Books.

Stunkard, A. J. (1988). Some perspectives on human obesity: Its causes. *Bulletin of the New York Academy of Medicine, 64,* 902–923.

Stunkard, A. J., Cohen, R. Y., & Felix, M. R. J. (1989). Weight loss competitions at the work site: How they work and how well. *Journal of Preventive Medicine, 18,* 460–474.

Stunkard, A. J., Felix, M. R. J., & Cohen, R. Y. (1985). Mobilizing a community to promote health: The Pennsylvania County Health Improvement Program (CHIP). In J. C. Rosen & L. J. Solomon (Eds.) *Prevention in health psychology* (pp. 143–190). Hanover, NH: University Press of New England.

Stunkard, A. J., Sorensen, T. I. A., Hanis, C., Teasdale, T. W., Chakraborty, R., Schull, W. J., & Schulsinger, F. (1986). An adoption study of human obesity. *New England Journal of Medicine, 314,* 193–198.

Suchman, E. (1964). Sociomedical variations among ethnic groups. *American Journal of Sociology, 70,* 319–331.

Suinn, R. M. (1971). *The application of short-term videotape therapy for the treatment of test anxiety of college students. Final Report.* Fort Collins: Colorado State University Press.

Suinn, R. M. (1977). Type A behavior pattern. In R. Williams & W. D. Gentry (Eds.), *Behavioral approach to medical treatment.* Cambridge, MA: Bellinger.

Suls, J. (1982). Social support, interpersonal relations, and health: Benefits and liabilities. In G. S. Sanders & J. Suls (Eds.), *Social psychology of health and illness* (pp. 255–277). Hillsdale, NJ: Erlbaum.

Suls, J., & Fletcher, B. (1985). The relative efficacy of avoidant and nonavoidant coping strategies: A meta-analysis. *Health Psychology, 4,* 249–288.

Suls, J., & Mullen, B. (1981). Life change in psychological distress: The role of perceived control and desirability. *Journal of Applied Social Psychology, 11,* 379–389.

Suls, J., & Sanders, G. S. (1989). Why do some behavioral styles place people at coronary risk? In A. Siegman & T. Dembroski (Eds.), *In search of coronary-prone behavior: Beyond Type A* (pp. 1–20). Hillsdale, NJ: Erlbaum.

Suls, J., Sanders, G. S., & Lebrecque, M. S. (1986). Attempting to control blood pressure without systematic instruction: When advice is counterproductive. *Journal of Behavioral Medicine, 9,* 567–578.

Suls, J., & Wan, C. K. (1989). The relationship between Type A behavior and chronic emotional distress: A meta-analysis. *Journal of Personality and Social Psychology, 57,* 503–512.

Suls, J., Wan, C. K., & Sanders, G. S. (1988). False consensus and false uniqueness in estimating the prevalence of health-protective behaviors. *Journal of Applied Social Psychology, 18,* 66–79.

Surwit, R. S., & Feinglos, M. N. (1983). The effects of relaxation on glucose tolerance in non-insulin-dependent diabetes. *Diabetes Care, 6,* 176–179.

Surwit, R. S., & Feinglos, M. N. (1988). Stress and autonomic nervous system in Type II diabetes: A hypothesis. *Diabetes Care, 11,* 83–85.

Sutton, S. R., & Eiser, J. R. (1984). The effect of fear-arousing communications on cigarette smoking: An expectancy-value approach. *Journal of Behavioral Medicine, 7,* 13–34.

Sutton, S. R., & Hallett, R. (1988). Understanding the effects of fear-arousing communications: The role of cognitive factors and amount of fear aroused. *Journal of Behavioral Medicine, 11,* 353–360.

Sutton, S. R., & Kahn, R. L. (1986). Prediction, understanding, and control as antidotes to organizational stress. In J. Lorsch (Ed.), *Handbook of organizational behavior* (pp. 272–285). Boston: Harvard University Press.

Svarstad, B. L. (1976). Physician-patient communication and patient conformity with medical advice. In D. Mechanic (Ed.), *The growth of bureaucratic medicine: An inquiry into the dynamics of patient behavior and the organization of medical care.* New York: Wiley.

Swan, G. E., Carmelli, D., & Rosenman, R. H. (1988). Psychological characteristics in twins discordant for smoking behavior: A matched-twin-pair analysis. *Addictive Behaviors, 13,* 51–60.

Swan, G. E., & Denk, C. E. (1987). Dynamic models for the maintenance of smoking cessation: Event history analysis of late relapse. *Journal of Behavioral Medicine, 10,* 527–554.

Swaveley, S. M., Silverman, W. H., & Falek, A. (1987). Psychological impact of the development of a presymptomatic test for Huntington's disease. *Health Psychology, 6,* 149–157.

Sweda, M. G., Sines, J. O., Lauer, R. M., & Clarke, W. R. (1986). Familial aggression of Type A behavior. *Journal of Behavioral Medicine, 9,* 23–32.

Sweet, J. J., Breuer, S. R., Hazlewood, L. A., Toye, R., & Pawl, R. P. (1985). The million behavioral health inventory: Concurrent and predictive validity in a pain treatment center. *Journal of Behavioral Medicine, 8,* 215–226.

Swinehart, J., & Kirscht, J. (1966). Smoking: A panel study of beliefs and behavior following the PHS report. *Psychological Reports, 18,* 519–528.

Tagliacozzo, D. L., & Mauksch, H. O. (1972). The patient's view of the patient's role. In E. G. Jaco (Ed.), *Patients, physicians, and illness* (2nd ed., pp. 172–185). New York: Free Press.

Tapp, W. N., & Natelson, B. H. (1988). Consequences of stress: A multiplicative function of health status. *FASEB J, 2,* 2268–2271.

Tausig, M. (1982). Measuring life events. *Journal of Health and Social Behavior, 23,* 52–64.

Taylor, C. B., Bandura, A., Ewart, C. K., Miller, N. H., & DeBusk, R. F. (1985). Exercise testing to enhance wives' confidence in their husbands' cardiac capability soon after clinically uncomplicated acute myocardial infarction. *American Journal of Cardiology, 55,* 635–638.

Taylor, C. B., Houston-Miller, N., Ahn, D. K., Haskell, W., & DeBusk, R. F. (1986). The effects of exercise training programs on psychosocial improvement in uncomplicated postmyocardial infarction patients. *Journal of Psychosomatic Research, 30,* 581–587.

Taylor, L. A., & Rachman, S. J. (1988). The effects of blood sugar level changes on cognitive function, affective state, and somatic symptoms. *Journal of Behavioral Medicine, 11,* 279–292.

Taylor, S. E. (1979). Hospital patient behavior: Reactance, helplessness, or control? *Journal of Social Issues, 35,* 156–184.

Taylor, S. E. (1983). Adjustment to threatening events: A theory of cognitive adaptation. *American Psychologist, 41,* 1161–1173.

Taylor, S. E. (1986). *Health psychology.* New York: Random House.

Taylor, S. E. (1989). *Positive illusions: Creative self-deception and the healthy mind.* New York: Basic Books.

Taylor, S. E., & Aspinwall, L. G. (1990). Psychological aspects of chronic illness. In G. R. VandenBos & P. T. Costa, Jr. (Eds.), *Psychological aspects of serious illness.* Washington, DC: American Psychological Association.

Taylor, S. E., & Brown, J. D. (1988). Illusion and well-being: A social psychological perspective on mental health. *Psychological Bulletin, 103,* 193–210.

Taylor, S. E., & Clark, L. F. (1986). Does information improve adjustment to noxious events? In M. J. Saks & L. Saxe (Eds.), *Advances in applied social psychology* (Vol. 3). Hillsdale, NJ: Erlbaum.

Taylor, S. E., Falke, R. L., Shoptaw, S. J., & Lichtman, R. R. (1986). Social support, support groups, and the cancer patient. *Journal of Consulting and Clinical Psychology, 54,* 608–615.

Taylor, S. E., Helgeson, V. S., Reed, G. M., & Skokan, L. A. (in press). Self-generated feelings of control and adjustment to physical illness. To appear in a special issue of *Journal of Social Issues.*

Taylor, S. E., Kemeny, M. E., Reed, G. M., & Aspinwall, L. G. (in press). Assault on the self: Positive illusions and adjustment to threatening events. In G. A. Goethals & J. A. Strauss (Eds.),

The self: An interdisciplinary perspective. New York: Springer.

Taylor, S. E., Lichtman, R. R., & Wood, J. V. (1984a). Attributions, beliefs about control, and adjustment to breast cancer. *Journal of Personality and Social Psychology, 46,* 489–502.

Taylor, S. E., Lichtman, R. R., & Wood, J. V. (1984b). Compliance with chemotherapy among breast cancer patients. *Health Psychology, 3,* 553–562.

Taylor, S. E., Lichtman, R. R., Wood, J. V., Bluming, A. Z., Dosik, G. M., & Leibowitz, R. L. (1985). Illness-related and treatment-related factors in psychological adjustment to breast cancer. *Cancer, 55,* 2506–2513.

Taylor, S. E., & Thompson, S. C. (1982). Stalking the elusive "vividness" effect. *Psychological Review, 89,* 155–181.

Taylor, S. E., Wood, J. V., & Lichtman, R. R. (1983). *Life change following cancer.* Unpublished manuscript, University of California, Los Angeles.

Tehan, C. (1982). Hospice in an existing home care agency. *Family and Community Health, 5,* 11–20.

Telch, C. F., Agras, W. S., & Rossiter, E. M. (1988). Binge eating increases with increasing adiposity. *International Journal of Eating Disorders, 7,* 115–119.

Telch, C. F., & Telch, M. J. (1986). Group coping skills instruction and supportive group therapy for cancer patients: A comparison of strategies. *Journal of Consulting and Clinical Psychology, 54,* 802–808.

Temoshok, L. (1987). Personality, coping style, emotion and cancer: Towards an integrative model. *Cancer Surveys, 6,* 545–567.

Temoshok, L., Grade, M., & Zich, J. (1988). Public health, the press, and AIDS: An analysis of newspaper articles in London and San Francisco. In I. Corliss & M. Pittman-Lindeman (Eds.), *AIDS: Principles, practices, and politics* (pp. 525–542). New York: Harper & Row.

Temoshok, L., Heller, B. W., Sagebiel, R. W., Blois, M. S., Sweet, D. M., DiClemente, R. J., & Gold, M. L. (1985). The relationship of psychosocial factors to prognostic indicators in cutaneous malignant melanoma. *Journal of Psychosomatic Research, 29,* 139–153.

Temoshok, L., Peeke, H. V. S., & Mehard, C. W. (1988). Individual behavior differences related to induced tumor growth in the female Syrian hamster: Two studies. *International Journal of Neuroscience, 38,* 199–209.

Tempelaar, R., de Haes, J. C. J. M., de Ruiter, J. H., Bakker, D., van den Heuvel, W. J. A., & van Nieuwenhuijzen, M. G. (1989). The social experiences of cancer patients under treatment: A comparative study. *Social Science and Medicine, 29,* 635–642.

Tessler, R., & Mechanic, D. (1978). Psychological distress and perceived health status. *Journal of Health and Social Behavior, 19,* 254–262.

Theorell, T. (1974). Life events before and after the onset of a premature myocardial infarction. In B. S. Dohrenwend & B. P. Dohrenwend (Eds.), *Stressful life events: Their nature and effects.* New York: Wiley.

Thoits, P. A. (1982). Conceptual, methodological, and theoretical problems in studying social support as a buffer against life stress. *Journal of Health and Social Behavior, 23,* 145–159.

Thoits, P. A. (1986). Social support as coping assistance. *Journal of Consulting and Clinical Psychology, 54,* 416–423.

Thoits, P. A. (1987). Gender and marital status differences in control and distress: Common stress versus unique stress explanations. *Journal of Health and Social Behavior, 28,* 7–22.

Thomas, C. B. (1976). Precursors of premature disease and death: The predictive power of habits and family attributes. *Annals of Internal Medicine, 86,* 653–658.

Thomas, C. B., & Duszynski, K. R. (1974). Closeness to parents and the family constellation in a prospective study of Eve disease states: Suicide, mental illness, malignant tumor, hypertension, and coronary heart disease. *Johns Hopkins Medical Journal, 134,* 251–270.

Thompson, D. R., & Cordle, C. J. (1988). Support of wives of myocardial infarction patients. *Journal of Advanced Nursing, 13,* 223–228.

Thompson, D. R., Webster, R. A. Cordle, C. J., & Sutton, T. W. (1987). Specific sources and patterns of anxiety in male patients with first myocardial infarction. *British Journal of Medical Psychology, 60,* 343–348.

Thompson, R. F., & Glanzman, D. L. (1976). Neural and behavioral mechanism of habituation and sensitization. In T. J. Tighe & R. N. Leatron (Eds.), *Habituation* (pp. 49–94). Hillsdale, NJ: Erlbaum.

Thompson, R. F., & Spencer, W. A. (1966). Habituation: A model phenomenon for the study of neuronal substrates of behavior. *Psychological Review, 173,* 16–43.

Thompson, R. S., Rivara, F. P., & Thompson, D. C. (1989). A case-control study of the effectiveness of bicycle safety helmets. *New England Journal of Medicine, 320,* 1361–1367.

Thompson, S. C. (1981). Will it hurt less if I can control it? A complex answer to a simple question. *Psychological Bulletin, 90,* 89–101.

Thompson, S. C., Cheek, P. R., & Graham, M. A. (1988). The other side of perceived control: Disadvantages and negative effects. In S. Spacapan & S. Oskamp (Eds.), *The social psychology of health: The Claremont applied social psychology conference* (Vol. 2, 69–94). Beverly Hills, CA: Sage.

Thompson, S. C., Sobolew-Shubin, A., Graham, M. A., & Janigian, A. S. (1989). Psychosocial adjustment following a stroke. *Social Science and Medicine, 28,* 239–247.

Thoresen, C. E., & Mahoney, M. J. (1974). *Behavioral self-control.* New York: Holt.

Thorndike, E. L. (1898). Animal intelligence. *Psychological Monographs, 1* (whole No. 8).

Time. (1970, November 2). The malpractice mess, pp. 36, 39.

Timko, C. (1987). Seeking medical care for a breast cancer symptom: Determinants of intentions to engage in prompt or delay behavior. *Health Psychology, 6,* 305–328.

Timko, C., & Janoff-Bulman, R. (1985). Attributions, vulnerability, and psychological adjustment: The case of breast cancer. *Health Psychology, 4,* 521–544.

Tischenkel, N. J., Saab, P. G., Schneiderman, N., Nelesen, R. A., Pasin, R. DeC., Goldstein, D. A., Spitzer, S. B., Woo-Ming, R., & Weidler, D. J. (1989). Cardiovascular and neurohumoral responses to behavioral challenge as a function of race and sex. *Health Psychology, 8,* 503–524.

Tomkins, S. S. (1968). A modified model of smoking behavior. In E. G. Borgatta & R. Evans (Eds.), *Smoking, health and behavior* (pp. 165–188). Chicago: Aldine.

Tompkins, C. A., Schulz, R., & Rau, M. T. (1988). Post-stroke depression in primary support persons: Predicting those at risk. *Journal of Consulting and Clinical Psychology, 56,* 502–508.

Tomporowski, P. D., & Ellis, N. R. (1986). Effects of exercise on cognitive processes: A review. *Psychological Bulletin, 99,* 338–346.

Toynbee, P. (1977). *Patients*. New York: Harcourt Brace.

Triplet, R. G., & Sugarman, D. B. (1987). Reactions to AIDS victims: Ambiguity breeds contempt. *Personality and Social Psychology Bulletin, 13,* 265–274.

Trotta, P. (1980). Breast self-examination: Factors influencing compliance. *Oncology Nursing Forum, 7,* 13–17.

Tuomilehto, J., Geboers, J., Salonen, J. T., Nissinen, A., Kuulasmaa, K., & Puska, P. (1986). Decline in cardiovascular mortality in North Karelia and other parts of Finland. *British Medical Journal, 293,* 1068–1071.

Turk, D. C., Litt, M. D., Salovey, P., & Walker, J. (1985). Seeking urgent pediatric treatment: Factors contributing to frequency, delay, and appropriateness. *Health Psychology, 4,* 43–59.

Turk, D. C., & Meichenbaum, D. (in press). Adherence to self-care regimens: The patient's perspective. In R. H. Rozensky, J. J. Sweet, & S. M. Tovian (Eds.), *Handbook of clinical psychology in medical settings*. New York: Plenum.

Turk, D. C., Meichenbaum, D. H., & Berman, W. H. (1979). Application of biofeedback for the regulation of pain: A critical review. *Psychological Bulletin, 86,* 1322–1338.

Turk, D. C., & Rudy, T. E. (1988). A cognitive-behavioral perspective on chronic pain: Beyond the scalpel and syringe. In C. D. Tollison (Ed.), *Handbook of chronic pain management* (pp. 222–236). Baltimore, MD: Williams & Wilkins.

Turk, D. C., Rudy, T. E., & Salovey, P. (1986). Implicit models of illness. *Journal of Behavioral Medicine, 9,* 453–474.

Turk, D. C., & Speers, M. A. (1983). Diabetes mellitus: A cognitive-functional analysis of stress. In T. G. Burish & L. A. Bradley (Eds.), *Coping with chronic disease: Research and applications* (pp. 191–218). New York: Academic Press.

Turk, D. C., Wack, J. T., & Kerns, R. D. (1985). An empirical examination of the "pain-behavior" construct. *Journal of Behavioral Medicine, 8,* 119–130.

Turner, J. A. (1982). Comparison of group progressive-relaxation training and cognitive-behavioral group therapy for chronic low back pain. *Journal of Consulting and Clinical Psychology, 50,* 757–765.

Turner, R. J. (1981). Social support as a contingency in psychological well-being. *Journal of Health and Social Behavior, 22,* 357–367.

Turner, R. J., & Noh, S. (1988). Physical disability and depression: A longitudinal analysis. *Journal of Health and Social Behavior, 29,* 23–37.

Turnquist, D. C., Harvey, J. H., & Anderson, B. L. (1988). Attributions and adjustment to life-threatening illness. *British Journal of Clinical Psychology, 27,* 55–65.

Udry, J., Clark, L., Chase, C., & Levy, M. (1972). Can mass media advertising increase contraceptive use? *Family Planning Perspectives, 4,* 37–44.

Umberson, D. (1987). Family status and health behaviors: Social control as a dimension of social integration. *Journal of Health and Social Behavior, 28,* 306–319.

U.S. Bureau of the Census. (1987). *Statistical abstract of the United States: 1988.* Washington, DC: U.S. Government Printing Office.

U.S. Department of Health, Education, and Welfare and United States Public Health Service, Centers for Disease Control. (1964). *Smoking and health: Report of the advisory committee to the Surgeon General of the Public Health Service* (Publication No. PHS-1103). Washington, DC: U.S. Government Printing Office.

U.S. Department of Health, Education, and Welfare. (1979). *Healthy people: A report of the Surgeon General on health promotion and disease prevention* (USPHS Publication No. 79-55071). Washington, DC: U.S. Government Printing Office.

U. S. Department of Health and Human Services. (1981). *Alcohol and health.* Rockville, MD: National Institute on Alcohol Abuse and Alcoholism.

U.S. Department of Health and Human Services. (1986). *Utilization of short-stay hospitals* (USDHHS Publication No. 86-1745). Washington, DC: U.S. Government Printing Office.

U.S. Department of Health and Human Services. (1988). *National Center for Health Statistics, 1988.* Hyattsville, MD: U.S. Government Printing Office.

U.S. Department of Labor. (1988–1989). *Occupational outlook handbook* (Bulletin 2300). Washington, DC: U.S. Government Printing Office.

U.S. Public Health Service. (1982). *The health consequences of smoking: Cancer. A report to the Surgeon General: 1982* (Publication of Superintendent of Documents). Washington, DC: U.S. Government Printing Office.

Uzark, K. C., Becker, M. H., Dielman, T. E., & Rocchini, A. P. (1987). Psychosocial predictors of compliance with a weight control intervention for obese children and adolescents. *Journal of Compliance in Health Care, 2,* 167–178.

Valois, P., Desharnais, R., & Godin, G. (1988). A comparison of the Fishbein and Ajzen and the Triandis attitudinal models for the prediction of exercise intention and behavior. *Journal of Behavioral Medicine, 11,* 459–472.

VanderPlate, C., Aral, S. O., & Magder, L. (1988). The relationship among genital herpes simplex virus, stress, and social support. *Health Psychology, 7,* 159–168.

Van Egeren, L. F., Sniderman, L. D., & Roggelin, M. S. (1982). Competitive two-person interactions of Type-A and Type-B individuals. *Journal of Behavioral Medicine, 5,* 55–66.

Van Itallie, T. B. (1979). Obesity: Adverse effects on health and longevity. *American Journal of Clinical Nutrition, 32,* 2723–2733.

van Komen, R. W., & Redd, W. H. (1985). Personality factors associated with anticipatory nausea/vomiting in patients receiving cancer chemotherapy. *Health Psychology, 4,* 189–202.

Verbrugge, L. M. (1979). Female illness rates and illness behavior: Testing hypotheses about sex differences in health. *Women and Health, 4,* 61–79.

Verbrugge, L. M. (1980). Sex differences in complaints and diagnoses. *Journal of Behavioral Medicine, 3,* 327–356.

Verbrugge, L. M. (1985). Gender and health: An update on hypotheses and evidence. *Journal of Health and Social Behavior, 26,* 156–182.

Verbrugge, L. M. (1990). Pathways of health and death. In R. D. Apple (Ed.), *Women, health, and medicine in America: A historical handbook* (pp. 41–79). New York: Garland.

Vernon, D. T. A. (1974). Modeling and birth order in response to painful stimuli. *Journal of Personality and Social Psychology, 29,* 794–799.

Vernon, D. T. A., & Bigelow, D. A. (1974). Effect of information about a potentially stressful situation on responses to stress impact. *Journal of Personality and Social Psychology, 29,* 50–59.

Vinck, J., Arickx, M., & Hongenaert, M. (1987). Predicting interindividual differences in blood-pressure response to relaxation training in normotensives. *Journal of Behavioral Medicine, 10,* 395–410.

Vinokur, A., & Caplan, R. D. (1986). Cognitive and affective components of life events: Their relations and effects on well-being. *American Journal of Community Psychology, 14,* 351–370.

Vinokur, A., & Selzer, M. (1975). Desirable versus undesirable life events: Their relationship to stress and mental distress. *Journal of Personality and Social Psychology, 32,* 329–337.

Visintainer, M. A., Seligman, M. E. P., & Volpicelli, J. R. (1983). Helplessness, chronic stress, and tumor development. *Psychosomatic Medicine, 45,* 75 (Abstract).

Visintainer, M. A., Volpicelli, J. R., & Seligman, M. E. P. (1982). Tumor rejection in rats after inescapable or escapable electric shock. *Science, 216,* 437–439.

Visotsky, H. M., Hamburg, D. A., Goss, M. E., & Lebovitz, B. Z. (1961). Coping behavior under extreme stress. *Archives of General Psychiatry, 5,* 423–428.

Vogler, R. C., Common, J. V., & Weissbach, T. A. (1975). Integrated behavior change techniques for alcoholics. *Journal of Consulting and Clinical Psychology, 43,* 233–243.

Volgyesi, F. A. (1954). "School for Patients" hypnosis-therapy and psychoprophylaxis. *British Journal of Medical Hypnotism, 5,* 8–17.

Wadden, T. A., Luborsky, L., Greer, S., & Crits-Christoph, P. (1984). The behavioral treatment of essential hypertension: An update and comparison with pharmacological treatment. *Clinical Psychology Review, 4,* 403–429.

Wadden, T. A., Stunkard, A. J., & Brownell, K. D. (1983). Very low calorie diets: Their efficacy, safety and future. *Annals of Internal Medicine, 99,* 675–684.

Wagener, J. J., & Taylor, S. E. (1986). What else could I have done? Patients' responses to failed treatment decisions. *Health Psychology, 5,* 481–496.

Waggoner, C. D., & LeLieuvre, R. B. (1981). A method to increase compliance to exercise regimens in rheumatoid arthritis patients. *Journal of Behavioral Medicine, 4,* 191–202.

Wagner, P. J., & Curran, P. (1984). Health beliefs and physician identified "worried well." *Health Psychology, 3,* 459–474.

Waitzkin, H. (1985). Information giving in medical care. *Journal of Health and Social Behavior, 26,* 81–101.

Waitzkin, H., & Stoeckle, J. D. (1976). Information control and the micropolitics of health care. *Journal of Social Issues, 10,* 263–276.

Waldron, I. (1976). Why do women live longer than men? *Journal of Human Stress, 2,* 2–13.

Waldron, I., & Johnston, S. (1976). Why do women live longer than men? Part 2. *Journal of Human Stress, 2,* 19–30.

Wallston, B. S., Alagna, S. W., DeVellis, B. McE., & DeVellis, R. F. (1983). Social support and physical health. *Health Psychology, 2,* 367–391.

Wallston, B. S., & Wallston, K. A. (1984). Social psychological models of health behavior: An examination and integration. In A. Baum, S. E. Taylor, & J. E. Singer (Eds.), *Handbook of psychology and health* (Vol. 4, 23–54). Hillsdale, NJ: Erlbaum.

Wallston, K. A., Wallston, B. S., & DeVellis, R. (1978). Development of the Multidimensional Health Locus of Control (MHLC) scale. *Health Education Monographs, 6,* 161–170.

Walsh, D. C., & Gordon, N. P. (1986). Legal approaches to smoking deterrance. *Annual Review of Public Health, 7,* 127–149.

Waltz, M. (1986). Marital context and post-infarction quality of life: Is it social support or something more? *Social Science and Medicine, 22,* 791–805.

Wan, T. T. H., & Gray, L. C. (1978). Differential access to preventive services for young children in low-income urban areas. *Journal of Health and Social Behavior, 19,* 312–324.

Wanburg, K. W., & Horn, J. L. (1983). Assessment of alcohol use with multidimensional concepts and measures. *American Psychologist, 38,* 1055–1069.

Ward, M. M., Chesney, M. A., Swan, G. E., Black, G. W., Parker, S. D., & Rosenman, R. H. (1986). Cardiovascular responses in Type A and Type B men to a series of stressors. *Journal of Behavioral Medicine, 9,* 43–49.

Ward, S. E., Leventhal, H., & Love, R. (1988). Repression revisited: Tactics used in coping with a severe health threat. *Personality and Social Psychology Bulletin, 14,* 735–746.

Ware, J. E., Jr., Davies-Avery, A., & Stewart, A. L. (1978). The measurement and meaning of patient satisfaction: A review of the literature. *Health and Medical Care Services Review, 1,* 1–15.

Warner, K. E. (1977). The effects of the anti-smoking campaign on cigarette consumption. *American Journal of Public Health, 67,* 645–650.

Warner, K. E. (1981). Cigarette smoking in the 1970's: The impact of the anti-smoking campaign on consumption. *Science, 211,* 729–731.

Warner, K. E., & Murt, H. A. (1982). Impact of the antismoking campaign on smoking prevalence: A cohort analysis. *Journal of Public Health Policy, 3,* 374–390.

Warr, P., & Parry, G. (1982). Paid employment and women's psychological well-being. *Psychological Bulletin, 91,* 498–516.

Warwick, D. P., & Kelman, H. C. (1973). Ethical issues in social intervention. In Z. Altman (Ed.), *Processes and phenomena of social change* (pp. 377–418). New York: Wiley.

Watkins, J. D., Roberts, D. E., Williams, T. F., Martin, D. A., & Coyle, I. V. (1967). Observations of medication errors made by diabetic patients in the home. *Diabetes, 16,* 882–885.

Watkins, J. D., Williams, T. F., Martin, D. A., Hogan, M. D., & Anderson, E. (1967). A study of diabetic patients at home. *American Journal of Public Health, 57,* 452–459.

Watson, D., & Clark, L. A. (1984). Negative affectivity: The disposition to experience aversive emotional states. *Psychological Bulletin, 96,* 465–490.

Watson, D., & Pennebaker, J. W. (1989). Health complaints, stress, and distress: Exploring the central role of negative affectivity. *Psychological Review, 96,* 234–254.

Watters, J. K. (1987). *Preventing human immunodeficiency virus contagion among intravenous drug users: The impact of street-based education on risk behavior.* Unpublished manuscript, University of California, San Francisco.

Wayment, H. (1989). *Coping with a stressful event: Does it matter who your friends are?* Unpublished manuscript, University of California, Los Angeles.

Wechsler, H., Levine, S., Idelson, R. K., Rothman, M., & Taylor, J. O. (1983). The physician's role in health promotion: A survey of primary care physicians. *New England Journal of Medicine, 308,* 97–100.

Weidner, G., Archer, S., Healy, B., & Matarazzo, J. D. (1985). Family consumption of low fat foods: Stated preference versus actual consumption. *Journal of Applied Social Psychology, 15,* 773–779.

Weidner, G., & Matthews, K. A. (1978). Reported physical symptoms elicited by unpredictable events and the Type A coronary-prone behavior pattern. *Journal of Personality and Social Psychology, 36*, 1213–1220.

Weidner, G., Sexton, G., Matarazzo, J. D., Pereira, C., & Friend, R. (1988). Type A behavior in children, adolescents, and their parents. *Developmental Psychology, 24*, 118–121.

Weidner, G., Sexton, G., McLellarn, R., Connor, S. L., & Matarazzo, J. D. (1987). The role of Type A behavior and hostility in an elevation of plasma lipids in adult women and men. *Psychosomatic Medicine, 49*, 136–145.

Weil, P. A., & Stam, L. (1986). Transitions in the hierarchy of authority in hospitals: Implications for the role of the chief executive officer. *Journal of Health and Social Behavior, 27*, 17–29.

Weinberg, J., Diller, L., Gordon, W. A., Gerstman, L. J., Lieberman, A., Lakin, P., Hodges, G., & Ezrachi, O. (1977). Visual scanning training effect in reading-related tasks in acquired right brain damage. *Archives of Physical Medicine and Rehabilitation, 58*, 479–486.

Weinberger, M., Hiner, S. L., & Tierney, W. M. (1987). In support of hassles as a measure of stress in predicting health outcomes. *Journal of Behavioral Medicine, 10*, 19–32.

Weiner, B., Perry, R. P., & Magnusson, J. (1988). An attributional analysis of reactions to stigmas. *Journal of Personality and Social Psychology, 55*, 738–748.

Weiner, H. (1977). *Psychobiology and human diseases.* New York: Elsevier.

Weinstein, K. A., Davison, G. C., DeQuattro, V., & Allen, J. W. (1987). Type A behavior and cognitions: Is hostility the bad actor? *Health Psychology, 6*, 55–56 (abstract).

Weinstein, N. D. (1979). Seeking reassuring or threatening information about environmental cancer. *Journal of Behavioral Medicine, 2*, 125–140.

Weinstein, N. D. (1982). Unrealistic optimism about susceptibility of health problems. *Journal of Behavioral Medicine, 5*, 441–460.

Weinstein, N. D. (1983). Reducing unrealistic optimism about illness susceptibility. *Health Psychology, 2*, 11–20.

Weinstein, N. D. (1984). Why it won't happen to me: Perceptions of risk factors and susceptibility. *Health Psychology, 3*, 431–457.

Weinstein, N. D. (1987). Unrealistic optimism about susceptibility to health problems: Conclusions from a community-wide sample. *Journal of Behavioral Medicine, 10*, 481–500.

Weinstein, N. D. (1989). Effects of personal experience on self-protective behavior. *Psychological Bulletin, 105*, 31–50.

Weintraub, M. (1976). Intelligent noncompliance and capricious compliance. In L. Lasagna (Ed.), *Patient compliance.* Mt. Kisco, NY: Futura.

Weisenberg, M. (1977). Pain and pain control. *Psychological Bulletin, 84*, 1008–1044.

Weisenberg, M., Kegeles, S. S., & Lund, A. K. (1980). Children's health beliefs and acceptance of a dental preventive activity. *Journal of Health and Social Behavior, 21*, 59–74.

Weisman, A. D. (1972). *On death and dying.* New York: Behavioral Publications.

Weisman, A. D. (1977). The psychiatrist and the inexorable. In H. Feifel (Ed.), *New meanings of death* (pp. 107–122). New York: McGraw-Hill.

Weisman, A. D., & Worden, J. W. (1976–1977). The existential plight in cancer: Significance of the first 100 days. *International Journal of Psychiatry in Medicine, 7*, 1–15.

Weisman, C. S., & Teitelbaum, M. A. (1985). Physician gender and the physician-patient relationship: Recent evidence and relevant questions. *Social Sciences and Medicine, 20*, 1119–1127.

Weiss, S. M. (1988). Stress management in the treatment of hypertension. *American Heart Journal, 116*, 645–649.

Welch-McCaffrey, S. (1985). Cancer, anxiety, and quality of life. *Cancer Nursing, 8*, 151–158.

Wellisch, D. K. (1979). Adolescent acting out when a parent has cancer. *International Journal of Family Therapy, 1*, 230–241.

Wellisch, D. K. (1981). Intervention with the cancer patient. In C. K. Prokop & L. A. Bradley (Eds.), *Medical psychology: Contributions to behavioral medicine* (pp. 224–241). New York: Academic Press.

Wellisch, D. K., Gritz, E. R., Schain, W., Wang, H-J., & Siau, J. (1990). *Psychological functioning of daughters of breast cancer patients: I. Daughters and controls.* Manuscript submitted for publication.

Wellisch, D. K., Jamison, K. R., & Pasnau, R. O. (1978). Psychosocial aspects of mastectomy: II. The man's perspective. *American Journal of Psychiatry, 135*, 543–546.

Wesch, D., Lutzker, J. R., Frisch, L., & Dillon, M.

M. (1987). Evaluating the impact of a service fee on patient compliance. *Journal of Behavioral Medicine, 10,* 91–101.

Wesson, A. F. (1972). Hospital ideology and communication between ward personnel. In E. G. Jaco (Ed.), *Patients, physicians, and illness* (pp. 325–342). New York: Free Press.

Wethington, E., & Kessler, R. C. (1986). Perceived support, received support, and adjustment to stressful life events. *Journal of Health and Social Behavior, 27,* 78–89.

Wheaton, B. (1983). Stress, personal coping resources, and psychiatric symptoms: An investigation of interactive models. *Journal of Health and Social Behavior, 24,* 208–229.

Wheaton, B. (1985). Models for the stress-buffering functions of coping resources. *Journal of Health and Social Behavior, 26,* 352–364.

White, J. R., & Froeb, H. F. (1980). Small-airways dysfunction in nonsmokers chronically exposed to tobacco smoke. *New England Journal of Medicine, 302,* 720–723.

White, L. P. (1977). Death and the physician: *Mortuis vivos docent.* In H. Feifel (Ed.), *New meanings of death* (pp. 91–106). New York: McGraw-Hill

White, L. P., & Tursky, B. (1982). Where are we... where are we going? In L. White & B. Tursky (Eds.), *Clinical biofeedback: Efficacy and mechanisms* (pp. 438–448). New York: Guilford Press.

White, R. W. (1959). Motivation reconsidered: The concept of competence. *Psychological Review, 66,* 297–333.

Wiebe, D. J., & McCallum, D. M. (1986). Health practices and hardiness as mediators in the stress-illness relationship. *Health Psychology, 5,* 425–438.

Wiens, A. N., & Menustik, C. E. (1983). Treatment outcome and patient characteristics in an aversion therapy program for alcoholism. *American Psychologist, 38,* 1089–1096.

Wiklund, I., Oden, A., Sanne, H., Ulvenstam, G., Wilhemsson, C., & Wilhemsen, L. (1988). Prognostic importance of somatic and psychosocial variables after a first myocardial infarction. *American Journal of Epidemiology, 128,* 786–795.

Wilhelmson, L., Sanne, H., Elmfeldt, D., Tibbin, B., Grimby, G., & Wedel, G. (1975). A controlled trial of physical training after myocardial infarction. *Preventive Medicine, 4,* 491–508.

Wilkes, E. (1965). Terminal cancer at home. *Lancet, 1,* 799–801.

Willenbring, M. L., Levine, A. S., & Morley, J. E. (1986). Stress induced eating and food preference in humans: A pilot study. *International Journal of Eating Disorders, 5,* 855–864.

Williams, A. F. (1982). Passive and active measures for controlling disease and injury: The role of health psychologists. *Health Psychology, 1,* 309–409.

Williams, A. W., Ware, J. E., Jr., & Donald, C. A. (1981). A model of mental health, life events, and social supports applicable to general populations. *Journal of Health and Social Behavior, 22,* 324–336.

Williams, G. H., Croog, S. H., Levine, S., Testa, M. A., & Sudilovsky, A. (1987). Impact of antihypertensive therapy on quality of life: Effect of hydrocholothiazide. *Journal of Hypertension, 5*(Suppl.), S29–S35.

Williams, R. B., Jr. (1984). An untrusting heart. *The Sciences, 24,* 31–36.

Williams, R. B., Jr., & Barefoot, J. C. (1988). Coronary-prone behavior: The emerging role of the hostility complex. In B. K. Houston & C. R. Snyder (Eds.), *Type A behavior pattern: Current trends and future directions* (pp. 189–211). New York: Wiley.

Williams, R. B., Jr., Barefoot, J. C., Haney, T. L., Harrell, F. E., Jr., Blumenthal, J. A., Pryor, D. B., & Peterson, B. (1988). Type A behavior and angiographically documented coronary atherosclerosis in a sample of 2,289 patients. *Psychosomatic Medicine, 50,* 139–152.

Williams, R. B., Jr., Barefoot, J. C., & Shekelle, R. B. (1985). The health consequences of hostility. In M. A. Chesney & R. H. Rosenman (Eds.), *Anger and hostility in cardiovascular and behavioral disorders* (pp. 173–185). New York: Hemisphere/McGraw-Hill.

Wills, T. A. (1984). Supportive functions of interpersonal relationships. In S. Cohen & L. Syme (Eds.), *Social support and health* (pp. 61–82). New York: Academic Press.

Wills, T. A. (1986). Stress and coping in early adolescence: Relationships to substance use in urban school samples. *Health Psychology, 5,* 503–529.

Wills, T. A. (1987). Downward comparison as a coping mechanism. In C. R. Snyder & C. E. Ford (Eds.), *Coping with negative life events: Clinical and social-psychological perspectives* (pp. 243–268). New York: Plenum Press.

Wills, T. A., & Vaughan, R. (1989). Social support and substance use in early adolescence. *Journal of Behavioral Medicine, 12,* 321–340.

Wilson, G. T. (1984). Toward the understanding and treatment of binge eating. In R. C. Hawkins, W. J. Fremouw, & P. F. Clement (Eds.), *The binge-purge syndrome* (pp. 77–103). New York: Springer.

Wilson, G. T. (1985). Psychological prognostic factors in the treatment of obesity. In J. Hirsch & T. B. Van Italie (Eds.), *Recent advances in obesity research* (Vol. 4, pp. 301–311). London: Libbey.

Wilson, J. P., Smith, W. K., & Johnson, S. K. (1985). A comparative analysis of PTSD among various survivor groups. In C. R. Figley (Ed.), *Trauma and its wake: The study and treatment of post-traumatic stress disorder* (pp. 142–172). New York: Brunner/Mazel.

Wilson, R. (1963). The social structure of a general hospital. *Annals of the American Academy of Political and Social Science, 346,* 67–76.

Wilson, W., & Pratt, C. (1987). The impact of diabetes education and peer support upon weight and glycemic control of elderly persons with non-insulin dependent diabetes mellitus (NIDDM). *American Journal of Public Health, 77,* 634–635.

Windsor, R. A., Lowe, J. B., & Bartlett, E. E. (1988). The effectiveness of a worksite self-help smoking cessation program: A randomized trial. *Journal of Behavioral Medicine, 11,* 407–421.

Wing, R. R., Epstein, L. H., Nowalk, M. P., Koeske, R., & Hagg, S. (1985). Behavior change, weight loss, and physiological improvements in Type II diabetic patients. *Journal of Consulting and Clinical Psychology, 53,* 111–122.

Wing, R. R., Epstein, L. H., Nowalk, M. P., & Lamparski, D. M. (1986). Behavioral self-regulation in the treatment of patients with diabetes mellitus. *Psychological Bulletin, 99,* 78–89.

Wing, R. R., Epstein, L. H., Nowalk, M. P., & Scott, N. (1988). Self-regulation in the treatment of Type II diabetes. *Behavior Therapy, 19,* 11–23.

Wing, R. R., Epstein, L. H., Nowalk, M. P., Scott, N., Koeske, R., & Hagg, S. (1986). Does self-monitoring of blood glucose levels improve dietary competence for obese patients with Type II diabetes? *American Journal of Medicine, 81,* 830–836.

Wing, R. R., Koeske, R., Epstein, L. H., Nowalk, M. P., Gooding, W., & Becker, D. (1987). Long-term effects of modest weight loss in Type II diabetes patients. *Archives of Internal Medicine, 147,* 1749–1753.

Wing, R. R., Nowalk, L. H., Marcus, M. D., Koeske, R., & Finegold, D. (1986). Subclinical eating disorders and glycemic control in adolescents with Type I diabetes. *Diabetes Care, 9,* 162–167.

Wingard, D. L. (1982). The sex differential in mortality rates: Demographic and behavioral factors. *American Journal of Epidemiology, 115,* 205–216.

Winkelstein, W., Samuel, M., Padian, N., Wiley, J. A., Lang, W., Anderson, R. E., & Levy, J. (1987). Reduction in human immunodeficiency virus transmission among homosexual/bisexual men: 1982–1986. *American Journal of Public Health, 76,* 685–689.

Witenberg, S. H., Blanchard, E. D., McCoy, G., Suls, J., & McGoldrick, M. D. (1983). Evaluation of compliance in home and center hemodialysis patients. *Health Psychology, 2,* 227–237.

Wittrock, D. A., Blanchard, E. B., & McCoy, G. C. (1988). Three studies on the relation of process to outcome in the treatment of essential hypertension with relaxation and thermal biofeedback. *Behavior Research and Therapy, 26,* 53–66.

Wolf, S., & Wolff, H. G. (1947). *Human gastric function: An experimental study of a man and his stomach.* New York: Oxford University Press.

Wolinsky, F. D. (1978). Assessing the effects of predisposing, enabling, and illness-morbidity characteristics on health service utilization. *Journal of Health and Social Behavior, 19,* 384–396.

Wolinsky, F. D., Mosely, R. R. II, & Coe, R. M. (1986). A cohort analysis of the use of health services by elderly Americans, *Journal of Health and Social Behavior, 27,* 209–219.

Wolpe, J. (1958). *Psychotherapy by reciprocal inhibition.* Stanford, CA: Stanford University Press.

Wong, M., & Kaloupek, D. G. (1986). Coping with dental treatment: The potential impact of situational demands. *Journal of Behavioral Medicine, 9,* 579–598.

Wood, E. R. (1989). Evaluation of a hospital-based education program for patients with diabetes. *Journal of the American Dietetic Association, 89,* 354–358.

Woods, P. J., Morgan, B. T., Day, B. W., Jefferson, T., & Harris, C. (1984). Findings on a relationship between Type A behavior and headaches. *Journal of Behavioral Medicine, 7*, 277–286.

Woods, S. M., Natterson, J., & Silverman, J. (1966). Medical students' disease: Hypochondriasis in medical education. *Journal of Medical Education, 41*, 785–790.

Wool, M. S., & Greenberg, R. J. (1986). Assessment of denial in cancer patients: Implications for intervention. *Journal of Psychosocial Oncology, 4*, 1–14.

Worden, J. W., & Sobel, H. J. (1978). Ego strength and psychosocial adaptation to cancer. *Psychosomatic Medicine, 40*, 585–592.

Worden, J. W., & Weisman, A. (1975). Psychosocial components of lagtime in cancer diagnosis. *Journal of Psychosomatic Research, 19*, 69–79.

World Health Organization. (1968–1969). *Cancer around the world: World health statistics annual.* Geneva, Switzerland: World Health Organization.

World Health Organization European Collective Group. (1982). Multifactoral trial in the prevention of coronary heart disease. 2. Risk factor changes at two and four years. *European Heart Journal, 3*, 184–190.

Wortman, C. B. (1984). Social support and the cancer patient: Conceptual and methodological issues. *Cancer, 53*, 2339–2360.

Wortman, C. B., & Brehm, J. W. (1975). Responses to uncontrollable outcomes: An integration of reactance theory and the learned helplessness model. In L. Berkowitz (Ed.). *Advances in experimental social psychology* (Vol. 8, 278–336). New York: Academic Press.

Wortman, C. B., & Dunkel-Schetter, C. (1979). Interpersonal relationships and cancer: A theoretical analysis. *Journal of Social Issues, 35*, 120–155.

Wright, L. (1984, April). *A possible biochemical mechanism for explaining Type A related coronary artery disease.* Presented at the Michael Dinoff Memorial Lecture, University of Alabama, Tuscaloosa.

Wright, L. (1988). The Type A behavior pattern and coronary artery disease: Quest for the active ingredients and the elusive mechanism. *American Psychologist, 43*, 2–14.

Wurtele, S. K., Galanos, A. N., & Roberts, M. C. (1980). Increasing return compliance in a tuberculosis detection drive. *Journal of Behavioral Medicine, 3*, 311–318.

Wylie, R. C. (1961). *The self-concept: A critical survey of pertinent research literature.* Lincoln: University of Nebraska Press.

Wylie, R. C. (1979). *The self-concept.* Lincoln: University of Nebraska Press.

Wynder, E. L., Kajitani, T., Kuno, IJ, Lucas, J. C., Jr., DePalo, A., & Farrow, J. (1963). A comparison of survival rates between American and Japanese patients with breast cancer. *Surgery, Gynecology, Obstetrics, 117*, 196–200.

Young, J. W. (1980). The effects of perceived physician competence on patients' symptom disclosure to male and female physicians. *Journal of Behavioral Medicine, 3*, 279–290.

Young, L. M., & Powell, B. (1985). The effects of obesity on the clinical judgments of mental health professionals. *Journal of Health and Social Behavior, 26*, 233–246.

Young, R. F., & Kahana, E. (1987). Conceptualizing stress, coping, and illness management in heart disease caregiving. *Hospice Journal, 3*, 53–73.

Young-Brockopp, D. (1982). Cancer patients' perceptions of five psychosocial needs. *Oncology Nursing Forum, 9*, 31–35.

Yurenev, A. P., Tkachuk, V. A., Mazaev, A. V., Dubov, P. B., Dyakonova, E. G., Patrusheva, I. F., Menshikov, M. Y., Atakhanov, S. E., & Tkhostova, E. B. (1988). The hypertensive heart: Pathogenesis, variants, and prognostic value. *Health Psychology, 7*(Suppl.), 105–111.

Zajonc, R. (1965). Social facilitation. *Science, 149*, 269–274.

Zarski, J. J., West, J. D., DePompei, R., & Hall, D. E. (1988). Chronic illness: Stressors, the adjustment process, and family-focused interventions. *Journal of Mental Health Counseling, 10*, 145–158.

Zastowny, T. R., Kirschenbaum, D. S., & Meng, A. I. (1986). Coping skills training for children: Effects on distress before, during, and after hospitalization for surgery. *Health Psychology, 5*, 231–247.

Zautra, A. J., Okun, M. A., Roth, S. H., & Emmanual, J. (1989). Life stress and lymphocyte alterations among patients with rheumatoid arthritis. *Health Psychology, 8*, 1–14.

Zborowski, M. (1952). Cultural components in responses to pain. *Journal of Social Issues, 8*, 16–30.

Zborowski, M. (1958). Cultural components in response to pain. *Journal of Social Issues, 8*, 16–30.

Zich, J., & Temoshok, L. (1987). Perceptions of social support in men with AIDS and ARC: Relationships with distress and hardiness. *Journal of Applied Social Psychology, 17,* 193–215.

Zimbardo, P. G. (1969). The human choice: Individuation, reason, and order versus deindividuation, impulse, and chaos. In W. J. Arnold & D. Levine (Eds.), *Nebraska symposium on motivation.* Lincoln: University of Nebraska Press.

Zimbardo, P. G., Ebbesen, E. B., & Maslach, C. (1977). *Influencing attitudes and changing behavior.* Reading, MA: Addison-Wesley.

Zimmerman, M. (1979). Peripheral and central nervous mechanisms of nociception, pain and pain therapy: Facts and hypotheses. In J. J. Bonica, J. C. Liebeskind, & D. G. Albe-Fessard (Eds.), *Proceedings of the Second World Congress on Pain: Vol. 3. Advances in pain research and therapy* (pp. 3–34). New York: Raven Press.

Zimmerman, R. (1983). *Preventive health attitudes and behaviors: A test of three models.* Unpublished doctoral dissertation, University of Wisconsin, Madison.

Zimmerman, R. S., Safer, M. A., Leventhal, H., & Baumann, L. J. (1986). The effects of health information in a worksite hypertension screening program. *Health Education Quarterly, 13,* 261–280.

Zohman, L. R. (1981). *Beyond diet: Exercise your way to fitness and heart health.* Englewood Cliffs, NJ: CPC International.

Zola, I. K. (1964). Illness behavior of the working class: Implications and recommendations. In A. Shostak & W. Gomberg (Eds.), *Blue collar world: Study of the American worker* (pp. 350–362). Englewood Cliffs, NJ: Prentice-Hall.

Zola, I. K. (1966). Culture and symptoms—An analysis of patient's presenting complaints. *American Sociological Review, 31,* 615–630.

Zola, I. K. (1973). Pathways to the doctor—From person to patient. *Social Science and Medicine, 7,* 677–689.

Zonderman, A. B., Heft, M. W., & Costa, P. T., Jr. (1985). Does the illness behavior questionnaire measure abnormal illness behavior? *Health Psychology, 4,* 425–436.

Zucker, R. A., & Gomberg, E. S. L. (1986). Etiology of alcoholism reconsidered: The case for a biopsychosocial process. *American Psychologist, 41,* 783–793.

Zuckerman, M. (1971). Dimensions of sensation seeking. *Journal of Consulting and Clinical Psychology, 36,* 45–52.

Glossary

acupuncture   A technique of healing and pain control developed in China in which long, thin needles are inserted into designated areas of the body to reduce discomfort in a target area of the body.

acute disorder   An illness or other medical problem that occurs over a short period of time, is usually the result of an infectious process, and is reversible.

acute pain   Short-term pain that usually results from some specific injury.

adherence   The degree to which an individual follows a recommended health-related or illness-related recommendation.

adrenal glands   Two small glands, located on top of the kidneys, that are part of the endocrine system and secrete several hormones, including cortisol, epinephrine, and norepinephrine, that are involved in responses to stress.

aerobic exercise   High-intensity, long-duration, and high-endurance exercise, believed to contribute to cardiovascular fitness and other positive health outcomes. Examples are jogging, bicycling, running, and swimming.

aftereffects of stress   Performance and attentional decrements that occur after a stressful event has subsided; believed to be produced by the residual physiological, emotional, and cognitive draining in response to stressful events.

AIDS (Acquired Immune Deficiency Syndrome)   Progressive impairment of the immune system by the human immunodeficiency virus (HIV); a diagnosis of AIDS is made on the basis of the presence of one or more specific opportunistic infections.

AIDS antibody testing   A blood test that assesses whether or not an individual has developed antibodies to the HIV virus, which indicates whether or not the person has been infected by the HIV virus.

AIDS-related complex (ARC)   A lesser clinical syndrome, similar to AIDS, that results from the HIV virus; usually involves enlargement of the lymph nodes, fatigue, and other symptoms; may precede the development of AIDS.

alcoholism   State of physical addiction to alcohol that manifests through such symptoms as stereotyped drinking, drinking to maintain blood alcohol at a particular level, experiencing increasing frequency and severity of withdrawal, drinking early in the day and in the middle of the night, a sense of loss of control over drinking, or a subjective craving for alcohol.

angina pectoris   Chest pain that occurs because the muscle tissue of the heart is deprived of adequate oxygen or because removal of carbon dioxide and other wastes interferes with the flow of blood and oxygen to the heart.

anorexia nervosa   A condition produced by excessive dieting and exercise that yields body weight grossly below optimal level, most common among adolescent girls.

anticipatory nausea   Nausea that occurs prior to a noxious event that typically produces nausea and vomiting, such as chemotherapy, because it has been conditioned to the stimuli previously associated with the noxious event.

appraisal delay   The time between recognizing that a symptom exists and deciding that it is serious.

assertiveness training   Techniques that train people how to be appropriately assertive in social situations; often included as part of health behavior modification programs, on the assumption that some poor health habits, such as excessive alcohol consumption or smoking, develop in part to control difficulties in being appropriately assertive.

arthritis   Inflammation of the joints; arthritis consists of about eighty diseases that attack the joints and other connective tissues.

at risk   State of vulnerability to a particular health problem by virtue of heredity, health practices, or family environment.

atherosclerosis   A major cause of heart disease; caused by the narrowing of the arterial walls due to the formation of plaques that reduce the flow of blood through the arteries and interfere with the passage of nutrients from the capillaries into the cells.

autoimmune disorders   Disorders in which the immune system falsely recognizes its own healthy tissue as an invader and attacks and destroys it; believed to be implicated in diabetes, arthritis, and lupus, for example.

autonomic nervous system   That part of the nervous system that controls the activities of visceral organs that typically cannot be controlled voluntarily; composed of the sympathetic and parasympathetic nervous systems.

avoidant (minimizing) coping style   The tendency to cope with threatening events by withdrawing, minimizing, or avoiding them; believed to be an effective short-term, though not an effective long-term, response to stress.

behavioral assignments   Home practice activities that clients perform on their own as part of an integrated therapeutic intervention.

behavioral health   An interdisciplinary subspecialty within behavioral medicine that is concerned with the maintenance of health and the prevention of illness and dysfunction in healthy persons.

behavioral immunization   Programs designed to inoculate people against adverse health habits by exposing them to mild versions of persuasive communications designed to get them to engage in a poor health practice and giving them techniques that they can use to respond effectively to these efforts.

behavioral inoculation   see **behavioral immunization**

behavioral medicine   The broad, interdisciplinary field concerned with behavioral aspects of health, illness, and related dysfunctions, to which many other disciplines, including health psychology, make specific contributions.

biofeedback   A method whereby an individual is provided with ongoing specific information or feedback about how a particular physiological process operates, so that he or she can learn how to modify that process.

biomedical model   The viewpoint that illness can be explained on the basis of aberrant somatic processes, and that psychological and social processes are largely independent of the disease process; the dominant model in medical practice until recently.

biopsychosocial model   The view that biological, psychological, and social factors are all involved in any given state of health or illness.

blood pressure   The force that blood exerts against vessel walls.

body image   The perception and evaluation of one's body, one's physical functioning, and one's appearance.

breast self-examination   Monthly practice of checking the breasts to detect alterations in the underlying tissue; a chief method of detecting breast cancer.

broad-spectrum, or multimodal, cognitive-behavioral therapy The use of a broad array of cognitive-behavioral intervention techniques to modify an individual's health behavior.

buffering hypothesis The hypothesis that coping resources are useful primarily under conditions of high stress and not necessarily under conditions of low stress.

bulimia An eating syndrome characterized by alternating cycles of binge eating and purging through such techniques as vomiting or extreme dieting.

carcinogens Any substances that cause cancer.

cardiac invalidism A psychological state that can result after a myocardial infarction or diagnosis of coronary heart disease, consisting of the perception that a patient's abilities and capacities are lower than they actually are; both patients and their spouses are vulnerable to these misperceptions.

cardiac rehabilitation An intervention program designed to help heart patients achieve their optimal physical, medical, psychological, social, emotional, vocational, and economic status after the diagnosis of heart disease or a heart attack.

cardiopulmonary resuscitation (CPR) A method of reviving the functioning of heart and lungs after a loss of consciousness in which the patient's pulse has ceased or lungs have failed to function appropriately.

cardiovascular system The transport system of the body responsible for carrying oxygen and nutrients to the body and carrying away carbon dioxide and other wastes to the kidneys for excretion; composed of the heart, blood vessels, and blood.

catecholamines The neurotransmitters epinephrine and norepinephrine that promote sympathetic nervous system activity; believed to be released in substantial quantities during stressful times.

catharsis The experience of emotionally venting about some highly stressful or traumatic experience.

causalgia A burning pain that may appear after a wound has healed.

central control mechanism A mechanism in the brain that interprets sensory experience as painful or not; the central control mechanism may ac-

tually influence the flow of some patterns of stimulation and inhibit others.

cerebellum Part of the hindbrain responsible for the coordination of voluntary muscle movement, the maintenance of balance and equilibrium, and the maintenance of muscle tone and posture.

cerebral cortex The main portion of the brain, responsible for intelligence, memory, and the detection and interpretation of sensation.

chemotherapy A treatment for advanced cancers, involving injections of often highly toxic chemicals that produce a variety of unpleasant side effects.

chronic illnesses Illnesses that are long-lasting and usually irreversible.

chronic pain Pain that may begin after an injury, but which does not respond to treatment and persists over time.

chronic strain Stressful experience that is a usual but continually stressful aspect of life.

classical conditioning The pairing of a stimulus with an unconditioned reflex, such that over time, the new stimulus acquires a conditioned response, evoking the same behavior; the process by which an automatic response is conditioned to a new stimulus.

clinical pains Pains that have clinical significance because they produce suffering but without necessarily any clear underlying physiological basis.

clinical thanatology The clinical practice of counseling people who are dying on the basis of knowledge of reactions to dying.

cognitive-behavior therapy The use of principles from learning theory to modify the cognitions and behaviors associated with some behavior to be modified; cognitive-behavior approaches are used to modify poor health habits such as smoking, poor diet, and alcoholism.

cognitive costs hypothesis A theory of stress that maintains that events are stressful to the extent that they tax perceptual and cognitive resources, draw off attention, or deplete cognitive resources for other tasks.

cognitive restructuring A method of modifying internal monologues in stress-producing situations; clients are trained to monitor what they say to themselves in stress-provoking situations and then to modify their cognitions in adapative ways.

colleague orientation Physician orientation toward gaining the esteem and regard of one's colleagues; fostered by any health care provider arrangement that does not involve direct reimbursement of physicians by patients.

comprehensive intervention model A model that pools and coordinates the medical and psychological expertise in some well-defined area of medical practice so as to make all available technology and expertise available to a patient; the pain center or pain clinic is one example of a comprehensive intervention model.

confrontative (vigilant) coping style The tendency to cope with stressful events by tackling them directly and attempting to develop solutions; may ultimately be an especially effective method of coping, although it may produce accompanying distress.

contingency contracting A procedure in which an individual forms a contract with another person, such as a therapist, detailing what rewards or punishments are contingent on the performance or nonperformance of some target behavior.

controlled drinking skills Training in discriminating blood alcohol level so as to control extent of drinking; may also include coping skills for dealing with situations that are high risk for high alcohol consumption; see also **placebo drinking.**

control-enhancing interventions Interventions with patients who are awaiting treatment to enhance their perceptions of control over those treatments.

conversion hysteria Viewpoint originally advanced by Freud that specific unconscious conflicts can produce physical disturbances symbolic of the repressed conflict; no longer a dominant viewpoint in health psychology.

coping The process of trying to manage demands that are appraised as taxing or exceeding one's resources.

coping outcomes The beneficial effects that are thought to result from successful coping; these include reducing stress, adjusting more successfully to it, maintaining emotional equilibrium, having satisfying relationships with others, and maintaining a positive self-image.

coping resources Things available to a person that will help in the process of coping with stressful events; may include external factors, such as social support or money, and internal factors, such

as a resilient personality or a sense of personal control.

coping style An individual's preferred method of dealing with stressful situations.

coronary heart disease (CHD) A general term referring to illnesses caused by atheroslcerosis, which is the narrowing of the coronary arteries, the vessels that supply the heart with blood.

cost containment The effort to reduce or hold down health care costs.

cost effectiveness The formal evaluation of the effectiveness of some intervention relative to its cost and those of alternative interventions.

costs of coping The depletion of internal or external resources that occurs in response to attempting to manage stressful events.

counterconditioning Pairing some response with cues that previously evoked maladaptive behaviors followed by reinforcement; for example, relaxation training may be undertaken so that people will cope with social anxiety by relaxing instead of drinking.

counterirritation A pain control technique that involves inhibiting pain in one part of the body by stimulating or mildly irritating another area, sometimes adjacent to the area in which the pain is experienced.

covert self-control The manipulation and alteration of private events, such as thoughts, through principles of reinforcement and self-instruction.

craving A desire for some substance, such as alcohol or nicotine; when unsatisfied, craving may produce such symptoms as nervousness, restlessness, fatigue, and depression.

creative nonadherence The modification or supplementation of a prescribed treatment regimen on the basis of privately held theories about the disorder or its treatment.

daily hassles Minor daily stressful events; believed to have a cumulative effect in increasing the likelihood of illness.

death education Programs designed to inform people realistically about death and dying, the purpose of which is to reduce the terror connected with and avoidance of the topic.

delay behavior The act of delaying seeking treatment for recognized symptoms.

denial A defense mechanism involving the inability to recognize or deal with external threatening events; believed to be an early reaction to the diagnosis of a chronic or terminal illness.

detoxification The process of withdrawing from alcohol, usually conducted in a supervised, medically monitored setting.

diabetes A chronic disorder in which the body is not able to manufacture or utilize insulin properly.

diagnostic-related groups (DRGs) A patient classification scheme that specifies the nature and length of treatment for particular disorders; used by some third-party reimbursement systems to determine the amount of reimbursement.

dieticians Trained and licensed individuals who apply principles of nutrition and food management to meal planning for institutions such as hospitals or for individuals who need help planning and managing special diets.

digestive system The system of converting food into heat and energy and the process of supplying nutrients for growth and the repair of tissues.

direct effects hypothesis The theory that coping resources, such as social support, have beneficial psychological and health effects under conditions of both high stress and low stress.

discriminative stimuli Stimuli in an environment that are capable of eliciting a particular behavior; for example, the sight of food may act as a discriminative stimulus for eating.

disease prototypes Organized concepts of specific diseases based on their origins, duration, symptoms, and treatment; believed to guide the interpretation of symptoms.

distraction A pain control method that may involve either focusing on some stimulus irrelevant to the pain experience or reinterpreting the pain experience; redirecting attention to reduce pain.

double-blind experiment An experimental procedure in which neither the researcher nor the patient knows whether the patient received the real treatment or the placebo until precoded records indicating which patient received which are consulted; designed to reduce the possibility that expectations for success will increase evidence for success.

emotional regulation The attempt to control one's adverse emotional experiences in responding to stressful events; part of the coping process.

endocrine system A system of ductless glands that secrete hormones into the blood to stimulate target organs; interacts with nervous system functioning.

endogenous opioids Opiate-like substances produced by the body.

etiology The origins and causes of illness.

euthanasia Ending the life of a person with a painful terminal illness for the purpose of terminating the individual's suffering.

extinction training Pairing a stimulus with the absence of its customary response, so that, over time, the stimulus no longer evokes the response; extinction training is used in the treatment of alcoholism by pairing the presentation of alcoholic beverages with no consumption.

fear appeals Efforts to change attitudes by arousing fear to induce the motivation to change behavior; fear appeals are used to try to get people to change poor health habits.

fight-or-flight response A response to threat in which the body is rapidly aroused and motivated via the sympathetic nervous system and the endocrine system to flee or attack a threatening stimulus; the response was first described by Walter Cannon in 1932.

flooding A procedure in which clients are trained to let anxiety-arousing cognitions engulf or flood them; repeated contact with a fear-arousing image in the absence of actual aversive consequences is supposed to reduce anxiety.

focused or rapid smoking An early stage in stop-smoking programs, in which the smoker puffs on cigarettes at prescribed and frequent intervals and is instructed to attend to all of their unpleasant effects.

gate theory An integrative theory of pain which argues that structures in the central nervous system affect the operation of a gatelike mechanism in the spinal column that controls the flow of pain stimulation to the brain.

general adapation syndrome Developed by Hans Selye, a profile of how organisms respond to stress; the general adaptation syndrome is characterized by three phases: a nonspecific mobilization phase that promotes sympathetic nervous system activity; a resistance phase, during which the organism makes efforts to cope with the threat; and an exhaustion phase, which occurs if the organism fails to overcome the threat and depletes its physiological resources.

gout A form of arthritis produced by a buildup of uric acid in the body, producing crystals that become lodged in the joints; the most commonly affected area is the big toe.

grief A response to bereavement involving a feeling of hollowness and sometimes marked by preoccupation with the dead person, expressions of hostility toward others, and guilt over death; may also involve restlessness, inability to concentrate, and other adverse psychological and physical symptoms.

guided imagery A technique of relaxation and pain control in which a person conjures up a picture that is held in mind during a painful or stressful experience.

hardiness An individual difference characterized by a sense of commitment, a belief in personal control, and a willingness to confront challenge; believed to be a useful resource in coping with stressful events.

health behaviors Behaviors undertaken by people to enhance or maintain their health, such as exercise or the consumption of a healthy diet.

health belief model A theory of health behaviors; the model predicts that whether or not a person practices a particular health habit can be understood by knowing the degree to which the person perceives a personal health threat and the perception that a particular health practice will be effective in reducing that threat.

health beliefs Beliefs about the relation between particular health practices and particular health outcomes; includes beliefs about the severity of a health problem, the efficacy of measures designed to offset the problem, and one's efficacy in being able to carry through the health measure.

health habit A health-related behavior that is firmly established and often performed automatically, such as buckling a seat belt or brushing one's teeth.

health locus of control The perception that one's health is under personal control, is controlled by powerful others such as physicians, or is determined by external factors including chance.

health maintenance organization (HMO) An organizational arrangement for receiving health care services, by which an individual pays a standard monthly rate and then uses services as needed at no additional or at greatly reduced cost.

health promotion A general philosophy which maintains that health is a personal and collective achievement; the process of enabling people to increase control over and improve their health. Health promotion may occur through individual efforts, through interaction with the medical system, and through a concerted health policy effort.

health psychology The subarea within psychology devoted to understanding psychological influences on health, illness, and responses to those states, as well as the psychological origins and impacts of health policy and health interventions.

health risk appraisal A formal strategy that assesses an individual's health risks based on his or her heredity, health practices, or family environment and suggests changes designed to promote health.

helplessness The belief that one is powerless to effect change in one's environment.

holistic health A philosophy characterized by the belief that health is a positive state that is actively achieved; usually associated with the practice of certain nontraditional health practices.

home care Care for dying patients in the home; the choice of care for the majority of terminally ill patients, though sometimes problematic for family members.

homophobia The irrational fear and loathing of homosexuality; believed to underlie prejudicial and discriminatory behavior toward persons with AIDS.

hospice Institution for dying patients that encourages personalized, warm, palliative care.

hospice care An alternative to hospital and home care, designed to provide warm, personal comfort for terminally ill patients; may be residential or home-based.

hospital patient role A set of behaviors expected of hospital patients by hospital staff, characterized by cooperation, a pleasant demeanor, and not demanding extra care except under exceptional conditions.

human immunodeficiency virus (HIV) The virus that is implicated in the development of AIDS and ARC.

hyperglycemia A condition of excessive blood sugar, marked by drowsiness, labored breathing, and flushed and dry skin; can result in a coma.

hypertension Excessively high blood pressure that occurs when the supply of blood through the blood vessels is excessive, putting pressure on the vessel walls; a risk factor for a variety of medical problems, including coronary artery disease.

hypnosis A pain management technique involving relaxation, suggestion, distraction, and the focusing of attention.

hypoglycemia A condition marked by an excessively low level of blood sugar; marked by feelings of excitation, nervousness, and rapid and shallow breathing.

hypothalamus That part of the forebrain responsible for regulating water balance and controlling hunger and sexual desire; assists in cardiac functioning, blood pressure regulation, and respiration regulation; has a major role in regulation of the endocrine system, which controls the release of hormones.

iatrogenesis Adverse medical conditions or injuries that result from medical agents or institutions.

illness delay The time between recognizing that a symptom implies an illness and the decision to seek treatment.

illness representation (or schema) An organized set of beliefs about an illness or type of illness, including its nature, cause, duration, and consequences.

immunity The body's resistance to injury from invading organisms, acquired from the mother at birth, through disease, or through vaccinations and inoculations.

immunocompetence The degree to which the immune system functions effectively.

immunocompromise The degree to which the immune system responds suboptimally, because of either reduced numbers of cells or reduced functioning.

immunosuppression The degree to which the numbers of immune cells or their functioning are subdued; may occur in response to stress.

infant mortality rate The number of infant deaths per thousand infants.

John Henryism A personality predisposition to cope actively with psychosocial stressors; may become lethal when those active coping efforts are unsuccessful; the syndrome has been especially documented among lower income blacks at risk for or suffering from hypertension.

kidney dialysis A treatment for kidney disease; the process of cleansing the body of its wastes to remove excess salts, water, and metabolytes by circulating the blood through a machine that performs this function because the kidneys are unable to do so.

lay referral network An informal network of family and friends who help an individual interpret and treat a disorder before the individual seeks formal medical treatment.

learned helplessness A response to helplessness in which an individual not only learns to cease responding in an environment in which helplessness was initially experienced but also ceases to respond in new environments in which adaptive responses are possible.

life-skills-training approach A smoking-prevention program characterized by the belief that training in self-esteem and coping skills will boost self-image to the point that smoking becomes unnecessary or inconsistent with lifestyle.

lifestyle rebalancing Concerted lifestyle change in a healthy direction, usually including exercise, stress management, and a healthy diet; believed to contribute to relapse prevention after successful modification of a poor health habit, such as smoking or alcohol consumption.

living will A will prepared by a person with a terminal illness, requesting that extraordinary life-sustaining procedures not be used in the event that the ability to make this decision is lost.

locus of control Belief about whether reinforcements are controlled by one's self or the environment. Those with an internal locus of control see reinforcements as consequents of their own behavior, whereas individuals with an external locus of control see reinforcements as under the control of external factors or chance.

lymphatic system The drainage system of the body; believed to be involved in immune functioning.

lymphocyte suppression Suppression of the production and/or the numbers of lymphocytes in animals or humans; believed to occur in response to stressful events.

matching hypothesis The hypothesis that social support is helpful to an individual to the extent that the kind of support offered satisfies the individual's specific needs.

medical anthropology A biocultural discipline

within anthropology concerned with the biological and sociocultural aspects of human behavior and how the two interact to influence health and disease.

medical delay Delay in treating symptoms that results from problems within the medical system, such as faulty diagnoses, lost test results, and the like.

medical psychology A subfield within health psychology devoted to the study of psychological factors in the illness experience.

medical sociology A subfield within sociology devoted to the sociological perspective on health and illness, including the role of societal factors, social institutions, and social relationships in health and illness.

medical student's disease The relabeling of symptoms of fatigue and exhaustion as a particular illness resulting from learning about that illness; called medical student's disease because overworked medical students are vulnerable to this labeling effect.

medulla Section of the hindbrain responsible for the control of reflex activities of the body.

metabolic system The systems of the body that control digestion and urination.

midlife crisis Believed to occur around age 40, the midlife crisis, which often centers around job or relationship, is believed to stem at least in part from the realization of eventual death.

mind-body relationship The philosophical position regarding whether the mind and body operate indistinguishably as a single system or whether they act as two separate systems; the view guiding health psychology is that the mind and body are indistinguishable.

mixed-pain treatment program Pain treatment program that includes a wide variety of pain control methods, including methods to reduce operant pain.

modeling Learning gained from observing another person performing a target behavior.

monitoring/blunting The degree to which people deal with threat by scanning the environment for threat-relevant information or by ignoring threat-relevant information (blunting).

multiple regulation model A model of smoking that maintains that smoking regulates nicotine level in the body as well as factors that become conditioned to nicotine, such as emotional states of reduced anxiety or depression.

myocardial infarction Heart attack produced when a clot has developed in a coronary vessel, blocking the flow of blood to the heart.

negative affectivity A personality variable marked by a pervasive negative mood, including anxiety, depression, and hostility; believed to be implicated in the experience of symptoms, the seeking of medical treatment, and possibly also illness.

nervous system The system of the body responsible for the transmission of information from the brain to the rest of the body and from the rest of the body to the brain; it is composed of the central nervous system (the brain and the spinal cord) and the peripheral nervous system (which consists of the remainder of the nerves in the body).

neuralgia A sudden sharp pain along a nerve pathway for which no neurological basis can be found.

neurotransmitters Chemicals that regulate nervous system functioning.

nicotine fixed-effect theory A theory maintaining that smoking is reinforcing because nicotine stimulates reward centers in the nervous system and produces physiological arousal; now considered to be too simple a model of smoking.

nicotine regulation theory A theory maintaining that smoking occurs to regulate plasma nicotine level and is responsive to time since the last cigarette and to current plasma nicotine levels; now considered to be insufficient to explain smoking.

nonspecific immune mechanisms A set of responses to infection or disorder that is engaged by the presence of some biological invader.

nurse-practitioners Nurses who, in addition to their training in traditional nursing, receive special training in primary care so they may provide routine medical care for patients.

obesity An excessive accumulation of body fat, believed to contribute to a variety of health disorders, including cardiovascular disease.

occupational therapists Trained and licensed individuals who work with emotionally and/or physically handicapped people to determine skill levels and to develop a rehabilitation program to build on and expand these skills.

operant conditioning The pairing of a voluntary, nonautomatic behavior to a new stimulus through reinforcement or punishment.

operant pain Pain that is experienced by virtue of

having been paired with reinforcements for expressing pain, such as drugs, freedom from obligations, or financial compensation.

operant pain treatment program An inpatient program designed to reduce pain by withdrawing all reinforcements that have been paired with pain, such as attention, rest, or medication.

optimism A disposition to look on the more favorable side of happenings or possibilities; believed to be an effective coping resource.

osteoarthritis A form of arthritis that results when the articular cartilage begins to crack or wear away due to overuse of a particular joint; may also result from injury or other causes; usually affects the weight-bearing joints and is common among athletes and the elderly.

pain behaviors Behaviors that result in response to pain, such as cutting back on work or taking drugs.

pain center or pain clinic A setting in which all technologies to control pain are brought together to achieve successful management of intractable or chronic pain problems.

pain control The ability to reduce the experience of pain, report of pain, emotional concern over pain, inability to tolerate pain, or presence of pain-related behaviors.

pain-prone personality The belief that there is a constellation of personality traits that predisposes a person to experience chronic pain.

pain threshold The point at which an intensely applied stimulus is reported to be painful by a person.

palliative care Care designed to make the patient comfortable, but not to cure or improve the patient's underlying disease; often part of terminal care.

parasympathetic nervous system The part of the nervous system responsible for vegetative functions, conservation of energy, and damping down the effects of the sympathetic nervous system.

passive smoking, or secondhand smoke Smoke inhaled by nonsmokers as a result of exposure to smokers; believed to cause health problems such as bronchitis, emphysema, and lung cancer.

pathogen Any factor that compromises health. Pathogens may be biological, psychological, or social in nature.

patient consumerism Movement among medical patients to become active and informed participants in their own care.

patient education Programs designed to inform patients about their disorder and its treatment, and to train them in methods for coping with a disorder and its corresponding limitations.

patient orientation Orientation by physicians primarily toward the patient's psychological and medical welfare; fostered by private, fee-for-service care.

perceived stress The perception that an event is stressful independent of its objective characteristics.

person-environment fit The degree to which the needs and resources of a person and the needs and resources of an environment complement each other.

pessimistic explanatory style A chronic tendency to explain negative events as due to internal, stable, and global qualities of the self and to attribute positive events to external, unstable, and nonglobal factors; believed to contribute to the likelihood of illness.

phagocytosis The process by which phagocytes ingest and attempt to eliminate a foreign invader.

phantom limb pain Pain experienced in a place where an amputated limb used to be.

physical rehabilitation A program of activities for chronically ill or disabled persons geared toward helping them use their bodies as much as possible, to sense changes in the environment and in themselves so as to make appropriate physical accommodations, to learn new physical and management skills if necessary, to pursue a treatment regimen, and to learn how to control the expenditure of energy.

physical therapists Trained and licensed individuals who help people with muscle, nerve, joint, or bone diseases to overcome their disabilities as much as possible.

physicians' assistants Graduates of 2-year programs who perform routine health care functions, teach patients about their treatment regimens, and record medical information.

pituitary gland A gland located at the base of and controlled by the brain, which secretes the hormones responsible for growth and organ development.

placebo A medical treatment that produces an effect in a patient because of its therapeutic intent and not its nature.

placebo drinking The consumption of nonalcoholic beverages in social situations in which others are drinking.

placebo effect The medically beneficial impact of an inert treatment.

placebo-prone personality A constellation of attributes believed to predispose people to experiencing placebo effects; although the idea of a placebo-prone personality is now largely discredited, some personality characteristics do increase the likelihood that a person will show a placebo effect.

platelets Carried by the blood, they clump together to block holes in blood vessels and are implicated in blood clotting.

post-traumatic stress disorder A syndrome that results after exposure to a stressor of extreme magnitude, marked by emotional numbing, reliving aspects of the trauma, intense responses to other stressful events, and other symptoms such as hyperalertness, sleep disturbance, guilt, or impaired memory or concentration.

preferred provider organization (PPO) A network of affiliated practitioners that has agreed to charge preestablished rates for particular medical services.

premature death Death that occurs before the projected age of 75.

primary appraisal The perception of a new or changing environment as beneficial, neutral, or negative in its consequences; believed to be a first step in stress and coping.

primary prevention Measures designed to combat risk factors for illness before an illness ever has a chance to develop.

private, fee-for-service care The condition under which patients privately contract with physicians for services and pay them for services rendered.

problem drinking Uncontrolled drinking that leads to social, psychological, and biomedical problems resulting from alcohol; the problem drinker may show some signs associated with alcoholism, but, typically, problem drinking is considered to be a prealcoholic or a lesser alcoholic syndrome.

problem-solving strategies Active efforts to cope with stressful events through such methods as planning, organizing, seeking information, and developing solutions.

protection motivation model A theory maintaining that the motivation to protect one's self from a health threat depends on the magnitude of the threat, the likelihood of its occurrence, the belief that a particular response will be effective in overcoming the threat, and the self-perception that one can perform that response.

psychoimmunology The study of psychological influences on the immune system and of immunologic influences on psychological states.

psychological control The perception that one has at one's disposal a response that will reduce, minimize, eliminate, or offset the adverse effects of some unpleasant event, such as a medical procedure.

psychosomatic The belief that a biological condition is produced by psychological conflict.

quality of life The degree to which a person is able to maximize his or her physical, psychological, vocational, and social functioning; an important indicator of recovery from or adjustment to chronic illness.

reactance A psychological state that results when people feel their freedoms have been arbitrarily restricted by an external factor or agent; reactance is believed to contribute to nonadherence to treatment and to some adverse psychological reactions to hospitalization.

relapse prevention A set of techniques designed to keep people from relapsing to prior poor health habits after initial successful behavior modification; includes training in coping skills for high-risk-for-relapse situations and lifestyle rebalancing.

relaxation training Procedures that help people relax, which include progressive muscle relaxation and deep breathing; may also include guided imagery and forms of meditation or hypnosis.

renal system As part of the metabolic system, the renal system is responsible for the regulation of bodily fluids and the elimination of wastes; regulates bodily fluids by removing surplus water, surplus electrolytes, and waste products generated by the metabolism of food.

repression A psychological defense by which individuals unable to deal with their own anxiety due to threatening events push these impulses into the unconscious; as a coping style, repression involves ignoring or not dealing fully with threatening events.

respiratory system The system of the body responsible for taking in oxygen, excreting carbon dioxide, and regulating the relative composition of the blood.

rheumatoid arthritis A crippling form of arthritis believed to result from an autoimmune process, usually attacking the small joints of the hands, feet, wrists, knees, ankles, and neck.

role conflict Occurs when two or more social or occupational roles that an individual occupies produce conflicting standards for behavior.

role overload Occurs when an individual occupies too many social roles or the roles that he/she occupies require too many tasks or too much time.

secondary appraisal The assessment of one's coping abilities and resources and judgment as to whether they will be sufficient to meet the harm, threat, or challenge of a new or changing event; believed to be the second stage in the stress and coping response.

secondary gains Benefits of being treated for illness, including the ability to rest, to be freed from unpleasant tasks, and to be taken care of by others.

self-concept An integrated set of beliefs about one's personal qualities and attributes.

self-control A state in which an individual desiring to change behavior learns how to modify the antecedents and the consequences of that target behavior.

self-efficacy The perception that one is able to perform a particular action.

self-employed desensitization A procedure in which a client constructs a hierarchy of anxiety-arousing situations and then learns deep breathing and progressive muscle relaxation to practice as he or she moves through the hierarchy.

self-esteem A global evaluation of one's qualities and attributes.

self-observation and self-monitoring Assessing the frequency, antecedents, and consequents of some to-be-modified target behavior.

self-reinforcement Systematically rewarding or punishing the self to increase or decrease the occurrence of some target behavior.

self-talk Internal monologues; people tell themselves things that may undermine or help them implement appropriate health habits, such as "I can stop smoking" (positive self-talk), or "I'll never be able to do this" (negative self-talk).

sensation seeking A personality variable assessing an individual's tolerance for stimulation; some people are thrill-oriented whereas others prefer regularity and a lack of surprise.

separation anxiety Feelings of fear or extreme distress that result from separation from someone important, usually the mother.

set point theory of weight The concept that each individual has an ideal biological weight that cannot be greatly modified.

shaping Reinforcing successive approximations to a desired target behavior; for example, reinforcement may be used to gradually help people stop smoking by rewarding them for fewer and fewer cigarettes over time.

smoking prevention programs Programs designed to keep people from beginning to smoke, as opposed to programs that attempt to induce people to stop once they have already become smokers.

social engineering Social or lifestyle change through legislation; for example, water purification is done through social engineering rather than by individual efforts.

social influence interventions Smoking-prevention interventions that draw on the social learning principles of modeling and behavioral inoculation in inducing people not to smoke; youngsters are exposed to older peer models who deliver antismoking messages after exposure to simulated peer pressure to smoke.

socialization The process by which people learn the norms, rules, and beliefs associated with their family and society; parents and social institutions are usually the major agents of socialization.

social-skills training Techniques that teach people how to relax and interact comfortably in social situations; often a part of health-behavior modification programs, on the assumption that maladaptive health behaviors, such as alcohol consumption or smoking, may develop in part to control social anxiety.

social support Information from others that one is loved and cared for, esteemed and valued, and part of a network of communication and mutual obligation.

social workers Trained and licensed individuals who help patients and their families deal with problems by providing therapy, making referrals, and engaging in social planning; medical social workers help patients and their families ease transitions between illness and recovery states.

specific immune mechanisms A set of responses designed to respond to specific invaders; includes cell-mediated and humoral immunity.

spinal cord That portion of the central nervous system that transmits sensory and motor information to and from the brain and other parts of the body.

stages of dying A theory developed by Kübler-Ross which maintains that people go through five temporal stages in adjusting to the prospect of death: denial, anger, bargaining, depression, and acceptance; believed to characterize some but not all dying people.

stimulus control interventions Interventions designed to modify behavior that involve the removal of discriminative stimuli that evoke a behavior targeted for change and the substitution of new discriminative stimuli that will evoke a desired behavior.

stress Appraising events as harmful, threatening, or challenging, and assessing one's capacity to respond to those events; events perceived to tax or exceed one's resources are perceived as stressful.

stress carriers Individuals who create stress for others without necessarily increasing their own level of stress.

stress eating Eating in response to stress; stress eaters choose foods with high water content; approximately half the population increases eating in response to stress.

stressful life event An event that forces an individual to make changes in his or her life.

stress inoculation The process of identifying stressful events in one's life and learning skills for coping with them, so that when the events come up, one can put those coping skills into effect.

stress management A program for dealing with stress in which people learn how they appraise stressful events, develop skills for coping with stress, and practice putting these skills into effect.

stress markers Physiological changes, emotional reactions, or cognitive responses that are believed to be indicative of the amount of stress an individual is experiencing; stress markers are indirect measures of stress, since stress cannot itself be directly assessed.

stressor An event perceived to be stressful

stress-sensitive Showing excessive sympathetic nervous system activity in response to stress; believed to be an attribute of those at risk for coronary heart disease and those suffering from hypertension.

stroke A condition that results from disturbance in blood flow to the brain, often marked by resulting physical or cognitive impairments and, in the extreme, death.

sudden death syndrome An abrupt loss of life, believed to be caused by the combination of a preexisting biological weakness and an extremely stressful and unexpected event, producing feelings of extreme hopelessness or helplessness.

sudden infant death syndrome (SIDS) A common cause of death among infants, in which an infant simply stops breathing.

support group A group of individuals who meet regularly and usually share some common problem or concern; support groups are believed to help people cope because they provide opportunities to share concerns and exchange information with similar others.

symbolic immortality The sense that one is leaving a lasting impact on the world, as through one's children or one's work, or that one is joining the afterlife and becoming one with God.

sympathetic nervous system The part of the nervous system that mobilizes the body for action.

systematic desensitization A process by which an individual exposes one's self to fear-arousing stimuli graduated in intensity, with the idea of eliminating the anxiety response to the stimulus; may be used as a treatment for anxiety disorders, such as a fear of heights or snakes.

systems theory The viewpoint that all levels of an organization in any entity are linked to each other hierarchically and that change in any level will bring about change in other levels.

teachable moment The idea that certain times are better for teaching particular health practices than others; pregnancy constitutes a teachable moment for getting women to stop smoking.

terminal care Medical care of the terminally ill.

testicular self-examination The practice of checking the testicles to detect alterations in the underlying tissue; a chief method of detecting early testicular cancer.

thalamus That portion of the forebrain responsible for the recognition of sensory stimuli and the relay of sensory impulses to the cerebral cortex.

thanatology The study of death and dying.

theory of planned behavior Derived from the theory of reasoned action, this theoretical viewpoint maintains that a person's behavioral intentions and behaviors can be understood by knowing the person's attitudes about the behavior, subjective norms regarding the behavior, and perceived behavioral control over that action.

theory of reasoned action A model of behavioral intentions and behavior; in the health arena, it predicts that health behaviors are determined by individual attitudes toward a health action and subjective norms about the appropriateness of that action.

third-party reimbursement programs Arrangements by which individuals or physicians are reimbursed for expenses incurred for diagnosis and treatment or other health-related expenses; insurance companies usually constitute third-party reimbursement programs.

thought-stopping A technique in which an individual stops maladaptive thought patterns by having a therapist shout ''Stop!'' when the thought patterns occur or by personally alerting the self to stop when the thought patterns occur.

time management Skills for learning how to use one's time more effectively to accomplish one's goals.

treatment effectiveness Formal documentation of the success of an intervention.

Type A behavior syndrome A behavioral and emotional style marked by an aggressive, unceasing struggle to achieve more and more in less time, often in hostile competition with other individuals or forces; a risk factor for coronary artery disease. Hostility appears to be especially implicated as the risk factor.

unrealistic optimism The belief that one is less vulnerable to a variety of adverse events and more likely to incur a variety of positive events than is actually true; in the context of health, it refers to a falsely positive assessment of one's risk of developing major health problems.

utilization delay The time between deciding to seek treatment and actually doing so.

vicarious systematic desensitization or guided mastery Coping with anxiety by observing a model progressively moved through a hierarchy of anxiety-arousing situations successfully.

wellness A philosophical orientation toward health involving interventions to increase individual control over and improve health.

window of vulnerability The fact that, at certain times, people are more vulnerable to particular health problems. For example, early adolescence constitutes a window of vulnerability for beginning smoking.

worried well Individuals free from illness who are nonetheless concerned about their physical state and frequently and inappropriately use medical services.

yo-yo dieting The process of chronically alternating between dieting and regular eating, leading to successive weight gains and losses; over time, yo-yo dieters increase their chances of becoming obese by altering their underlying metabolism.

NAME INDEX

SUBJECT INDEX

PHOTO CREDITS